D0161751

ENCYCLOPEDIA OF AFRICAN-AMERICAN LITERATURE

Wilfred Samuels

Associate Editors
Loretta Gilchrist Woodard
Tracie Church Guzzio

An imprint of Infobase Publishing

Encyclopedia of African-American Literature

Facts On File, Inc.
An imprint of Infobase Publishing
132 West 31st Street
New York NY 10001

ISBN-10: 0-8160-5073-2
ISBN-13: 978-0-8160-5073-4

Library of Congress Cataloging-in-Publication Data
   Encyclopedia of African American literature / Wilfred D. Samuels, editor; Tracie Guzzio, associate editor, Loretta Gilchrist Woodard, associate editor.
       p. cm.
   Includes bibliographical references and index.
   ISBN 0-8160-5073-2 (acid-free paper)
   1. American literature—African American authors—Encyclopedias. 2. American literature—African American authors—Bio-bibliography—Dictionaries. 3. African American authors—Biography—Dictionaries. 4. African Americans—Intellectual life—Encyclopedias. 5. African Americans in literature—Encyclopedias. I. Samuels, Wilfred D. II. Guzzio, Tracie. III. Woodard, Loretta Gilchrist.
   PS153.N5E48 2007
   810.9'896073003—dc22   2006026140

Facts On File books are available at special discounts when purchased in bulk quantities for businesses, associations, institutions, or sales promotions. Please call our Special Sales Department in New York at (212) 967-8800 or (800) 322-8755.

You can find Facts On File on the World Wide Web at http://www.factsonfile.com

Text design by Rachel Berlin
Cover design by Takeshi Takahashi

Printed in the United States of America

VB KT 10 9 8 7 6 5 4 3 2 1

This book is printed on acid-free paper.

TABLE OF CONTENTS

INTRODUCTION

⤜⟶⟵⤛

We have always been imagining ourselves . . .
we are the subjects of our own narratives,
witnesses to and participants in our own
experience. . . . We are not, in fact, "other."
(Morrison, 208)

In this profoundly proud, eloquent, and bold
declaration, novelist Toni Morrison takes on those
"serious scholars" and new discoverers of what
she defines as a rich "Afro-American artistic presence" in Western culture in general and American
culture in particular. For many years Western
scholars considered the phrase *African-American
literature* to be either a myth or a contradiction
and either negated or dismissed the rich body of
writing by Americans of African descent.

As Olaudah Equiano declares in his 18th-cen-
tury autobiography, *The Interesting Narrative of
Olaudah Equiano, Or Gustavus Vassa, The African,
Written by Himself* (1789), black Africans brought
with them to the strange land of the "New World"
memories of their traditions of dance, music, and
poetry, which, planted in the British colonies of
North America in particular, took root in the new
songs they sang. Today those songs run deep like
a river in the souls of black folks and reverberate
and resound in the antiphonal call-and-response

style that constitutes the foundation and heartbeat
of the African-American literary tradition.

During the 17th, 18th, and 19th centuries,
unknown black bards, as James Weldon Johnson
recounts, placed their lips to the sacred fire of
poetry and created "sorrow songs" whose lyrics
responded to the dehumanization of the world of
chattel slavery, a world that, in the end, reduced
African Americans to "three-fifths other." In their
songs, they registered their personal humanity
and simultaneously humanized the troubled and
troubling world around them. The lyrics of such
songs as "Steal Away," "Swing Low Sweet Chariot,"
and "Motherless Child," as well as the didactic and
often humorous narratives and tales about Brer
Rabbit, Tar Baby, and High John de Conquer, commented on current conditions, passed on traditions, entertained, and offered lessons in morality
and virtue in the "broken tongue" that black people
created. But when exposed to the written texts and
more formal language of Western culture, African
Americans also put pen to paper to create works of
merit. For example, kidnapped between the ages
of seven or eight, Ethiopian-born Phillis Wheatley
confounded the community of her New England
"city upon a hill," the cradle of many Founding
Fathers, with her broadsides and eventually with

her *Poems on Various Subjects, Religious and Moral* (1773), the first known collection of poems to be published by an enslaved black person.

Witnesses to and participants in the horrific system of chattel slavery, early writers such as Olaudah Equiano, Frederick Douglass, and Linda Brent (Harriet Jacobs) wrote their way to freedom with the publication of their respective works, *The Interesting Narrative . . . ; Narrative of Frederick Douglass, An American Slave, Written By Himself* (1845); and *Incidents in the Life of a Slave Girl, Written by Herself* (1861), all three paradigms of a new genre: the slave narrative–black autobiography. These now-acknowledged classic texts are clear evidence of the way Africans and African Americans directly affected the development of Western literature and even intellectual history. Like the drafters of the Declaration of Independence and the U.S. Constitution, documents that undergird Western thought and philosophy, Equiano and Douglass have much to say about the true meaning of freedom, the rights of the individual (particularly in a democracy), and universal human rights. Many of these ideas were echoed and added to by other 19th-century African-American writers, of fiction and nonfiction, many of whom were fierce abolitionists, including William W. Brown, Nat Turner, Martin Delaney, Henry H. Garnet, and Frances Ellen Watkins Harper.

African Americans entered the 20th century with cadences of progression and precision grounded in determination, spirituality, and literacy. In *The Souls of Black Folk* (1903), which many consider the black master text or "the African-American book of the 20th century," William Edward Burghardt (or W. E. B.) DuBois, with, it seems, prophetic vision, succinctly captures African Americans' dogged journey from children of emancipation to youths "with dawning self-consciousness":

If, however, the vistas disclosed as yet no goal, no resting place, little but flattery and criticism, the journey at least gave leisure for reflection and self-examination; it changed the child of Emancipation to the youth with

dawning self-consciousness, self-realization, and self-respect. In those sombre forests of his striving his own soul rose before him, and he saw himself, darkly as through a veil; and yet he saw in himself some faint revelation of his power, of his mission. He began to have a dim feeling that, to attain his place in the world, he must be himself and not another. (368)

The result of this "striving in the souls of black folk" (371) was their "gift of story and of song"— the means by which they carved a place for themselves in the American cultural landscape. DuBois concluded, "And so by fateful chance the Negro folk-song—the rhythmic cry of the slave—stands today not simply as the sole American music, but as the most beautiful expression of human experience born this side of the seas. It still remains as the singular spiritual heritage of the nation and the greatest gift of the Negro people" (536–537). DuBois's task in *The Souls of Black Folk* was to claim, validate, and celebrate the contributions of African Americans, particularly in music, and to place them at the heart of American culture— indeed, at the heart of human culture.

Were he alive today, DuBois would undoubtedly be able to assess critically the last 100 years as a historical playing field on which African Americans— not only through their music, including blues, jazz, and particularly rap music, but also through their oral and written texts—re-envisioned, redefined, and re-represented themselves, not merely "darkly as through a veil" but also in the multifaceted spaces they created for themselves outside and inside the black/white paradigm imposed on them as a people, as writers, and as scholars of a more dynamic black world and culture.

In light of the racial realities and marginalization faced by African Americans, these accomplishments did not come easily. In fact, from a legal perspective, the double-conscious striving of African Americans lasted into the middle of the 20th century. when the Supreme Court rendered its 1954 decision in *Brown v. Board of Education of Topeka,* ostensibly tearing down the doctrine of "separate but equal" inherent in segregationist Jim Crow laws. Black writers, particularly Richard Wright, considered it their responsibility to fight the same battle for equality, as exhibited in their work.

The dilemma African-American writers faced throughout much of the 20th century is concisely outlined by Hoyt Fuller, a black scholar/critic and the editor of the *Negro Digest / Black World,* in his essay "Contemporary Negro Fiction" (1965), in which he responds to John W. Aldridge's contention that "the writing of novels is basically a process of assigning value to human experience" (322). Were all things equal, Fuller maintains, there would be no problem. However, a conflicting line is drawn, he concludes, because "in practice, if not in principle, the two major races in America often have different values, or at least different ways of interpreting the same values" (322). Fuller further argues, "... the reading public, which is white, must be cognizant first of the nature and purpose of literature in general before taking the further step toward the appreciation of that literature produced by Negroes. The failure or refusal of both critics and public to do this in the past has resulted in the attachment of stigma to the designation, 'Negro literature,' making it easy, when desirable, to dismiss much of this literature as inconsequential" (323). Fuller claims that "Negro literature" is often derided as "protest literature," because "if it deals honestly with Negro life, it will be accusatory toward white people, and nobody likes to be accused, especially of crimes against the human spirit" (324). Fuller concludes:

> The reading public must realize, then, that while it is the duty of any serious writer to look critically and truthfully at the society of which he is a part, and to reveal that society to itself, the Negro writer, by virtue of his identification with a group deliberately held on the outer edges of that society, will, if he is honest, call attention to that special aspect of the society's failure. (324)

Throughout the 20th century, the question for black writers, from James Weldon Johnson ("Preface," *The Book of American Negro Poetry*) and Langston Hughes ("The Negro Artist and the Racial Mountain") to Richard Wright ("Blueprint for Negro Writing"), James Baldwin ("Everybody's Protest Novel"), Ralph Ellison ("The Art of Fiction: An Interview"), and LeRoi Jones (Imamu Amiri Baraka), became the relationship between art and propaganda or polemics. While Ellison maintained that "The understanding of art depends finally upon one's willingness to extend one's humanity and one's knowledge of human life" (175), Baraka and the architects of the Black Arts Movement argued that "Black Art is the aesthetic and spiritual sister of the Black Power Concept. As such it envisions an art that speaks directly to the needs of and aspirations of Black America" (Neal, 257).

Even a cursory review of the 20th-century debate over the existence, much less the value, of an African-American literary tradition—often engaged in by white critics and scholars, including Robert Bone, C. W. E. Bigsby, Warren French, and Alfred Kazin—reveals that African-American writers occupied both sides of the debate. It fell to Bone to define with clarity not only what white Western scholars saw as the problem but also what the dilemma was for the African-American writer. Bone wrote in his now-classic text, *The Negro Novel in America* (1958):

> The Negro must still structure his life in terms of a culture to which he is denied full access. He is at once a part of and apart from the wider community in which he lives. His adjustment to the dominant culture is marked by a conflicting pattern of identification and rejection. His deepest psychological impulses alternate between magnetic poles of assimilation and Negro nationalism. (3–4)

Black scholars, particularly Darwin T. Turner and Hoyt Fuller, rushed to respond to Bone's partially correct but, they vehemently argued, flawed contention. On the one hand, although Fuller noted Bone's understanding of the central issues, he also conceded that generations of black writers have embraced "assimilationism." He writes, "It is true that some of the writers in the twenties and thirties, Walter White and Jessie Fauset among them, sought in their novels to illustrate how little difference there was between Negroes and whites, even going to the extent of presenting heroes and heroines white enough to pass. After all, it is natural for man to want to belong, really belong, to the society which nurtured him" (326). On the other hand, despite acknowledging Bone's "commendable effort," Turner, in "*The Negro Novel in America:* In Rebuttal," caustically took Bone to task for the "errors of fact and inference, inconsistencies and contradictions, supercilious lectures, and flippant remarks often in bad taste.... Unfortunately, not content to confine himself to the role of critic and historian of individual writers, [Bone] has presumed himself to serve as psychiatrist, philosopher, and teacher not only for all Negro writers but for all Negroes" (122).

Most scholars agree that in the 1960s and 1970s, the Black Aesthetics and Black Arts movements challenged the hierarchy with radical and militant voices that spoke cacophonously black, insisting that blacks were not victims but agents. For example, Baraka identified blacks as magicians who own the night. Despite this challenge, however, black writers and critics in general continued to value assimilationism, led, according to Professor Lawrence Hogue, by "elite/middle class African Americans" who were interested in racial uplift, in protesting racism, and in refuting negative images of African Americans. This [attitude] kept the black/white binary firmly, counterproductively, destructively, and "supremely in place." Here, Hogue echoes Baldwin who, in his critique of Wright's *Native Son,* "Everybody's Protest Novel," in which he derided the protest novel, argues that Bigger's tragedy is "that he has accepted a theology that denies his life; that he admits the possibility of his being sub-human and feels constrained, therefore, to battle for his humanity according to those brutal criteria bequeathed him at his birth" (23). According to Baldwin, Bigger seeks "acceptance within the present community" (23).

Hogue argues that the acceptance of a black/white binary "failed to engage and appreciate African American differences, rich cultural diversity and approaches to life that comprise American/African American life" (2). Ironically, it also created yet another paradigm, the elite or black middle-class norm/center, reducing African-American differences to a "singular formation."

Hogue demands that a wider net be cast—one that would include, embrace, and value the multivalent black voices and identities of African Americans, including "jazz/blues African Americans, Voodoo African Americans, working class African Americans, subaltern African Americans, modern African Americans and urban swinging African Americans" (2)—which, in the end, is concerned less with white racism and more with defining and constructing themselves as subjects with agency. Hogue calls for a more polycentric theoretical perspective to access and assess the African-American literary tradition and "to examine and discuss African Americans in terms of their own distinctions and traditions, to engage the polyvalent nature of African American literatures, history, and criticism" (2).

Returning now to the question of what DuBois might discover at the beginning of the 21st century in a new exploration of the "striving in the souls of black folks," it would be impossible to deny that he would discover a veritable vineyard in which, as unfettered and emancipated former chattel, African Americans flowered the American literary landscape with their gift of story, reaping a rich and bountiful harvest that runs the gamut from autobiography and slave narrative to slam poetry; hip-hop and rap narratives; black erotica and experimental fiction; blues drama and novels; baby mamma drama fiction; gay, lesbian, detective, and science-fiction popular best sellers; feminist, womanist, and Africana Womanism voices; African-American–Caribbean voices; modernist and postmodernist voices; the humorous tales of Jesse B. Semple; and the bitingly satirical voice of *The Boondocks* comic strip. No doubt, he would, indeed, say "amen" to Morrison's claim with which this introduction began: that African Americans "have always imagined" themselves.

Moreover, DuBois would find the now-undeniable progress and contributions made by African Americans in their efforts to create and validate an African-American literary tradition emblematized in the history-making publication of several anthologies by major presses, specifically the *Norton Anthology of African American Literature* (1997), *Call and Response: The Riverside Anthology of the African American Literary Tradition* (Riverside, 1997), *Cornerstones: An Anthology of African American Literature* (St. Martin's, 1996), and *Trouble the Water: 250 Years of African American Poetry* (Mentor Books 1997), as well as major reference works such as *The Oxford Companion to African American Literature* (1997) and Macmillan's *African American Literary Criticism, 1773 to 2000* (1999). Equally significant are major electronic productions, such as the Encarta Africana multimedia encyclopedia maintained by Harvard's Professors Henry Louis Gates and Kwame Anthony Appiah at Africana.com; the related site *Encyclopedia Africana,* managed by Henry DuBois (W. E. B. DuBois's grandson); and the online Oxford African American Studies Center.

African-American writers of serious and popular literature have never been more influential. They are interviewed on *Good Morning America* and *The Today Show,* as well as *Sixty Minutes.* Their works are regularly selected and celebrated by members of Oprah's Book Club; reviewed in the *New York Times Book Review, Publications of the Modern Language Association, African American Review,* and *Callaloo;* promoted in *Black Issues Book Review;* and taught on college and university campuses across the country. African-American writers are noted for embracing, validating, and proclaiming an America that is diverse, beautiful, and complex.

ABOUT THIS BOOK

The *Encyclopedia of African-American Literature* covers the entire spectrum of the African-American literary tradition, from the 18th-century writings of pioneers such as Equiano and Wheatley to 20th-century canonic texts to the finest of today's best-selling authors. This volume includes entries on major and minor writers, including writers of fiction and nonfiction, poets, dramatists, and critics, as well as entries on the finest works of African-American literature, from all genres and time periods.

Browsers will find entries on all the canonical autobiographers, novelists, and poets, including Maya Angelou, Amiri Baraka, Charles Chesnutt, Paul Laurence Dunbar, Zora Neale Hurston, Paule Marshall, Toni Morrison, Alice Walker, John Edgar Wideman, and August Wilson. The volume also highlights a host of emerging (in some cases already award-winning) literary voices, such as Jeffrey Reynard Allen, Toi Derricotte, Pearl Cleage, Thomas Glade, E. Lynn Harris, William Henry Lewis, Sapphire, Danzy Senna, and Trey Ellis, and popular fiction writers, such as Jerome Dickey, Omar Tyree, and Zane, whose works are readily available and whose readers are numerous and diverse. Finally, this volume includes discussions of the major critical and theoretical schools and scholars that have influenced the perception and reception of this body of material, as well as entries on important terms, themes, historical events, and more. Entries are cross-referenced for ease of use.

Given the successful movement toward validation and inclusivity witnessed today, the editors found it imperative to include a handful of representative voices from hip-hop culture, and specifically from rap poetry. Our intention does not signal, in any way, a decision to be blind to, supportive of, or cavalier about the pervasive colonialist, nihilistic, oppressive, drug-promoting, homophobic, lust-filled, and misogynist messages of many rap videos and lyrics, often, but not exclusively, by gangster rappers. Such messages proclaim, as bell hooks notes, that "Blackness represents violence and hate" (53). We do not mean to endorse such particular views or ideologies.

However, we recognize that hip-hop culture is firmly rooted in the call-and-response cadence that undergirds African-American culture in general and the African-American literary tradition specifically and that can be heard in everything from Negro spirituals, work songs, blues, and jazz to the poetry of Langston Hughes, Maya Angelou,

Nikki Giovanni, and Kevin Young. Ultimately, what attracts us to hip-hop culture and rap is the seeming continuity and resonance between it and the Black Arts Movement apparent in the often raw, unveiled, and unsilenced voices of many hip-hop artists, including Tupac Shakur, Queen Latifah, and Public Enemy, who use their lyrics, poetry, and fiction as social and political vehicles of comment. As critic Mel Donalson maintains, "Much like poets Amiri Baraka, Haki Madhubuti, Gil Scott Herron, and Nikki Giovanni, who sought to use the Black Arts Movement as a vehicle for black consciousness and liberation, Public Enemy and the new black youth culture sought to empower their generation and the black community through rap lyrics and hip-hop sounds."

In summary, we have chosen to include more than just the best-known authors of the African-American canon. Indeed, our emphasis is on new and emerging writers, who, we are convinced, are equally and totally committed to speaking the unspeakable; we also call attention to what Hogue identifies as the more "polyvalent nature of African American literature, history and criticism" (2), not only to distinguish the *Encyclopedia of African-American Literature* from other reference works but also, in our view, to provide some of its most significant value.

SELECTED BIBLIOGRAPHY

Baldwin, James. "Everybody's Protest Novel." In *Notes of a Native Son.* Boston: Beacon Press, 1955, 13–22.

Bigsby, C. W. E., ed. *The Black American Writer.* Vol. 1, *Fiction.* Deland, Fla.: Everett/Edwards, 1969.

Bone, Robert. *The Negro Novel in America.* New Haven, Conn.: Yale University Press, 1958.

Donalson, Mel. Interview. Pasadena, Calif.: June 20, 2006.

DuBois, W. E. B. *The Souls of Black Folk.* In *W. E. B. DuBois: Writings.* New York: Library of America College Edition, 1986, 357–546.

Ellison, Ralph. "The Art of Fiction: An Interview." In *Shadow and Act.* New York: Vintage Books, 1972, 167–183.

Fuller, Hoyt. "Contemporary Negro Fiction." *Southern Review* 50 (1965): 321–335.

Hogue, Lawrence W. *The African American Male, Writing, and Difference: A Polycentric Approach to African American Literature, Criticism and History.* Albany: State University of New York Press, 2003.

hooks, bell. *Salvation: Black People and Love.* New York: William Morrow, 2001.

Morrison, Toni. "Unspeakable Things Unspoken: The Afro-American Presence in American Literature. In *Toni Morrison,* edited by Harold Bloom, 201–230. New York: Chelsea House Publishers, 1990.

Neel, Larry. "The Black Arts Movement." In *The Black Aesthetics,* edited by Addison Gayle, 256–274. New York: Doubleday & Company, 1972.

Turner, Darwin T. "*The Negro Novel in America:* In Rebuttal." *College Language Association Journal* 10 (1966): 122–134.

ACKNOWLEDGMENTS

When I began this project, family members, friends, and colleagues lauded me for taking on such a monumental task. In fact, while some profusely wished me good luck and best wishes, others candidly warned that I was taking on a herculean task. This was indeed a challenging project. However, it was also a rewarding one.

First of all, the associate editors and I completed the journey with the encouragement, support, and, above all, patience of our editor Jeff Soloway, without whom we would never have crossed the finish line.

As chief editor I must also express similar thanks and appreciation to my incredible team of associate editors, Mel Donalson, Tracie Guzzio, and Loretta Gilchrist Woodard, who more than rose to the occasion, going the extra mile to ensure continued progress and the production of the highest quality work. Equally important are contributors G. Winston James, Lynda Koolish, Howard Ramsby III, Beverly Tate, Terry Rowden, Gloria Cronin, Warren Carson, Robert Dowling,

Keith Byerman, Kim Hai Pearson, Brian Jennings, Jerry Ward, E. Ethelbert Miller, Julia Galbus, Clenora Hudson Weems, Michael Poindexter, William Graves, Ronald G. Coleman, France Davis, and librarians Curley Jones and Marie Paiva, whose effusive support, commitment, and contributions never lagged. They are living testimonies to unconditional love, friendship, and enduring collegiality.

Needless to say, I could not have accomplished this project without the assistance I received with the day-to-day tasks of managing it. I thank the many student assistants who worked with me over the past three years, including Kindra Briggs, Ryan Dixon, Robyn Lemon, Christine Pak, Carlos Perez, Rich Roberts, Edward L. Robinson, Brooke Shiffler, Erik Ludwig, and Rondell Nelson Richards, who did everything from setting up and maintaining grids to corresponding with contributors and potential contributors, doing library work, and typing. In other words, they served as my army and navy. They deserve the medals.

A TO Z
ENTRIES

Aasim, Afrika Bambaataa (1960–)

Often called the "Godfather of Hip-Hop," Afrika Bambaataa Aasim, familiarly known as Bam, was born in the Bronx, New York on April 10, 1960. Many say his given name at birth was Kevin Donovan, but in an interview Bam states, "This Kevin Donovan, they be wanting to swear that person is me. That's a Godfather of mine who used to be in the gangs with me. But they don't know what's what. So, they are caught up in their belief system" (Banjoko). During his early teens Bam became interested in music and became a D.J. He also became a founding member of the Savage Seven, a street gang based in the Bronxdale Projects. Bam's gang grew quickly and eventually became known as the Black Spades.

Becoming fascinated with the warrior tradition of the Zulus, which he learned about from his wide studies on African history, Michael Caine's film *Zulu,* and a trip to Africa, Bam took the name Bambaataa Aasim, which means "affectionate leader" in English. Bam's leadership qualities and potential were evident even in his childhood, but the question was what direction would his leadership take. The direction of gang leader was not positive, but it was apparent that leadership was always in him; perhaps because of his Jamaican ancestry his legacies were tied to MARCUS GARVEY, the leader of the Universal Negro Improvement Association (UNIA), which some historians consider the largest black mass movement in 20th-century America before Martin L. King, Jr.'s Southern Christian Leadership Conference.

Around 1973, when Black Spades began to fade, Bam started his own performing group, called Zulu Nation. Although Bam established a different direction for this organization from that of the Black Spades, he designed objectives that were fundamentally quite similar. For example, knowing that the gang life he had lived as a member of Black Spades was essentially an outlet for young people in the ghetto, Bam wanted his new organization to serve a similar objective; significantly, however, instead of crime, he emphasized creativity. Well grounded in African history, Afrocentric thought, spirituality, health-consciousness, and the culture surrounding disk jockeying, which remained dear to him, Bam identified five elements of black culture he would later call hip-hop as the centerpiece of the Zulu Nation. These elements included the following: emceeing (rapping), disk jockeying, writing (aerosol art/graffiti), dancing (including several forms, breaking, up-rocking, popping, and locking), and knowledge, particularly knowledge of self, which held the other four elements together.

Knowledge of self was to be the primary function of hip-hop; emceeing was to be used to communicate—to get a message across. Disk jockeying was an equally important venue of communication as Bam and others used it to play speeches by MALCOLM X, MARTIN LUTHER KING, JR., and other sociopolitical voices over the beat of the music they were playing. Writing was used to express some political or ideological message or as an expression of cultural creativity. Dance forms were to be valued as cultural expressions as well, similar to the way the Brazilian martial arts form capoeira was used to celebrate the influences and retention of African culture in South America.

Knowledge of self and the world that blacks lived in was inspired by the society and culture in which hip-hop was born. Bam's transformation from gang leader into the "Godfather of Hip-Hop" was inspired by several sources of knowledge; he credits in particular the Honorable Elijah Muhammad and the Nation of Islam for introducing him to knowledge of self and the significance of the time he was living in. Consequently, it was not surprising that demands for the emergence of new civil rights and nationalist organizations, as well as cries for black power prevalent during the 1960s and 1970s, echoed in the world of hip-hop culture within the black community.

The growth of disk jockeying in the late 1970s laid the foundation for the new phenomenon of "battles" between groups based solely on the loudness of the music. Bam transformed the nature of the D.J. battle when he began to have D.J.'s take turns to determine who was the best. Each D.J. would play for an hour, and then the listeners would choose their favorite. This metaphoric battle and competition ran over into the other areas of hip-hop as well, such as rap battles and break dancing battles.

Bam began his recording career in 1980 with Paul Winley Records. However, the experience proved to be an unhappy one, and he decided to leave the company. By 1981 Bam had moved from doing house and block parties, where he would connect his equipment to the streetlight, to shows at the Audubon Ballroom. In 1982 Bam released the hip-hop album *Planet Rock,* which changed not only hip-hop but also music in general. Bam called the new sound electro funk. He gave credit to James Brown, Parliament, and Sly and the Family Stone, musical groups that were popular during the 1960s and 1970s, the zenith of the BLACK ARTS MOVEMENT, as the sources of his musical inspira-

tion. By 1986 Bam and the Zulu Nation became global ambassadors, spreading hip-hop throughout the world by taking their first trip to Europe, where they performed in Paris and were eagerly received by European youth. Two years later, in 1988, Bam released the album *The Light,* on which he performed with Nona Hendryx, UB40, Boy George, George Clinton, Bootsy Collins, and Yellowman.

In 1990, *Life* magazine named Afrika Bambaataa one of the most important Americans of the 20th century. During this time he and other artists were hard at work fighting against apartheid in South Africa. He played an instrumental role in this effort by putting on a concert in London, which raised £30,000, for the African National Congress in support of the release of Nelson Mandela. Seven years later, in 1997, Bam founded his own record label, Planet Rock, and began disk jockeying at Hot 97, a New York–based radio station.

For the past 20 plus years, Bam has released at least one record every other year. He has been influential in the music careers of both hip-hop and rhythm-and-blues groups, including New Edition, QUEEN LATIFAH, MOS DEF, and many others.

BIBLIOGRAPHY

Banjoko, Adisa. "The Godfather Speaks: Up Close with Afrika Bambaataa." *Lyrical Swords.* Available online. URL: www.lyricalswords.com/articles/africabambaataa.html. Accessed February 14, 2007.

Alim BakenRa

Adams, Jenoyne   (n.d.)

Dancer, poet, journalist, and novelist Jenoyne Adams is a native Californian. Born the daughter of Virgil Adams and Bertha Degan Adams, she was raised in San Bernardino, California. She attended California State University at Fullerton, where she majored in political science, and she continued her studies at St. Mary's University, where she earned her first degree. Adams established a career as a journalist while working as a reporter for the *San Bernardino Reporter,* one of the largest African-American newspapers in Southern California.

Adams received critical acclaim with the publication of her first novel, *Resurrecting Mingus* (2001), which tells the story of Mingus Browning, a successful, young, beautiful lawyer whose personal, romantic life falls apart simultaneously with her parents' marriage after 35 years. Mingus must come to grips with the fact that her African-American father is leaving her Irish mother for a black woman. Mingus finds herself in a tripartite family whirlwind that threatens to tear her apart, as she must choose between the father she has always loved (she is a daddy's girl) and the mother she also loves and may have to defend during the divorce proceedings; all the while she endures the antics of her sister, Eva, with whom she has had a lifelong sibling rivalry.

Thus, in *Resurrecting Mingus,* Adams explores a variety of themes—including biracialism, sibling rivalry, parental relationships, love, trust, and infidelity—and the protagonist's efforts to confront these various issues directly as she attempts to experience, at a critical juncture in her own life when she must venture on a new quest for romantic wholeness (i.e., should she date black or white men), a variety of romantic relationships. Though race remains central in each of Mingus's relationships, what ultimately matters is her own psychological wholeness, which requires that she maintain a positive sense of self. She must confront her life of liminality, due largely to her biracial identity; find wholeness, including romantic wholeness; and embrace her total self. Although in this sense *Resurrecting Mingus* resonates thematically with TERRY MCMILLAN's novels, Adams was lauded by critics for her raw images and poetic prose. Describing it as a "stunning debut novel," the reviewer for *Booklist* praised Adams for her "vivid and direct" (910) style.

Adams's second novel, *Selah's Bed* (2003), explores issues of reconciliation and forgiveness. The story focuses on Selah Wells, who, though married to a pastor, Parker, continues to seek confirmation and fulfillment through sex. The victim of childhood neglect and abuse, Selah clearly suffers from issues of self-esteem. Her grandmother, Mama Gene, raised her because Ruthelen Mae, her biological mother, was addicted to drugs and consequently was only a fleeting presence in young Selah's life. Selah's need for affection leads to her exploitation and rape by the time she is 14. When she falls in love with Parker, a minister's son, and becomes pregnant out of wedlock, Selah struggles with the issue of abortion, its moral and personal implications. Although she turns to photography as a vehicle of empowerment through art, Selah is unable to transcend the childhood scars that leave her with an unfinished sense of self and the need for validation through sex. Although *Selah's Bed* is not as strong as *Resurrecting Mingus,* most critics agree that Adams is well on her way to becoming an important writer.

Adams is the recipient of the prestigious PEN USA Fellow award. Currently, she is a writing consultant for Voices in Harmony, an organization that helps at-risk and underserved youths write and produce plays on important social issues. She is married to novelist MICHAEL DATCHER and pursuing a master's degree in creative writing in the graduate program at University of Southern California.

Beverly A. Tate

Afrekete: An Anthology of Black Lesbian Writing   (1995)

Edited by Catherine E. McKinley and L. Joyce DeLaney and published by Doubleday and Co., Inc., *Afrekete: An Anthology of Black Lesbian Writing* brings together 20 selections of fiction, nonfiction, and poetry from women writing in the United States, Canada, the Caribbean, Australia, and Europe. *Afrekete* weaves together these seemingly divergent traditions and celebrates the multiplicity of voices and experiences of black lesbians in all their depth and variety while pointing critically to complicated and ever-changing considerations of black lesbian identity and experience.

The editors tease readers into remembering that black lesbians, like other people, have complex and remarkable stories in their lives. The notion that real lives and real stories, unlike the politics of identity, are not so simple that they can be told from one point of view or one mind is crucial to understanding this collection. Issues of race and sexual orientation inform the selections as they do life—unexpectedly but often joyously.

The title is taken from AUDRE LORDE's "Tar Beach," an excerpt from her biomythography *ZAMI: THE SPELLING OF MY NAME,* that introduces the character Afrekete. Afrekete is the mythical lover who is born in the South but migrates north to Harlem, where she appears in the life of young Audre, helping her collect the "journey-woman pieces of herself"—the immediate intersections of identity and experience—which allow her to chart a life course.

Lorde's work in this anthology—beginning with the autobiographical "Tar Beach," which chronicles the arrival of Afrekete into Audre's early gay life, and ending with her poem "Today Is Not the Day," written just months before her death in 1992—offers both dynamic form and thematic considerations to the 18 other voices speaking their stories.

Other contributors include Michelle Cliff, Carolivia Herron, Alexis DeVeaux, Jacqueline Woodson, SAPPHIRE, the activist and publisher Barbara Smith, Linda Villarosa (former executive editor of *ESSENCE*), and the filmmaker Michelle Parkerson.

BIBLIOGRAPHY

Ball, M. Charlene. "Old Magic and New Fury: the Theaphany of Afrekete in Audre Lorde's 'Tar Beach.'" *NWSA Journal* 13, no. 1 (2001): 61–85.

Janet Bland

African American Review

African American Review is one of the leading journals in African-American literary and cultural studies. It was established in 1967 as *Negro American Literature Forum,* published by the Indiana State University School of Education. Originally a mimeographed newsletter, it had an initial audience among teachers who were bringing black writing into the classroom, often for the first time. As John F. Bayliss, the founder and first editor, said in the inaugural issue, "Perhaps one of the most urgent features of Negro American Literature Studies at the moment is that they be popularized among teachers at all levels of education. At school level, integration of material is a 'must'; at college level, this latter point may be debatable" (1). Since Indiana State University was established as the state normal school, it is surprising that the journal had a pedagogical emphasis.

What is perhaps more surprising is that the first issue was oriented more toward an academic audience than its sources and editorial stance would suggest. In addition to a tribute to LANGSTON HUGHES by DARWIN TURNER, it included a short commentary by James A. Emanuel titled "The Future of Negro Poetry," two short articles on *NATIVE SON,* a checklist of African-American periodicals and journals, and a review by Blyden Jackson of Seymour Gross's *Images of the Negro in American Literature.* The list of contributors suggests that a group of scholars was already in place to help shape the critical development of the field by means of such a journal. Perhaps the most significant piece in the issue was "Some Queries about Negro American Literature" by J. S. Lowry. The questions it posed were crucial ones for literature that was often at that time associated with politics and social critique: What determines the category, the standards of evaluation, and the status within literature generally? These, of course, continue to be central issues for African-American literary analysis.

As the journal developed into a large-format publication under Bayliss and later Hannah Hedrick, it maintained its dual role as pedagogical resource and a site of professional criticism. The first major shift came in the spring 1977 issue, when Joseph Weixlmann became editor. He changed the name to *Black American Literature Forum,* reflecting a shift in perspective; moreover, all of the articles were analytical pieces clearly designed for an audience of literary critics. Academic book reviews were included, and special issues were introduced on CLARENCE MAJOR, fiction, and women writers.

In 1991, the journal received a Lila Wallace–Reader's Digest Foundation Grant to develop strategies for expanding its readership. One result was a change in name to *African American Review,* designed to reflect an expansion of the emphasis to incorporate African-American expressive culture generally. Out of this change came special issues on black music, jazz, the black church, and theater. In addition, the journal's cover made full-color use of the work of African-American visual artists. In addition to the Lila Wallace grant, *African American Review* has won three American Literary Magazine Awards for editorial content and several NEA grants, and it serves as the official publication of the Black American Literature Division of the Modern Language Association. In 2001, its base of operations was moved to St. Louis University; in 2004 Joycelyn Moody became editor.

BIBLIOGRAPHY

Bayliss, John F. "Editorial," *Negro American Literature Forum* 1, no. 1 (1967): 1.

Keith Byerman

Ai   (Florence Anthony) (1947–   )

Florence Anthony's discovery of the poet within herself began, she believes, at her birth on October 21, 1947, in Albany, Texas. While Florence Anthony was aware of the unique cultural background she inherited from her African-American, Choctaw, Irish, Dutch, and Southern Cheyenne mother, she was 26 when she learned about her Japanese father. As a result of this discovery and her lack of affinity with either African-American or white students at her integrated Catholic grade school, Florence Anthony became Ai, which means "love" in Japanese. To pursue her interest in and validate her newfound heritage, Ai earned her B.A. in Japanese from the University of Arizona in 1964 and developed her professional interest in poetry. In 1971, she earned an M.F.A. from the University of California at Irvine.

In her first collection of poems, *Cruelty* (1972), Ai introduced the style, a series of dramatic monologues, that continues to dominate her work. Equally important, however, are her diverse speakers, who deal with themes and subjects ranging from abortion to domestic violence, generally considered social taboos. The one thing these speakers have in common is their lower-class status and struggle for survival. Ai's honest portrayal of these personas and their thoughts often forces readers into the uncomfortable position of relating with the child abuser, the battered wife, or the father of an aborted child. Despite the harsh criticism she received for the violent nature and language of her work, Ai has not wavered from her use of graphic representations of violence and her focus on the body in her work for more than 20 years and seven texts.

Although similar to *Cruelty* in style, specifically in its use of dramatic monologues, Ai's second collection of poems, *Killing Floor* (1973), features disparate narrators. Instead of focusing on the voiceless, poverty-stricken, and socially ousted, *Killing Floor* features speakers who are popular cultural and historical icons: Marilyn Monroe, Leon Trotsky, and Ira Hayes. Other characters—a son who must deal with a senile father, a murderous 14-year-old boy, and a crazy Indian bride—have unusual qualities that color their experience and portrayals. Ai's use of genocide, cannibalism, necrophilia, and murder to connect private evils with public degradation continues in her next collection, *Sin* (1986). The religious overtone of the title draws together the diverse cast of speakers, ranging from John F. Kennedy to an unnamed priest, as each tries to justify his previous actions, rooted in a desire for power, and the need to escape the guilt associated with "sin." Viewed as a chorus, the speakers in *Sin* represent Ai's critique of the many institutions that she believes dominate society, especially religion and politics. In *Fate* (1991) and *Greed* (1993), Ai completes her undeclared objective of progressing from giving voice to the unnamed to speaking for the idols of American culture. However, the characters in these two collections, Elvis Presley, James Dean, and Jimmy Hoffa, do not speak as individuals; instead, they become the collective representation of American values.

While Ai's poetry has often earned harsh criticism, her plain, direct style has brought her accolades. Aside from winning the Bunting Fellowship, an American Book Award, a Guggenheim Fellowship, and the Lamont Prize, Ai's *Vice: New and Selected Poems* (1999) won the sought-after National

Book Award. Currently a professor at Oklahoma State University, where she is researching the history of her relatives, members of the Choctaw and Southern Cheyenne tribes in Oklahoma, Ai is planning to use this material to write a memoir.

BIBLIOGRAPHY

Ingram, Claudia. "Writing the Crises: The Development of Abjection in Ai's Dramatic Monologues." *LIT: Literature Interpretation Theory* 8, no. 2 (October 1997): 173–192.

Kilcup, Karen. "Dialogues of the Self: Toward a Theory of (Re)Reading Ai." *Journal of Gender Studies* 7, no. 1 (1998): 16–21.

Cassandra M. Parente

AIDS

The presence of AIDS in black literature, thematic, linguistic, and central to setting, can be read as part of a longer tradition of bearing witness to the calamities that have affected black people dating back to the transatlantic slave trade. Both contemporaneous autobiographical accounts of slavery by such authors as OLAUDAH EQUIANO and FREDERICK DOUGLASS and recent interpretations by TONI MORRISON (*BELOVED*, 1987) and CHARLES JOHNSON (*MIDDLE PASSAGE*, 1990) underscore the importance of understanding slavery as a test of black survival. Similarly, given the high incidences of AIDS in present-day black communities, texts in black literature that examine AIDS are similar to texts about slavery in speaking to the threat posed to black individuals and the community at large.

Black literature about AIDS is a form of truth telling. It involves being honest about a host of ills, namely homophobia, that are at the heart of black culture and life today. It is not surprising, then, that much of the black literature about AIDS has sprung from the pens of black gay men. Because their community has been decimated by the AIDS crisis, black gay men are determined to call to public attention their experiences as HIV-positive subjects, as well as on their relationships with individuals who have died from the disease.

Most writing about AIDS in black literature constitutes a political act whereby the author asserts his, generally speaking, gay identity proudly, in a fashion that does not detract from his blackness or his place in the black community. Authors such as MELVIN DIXON, Joseph Beam, and MARLON RIGGS have chronicled their efforts at successfully being part of both communities. That these individuals have also claimed HIV-positive identities is significant as well, since HIV/AIDS can be a taboo subject in black communities: A person with AIDS is often encouraged not to speak, and certainly not to write, about it. That these authors and others have defied this ideology is a testament not only to the viability of bearing witness to crisis but also to the importance of speaking truth to power.

AIDS in black literature takes many forms, from fiction to autobiography. Author E. LYNN HARRIS, whose work holds immense appeal in black communities, includes an AIDS plotline in his novel *Just as I Am* (1994). The entire second half of the novel is devoted to the story of Kyle Benton, best friend to the novel's protagonist, who learns he is HIV positive. Harris describes how Benton's friends care for him during his illness and up to the moment of his death. Benton remains an inspiring figure in this series of novels by Harris, even being reincarnated for a brief appearance at the conclusion of *Abide with Me* (1999), a later book in the series.

JAMES EARL HARDY is best known for the B-Boy Blues series of novels, the tale of two men falling in love in urban New York City. In *The Day Eazy-E Died* (2001), Hardy integrates an AIDS plotline into the narrative. The novel is set during two weeks in March 1995, when the central character Raheim, learns that one of his favorite rappers, Eazy-E, has developed AIDS and is dying. While Raheim grapples with this news, he is informed that his former lover David is in a Bronx hospital, also stricken with AIDS. In response, Raheim seeks HIV testing and counseling. This action mirrors that of many urban black youths, particularly black males, following the real-life HIV diagnosis and subsequent death of Eazy-E (Eric Wright).

The B-Boy Blues series is distinguished by the writing style Hardy uses, incorporating an abundance of slang, specifically hip-hop vernacular, to lend the books verisimilitude and street flavor. By virtue of their identification as B-Boy's (a term associated with break dancers in urban culture), the characters in his novels most likely would use this language; as a result, Hardy's linguistic code shifting is appropriate. Additionally, individuals who might not be inclined to read literature written solely in standard English are reading these books, and in the case of *The Day Eazy-E Died,* they are perhaps coming to a better understanding of AIDS pathology. This is how AIDS in black literature is an example of art that not only is political but also can save lives.

The popular science-fiction author SAMUEL DELANY also plays with the complexities of language in an attempt to incorporate AIDS into his work. For instance, in his novella *The Tale of Plagues and Carnivals, or: Some Informal Remarks towards the Modular Calculus, Part Five* (1985), Delany writes, "AIDS is like . . . the wrath of Khan" (187); Delany's statement has dire and potentially galvanizing meaning for fans of science fiction.

Perhaps no other black gay author has contributed more to discussions of AIDS in black literature than ESSEX HEMPHILL. Hemphill, who died from AIDS in 1995, wrote about the disease in a variety of forms, including poetry, performance pieces, and essays. In his poem "Now We Think," he details how the reality of AIDS has altered his sex practices. In the landmark film "Tongues Untied," he freely discusses his thoughts not only as a black gay man, but as a black gay man living with AIDS. One of Hemphill's more poignant comments on the culture and reality of AIDS is his essay "Does Your Mama Know About Me?," wherein he contends

Some of the best minds of my generation would have us believe that AIDS has brought the gay and lesbian community closer and infused it with a more democratic mandate. That is only a partial truth that further underscores the fact that the gay community still operates from a one-eyed, one-gender, one-color perception of "community" that is most likely to recognize blond before black but seldom the two together.

Some of the best minds of my generation believe AIDS has made the gay community a more responsible social construction, but what AIDS really manages to do is clearly point out how significant are the cultural and economic differences between us; differences so extreme that black men suffer a disproportionate number of AIDS deaths in communities with very sophisticated gay health care services. (40–41)

Although this essay was published more than a decade ago, it maintains relevance and currency, particularly in highlighting the socioeconomic disenfranchisement and racism prevalent in gay communities.

Although the *Norton Anthology of African American Literature* concludes with excerpts from Essex Hemphill's poetry, the chosen excerpts focus more on his black gay subjectivity than on his work on AIDS or his status as HIV positive. The bibliography prefacing those excerpts does not mention that he died from AIDS. Such avoidance is indicative of the silence surrounding AIDS in black communities, a silence to which Hemphill's work, and that of others contributing to discussions of AIDS in black literature, speaks.

Whether situated in a fictive narrative or discussed in the form of autobiography, AIDS in black literature is an indication that blacks are aware of the disease's reality and are creating art in response to it.

BIBLIOGRAPHY

Delany, Samuel R. *The Tale of Plagues and Carnivals, or: Some Informal Remarks towards the Modular Calculus, Part Five. Flight from Neveryon.* Hanover, N.H.: Wesleyan University Press, 1985.

Gates, Henry Louis, and Nellie Y. McKay, eds. *The Norton Anthology of African American Literature.* New York: W. W. Norton, 1997.

Hardy, James Earl. *The Day Eazy-E Died.* Los Angeles: Alyson, 2001.

Harris, E. Lynn. *Abide with Me.* New York: Double-day, 1999.

———. *Just as I Am.* New York: Doubleday, 1994.

Hemphill, Essex. *Ceremonies.* New York: Plume, 1992.

Chris Bell

Alexander, Will　(1948–　)

The poet, dramatist, essayist, and visual artist Will Alexander was born in Los Angeles, California, on July 27, 1948, to devout Christian parents Will Alexander, Sr., an employee of the Department of Water and Power, and Birdie Alexander. Although he was raised in the heart of South Central Los Angeles, at 116th Street and Avalon Boulevard, Alexander's parents moved before that location became the site of the 1965 Watts Rebellion. Not allowed to wander far from his mother's watch while his father was at work, Alexander spent a good deal of time playing safely alone for hours; perhaps this became the root of his steadfast, independent, and self-paced development as a fine artist. A graduate of Los Angeles's Washington High School, Alexander studied sociology at Harbor College and earned a B.A. in English and creative writing from University of California at Los Angeles, in 1972.

The Alexanders prevented Will, their only son, from reading anything but the Bible during his childhood. A slow learner, Alexander did not fully grasp reading until he was eight and a half; although he later discovered that this experience was typical of many black males, by age 11 he doubted his own intellectual ability. However, in his early teens, Alexander, who had grown tired of his parents' restriction, was repulsed by what he considered the superficiality of the churchgoers he knew. Left with a spiritual void, Alexander, like Arthur Rimbaud, whose work influenced him, concluded that he was being suffocated by his Christian beliefs. During his teenage years, Alexander became an avid reader of leftist political writings, played sports, and collected jazz albums. At 13, he first heard what he called the "planetary power" of Eric Dolphy, McCoy Tyner, John Coltrane, and Jackie McLean. At 16, his jazz collection, which grew to nearly 3,000 records over time, consisted of two albums—Cannonball Adderly's *Nippon Soul* and Coltrane's *Olé.*

Insatiably curious, Alexander educated himself by reading. His informal teachers were the painter Chaïm Soutine and surrealist writers Antonin Artaud, André Breton, BOB KAUFMAN, Philip Lamantia, and Octavio Paz. Listening to them, Alexander built his own energy circle, found his own voice, and wrote his first poem at 18. By the time he entered the University of California, he was writing daily. However, by the time he earned his degree, he had ceased writing, unable to consider himself a true writer. He chose instead to study independently art, music, and literature that, he was convinced, would provide him with the self-respectable level of artistic development he desired.

By 1987, when he published *Vertical Rainbow Climber,* his first collection of poems and drawings, Alexander had developed his own perspective on language, which, he concluded, must be simultaneously grounded and take flight, a combination that he could only achieve by working with palpable subject matter. He found support for this philosophy in the African concept of animism, which, grounded in the Nubian epistemology, teaches that everything is alive. Alexander came to see language as an agent of change that advances and heightens individual and collective consciousness for spiritual realignment to life.

Alexander has published, a collection of short fiction, *Arcane Lavender Morals* (1994); a play, *Conduction in the Catacombs* (1997); a collection of essays, *Towards the Primeval Lightning Field* (1999); and five collections of poetry: *Vertical Rainbow Climber* (1987), *The Stratospheric Canticles* (1995), *Asia and Haiti* (1995), and *Above the Human Nerve Domain* (1999).

Early on, critics described Alexander as the writer of "seeming nightmare idiom"; however, his publication in such literary journals as *CALLALOO, Exquisite Corpse, Hambone,* and *Sulfur* garnered a wider general readership and brought broader critical attention. In time, he would be called a surrealist, black postmodernist, neosurrealist, innovative American poet, supra-pan-African surrealist, experimental poet, a fine Black poet, and one of the greatest living poets.

In his works Alexander explores language, the transmutation of being through language, the philosophy of mathematics, the transmutation of leadership from adversarial to divine, dizzying alchemical movement, and the states of break-through, seepage, and blankness. In an introduction to Alexander's *Towards the Primeval Lightning Field,* Andrew Joron claims, "This pre-Romantic idea of the imagination as 'the link of links' still dwells in the thought and practice of Alexander. Here, the energy of the imagination has not yet been harnessed (as it would be in Romanticism) to the goals of bourgeois subjectivization."

Alexander's subsequent works include three collections of poems (*Impulse & Nothingness* [Green Integer], *Exobiology as Goddess* [2005, Manifest Press], and *Sri Lankan Loxodrome* [2002, Canopic Press]); a trilogy of novels, *Sunrise in Armageddon* [2006, Spuyten Duyvil]); the novella *Alien Weaving* (2002, Green Integer); and a collection of essays, *Singing in Magnetic Hoof-beat.* Alexander's visual artistry includes covers and illustrations for books and magazines, exhibitions, and privately collected paintings and drawings. In his hometown Los Angeles, as the lead artist for Theatre of Hearts/Youth First, he engages at-risk youngsters in finding their voice through the arts.

BIBLIOGRAPHY

Caples, Garrett. "The Impossibility of Will Alexander's Prose." *Facture* 2 (2001): 209–216.

———. "Is the Analysis Impure?" *Lingo* 7 (1997): 74–76.

Hejinian, Lyn, and David Lehman. *The Best American Poetry 2004.* New York: Simon & Schuster, 2004.

Koolish, Lynda. *African American Writers: Portraits and Visions.* Jackson: University Press of Mississippi, 2001.

Marshall, Kerry James. *Mementos.* Chicago: Renaissance Society at the University of Chicago, 1998.

Mullen, Harryette. "A Collective Force of Burning Ink: Will Alexander's *Asia & Haiti.*" *Callaloo* 22, no. 2 (1999): 417–426.

———. "Hauling up Gold from the Abyss: An Interview with Will Alexander." *Callaloo* 22, no. 2 (1999): 391–408.

Nielsen, Aldon Lynn. "Will Alexander's 'Transmundane Specific.'" *Callaloo* 22, no. 2 (1999): 409–416.

Tuma, Keith. "Noticings." *Sulfur* 39 (Fall 1996): 171–173.

Merilene M. Murphy

Allen, Jeffery Renard   (1962–   )

Born in Chicago, Illinois, Jeffery Renard Allen earned a B.A. (1986), an M.A. (1988), and a Ph.D. (1992), all in English, from the University of Illinois at Chicago. Since 1992, he has taught at Queens College of the City University of New York, where he specializes in African-American literature and creative writing.

In addition to a collection of poems, *Harbors and Spirits* (1999), Allen has published a number of individual and as yet uncollected poems in a number of magazines and journals, including CALLALOO, AFRICAN AMERICAN REVIEW, and the *Literary Review.* Allen has also published short fiction in journals such as the *Antioch Review* and the *Notre Dame Review.* In 2000, Allen published his debut novel, *Rails under My Back,* to wide critical acclaim, garnering the Whiting Writer's Award (2002), the *Chicago Tribune's* Heartland Prize for Fiction (2000), and the Pioneering Achievements in Fiction award from the African American Literature and Culture Society (2001). In addition, *Rails under My Back* was named a *New York Times* Notable Book (2000), was one of the Year's 25 Best Books in *The Village Voice* (2000), and was the *Chicago Tribune's* editor's pick among the Year's Best 10 Books (2000). *Rails* was also a selection of the Book-of-the-Month Club and the Quality Paperback Book Club for 2000. Subsequent works include a collection of poems titled *Stellar Places* as well as several fictional works.

Rails under My Back is a long family chronicle that focuses on the younger generation of the Griffith and Simmons families. However, it is more than just a fictional life story in the usual sense, for it contains a variety of literary elements that are frequently absent from much of the popular literature in contemporary America. These elements include storytelling in the black male tradition, a narrative complexity that ranks Allen among the best of the modern and postmodern literary stylists, and a concern for character and place that recalls some of the most significant works in the American literary canon. At the same time, Allen treads into the popular province of the comic and the violent, showing that he knows well the contemporary dimensions of the lives of the people about whom he writes.

The narrative voice is largely that of Hatch Jones, a present-generation character who tries to arrive at some sense of himself and his family in the aftermath of a painful past and as a victim of more recent familial fractures and dysfunction. Allen deals deftly with the Great Migration of blacks from South to North and the resulting changes in their economic and emotional fortunes. He also deals with contemporary urban plagues like drug abuse, intraracial crime and violence, and neighborhood blight that have devastated so many black families. What makes the devastation so intense for this family is that members of the present generation have received double doses of heritage: Their fathers are brothers who married two sisters. The tragedy associated with all these occurrences is most clearly seen in the life of Hatch's double first cousin, Jesus Jones, a proverbial lost child in the jungle of drugs, alcohol, and violence, reminiscent of CLAUDE BROWN's character in *Manchild in the Promised Land*.

Stylistically, there is a mélange of narrative styles that are often complex and nonlinear. Sometimes other characters intrude on Hatch Jones's narration; at other times, a newspaper clipping, a page torn from a Bible, or an obituary notice propels the narrative. Often, an omniscient narrator provides clarity or, more often than not, deliberately adds greater confusion. Just as frequently, lines blur between people and places. Allen handles all of these strategies with great skill. The text also confirms that Allen is a lover of words and of storytelling in its most artistic sense.

Thematically, Allen explores the results of deferred dreams in the context of the African-American quest for America's promise. Other themes include the importance of the extended family, suffering, reconciliation, and the journey toward fulfillment. Moreover, the South as a touchstone for African Americans figures prominently in the novel. Allen is clearly aware of the African-American literary tradition, and he is deeply rooted in the elements of the culture.

BIBLIOGRAPHY

Carson, Warren J. Review of *Rails under My Back. AALCS Newsletter* 6, no. 1 (May 2002): 5–6.

Channer, Colin. Review of *Rails under My Back. Minneapolis Star Review*, April 2000.

Tate, Greg. Review of *Rails under My Back. Village Voice Literary Supplement*, February 2000.

Warren J. Carson

Angelou, Maya   (née Margeurite Johnson) (1928–   )

Acclaimed for her serial autobiographies, poetry, and public performance lectures, Maya Angelou was born Marguerite Johnson in Saint Louis, Missouri, to Bailey Johnson, a navy dietitian, and Vivian Johnson, a cocktail hostess. In 1931 Maya and her brother, Bailey, were sent to Stamps, Arkansas, to live with their grandmother, Annie Henderson. Later, in 1936, while living in St. Louis, Angelou was raped by her mother's boyfriend, who was subsequently found kicked to death in a vacant lot. Fearing her confession had literally killed him, she became ill and was sent back to Stamps suffering from voluntary mutism. During this time she read prodigiously and discovered poetry. In 1944 she dropped out of high school in San Francisco, where she lived with her mother; worked as the first black trolley car conductor; and gave birth to her son, Guy. She married Tosh Angelou in 1949, later worked as a singer at the Purple Onion nightclub in San Francisco, and soon thereafter dissolved the marriage. She toured Europe from 1954 to 1955 with the Everyman's Opera Company's production of *Porgy and Bess,* joined the Harlem Writers Guild in 1959, worked as the northern coordinator for the Southern Christian Leadership Conference in 1960, and helped write and produce, in collaboration with Godfrey Cambridge, the famous fundraiser *Cabaret for Freedom.*

In 1961 Angelou moved to Africa with Vusumzi Make, an African freedom fighter; as that relationship began to fail, she worked at the University of Ghana, the Ghanaian Broadcast Corporation, and eventually at the *Ghanian Times.* In 1970, after the publication of *I Know Why the Caged Bird Sings,* she became a writer-in-residence at the University of Kansas, received a Yale University Fellowship, and, in 1973, married Paul Du Feu. That marriage ended in 1980. Maya Angelou has been a cook, streetcar conductor, BLUES singer, dancer, madam, actress, activist, teacher, playwright, writer, film director, television writer, producer, acclaimed public lecturer, autobiographer, poet, and writer of children's literature. She has produced six serial autobiographies, numerous books of poetry, recordings, film scripts, screenplays, essays, and children's books.

Beginning in 1970 with the acknowledged literary classic *I Know Why the Caged Bird Sings,* she published more than 30 books, including *Just Give Me a Cool Drink of Water 'Fore I Die* (1971), *Gather in My Name* (1974), *Oh Pray My Wings Are Gonna Fit Me Well* (1975), *Singin' and Swingin' and Gettin' Merry like Christmas* (1976), *And Still I Rise* (1978), *Phenomenal Woman* (1978), *The Heart of a Woman* (1981), *Shaker, Why Don't You Sing* (1983), *All God's Children Need Traveling Shoes* (1986), *Poems: Maya Angelou* (1986), *I Shall Not Be Moved* (1990), "On the Pulse of the Morning" (1993; poem delivered at President Bill Clinton's inauguration), *Wouldn't Take Nothing for My Journey Now* (1993), *The Complete Collected Poems of Maya Angelou* (1994), *A Brave and Startling Truth* (1995), *Even the Stars Look Lonesome* (1997), and *A Song Flung Up to Heaven* (2003). In addition, Angelou's children's stories include *Mrs. Flowers* (1986), *Life Does Not Frighten Me* (1993), *My Painted House, My Friendly Chicken, and Me* (1994), and *Kofi and His Magic* (1996).

Angelou has been a prolific film script and screenplay writer. Her list of achievements in this category include *Cabaret for Freedom* (1960; musical review written and produced in collaboration with Godfrey Cambridge), *The Least of These* (1966; two-act drama), *Blacks, Blues, Black* (1968; PBS documentary), *All Day Long* (1974; film script, American Film Institute), *The Legacy* (1976; Afro-American Television Special), *The Inheritors* (1976; Afro-American Television Special), *I Know Why the Caged Bird Sings* (1979; with Leonora Thuna, film), *Sister, Sister* (1982; drama for NBC-TV), and *Down in the Delta* (1990; film director). She also has a music CD, *Music, Deep Rivers in My Soul* (2003).

Angelou's poetics are informed by her public persona and several uniquely African and African-American models: the African griot who performs public poetic utterance on behalf of the group, the African-American preacher, and the civil and women's rights political apologists. Academicians and purists who fail to understand her style consistently devalue her poetry as too popular, too propagandistic, and too public. Most have failed to take seriously "On the Pulse of the Morning," one of her best-known poems, as a highly performative postcolonial protest poem that speaks back powerfully to the white male poet Robert Frost, her predecessor, whose universal "We" she displaces with her catalog of vastly different American auditors such as "The Sioux" and "The Catholic." The poems most beloved by her readers and listeners are "And Still I Rise" and "Phenomenal Woman," now much anthologized and reprinted. Critics of Angelou's poetry who judge it from within the rhetorical traditions of African and African-American cultural traditions generally appreciate the orality, representationality, and public dimension of her poetry far more than those for whom poetry is an individualist academic genre privately read and privately experienced.

Most significant are Angelou's serial autobiographies. Since there is no precedent in American literary history of a writer, white or black, whose predominant contribution to American letters is in serial autobiographical form, the literary establishment seems confused as to how to evaluate this literary phenomenon and its popularity. Taken together, the six volumes stage the ethnogenesis of a representative 20th-century black female consciousness. *I Know Why the Caged Bird Sings* (1970), published when Angelou was 41 years old, garnered impressive academic reviews and marked a new era in black consciousness with its rehearsal of black femininity and the dignity of southern black lives lived amidst appalling racism and economic peonage. *Gather Together in My Name* (1974) presents Maya as a young black woman struggling for economic and emotional security in segregated post–World War II America, and *Singin' and Swingin' and Gettin' Merry like Christmas* (1976) shows her married and raising a child in the 1950s, trying to establish a career on the stage, and regularly encountering mainstream white racism. *The Heart of a Woman* (1980) shows a mature Maya who is mostly accounting for her roles as black mother and black woman. *All God's Children Need Traveling Shoes* (1986) presents Maya the poet, musician, and performer as a journalist in Ghana and as an expatriate exploring the promises of Pan-Africanism among black American returnees. Perhaps the most literary of these works since her first autobiography, this volume forges links with her ancestors and the slave past. It also records the history of the "lost generation" of African-American expatriates in Ghana and provides portraits of many African dignitaries in the Nkrumah era, in the midst of an African cultural renaissance. Though Angelou's search for an African identity ultimately eludes her, she nevertheless finds the accepting spiritual presence of her slave ancestors. *A Song Flung Up to Heaven* (2002), the sixth volume, begins with her return from Africa to work with MALCOLM X, her miserable sojourn in Hawaii after his assassination; her recruitment by MARTIN LUTHER KING; her experience of King's assassination; her presence in Watts, Los Angeles, during the riots; and her move to New York to find her way as a writer among such black intellectuals as JAMES BALDWIN, PAULE MARSHALL, ROSA GUY, Abbey Lincoln, and Max Roach. This volume is a *künstlerroman* containing the account of her beginnings as a writer during the height of the BLACK ARTS MOVEMENT as she began working on the manuscript of *I Know Why the Caged Bird Sings*.

Angelou's autobiographies mostly follow the classic pattern of black autobiography: the journey out, the quest, the achievement, and the return home. All six of her serial first-person narratives arise directly from the aesthetics and traditions of the slave narrative, the blues, the contemporary African-American journey narrative, and formal autobiography. Each is characterized by an affirmative pattern of moral growth and the reconstruction of the collective myth of black female identity. As blues traveler she confronts being afraid and bereft through sheer style and courage and offers picaresque progression experiences. Her sympathies range across history, class, color lines, communities, and whole continents. Recurring themes include the role of the black mother, eternal nostalgia for home, racial wounds, racial freedom, sister friends, the call of Africa, the slave presence, black female sexuality, WOMANIST values, dramatic confrontations, and accumulating wisdom. The volumes all merge history, fact, fiction, poetry, and religious experience. She always provides a clear map of the inner racial surfaces of American cultural history. Her gifted prose combines remarkable metaphors, rich dialogues, vivid street scenes, brilliant social portraiture, memorable anecdotes, self-parody, and spiritual insights. However, her enduring project is the ethnogenesis of black womanhood. She is credited with developing serial autobiography as a significant literary form within American letters.

Angelou has received more than 20 honorary degrees from such prestigious academic institutions as Brandeis University, Brown University, University of South Carolina, University of North Carolina at Greensboro, Lawrence University, Wake Forest University, University of Durham, and Columbia University. Her long list of awards, fellowships, and recognitions include a Rockefeller Foundation Fellowship; the *Ladies' Home Journal* Woman of the Year Award, 1975; a lifetime appointment as the Reynolds Professor of American

Studies at Wake Forest University (1981); inaugural poet for President Bill Clinton (1993); the United States of America, Congressional Record, 104th Congress, House of Representatives, Tribute to Maya Angelou by the Honorable Kweisi Mfume, Maryland Congressman (1996); the Board of Governors, University of North Carolina, "Maya Angelou Institute for the Improvement of Child & Family Education" at Winston-Salem State University, Winston-Salem, North Carolina (1998); lifetime membership to the National Women's Hall of Fame (2002); a Grammy for Best Spoken Word Album (1994); the Spingarn Award, NATIONAL ASSOCIATION FOR THE ADVANCEMENT OF COLORED PEOPLE (1994); the Southern Christian Leadership Conference of Los Angeles & Martin Luther King, Jr. Legacy Association National Award (1996); The New York Black 100, Schomburg Center & The Black New Yorkers (1996); the Black Caucus of American Library Association, Cultural Keepers Award (1997); a Lifetime Achievement Award for Literature (1999), and the Presidential Medal of Arts (2000).

Angelou currently maintains a rigorous writing, teaching, lecturing, performing, consulting, and media appearance schedule.

Gloria L. Cronin

Annie John   Jamaica Kincaid (1983)

At the end of JAMAICA KINCAID's short novel, *Annie John,* the heroine, Annie, whose coming-of-age story the novel records, explains, while describing her parents, "I suppose I should say that the two of them made me with their own hands. For most of my life, when the three of us went anywhere together I stood between the two of them or sat between the two of them. But then I got too big. . . . And so now they are together and here I am apart. I don't see them now the way I used to, and I don't love them now the way I used to. . . . [I]t is I who have changed" (133). Metamorphosis, growth, change, independence, and rebirth are the central themes of this bildungsroman, which begins with the heroine's concern and curiosity

about death and ends with her emergence as a 17-year-old who embarks on a journey from Antigua, her island home, to England, the motherland of British subjects like Annie.

Annie is the love (and only) child of Annie, her mother, and Alexander John, who is 35 years older than his wife. Through age 12, Annie is the apple of her parents' eyes, and her mother particularly dotes on her, attempting literally to shape and mold her, gently caressing and kissing her daily when she returns home from school. "I was ever in her wake," Annie states. "When my eyes rested on my father, I didn't think very much of the way he looked. But when my eyes rested on my mother, I found her beautiful" (18), Annie confesses. Annie sleeps in a bed her carpenter father made for her, and she wears clothes her mother, a seamstress, had sewn just for her.

Throughout her childhood and early teenage years, Annie is thoroughly baptized in the dual cultures that form her legacy. She eats breadfruit, banana fritters, pepper pot, salt fish, and porridge; she celebrates Queen Victoria's birthday and reads the works of John Milton. She develops special friendships with Gweneth and The Red Girl, while navigating through and mastering with ease the established colonial educational system imposed on the Antiguan natives, literally sitting at the head of her class as prefect, winning the respect and envy of her uniform-clad peers in her all-girl school. She observes her parents making love and learns about her own sexuality. She observes, but does not quite understand, obeah, the traditional African religion practiced by her parents and particularly by her maternal grandmother, who comes to their home when Annie is sick to heal her with traditional folk medicine.

As in the stories in Kincaid's *At the Bottom of the River* (1983) and her autobiographical novel, *The Autobiography of My Mother* (1996), ever present in *Annie John* is the heroine's alienation from her community, parents, and particularly her mother. The tension in their mother-daughter relationship becomes tangible by Annie's 12th birthday, when her previously doting mother ("when I gave her herbs, she might stoop down and kiss me on my lips and then on my neck" [25]) begins ushering her from the self-created safety of childhood (she hid her favorite books and the marbles she was not allowed to play with under her house) into adolescence and young womanhood—into "young lady business" (27). When Annie seeks to have a dress made from the same material as her mother's, as she had always done, her mother tells her; "It is time you had your own clothes. You just cannot go around the rest of your life looking like a little me" (26). When her mother sees Annie talking to a group of boys after school one day, she calls her a slut, to which Annie responds, "like mother like daughter" (102).

At the end of the novel, Annie's parents provide or perform the appropriate rituals—bathing, dressing, braiding her hair, eating, and so forth—necessary to complete her rites of passage into young womanhood. As she walks through her village to the ship that will take her away, Annie passes the significant sites where, as a novice, she had been guided and shaped by the appropriate ritual priests/priestess: Miss Dulcie's (the seamstress), the schoolhouse, church (where she had been christened), the store, the pharmacy (where she had gone on errands for her mother), the doctor's office, the bank (where she had saved her weekly allowance). She recalls, "As I passed all these places, it was as if I were in a dream. . . . I didn't feel my feet touch ground, I didn't even feel my own body" (143). Upon parting, Annie's mother proudly tells her, "Of course, you are a young lady now, and we won't be surprised if in due time you write to say that one day soon you are to be married" (136). Annie curtly responds, "How absurd!" (136).

Reviewing *Annie John* for the *New York Times Book Review,* Susan Kenney wrote, "I can't remember reading a book that illustrates [the results of growing up] more poignantly than *Annie John.* . . . [Annie John's] story is so touching and familiar it could be happening in Anchorage, so inevitable it could be happening to any of us, anywhere, any time, any place. And that's exactly the book's strength, its wisdom and its truth" (Kenney, 7).

BIBLIOGRAPHY

Kenney, Susan. Review of *Annie John. New York Times Book Review,* 17 April 1985, p. 6ff.
Kincaid, Jamaica. *Annie John.* New York: Farrar, Straus and Giroux, 1985.

Wilfred D. Samuels

Another Country   **James Baldwin** (1962)

Divided into three sections, Baldwin's third novel, *Another Country,* begins by introducing Rufus Scott, a black jazz musician who mysteriously commits suicide by the end of the first section, although he remains the focus of the narrative throughout the remaining two sections. In the end, *Another Country* is a novel about sexual and racial identities. Rufus Scott, who is uncertain about his sexual orientation and frustrated by being a southern, black American male, is involved with Leona, a white southerner who is seeking to escape her failure as both wife and mother. Their physically and mentally debilitating and dysfunctional relationship, the consequence of poor self esteem, leads Scott to jump to his death from a bridge and to Leona's breakdown and institutionalization.

Baldwin develops *Another Country,* criticized for what was seen as its flawed form, around the life experiences of its richly eclectic characters, who, like Rufus, are also engaged in a process of self-discovery and, in Baldwinesque form, a process of finding meaningful love. Vivaldo, Rufus's best friend, is a struggling writer and former student and a friend of novelist Richard Salenski. Richard's socially conscious wife and the mother of their two boys, Cass, disillusioned by her husband's nominal success in writing a "popular" novel, has an affair with Eric, an actor from Alabama and Rufus's erstwhile lover. Eric, meanwhile, is awaiting the arrival of his current young homosexual lover, Yves, from France, where the two met while Eric was living abroad. Completing the group, Ida, Rufus's sister and Vivaldo's lover, has a short-lived affair with Ellis, the white promoter who promises to help get her singing career off the ground.

Baldwin exposes the characters' inability to connect with one another and links these failings to the inability of multiple races, sexualities, nationalities, and classes to establish common ground. The novel, vacillating between both time period and location, is set in Greenwich Village, Harlem, France, and Alabama. Using loosely connected, almost jazzlike episodes, the novel traces the multiple affairs—homosexual, heterosexual, bisexual, and interracial—of Rufus's surviving acquaintances as they attempt to understand and come to terms with his untimely death and simultaneously deal with their own shortcomings. The characters find redemption as they attempt to reconcile the failure of both Rufus's and their own dreams.

A distinctly postmodern work, Baldwin's intensely psychological novel serves as a testament to the difficulties of self-love while disrupting and challenging America's sexual and racial norms. Baldwin posits the idea of "another country" as an individually created locale, free of the restraints of time and place as well as socially constructed identities.

Because of the graphic representation of sexuality in *Another County,* Baldwin was the subject of an FBI investigation following the complaints it received from numerous American readers. Further, many critics have argued that the distorted identities of the characters are a direct result of Baldwin's inability to define his own boundaries. Notably, Robert A. Bone cites Baldwin's narcissism for the failure of the characters in *Another Country.* He contends that the author "does not know where his own psychic life leaves off and that of his characters begins" (236). However, Charles Newman, comparing Baldwin to Henry Adams, places *Another Country* within the larger spectrum of the American literary tradition. According to Newman, in *Another Country,*

the legend of America as refuge for the oppressed, opportunity for the pure in heart, is invoked only to be exposed. From the very first, [Baldwin] is saying our vision has been parochial. We have not accounted for the variety of man's motives, the underside of our settlers, the costs of a new life. . . . If *Another Country* is formless, it is so because it rejects the theories of history available to it. (97)

BIBLIOGRAPHY

Bone, Robert A. *The Negro Novel in America.* New Haven, Conn.: Yale University Press, 1965.

Newman, Charles. "The Lesson of the Master: Henry James and James Baldwin." In *James Baldwin; A Collection of Critical Essays,* edited by Keneth Kinnamon, 52–65. Englewood Cliffs, N.J.: Prentice Hall, Inc., 1974.

Ohi, Kevin. "'I'm not the boy you want': Sexuality, 'Race' and Thwarted Revelations in Baldwin's *Another Country.*" *African American Review* 33 (1999): 261–281.

Tuhkanen, Miko. "Binding the Self: Baldwin, Freud and the Narrative of Subjectivity." *GLQ: A Journal of Lesbian and Gay Studies* 7 (2001): 553–591.

David Shane Wallace

Ansa, Tina McElroy   (1949–   )

Novelist Tina McElroy Ansa was born in Macon, Georgia, on November 18, 1949. After graduating from Spelman College (1971), Ansa worked for the *The Atlanta Journal-Constitution* and the *Charlotte Observer.* Since 1990 she has been a writer-in-residence at Spelman and freelance writer for magazines and newspapers, including *ESSENCE, Ms.,* and *The Los Angeles Times.* In 1978, she married Jone'e Ansa, a filmmaker. They reside in St. Simons Island, Georgia, and have one daughter.

Though she has written in several genres, Ansa is best known for her fiction, which is set in the southern fictional town of Mulberry, Georgia. Her first novel, *Baby of the Family* (1989), is the coming-of-age story of Lena McPherson. Born with a caul—a veil left by the membrane of the amniotic sac, which, according to folk belief, endows its owner with second sight—Lena is able to see and communicate with ghosts. Familiar with this folk belief, the delivery nurse gives Lena's mother,

Nellie, a tea to protect Lena from being plagued by her gift. However, dismissing the belief as mere superstition, Nellie discards the tea and caul. As a result, Lena is troubled by ghostly visits through which, in the end, she learns about African-American traditions and folk medicine. *The New York Times* named *Baby of the Family* a "Notable Book of the Year" in 1989, and the Ansas are converting this novel into a film.

Ansa's second novel, *Ugly Ways* (1993), is told largely through flashbacks. After the death of Esther "Mudear" Lovejoy, her husband and their three daughters attempt to recall memories of her. During the early years of Mudear's marriage, her husband physically and emotionally abused her. Eventually, to retaliate, Mudear refuses to work, forcing her daughters fundamentally to raise themselves, thereby becoming independent. Although she is already dead at the beginning of the novel, Mudear's spirit eavesdrops on her daughters' conversations about her. Mudear's ghostly presence accentuates her influence and emotional hold over her daughters. Ansa confirms that her intention was to make Mudear a character who subverts prevailing stereotypes about African-American mothers. She states, "I wanted to see more complexity. What happens if you don't have this strong kind of mother?" (Peterson 54). Ansa was nominated for a NATIONAL ASSOCIATION FOR THE ADVANCEMENT OF COLORED PEOPLE Image Award and the African American Blackboard List named the novel Best Fiction in 1994.

In Ansa's third novel, *The Hand I Fan With* (1996), readers are reunited with Lena McPherson, now a single, 45-year-old wealthy businesswoman. When Lena and Sister, her best friend from New Orleans, conjure a man, Herman, a ghost who has protected Lena from bad ghosts all her life, answers the call. Through her relationship with Herman, Lena is able to have an erotic spiritual experience and to conquer the powers of the veil, which had made it impossible for her to be intimate with men. Lena adored and admired her mother, but like the other Lovejoy women, she too must overcome the error of her mother's judgment.

Like *Baby of the Family* and *Ugly Ways*, which deals with family conflicts, Ansa's novel *You Know*

Better (2002) is the story of three generations of women, the Pines. LaShawndra is a sexually promiscuous 18-year-old who runs away from home. Sandra, her mother, is more concerned with her looks, her romantic relationship, and her career than she is about her daughter. Sandra does not search for her daughter, but Lily, LaShawndra's grandmother, does. As in the other novels, ghosts' visits play a significant role in guiding the living in *You Know Better*. Also, Ansa continues to empower her female characters by giving each one, through the narrative technique, a distinct voice.

Although not purely autobiographical, Ansa admits that her work "is informed by where I come from and who I am" (Montgomery). She admits further that her mother, Nellie—who has the same name as Lena McPherson's mother—has influenced her art. Of her narrative technique, Ansa says, "my literary voice [is] my 'mother language'. . . . [It] was through my mother's voice that I learned language could be funny, that it could be painful, that it could be sympathetic, biting, stinging, that it could be wise" (Ansa, 194). This "mother language" is reflected in her four novels. Ansa's talent is her ability to present strikingly realistic portraits of supernatural entities and events, to construct picturesque settings, and to reveal the emotional complexities of middle- to upper-class African-American women.

BIBLIOGRAPHY

Ansa, Tina McElroy. "Finding Our Voice." *Essence,* May 1995, pp. 194–195.

Montgomery, Georgene Bess. "Author Interview." bookreporter.com. Available online. URL: http://www.readinggroupguides.com/guides3/you_know_better2.asp#interview. Accessed September 28, 2006.

Peterson, V. R. "Tina McElroy Ansa a Real Mother's Tale." *Essence,* December 1993, p. 54.

Tara Green

Attaway, William   (1911–1986)

Novelist and scriptwriter William Attaway was born in Greenville, Mississippi, on November 19,

1911. His parents, William and Florence Attaway, both professional people, a doctor and teacher, respectively, relocated to Chicago in 1916. There Attaway began writing, later attending the University of Illinois, where he graduated in 1936.

Attaway's earliest forays into imaginative literature included plays written for his sister Ruth's theater group and the draft of a novel that was refused by his college dean in lieu of the prescribed academic work. Later, Attaway had a play, *Carnival* (1935), produced at the University of Illinois, and his short story "The Tale of the Blackamoor" appeared in Dorothy West's *Challenge* in 1936.

Attaway is best known for his two novels, *Let Me Breathe Thunder* (1939) and *Blood on the Forge* (1941). Both reflect the proletariat concerns of the period, but neither work achieved much public success. The most striking feature of *Let Me Breathe Thunder* is that its central characters, Step and Ed, are white. They are rootless men in search of their dreams and no doubt the kinds of men Attaway encountered during his days as a hobo while on hiatus from college during the early 1930s. The novel is narrated by Ed who picks up their story as they are leaving New Mexico en route to Seattle with a young Mexican boy, Hi Boy, who adopts Step and Ed as his guardians. Much of the narrative concerns the experiences of the rootless as they seek to establish some permanence in their lives. Theirs is a harsh world of like-minded men who live precariously from day to day, working hard, living hard, and often dying hard without ever realizing their dreams. In the case of Step and Ed, the harshness of their lives is, over time, tempered by their care of and concern for Hi Boy, whom they eventually lose to a tragic death.

Let Me Breathe Thunder bears a striking resemblance in subject matter and tone to one of its contemporaries, Steinbeck's *Of Mice and Men.* Additionally, the novel was no doubt informed by Attaway's own experiences on the road as well as his involvement in the Federal Writers Project. However, Attaway brings to bear on the novel's situation a dual perspective of rootlessness—having been black and a hobo—that lifts the novel well above the derivative or simply a tract of the period.

Blood on the Forge, Attaway's second novel, in many ways furthers the author's interest in the restlessness of the human spirit. Moreover, the novel is indeed protest fiction, but protest fiction that is artistically rendered. Here race is a prime factor: The three brothers, Big Mat, Chinatown, and Melody Moss, are doubly victimized by their race and class. In the novel, Attaway focuses on the more negative aspects of the sharecrop system in the South and the equally damning aspects of life in the North on the other side of the Great Migration. The brothers' physical and spiritual destruction at the hands of freedom shows the novel's strong kinship to Richard Wright's *Native Son,* which clearly both influenced and overshadowed *Blood on the Forge.* Still, *Blood on the Forge* is an important portrayal of the effects of rootlessness on African Americans who cast their lots with life in the so-called "promised land" of the North; again, Attaway's dual perspective on rootlessness informs the work significantly.

Because neither novel sold well, Attaway abandoned novel writing in favor of writing musical compositions and scripts for various media, including "One Hundred Years of Laughter," a 1966 television special on black humor. An additional short story, "Death of a Rag Doll," appeared in 1947, and shortly before his death in 1986 Attaway had completed work on the script for "The Atlanta Child Murders." Regardless of genre, Attaway's work is that of a perfectionist. In general, his narratives are unencumbered by subplots, and he demonstrates a high level of sophistication in weaving together protest and symbolic imagery. Also, Attaway's importance as a chronicler of the Great Migration should not go unnoted. As one of the several black writers who dealt with that aspect of African-American life, Attaway stands out for his sophisticated handling of literary naturalism through his black characters.

BIBLIOGRAPHY

Carson, Warren J. "Four Black American Novelists, 1935–1941." Master's thesis, Atlanta University, 1975.

Klotman, Phyllis R. "An Examination of Whiteness on Blood on the Forge." *CLAJ* 16 (1974): 101–109.

Young, Stanley. "Tough and Tender: Review of Let Me Breathe Thunder." *New York Times Book Review,* 25 June 1939.

Warren J. Carson

Aubert, Alvin   (1930–   )

Poet, playwright, founder of the black literary journal *Obsidian,* editor, publisher, and literary critic Alvin Aubert was born in Lutcher, Louisiana, on March 12, 1930. He was the youngest of Albert and Lucille Roussel Aubert's seven children. At age 14, he dropped out of high school and later joined the U.S. Army, where he remained until 1954. In 1947, he completed his high school general equivalency diploma and in 1955 entered Southern University in Baton Rouge, Louisiana, where he received his B.A. in English in 1959. A year later, he earned his M.A. in English from the University of Michigan and later pursued two years of graduate work at the University of Illinois. An educator since 1960, Aubert has taught African-American literature and creative writing at Southern University in Baton Rouge, the University of Illinois, the University of Oregon, and the State University of New York, Fredonia. Currently, he is professor emeritus at Wayne State University in Detroit, where he taught creative writing and African-American literature and served two years as interim chair of the department of Africana studies; he lives with his wife, Bernadine Tenant.

In 1975, Aubert founded and edited the journal *Obsidian: Black Literature in Review,* which provided many aspiring writers in the 1970s and 1980s an opportunity to publish their works. The editorial board included Kofi Awooner, ERNEST GAINES, Blyden Jackson, SAUNDERS REDDING, and DARWIN T. TURNER. After it ceased publication in 1982, the journal was reissued as *Obsidian II* in 1986. *Obsidian III: Literature in the African Diaspora* is now a semiannual journal of contemporary poetry, fiction, drama, and nonfiction prose aimed at publishing works in English by and about writers of African descent. Housed at North Carolina State University, this outstanding journal, under the leadership of Joyce Pettis and its former editors, Gerald Barrax and Afaa M. Weaver, continues to debut the works of many scholars and creative writers worldwide.

An award-winning poet, Aubert has published his work in a number of journals and anthologies since 1966. Though he was criticized in the 1970s for not embracing the BLACK ARTS MOVEMENT, his poetry is nevertheless distinguished by his attention to craft and his focus on personal experiences, rich in the use of Louisiana folk culture and diction. His first poetry collection, *Against the Blues* (1972), deals with his childhood in Louisiana, and *Feeling Through* (1975) reflects on military experiences, knowledge of African-American writing, and adolescence. Of his second volume, Jerry Ward observes that the poems "are informed by clarity, wit, and the easy rhythmic flow of human speech" (2). Both *South Louisiana: New and Selected Poems* (1985) and *If Winter Come: Collected Poems, 1967–1992* (1994) include a diverse range of experiences. His latest collection, *Harlem Wrestler, and Other Poems* (1995), incorporates many of his previous themes and continues with personal reflections on national holidays, retirement, self-awareness, and maturing romance.

Aubert has received numerous awards, grants, and honors. At the University of Michigan he was a Woodrow Wilson Fellow in 1959, a 1968 Bread Loaf Scholar in poetry, and a recipient of two creative writing fellowship grants from the National Endowment for the Arts for his poetry in 1973 and 1981. He also received an Editors Fellowship Grant in 1979 from the Coordinating Council of Literary Magazines to publish *Obsidian* and received the 1988 *CALLALOO* Award for his contribution to African-American cultural expression. In 2001 he was the inaugural recipient of the Xavier Activist for the Humanities Award.

Aubert has donated his papers and records of *Obsidian* dating from its founding in 1975 to Xavier University Library of New Orleans. In addition, he has given more than 2,500 volumes on the creative writing of African Americans, one of the largest gifts by a single donor, and many rare books published by the now-defunct BROADSIDE PRESS of Detroit.

BIBLIOGRAPHY

Martin, Herbert Woodward. "Alvin Aubert: *South Louisiana: New and Selected Poems.*" *Black American Literature Forum* 21, no. 3 (Fall 1987): 343–348.

Ward, Jerry W., Jr. "Alvin Aubert: Literature, History, Ethnicity." *Xavier Review* 7, no. 2 (1987): 1–12.

Loretta G. Woodard

Autobiography of An Ex-Colored Man, The
James Weldon Johnson (1912)

When the unnamed protagonist and narrator of James Weldon Johnson's *Autobiography of an Ex-Colored Man* discovers he is categorized as "colored," the realization, he explains, marks "the miracle of my transition from one world into another" (785). The son of a light-skinned African-American mother and a white, Southern father, the narrator finds himself subject to the prejudices of a caste system that categorizes any person with "one drop" of black blood as African-American. Johnson uses his protagonist's precarious racial position to explore American race relations in the early 20th century. As Johnson develops the racial tension of the novel, he also probes the psychological effects this tension has on the narrator's identification with both the white and black races.

After his schoolteacher publicly identifies him as a Negro, the narrator is cast out from the circle of white children and is unwilling to consort with the black children; instead, he develops an absorbing passion for the piano as a means of alleviating his loneliness. The narrator carries these two legacies of his childhood—racial alienation and musical interest—with him as he journeys through the United States and Europe in search of a satisfying life. He seeks an identity through different roles in a variety of black communities: as a student at Atlanta University, a cigar maker in the middle class black community of Jacksonville, Florida, a master ragtime player in the black New York nightclub scene; and finally, a collector of black folk music in rural Georgia. Certain attitudes and actions of the narrator, however, suggest his unwillingness to identify fully with African Americans. The black underclass of Atlanta, for example, unsettles him, as does the sight of a white woman with a dark-skinned black man in a New York nightclub. Likewise, although he reaches the pinnacle of black folk culture as the best ragtime player in New York, he plays for predominantly white audiences before accompanying a white benefactor to Europe as his personal pianist.

A renewed commitment to African Americans and African-American culture briefly leads the narrator back to the South, where he hopes to help uplift the black race by collecting folk songs. However, when he witnesses the brutal lynching of a black man in Macon, Georgia, and the "shame at being identified with a people that could with impunity be treated worse than animals" (853), he leaves the South. Returning to New York, he successfully passes into the white community, adopts its goal of making money, marries a white woman, and raises two children who know nothing of their racial heritage. The novel concludes with the narrator thinking admiringly of the dedicated African-American activists and wondering wistfully whether he has "chosen the lesser part" by selling his "birthright for a mess of pottage" (861).

Published anonymously and with little fanfare in 1912, *The Autobiography of an Ex-Colored Man* sold poorly. When Johnson republished the novel in 1927—this time with his authorship acknowledged and the British spelling "coloured" in the title—it was more widely read and more warmly received. Published at the peak of the Harlem Renaissance, the second edition found a reading public that was more attuned to the issues Johnson addressed. Indeed, the novel had anticipated a number of the concerns of the Harlem Renaissance, including the celebration of African-American folk culture, a vibrant black urban life emerging in the North, and the struggle toward an African-American racial identity. More important, with the portrayal of a light-skinned African-American protagonist, Johnson followed in the tradition of the "tragic mulatto" established by such writers as William Wells Brown, Frances Harper, and Charles Chesnutt, reinvigorating the conventions with a rich psychological complexity that would influence later authors such as WALTER WHITE, JESSIE FAUSET, and NELLA LARSEN. Johnson's protagonist is the first major fictive representation of W. E. B. DuBois's concept of double consciousness, and this nameless searching soul would serve as a prototype of sorts for RALPH ELLISON's protagonist in *INVISIBLE MAN* (1952).

In the end, *The Autobiography of an Ex-Colored Man*'s complex blend of styles—picaresque, psychological realism, social protest, and autobiography—speaks to Johnson's artistry. More than any other aspect of the work, however, the narrator's characterization gives the novel its power. A highly ironic character, he describes his reason for telling his story as a "savage and diabolical desire to gather up all the little tragedies of my life, and turn them into a practical joke on society" (778). Despite his attempts to maintain this detached ironic distance from his story, his inability to live comfortably with his decisions marks him, instead, as the object of the author's irony. The protagonist's inability to control fully his own narrative mirrors the numerous contradictions in his personality. He is alternately a man of astonishing brilliance and absurd naiveté, of strong voice and weak will, of determination and vacillation, of racial commitment and racial renunciation. The last of these contradictions, in particular, has led some readers to take issue with the novel and even mistake Johnson for his narrator, but it is this rich ambiguity of characterization and range of possible interpretations that has engaged new generations of readers and assured the novel a place of prominence in American literature.

BIBLIOGRAPHY

Fleming, Robert E. *James Weldon Johnson.* Bloomington: Indiana University Press, 1987.

Greene, J. Lee. *Blacks in Eden: The African American Novel's First Century.* Charlottesville: University Press of Virginia, 1996.

Johnson, James Weldon. *The Autobiography of an Ex-Colored Man.* In *The Norton Anthology of African American Literature,* edited by Henry Louis Gates, Jr., and Nellie Y. McKay, 777–861. New York: W. W. Norton, 1997.

Price, Kenneth M., and Lawrence J. Oliver, eds. *Critical Essays on James Weldon Johnson.* Critical Essays on American Literature. New York: G. K. Hall, 1997.

Andrew B. Leiter

Autobiography of Malcolm X, The
Malcolm X, with the assistance of Alex Haley (1965)

In this classic autobiography, MALCOLM X chronicles a life that epitomizes in every way LANGSTON HUGHES's speaker in "Mother to Son," who declares at the beginning of the poem, "Life for me ain't been no crystal stairs." Malcolm titles the first chapter of his autobiography "Nightmare," and he describes his "earliest vivid memory" as the "nightmare night in 1929" when he was "suddenly snatched awake into a frightening confusion of pistol shots and shouting and smoke and flames. . . . Our home was burning down around us. We were lunging and bumping and tumbling all over each other trying to escape" (3). Like RICHARD WRIGHT in *BLACK BOY,* Malcolm in the *Autobiography* bears witness to the atrocities and destructiveness of American racism, particularly to young African-American males growing up in a Jim Crow–dominated America. In the *Autobiography,* Malcolm revisits his lived experiences, dividing them into three distinct stages, which are clearly demarcated by the personal transformation, metamorphosis, and accompanying name changes he undergoes as he moves from a life as almost orphaned to life as a street hustler to a spiritual life shaped by Islamic teachings and beliefs.

Born in Omaha, Nebraska, on May 19, 1925, to Reverend Earl and Louise Little, Malcolm, one of eight children, became (in part because of his light skin) the dearly beloved child of his father, an itinerant minister and leader-organizer for MARCUS GARVEY's "Back to Africa" Universal Negro Improvement Association (UNIA) movement in Lansing, Michigan. Reverend Little's involvement with what many "good Christian white people" (1)—including members of the Black Legionnaires and Ku Klux Klan—considered a troublemaking, radical black movement led to his violent murder during which his badly beaten body, run over by a streetcar, was almost cut in two. Although Malcolm was six, he recollects the nightmare of it all. Malcolm records the tragic consequences caused by the deterioration and eventual separation of his family, including his mother's mental breakdown and the inevitable separation of his family, when he and his siblings were placed in foster care. Despite the ensuing instability in his young life, Malcolm excelled educationally and even became president and valedictorian of his eight-grade class. However, Malcolm's aspiration to become a lawyer by profession was discouraged by his English teacher, who told him, "you have got to be realistic about being a nigger. A lawyer—that's no realistic goal for a nigger. You need to think about something you *can* be" (36).

After dropping out of school during his teenage years, Malcolm relocated to Boston to live with his half sister, Ella. There, he was introduced to the black middle class, which he rejected outright for city life and particularly the black underclass life he found in the Roxbury section of Boston. Employed first as a shoeshine boy at the Roseland State Ballroom—where he learned to lindy hop, conked his hair, and was tutored by his new streetwise friend Shorty—and later as a waiter on the railroad, traveling the eastern corridor from Boston to New York on the "Yankee Clipper," he fell prey to and embraced the underworld of criminality, drugs, and burglary that dominated his Harlem environment. To immerse himself fully in his new lifestyle, Malcolm, at age 17, moved from Boston to Harlem, where his new surrogate fathers, including Charlie Small and West Indian Archie, schooled him "in such hustles as the numbers, pimping, con games of many kinds, peddling dope, and thievery of all sorts, including armed robbery" (83). Malcolm confesses, "A roll of money was in my pocket. Every day, I cleared at least fifty or sixty dollars. In those days . . . this was a fortune to a seventeen-year-old Negro. I felt, for the first time in my life, that great feeling of *free!*" (99). Thus, hustling, Malcolm was convinced at this stage of his life, provided an avenue through which he could challenge the world that insisted on emasculating him. Sidone Smith

argues, "through criminality, he [Malcolm] recovers his manhood"; he is no longer the "mastered but the master" (79). After learning his lessons well, Malcolm, whose street name was "Detroit Red," eventually landed in prison, having "sunk to the very bottom of the American white man's society" (150), where he remained from 1946 to 1952.

While in prison Malcolm reeducated himself by reading the dictionary and the works of the old philosophers, "Occidental and Oriental," and was introduced to the teachings of Elijah Muhammad, the leader of the Nation of Islam (NOI), the Black Muslims. According to Michael Eric Dyson, "Malcolm was drawn to the Nation of Islam because of the character of its black nationalist practices and beliefs: its peculiar gift for rehabilitating black male prisoners; its strong emphasis on black pride, history, culture, and unity; and its unblinking assertion that white men were devils" (Dyson, 6). Literacy, for Malcolm, as for FREDERICK DOUGLASS, became his key to his desired freedom and transformation. Malcolm writes, "I knew right there in prison that reading had changed forever the course of my life" (*Autobiography,* 179). Upon his release, Malcolm, who at his conversion to Islam changed his name from Malcolm Little to Malcolm X and was personally mentored by Elijah Muhammad, his new surrogate father, became the assistant minister of the Detroit Temple Number One, a minister of Harlem's Temple Number Seven, and, within a short time, the NOI's most visible leader and powerful spokesperson, preaching to the black masses across the nation that "Our *enemy* is the *white man!*" (251). This transformation began the second phase of his life.

Distraught when a personal rift between him and Elijah Muhammad—over Muhammad's alleged extramarital affairs, as well as their growing political differences—led to his ouster and silencing, Malcolm took the requisite pilgrimage, the Hajj, to the Muslims' holy city, Mecca. This spiritual journey initiated the final phase of Malcolm's life; he became El-Hajj Malik El Shabazz. In Mecca, where he had witnessed "The people of all races, color coming together as one!" (338), Malcolm discovered the true brotherhood of humankind as taught by orthodox Islam, which encourages everyone, irrespective of race or color, to honor the same God, Allah. Returning to America, after also visiting Africa and the Arab nations, Malcolm began teaching that "if racism could be removed, America could offer a society where rich and poor could truly live like human beings" (371). Before leaving on his pilgrimage, he had founded the Moslem Mosque, Inc., to work within the American mainstream and more cooperatively with extant civil rights leaders. Reflecting on his metamorphosis from Malcolm Little to Malcolm X to El Shabazz, Malcolm concluded, "it is only after the deepest darkness that the greatest joy can come; it is only after slavery and prison that the sweetest appreciation of freedom can come" (379).

Malcolm X was assassinated in February 1965 at the Audubon Ballroom in New York City, where he had gone to talk about the Organization of African Unity (OAU), which he had founded. He was married to Betty (Sanders) Shabazz, the mother of his six daughters: Attallah, Qubilah, Ilyasah, Gamilah, and Malaak and Malika, twin girls.

The Autobiography of Malcolm X not only records Malcolm X's effort to assess and even shape his historical and personal importance but also reveals his complexity as an individual who, as Dyson notes, was willing, in his quest for truth, "to be self-critical and to change his direction [which is] an unfailing sign of integrity and courage" (Dyson, 17). Malcolm X has been resurrected as an important icon at the end of the 20th century. His influence and ideas continue to be felt. He is, says Robin Kelly, "a sort of *tabula rasa,* or blank slate, on which people of different positions can write their own interpretation of his politics and legacy" (1236).

BIBLIOGRAPHY

Dyson, Michael Eric. *Making Malcolm: The Myth and Meaning of Malcolm X.* New York: Oxford University Press, 1995.

Kelly, Robin. "Malcolm X." In *Africana: The Encyclopedia of the African and African American Experience,* edited by Kwame Anthony Appiah and Henry Louis Gates, Jr., 1233–1236. New York: Basic Civitas Books, 1999.

Malcolm X, with the assistance of Alex Haley. *The Autobiography of Malcolm X.* New York: Ballantine Books, 1965.

Smith, Sidone. *Where I Am Bound: Patterns of Slavery and Freedom in Black American Autobiography.* Westport, Conn.: Greenwood Press, 1974.

Wilfred D. Samuels

Autobiography of Miss Jane Pittman, The
Ernest Gaines (1971)

One of ERNEST GAINES's most popular novels, *The Autobiography of Miss Jane Pittman* has as its title character one of African-American literature's most memorable characters. The novel spans Jane's entire life—all 110 years. Her "autobiography" is recounted to an African-American high school teacher collecting oral personal histories. His voice frames the narrative, but Jane's artful storytelling becomes the core of the novel. Her history marks the years between the Civil War and the CIVIL RIGHTS MOVEMENT of the 1960s. Jane's transformation from slave to free woman illustrates the changes in American society over the span of her lifetime. In genre, the work is a neo–slave narrative, modeling itself after the thousands of oral and written narratives of former slaves but presented in a contemporary fictional form. The purpose of such novels, including TONI MORRISON's *BELOVED*, is to highlight the connections between the past horrors of slavery and the present problems of racism.

Jane's account begins with her life as a slave named Ticey at the close of the Civil War. A Yankee soldier befriends her and suggests that she take a new name to represent her new freedom. She chooses the given name Jane and, in the tradition of true slave narratives, pays respect to the soldier who helped her by taking his surname, Brown. For a time, she dreams of moving North to the "promised land," but after federal troops leave the South, following Reconstruction, Jane is convinced that the North holds little more promise of freedom than the South. Jane's life is also disrupted by family tragedy: Racists murder an adopted son, and her husband is killed in an accident.

The Autobiography of Miss Jane Pittman represents the numerous stories of slave life that have been silenced in history. Though a fictional persona, Jane embodies both the triumph and the suffering of many unknown, but real, men and women. The closing scene of the novel, where Jane finally drinks from a "whites only" fountain, portrays the victory of the African-American spirit over adversity.

Tracie Church Guzzio

B

Baker, Houston A., Jr. (1943–)

Born and raised in "racist, stultifying" Louisville, Kentucky, Houston Baker is one of the preeminent scholars and critical theorists of African-American literature in the United States today. Over the course of his career, Baker has published numerous theoretical works, scores of scholarly essays, and several works of poetry and edited scholarly collections, including his anthology *Black Literature in America* (1971). He served as the first black president of the Modern Language Association of America. He has held teaching appointments at numerous prestigious universities, including Yale (1968–1970), University of Virginia (1970–1974), University of Pennsylvania (1974–1998), and Duke University (1998–present). He received his B.A. from Howard University in 1965 and his Ph.D. from the University of California at Los Angeles in 1968.

In his poetry, Baker presents the Louisville of his childhood as a socially complicated site where, on the one hand, economic decline and white racism led to intense feelings of "hatred, bitterness, longing." On the other hand, the same site was significant because it provided Baker with a real sense of communality with his predecessors. Baker writes in "This Is Not a Poem," "Had you been there while I was growing up, or / Even in the thin / worn time of their decline, / I would have introduced you. / Allowed you to share the fine

goodness of ancestral / Caring." The constant pull between the hatred of racism and appreciation of communality rooted in a specific location is characteristic of Baker's critical output.

Whereas his dissertation and first publications focused on Victorian poetry, throughout the majority of his career Baker's work has been centrally concerned with theoretical paradigms for studying vernacular literatures. Baker argues that canons that are built not on conventional works of high literary and cultural value but written in what he calls "standard" language require their own individuated modes of criticism. The study of African-American literature, he concludes, needs to follow principles rooted in African-American aesthetic experience. The BLUES, then, and specifically blues musicians like Robert Johnson "at the crossroads," become generative figures for making meaning out of African-American art. When combined with the philosophical, social, and linguistic considerations of "high" theorists like G. W. F. Hegel and Karl Marx and of contemporaries like Jacques Derrida and Fredric Jameson, Baker's approach puts the sociocultural significance of the art into dialogue with works written in "standard" languages. As Baker states in one of his seminal works, *Blues, Ideology, and Afro-American Literature: A Vernacular Theory* (1984), "Afro-American culture is a complex, reflexive enterprise which finds its proper figuration in blues conceived as a matrix. . . . The matrix is a point of ceaseless input and output, a web of intersecting, crisscrossing impulses always in productive transit" (3).

In more recent works, Baker has turned to questions of cross-cultural and cross-linguistic hybridities in which language is multiply marked by intersecting and mutually influential matrices. Rap music, modernism, and the HARLEM RENAISSANCE are all subjects of critique, as Baker looks at ways in which vernacular languages existing on the periphery of American literature come into contact with, influence, and are influenced by a standardized, "central" American canon. In *Turning South Again* (2001), Baker critiques modern notions of citizenship as he analyzes the place of the plantation economy in the work of BOOKER T. WASHINGTON, and he draws parallels between the constraints on black mobility at the turn of the century and the contemporary "prison-industrial" complex.

Unlike the conventional model of an American academic involved only in intellectual endeavors, Baker has been extremely active in forging relations with the multiple communities of which he is a part. The importance of pedagogy in high school has led to programs whereby university instructors and high school teachers exchange knowledge. Baker has also stressed the need for literacy programs in the inner cities, as well as the need to adopt a critical stance resisting the ways racial formation is used to continue to deprive people of color in the United States. In short, the "invitation to inventive play" (14) that Baker offers in *Blues, Ideology, and Afro-American Literature* continues to address imperative contemporary concerns across the American landscape.

BIBLIOGRAPHY

Baker, Houston. *Black Literature in America.* New York: McGraw-Hill, 1971.
———. *Black Studies, Rap, and the Academy.* Chicago: University of Chicago Press, 1993.
———. *Blues, Ideology, and Afro-American Literature: A Vernacular Theory.* Chicago: University of Chicago Press, 1984.
———. *Turning South Again: Re-thinking Modernism/Re-reading Booker T.* Durham, N.C.: Duke University Press, 2001.

Keith Feldman

Baldwin, James   (1924–1987)

James Baldwin, fiction writer, essayist, dramatist, and poet, was born in Harlem, in New York City, in 1924. Growing up in the inner city had a profound influence on his life and writing, often serving as a literary and spiritual touchstone for his later works. Baldwin attended DeWitt Clinton High School, where he became inspired by HARLEM RENAISSANCE poet and teacher COUNTEE CULLEN. After his graduation in 1942, he met and became influenced by RICHARD WRIGHT. During the 1950s and 1960s, Baldwin was not only an important fiction writer but also became, through his provocative essays, a reckoning force in the struggle for civil rights. Baldwin later moved to Europe in an effort to distance himself from America's racism and homophobia.

Baldwin's first novel was the autobiographically charged GO TELL IT ON THE MOUNTAIN (1953). In it, he introduces a young African-American male, John Grimes, who struggles to determine his place in an extended dysfunctional family; moreover, John struggles to define his racial, sexual, and religious difference within a society that demands sameness. Baldwin would examine these themes in all of his subsequent novels and stories. Baldwin's next novel, *Giovanni's Room* (1956), explores homosexuality in terms that few writers have matched either before or since. David, the protagonist, is a young American sailor who finds himself at the crossroads of sexuality. Ultimately, David is unable to accept his attraction to male flesh or acknowledge his true feelings for Giovanni. For Baldwin, it is not homosexuality per se that is the destructive force but the absence of honesty and truth in human relationships, sexual or otherwise. This is the central theme of ANOTHER COUNTRY (1962), his third and perhaps most controversial novel.

Baldwin's novels and stories of the 1960s, ANOTHER COUNTRY, *Going to Meet the Man* (1965), and *Tell Me How Long The Train's Been Gone* (1968), extend his preoccupations with various crossings between race and sexuality. In addition, Baldwin begins to construct an extended definition of black manhood, a project that would continue throughout the remainder of his published works. Moreover, these novels become meditations on the necessity of truth and honesty in human relationships. He also wrote two plays during this time, *The Amen Corner* (1968) and *Blues for Mister Charlie* (1964), which were well received by audiences.

The 1970s saw Baldwin's career as novelist begin to wind down, but not until he produced *If Beale Street Could Talk* (1974) and his last novel, *Just above My Head* (1979), two very different novels that, at the same time, are variations on the themes, character types, and situations that constitute his canon. Indeed, *Just above My Head* is culminatory in scope and treatment as Baldwin attempts to crown his previous achievements by producing the quintessential narrator/witness, Hall Montana; the fully composite black homosexual artist in society, Arthur Montana; the victim-made-whole through the renouncing of religion and the acceptance of truth, Julia Miller; and young black males striving, but often failing, to make their way in a society that uses but neither values nor understands them, the Trumpets of Zion.

Beginning in the 1950s, Baldwin's essays appeared regularly in leading literary magazines and intellectual journals, including *Harper's, The New Yorker, Esquire,* and *Partisan Review.* Not only were his topics timely and his analyses far-reaching, but also the combination of an elegant prose style and a driving fury seething just below the surface established Baldwin as a true public intellectual and an ardent spokesperson for civil rights. Notable among these essays is "EVERYBODY'S PROTEST NOVEL," in which Baldwin argues for artistic freedom for black writers, especially from the mantra of the protest tradition presided over by RICHARD WRIGHT. Likewise, "The Fire Next Time" put white America on notice and prophesied correctly the turmoil that the civil rights struggle would become during the 1960s.

Baldwin's last published works also include a brief selection of his poems, *Jimmy's Blues* (1985),

and the essay collections *The Devil Finds Work* (1976) and *The Evidence of Things Not Seen* (1985). Among his unpublished manuscripts are two that he was working on at the time of his death, "Harlem Quartet" and "The Welcome Table." Though these late works offer little that is new in terms of Baldwin's approach or concerns, they confirm his continued focus on the things that had made his writing provocative and alluring in the first place.

James Baldwin is not easily categorized as a writer. He is modern in many ways and both traditional and contemporary in many others; that he wrote in so many varied genres does not make such categorization easier. For example, although he broke with protest writing in the mid-1950s, much of Baldwin's work continues in the protest vein, yet some of the works, especially *If Beale Street Could Talk* and *Just Above My Head,* transcend protest and become almost meditative. Similarly, many of the essays, though they do offer protest, tend to be cast more broadly as protests of the human condition. Stylistically, Baldwin is a probing, incisive writer who examines every nook and cranny of the matter at hand in an effort to get at the essence of truth, regardless of how elusive it is. His style is often dismissed as repetitive and as evidence of poor control, but the final revelations, regardless of how brief, show how Baldwin adds to the clarity of his examination cubit by cubit. In addition, Baldwin's texts have frequently been regarded as "preacherly," owing much to his early experience as a child preacher in the fire-baptized church. Even so, there is a sincerity about Baldwin's work, and doubtless he was committed to exposing the whole truth, often at great personal expense. Also, music—most often jazz, BLUES, and gospel—pervades Baldwin's texts, and just as often the meditation turns to musicality, musicianship, and the role and special challenges of the musician as artist. Finally, Baldwin's lifelong project was the construction of a definitive statement on black manhood, a definition he sought to establish through both fictional and nonfictional means.

Critical appreciation for James Baldwin has been widespread, but until recently the attention has been devoted mostly to the earlier works, while the later works have often been neglected. There are a number of interviews, reviews, articles, essays, full-length studies, biographies, and literary biographies of Baldwin. Likewise, Baldwin has been the subject of many doctoral dissertations, conference presentations, and symposia. His work continues to be in print and appears as part of the Library of America series.

Clearly, James Baldwin was one of the most important writer/activists of the 20th century. He never wavered from what he perceived as the essential role of the artist—to expose the truth and present it for consumption—and he never abdicated his responsibility as one who was charged by his gift of talent to serve humankind through his art. More to the point, Baldwin occupied an important place in the continuing development of the black masculinist tradition in African-American writing by both extending and transcending protest literature. He died in France in 1987.

BIBLIOGRAPHY

Campbell, James. *Talking at the Gates.* New York: Viking, 1991.

Leeming, David. *James Baldwin.* New York: Knopf, 1994.

Miller, Quentin, ed. *Re-Viewing James Baldwin: Things Not Seen.* Philadelphia: Temple University Press, 2000.

O'Daniel, Therman B., ed. *James Baldwin: A Critical Evaluation.* Washington, D.C.: Howard University Press, 1981.

Troupe, Quincy, ed. *James Baldwin: A Legacy.* New York: Touchstone, 1989.

Weatherby, W. J. *James Baldwin: Artist on Fire.* New York: Laurel, 1989.

Warren J. Carson

"Ballad of Remembrance, A"
Robert Hayden (1948, 1962)

Transcending the didacticism of ROBERT HAYDEN's *Heart-Shape in the Dust* (1940), "A Ballad of Remembrance" presages his later modernist experimentation. Occasioned by Hayden's 1946 encounter in New Orleans with Mark Van Doren, "A Ballad"—first published in 1948 and revised and published again in 1962—dramatizes Hayden's effort to confront the legacy of slavery that threatened to silence the poet's voice.

"A Ballad's" surrealistic imagery depicts a Mardi Gras tradition, a parade led by a degradingly comic Zulu king figure:

> Quadroon mermaids, Afro angels, black
>   saints
> balanced upon the switchblades of that air
>   and sang. . . . (1–3)

A quantifier central to America's system of chattel slavery, "Quadroon" posits "race," a tenacious historical artifact, as a natural division of human existence. "Quadroon" renders the biracial female slave's body as exotically monstrous—it is one-quarter "Negro" and three-quarters "other"—even before the word "mermaid" is juxtaposed to intervene. The 1948 version associates the "Quadroon mermaids" with "the minotaurs of edict" (38). Slavery's institutions and their Jim Crow successors monstrously split humanity, defining some individuals as only partially human. Institutions policed and citizens internalized such division, rendering New Orleans a "schizoid city" (42).

Singing as "mermaids," "angels," and "saints," marchers leave humanity silent, proclaiming and inscribing slavery's enduring influence. Echoing this song, the "Zulu king" and "gun-metal priestess" perpetuate their burdensome legacy and history: The line "Accommodate, muttered the Zulu king" suggests a grotesque attempt to personify racism's caricatures (20). With almost silenced voice (*mutter* derives from the Latin for "mute"), oppression speaks. Embracing the inhumanity racism fantasizes, the priestess ironically voices her capture by the racism she would protest:

> Hate, shrieked the gun-metal priestess
> from her spiked bellcollar curved like a
>   fleur-de-lis:
> As well have a talon as a finger, a muzzle
>   as a mouth. . . . (23–25).

After the parade disperses, the "dance," extending the past into the present, "continued—now

among metaphorical / doors, coffee cups floating poised / hysterias . . ." (29–31). Conceptually,
segregation ("doors") becomes "metaphorical."
Hayden and Van Doren, while attempting to open
such doors by having coffee together in several
French Quarter restaurants, found that segregation laws made it virtually impossible for them to
do so (McClusky, 161). This biographical "dance"
with hysteric racism translates as poetic crisis.
Spellbound by this racist history, the poet cannot
voice his humanity to announce that history's possible demise.

Van Doren delivers the poet from the "dance"
and the parade, which surged as "a threat / of
river" (15–16):

> *Then you arrived, meditative, ironic,*
> *richly human; and your presence was shore*
> *where I rested*
> *released from the hoodoo of that dance,*
> *where I spoke*
> *with my true voice again. (34–37)*

Encountering another's humanity, the poet regains
what the 1948 version calls his "human voice," and
"the minotaurs of edict dwindle feckless, foolish"
(37, 38). In the end, "A Ballad" exemplifies Hayden's
continued faith that humanism may be neither fu-
tilely utopian nor perniciously ideological.

BIBLIOGRAPHY

Chrisman, Robert. "Robert Hayden: The Transition
Years, 1946–1948." In *Robert Hayden: Essays on
the Poetry,* edited by Laurence Goldstein and Robert Chrisman, 129–154. Ann Arbor: University of
Michigan Press, 2001.

Hayden, Robert. "A Ballad of Remembrance." 1962.
In *Collected Poems,* edited by Frederick Glayshere.
New York: Liveright Publishing Corporation,
1985.

McClusky, Paul. "Robert Hayden: The Poet and His
Art: A Conversation." In *How I Write / 1,* 133–213.
New York: Harcourt Brace Jovanovich, 1972.

Williams, Pontheolla T. *Robert Hayden: A Critical
Analysis of His Poetry.* Urbana and Chicago: University of Illinois Press, 1987.

Robert S. Oventile

Bambara, Toni Cade   (1939–1995)

Novelist, essayist, short story writer, activist, and
screenwriter Toni Cade Bambara was a prolific
artist and a spokesperson for issues affecting
black women. She was born Mitona Mirkin Cade
to Helen Brent Henderson Cade in New York City
on March 25, 1939. She grew up in Harlem, Bedford-Stuyvesant in Brooklyn, and Queens. She
took the name Toni when she entered school and
added the name Bambara later when she found
it on a sketchbook belonging to her great-grandmother. She attended the public schools of New
York and then entered Queens College to study
theater arts and English. After receiving her degree
in 1959, she continued her education at the University of Florence, where she studied commedia
dell'arte, and in Paris at École de Pantomime Eti-
enne Decroux. She returned to the United States
to complete an M.A. at City College in 1964. She
undertook additional work in linguistics at New
York University and New School for Social Research. She did doctoral work at State University
of New York, Buffalo.

During this period Bambara was also involved
in community activism. During college she worked
as a social investigator for the New York Depart-
ment of Social Welfare and then for Metropolitan
Hospital and Colony House Community Center.
Later, she was part of the SEEK program of City
College and the New Careers Program in Newark,
New Jersey.

Her first short story, "Sweet Town," published
while she was a student, received the John Golden
Award for fiction. In 1970, she published *The Black
Woman,* an anthology of poetry, essays, and stories
by Nikki Giovanni, Alice Walker, Audre Lorde,
and others. Her second collection, *Tales and Stories for Black Folks,* included works by both established African-American authors and students of
Livingston College of Rutgers University, where
Bambara was teaching at the time.

In 1972, she published *Gorilla, My Love,* a collection of stories written between 1959 and 1970.
They were narrated in the voices of black women
of different ages, from childhood to maturity,
and had both northern urban and southern rural
settings. They made considerable use of the oral

tradition and are distinguished by the speech patterns of the narrators. In "The Lesson," "My Man Bovanne," and the title story, she affirms the experiences of the black community and especially the women in it.

During the period after this publication, she traveled to Cuba and Vietnam and established ties to women's organizations in those countries. She also moved to Atlanta with her daughter. In 1977, she published her second collection of stories, *The Sea Birds Are Still Alive*, which was influenced by these experiences. The key characters of several of the stories are community activists who must come to terms with the complexities of a black community pulled in different directions while still suffering the effects of racism. Within the community, there is conflict over political and gender issues. The heroic figures are women who try to engage these concerns while moving the community forward.

In her first novel, *The Salt Eaters* (1980), Bambara continues this theme through the story of Velma Henry, a southern activist who is trying to hold together the centripetal forces of the social movements in her community. Because each group believes its cause is most important, they refuse to cooperate and thus effectively eliminate the possibility for social change. In despair, Velma attempts suicide but is resuscitated through the efforts of the faith healer Minnie Ransom. The message of the text is that life inherently involves change and that there is no secure, fixed identity for either self or community. Life, according to Bambara in this work, is a constant process of re-creation. *The Salt Eaters* won the 1981 America Book Award.

Bambara began working in other genres after the publication of the novel. In line with her training in theater, she had been writing screenplays for several years. *Zora* had been produced in Boston in 1971, *The Johnson Girls* by NET in 1972, and *Transactions* by Atlanta University in 1979. In 1981, ABC produced *The Long Night*. Bambara also adapted TONI MORRISON's novel *Tar Baby* in 1984. Her most important film project was *The Bombing of Osage* in 1986, which tells the story of MOVE, a radical black organization that was the target of police action, including a bomb, which killed several people, including children, and destroyed much of the neighborhood. It won awards for best documentary from both the Pennsylvania Association of Broadcasters and the National Black Programming Consortium.

In 1993, she was diagnosed with colon cancer and underwent extensive treatment. She continued to work, however, focusing her attention on Louis Massiah's documentary *W. E. B. DuBois: A Biography in Four Voices*, which was produced in early 1995. She died on December 9 of that year.

A collection of her essays and stories, *Deep Sightings and Rescue Missions*, was edited by TONI MORRISON and published by Pantheon in 1996. Three years later, the same press brought out *Those Bones Are Not My Child*, also edited by Morrison. This novel was the result of 12 years of research into the Atlanta child murders, which occurred in the early 1980s, and traces one family's dealings with corruption, cover-up, and incompetence in the investigation.

BIBLIOGRAPHY
Schirack, Maureen. "Toni Cade Bambara, 1939–1995." Available online. URL: http://www.edwardsly.com/bambara.htm. Accessed September 28, 2006.

Keith Byerman

Banneker, Benjamin   (1731–1806)
A social critic, inventor, almanac compiler, astronomer, mathematician, and poet, Benjamin Banneker was, like PHILLIS WHEATLEY and OLAUDAH EQUIANO, living evidence to debunk prevailing 18th-century ethnic notions about the innate inferiority of Africans and their descendants. Even the framer of the Declaration of Independence, Thomas Jefferson, wrote, in *Notes on State of Virginia*, that blacks, "in reason [are] much inferior [to whites] as I think one could scarcely be found capable of tracing and comprehending the investigations of Euclid; and in imagination they are dull tasteless, and anomalous" (139). Banneker, the son and grandson of former slaves and a farmer by profession, was born free on November 9, 1731, on a farm near the Patapsco River, a short distance

from Baltimore, Maryland. Although his family's background is not well known, he is thought to be the son and grandson of native Africans by some biographers, whereas others believe he is the grandson of Mollie Welsh, "an English woman of the servant class" (Baker 101).

Banneker's interest in mathematics and science made him, according to RICHARD BARKS-DALE and Keneth Kinnamon, "the foremost Black intellectual of the eighteenth century" (49). His friendship with members of the Ellicott family, prominent Quaker merchants who recognized his genius, provided Banneker with access to the scientific instruments, which he used to develop his curiosity in and explore engineering and the physical sciences, particularly astronomy. By age 20, Banneker invented what many consider the first American clock, which he carved with a pocketknife from a piece of wood. According to Henry E. Baker, Banneker's clock "stood as a perfect piece of machinery, and struck the hours with faultless precision for a period of 20 years" (106). By age 60, the primarily self-taught Banneker published his first *Banneker's New Jersey, Pennsylvania, Delaware, Maryland and Virginia Almanac or Ephemeris* (1791). Unlike many of his contemporary fellow astronomers, Banneker successfully predicted the solar eclipse of April 1789. Banneker's *Almanac,* although short lived, was viewed favorably along with its rival, *Poor Richard's Almanac,* which was published by the better-known inventor-statesman Benjamin Franklin.

Recognizing Banneker's genius, President George Washington appointed him, along with Major Andrew Ellicott, to a commission headed by the French civil engineer Pierre Charles L'Enfant to survey the Federal Territory, the future District of Columbia, Washington, D.C. Announcing Banneker's appointment, the Georgetown *Weekly Ledger* (March 12, 1791) called Banneker "an Ethiopian," noting that his "abilities as surveyor and astronomer already prove that Mr. Jefferson's concluding that that race of men were void of mental endowment was without foundation" (Baker, 121). As Winthrop Jordan points out in *White Over Black,* "Ironically, Banneker's nomination had come from the Secretary of State, Thomas Jefferson" (450).

Although Banneker is credited with writing poetry, his verses, primarily mathematical and scientific riddles, pale in comparison to the works of better-known 18th-century poets GEORGE MOSES HORTON and Phillis Wheatley. His poem in which a vintner hires a cooper to make a bathtub is exemplary.

> *The top and the bottom diameter define*
> *To bear that proportion as fifteen to nine,*
> *Thirty-five inches are just what I crave,*
> *No more and no less, in depth will I have;*
> *Just thirty nine gallons this vessel must hold,—*
> *Then I will reward you with silver or gold.*

The speaker's ultimate concern is found in the final couplet:

> *Now my worthy friend, find out, if you can,*
> *The vessel's dimensions and comfort the man!*
> *(Loggins, 40)*

Banneker's greatest literary legacy, however, is the letter exchange he engaged in with Jefferson. Not only aware Jefferson's public stance and published theory on the innate inferiority of blacks but also certain that he was living proof to the contrary, in 1791 Banneker sent Jefferson a copy of his *Almanac* with a cover letter in which he politely chided the Secretary of State:

> Sir, if these are sentiments of which you are fully persuaded, I hope you cannot but acknowledge, that it is the indispensable duty of those, who maintain for themselves the rights of human nature, and who possess the obligations of Christianity, to extend their power and influence to the relief of every part of the human race, from whatever burden or oppression they may unjustly labor under. . . . Sir, I have long been convinced, that if your love for yourselves, and for those inestimable laws, which preserved to you the rights of human nature, was founded on sincerity, you could not but be solicitous, that every individual,

of whatever rank or distinction, might with you equally enjoy the blessings thereof." (Banneker, 51)

Banneker unabashedly informed Jefferson that the "train of absurd and false ideas and opinions which so generally prevails with respect to the Negro should now be eradicated. Jefferson's response conveys a sense of sincerity: "no body wishes more than I do to see such proofs as you exhibit, that nature has given our black brethren, talents equal to those of the other colours of men." (quoted in Baker, 110–111)

Committed to peace and justice, Banneker suggested in an *Almanac* essay that the U.S. government add to the president's cabinet a secretary of peace to offset the existing Department of War. Banneker died in October 1806.

BIBLIOGRAPHY

Baker, Henry E. "Benjamin Banneker, The Negro Mathematician and Astronomer." *Journal of Negro History* 3 (April 1918): 99–118.

Banneker, Benjamin. "Letter to Thomas Jefferson." In *Black Writers of America*, edited by Richard Barksdale and Keneth Kinnamon, 50–52. New York: Macmillan Company, 1972.

Barksdale, Richard, and Keneth Kinnamon, eds. *Black Writers of America*. New York: Macmillan Company, 1972.

Jefferson, Thomas. *Notes on the State of Virginia*. Edited by William Peden. Chapel Hill: University of North Carolina Press, 1955.

Jordan, Winthrop. *White Over Black: American Attitudes Toward the Negro, 1550–1812*. New York: W. W. Norton, 1968.

Loggins, Vernon. *The Negro Author: His Development in American to 1900*. Port Washington, N.Y.: Kennikat Press, 1931.

Wilfred D. Samuels

Baraka, Amiri   (Everett LeRoi Jones)
(1934–   )

Prolific essayist, dramatist, short story writer, poet, music critic, popular culture historian, and political activist, Amiri Baraka was born Everett LeRoi Jones to middle-class parents in Newark, New Jersey. His father, Colt Leroy Jones, was a postal supervisor, and his mother was a social worker. After graduating from high school, where he had amused himself by writing comic strips and science fiction stories, he spent two years at Rutgers University before transferring to Howard University, where he received a B.A. degree in English in 1954. After his graduation, Baraka spent three years in the U.S. Air Force, from which he was dishonorably discharged for submitting poetry to alleged communist publications.

In 1957 Baraka moved to Greenwich Village, where he became "the most talented Black among the Beats" (Redmond, 323); married Hettie Cohen, a Jewish woman with whom he edited *Yugin;* and became a music critic, primarily of jazz, for such publications as *Downbeat, Jazz Review,* and *Metronome.* He also founded Totem Press, which published the works of such writers as Allen Ginsberg and Jack Kerouac. Throughout the late 1950s, Baraka, known for his vigorous language and images, was not, for the most part, ideologically driven. However, in 1960 he was invited to Cuba, where he met with artists and writers who were discussing the political ramifications of art and revolution. Returning to an America deeply in the throes of the Civil Rights movement led by MARTIN LUTHER KING, JR., which was morphing into a Black Power movement headed by MALCOLM X, Baraka began to systematically integrate his art and politics, particularly Black Nationalism, in order to denounce white racism and oppression.

From 1961 to 1964 Baraka published *Preface to a Twenty-Volume Suicide Note* (1963) and coedited, with Diane DiPrima, *Floating Bear,* a literary newsletter; he explored, biographically and thematically, his mistrust for European-American society and culture in two plays: *The Slave* (1964) and *The Toilet* (1964). Using African-American music as a vehicle in *Blues People: Negro Music in White America* (1963), he traced the transformation of Africans into American slaves. Also in 1964 Baraka established his reputation as a playwright when his controversial Obie Award–winning play, *Dutchman* (1963), was produced off-Broadway at the Cherry Lane Theater in New York City. Eventually made into a film, this play, through its main characters, Clay and Lula, suggests, as DARWIN T. TURNER points out, "the manner in which the white world destroys the black who intellectually has become a threat; simultaneously, it denounces the black who chooses to use his knowledge in sterile pursuits rather than directing it toward the destruction of oppression" (18). Despite the anger his work expresses, Baraka remained committed, until he was deeply affected by the assassination of MALCOLM X in 1965, to Western aesthetics, specifically Western use of language.

Following Malcolm X's death, however, Baraka revised his artistic perspective and commitment, prioritizing a more functional art as demanded by a traditional African and black aesthetic. Together with LARRY NEAL he spearheaded the BLACK ARTS MOVEMENT and founded the short lived Black Arts Repertory Theater in Harlem to produce agitation-propaganda (agitprop) plays and poetry that strictly addressed the needs and liberation of black people. Baraka and Neal identified the utilitarian function of art in the black community in their respective works, "Black Art" and the "Black Arts Movement." Baraka announced the urgency for transition and revolution in "SOS"—"Calling all black people / . . . Wherever you are. . . . / . . . come in, black people, come / on in"—and penned "Black Art," which became the movement's manifesto: "Poems are bullshit unless they are / teeth or trees or lemons piled / on a step. . . . We want 'poems that kill.' / Assassin poems. Poems that shoot / guns." Neal explained:

> Neal pronounced that "The Black Arts Movement is radically opposed to any concept of the artist that alienates him from his community. Black Art is the aesthetic and spiritual sister of the Black Power concept, as such, it envisions an art that speaks directly to the needs and aspirations of Black America. In order to perform this task, the Black Arts Movement proposes a radical reordering of the western cultural aesthetic" (257).

In 1968 Baraka and Neal coedited *Black Fire*, the signature anthology of black revolutionary literature. Baraka's play *Home on the Range* was performed as a benefit for the Black Panther Party. In 1969 his *Great Goodness of Life* became part of the *Successful Black Quartet* off-Broadway, and his play *Slave Ship* was widely reviewed.

In New Jersey Baraka became a leading political voice; he founded and chaired the Congress of African People, a nationalist Pan-Africanist organization, and was one of the chief organizers of the National Black Political Convention, which convened in Gary, Indiana. He also founded Spirit House Players and produced two plays, *Police* and *Arm Yrself or Harm Yrself,* that addressed police brutality in urban black communities. In addition, Baraka divorced from Hettie Cohen, with whom he had fathered two children; married Sylvia Robinson (Amina Baraka), an African-American with whom he fathered five children; became a Muslim; changed his name to Imamu Amiri Baraka; and committed himself completely to black liberation and Black Nationalism. He assumed leadership of Kawaida, founded to promote the ideology of Black Muslims and Black Nationalism and, from 1968 until 1975, was the chairman of the Committee for Unified Newark, becoming, as Eugene Redmond noted, "the most influential of the young activist poets" of his generation (12).

In 1974, disappointed and disgruntled with both Islamic and Black Nationalist ideology, Baraka dropped Imamu ("teacher") from his name and soon thereafter embraced a more Marxist-Leninist position. In 1983 he and Amina edited *Confirmation: An Anthology of African American Women,* which won an American Book Award from the Before Columbus Foundation, and in 1987 they published *The Music: Reflections on Jazz and Blues.* Baraka independently published his life story, *The Autobiography of LeRoi Jones / Amiri Baraka,* in 1984.

Baraka has won numerous literary prizes, including a Guggenheim Foundation Fellowship, a National Endowment of the Arts Grant, the PEN / Faulkner Award, the Rockefeller Foundation Award for Drama, and the Langston Hughes Award from the City University of New York. He has held teaching positions at various universities, including the New School for Social Research, the University of Buffalo, Columbia University, Yale University, and San Francisco State University. Most recently, he served as the Poet Laureate of New Jersey until he was removed for writing poetry that some critics considered anti-Semitic.

Like W. E. B. DuBois, JAMES BALDWIN, and RICHARD WRIGHT, Amiri Baraka is one of the most important writers and cultural critics of 20th-century America. He has striven, with the same force of his rejection of European-American society and cultural norms, to create a more didactic art that reflects clearly the values of African-American culture, the richness of its history, and the complexity of its multifaceted community.

BIBLIOGRAPHY

Baraka. Amiri. *The Autobiography of Le Roi Jones / Amiri Baraka.* New York: Freundlich Books, 1984.

Bentson, Kimberly. *Baraka: The Renegade and the Mask.* New Haven: Yale University Press, 1976.

Jones, Leroi. *The Baptism: the Toilet.* Evergreen Playscript. New York: Grove Press, 1967.

Neal, Larry. "The Black Arts Movement." In *The Black Aesthetics,* edited by Addison Gayle, 257–274. Garden City, N.Y.: Anchor Books, 1972.

Redmond, Eugene. *Drumvoices: The Mission of Afro-American Poetry,* Garden City, N.Y.: Anchor Books, 1976.

Turner, Darwin T., ed. *Black Drama in America.* Greenwich, Conn.: Fawcett Publications, 1971.

Raymond E. Jannifer

Barksdale, Richard K.   (1915–1993)

Richard K. Barksdale, the son of Simon and Sarah Brooks Barksdale, the brother of Phillips, Mason, and Clement, was born October 31, 1915, in Winchester, Massachusetts. A Phi Beta Kappa graduate of Bowdoin College in Brunswick, Maine (1937), Barksdale received two master's degrees in English, one from Syracuse University (1938) and the other from Harvard University (1947). In 1951, he became the second African American to earn a Ph.D. degree in English from Harvard. Bowdoin awarded him an honorary doctor of humane letters degree in 1972.

Barksdale began his illustrious teaching and administrative career in the Deep South at several historically black colleges and universities (HBCUs), including Southern University, Tougaloo College, North Carolina Central University, and Morehouse College. The culmination of these HBCU achievements was his appointment as professor of English and dean of the graduate school at Atlanta University. In 1971, Barksdale joined the faculty of the University of Illinois at Champaign-Urbana as professor of English and graduate dean. He remained there until his retirement as professor emeritus in English in 1986. After retiring, Barksdale became distinguished visiting professor at numerous colleges and universities, his appointments including the Langston Hughes Visiting Professorship in American and African-American Literature at the University of Kansas (spring 1986), Tallman Visiting Professor of English Literature at Bowdoin College (fall 1986), visiting professor in African-American Literature at Grinnell College (April 1987), the United Negro College Fund Distinguished Scholar at Rust College (spring 1988), and visiting professor in African-American Literature at the University of Missouri, Columbia (fall 1988).

The author of many articles on the African-American literary tradition, Barksdale's work appeared in numerous scholarly journals, including the COLLEGE LANGUAGE ASSOCIATION JOURNAL, *Phylon, Black American Literature Forum,* and the *Western Humanities Review.* Coeditor, with Keneth Kinnamon, of the first BLACK AESTHETICS anthology, BLACK WRITERS OF AMERICA: A COMPREHENSIVE ANTHOLOGY (Macmillan, 1972), Barksdale is credited with having greatly influenced the Black Aesthetics perspective of CALL AND RESPONSE: THE RIVERSIDE ANTHOLOGY OF THE AFRICAN AMERICAN LITERARY TRADITION (Houghton Mifflin, 1997), edited by Patricia Liggins Hill, Bernard W. Bell, Trudier Harris, William Harris, R. Baxter Miller, and Sondra A. O'Neale, with Horace A. Porter.

Barksdale is also the author of *Langston Hughes: The Poet and His Critics* (1977) and his swan-song collection of selected essays, *Praisesong of Survival: Lectures and Essays, 1957–1989* (University of Illinois Press, 1992), in which his defining, signature essay, "Critical Theory and Problems of Canonicity in African American Literature" presents his insightful message; "African American literature cannot effectively survive critical approaches that stress authorial depersonalization and the essential unimportance of racial history, racial community, and racial traditions."

Barksdale was one of the founding presidents of the COLLEGE LANGUAGE ASSOCIATION (1973–1975), a major organization for blacks who taught English, as the doors of the segregated Modern Language Association were still closed to them at that time. He was also one of the founding presidents of the Langston Hughes Society (1981–1983), which granted him the Langston Hughes Prize in 1986. In 1989, he received three major awards: the Therman B. O'Daniel Distinguished Educator Award presented by the Middle Atlantic Writers Association, the National Council of Teachers of English Black Caucus Distinguished Educator Award, and the Olaudah Equiano Distinguished Award for Pioneering Achievements in African American Literature and Culture. He was a distinguished member of the advisory committee for the Mellon Humanities Program for Black Colleges from 1975 to 1979, the Graduate Record Examination Administrative Board from 1976 to 1978, and the University of Illinois Press Board from 1982 to 1986. He was also a consultant for the Ford Foundation from 1968 to 1970; the Commission on Higher Education, North Central Association from 1973 to 1986; and the National Endowment for the Humanities in 1983.

Barksdale was married to Mildred Barksdale (1922–2000), the first black to receive the rank of professor at Georgia State University in Atlanta, who joined him at the University of Illinois at Urbana-Champaign as assistant dean of the College of Liberal Arts and Sciences. He was the father of four children—Maxine, Richard Jr. (deceased), Calvin, and James—and seven grandchildren—Nikomis, James Jr., Adam, Andrew, Kirby, Nathan,

and Samuel. Although trained as a British Victorian scholar, Barksdale was, during the 20th century, one of the major literary and critical voices of the African-American literary tradition, particularly as a black literary historian and Black Aesthetic theorist and critic, having written in the area for nearly four decades. His literary legacy lives on, as it continues to expand and influence indelibly the broader literary world and the Africana literary tradition in particular.

Clenora Hudson-Weems

Barlow, George   (1948–)

Although born in Berkeley, poet George Barlow grew up in Richmond, California. After receiving his B.A. in English from California State University, Hayward (1970), he completed an M.F.A. degree in English from the University of Iowa (1972), where he was a Woodrow Wilson Fellow and a Ford Foundation Fellow. Returning to the University of Iowa after teaching courses in creative writing and African-American literature at DeAnza College and Contra Costa College for more than a decade, Barlow received an M.A. degree in American studies in 1992.

Barlow has published two collections of poems, *Gabriel* (1974), a Broadside Press publication, and *Gumbo* (1981), which was published by Doubleday as a 1981 National Poetry Series selection (selected by ISHMAEL REED). He coedited, with Grady Hillman and Maude Meehan, *About Time III: An Anthology of California Prison Writing* (William James Associates, 1987). His poetry is included in such major anthologies as *Trouble the Water* (1997), edited by Jerry Ward; *In Search of Our Color Everywhere* (1994), edited by E. ETHELBERT MILLER; and *The Garden Thrives: Twentieth Century African American Poetry* (1996), edited by CLARENCE MAJOR. His work has also been published in such leading journals as *The American Poetry Review, Obsidian, CALLALOO,* and *The Iowa Review.*

Although he cannot be placed fully within the camp of the BLACK ARTS MOVEMENT and its major architects, thematically Barlow's poetry resounds with many of the central tenets of this movement, particularly its celebration of the African-American community, black family, history, culture, and black masculinity. However, his work is not unlike that of the more traditionalist ROBERT HAYDEN in its approach to these themes. For example, Barlow is interested in paying homage to black slaves who made a difference, as Hayden does in "Gabriel," "Frederick Douglass," and "The Ballad of Nat Turner."

Barlow makes this celebration his primary task in the title poem of his first published collection of poems, "Gabriel," a praisesong for the heroic life and action of Gabriel Prosser. An educated, rebellious blacksmith-slave, Prosser is credited with attempting to lead a slave revolt in Richmond, Virginia, with, according to Herbert Aptheker, more than a thousand "conscious revolutionist[s]" in 1800. The planned insurrection was literally washed out by torrential rains, as Barlow chronicles: "Wind, rain, / cracks in the sky: / a stranger storm / has come to stop / the march; / high water / splashing from hell; / . . . / Gabriel / & one thousand armed blacks / can't cross / into Richmond." Prosser and several of his followers were hung for their revolutionary plot.

However, unlike Hayden, who focuses on Gabriel's death in his poem, Barlow concentrates on the totality of his character's life, emphasizing from the outset Gabriel's complexity as a black man-slave-rebel-leader-trumpeter. "He is Gabriel; / black man & slave; / blacksmith / rebel leader; / Thom Prosser's nigger; / black man, armed & thinking, blending with the landscape, plotting in the swamp." Consequently, Barlow's Gabriel trumpets "death / in life / & life in death." Like John the Baptist, Gabriel is prophet preparing the way for the ultimate revolutionary and liberator, Nat Turner: "Our own substance / black flesh, black bone / black fiber & liquid— / a newborn warrior— / our son, *Nat! Nat Turner.*" Born in Virginia in 1800, the year of Prosser's failed revolt, Turner led a successful slave insurrection in Southampton County 30 years later.

Barlow's signature style, rhythm, and themes are deeply submerged in black culture, particularly music, from folk ditties, Negro spirituals—W. E. B. DuBois's "sorrow songs"—and the BLUES to contemporary rhythm-and-blues and jazz. He successfully incorporates these styles by using antiphonal narrators, or call and response: (*"Steal Away, brother, steal away* / question & question / *Run away, run away"*), song titles and lyrics ("Bitch's Brew," *"Hear it in the dark / Here is the spirit in the dark"*), and musicians (Aretha, Mahalia, Nina, B. B., Otis, Sam, Billie, Diz, and Bird). Barlow seems to suggest that music is the single most important means to both knowledge and understanding of black culture and community, which Barlow demands that we "*feel* . . . in the spirit / *feel* . . . in the dark." In the spirit in the dark one can descend into memory (to "re / remember," to use a TONI MORRISON trope) to experience continuity, the fluidity of the past and present. Black history, the history that records Prosser's experience, is, unlike linear Western history, synchronic, like the planting and harvesting seasons that beat out the rhythms of traditional life and record ritual praise songs for heroic communal members. Like Prosser, Barlow becomes cultural trumpeter, a spirit in the dark.

Not surprisingly, Barlow's work is replete with humor and the language of signifying, as is clearly seen in "The Place Where He Arose," with its focus on an urban, cool, posed, styling, profiling brother-man, determined to register his presence—his proud black male self—into a world that often chooses to ignore and, even worse, erase him.

> brother-man be out there . . .
> he ain't no linear dude
> so why should he
> stroll between the lines
> of the crosswalk . . .

Like Prosser; like Barlow's brother, Mark ("gliding gazelle-like"); like his father, Andy, with his "spit – shined shoes"; like the "low-ridin army" cruising in cars inscribed with such names as *"Prisoner of Love," "Duke of Earl,"* and *"Fireball,"* this "dapper dude," Barlow's speaker, screams silently and loudly, is a man:

> dead up in there
> always been here

he is
what it is.

The recipient of numerous awards, Barlow has a wife, Barbara, and two children, Erin and Mark. Barlow is a member of the English and American studies faculties at Grinnell College.

BIBLIOGRAPHY

Aptheker, Herbert. *American Negro Slave Revolts.* New ed. New York: International Publishers, 1974, 219–226.

Redmond, Eugene. *Drumvoices: The Mission of Afro-American Poetry, A Critical History.* Garden City, N.Y.: Anchor Press, 1976.

Wilfred D. Samuels

Beatty, Paul (1962–)

Once described by ISHMAEL REED as possessing "the guts and verve of a Tiger Woods on paper," the poet and novelist Paul Beatty, who fuses references to elite, hip-hop, and street cultures with equal dexterity, has elicited high praise from literary peers and critics alike. Beatty, who was born in Los Angeles in 1962, earned his advance degrees in the east—an M.F.A. in creative writing from Brooklyn College and an M.A. in psychology from Boston University.

In his first published volume of poetry, *Big Bank Take Little Bank* (1991), Beatty displayed the facility with language, humor, and incisive cultural observations that have become his hallmark. In the poem "Darryl Strawberry Asleep in a Field of Dreams," he comments on America's favorite pastime, baseball, while raising larger questions about the uneven nature of the country's euphemistic playing fields: "*is this heaven / no its iowa / is this heaven / no its harlem / . . . / do they got a team / aint sure they got dreams / damn sure aint got a field / or crops that yield.*"

Beatty's second collection, *Joker, Joker Deuce* (1994) includes such titles as "Big Bowls of Cereal" and "Verbal Mugging." In the latter, the writer, who is also a performance artist, shares his observations on how to play the performance poetry game suc-

cessfully. In "About the Author," one of his most scathingly satirical pieces, he dares to imagine the iconic MARTIN LUTHER KING, JR., caught up in the celebrity endorsement game that has ensnared other vaunted figures: "this is mlk . . . yes suh / i thank god i wear air integrationists / crossover trainers by nike / hallelujah." Virtually nothing is sacred within Beatty's literary world.

While the critical responses to Beatty's poetry have been strong, his novels have generated even higher levels of praise. His first, *The White Boy Shuffle* (1996), features protagonist Gunnar Kaufman, an African American with some of the most embarrassing yet comical ancestors in black literary history. Among them are a freeborn choreographer who dances his way into slavery, a servant so dedicated to his master that no one has the heart to tell him that his master has died, and a music promoter who only handles white Motown wannabes. When Gunnar's mother realizes that her children consider themselves different from inner-city black youths, she moves them from predominantly white Santa Monica to a tough section of Los Angeles. There the book-smart, former suburbanite struggles to fit in until he asserts his poetic voice, learns he has a jump shot, and by novel's end becomes a reluctant messiah for his people.

All of this occurs as he is surrounded by an outlandish cast of friends (including a fellow basketball player who worships Mishima) and antagonists (such as young, black sexual terrorists Betty and Veronica) who are also trying to find a place for themselves in a world in which difference is generally a liability. Richard Bernstein of the *New York Times* declared Beatty to be "a fertile and original writer, one to watch" (25).

Tuff, Beatty's second novel (2000), received a similarly glowing reception. Its male protagonist is 19-year-old, 320-pound Winston "Tuffy" Foshay, whose run for city council allows the always acerbic Beatty to pick apart every aspect of politics, from voter apathy to campaign strategies. Yet he ends this novel on a hopeful note. Again, his protagonist lives in a world populated with a variety of over-the-top characters. Still, even some of those who applaud Beatty's brilliance believe the best is yet to come from this young writer. Reed, for example, who praises Beatty's "extraordinary eye for detail," suggests that Beatty follow the path "paved by his predecessors, Chester Himes, John O. Killens and John A. Williams . . . [,] think the unthinkable" and step away from characters who are "police lineup chic" (1). Reed's perspective is generally outweighed by other critics who have already called Beatty the new RALPH ELLISON because of his deft handling of issues of race, gender, and identity.

Beatty, who says he writes because he's "too afraid to steal, too ugly to act, too weak to fight, and too stupid in math to be a Cosmologist," lives and works in New York City.

BIBLIOGRAPHY

Bernstein, Richard. "Black Poet's First Novel Aims the Jokes Both Ways" *New York Times,* 31 May 1996, c25.

Furman, Andrew. "Revisiting Literary Blacks and Jews." *The Midwest Quarterly* 45, no. 2 (Winter 2003): 131–147.

Mosely, Walter. "Joker, Joker, Deuce." Review *Publishers Weekly,* 2 February 1994. Available online. URL: http://reviewpublishersweekly.com/bd.aspx?/sbn=0140587233&pub-pw. Accessed February 16, 2007.

Reed, Ishmael. "Hoodwinked: Paul Beatty's Urban Nihilists." *Village Voice Literary Supplement,* April–May 2000. Available online. URL: http://www.villagevoice.com/specials/ULS/167/read.shtml. Accessed February 14, 2007.

Selinger, Eric Murphy. "Trash, Art, and Performance Poetry." *Parnassus: Poetry in Review* 23, no. 1/2 (1998): 356–358.

Svoboda, Terese. "Try Bondage." *Kenyon Review* (Spring 1995): 155–157.

Deborah Smith Pollard

Beckham, Barry   (1944–   )

The novelist and book publisher Barry Beckman was born in Philadelphia, Pennsylvania, on March 19, 1944, to Clarence and Mildred (William) Beckham. At age nine, he moved with his mother to a black section of Atlantic City, New Jersey, which offered him a wealth of cultural exposure. He attended interracial public schools and graduated from Atlantic City High School. While there, he enjoyed the popularity of his peers and read such writers as JAMES WELDON JOHNSON, RICHARD WRIGHT, and CHESTER HIMES. In 1962 he entered Brown University as one of only eight black members of the freshman class. Inspired by the craft of novelist John Hawkes, Beckham began writing his first book, *My Main Mother,* in his senior year. In 1966 he graduated with a B.A. in English, married, and briefly attended Columbia University College of Law on a scholarship. Beckman has taught and served as director of the graduate writing program at Brown University and as writer-in-residence at Hampton University. Since 1997, Beckham has been married to Monica Scott of Washington, D.C.

In 1969 Beckham, at age 25, completed *My Main Mother,* which won him praise for having "penetrating personal insight." Set in an abandoned wooden station wagon, *My Main Mother* presents the psychological profile of a young man driven to matricide by his mother's avarice, promiscuity, betrayal, and abuse of his personal things. As the protagonist, Mitchell Mibbs, relives his experiences through flashbacks while in rustic Maine, in Harlem, at an Ivy League college, and during his Uncle Melvin's funeral in Boston, Beckham successfully unravels the psychological complexity of a lonely young man who quests for love, attention, and respect, suggesting the extent to which people will go to be recognized as human beings.

In 1972 Beckman published *Runner Mack,* his most accomplished work; it was nominated for a 1973 National Book Award. In *Runner Mack,* Henry Adams, an aspiring black baseball player, encounters several agents of racial oppression: big business, the military, and professional sports. Adams is convinced that baseball, his forte, is an objective venue to his desired success. However, the fast-talking revolutionary Runner Mack forces Adams to confront what he sees as Adams's false perception, shaking Adams's convictions. As Adams grows and seeks personal fulfillment and identity in an oppressive society, Mack continues to have an impact on him—one that is likened to the force of a Mack truck.

Holloway House released *Double Dunk* (1980), which was initially rejected by other publishers. A novelized biography of the Harlem basketball legend Earl "the Goat" Manigault, the inventor of the double dunk shot, *Double Dunk* chronicles Earl's life as he succumbs to heroin addiction and petty crimes before making a miraculous recovery while in jail. Once out, Manigault forms his own summer Goat Tournament for youngsters. With a masterful blend of the stream-of-consciousness technique and street dialogue, Beckham, like CLAUDE BROWN, shows how a black man who grew up in mean urban streets can transcend the adversities he has to face, give back to the community, and live his dreams through others. In 1996, *Rebound,* the movie based on Earl Manigault's life, aired on HBO, featuring Don Cheadle, Forest Whitaker, Eriq LaSalle, Loretta Devine, James Earl Jones, and Kareem Abdul-Jabbar.

Beckman's difficulties with publishers encouraged him to take matters into his own hands. In 1982, with the assistance of students from Brown, he compiled, edited, and published the first edition of *Black Student's Guide to Colleges,* which was well received in the academy. In 1989, in Maryland, he founded Beckham House Publishers (now called the Beckman Publications Group), a major black-oriented book company.

Before launching his career as a writer, Beckham worked as an assistant editor of New York's *Chase Manhattan News.* In July 1999 he published his long-awaited novel, *You Have a Friend: The Rise and Fall and Rise of the Chase Manhattan Bank.* It became the first serialized full-length book to be published on the Internet. A compelling narrative combining historical events, *You Have a Friend* details a richly textured social history of corporate America. Beckham presents, from firsthand experience as a Chase public relations writer, a portrait that goes beyond mere institutional history and focuses on landmark characters and events. One of the dominant themes throughout the novel is the inability of the Chase Manhattan Bank to define itself with authority during the 1960s and the 1970s, two of the most turbulent decades of the bank's existence.

Beckman has been published in *Black Review, Brown Alumni Monthly, Esquire, Intellectual Digest,* and *New York Magazine.* Beckman published the novel *Will You Be Mine?* in 2006.

BIBLIOGRAPHY

Loeb, Jeff. "Barry Beckham." In *The Oxford Companion to African American Literature,* edited by William L. Andrews, Frances Smith Foster, and Trudier Harris, 55. New York: Oxford University Press, 1997.

Umphlett, Wiley Lee. "The Black Man as Fictional Athlete; 'Runner Mack,' the Sporting Myth, and the Failure of the American Dream." *Modern Fiction Studies* 33, no. 1 (Spring 1987): 73–83.

Watkins, Mel. Introduction to *Runner Mack.* New York: Morrow, 1972. Washington, DC: Howard University Press, 1983.

Loretta G. Woodard

Beloved   Toni Morrison (1987)

According to critics, *Beloved* fits into the subgenre of African-American literature known as the "neo-freedom or neo-slave narrative." The immediate setting is Ohio in 1873–1875. The plot unfolds through flashbacks and the narrative voices of the central characters, primarily Sethe Suggs, who, at age 13, was taken as a slave to Sweet Home, a Kentucky plantation owned by the Garners. Mr. Garner was a relatively benevolent slave master, but upon his death, his cruel relative "Schoolteacher" replaces him. Although Sethe and the other slaves, Paul A, PAUL D, Paul F, Sixo, Halle (Sethe's husband), and their children, resolve to escape, only Sethe and her children succeed. Eventually, they arrive in Cincinnati, at 124 Bluestone Road, where BABY SUGGS, Sethe's mother-in-law, lives. Surviving the arduous journey, after giving birth along the way to her fourth child, Denver, Sethe enjoys 28 free days—loving her children in a way she had not before dared—before slave catchers locate them and attempt to return them to slavery. Sethe sets out to kill her children and then commit suicide, but manages only to kill her "already crawling" but not yet named baby girl. After serving time for her crime, Sethe returns to Bluestone Road to continue her life, while attempting to keep the past "at bay."

At the beginning of the novel, Sethe, Denver (now 18), and the sad, spiteful spirit of Sethe's murdered baby girl are living at 124 Bluestone Road when Paul D—who had been captured during the attempted escape from Sweet Home, sold South, and eventually consigned to a chain gang—joins them. He immediately drives away the spirit child, only to have it return in the flesh, the identical age she would have been had she lived. Identifying herself as B-E-L-O-V-E-D, the letters written on her gravestone, the fleshly ghost personifies the composite desire that deprivation under slavery fomented. A highly disruptive presence, Beloved not only seduces Paul D and drives him away but also sets about draining the life out of Sethe, her guilt-ridden mother, who is eventually rescued and saved by a communal exorcism.

The other major characters include Baby Suggs, the spiritual center of the free black community, and Denver, its symbolic future. Baby Suggs is also the ancestral presence Denver must invoke to save Sethe's life. Present only in the memories of Sethe and Paul D, Sixo is the most apparent symbol of physical resistance in the novel. In one detailed confrontation with Schoolteacher, Sixo is beaten; in another he is killed during an escape attempt when Schoolteacher realizes that he will never be a willing slave. Ella, along with Stamp Paid, operates the Underground Railroad station, the venue through which Sethe and her children successfully arrive at 124 Bluestone Road. Ella, a former slave who had been made the sex object for a slave owner and his son, measures life's atrocities against what the two did to her. She leads the communal exorcism that saves Sethe's life. Born Joshua, Stamp Paid renamed himself after being forced to give his wife over as concubine to his master's son. When Stamp Paid shows Paul D the newspaper clipping with the record of Sethe's heinous deed and resulting arrest, he enhances the wedge between Paul D and Sethe that Beloved's presence had set in place. Shortly after Paul D confronts Sethe with this in-

formation, Sethe realizes that Beloved is, indeed, her daughter.

In addition to portraying a previously missing black historical subject, TONI MORRISON aims with *Beloved* to depict the inner lives of blacks who were victimized by New World slavery. She addresses questions concerning self-identity, manhood, motherhood, womanhood, sexual and reproductive exploitation, love, and desire. She makes actual historical events part of the narrative, displaying her extensive knowledge of African and African-American folklore. *Beloved* received unprecedented critical acclaim and attention for a work by an African-American writer. The novel garnered for Morrison a Pulitzer Prize in 1988 and was largely responsible for her Nobel Prize for literature in 1993. In 2006, a panel of critics assembled by the *New York Times* named *Beloved* the best work of American fiction published in the last 25 years.

BIBLIOGRAPHY

Andrews, William L., and Nellie Y. McKay, eds. *Toni Morrison's Beloved: A Casebook.* New York: Oxford University Press, 1999.

Bloom, Harold, ed. *Beloved;* Modern Critical Interpretations. Philadelphia: Chelsea House, 1999.

Plasa, Carl, ed. *Toni Morrison's Beloved.* New York: Columbia University Press, 1999.

Solomon, Barbara H., ed. *Critical Essays on Toni Morrison's Beloved.* Critical Essays on American Literature. New York: G. K. Hall, 1998.

Lovalerie King

Belton, Don   (1956–   )

Although Don Belton's family moved into an integrated Philadelphia neighborhood two years after the Supreme Court ruling in *Brown v. Board of Education of Topeka,* which declared illegal "separate but equal" practices in the United States, he grew up in the Hill District of Newark, New Jersey, cared for by his grandmother, before the riots of 1967. Slipping through the cracks of imprisoning spaces to which Newark's "black boys" were often consigned (unlike his brothers and nephew),

Belton attended Philadelphia's Penn Charter, a private Quaker school, before attending and graduating from Vermont's Bennington College and later Virginia's Hollins College. In his personal narratives Belton speaks lovingly and proudly of his grandparents and great-grandparents. For example, in the introduction to *Speak My Name* (1995), Belton speaks the name of his great-great-great-grandfather, Albert Stone, a Virginia slave, master hunter, and equestrian who taught dignity to white men with his stellar character, will, and determination as a member of a race that, although it "had lost everything . . . still had the heroism to re-create itself in a lost new world" (3). Born the third son of a father whose name he fails to mention at first—although it is later given as Charles, Belton writes, "My father worked himself to death, a man from whom I inherited a legacy of masculine silence about one's own pain going back seven generations" (3). Before publishing his first novel, *Almost Midnight* (1986), Belton worked as a reporter for *Newsweek* magazine and taught creative writing at the University of Colorado at Boulder.

Although Martha and Peanut are the central characters of *Almost Midnight,* their narratives center around the life and impact of their father, Reverend Daddy Poole, a biracial former spiritual leader, preacher, millionaire incestuous pimp, numbers runner, and drug dealer, who, "as old as Methuselah," lies on his deathbed at the beginning of the novel. Although Peanut hates Poole with a vengeance and welcomes his death, Margaret, her half sister, whom Poole raises after she was abandoned by her mother, Poole's most prized prostitute, believes he is invisible and, indeed, "that he is God and won't die" (37). Martha will not abandon Poole or curse him, as Peanut does, on his deathbed, despite the horrific stories of abuse, neglect, incest, and exploitation that, she knows from personal experience, can be attributed to him. Peanut, considering her father a soulless man, tells Martha, "Your daddy got to pay for the shit he dealt women" (28). Martha remains suspicious of Peanut's motives, convinced that Peanut is interested purely in developing further the lesbian relationship they, as young women who were sexually abused by their father, had explored together. Peanut refutes this:

"I don't believe in living in the past. This ain't even about the past really. It's about all the stories of the women what lived it—and seen—coming together into one story" (25).

During his young adulthood, Poole, the son of a Louisiana prostitute and voodoo priestess, Mozelle, who had given him up for adoption, finds his mother, who by then had become well known for giving "spells to people to perform good or evil" (129). She takes him and at first trains him to "identify those plants used for healing and divination and [tells] him of their different uses" (131). Later, becoming the oracle of the snake, she performs the proper rituals to empower him with her magical gifts. In Newark, the Eden to which they migrate with great expectation, Poole is loved and feared by the members of his Metaphysical Church of the Divine Investigation, his prostitutes, and his children because of his knowledge of the occult, specifically voodoo and other forms of African traditional religious beliefs and practices, that he inherited from his mother. "You could pay to have private sessions with him, and there was a time he sold cures and spells for everything from TB to love trouble. . . . [H]e sold magic powders and potions with names like Lucky Jazz, Get Away and Easy Life" (47). In the end, however, neither his knowledge nor his daughter can save him from death, which comes at midnight.

Ultimately, *Almost Midnight* is about self-empowerment: "you must read the scripture of your own heart." This is particularly true of women, who in the novel too often seem to be totally dependent on men, who exploit and abuse them; this gives the novel a feminist twist. It is also about black migration from the South to the North and the inevitable disappointment blacks encounter when their naively imagined primordial space turns out to be a nightmare. Ironically, before migrating to Newark, Poole envisions it as a place "where gas-powered automobiles were plentiful and parks with lakes and fine trees lay in the thick of granite and limestone" (135). A postmodern world of alienation and destruction, Newark is a place where deferred dreams were manifested in "the conflagration of the 1967 riots" and attested to with "burning streets and burned-out, gutted-out stores and houses, [and] mothers and babies shot up on their own porches" (32). Belton writes, "Today, Newark is a ghost of a city" (1995, 223).

Although he has not published a second novel, Belton, proudly embracing his homosexuality like ESSEX HEMPHILL, stands in the vanguard with black male writers who "chorus a black masculinist movement, speaking their names, demanding their right to self identification, describing their lived experiences and challenges of oppression while confronting a racism so covert and insidious" (1995, 225), while celebrating their successes and victories. He does so in the book he edited, *Speak My Name: Black Men on Masculinity and the American Dream* (1995). His fiction has been anthologized in *Calling the Wind: A Twentieth Century Anthology of the African American Fiction,* edited by CLARENCE MAJOR, and *Breaking Ice: An Anthology of African American Fiction,* edited by TERRY MCMILLAN.

BIBLIOGRAPHY

Belton, Donald. *Almost Midnight.* New York: Beach Tree Books, 1986.
———, ed. *Speak My Name: Black Men on Masculinity and the American Dream.* Boston: Beacon Press, 1995.

Wilfred D. Samuels

Bennett, Hal (1930–)

Hal Bennett was born George Harold Bennett on April 21, 1930, in Buckingham, Virginia; he was reared and educated in Newark, New Jersey. At age 16, he became a feature writer for the *Newark Herald News.* He served in the U.S. Air Force as a writer for the public information division during the Korean War (1950–1953). Taking advantage of the G.I. Bill, he moved to Mexico and attended Mexico City College. There, Bennett became a fellow of the Centro Mexicano de Escritores. In 1961, Obsidian Press published his books *The Mexico City Poems* and *House on Hay.* Doubleday published his *Wilderness of Vines* (1966), which won him a fiction fellowship to the Bread Loaf Writer's Conference and which Bennett, in an interview, described as influ-

enced by the musical arrangement of Beethoven's *Ninth Symphony.* He next published *The Black Wine* (1968) and *Lord of the Dark Places* (1970). In 1970 Bennett was selected most promising writer by *Playboy* magazine for his short story "Dotson Gerber Resurrected." He received the Faulkner Award in 1973. His other books include *Wait until the Evening* (1974), *Seventh Heaven* (1976), and a collection of short stories, *Insanity Runs in Our Family* (1977), all published by Doubleday.

Always a man who likes to distort tradition, order, and standards to show that deeper meaning and understanding dominate life and that one need only be willing to search to find them, Bennett authored numerous titles under the pseudonyms Harriet Janeway and John D. Revere. In 1979 New American Library published *This Passionate Land* (Janeway) and Pinnacle published the five-set assassin series (Revere): *The Assassin* (1983), *Vatican Kill* (1983), *Born to Kill* (1984), *Death's Running Mate* (1985), and *Stud Service* (1985). In 1983 CALLALOO awarded Bennett its annual award for fiction. His work has also been published in the *Virginia Quarterly Review* and *Negro Digest* (BLACK WORLD). In 1997 Turtle Point Press republished Bennett's *Lord of Dark Places.*

Bennett often worked within the ideological framework of the BLACK AESTHETICS MOVEMENT. Characters in his novel constantly move from one location to the next searching for freedom. According to James Miller, many of Bennett's characters shuttle back and forth, representing the saga of African Americans who sought a new life through migration from the South to the North and from the rural country to the urban, industrial city. With that migration comes new ways of adapting and adjusting to new communities, people, customs, and beliefs. In his novels, Bennett challenges traditional Christian symbols and images by presenting protagonists who exercise agency in their lives to create valued, valid, and empowered individuals.

BIBLIOGRAPHY

Miller, James A. "Bennett, Hal." In *The Oxford Companion to African American Literature,* edited by William L. Andrews, Frances Smith Foster, and

Trudier Harris, 57–58. New York: Oxford University Press, 1997.

Newman, Katherine. "An evening with Hal Bennett: An Interview." *Black American Literature Forum* 21, no. 4 (Winter 1987): 357–378.

Jerome Cummings

Berry, Venise T. (1955–)

Venise Berry has devoted much of her professional life to attempting to demonstrate how the media portrays African Americans. "Stereotypical ideals and attitudes have been formed and solidified over decades into accepted ideologies and norms about African Americans," writes Berry in her groundbreaking book *Mediated Messages and African-American Culture: Contemporary Issues* (1996).

While growing up in Des Moines, Iowa, where she was born in 1955, Berry became fascinated with the media. She attended the University of Iowa, where she received a bachelor's degree in journalism and mass communication (1977) and a master's degree in communication studies (1979). Although she began her professional media career in radio news in Houston, Texas, Berry left the airwaves and entered the academic world, teaching at Huston-Tillotson College while pursuing a doctorate at the University of Texas, Austin. She wrote the first drafts of her debut novel, *So Good* (1996), in a scriptwriting class. After receiving her doctorate in radio, television, and film in 1989, Berry adapted the screenplay for publication as a novel but found no interested publishers.

In the meantime, Berry returned to the University of Iowa School of Journalism and Mass Communication in 1990, where she became the first African American to receive tenure in 1997. Her research in the areas of media, youth, and popular culture and African-American cultural criticism reflects an intersection of her experiences as both a practitioner and an observer of mediated messages: "Although I don't believe that the media have an all-encompassing power or control over their audience, I do recognize that they serve as a primary source of communication in this country, and, therefore, their images and ideals can af-fect specific people, at specific times, in specific ways, depending on the context of the situation" (Berry, viii).

Berry's commercial publishing endeavors coincided with the publishing industry's increasing interest in African-American contemporary fiction, enhanced by the success of TERRY MCMILLAN's novel *Waiting to Exhale*. Securing an agent and a publisher, Dutton, Berry published *So Good* (1996), which focuses on the relationships of single and married 30-something African-American women with careers and male-female relationship problems. Reflected in the story are Berry's trademarks of media criticism, intellectual discussions of current issues, and intelligent protagonists. Lisa, the heroine, pursues both a doctorate and a good man. Her sister, Danielle, and her longtime friend Sundiata round out the cast of central characters. Although Danielle is married to a loving husband, she is not sexually satisfied and has an affair. Through Sundiata's husband, a Nigerian, Berry is able to explore cultural conflicts. Critics describe Berry's writing style as nonliterary and journalistic, but they have lauded her storytelling abilities and wit. *So Good* was a *Blackboard* best seller and an alternate selection of the Literary Guild.

In her second novel, *All of Me: A Voluptuous Tale* (2000), Berry focuses on the experiences of her heroine, Serpentine Williamson, an overweight, ambitious news reporter who is tormented by the stereotypes and labels thrust upon her by society. Serpentine's self-esteem finally collapses under the pressure. Berry thoughtfully explores the unconditional self-love Serpentine must embrace while recovering. *All of Me* garnered a 2001 Honor Book Award from the Black Caucus of the American Library Association and the 2001 Iowa Author Award from the Public Library Foundation in Des Moines.

In *Colored Sugar Water* (2002), Berry takes a sharp departure from her previous novels, yet some familiar strains continue. Protagonists Lucy Merriweather and Adel Kelly are best friends, 30-something professional black women with male-female relationship problems. However, Berry uses them and the men in their lives to adeptly explore issues related to religion. What is the right faith? How can one find spiritual fulfillment?

Berry's commercial publishing ventures have not overshadowed her scholarly work. *Mediated Messages and African-American Culture: Contemporary Issues* (1996), coedited with Carmen L. Manning-Miller, was published almost simultaneously with *So Good.* Contributors examine the media's images and messages about African Americans. In 1997, *Mediated Messages* received the Meyers Center Award for the Study of Human Rights in North America. In addition to continuing to teach in the School of Journalism and Mass Communication at the University of Iowa, Berry published *The 50 Most Influential Black Films* (2001), coauthored with her brother, S. Torriano Berry, a professor of film studies at Howard University. Capturing the historical and social contexts of movies starring and largely produced by African Americans since the start of the film industry, the book is a valuable resource, particularly for media scholars.

BIBLIOGRAPHY
Berry, Venise T., and Carmen L. Manning-Miller, eds. *Mediated Messages and African American Culture: Contemporary Issues.* Thousand Oaks, Calif.: Sage Publications, 1996.

Townes, Glenn R. "When It Feels Good." *Pitch Weekly,* 6–12 February 1997, 46.

Vanessa Shelton

Big Sea, The   Langston Hughes (1940)

The Big Sea is the first of Langston Hughes's autobiographical texts, preceding *I Wonder as I Wander* (1957). Probably the best-known and most prolific writer of the Harlem Renaissance, Hughes offers, in *The Big Sea,* insight into his development as an artist and a major literary figure. The work covers his early years, from his childhood in Kansas through his years as a mess boy on a merchant ship to his impressions of the Harlem Renaissance.

Hughes divides *The Big Sea* into three parts. In Part I, he begins with his departure for Africa on the S.S. *Malone,* a merchant ship, at 21 years old.

Born James Mercer Langston Hughes in Joplin, Missouri, in 1902, Hughes grew up in Lawrence, Kansas. Although he knew his parents, Carrie Langston Hughes and James Nathaniel Hughes, his maternal grandmother primarily raised him until he was 12 years old. After Hughes was named class poet of his elementary school in Kansas, he wrote for the Central High School magazine in Cleveland, Ohio. In the remaining chapters of Part I, Hughes recalls his trips to Mexico to visit his estranged father, and Columbia University, which he left after his first year to write and work. Both were unpleasant experiences. Fearing a life of dull, physical labor, Hughes joined the merchant marine.

In Part II of *The Big Sea,* Hughes recounts his exploits in Africa and the West Indies, where his coworkers took economic and sexual advantage of the indigenous population. In Paris, France, he worked as a dishwasher, spending his days "writing poems and having champagne for breakfast" (163). Hughes concludes Part II with his entry into the literary world of Harlem. After being "discovered" by poet Vachel Lindsay while he was working as a busboy at the Wardman Park Hotel, Hughes entered the Opportunity magazine literary contest, winning the poetry prize. At the awards banquet, Hughes met Carl Van Vechten, who became instrumental in the publication of *The Weary Blues,* Hughes's first poetry collection.

In Part III, the concluding section of *The Big Sea,* Hughes recalls his life in Harlem during the "Black Renaissance," his college experience at Lincoln University in Pennsylvania, and his travels through the American South. Hughes offers commentaries on Jean Toomer's racial politics, A'Lelia Walker's extravagant parties, Carl Van Vechten's controversial novel *Nigger Heaven,* and Hughes's own difficulties with his collection of poems *Fine Clothes to the Jew.* Additionally, Hughes critiques the all-white faculty at his alma mater, Lincoln University, as well as the patronage system that fueled the Harlem Renaissance. The final chapter of *The Big Sea* discusses the quarrel that signaled the end of his friendship with Zora Neale Hurston and their collaboration on the play *Mule Bone.* The break seemed emblematic of the end of the

Harlem Renaissance, and Hughes's postscript to the autobiography notes the close of the era.

Hughes's *The Big Sea* provides a unique and intimate look into the Harlem Renaissance, taking the reader beyond the propaganda and manifestos. It offers not only a glimpse of the glittering existence of the literati but also an uncompromising look into the daily struggles of the young artist during Harlem's heyday.

BIBLIOGRAPHY

Berry, Faith. *Langston Hughes: Before and Beyond Harlem.* Westport, Conn.: L. Hill, 1983.

Haskins, James. *Always Movin' On: The Life of Langston Hughes.* Trenton, N.J.: Africa World Press, 1993.

Hughes, Langston. *The Big Sea: An Autobiography.* New York: A. A. Knopf, 1940.

———. *I Wonder as I Wander: An Autobiographical Journey.* New York: Rinehart, 1956.

Rampersad, Arnold. *The Life of Langston Hughes.* New York: Oxford University Press, 1986.

Barbara Wilcots

Black Aesthetic

This movement represents the attempt to formulate theories to govern the production of African-American artistic expression in relation to the evolving nature of black life in the United States in the aftermath of the organized movement for civil rights in the 1960s. When the racial designation and self-identity of African Americans underwent a radical change (from "Negro" to "black") after the declaration of "black power," many of the younger, more militant voices of the artistic community called for a redefinition and new direction for black literature. Proponents of the Black Aesthetic sought to influence the development of black expressive works by insisting that black writers adhere to the nationalistic principles that had emerged as the most visible, if not dominant, mode of black intellectual thought. Just as the BLACK ARTS MOVEMENT served as the cultural arm of the BLACK POWER movement, the Black Aesthetic was an attempt to dictate the content, style, and form of African-American writing so that the works produced by writers from the black community would adhere to black revolutionary principles. As a result, Black Aesthetic advocates most often proclaimed that black works had to be relevant to black political causes; they had to actively seek to improve the social conditions of the black masses.

The most widely discussed Black Aesthetic documents include the seminal nationalist anthology *BLACK FIRE* (1968), edited by AMIRI BARAKA and LARRY NEAL, which includes Neal's famous afterword, "And Shine Swam On," in which he writes, "Finally, the black artist must link his work to the struggle for his liberation and the liberation of his brothers and sisters. . . . The artist and the political activist are one. They are both shapers of the future reality. Both understand and manipulate the collective myths of the race. Both are warrior priests, lovers and destroyers. For the first violence will be internal—the destruction of a weak spiritual self for a more perfect self" (655–656). For Neal, the goal of the black artist was to help destroy the "double consciousness"—the source of tension "in the souls of black folks."

Among some of the other important publications containing Black Aesthetic writings are ADDISON GAYLE, JR.'s collection of essays, *The Black Aesthetic* (1971), and STEPHEN HENDERSON's anthology, *Understanding the New Black Poetry* (1972). Gayle's volume applies Black Aesthetic principles to various genres of black artistic expression while offering essays that explore Black Aesthetic thought of writers and scholars from earlier generations, such as W. E. B. DuBois, ALAIN LOCKE, and LANGSTON HUGHES. With this volume the term *Black Aesthetic* became the formal designation for the theoretical ideas that would govern "committed" black writings. Henderson's introduction to his anthology, "The Form of Things Unknown," represents one of the most important detailed, theoretical discussions of "black" poetry in the history of the literary tradition to date, one that attempts to explore the historical development of Black Aesthetic concerns in the poetry itself as opposed to separating the works of recent writers from their historical roots.

Although the term *Black Aesthetic* is most often associated with the theoretical thought that shaped primarily the poetry, drama, and nonfiction prose produced during the Black Arts Movement, Black Aesthetic thought is best understood when examined as part of the continuum of African-American critical concerns about the nature and purpose of the literature and art of African Americans. Some critics, including Reginald Martin, have argued that the Black Aesthetic during the 1960s is only one of several phases of Black Aesthetic thought, ranging from the articulation of freedom cries by slaves and former slaves during the antebellum period and beyond, to negotiations of civil liberties and rights through the 20th century until the end of the Civil Rights movement; the third phase covered only a short period of years during the 1960s.

Nevertheless, today the Black Aesthetic, as well as the Black Arts Movement as a whole, is often narrowly defined and characterized by its most extreme or problematic pronouncements. Even Larry Neal had revised many of his earlier views before his untimely death in 1981. Many of those who were at the forefront of developing Black Aesthetic thought were poets and dramatists, but as DARWIN T. TURNER has noted, the theory of the art actually preceded the art itself, a progression that, in retrospect, was possibly the movement's tragic flaw.

BIBLIOGRAPHY

Fabio, Sarah Webster. "Tripping with Black Writing." In *Within the Circle: An Anthology of African American Literary Criticism from the Harlem Renaissance to the Present,* edited by Angelyn Mitchell, 224–231. Durham, N.C.: Duke University Press, 1994.

Gayle, Addison, Jr. *The Black Aesthetic.* New York: Doubleday, 1971.

Henderson, Stephen. "The Form of Things Unknown." Introduction to *Understanding the New Black Poetry: Black Speech and Black Music as Poetic References,* 3–69. New York: William Morrow, 1972.

Jones, LeRoi, and Larry Neal. *Black Fire: An Anthology of Afro-American Writing.* New York: William Morrow, 1971.

Seibles, Timothy. "A Quilt in Shades of Black: The Black Aesthetic in Twentieth-Century African American Poetry." In *A Profile of Twentieth-Century American Poetry,* edited by Jack Myers and David Wojahn, 158–189. Carbondale: Southern Illinois University Press, 1991.

Reggie Young

Black American Literature: Essays, Poetry, Fiction, Drama Darwin T. Turner, ed. (1970)

Formerly published in separate volumes (by C. E. Merrill in 1969), *Black American Literature: Essays, Poetry, Fiction, Drama* was a central part of a core of anthologies of black writing for college and university classrooms during the 1970s and 1980s. This anthology was part of a growing body of material used in the scholarship and research of developing programs and departments in African-American studies. In the introduction to the selection of 15 essays, DARWIN T. TURNER provides historical background and analysis of essays ranging from Jupiter Hammon's "Address to Negroes in the State of New York" (1787) to Eldridge's "The White Race and Its Heroes" (1968). Within this 181-year span of essays, Turner demonstrates that black essayists have evolved from insisting on black inclusion in American democracy to questioning the standards on which democracy rests. Turner's design is also to include examples that do not focus on race, such as the essay "Letter XI" by William Wells Brown, from his 1852 collection *Three Years in Europe; or, Places I Have Seen and People I Have Met.*

The selections in volume 2 of Turner's anthology point to the developing subject matter and style of such poets as Lucy Terry (whose poem "Bars Fight" [1746] was the first known poem written by a black American), PHILLIS WHEATLEY, and GEORGE MOSES HORTON. Turner observes that later poets, like those from the HARLEM RENAISSANCE, were given the opportunity to come together as artists and become "aware of the ideas circulating among artists of their own race" (160).

This mingling is reflected in the racial pride in such poems as "Africa" (CLAUDE MCKAY) and "Dream Variation" (LANGSTON HUGHES). Turner includes a sampling of his own poetry from his collection, *Katharsis* (1964), and poems by Don Lee (HAKI MADHUBUTI) and LeRoi Jones (AMIRI BARAKA).

Turner's inclusion of more short stories from early writers than later ones in volume 3 stems from his concern that students of black literary history might have less access to early stories like PAUL LAURENCE DUNBAR's "The Mortification of the Flesh" (1901), WALLACE THURMAN's "Cordelia the Crude" (1926) or FRANK YERBY's "My Brother Went to College" (1946). Turner's other selections are stories that may not be included in other anthologies: RALPH ELLISON's "Mister Toussan" (1941) and WILLIAM MELVIN KELLEY's "The Only Man on Liberty Street" (1963).

The final section of this anthology is devoted to drama, the genre in which black writers have had the least "opportunity for recognition," according to Turner. In response to this dearth, Turner, a scholar in American theater, offers an extensive introduction to such plays as Randolph Edmonds's *Nat Turner* (1943) and Kingsley B. Bass Jr.'s *We Righteous Bombers* (1969).

This anthology includes thorough introductions to each genre, informative explanatory sections to each author, and extensive bibliographies. It reflects Turner's dedication and legacy as an exemplary scholar of African-American literature and criticism, his devotion to students, and his consistent support of the craft of teaching. Turner, whose memory is honored with a number of scholarships, was 18 when he completed an M.A. at the University of Cincinnati in 1949. When he was awarded the Ph.D. from the University of Chicago, Turner had taught at Clark College (now Clark Atlanta University) and Morgan State College (now Morgan State University). His academic career, which included numerous administrative positions, extended over 40 years, the last 20 of which were spent as chair of the African American World Studies Program at the University of Iowa.

BIBLIOGRAPHY

Turner, Darwin T. *Black American Literature: Essays, Poetry, Fiction, Drama.* Columbus, Ohio: Charles E. Merrill, 1970.

———. *Black Drama in America: An Anthology.* Washington, D.C.: Howard University Press, 1994.

———. *Katharsis.* Wellesley, Mass.: Wellesley Press, 1964.

Australia Tarver

Black Arts Movement   (1965–1974)

The Black Arts Movement continued the tradition of revolutionary writing by African Americans. According to LARRY NEAL, African-American "traditions, the politics, art, culture . . . have always been democratic and because of this—in the context of chattel slavery, reaction, white supremacy, racism, national oppression—our traditions are revolutionary" (Neal, xiv). The literature of the Black Arts Movement spoke specifically to African Americans. Black Arts Movement artists called for African-American self-determination, self-respect, and self-defense. Participants sought to create a revolutionary art that exposed the white power structure that condoned violence directed against blacks and perpetuated institutional and social racism.

The architects of this movement sought to transform American culture in general and specifically African-American culture. LeRoi Jones (AMIRI BARAKA), Larry Neal, SONIA SANCHEZ, NIKKI GIOVANNI, Don Lee (HAKI MADHUBUTI), ADDISON GAYLE, HOYT FULLER, and many others used their poetry, plays, essays, and work in other genres to define the African-American aesthetic, identity, and black art. They also were interested in creating an art that would "educate and unify black people in our attack on an anti-black racist America" (Neal, x). Black Arts Movement artists used their art as a blueprint for the revolution they hoped would aid the liberation of black people in the United States and across the diaspora. In addition to paying homage overtly to African-American history, African-American leaders, and the African ancestral past, these writers attempted to create a "symbolism, mythology, critique, and iconology" specific to black culture and separate from the dominant white culture (Neal, 62).

The Black Arts Movement succeeded in increasing black-operated and financed publishing houses and journals. BROADSIDE PRESS, for example, was one of four black publishing houses operating in the 1960s. African-American journals such as *The Journal of Negro Poetry, Black Scholar, Negro Digest,* (BLACK WORLD) *Liberator,* and *Black Theater* provided black artists with a forum in which to share their work and discuss extant political and social problems and possible resolutions, central to which were reclaiming black history, asserting pride in blackness, insisting on the liberation of blacks in American society, and reconstructing the image of blackness in mainstream American art, media, music, and literature.

Writers of the Black Arts Movement sought to validate black vernacular, as noted by DUDLEY RANDALL in his introduction to *The Black Poets.* Dudley Randall explains that the writers used the language of "the folk, the streets, to jazz musicians, the language of black people for their models" (Randall, xxvi). The directness of the language allowed them to make an unmistakable plea to all African Americans to rise up and fight all oppressive forces, with violence if necessary, in order to free African Americans from the evils of segregation, educational and employment discrimination, disenfranchisement, and white violence. Also, they often used drama as a vehicle to convey their message and validate black language. In addition to the formation of the Black Arts Repertory Theatre/School to meet this goal, there was an increase in community-based black theaters that provided a forum for black playwrights, actors, and directors to develop their craft.

Also, during the Black Arts / BLACK POWER MOVEMENT, black recording artists, including Aretha Franklin, Marvin Gaye, Stevie Wonder, James Brown, Gil Scott Heron, and Curtis Mayfield, wrote and performed socially and politically conscious songs. Franklin's "Think," Brown's "Say

It Loud I'm Black and I'm Proud," Gaye's "Inner City Blues (Make Me Want to Holler)," Wonder's "Living for the City," Mayfield's "We the People Who Are Darker Than Blue," and Gil Scott Heron's "The Revolution Will Not Be Televised" became anthems, of a sort, during this period.

Writers and the artists of the Black Arts Movement were directly influenced by the political rhetoric of key black political figures including MARTIN LUTHER KING, MALCOLM X, Stokely Carmichael, Huey P. Newton, and Bobby Seale. Malcolm X, with his call for black self-determination, was most influential. Writers were also concerned with the violence, both internal and external to the United States, of the period, including the Vietnam War, the black liberation struggle throughout the African continent, the assassinations of Malcolm X in 1965, Medgar Evers in 1963, Martin Luther King in 1968, and many others. In fact, following the assassination of Malcolm X, according to Sonia Sanchez, in the film "Not a Rhyme Time 1963–1986," LeRoi Jones (Amiri Baraka) sent letters to black writers, painters, musicians, social/political critics, and so forth, asking them to work within the black community, help organize the masses, and create the functional art associated with the Black Arts Movement.

The writers of the Black Arts Movement acted as a voice for the displaced and poor black masses in the United States during the 1960s and 1970s. However, the various factions of the Black Arts / Black Power movement and Civil Rights movement used differing ideological perspectives to structure their work. The Black Arts Movement authors more often than not defined themselves and constructed their work through the lens of Marxism, cultural nationalism, or Pan-Africanism.

The Black Arts Movement came to a climax around 1974 for a number of reasons, including government harassment of the artists and a move away from interest in Black Arts / Black Power within the academy. Also, several artists became targets of COINTELPRO, a counterintelligence program of the FBI that attempted to neutralize perceived "Black Nationalist Hate Groups." Despite attempts to downplay the significance of the Black Arts Movement to African-American literature, particularly within certain quarters of the academy, it was truly the most African American–centered and revolutionary movement in African-American art and culture during the 20th century. The artists raised black consciousness, instilled pride in blackness, and influenced the shift in the national spotlight onto the evils of American racism and its effects on African Americans. Today, many Black Arts Movement artists, including Giovanni, Sanchez, Madhubuti, and Baraka, continue to pursue their art, are ardent activists, and serve as mentors to a younger generation of African-American artists.

BIBLIOGRAPHY

Baraka, Amiri. "It's Nation Time." In *Black Fire: An Anthology of African American Writing.* New York: William Morrow and Company, 1968.

Gayle, Addison. *The Black Aesthetic.* New York: Doubleday, 1971.

Hampton, Henry. *Not a Rhyme Time, 1963–1986.* Film. Blackside, 1999.

Neal, Larry. *Visions of a Liberated Future: Black Arts Movement Writings.* New York: Thunder's Mouth Press, 1989.

Randall, Dudley. *The Black Poets.* New York: Bantam Books, 1971.

Deirdre Raynor

Black Boy   Richard Wright   (1945)

An innovative genius, RICHARD WRIGHT, author of the classic novel *NATIVE SON* (1940), was born on September 4, 1908, in Natchez, Mississippi, where, while growing up, he became aware of "the ethics of living Jim Crow," confronting and combating (usually through deception) the racism and segregation he encountered, from places of employment to the public library from which he was legally barred. In *Black Boy* (1945), the first part of a longer autobiographical work, *American Hunger,* Wright documents the atrocities of his poverty-ridden life, symbolized by his incessant hunger; the instability his family had to endure after his father, a sharecropper, abandoned them,

and the insecurity and fragmentation that marred the family's life when his mother became permanently disabled, forcing them to seek sanctuary in the homes of various family members.

Black Boy begins with four-year-old Richard setting fire to the curtains in the family home, partly to combat his boredom and partly to rebel against his restrictive parents, who had forbidden him from touching the curtains. Naively, he takes refuge under the burning house to escape punishment, only to be found and severely beaten by his parents, who were frightened by their inability to find him. The adult Wright reports, "I was lashed so hard and long that I lost consciousness. I was beaten out of my senses. . . . A doctor was called" (13).

Wright, whose *Black Boy,* like the best slave narratives, moves beyond the personal narrative of an individual to represent the general experience of the black southern masses, suggests that the life of black sharecroppers living in the South at the turn of the 20th century was not unlike that of former slaves, for whom the quest for freedom was paramount. He further reveals, through his parents' brutal response, a form of misplaced aggression, the way some blacks internalized their oppression. The child's psychological damage and sense of betrayal are symbolized in young Richard's dream: "Whenever I tried to sleep I would see huge wobbly white bags, like the full udders of cows, suspended from the ceiling above me. . . . I could see the bags in the daytime with my eyes open and I was gripped by the fear that they were going to fall and drench me with some horrible liquid" (13).

Not surprisingly, the adult Wright would broodingly write;

> After I had outlived the shock of childhood, after the habit of reflection had been born in me, I used to mull over the strange absence of real kindness in Negroes, how unstable was our tenderness, how lacking in genuine passion we were, how void of great hope how timid our joy, how bare our traditions, how hollow our memories, how lacking we were in those intangible sentiments that bind man to man and how shallow was even our despair (45).

Throughout *Black Boy,* Wright uses whiteness, like the threatening white bags that hover above the child's head, as a metaphor for the endemically oppressive world he knows intimately—found not only in the dichotomized society he must endure but also often in the biracial home of family members, especially his white-looking grandmother. His naive "black boy," and later young adult Richard, must escape. For example, by age nine Richard learns a lesson about the power of whiteness while living in Elaine, Arkansas, with his Aunt Maggie and Uncle Hoskins, proprietors of a black saloon, with whom his mother had sought sanctuary. When covetous whites kill Uncle Hoskins, the entire family is forced to flee in the middle of the night out of fear that they, too, will be killed. Wright recalled;

> I did not know when or where Uncle Hoskins was buried. Aunt Maggie was not even allowed to see his body nor was she able to claim any of his assets. Uncle Hoskins had simply been plucked from our midst and we, figuratively, had fallen on our faces to avoid looking into that white-hot face of terror that we knew loomed somewhere above us. This was as close as white terror had ever come to me and my mind reeled (64).

Unlike the black masses of Mississippi, Arkansas, and Tennessee, whose enforced obsequiousness and self-deprecation before white people he had grown to detest, Richard developed a rebellious spirit, becoming an outcast even among family members who, seeking to protect him, insisted that he, too, defer to his "Jim Crow station in life" (274). The clear exception was the well-crafted buffoonery that Wright employs, for example, to gain access to the public library and the "strange world" of books, for which he hungered upon discovering that words could be used as weapons—as the vehicle to self actualization and true freedom. In 1927, Wright migrated to Chicago—the North—where, he was convinced, "life could be lived in a fuller and richer manner" (281).

Black Boy, which ends with Wright's departure, at age 18, from the American South, surpassed the success of NATIVE SON and *Uncle Tom's Children* (1938), a collection of short stories about Jim Crow life in the South. For most critics, black and white, it was an angry—almost too angry—book. In March 1945, *Black Boy* received the Book-of-the-Month Award. In 1992, Library of America published Wright's complete original work, *Black Boy* together with *American Hunger,* which covers his experiences in the North.

BIBLIOGRAPHY

Gates, Henry Lous, Jr., and K. A. Appiah, eds. *Richard Wright.* New York: Amistad, 1993.
Wright, Richard. *Black Boy.* New York: Perennial Library, 1966.

Linda Johnson

Black Fire: An Anthology of Afro-American Writings   LeRoi Jones (Amiri Baraka) and Larry Neal, eds.   (1968)

AMIRI BARAKA and LARRY NEAL, leading architects of the BLACK ARTS MOVEMENT, edited *Black Fire,* selecting writers whose nationalist leanings resonated with their ideological prescription for the production of a more utilitarian, functional art with emphasis on the political interconnectedness of the artist/writer and the black community. Most of the writers were driven by a sense of urgency for change, one Baraka announced in his May Day poem "SOS": "Calling all black people, man woman child / Wherever you are, calling you, urgent, come in." Baraka declared in the foreword that black artists are black magicians, wizards, and bards whose role, as founding fathers and mothers of a new black nation, was to destroy Western culture as it existed and fulfill the immediate needs and well-being of the black community. Convinced that new writers were adhering to this admonition, Baraka celebrated: "We are beings of goodness, again. We will be righteous, and teaching" (xvii).

Neal explained, in his manifesto "The Black Arts Movement," "The cultural values inherent in western history must either be radicalized or destroyed. . . . In fact, what is needed is a whole new system of ideas" (188). Like Baraka, he, too, wanted the black artist to "Clean out the world for virtue and love." Neal further explained, "The Black Arts Movement is radically opposed to any concept of the artist that alienates him from his community. Black Art is the aesthetic and spiritual sister of the Black Power concept. As such, it envisions an art that speaks directly to the needs and aspiration of Black America.... The Black Arts and the Black Power concept both relate to the Afro-American's desire for self-determination and nationhood." Neal further explained, "A main tenet of the Black Power concept is the necessity for Black people to define the world in their own terms. The Black artist has made the same point in the context of aesthetics" (187).

As editors Baraka and Neal selected for inclusion in *Black Fire* writers and works that met their criteria, including James T. Stewart, Calvin C. Hernton, Sun-Ra, David Henderson, Sonia Sanchez, and Yusef Imam. The included essays bore titles that denoted the authors' perspective, for example, Stewart's "The Development of the Black Revolutionary Artist" and Stokeley Carmichael's "Toward Black Liberation." Revolutionary fiction and samplings of agitprop drama popularized by Baraka were also included, such as Neal's "Sinner Man Where You Gonna Run To?," Jimmy Garrett's "We Own the Night," and Ed Bullins's "How Do You Do." Much like the Calvinist settlers of colonial America who were convinced God had sent them on an "errand into the wilderness" to establish a "city upon a hill," Baraka closes his foreword with a resonant sense of mission: "We are presenting, from God, a tone, your own. Go on. Now" (xvii).

BIBLIOGRAPHY

Baraka, Amiri, and Larry Neal, eds. *Black Fire: An Anthology of Afro-American Writings.* New York: Bobbs Merrill, 1968.

Neal, Larry. "The Black Arts Movement." In *The Black American Writer.* Vol. 2: *Poetry and Drama,* edited by C. W. E. Bigsby, 187–202. New York: Penguin Books, 1969.

Wilfred D. Samuels

Black Issues Book Review (BIBR)

In the first published volume of *Black Issues Book Review* (*BIBR*) (January–February 1999), the editors declared, "So it is with great pride that Cox, Matthews & Associates, Inc., presents the first issues of a magazine passionately devoted to books by and about the people of the great African diaspora." Despite this stated global mission, *BIBR* was also to be "the premiere source of information and news about books for the African American audience." The staff included president and editor in chief William E. Cox, executive editor Susan McHenry, and editorial advisers E. Ethelbert Miller, Angela Dodson, Wanda Coleman, and Sheila Walker.

Cox explained that *BIBR* would not be a traditional review in which critics offered lofty opinions about books. Instead, *BIBR* would be "a community-in-print, where readers and writers exchange ideas about the many ways in which particular books move us." *BIBR* would also celebrate music, visual arts, films, dance, and other models of spirituality, health and healing, sports, science, politics, economics—"indeed every fact of life we think and write about as black people" (5). In summary, *Black Issues Book Review* was committed to examining the range of issues that shape and define black culture. "New times, new challenges and new publication attuned to it all" (7).

Each issue of *BIBR* includes news and articles placed within seven categories: (1) "Between the Lines," which offers news from the publishing industry; (2) "Market Buzz," which focuses on trends in the industry; (3) "Book Bytes," which offers information about the Internet and publishing; (4) "Faith," which focuses on inspirational, motivational, and spirituality texts; (5) "Eye," which focuses on art and coffee table books; (6) "Self Publishing," which provides advice from self-publishing experts and highlights up-and-coming self-publishing authors; and (7) "Tribute" a focus on a major author whose legacy is generally well established. The author usually appears on the cover of the magazine.

Science fiction writer Octavia Butler graced the cover of the first issue, which also included a memorial to MARGARET WALKER ALEXANDER (1915–1998); an interview with CHARLES JOHNSON, the author of MIDDLE PASSAGE, "The Politics of African American Scholarship," an essay by the coauthor of Africans in America HENRY LOUIS GATES, JR., and book reviews of works by Caribbean writer EDWIDGE DANTICAT and TREY ELLIS, the author of Platitude. BIBR's breadth was further validated with articles on MARTIN LUTHER KING, JR., Thurgood Marshall, JUNE JORDAN's Affirmative Acts: Political Essays (Anchor Books, Doubleday 1998), and Ruby Dee and OSSIE DAVIS, who celebrated their 50th anniversary with the publication of With Ossie and Ruby: In This Life Together (New York: William Morrow and Company, 1998). Other book articles of interest included one on The Tribal Art of Africa and one on black bookstore owner Clara Villanova, who had moved her Hue Man Experience Bookstore from Denver, Colorado, to Harlem, New York.

Wilfred D. Samuels

Black Nationalism

As defined by many scholars and critics, Black Nationalism refers to the belief that black people share a common culture and worldview, have a common destiny, and have a common experience. The concept of a self-defined, self-sufficient state, which is of the black politic and exists independently of any other state, is also foundational to the ambitions of Black Nationalism. The multiple aspects of this brand of nationalism include economic self-sufficiency, political sovereignty, and a social if not cultural existence based on the identity and initiative of the black politic. While overcoming the racism and discrimination of America is a goal, Black Nationalism seeks to forge a state that embodies collective thought, interests, and positive self-perceptions of its people. Generally, these perceptions include community-mindedness, spiritual affinity, and brotherhood and sisterhood. This is the aspect of Black Nationalism that many black writers of the 1960s, and specifically those who aligned themselves with the BLACK ARTS MOVEMENT led by

AMIRI BARAKA, HAKI MADHUBUTI, and LARRY NEAL, among many others, embraced as part of their desire for black empowerment.

Historically, Black Nationalism advocated by these writers had its roots in the emigrationist and separatist ideas and activities popular among 19th-century black Americans and promoted by MAULANA KARENGA in the mid-20th century. The historic record of emigrationist thought in America includes a 1773 petition by blacks from Massachusetts to the state legislator expressing a desire to be settled in some part of Africa. A similar petition requesting assistance in immigrating to Africa came from Prince Hall, a Methodist preacher during the same era. A 1789 letter from the Free African Society (a black fraternal organization) of Newport, Rhode Island, to its brother organization in Philadelphia suggested the serious consideration of a return-to-Africa movement. No action ensued immediately after this correspondence, but the idea was not lost.

In 1808, Paul Cuffee, an independently wealthy merchant, captain, and shipbuilder from Massachusetts, also conceived an idea of repatriation. He had the support of many black New Englanders who were interested in starting colonies in Africa. In 1811 he became a cosponsor of an exploratory trip to Sierra Leone. Although temporarily deterred by the War of 1812 until 1815, the idea was realized when Cuffee financed the transportation of 38 black men, women, and children to Sierra Leone at an expense of $3,000 to $4,000 to himself.

Separatist and emigrationist thought was institutionalized by such organizations as the Haytian Emigration Society and the American Colonization Society (ACS) in addition to Cuffee. Blacks formed the Haytian Emigration Society, with chapters in Baltimore, Boston, Cincinnati, New York, and Philadelphia, through which 6,000 blacks migrated to Haiti in the 1820s. Similarly, established from December 1817 to January 1818, under the auspices of Thomas Jefferson and other leading mainstream politicians, the American Colonization Society's central goal was to repatriate Africans to Liberia, a new American colony. This initiative was a fund-raising organ that would finance the transportation of people back to Africa and establish colonies and Christian missions there. From 1821 to 1830, 1,420 blacks emigrated. The ACS took on a diverse contingent of supporters and dissenters. Major objections to its objectives came even from blacks who favored emigration, such as Martin R. Delany, who objected to white control of the organization. Nonetheless, from 1817 to 1865, 147 ships set sail for Liberia, and 18,959 blacks emigrated.

Influenced by the emigrationist ideas of Lewis Woodson, a former Virginia slave, several major 19th-century black leaders, including T. Holly, Samuel Ringgold Ward, Henry Highland Garnet, Alexander Crummell, and MARTIN R. DELANY, among others, supported emigration and espoused Black Nationalist ideology. Delany, a physician, and a journalist, coined the phrase "Africa for the Africans" in 1854. Although the Civil War and black American aspirations of liberation led Delany to change his stance on emigration, join the Union forces, and recruit many blacks for military service, Delany would once again revert to the idea of emigration; he supported the South Carolina–based Liberian Exodus and Joint Stock Steamship Company after the reconstruction period. The Liberian Exodus and Joint Stock Steamship Company acquired the *Azors,* which made one voyage in 1878 before the company went bankrupt. Another prominent figure in the emigration scene of the mid- to late 1800s was Alexander Crummell, a missionary to Liberia whom many critics consider the father of Pan-Africanism. Crummell asserted that all people have a relation and a duty to the land of their fathers, in this case meaning Africa.

However, perhaps the most famous of Black Nationalists by way of emigration was MARCUS GARVEY. This Jamaican-born Pan-Africanist propounded the idea of "Africa for the Africans." Though he never spearheaded any emigration movements directly, he did organize 6 million Africans in 33 chapters of the Universal Negro Improvement Association (UNIA). Although 20th-century black writers did not outright embrace an emigrationist agenda, they spoke in terms of building a black nation—a black world, as Madhubuti's speaker demands in "We Walk the Way of the New World," that leads to morality and cleanliness: "We walk in cleanliness / the newness of it all / becomes us" (Randall, 309). Maulana Karenga's Pan-African holiday, Kwanzaa, a cultural holiday of seven days of observation, and his doctrine of *Nguzu Saba,* the "Seven Principles of Blackness," to guide Kwanzaa celebration, are a clear example of the impact Black Nationalist ideas continue to have not only on African Americans but globally.

BIBLIOGRAPHY

Berry, Mary Francis, and John Blassingame. *Long Memory: The Black Experience in America.* New York: Oxford University Press, 1982.

Franklin, John Hope, and Alfred Moss, Jr. *From Slavery to Freedom: A History of African Americans,* Vols. 1 and 2. 7th ed. New York: Knopf, 1994.

Randall, Dudley, ed. *The Black Poets.* New York: Bantam Books, 1971.

Gwinyai P. Muzorewa

Black No More   **George Schuyler** (1931)
GEORGE SCHUYLER's first novel, *Black No More,* originally published in 1931 by Macaulay and reissued in 1989 by Northeastern University Press, is generally considered the first full-length satire by an African American and perhaps the first African-American science fiction novel. Moreover, its satirical importance includes its open, yet humorous, critique of the New Negro movement (during which it was published) and the absurdities of race matters from both sides of the color line. Schuyler addresses the political issues for which he was best known: America's social stratification based on race and its obsession with racial differences. While society searched for a solution to the "race problem," Schuyler, as a minority voice, insisted that race was in fact not the problem at all. His satire is aimed specifically at myths of racial purity and white supremacy, presenting ways in which the perpetuation of racism serves economic purposes foremost; greed is the primary motivation of his characters, black and white. He presents

caricatures of organizations, such as the NATIONAL ASSOCIATION FOR THE ADVANCEMENT OF COLORED PEOPLE, the Ku Klux Klan, and the Urban League, and their leaders as hustlers in different shades.

In the preface, Schuyler dedicates *Black No More* to all of the "pure Caucasians" of the world, setting up any such readers for a shock. He then introduces Max Disher, a brown trickster; Bunny Brown, his sidekick; and the racist environment in which they live. Max is rejected by a racist white woman, Helen, who is entertained by black cabaret performers but is repulsed at the idea of dancing with a black man. This rejection sends Max to Dr. Crookman, founder and inventor of Black-No-More, Inc., where all traces of blackness are removed; here Max becomes Matt, "white" man. The remainder of the novel traces Matt's adventures as a Caucasian: He marries Helen and, with Bunny (also transformed), infiltrates the major racist organization of the country, extorting millions of dollars and finally fleeing to Europe.

In addition to the exploits of Max/Matt, the reader is also privy to the effects of the runaway success of Black-No-More, Inc., on American society. As the population takes advantage of this solution to the race problem, black race leaders are put out of the "leadership" business; as America loses its cheap black labor, an increasingly violent labor situation erupts; and lying-in hospitals are created to secretly change the growing number of mixed-race babies to white. In an attempt to decipher a "proper" race hierarchy, scientists discover that more than half of the Caucasian population has "tainted" black blood, including those who have most advocated racial purity. Just as America goes wild with frenzy, Dr. Crookman brings order back to society by announcing that that the "newly" white are actually two to three shades lighter than "real" Caucasians. Suddenly white is no longer right, and sales boom for skin-darkening lotions; "normality" returns with the ideology "black is beautiful." Schuyler makes clear that there are definite advantages to possessing white skin in America, but human nature does not change purely because of skin color.

Adenike Marie Davidson

Black Power

In 1966 Stokely Carmichael (aka Kwame Ture), coined the term "Black Power" during a period of incarceration in Greenwood, Mississippi. James Meredith had been conducting his Walk Against Fear from Memphis to Jackson that summer. A sniper had shot Meredith, the first African-American student to integrate the University of Mississippi, during his solitary march. MARTIN LUTHER KING's Southern Christian Leadership Conference (SCLC), Floyd McKissick's Congress of Racial Equality (CORE), and Carmichael's Student Nonviolent Coordinating Committee (SNCC) decided to continue the march. When they set up camp in Greenwood, Carmichael was arrested. When he emerged from custody, he said, "This is the 27th time I've been arrested. We've been saying freedom for six years. What we are going to start saying now is Black Power." He began to use the term in a series of speeches for his organization.

As a terminology, Black Power had been used before by RICHARD WRIGHT and by the former U.S. congressman Adam Clayton Powell, but it was Carmichael's fiery rhetoric that made it famous. Carmichael's idea of Black Power implied a rejection of and separation from the social and economic systems into which African Americans had sought to be integrated. He oversaw the redefinition of what had been seen as a consensual national value system as a white value system, from which African Americans, particularly the younger generation, were alienated.

Carmichael's Black Power slogan raised the issue of the right of African Americans to define their identity on their own terms. Carmichael believed that asking blacks to appeal to the white power structure as a vehicle for change was ineffective and demeaning. Real change, he argued, required that blacks develop the necessary economic and political muscle themselves. Just as the CIVIL RIGHTS MOVEMENT, under King's leadership, was achieving its greatest successes, militant blacks like Carmichael and MALCOLM X were questioning the fundamental premises of nonviolent civil disobedience. Integration, they concluded, must no longer be viewed as a positive solution to racism and segregation, as whites and blacks had few interests in common and whites were unable to speak for blacks.

King recalled that shortly after Carmichael's release from jail in Greenwood he mounted a platform and declared, "What we need is Black Power," and Willie Ricks, his SNCC colleague, shouted to the crowd, "What do we want?" The crowd roared back, "Black Power." King said, "This call and response continued over and over again for some time as [Carmichael] strutted around the podium thrusting his fist into the air" (34). His followers embraced the idea that power was the "only thing respected in the world" (35). Carmichael told them to "Begin building independent political, economic, and cultural institutions that they control and use as instruments of social change in the US."

Carmichael's followers embraced the ideology of Black Power and saw it as a call for African Americans to unite, to recognize their shared heritage, and to build a sense of community. Carmichael began to convince them that "Before a group can enter society, it must first close ranks. By this we mean that group solidarity is necessary before a group can operate effectively from a bargaining position of strength in a pluralistic society" (44). From the Greenwood rally on, definitions of the precise meaning of Black Power varied within the movement. It came to encompass the black nationalistic and revolutionary organizations and ideologies of the late 1960s and 1970s and marked a break from the Civil Rights movement in rhetoric and organizing style.

Black Power also represented a rejection of the conciliatory leadership style of King, Roy Wilkins, and Whitney Young. More important, Black Power became a rallying cry for young urban black males, who felt increasingly isolated from King and his mass movement, particularly his nonviolence and nonconfrontational leadership style. They believed that King's Civil Rights movement's main thrust of eliminating racial segregation and winning the right to vote in the South had largely ignored the economic problems of vast numbers of African Americans in the urban ghettoes of the rest of the United States.

Although consensus on the meaning of Black Power was never reached within the movement, its articulation in 1966 by Carmichael and others marked a shift in the U.S. black freedom struggle. It quickly became associated with the more militant and radical groups of the Black Social Protest Movement that emerged after the assassinations of Malcolm X and King. These more militant and radical groups viewed the traditional Civil Rights movement as too pacifist and slow to anger. National conferences on Black Power began to be held in various cities throughout the United States; delegates adopted a number of resolutions including, among other things, a boycott of the military by African-American men, self-defense training for African-American youth, and the division of the country into separate black and white nations.

As a political idea, Black Power derived from a long tradition of BLACK NATIONALISM dating back to late 19th- and early 20th-century leaders, such as Henry McNeil Turner and MARCUS GARVEY. Black Power generally meant the empowerment of African Americans and, in some cases, outright separatism. Classical Black Nationalistic theory argues that blacks must unite, gain power, and liberate themselves, not ask for freedom to be granted to them from racist whites. Most of these black militants and radicals of the late 1960s considered themselves followers of the philosophical ideals of Malcolm X, who argued eloquently that African Americans should strive for self-determination rather than integration and that they had the right to defend themselves "by any means necessary" against violent attacks from racist whites.

In *Black Power* (1967), which Carmichael wrote with Charles Hamilton, professor of political science at Columbia University, the author, explained that Black Power was "A call for black people in this country to unite, recognize their common heritage, and build a sense of community. It is a call for black people to define their own goals, to lead their own organizations" (44). On his own, Carmichael's call became increasingly more provocative. He said that "When you talk about Black Power, you talk about building a movement that will smash everything Western civilization has created."

Hamilton said that as civil unrest began to flare in Detroit, Michigan, and Newark, New Jersey, Carmichael's words eventually began to be associated with race riots and guns and "burn baby burn," a slogan adopted by urban dwellers, who called on blacks to riot, to burn down their often less-than-human living spaces in ghettos (spaces of hopelessness and despair) across America from California to New York. Images of young people on television singing "We Shall Overcome" began to be replaced with pictures of angry young people in black berets, with raised fists, and men with guns. In 1966 and 1967 Carmichael lectured at campuses around the United States and traveled abroad to several countries, including North Vietnam, China, and Cuba. He made perhaps his most provocative statement of all in Havana: "We are preparing groups of urban guerrillas for our defense in the cities. It is going to be a fight to the death."

Although Black Power quickly became associated in the eyes of the national media with violence, the term mainly referred to African Americans' self-reliance, racial pride, and economic and political empowerment. According to Carmichael,

> We are on the move for our liberation. We're tired of trying to prove things to white people. We are tired of trying to explain to white people that we're not going to hurt them. We are concerned with getting the things we want, the things we have to have to be able to function. The question is, Will white people overcome their racism and allow for that to happen in this country? If not, we have no choice but to say very clearly, "Move on over, or we're going to move over you."

Many black writers, particularly proponents of the BLACK AESTHETICS and BLACK ARTS movements, such as AMIRI BARAKA, HAKI MADHUBUTI, SONIA SANCHEZ, NIKKI GIOVANNI, SARAH WEBSTER FABIO, and CAROLYN RODGERS, conceptually embraced Black Power. LARRY NEAL explained in his now-classic essay "The Black Arts Movement" that the movement was the aesthetic sister of the Black Power movement. As the editor of *Negro Digest/ BLACK WORLD,* HOYT FULLER promoted Black Pow-

er's fundamental ideals. DUDLEY RANDALL founded BROADSIDE PRESS to publish works that promoted and celebrated the political message, goals, and objectives of Black Power.

BIBLIOGRAPHY
Carmichael, Stokeley, and Charles Hamilton. *Black Power: The Politics of Liberation.* New York: Vintage, 1967.

Gayle, Addison, Jr., ed. *The Black Aesthetics.* Garden City, N.Y.: Anchor Books, 1972.

King, Martin Luther, Jr., *Where Do We Go from Here: Chaos or Community.* New York: Bantam Books, 1968.

Raymond Janifer

Black World   (*Negro Digest*)

At the height of the BLACK ARTS MOVEMENT no other outlet celebrated "blackness"—with a global/ Pan-Africanist emphasis—more vociferously than did the editors of *Black World,* a part of the publishing empire that John H. Johnson (1918–2005), the grandson of slaves, successfully built in Chicago, Illinois. In fact, Johnson began his pioneering journalistic and business venture of *Negro Digest,* "A Magazine of Negro Comment," with a $500 loan, borrowed with his mother's furniture as collateral, on November 1, 1942. Founding *Negro Digest,* Johnson, a recipient of relief during the Great Depression, wrote in his autobiography, *Succeeding against the Odds,* was his means of achieving his dream of getting "some of the good things of this life" (3).

Patterned after the mainstream's *Reader's Digest, Negro Digest* opened, Johnson retrospectively concluded, "a vein of pure black gold" (3) and became the forerunner to the Johnson Publishing Company's commercially successful signature magazines, *Ebony* (founded in 1945) and *Jet* (founded in 1951). In his introduction to the inaugural issue, Johnson explained, "*Negro Digest* is published in response to a demand for a magazine to summarize and condense the leading articles and comment on the Negro now current in the press of the nation in ever increasing volume." Johnson further explained, "*Negro Digest* is dedicated to the development of interracial understanding and promotion of national unity. It stands unqualifiedly for the winning of [World War II] and the integration of all citizens into the democratic process (Johnson, 122). Contributors to this first issue included WALTER WHITE and LANGSTON HUGHES. Johnson discontinued *Negro Digest* in 1951, at which time the magazine's circulation had been eclipsed by *Ebony.*

However, wishing to meet the needs of the growing black political consciousness of the 1960s post–CIVIL RIGHTS MOVEMENT, growing demands for black power, and, as Johnson wrote, "to promote the works of Black writers and artists" (Johnson, 288), Johnson Publishing Company resurrected *Negro Digest* in the late 1960s. In 1970 its managing executive editor, HOYT FULLER, renamed it *Black World,* illustrating his more global and nationalistic perspective. Fuller's support for the BLACK AESTHETICS proposed by LARRY NEAL, ADDISON GAYLE, and AMIRI BARAKA clearly stood at the opposite end of the political spectrum from Johnson and the position he articulated in the introduction to his inaugural issue.

Fuller recorded his view on the direction of African-American literature in his now-classic essay "The New Black Literature: Protest or Affirmation," in which he wrote,

> There is a revolution in black literature in America. It is nationalistic in direction, and it is pro-black. That means, in effect, that it is deliberately moving outside the sphere of traditional Western forms, limitations, and presumptions. It is seeking new form, new limits, new shapes, and much of it now admittedly is crude, reflecting the uncertainty, the searching quality of its movement. But, though troubled and seeking, it is very, very vital" (Fuller, 327).

Above all, Fuller used the pages of each issue of *Black World* not only to shape the direction of this movement but to give its architects a venue for their voices.

Under Fuller's leadership, African-American writers graced many of the covers of issues of *Negro Digest and Black World.* For example, while an image of a very young LeRoi Jones (Baraka) greets reader on the cover of *Negro Digest* January 1969, and pictures of CAROLYN RODGERS and SAM GREENLEE appears on the cover of its June 1969 issue, an image of a more mature RALPH ELLISON is on the cover of *Black World*'s September 1970 special issue on Ellison's literary work and status. A smiling drawing of a graying, expatriate CHESTER HIMES appears on the cover of the March 1972 issue of *Black World.* More important, Fuller provided annual special issues on each genre: theatre, fiction, poetry; introductions and interviews with emerging black writers such as MARI EVANS, AUDRE LORDE, and JOHN EDGAR WIDEMAN, and SONIA SANCHEZ; and monthly features and sections such as "Perspectives," "Commentaries," and "Books Noted" to provide readers with relevant information about the direction of African-American literature, authors, new publications, conferences, debates, and criticism. *Black World* was the first magazine to publish the works of many of the poets of the BLACK ARTS MOVEMENT. Critics and scholars such as STEPHEN HENDERSON and Gayle used its pages to debate and test their theories on the Black Aesthetic.

As Clovis E. Semmes points out, "It is in *Negro Digest/Black World* that we begin to see scholars coin and develop the concepts of Afrocentric and African-centered analysis. In fact, there is a sustained effort to probe the epistemological foundation of a Black perspective in numerous areas of intellectual inquiry" (xii). Johnson Publishing Company discontinued *Black World* in 1976, at which time its circulation had dropped from 100,000 to 15,000.

BIBLIOGRAPHY

Fuller, Hoyt. "The New Black Literature: Protest or Affirmation." In *The Black Aesthetic,* edited by Addison Gayle, 327–348. New York: Anchor Books, 1972.

Johnson, John H., with Lerone Bennett, Jr. *Succeeding against the Odds.* New York: Warner Brothers, 1989.

Semmes, Clovis E., comp. *Roots of Afrocentric Thought: A Reference Guide to* Negro Digest / Black World,

1961–1976. Westport, Conn.: Greenwood Press, 1998.

Wilfred D. Samuels

Black Writers of America: A Comprehensive Anthology Richard K. Barksdale and Keneth Kinnamon, eds. (1972)

In 1972, coeditors RICHARD K. BARKSDALE and Keneth Kinnamon, colleagues at the University of Illinois–Urbana, introduced the first BLACK AESTHETIC anthology, *Black Writers of America: A Comprehensive Anthology.* This anthology was instrumental in advancing the writings of major 20th-century writers through the early 1970s, paying particular attention to the social, political, and cultural revolution of the CIVIL RIGHTS MOVEMENT, the BLACK POWER movement, and the BLACK ARTS MOVEMENT, which, in combination, led to the demand for and validation of a well-defined Black Aesthetics movement for African-American literature and culture.

Black Writers of America covers works by major authors, beginning with the slave narrator OLAUDAH EQUIANO, who published his commercially successful autobiography, *The Interesting Narrative of the Life of Olaudah Equiano or Gustavus Vassa, The African, Written by Himself* during the 18th century, and continuing with such writers as PHILLIS WHEATLEY, BENJAMIN BANNEKER, FREDERICK DOUGLASS, DAVID WALKER, NAT TURNER, HENRY HIGHLAND GARNET, FRANCES WATKINS HARPER, CHARLES CHESNUTT, PAUL LAURENCE DUNBAR, W. E. B. DUBOIS, BOOKER T. WASHINGTON, JAMES WELDON JOHNSON, CLAUDE MCKAY, LANGSTON HUGHES, COUNTEE CULLEN, RICHARD WRIGHT, MARCUS GARVEY, ALAIN LOCKE, ZORA NEALE HURSTON, MARGARET WALKER, RALPH ELLISON, GWENDOLYN BROOKS, JAMES BALDWIN, PAULE MARSHALL, ERNEST J. GAINES, MARI EVANS, ETHERIDGE KNIGHT, Don L. Lee (HAKI MADHUBUTI), SONIA SANCHEZ, NIKKI GIOVANNI, NATHAN HARE, MARTIN LUTHER KING, JR., and MALCOLM X.

Editors Barksdale and Kinnamon provide excellent biographical introductions for each author, appropriately establishing the social and intellectual context of their lives and works. Additionally they provide useful, updated bibliographies for each author. The anthology is divided into six chronological periods: "The Eighteenth-Century Beginnings," "The Struggle against Slavery and Racism: 1800–1860," "The Black Man in the Civil War: 1861–1865," "Reconstruction and Reaction: 1865–1915," "Renaissance and Radicalism: 1915–1945," and the "Present Generation: Since 1945." The editors identify the major African-American writers for all except one of those periods, the Civil War era of 1861–1865, where the emphasis is on works that reflect African Americans' involvement in and response to the war.

Each chronological period is divided into chapters, which precisely delineate the focus of the works in the respective chapter, ranging from JUPITER HAMMON and Banneker under the heading "A Poet and an Intellectual" to King, and Malcolm X under the heading "Racial Spokesmen." These precise, descriptive headings may be used to assist the teacher or scholar of the African-American literary tradition in their selections and instruction. Finally, each section closes with folk literature, including tales, spirituals, work songs, fables, and BLUES, carefully selected to reflect the mood of the era.

Black Writers of America: A Comprehensive Anthology's holistic, inclusive structural and thematic depth and breadth has made it a classic in African-American scholarship, as well as a model for other anthologies in the rich tradition of Black Aestheticism. It continues to be lauded by many scholars in African-American literary studies, including the editors of CALL AND RESPONSE: THE RIVERSIDE ANTHOLOGY OF THE AFRICAN AMERICAN LITERARY TRADITION, a more recent anthology that continues its legacy.

Alexander Bell

"Blueprint for Negro Writing" Richard Wright (1937)

Originally published in the short-lived left-wing magazine *New Challenge*, RICHARD WRIGHT's essay "Blueprint for Negro Writing" has become, over the more than six decades since it appeared, one of the most widely read and influential works of African-American cultural criticism. In this essay, Wright attempts to formalize what he considered to be the appropriate ideological "perspective" for African-American literature and to argue that black creative writing should be accorded a normative centrality in the lives of African Americans. Wright bemoans the fact that, for African Americans, "the productions of their writers should have been something of a guide in their daily living is a matter which seems never to have been raised seriously" (Wright, 37).

In one of the best known and most controversial passages in the essay, Wright asserts that

> Generally speaking, Negro writing in the past has been confined to humble novels, poems, and plays, prim and decorous ambassadors who went a-begging to white America. They entered the Court of American Public Opinion dressed in the knee-pants of servility, curtsying to show that the Negro was not inferior, that he was human, and that he had a life comparable to that of other people. For the most part these artistic ambassadors were received as though they were French poodles who do clever tricks (37).

Alternatively, Wright argues, "Negro writers should seek through the medium of their craft to play as meaningful a role in the affairs of men as do other professionals" (47–48). Wright provocatively suggests that it was just such meaningfulness that African-American literature had failed to achieve because of the insular and racially compromised nature of the writings of the HARLEM RENAISSANCE, or what he slightingly refers to as the "so-called Harlem school of expression" (47).

Although the Marxist perspective that informs much of the essay would diminish in the subsequent years of Wright's career as a reflection of his disillusionment with the Communist Party, the call for a socially engaged literary practice that this essay presents would characterize Wright's work until his death in 1960.

BIBLIOGRAPHY

Bigsby, C. W. E. "Richard Wright and His Blueprint for Negro Writing." *PN Review* 19 (1980): 53–55.

Wright, Richard. "Blueprint for Negro Writing." In New *Challenge* 2 (Fall 1937): 53–65. Reprinted in *Richard Wright Reader,* edited by Ellen Wright and Michel Fabre. New York: Harper and Row Publishers, 1978.

Terry Rowden

blues

Music is a focal point in African-American literary traditions. The close relationship of music and literature has its beginning in both West African cultural contexts that made music a part of daily life and an American tradition of denying enslaved African Americans literacy and thus restricting their exposure to written communication. Within this artistic and social framework, musical and oral expressions were the most accessible artistic forms for enslaved African Americans.

As the blues emerged as an identifiable musical style around the end of the 19th century, black communities were struggling to enter the wage labor force with little, if any, support. Blues began in the lives of formerly enslaved blacks, most with experience as agricultural workers, in rural southern portions of the United States. Work songs and field hollers, with their respective focus on communal and individual voices, were precursors of this early, mostly unrecorded, rural/folk period. At its outset, blues emphasized the articulation of personalized experience, usually using the first person, for individual or communal benefit. As recordings and performances took musical artists out of their home communities, the classic/vaudeville blues period (at its height in the 1920s) signaled the genre's inclusion in the mainstream American music industry. Blues songstresses such as Ma Rainey, Mamie Smith, and Bessie Smith were catapulted into fame. Urban blues reflects the lives of blacks firmly entrenched in industrialized post–Great Migration life and relies heavily on electronic instrumentation. Urban blues dominates the contemporary global music industry, but styles from all of these periods are still performed.

Each of these periods in blues development continues to influence African-American literature, and across the various blues subgenres and regional styles, several patterns in theme and philosophy can be identified. Among them are

1. a belief that the artful rendering of painful experience can be transforming;
2. an affirmation of the community, often through the personal voice (e.g., "I" = "we");
3. a use of music for social criticism, frequently in a covert manner;
4. an exploration of various aspects of adult romantic and sexual relationships;
5. a willingness to dwell in stark reality;
6. a reliance on personal power in the face of challenge;
7. an "acceptance of the contradictory nature of life" (Kalamu ya Salaam); and
8. a sharp attention to the consequences of travel and movement.

African-American writers, such as Jayne Cortez, RALPH ELLISON, and STERLING BROWN, have sought to define the blues and its importance to African-American culture. Cortez addresses the paradigmatic potential of the blues with her claim that "The [b]lues talks about and has respect for the struggles of the past and is definitely concerned with the present and the future. It talks about Black culture and reinvestigates the African experience as encountered all over the world" (*Taking the Blues Back Home,* 1). According to Ellison, "The blues is an impulse to keep the painful details and episodes of a brutal experience alive in one's aching consciousness, to finger its jagged grain, and to transcend it, not by the consolation of philosophy but by squeezing from it a near-tragic, near-comic lyricism. As a form, the blues is an autobiographical chronicle of personal catastrophe expressed lyrically. . . . They at once express both the agony of life and the possibility of conquering it through sheer toughness of spirit (*Shadow and Act,* 78). As an early critic of the blues, Brown sought to validate

its literary impact and importance. He noted, "The images of the [b]lues are worthy of a separate study. At their best they are highly compressed, concrete, imaginative, original. . . . With their imagination they combine two great loves, the love of words and the love of life. Poetry results" (239).

Brown, as well poets such as LANGSTON HUGHES, sought not only to define the blues and its importance to African-American culture but also to incorporate the blues thematically and structurally into his works. Brown's poem "Ma Rainey" (1932) provides an excellent example of how African-American writers have borrowed from blues themes and philosophies. Keen in his poem is the idea that the blues artist speaks for his or her community. First, Rainey is able to draw people from "little river settlements," "blackbottom cornrows," and "lumber camps" to come together for her performance. The singer and audience establish a real sense of community through call and response, perhaps the centerpiece of black orality:

> O Ma Rainey
> Sing yo' song. . . .
> Sing us 'bout de hard luck
> Roun' our do':
> Sing us 'bout de lonesome road
> We mus' go.

Critically important to her listeners' sense of unity and community is the cadence of Ma's song; her vocabulary and vernacular speak and reflect their voice, allowing them to validate and empower one another's experience, despite the struggles they have known individually and communally. Ma Rainey's song provides catharsis; it provides listeners with the needed strength and determination to go forward in spite of whatever disasters, natural or human, they might encounter along their "lonesome road," clearly a metaphor for life.

Indeed, the poetic quality of blues lyrics themselves has been a resource for nonmusical authors. Poets have also mimicked the rhythms, repetition, call and response, and AAB verse form of blues songs from the "New Negro" HARLEM RENAISSANCE era (e.g., Hughes's first collection of poetry, *The Weary Blues*), to poets of the BLACK AESTHETICS movement, to the collection of poetry titled *Blues Narrative* (1999) by STERLING PLUMPP, a native of Mississippi (considered to be central in the birth of the blues). The blues has influenced all African-American literary genres, as can be seen in the works of JAMES BALDWIN, AUGUST WILSON, ED BULLINS, ZORA NEALE HURSTON, Ellison, GAYL JONES, Stanley Crouch, ALICE WALKER, ARTHUR FLOWERS, TONI MORRISON, ISHMAEL REED, ANN PETRY, LEON FORREST, SHERLEY A. WILLIAMS, and many others.

Given the dynamic and pervasive influence of the blues in American and African-American literature throughout the major monumental shifts in black people's lives: enslavement, emancipation, Reconstruction, the Great Migration, the Civil Rights movement, and the contemporary Information Age, many African-American literary scholars have attempted to identify, design, and define what some have called a "blues aesthetic." In doing so, scholar-critics and writers such as ALBERT MURRAY, Angela Davis, AMIRI BARAKA, LARRY NEAL, Sherley A. Williams, HOUSTON A. BAKER, JR. and STEPHEN HENDERSON illustrate that the blues has the power to forge not only an individual's voice but also a community's evaluation of what constitutes "art" and "literature."

BIBLIOGRAPHY

Baker, Houston A., Jr. *Blues, Ideology, and Afro-American Literature: A Vernacular Theory.* Chicago: University of Chicago Press, 1984.

Brown, Sterling. "The Blues as Folk Poetry." In *Folk-Say: A Regional Miscellany,* edited by B. A. Botkin. Norman: University of Oklahoma Press, 1930.

Cortez, Jayne. *Taking the Blues Back Home.* Album. 1996.

Davis, Angela. *Blues Legacies and Black Feminism.* New York: Pantheon, 1998.

Ellison, Ralph. *Shadow and Act.* New York: Vintage Books, 1972.

Jimoh, A. Yemisi. *Spiritual, Blues, and Jazz People in African American Fiction: Living in Paradox.* Knoxville: University of Tennessee Press, 2002.

Jones, Gayl. *Liberating Voices: Oral Tradition in African American Literature.* New York: Penguin, 1991.

Jones, LeRoi. *Blues People: Negro Music in White America.* New York: Morrow Quill, 1963.

Murray, Albert. *The Hero and the Blues.* New York: Vintage, 1973.

Tracy, Steven C. *Langston Hughes and the Blues.* Urbana: University of Illinois Press, 1988.

———. *Write Me a Few of Your Lines: A Blues Reader.* Amherst: University of Massachusetts Press, 1999.

Ya Salaam, Kalamu. *What is Life?: Reclaiming the Black Blues Self.* Chicago: Third World Press, 1994.

Kimberly N. Ruffin

Boles, Robert   (1942–   )

Although he has lived mostly in New England, Robert Boles was born in Chicago in 1942. The son of an architect who worked for the State Department, Boles spent most of his early years outside the United States. A medic for the U.S. Air Force from 1960 to 1962, he worked for several years as a reporter and photographer for the Yarmouth *Register* upon his return. These varied experiences inform the often-exhausting displays of cultural capital and worldliness in both of Boles's novels, *The People One Knows* (1964) and *Curling* (1968). Still, these novels stand as two of the most self-assuredly cosmopolitan and discursively original works in 20th-century African-American fiction.

The People One Knows (1964), loosely based on Boles's experiences as a medic, tells the story of Saul Beckworth, the young biracial son of a white father and an African-American mother, as he recuperates under psychiatric observation in an army hospital in France after a failed suicide attempt. Beckworth's account of this experience is interspersed with surrealistic dreams and disturbing memories of his experiences in the American South, where he grappled with the complications of what the jacket of the first edition describes as "how it feels to cross the murky division of races."

Boles's second novel, *Curling* (1968), presents the story of Chelsea Meredith Burlingame, a black man who is adopted into a wealthy white New England family as an infant. The novel follows the incongruously named Chelsea as he attempts and often fails to relate to the white members of his family; his various white friends and lovers, including a sister and a lover both named Anne; and the black people who cross his path as both aliens and, as his buying of a building in a Boston ghetto suggests, the bearers of potential salvation. Over a series of increasingly intense and frustrating encounters, Chelsea is forced to find ways to integrate the privilege that he has no desire to repudiate into his identity as a black man in a society that can see him only as an attractive but essentially threatening anomaly. His condition is symbolized by the game that gives the novel its title, a game played on ice, generally in countries that have few blacks, in which heavy stones with handles are slid toward a target.

Despite critical acclaim from figures as prominent as Kurt Vonnegut, who declared *The People One Knows* to be the most significant debut novel since Truman Capote's *Other Voices, Other Rooms,* Boles's novels were too singular to be easily assimilated into the black literary culture of the post–CIVIL RIGHTS MOVEMENT era and stood little chance of appealing to critics and readers whose tastes had been shaped by the dictates of BLACK NATIONALISM and the notions of a BLACK AESTHETIC that grew from them. Although Boles has not published another novel, he continued to publish short fiction. His stories have appeared in *The New Yorker, Tri-Quarterly,* LANGSTON HUGHES's anthology *The Best Short Stories by Black Writers: The Classic Anthology From 1899 to 1967,* and *Calling the Wind: Twentieth-Century African-American Short Stories,* edited by CLARENCE MAJOR.

BIBLIOGRAPHY

Southgate, L. *Black Plots and Black Characters: A Handbook for Afro-American Literature.* Syracuse, N.Y.: Gaylord Professional Publications, 1979.

Terry Rowden

Bonair-Agard, Roger   (1969–   )

A native of Trinidad and Tobago who resides in Brooklyn, New York, Roger Bonair-Agard has emerged as one of the progenitors of what is being heralded as a renaissance of black poetry and spoken-word performance. Bonair-Agard immigrated to the United States in 1987 to attend Hunter College as a pre-law student and changed gears just one week before his law school entrance exam. He channeled his energies toward becoming a poet, embracing poetry with a dedication to craftsmanship as well as an honesty and passion that made him instantly recognizable as a new and enduring poetic voice.

The intersections of his Caribbean heritage, his American present, and his global awareness are ever-present influences in his work, which reflects on male-female relationships, family, island life, and the sociopolitical issues facing the black diaspora. His most notable and frequently anthologized poems are "How the Ghetto Loves Us Back," "Love in a Time of Revolution Is Hard Work (Poetz)," and "Song for Trent Lott." Though Bonair-Agard is a prominent voice in the slam movement, which emphasizes both the writing and performance of poetry, he recognizes its limitations in determining the best poet from a myriad of poetry performers. Along with Lynne Procope and Guy LeCharles Gonzales, he founded the Louder Arts Project to concentrate on the writing of poetry rather than its performance. Louder Arts also seeks to foster a sense of community awareness, conducting poetry workshops for youths and homeless communities. He is also affiliated with the Community-Word Project and Youth Speaks, which are art-in-education programs for younger poets.

Bonair-Agard's poetic craft has received national and international recognition. Named Nuyorican Fresh Poet of the Year in 1998, he coached the Nuyorican Poets Café's team to its first national championship that same year and coedited *Burning Down the House* (2000), an anthology of the poems written by the championship team. He has also appeared on HBO's *Def Poetry Jam,* the *MacNeil/Lehrer NewsHour,* and CBS's *60 Minutes.* His first full-length collection, *Chaos Congealed,* was published in 2004.

Candace Love Jackson

Bonner, Marita Odette   (1899–1971)

Playwright, short story writer, and essayist, Marita Bonner was one of the most interesting, versatile, and talented figures in the theatre movement during the HARLEM RENAISSANCE. An innovator in form and thesis, she was ahead of her time; her works would later influence such playwrights as LORRAINE HANSBERRY, ADRIENNE KENNEDY, and NTOZAKE SHANGE. Despite her small literary output, particularly her lack of plays, Bonner used the stage as a platform to address a wide range of social issues related to gender, class, and race.

Bonner was born in Boston, Massachusetts, on June 16, 1899, to Joseph Andrew and Mary Anne (Noel) Bonner. Younger than her three siblings, Bernice, Joseph, and Andrew, she was educated at Brookline High School, where she excelled in musical composition and German and contributed regularly to *The Sagamore*, a student magazine. Between 1918 and 1922 Bonner attended Radcliffe College, where she studied English and comparative literature and was admitted into the highly competitive writing seminar of Charles T. Copeland, who cautioned her not to be a "bitter" writer. His reprimand, which she called "a cliché to colored people who write" (Roses and Randolph, 181), further fueled her determination to become a writer and to protest the social ills of America. In her senior year at Radcliffe, Bonner began teaching at Cambridge High School in Boston. After graduating, she taught at Bluefield Colored High School in Bluefield, West Virginia, and at Armstrong Colored High School in Washington, D.C.

While in D.C., Bonner attended poet and playwright GEORGIA DOUGLAS JOHNSON's famous S Street Salon, a weekly writers' group, where she was encouraged and inspired by other writers and playwrights, including MAY MILLER, ZORA NEALE HURSTON, LANGSTON HUGHES, ALAIN LOCKE, COUNTEE CULLEN, JESSIE FAUSET, JEAN TOOMER, S. Randolph Edmonds, Willis Richardson, and her close friend and mentor Johnson. Although Bonner devoted much of her literary career to writing fiction, she began writing plays during this period. She used her experimental plays to voice her concern with the racial, class, and gender inequities she was convinced blacks faced. She echoed this concern in her 1925 landmark autobiographical essay, "On Being Young—A Woman—and Colored."

Published in *OPPORTUNITY* and written in black dialect, Bonner's first play, *The Pot Maker: A Play to Be Read* (1927), which suggests a strong influence by Georgia Douglas Johnson, indicts, through the main character, who feels "devalued" as a woman, the infidelity often found in oppressive, poverty-ridden environments. Praised as her masterpiece and most ambitious work, *The Purple Flower: A Phantasy That Had Best Be Read* (1928) takes place in a fictional world that allegorically represents race relations in America. The characters are convinced that only a violent revolution in a racist America will free them from their plight and ensure the survival of the NEW MAN. Written three decades before the turbulent 1960s, *The Purple Flower*, as critics note, signaled Bonner's prophesy of vast changes in America, setting the stage for such writers as Lorraine Hansberry, AMIRI BARAKA, SONIA SANCHEZ, and ED BULLINS (Brown-Guillory, 18).

In Bonner's last known existing play, *Exit, an Illusion* (1929), she probes the popular HARLEM RENAISSANCE theme of "passing," in which light-skinned blacks deny their black identity to become white-identified. Passing is a major theme for the central characters in JAMES WELDON JOHNSON's *The AUTOBIOGRAPHY OF AN EX-COLORED MAN* and ALICE DUNBAR-NELSON's *Gone White*. Bonner's later one-act plays won the $200 first prize for best play in the 1927 *CRISIS* magazine contest. *Muddled Dreams*, a fourth play, has not been located. Bonner joined the Washington Krigwa Players, but the company did not produce her prize-winning plays.

As the subtitles of Bonner's first two plays suggest, she apparently intended them to be read, which may explain why they were never produced during her life. Some critics speculate that they were considered too avant-garde, which not only set them apart from the plays of her contemporaries but also necessitated numerous technological challenges to stage them. Nevertheless, they were read and appreciated by several artists of the Harlem Renaissance and were most influential to later writers such as TONI MORRISON, ALICE WALKER, GLORIA NAYLOR, TONI CADE BAMBARA, and GAYL JONES (Roses and Randolph, 166).

After Bonner married accountant William Almy Occomy, a Rhode Island native and Brown University graduate, she moved to Chicago in 1930. Shortly after the marriage, Bonner ceased writing drama to raise her family of three children—William Almy, Jr., Warwick Gale Noel, and Marita Joyce—and to focus exclusively on writing fiction. For her work she received literary recognition in CRISIS and OPPORTUNITY. While her Chicago stories from 1933 on reflect new subject matter, those written between 1937 and 1941, "On the Altar," "High Stepper," "One True Love," "Stones for Bread," "Reap It as You Sow It," and "Light in Dark Places," continue to center on prejudice and oppression, as did her earlier plays and essays.

In 1941, Bonner stopped writing and began teaching in Chicago's public school system, including Phillips High School and the Doolittle School for educationally challenged children. Aside from family commitments and teaching, as some critics note, Bonner abandoned her writing to devote much of her time and energy to the Christian Science Church. On December 6, 1971, Bonner died in Chicago as a result of injuries she sustained in a fire in her apartment.

BIBLIOGRAPHY

Brown-Guillory, Elizabeth. *Their Place on the Stage: Black Women Playwrights in America.* Westport, Conn.: Greenwood, 1988.

Burton, Jennifer, ed. *Zora Neal Hurston, Eulalie Spence, Marita Bonner, and Other Plays: The Prize Plays and Other One-Acts Published in Periodicals.* New York: G. K. Hall, 1996.

Flynn, Joyce, and Joyce Occomy Stricklin, eds. *Frye Street and Environs: The Collected Works of Marita Bonner.* Boston: Beacon Press, 1987.

McKay, Nellie. "'What Were They Saying?': Black Women Playwrights of the Harlem Renaissance." In *The Harlem Renaissance Re-examined,* edited by Victor A. Kramer, 129–147. New York: AMS, 1986.

Roses, Lorraine E., and Ruth E. Randolph. "Marita Bonner: In Search of Other Mothers' Gardens." *Black American Literature Forum* 21, no. 1–2 (Spring–Summer 1987): 165–183.

Loretta G. Woodard

Bontemps, Arna Wendell   (1902–1972)

Arna Wendell Bontemps was born in Alexandria, Louisiana, on October 13, 1902, to Paul Bontemps, a bricklayer and musician, and Maria Pembroke Bontemps, a schoolteacher. The older of two children (his sister was named Ruby), he was named Arnaud, but his name was later shortened to Arna, probably because it was easier to pronounce. His French surname came from his father, who was born in Avoyelles Parish, Louisiana. Bontemps grew up in Los Angeles, California, where the family migrated when he was a small child. His mother died nine years after their arrival.

During his early teenage years, Bontemps, who had been the only African American in his kindergarten class, was sent to a white boarding school to counteract the worldly influence his father believed Bontemps's great uncle, Buddy Jo Ward, was having on his only son. In 1923, Bontemps graduated from Pacific Union College, a parochial college operated by the Seventh-Day Adventist church, with which the family was affiliated.

Bontemps was an influential and significant member of the HARLEM RENAISSANCE literati and had a close relationship with his best friend and collaborator, LANGSTON HUGHES. Many of the themes of his work, his "integrative approach" to African-American writing, his attitude toward folk material and Africa, and his racial protest, reflect the primary concerns of Harlem Renaissance literature. Generally, the thematic, structural and writing style of his poetry, fiction, and nonfiction demonstrate the depth of Bontemps's feeling for and commitment to celebrating the cultural significance of African-American contributions to American culture. Although Bontemps was physically removed from the South, he maintained a longing and appreciation for his southern ethnic heritage. This admiration formed the basis for his collected work.

Bontemps published his works in the literary magazines CRISIS and OPPORTUNITY, winning awards and honors. In 1931, Bontemps, by then the father of two, published *God Sends Sunday*. However, by then, feeling the pinch of the Great Depression, Bontemps had left Harlem to find employment, going to Oakwood Junior College, the historically black college established by the Adventist Church in Huntsville, Alabama, where he had a heavy teaching load. Bontemps's experience was further compounded by life in northern Alabama, which had been affected by the Scottsboro trials. The case of the "Scottsboro boys" offers a clear example of the injustices southern blacks experienced under what RICHARD WRIGHT called the "ethics of living Jim Crow." When nine innocent African-American youths, hitchhikers (hobos) on an open freight train traveling through Alabama, were arrested, accused, tried, and found guilty of allegedly raping two white girls, also illegal passengers onboard the same freight train, the black community, led by the NATIONAL ASSOCIATION FOR THE ADVANCEMENT OF COLORED PEOPLE (NAACP), vociferously came to their defense. The young men's convictions, which were in most cases eventually overturned, were appealed all the way to the Supreme Court. Recognized as important spokespersons, African-American writers such as Bontemps and particularly LANGSTON HUGHES were often in the vanguard of protestors and challengers of the blatant injustices blacks suffered in a world deemed "separate but equal."

Nevertheless, Bontemps continued writing to Langston Hughes and borrowing library books by mail; this correspondence, along with his friendship with Hughes and others who were considered revolutionaries, aroused the suspicion of both blacks and whites. Considering Bontemps's reading material "race-conscious and provocative trash," Oakwood's president demanded that he publicly burn his small library. At the end of the following term, Bontemps returned to California, where he completed *Black Thunder,* which he wrote while living in deplorable conditions.

Bontemps later moved to Chicago's South Side and began working at Shiloh Academy, another Seventh-Day Adventist school from which he was forced to resign for reasons similar to the ones that lost him his job at Oakwood College. Bontemps then began working for the Works Project Administration (WPA). In Chicago, Bontemps was well received. The Chicago Chapter of the National Negro Congress featured a symposium on *Black Thunder* and hosted a reception for him at Lincoln Center. While there, he and COUNTEE CULLEN collaborated on the drama *St. Louis Woman;* in 1937 he published *Sad Faced Boy,* a children's novel.

An award to the Graduate Library School of the University of Chicago and a Julius Rosenwald Fund Fellowship for creative writing turned Bontemps's life around. He traveled to the Caribbean and later produced *Drums at Dusk* (1939), a historical romance about the Haitian revolution. Although he briefly returned to Harlem to live in 1942, Bontemps moved to Nashville, Tennessee, to become librarian at Fisk University. Six months later, he received his M.S. degree from Chicago's Library School. Bontemps remained at Fisk from 1943 to 1966, publishing a novel, *Chariot in the Sky: The Story of the Fisk Jubilee Singers* (1951). Fisk provided emotional solace and an environment where his craving for cultural identity and roots could be satisfied. His correspondence with CARL VAN VECHTEN resulted in Fisk's acquiring the George Gershwin Collection, which became the first significant acquisition to the famous "Negro Collection" Bontemps built during his tenure as chief librarian.

At age 64, Bontemps took a sabbatical from Fisk and went to the University of Illinois's Chicago Circle campus, which offered him a tenure-track position as an associate professor in American literature at a salary three times his highest pay at Fisk. In 1969 he went to the University of Wisconsin at Madison and later was named curator of the James Weldon Johnson Collection at Yale University. While at Yale he taught courses in African-American literature, including one on the Harlem Renaissance; he also published the anthology *The Harlem Renaissance Remembered* (1972), as well as a collection of short stories, *A Summer Tragedy and Other Stories* (1973).

In 1971 he was asked to serve as "Writer in Residence" at Fisk University. In 1972 he was invited to speak by the library section of the Louisiana Education Association in Alexandria, his birthplace. He accepted, since he had plans for an autobiography, "A Man's Name," which he had already outlined, and he wanted to do research there and in surrounding towns. On May 27, 1973, Berea College bestowed upon him his second honorary doctoral degree; the first was awarded by Morgan State University. Bontemps died on June 4, 1973; his funeral was held in the Fisk University Chapel. After his death, Alexandria, Louisiana, honored him by restoring his family home and establishing the Arna Bontemps Museum.

BIBLIOGRAPHY

Bontemps, Arna W. *Black Thunder.* New York: Macmillan, 1936.

———. *God Sends Sunday.* New York: Harcourt, 1931.

Bontemps, Arna W. and Langston Hughes, eds. *The Poetry of the Negro, 1746–1949: An Anthology.* New York: Doubleday, 1949.

———, eds. *The Book of Negro Folklore.* New York: Knopf, 1958.

Betty Taylor-Thompson

Boyd, Melba Joyce (1950–)

One of the major figures of the Detroit School of African American poets, which emerged from the BLACK ARTS MOVEMENT of the 1960s, Melba Joyce Boyd was born on April 2, 1950, to parents Dorothy Wynn Boyd and John Percy Boyd, Sr. Boyd grew up and was educated in Michigan, receiving her B.A. and M.A. degrees in English and communication from Western Michigan University (1971 and 1972) and her doctor of arts (D.A.) from the University of Michigan (1979).

Boyd has produced a prodigious body of work since her first book, *Cat Eyes and Dead Wood* (1978), which was followed by five other volumes of poems, including *Song for Maya* (1983) (published in Germany as *Lied fur Maya* [1989]), *Thirteen Frozen Flamingoes* (1984), *The Inventory of Black Roses* (1989), *Letters to Che* (1996), and *The Province of Literary Cats* (2002). Her poetry has been translated into German, Italian, and Spanish. Boyd edited, along with M. L. Liebler, *Abandon Automobile: Detroit City Poetry 2001.*

In addition to her work as a poet, Boyd is also a literary biographer. Her first offering in this direction was *Discarded Legacy: Politics and Poetics in the Life of Frances E. W. Harper, 1825–1911* (1994). An internationally known poet and novelist, FRANCES HARPER played a significant role in the abolitionist and feminist movements of the 19th century. Boyd's pioneering work on this important author's novel *Iola Leroy, or Shadows Uplifted* (1892), one of the earliest best-selling novels by an African-American author, revived research on Harper's work and helped restore her to her rightful place along with William Wells Brown, Martin Delaney, SUTTON GRIGGS, and BOOKER T. WASHINGTON. Boyd introduces and exposes Harper's work to a new generation of readers. As Ann DuCille, writing in *The Women's Review of Books,* observes, "Boyd proves herself a literary historian of the first order in this scrupulously researched biography" (15).

In 2003, Boyd published another pioneering work, *Wrestling with the Muse: Dudley Randall and Broadside Press.* As she does in her work on Harper, in this text Boyd uncovers a neglected but important aspect of American and African-American literary history. DUDLEY RANDALL (1914–2000) was the founder of the most significant poet's small press of the 1960s. The Detroit-based BROADSIDE PRESS published, over the course of two decades, some 95 titles and introduced such important 20th-century African-American poets as HAKI MADHUBUTI, NIKKI GIOVANNI, SONIA SANCHEZ, AUDRE LORDE, and ETHERIDGE KNIGHT to the reading public. Each poet became an important voice of the Black Arts Movement. In addition, in 1995 Boyd produced a documentary film on Randall's life, *The Black Unicorn,* which complemented her published biography. Boyd, a former assistant editor at Broadside Press, brings firsthand knowledge and legitimacy to her work on Randall and Broadside Press. According to biographer Arnold Rampersad, *Wrestling with the Muse* is "a richly creative exploration" of Randall's "remarkable life as a poet and creative visionary."

In her poetics, Boyd employs a spare, sharp verse whose vernacular style and generally short lines are informed by a wide-ranging sensibility that is rooted in American contemporary urban experiences. Boyd's declarative sentences are made powerful through her jagged, fragmented, style. Her poems often praise the urban landscape for just those things that seem most unexpected. The grittiness, the anonymity, and the visual and aural noise of this environment find their way into her poems as monumental icons; "the crowd wears sunglasses" offers an excellent example, describing "the city" as a complicated place where

> . . . the need
> for greed
> weaves pain
> into fear
> into a slow
> kill.

Despite its complexity, the vibrant and electrifying city must also be associated with fear and slow death.

Equally important, as observers and commentators, Boyd's speakers are deeply informed about the endemic class and racial conflicts in modern America. Consequently, through her speakers Boyd often directly and unabashadedly addresses the ills of American modernity and the African-American community, such as drugs, homelessness, police brutality, disfranchisement, and white privilege in a racialized society, as she does in "We Want Our City Back":

> We don't want police
> harassing the homeless
> for being without a lease.

Mock-irony, a distinct feature of African-American modernism, creates the tension that drives this poem forward, successfully creating the cacophony that marks inner city life.

Boyd's poetics are grounded in the primacy of the images she creates that seem to mount up like skyscrapers in an urban skyline. Boyd draws these images from the rich diversity found in the modern urban environment, juxtaposing them against one another to produce unexpected, exciting, and rich associations. This is true in poems that deal with both public and private subjects, such as "passion. joy. peace":

> your gift of
> 3 words

> etched in gold
> on 3 pastel
> stones.

Since receiving her doctor of arts in English from the University of Michigan in 1979, Boyd has taught at the University of Iowa, Ohio State University, and the University of Michigan–Flint. She joined the faculty of Wayne State University in 1996 and is currently a professor in the department of Africana studies. She is also an adjunct professor at the Center for Afroamerican and African Studies at the University of Michigan–Ann Arbor. Boyd continues to publish poetry and scholarly articles widely, both in the United States and in Europe, and has received numerous awards. She lives with her family in Detroit.

BIBLIOGRAPHY

Boyd, Melba Joyce, and M. L. Liebler, eds. *Abandon Automobile: Detroit City Poetry 2001.* Detroit: Wayne State University Press, 2001.

———. *The Black Unicorn: Dudley Randall and the Broadside Press.* (Film) 1995.

———. *Discarded Legacy: Politics and Poetics in the Life of Frances E. W. Harper (1825–1911).* Detroit: Wayne State University Press, 1994.

———. *The Province of Literary Cats.* Detroit: Past Tents Press, 2002.

———. *Wrestling with the Muse: Dudley Randall and Broadside Press.* New York: Columbia University Press, 2003.

DuCille, Ann. "Trials and Triumphs of Reconstruction." *Women's Review of Books* (Autumn 1994): 13–15.

Rampersad, Arnold. "Wrestling with the Muse." Columbia University Press Web site. Available online. URL: www.columbia.edu/cu/cup/catalog/data/023113/0231130260.htm. Accessed September 29, 2006.

Geoffrey Jacques

Boykin, Keith   (1965–)

Activist author and lecturer Keith Boykin was born in St. Louis, Missouri, to William Boykin, a small-business owner, and Shirley Hayes, a federal government employee. A 1992 graduate of Harvard Law School, Boykin served two years as special assistant and director of specialty press for President Clinton, acting as the principal liaison and spokesperson between the White House and the minority media, including the African-American and gay media. Currently, he serves as executive director of the National Black Gay & Lesbian Leadership Forum. He lives in New York City.

In 1992 Boykin worked on the Democratic primary in New Hampshire for Governor Bill Clinton and, later that year, moved to Little Rock to work on the presidential campaign. Boykin continued to work in Little Rock on inaugural functions after Clinton was elected president of the United States until 1993, when the president brought him to Washington, D.C. as special assistant to the president, first as the director of news analysis and then as director of specialty press. Boykin left his post in 1995 to write *One More River to Cross* (1997), his autobiography, which chronicles his struggles with being black, middle class, and gay in America.

One More River to Cross presents a strong social commentary on the complex realities black lesbians and gay men face within gay white and straight black communities. Boykin introduces himself as an imaginative and intuitive child raised in a typical middle-class St. Louis suburb in a strong, supportive family. However, he is made to confront the dichotomy of being black and gay in America when he attends predominantly white elementary and middle schools. The Boykin family lives in a white suburb, while the black children who attend the public schools are poor and are bused from the outskirts of the city. On fitting in, he recalls that, although he was not certain what made him different, he knew it was something more ingrained and impenetrable than the exterior of his skin and class.

Boykin graciously fumbles through sexual growing pains, dating a few girls in high school and allowing them to temper his effeminate manners. More important, arriving at high school in Clearwater, Florida, he noted that white girls would not befriend with him because he was

black, and black girls would not because he was not black enough. These social commentaries and nuances in the fabric of accepted American norms gain even greater credibility when Boykin points to the black stereotypes in popular television shows and other media. Further, while chronicling his own experiences, he researches history, the language of the CIVIL RIGHTS MOVEMENT, and speeches, testimonies, and quotes made by prominent black figures, such as historian Roger Wilkins and the Reverend Jesse Jackson, for notions of stereotypes and their perpetuating ability to create a false sense of black identity in America. He canvasses church leaders, gay political leaders, and other black gays and lesbians on issues of faith, family, and discrimination, using their views to determine what discrepancies, both real and imagined, prevent a coalition of blacks and gays. While Boykin's research suggests that blacks are less homophobic than whites, despite the coarse rhetoric of rap lyrics and ardent doctrines, he suggests that both conservative political and religious forces equally perpetuate tolerance for racially motivated homophobia in America.

Boykin's portrayal of what it means to be black and gay offers an extraordinary insight into a community that challenges America's acceptance of its minorities, both racial and sexual. A black homosexual remains invisible to or is unaccepted by both black straight and white gay groups. *One More River to Cross* explores historical and contemporary political and religious themes to gain access into roles of black leadership, cultural function, tolerance, domination, and racial marginalization in America. His second nonfiction publication, *Respecting the Soul: Daily Reflections for Black Lesbians and Gays,* received the prestigious Lambda Literary Award.

BIBLIOGRAPHY

Greene, Beverly, ed. *Ethnic and Cultural Diversity among Lesbians and Gay Men: Psychological Perspectives on Lesbian and Gay Issues.* Vol. 3. Thousand Oaks, Calif.: Sage Publications, 1997.

Hawkeswood, William G. *One of the Children: Gay Men in Black Harlem.* Berkeley: University of California Press, 1996.

Reid-Pharr, Robert F., ed. *Black Gay Man: Essays.* New York: New York University Press, 2001.

Lawrence Potter

Bradley, David (1950–)

Like many African-American writers, David Bradley centers his work on essential questions pertaining to family, community, history, and racism. Bradley's work is distinguished by its immediacy and the profound effect of his awareness and treatment of the intersection between the burdens of history and the difficult promises of individual existence. His first book, *South Street* (1975), written while he was an undergraduate, went out of print soon after publication. His second novel, *The Chaneysville Incident* (1981), winner of the PEN/Faulkner Prize and a Book-of-the-Month Club Alternate Selection, quickly established Bradley's reputation as a major 20th-century African-American author.

David Bradley, the only son of Reverend D. H. Bradley and Harriet M. Jackson Bradley, was born and raised in Bedford, Pennsylvania, where he attended public school. He graduated from Bedford Area High School in 1968 and attended the University of Pennsylvania as a creative writing and English major, graduating summa cum laude in 1972. He attended the University of London, studying at the Institute for United States Studies; in 1974, he received his M.A. in area studies, United States, from Kings College, London. Bradley had begun in earnest his study of 19th-century American history, laying the foundation for what would become *The Chaneysville Incident,* a novel he planned to center around the local legend of 13 runaway slaves he had heard in Bedford.

Bradley became interested in this legend when his mother, while researching the history of Bedford's black community for the local bicentennial, came across the story and then found the actual graves of the fugitive slaves in Bedford County. Mrs. Bradley's discovery confirmed the well-known legend: While making their way to freedom through Bedford on the Underground Railroad, 13 fugitive slaves asked to be put to death to avoid their impending recapture. Although Bradley first recorded the story of their tragic choice in his unpublished collection of short stories, written while he was in college, his interest in this legend did not end there. He would make it central to the narrative of *The Chaneysville Incident.*

Bradley wrote four versions of *The Chaneysville Incident* over a 10-year period. The final version is a compelling story of a young black man's search for meaning in the history of his family, particularly his father, and his community. The protagonist, John Washington, a young black history professor living in Philadelphia, returns home to Chaneysville to care for and then bury his surrogate father, Jack Crawley. While home, John visits his parents' house, where he examines the historical documents, papers, and journals of his late biological father, Moses. Through this research, John works toward a better understanding of his father's suicide and its connections to the death of the 13 fugitive slaves many years before. Through a process of self-discovery and examination, involving Judith, the white psychiatrist he is dating, John comes to a deeper understanding of the true meaning of communal and personal history. By comprehending what led the fugitive slaves to forfeit their lives, John comes to understand why his father, Moses, chose to take his own life.

In *The Chaneysville Incident* Bradley weaves numerous stories together into a central narrative thread. Central characters John and Jack are storytellers, weavers of a good yarn. John's return home begins a series of memories and flashbacks—to his own childhood and adolescence and to other stories told by Jack. In a multiplicity of telling and remembering, Bradley weaves together John's memories, Jack's stories, Moses' history, conversations with Judith, and John's vision of the Chaneysville incident into a narrative tapestry depicting the violence and cruelty that not only often typified slavery but also typifies life within a racist culture.

A former Temple University professor and currently a visiting faculty member at the University of Oregon, Bradley has also written eight screenplays. Frequently writing on topics pertaining to the African-American experience, Bradley has been a consistent contributor to *The New Yorker,* the *New York Times Magazine,* the *Los Angeles Times, Esquire,* the *Philadelphia Inquirer Magazine,* and *The Village Voice.* In addition to his PEN/Faulkner, Bradley has been awarded a Guggenheim Fellowship for fiction and a National Endowment for the Arts Literature Fellowship for nonfiction; he was a Lila Wallace–Reader's Digest Visiting Writer Fellow.

BIBLIOGRAPHY

Blake, Susan L., and James A. Miller. "The Business of Writing: An Interview with David Bradley." *Callaloo* (Spring–Summer 1984): 19–39.
Ensslen, Klaus. "Fictionalizing History: David Bradley's *The Chaneysville Incident.*" *Callaloo* (Spring 1988): 280–296.

Janet Bland

Braithwaite, William Stanley Beaumont
(1878–1962)

Boston-born William Braithwaite, whose parents, Emma DeWolfe and William Smith Braithwaite, were West Indians, was best known as an editor, critic, and anthologist. Left practically destitute at age 12 by the death of his father, having previously grown up in a fairly prosperous home where he was tutored in French, Braithwaite, who was forced to seek employment to help meet the daily needs of the family, was self-educated for the most part, although he later received honorary degrees from Atlanta University and Talladega College and held a chair as professor of creative literature at Atlanta University. Braithwaite's intelligence, brilliance, and scholarly productivity placed him among peers W. E. B. DuBois and James Weldon Johnson, although not necessarily in the vanguard with such pioneering turn-of-the-century black writers as Paul Laurence Dunbar and even Charles Chesnutt, who, at first, distanced himself from his black identity in order to publish. Preceding the younger generation of Harlem Renaissance writers such as Langston Hughes, Zora Neale Hurston, and Wallace Thurman, who were, as Hughes notes in "The Negro Artist and the Racial Mountain," interested in embracing and celebrating the complete spectrum of black identity and culture in their works, Braithwaite did not wish to be viewed as a "Negro poet"—a "race poet." In fact, he encouraged the younger poets of the Harlem Renaissance, specifically Claude McKay, to submit for publication only works that did not signal their racial identity. Braithwaite, whom Robert Bone identified, along with DuBois, as a member of the conservative black faction, accused Hughes and his peers, with the exception of Jean Toomer, the author of *Cane,* of "glorifying the lowest strata of Negro life, pandering to sensationalism, and succumbing to the influence of white Bohemia" (95).

Becoming familiar with British lyricist poets while working in a printing shop, Braithwaite began to value and to write poetry in that tradition, bemoaning the legitimatization of the minstrel's mask and voice, black dialect, imposed on Dunbar, Johnson, and Chesnutt. Braithwaite became editor of the *New Poetry Review* and a regular contributor to such mainstream journals as the *Forum, Century, Scribner's,* and *Atlantic Monthly.* He was, for many years, the leading book reviewer for the *Boston Transcript.* His most significant literary contributions, however, were his annual *Anthology of Magazine Verse and Yearbook of American Poetry,* published from 1913–1929, which included not only poems focused on such traditional themes as truth and beauty but also his critical literary analyses and reviews. He published the work of many American modernist poets, including Vachel Lindsay and Carl Sandburg, before they became well known.

His personal work includes three volumes of poetry: *Lyrics of Life and Love* (1904), *The House of Falling Leaves* (1908), *Sandy Star* (1926), and *Selected Poems* (1948). In addition, he wrote his autobiography, *The House under Arcturus* (1940), and a biography of the Brontes, *The Bewitched Parsonage* (1950). His celebration of Keats's birthday, "October XXIX, 1795" (1908), is exemplary of his nonracial, more traditional themes, as seen in its last stanza:

> And with these blazing triumphs spoke one voice
> Whose wistful speech no vaunting did employ:
> 'I know not if 'twere by Fate's chance or choice
> I hold the lowly birth of an English boy;
> I only know he made man's heart rejoice
> Because he played with Beauty for a joy!"

Perhaps Braithwaite, winner of the Spingarn Medal in 1918, would have readily applied to himself his critique of Toomer in his "The Negro in American Literature," which Locke included in his anthology *The New Negro:* "He would write just as well, just as poignantly, just as transmutingly, about the peasants of Russia, or the peasants of Ireland, had experience brought him in touch with their existence. . . . Jean Toomer is a bright and morning star of a new day of race in literature."

BIBLIOGRAPHY

Bone, Robert. *The Negro Novel in America.* Rev. ed. New Haven: Yale University Press, 1958.

Braithwaite, Benjamin Stanley. "The Negro in American Literature." In *The New Negro,* edited by Alain Locke, 29–53. New York: Atheneum, 1968.

Wilfred D. Samuels

Broadside Press

Founded by the poet DUDLEY F. RANDALL, the editor and publisher, in Detroit, Michigan, in 1965, Broadside Press, most critics agree, was vital to the success the BLACK ARTS MOVEMENT and its major poets during the 1960s and 1970s. A librarian who was aware of the importance of copyrighting as a means of protecting intellectual property, Randall founded Broadside to protect his first published work, "Ballad of Birmingham," which Jerry Moore, a folk singer, had also set to music as "Dressed All in Pink." The two poems formed the beginning of the Broadside Series and the genesis

of Broadside Press. Although for the first five years Broadside Press was a one-man operation, housed in Randall's basement and study, Broadside Press would become a company that kept outgrowing its space.

In many ways, *For Malcolm: Poems on the Life and Death of Malcolm X* (1967), which Randall coedited with visual artist Margaret Burroughs and which was inspired by MARGARET WALKER's poem "For Malcolm," witnessed the true genesis of Broadside Press as a viable and valuable publishing vehicle. *For Malcolm* was the outcome of the radical and contentious debate among black writers about the functional role of art and propaganda that took place during the 1966 Fisk Writers Conference at Fisk University, during which the more traditionalist ROBERT HAYDEN (who described himself as a poet first and foremost) and the supporters of a black aesthetics clashed head on. The symbolic importance of the life and death of MALCOLM X was the sole space in which the various camps found common ground.

The response to Randall and Burroughs's call for works on Malcolm X, which would be published in an anthology, was electric and eclectic. Even Hayden submitted an entry, "El Hajj Malik, El Shabazz." The list of those who responded reads like a "Who's Who" list among black writers of the 1960s and 1970s: GWENDOLYN BROOKS, LeRoi Jones (AMIRI BARAKA), Margaret Walker, OSSIE DAVIS, CLARENCE MAJOR, TED JOANS, MARI EVANS, Julia Fields, SONIA SANCHEZ, DAVID HENDERSON, and LARRY NEAL, among many others. As MELBA JOYCE BOYD notes, "The divergent political perspectives and broad range of literary styles that characterized the anthology foreshadowed the profiles of future Broadside Press authors" (144).

For Malcolm would also be instrumental in attracting many of the poets who became the major architects of the BLACK ARTS MOVEMENT, particularly Don L. Lee (HAKI MADHUBUTI), NIKKI GIOVANNI, James Emmanuel, and ETHERIDGE KNIGHT, who was in Indiana State Prison when he first contacted Randall. Madhubuti's early best-selling books were published by Broadside Press, including *Black Pride* (1968), *Think Black* (1968), and *Don't Cry, Scream* (1969), which has the distinction of being Broadside's first hardcover publication. Randall also created an audio series, Broadside Voices, of poets reading their own books on tape.

Although the 1960s witnessed a proliferation of black presses, including Lee's (Madhubuti's) THIRD WORLD PRESS in Chicago and Baraka's Jihad Press in New Jersey, as Randall himself concluded, "Broadside set the precedent" (quoted in Boyd, 235). As Randall further explained, "There was something further in the air in the '60s, and the poetry was new too. . . . The political climate, the sit-ins and the civil demonstrations focused attention on the black revolt. Poetry is more emotional than prose, and it was time for emotions" (235).

BIBLIOGRAPHY

Boyd, Melba Joyce. *Wrestling with the Muse: Dudley Randall and the Broadside Press.* New York: Columbia University Press, 2003.

Gayle, Addison, ed. *The Black Aesthetic.* Garden City, N.Y.: Anchor Books, 1972.

Wilfred D. Samuels

Brooks, Gwendolyn   (1917–2002)

Gwendolyn Brooks was born on June 7, 1917, in Topeka, Kansas, to schoolteacher Keziah Corinne Wims and janitor David Anderson Brooks. The family moved to Chicago five weeks later, where she was raised. She graduated from high school and completed her formal education at Wilson Junior College in 1936 and then worked for a short time as a maid and secretary. Two years later she joined Chicago's NATIONAL ASSOCIATION FOR THE ADVANCEMENT OF COLORED PEOPLE Youth Council, and a year later she married Henry Lowington Blakely II. The young couple lived in a kitchenette apartment (similar to the one described in her novel MAUD MARTHA) at 63rd and Chaplain in Chicago above a real-estate agency.

Like LANGSTON HUGHES and JAMES WELDON JOHNSON, who would critique her work and mentor her, Brooks is best known for her poetry. Her first poem appeared in *American Child* magazine when Brooks was only 13. Three years later JAMES WELDON JOHNSON had read and critiqued her poetry. When she graduated from high school in 1935, she was already a regular contributor to the weekly variety column of *The Chicago Defender,* a black newspaper, in which she also published a number of her poems.

Brooks studied poetry with Inez Cunningham Stark at a community art center on the South Side of Chicago. She would later teach creative writing to one of the South Side's best-known youth "gangs," the Blackstone Rangers. Winning the Midwestern Writers' Conference poetry award in 1943 led to the publication of her first collection of poems, *A Street in Bronzeville* (1945). Her other collections include *Annie Allen* (1949), *Maud Martha* (1953), *The Bean Eaters* (1961), and *In the Mecca* (1968). In 1950 Brooks became the first black writer to win a Pulitzer Prize for poetry (for *Annie Allen*). She also published *Bronzeville Boys and Girls* (1956), poems for children. During this period she also wrote reviews and articles that were published in the *New York Times, Negro Digest,* and the *New York Herald Tribune.* She represented in a variety of poetic forms the human condition from a black perspective. Much of her work concentrates on the people who live in a small Chicago community.

Brooks's first book of poetry, *A Street in Bronzeville,* celebrates the ordinary lives of a group of ordinary urban dwellers who live in a community that resembles Chicago's South Side. Brooks sacrifices overt protest in favor of focusing on the everyday lives of preachers, gamblers, maids, beauty shop owners, and other members of the black community of Bronzeville. In "the mother," for example, she provides an extraordinarily sensitive treatment of a woman's afterthoughts about having experienced multiple abortions. "The Sundays of Satin-Legs Smith" takes the reader through a typical Sunday in the life of a Bronzeville man who relishes that day in particular when he can dress in his zoot suit and strut through the community. The poem tracks Satin-Leg Smith's personal history of social and economic deprivation while celebrating the minor triumph represented by his ordinary Sunday pleasures—from his coffee and rolls for breakfast, to the BLUES he hears as he strolls through the community, to an evening capped by a completely satisfying date with a soft, willing woman.

Annie Allen (1949) renders the story of an ordinary black woman in four parts: "Notes from the Childhood and the Girlhood," "The Anniad," "Appendix to the Anniad," and "The Womanhood." Set in Chicago, the centerpiece of the collection, "The Anniad," is a mock epic that alludes to Homer's *The Iliad* and Virgil's *The Aeneid*. Through Annie's urban black female consciousness, Brooks takes the reader from Annie's early life through the disillusionment of marriage and other life experiences. Annie's search for self and for romantic love unfolds in the form of a ballad of desire and experience that culminates a lesson of self-esteem and self-reliance in the final section, "The Womanhood." The mock epic and, indeed, the entire collection cover many of the same concerns that Brooks later tackles in her only novel, *Maud Martha*.

Maud Martha deals with the developing consciousness of a young girl living in a northern city during the period before, during, and after World War II. Composed of 34 very poetic sketches, the novel provides an application of double-consciousness, which Brooks expands by presenting a title character and protagonist who must overcome her feelings of rejection in a world that values whiteness (light skin), maleness, European features, and "good hair" over blackness (dark skin), femaleness, African features, and coarse hair. In effect, Maud experiences and exhibits "multiple consciousness." In some ways *Maud Martha* is akin to the realism of ZORA NEALE HURSTON's classic *THEIR EYES WERE WATCHING GOD* (1937) in its focus on a woman's journey of self-discovery and her growing awareness of her own agency.

Brooks's literary career took a decided turn after she attended a Black Writers' Conference at Fisk University in 1967 and interacted with a number of artists involved with the BLACK ARTS MOVEMENT. She credits these younger artists with helping her gain greater awareness about American society and about herself. In the 1970s she became a consultant in American literature for the Library of Congress and was named poet laureate of Illinois. Brooks taught in a number of colleges and universities, including Chicago's Columbia College, the University of Wisconsin at Madison, and City University of New York. Her career as author, teacher, and community activist spanned almost 70 years. She died on December 3, 2000.

BIBLIOGRAPHY

Bloom, Harold, ed. *Gwendolyn Brooks.* Philadelphia: Chelsea House, 2000.

Bolden, Barbara Jean. *Urban Rage in Bronzeville: Social Commentary in the Poetry of Gwendolyn Brooks, 1945–1960.* Chicago: Third World Press, 1999.

Bryant, Jacqueline, ed. *Gwendolyn Brooks's Maud Martha: A Critical Collection.* Chicago: Third World Press, 2002.

Gayles, Gloria Wade. *Conversations with Gwendolyn Brooks.* Jackson: University Press of Mississippi, 2003.

Kent, George E. *A Life of Gwendolyn Brooks.* Lexington: University Press of Kentucky, 1990.

Melhem, D. H. *Gwendolyn Brooks: Poetry and Heroic Voice.* Lexington: University Press of Kentucky, 1987.

Mootry, Maria K., and Gary Smith, eds. *A Life Distilled: Gwendolyn Brooks: Her Poetry and Fiction.* Urbana: University of Illinois Press, 1987.

Wright, Stephen Caldwell, ed. *On Gwendolyn Brooks: Reliant Contemplation.* Ann Arbor: University of Michigan Press, 1996.

Lovalerie King

Brothers and Keepers
John Edgar Wideman (1984)

Following the arrest of his brother, Robby, for murder, novelist JOHN EDGAR WIDEMAN began taking a new direction with his literary career. Seeking to understand the reasons behind his brother's descent into a life of crime and eventually life imprisonment, Wideman explored the intersections of family, race, and history in America. The result was the autobiographical account of his own journey and Robby's incarceration in *Brothers and Keepers*. Wideman had drawn a fictional account of some of these events in the short story cycle *Damballah*

(1981), published three years before *Brothers and Keepers* appeared. *Brothers and Keepers* develops some of the same themes of *Damballah* but further extends Wideman's critique of America, especially his claim that the numbers of African-American males incarcerated reveals the connection between the past and the present: Slavery is the historical equivalent of Robby's prison life. Wideman reaches this conclusion in his short story "The Beginning of Homewood" in *Damballah,* when he imagines the life of an ancestor, a slave, who committed a crime by running away, juxtaposed with that of Tommy (the fictional persona of Robby). Both the slave and the prisoner are chained like outlaws, but they are really the victims in a larger economic, social, and racial drama.

As Wideman traces the historical, cultural, and personal forces that led to Robby's downfall, he reconciles himself to his own troubled past and to the family and community that he fled as a young writer and academic. This flight away from home and racial identity marks Wideman's own double-consciousness in the work. And though Robby is acknowledged by the society as being the "criminal," Wideman discovers that he himself has been the one that has acted like a "fugitive." Turning his back on his African-American community has alienated Wideman from himself. John and Robby both suffer from the limitations imposed on them by a racist America. While it appears that Wideman has beaten the system, he has sacrificed his personal history to do so. The promise of American middle-class success has seduced him away from his family and the Homewood neighborhood of his youth. Robby stayed behind, a statistic of urban desolation, impoverishment, drug use, and crime, though *Brothers and Keepers* shows that this was not always the life that Robby saw before him. Like his brother, Robby had dreams, talent, and intelligence—all ravaged by a society that refused to see beyond the color of his skin.

While Wideman recognizes Robby's own responsibility in the direction that his life ultimately took, he cannot overlook the "keepers" who resolutely refuse to acknowledge Robby's humanity. The keepers include the guards who control Robby's movements, but the keepers are also the guardians of American institutions who control the perceptions that this society holds of black men and women. On a visit to the prison, Wideman marks the way that the guards treat his children, his wife, and his mother. Treated like prisoners themselves, Wideman realizes his inability to make the world see beyond race. His mother also remembers Robby's friend, Garth, who died after a long illness. Unable to get adequate health care because he was poor and black, Garth lingers through terrible pain. Little is done to comfort him, and the system seems to abandon him. It is the loss of young, black male lives to a world that ignores them that embitters Wideman's mother most.

The structure of the work embodies Wideman's commitment to the communal voice, to the notion that "all stories are true"—the title of one of his short story collections. The work is divided into three sections; the voices of Wideman, his mother, and Robby moderate the different sections. The three distinct points of view offer a more complete observation of the circumstances that brought Robby to prison. But the different voices also remind us that there is no one singular African-American experience, and until America understands and accepts the humanity of African Americans, the past will continue to haunt the present.

BIBLIOGRAPHY

Wideman, John Edgar. *Brothers and Keepers.* New York: Holt, Rinehart and Winston, 1984.
———. *Damballah.* London: Allison & Busby, 1984.

Tracie Church Guzzio

Brother to Brother: New Writings by Black Gay Men   Essex Hemphill, ed.   (1991)

Brother to Brother is an emotive journey of discovery on what it means to be black and gay. In his introduction, ESSEX HEMPHILL states that if there had been a book about black gay men available to him during his own youth, such as *In the Life: A Black Gay Anthology* (1986), he would not have had to create still another mask. The historical communities of silence that reared black gay men, silence's accountability for the AIDS epidemic among blacks, and the misconstrued representation of black homosexuals by the media led Hemphill to publish a generous anthology as an offering to others like him. He dedicates the anthology to his lover, Joseph Fairchild Beam, editor of *In the Life,* who died from an AIDS-related illness in 1988. In Hemphill's poem to Beam, "When My Brother Fell," his speaker says, "it's too soon to make monuments" for sons of AIDS (111). *Brother to Brother* is greater than any monument. The poems, short stories, interviews, and essays are testimonies of love, strength, and courage and give a powerful representation of the black gay male amid self-discovery and the development of a collective consciousness often chastised by silence and deadly change.

"When I Think of Home," Section I of the anthology, opens with "Sacrifice," a metaphorical birth of homosexuality in the black American race. The title of Adrian Stanford's poem alone is resonant of the black man's self-sacrifice to America and all that is owing to his own loss of identity. The poem is powerfully imagistic in its sense of duality. The effeminate identity of the son could be the father's second sacrifice. The question is, can the father choose to eliminate his gay son? Or is the title's image of sacrifice a forecast for the socially imposed silence on the gay black son? Is a strong sense of community possible for the black homosexual?

Family is community for many African Americans, who may not have a clear national identity. Coming out represents an even greater challenge for the African-American male, as he admittedly sacrifices the very foundation that birthed and strengthened his fortitude for becoming a man. A touching story, "The Jazz Singer," by Charles Henry Fuller, illustrates the lonely awkwardness of an adolescent discovering his homosexuality. By personifying the jazz singers his parents listen to, singers like Ella Fitzgerald, Bessie Smith, Billie Holliday, Lena Horne, and Sarah Vaughn, the boy adheres to the music of his family, yet he stands in opposition to his father's sense of masculinity. The father does soften to his discovery of his son

dressed up in women's clothing, but he sternly warns his son that there are things in this world a black man simply cannot be (6).

"Daddy Lied," a somber poem by Rory Buchanan, reconciles the silence and its irrational sensibilities as belonging to the past. Buchanan's father raised him as his father's father had done: according to a silent code of manhood. Silence serves as a refrain in the African-American community. Like music, the sustained pause is a somber unspoken embrace. "Letter to Gregory" by Alan Miller broadens the notion of community and its quiet embrace in a moving eulogy for a young man killed in "the unyielding appetite of the harshest / light . . ." by a drive-by shooter (29). Miller's use of photographs offers an intimate remembrance of Gregory and an emotive mourning over the decline of the African-American community to violence and infighting.

Essex Hemphill challenges notions and representations of family in his poem "Commitments." Like Miller, Hemphill uses photographs to show the quiet legacy of the homosexual youth as he stands among his relatives, seated beside them at the picnic table and at holiday dinners. Hemphill uses the poem to challenge his community, his family, regarding their "conditional" commitment to the child represented in those family photographs. He says, essentially, that the homosexual has always been there among his family, but where, father, mother, aunt, and uncle, have you been?

Self-empowerment finally seems to reign for the gay black man in "At 36," a story by Charles Harpe. Here, Harpe is at the age he had always found captivating and secure in a homosexual. Homosexuality is no longer an issue for him, yet he is in a place of forgiveness (53). The lack of love, the desire to be loved, and low self-esteem are common traits in the otherwise diverse community of gay men. The desperate need for love continues "At 36," as long as a lack of understanding and stability in the African-American community in general persists.

"Baby, I'm for Real," Section II, chronicles the voices of lovers and the development of a gay black community. "Comfort," a poem by Don Charles, addresses the warmth of things familiar, the comfort of likeness, of history, and shared experience.

"Safe Harbour," a poem by David Frechette, is a metaphor for the rescue of a lover's arms against the "tidal wave of woes" the black homosexual would face outside his lover's embrace. "Names and Sorrows," a poem by D. Rubin Green, chronicles the myriad discrepancies and problems of black-on-white gay love. All three poems are emblematic of the carving out of a new community. Many black gay men are estranged from their families. The conciliatory tone of Charles's "Comfort" is tempting to a gay black male adrift from a community he had always known. Frechette's poem too draws a cold, unforgiving heterosexual world, while Green goes deeper into blackness, addressing ostracism by chanting some of the taboos a black man who loves a white man must turn over in his mind.

The exterior world's impression of the black male preys on the identity of the black homosexual. "Couch Poem" by Donald Woods juxtaposes the complex mask a professional gay man wears throughout his day, against his true personal yearnings, sense of place, and comforts (64–67). "Hey, Brother, What's Hap'nin?," a short story by Cary Alan Johnson, further challenges the figurative roles gay black men must play. By reestablishing dominant and effeminate manners, Johnson throws all the white definitions away and establishes the boy next door as the ideal. The boy next store is both something to be and someone to pine after. "Jailbait," a poem by Don Charles, denies the boy next store the ability to know what his needs are and what he could be representing to the older, wiser black homosexual.

"Hold Tight Gently," Section III, broadens the black homosexual community to include friends and caregivers. "It Happened to Me," a nonfiction account by Roger V. Pamplin, Jr., shows the rationale and behavior that led Pamplin to be tested for HIV and learn he is positive. Part of the rationale seems to be a lack of communication filtering over from the gay white community. Pamplin survives PCP pneumonia and, at the time of his writing this piece, owes his defeat of death to the support of friends and his faith in God. He initially goes from being angry with God to having an even greater sense of purpose. Through Pamplin's piece, oth-

ers can learn to be safe and the black gay community can become strengthened. "The Scarlet Letter, Revisited: A Very Different AIDS Story," by Walter Rico Burrell, follows a diary account of the author's AIDS-related illnesses. Caught between hostile, fearful medical and pharmaceutical communities and a tolerant and loving community of a doctor and one friend, Burrell undergoes the trials of AZT. Through the delirium of the drug, he tells his family history, the dichotomy of his father's sense of place in the world (black and economically successful was rare), and the social constrictions of being black. The physical and emotional closeness he shares with his father is something he wishes to pass on to his own children, especially to his son. Burrell openly discloses his ex-wife's hatred for him and his lifestyle and his son's rejection of him, and he reconciles that he may just "leave this life still longing for love" given the limited though warm community in which he resides (135). "Remembrance," a prose piece by Kenneth McCreary, chronicles the love, dedication, and profound aloneness that the caregiver experiences following the loss of a lover or friend to AIDS. The sadness is found in the fact that in the weeks following the death, perhaps even in years to come, rediscovered items belonging to the deceased will echo a life left to be remembered.

"The Absence of Fear," section IV, begins with Adrian Stanford's famous "Psalm for the Ghetto." Stanford's emotive call for coalition within the black culture for the survival of the black intellect transitions into the essay "True Confessions: A Discourse on Images of Black Male Sexuality." Here, Isaac Julien and Kobena Mercer object to laws against pornography for their overriding white representation and its lack of libertarian arguments. Julien and Mercer further discuss "black male gender roles" and "a multiplicity of identities" to contribute to the coalition for a true black intellectual and sexual identity.

Essex Hemphill and Joseph Beam look to the contributions of black literary icons LANGSTON HUGHES and JAMES BALDWIN and to contemporary artists' depictions of their works in search of a cornerstone to define the black homosexual intellect. Roy Simmons discusses some of the social, intellectual, and literary biases black gay intellectuals face, while Charles Nero looks "Toward a Black Gay Aesthetic" development in literature with the premise of finding a positive black identity that renders the life of a black homosexual as "visible" and "valid" (229). The search for a positive, true figure, one fully realized by family and by the broader community, is what brings this collection together. What the Hemphill collection provides, beyond the search for community, is a notable literary text for young gay men to read and learn by.

Lawrence Potter, Jr.

Brown, Claude (1937–2002)

Writer and autobiographer Claude Brown was born on February 23, 1937, in Harlem, New York. He is best known for his novelistic autobiography, *Manchild in the Promised Land* (1960), which, according to Macmillan, its publisher, has sold more than 4 million copies and has been translated into 14 languages. He is also the author of *The Children of Ham* (1976), a children's book.

By age eight Brown was already living the troubled life associated with many urban poverty-stricken blacks of his generation.

Brown spent most of his youth in and out of juvenile detention centers and correctional schools for boys, specifically Warwick and Wiltwyck, because of his delinquent lifestyle and street life of stealing, fighting, and dabbling in drugs and alcohol. He was a charter member of a gang by the time he was 10. At Warwick, he says, "I was ready to stay there for a long time and live real good. I knew how to get along there. I'd had a place waiting for me long before I came. If I'd known Warwick was going to be as good as it turned out to be, I would never have been so afraid. As a matter of fact, I might have gotten there a whole lot sooner."

Brown's criminal lifestyle was to be expected given the often-negative consequences of inner city life—the Harlem he grew up in was one of the fiercest inner cities in the United States—but it was also due to the choices he made. His father, a dock-worker, frequently beat him and was by no means a positive example or father figure. His mother, a good-hearted woman, was always there for him, but she seemed weak when he needed her the most. However, his family had some sense of unity, although there was little income and minimal opportunities for the young Sonny, as he was called. Inevitably, to succeed, Brown turned to the streets, where drugs, prostitution, and violence dominated and contaminated the neighborhood, although he was well aware of the potential consequences. Brown's illicit lifestyle took a deep turn when, at 13 years of age, he was shot in the abdomen during a robbery. This incident became a turning point in his life. Brown, with the encouragement of a friend and a school psychologist, abandoned his criminal behavior, completed high school, and enrolled at Howard University in Washington, D.C., where the award-winning novelist TONI MORRISON was one of his teachers.

Brown wrote about what he knew best: his own life experiences. He confessed, "I didn't know anything other than my own life, so that was what I wrote. . . ." In *Manchild in the Promised Land* his major themes run the gamut from the appeal of the Nation of Islam (the Black Muslims) in the African-American community to homosexuality and the quest for masculine identity, the significance of education to black liberation, and conflicts between southern values and urban inner-city life. By the end of the book his main character has, despite the many challenges he faces, empowered himself, much like FREDERICK DOUGLASS and RICHARD WRIGHT. Unlike "Pimp," his younger brother who became a drug addict, Brown transcended, significantly through education, rather than sank beneath the cracks and insurmountable odds of ghetto life.

Not surprisingly, critics view *Manchild in the Promised Land* as a 20th-century slave narrative. According to Sidone Smith, "*Manchild* is an exposé of the slave system as the slave narrative and Wright's *Black Boy* were exposés of the slave system of the South. Brown . . . vividly portrays the brutal reality of life in Harlem" (157). Brown returned to Harlem after completing his formal education; he lived there until his death. He also established and operated a mentoring program for Harlem's youth and an intensive residential treatment program to help turn young people's lives around, much as he had done for himself.

BIBLIOGRAPHY

Boyd, Herb. "Claude Brown-Tribute." *Black Issues Book Review* 4, no. 3 (May/June 2002): 80.

Smith, Sidone. *Where I'm Bound.* Westport, Conn.: Greenwood Press, 1974.

Carlos Perez

Brown, Frank London   (1927–1962)

Novelist, journalist, and activist Frank London Brown was born in Kansas City, Kansas, to parents Frank London Brown, Sr., and Myra Myrtle Brown Frank London in October 1927. Brown, who grew up in Chicago, graduated from Roosevelt University in 1951, after also attending Wilberforce University. He attended Kent College of Law and received a M.A. degree from the University of Chicago in 1960. He pursued doctoral studies at the University of Chicago with the Committee on Social Thought. Brown had various interests; he was a labor organizer and a jazz musician who was closely connected with the Chicago jazz music scene. He performed with such musicians as Thelonious Monk, Dizzy Gillespie, and Gene Ammons.

Brown's novels include *Trumbull Park* (1959) and *Mythmaker* (1969). Brown was also known for his short stories, which appeared in *Chicago Magazine,* the *Chicago Review, Down Beat, Ebony, Negro Digest, Southwest Review,* and the *Chicago Review Anthology.*

Brown's most famous work, *Trumbull Park,* is based on true events. From the mid-1950s to the mid-1960s, Trumbull Park Homes was a government program designed to end segregation forcibly. The resistance against black families moving into a white residential area was "massive and intractable" (Washington, 32), turning the area into a war zone. Homemade bombs were lobbed into the housing development every night, and blacks were prevented from using any of the neighborhood churches, parks, or stores. In *Trumbull Park,* when Buggy and Helen Martin move into Trumbull Park Homes, they are faced with malice and violence. Rather than focus solely on the anger that the Martins clearly feel about the ongoing hostility, Brown shows the strain and consequence on his characters of having to face constant violence with nonviolence. He shows the Martins' day-to-day life, further humanizing them. Brown's greatest skill in telling the Martins' story is the authentic representation of black life, dialogue, and idiom. Brown depicts "thoroughly respectable" (79), "intelligent, hardworking, and stable" (79) black families. They are not merely interested in their ability to imitate whites.

Mythmaker, Brown's second novel (also his M.A. thesis), which was published posthumously, is set on Chicago's South Side; it is less optimistic than *Trumbull Park.* The main character, Ernest Day, briefly escapes the ghetto, only to be forced back to it in disillusionment and despair. Day's quest to find his identity and place to live in the world is illustrated in his struggle against failure and ruin.

Brown was awarded the John Hay Whitney Award for *Trumbull Park.* He died of leukemia on March 12, 1962, in Illinois.

BIBLIOGRAPHY

Fleming, Robert E. "Overshadowed by Richard Wright: Three Black Chicago Novelists." *Negro American Literature Forum* 7, no. 3 (Autumn 1973): 75–79.

Washington, Mary Helen. "Desegregating the 1950s: The Case of Frank London Brown." *Japanese Journal of American Studies* 10 (1999): 15–32.

Kim Hai Pearson
Brian Jennings

Brown, Sterling Allen   (1901–1989)

Intellectual, educator, mentor, folklorist, cultural guardian, and poet, Sterling Allen Brown was born in Washington, D.C., the son of Sterling Nelson Brown, a former slave and a Howard University professor of theology. A graduate of Dunbar High School, where his teachers included novelist JESSIE REDMON FAUSET, Brown was educated at Massachusetts's Williams College, where he received his B.A. degree Phi Beta Kappa, and at Harvard University, where he received an M.A. degree in English. During the Great Depression, Brown, who had been book review editor for OPPORTUNITY, became the editor of *Negro Affairs* for the Federal Writers' Project of the WPA (1936–1939) and a staff member for the Carnegie-Myrdal Study of the Negro (1939). His work appeared in the *New Republic, The Journal of Negro Education, CRISIS, Phylon,* and the *Massachusetts Review.* Although late in his career as an educator he became a visiting professor at New York University and Vassar College, Brown spent most of his academic life in historical black colleges and universities, including Lincoln University, Fisk University, and particularly Howard University, where he was on the English faculty for 40 years.

Brown published his first collection of poems, *SOUTHERN ROAD,* in 1932. His second collection, *The Last Ride of Wild Bill,* was published more than 40 years later, in 1973. His final collection of poems, *The Collected Poems of Sterling A. Brown,* was published by BROADSIDE PRESS in 1980. Given Broadside's association with the main poets of the BLACK ARTS MOVEMENT, primarily Don L. Lee (HAKI MADHUBUTI), SONIA SANCHEZ, and ETHERIDGE KNIGHT, this was quite a statement by the senior poet and "dedicated genius," as HOUSTON BAKER called Brown (92).

Between publishing his collection of poems and working for the WPA, Brown established himself as an authority on the black writer in America and on the subject of blacks as characters and stereotypes in American literature in such now-classic scholarly works as *The Negro in American Fiction* (1937) and *Negro Poetry and Drama* (1937). As the senior editor, Brown, along with Arthur P. Davis and Ulysses Lee, compiled the pioneering comprehensive anthology on African-American literature *The NEGRO CARAVAN* (1941).

As Baker has noted, during this period Brown was mining the BLUES, a form indigenous to black southern culture that was, ironically, deemed of lesser importance by the black intelligentsia leaders of the HARLEM RENAISSANCE, including ALAIN LOCKE and W. E. B. DUBOIS. As the editors of *CALL AND RESPONSE* noted, "Brown was in the academy but never completely of it" (993). Nor was he a full-fledged member of the Harlem Renaissance, although Locke would eventually describe Brown as a true Negro folk poet like LANGSTON HUGHES and ZORA NEALE HURSTON, who wanted to make the individuals Hughes called the "low down folks" and "the so-called common element" (900), the true representative of the "New Negro Movement" and thus the most credible agent of black culture. Brown, although himself a member of DuBois's "Talented Tenth" of the black middle class, used his work to celebrate the "unwashed" masses, whom, ultimately, he saw as his best teachers.

As the poems in *Southern Road* reveal Brown found more than humor and pathos in poetry written in black dialect, the genre he embraced after living in Lynchburg, Virginia, where he taught at Virginia Seminary and College. In fact, as Cornel West and Henry L. Gates, Jr., point out, Brown "resuscitated dialect poetry, a genre that had been confined to what one critic called 'the waste-bins of minstrelsy'" (119). It had been abandoned by even JAMES WELDON JOHNSON, the distinguished scholar and poet known best for his celebration of black folk culture in *God's Trombones: Seven Negro Sermons,* who had also written in dialect. Brown saw the black folk tradition as the foundation of African-American literary tradition.

Brown's poetry reveals his careful attention to black speech, his validation of black folklore and myth, and his preservation of black culture in its multifaceted form, particularly music: spirituals, jazz, work songs, and specifically the blues. The recipient of a Guggenheim Fellowship, Brown was given an honorary doctorate by Howard University, due, Gates and West claim, to the lobbying of many of his students who had gone on to become the leaders of the Black Arts Movement.

BIBLIOGRAPHY

Baker, Houston A. *Modernism and the Harlem Renaissance.* Chicago: University of Chicago Press, 1987.

Brown, Sterling A. *The Collected Poems of Sterling A. Brown, Selected by Michael Harper.* New York: Harper & Row Publishers, 1983.

Gates, Henry Louis Jr., and Cornel West. "Sterling A. Brown: The Vernacular Poet." In *The African American Century: How Black Americans Have Shaped Our Country,* 119–121. New York: Free Press, 2000.

Hughes, Langston. "The Negro Artist and the Racial Mountain." In *Call and Response: The Riverside Anthology of the African American Literary Tradition,* edited by Patricia Liggins Hill, et. al., 899–902. Boston: Houghton Mifflin Company, 1998.

Wilfred D. Samuels

Brown Girl, Brownstones Paule Marshall (1959)

PAULE MARSHALL's *Brown Girl, Brownstones* (1959) is regarded by many scholars as the beginning of contemporary African-American women's writing. According to BARBARA CHRISTIAN, in *Brown Girl, Brownstones,* Marshall "dramatized the idea that racism is insidious not only in its impact on a person's definition of self as black or white, but also as male and female. . . . Because of the novel's insistence on the relationship of woman as self and as part of a community, it prefigured the major themes of black women's fiction in the 1970s: the black woman's potential as a full person and necessarily as major actor on the social, cultural, and political issues of our times" (104–105).

Through her rich language, vivid characterizations, and unique social contexts, Marshall gave voice to black women and the Caribbean immigrant community. Set in Brooklyn from the late 1930s to World War II, this autobiographical first novel chronicles the coming of age of Selina Boyce. The daughter of Barbadian immigrant parents, Selina is bright and rebellious. Her mother, Silla, is a hard-working, unsentimental woman

for whom the United States promises prosperity. Subconsciously admiring her mother's strength, Selina rejects her materialism. Her father, Deighton, alternately fantasizes about instant American success and returning home to the Caribbean. Selina both adores her father and regrets his delusional approach to life. In the novel, Selina and the reader are educated about love, sacrifice, and African-American history. Marshall's focus on a black girl as protagonist, her exploration of gender dynamics within the black community, and her celebration of black immigrant communities quietly revolutionized American and African-American literature.

Though the novel was well received and earned Marshall a Guggenheim Fellowship in 1960, it did not become a commercial success until interest in black women writers heightened in the early 1970s; it gained widespread recognition only when it was reprinted in 1981.

BIBLIOGRAPHY

Christian, Barbara. *Black Feminist Criticism: Perspective on Black Women Writers.* New York: Pergamon Press, 1985.

Marshall, Paule. *Brown Girl, Brownstones.* New York: Random, 1959.

Elizabeth McNeil

Bullins, Ed (1935–)

Ed Bullins (Kingsley B. Bass) was born in Philadelphia, Pennsylvania, on July 2, 1935, to Edward and Bertha Marie (Queen) Bullins. His mother, a civil servant, tried to instill middle-class values in her son. After attending a predominantly European-American elementary school, where he was a very good student, Bullins, who spent his summers vacationing in Maryland farming country, transferred to an inner-city school as a junior high student. He soon became involved in street gang activities. In one confrontation he was stabbed in the heart and pronounced dead, but he was miraculously resuscitated. Although he attended Philadelphia's infamous Benjamin Franklin High School, he would drop out before graduating. He joined the U.S. Navy, serving from 1952 to 1955. While in the navy, where he won a lightweight boxing championship, Bullins embarked on a self-education program through reading. After his discharge in 1958, he moved to Los Angeles; earned his graduate equivalency diploma; began writing fiction, essays, and poetry; and resumed his formal studies at Los Angeles City College. In 1964 he moved to the San Francisco Bay area and, while registered in a college writing program at San Francisco State College, he began writing plays because, as he later explained, "I came to realize that only closed circles of African Americans read fiction."

Although he would later go on to earn a bachelor of arts from Antioch University in 1989 and an M.F.A. from San Francisco State University in 1994, Bullins, in the late 1960s, emerged as one of the leading and most prolific playwrights of the BLACK ARTS MOVEMENT, whose leaders sought to define a genuinely BLACK AESTHETIC based on the politics of BLACK NATIONALISM and a skillful reconstruction of African-American folklore. This movement was spearheaded by ADDISON GAYLE, LARRY NEAL, NIKKI GIOVANNI, SONIA SANCHEZ, AMIRI BARAKA, and HOYT FULLER, among others. In "Towards a Black Aesthetic," Fuller explains that during the 1960s black writers desired a system of isolating and evaluating the artistic works of African Americans that reflect the special character and imperatives of their experiences. For Fuller, these writers created, through the Black Arts Movement, a way of perceiving African-American art forms as containing more than aesthetic beauty, as demanded by European aesthetics. Their functional art would be a liberating force through which African Americans could reclaim their personal and cultural beauty through their art. Neal argued, in "Visions of a Liberated Future," that drama was a prime vehicle for achieving the specific goals of the Black Aesthetic.

As a dramatist, Bullins was strongly influenced by the major tenets and themes of the Black Arts Movement, including beauty, love, power, and revolution. He, Bobby Seale, Huey Newton, and ELDRIDGE CLEAVER founded Black House, a militant cultural-political organization, and he briefly aligned himself with the Black Panther Party, where he was appointed minister of culture. Although Bullins wanted to promote Kawaida, the cultural nationalism championed by MAULANA KARENGA, other Black Panther members wanted a more revolutionary ideology promoted in African-American art, one that called for armed rebellion.

In August 1965, Bullins made his theatrical debut in San Francisco at the Firehouse Repertory Theater with three one-act plays: *How Do You Do, Dialect Determinism or The Rally,* and *Clara's Ole' Man.* Although he initially considered leaving the United States following his philosophical disagreement with Eldridge Cleaver, Bullins moved to New York City to become playwright in residence and associate director at Robert Macbeth's New Lafayette Theater in Harlem. He also headed the New Lafayette's Black Theater Workshop and edited its *Black Theater Magazine.* For the next 10 years Bullins became one of the most powerful and controversial voices on the off-Broadway stage and, along with Baraka and Neal, one of the most influential playwrights of the Black Arts Movement. Later, he also directed the Writer's Unit Playwrights Workshop for Joseph Papp at the Public Theater and the Playwrights Workshop at Woodie King's New Federal Theater in New York City.

Bullins is perhaps best known for his first full-length play, *In the Wine Time* (1968), which examines the scarcity of options available to African Americans, especially the urban poor. It became the first in a series of plays focused on a group of young friends growing up in America in the 1950s, which he called the Twentieth Century Cycle. The other plays in this cycle are *The Corner* (1968), *In New England Winter* (1969), *The Duplex* (1970), *The Fabulous Miss Marie* (1971), *Homeboy* (1976), and *Daddy* (1977). His other notable works include *Goin' A Buffalo* (1968); *Salaam, Huey Newton, Salaam* (1991); *The Hungered One* (1971), a collection of stories; and *Reluctant Rapist* (1973), a novel. In *Ed Bullins: A Literary Biography* (1977), Samuel Hay describes Bullins as a playwright with a revolutionary bent who, despite this inclination, became an artist who has displayed some of the more deeply ignored representations of African-American life.

Beginning in 1975 Bullins received critical acclaim, including an Obie Award and the New York Drama Critics Award for *The Taking of Miss Janie,* a play about the failed alliance of an interracial group of 1960s political idealists. He has also received a Vernon Rice Desk Drama Award, Guggenheim fellowships, and Rockefeller Foundation and National Endowment for the Arts playwriting grants. True to his Black Nationalistic aesthetic leanings, Bullins's naturalistic plays incorporate elements of African-American folklore, especially "street" lyricism, and interracial tension.

In 1995 Bullins was appointed professor of theater at Northeastern University in Boston. His most recent work, *Boy X Man,* is a memory play about a man looking back on his childhood and the process of growing up. He strains to come to grips with not ever having understood his mother and with having failed to say thank you to a stepfather who has been as much of a father to him as any man could have ever been. Bullins remains continually concerned with getting important themes across to his audience through his plays, and he believes that theater must be revolutionary in order for African-American art to be successful.

BIBLIOGRAPHY

Branch, William B., ed. *An Anthology of Contemporary African American Drama.* New York: Penguin, 1992.

Hay, Samuel. *Ed Bullins: A Literary Biography.* Detroit: Wayne State University Press, 1997.

Hatch, James V., ed. *Black Theater USA: Plays by African Americans.* New York: Free Press, 1996.

Neal, Larry. *Visions of a Liberated Future.* St. Paul, Minn.: Thunder's Mouth Press, 1989.

Raymond E. Janifer

Bum Rush the Page: A Def Poetry Jam
Tony Medina and Louis Reyes Rivera, eds.
(2001)

Bum Rush the Page introduces the United States and the world to recent African-American history through the fresh, sometimes youthful, voices of black poets, artists, literary thinkers, urban translators, musicologists, and revelers. The collection offers the emotions of a community rocked by high crime and violence, urban expressions of hip-hop, and an emergence of class consciousness. The poems are about the "politics of being Black, from civil rights to Black Power, to the new sense of self" and empowerment for future African-American communities, as SONIA SANCHEZ writes in her introduction to the collection (xvi).

In the introduction, Tony Medina contends that the aggressive-progressive intrusion of the media, its hyper-insensitivity, its ugly talk show voyeurism, nearly lost the new African-American poets to the slam; it nearly limited the form to the "spoken word—that which lives in performance" (xx). Medina's argument is not new. RALPH ELLISON presents it symbolically in the boxing ring scene in the opening chapter of *INVISIBLE MAN* (1952). The voices of *Bum Rush* belong to the page, to the solace of the written word. Through their more global perspectives, the poets share social and political concerns over race and gender; engage in struggles over art, place, and self; and "celebrate life, language, and poetry" and cultural creativity (xxi).

Whereas the poetic tones in *Bum Rush* are seductive, prominent, and savvy, the voices form a collective witness to artistic growth, political history, states of exile, and sexual and educational liberation. They are, as YUSEF KOMUNYAKAA argues, "textured by popular-culture references and multiple levels of diction—erudite and street-smart" (xii). While steeped in colloquialisms, sometimes to achieve poetic beat, the open and sometimes genderless verse reveals an international youth spawned by a global market. For example, in "New York Seizures," EUGENE B. REDMOND captures the confused nature of the African American as singular amid globalization's recipe for soup (a melting pot):

> A Puerto Rican speaks Voodoo with an
> African accent;
> A European speaks African with a Spanish
> accent;
> A West Indian yawns in Yiddish and curses
> in Arabic;
> An African speaks English in silence. (184)

Like Redmond, Felice Belle narrows the hypocrisy of having a global voice by revealing the absurd sounds of a national voice. By listing the historical lies and myths that cultivate such a crazy notion, "Exceptions" regenerates cultural fads to demystify the African American's lack of participation in the white global economy (163–166).

While AMIRI BARAKA testifies that the artist's blood courses naturally (perhaps fatedly) through the African American (264), GWENDOLYN BROOKS creates physical and tangible metaphors so readers can envision the human and artistic challenge of community development and extension in "Building" (xxix). Poet and dramatist Carl Hancock Rux simply turns contemporary artistic challenges on their head. Turning phrases that are sometimes maudlin, other times musical, Rux relies on the universal language—music—to continue the collection's thematic thread of a media-developed sense of place and its illusionary results. The effect of working with two artistic mediums—mixing poetry and music—perhaps mimics blending and the death of individual cultural esteem in America:

> am Belial . . .
> Nostrils wide open, veins hungry, mouthing
> incantations to Spanish Key on trumpet
> reading Faust out loud
> drunk on Moett. (116)

Many of the poems address such social and political issues as drive-by shootings, the threat of AIDS, and police brutality.

In *Bum Rush,* these contemporary problems, attributable directly and indirectly to the history of racism and discrimination, are often described or attested to by the collection's youngest, most novice poets. However, the youthfulness of the chorus does not detract from the literary potency of the political verses. They address the upsurge of gangs in the 1980s and 1990s in poems like "Bullet Hole Man" and "Bensonhurst" (110, 243), offering fresh insight into this intraracial class warfare in black America. These brave poems are often somber, morose, and emotional. Other poems, such as "Complected" and "The Tragic Mulatto Is Nei-

ther," address the struggle with cultural and artistic identity, contributing to the poetic canon generated by "complected" American poets long ago (154–158). Also, there are commemorative poems that acknowledge, celebrate, and express appreciation of social and literary icons who not only influenced but also mentored the younger generation of poets.

BIBLIOGRAPHY
Braithwaite, Wendy. *Motion in Poetry.* Toronto: Women's Press, 2002.

Komunyakaa, Yusef, Foreword. In *Listen Up! Spoken Word Poetry,* edited by Zoë Angelesey New York: Ballantine Publishing Group, 1999.

Lawrence T. Potter

Butler, Octavia E.   (1947–2006)

Octavia Estelle Butler was born in 1947 to Laurice Butler and Octavia M. Guy in Pasadena, California. She was an only child whose father died when she was a baby. Her mother, grandmother, and other close relatives raised her in a racially diverse neighborhood that was nonetheless unified in its fight for economic survival. Butler characterized herself as an introspective daydreamer. She had to overcome dyslexia, and she started writing at a young age to deal with her boredom and loneliness. As a young teenager, she was interested in science fiction because it appealed to her sense as an alienated or "out kid." In 1968 she earned an associate of arts from Pasadena City College. She then studied at California State University, Los Angeles, and the University of California at Los Angeles but did not study creative writing formally, opting instead to take writing classes at night. She received further creative writing training in the Open Door Program of the Screen Writers Guild of America in the 1960s and 1970s and the Clarion Science Fiction Writer's Workshop in 1970. Butler also devoted time to researching biology, genetics, and physical science.

Butler has written both novels and short stories. The Patternist series consists of *Wild Seed* (1980), *Mind of My Mind* (1977), *Patternmaster*

(1976), *Clay's Ark* (1984), and *Survivor* (1978). *Kindred* (1979) was a departure from the Patternist series exploring miscegenation, slavery, and powerlessness. The Xenogenesis series includes *Dawn* (1987), *Adulthood Rites* (1988), and *Imago* (1989); this trilogy was republished in 2000 as *Lilith's Brood.* Her Parable series is made up of PARABLE OF THE SOWER (1994) and *Parable of the Talents* (1998). Her short works are "Speech Sounds," the oft-anthologized "Bloodchild," and a collection of short works, *Bloodchild and Other Stories.*

Her best known novel, *Kindred,* is about a black woman, Dana, who lives in the Los Angeles suburbs with her white husband in the 1970s. She is pulled out of her life and into the past by a white ancestor in great need. Many of Butler's novels explore complex issues of race, power, and gender. Most of the characters in her novels have immense powers that they have to learn to control because the powers are nearly as threatening as outside forces are. In her Parable novels, Butler addresses drug use and other factors that beset African-American communities in the 20th century. Butler uses science fiction as a vehicle to examine social issues, relationships, identity, class, and gender with artistry and originality.

Butler won the Hugo award in 1984 for "Speech Sounds." She won a second Hugo in 1985, as well as a Nebula in 1984, for "Bloodchild." Butler was awarded the MacArthur Foundation "genius grant" in 1995. In 1999, she won the Nebula award for best science fiction novel of the year for *Parable of the Talents.* She received the PEN Center West Lifetime Achievement Award in 2000.

BIBLIOGRAPHY

Becker, Jennifer. "Octavia Butler." *Voices From the Gaps.* May 17, 1997. Department of English, University of Minnesota, Minneapolis. Available online. URL: http://voices.cla.umn.edu/vg/Bios/entries/butler_octavia_estelle.html. Accessed September 29, 2006.

Kim Hai Pearson
Brian Jennings

Cain, George (1943–)

Harlem-born George Cain attended public and private schools in New York City. Although he attended Iona College in New Rochelle on an athletic scholarship, he left during his junior year and traveled to California, Mexico, and Texas, where he was imprisoned. After his release, he returned to New York, where he wrote his autobiographical novel, *Blueschild Baby* (1970), revealing his painful and self-destructive life as a heroin addict and his effort to become and stay clean.

Blueschild Baby begins with George, the protagonist, experiencing withdrawal while desperately searching for a fix and fearing an encounter with the police, as he is a parolee who has no desire to return to prison. "A sickness comes over me in this twilight state, somewhere between wake and sleep, my nose runs and my being screams for heroin" (1), announces the narrator at the beginning, setting in motion the roller-coaster ride that lasts the entire length of the novel. Through the narrator's eyes, the reader experiences firsthand the subterranean labyrinth of Harlem's drug world and its concomitant illegal activities and behavior, including robbery, rape, murder, exploitation, deception, looting, and strains of animalistic instinct-related behavior: Everyone struggles to be among the surviving fit. In this "land of black people" (9), buildings are inhabited by "people trying to escape the day. On every landing they sat. Men and women alone, together, bowed heads, smelling of themselves and cheap wine" (22). Imprisoned by fate in their jungle existence, these "dead people" sometimes rebel, as their history of riots reveals, including the Newark riot of the 1960s, which Cain chronicles.

In recalling his childhood, however, and particularly his love for his grandmother, Nana; his close relationship with his parents, particularly his mother; and his first love, Nandy, who "fired [his life] with purpose" (150), George reveals that this environment was not always a tomb for the living. As he successfully navigates through several critical rites of passage that lead to young adulthood and manhood, George attends the prestigious and "very private" Brey Academy, proudly wearing the school blazer, where he "loved the library with endless volumes, furnished darkly, mahogany, musty, and dim. Giant windows looking on the street and park" (157). At Brey he excels in academics and sports. His proud black community, which "watched and prayed" over him, consider him "the chosen one" (160). When the building he was born in burns for the second time, precipitating the death of his grandmother, George, feeling defeated, abandons his near-stellar youth and promising future and walks directly into what seems like the inevitable: a life of drug abuse. He, too, will become one of the "dead people." However, convincing himself that he is "[t]rapped in a prison of [his] own making" (116), George, with the help of Nandy, embarks on the painful, three-day process of detoxification. Liberated at the end of the novel, he buys a necklace with a monkey's head from a street vendor. The jewelry reminds him of the addiction that, he knows, will always haunt him. "I buy it and throw it on. He hangs round my neck and the hunger [for heroin] shall always be a threat" (185).

Blueschild Baby and Cain were showered with accolades. Reviewers compared *Blueschild Baby* to *Native Son* and lauded its style for its blues resonances. According to Houston Baker, "As a fictional autobiography, it stands at the far end of the tradition that begins with the narrative of Briton Hammon, matures in the work of Frederick Douglass, expands with James Weldon Johnson's *Autobiography of an Ex-Colored Man,* and received acknowledgment during the early sixties in the works of Claude Brown and Malcolm X" (89). Cain, who continues to live in Bedford Stuyvesant, never published a second novel.

BIBLIOGRAPHY

Baker, Houston A. *Singers of Daybreak: Studies in Black American Literature.* Washington, D.C.: Howard University Press, 1983.

Cain, George. *Blueschild Baby.* New York: Dell, 1970.

Michael Poindexter

Caldwell, Benjamin (Ben) (1937–)

Playwright, essayist, poet, and graphic artist, Benjamin Caldwell was born in Harlem, New York, on September 24, 1937, the seventh of nine children. Encouraged by a junior high school guidance counselor, he attended the School of Industrial Arts in New York City to become a commercial artist, but in 1954, after his father's death, he was forced temporarily to abandon his dreams of an art career to help support his family financially. While painting and drawing to supplement his income, Caldwell also wrote plays and essays. From 1965 to 1966, Caldwell lived in Newark, New Jersey, where he was influenced by AMIRI BARAKA and his repertory group, the Spirit House Players. Though he returned to New York City before the end of 1966, Caldwell's "Newark Period" was the beginning of his most prolific career as a playwright.

A recipient of the Guggenheim Fellowship for playwriting (1970), Caldwell wrote more than 50 plays at the height of the BLACK ARTS MOVEMENT, which have been performed all over Harlem as well as by the Black Arts Alliance in San Francisco and throughout the United States. Employing the revolutionary rhetoric common to the period, Caldwell's one-act dramas, described as "agitprop cartoons" or "parodic vignettes," satirize not only white racism but also African Americans who emulated whites, were unduly materialistic, or anchored themselves to stereotypes. Critics note that Caldwell's greatest power is his ability to communicate racial issues with both a superb economy of dramaturgy and mordancy (Grant, 117).

Caldwell's critically acclaimed one-act comedy *Prayer Meeting: or, the First Militant Minister* (1967) was first performed at the Spirit House Theatre under the title *Militant Preacher.* It was later retitled and performed off-Broadway in *"A Black Quartet: Four New Plays,"* along with plays by RONALD MILNER, ED BULLINS, and Baraka. Praised for its satire, the play uses a comic premise to dramatize the political message that black people must be willing to struggle actively for their rights and that they should not expect an easy accommodation within white society. *Militant Preacher* is about the conversion of a passive, "UNCLE TOM" preacher (see SAMBO AND UNCLE TOM). While praying to God for assistance in dealing with a potentially volatile congregation, angry over the murder of a black teenager by the police, the preacher receives an answer from God, in the form a thief hiding in his home who pretends to be the voice of God. The preacher adheres to God's demand, becomes a black militant, and leads his parishioners to City Hall in protest.

Caldwell's other plays, which examine such themes as the exploitation of blacks, Christianity, materialism, gullibility, entrapment, and birth control, include *The Job* (1966), *The Wall* (1967),

Mission Accomplished (1967), *Riot Sale, or Dollar Psyche Fake-Out* (1968), *Top Secret, or A Few Million After B.C.* (1968), *The Fanatic* (1968), *Recognition* (1968), *Unpresidented* (1968), *Hypnotism* (1969), *Family Portrait (or My Son the Black Nationalist)* (1969), *The King of Soul, or the Devil and Otis Redding* (1969), *Runaround* (1970), *All White Castle* (1971), and *Rights and Reasons* (1973).

In 1982, Caldwell's collection of skits and monologues, *The World of Ben Caldwell: A Dramatized Examination of the Absurdity of the American Dream and Subsequent Reality,* was produced off-Broadway by the New Federal Theatre (NFT), featuring Reginald Vel Johnson, Garrett Morris, and Morgan Freeman. While Mel Gussow of the *New York Times* reported that Caldwell showed such deftness and caustic cleverness in these sketches that he might well consider writing material for Richard Pryor (13), Stanley Crouch noted that "Caldwell's strong suit is a great ability to stitch together fabrics of rhetoric ranging from bureaucratic to black bottom barber shop" (104).

In addition to drama, Caldwell has written essays and poetry; he served as a contributing editor of the short-lived periodical *Black Theater,* published intermittently by the New Lafayette Theatre in Harlem. Since the early 1980s, Caldwell has turned his interest to the visual arts, participating in New York's Kenkeleba Gallery exhibit in 1983, connecting the media of painting and jazz with such talented artists as Camille Billops, FAITH RINGGOLD, Romare Bearden, and Norman Lewis. Though a fire swept through Caldwell's Harlem apartment in 1991, destroying more than four decades' worth of manuscripts, paintings, and memorabilia, he has returned to writing monologues and sketches and has completed a series of portraits on African-American men and women.

Labeling Caldwell a gifted playwright, DARWIN T. TURNER credits him, along with ALICE CHILDRESS, LORRAINE HANSBERRY, JAMES BALDWIN, DOUGLAS WARD, ADRIENNE KENNEDY, and many others, with bringing Afro-American drama "from minstrelsy, apology, and defense to awareness and assertion" (23). Caldwell's short satirical plays, though not in vogue today, delivered a powerful message that reflected the nationalistic fervor that prevailed among the architects of the Black Arts Movement and many of his contemporaries.

BIBLIOGRAPHY

Crouch, Stanley. "Satireprop." *Village Voice,* 27 April 1982, p. 104.

Grant, Nathan L. "Caldwell, Ben." In *The Oxford Companion to African American Literature,* edited by William L. Andrews, Frances Smith Foster, and Trudier Harris, 116–117. New York: Oxford University Press, 1997.

Gussow, Mel. "Federal Office 'World of Ben Caldwell.'" *New York Times,* 10 April 1982, p. 13.

Turner, Darwin T., ed. *Black Drama in America: An Anthology.* Greenwich, Conn.: Fawcett, 1971.

Loretta G. Woodard

Callaloo: A Journal of African American Diaspora Art and Letters

Callaloo has continually served as one of the premier publications for African Americans and people of African descent throughout the African diaspora. It is impossible to consider black artistic concerns without referring to works published in this acclaimed journal. CHARLES JOHNSON has called *Callaloo* "a resource scholars and creators will find crucial for understanding contemporary black literary practice," and THOMAS GLAVE sees the journal "propelling our traditions into brilliancies far beyond the easy, the simple, [and] the not-brave."

Callaloo was founded in 1976 at Southern University at Baton Rouge by Charles Henry Rowell, Jr., as a vehicle for raising artistic, critical, and theoretical issues of the experience of blacks in the South. Rowell writes in the inaugural issue, "[Black South experiences] have meanings. And as such they merit creative attention. They are rich material for today's Black South writers, who more than our brothers and sisters in the North, are closely fixed to our roots." In 1977, the journal became quarterly and moved to the University of Kentucky, where it broadened its scope to include a more comprehensive focus on African-American literature throughout the United States. With its 1986 move to the University of Virginia, the journal's breadth again expanded to its current status. *Callaloo* now sets out to address the whole of African diaspora experience, including in Central and South America, the Caribbean, and Europe. Now housed at Texas A&M University, *Callaloo* is a nexus for black artistic culture in the United States and elsewhere.

The journal has a long history of devoting issues to prominent writers, artists, critics, and genres. Most issues have sections presenting poetry, fiction, literary nonfiction, visual artwork, criticism, and bibliography. Maryse Condé, RITA DOVE, ERNEST J. GAINES, Nicolas Guillen, Wilson Harris, LANGSTON HUGHES, LARRY NEAL, JAY WRIGHT, RICHARD WRIGHT, and dozens of other individual authors have been comprehensively examined in *Callaloo*. An example of the close examination the journal publishes is a special section of a 1990 issue addressing the work of poet and professor MICHAEL HARPER. Fourteen recent poems by Harper were reprinted, followed by a lengthy interview conducted by Rowell; essays written by Robert B. Stepto, Niccolo N. Donzella, Anthony Walton, Robert Dale Parker, Herman Beavers, Suzanne Keen, John S. Wright reflected on the various manners in which Harper had influenced their work as scholars, poets, and Americans. Closing the section is an extended essay by John F. Callahan on Harper's friendship songs. Harper's work is given a well-rounded and multiperspective presentation.

Additionally, special issues have addressed women's poetry, Native American literature, Puerto Rican women writers, postcolonial discourse, Caribbean literature, jazz poetics, and other literary and theoretical concerns, both contemporary and historical. Rowell continues to serve as editor, and the contributing and advisory editors include some of the most prominent talents in African-American letters: Thadious Davis, YUSEF KOMUNYAKAA, Robert B. Stepto, Derek Walcott, and JOHN EDGAR WIDEMAN, are among the many in the journal's esteemed editorial community.

Making Callaloo: 25 Years of Black Literature, a capstone book, was published in 2002. Edited by Rowell, this is a collection of more than 50 of the most important works published in the journal's first quarter century. RALPH ELLISON's "Cadillac Flamb" excerpt from his posthumous novel *Juneteenth* and OCTAVIA BUTLER's oft-read "The Evening, the Morning, and the Night" are both reprinted, as is a section of SAMUEL R. DELANY's *Shoat Rumblin'.* The book, a useful and valid representative selection, underlines *Callaloo*'s critical importance to black literary culture in the United States and elsewhere today.

Keith Feldman

Call and Response: The Riverside Anthology of the African American Literary Tradition Patricia Liggins Hill, et al., eds. (1997)

A signature publication for Houghton Mifflin (Boston and New York), a major academic press, *Call and Response* was edited by Patricia Liggins Hill, general editor, Bernard W. Bell, Trudier Harris, William Harris, R. Baxter Miller, and Sondra A. O-Neale, with Horace A. Porter. Unlike the more canonical, Eurocentric *Norton Anthology of African American Literature, Call and Response* is the first BLACK AESTHETIC–based anthology to be published since *BLACK WRITERS OF AMERICA: A COMPREHENSIVE ANTHOLOGY* (1971), edited by RICHARD K. BARKSDALE and Keneth Kinnamon. For the most part, its works and authors are committed to promoting a more authentic criterion for black art.

Call and Response is structured both chronologically and thematically. It is divided into six parts. Each section focuses on a distinct feature of African-American history and culture: 1619–1808 (Slavery as Racial and Religious Oppression), 1808–1865 (The Quest for Freedom), 1865–1915 (Escaping Slavery to Reconstruction and Post-Reconstruction), 1915–1945 (The Harlem Renaissance and Reformation), 1945–1960 (Post–Harlem Renaissance and Post-Reformation), and 1960 to the present (Social Revolution, the New Renaissance, and the Second Reconstruction). This division not only indicates the editors' emphasis on the history of oppression known by New World

Africans and their progeny but also celebrates African Americans' history of transcendence. *Call and Response* comes with an accompanying CD, which includes BOOKER T. WASHINGTON's original 1895 "Atlanta Exposition Address," as well as "The Message," a rap song popularized by Grandmaster Flash and the Furious Five.

Each section contains selections from both the oral and written tradition, including proverbs, folk tales, slave narratives, music, orations, fiction, poetry, and essays. A truly inclusive volume in reference to the contributors and their works, *Call and Response* also presents both traditional and evolving theories. Contributors are vast; ideologies are vast as well, ranging from OLAUDAH EQUIANO, who signaled the earliest stages of the African-American literary tradition in the 18th century, to key abolitionist orators of the 19th century, including to Washington's 1895 conciliatory speech at the Atlanta Exposition, in which he advocates harmonious racial segregation with white supremacy and black subservience, to HARLEM RENAISSANCE writers, including CLAUDE MCKAY, who writes in the spirit of the "New Negro," the spirit of militancy and rebellion, to the new Renaissance writings of the 1960s, characterized as the BLACK ARTS MOVEMENT, led by AMIRI BARAKA and LARRY NEAL. The range of writers since the 1960s is vast, including notable black women fiction and nonfiction writers. TONI MORRISON, Pulitzer Prize–winning author of *BELOVED*, leads this category. In addition to the informative and comprehensive introductions to the various historical eras, *Call and Response* offers valuable information about each author and his or her theoretical persuasion.

Finally, the headnotes provided by Hill are both detailed and scholarly, placing the African-American experience within a historical, sociopolitical, and economic perspective. *Call and Response* has emerged as a significant volume, documenting the truly holistic African-American literary experience from its humble beginnings to the present. Within three months of its release in 1997, *Call and Response*, a massive volume of 2,039 pages, commanded a second printing.

Clenora Hudson Weems

Campbell, Bebe Moore (1950–2006)

Born and raised in Philadelphia, Pennsylvania, the daughter of George Linwood Peter Moore and Doris Carter Moore, Bebe Moore Campbell, novelist and freelance journalist, received a bachelor of science degree in elementary education from the University of Pittsburgh. Although known nationally as an outstanding novelist, Campbell's memoir, *Sweet Summer: Growing Up With and Without My Dad* (1989), was her first published book. Her coming-of-age story details the summers she spent in the South with her father, a paraplegic: "I was seven years old, sitting on the front steps waiting for my daddy to come and take me to summer. I can't remember when this waiting for my father began. . . . All I know is, it became an end-of-June ritual, an annual event, something I could set my clock by, set my heart on." The most poignant description in the novel is when she tells her childhood friend, Carol, about her father: "Didn't she know that my father was a royal king, plowed down by an enemy in the heat of the battle? Didn't she realize that he was good, completely good, and that his survival was a testimony to his nobility and fortitude?" Campbell's memoir is often lauded for its positive portrayal of a black father-daughter relationship.

In 1999 Campbell published *Your Blues Ain't Like Mine*, her first novel in which, like her memoir, the setting is the South and the North. It is loosely based on the true story of Emmett Till, a 14-year-old boy who was brutally murdered in Mississippi in 1955. This powerful novel begins during the early civil rights era, when a poor white man, Floyd Cox, murders a black teenager, Armstrong Todd: "Delotha [Armstrong Todd's mother] stared at the battered and swollen body of her son, spread out on the funeral parlor table. A strange odor she couldn't place hovered in the air." The novel follows the lives of Delotha and Wydell Todd from the South and to the North, as well as explores how the small town of Delta handles the murder of their son, Armstrong, as well as its own racist past. Campbell's exploration of the racism in the South is contrasted with the story of the vast black migration to Chicago, which the migrants equate with going to heaven. However, Delotha and

Wydell Todd discover that although racism is not as overt in the North as it is in the South, it is visible through the prevailing violence: "He [Wydell] passed the street where he and Delotha had rented a kitchenette when they first moved to Chicago. They'd shared a bathroom with three other families who'd come up from Mississippi. The area had been hit hard by the riots and had deteriorated badly." The cramped living quarters, the riots, and their aftermath symbolize, as LANGSTON HUGHES suggests in his signature poem, deferred dreams. Campbell's novel was voted *New York Times* notable book of the year, and it was the winner of the NATIONAL ASSOCIATION FOR THE ADVANCEMENT OF COLORED PEOPLE Image Award for Literature.

In her next two novels, Campbell explores the complexity of black familial relationships and their impact on communities. The theme of *Singing in the Comeback Choir* (1999) is forgiveness. The protagonist, Maxine McCoy, a popular talk show host, returns to Philadelphia, the neighborhood of her childhood, to become the caretaker of her grandmother, Lindy. In the end Maxine must not only deal with her grandmother's addictions but also face the hopelessness of the blighted community in which she and her neighbors live. Campbell next published *What You Owe Me* (2001), in which the central focus is on parent-child relationships; however, Campbell also explores the theme of the complex and often contentious relationship between blacks and Jews.

In her children's book, *Sometimes My Mommy Gets Angry* (2003), Campbell turns her attention to mental health as an issue in the African-American community. She describes how a young girl, Annie, copes with her mother's frightening and depressing mental illness. The book won the National Association for the Mentally Ill (NAMI) Outstanding Literature Award for 2003. In 2003 Campbell also wrote her first play, *Even with the Madness,* which also explores issues of mental illness and family.

Although known nationally for her novels, Campbell has also written a nonfiction text, *Successful Women, Angry Men* (1986), in which she offers advice for men and women on coping with relationships. To write this book, Campbell interviewed more than 100 couples. A regular on National Public Radio, Campbell has written for the *New York Times Book Review,* and her articles have been published in such well-known black popular magazines as ESSENCE, *Ebony,* and *Black Enterprise.* She has a daughter, Maia, and was married to her husband, Ellis Gordon, Jr., for more than 22 years. Bebe Moore Campbell (Gordon) died on November 27, 2006, from complications related to brain cancer.

Beverly A. Tate

Cavalcade: Negro American Writing from 1760 to the Present Arthur P. Davis and J. Saunders Redding, eds. (1971)

Arthur P. Davis and J. Saunders Redding, the seasoned literary giants of the African-American literary tradition who compiled this groundbreaking anthology, made their objectives lucidly clear in their general introduction. Although there had been several collections of "Negro American Writing," they argued, "none had served as a pedagogical function for students," even the most recent ones. They wrote, "None shows the evolution of this writing as literary art. None provides the historical context that makes meaningful the criticism of this writing as the expression of the American Negro's special experience and as a tool of social and cultural diagnosis" (xvii). The editors' objective, therefore, was to offer a comprehensive volume of more than 200 years of literary contributions by African Americans.

Moreover, Davis, who had joined with Sterling A. Brown and Ulysses Lee to edit the groundbreaking forerunner, *The* NEGRO CARAVAN, three decades before, and Redding made it explicitly clear that they had sought to compile "a balanced and impartial account" in making their selections. They assured that "No author has been left out because we disagree with his critical attitude, or his politics, or his stand on certain issues"; and, conversely, "no author had been included because he happens to think as we do" (xvii).

Davis and Redding found it important to explain their use of the term "Negro writing." Although most black writers, they argued, wrote out of a DuBoisian "double consciousness"—Negro and American—there were those, STANLEY BRAITH-WAITE and FRANK YERBY, for example, who "write like whites." In fact, the anthologists conclude, "the entire stock of their referent is white, Anglo Saxon-American derived" (xvii). However, the "twin rooted" majority finds that whereas "one root is nourished by the myths, customs, culture and values traditional in the Western world, the other feeds hungrily on the experiential reality of blackness" (xvii). The writers in this group have a special vision and mission: "In their work they combine the sermon and the liturgy, the reality and the dream" (xvii).

Davis and Redding offered a new paradigm for examining and discussing African-American literature. Moving chronologically from slavery to the 1970s, they divided their work into four major periods: pioneer writers (1760–1830), freedom fighters (1830–1865), accommodation and protest (1865–1910), and integration versus Black Nationalism (1954–present). They included short stories, novels, essays, plays, biographies, and autobiographies and prefaced each section with a critical introduction and bio-bibliographical headnotes for each author. In designing this specific format, Davis and Redding established a paradigm that, with the exception of a few variations based on ideological perspectives or thematic emphasis, continues to dominate the mapping of the African-American literary tradition through the publication of *The Norton Anthology of African American Literature* (1997), edited by HENRY LOUIS GATES, JR., and colleagues and *CALL AND RESPONSE: THE RIVERSIDE ANTHOLOGY OF THE AFRICAN AMERICAN LITERARY TRADITION* (1998), edited by Patricia Liggins Hill and colleagues.

Despite their claimed impartiality and their coverage of integration and Black Nationalism, Davis and Redding registered, with their use of the word "Negro" in the title of their pioneering work, their association with ties to historically black colleges and their commitment to a more academic and Western aesthetic. Significantly, *Cavalcade* appeared just when the BLACK ARTS MOVEMENT and the BLACK AESTHETICS movement were reaching their apotheosis among black writers and critics. However, the editors chose not to use the labels "Afro-American literature," "black American literature," or "black American writers," unlike succeeding compilers such as RICHARD BARKSDALE and DARWIN T. TURNER. Davis, University Professor at Howard University, and Redding, Ernest I. White Professor of American Studies and Humane Letters at Cornell University, aligned themselves more with white critic Robert Bone, who, in his historically important work *The Negro Novel in America,* divided writers of the black literary tradition into two basic camps: assimilationism and Negro nationalism (Bone, 7).

In 1992 Howard University Press added scholar-critic Joyce Ann Joyce to the original compilers and updated its now-classic text by issuing *The New Cavalcade: African American Writing from 1760 to the Present,* volumes 1 and 2. The first volume covers contributions through 1954, the second volume from 1954 to the 1980s.

BIBLIOGRAPHY

Bone, Robert A. *The Negro Novel in America.* New Haven: Yale University Press, 1958.

Davis, Arthur P., and J. Saunders Redding, ed. *Cavalcade: Negro American Writing from 1760 to the Present.* Boston: Houghton Mifflin Company, 1971.

Wilfred D. Samuels

Cave Canem

Established by poets TOI DERRICOTTE and COR-NELIUS EADY in 1996, Cave Canem began as a retreat and writer's workshop for African-American poets. According to the program's Web site, it was "designed to counter the under-representation and isolation of African American poets in writers' workshops and literary programs" (http://www.cavecanempoets.org).

Derricotte, Eady, and Sarah Micklem, Eady's wife, found the name and symbol for the retreat while on vacation in Italy. In Pompeii, at the entrance to the House of the Tragic Poet, they came across the mosaic of a black dog and an inscription that read: "cave canem," Latin for "beware of the dog." They adopted the words and mosaic as their symbols that illustrated the most important tenet of the retreat—it was to be a safe haven for black poets.

At its onset, Cave Canem was an all-volunteer effort. Its only component was the weeklong summer workshop, where fellows were invited to study with reputable African-American poets while completing an intensive writing regimen throughout the week. Many notable poets have taught at Cave Canem, including SONIA SANCHEZ, Elizabeth Alexander, AL YOUNG, YUSEF KOMUNYAKAA, and LUCILLE CLIFTON.

Fifty-two fellows are invited to the workshop each year. The founders decided early on to keep the number of fellows to a minimum so that the retreat would remain close-knit. The fellows attend the retreat for three sessions and have a five-year span in which to complete them. Cave Canem does not adhere to any particular school of poetry; its fellows are from various backgrounds and write in numerous voices and styles.

Since 1996, with the help of volunteers and the program's director, Carolyn Micklem, the summer retreat has flourished into the Cave Canem Foundation. In addition to the original workshop, the foundation holds numerous public readings as well as regional workshops designed to reach writers who may not have the opportunity to attend the summer workshop.

In 1999, Cave Canem began sponsoring a first-book contest for African-American writers whose work has not been published by a university or commercial press. Each year, the directors also publish an anthology featuring the work of fellows and faculty who attend the summer retreat. In 2006 the *Cave Canem Reader* was published to commemorate the organization's 10th anniversary.

Remica L. Bingham

Celestine, Alfred Bernard (1949–)

Born in Los Angeles, California, to Alfred and Irene Jane Celestine, Al Celestine graduated from Sherman E. Burroughs High School in Ridgecrest, California, in 1967. He attended Fresno State, the University of California at Riverside (UCR), and University of California, Berkeley, majoring in sociology. During his undergraduate studies at UCR, Celestine became a student activist. He led the black student union in its effort to prevent UCR's chancellor from dismantling its pioneering, degree-granting Black Studies Department. Totally committed to validating and promoting black culture during the BLACK ARTS MOVEMENT, Celestine produced plays, sponsored poetry readings, and invited well-known writers, including the poet AMIRI BARAKA, to UCR's campus; he also published a student literary journal.

After publishing his first poem in an Ohio State University journal, Celestine published *Confessions of Nat Turner,* his first collection of poems, in 1978, with Many Press. The themes in *Confession* remain central to his work: political activism, celebration and critique of black life and black identity, and personal quest for sexual identity. Rich in irony, Celestine's poetry, often impressionistic or Haiku-like, demands the reader's total engagement; generally, his speakers leave little or no wiggle room. For example, in a poem from *Confessions* that critiques and celebrates the BLACK POWER movement of the 1960s, Celestine writes, "silence died? / what funeral, / yesterday's black man"; the rich irony found in the last line forces readers to think about the validity and complexity of this movement and its demand that the heretofore silent and nearly invisible American Negro morph into a more African-centered, self-identified black man.

In a poem concerned with the quest for personal identity and sexuality, the speaker celebrates and records salient rituals of the black church, while critiquing what for him is the suffocating oppressiveness of Christianity from which the adolescent speaker must escape, exploring and suggesting the complexity of black ideological, spiritual, and generational shifts—resonating, as he does, with central themes in the works of JAMES BALDWIN, particularly *GO TELL IT ON THE MOUNTAIN:*

> *. . . And again: Big Mama in whom the Lord*
> *Sang now and then like a magpie*
> *Testified.*
> *Rolled in red dust of the threshing floor.*

Celestine's poems are reflective—autobiographical. He is interested in exploring significant episodes of his life and the African-American past. In "A Walk in the Winter Rain," his speaker declares, "This poem has a pain worth looking at. / Its best lines wake at the crack of daybreak / carrying the wastes of night to the page." In "The Letters and Numbers of Straw," published in the *James White Review* with the works of ESSEX HEMPHILL, the speaker candidly discusses his sexuality: "I was schooled in sex: first women, then men." What remains important to him in the end, however, is the sanctity of his own voice and his independence: "both / gave out diplomas, / but I tore them up." His speaker in "The Witchdoctor's Wife Looks Towards the New World" imagines the Middle Passage—"In the hold of memory events packed / Together so tightly are stories lost"—surmising the possible devastation of stories lost.

Ultimately, though, Celestine is concerned throughout his work with the role of the artist, in particular the black artist, who must work within the boundaries of the language of former oppressors to find self validation and worth:

> I don't know if I make myself clear.
> English the language you tried to teach me
> Its Word is unkempt in the House on Fleet
> Street.
> . . . .
> I'm not-looking, before the words
> slowly disappear from sight. I am Caliban.

In 1975, Celestine became an expatriate, moving to London, England, where he continues to live and where he completed, though never published, *Nights of Gethsemane*, his first novel.

Wilfred D. Samuels

Celie

is the heroine in Alice Walker's award-winning novel-turned-screenplay *The Color Purple*. Written in epistolary form, the novel invites readers to share in Celie's transformation from a helpless abused teenage girl to an audacious, independent businesswoman. At the beginning of the novel, Celie is described as a 14-year-old girl who is continuously raped by her stepfather. She is pregnant for the second time with his child. He has threatened her into silence and made her feel she is complicit in his nefarious act: "*You better not never tell nobody but God. It'd kill your mammy*" (3). Her belief in God becomes her sanctuary, and her letters to him her lifeline.

To rob her of any remaining self-esteem, Celie's stepfather tells her she is ugly, stupid, and old. To cover his abuse, he puts the baby up for adoption and marries Celie off to Mr. ____. In her father's transaction with Mr. ____, Celie becomes no more than the property of men, a bondswoman. Walker creates Celie's identity as slave through the setting, particularly the porch, where she stands silently to be examined during the transaction. The porch becomes a symbolic slave auction block where Celie is denied voice or agency. She is equated with the cow she takes as dowry to Mr. ____'s property. In the end, they are both only chattel, a source of profit for their owner, Mr. ____.

Significantly, other women in the community provide models for Celie and enhance Celie's transformation through their varied experience as she shapes and molds a new identity. Sofia, Mr. ____'s daughter-in-law, represents the freedom and strength Celie seeks; she is a powerful, self-defining black woman who refuses to be domestically obedient to her husband, Harpo, Mr. ____'s son. Sofia, who has been abused by her stepfather, refuses to be abused by Harpo, whose eyes she blackens when he tries to beat her.

Shug Avery, Mr. ____'s former lover who returns into his life after he marries Celie, is equally crucial to Celie's transformation. Shug teaches Celie to appreciate herself physically, spiritually, and emotionally and to stop being Albert's (Mr. ____'s real name) metaphoric mule. Shug opens Celie's eyes to her complex self as woman. As a consequence, Celie begins to learn the true meaning of what it is to love and be loved. Through a lesbian relationship and the deepening friendship, Celie embarks on a path to healing and wholeness. She states, "My life stop when I left home, I think. But then I think again. It stop with Mr. ___ maybe, but it start up again with Shug" (85). The sense of value that Celie gets from Shug helps form the foundation on which she builds the courage not only to stand up to Mr. ___ but also to leave his house and create a life for herself.

Finally, Celie's relationship and friendship with her sister, Nettie, ensures Celie's ultimate transformation. Nettie writes letters (which Albert keeps from Celie) while she is serving as a missionary in Africa. She desperately tries to find and reconnect with her sister and ultimately helps Celie reshape and redefine her identity and reshape her image of God. Once Nettie reenters Celie's life, Celie no longer needs to keep secrets that only God can know. Nettie successfully "conveys to Celie her belief that Celie is of value" (Proudfit, 23). Upon her return to the United States, Nettie joins Celie to become a family, which includes Celie's children, Adam and Ophelia, who had been adopted by Nettie's Christian surrogate family that took her to Africa.

At the end of the novel, Celie emerges transformed by a combination of Albert's red rage and Shug's BLUES in order to redefine herself as purple: the color of God, creation, and power. Perhaps she is transformed by love of self and family. Walker makes the transformative power of love the central theme of the novel.

BIBLIOGRAPHY

Bloom, Harold, ed. *Modern Interpretations: Alice Walker's* The Color Purple. Philadelphia: Chelsea House Publishers, 2000.

Brown-Clark, Sarah. "The Community of Black Women in *The Color Purple.*" In *Women in History, Literature, and the Arts: A Festschrift for Hildegard Schuttgen in honor of her Thirty Years of Outstanding Service at Youngstown State University,* edited by Lorrayne Y. Baird-Lange and Thomas Copeland, 295–305. Youngstown: Youngstown State University, 1989.

Proudfit, Charles. "Celie's Search for Identity: a Psychoanalytic Developmental Reading of Alice Walker's *The Color Purple.*" *Contemporary Literature* 32 (Spring 1991): 12–37.

Ross, Daniel. "A Fairy-Tale Life: The Making of Celie in Alice Walker's *The Color Purple.*" In *Teaching American Ethnic Literatures: Nineteen Essays,*
159–174, edited by John R. Maitino and David R. Peck. Albuquerque: University of New Mexico Press, 1996.

Walker, Alice. *The Color Purple.* New York: Pocket Books, 1982.

———. *In Search of Our Mothers' Gardens.* New York: Harcourt Brace & Company, 1983.

LaJuan Simpson

Channer, Colin   (1963–)

Jamaican born and a naturalized American citizen, Colin Channer is a journalist and musician who lives in the Fort Greene section of Brooklyn. After graduating from high school, Channer migrated to America at age 19; he later earned a degree in media communication from Hunter College of the City University of New York. Like G. WINSTON JAMES and Patricia Young, as well as CLAUDE MCKAY, JAMAICA KINCAID, and PAULE MARSHALL before them, Channer joins a group of Caribbean writers who, after becoming American citizens, meld their medley of accents and cultures to augment, supplement, and expand the chorus of voices that join to create the black experience in America and, consequently, that proclaim a more dynamic African-American literary tradition and experience.

Channer does exactly this in *Waiting in Vain* (1998), his debut novel that is at once a postmodern romance (though some may even argue it is a sentimental novel), black erotic novel, black postcolonial novel, and existential novel. These varied genres and their related themes emerge from the torrid love affair that Jamaican Adrian "Fire" Heath, an artist/writer, and Sylvia Lucas, a writer/editor, develop after their accidental (or fated) meeting in New York City. Fire is closer to Janie's TEA CAKE in *THEIR EYES WERE WATCHING GOD* and Sethe's Paul D in *BELOVED* than to CELIE's Mr.____ in *THE COLOR PURPLE.* After she gets to know Fire, Sylvia concludes that he has "more than the strength of a man. He also had the strength of a woman. A penis as a totem could not fully represent him. For he was more than the giver of pleasure. He was the giver of life" (65). Fire, who had been celibate when he first meets Sylvia, confesses that the time they have spent together has led him to "know how Dizzy must have felt when he heard Bird play the first time, like, 'Yeah, this is the sound I've been searching for inside myself'" (70–71).

Despite the infinite possibilities Fire and Sylvia think they might offer each other, their professional lives, close friends, other sexual relationships and commitments, and philosophies on love and life affect their lives and relationship. Although they are intermittently able to meet each other's needs, physically and emotionally, they are unable, at first, to commit to each other and so go separate ways. After a mountain of individual trials and tribulations, however, they find each other again, pledge their love, and commit to spend a lifetime together. "Every day won't be like this, you know. Happy and sweet," Fire reminds Sylvia. She responds, "I know that. But these will be the moments that we'll live for."

Waiting in Vain is more than a mushy novel, however. Channer's characters move, like postmodern nomads, across borders, from Jamaica to London to Paris to New York, as easily as they take the A train from uptown to downtown Manhattan. They are at home speaking Jamaican patois and listening to Charlie Parker, Bob Marley, or Al Green. They are able to enjoy and critique hip-hop music; drive through Brooklyn's Prospect Park, Chinatown, or Soho; or land at New York's Kennedy Airport or London's Heathrow and walk through the marketplace in Brixton. In doing so they come to the realization, in the end, that "Everything in life is a struggle, and the greatest one of all is holding that commitment to keep struggling no matter what. Cause when you lose that one, you can easily lose it all" (323). *Waiting in Vain* was received with rave reviews.

At the end of the 20th century and the beginning of the 21st century, Channer simultaneously registers, validates, and challenges the true complexity of the many borders that make up the black literary tradition of the black diaspora. During his eulogy for his friend, Fire declares,

> And I'm not a Rastaman. But that shouldn't matter, because we are here today in the name of love. And love is bigger than religion. For religion was made by man . . . and love was made by God. So let us walk together and make a joyful noise and sing that song that binds every one of us who came across the Atlantic in the belly of the whale—"Amazing Grace." (320)

Fire seems to speak for Channer in his plea: "let us walk together and make a joyful noise." Channer, whose second novel, *Satisfy My Soul,* was published in 2000, seems here to be reaching out to all black writers, maybe even specifically African-American writers, on the threshold of the 21st century.

BIBLIOGRAPHY
Channer, Colin. *Waiting in Vain.* New York: One World, 1998.

Wilfred D. Samuels

Chant of Saints   Michael S. Harper and Robert B. Stepto, eds. (1979)

Three years in the making, *Chant of Saints* is experimental in form and content. The editors' main goal was to present the "contributing authors and artists in a substantial and varied way" (xiv). To accomplish this goal, *Chant* includes only a few essays, created specifically for it, trying to avoid being a collection of social commentary or scientific documents about the black experience. Fundamentally, *Chant* seeks to capture facets of black experience by focusing on music, metaphor, images, and lyric. *Chant* negotiates between its roles of documenting black art and culture in the 1970s and contextualizing writers and artists as being "mobile in time" (xvi).

Chant's uniqueness lies in the editors' experiment with the genre of the anthology by moving away from the generic categories: fiction, poetry, and drama. For example, critical essays on a given writer's work are complemented by interviews with the writers. Consequently, interviews with writers and poets like TONI MORRISON, LEON FORREST, GAYL JONES, Derek Walcott, and RALPH ELLISON and essays on their works are included in the collection. *Chant* also includes poetry by Jones, ROBERT

HAYDEN, and JAY WRIGHT. In addition to the novel excerpts, short stories, and commentary, *Chant* has art sprinkled throughout, including black-and-white photographs of sculpture by Richard Hunt and paintings by Richard Yarde. Romare Bearden's collages, reproduced in full-color plates with an introduction by Ralph Ellison, add to the uniqueness of this anthology. Finally, four essays about music and culture complete the editors' documentary and, indeed, celebration of African-American culture and cultural contributions during the last quarter of the 20th century.

Chant of Saints does not pretend to provide a comprehensive or monolithic representation of the black experience. Rather, it opens a dialogue about which works should be in the canon while attempting primarily to present works that, according to the editors, are superior in multiple disciplines. In many ways *Chant* echoes ALAIN LOCKE's pioneering anthology on the HARLEM RENAISSANCE, *The New Negro*. However, structurally, *Chant* goes further, as its very title, taken from BLUES lyrics, suggests.

BIBLIOGRAPHY

Harper, Michael S., and Robert B. Stepto, eds. *Chant of Saints: A Gathering of Afro-American Literature, Art, and Scholarship.* Urbana: University of Illinois Press, 1979.

Kim Hai Pearson
Brian Jennings

Chase-Riboud, Barbara   (1939–   )

Barbara Chase-Riboud was born in 1939 in Philadelphia to Charles Edward and Vivian May West. She showed promise at a young age, developing skills in music, art, and writing; she took art classes at both the Philadelphia Museum of Art and the Fletcher Memorial Art School when she was seven years old. She earned her bachelor of fine arts degree at Temple University and her master of fine arts at Yale University in 1960. After graduating, she worked as a sculptor in Paris, where she won a number of awards for her artwork, which featured silk, wool, textiles, and cast and polished bronze. She also studied art in Rome on the John Hay Whitney Fellowship. While living in Paris, she met and married photo journalist Marc Edward Riboud. They had two children, Alexis and David. They divorced in 1981, and Chase-Riboud married Sergio Tosi. Chase-Riboud is an expatriate, living in France and Italy. She continues to write, garnering critical and popular attention for her novels, *Sally Hemings* and *Echo of Lions.*

Chase-Riboud has written poetry as well as novels. Her poetry is collected in *From Memphis and Peking* (1974) and *Portrait of a Nude Woman as Cleopatra* (1987). Her novels include *Sally Hemings* (1979), *Valide: A Novel of the Harem* (1988), *Echo of Lions* (1989), *Hottentot Venus* (2003), and *The President's Daughter* (1995). She has also written book reviews for the *Washington Post.* Two of Chase-Riboud's novels have been the subjects of copyright infringement litigation. Granville Burgess, a playwright, infringed on Chase-Riboud's copyright to *Sally Hemings,* a historical novel about Thomas Jefferson's romantic relationship with a slave named Sally Hemings. Later, the film *Amistad,* by Steven Spielberg, appeared to relate the same story as Chase-Riboud's *Echo of Lions;* however, Chase-Riboud did not pursue litigation because she felt that no wrong was done.

Travel figures largely in Chase-Riboud's poetic work. In addition to exploring alienation, distance, change, and discovery, several of her works resonate with a celebration of erotic love, passion, and sensuality. Figures of couples permeate her work, appearing in her poems, novels, and sculptures. She often joins opposing forces together, such as male/female and black/white, because they are simultaneously "banal and impossible." Her novel *Sally Hemings* explores a number of contradictions and problematic dynamics in the United States's history of miscegenation. While developing a novel that dramatizes a 38-year affair between Thomas Jefferson and Sally Hemings, Chase-Riboud also examines a relationship fraught with the inevitable tension stemming from Hemings's multiple roles as Jefferson's lover, victim, and property and mother of his children. Chase-Riboud's *Sally Hemings* drew a great deal of attention when it first appeared, eclipsing the warm critical reception for her first volume of poetry, *From Memphis and Peking*. *The President's Daughter* is the sequel to *Sally Hemings,* relating the tale of one of Hemings and Jefferson's daughters.

Chase-Riboud has won several awards for her art, poetry, and writing. In addition to the John Hay Whitney Fellowship, she won the Janet Heidinger Kafka Prize for Excellence in Fiction by an American Woman in 1980. In 1988 she won the Carl Sandburg Prize as best American poet. She has also won a National Fellowship of the Arts. Chase-Riboud continues to live in Paris, France, and is currently working on the third novel in her Sally Hemings series.

BIBLIOGRAPHY

Munsch, Andrew, and Greg Wilmer. "Barbara Chase-Riboud." *Voices from the Gaps.* October 19, 1998. Department of English, University of Minnesota, Minneapolis. Available online. URL: http://voices.cla.umn.edu/vg/Bios/entries/chaseribaud_barbara.html. Accessed September 29, 2006.

Selz, Peter, and Anthony F. Janson. *Barbara Chase-Riboud, Sculptor.* Edited by Harriet Whelchel. New York: Abrams, 1999.

Kim Hai Pearson
Brian Jennings

Chesnutt, Charles W.   (1858–1932)

Born to free parents in Cleveland, Ohio, in 1858, Charles Waddell Chesnutt was fascinated at an early age by the stories and folktales he heard in his father's store. The family returned to the South after the end of the Civil War. His mother and father had left Fayetteville, North Carolina—their hometown—in 1856. Both his maternal and paternal grandfathers had been the white masters of their respective children. Set free and given a small inheritance, Chesnutt's parents had left the South for the freedom of the North, but as inhabitants of the "color line," they did not find themselves free from prejudice (often from other African Americans) in Ohio. His parents' struggles, as well as his own as a light-skinned African American, informed much of Chesnutt's work, especially his stories of "pass-ing" African Americans and the price they paid for hiding their true identities. Chesnutt's writing also emphasizes the problems faced by families like his own living in the tumultuous South following the Civil War and later the Reconstruction.

Chesnutt was a stellar student and eventually became a teacher and then a principal, all at a relatively young age. In 1878 he married Susan Perry. Soon after, in the wake of growing racial hostility in North Carolina (where Chesnutt had lived most of his life), the couple moved to Cleveland, Chesnutt's birthplace. He worked various jobs while developing his writing, producing several stories. As the father of two young daughters, however, he could not risk living solely by his writing. A literary career did not hold much promise for African Americans in the 1880s.

Chesnutt passed the Ohio bar exam in 1887 and later opened his own legal stenography business. In the same year, "The Goophered Grapevine" appeared in *Atlantic Monthly.* He also worked steadily on a novella, called "Rena Walden." Despite numerous revisions, he could not find a publisher for the piece, but he continued to write short fiction, and by 1890 he accumulated enough stories to consider a collection. Initially, there was no interest in such a collection until editor Walter Hines Page suggested to Chesnutt that he gather the "conjure" stories together. Chesnutt composed four new "conjure" tales and included three older ones for *The Conjure Woman,* published in 1899. Later the same year, another collection, *The Wife of His Youth and Other Stories of the Color Line,* appeared. With the success of the two collections, Chesnutt felt confident enough in the progress of his writing career to close the stenography business.

Intent on producing a novel, Chesnutt returned to "Rena Walden" and by 1900 found a publisher interested in the revised manuscript, *The House behind the Cedars.* The novel failed to find an audience, and while it did garner some critical attention, it did not, in the opinion of many reviewers, live up to the previous short story collections. Nevertheless, Chesnutt attempted another novel the following year, *The Marrow of Tradition* (1901). Based on the Wilmington, North Carolina, massacre in 1898, the work drew controversial attention.

While most critics thought that the novel was well written, many condemned its themes and subject matter. The content was too inflammatory and the portrait of southern violence and the dilemma of miscegenation too provocative. Chesnutt's well-known and respected editor, William Dean Howells, called the novel "bitter." The financial failure of *The Marrow of Tradition* forced Chesnutt to reopen his stenography business.

Although Chesnutt continued to write over the next few years, he found little success. One short story, "Baxter's Procrustes," was published in 1904 in the *Atlantic Monthly*. Another novel, *The Colonel's Dream,* appeared the same year. Neither work made a substantial impact on Chesnutt's career; subsequently, he did not return to writing. At his death in 1932, he left behind six unpublished novels, including *Mandy Oxendine,* which finally saw print in 1997. Chesnutt's influence on the development of African-American fiction, the American short story, and the next generation of writers, which would constitute the New Negro movement and the Harlem Renaissance, cannot be underestimated. He remained a critical voice for American history and culture throughout his lifetime. In 1915, he opposed the screening of D. W. Griffith's *The Birth of a Nation* in Cleveland, Ohio, where he was still a resident. Based on the novel *The Clansmen* by Thomas Dixon, who was a contemporary of Chesnutt's, the film and the story represented the violent and racist attitudes engendered by southern history that Chesnutt had spent his career trying to dismantle. Four years before his death, he was awarded the National Association for the Advancement of Colored People's Spingarn Medal celebrating his service to African-American life, art, and culture.

Although Chesnutt never achieved the literary reputation that he desired in his lifetime, his contribution to a deeper understanding of race relations in America following the Civil War was profound. He believed that it was his mission as a writer to "educate" white America about the culture and life of African Americans, both historically and in his own era. His work critically engaged the popular literature of the time in a process of African-American "signifying." *The Marrow of Tradition* draws on character types and themes found in Twain's *Pudd'nhead Wilson,* and both *The Conjure Woman* and *The Wife of His Youth* contain stories that directly refute the portrait of African-American life depicted by novelists of the South. The work of plantation writers like Joel Chandler Harris, Thomas Nelson Page, and Dixon had a wide readership and provided the American public with a picture of the South that was often romantic. Their work especially illustrated a dangerous nostalgia or distortion of history. Chesnutt's writing countered this vision with sociopolitical realism and, sometimes, satirical humor. Chesnutt belonged to the same group as Twain, Henry James, Sarah Orne Jewett, and Kate Chopin: American literary realists who were at one time edited by Howells.

Howells's penchant for dialect partially explains his fondness for Chesnutt's work. The editor especially admired the stories of *The Conjure Woman* and Chesnutt's ability to reflect accurately the African-American vernacular tradition. The seven stories that constitute this collection are presented in a frame narrative constructed around the characters of Annie, John, and Uncle Julius. John is a carpetbagger who has traveled to the former McAdoo plantation with the intent of purchasing the land and revitalizing its vineyards. He has been instructed to go South for the climate in the hopes that it will help the health of his wife, Annie. Uncle Julius is a former slave of the plantation who still inhabits the space. At first he appears as a counterpart to Harris's infamous Uncle Remus. He does begin to spin tall tales, or folk narratives, in the manner of Uncle Remus. But in John's eyes, the goal of the storytelling is financial reward. To a more critical reader, Julius's stories reveal a more nuanced tricksterism. Julius does often receive some benefit from his tales; he often tells them to forestall an event that will impede his own objectives, as is the case in "The Goophered Grapevine." But these transformation tales also allow Julius to revise the history of the South that John and America think they know. Symbolically, the slaves in the tales represent the post-Reconstruction lives of African Americans—held in economic slavery by the policies of the American government and by racism and white supremacy. Julius's tales not only condemn slavery but also criticize the system that continued to disenfranchise and displace African Americans in Chesnutt's day.

John fails to see the true purpose of Julius's stories. As a northern opportunist, he understands only the financial importance of the land and its people to his own prosperity. His blindness signifies the country's inability to see the damage done by past oppression and prejudice. Nevertheless, Julius's tales should affect the reader more in the manner that they do Annie. The storytelling is sometimes meant to ease Annie's suffering, as does "Sis Becky's Pickanniny," a tale about a slave mother (Sis Becky) and son (little Mose) who are reunited through the conjuring skills of Aun' Peggy, a "conjuh 'oman." As such, "conjure" stories offer magic remedies and ways for those living in the present to heal from the diseases of slavery and racism.

The nine short stories that make up *The Wife of His Youth and Other Stories of the Color Line* are more varied in their tone and style. In the titular piece, Chesnutt examines attitudes toward light-skinned blacks living in Groveland (Cleveland), Ohio. The lighter, middle-class African Americans form "Blue Vein Societies" as an exclusive act against their darker brethren. In doing so, some members have turned their backs on their past and their identities. Though not a true "passing" story, the work criticizes anyone who forgets the prices paid for African-American freedom by men and women of all hues. "The Sheriff's Children" considers the moral problems of miscegenation in the post-Reconstructionist South. Having fathered two children—one by a white woman, one by a black—the sheriff epitomizes the historical implications of mixed-race couples and their children. Symbolically, the South is the father of both children, accountable to both futures. Its inability to care for and nurture all of its children results in the tragedy at the end of the story. Believing she is protecting her father, the sheriff's innocent, white daughter shoots and kills the darker, half brother she never knew. The racial violence exacts a ritual reenactment of race

relationships in the South as well as the inevitable violence that results from the failure to accept the responsibilities of the past. Another story, "The Passing of Grandison," written in the vein of some of the "conjure" tales, uses satirical humor to illustrate the tricksterism and intelligence of slaves. Grandison outwits nearly every white man in the story to bring his entire family North to freedom, all the while pretending to be the "happy darky" embodied by a figure like Uncle Remus.

Chesnutt's first novel, *The House behind the Cedars,* presents a story of "passing" but stops short of being a typical "tragic mullato/a" tale. Another work set in Groveland, the novel follows the lives of a brother and sister, John and Rena Walden. John has been passing for some time and returns home to convince his sister to do the same. After all, John seems happy and content in his decision. Chesnutt points out that such a decision is not without its consequences. When Rena finds love, she is unable to share the truth of her identity. Some part of her will always be hidden. After she is revealed to her love, George Tyron, he dismisses her. Heartbroken, she tries to rebuild her life. For a while she finds peace, but she ultimately succumbs to illness. Tyron realizes his mistake too late, and before he can ask for forgiveness and confess his love, Rena has died. Chesnutt uses the love affair to suggest that passing and miscegenation do not just affect African Americans. The moral problem of the culture leads to suffering for whites and blacks alike. Love cannot overcome racism or the lie of passing.

The Marrow of Tradition remains one of Chesnutt's finest achievements and a powerful social / protest novel of African-American literature. Like *The House behind the Cedars,* it considers the issues of passing and miscegenation, but operating at its center is the Wilmington massacre of 1898 (Wilmington, North Carolina, is recast here as Wellington). The massacre was the result of political maneuvering that used lynching as a terrorist tactic to determine an important election. The work also engages Twain's *Pudd'nhead Wilson* and questions the accident of birth and the fate of race in determining a person's worth in American society. Though the work never successfully "educated" the white population about the problem of race in America, it did contribute to the growth and development of the African-American novel, particularly in its ability to uncover the truth in history's darkest corners, presenting the hidden or silenced African-American perspective, a function characteristic of all of Chesnutt's work.

BIBLIOGRAPHY

Andrews, William. *The Literary Career of Charles W. Chesnutt.* Baton Rouge: Louisiana State University Press, 1980.

Brodhead, Richard, ed. *The Journals of Charles W. Chesnutt.* Durham, N.C.: Duke University Press, 1993.

Duncan, Charles. *The Narrative Craft of Charles Chesnutt.* Athens: Ohio University Press, 1998.

Ellison, Curtis W., and E. F. Metcalf. *Charles W. Chesnutt: A Reference Guide.* Boston: G. K. Hall, 1977.

McElrath, Joseph, and Robert Leitz, III, ed. *"To Be an Author": Letters of Charles W. Chesnutt, 1899–1905.* Princeton, N.J.: Princeton University Press, 1997.

Pickens, Ernestine Williams. *Charles W. Chesnutt and the Progressive Movement.* New York: Pace University Press, 1994.

Render, Sylvia Lyons. *Charles W. Chesnutt.* Boston: Twayne, 1980.

Sundquist, Eric. *To Wake the Nations: Race in the Making of American Literature.* Cambridge, Mass.: Belknap Press, 1993.

Wideman, John Edgar. "Charles Chesnutt and the WPA Narratives: The Oral and Literate Roots of Afro-American Fiction." In *The Slave's Narrative,* edited by Henry Louis Gates, Jr., and Charles Davis, 59–78. New York: Oxford University Press, 1985.

Wonham, Henry. *Charles W. Chesnutt: A Study of the Short Fiction.* New York: Twayne, 1998.

Tracie Church Guzzio

Childress, Alice   (1916–1994)

A pioneer in the theater, as well as an actress, director, novelist, playwright, columnist, essayist, lecturer, and theater consultant, Alice Childress was a versatile writer-playwright who boldly explored controversial racial and socioeconomic issues that portray the masses of poor or "ordinary" people struggling to overcome insurmountable obstacles in America. Through innovative characters and themes, and by writing frankly and realistically, she challenged her audiences and made lasting impressions on them for more than four decades. Additionally, she paved the way for such talented black women playwrights as LORRAINE HANSBERRY, SONIA SANCHEZ, ADRIENNE KENNEDY, NTOZAKE SHANGE, and Elizabeth Brown-Guillory.

Childress was born on October 12, 1920, in Charleston, South Carolina. She grew up in Harlem, raised by her maternal grandmother, Eliza Campbell White, who stimulated her interest in reading, writing, and storytelling. Her grandmother also took her often to Wednesday night testimonials at the Salem Church of Harlem, where Childress heard many accounts of the troubles of poor people, mostly women, that would later become major themes for her literary works, especially her plays. Childress attended Public School 81, the Julia Ward Howe Junior High School. Although she attended Wadleigh High School, she only completed three years because of the death of her grandmother and mother. To continue her education, she frequented the public library, often reading two books a day. This allowed her to evaluate form carefully and to develop her craft in the various mediums that she would later explore.

In 1935, Childress gave birth to her only child, Jean R. Childress, whose father was Childress's first husband, actor Alvin Childress. In the 1940s, after the marriage dissolved, Childress held various jobs, including those of insurance agent and domestic worker, to support herself and her daughter. Childress's varied experiences provided her with a reservoir of materials to draw upon as she pursued a career in writing and acting. She explained, "My writing attempts to interpret the 'ordinary' because they are not ordinary. Each human is uniquely different. Like snowflakes, the human pattern is never cast twice. We are uncommonly and marvelously intricate in thought and action, our problems are most complex and, too often, silently borne" (Childress 112).

Also in the 1940s, Childress helped found the American Negro Theatre (ANT), to nurture the dreams and hopes of aspiring black playwrights, actors, and performers. (It later influenced such actors as Sidney Poitier, OSSIE DAVIS, Ruby Dee, and Frank Silvera, among others.) For almost a decade, Childress studied and worked with ANT, both on and off-Broadway, as an actress, playwright, personnel director, and coach. She appeared in *On Strivers Row* (1940), *Natural Man* (1941), and *Anna Lucasta* (1944), in which she originated the role of Blanche, for which she was nominated for a Tony award. In 1949, Childress directed and starred in her one-act play *Florence;* produced by ANT and set in a Jim Crow railway station in a small southern town, the play treats the issue of stereotyping.

Childress was not only very productive as an author during the 1950s but also gained recognition for several pioneering achievements. She negotiated all-union off-Broadway contracts in Harlem. She also produced two plays at Club Baron Theatre in Harlem, *Just a Little Simple* (1950), an adaptation of stories by LANGSTON HUGHES, and *Gold through the Trees* (1952), these were the first two plays by a black woman to be produced professionally on the American stage. She became the first black woman to win the Obie Award for the best original off-Broadway play during the 1955–56 season with the production of her first full-length play-within-a-play, *Trouble in Mind* (1955), whose title is taken from a BLUES song of the same name. A Broadway production of *Trouble in Mind,* scheduled for April 1957, was never performed because Childress refused to make changes in theme and interpretation to appease white producers and audiences. Her plays were optioned for Broadway 11 times, and each time Childress would not compromise.

In 1957 Childress married her second husband, Nathan Woodard, a professional musician who frequently composed music for her plays. For the next three decades, she continued her interest in drama and became one of America's most prolific dramatists. During this time, she wrote *Wedding Band: A Love/Hate Story in Black and White* (1966). Considered her finest full-length play, it was first produced by the Mendelssohn Theatre at the University of Michigan (1966) and was nationally broadcast on ABC television; a 1972 New York Shakespeare Festival production starred Ruby Dee and James Broderick. Other plays include *The World on a Hill* (1968); *Young Martin Luther King* (1969); *String* (1969); *Wine in the Wilderness* (1969), considered "a classic piece of contemporary black theatre" (Bailey, 34); and *Mojo: A Black Love Story* (1970). Childress also wrote plays for children: *When the Rattlesnake Sounds* (1975), *Let's Hear It for the Queen* (1976), *Sea Island Song* (1977), *Gullah* (1984), and *Moms* (1987).

Childress received numerous awards for her innovative achievements and genuine dedication to the theater. In addition to being a writer in-residence at the MacDowell Colony in Peterborough, New Hampshire (1965), and a playwright-scholar at the Radcliffe Institute for Independent Study (1966 and 1968), she received a Rockefeller grant (1967), a John Golden Fund for Playwrights grant (1975), the Paul Robeson Award for Outstanding Contribution to the Performing Arts from the Black Filmmakers Hall of Fame (1977), and the Virgin Islands Film Festival Award. Alice Childress Week was officially observed in Columbia and Charleston, South Carolina, for the opening of *Sea Island Song* (1977). She was also the recipient of the Radcliffe/Harvard Graduate Society medal (1984), the African Poets Theatre Award (1985), the AUDELCO Award (1986), the Harlem School of the Arts Humanitarian Award (1987), and the Lifetime Career Achievement Award from the Association for Theatre in Higher Education (1993). Childress died of cancer August 14, 1994, in Manhattan.

BIBLIOGRAPHY

Bailey, Peter. "Stage: Contemporary Black Classic Theatre." *Black Collegian* 14 (January/February 1984): 34.

Brown-Guillory, Elizabeth. "Alice Childress, Lorraine Hansberry, Ntozake Shange: Carving a Place for Themselves on the American Stage." In *Their Place on the Stage: Black Women Playwrights in America.* 25–49, 52–64, 137–140. Westport, Conn.: Greenwood, 1988.

———. "Childress, Alice." In *Notable Women in the American Theatre: A Biographical Dictionary,* edited by Alice M. Robinson, Vera Mowry Roberts, and Milly S. Barranger, 126–130. Westport, Conn.: Greenwood, 1989.

Childress, Alice. "A Candle in Gale Wind." In *Black Women Writers (1950–1980): A Critical Evaluation,* edited by Mari Evans, 111–116. New York: Doubleday, 1984.

Jennings, La Vinia Delois. *Alice Childress.* New York: Twayne, 1995.

Killens, John O. "The Literary Genius of Alice Childress." In *Black Women Writers (1950–1980): A Critical Evaluation,* edited by Mari Evans, 129–133. New York: Doubleday, 1974.

Loretta Gilchrist Woodard

Christian, Barbara   (1943–2000)

Literary critic, scholar, and distinguished professor, Barbara Christian was an important voice in acknowledging the contribution of black women to the formation of the African-American literary canon and to American literature. Born in St. Thomas, Virgin Islands, Christian studied in the United States and received her doctorate in English at Columbia University in 1970. A serious political activist, Christian dedicated her life to fighting openly for and about the rights of black women and other women of color, yet her importance to African-American literature and studies responds to her focus on educating people about the value and worth of black women writers.

Writers like Toni Morrison and Alice Walker, who were receiving little critical attention, and writers like Frances Ellen Watkins Harper, Zora Neale Hurston, Nella Larsen, and Jessie Fauset, whose works had been relegated to obscurity, became significant literary figures thanks in large part to the scholarly work Christian did in revealing their novels to the literary world in her book *Black Women Novelists: The Development of a Tradition, 1892–1976* (1980). Moreover, Christian uncovered an important tension between presenting the voices of black women writers and critically assessing those writers' voices without silencing them—subsuming them into dominant and often exclusionary modes of abstract philosophical thought. Christian's numerous books and articles remain central to studies of African-American women novelists, essayists, and scholars, and of black feminist criticism, as well as the study of American literature.

Best known for her critique of literary critics and the role they play in the reading public's consumption and exposure inside and outside academia to black women's works, Christian charged that literary critics were becoming elitist and exclusionary—manipulating and using language in ways that silenced the voices of both black women writers and the scholars who refused to participate in those normalizing discourses. In "The Race for Theory" (1987), she examines what she terms "the takeover" of the literary world by "Western Philosophers from the old literary elite" who turned literary works representing a writer's labor-intensive creative and artistic expression into texts (products devoid of creative meaning) made to fit into scripted, self-serving vehicles for furthering the critics' own professional purposes. In this essay, Christian articulates a presence for the voices of those writers, particularly black women writers and other women writers of color, whose works were once neglected by the literary elite and then misappropriated for academic and personal gain.

Christian extends her discussion of what she sees as the disturbing pattern in literary criticism to the larger project of the struggle of black women for recognition of their presence in both the American and the African-American literary canon and in the larger world. As a central work of black feminist criticism, a literary and social movement raising the awareness and presence of black women's literature and thought, Christian's landmark collection, *Black Feminist Criticism: Perspectives on Black Women Writers* (1985), examines creative voices of black women from the 19th and 20th centuries by illuminating the social and cultural matrices from which these creative voices arise. Christian calls for critical approaches that come from the work itself—approaches examining the realities of these works' contexts as they appear in the work rather than creating or imaging a world to fit into some abstract theory only a few can decipher.

In a career spanning more than 30 years, Christian's own critical portfolio comes from a perspective acutely aware of the intersections of race, class, and gender on the lives of the black women novelists she studies, as well as her own reading as a black feminist critic—a field and discipline she helped create. While Christian levied sharp criticism on literary theorists, she did not turn away from literary theory; she embraced it in her own work, including *Female Subjects in Black and White: Race, Psychoanalysis, Feminism* (1997), edited with Elizabeth Abel and Helen Moglen, examining the complexities of applying psychoanalysis to readings by women writers, specifically women writers of color. In this work, as in others, Christian's analysis was not a catalogue of fixed theories that she read through the work but a project of actively theorizing to understand not only what each writer writes and why the writer writes, but also to illuminate ways to understand the writer and the work itself. She weaves her personal experience with the experience of theorizing and creates analyses that show a partnership between theorist and writer.

Christian dedicated her life to making the world aware of the work of black women novelists and other women of color as well as furthering studies on the intersections of race, gender, and class in these women's lives, all evidenced by her help in establishing the African-American studies department at the University of California at Berkeley and her position as chair of Berkeley's Ethnic Studies Department. Christian took her personal passion and made it a central feature of a life steeped in social consciousness and conscious activism and in doing so left a legacy of important critical thought that will continue to inform studies in not only African-American literature but American literary studies as a whole.

BIBLIOGRAPHY

Christian, Barbara. *Black Feminist Criticism: Perspectives on Black Women Writers.* New York: Teachers College Press, 1985.

———. *Black Women Novelists: The Development of a Tradition, 1892–1976.* Westport, Conn.: Greenwood, 1980.

———. "Fixing Methodologies: *Beloved.*" In *Female Subjects in Black and White: Race, Psychoanalysis, and Feminism,* edited by Elizabeth Abel, Barbara Christian, and Helen Moglen, 363–370. Berkeley: University of California Press, 1997.

———. "The Race for Theory." *Cultural Critique* 6 (Spring 1987): 51–63.

Gena Elise Chandler

Civil Rights movement   (1954–1965)

For many critics the Civil Rights movement officially began with the unanimous Supreme Court decision in *Brown v. Board of Education of Topeka,* on May 17, 1954. This Supreme Court ruling declared that separate was not equal and opened the doors for school integration, overturning *Plessy v. Ferguson* (1896), which had approved school segregation as legal and constitutional almost 60 years earlier. The next 11 years changed the course of history, especially as life was lived in the southern United States. Parallel worlds that supported a Jim Crow environment were legally challenged, as ordinary citizens rose to the demands of these extraordinary times. Other important markers of the genesis of this movement are Emmett Till's lynching in Money, Mississippi, in August 1955 (for allegedly whistling at or saying something to a white woman), and the Montgomery, Alabama, bus boycott, which began in December 1955 and lasted 381 days. Both events attracted national attention in the movement's early days. The latter event launched MARTIN LUTHER KING, JR., as the spokesperson for the nonviolent agenda of the movement.

In subsequent years, the Civil Rights movement was associated with several other important historical events, including the integration of public school systems across the South, the sit-in movement, the freedom rides, the assassination of Medgar Evers, and the March on Washington. In the fall of 1957, nine black students integrated the previously all-white Central High School in Little

Rock, Arkansas, but they needed the supportive presence of more than 1,000 troops from the 101st Airborne Division of the U.S. Army to do so. School integration throughout the South did not come swiftly, and after schools were integrated, social activities lagged behind. In May 2002 Taylor County High School in central Georgia voted to hold its first integrated prom.

On February 1, 1960, four young male students at North Carolina A&T State University in Greensboro, North Carolina, walked the few blocks to the downtown Woolworth's to sit at the counter to order coffee. Their simple action launched a wave of sit-ins across the South. Within weeks, students from historical black colleges and universities were sitting in at counters asking for service where black citizens had traditionally been denied. Leaders of the sit-ins in various cities became leaders of the Student Non-violent Coordinating Committee (SNCC), which was formed at Shaw University in Raleigh, North Carolina, in April 1960.

In May 1961, national attention was directed toward the Freedom Riders, especially after their bus was attacked and burned in Anniston, Alabama, and further violence erupted at stops in Montgomery and Birmingham. In 1963, people around the globe watched and listened for news of Birmingham—from the hosing of the black citizens to the police attack dogs to the jailing of men, women, and children who participated in what were supposed to have been peaceful demonstrations. In June 1963, NATIONAL ASSOCIATION FOR THE ADVANCEMENT OF COLORED PEOPLE activist Medgar Evers was assassinated as he walked from his car toward his front door in Jackson, Mississippi. His killer roamed free for more than 30 years before being convicted and sentenced. Equally important is the historically successful March on Washington in August of 1963, where King delivered his "I Have a Dream" speech, and the bombing, a few weeks later, of Birmingham's 16th Street Baptist Church, in which four young girls attending Sunday school were killed.

Freedom Summer 1964 flooded Mississippi with college students from all over the country who volunteered their time in direct action with Freedom Schools for the children and voter reg-

istration drives for the adults. The summer was plagued by an FBI search for three young men—James Chaney, Andrew Goodman, and Michael Schwerner—who were reported missing in June and whose bodies were found in August. The voter registration drive culminated in members of the Mississippi Freedom Democratic Party attempting to seat themselves in Atlantic City, New Jersey, at the National Democratic Convention. Though unsuccessful in 1964, their actions paved the way for integrated representations from southern states in all subsequent national political conventions.

The last hurrah of the modern Civil Rights movement took place in March 1965 with the successful walk from Selma to Montgomery; an estimated 25,000 people joined in this final triumphant moment on Dexter Avenue in front of the steps of the state capitol to listen to speeches delivered by the movement's leaders, who, as it turned out, were assembled for the last time. Within hours, a voting rights bill was journeying through the corridors of the nation's capitol to becoming law.

The Civil Rights movement was responsible for massive gains for black Americans in the erosion of the Jim Crow South. Many people died, while others went to prison, boycotted both transportation and businesses, marched in the streets, and organized themselves in the hopes of achieving a better tomorrow. Despite the many famous leaders associated with this movement, including King and Jesse Jackson, it would not have been a success without the courage and labor of thousands of unnamed and unknown ordinary citizens.

Significantly, the Civil Rights movement became and remains an important setting and theme in African-American literature. Virtually every black writer writing during the last half of the 20th century, from MAYA ANGELOU, JAMES BALDWIN, and AMIRI BARAKA to JOHN EDGAR WIDEMAN and JOHN A. WILLIAMS, address this movement in their works. For example, it provides the major backdrop for ERNEST GAINES's novels *The AUTOBIOGRAPHY OF MISS JANE PITTMAN* (1971) and *A Gathering of Old Men* (1983) and is a central theme in the short stories of ALICE WALKER and a critical rite of passage for the heroine of her novel *Meridian* (1976). MARGARET WALKER's collection of poems

Prophets for a New Day (1970) focuses on historical events from this movement.

BIBLIOGRAPHY

King, Martin L., Jr. *I Have A Dream: Writings and Speeches That Changed the World.* Edited by James M. Washington. San Francisco: Harper Collins Publishers, 1986.

Lewis, Anthony. *Portrait of a Decade: The Second American Revolution.* New York: Bantam Books, (with *The New York Times*) 1965.

Williams, Juan. *Eyes on the Prize: America's Civil Rights Years: 1954–1965.* New York: Viking Penguin, 1987.

Margaret Whitt

Cleage, Pearl Michelle   (1948–   )

Award winning author, dramatist/poet and one of the nation's most produced African-American woman playwrights, who said she writes to "find solutions and pass them on . . . and to find language and to pass it on," Pearl Cleage was born on December 7, 1948 in Springfield, Massachusetts; she grew up in Detroit, Michigan. Her father, the late Reverend Albert Buford Cleage, was a prominent minister who founded his own denomination, the Pan African Orthodox Christian Church, changed his name to Jaramogi Abebe Agyeman, and, in 1962, ran for governor of Michigan on the Freedom Now ticket. Her mother, Doris Graham Cleage, was an elementary school teacher. Pearl is the youngest of two daughters.

Cleage studied playwriting at Howard University in Washington, D.C., from 1966 to 1969 and produced two one-act plays as a student. She left Howard to marry Michael Lomax, an Atlanta politician, and to move to Atlanta. They divorced in 1979. Cleage received her bachelor of arts degree from Atlanta's Spelman College in 1971 and continued graduate study at Atlanta University. In Atlanta, she established an impressive list of media achievements, including serving as a host on an Atlanta-based community affairs program, as director of communications for the city, and as press secretary for Mayor Maynard Jackson.

Cleage began her playwriting career in the 1980s with productions of her plays *Puppetplay, Hospice, Good News,* and *Essentials.* Since the early 1980s, she has drawn national attention for her works *Chain, Late Bus to Mecca,* and *Flyin' West,* which chronicle the lives of pioneer black women at the turn of the century, and for *Blues for an Alabama Sky.* Her other theatrical works include *Bourbon at the Border,* a full-length drama commissioned by and premiered at the Alliance Theatre in 1997 under the direction of Kenny Leon, a frequent collaborator and Alliance artistic director.

Although Cleage frequently performs her work on college campuses, *Blues* was part of the Cultural Olympiad in Atlanta in conjunction with the 1996 Olympic games. During the 1992–93 season, under the direction of longtime collaborator Leon, *Flyin' West* was produced at more than a dozen venues nationwide, including the Kennedy Center in Washington, D.C., the Brooklyn Academy of Music, the Indiana Repertory Company, Crossroads Theatre Company, the Alabama Shakespeare Festival, the St. Louis Black Repertory Theatre, and the Long Wharf Theatre, making it one of the most produced new plays in the country that year. In 1983, Cleage garnered five AUDELCO awards for Outstanding Achievement off-Broadway for her play *Hospice.*

Cleage has received grants from the NEA, the City of Atlanta Bureau of Cultural Affairs, and the Georgia Council for the Arts. Her exploration of topics such as race and gender issues forces readers to stand at attention and heed her clarion call. She does so in many of her collected essays found in *Mad at Miles: A Black Woman's Guide to Truth* (Cleage Group, 1990), *Deals with the Devil and Others Reasons to Riot* (One World/ Ballantine, 1993), and *The Brass Bed and Other Stories* (Third World Press, 1996). In *Mad at Miles,* Cleage candidly describes her objectives as a writer: "I am writing to expose and explore the point where racism and sexism meet. I am writing to help myself understand the full effects of being black and female in a culture that is both racist and sexist. I am writing to try and communicate that information to my sisters and then to any brothers of good will and honest intent who will take the time to listen."

Cleage's first novel, *What Looks like Crazy on an Ordinary Day* (1998), is centered on the odyssey of a woman who is diagnosed with HIV and the way she interacts with people who either alienate her or love her. It was selected by the Oprah Book Club in October 1998 and appeared on the *New York Times* best seller list for nine weeks. It also was a Black Caucus of the American Library Association Literary Award winner. Cleage is also the author of a second novel, *Wish I Had a Red Dress.* Her highly anthologized work can be found in *Double Stitch: Black Women Write about Mothers and Daughters* (1991), *Black Drama in America* (1994), *Contemporary Plays by Women of Color* (1995), and *Bearing Witness: Contemporary Works by African American Women Artists* (1996). The Theatre Communications Group published an anthology of her plays, *Flyin' West' and Other Plays* (1999).

While simultaneously publishing essays in such popular magazines as *ESSENCE, Ms., Vibe,* and *Rap Pages,* Cleage contributed essays to several mainstream venues, including the *New York Times Book Review,* in which she published "Good Brother Blues." Currently, she is a contributing editor to *Essence* magazine. The accomplished playwright, cofounder of the literary magazine *Catalyst,* and speaker has taught at Spelman College and Smith College. Random House published her third novel, *Some Things I Never Thought I'd Do,* in 2004. Based in Atlanta, Cleage is the mother of a daughter, Deignan, and the wife of Zaron W. Burnett, Jr.

BIBLIOGRAPHY

"Blues for an Alabama Sky." *American Theatre,* 17 July 1996.
Clease, Pearl. *Mad at Miles.* Atlanta: Cleage Group, 1990.
Giles, Freda Scott. "The Motion of Herstory: Three Plays by Pearl Cleage." *African American Review* 31, no. 4 (Winter 1997): 709–712.
Roberts, Tara. "Pearls of Wisdom." *Essence,* December 1997.
Turner, Darwin T., ed. *Black Drama in America: An Anthology.* Washington, D.C.: Howard University Press, 1994.
Washington, Elsie, "Pearl Cleage." *Essence,* September 1993.

Jeannine F. Hunter

Cleaver, Eldridge   (1935–1989)

A native of Little Rock, Arkansas, Eldridge Cleaver became, during the 1960s, a spokesperson for the revolutionary Black Panther Party, founded by Huey P. Newton and Bobby Seale in Oakland, California. As the minister of defense, Cleaver became its most articulate spokesperson, in the way MALCOLM X did for the Nation of Islam. Cleaver, who, like Malcolm X, had converted to Islam while in prison, declared his interest in one of two things: the total liberation of black people or total destruction for America, as did such writers of the BLACK ARTS MOVEMENT as AMIRI BARAKA, HAKI MADHUBUTI (Lee), and NIKKI GIOVANNI. Cleaver was also the Black Panthers' candidate for the office of president of the United States.

More important, however, the Black Panther's general Marxist platform called for full employment and decent housing for blacks, the end of oppression and police brutality endemic in the black community, and the establishment of educational and liberation centers. The Black Panthers established breakfast programs, day care centers, and medical care for the underclass. They published the radical newspaper *The Black Panther* to promulgate their philosophy and ideology. Considered armed revolutionaries, the Panthers lived under the watchful eyes of the Oakland Police Department and the FBI, which infiltrated the organization because of its radical philosophy and militant leaders. When an Oakland police officer was killed during an FBI raid and ensuing gun battle, Cleaver, like a fugitive slave running to freedom, fled the United States; he remained exiled for seven years in a variety of Third World countries.

Cleaver is best known for his neo–slave narrative/autobiography *Soul on Ice* (1968), written while he was in California's Folsom Prison, sentenced there in 1954 for possession of marijuana. Coming as it did during the same year the Supreme Court handed down its history-changing decision in *Brown v. Board of Education,* outlawing segregation, Cleaver's imprisonment, he argues in *Soul,* awakened him to his "position in America" and he "began to form a concept of what it meant to be black in white America" (3). His awakening, he further argues, enlightened him to the way whites had been able to oppress black males. His dysfunctionality surfaces in his justification for raping white women:

> . . . and when I considered myself smooth enough, I crossed the tracks and sought out white prey. I did this consciously, deliberately, willfully, and methodically—though looking back I see that I was in a frantic, wild, and completely abandoned frame of mind. Rape was an insurrectionary act. It delighted me that I was defying and trampling upon the white man's law, upon his system of values, and that I was defiling his women—and this point, I believe was the most satisfying to me because I was very resentful over the historical fact of how the white man has used black women. I was getting revenge. (1968, 14)

Using a narrative voice that recalls those of FREDERICK DOUGLASS, MAYA ANGELOU, JAMES BALDWIN, W. E. B. DuBois, RALPH ELLISON, MALCOLM X, and RICHARD WRIGHT, Cleaver also seeks to create a self beyond that of criminal other—to offer a candid, critical vision on the status of the United States, generational shifts, and the need for reform, particularly in the essay "The White Race and Its Heroes." Warning that there is a crisis in communication between the older and younger white generations, Cleaver writes:

> What has suddenly happened is that the white race has lost its heroes. Worse, its heroes have been revealed as villains and its greatest heroes as the arch-villains. The new generations of whites, appalled by the sanguine and despicable record carved over the face of the globe by their race in the last five hundred years, are rejecting the panoply of white heroes, whose heroism consisted in erecting the inglorious edifice of colonialism and imperialism. (1968, 68)

In the end, writing becomes for Cleaver, much like it had for Angelou, Malcolm, and Wright, a venue to the existential self. Like them, he discovers what Sidone Smith calls "the curative power of the act of writing autobiography" (153). Cleaver wrote, "I started to write [to] save myself. I realized that no one could save me but myself. . . . I had to seek out the truth and unravel the snarled web of my motivations. I had to find out who I am and where I want to be, what type of man I would be, and what I could do to become the best of which I was capable" (1968, 15).

Soul on Ice sold millions of copies and was critically acclaimed. Cleaver would follow his award-winning text with the less successful *Soul on Fire* (1978), in which he delineates his conversion to Christianity. The book's dedication reveals how far Cleaver had moved philosophically from his previous militant position as a member of the Black Panthers and revolutionary leader: "This book is dedicated to the proposition that all human beings are created equal—in sin—with the God-given capacity to rise above themselves. From the depths of the pit of despair we can ascend to sublime heights of hope and fulfillment" (dedication, *Soul on Fire*). Before his death in 1989, Cleaver had also become a member of the Church of Jesus Christ of Latter Day Saints.

BIBLIOGRAPHY

Cleaver, Eldridge. *Soul on Fire.* Waco, Tex.: World Books, 1978.
———. *Soul on Ice.* New York: Dell Publishers, 1968.
Smith, Sidone. *Where I Am Bound.* Westport, Conn. Greenwich Press, 1974.

Wilfred D. Samuels

Clifton, Lucille Sayles (1936–)

Born in 1936 in Depew, New York, to Samuel L. Sayles, a steel worker, and Thelma Moore Sayles, a homemaker, poet Lucille Clifton grew up in Depew and Buffalo, a child of the Great Migration of southern blacks to the industrial North. Though her southern-born African-American parents had little formal education, they both read voraciously, and Lucille's mother wrote poetry in iambic pentameter. Although it was very different from the sort of verse Clifton would go on to write, her mother's writing nevertheless provided an important example for the future poet.

Clifton was not only the first in her family to graduate from high school but also the first to attend college. Poor grades cost her the scholarship she received from Howard University, however, and her subsequent enrollment at Fredonia State Teachers' College lasted but a few months. Although she would later become a professor of creative writing and eventually hold a chaired professorship at St. Mary's College of Maryland, Clifton chafed at the restrictions placed on her as a student and chose to pursue her education on her own.

In 1958 she married Fred Clifton, who was completing his senior year at the University of Buffalo. The couple lived in Buffalo for about a decade while Fred, a yogi with wide-ranging philosophical interests, pursued a Ph.D. in philosophy at the university. Lucille, who worked for the first several years of her marriage as a claims clerk for the New York State employment office, had six children between 1961 and 1967. All the while, she was writing poems, with an eye toward someday publishing them.

For Clifton, 1969 proved to be a professional turning point. After the poet ROBERT HAYDEN received a letter and sample poems from Clifton, he shared the poems with the poet Carolyn Kizer, who entered the poems in the YW-YMCA Poetry Center Discovery Award competition. By now Fred and Lucille Clifton were living in Baltimore, where Fred was educational coordinator for the Model Cities Program and Lucille worked for the U.S. Office of Education. Clifton did not know that she was entered in the contest, so her selection as the winner came as a surprise. The Discovery Award drew the attention of Random House, which then published her first book, *Good Times* (1969), as well as two subsequent poetry collections and her memoir.

In brief, often elegiac poems about urban black life, *Good Times* demonstrated clarity of style and an incisive social awareness that would become hallmarks of Clifton's poetry. *The New York Times* named the volume one of 10 notable books of 1969. This was the same year, coincidentally, that Clifton published the first of some two dozen picture books for children. No longer a civil servant who wrote on the side, she was now managing two professional writing careers.

Clifton followed her debut poetry success with *Good News about the Earth* (1972), a book reflecting the activist spirit of the BLACK ARTS MOVEMENT. As the women's movement gathered momentum in the 1970s, an increasingly self-confident and self-consciously female persona took shape in her poems as well as in her memoir, *Generations* (1976). In *An Ordinary Woman* (1974) and *Two-Headed Woman* (1980), a feminist spirituality surges through her poems. Her private spiritual experiences—notably her supernatural communications with her deceased mother—became central to her vision of the world.

After the publication of *Two-Headed Woman*, however, Clifton did not publish another poetry book for seven years. Important changes in her life—the death of her husband at age 49 in 1984 and a move to California in order to teach at the University of California at Santa Cruz—no doubt contributed to this quiet period. In 1987 she re-emerged with the publication of *Next*, a bold collection of elegiac poems, and *Good Woman: Poems and Memoir, 1969–1980*, a compilation of her first four poetry volumes and memoir. In 1988, she published a limited-edition chapbook, *Ten Oxherding Pictures*. Around the same time, she returned to Maryland and began teaching at St. Mary's College, where she has held a position ever since.

The books she would write in the next decade reveal that her spirituality and mortality were now the definitive core around which her poetry revolved. Between 1991 and 2000, despite bouts with breast cancer and kidney failure, she published four volumes of poetry: *Quilting* (1991), *The Book of Light* (1993), *The Terrible Stories* (1996), and *Blessing the Boats: New and Selected Poems, 1988–2000* (2000). More and more, she was able to use her own life experience as a template for meditations on social injustice, African-American history, and the innate strength of womanhood.

Though her books have earned her the National Book Award for Poetry in 2000 and an appointment to the previously all-white board of chancellors of the Academy of American Poets in 1999, Clifton is a voice speaking from, and for, the racial and social margins of American society. Her writing reveals her strong social conscience and broad awareness of human suffering. Blackness and femaleness are at one with her art's humanity. Clifton asks us to see individual experience, race, and gender not as qualifiers limiting a person's ability to relate to others but as revelations of selfhood that open up new possibilities of communication, communion, and collective action.

The new poems in *Blessing the Boats: New and Selected Poems, 1988–2000* mourn the cruelties that humans inflict on one another and decry the violent legacy that today's children have inherited from their elders. Preoccupied with mortality, the persona Clifton adopts in these poems is nevertheless drawn to the wondrous possibilities that life holds for each person, each generation. Her poems make it clear that she still believes in the restorative power of love, though she acknowledges, in her indictments of social injustice, that love for one's fellow humans is often in woefully short supply.

Hilary Holladay

Coleman, Wanda (1946–)

Born Wanda Evans to George and Lewana Evans in Watts, and raised in South Central Los Angeles, California, Coleman remains today an important literary and the existential voice of this West Coast community, specifically in relation to the socioeconomic and political uprisings associated with this area: the Watts Revolt (1965), which she experienced first hand as a young adult, and the south central Los Angeles rebellion (1992), a conflagration that took place after the Rodney King verdict was announced. Influenced by MAULANA KARENGA's nationalist Us Organization, Coleman began writing poetry at age 15, embracing and validating the functional purpose of art prescribed in Karenga's Kawaida theory of social change for

African-American life and culture. Identifying in an interview her desire to write, Coleman added, "And through writing control, destroy, and create social institutions. I want to wield the power that belongs to the pen," affirming, on the one hand, her dedication to "the cause" and the political principles of the BLACK ARTS MOVEMENT, while echoing on the other hand, RICHARD WRIGHT in *BLACK BOY*. After attending college for two years, Coleman left to serve as writer-in-residence at Studio Watts from 1968 to 1969. In addition to working as a recruiter for Peace Corps/VISTA, Coleman was a staff writer for NBC's *Days of Our Lives,* winning, in 1976, an Emmy Award for best writing in a daytime drama.

Coleman, an eclectic poet, short story writer, and performer, is the author of one novel, *Mambo Hips and Make Believe* (1999), and several collections of poetry and stories, including *Art in the Court of a Blue Fag* (1977), *Mad Dog Black Lady* (1979), *Imagoes, Heavy Daughter Blues: Poems and Stories* (1987), *A War of Eyes and Other Stories* (1988), *Dicksboro Hotel and Other Travels* (1989), *African Sleeping Sickness: Stories and Poems* (1990), and *Hand Dance* (1993). Coleman's *Bathwater Wine* won the 1999 Lenore Marshall Poetry Prize, and her *Mercurochrome: New Poems* made her a bronze-metal finalist at the National Book Awards in 2001. Her *Love-Ins with Nietzsche,* published as a chapbook, was nominated for the Pushcart Prize (2000).

In her poetry, Coleman records and celebrates the complex and dynamic history of African Americans found in the entire spectrum of the black experience, encompassing everything from black urban life and family structure, the often painful journey from childhood to young adulthood, and the inevitable destructiveness of racial oppression to an unabashed treatment of lesbianism, a celebration of blackness, and the artist's quest for identity and form. For example, set in the 1960s, a period dominated by African-American music and dance ("hully gully shimmy peanut butter"), "At the Record Hop" preserves black youth culture. Attending a record hop held in her junior high school gym, the speaker looks on as "bobby-soxers exchange clandestine feels / in dark hallways . . . / young black bodies humped hard." Ironically, she is unable to participate in this important sexual rite of passage because she unexpectedly begins her own initiation into womanhood: "menstrual red stains white pleated skirt / catching on to 2-tone socks." The consequence is, for the novice, painful, as she remains "the only girl not asked to dance." Through her youthful speaker, who at the end ponders "why boys don't like me," Coleman explores the often paradoxical experiences of puberty, a theme and treatment that move the poem beyond the racial specificity Coleman cherishes.

In contrast, although it, too, is about rituals and puberty—about "coming into manhood"—"Emmett Till" explores myopia by focusing on the blind and senseless destruction caused by racism. The poem accurately recalls the 1955 death of Emmett Till, a 14-year-old Chicago youth who was lynched and thrown into the Mississippi River while visiting his grandparents, ostensibly for committing oracular rape: "that hazel eye sees / the woman / she fine mighty fine / she set the sun arising in his thighs / . . . and he let go a whistle / . . . but she be a white woman. but he be / a black boy." Till pays a horrific price for his crime, his lust-filled whistle: "his face smashed in / lord! lord! / his body beaten beyond recognition."

Coleman is best known for the gutsy, raw, unpretentious language of her poems about the complexity of women and multifaceted character of urban life—the life of the ghetto—with which she strongly identifies. In these poems, she gives voice to the often marginalized—for example the lesbian, prostitute, the john or pimp—as she does in "Sweet Mama Wanda Tells Fortune for a Price." Returning to walk the street after servicing a customer, the prostitute speaker reflects, "outside i count my cash / it's been a good night / the street is cold / i head east / i am hungry / i smile." Clearly, prostitution, for the speaker, is a respectable and legitimate way of making a living, of putting food on her table. She heads east, ready to meet head-on and embrace without fear a new day. Ebullient from the joy of her existential act and sense of agency, she smiles.

In the end, Coleman's work, poetry and fiction, is dominated not only by her concern with women's lives and issues but fundamentally by dynamic love, which forms the central theme of her work. Often, she uses this theme in conventional ways, running the gamut from the purely physical and erotic to the psychological, emotionally fulfilling, and racial. For example, self-love and a celebration of blackness is the central theme in "Coffee," in which the speaker unabashedly and humorously recalls with fond memory her love for the coffee her Aunt Ora made, "in the / big tin percolator," and served to her and her playmates in "thick / white fist-sized mugs." The children love coffee "better than chocolate," despite a neighbor's warning that "young colored children" should not drink coffee because "it made you get blacker / and blacker." With their act, the children confirm the popular folk rhyme, "the blacker the berry the sweeter the juice," and affirm the mantra of the 1960s: "black is beautiful." As Lynda Koolish points out, Coleman forces "readers to reexamine their own attitudes about sexuality and race" (26).

In Coleman's short story "Lonnie's Cousin," a young mother and wife, trapped in an unfulfilling interracial marriage, is seduced by her neighbor's cousin. Claiming, at first, that she has been "hexed" by her pursuer, the wife confesses her infidelity to her husband, who, upon hearing her story for the first time, insists on hearing it over and over again. Although she reveals her own complicity in the process of retelling her story, which she embellishes with each new narration, the speaker succeeds in seducing her husband in the end, infusing new life into their heretofore less than exciting marriage.

Coleman's work has been published in such well-known magazines and journals as *Antioch Review, Crab Orchard Review, Obsidian,* and *Zyzzyva.* Her poems and short stories have been included in *Best American Poetry* (1988); *Trouble the Water,* edited by Jerry Ward; and *Breaking Ice,* edited by TERRY MCMILLAN. The mother of a son, Coleman has received fellowships from the Guggenheim Foundation and the National Endowment for the Arts.

BIBLIOGRAPHY

Karenga, Maulana. *Kawaida Theory: An Introductory Outline.* Inglewood, Calif.: Kawaida Publications, 1980.

Koolish, Lynda, comp. *African American Writers, Portraits and Visions.* Jackson: University Press of Mississippi, 2001.

Magistrate, Tony, and Patricia Ferreira. "Sweet Mama Wanda Tells Fortunes: An Interview with Wanda Coleman." *Black American Literature Forum* 24, no. 3 (Fall 1990): 491–507.

Wilfred D. Samuels

College Language Association Journal, The (CLAJ)

Founded in 1957, *The College Language Association Journal* is published by the College Language Association (CLA), a predominantly black organization of college professors that began in 1937. CLA grew out of correspondence between then-leading scholars of African-American literature and culture, professors Hugh M. Gloster and Gladstone Lewis Chandler, which culminated in a meeting of eight English professors who initially named the organization the Association of English Teachers in Negro Colleges. However, in 1941, the organization's name was changed to the Association of Teachers of Languages in Negro Colleges to encompass both literature and foreign languages. In yet another effort to broaden the organization's scope to include all academics interested in scholarship on languages and literature, including that written by and about African Americans, the name was changed, in 1949, to the College Language Association.

To extend opportunities for more scholarly exchange, CLA's Planning Board founded, in 1957, *The College Language Association Journal (CLAJ)* as CLA's official organ of printed scholarship in literature and languages. *CLAJ* continues to serve multiple functions: providing information about annual CLA conventions, publishing the president's annual convention address, informing readership of CLA member publications, offering job placement service listings in languages and literature, encour-

aging the historical continuity of CLA by paying tribute to its prominent scholars and supporters who have passed on, encouraging undergraduate and graduate students through its essay and study abroad competitions, using its book reviews and lists to keep its readership updated on scholarship in the field, helping preserve the interest and support in historically black colleges and universities, and including articles on pedagogy. Published quarterly, *CLAJ* offers publication opportunities to members and subscribers. Much of the history of CLA and *CLAJ* is available at the Clark Atlanta University Center Archives.

Australia Tarver

Color Purple, The   Alice Walker   (1982)

ALICE WALKER's Pulitzer Prize–winning novel, *The Color Purple,* tracks the torturous journey of CELIE, a rural black female adolescent, toward womanhood and self-awareness. In a larger vein, Walker's third novel offers her vision of the possibility for healthy, cooperative relationships between women and men. *The Color Purple* quickly became a subject of controversy for its explorations of abusive and otherwise problematic relationships between black men and women. If LANGSTON HUGHES's "Negro artist" had to confront the "racial mountain," Walker and other black women writers have had to confront the racial and "gender mountain."

An epistolary novel (composed of letters from Celie to God and to her younger sister, Nettie, and from Nettie to Celie), *The Color Purple* is set for the most part in rural Georgia, though some scenes take place in Memphis, Tennessee, and Africa. Celie's first letter, written when she is 14, tells of her sexual and emotional abuse at the hands of Alphonso, the man she believes to be her father. He not only impregnates her but also refuses to allow her to keep either of the two children he fathers; he admonishes her to tell no one but God. The situation, including the separate sleeping quarters for Celie and Nettie, invokes the slaveholder/bond-woman relationship of freedom narratives, and Celie's inner transformation parallels the outer physical transformation from slavery to freedom. After her mother dies, Celie's stepfather arranges her marriage to a much older man, Albert, continuing her involuntary servitude. Left alone to fend off her "father's" advances, Nettie runs away and joins Celie in her new home, but Albert throws Nettie out when she soundly rebuffs his sexual advances. Nettie is, coincidentally and miraculously, taken in by the missionary couple who is raising Celie's "stolen" babies; Nettie subsequently travels with the family to Africa. In her pre-enlightenment letters, Celie refers to her husband simply as Mr. _____. She does not learn his first name until Shug Avery, his BLUES-singing lover, arrives.

Celie develops a meaningful relationship with Shug Avery, whom she nurses back to physical health after Albert moves her into their home. Celie and Shug become first friends and then lovers. Walker stresses reciprocity in the relationship between Shug and Celie; each woman helps the other toward physical, psychological, and spiritual health. In a parallel movement that many of her harshest critics seem to miss, Walker also depicts a similar transformation in the male characters, particularly Albert. The new community that Walker imagines is cooperative and egalitarian. In a series of events that befits the optimistic fable (almost utopian) quality of the novel, Alphonso dies, Celie and Nettie inherit the property that their real father left for them, and the two sisters are subsequently reunited when Nettie returns from Africa with Celie's children.

In addition to the Pulitzer Prize, *The Color Purple* garnered for Walker the prestigious National Book Award. The 1985 film version, directed by Steven Spielberg, was nominated for an Academy Award. The novel has since become a mainstay of the African-American literary tradition.

BIBLIOGRAPHY

Bloom, Harold, ed. *The Color Purple.* Modern Critical Interpretations Series. Philadelphia: Chelsea House Publishers, 2000.

Bobo, Jacqueline. "Watching *The Color Purple:* Two Interviews." In *Black Women as Cultural Readers,* 91–132. New York: Columbia University Press, 1995.

Dieke, Ikenna, ed. *Critical Essays on Alice Walker.* Westport, Conn.: Greenwood Press, 1999.

Gates, Henry Louis, Jr., and Kwame Anthony Appiah, eds. *Alice Walker: Critical Perspectives Past and Present.* Amistad Literary Series. New York: Amistad, 1993.

Lauret, Maria. *Alice Walker.* New York: St. Martin's Press, 2000.

Lovalerie King

Colter, Cyrus   (1910–   )

Before winning the University of Iowa Prize School of Letters Award for Short Fiction in 1970, Colter, then a 60-year-old attorney, had been a commissioner of commerce for Chicago, Illinois. Born in Noblesville, Indiana, the second child of James Alexander Colter and Ethel Marietta Bassett Colter, Colter attended Youngstown, Ohio's Rayen Academy and Youngstown University. He received his L.L.B. degree from Chicago-Kent College of Law. He had worked for both the YMCA and YWCA, served as deputy collector of internal revenue, and was a captain in the U.S. Army before serving as assistant commissioner of commerce and then commissioner of public utilities in Chicago. In 1973, Colter became the Chester D. Tripp Professor of Humanities and chairman of the department of African-American studies at Northwestern University in Evanston, Illinois. The University of Illinois, Chicago Circle, conferred on him the honorary degree of doctor of letters in 1977.

Convinced that his short story, "The Beach Umbrella," identified Colter as a "master in theme and style from the very beginning of his career" (O'Brien, 17), the Friends of Literary Prize and the Patron Saints Award of the Society of Midland Authors joined the University of Iowa in recognizing Colter with accolades and awards for the lead story in his collection *The Beach Umbrella,* (1970). Previously, Colter had made the Honor Roll of *Best American Short Stories* in 1962 and 1967. His stories had also appeared in *The Best Short Stories by Negro Writers* (1967).

The author of four novels—*The River of Eros* (1972), *The Hippodrome* (1973), *Night Studies*

(1979), and *A Chocolate Soldier* (1988)—Colter, whose favorite novel is *Crime and Punishment* and whose favorite philosophers are Thomas Hobbes and B. F. Skinner, prefers to avoid racial themes and social issues in his work. Instead, he is interested in more existential and deterministic experiences: the condition of merely being a human being. When asked by John O'Brien if he felt his art "must be used in some way to effect changes in society," Colter candidly responded, "I can't say that I do. . . . What I am trying to do when I'm writing is to get down on paper what I see and feel, and it's very possible that it has no social value at all. I'm not sure, and I really don't care too much actually" (21).

Like Camus's Sisyphus, Colter's characters are caught in situations over which they have no real control. They are determined. Colter explains his view of the human condition: "we are here as effects of certain causes about which we have nothing to do, and that these causes determine what we are and what we shall be. . . . We are caught in this bind, and we go inexorably down this course which is willed for us by these causes that we had no control of" (22). This is true of Mary in "Mary's Convert," Mildred in "The Lookout," and Verna in "A Man in the House," who are all unable to change their lot, circumstances, class, or environment. None of these characters can control or determine the outcome of their lived experiences. This is also true of Elijah of "The Beach Umbrella," whose desperate search for love and human compassion remains untenable.

Although the characters in the 14 stories in *The Beach Umbrella* are black, the personal stories are all deterministic; race plays little or no significant role in the characters' experiences which include stories about guilt, loneliness, love, alienation, and a lack of communication. These themes also characterize Colter's novels. For example, in his tragedy *The Rivers of Eros*, Clotilde Pilgrim, a grandmother who thinks she has done everything to protect her 16-year-old granddaughter from making the same mistakes she has made, learns that her granddaughter is involved in an affair with a married man. Driven by guilt and fear, Clotilde kills her granddaughter to avoid seeing history repeat itself.

When he received the Iowa Prize for short fiction, Colter was described as "what a writer is and always has been—a man with stories to tell." Colter has lived up to this description for more than four decades.

BIBLIOGRAPHY

O'Brien, John. *Interviews with Black Writers.* New York, Liveright. 1973.

Wilfred D. Samuels

Conjure-Man Dies: A Mystery Tale of Dark Harlem, The   Rudolph Fisher (1932)

The Conjure-Man Dies, RUDOLPH FISHER's second novel, holds the distinction of being the first African-American detective novel and, for some critics, psychological thriller. When Harvard-educated N'Gana Frimbo, an African "conjure man" who plies his trade in Harlem, turns up dead, Harlem's Detective Perry Dart and Dr. John Archer, a physician who assists homicide detectives, are called in to help solve the case. In the end, however, Frimbo, who it is discovered is very much alive, helps solve the mystery and find his would-be killer.

The novel's strength is Fisher's complex characters. Frimbo, besides being an intelligent Harvard graduate and student of philosophy, is also an African king who suffers from paranoia and, as conjurer, seeks to "escape the set pattern of cause and effect" (268). Frimbo engages John Archer, a medical doctor who is incapable of using language that falls outside his medical profession, so his speech is esoteric and archaic. Perry Dart, "the newly appointed champion of the law" (98), is Harlem's first black patrolman to be promoted to detective. According to the narrator, Dart has been chosen because "his generously pigmented skin rendered him invisible in the dark, a conceivable great advantage to a detective who did most of his work at night" (14). This description of Dart gives insight into the humor Fisher successfully weaves into his entire text. Fisher juxtaposes his more intelligent characters—perhaps representatives of ALAIN LOCKE's class of "thinking Negro"—with stereotyped urbanites such as Bubber Brown, a would-be private detective; Jinx Jenkins, his friend; Spider Webb, a numbers runner; Doty Hicks, a drug addict; and Samuel Crouch, the undertaker. Placed together in Harlem, these characters create a medley of vision, intrigue, and laughter.

From the opening pages of *The Conjure-Man Dies,* Fisher presents readers, as did CARL VAN VECHTEN in *NIGGER HEAVEN* and CLAUDE MCKAY in *HOME TO HARLEM,* with a panoramic view of the New Negro's black mecca, particularly the night street life scene that "sprouted . . . like fields in spring," as camel hair-clad men and musk-rat-wrapped women eagerly seek "the voracious dance halls" (3). Exemplary is the Hip-Toe Club on Lenox Avenue, a cabaret frequented by dandies, dope users and peddlers, and number runners, where blues and jazz beat the rhythms and blare the exotic sounds of the Jazz Age. Fisher's description of this sexually liberated, primitive setting also resonates with NELLA LARSEN's more middle-class oriented novels, *Quicksand* (1928) and *Passing* (1929). Fisher writes,

> In the narrow strip of interspace, a tall brown girl was doing a song and dance to the absorbed delight of the patrons seated nearest her. Her flam chiffon dress, normally long and flowing, had been caught up bit by bit in her palms, which rested nonchalantly on her hips, until now it was not so much a dress as a sash, gathered about her waist. (102)

By making the central figure of his novel a conjure man, whom he ironically pairs with a formally trained medical doctor, Fisher records, preserves, and to some degree celebrates black folk culture as did CHARLES CHESNUTT in *The CONJURE WOMAN AND OTHER STORIES,* and as ZORA NEALE HURSTON, LANGSTON HUGHES, WALLACE THURMAN, and ERIC WALROND and other HARLEM RENAISSANCE luminaries, were interested in doing. In *The Conjure-Man Dies,* Fisher's Hicks explains that he has gone to see Frimbo, known for his potent spells, because his brother's former wife had hired Frimbo to kill Spat, her former abusive husband who is also Hicks's brother. Doty explains: "Frimbo's a conjure man. He can put spells on folks. One kind o'spell to keep 'em from dyin'. . . . Another kind to set 'em to dyin—misery all in through here, coughin' spell, night sweats, chills and fever, and wastin' away. That's what he was doin' to Spats" (113). Frimbo's urban city dweller customers all believe in the power of the African traditional religion practiced by Frimbo's family in Africa and passed down to him as his inheritance.

For the most part, *The Conjure-Man Dies* was well received. ARNA BONTEMPS and COUNTEE CULLEN adapted it for the stage as a Federal Theatre Project. It is considered a forerunner to the detective novels of CHESTER HIMES and contemporary novelist WALTER MOSLEY. According to Arthur P. Davis, *The Conjure Man Dies* is a conventional thriller that "has all of the customary trappings of the type: the red herrings, the false starts, the least likely suspect, and a team of detectives—one amateur, the other official police" (103).

BIBLIOGRAPHY

Davis, Arthur P. *From the Dark Tower, Afro-American Writers 1900–1960.* Washington, D.C.: Howard University Press, 1981.

Fisher, Rudolph. *The Conjure-Man Dies: A Mystery Tale of Dark Harlem.* New York: Arno Press and The New York Times, 1971.

Wilfred D. Samuels

Conjure Woman and Other Stories, The
Charles W. Chesnuttt (1899)

CHARLES W. CHESNUTT published "The Goophered Grapevine," his first short story, in the prestigious *Atlantic Monthly* in 1877. Twenty-two years later, it became the lead story in his first collection, *The Conjure Woman and Other Stories* (1899). William Dean Howells favorably reviewed the collection, but Chesnutt's African-American identity was not immediately revealed. That Chesnutt, who saw literature as "a weapon that could defeat racism" (Gates, 116), set out to accomplish his established goal of using literature as a venue for moral progress in America with the stories in *The Conjure Woman and Other Stories* is readily visible.

Set in the fictional postbellum community of Pasteville, North Carolina (Chesnutt's fictional Fayetteville), the seven frame stories in the book provide southern local color of the past told in the heavy North Carolinian black dialect of Uncle Julius McAdoo, a shrewd former field hand slave, who enriches his recollection of the plantation with conjure and voodoo tales and folk practices and beliefs. Uncle Julius tells his stories to John, the primary narrator, an Ohioan who has gone south after the Civil War to invest in a vineyard and to find a hospitable climate for his ailing wife, Annie. Upon meeting the prospective owners for the first time, Uncle Julius advises them against the purchase, relating the strange and tragic events caused by the gopher, or hoodoo, placed on the vineyard by its former owner, Colonel McAdoo, to keep his slaves from stealing his valued and price-less scuppemong grapes. Aware of Julius's own personal interest in the property and the profits he might have already realized from the land, John purchases it nevertheless and hires Uncles Julius as his coachman.

In his role as griot, or storyteller, Uncle Julius illuminates the darker side of the peculiar institution, slavery. Unlike the loyal and obsequious slave Friday, who yearns to return to the "good ole days" of slavery, Julius topples it from its benign pedestal. Images of bartering human flesh and the lawless appropriation of human bodies surface throughout Uncle Julius's recollection. We see this, for example, in "Sis' Becky's Pickaninny." Although it means she will be separated from her infant, Little Mose, Sis Becky, already separated from her husband, is traded by her master, Colonel Penddleton, for a racehorse. The colonel's action confirms Sis Becky's status not only as voiceless property but specifically as chattel, as beast of burden. Similarly, when he returns to the slave quarters after being "lent out" to his master's children, Sandy of "Po' Sandy" discovers that his master has swapped his wife for a new female slave. Sandy reveals that commodified black bodies are important only for their exchange value. Mars Marrabo "pays" Sandy one dollar to compensate for having separated his family.

Finally, the expediency of black life is found in the exploitation of Henry in "The Goophered Grapevine." After he unknowingly eats the goophered grapes, Henry is kept alive by Aunt Peggy's conjuration, a sap made from the vine, which she instructs him to rub on his head. Although he does not die, Henry takes on the properties of the vine, becoming young and strong during the spring but old and infirm during the fall. Aware of Henry's dilemma, Marse Dugal McAdoo devises a plan in which he sells Henry at the height of his virility and buys him back when his body goes dormant like the vineyard. His scheme brings him a profit of $5,000 in five years. As critic Robert Bone notes,

> Beneath the comic surface of the tale is a lesson in economics of slavery. The slaves were in fact worth more in the spring, with the growing season still to come; in the fall prices declined, for an owner was responsible for supporting his slaves through the unproductive winter season. These fluctuations in price underscore the slave's status as commodity; his helpless dependence on the impersonal forces of the market. The target of Chesnutt's satire is the dehumanizing system that reduced the black man to the level of the crops that he was forced to cultivate. (85)

In the end, Uncle Julius indicts multifaceted slavery, while enriching his tales with conjure, voodoo, and folk practices and beliefs. Julius is clearly patterned after the paradigmatic African folk hero, the trickster. More important, however, Uncle Julius, in action and narration, moves beyond chronicling horrific slavery. As griot, he simultaneously records and celebrates the slaves' successful conversion of their marginalizing site of oppression and deprivation into a space of resistance and radical possibilities. For example, the bond between Sandy and his second wife, Tennie, a conjure woman, is so strong that rather than be sold into slavery he allows her to convert him into a tree during the day. At night, she reconverts him into her mate and companion. Also, rather than let Little Mose, Sis Becky's son, pine away, Aunt

Jane, his surrogate mother, has Aunt Peggy convert Mose into a hummingbird and later a mockingbird. On both occasions, Mose is able to fly to his mother, whom he finds grieving as well on a distant plantation. Mose sings to Becky, who, recognizing his voice, is soothed and comforted by his plaintive song. Mother and child are reunited in the end as a result of the joint effort of the extended family structure created and maintained in the slave quarters. Most important is Aunt Peggy's role as conjurer. Her empowerment is derived from her familiarity and relationship with nature, which she is able to harness and directly influence. Even the slave master, Marse Dugal, retains her service.

Through his treatment and characterization of Uncle Julius and Aunt Peggy, Chesnutt unmasks and validates a complex social structure within the slave community. Both affirm that slaves had a rich and animated life of their own in which they found creative ways of exercising control over their daily lives by exorcizing the master's gaze. Theirs was a self-sufficient world that turned inward to reproduce and continue its own culture, one that was firmly grounded in orality and antiphonality, the sound of blackness. According to HOUSTON BAKER, Uncle Julius "presents a world in which 'dialect' masks the drama of African American spirituality challenging and changing disastrous transformation of slavery" (44). In 1928, the NATIONAL ASSOCIATION FOR THE ADVANCEMENT OF COLORED PEOPLE awarded Chesnutt its Spingarn Medal for his pioneering work as a literary artist depicting the life and struggles of Americans of Negro descent, and for his long and useful career as scholar, worker, and freeman in one of America's greatest cities.

BIBLIOGRAPHY

Baker, Houston A., Jr. *Modernism and the Harlem Renaissance.* Chicago: University of Chicago Press, 1987.

Bone, Robert. *Down Home: A History of Afro-American Short Fiction from Its Beginnings to the End of the Harlem Renaissance.* New York: G. P. Putnam's Sons, 1975.

Gates, Henry L., Jr. *The Signifying Monkey: Towards a Theory of Afro-American Literary Criticism.* New York: Oxford University Press, 1988.

Wilfred D. Samuels

Cooper, J. California   (1940–)

Prolific short story writer, novelist, and playwright, J. California Cooper was born in Berkeley, California, in 1940. Cooper says that she has always "just liked stories" and that she remembers writing plays she performed for friends and family when she was only five years old. She started her writing career as a playwright in the 1970s, eventually writing 17 plays, some of which were performed by the Berkeley Black Repertory Theater. She was honored as the Black Playwright of the Year in 1978 for her play, *Strangers.* In the 1980s, Cooper's short stories caught the attention of fellow writer ALICE WALKER, who was impressed by Cooper's "strong folk flavor." Cooper's short story collection *A Piece of Mine* (1984) became the first work published by Walker's Wild Tree Press. In all, Cooper has published six collections of short stories, *A Piece of Mine* (1984); *Homemade Love* (1986), which won her the American Book Award; *Some Soul to Keep* (1987); *The Matter Is Life* (1991); *Some Love, Some Pain, Sometime: Stories* (1996); and *The Future Has a Past: Stories* (2001), along with three novels, *Family: A Novel* (1991), *In Search of Satisfaction* (1994), and *Wake of the Wind* (1998). Her work has also won the James Baldwin Award (1988) and the Literary Lion Award of the American Library Association (1988).

Compared to such African-American authors as LANGSTON HUGHES and ZORA NEALE HURSTON, Cooper focuses most of her stories on the everyday foibles of common people. The settings are usually rural, and the time periods vary from colonial America to contemporary times, highlighting the African-American experience. Each work tackles the human condition and the ways in which people have tried to understand the complexities of life. Cooper seems most concerned with sharing stories that illuminate the moral dilemmas that people face every day, as her mostly African-American female protagonists deal with issues of racism, sexism, and poverty. Moreover, she writes fables that reflect her Christian ethic. She told the *Washington Post:* "I'm a Christian. That's all I am. If it came down to Christianity and writing, I'd let writing go. God is bigger than a book" (Wiltz, 1).

These basic themes serve as the template for her fiction. *A Piece of Mine* collects 12 stories that focus on how women overcome abusive or loveless relationships with men. *Homemade Love* features 13 tales in which characters enumerate the choices they have made to find, keep, and support love in their lives—some successfully, some not. *Some Soul to Keep* is a collection of five longer pieces in which Cooper discusses the highs and lows of black womanhood, from the joys and difficulties of being a wife and mother to learning how to deal with loneliness. In *The Matter Is Life,* Cooper weaves eight tales that pay close attention to the choices that people make when dealing with the uncertainties of life. Her first novel, *Family,* is a close examination of the physical, mental, and spiritual effects of slavery, as a ghost-mother narrator, Clora, watches the pursuits of her children and their descendents from slavery to emancipation. Cooper's second novel, *In Search of Satisfaction,* also picks up the subject of slavery and its aftermath but is more fable-like, as Satan himself watches over the missteps of half-sisters Ruth and Yinyang. Cooper returns to theorizing about the ins and outs of love with a collection of 10 tales titled *Some Love, Some Pain, Sometime,* creating protagonists who learn to love not only others but themselves. *Wake of the Wind* (1998), Cooper's third novel, focuses on the lives of Lifee and Mordecai, a former slave couple working to build their lives in the oppressive postbellum South. In *The Future Has a Past,* Cooper writes stories that show the harsh consequences of losing the sense of history, a history she sees as necessary for securing a brighter future.

Cooper belongs to the great emergence of black women writers that began in the 1970s. Like her contemporaries, she has offered an intimate look into the lives of African-American women. She has received much acclaim for her narrative style, which shows the cadences and folkways of black women. Her use of first-person narrative with characters who speak directly to the reader is one of her hallmarks. Writer and critic TERRY McMILLAN says that Cooper's narrative technique "give[s] you the feeling that you're sitting on the front porch with the narrator, somewhere in the South; it's hot and humid, she's snapping beans, you're holding the bowl and she's giving you the inside scoop on everybody" (23). Cooper employs narrators that not only share stories (usually the tales center around people other than the narrators) but also offer their own take on the situations, revealing personal frailties, biases, or feelings. With this approach, Cooper creates an intimacy between the teller and the reader. Her style has been called "folksy," "down-home," and "gossipy." In "Down That Lonesome Road" from *Homemade Love,* for example, the character Bertha begins the story about how she paired up her lonely cousin with one of her widowed friends, saying: "First off, let me let you know, I am not a gossip! Can't stand em! I'm known for that! I don't tell nobody's business . . . and I know everybody's!" (141). The narrators are not always the most knowledgeable, however, nor do they always learn the moral Cooper weaves in the tales. For instance, Nona, the narrator of "Friends, Anyone?" in *The Matter Is Life,* bemoans how her former husband and best friend have "betrayed" her by marrying despite Nona's admitting to cheating on her husband, abandoning her twin daughters because they are handicapped, and manipulating friends and family for her own desires. Like Hurston, Cooper provides context for her tales: The teller is just as important as the story itself, making Cooper a consummate storyteller within the African-American tradition.

BIBLIOGRAPHY

Gates, Henry Louis, Jr. "Shattering Family Myths." *Newsday,* 27 January 1991, p. 23.

McMillan, Teri. "Life Goes On, and Don't You Forget It!" *New York Times,* 8 November 1987, p. 23.

Wiltz, Teresa. "The Writer Who Talks to Frogs." *Washington Post,* 26 October 2000, c1.

Stephanie Powell Hankerson

Corbin, Steven   (1953–1995)

Steven Corbin was born in 1953 in Jersey City, New Jersey. Although he left before graduating, Corbin attended the University of Southern California film school and was at one time a fiction-writing instructor at University of California, Los Angeles. His three published novels, *No Easy Place to Be* (1989), *A Hundred Days from Now* (1994) and *Fragments That Remain* (1995), function as a trilogy reflecting, celebrating, and critiquing contemporary black gay male culture and identity as well as the cultural history from which it stems.

Corbin's first book, *No Easy Place to Be*, is a historical novel that explores the lives and relationships of the Brooks sisters, three very different African-American women, in 1920 Harlem. Corbin's account of the emotional and sexual travails of Miriam, a nurse and militant Garveyite; Velma, a sophisticated and sexually adventurous "New Negro" writer; and Louise, a light-skinned Cotton Club showgirl who ultimately finds the problems of being a white-black woman too intense and "passes" over into the white world, presents a provocative vision of the intersection of racial and sexual identities in the HARLEM RENAISSANCE. With its in-depth exploration of Garveyism, the politics of skin color, white literary patronage and the "vogue" for black authors, and the emergence of a recognizable homosexual and bisexual subculture in 1920s New York, the novel brings the period to life while reflecting and utilizing the discursive construction and critical legitimation of the Harlem Renaissance as a site for academic inquiry that has taken place over the last two decades.

Reminiscent of JAMES BALDWIN's GO TELL IT ON THE MOUNTAIN, Corbin's second novel, *Fragments That Remain*, tells a multigenerational story of emotional and physical abuse as it is experienced in the family of a successful black actor, the dark-skinned but blue-eyed Skylar Whyte. Concurrently, the novel explores the issue of interracial gay attraction in its depiction of the deteriorating relationship between Skylar and his white lover, Evan Cabot. By telling the story from the perspectives of Skylar, his mother, his father, his brother Kendall, and Evan in individual chapters, the novel offers a complex and ultimately non-judgmental exploration of truth, memory, and forgiveness and their effects on the formation of personality and, more problematically, sexual preference.

Corbin's last novel, *A Hundred Days from Now*, which was nominated for a 1994 Lambda Literary Award for gay male fiction, tells the story of Dexter Baldwin, an openly gay HIV-positive African-American screenwriter, whose relationship with Sergio Gutierrez, a closeted Mexican-American millionaire who is dying from AIDS, devolves into a disturbing tangle of self-hatred, homophobia, and emotional sadomasochism as Dexter attends to Sergio during the 100 days that it will take to discover if the experimental bone marrow transplant that he has received from his identical twin brother will cure or arrest the progress of his disease. Published in the year before Corbin's death, this bleak novel may reflect aspects of Corbin's own losing struggle with AIDS, from which he died on August 31, 1995, in New York City.

Although the critical response to Corbin's novels has been mixed and he never received the popular recognition from either gay or mainstream readers accorded his contemporaries E. LYNN HARRIS and JAMES EARL HARDY, at his best Corbin adroitly walks the line between serious and popular fiction while exploring almost the entire range of issues found in contemporary gay men's fiction. Corbin's short fiction has appeared in the collections *Breaking Ice: An Anthology of Contemporary African-American Fiction, More Like Minds, Frontiers, Streetlights: Illuminating Tales of Urban Black Experience, Sundays at Seven: Choice Words from a Different Light's Gay Writers Series*, and *Black Like Us: A Century of Lesbian, Gay and Bisexual African American Fiction*.

BIBLIOGRAPHY

Duplechan, Larry. "Steven Corbin." *BLK* (1992): 11–23.

Oliver, Myrna. "Steven Corbin: Novelist and AIDS Activist." *Los Angeles Times*, 3 September 1995, p. A26.

Terry Rowden

Cornish, Sam (1935–)

A prolific poet, editor, and juvenile author, Cornish was born in Baltimore, Maryland. He left high school during his freshman year but later attended Goddard College and Northwestern University. He served in the U.S. Army Medical Corps from 1958 to 1960. After returning from the military service, Cornish worked as a writing specialist for the Enoch Pratt Library, where he edited *Chicory* with Lucian W. Dixon. In 1968 Cornish received both a National Endowment for the Arts grant and the poetry prize from the Humanities Institute of Coppin State College. In 1969 he moved to Boston, where he became an education specialist on projects emphasizing creative writing for children. He served as a special consultant to the Educational Development Center in Newton, Massachusetts, where he worked on the Open Education Follow Through Project from 1973 to 1978.

Cornish has produced a large body of work, beginning with his first widely accepted collection of poetry, *Generations, and Other Poems* (1964), which he published through his own Beanbag Press. His other notable collections are *Sam's World: Poems* (1978), *Song's of Jubilee: New and Selected Poems, 1969–1983* (1986), and *Folks Like Me* (1993). AMIRI BARAKA and LARRY NEAL included him in their history-making anthology, *BLACK FIRE: AN ANTHOLOGY OF AFRO-AMERICAN WRITING* (1968) as did CLARENCE MAJOR in his *New Black Poetry* (1969). Cornish is also the author of four books for young adults: *Your Hand in Mine* (1970), *Grandmother's Pictures* (1974), *My Daddy's People Were Very Black* (1976), and *Walking the Streets with Mississippi John Hurt* (1978). In addition, he has published a memoir, simply titled *1935* (1990).

Cornish's breakout collection of poetry, *Generations,* is an attempt to write a universal collection that deals with the triple axes of African-American literature, kinship, and history. Going beyond physical bonds, kinship is "social bonding, a recognition of likeness in context, concern, need, liability, and value." This theme is expressed in "Harriet Tubman #2," a celebration of Tubman and her mother, and their survival:

> Lord, while I sow earth or song
> the sun goes down. My only mother
> on a dirt floor is dying. . . .
> I think
> of the children
> made in her and sold. (Generations, 10)

The harsh, though natural rhythms of life ("sow earth" "sun goes down," "mother . . . dying") are dishonored by the commodification of procreation itself ("the children / made in her and sold") yet revered for representing the persistence of the will to live.

In *Folks Like Me,* Cornish continues his theme of kinship, expanding it to "African Americans of all descriptions—working people, entertainers, disaffected radicals, sober churchgoing folk—and they step forth one after the other from the decades of our century to present their testimony." It is Cornish's deep commitment to kinship that allows this variety of voices to emerge. The expression of kinship—the African-American experience—can be found in his brief yet poignant poem "Negro Communists":

> When white
> workers find
> hotel rooms
> the Negro worker
> hits the street. (Folks Like Me, 48)

Here, Cornish's speaker registers his support for the working class, the proletariat, who must unite, as the Communists demand, with the other workers of the world. Cornish's black worker must protest, "hit the street," in order to not sit quietly and be discriminated against or oppressed. Although the speaker seems to embrace communist ideology, however, there is an ironic twist, as the white worker, although a member of the proletariat, still enjoys privileges the black worker does not because he is able to "find / hotel rooms." The white worker is not as alienated, in the end, as the black worker, who is left "outdoors," as TONI MORRISON might say. To the white reader, this poem may be slightly confusing, but the African-American reader already knows the ending by the third line. In the end, however, the workers have a common bond. Currently, Cornish teaches at Emerson College in Boston in the department of writing, literature, and publishing.

BIBLIOGRAPHY

Cornish, Sam. *Folks Like Me.* Cambridge, Mass.: Zoland Books, 1993.

———. *Generations, and Other Poems.* Baltimore: Beanbag Press, 1964.

———. *Songs of Jubilee: New and Selected Poems.* Greensboro, N.C.: Unicorn Press, 1986.

Doreski, C. K. "Kinship History in Sam Cornish's *Generations.*" *Contemporary Literature* 33, no. 4 (1992): 665–687.

Metzger, Linda, et al., eds. *Black Writers: A Selection of Sketches from Contemporary Authors.* Detroit: Gale Research, 1989.

Ryan Dickson

Corregidora   Gayl Jones (1975)

This critically acclaimed novel begins with Ursa Corregidora's miscarriage of her child and a disruption of the path her foremothers have ordained for her. Ursa is the descendant of Portuguese slave owner Corregidora, who prostituted both Ursa's great-grandmother and grandmother and impregnated, in turn, both her great-grandmother and his own daughter. Ursa's responsibility, as was her mother's before her, is to create a girl child who can be a living evidence of this history of slavery and sexual violence. Ursa is constantly told, "the important thing is making generations. They can burn the papers but they can't burn conscious, Ursa. And that what makes the evidence. And that's what makes the verdict" (22). With her miscarriage and subsequent hysterectomy, Ursa can no longer fulfill the expectation of both bearing witness and giving birth to a new witness. The novel explores Ursa's struggle to understand the agency, if any, she has in the world without this assigned reproductive role.

Critics have focused on the means by which Jones explores the trauma of slavery and on the ties between black mothers and daughters who carry the psychic scars of a history of sexual violence and oppression. Most critics have been interested in the role of the BLUES as a mode of agency and expression for Ursa, who uses the blues to express her feelings about relationships between black men and women that she cannot successfully articulate otherwise. With her stark prose style, Jones often has her characters exchange what she calls "ritualized dialogue," a patterned exchange of dialogue that mirrors blues syntax. Ursa moves from the ritualistic recounting of her foremother's histories to her own unproductive rituals with men—particularly with her former husband, Mutt. Jones values the power of family histories and rituals in relationships, but she also explores the ways that such patterns can be oppressive.

Gayl Jones has been critiqued for presenting pathological stereotypes of black men and women. Such criticisms, however, cannot diminish the novel's power and contribution to black literature. With its focus on the violence in the lives of African-American women and men, its exploration of how the trauma of slavery continues to have effects in the 20th century, and its treatment of a blues aesthetic as an important social and psychological tool, *Corregidora* is one of the most important works of African-American literature at the end of the 20th century.

BIBLIOGRAPHY

Dubey, Madhu. "Gayl Jones and the Matrilineal Metaphor of Tradition." *Signs: Journal of Women in Culture and Society* 20, no. 2 (Winter 1995): 245–267.

Harper, Michael. "Gayl Jones: An Interview." In *Chant of Saints,* edited by Michael S. Harper and Robert B. Stepto, 352–375. Champaign: University of Illinois Press, 1979.

Rushdy, Ashraf H. A. "Relate Sexual to Histori-
    cal: Race, Resistance, and Desire in Gayl Jones's
    Corregidora." *African American Review* 34, no. 2
    (Summer 2000): 273–297.
Tate, Claudia C. "*Corregidora*: Ursa's Blues Med-
    ley." *Black American Literature Forum* 13 (1979):
    139–141.

Rebecca Wanzo

Corrothers, James D.   (1869–1917)

Although James D. Corrothers's career predated the HARLEM RENAISSANCE, many themes in his work and recurring struggles in his life prefigured the spirit and strivings of the Renaissance. W. E. B. DuBois's comment that Corrothers's death was a "serious loss to the race and to literature" suggests that during his lifetime Corrothers had gained a significant readership.

Corrothers was born in Chain Lake settlement, a small rural southwest Michigan community of free blacks and former fugitive slaves. Corrothers received a strong fundamental education in the nearby South Haven public schools, where he was the only black student. South Haven and surrounding southwest Michigan towns where Corrothers tried to make a living did not offer him the opportunities he needed after his schooling. So after doing mill and dock work on Lake Michigan in Muskegon, Corrothers stowed away on a steam barge bound for Chicago, on the opposite shore of Lake Michigan. Corrothers also traveled through Indiana and Ohio, working at odd jobs and intending to save money to attend college.

In Springfield, Ohio, Corrothers found work and time to pursue his writing. His poem "The Deserted Schoolhouse" appeared in the Springfield *Champion City Times.* Whites' general reaction of disbelief that Corrothers actually wrote the poem was an ominous portent of the difficulties he would face his entire life when pursuing his passion for writing. After leaving Ohio, Corrothers moved to Chicago. There, he resorted to a series of menial jobs because he was unable to secure a publisher. While working as a bootblack in a white-owned barbershop, Corrothers discussed literature with a distinguished-looking customer, who happened to be Henry Demarest Lloyd, whose father-in-law owned the *Chicago Tribune.* After their barbershop discussion, Corrothers's poem "The Soldier's Excuse" appeared in the *Tribune.* Subsequently, Corrothers was offered a job as a porter in the *Tribune's* counting room. This was also menial work, but it was more secure than any job Corrothers had previously held.

In early 1893 many black artists were drawn to the Chicago area, anticipating the 1893 Columbian Exposition. In Chicago, Corrothers met poet PAUL LAURENCE DUNBAR, who was secretary to FREDERICK DOUGLASS during the Exposition. Corrothers learned that Dunbar was also struggling to get his work published. In 1894 Corrothers married Fanny Clemens, and, as a result of her efforts, Corrothers was paid for his writing for the first time. His wife sold one of his articles to the *Chicago Daily Record.* Despite this success, steady income from writing still eluded him.

In 1896, desperate for income, Corrothers created a sketch of a character named Sandy Jenkins, a streetwise self-taught black man who spoke in "Negro dialect." The editors of the *Chicago Evening Journal* published the story, titled "De Carvin," and insisted that Corrothers write more sketches of Jenkins. The reception of "De Carvin" prompted Corrothers to change his opinion of dialect writing, which he had always considered demeaning. In his autobiography, *In Spite of the Handicap* (1917), Corrothers recorded his newfound insight that African-American dialect "was splendid material which I had overlooked, and which all Negroes but Dunbar had allowed to go begging."

Eventually, Corrothers's devotion to his religious faith drew him to the ministry. Shortly after he received a pastoral assignment in Bath, New York, his wife and youngest son died. After taking his post at the African Methodist Episcopal church in Bath, Corrothers returned to writing to supplement his salary. To satisfy the appetites of American readers at the turn of the century, Corrothers contributed Negro dialect poetry to leading magazines, culminating with the publication of a series of sketches of Sandy Jenkins, the character he created in 1896. These sketches were collected into his first book, *The Black Cat Club* (1902).

Most of Corrothers's dialect poetry appeared in newspapers and periodicals intended for white readers, reflecting the demands of white editors and the pervasive plantation stereotypes that white readers preferred. As Corrothers's literary career gained momentum, the heyday of African-American dialect writing was coming to an end. Defining a new agenda for African-American poetry in *The Book of American Negro Poetry*, JAMES WELDON JOHNSON assailed dialect poetry as "an instrument . . . incapable of giving the fullest interpretation of Negro character and psychology." In publications intended for African-American readers, Corrothers could ignore the demand for Negro dialect and plantation stereotypes and explore the theme that preoccupied him throughout his life—the paradox between the American Dream and African-American oppression.

In 1906 Corrothers married Rosina B. Harvey, and in 1913 he moved his wife and sons to Philadelphia. Corrothers devoted himself to the ministry, serving Baptist congregations in New Jersey, Michigan, and Virginia, and a Presbyterian congregation in Pennsylvania. During this time Corrothers continued to write and publish. *In Spite of the Handicap* was published in 1916, one year before his death. As the title suggests, the handicap of racial oppression figures prominently in Corrothers's life. It also serves as an apt metaphor for the limitations that curtailed Corrothers's productivity as a writer.

BIBLIOGRAPHY

Barton, Rebecca Chalmers. *Witnesses for Freedom: Negro Americans in Autobiography.* New York: Harper, 1948.

Bruce, Dickson D., Jr. *Black American Writing from the Nadir: The Evolution of a Literary Tradition, 1877–1915.* Baton Rouge: Louisiana State University Press, 1989.

———. "James Corrothers Reads a Book: Or, the Lives of Sandy Jenkins." *African American Review* 26, no. 4 (Winter 1992): 665–673.

Gaines, Kevin. "Assimilationist Minstrelsy as Racial Uplift Ideology: James D. Corrothers' Literary Quest for Black Leadership." *American Quarterly* 45, no. 3 (September 1993): 341–369.

Payne, James Robert. "Griggs and Corrothers: Historical Reality and Black Fiction." *Exploration in Ethnic Studies* 6 (January 1983): 1–9.

Veta S. Tucker

Cotter, Joseph Seamon, Jr.   (1895–1919)

Born in Louisville, Kentucky, to poet JOSEPH SEAMON COTTER, SR., and Maria F. Cox, Joseph Cotter, Jr., was encouraged from a young age to write poetry. He attended Fisk University where he worked on the *Fisk Herald*, a literary magazine, before tuberculosis forced him to return home. Back in Louisville, he worked for a local newspaper, the *Leader*, and wrote poetry, steering clear of the dialect tradition established by contemporary PAUL LAURENCE DUNBAR and adopted by his father.

Considered an important forerunner to the writers of the HARLEM RENAISSANCE, Cotter published a collection of 25 somewhat autobiographical poems, *The Band of Gideon and Other Lyrics* (1918; reissued in 1969), before his death at age 23 of tuberculosis. CRISIS magazine published his one-act play, *On the Field of France*, in 1920. Between 1921 and 1922, the *A.M.E. Zion Quarterly Review* published several of his poems, and *Poems,* a collection of 14 poems, was also published posthumously in 1922.

As his poetry reveals, Cotter's models, like those of CLAUDE MCKAY and COUNTEE CULLEN, were the British romantics, particularly Keats. Cotter experimented with form and subject matter, ranging from social commentary about World War I to postwar race relations in America. His "Is It Because I Am Black?" discusses the latter:

Why do men smile when I speak,
And call my speech
The whimpering of a babe
That cries but knows not what it wants?
Is it because I am black?

Why do men sneer when I arise
And stand in their councils,
And look them eye to eye,
And speak their tongue?
Is it because I am black?

Cotter clearly criticizes Western culture's propensity to conflate color with intelligence, as did such great thinkers as David Hume, Immanuel Kant, John Locke, and George Wilhelm Friedrich Hegel. As EUGENE REDMOND concludes, Cotter "shows a sharp awareness . . . of the plight of blacks and an even sharper ability to express that plight" (168).

BIBLIOGRAPHY

Gates, Henry L., Jr. "Writing 'Race' and the Difference It Makes." In *'Race.' Writing and Difference*, 1–20. Chicago: University of Chicago Press, 1985.

Mason, Julian. "Who Was Joseph Seamon Cotter, Jr.?" *The Southern Literary Journal.* 23, no. 1 (Fall 1990): 104–106.

Redmond, Eugene. *Drumvoices: The Mission of Afro-American Poetry. A Critical History.* Garden City, N.Y.: Anchor Books, 1976.

Kim Hai Pearson
Brian Jennings

Cotter, Joseph Seamon, Sr.   (1861–1949)

Joseph Cotter was born in 1861 in Bardstown, Kentucky, to Michael Cotter and Martha Vaughan. Cotter's mother often told him stories and plays that she made up while working around the house, presumably giving Cotter his love of storytelling. Cotter had little formal education; he had to leave school in the third grade to help his mother. He worked a number of odd jobs, including prize-fighting, bricklaying, ragpicking, and whiskey distilling. Cotter was smaller than many of the men he worked with, but because he was a storyteller he escaped being harassed by his fellow workers. At age 22, after studying hard in only two sessions of night school at the primary level, Cotter was considered ready to teach. He taught English literature and composition at Louisville's Colored Ward School. He founded and served as principal of Paul L. Dunbar School and later was the principal of Samuel Taylor Coleridge School. He was a major voice in his community, serving as the director of the Louisville Colored Orphan's Home Society while belonging to the NATIONAL ASSOCIATION FOR THE ADVANCEMENT OF COLORED PEOPLE, the Story Teller's League, the Negro Educational Association, and the Author's League of America. He married Maria F. Cox in 1891; tragically, they lost both of their children, including the poet JOSEPH S. COTTER, JR., to tuberculosis.

Best known for his poetry, Cotter began publishing his work at the end of the 19th century. Despite an admirable reputation, he was overshadowed by giants PAUL LAURENCE DUNBAR, JAMES WELDON JOHNSON, CHARLES CHESNUTT, and W. E. B. DuBOIS. EUGENE REDMOND nonetheless identifies Cotter as "one of the most gifted and prolific writers of his era" (104). Cotter published *A Rhyming* (1895), *Links of Friendship* (1898), *A White Song and a Black One* (1909), and *Negro Tales* (1912). His play *Caleb, the Degenerate* was published in 1903. In 1938 Cotter published *Collected Poems*. Cotter's writing is characterized by variety, touching on such diverse areas as moral lessons, folk tales, philosophy, satire, tragedies, and reflections about people. According to the editors of *The NEGRO CARAVAN,* Cotter's poetry falls under several categories: that of the schoolmaster, that of teller of tales for children, and that of race leaders. Moreover, they identified his dialect poetry as "more racially critical" than Dunbar's (343). His poetry is a journey of discovery into human nature.

Although criticized for his precision and intellectual angle (his play *Caleb, the Degenerate* was written in blank verse), Cotter's poetry also beautifully captures people's language and stories. "Tragedy of Pete," which won an *OPPORTUNITY* poetry prize, is exemplary. When Pete, who enjoys getting drunk at the local bar with his friends, "Both day and night," is told, after his Bible-carrying wife is killed in a car accident, that she was drunk, Pete murders her accuser. Standing before the judge, Pete proudly confesses, "I raised my knife / And drove it in / At the top of his head / And the point of his chin." Pete willingly asks to be sent to the electric chair. Having defended his wife's honor, he has behaved chivalrously and can die with dignity. *Caleb, the Degenerate,* although never performed, was a response to Thomas Dixon's *The Clansmen,* which attacked African Americans and praised the Ku Klux Klan.

BIBLIOGRAPHY

Brown, Sterling, et al., eds. *The Negro Caravan.* New York: Dryden Press, 1941.

Page, James A. "Cotter, Joseph Seamon, Sr." In *Selected Black American Authors,* 178–180. Boston: G. K. Hall, 1977.

Redmond, Eugene. *Drumvoices, the Mission of Afro-American Poetry.* New York: Anchor Books, 1976.

Kim Hai Pearson
Brian Jennings

Crawford, Janie

The protagonist of ZORA NEALE HURSTON's *THEIR EYES WERE WATCHING GOD,* Janie Crawford moves through two marriages before finding love in her third marriage, to TEA CAKE (Vergible Woods). In her marriage to Logan Killicks, her first husband, Janie, who had been influenced by her image of love while daydreaming under a pear tree, quickly learns that marriage and love are not necessarily the same. Interested more in his land and in having a wife who at best is a helper and at worst a slave, Killicks, who has been selected for Janie by her grandmother, does not fulfill Janie's romantic ideal.

When Joe Starks offers her the opportunity to abandon her loveless marriage, Janie leaves with him, marries him, and commits to helping him fulfill his vision of being a major player in Eatonville, Florida, a town made "all outa colored folks" (28). Reality sets in quickly when they arrive in Eatonville, where Joe, immediately after he is elected mayor, silences Janie's voice. Although Janie is identified as "Mrs. Mayor," Joe never allows her to ask questions or express her opinions; instead, he tells the community what he expects of her: "she's uh woman and her place is in de home" (69). Although he does allow Janie to help him run the community store, Joe forbids her from participating in the communal rituals engaged in by locals (mostly men) who frequent their porch to talk. Initially, Janie conforms and sits silently on the pedestal Joe creates and assigns her to. However, when she finally talks back to Joe, insisting that he not use his loud voice to belittle her, she empowers herself and wins the respect of the community. By the time Joe dies, Janie, now fully in control of her life, is well on her way to blossoming into a more fully realized individual.

Janie's life changes forever when Tea Cake, a younger man, walks into the store; they develop a reciprocal friendship based on respect. Unlike Killicks and Starks, Tea Cake provides her with laughter and companionship; he talks with her, plays checkers with her, and takes her fishing. Above all, he respects her thoughts and opinions, creating, in the end, a relationship that, from its genesis, is balanced, competitive, and friendly. Janie falls in love for the first time in her life and is able to embrace Tea Cake as the "bee to her blossom"—the fulfillment of her lifelong search for her pear tree ideal.

Janie leaves Eatonville and follows Tea Cake to the Florida Everglades, where they seek to work out a meaningful friendship and successful marriage. Their love is tested when, caught in a hurricane, Tea Cake is bitten by a rabid dog as he attempts to protect Janie, forcing Janie to kill him in self-defense. Janie knows the Tea Cake she kills is no longer the man she loved. Without Tea Cake, Janie can no longer live in the muck. She returns to Eatonville, where she attempts to work through her grief and enjoy the freedom she had come to know in her marriage to Tea Cake. In Eatonville, Janie continues to feel Tea Cake's presence. She embraces the memory of their life together and, above all, herself, convinced that the horizon is not out there, off in the distance; it is within.

BIBLIOGRAPHY

Hurston, Zora Neale. *Their Eyes Were Watching God.* New York: Perennial Classics, 1998.

Margaret Whitt

Crisis, The

First published in November 1910 as the official organ of the NATIONAL ASSOCIATION FOR THE ADVANCEMENT OF COLORED PEOPLE (NAACP), *The Crisis* magazine was meant to serve as the "record of the darker races." W. E. B. DuBois, its first editor, retained this position until 1934. Ten years later he returned to edit the magazine for another four years, until 1948. More than 90 years after its beginning, *The Crisis* is still in publication, making it one of the oldest black periodicals in America. In its present status, it is legally separate from and may not represent the official position of the NAACP.

The title of the magazine was taken from James Russell Lowell's 1844 poem "The Present Crisis." Though the title emerged from a casual conversation among people who would be involved in the magazine's early days, Lowell's beginning line— "When a deed is done for Freedom"—suggests the early mission of the magazine, which was to be an articulate vehicle for civil rights. According to DuBois, it succeeded in those early days because of its attention to news published under the heading "Along the Color Line," "blazing editorials" that irritated friends and alarmed foes, and an increasing number of pictures, many in color, of African Americans. In the early days in white papers, pictures of African Americans usually appeared only when alleged wrongdoing was charged. By 1916, *The Crisis* was self-supporting. Circulation grew faster than the membership rolls of the NAACP.

From the beginning, DuBois's agenda was always political; he had help in this area from JAMES WELDON JOHNSON and WALTER WHITE, in particular. Early on, the magazine was used to promote the literary talents of many young, unrecognized, and unsung black writers. JESSIE FAUSET became literary editor in 1919. In that role until 1926, she was responsible for bringing the pages of *The Crisis* to life with the works of artists who would become the outstanding talents of the HARLEM RENAISSANCE. For example, the first published poem by 19-year-old LANGSTON HUGHES, "The Negro Speaks of Rivers," appeared in the magazine in 1921. Among the luminaries to seek and be sought for the pages of *The Crisis* were JEAN TOOMER, CLAUDE MCKAY, ARNA BONTEMPS, and COUNTEE CULLEN.

In 1924, *The Crisis* initiated a contest—with the Amy Einstein Spingarn Prizes in Literature and Art—to attract new talent and foster the growth of the burgeoning black arts in Harlem. During the first half of the 20th century, *The Crisis,* with its rich literary offerings in poetry, fiction, and plays, and its assorted personal, literary, cultural, and social essays, was a periodical of immense influence; it was an integral component of the African American's educational development.

BIBLIOGRAPHY

Bontemps, Arna. ed. *The Harlem Renaissance Remembered.* New York: Dodd, Meade, 1972.
Wilson, Sondra Kathryn, ed. *The Crisis Reader: Stories, Poetry, and Essays from the N.A.A.C.P's* Crisis *Magazine.* New York: Modern Library, 1999.

Margaret Whitt

Cullen, Countee (1903–1946)

Countee Cullen was born Countee Leroy Porter, but his birthplace is uncertain. Though Ida Mae Cullen, his widow, claimed he was born in Louisville, Kentucky, Cullen sometimes claimed New York as his birthplace. (Other sources claim his birthplace was Baltimore.) At age 15, Cullen was adopted by the Reverend and Mrs. Frederick A. Cullen of the Salem Methodist Episcopal Church in Harlem. In his adoptive father's library, Cullen began his early study of books and literature, a study that would serve him well in his career as one of the most prominent poets of the HARLEM RENAISSANCE. In 1918, he enrolled at DeWitt Clinton High School, a predominantly white boys' school in New York, where he eventually became the editor of *Magpie,* the school's literary magazine. It was at Dewitt Clinton that Cullen found a passion for the 19th-century English poet John Keats. The profound impact Keats had on Cullen as a poet was voiced by ARNA BONTEMPS years later in *The Harlem Renaissance Remembered.* When the two first met, Cullen told him "that John Keats was his god."

In 1922, Cullen entered New York University and began his career as a published poet. In 1923 and 1924, respectively, he won second prize and first honorable mention in the national Witter Bynner Poetry Contest for his "Ballad of the Brown Girl" and "Spirit Birth." During this period, Cullen's poems appeared in many periodicals, including OPPORTUNITY, CRISIS, *Bookman, Poetry, Harper's,* and *The Nation.* In 1925 he won the Witter Bynner contest, graduated Phi Beta Kappa from NYU, and enrolled in Harvard University. In the same year, Cullen's first collection of poetry, *Color,* appeared and was critically acclaimed primarily for its poignant and sincere treatment of racial themes. One of the most famous poems of the volume, "Yet Do I Marvel," ends with a couplet that quickly became one of the most quoted in the English language: "Yet do I marvel at this curious thing: / To make a poet black, and bid him sing!"

After graduating from Harvard in 1926, Cullen began to write the column "The Dark Tower" for *Opportunity,* and he soon became the magazine's assistant editor. In 1927 Cullen published *Caroling Dusk,* an important anthology of African-American poets ranging from PAUL LAURENCE DUNBAR to the then 18-year-old Lula Lowe Weeden. This year also saw the publication of Cullen's *Copper Sun* and *Ballad of the Brown Girl.* Though generally well received, many critics agreed that these works did not match the quality of *Color.* In April 1928, Cullen married Yolande, his longtime sweetheart and the daughter of the prominent writer and activist W. E. B. DuBois. Soon after the wedding, Cullen traveled to France on a Guggenheim Fellowship. Here, Cullen wrote and studied French literature at the Sorbonne. When Yolande joined him in Paris in July 1928, the couple decided to end the relationship. Cullen stayed in France and completed his *The Black Christ and Other Poems.* Published in 1930, *The Black Christ* was not well received by the critical community. Reviewers argued that Cullen's later work lacked the intensity of his earlier volumes.

Cullen returned to the United States and divorced his wife in 1930. He soon set out to write the novel *One Way to Heaven,* a satirical work published in 1932. Offered a professorial position at Dillard University in New Orleans in 1934, Cullen declined the position and accepted a job as a French teacher at Frederick Douglass Junior High School. Though he continued to write and give lectures, Cullen's only major work over the next decade include the book of poetry *The Medea, and Some Poems,* the children's books *The Lost Zoo* and *My Lives and How I Lost Them,* and the posthumous *On These I Stand.* Cullen married Ida Mae Roberson in 1940 and died of uremic poisoning in 1946.

Sometimes called (along with LANGSTON HUGHES) the "poet laureate" of the HARLEM RENAISSANCE, Countee Cullen differed from such African-American contemporaries as Hughes and JEAN TOOMER in that he did not turn to jazz, BLUES, or a more modern free-verse style in his poetry. He relied on more classical and romantic models throughout his life, but, like Toomer, he fervently rejected the title "Negro" or "Black" poet and wished to be known only as an "American" poet. As such, he stated in his foreword to *Caroling Dusk* that "the attempt to corral the outbursts of the ebony muse into some definite mold to which all poetry by Negroes will conform seems altogether futile and aside from the facts." Though his career as a poet had long since faded by the 1940s, Cullen remains an important figure in African-American literature.

BIBLIOGRAPHY

Bontemps, Arna Wendell, ed. *The Harlem Renaissance Remembered.* New York: Dodd, Mead & Co., 1972.

Early, Gerald, ed. *My Soul's High Song: The Collected Writings of Countee Cullen.* New York: Anchor Books, 1991.

Ferguson, Blanche E. *Countee Cullen and the Negro Renaissance.* New York: Dodd, Mead & Co., 1966.

Turner, Darwin T. *In a Minor Chord: Three Afro-American Writers and Their Search for Identity.* Carbondale: Southern Illinois University Press, 1971.

Jeremy Gregersen

Danner, Margaret Esse (1915–1984)

Poet, editor, and community activist Margaret Esse Danner was born in Pryorsburg, Kentucky, on January 12, 1915, to Caleb and Naomi Esse Danner. Her family moved to Chicago, where she attended Englewood High School and studied poetry at Loyola College, Roosevelt University, and Northwestern University. While in Chicago, from 1951 to 1957, Danner worked for *Poetry: The Magazine of Verse* as an editorial assistant and an assistant editor with Karl Shapiro and Paul Engle, who nurtured her creativity as a poet. She was a poet-in-residence at Wayne State University in 1961, at Virginia Union University in 1968–69, and at LeMoyne-Owens College in Memphis, Tennessee. She established Boone House Writers in 1962–64 and met such other notable poets as DUDLEY RANDALL, ROBERT HAYDEN, NAOMI LONG MADGETT, HOYT FULLER, and OWEN DODSON. Together, Boone House and Randall's Broadside Press made Detroit a key part of the BLACK ARTS MOVEMENT and made Danner's poetry a central focus in the movement.

In 1945, by winning second prize in the poetry workshop of the Midwestern Writers Conference at Northwestern University, Danner gained national recognition. However, she did not become a prominent poet until the 1950s. In 1951 Danner was awarded a John Hay Whitney Fellowship and a trip to Africa for four poems in a series titled "Far from Africa," which she took in 1966 when she went to read her poetry at the World Exposition of Negro Arts in Dakar, Senegal. Danner's African poems have won praises for their form and exact images.

Danner is the author of five volumes of poetry: *To Flower* (1962); *Poem Counterpoem,* with Dudley Randall (1966); *Impressions of African Art Forms* (1968); *Iron Lace* (1968); and *The Down of a Thistle: Selected Poems, Prose Poems and Songs* (1976). Her speakers in these poems protest against white racism and its effects on African Americans, as well as address subjects ranging from the CIVIL RIGHTS MOVEMENT to old age to black heritage. "The Elevator Man Adheres to Form," in which the black male character has a Ph.D. but operates an elevator and has become too passive, is one of her most anthologized poems. One of her most successful protest poems is "The Endangered Species"; the endangered species is a black pearl, which is less valued because it is "such a sooty stone." Danner also edited two anthologies of poetry, *Brass Horses* (1968) and *Regroup* (1969).

Danner received several grants and awards. She has received grants from the Women's Auxiliary of Afro-American Interests (1950), the African Studies Association (1950), the American Society of African Culture (1960), the African Studies Association Award (1961), the Harriet Tubman Award (1965), and the Poets in Concert Award (1968). She was a touring poet with the Baha'i Teaching

Committee (1964–1966). In 1973, Danner was among 18 prominent black women poets invited to read from her works at the Phillis Wheatley Poetry Festival, organized by poet and novelist MARGARET WALKER and held at Jackson State College (now University).

Writing over several decades, Danner was a meticulous poet who made a significant contribution to African-American literature and to the Black Arts Movement. Like that of GWENDOLYN BROOKS, MARI EVANS, NIKKI GIOVANNI, SONIA SANCHEZ, and LANGSTON HUGHES, Danner's work addresses issues that connect African Americans to their heritage and culture. Danner died in Chicago on May 1, 1986.

BIBLIOGRAPHY

Aldridge, June M. "Margaret Esse Danner." In *Dictionary of Literary Biography.* Vol. 41: *Afro-American Poets Since 1955,* edited by Trudier Harris and Thadious M. Davis, 84–89. Detroit: Gale, 1985.

Carson, Sharon. "Danner, Margaret Esse." In *The Oxford Companion to African American Literature,* edited by William L. Andrews, Frances Smith Foster, and Trudier Harris, 199–200. New York: Oxford University Press, 1997.

Bailey, Leonard Pack, ed. *Broadside Authors and Artists: An Illustrated Biographical Directory.* Detroit: Broadside, 1974.

Loretta G. Woodard

Danticat, Edwidge   (1969–   )

Born in Port-au-Prince, Haiti, on January 19, 1969, to André and Rose Danticat, Edwidge Danticat spent formative childhood years living with a beloved aunt and uncle in Haiti under the Duvalier dictatorship until 1981. The danger of being a writer under his dictatorship seeped into her writing style, creating a tension between the brutal honesty of her stories and the lyricism of her prose.

When Danticat was two, her father left for New York to begin a better life; her mother followed two years later, in 1973, to join him. In 1981 Edwidge and her brother came to Brooklyn, New York, where her father worked as a cab driver and her mother was a textile worker. She and her brother arrived to find two new brothers. She notes, "When I first came [to America], I felt like I was in limbo, between languages, between countries" (Farlay, 1). Her liminal experience and status augmented the incandescent quality of her writing.

Quiet during junior high and high school, Danticat turned to writing to express herself and her coming of age in English rather than in her native Creole and school-learned French. She wrote in journals and began writing for a local newspaper. The native Creole flavored her English in ways that proved helpful to her writing career. She planned to become a nurse or a doctor, but the pull of the written word proved too strong. She earned a bachelor of arts degree in French literature from Barnard College; as an undergraduate, she began writing stories that eventually became part of *Krik? Krak!* (1995), her second book, which explores the lives of Haitians and Haitian Americans before democracy in Haiti.

She later earned a master of fine arts degree from Brown University (1993), out of which came her first book, *Breath, Eyes, Memory* (1994). Of this book, she says, "I first started writing [it] when I was still in high school after writing an article for a New York City teen newspaper about my leaving Haiti and coming to the United States as a child. . . . The story just grew and grew and as it grew I began to weave more and more fictional elements into it and added some themes that concerned me." These themes include

migration, the separation of families, and how much that affects the parents and children who live through that experience, . . . the political realities of Haiti—as a young girl felt and interpreted them—and how that affected ordinary people, the way that people tried to carry on their daily lives even under a dictatorship or post-dictatorship. Finally, I wanted to deal with mother-daughter relationships and the way that mothers sometimes attempt to make themselves the guardians of their daughter's sexuality." ("conversation")

It is a book told in four fragments, an imitation of how Sophie, the narrator and a new speaker of English, would have told the story in English.

Her third novel, *The Farming of Bones* (1999), narrates Trujillo's massacre of 20,000 Haitians in 1937 through the eyes of Amabelle Desir, a young peasant girl in service to a Dominican family. The story traces Amabelle's journey from service to slaughter, recounting numerous tales of horror along the way, and yet maintains a lyric beauty that, as Christopher John Farley notes, "confronted with corpses, has the cold-eyed courage to find a smile."

Published in October 2002, *Behind the Mountains* was her first foray into the realm of young adult fiction. It is told through the journal entries of a young Haitian girl, separated from her father because he has moved to New York seeking enough money to bring his family to him and to freedom. In beautiful, fresh, practiced English, Celiane narrates her family's journey from the political strife of Haiti to the harsh realities of black life in Brooklyn, New York. Not directly autobiographical, the story still draws on Danticat's own experience of immigration and adjustments to the United States. Danticat's third such novel, *The Dew Breaker* (2005), has also been highly acclaimed.

Danticat has taught creative writing at New York University and has worked with filmmaker Jonathan Demme on documentaries about Haiti. In addition to her novels, she wrote a travel narrative, *After the Dance: A Walk through Carnival in Jacmel, Haiti* (2002), in which she takes her readers to the core of Carnival—the spiritual origins and implications that reach far beyond the surface appearance of hedonism. Bringing her lyric voice and practiced eye to nonfiction, Danticat creates a travel narrative to rival most fiction for beauty and provocative style.

In addition to her own works, including more than 20 short stories and essays published in magazines and newspapers, Danticat worked as editor on *The Butterfly's Way: Voices from the Haitian Dyaspora* (2001) and *The Beacon Best of 2000: Great Writing by Women and Men of All Colors and Cultures.* Danticat's voice will resonate throughout U.S. and African-American literature as well as the literature of the diaspora. Her awards include the Caribbean Writer (1994), the Woman of Achievement Award (1995), the Pushcart Short Story Prize, Best Young American Novelist for *Breath, Eyes, Memory* (by *Granta*) (1996), the American Book Award for *The Farming of Bones* (1999), fiction awards from *Essence* and *Seventeen Magazine,* and Oprah Winfrey's book-of-the-month club for *Breath, Eyes, Memory;* she was a finalist for the National Book Award for *Krik? Krak!* (1995).

BIBLIOGRAPHY

"A Conversation with Edwidge Danticat." Available online. URL: http://www.randomhouse.com/vintage/danticat.html. Accessed February 14, 2007.
Farley, Christopher John. "Smiling amid Corpses." *Time,* 7 September 1998, p. 1.

Shauna Lee Eddy-Sanders

Dash, Julie   (1952–)

An independent filmmaker and feminist voice, Julie Dash has often articulated the significance of film as a cultural and political tool. She once wrote, "One of the ongoing struggles of African American filmmakers is the fight against being pushed, through financial and social pressure, into telling only one kind of story. . . . We have so many stories to tell. It will greatly enrich American filmmaking and American culture if we tell them" (25).

Born in New York City in 1952, Dash grew up in the Queensbridge Housing Projects, developing a passion for films while in high school and studying film production at the Studio Museum of Harlem. She attended City College of New York to study psychology but changed her major to film and television production, receiving a B.A. in 1974. Traveling to Los Angeles, she studied at the American Film Institute, where she completed a feature-length script titled "Enemy of the Sun," and then she completed graduate work in film production at University of California, Los Angeles. While there, Dash completed an experimental dance film, titled *Four Women,* based on a Nina Simone song. The film won the 1977 Golden Medal for Women in Film at the Miami International Film

Festival; in the same year, her film *Diary of an African Nun*, inspired by an Alice Walker short story, earned the Directors Guild Award at the Los Angeles Film Exposition.

In 1981, Dash received a Guggenheim grant to develop a series of films on black women. This support led to her writing, producing, and directing *Illusions* (1983) and the early stages of research for *Daughters of the Dust* (1991). *Illusions*, a 30-minute short work, focuses on two black women working at a Hollywood studio during World War II. In the lead role, Lonette McKee portrays a woman passing for white in order to work as a studio executive; at the same time, another black woman works behind the scenes as the dubbed-in singing voice of white actresses. The film gained critical praise and the distinction of being named Best Film of the Decade in 1989 by the Black Filmmakers Foundation. Additionally, Dash's screenplay for the short film was published in Phyllis Rauch Klotman's *Screenplays of the African American Experience* (1991).

Receiving a wider audience and extensive critical adulation, *Daughters of the Dust* appeared after years of misfires and struggles to complete the work. Set in the early years of the 20th century in South Carolina and Georgia's Gullah Islands, the film presents the celebration of the Peazant family prior to their journey to the North. Told in an unconventional visual style, the film gives a particular emphasis to the women in the family, creating a mosaic portrait of the cultural, spiritual, historical, and emotional elements that both connect and collide. Serving as the writer and director, Dash provides a story that echoes the important link between past and present, as she weaves together stunning images, music, and voice-overs in a layered treatment of black women characters. As one critic surmised, "the film is an extended, wildly lyrical meditation on the power of African cultural iconography and the spiritual resilience of the generations of women who have been its custodians" (Holden, C19). With its remarkable cinematography, the film is a moving and unforgettable exploration of the beauty and complexities of black women. *Daughters of the Dust* received the *Filmmakers Magazine* honor of being named one of the 50 most important independent films ever made. In 1992 Dash published a book titled *Daughters of the Dust: The Making of an African American Woman's Film*, which contains the screenplay and commentary by Toni Cade Bambara and bell hooks.

After publishing *Daughters of the Dust*, Dash obtained a Fulbright Fellowship, which allowed her to travel to London to collaborate on a screenplay with Maureen Blackwood of Sankofa, a Black British film collective. By the mid-1990s, Dash was back in America working on various projects, including music videos and cable television films such as *Subway Stories* (1996), *Funny Valentines* (1998), *Incognito* (1999), *Love Song* (2001), and *The Rosa Parks Story* (2002).

BIBLIOGRAPHY

Cooper, India. "Julie Dash." In *Facts On File Encyclopedia of Black Women in America: Theater, Arts, and Entertainment*, edited by Darlene Clark Hine, 86–87. New York: Facts On File, 1997.

Dash, Julie. *Daughters of the Dust: The Making of an African American Woman's Film*. New York: New Press, 1992.

Donalson, Melvin. *Black Directors in Hollywood*. Austin: University of Texas Press, 2003.

Holden, Stephen. "Daughters of the Dust." *New York Times Film Review*, 16 January 1992, p. C19.

Melvin Donalson

Datcher, Michael   (1967–   )

Born Michael Gerald Cole in 1967, in Chicago, Illinois, Michael Datcher began his early childhood in Fort Wayne, Indiana, before his family moved to Long Beach, California, where he completed his secondary education. He pursued athletics, specifically basketball, through the college level. A mishap in admissions forms caused him to receive a letter of acceptance to the University of California at Berkeley (UCB), where he earned a bachelor of science degree in psychology in 1992. While at UCB, Datcher became involved in student protests and activism. On lecture circuits he spoke most often about his involvement in the student protests against

Berkeley's administration to stop all funding to the Apartheid-run government of South Africa. Also while attending UCB, he edited *My Brother's Keeper: Blackmen's Poetry Anthology* (1992), which, published by Small Press Distributors, includes an introduction by Pulitzer Prize winner YUSEF KOMUNYAKAA. In 1994, Datcher earned his master's degree in African-American literature from the University of California, Los Angeles.

Datcher's work, including hip-hop, rap, poetry jam, and post–BLACK AESTHETICS literature, has been featured in *Testimony: Young African Americans on Self-Discovery and Black Identity* (Beacon Press, 1995), *Soulfires: Young Black Men on Love and Violence, Body and Soul* (Penguin, 1996), and *Catch the Fire: A Cross Generational Anthology of Contemporary African-American Poetry* (Riverhead Books, 1998). He has written for *VIBE,* the *Los Angeles Times,* the *Washington Post, Baltimore Sun,* BLACK ISSUES BOOK REVIEW, and the *Pacific News Service.* He served as former editor-In-chief of *Image* magazine and as an editorial writer for the *Los Angeles Sentinel.*

In 1993 Datcher received NATIONAL ASSOCIATION FOR THE ADVANCEMENT OF COLORED PEOPLE's Walter White Award for commentary. Also in 1993, he became director of literacy programs for the Los Angeles World Stage Anansi Writer's Workshop, a poet's chance to submit and perform original work and allow feedback from the audience. In 1996 Black Worlds Press published his coeditorial work *Tough Love: Cultural Criticism and Familial Observations on the Life and Death of Tupac Shakur.* Michael Datcher also edited *Black Love* (1999), which was published by the Beyond Baroque Foundation. In 2001–2002, the J. Paul Getty Museum commissioned Datcher to write and direct a full-length play. That product became *SILENCE.* Currently, he serves on the California Art's Council's Poet Laureate Review Panel and is a board of directors member for PEN Center USA West.

His memoir, *Raising Fences: A Black Man's Love Story* (Riverhead Books, 2001), represents a life and culture of black American life of the 1980s and early 1990s. He tells of his adoption, his unknown father, and two relationships with vastly different outcomes. It illustrates his dedication to his writing and offers a personal message that a positive and supportive family life can exist in today's society. One of the gifts of this book is its demonstration that cultural expression and communication have evolved beyond just printed words and that there can be honest communal emotion, action, and meaning past the mere surface.

BIBLIOGRAPHY

Baran, Michelle. "Author Promotes Dream in 'Raising Fences.'" *Daily Bruin Online.* April 3, 2001. Available online. URL: http://www.dailybruin.ucla.edu/news/articles.asp?ID=3489. Accessed October 2, 2006.

"Michael Datcher." Contemporary Authors Online. The Gale Group, 2002. Available by subscription.

Jerome Cummings

Davis, Ossie　(1917–2005)

An author, actor, director, and activist, Ossie Davis has become an African-American icon of achievement. Born in Cogdell, Georgia, in 1917, his family had to travel to the city of Waycross for him to receive a formal education. The results of that education surfaced at an early age, when he began writing plays and acting in high school. Earning a place at Howard University in 1935 for undergraduate studies, he hitchhiked north to attend the school, studying with black critic-professor ALAIN LOCKE, who encouraged Davis to relocate to New York to follow his dream to become a playwright.

Taking the train to New York, Davis worked an assortment of jobs as he eventually joined the Rose McLendon Players of Harlem, making his stage debut as an actor with that company in 1941. Caught between writer's block and patriotic duty, he enlisted in the military and was trained to work in the Walter Reed Hospital's Army Medical Center in Washington, D.C., before being later stationed at an army hospital in Liberia. After the war and back in New York, he won the title role of *Jeb* in 1946, where he costarred with actress Ruby Dee. The two married in 1948, having three children and a long career in the performing arts, often working together. Celebrating their 50th anniversary and decades in entertainment and politics, they coauthored a joint memoir titled *With Ossie and Ruby: In This Life Together* (1998).

Working as an actor in the late 1940s and 1950s in such plays as *Anna Lucasta* (1946), *A Long Way from Home* (1948), *Stevedore* (1949), *Green Pastures* (1951), *No Time for Sergeants* (1956) and *A Raisin in the Sun* (1959), Davis also wrote the one-act plays *Clay's Rebellion* (1951), about the 1906 Brownsville, Texas, racial violence; *Alice in Wonder* (1952), focusing on a black entertainer who is pressured to testify against a black political leader at anticommunist hearings; and *What Can You Say, Mississippi?* (1955), responding to the Emmett Till murder case. But it was Davis's full-length play *Purlie Victorious* (1961) that finally brought him a wide acclaim as a playwright. The result of five years of work, the play is a comedy that examines the ludicrous nature of racial stereotypes as it follows a black preacher who attempts to form a racially integrated church in the segregated South. The successful play went on to be adapted into the film *Gone Are the Days* (1963) and later the musical play *Purlie* (1970), which was nominated for a Tony Award as Best Musical.

In the 1950s, Davis also extended his efforts into film and television. His film appearances included *No Way Out* (1950), *Fourteen Hours* (1951), and *The Joe Louis Story* (1953), as well as a television version of *The Emperor Jones* (1955).

It was also in the early 1950s that Davis's radicalism went beyond writing, as he and Ruby Dee became involved personally and professionally with people, events, and productions deemed "leftist." Davis and Dee survived the guilty-by-association labels, as they supported accused friends who were kept from working by the anticommunist blacklisting. But Davis's commitment to fairness was just as intense when responding to racial issues. Working with organizations such as the National Association for the Advancement of Colored People, CORE, and the Urban League, he was viewed as a stalwart leader and voice for the cause of human rights. Davis observed, "Ruby and I . . . We took a lot of chances, but we never bluffed, or postured, or pulled rank unless we had to. To-

gether we met the cataclysmic changes rushing at us from all sides—efforts to unionize the hospitals; the antiwar demonstrations; the dogs and fire hoses in Birmingham; the funerals and the turmoil when Kennedy, Malcolm, and later, King, were assassinated" (Davis and Dee, 347). In 1963, he served as the master of ceremonies for the March on Washington. Later in the decade he delivered the eulogies for both Malcolm X and Martin Luther King, Jr. In the 1970s he cochaired, along with Dick Gregory, the Committee to Defend the Panthers, and Davis chaired the Committee to Defend Angela Davis.

The 1970s, however, developed as a creative era for Davis, as he added film directing to his credits by completing *Cotton Comes to Harlem* (1970), *Kongi's Harvest* (1971), *Black Girl* (1972), and *Countdown at Kusini* (1976). Other than the commercial success of *Cotton Comes to Harlem,* which was based on a novel by Chester Himes, Davis's efforts as a film director never reached the same level of popularity as his acting over the decades. Davis has appeared in more than 25 films, including *The Cardinal* (1963), *A Man Called Adam* (1966), *The Scalphunters* (1968), *Let's Do It Again* (1975), *School Daze* (1988), *Do the Right Thing* (1989), *Malcolm X* (1992), *The Client* (1994), and *Get on the Bus* (1996).

On the small screen, audiences saw Davis in recurring roles in television series, including *The Defenders* (1963–65), *B. L. Stryker* (1989–90), *Evening Shade* (1990–94), and *The Client* (1995–96), as well as in the miniseries *King* (1978), *Roots: The Next Generation* (1978), and *Alex Haley's Queen* (1993). His roles in television movies were just as numerous over the years; he appeared in *Teacher, Teacher* (1969), *Freedom Road* (1979), *Miss Evers' Boys* (1997), and *Twelve Angry Men* (1997).

Concurrently, as he performed on screen, he continued writing in various mediums. He penned several plays, namely *Curtain Call, Mr. Aldridge, Sir* (1963), *Escape to Freedom: The Story of Frederick Douglass, A Play for Young People* (1976), and *Langston: A Play* (1982). His young adult novel, *Just Like Martin,* set during the historical period of the 1963 March on Washington, appeared in 1992.

With a bounty of awards and honors for his writing, acting, and activism, Davis, along with wife Ruby Dee, won the Presidential Medal for Lifetime Achievement in the Arts in 1995. In his memoir, Davis aptly reflected on the foundation of his life as an author:

> It wasn't a matter of whether I had the talent, but of whether I was free enough, strong enough, bold enough, and confident enough to use it—to summon up at will, from memory and imagination, the authority and the power to assert myself, to stop hiding behind the ready smile of a free and easy good nature . . . and dare to become the man I was meant to be. . . . Such is the redemptive power of trying to become an artist. I couldn't be an artist unless first I became a man! (Davis and Dee, 397).

BIBLIOGRAPHY

Davis, Ossie, and Ruby Dee. *With Ossie and Ruby: In This Life Together*. New York: Morrow and Co., 1998.

Hatch, Shari Dorantes, and Michael R. Strickland, eds. *African-American Writers: A Dictionary*. Santa Barbara, Calif.: ABC-Clio, 2000.

McIntosh, Susan, and Greg Robinson. "Ossie Davis." In *Encyclopedia of African-American Culture and History*. Vol. 2, edited by Jack Salzman, David Lionel Smith, and Cornel West, 723–724. New York: Simon and Schuster, 1996.

Melvin Donalson

Delany, Samuel R. (1942–)

In a publishing career that has lasted more than 40 years, Samuel Delany has come to be recognized as one of the most significant and original writers of his generation across an astonishing variety of genres. After having quickly made his mark in the world of science fiction, he has gone on to become an increasingly recognized and esteemed figure in the worlds of gay and lesbian literature, literary theory, and, belatedly, African-American literary culture.

Born April 1, 1942, in New York City to Samuel R. Delany, Sr., and Margaret Carey Boyd, the owners of a successful Harlem funeral parlor, Delany was given an education reflecting this relatively privileged background. Attending the exclusive Dalton Elementary School and the Bronx High School of Science, he was exposed early in his life to a wide range of artistic and cultural influences. Despite his homosexuality, in 1961 he married the brilliant Jewish poet Marilyn Hacker, whom he had met at Bronx High and with whom he would edit the science-fiction journal *Quark*. Although the marriage would soon evolve into an unconventional pairing of essentially independent creative artists, they would remain married until 1975. These varied influences no doubt shaped the cosmopolitanism and unconventionality that has characterized his writing and may have contributed to his decision to write outside of the confines of realism and social protest that most African-American writers of the period were deploying. Another element in Delany's willingness to place himself outside the mainstream of African-American writing was his awareness and acceptance of his homosexuality and his commitment to making the radical themes of sexuality and homosexuality prominent components of his work.

After publishing his first novel, *The Jewels of Aptor* (1962), at age 19 and completing his landmark series *The Fall of the Towers* in 1971, Delany was almost immediately recognized as both a prodigy and an important new voice in the field. Reflecting this recognition by the science-fiction community, Delany would go on to win four Nebula awards, most notably for the books *Babel-17* (1966) and *The Einstein Intersection* (1967), and two Hugo Awards. In 1979 Delany published *Tales of Neveryon*, the first book in his celebrated fantasy series, in which he combines elements of the often critically castigated sword-and-sorcery genre with explorations of contemporary issues like AIDS and feminist theories of gender relations. This book was followed by *Neveryona* (1983), *Flight from Neveryon* (1985), and *The Bridge of Lost Desire* (1987). In 1984, he published one of his most acclaimed and academically recognized works of science fiction, the neo–slave narrative *Stars in My Pocket like Grains of Sand.*

Transgressive themes have characterized Delany's output from the beginning, as evidenced by his often sexually explicit science-fiction texts. Even more controversially, Delany has explored the world of pornography in such novels as *The Tides of Lust (aka Equinox)* (1973) and *Hogg* and created provocatively sexualized social worlds in his best-selling novel *Dhalgren* (1975), the work that many critics consider his masterpiece, and the AIDS picaresque, *The Mad Man* (1994). He also offers personalized accounts of his life as a sex radical and theorist of sexuality in his autobiographical works *The Motion of Light in Water: Sex and Science Fiction in the East Village* (1988, rev. and expanded edition 1990) and *Times Square Red, Times Square Blue* (1999). These books laid the groundwork for Delany's recognition by the gay and lesbian creative and intellectual community as a major voice in the creation of a counternarrative to heteronormative cultural politics.

With such texts as *The Jewel-Hinged Jaw: Notes on the Language of Science Fiction* (1977), *Starboard Wine: More Notes on the Language of Science Fiction* (1984), and *Silent Interviews: On Language, Race, Sex, Science Fiction, and Some Comics* (1994), Delany has also established himself as one of the most prolific and authoritative critics and theorists on science fiction. These critical texts and the teaching positions that he has had over the years at such universities as the State University at Buffalo, Cornell University, the University of Massachusetts at Amherst, and most recently at Temple University, reflect Delany's increasingly prominent status as an academic.

BIBLIOGRAPHY

Fox, Robert Elliot. *The Conscientious Sorcerers: The Black Postmodernist Fiction of LeRoi Jones / Amiri Baraka, Ishmael Reed, and Samuel R. Delany.* New York: Greenwood Press, 1987.

Sallis, James, ed. *Ash of Stars: On the Writing of Samuel R. Delany.* Jackson: University Press of Mississippi, 1996.

Slusser, George E. *The Delany Intersection: Samuel Delany Considered as a Writer of Semi-precious Words.* San Bernardino, Calif.: Borgo Books, 1977.

Terry Rowden

Demby, William   (1922–   )

Born on Christmas Day to William and Gertrude Demby of Clarksburg, West Virginia's coal mining region, Demby enjoyed, with his siblings, the ethnically diverse, middle-class lifestyle his father, a file clerk for Hopewell Natural Gas Company, was able to provide. Demby attended West Virginia State College, where his teachers included the distinguished poet MARGARET WALKER, after graduating from Langley High School. Leaving to serve in the U.S. Army during World War II, Demby completed his education at Fisk University, where he studied with ROBERT HAYDEN, a major voice in African-American poetry. Moving to Italy, where he had been stationed during the war, Demby studied art history and became, like RICHARD WRIGHT, FRANK YERBY, and JAMES BALDWIN, an expatriate. He married an Italian, Lucia Drudi, with whom he fathered a son, James. Returning to the United States in 1969, he taught at the College of Staten Island of the City University of New York, retiring in 1989.

Demby is the author of four novels: *Bettlecreek* (1950), *The Catacombs* (1950), *Love Story Black* (1978), and *Blueboy* (1979). Written while he was an expatriate, the first two novels are the better known of the four. In *Bettlecreek,* when white recluse William Trapp catches Johnny Johnson in one of his apple trees, he invites him into his home for cider. Johnny and his Nightrider gang members had gone to the orchard to steal apples and harass the well-known hermit. The odd couple not only develop a special friendship but are also joined by Johnny's uncle, David Diggs, who comes looking for his missing nephew, in a relationship that transcends the racial taboos of their segregated West Virginia community. By the end of novel, Trapp leaves his isolated world to rejoin the larger community through his altruistic acts.

When Johnny returns to Bettlecreek from Pittsburgh, he is anxious to reunite with Trapp and his friends; however, when he is challenged to choose between them, he chooses the gang. The novel ends when Johnny kills Trapp, who has been falsely accused by the community of molesting a young girl, while attempting to burn down Trapp's house as part of the gang's rites of passage. At the end of the novel, David leaves Detroit in search of a better life; however, the ending gives the impression that he will never escape the pessimistically determined life that humans are inevitably bound to suffer, reflecting the novel's naturalistic bend. Demby suggests through his main characters that, irrespective of this given, everyone must create a meaningful life, as does Bill Trapp when he leaves his isolated world and reenters his community.

Set in Rome, *The Catacombs,* in which death and resurrection are dominant tropes of the chaotic worlds of the characters, is narrated by an expatriate novelist who examines the lives of a nun and an actress who is romantically involved with the Count, her aristocratic lover. Similarly, *Love Story Black* centers on Edward, a black writer-professor (also an expatriate and a teacher at New York City College) as a central character. As critics point out, the narrator characters of both novels serve as Demby's alter ego. They deliver, in the end, the same message about the inevitable publication of the great or ideal novel.

Although the critical response to *The Catacombs* was mixed, Demby received international praise for *Bettlecreek,* admired because, despite its black characters, it moved beyond racial issues and concerns with its focus on William Trapp and the themes of death, resurrection, youth, and old age. Critics also lauded its naturalistic and existential focus.

BIBLIOGRAPHY

Hansen, Klaus P. "William Demby's *The Catacombs: A Latecomer to Modernism.*" In *The Afro-American Novel Since 1960,* edited by Peter Bruck and Wolfgan Karrer, 1234–1243. Amsterdam: B. R. Gruner, 1982.

Margolies, Edward. "The Expatriate as Novelist." In *Native Son: A Critical Study of Twentieth Century Black American Authors,* 173–189. Philadelphia: Lippincott, 1968.

O'Brien, John. *Interviews with Black Writers,* 34–53. New York: Liveright, 1973.

James Celestino

Derricotte, Toi   (1941–   )

In an interview with Charles Rowell, Toi Derricotte revealed that she "believe[s] we are prisoners of what we don't know, of what we don't acknowledge" (655). Perhaps this is why her poetry gives voice to experiences that are labeled taboo, such as the physical aspects of birth, sex, and death. Through her experimentation with topics and language, Derricotte has played a significant role in the development of African-American literature.

Born in 1941 in Detroit, Michigan, Derricotte took many years to develop an interest in being a poet. Married in 1962 to artist Clarence Reese, Derricotte worked as a teacher for Manpower, an educational organization established by the federal government, while completing her B.A. in special education at Wayne State University. By the time she received her degree, she was divorced. After her graduation, Derricotte worked with remedial readers and emotionally and mentally disabled students in the Detroit and New Jersey school systems. In 1967 she married banking consultant Clarence Bruce Derricotte. She received her M.A. in English and creative writing from New York University in 1984.

However, while her professional interest in poetry developed slowly, her personal experiences that were central to her poetry began at a very young age. For example, Derricotte's prominent interest in death, evident in her first collection, *The Empress of the Death House* (1978), appears to have begun with her father's career as a mortician, her encounters at a Catholic grade school, and her experiences at her grandparents' funeral home. The poems in this collection depict a morbid sense of death that is often unspoken. Further, the graphic language she uses in her depictions broke with traditional expectations for women's poetry to avoid explicit sexuality. Derricotte avoids sentimentality, choosing to use language that allows her to explore honestly death, violence, sexuality, and racism.

While Derricotte explores the universal fear of death in *The Empress of the Death House,* she also uses as central themes exclusive female experiences and anger about the dismissive treatment of women. The portrayal of African-American female victims and survivors is a theme that persists in Derricotte's work. In fact, Derricotte's second collection, *Natural Birth* (1983), focuses almost exclusively on female experiences. In this text, she explores the pain and degradation experienced in childbearing. Much of this poetry is again based on personal experience. After her divorce, Derricotte gave birth to her son, Anthony, in a home for unwed mothers. From this solely female experience, Derricotte broadens her focus, returning to the universal experiences of fear and ecstasy that transcend gender roles.

Derricotte again challenged borders when, in 1989, she published *Captivity.* This collection of poetry uses the aftermath of slavery in contemporary African-American lives to begin a discussion of abuse within the family and racism in society. As W. E. B.DuBois argued, African Americans are forced to experience a double consciousness: the sense of measuring themselves through the eyes of others and forcing the realities that do not coincide with the idealized portrait of human behavior to remain hidden. Derricotte's goal in *Captivity* is to begin to unravel the binds of double consciousness through a candid examination of the silenced issues that arise within the lives of African Americans.

Derricotte's fourth collection, *Tender,* upholds the tradition she began in her first text: Her poems use plain but precise language to explore issues of violence, sexuality, and racism. One of the most interesting characteristics of this collection is that all of the poems emanate from the title poem. In this short poem, Derricotte questions the meaning of the word *tender*, which is used to describe both meat and family. Derricotte also begins to discuss in this work the issue of "passing," which she more thoroughly explores in her prose work *The Black Notebook* (1997). Composed of selections from the journal she kept for more than 20 years, *The Black Notebook* focuses on the complex search for identity by a black woman who is light enough to pass.

Compared to Doris Lessing's *The Golden Notebook, The Black Notebook* offers a unique perspective on the racial divide by discussing Derricotte's ability and choice to pass as white in certain situations. As Derricotte dangles between hating her blackness and not being black enough, we begin to see her develop as a 20th-century multicultural woman writer.

Toi Derricotte currently works as an associate professor at the University of Pittsburgh. Aside from the texts previously mentioned, she has been published in numerous anthologies and in periodicals such as *American Poetry Review, Poetry Northwest,* and *Northwest Review.* Derricotte has received many awards, including the Distinguished Pioneering of the Arts Award from the United Black Artists, the Paterson Poetry Prize, two Pushcart Prizes, the Folger Shakespeare Library Poetry Book Award, two National Endowment for the Arts Fellowships, and the Lucille Medwick Memorial Award from the Poetry Society of America. Derricotte not only works to improve her own writing but is also a cofounder of Cave Canem, the first workshop for African-American poets. As her voice continues to develop, only the future will determine the significance of Derricotte's work on the African-American literary canon.

BIBLIOGRAPHY

Rowell, Charles. "Beyond Our Lives: An Interview with Toi Derricotte." *Callaloo* 14, no. 3 (Summer 2003): 654–664.

Cassandra Parente

Dessa Rose **Sherley Anne Williams** (1986)
Sherley Anne Williams is best known for *Dessa Rose,* a novel based on the fictional meeting of two historical figures: a pregnant black woman who helped lead a slave uprising while chained in a coffle and a North Carolina white woman who gave sanctuary to slaves. As their lives become entangled (their unexpected friendship made possible by the latter's painfully evolving consciousness regarding slavery, patriarchy, and

class), the history of black women and white women is reinscribed. Without sentimentalizing or denying, Williams also reinscribes the hideous and unspeakable, as in the scene in which Harker kisses tenderly and reclaims as beautiful Dessa's whipscarred, branded thighs.

Based on a blues structure of repetition and variation of a central motif, the novel begins with a prologue full of laughter and desire—Dessa's memory of her husband, Kaine, whose talk was "as beautiful as his touch . . . his voice high and clear as running water over a settled stream bed, [who] walked the lane between the indifferently rowed cabins like he owned them, striding from shade into half-light as if he could halt the setting sun." But her dream reverie is abruptly and brutally shattered by a second memory: Kaine's murder. The novel chronicles Dessa's retaliation, subsequent captivity, and interrogation; her resistance and escape; and her growing love not only for Nathan and Harker but also for Ruth/Rufel, the young white woman who gives Dessa sanctuary on the half-ruined Alabama plantation where she herself has been abandoned by her riverboat gambler husband. The call-and-response tradition also figures centrally in the novel, particularly in Dessa's jail cell communiqués to the slaves with whom she orchestrates her escape plans—the singing that Adam Nehemiah, to his later great regret, dismisses as "quaint piece[s] of doggerel."

The importance of names and of living in a world of self-authored names and perceptions, central to all of Williams's work, is clarified in the beauty of names that are meant to be savored—Kaine, who "was the color of the cane syrup taffy they pulled and stretched to a glistening golden brown in winter," but whose name also suggests the tormented Biblical mark of Cain (60); Nathan, a name clearly in homage to fugitive slave Nat Turner; Rufel/Ruth, whose name suggests a sorrow of biblical proportions; and most of all, Dessa, first known as Odessa, whose name suggests, among other things, the words odyssey, ode, odious, and odor, each of which is a signifier in Dessa's story.

Misappropriations of both names and stories abound in this novel. Adam Nehemiah, in trying to rewrite Dessa's story according to his own stubborn

misinterpretation of the facts—the white amanuensis disrobed for all to see—attempts to reenslave Dessa figuratively as well as literally when he either refers to her by some truly foul epithet like "darky," "raging nigger bitch," or "she devil" or insists on reconstructing her name as "Odessa." But Dessa, in a powerful act of symbolic understatement, demands that her name is "Dessa, Dessa Rose. Ain't no O to it." As critic Adam McKible, expounding on Mae Henderson's brilliant essay "Speaking in Tongues" (1989), comments, "by calling Dessa out of her name, Nehemiah attempts to asserts his social dominance and deny Dessa's humanity. The 'O' he adds to her name is the "O" of Otherness and objectification, as well as the zero of nonbeing or worthlessness. . . . Her insistence on the name Dessa disrupts Nehemiah's fiction and rewrites her narrative" (233). Later in the novel, Nehemiah's misnaming is echoed transformatively, when Ruth, chagrined, realizes that she has misappropriated both Dorcas's history and her name and has nearly done the same to Dessa.

BIBLIOGRAPHY

McKible, Adam. "'These Are the Facts of the Darky's History': Thinking History and Reading Names in Four African American Texts." *African American Review* 28, no. 2 (Summer 1994): 223–235.
Williams, Sherley Anne. *Dessa Rose.* New York: Morrow, 1986.

Lynda Koolish

Devil in a Blue Dress   Walter Mosley (1990)

WALTER MOSLEY's impressive career as a popular American author began with the publication of his first novel, *Devil in a Blue Dress* (1990). Taking its place within the commercial genre of detective novels, *Devil in a Blue Dress* was the first in a series of seven novels presenting the exploits of recurring hero-protagonist Easy Rawlins, a black everyman and reluctant private investigator.

In the novel, which is set in Los Angeles in 1948, Ezekiel "Easy" Rawlins, who migrated from Houston, works at the Champion Aircraft Factory. With no family ties, Easy loves the comfort and security of his house, but after a confrontation with his foreman, Easy loses his job. With the help of his friend Joppy, Easy gets a job with Dewitt Albright, a white man who hires him to find Daphne Monet, a white woman who socializes in the black section of the city. Needing to keep his house, Easy takes the job and slowly finds himself pulled into a volatile world of ambitious, wealthy, and violent people.

When an acquaintance is killed during Easy's search, the police harass him, looking to charge him with the murder. Then Daphne contacts Easy, presenting herself as a woman in danger and in need of his help. When he extends himself, a white man turns up dead, and Daphne disappears, leaving Easy to face both Albright and the police. Feeling pressure from both sides, Easy calls for his friend Raymond "Mouse" Alexander to come to town and back him up. Hearing that Daphne Monet associates with a black bootlegger named Frank Green, Easy begins looking for him. Unfortunately, more dead bodies show up. Easy then learns that Daphne is connected to the two white men running for mayor: Matthew Teran and Todd Carter. It soon becomes evident that the former is a pedophile and the latter is Daphne's former lover who wants her back, forgiving the $30,000 she took from him.

When the mysterious Daphne contacts Easy again, he tries to get her out of town, but she refuses until she sees Frank Green, who is later found dead. Taking her to a safe house, Easy becomes Daphne's lover, and she reveals her incestuous past with her father. Shortly thereafter, Easy is outmuscled by Albright and Joppy, who are partners in crime and murder, and they take Daphne to force her to repay the $30,000. Easy traces them down, shooting Albright while Mouse kills Joppy. At this point, Easy hears the truth about Daphne: Her real name is Ruby Hanks and she is actually black, passing and living in white society. Frank Green was Daphne's half-brother who kept the secrets about their common past and background.

Splitting the money with Easy and Mouse, Daphne confesses to Easy that she shot Matthew Teran, partly because of his sexual abuse of a little

boy. Daphne asks Easy to let her go away on her own and to take care of the abused boy (whom Easy raises as his son in later novels). With mixed emotions about her, Easy concedes, as Mouse reminds him that Daphne will never find peace until she accepts who she is racially. Mouse also warns Easy to remain black in his thinking and aspirations.

Stylistically, *Devil in a Blue Dress* renders the necessary elements of the detective genre story: murdered victims, first-person narration, terse dialogue, generous physical action, and an informal diction rooted in slang. Negotiating a morally ambiguous world, Easy, similar to most detective-protagonists, is introspective, leaning toward male chauvinistic attitudes, while possessing abilities in deductive reasoning, critical analysis, and metaphorical language.

Beneath the genre trappings, however, there are discernible themes that emanate in this novel. One of the more interesting ones revolves around Daphne Monet; specifically, a denial of her racial self leads to emotional chaos, psychological confusion, and spiritual emptiness. Despite the possible social and material advantages of "passing," particularly during the 1940s, the price of denying her blackness is too high to pay.

Complementing that theme, the novel serves as a barometer for the ethnic and cultural relationships in Los Angeles after World War II. As black migrants came to the city for better jobs and opportunities, they moved into de facto segregated neighborhoods as racial lines were drawn between communities. The novel recounts the black business and cultural center of the city's Central Avenue, a site of black entrepreneurship and artistic expression, particularly in music. The nearby enclaves of Hollywood, Santa Monica, and Malibu remain distant worlds for Easy and other black Angelinos. Easy remains aware of where he should and should not travel after dark, comprehends the racial profiling of the police; and understands the inextricable connection between race and class. Demonstrating this last point, Easy appreciates his relationship with Primo, a Mexican-born American, when he reflects, "Primo was a real Mexican, born and bred. That was back in 1948, before

Mexicans and black people started hating each other. Back then . . . a Mexican and a negro [sic] considered themselves the same . . . just another couple of unlucky stiffs left holding the short end of the stick" (177).

Devil in a Blue Dress emerges as an entertaining novel that carries serious messages about identity, ambition, friendship, and morality. Walter Mosley achieved an outstanding first novel that won awards and the praise of then President Bill Clinton. Following *Devil in a Blue Dress,* Mosley went on to present the development of Easy Rawlins as a private detective and a private man in eight additional works: *A Red Death* (1991), *White Butterfly* (1992), *Black Betty* (1994), *A Little Yellow Dog* (1996), and *Bad Boy Brawly Brown* (2002), *Six Easy Pieces* (2003), *Little Scarlet* (2004), and *Cinnamon Kiss* (2005). His novel *Gone Fishin'* (1997) is not a detective novel but explores the teenage friendship and experiences between Easy and Mouse before the former moves to Los Angeles.

BIBLIOGRAPHY

Walter Mosley. *Devil in a Blue Dress.* New York: Pocket Books, 1990.

Melvin Donalson

Dickey, Eric Jerome   (1962–   )

Eric Jerome Dickey is the author of 10 novels, all of which explore contemporary relationships among African Americans. Originally from Tennessee, Dickey is a graduate of Memphis State University (now the University of Memphis) in computer systems technology. He has worked at Federal Express and Rockwell (now Boeing) and as a substitute teacher and a stand-up comedian. He is, however, best known as an author, having established himself as one of the most popular African-American male authors of the late 20th and early 21st centuries, a feat he has accomplished in just under 10 years.

His works include *Sister, Sister* (1996), *Friends and Lovers* (1997), *Milk in My Coffee* (1998), *Cheaters* (1999), and *Naughty or Nice* (2003). He has also contributed short stories to the collections *Got to Be Real: Four Original Love Stories* (2000) and *Gumbo: A Celebration of African American Writing* (2002). In his works, Dickey's primary concern is the trials and travails that come with the search for long-lasting love. His characters often struggle in their relationships, their respective dramas and crises serving as a testament to the real-life predicaments of many of Dickey's readers. Although the characters may express a desire for intimacy and affection, monogamy is often an unattainable fantasy for them, and the vast majority willfully seek out and engage in extramarital dalliances. A quick survey of Dickey's titles (e.g., *Cheaters* and *Liar's Game* [2000]) bears this out.

Most of the novels are set in Los Angeles, the city Dickey calls home. The focus is largely on middle-class African Americans, conspicuous consumption, and a healthy dose of brand name dropping are mainstays in his novels. The world Dickey depicts is undeniably one of young, upwardly mobile African Americans. While there are cultural exchanges with whites, particularly in *Milk in My Coffee,* which chronicles an interracial romance, the novels are grounded in their depictions of African Americans.

Perhaps Dickey's work is most noteworthy because of his skill at "adopting" female voices. Readers and reviewers are consistently impressed with Dickey's technique of crafting "believable" female characters. Evidence of this is Dickey's popularity among reading groups organized by African-American women, as well as women's reliable presence at the author's book signings. An additional reason for his success might lie in the language he uses. His characters engage in snappy dialogue replete with profanities. Such language is authentic for many of Dickey's readers, rendering the characters all the more believable and true to life.

All of Dickey's novels have been best sellers, appearing on the *Blackboard, Wall Street Journal,* and *New York Times* lists, among others. A 2004 *New York Times* article noted that Dickey sells more than 500,000 novels a year. Dickey's success is proof that contemporary African-American readers are hungry for fictive renderings of aspects of their daily lives, particularly their relationships.

Chris Bell

Different Drummer, A
William Melvin Kelley (1959)

The unconventional approach of WILLIAM MEL-
VIN KELLEY's first novel, *A Different Drummer,*
challenges the definition of a "black" story as it
encourages people to consider the ways in which
human relationships are intertwined despite apparent cultural differences. Kelley anchors the
story of a mass exodus of blacks from a mythic
southern state, Sutton. While the plot hinges on
the actions of Tucker Caliban, a black chauffeur
who works for the family that enslaved his predecessors, it unfolds through the voices of several white characters, including Harry Leland, a
young boy trying to make sense of the messages
he receives about race as he maintains a friendship
with Tucker. Kelley mixes multiple white narrators with a variety of styles and references—storytelling, the Bible, letters, dialogue, diary entries,
William Shakespeare, and magazine clippings—to
tell this remarkable story.

Mister Harper, a white retired army officer vol-
untarily confined to a wheelchair, relays the story
that embodies the novel's central theme: the power
of family history. An African rumored to be a former chief escapes into the wilderness with a baby
upon the arrival of a slave ship to Sutton. When he
is eventually found, the runaway, known only as
"the African," is shot and killed by Dewitt Willson,
who enslaves the child, the "First Caliban," who
begins Tucker's family history. Many years later
Tucker purchases some of the land on which his
enslaved ancestors worked, determined that his
child will not have to work for the Willsons. He
proceeds to destroy the land, kill the farm animals,
set fire to his home, and leave with his family to an
undisclosed location. His cathartic action mystifies
and angers whites while inspiring all of the state's
black residents to leave as well. Harper concludes
that it is "something special in [Tucker's] blood"
that fuels his deeds.

Kelley contrasts Tucker, who refuses to support the fictional National Society for Colored
Affairs (NSCA), a leading organization interested
in the advancement of black people, with Reverend Bennett Bradshaw, an Ivy League–educated

northerner who has a keen interest in such organizations. Tucker explains to his wife, Bethra,
that the "[NSCA] ain't working for my rights.
Ain't nobody working for my rights; I wouldn't
let them. . . . Ain't none of my battles being fought
in no courts. I'm fighting all my battles myself"
(111). Bradshaw, who works for the civil rights
group Tucker refuses to support, later establishes
the Resurrected Church of the Black Jesus Christ
of America, Inc. Despite his efforts to help liberate
blacks and learn from the influence Tucker has on
them, Bradshaw is convinced Tucker's leadership
is ultimately obsolete. He remarks, "Did you ever
think that a person like myself, a so-called religious
leader needs the Tuckers to justify his existence?"
Ironically, angry over the loss of all the blacks,
whites scapegoat and lynch Bradshaw, although he
has nothing to do with the black emigration.

Phyllis R. Klotman describes Bradshaw's lynching as "an ironic dénouement which reinforces
Kelley's theme: individual black men of courage
and integrity can be *natural* leaders who, regardless of the moral imperatives of the larger society,
will by their example effect real change in the conditions of black people" (63). Bernard Bell offers
a similar assessment, claiming that the novel "affirms self-reliance and moral courage as the imperatives for social change" (300). Yet the novel's
commentary on the source and efficacy of leadership is only one of its themes. Kelley also delves
into the role of friendship, family relationships,
and formal education in the lives of his black and
white characters.

Kelley's stylistic complexity and unconventional narrative strategies serve as an interesting
answer to the misguided (and oftentimes malicious) claims that African American writers would
only obtain a "universalist" appeal if they were to
write about the lives of nonblack characters. While
A Different Drummer certainly shows an African-
American male writer's flexibility in portraying
the perspectives of white male, white female, and
black female characters, it also debunks the notion that stories about black characters, regardless
of their narrators, are less capable of dealing with
"universal" themes.

BIBLIOGRAPHY

Adams, Charles H. "Imagination and Community in W. M. Kelley's *A Different Drummer.*" *Critique: Studies in Contemporary Fiction* 26, no. 1 (1984): 26–35.

Bell, Bernard W. *The Afro-American Novel and Its Tradition.* Amherst: University of Massachusetts Press, 1974.

Klotman, Phyllis R. "'Tearing a Hole in History': Lynching as Theme and Motif." *Black American Literature Forum* 19, no. 2 (1985): 55–63.

Rodgers, Lawrence R. *Canaan Bound: The African-American Great Migration Novel.* Urbana: University of Illinois Press, 1997.

Sundquist, Eric J. "Promised Lands: A Different Drummer." *Triquarterly* (Winter/Summer 2000) 107–108, 268–284.

Williams, Gladys M. "Technique as Evaluation of Subject in *A Different Drummer.*" *CLA Journal* 19 (1975): 221–237.

Kimberly N. Ruffin

Dixon, Melvin   (1950–1992)

Writer, poet, educator, translator, and activist Melvin Dixon was born in Stamford, Connecticut, in 1950. Dixon's writing explores what it means to be both an African-American male and gay. Writing was a freeing agent that allowed Dixon to tackle issues that had been ignored in contemporary African-American literature. His work is straightforward and unashamedly honest. He set the stage for such writers as E. LYNN HARRIS and JAMES EARL HARDY, whose work also explores identity and sexuality.

Dixon began a love affair with the power of language at an early age. Dixon graduated from Wesleyan University with a B.A. in American studies (1971), and went on to receive his Ph.D. from Brown University (1975). By this time, Dixon's thirst for writing had been established. He traveled to the Caribbean, Paris, West Africa, Haiti, and Europe, researching such notable writers as James Wright, Jacques Roumain, and Leopold Senghor, the former president of Senegal. As his writing talent developed, Dixon received various accolades, including a French Government Fellowship, a Ford Foundation Postdoctoral Fellowship, and a Scholar-in-Residence Fellowship from the Schomburg Center for Research in Black Culture.

Establishing himself as an educator early on, Dixon accepted a position as assistant professor of English at Williams College (1976). After his tenure there, he accepted a position in the English department at Queens College, City University of New York (1980), where he taught until his death (1992).

During his time as an educator, Dixon wrote poems, stories, novels, essays, and critical studies and even translated French literature. He translated and published *Drumbeats, Masks, and Metaphor: Contemporary Afro-American Theatre* (1983) and *The Collected Poems of Leopold Sedar Senghor* (1991). Dixon's *Climbing Montmartre* (1974) examines the black American expatriate experience in France. He published another book of poetry titled *Change of Territory* (1983).

Love's Instruments (1995) was published after Dixon's death. The work displays Dixon's talents as a lyrical poet and establishes him as an intellectual. He courageously writes about his struggle with AIDS. The seminal poem in the book, "Aunt Ida Pieces a Quilt," is a loving tribute to the lives lost in the AIDS epidemic. The story is told from the point of view of a grandmother who is gathering the belongings of her great-nephew, who has died. She is piecing together a panel to send to the AIDS Memorial in Washington, D.C. In the introduction to the book, Elizabeth Alexander writes that these poems "accrue further meaning in the context of both the literature of this plague and the premature loss of their author." MICHAEL HARPER adds, "Dixon's poems are receptacles and illuminations, anodynes and tropes, the distillations of a fully lived and truncated life of study and experience."

Dixon's novels articulate his interest in and understanding of the African-American experience. His first novel, *Trouble the Water* (1989), for which Dixon won the Nilon Excellence in Minority Fiction Award, deals with black life in the South. This historical journey to uncover the pain of this past life for African Americans was most likely based on Dixon's own parents, who migrated from the South before Dixon's birth. Dixon's second novel, *Vanishing Rooms* (1991), places a love story at the center of urban violence in a New York City borough. Both novels have a contemporary feel, and Dixon's skill at infusing history into his novels is masterful. His novels illuminate the connection of the present to the past.

Dixon also delved into the world of critical study and published *Ride Out the Wilderness: Geography and Identity in Afro-American Literature* (1987), which explored African-American literature. Marcellus Blount of the *Southern Review* writes that Dixon takes us into the places of refuge, those conquered spaces and imagined havens that mark the African-American voyage from slavery to freedom; and still he lingers along the way to reinterpret several writers in this newly revised canon. Dixon revisits the work of such notable writers as FREDERICK DOUGLASS, HARRIET JACOBS, JEAN TOOMER, RALPH ELLISON, and AMIRI BARAKA (LeRoi Jones), to name a few, and connects their shared experiences.

Dixon's work examines life in its most intricate form. To him, his sexuality was not static. It was an aspect of his constantly evolving identity as an African-American male. As in the work of JAMES BALDWIN, Dixon's incarnation as various symbols within his work illuminates his ultimate need to explore what it means to be an African-American male who also happens to be gay. By the time of his death, Dixon had already created a body of work that represented his passion for life and thirst for knowledge. And much like the late Joseph Beam, Dixon, in his life and work, frames a time in African-American literature that will be discussed for many years.

BIBLIOGRAPHY

Morrow, Bruce, and Charles H. Rowell, eds. *Shade: An Anthology of Fiction by Gay Men of African Descent*. New York: Avon, 1996.

Nelson, Emanuel S. *Contemporary African American Novelists*. Westport, Conn.: Greenwood Publishing Group, 1999.

Paul W. Rodgers III

Dodson, Owen Vincent   (1914–1983)

Although born too late to become a meaningful voice during the HARLEM RENAISSANCE and overshadowed by the popularity of RICHARD WRIGHT's fiction, Brooklyn-born Dodson succeeded in winning the attention of major critics, who compared him as poet to Robert Frost and Carl Sandburg. This secured a place for Dodson within the African-American literary tradition, if not in the mainstream literary tradition. With a B.A. from Bates College and an M.F.A. in playwriting from Yale School of Drama, Dodson became a well-known dramatist and director, primarily at historically black colleges and universities, while achieving distinction as a novelist and poet. For most of his professional career, he was associated with the drama department at Howard University. Dodson took the Howard University Players on a successful tour, sponsored by the State Department, of Scandinavia and Germany in 1949. DARWIN T. TURNER credits Dodson with "contributing significantly in Negro college theatre, a little-known but important training ground for black playwrights and performers" (95).

Dodson gained attention with the production of his first and best-known play, *Divine Comedy,* based on the life of African-American prophet, spiritual and social leader, and founder during the Great Depression of "heavens" or peace missions, Father Divine (George Baker). In an interview with John O'Brien, Dodson said his play, which received a Maxwell Anderson Verse Play award in 1938, was received with "raptures of pleasure" (59). *Divine Comedy* and Dodson's *Garden of Time*, a drama about Medea, were produced at Yale University during the 1930s. Several of his plays and operas were later produced at the Kennedy Center. Dodson's first novel, *Boy at the Window* (1951), about a boy growing up, as he had done, in Brooklyn in the 1920s who must come to grips with the death of his mother, was republished as *When Trees Green*. He won a *Paris Review* prize for "The Summer Fire"; the *Review* also included it among its best short stories (1961).

Scholars and critics agree that *Powerful Long Ladder* (1946), the first of Dodson's three published collections of poems, represents his best work. EUGENE B. REDMOND's observation in *Drumvoices,* "There is not one poem in the book that cannot be aesthetically or stylistically called 'poetry'" (285), is universally shared by Turner, Charles T. Davis, and ROBERT HAYDEN. Dodson is lauded for the poems effectively written in "Negro folk speech," including the BLUES, on the one hand; on the other hand, his signature poems written during World War II, in which inner and spiritual turmoil, anguish, and death are major themes, have been acclaimed for their powerful tropes and conceits. "Black Mother Praying," in which the speaker prays for peace, not only for the war in which her son and other black sons are fighting and dying but also, ironically, for peace in the urban streets of America, where "freedom is being crossed out"—where black males are being lynched—is exemplary of both styles.

> Lord, I'm gonna say my say real quick and
> simple:
> You know bout this war that's bitin the skies
> And gouging out the earth.
> (Powerful Long Ladder 8)

Dodson's vision of a world in which, as he tells O'Brien, "people are people, they are not black or white or anything. They are themselves. People. And they have their own worth" (57) is shared by the mother at the end of her prayer: "Lord, let us all see the golden wheat together." Dodson's other collections of poems are *The Harlem Book of the Dead* (1978) and *The Confession Stone: Song Cycles,* which, "filled with stories, diaries, and re-membrances of Jesus," Dodson described as "my most dedicated work" (O'Brien, 58). The recipient of a Rosenwald and a Guggenheim Fellowship, Dodson rejected the philosophy of the architects of the BLACK ARTS MOVEMENT, declaring, "The Black writer has no obligation to 'blackness'" (O'Brien, 57).

BIBLIOGRAPHY

Davis, Charles T., and Daniel Walden, eds. *On Being Black: Writings by Afro-Americans from Frederick Douglass to the Present.* Greenwich, Conn.: Fawcett Publications, 1970.

Hayden, Robert, ed. *Kaleidoscope: Poems by American Negro Poets.* New York: Harcourt, Brace and World, 1967.

O'Brien, John, ed. *Interviews with Black Writers.* New York: Liveright, 1973.

Redmond, Eugene. *Drumvoices: The Mission of Afro-American Poetry: A Critical History.* Garden City, N.Y.: Anchor Books, 1976.

Turner, Darwin T., ed. *Black American Literature: Poetry.* Columbus, Ohio: Charles E. Merrill Publishing Company, 1969.

Wilfred D. Samuels

Douglass, Frederick   (1818–1895)

Born into slavery in 1818, Frederick Douglass transformed himself from an illiterate slave into a leading abolitionist orator, influential journalist, and well-known public speaker who was celebrated in Europe and received in the White House. His three autobiographies, *Narrative of the Life of Frederick Douglass, an American Slave* (1845), *My Bondage and My Freedom* (1855), and *Life and Times of Frederick Douglass* (1893), not only are the finest examples of what came to be known as the slave narrative, but also placed Douglass among such 19th-century literary giants as Ralph Waldo Emerson, Henry David Thoreau, and Walt Whitman in affirming the importance of the first-person narrative voice as the essential literary representation of American identity and individualism.

Frederick Douglass was born Frederick Augustus Washington Bailey in Tuckahoe near Easton, Talbot County, Maryland. His mother, Harriet Bailey, was a literate slave who died when he was seven while his father was reported to be his mother's white master, a member of the Auld family. Douglass spent the first six years of his life with his grandmother before being sent to Wye House, where he came to understand and experience the many injustices and horrors of the slave system. From here Thomas (one of many possible fathers) and Lucrecia Auld would send him to Baltimore in 1826 to live with Thomas's brother, Hugh, to be a companion to Hugh Auld's young son, Tommy. In Baltimore young Frederick learned to read, initially aided by his mistress but later by sneaking into the Auld's library and reading whatever he could find, including the *Baltimore American, The Columbian Orator,* and the Bible. He would also work on his penmanship in the margins of Tommy's discarded copybooks and trick white boys on the street into writing or reading contests to aid in his learning.

As his knowledge and independence grew, Douglass was sent back to Thomas Auld in St. Michael's, Maryland, where, gaining a reputation as a problem slave, he was sent to live with Edward Covey, who was paid to break rebellious slaves. After a particularly vicious beating, Douglass was able to stand up to Covey, in one instance beating the slave breaker to such an extent that his victory over Covey was a major turning point of self-awareness and empowerment.

After his involvement in an escape plan with five other slaves, Douglass was sent back to Baltimore, where he made his escape. In September 1838, with the help of a freedwoman, Anna Murray, who would later become his wife, he disguised himself as a sailor and boarded a train to New York. He and Anna were married in New York and then, with help from an Underground Railroad agent, they moved farther north to their new home in New Bedford, Massachusetts. He traveled under the name Frederick Johnson, but upon arriving in New Bedford he found that Johnson was far too common a name, so he took the name Douglass from a character in Sir Walter Scott's *Lady of the Lake.*

In New Bedford Frederick Douglass first subscribed to William Lloyd Garrison's antislavery *Liberator:* In the summer of 1841 Douglass attended an antislavery convention organized by Garrison in Nantucket, where Douglass was approached by William C. Coffin, who asked him first to speak to the convention and, after Douglass's wildly successful speech, to become an agent for the Massachusetts Anti-Slavery Society.

In 1845, Douglass wrote down the story of his life that he had been recounting in his orations over the previous four years. The resulting book, *Narrative of the Life of Frederick Douglass, an American Slave,* was a best seller on two continents and became the most significant writing of his entire career. His narrative is remarkable for its content, its stylistic sophistication, and its extensive detail and documentation (naming specific people, places, and events), and it serves as both a life story and a historical document of the times. Clearly influenced by the wide range of reading material Douglass found in the homes of his servitude, *Narrative of the Life of Frederick Douglass* employs eloquent figurative language, classic rhetorical structures, sophisticated sentence structure, and vivid details to paint the brutal and inhumane picture of life under slavery. In the wake of such successful publication, his fear of recapture grew, and he fled to England, where he spent the next two years lecturing throughout the British Isles before British friends arranged through an attorney to pay Thomas Auld $750 for Frederick Douglass's freedom. Thus, he sailed home to America in the spring of 1847 as a free man.

Upon returning to America, he began his career as a publisher with his own antislavery newspaper, the *North Star,* which, along with other publications at this time, signaled his independence from white-controlled antislavery organizations. While publishing and editing his paper, Douglass also served as the Rochester, New York, station agent for the Underground Railroad, helping many other former slaves to freedom. In 1848, he would be the only man invited to speak to the Seneca Falls Women's Rights Convention; a forward-looking social reformer, Douglass enthusiastically supported the women's movement in addition to the antislavery movement.

The *North Star* would change its name to *Frederick Douglass' Paper* in June 1851 while adhering to Douglass's insistence on the highest editorial standards, but the paper continued to struggle financially. In 1858, Douglass established *Douglass' Monthly,* an abolitionist magazine primarily aimed at the British audience, in hopes of raising financial support for the cause.

Throughout the 1850s, Douglass was at the center of the abolitionist cause, working with such notables as Sojourner Truth and Harriet Beecher Stowe. By 1855 he had revised and republished his autobiography as *My Bondage and My Freedom,* inserting into this second version more of his own philosophies and feelings than he had in the *Narrative*. It was also during this time that Douglass continued his friendship with John Brown, who would lead 18 followers in a doomed attack on the arsenal at Harper's Ferry in October 1959. As the survivors of the raid were being executed, public opinion called for an expanded prosecution in Virginia of Brown's friends and supporters, including Frederick Douglass. Douglass was able to escape to Canada and then to Scotland, where he lectured on the Harper's Ferry Raid. While Congress investigated Brown's supporters, none were implicated by Brown, and the issue was pushed off the public stage by the Lincoln-Douglas debates. Douglass was able to return to America soon after.

During the Civil War Douglass became a strong supporter of President Lincoln, particularly after the Emancipation Proclamation of 1863. Douglass was summoned to the White House by Lincoln several times to address the condition of blacks in the south, and he was the first black man to attend an inauguration (Lincoln's second) as an invited guest.

After the Civil War, Douglass continued his work for African Americans as they moved beyond the bonds of slavery and toward the hope of full freedom and all the entitlements of citizenship. Universally recognized as both a valuable spokesman and leader for black Americans, Douglass fought for the enactment of the Thirteenth, Fourteenth, and Fifteenth Amendments to the U.S. Constitution. Douglass served as U.S. marshall for the District of Columbia from 1877 to 1881, and then as recorder of deeds for the District of Columbia from 1881 to 1886. As perhaps the ultimate recognition of his importance on the national scene, Douglass served as the U.S. minister to Haiti from 1889 to 1891. A voice for individual achievement and universal freedom, and arguably one of the finest American orators of the 19th century, Frederick Douglass died in Washington, D.C., on February 20, 1895.

BIBLIOGRAPHY

Blassingame, John W., ed. *The Frederick Douglass Papers.* New Haven: Yale University Press, 1979.

Douglass, Frederick. *Narrative of the Life of Frederick Douglass: An American Slave. Written by Himself.* New York: Signet, 1968.

Gates, Henry Louis, Jr., ed. *The Classic Slave Narratives.* New York: New American Library, 1987.

McFeely, William S. *Frederick Douglass.* New York: Norton, 1991.

Janet Bland

Dove, Rita Frances   (1952–   )

Acclaimed poet, novelist, performer, and playwright Rita Dove stands as a pillar in contemporary literature. Not only was she the first African-American U.S. Poet Laureate and Consultant in Poetry at the Library of Congress, but she also won a Pulitzer Prize for her collection *Thomas and Beulah.*

Born in 1952 in Akron, Ohio, Dove is the daughter of Elvira and Ray Dove, one of the first African-American research chemists. Dove's creative and scholarly pursuits began at an early age. After visiting the White House as a Presidential Scholar in high school, she attended Miami University as a National Merit Scholar, graduating summa cum laude in 1973. Following this, Dove received a Fulbright Fellowship and attended the Universität Tübingen in West Germany for two semesters. Recognizing her passion for creative writing, Dove attended the University of Iowa Writers' Workshop, where she earned her master of fine arts degree in 1977. While there, Dove met and married the German writer Fred Viebahn and, in 1983, their daughter Aviva Chantal Tamu Dove-Viebahn was born. After teaching creative writing at Arizona State University from 1981 to 1989, Dove became the Commonwealth Professor of English at the University of Virginia in Charlottesville, where she now lives with her husband and daughter.

Dove's literary and academic successes are too numerous to list. She has received more than 20 honorary literary doctorates from institutions such as Miami University, Notre Dame, The University of Akron, Columbia University, and State University of New York at Brockport. Besides her aforementioned laurels, Dove has also received the

2003 Emily Couric Leadership Award, a Guggenheim Fellowship, the Portia Pittman Fellowship, a Bellagio Residency, an Ohio Governor's Award, the Lavan Younger Poet Award from the Academy of American Poets, the NATIONAL ASSOCIATION FOR THE ADVANCEMENT OF COLORED PEOPLE Great American Artist Award, the Harvard University Phi Beta Kappa Poetry Award, the Carl Sandburg Award, the Heinz Award in the Arts and Humanities, the National Humanities medal from the U.S. government, the 1998 Levinson Prize from *Poetry,* and myriad other awards, grants, and honors.

Dove's often-stated belief that poetry should be accessible to all is evident in the themes and language of her poetry. Often considered autobiographical, her poetry teaches readers to see the beauty in everyday aesthetics. Beginning with the publication of her first two chapbooks, *Ten Poems* (1977) and *The Only Dark Spot in the Sky* (1980), this has been a quality Dove has established throughout her career. In 1980 she published her first collection of poetry, *The Yellow House on the Corner,* which introduced readers to Dove's use of dramatic monologue and narrative. Aside from her eloquent and accurate depiction of historical issues such as slavery and freedom, Dove's work uses biblical allusions to transcend racial boundaries and establish a universal humanity that allows for a connection between master and slave.

After producing another chapbook that emphasized the musicality of her poetry, *Mandolin* (1982). Dove published her second collection of poetry, *Museum.* Dove describes the spirit of her book as the feeling she had while traveling in Europe: "I was a Black American, and therefore I became a representative for all of that. And I sometimes felt like a ghost, I mean, people would ask me questions, but I had a feeling that they weren't seeing *me,* but a shell" (Robin and Ingersoll, 233). Though both praised and criticized for its universal quality and avoidance of personal issues, the precise craft and detailed imagery have fostered a high regard for *Museum.*

Dove's third poetry collection would not face such mixed reviews. *Thomas and Beulah* became the second Pulitzer Prize–winning book by an African-American poet. This book is divided into two sections: "Mandolin," the first section of 23 poems, deals with Thomas, a migrant from Tennessee traveling north in the early 1900s; the second 21 poems, titled "Canary," are about Beulah, a woman born in 1904 in Georgia. Based on the lives of Dove's maternal grandparents, *Thomas and Beulah's* organization shows both sides of a relationship between a man and woman. The poems move readers through the experiences of the two characters—youth, marriage, parenthood, and death. Through lyric and biography, Dove again focuses on the small everyday happenings, giving them meaning that transcends race and gender, making them universal and meaningful to all readers.

Dove's next collection, *Grace Notes* (1989), which followed the publication of her chapbook *The Other Side of the House* (1988), was also highly praised. Largely autobiographical, using ordinary language, the poetry in *Grace Notes* comments on middle-class black life. Dove shifted her focus in her next collection, *Mother Love* (1995), which explores mother-daughter relationships through the Demeter/Persephone myth. Rather than being sentimental, Dove uses sonnets to focus on the pain and separation that occurs throughout the motherhood cycle. Throughout the text, her poems change speakers so that readers can experience the emotions and thoughts of the various personas, as they can in *Thomas and Beulah.* Stephen Cushman describes Dove's work as valuing "both meter and variation, regularity and irregularity, rule and exception" (134), commenting that these pairings allow readers to register the fluctuations of their own lives.

Dove's collection *On the Bus with Rosa Parks* (1999) uses American mythology and history to illuminate characters in their ordinariness. Though some critics have cited a few weak poems, most praised Dove's use of simple yet exact language and the poems' lyrical quality. Further, the collection was nominated for the National Book Critics Circle Award.

Aside from these collections, Dove's work has been translated into Hebrew, French, Norwegian, and German. She has also published her laureate lectures, *The Poet's World*. In her goal to make poetic language speak to the masses, Dove has experimented with other genres. In 1985, Dove published a collection of short stories titled *Fifth Sunday* as a part of the CALLALOO fiction series. In their portrayal of African-Americans lives in various settings, many of the stories featured in the text foreshadow her poetry. While praised for its style, the book generally received mixed reviews, but most highlighted the qualities of the text as promising of future publications.

Dove ventured outside of genre boundaries again with the publication of a novel, *Through the Ivory Gate* (1992). The story revolves around a young black woman, Virginia King, who returns to her hometown to serve as an artist-in-residence at an elementary school. Flashing from the present to the past, the narrative follows Virginia through a series of painful memories, encounters with prejudice, and shattered relationships.

In 1994, Dove returned to the issue of slavery in her full-length play, *The Darker Face of the Earth: A Verse Play in Fourteen Scenes*. Using slavery as a frame, Dove creates her own version of the Oedipus tragedy. Described by Theodora Carlisle in AFRICAN AMERICAN REVIEW as "imaginative, deeply compassionate, electric with erotic power, and unflinching in its honesty" (147), Dove's powerful play has been embraced by many scholars and critics. The play had its world premiere in 1996 at the Oregon Shakespeare Festival and has been staged several times since.

Dove has made significant contributions not only to African-American literature but to all of humanity by the gestures she has made to reach the community through language. Dove has hosted *Sesame Street* and produced a nationally televised show about poetry, *Shine Up Your Words: A Morning with Rita Dove* for elementary school children. Dove has made appearances on NBC's *Tonight Show*, read her poetry at the White House, and wrote the text for Alvin Singleton's symphony "Umoja—Each One of Us Counts," which was performed during the opening festivities of the Olympic Games held in Atlanta. Further, Dove's continued passion for writing is apparent in her

dedication to giving writers an opportunity to publish their works, as she is an advisory editor to more than six literary journals, including *Callaloo, Gettysburg Review,* and *Mid-American Review.*

Given Dove's many achievements during her career and the impact she has had throughout the arts and humanities, the concluding lines of her "Lady Freedom among Us" seem also to ring true of Dove herself:

> *no choice but to grant her space*
> *crown her with sky*
> *for she is one of the many*
> *and she is each of us.*

BIBLIOGRAPHY

Carlisle, Theodora. "Reading the Scars: Rita Dove's 'The Darker Face of the Earth.'" *African American Review* 34, no. 1 (Spring 2000): 135–151.
Cushman, Stephen. "And the Dove Returned." *Callaloo* 19, no. 1 (1996): 131–134.
Pereira, Malin. *Rita Dove's Cosmopolitanism.* Champaign: University of Illinois Press, 2003.
———. "'When the pear blossoms / cast their faces on / the darker face of the earth': Miscegenation, the Primal Scene, and the Incest Motif in Rita Dove's Work." *African American Review* 36, no. 2 (Summer 2002): 195–212.
Rubin, Stan, and Earl Ingersoll. "A Conversation with Rita Dove." *Black American Literature Forum* 20, no. 6 (Fall 1986): 227–240.
Steffen, Therese. *Crossing Color: Transcultural Space and Place in Rita Dove's Poetry, Fiction, and Drama.* Oxford: Oxford University Press, 2001.
Vendler, Helen Hennessy. *The Given and the Made: Strategies of Poetic Redefinition.* Cambridge: Harvard University Press, 1995.

Cassandra Parente

DuBois, W(illiam) E(dward) B(urghardt) (1868–1963)

W. E. B. DuBois stands as the preeminent African-American intellectual, scholar, journalist and political activist of the 20th century. The first African American to receive a Ph.D. from Harvard University, DuBois was a founder of the NATIONAL ASSOCIATION FOR THE ADVANCEMENT OF COLORED PEOPLE (NAACP), editor of *The Crisis* magazine, author of more than 20 books, founder and editor of five journals and magazines, and an American Labor Party candidate for the U.S. Senate. DuBois's most enduring legacy is recorded in his now-classic text, *The Souls of Black Folks* (1903), a study of African-American history and discourse and the source of his original formulations of double consciousness, the talented tenth, and the problem of the color line, which continue to have an enormous, if hotly contested, influence.

W. E. B. DuBois was born in Great Barrington, Massachusetts, on February 23, 1868, to Alfred DuBois and Mary Silvinia Burghardt. Raised primarily by his mother, DuBois spent his early years excelling at local schools, developing his skill as a journalist (submitting articles to the *Springfield Republican* and the *New York Globe*), and working odd jobs to supplement his mother's modest income. Though DuBois distinguished himself as an outstanding student (he was valedictorian at his high school graduation) and had hopes of attending Harvard University, town leaders of Great Barrington had other intentions, granting DuBois a scholarship to attend an all-black educational institution, Fisk University, in Nashville, Tennessee. His years at Fisk University marked his first encounter with a substantial black community and would prove formative for his later thought regarding the sources of African-American culture (the Negro spirituals) and the importance of higher education as a training ground for black leadership (the "talented tenth"). Entering Fisk in 1885, DuBois completed an A.B. in three years' time and continued on to pursue his dream of studying at Harvard University, where he was admitted as a junior in 1888; he received a second B.A. cum laude in philosophy in 1890 and an M.A. in history in 1891.

At Harvard DuBois met, studied with, and befriended the leading scholars of his day—William James, Josiah Royce, Albert Bushnell Hart, and George Santayana—and began to garner recognition as a young scholar and orator of exceptional talent and skill. In 1892, DuBois won a Slater Fund Fellowship to pursue graduate study in history and economics at the Friedrich Wilhelm University, later Berlin University. The year 1893 marked a major turning point in DuBois's life and, while a student in Germany and on the occasion of his 25th birthday, he dedicated himself to the improvement of African Americans. After two years of study in Germany, DuBois ran out of money and, unable to finish his graduate studies or receive his degree from a German university, returned to the United States, where he finished his doctorate at Harvard University, becoming the first African American to receive a Ph.D. from that institution. His doctoral dissertation, *The Suppression of the African Slave Trade to the United States of America, 1638–1870* (1896), was published as the first volume in the Harvard Historical Monograph Series.

Beginning in 1894, DuBois took a series of academic positions for varying lengths of time at Wilberforce University (1894–1896), the University of Pennsylvania (1896–1897), and Atlanta University (1897-1910, and later from 1933–1944), where he would have his longest tenure. During this initial 16-year period, DuBois established himself as a prolific scholar and meticulous researcher, publishing his groundbreaking sociological study, *The Philadelphia Negro: A Social Study* (1899), as well as his greatest work, *The Souls of Black Folk: Essays and Sketches* (1903). During this same period, DuBois supervised the Atlanta University conferences on the sociological dimensions of African-American life, which resulted in the publication between 1898 and 1914 of 16 reports on the political, economic, educational, religious, and social status of African Americans. This research became the foundation for the future academic discipline of African-American studies. DuBois also founded and edited three journals during this time, *The Moon* (1905–1906), *The Horizon: A Journal of the Color Line* (1907–1910), and *The Crisis: A Record of the Darker Races* (1910–1919; 1934), a monthly magazine for the NAACP.

During the years 1895 to 1915, DuBois began a historic and protracted ideological struggle with BOOKER T. WASHINGTON, founder and president of Tuskegee Institute and then a recognized black spokesman on the "Negro Problem," over the leadership of African Americans. In favor of liberal arts training and social and political activism for full citizenship rights of African Americans, DuBois rejected Washington's advocacy of vocational education, social compromise, and political accommodation. He penned his most critical assessment of Washington's leadership and its shortcomings in the third chapter of *The Souls of Black Folk,* titled "Of Booker T. Washington and Others." This criticism led to both enmity between the two men and the emergence and organization in 1905 of the Niagara movement, a gathering of African-American leaders who shared DuBois's opposition to Washington's leadership and philosophy. The Niagara movement ended just months before the creation of the NAACP in 1909, an organization initially created and led by white Americans sympathetic to the plight of African Americans that now stands as the premier and predominantly African-American civil rights organization in the United States.

In 1910, the NAACP hired DuBois as the director of publication and research, and he subsequently founded and edited *The Crisis* from 1910 to 1934. During his nearly 20-year tenure as editor, DuBois discovered his métier in writing *Crisis* editorials and articles and cemented his reputation as a scholar and leader of national standing regarding the problem of race. He displayed an unparalleled intellectual grasp of the variety and complexity of problems generated by the color line. In editorials that gave impassioned yet measured voice to the strange meaning of being black in America, DuBois addressed the segregation of black troops during the World War I, the epidemic of lynching, Jim Crow laws, voting rights for women, the civil rights policies of American presidents, and the cultural and literary achievements of African-American artists. DuBois was not above delivering the occasional jeremiad against prominent African-American leaders who failed to meet his expectations for leadership. In 1924 he directed a series of withering and acerbic editorials and essays against Marcus Garvey, founder of the Universal Negro Improvement Association and the *Black Star Line,* whose commercial projects and

leadership of a growing grassroots movement among working-class blacks DuBois found both troubling and questionable. In 1934 DuBois directed similar criticism against the policies of the NAACP's board, both its advocacy of integration and its reluctance to adopt more radical measures in the fight against racial injustice in America. This last series of editorials led to DuBois's resignation as editor of *The Crisis.*

DuBois's reputation as a scholar and African-American leader reached far beyond national boundaries. As early as 1900, DuBois attended the first Pan-African Conference in London, a gathering of delegates of African descent from around the world. In a speech titled "Address to the Nations of the World," DuBois formally announced that "the problem of the twentieth century is the problem of the color-line," a phrase that would be often repeated and puzzled over for the next century. In the nearly 45 years that followed, DuBois organized five more Pan-African conferences (1919, 1921, 1923, 1927, and 1945) in Europe and America, earning him the title "the Father of Pan Africanism." DuBois was also internationally known and respected for his principled stands against American and European racism, imperialism, colonialism, and economic exploitation, yet his views and organizing activities on behalf of peace and civil rights were less well received and tolerated in the United States. Frequently asked to speak and visit in Poland, the Soviet Union, China, Japan, and Africa, DuBois was not shy of criticizing America's racial practices or appealing to socialist and communist nations to support the ongoing struggle of African Americans for civil rights in America. His outspokenness earned him the label of communist sympathizer and resulted in the loss of his passport from 1952 until 1958, when a Supreme Court ruling allowed him to regain it. In 1959, DuBois embarked on a world tour that included Europe, Eastern bloc nations, and China, where, on his 91st birthday, with the help of Mao Zedong and Zhou Enlai, he broadcast an address to Africa on Radio Beijing.

DuBois's major writings from 1935 until 1960 reflect the enormous breadth of his thought and social and political concerns. In 1935 DuBois published *Black Reconstruction,* a voluminous historical reexamination of the role of African Americans in the restoration of the South with a decidedly Marxist analysis. In 1940 he published *Dusk Dawn: An Essay toward an Autobiography of a Race Concept,* what might be considered the third in a series of four autobiographical books about his life. In *Color and Democracy: Colonies and Peace* (1945) and *The World and Africa: An Inquiry* (1947), on the part that Africa has played in world history, DuBois presented a more global view of discrimination and injustice and critically examined the continuing problem of race in a postwar world. DuBois also experimented with fiction, writing a trilogy of novels titled The Black Flame (*The Ordeal of Mansart* [1957], *Mansart Builds a School* [1959], and *Worlds of Color* [1961]). In his final years, DuBois began work, for a second time, on the *Encyclopedia Africana* and completed a final autobiography titled *The Autobiography of W. E. B. DuBois: A Soliloquy on Viewing My Life from the Last Decade of Its First Century.*

In 1961, at age 93, DuBois left the United States and accepted an invitation from President Kwame Nkrumah to take up residence in Accra, Ghana, an independent African republic. In 1963 DuBois formalized his status as a citizen of Ghana, and on August 27, the eve of the March on Washington and MARTIN LUTHER KING, JR.'s "I have a Dream" speech, DuBois died in Ghana at age 95. DuBois was married twice, first to Nina Gomer, from 1896 until her death in 1950, and then to Shirley Graham, a teacher, playwright, and civil rights activist, from 1951 until his death in 1963. DuBois fathered two children, Burghardt Gomer DuBois (1897–1899) and Nina Yolande DuBois (1900–1961), and adopted David Graham, the son of Shirley Graham DuBois.

BIBLIOGRAPHY

Aptheker, Herbert. *The Literary Legacy of W. E. B. DuBois.* New York: Kraus International Publications, 1989.

DuBois, W. E. B. *The Autobiography of W. E. B. DuBois: A Soliloquy on Viewing My Life from the Last Decade of Its First Century.* New York: International Publishers, 1968.

————. *The Souls of Black Folk: One Hundred Years Later.* Edited by Dolan Hubbard. Columbia: University of Missouri Press, 2003.

Early, Gerald, ed. *Lure and Loathing: Essays on Race, Identity, and the Ambivalence of Assimilation.* New York: Penguin Press, 1993.

James, Joy. *Transcending the Talented Tenth: Black Leaders and American Intellectuals.* New York: Routledge, 1997.

Lewis, David Levering. *W. E. B. DuBois: Biography of a Race, 1868–1919.* New York: Henry Holt and Company, 1993.

————. *W. E. B. DuBois: The Fight for Equality and the American Century, 1919–1963.* New York: Henry Holt and Company, 2000.

Marable, Manning. *W. E. B. DuBois: Black Radical Democrat.* Boston: Twayne Publishers, 1986.

Rampersad, Arnold. *The Art and Imagination of W. E. B. DuBois.* New York: Schocken Books, 1976, 1990.

Reed, Adolph L., Jr. *W. E. B. DuBois and American Political Thought: Fabianism and the Color Line.* New York: Oxford University Press, 1997.

Zamir, Shamoon. *Dark Voices: W. E. B. DuBois and American Thought, 1888–1903.* Chicago: University of Chicago Press, 1995.

Marcus Bruce

Due, Tananarive   (1966–   )

(pronounced tah-nah-nah-REEVE doo) Novelist Tananarive Due blends spine-tingling storytelling and evocative prose in her works, which have been classified as horror writing and genre science fiction or speculative fiction. Born in 1966 in Tallahassee, Florida, Due is one of three daughters of John Due and Patricia Stephens Due, who met as students at Florida A&M University (FAMU) and married in 1963.

Due studied journalism and literature at Northwestern University and later earned her master's in English literature from the University of Leeds, England, where she specialized in Nigerian literature as a Rotary Foundation Scholar. She has taught at the Clarion Science Fiction and Fantasy Writers' Workshop at Michigan State University, the University of Miami, and the summer Imagination creative writing conference at Cleveland State University.

Her novels are *The Between* (1995), *My Soul to Keep* (1997), and its sequel, *The Living Blood* (2001), a folklore-laden and suspense-filled tale that is both powerful and poignant. Set in the United States and Ethiopia, *The Living Blood,* which received a 2002 American Book Award, chronicles the unfolding of an ancient secret. In 2000, actor Blair Underwood shot footage in Lalibela, Ethiopia, as part of her effort to make the film version of *My Soul to Keep.* Noted as one of the Best Books of the Year by *Publishers Weekly* magazine, *My Soul to Keep* also garnered a nomination from the Horror Writers Association for the Bram Stoker Award for Outstanding Achievement in a Novel. *The Between* was nominated for the Bram Stoker Award for Outstanding Achievement in a First Novel. *Publishers Weekly* also named *The Living Blood* one of the best novels of the year.

Due also contributed to the anthology of science fiction stories and essays *Dark Matter: A Century of Speculative Fiction from the African Diaspora* (2000), edited by Sheree R. Thomas, and *Best Black Women's Erotica* (2001), a showcase of original, erotic literature edited by Blanche Richardson. Due's short story "Patient Zero" was included in two best-of-the-year science fiction anthologies for the year 2000—*Year's Best SF 6,* edited by David G. Hartwell, and *The Year's Best Science Fiction: 17th Annual Collection,* edited by Gardner R. Dozois.

Known for her style of supernatural suspense, Due is thought to be among a cadre of African-American writers who are redefining the genre. She acknowledges being influenced by writers such as Octavia E. Butler, Franz Kafka, Toni Morrison, and Stephen King.

Due's richly vibrant collection of writing also consists of news stories and columns published in newspapers through the years. The storyteller worked as a full-time journalist as she crafted her fiction writing. At *The Miami Herald,* the former features writer helped the lovelorn through her syndicated column on relationships. In 1993, her story on Hurricane Andrew's impact on children was part of coverage that garnered a Pulitzer Prize for the *Herald.* The paper received the prize for public service for helping readers cope with the hurricane's devastation and showing how lax zoning, inspection, and building codes contributed to the storm's effects. Before working full time at the *Herald,* Due interned at *The New York Times* and *The Wall Street Journal.*

Due's foray into historical fiction resulted in *The Black Rose* (2000), an examination of the life of Madame C. J. Walker, who, though born a slave on a Louisiana plantation in 1867, rose from indignity and poverty to create a beauty empire. She also was a leading philanthropist and activist in many causes, including antilynching campaigns and efforts to desegregate the military. *The Black Rose,* based on research started by late author Alex Haley, earned Due an Image Award nomination from the National Association for the Advancement of Colored People.

One World/Ballantine published Due's family civil rights memoir, *Freedom in the Family: A Mother-Daughter Memoir of the Fight for Civil Rights,* in 2003. Coauthored with her mother, *Freedom in the Family* recalls the novelist's childhood as the daughter of a civil rights activist, Patricia Stephens Due, who details her own involvement in the Civil Rights movement. In 1960, when Patricia Stephens Due was a 19-year-old freshman at FAMU, she and five classmates purposely tried to break the color barrier at the segregated lunch counter of the Tallahassee Woolworth's store. The students ordered food, were refused service and were asked to leave. Patricia Stephens Due spent 49 days in jail for sitting in at the lunch counter, an incident recognized as the first "jail-in" of the student sit-in movement. The novelist's father, John Due, was a law student at FAMU, where he assisted fellow students and participated in freedom rides. After he passed the bar exam, John Due represented the Congress of Racial Equality and other civil rights organizations as well as individuals such as a St. Augustine dentist who was brutally beaten by the Ku Klux Klan.

The author started a scholarship fund in her parents' names at their alma mater and her birthplace from the proceeds of the sale of *Naked Came the Manatee* (1997). Thirteen writers penned the comic thriller. The writers, including Dave Barry, Carl Hiaasen, and Elmore Leonard, all of whom had ties to South Florida, each wrote a chapter and passed on the book to the next contributor.

In 2003 Atria Books published Due's supernatural novel *The Good House,* set in a haunted house in the Pacific Northwest. Due and her husband, the television and science fiction writer Steven Barnes, make their home in Longview, Washington. They married in 1998.

BIBLIOGRAPHY

Contemporary Black Biography: Profiles from the International Black Community. Vol. 30. Detroit: Gale Group, 2002.

Jeannine F. Hunter

Dumas, Henry   (1934–1968)

Henry Dumas's preteen years spent in his native state of Arkansas, combined with his experience of living in Harlem as a young adult, are key elements in his work as a writer. But more important to Dumas's legacy is the story of his tragic death at age 33, when he was gunned down by a transit officer in a New York subway in a reputed case of mistaken identity. Before his death, Dumas attended Rutgers University and participated in the CIVIL RIGHTS MOVEMENT in the South while developing his skills as a poet and fiction writer. In 1967 Dumas took a position at Southern Illinois University (SIU), where he worked in a support service program. During his brief tenure at SIU, Dumas became a colleague and friend of fellow teacher and writer EUGENE REDMOND, who has worked tirelessly since Dumas's tragic death to promote his works and nurture his legacy as a writer.

Although little of his work was published during his lifetime, it is due to Redmond's advocacy that six books by Dumas have appeared since his death. The first, *Ark of Bones,* a short story collection, appeared in 1970, and a poetry collection, *Poetry for My People,* also appeared that year. Both books were initially published by Southern Illinois University Press under the editorship of Redmond and Hale Chatfield, one of Dumas's professors at Rutgers, and both were reissued by Random House in 1974, under TONI MORRISON's editorship; the book of poems was retitled *Play Ebony, Play Ivory.* Redmond also served as editor of two more Random House publications of Dumas's works: *Jonoah and the Green Stone,* an unfinished novel (1976), and *Rope of Wind and Other Stories* (1979). Dumas's works were made available for a new generation of writers in *Goodbye, Sweetwater* (1988) and *Knees of a Natural Man* (1989), both also edited by Redmond.

"Ark of Bones," Dumas's most widely circulated story, depicts two youths who encounter a mysterious "ark" on the Mississippi River. This and other works of Dumas's fiction, such as "Rain God," "Six Days You Shall Labor," "Fon," "The Voice," and "A Boll of Roses," explore African-American life through the author's mythic vision. *Jonoah and the Green Stone,* similar to "Ark of Bones," draws on biblical narratives to comment on the present social plight of African Americans. Dumas intended the novel to be part of a trilogy, one that shows a boy, Jonoah, surviving one of the worst floods of the Mississippi in memory, becoming involved in both civil rights and the street life of Harlem in the North after growing up, and then returning to the South to aid his adopted family in their struggle against racial oppression. Dumas's work is not limited to southern settings, as several of his better stories take place in Harlem. In "The Voice," for example, Dumas again addresses the question of black spirituality by exploring the lives of a group of urban youths who have lost their leader. The spiritual power of black music is also the focus in "Will the Circle Be Unbroken," but this time the religious ritual portrayed is not one that shares any connection with a Judeo-Christian origin; it is a purely African rite that draws on the cosmic forces of black music to build a protective wall for African Americans against the cultural aggressions of nonblacks.

Various strains of BLUES are found in Dumas's poetry, from tightly structured lyrical blues poems to poems in open forms that are nevertheless steeped in blues rhythms and idioms. Some of the poems take the form of blues lyrics—a section of *Play Ebony, Play Ivory* is titled "Blues Songs"— while others, shaped by the poet's usage of vernacular speech, speak to readers in the familiar tones of "back home." "Knees of a Natural Man," for example, portrays a day in the life of a transplanted country boy in the big city. The voice in the poem represents the millions of black voices recalling the difficult transition from a rural to an urban lifestyle. Rivers are also of particular significance in Dumas's poetry; growing up near the Mississippi, he may have been influenced by LANGSTON HUGHES's use of rivers in poems such as "The Negro Speaks of Rivers." In "Afro-American" the poet says "my black mother is a long-haired sensuous river / where the Kongo flows into the Mississippi," and as in Hughes's poem a connection is made between Africa ("the Kongo") and the Mississippi River.

As a writer associated with the BLACK ARTS MOVEMENT, Henry Dumas wrote during a time when many African-American writers were starting to embrace Africa as a cultural motherland, while rejecting Christianity as "the white man's religion," but Dumas did not reject the religious practices of the majority of the culture. His cosmology draws from Islam, Hinduism, Buddhism, the Old Testament, Native American spirituality, and black American hoodoo, as well from various diverse forms of African religious thought, such as Akan, Dagon, and Yoruba. Instead of totally rejecting Christianity in works such as "Ark of Bones," he blurs the lines between African cosmology and Christian beliefs. Not only do the spiritual realism and depictions of African-American life in pastoral settings set the stage for writers such as Morrison, GLORIA NAYLOR, ERNEST GAINES, and RANDALL KENAN, but his stories and poems also anticipate the experimental writers who would later emerge in the tradition such as CLARENCE MAJOR, NATHANIEL MACKEY, and HARRYETTE MULLEN. Morrison's borrowing of the name of Dumas's birthplace, Sweet Home, Arkansas, for the plantation setting in *BELOVED* serves as an indication of Dumas's importance to the writers of the Black Arts Movement and beyond.

BIBLIOGRAPHY

Collier, Eugenia. "Wisdom in *Goodbye, Sweetwater*: Suggestions for Further Study." *Black American Literature Forum* 22 (Summer 1988): 192–199.

Redmond, Eugene B. Introduction. "The Ancient and Recent Voices within Henry Dumas." In *Goodbye, Sweetwater: New and Selected Stories*, by Henry Dumas. New York: Thunder's Mouth, 1988.

———. Introduction. "Poet Henry Dumas: Distance Runner, Stabilizer, Distiller." In *Knees of a Natural Man: The Selected Poems of Henry Dumas.* New York: Thunder's Mouth Press, 1989.

Taylor, Clyde. "Henry Dumas: Legacy of a Long-Breath Singer." *Black American Literature Forum* 22 (Summer 1988): 353–364.

Werner, Craig. "Dumas, Nationalism, and Multicultural Mythology." *Black American Literature Forum* 22 (Summer 1988): 394–399.

Williams, Dana A. "Making the Bones Live Again: A Look at the 'Bones People' in August Wilson's *Joe Turner Come and Gone* and Henry Dumas's 'Ark of Bones.'" *CLA Journal* 42 (1999): 309–319.

Reggie Young

Dunbar, Paul Laurence   (1872–1906)

One of the two best-selling turn-of-the-century American poets, black or white, Paul Laurence Dunbar is best known for being the finest African-American composer of black dialect poetry. Also the author of a notable body of traditional English poetry, numerous short stories, three novels, essays, songs, and Broadway musicals, Dunbar never fully enjoyed his fame; he resented the insistence of white publishers, critics, and consumers that he produce more of his celebrated "minstrelized" dialect work and less traditional, "literary" verse.

Dunbar was born in Dayton, Ohio, to Joshua Dunbar and Matilda Glass Burton Murphy, both former Kentucky plantation slaves. Although he was the only black student in his high school, Dunbar's consummate charm and extracurricular activities made him a popular addition to the student body: He served as editor in chief of his school newspaper, he was the president of the school literary society, he founded and edited a black newspaper, he published his first poem at age 16 in the *Dayton Herald,* and he edited and contributed to the *West Side News* and the black journal *Tattler,* two of the future aviator Orville Wright's earliest experiments. Dunbar's popularity in school along with his literary successes understandably, if naively, led him to expect great professional rewards after graduation in 1891. But after a failed search for suitable employment and lacking the funds for college, Dunbar resigned himself to working locally as an elevator operator—a job that afforded him time to compose and submit poetry and short stories to local periodicals.

On the strength of his early work, a former teacher invited Dunbar to address the 1892 meeting of the Western Association of Writers. His masterful performance convinced the association to grant him membership, and the poet James Newton Matthews, who was in attendance at the meeting, wrote a piece on the unknown black poet that circulated widely throughout the Midwest. Prominent midwestern newspapers were quick to respond and invited Dunbar to submit his work for publication to a wider audience. One year after the Dayton speech, Dunbar published his debut volume of poetry, *Oak and Ivy* (1893), a collection of 56 poems that sold remarkably well. His abilities as a public speaker only improved with time, and after a successful publicity tour through Ohio and Indiana, the elevator operator from Dayton secured a devoted regional following.

In 1893, the *Dayton Herald* sent Dunbar on assignment to the Chicago World's Columbian Exposition. There, Dunbar met and deeply impressed FREDERICK DOUGLASS, who arranged for the young poet to read "The Colored Soldiers" on Negro American Day. In attendance were the lawyer Charles A. Thatcher and the psychiatrist Henry A. Tobey, who became lifelong supporters of Dunbar's career. Dunbar remained in Chicago for a short period, hoping to take advantage of the opportunities of the growing literary center. Though he spent some time as Douglass's secretary, the only other jobs he could find in that city were as a bathroom attendant and elevator operator. Disillusioned by Chicago's racial intolerance, he soon returned to Dayton, where, unable to sup-

port either his mother or himself, Dunbar began to exhibit suicidal tendencies.

His self-esteem stabilized in 1895, however, when he published, with financial support from Thatcher and Tobey, his second collection of poetry, *Majors and Minors* (1895). This volume caught the attention of the United States's most influential literary critic of the period, the "Dean of American Letters" William Dean Howells, whose review in the June 20, 1896, edition of *Harper's Weekly* established Dunbar as a foremost American poet. Subsequent sales allowed Dunbar to devote more time to writing and touring the countryside.

Howells voiced a sentiment in his *Harper's* piece that would haunt Dunbar to his death. The title *Majors and Minors* referred to his two poetic forms. Whereas the "majors" are poems written in standard English verse, the "minors" are written in dialect. On this duality, Howells remarked that the majors, aside from the fact that Dunbar was of pure black ancestry, are "not . . . specially notable," but rather, "it is when we come to Mr. Dunbar's Minors that we feel ourselves in the presence of a man with a direct and a fresh authority to do the kind of thing he is doing." Though the review ensured popular success, Dunbar later admitted that Howells's good intentions consigned him to the dustbin of dialect poetry. He submitted many standard English poems to journals after *Majors and Minors,* but editors continuously rejected them and responded with calls for more "minors."

In 1896 Dunbar signed with Major James Burton Pond's lecture bureau, a management agency that also boasted Frederick Douglass, George Washington Cable, and Mark Twain. Pond arranged for Dunbar's next and most highly acclaimed book, *Lyrics of Lowly Life* (1896), to be published by Dodd, Mead and Company, one of the most prominent American imprints, and introduced with a tribute by Howells. After a national tour, Dunbar toured England, thus securing an international audience as well.

Back in the United States, Dunbar landed first in New York and then in Washington, D.C., where he was offered a post at the Library of Congress. In New York, he collaborated on a Broadway musical, *Clorindy; or, The Origin of the Cake Walk,* with the renowned Broadway composer Will Marion Cook. Dunbar's naturalistic novel *The SPORT OF THE GODS* (1901 in *Lippincott's;* 1902 in book form) contains a series of New York chapters that were inspired by his time in that milieu. Set in New York's Tenderloin, located just southwest of the Broadway theater district, these chapters uniquely explore the gambling, drinking, and ragtime music offered in what JAMES WELDON JOHNSON later termed the "black Bohemia" of the 1890s, not Harlem as many critics mistakenly assume. Dunbar renders New York as alluring but ultimately lethal for all but the most resourceful migrants. Dunbar's New York experience was bittersweet; though a number of his musicals and vaudeville shows were lucrative, black reviewers began labeling him "the Prince of the Coon Song Writers" for his perpetuation of 19th-century black stereotypes.

On March 6, 1896, Dunbar secretly married the short story writer and teacher Alice Ruth Moore. Dunbar had suffered from poor health since he was a child, and by the time of his marriage and at the height of his literary success, his health took a substantial turn for the worse. Regardless of these setbacks, he continued to write at a furious pace, and in 1898 he published his first novel, *The Uncalled,* and his first collection of short stories, *Folks from Dixie.* In 1899 two collections of his poetry appeared, *Lyrics of the Hearthside* and *Poems of Cabin and Field.* As in *Majors and Minors,* in *Lyrics of the Hearthside* Dunbar placed the necessary dialect poems at the end of a body of finely crafted standard English verse.

In May 1899 Dunbar was diagnosed with pneumonia. Toggling back and forth from major literary centers like New York and Washington, D.C., to the salubrious climes of the Catskills and Colorado, Dunbar continued to write poems, short stories, and essays for periodicals like the *Lippincott's Monthly,* the *Century,* the *Independent, Harper's Weekly,* and the *Saturday Evening Post.* While in Colorado, he published *The Love of Landry* (1900), a western of scant literary value; in that same year, he published *The Strength of Gideon and Other Stories,* containing realistic portraits of both blacks and whites corrupted by racist American institutions. In 1901 Dunbar published *The Fanatics,* a

portrait of white sectional tension and racism during the Civil War.

Despite skyrocketing sales and critical acclaim, Dunbar's health declined rapidly, and he drank to ease the pain. In 1902 he and Alice separated, mainly because of his alcoholism, which led to outrageous rants, and his increasingly violent spousal abuse, which had always been a problem but culminated in a vicious episode that year. Soon after his breakup with Alice, he moved back to New York and continued to write at a fantastic rate. A year after *The Sport of the Gods* appeared as a book in 1902, he published *Lyrics in Love and Laughter,* which includes tributes to the leading black activists Frederick Douglass and BOOKER T. WASHINGTON as well as many autobiographical poems that allude to his illness and the times he spent convalescing in the Catskills, Colorado, and New England. In "The Poet" he laments his audience's insatiable demand for dialect poetry— a "jingle in a broken tongue"—as opposed to his standard English verse, which was the source of his artistic pride.

In the fall of 1903, a combination of poor physical and mental health compelled Dunbar to return to his mother's home in Dayton. In that year his collection of short stories *In Old Plantation Days* came out, which included a series of relatively benign stories of Old South plantation life, concretizing, in the eyes of many critics, his status as an UNCLE TOM (see SAMBO AND UNCLE TOM). More recently, scholars have revisited these tales, arguing they contain more subversive comments on black life than originally believed. His next collection, *The Heart of Happy Hollow,* depicts crooked white politicians and confidence men victimizing blacks. Dunbar's widely anthologized tale of southern race violence and mistaken identity, "The Lynching of Jube Benson," appears in this collection. Dunbar published three more volumes of verse, *Li'l Gal* (1904), *Lyrics of Sunshine and Shadow* (1905), and *Howdy Honey, Howdy* (1905), before his death on February 9, 1906. *Joggin' Erlong* was published posthumously that year and includes the last poem he ever wrote, "Sling Long."

Dunbar's standard English poem "We Wear the Mask" (included in *Lyrics of Lowly Life*) is perhaps his most important contribution to the African-American literary tradition. In it Dunbar voices his blueprint for survival in a white-dominated world, later echoed in the work of major 20th-century African-American writers like RALPH ELLISON, JAMES BALDWIN, and JOHN EDGAR WIDEMAN. The first stanza reads,

> "We wear the mask that grins and lies, / It hides our cheeks and shades our eyes,— / This debt we pay to human guile; / With torn and bleeding hearts we smile, / And mouth with myriad subtleties."

Here, Dunbar removes the mask that hides his "tears and sighs" in favor of a proud and smiling façade to reveal the tortured soul within. Like the smile plastered on his false exterior, Dunbar's body of work has been progressively mined for the "myriad subtleties" he alludes to, and the project will continue as the understanding of his multifaceted writing grows. "We Wear the Mask" confronts problems of human identity in universal as well as racial terms. Our very existence, Dunbar seems to say, depends on our ability to present a dignified front in the face of life's injustices.

BIBLIOGRAPHY

Dunbar, Alice Ruth Moore. *The Poet and His Song.* Philadelphia: AME Publishing House, 1914.

Gayle, Addison, Jr. *Oak and Ivy: A Biography of Paul Laurence Dunbar.* Garden City, N.Y.: Anchor/ Doubleday, 1971.

Martin, Jay, ed. *A Singer in the Dawn: Reinterpretations of Paul Laurence Dunbar.* New York: Dodd, Mead, 1975.

Robert M. Dowling

Dunbar-Nelson, Alice   (1875–1935)

Alice Dunbar-Nelson was a prolific writer, yet she left few details regarding her background prior to her emergence as an author. She was born Alice Ruth Moore on July 19, 1875, in New Orleans, and although her visage on her first published volume represents middle-class respectability, she was born in a poor, working-class neighborhood. Alice was the second daughter of a washerwoman, Patsy Wright, a biracial former slave. Monroe Moore, probably a white laborer, is her father. She graduated from Southern University's high school division at 14 and entered Straight University, where she trained to become a teacher and transformed herself into a cultured society belle and a self-proclaimed Creole. By age 17 she had both graduated and submitted manuscripts for publication.

In addition to being a schoolteacher, Alice was an occasional bookkeeper-stenographer and a devoted club woman, a charter member of the Phyllis Wheatley Club, newspaper and current events chairperson of the New Orleans branch of the Woman's Era Club, and the New Orleans correspondent and local sales agent for the *Woman's Era.* She also wrote a weekly women's column for the *Journal of the Lodge.* In 1893 she won third place in two short story contests, and in 1895, at age 20, her first volume, *Violets and Other Tales,* appeared in print.

Violets and Other Tales is a collection of short stories, poems, essays, and prose poems. It was widely and favorably reviewed as a testament of racial uplift and an excellent representation of the black race. In this first work, Dunbar-Nelson introduces the reader to her favorite theme, New Orleans and Creole society, one she would return to in most of her published artistic writing. What she does not explore is the color line, and very few of her characters are racially marked. Dunbar-Nelson was adamant about keeping politics out of art, which many critics suspect may be one reason that she is rarely examined as a writer. Yet this attitude did not prevent her from performing duties as a "race" woman. Her journalism and club work showed her commitment to racial uplift, and although she was able to pass for white, her marriages are also a testament to her race work.

Her picture accompanied her first volume, and after seeing this image, PAUL LAURENCE DUNBAR began to court her. Theirs was a three-year romance—two of which were by correspondence only—that ended with an elopement in 1898. Although their relationship was unstable from the very beginning, with frequent sexual and physical abuse, Paul and Alice saw themselves as the black Elizabeth Barrett and Robert Browning. Her second book, *The Goodness of St. Rocque and Other Tales* (1899), was a companion piece to her husband's *Poems of Cabin and Field.* After her marriage, Dunbar-Nelson acquired her husband's agent and publisher and became forever known as Mrs. Dunbar, despite her publication history prior to their union and her two subsequent marriages after his death. In *The Goodness of St. Rocque,* she more fully develops the themes initiated in her first collection, but she also focuses strictly on the short story. She admitted that this form was most representative of her work, and she only sporadically produced poems after the first volume; how much this shift to prose had to do with her marriage to a famous poet is unknown. *The Goodness of St. Rocque* is usually read as local-color fiction, but again her characters are not racially marked. Instead of race, she examines class conflicts. Gloria T. Hull suggests that Dunbar-Nelson "used class as a psychological metaphor to replace race in her writings" (55). Perhaps it is equally important to see Dunbar-Nelson as instrumental in establishing a short story tradition in African-American literature.

In 1900, she published a "playlet" in *The Smart Set* titled *The Author's Evening at Home*—one of only two attempts at drama. Her marriage to Dunbar lasted until 1902, when she separated from him after a violent argument. Although he tried for four years to reconcile, they were still estranged when he died in 1906 of tuberculosis. Dunbar-Nelson did not attend his funeral but became a devoted widow, keeping his name alive by taking his material on the lecture circuit and reading poems and selections from his novels.

Dunbar-Nelson blossomed after her separation from her well-known husband. She returned to teaching and scholarship, studied at the University of Pennsylvania and Cornell, and published an article on Milton in 1909. She continued to write fiction, mostly short stories but also a couple of unsuccessful novel manuscripts that never found a publisher. While teaching at Howard High School, she secretly married a younger man, Arthur Callis, in 1910. Little is known about this union ex-

cept that it was short-lived. In 1916, she married Robert J. Nelson, a journalist and widower. They met while she was editing *Masterpieces of Negro Eloquence* (1914), a collection of great speeches delivered by African Americans as rhetorical inspiration for the younger generation; from 1920 to 1922 they published the Wilmington *Advocate,* a liberal African-American newspaper.

In 1920, she edited *The Dunbar Speaker and Entertainer,* a collection of her late husband's work. Her marriage to Nelson seemed to propel her into politics more than literary pursuits, although she continued to submit pieces without much success (a one-act play, *Mine Eyes Have Seen,* was published in 1918 in *The Crisis*) and was very productive with journalism pieces. She was the first African-American woman to be named a member of the Republican State Committee. In 1921, she was also a member of the delegation that presented racial concerns to President Harding at the White House, and she headed the Anti-Lynching Crusade in Delaware.

Dunbar-Nelson returned to poetry during the New Negro movement, attempting to adapt her style to the new political age. Although her work was accepted in African-American periodicals such as *The Crisis* and *Ebony and Topaz,* she was still unable to make a literary name for herself. She is included in James Weldon Johnson's anthology, *The Book of American Negro Poetry* (1931). Strangely, her reputation is fixed as a poet during this period, although she produced far more prose.

Although she experimented with several genres—poetry, short story, drama, novel, and nonfiction—Dunbar-Nelson's diary, Hull suggests, may be her most important work. Written between 1921 and 1931 and reprinted as *Give Us Each Day,* Hull states that "it serves to illuminate what it meant to be a black woman/writer in earlier twentieth-century America, while providing the accompanying background and contexts" (97).

Dunbar-Nelson emerged as a writer at a time when the Victorian woman was becoming the "New Woman, Race Woman," who was encouraged by the National Association of Colored Women (NACW), the *Women's Era,* and The Congress of Colored Women of the United States to "Confront the various modes of their oppression" (Carby, 303). This environment placed great stress on the African-American woman, as racial uplift ideology demanded a certain social conservatism and adherence to domesticity, marriage, and motherhood. In her diary, Dunbar-Nelson uses a distinct and original voice not found in her public literary pursuits. She reveals the details of financial stresses of the black middle class, which was based more on education and breeding than money. She also bares her personal doubts and fear regarding her talents as a writer and lack of success with publications. Most illuminating, she exposes an active black lesbian network of which she was a member. The diary ends with the appointment of Nelson to a government position, a welcome relief from financial precariousness.

Alice Dunbar-Nelson died on September 18, 1935, of heart trouble. Only recently has her reputation as a talented writer been rescued from the shadows of her famous first husband.

BIBLIOGRAPHY

Alexander, Eleanor. *Lyrics of Sunshine and Shadow: The Tragic Courtship and Marriage of Paul Laurence Dunbar and Alice Ruth Moore.* New York: New York University Press, 2001.

Carby, Hazel. "On the Threshold of Woman's Era: Lynching, Empire, and Sexuality in Black Feminist Theory." In *"Race," Writing, and Difference,* edited by Henry L. Gates, 301–316. Chicago: University of Chicago Press, 1986.

Hull, Gloria T. *Color, Sex, and Poetry: Three Women Writers of the Harlem Renaissance.* Bloomington: Indiana University Press, 1987.

———, ed. *The Works of Alice Dunbar-Nelson.* 3 vols. New York: Oxford University Press, 1988.

Adenike Marie Davidson

Dust Tracks on a Road
Zora Neale Hurston (1942)

ZORA NEALE HURSTON took the title for her autobiography, *Dust Tracks on a Road,* from a folk saying she often heard as a child from her mother. Blending autobiographical narrative, essay, folk-loric elements, and double-voiced discourse, Hurston addresses a range of topics—her childhood, family, love, friendship, race, research, religion, and many of her own publications. She poetically and uniquely lays out her purpose for writing *Dust Tracks* when she writes, "I have memories within that come out of the material that went to make me. . . . So you will have to know something about the time and place where I came from, in order that you may interpret the incidents and directions of my life" (11). She proceeds, at the beginning of *Dust Tracks,* to provide a vivid background about the place of her birth, the all-black town of Eatonville, Florida, and immediately situates herself in a place and time of historical and cultural significance.

In Chapter 2, "My Folks," Hurston introduces her parents and sets the stage for her own birth in Chapter 3, "I Get Born," where she emerges as a mystical, bright, imaginative, determined child in tune with her environment and surrounded by the people who helped shape her personality. Chapter 4, "The Inside Search," describes the world of Zora's inquisitive young mind, and Chapter 5, "Figure and Fancy," highlights the folk culture of Joe Clarke's storefront porch with its "lying sessions"—which became a central metaphor in her collected work. Chapter 6, "Wandering," presents a heart-wrenching account of the death of Hurston's mother, while Chapter 7, "Jacksonville and After," recounts the constant bickering with her stepmother, which ultimately drives her away from home and into a new world of adventure and success.

The remaining chapters in *Dust Tracks* provide an engaging portrait of Hurston as a woman who is continually in the process of asserting her own authenticity. Chapters 8 through 10, "Backstage and the Railroad," "School Again," and "Research," depict Hurston's endless struggle to survive on her own, to refine herself, and to pursue her creative interests. She writes at the beginning of "Backstage and Railroad," "There is something about poverty that smells like death. Dead leaves dropping off the heart like leaves in a dry season and rotting around the feet" (116). In "Research" Hurston boldly confesses, "In New Orleans, I delved into Hoodoo, or sympathetic magic. . . . I learned the routines for making and breaking marriages; driving off and punishing enemies; influencing the minds of judges and juries in favor of clients; killing by remote control and other things" (191). In Chapter 11, "Books and Things," Hurston discusses the different genres she attempted to publish and the financial challenges she faced as she attempted to bring her work to fruition. After noting that she had written her award-winning novel *Their Eyes Were Watching God* (1937) in Haiti, Hurston wrote, "It was dammed up in me, and I wrote it under internal pressure in seven weeks. I wish that I could write it again. In fact, I regret all of my books" (212).

In "My People! My People!," the chapter that critics often find problematic, Hurston provides her ambiguous pronouncements about race and race consciousness. For example, she writes, "The bookless [blacks] may have difficulty in reading a paragraph in a newspaper, but when they get down to 'playing the dozens' they have no equal in America, and, I'd risk a sizable bet, in the whole world" (217). Nevertheless, as Robert Hemenway points out in his introduction, "Hurston's nonconfrontational strategy was not unusual for the period, but modern readers should know that *Dust Tracks* sacrifices truth to the politics of racial harmony" (xiii). Chapter 13, "Two Women in Particular," reveals Hurston's special friendships with writer Fannie Hurst and singer Ethel Waters. Chapters 14 and 15 share her candid views on love and religion. Hurston concludes *Dust Tracks* with "Looking Things Over," in which she examines political and international affairs.

Written at the urging of Bertram Lippincott, her editor, while she was in California working in the movie industry, *Dust Tracks* was, upon publication, criticized for its unreliability, inconsistencies, fragmentation, unconventionality, and assimilationist perspective. Despite what some critics saw as its shortcomings, however, *Dust Tracks* received the Anisfield-Wolf Book Award from *Saturday Review* for its contribution to race relations. A reviewer for *The New Yorker* called *Dust Tracks* a "warm, witty, imaginative . . . rich and winning book by one of our genuine, grade A folk writers"

(71). In his often unflattering chapter on Hurston in *In a Minor Chord,* DARWIN T. TURNER wrote that *Dust Tracks* illustrates her "artful candor and coy reticence . . . her irrationalities and extravagant boasts which plead for the world to recognize and respect her" (91).

In more recent editions of *Dust Tracks,* several chapters previously altered or omitted have been restored. Along with the original chapters, these new additions offer tremendous insight into the complex portrait of an individual and a writer who rose from poverty to a place of prominence among such leading artists and intellectuals of the HARLEM RENAISSANCE as ALAIN LOCKE, LANGSTON HUGHES, DOROTHY WEST, NELLA LARSEN, CLAUDE MCKAY, GEORGIA DOUGLAS JOHNSON, COUNTEE CULLEN, and W. E. B. DUBOIS.

BIBLIOGRAPHY

Hurston, Zora Neale. *Dust Tracks on a Road.* Philadelphia: J. B. Lippincott, 1942.

Rayson, Ann L. "*Dust Tracks on a Road:* Zora Neale Hurston and the Form of Black Autobiography." *Negro American Literature Forum* 7 (1973): 39–45.

Review of *Dust Tracks on a Road. New Yorker,* 14 November 1942, p. 71.

Turner, Darwin T. *In a Minor Chord: Three Afro-American Writers and Their Search for Identity.* Carbondale: Southern Illinois University Press, 1971.

Loretta G. Woodard

Dutchman   Amiri Baraka (1964)

A brutal, haunting, and allegorical commentary on race in America, *Dutchman* remains AMIRI BARAKA's most frequently performed and most celebrated work. Written when the poet and dramatist was known as LeRoi Jones, the play, which follows one man's symbolic descent into the hellish reality of black life, was first produced off-Broadway in 1964. It later won the Obie award. A film version appeared in 1967. The title alludes to the ghost ship, the *Flying Dutchman,* forever cursed to repeat its voyage. Baraka suggests that African Americans, like the legendary ship, continue to repeat and relive the experiences of the Middle Passage and slavery, even in the modern world and particularly in the urban environment in which a majority of African Americans live. This is also echoed by the recognition of the role of the Dutch in the growth and impact of the slave trade on world history. The play argues that African Americans, like the main character, Clay, remain in a perpetual slavery because of white, European supremacy and domination, represented by Lula, the white female character.

The play also structures its themes around the stereotypes of the African-American male, the white woman, and the history of lynching. Clay's attraction to Lula, who first flirts with him on a subway train and then initiates his communal murder, reenacts a ritualized violence endemic to race relations in America. She is attracted to his "primitive" sexuality and tries to entice him into a dangerous encounter. Her eating an apple highlights her image as a dangerous and mythic temptress. Her sexuality, her power, her race, and her seemingly "liberal" nature control the movement of the subway train and its passengers. She represents the forces in America that dominate the ideology of the nation from its inception to the CIVIL RIGHTS MOVEMENT of the 1960s.

The issues current to the 1960s and to the original production of *Dutchman* are reflected in some of the other racial politics Baraka also explores in the play. For example, Clay at first assumes that Lula might be a "hippie" by her dress. The liberal viewpoint that her image implies to him puts him at ease, and she even gains his trust for a few moments. Yet she and, by extension, her left-wing politics betray him. It is this facet of her image that Baraka indicates might be the most dangerous. The play cautions that such well-meaning whites are really disguised racists, using their rhetoric and their governmental policies to further damage and destroy the soul of the African American. But Clay is implicated in his own demise in this reading of the play by his willingness to assimilate to white attitudes and values and to let his identity be defined by others. In this act, he negates not only himself but also his past, his race, and his community. Instead of being a pawn in such a self-destructive

plan, Baraka suggests, Clay should embrace his rage and its revolutionary possibilities. Lula's attempts to "unmask" Clay, to show what is behind his polite facade, ultimately lead to his downfall but simultaneously, for a moment at least, liberate the man by forcing him to confront his identity. Like any other profound tragic hero, Clay is fated to die, but in the last moments of his life, his enlightenment, his refusal to let his life be determined by white culture and history, finally allows the metaphorical slave to find freedom.

BIBLIOGRAPHY

Ceynowa, Andrzej. "The Dramatic Structure of *Dutchman*." *Black American Literature Forum* 17, no. 1 (1983): 15–18.

Kumar, Nita N. "The Logic of Retribution: Amiri Baraka's *Dutchman*." *African American Review* 37, no. 2–3: (Summer–Fall 2003): 271–279.

Tate, Greg. "How We Talk about Race." *American Theater* 17, no. 5 (2000): 44–46.

Tracie Church Guzzio

Dyson, Michael Eric (1958–)

Preacher, ethicist, professor, cultural critic, and public intellectual, Michael Eric Dyson was born in Detroit, Michigan, in 1958, the son of an auto worker father and a mother who worked in the city school system. He reveals his roots and motivation in *I May Not Get There with You* (2000): "Although I grew up on the street, it was the rich tradition of the black church that saved me and led me to the world of words and ideas. . . . [A]s a teacher, writer, and man of the church, I have traveled around the country speaking to large audiences, many of them young people, and I have witnessed a great need." Although Dyson had become a teen father by the time he graduated high school in 1976, he became a Baptist minister after attending divinity school in Tennessee. He began college at age 21, and, after earning his bachelor's degree, received a fellowship at Princeton University, where he earned his masters and doctoral degrees in religion. He has taught at several major institutions, including the University of North Carolina at Chapel Hill, Columbia

University, and DePaul University. He is currently the Avalon Foundation Professor in the humanities and African-American studies at the University of Pennsylvania.

In 1993, Dyson, a former welfare teen father, published *Reflecting Black: African-American Cultural Criticism,* a collection of essays in which he provides dynamic conversations and insights on a variety of topics, including black masculinity. With the publication of numerous essays and several books between 1993 and 2000, including the notable *Race Rules: Navigating the Color Line* (1996), Dyson emerged as a popular public black intellectual. Part rapper, preacher, and academic theoretician, Dyson brings together the worlds of black American culture, mainstream popular culture, and academic writing. His cultural bilingualism combines the poetics of black vernacular and black music forms such as rap and gospel with scholarly language. With his mastery of the spoken and written word, Dyson explores the contemporary critical relevance of the subjects crucial to him—race, gender, class, sexuality, religion, and popular culture—with a zeal and fluidity that has made him one of the most compelling voices in recent history.

Dyson is a fiery orator with a keen ability to convey sophisticated insights in accessible, creative language, a quality evidenced by his prolific writing in a wide array of academic and mainstream publications and his many lively interrogations of political and cultural events on television. Dyson has appeared on such talk shows as *Oprah, Charlie Rose,* and *Politically Incorrect.* He contributes regularly to such black popular magazines as ESSENCE and *Savoy,* the music magazines *Rolling Stone* and *Vibe,* and newspapers including *The Chicago Sun Times, The New York Times,* and *The Washington Post.* In addition, Dyson is a much sought-after public speaker at universities and on national radio programs.

Dyson's significant intensive work, which he has referred to as "bio-criticism," demonstrates rigorous research and insightful social criticism. In several of his books, Dyson translates the complexity of several key black male figures. With his pro-

vocative *Making Malcolm: The Myth and Meaning of Malcolm X* (1995), Dyson established himself further as an astute, scholarly cultural critic with his exploration of the appeal of MALCOLM X to African-American men of recent generations. In his study on the late rapper TUPAC SHAKUR: *Holler If You Hear Me: Searching for Tupac Shakur,* Dyson explores Shakur's poetic rap genius and the rapper's problematic public "gangsta" persona. His best-selling *I May Not Get There With You: The True Martin Luther King, Jr.* (2000) is a compelling examination of MARTIN LUTHER KING, JR., that illuminates the radicalism of his political and moral vision, yet offers a complex portrait of King as a cultural myth and human being. Dyson is currently at work on a cultural biography about the singer Marvin Gaye. His work thus far has received numerous awards, including the selection as a *New York Times* Notable Book for *Making Malcolm* and the selection of *Holler If You Hear Me* as one of the best books of 2001 by *Publisher's Weekly,* among many others.

BIBLIOGRAPHY

Dobrin, Sidney. "Race and the Public Intellectual: A Conversation with Michael Eric Dyson." In *Race, Rhetoric, and the Postcolonial,* edited by Gary A. Olsen and Lynn Worsham, 81–128. Albany: State University of New York Press, 1999.

Dyson, Michael Eric. *Between God and Gangsta Rap: Bearing Witness to Black Culture.* New York: Oxford University Press, 1996.

———. *Holler If You Hear Me: Searching for Tupac Shakur.* New York: Basic Civitas Books, 2001.

———. *I May Not Get There with You: The True Martin Luther King Jr.* New York: Free Press, 2000.

———. *Making Malcolm: The Myth and Meaning of Malcolm X.* New York: Oxford University Press, 1995.

———. *Race Rules: Navigating the Color Line.* Reading, Mass.: Addison-Wesley, 1996.

———. *Reflecting Black: African American Cultural Criticism.* Minneapolis: Minnesota University Press, 1993.

Reid, Calvin. "Michael Eric Dyson: Of Hers and Hip Hop." *Publishers Weekly,* 21 February 2000. Formerly available online. URL: http://publisher-sweekly.reviewsnews.com.

Spivey, Angela. "Speaking in Tongues." Interview with Michael Eric Dyson. *Endeavors,* December 1995.

Available online URL: http://research.unc.edu/endeavors/end 1295/tongues.htm. Accessed February 14, 2007.

Stephanie Dunn

E

Eady, Cornelius (1954–)

An award-winning poet and playwright, Cornelius Eady was born in Rochester, New York, in 1954. He has taught poetry at several places, including State University of New York at Stony Brook, where he directed the poetry center; City College of New York; Sarah Lawrence College; New York University; The College of William and Mary; and American University. Along with Toi Derricotte, he is the cofounder of Cave Canem, a summer workshop and retreat for African-American poets.

Eady has written poetry for more than two decades, including the volumes of poetry *Kartunes* (1980), *Victim of the Latest Dance Craze* (1986), the Pulitzer Prize nominee *The Gathering of My Name* (1991), *You Don't Miss Your Water* (1995; an adaptation was performed in June 1997), *The Autobiography of a Jukebox* (1997), and *Brutal Imagination* (2001; first performed as a workshop production with Diedre Murray in October 2000).

One of the best poems in *The Gathering of My Name* is "Thelonious Monk." Through language, Eady duplicates the deliberate playfulness of Monk's rhythmic music with monosyllabic lines to create a broken narrative that allows him to pay homage to a great musician. By cleverly infusing the voice of Monk and first-person narrative, Eady permits Monk to explain what he was trying to accomplish in his music, when he writes:

"I know what to do with math. / Listen to this. It's / Arithmetic, a soundtrack. / The motion / Frozen in these lampposts, it / Can be sung."

In Eady's fourth "exquisitely constructed" and emotionally charged volume of poems, *You Don't Miss Your Water,* he meditates on his father's illness and death ("I Know I'm Losing You" and "Fetchin' Bones"); his lies, infidelities, and secrets about a half-sister with the same last name ("Papa Was a Rolling Stone"); and his bitterness toward a darker-skinned son ("A Little Bit of Soap") and the unmarried mother ("Motherless Children"). Related through strong images, references to African-American music, and heartfelt honesty, the poems weave an intense, powerful, personal tale of an artist who attempts to come to terms with specific childhood memories.

The National Book Award finalist, *Brutal Imagination,* is based on the true story of Susan Smith, who, to cover her infidelity, murdered her two sons and invented a black kidnapper-murderer as the perpetrator of her crime. The dominating theme of the two cycles of poems is the subject of the black man in white America. Combining subtlety; charged, harsh images; the sweetly ordinary; and street idiom with elegant inversions, Eady's inventiveness, his deft wit, and skillfully targeted anger capture the vision of the black man in the white imagination in such poems as "How I Got Born," "Who Am I," "My Face," "The Law," and "Composite." At the center of the second cycle, "Running Man," is the black family and its inevitable division and fragmentation by racism and classism, which is the central theme in "When He Left," "Failure," "Liar," and the title poem, "Running Man."

Eady's many honors and awards include an NEA Fellowship in Literature (1985), a John Simon Guggenheim Fellowship in Poetry (1993), a Lila Wallace-*Readers Digest* Traveling Scholarship to Tougaloo College in Mississippi (1992–1993), a Rockefeller Foundation Fellowship to Bellagio, Italy (1993), and The Prairie Schooner Strousse Award (1994). *Running Man,* a music-theater piece cowritten with jazz musician Diedre Murray, was awarded an Obie (1999).

Although Eady's works have not garnered the critical attention they so richly deserve, he is "a phenomenal talent," who has emerged among his contemporaries QUINCY TROUPE, YUSEF KOMUNYAKAA, KALAMU YA SALAAM, E. ETHELBERT MILLER, LUCILLE CLIFTON, and RITA DOVE as one of the most skilled and sensitive African-American writers. Using his full range and voice, Eady's poems reverberate with a BLUES rhythm that captures the heartbeat of black America. His next volume of poetry is *New Selected Poems* (2005).

BIBLIOGRAPHY

Pettis, Joyce, ed. *African American Poets: Lives, Works, and Sources.* Westport, Conn.: Greenwood Press, 2002.

Loretta G. Woodard

Elder, Lonne, III   (1941–1996)

Although Lonne Elder was born in Americus, Georgia, he grew up in Newark, New Jersey, where he was reared by an aunt and uncle after the death of both parents left him an orphan. As a teenager, Elder accompanied his uncle, a numbers runner, while he collected betting slips. After graduating high school, Elder briefly attended New Jersey State Technical College but left before completing his first year. He was subsequently drafted into the army and stationed at Fort Campbell in Kentucky. While in Kentucky, Elder met poet ROBERT HAYDEN, then a professor at Fisk University, who became a very important mentor-educator to him. In 1953, after completing his stint in the army, Elder moved to Harlem where he roomed with dramatist DOUGLAS TURNER WARD, became actively involved with the Harlem Writer's Guild headed by novelist JOHN O. KILLENS, and studied all aspects of the theater. Ward would, in the end, have the greatest influence on Elder, who worked part time as an actor, playing his first role as Bobo in a production of LORRAINE HANSBERRY's *A RAISIN IN THE SUN.*

Although his first play, *A Hysterical Turtle in a Rabbit's Race,* remains unpublished, Elder gained attention for his second play, *Ceremonies in Dark Old Men* (1969), which was first read and staged in 1965 at New York's Wagner College on Staten Island. With funding secured from the successful reception of *Ceremonies,* Elder formally studied drama and filmmaking at Yale University from 1965 to 1967. Elder's third play, *Charade on East Fourth Street,* was performed at Expo '67 in Montreal, Canada. Also during this period, he worked with the Negro Ensemble Company, headed by his former roommate; he acted in Ward's *Day of Absence* before the company produced his *Ceremonies* at the St. Mark's Playhouse in 1969.

A two-act play set in a near-defunct barber shop on Harlem's 126th Street, *Ceremonies in Dark Old Men,* Elder's best-known work, is centered around the fragmentation of the Parker family, father Russell Parker and siblings Theo, Bobby, and Adele, following the death of the mother. Tired of her unsolicited role as the family's sole breadwinner, Adele sets an ultimatum for the unemployed males, demanding they find employment within six days and become responsible contributors to the operation of their home. She informs them that, unlike her mother, she has no intention of working herself to death while they loaf around. As the days pass, Parker unsuccessfully searches for work and spends time playing checkers with his retired friend, William Jenkins, whom he has never beaten in their weekly marathons. Theo, the oldest son, engages in a get-rich-quick bootlegging and numbers running scheme with streetwise Blue Haven, "Prime Minister of the Harlem Decolonization Association, while Bobby, the youngest sibling, further hones his skills and reputation as a professional shoplifter and thief.

By the end of the play, the family is totally fragmented. Although Theo and Parker experience a modicum of success with their Black Lightening bootlegging business, their expected rewards are not readily forthcoming; Theo ends up working harder than ever before, and Parker is deceived by a young lover who spies for their competitor. Adele finds herself in an abusive relationship, and Bobby, whose shoplifting talents are totally exploited by Blue, is shot and killed by security guards. Ironically, on the day Bobby is killed, his father finally beats his best friend at chess.

Although Elder explores the inevitable consequences of a depraved urban life, specifically through Blue, *Ceremonies in Dark Old Men,* unlike the mid-century paradigmatic play *A Raisin in the Sun* or the militant agitprop drama popularized by AMIRI BARAKA and ED BULLINS during the BLACK ARTS MOVEMENT, is not fundamentally about American racism or oppression in the post–civil rights era. Elder turns his camera inward to examine issues that threaten the existence and strength of the black family as a unit. Economics, class, and even gender roles and issues seem to supersede any concern with race Elder might have had. Although they do so through illegitimate means, Theo and his endorsing father pursue, blindly and selfishly, the American Dream. Both Theo and Blue unsympathetically exploit Bobby, who is learning disabled, leading to Bobby's death. Adele's quest for independence from her father and brothers and for a meaningful romantic relationship in her life is achieved, in the end, with a terrible price. Questions of existential responsibility abound. Nonetheless, the viewer is left with the conviction that the friendship that Parker and Jenkins share will, in the end, provide balm in the Parker family's Gilead.

In 1969 *Ceremonies in Dark Old Men* was nominated for the Pulitzer Prize. It won the Outer Circle Award, the Drama Desk Award, the Vernon Rice Award, the Stella Holt Memorial Playwright Award, and the Los Angeles Drama Critic Award.

BIBLIOGRAPHY

Cherry, Wilsonia E. D. "Lonnie Elder III." In *Dictionary of Literary Biography* Vol. 38: *Afro-American Writers after 1955,* edited by Thadious M. Davis and Trudier Harris, 97–103. Detroit: Gale Research Company, 1985.

Wilfred D. Samuels

Ellis, Trey (1962–)

Novelist, screenwriter, and journalist Trey Ellis was born in 1962 in Washington, D.C., the son of a psychiatrist and a psychologist. After attending the acclaimed private school Phillips Academy, in Andover, Massachusetts, Ellis graduated from Stanford University. Ellis has published three novels—*Platitudes* (1988), *Home Repairs* (1992), and *Right Here Right Now* (1999)—and written several screenplays, including the *Inkwell* (1992) and the HBO film *The Tuskegee Airmen,* for which he was nominated for an Emmy.

Ellis's debut novel, *Platitudes,* was published to great acclaim. The novel records the writing collaboration of two black novelists—the failing black experimental novel writer DeWayne Washington and the successful feminist novelist Isshee Ayam—in the coming-of-age story of two black middle-class teenagers, Dorothy and Earle, growing up in New York City in the 1980s. The novelists engage in ideological battles while they alternate writing the tragic comedy of Dorothy and Earle's story. Although the novel ostensibly focuses on illuminating the lives of the black middle class, it is also engaged with debates within the African-American literary tradition between realist and experimental fiction, the latter of which is associated with such writers as ISHMAEL REED, CLARENCE MAJOR, and JOHN EDGAR WIDEMAN.

Ellis explores this subject in greater detail in "The New Black Aesthetic," a manifesto of sorts written for CALLALOO the year after *Platitudes* was published. In the essay, Ellis argues that the hope of an African-American literary tradition lies with writers and artists like himself, who draw on the totality of their lived experience. Unlike the previous generations, who chose to mine and incorporate the traditions of African-American culture, the artists of this new generation draw inspiration from Shakespeare as well as H. Rap Brown.

His next novel, *Home Repairs,* traces the adventures of a young black man as he rises from middle-class geekdom to fame as the host of a home repair show. Written as a series of journal or diary entries, the novel challenges stereotypes of American black men. His third novel, *Right Here Right Now,* is a satire of the new age and self-help movements.

BIBLIOGRAPHY

Favor, Martin J. "'Ain't nothin' like the real thing, baby': Trey Ellis's Search for New Black Voices." *Callaloo* 16, no. 3 (June 1993): 694–705.

Nicolé N. Aljoe

Ellison, Ralph   (1914–1994)

Despite his humble beginnings in Oklahoma, Ralph Waldo Ellison will be remembered as one of the most significant writers of the 20th century. Though he only published one major novel in his lifetime, the epic INVISIBLE MAN, Ellison produced a wealth of critical and autobiographical essays, reviews, and short stories. *Invisible Man* garnered the National Book Award, making Ellison the first African-American author to win the prize, but Ellison could never achieve another artistic tour de force like his first novel.

Born to Lewis and Ida Ellison in Oklahoma City on March 1, 1914, Ellison seemed destined for a life beyond the expectations of most African Americans of the time. His father named the child after his favorite poet, Ralph Waldo Emerson, hoping that his son would somehow live up to the great American writer's legacy. It was a substantially optimistic dream for young Ellison, given his family's past: His paternal grandfather had been a slave, and his mother's parents had been sharecroppers. Nevertheless, the Ellisons were determined to give their sons (Ralph and his younger brother, Herbert) a diverse and significant education. The death of Ellison's father in an accident in 1916 left the family nearly destitute. Ida worked as a domestic, and the family settled above a church. Ida educated the children by any means available, bringing home discarded books and magazines from her various jobs.

Oklahoma was segregated during Ellison's childhood years. The African-American schools in Oklahoma tended to support a strong curriculum for their students, including not only traditional and classical sources for reading but also African-American poetry and music. In elementary school, Ellison was first exposed to a musical education. His love and passion for music would stay with him throughout his lifetime, influencing both his fiction and his criticism. Ida presented him with his first musical instrument, a cornet, when he was eight years old. Unable to afford formal musical training outside of the public schools, Ellison traded work for private lessons. He also spent a great deal of time painting and drawing, and even before his teen years, he wrote stories at his typewriter. Well before he graduated high school, Ellison was on his way to becoming a "Renaissance man." Upon graduation in 1933, Ellison headed to the Tuskegee Institute in Alabama, where he had received a music scholarship. Even though he had grown up in segregated Oklahoma, he was not fully prepared for life as an African-American male in the Deep South. Before he arrived at the school, white detectives who found him hitching a ride on the train beat him up.

Tuskegee offered Ellison the tools to achieve the lifestyle he dreamed of: being a composer and musician like Duke Ellington or Louis Armstrong, both personal heroes of Ellison's. Although he trained in classical music at the institute, he loved jazz and swing. Both styles found their way into his own compositions, but his music professor disliked these contemporary forms. Soon, Ellison began to rebel against the provincial curriculum and attitudes that he found in most of the faculty and the student body of Tuskegee. He found respite in his literature courses and discovered the work of T. S. Eliot. The modernist style and content of Eliot's poetry would later influence Ellison's *Invisible Man*. In 1936, at the end of his junior year, he left Tuskegee for New York City. He never returned to complete his degree.

Instead, Ellison decided to stay in Harlem and study sculpture with the famed HARLEM RENAISSANCE artist, Augusta Savage. While at Tuskegee, Ellison had met the "New Negro" critic ALAIN LOCKE. Ellison ran into Locke at a YMCA in New York City the following year. Locke introduced the young Ellison to one of Harlem's most influential figures, LANGSTON HUGHES. Hughes, in turn, introduced Ellison to Duke Ellington (whom Ellison had briefly met at Tuskegee) and to RICHARD WRIGHT. Both encounters influenced the rest of Ellison's life. Ellington offered Ellison a chance to play with his band but later had to cancel. This missed opportunity to play the trumpet in a New York City big band led Ellison to reconsider his goals, and the developing friendship with Wright gave Ellison access to the Harlem literati. It also brought him to the Harlem headquarters of the American Communist Party.

While never a member of the party, Ellison did write pamphlets for the organization and published pieces in the *New Masses*. He also found work writing for the Federal Writers Project. As part of the work for the project, Ellison was required to collect African-American folklore and slave narratives. At this time many of the ideas and images that would later be found in *Invisible Man* took form. Over the next couple of years, several of Ellison's short stories were published. By 1938 Ellison was married (to Rose Poindexter) and was well on his way to becoming a writer. As the managing editor of *Negro Quarterly* in 1942, Ellison was also able to help nourish the careers of other young writers.

The beginning of World War II forced Ellison to put his writing career on hold. He enlisted with the merchant marine, but, nevertheless, he was able to publish several of his most renowned short stories, including "King of the Bingo Game" and "Flying Home." In "King of the Bingo Game" an unnamed protagonist (a precursor to the nar-rator of *Invisible Man*) fights to aid his ailing wife by playing for money on a wheel of fortune. Having coming north looking for work, the man represents the thousands who were led by their dreams to a false "promised land." Unable to beat the odds, which clearly have been stacked against him, the man loses his mind. Historical and cultural forces are in control of his identity and his future. Similar themes can be found in "Flying Home." Though a young Tuskegee pilot believes he has finally found a way to break free from the forces that confine him to the ground below, he is sent crashing back earthward after his plane hits a bird—a "jim" crow.

By the end of the war, Ellison had gained solid ground as a writer, but his personal life suffered dramatically. In 1945 he divorced Rose. The previous year Langston Hughes had introduced Ellison to Fanny Buford, a writer and JAMES WELDON JOHNSON's former secretary. The two married in 1946, and Fanny worked as Ellison's unofficial editor for the remainder of his life. After the war, Ellison wrote and supported himself and his wife through counseling work in a psychiatric clinic and as a stereo repairman. Ellison also began work on the novel that would become *Invisible Man*.

In 1952 Random House published *Invisible Man*. The novel received accolades from nearly every important literary voice in the country. Some criticized it, however, for its negative portrayal of the American Communist Party. The novel has since gone on to win dozens of awards and a substantial body of criticism. Besides the National Book Award, Ellison received the Rockefeller Foundation Award in 1954 and the Chevalier de l'Ordre des Artes et Lettres and the Medal of Freedom in 1969. By the end of the century, *Invisible Man* was included on many critics' lists as one of the most significant works of American literature.

Ellison began work on his second novel almost immediately after the publication of *Invisible Man*. Some sections of the novel were published as short stories, but a fire destroyed the manuscript in 1967. Ellison tried to reconstruct the novel for the rest of his life. After his death in 1994, the executor of his literary estate, John Callahan, and Fanny worked on bringing the pieces of the work together, eventually published posthumously in 1999 as the novel *Juneteenth.*

Even though a second novel was not published during his lifetime, Ellison produced a staggering amount of writing in the form of short stories, reviews, and criticism. His essays on literature, art, culture, democracy, and jazz remain some of the most lucid and sophisticated commentary on American society. "Richard Wright's Blues" is considered one of the most important critiques of the writer's work, even though Ellison had a falling out with his former friend in the 1940s. Essays like "The Charlie Christian Story" offer insightful discussions on the role of African-American art, especially jazz, in mainstream American culture. Ellison's essays were collected and published in two separate works during his lifetime, *Shadow and Act* in 1964 and *Going to the Territory* in 1986.

Ellison's critical success as an African-American writer waned in the 1960s partly because of the interpretation of his work as "anti-political." Writers and critics of the BLACK ARTS MOVEMENT preferred the overt political messages of Wright to Ellison. LARRY NEAL specifically targeted Ellison during this era, echoing other sentiments about Ellison that suggested he was an Uncle Tom (see SAMBO AND UNCLE TOM) because he refused to take a public stand on the civil rights issues of the 1960s. The critic revised his position on Ellison by 1990, saying that Ellison "countered" the dark portrait of African-American life illustrated by Wright with an image of men and women that was "profoundly human and blessed with a strong, spiritually sustaining culture."

Ellison may have lived a quiet life publicly, but he continued to write until his death. He also spent the last 20 years of his life teaching. After receiving honorary doctorates from schools such as Harvard, the College of William and Mary, Rutgers University, Tuskegee, and the University of Michigan, Ellison settled in at New York University, where he served as the Albert Schweitzer Professor of the Humanities from 1970 to 1979. In 1979, NYU named him professor emeritus. He continued to live in Harlem until his death on April 16, 1994. Besides *Juneteenth,* two other works were published posthumously: *Flying Home and Other Stories* and *Trading Twelves: Selected Letters of Ralph Ellison and Albert Murray.* The two writers had been corresponding since their days at Tuskegee together (though they were several years apart). Their letters reflect a lifetime spent analyzing American culture and literature and the role of the African-American artist.

Ellison's life illuminates the "infinite possibilities" that the narrator of *Invisible Man* believes are hidden in the darkness that has shrouded the history of African Americans—the "invisibility" of their life in the mainstream consciousness. The epic work's landscape is American culture and history. Its examination of democracy and the quest for identity are prototypically American in the tradition of the great writers Ellison loved, such as Mark Twain, Ernest Hemingway, and especially Herman Melville. But Ellison's unnamed protagonist, unlike the heroes of other classic American novels, is left still wondering who he is and where he belongs. Having traveled through the history of African Americans during the course of the narrative—through slavery, the Reconstruction, the Great Migration, BLACK NATIONALISM, the dawn of the civil rights era—the titular character remains invisible still. Carrying the baggage of the past— the SAMBO doll, the leg irons, and so forth—he searches for a means to move forward, changing his identity, like the trickster Rinehart, until the world is enlightened and can finally comprehend the importance of African-American life in the scheme of American history. Ellison's love of music, his love of his culture and its stories, imbues the novel with the same "profoundly human" quality that he found in the BLUES, slave narratives, and African-American folklore. His novel remains a testament to that spirit even though its readers may feel that the narrator is still waiting somewhere—underground—for the future to arrive.

BIBLIOGRAPHY

Baker, Houston. *Blues, Ideology, and Afro-American Literature: A Vernacular Theory.* Chicago: University of Chicago Press, 1984.

Benston, Kimberly W., ed. *Speaking for You: The Vision of Ralph Ellison.* Washington, D.C.: Howard University Press, 1987.

Butler, Robert J., ed. *The Critical Response to Ralph Ellison.* Westport, Conn.: Greenwood Press, 2000.

Callahan, John. "'Riffing' and Paradigm Building: The Anomaly of Tradition and Innovation in *Invisible Man* and *The Structure of Scientific Revolutions.*" *Callaloo* 10, no. 1 (1987): 91–102.

Graham, Mayemma, and Amritjit Singh, eds. *Conversations with Ralph Ellison.* Jackson: University Press of Mississippi, 1995.

Jackson, Lawrence. *Ralph Ellison: Emergence of Genius.* New York: John Wiley and Sons, 2002.

Neal, Larry. "Ellison's Zoot Suit." In *Speaking for You: The Vision of Ralph Ellison,* 105–124. Washington, D.C.: Howard University Press, 1990.

O'Meally, Robert. *The Craft of Ralph Ellison.* Cambridge, Mass.: Harvard University Press, 1980.

Porter, Horace. *Jazz Country: Ralph Ellison in America.* Iowa City: University of Iowa Press, 2001.

Rowell, Charles. "Remembering Ralph Ellison." Special Edition of *Callaloo* 18, no. 2 (1995): 249–320.

Tracie Church Guzzio

Equiano, Olaudah (Gustavus Vassa)
(c. 1745–1797)

Although his life spanned the second half of the 18th century and for most of his adult life he lived and worked in England, Olaudah Equiano made a profound contribution to modern African-American literature. His legacy remains significant—and controversial—into the 21st century. His major literary achievement was *The Interesting Narrative of the Life of Olaudah Equiano, or, Gustavus Vassa, the African.* Published in 1789, this work, an important contribution to the campaign to abolish the British slave trade, was in part autobiography, voyage narrative, conversion narrative, and political treatise. In combining these, Equiano perfected the autobiographical form that was later to be known as the slave narrative.

In *Narrative of the Life,* Equiano tells us that he was born in 1745 in Essaka in the province of Eboe, identified by modern scholars as the thospeaking region of modern Nigeria. Equiano gives us a detailed account of life in Essaka, his traditional village, before telling how he and his sister

were abducted by slave traders, taken on the long journey to the coast, and put aboard a slave ship bound for the Americas. The famous passages that follow describe the horrors of the Middle Passage, in which "the shrieks of the women, and the groans of the dying, rendered the whole a scene of horror almost inconceivable." Having crossed the Atlantic, Equiano was taken first to Barbados and then to Virginia. There he was sold to Michael Pascal, a lieutenant in the Royal Navy.

Equiano's description of his African childhood, his abduction, and his voyage in the Middle Passage is a rare and celebrated firsthand narrative of life in an African village prior to European colonization, as well as an eyewitness account of the horrors of the slave trade. In Equiano's time, these vivid and detailed episodes provided direct evidence that could be used in the abolition campaign. For readers in later generations, particularly for descendents of those who suffered slavery, Equiano's accounts offer a personal point of connection between Africa and the New World. Recent research by Vincent Carretta, however, has suggested that Equiano was not born in Africa but in South Carolina, then a British colony in North America. According to Carretta, Equiano may never have visited Africa, and the early parts of his *Narrative of the Life* may well be rhetorical exercises in oral history rather than his true personal history. Carretta's evidence, a baptismal record and a muster roll, strongly suggests that, before the publication of the *Narrative of the Life* in 1789, Equiano was in the habit of telling employers and officials that he was born in South Carolina. Nevertheless, the evidence, although intriguing, is not yet overwhelming, and many readers continue to accept Equiano's account of his African nativity as told in the *Narrative of the Life.* It seems likely that the truth about Equiano's birth and early life will never be known for certain.

What is certain are Equiano's later achievements, which are both outlined in detail in the *Narrative of the Life* and supported by a wealth of external evidence. As Pascal's slave, the young Equiano spent about six years on a ship in the Royal Navy. During this time he saw action in the war with France, but more important, the relative freedoms of shipboard life meant that he was able to learn to read and write. Swindled out of his wages and prize money in 1763, Equiano was suddenly sold to Robert King, a Quaker merchant in Montserrat. His literacy and his maritime training protected him from the harshest forms of servitude, however, and by petty trading and hard saving, Equiano raised enough cash to buy his own freedom, which he did on July 11, 1766: "the happiest day I had ever experienced."

As a free man, Equiano spent 20 years involved in a variety of mostly maritime occupations, from ship's steward to hairdresser. He was extremely well traveled in both Europe and the New World, and he even joined an expedition toward the North Pole in 1773. In 1774, he underwent a conversion to Methodism and, shortly after, was briefly involved in a project to settle a colony on the Mosquito Coast (modem Nicaragua). Equiano's role in buying slaves for this colony and the eagerness with which he sought to convert the Native Americans to his newfound faith have been seen as problematic by modem commentators. In the 1770s, however, early abolitionists mostly agreed that abolition should go hand in hand with evangelization. Equiano thus acted entirely within the expectations of his age.

In the 1780s an organized abolition campaign was instituted in London, and Equiano quickly became involved. As early as 1774, he had been in touch with the slavery campaigner Granville Sharp. In 1785, Equiano began to write letters to campaigners and prominent figures in British political life. The following year, he was appointed as a Commissary of Provisions and Stores to the project, supported by the British government, to resettle poor black Londoners in Sierra Leone in West Africa. Equiano thus became the first black civil servant in British history. However, he soon realized that the scheme was heading for disaster because of corruption and incompetence. When he tried to remedy the situation, he was fired. After this, he devoted all his attention to the abolition movement, and in May 1789 the *Narrative of the Life* was published to much critical acclaim. Equiano vigorously promoted the book on an exhausting lecture tour around the British Isles.

In 1791, the first U.S. edition was published, the same year that Equiano married Susanna Cullen in Cambridgeshire. Equiano spent the last six years of his life promoting his book and the cause of abolition. He died on March 31, 1797, a full 10 years before the British and American slave trades were abolished, 40 years before slavery was ended in British colonies, and 68 years before the abolition of slavery in the United States. Although Equiano did not live to see these events, his *Narrative of the Life* played an important part in bringing them about.

BIBLIOGRAPHY

Carretta, Vincent. *Equiano, the African: Biography of a Self-Made Man.* Athens: University of Georgia Press, 2005.

———. "Olaudah Equiano or Gustavus Vassa? New Light on an Eighteenth-Century Question of Identity." *Slavery and Abolition* 20, no. 3 (December 1999): 96–105.

Costanzo, Angelo. *Surprizing Narrative: Olaudah Equiano and the Beginnings of Black Autobiography.* New York: Greenwood Press, 1987.

Equiano, Olaudah. *The Interesting Narrative and Other Writings.* Edited by Vincent Carretta, 2nd ed. New York and London: Penguin, 2003.

Samuels, Wilfred. "Disguised Voice in *The Interesting Narrative of Olaudah Equiano.*" *Black American Literature Forum* 19 (1985): 64–69.

Sandiford, Keith. *Measuring the Moment: Strategies of Protest in Eighteenth-Century Afro-English Writing.* London: Associated University Presses, 1988.

Walvin, James. *An African's Life: The Life and Times of Olaudah Equiano, 1745–1797.* Washington: Cassell, 1998.

Brycchan Carey

Essence

The maiden issue of *Essence* magazine appeared in May 1970, promising to "delight and to celebrate the beauty, pride, strength, and uniqueness of all Black women." For the next 30 years, *Essence* was a leading incubator of journalistic and literary writers as well as a major showcase for the published work of new and established authors, particularly black women.

As of 2004, *Essence*'s seven editors in chief have been black women: Ruth Ross (who came up with the name), Daryl Alexander, Monique Greenwood, Diane Weathers, Ida Lewis, Marcia Gillespie, and Susan Taylor. The last three are probably the most recognized in the industry and by the readership. Ida Lewis, a pioneer black woman reporter with *The Washington Post, Meet the Press,* and *L'Express* in Paris, founded, published, and edited *Encore American and Worldwide News.* Marcia Gillespie's 10-year leadership put the magazine on the map, building circulation up to near a half million, advocating for social justice, and articulating a feminist vision rooted in black women's experience. She later became editor in chief of *Ms.*

Susan Taylor was the iconic *Essence* woman, having an uncanny knack for connecting across gender and class lines. Most significantly, she specifically fostered black writers and writing. She organized writers' conferences, facilitated staff editors' execution of book contracts, and saw that *Essence* regularly featured high-caliber fiction, nonfiction, and poetry by and about black people.

The list of writers who either developed their craft with *Essence* or were recognized and promoted in its pages includes literary icons TONI MORRISON, ALICE WALKER, TONI CADE BAMBARA, NIKKI GIOVANNI, JOHN EDGAR WIDEMAN, JUNE JORDAN, ALEXIS DEVEAUX, and EDWIDGE DANTICAT. Other authors who published in *Essence* as they built noteworthy careers include BEBE MOORE CAMPBELL, JILL NELSON, Benildy Little, Harriette Cole, Jessica Harris, Pulitzer Prize winners Isabel Wilkerson and EDWARD P. JONES, NELSON GEORGE, TERRY MCMILLAN, Doris Jean Austin, ARTHUR FLOWERS, Valerie Wilson Wesley, Rosemarie Robotham, and many more.

"*Essence* was founded by . . . Clarence O. Smith, Jonathan Blount, Cecil Hollingsworth and myself, four brash young men with no experience in magazine publishing," wrote *Essence* publisher and chief executive officer Edward Lewis ("In Celebration"). Smith and Lewis stayed the course, guiding Essence Communications for 30 years through diversification into television, book publishing, branded merchandising, and *Latina,* a magazine for Hispanic women. In October 2000, they made a deal creating Essence Communications Partners, allowing Time Warner to acquire 49 percent of the company. This signaled the end of the founding era, when *Essence*'s sensibility sprang from the pre-1960s African-American ethos manifested in the BLACK ARTS MOVEMENT and the entrepreneurship that created *Essence.*

BIBLIOGRAPHY

Lewis, Edward. "In Celebration of our Twentieth Anniversary." *Essence* 21, no. 1 (May 1990): 20–21.

Judy Dothard Simmons

Evans, Mari   (1923–)

Poet, dramatist, short fiction writer, children's writer, editor, essayist, and lecturer Mari Evans was born in Toledo, Ohio, on July 16, 1923. She attended the public schools of Toledo and the University of Toledo, where she studied fashion design. Instead of pursuing a career in fashion design, however, Evans began her professional career as a writer and editor, working for a chain manufacturing company for three years. This provided her with a range of creative freedom and discipline. She worked as producer, director, and writer for the television program "The Black Experience" for WTTV, Channel 4, in Indianapolis (1968–73). Evans has held teaching positions at Purdue University (1969–70); Indiana University at Bloomington (1970–78); Purdue University, West Lafayette (1978–80); Cornell University (1981–85); and State University of New York, Albany (1985–86), and she was a writer-in-residence at Spelman College (1989–90). In addition to teaching, Evans has lectured extensively throughout the country and served as a consultant for such agencies as the National Endowment for the Arts (1969–70) and the Indiana State Arts Commission (1976–77).

Inspired by her father and influenced by LANGSTON HUGHES, Evans is noted as a "powerful poet" whose poetry has "a strong social commitment and a marked clarity of poetic vision" (Peppers, 117). Like that of her contemporaries in the

BLACK ARTS MOVEMENT, AMIRI BARAKA, SONIA SANCHEZ, NIKKI GIOVANNI, HAKI MADHUBUTI, ASKIA M. TOURÉ, and ETHERIDGE KNIGHT, Evans's poetry is grounded in the social and political realities of the black community. Highly experimental, it embraces historical, political, and romantic love themes. Her volumes include *Where Is All the Music?* (1968), with its memorable "Black jam for dr Negro"; *I Am a Black Woman* (1970), which includes the popular "Who Can Be Born Black"; *Whisper* (1979); her most innovative work, *Nightstar: 1973–1978* (1981); and *A Dark and Splendid Mass* (1992). The poems in *A Dark and Splendid Mass* represent a new development in Evans's poetic style; they are short romantic praises of the uncommon courage of ordinary black people as victim-survivors or heroes.

In addition to poetry, Evans has written in other genres. Her fiction for children, *J. D.* (1973), *I Look at Me!* (1974), *Rap Stories* (1974), *Singing Black* (1976), and *Jim Flying High* (1979), represents a wholesome focus on the black community. Her dramas are *River of My Song* (first produced in 1977), *Portrait of a Man* and *Boochie,* a one-woman performance (both 1979); the musical *Eyes,* adapted from ZORA NEALE HURSTON'S *THEIR EYES WERE WATCHING GODS* (first produced 1979); and *New World,* a children's musical (1984).

In 1984, Evans edited and contributed to *Black Women Writers (1950–1980): A Critical Evaluation,* a landmark work centering on 15 contemporary black writers, including MAYA ANGELOU, GWENDOLYN BROOKS, AUDRE LORDE, ALICE CHILDRESS, LUCILLE CLIFTON, TONI MORRISON, PAULE MARSHALL, SONIA SANCHEZ, ALICE WALKER, and MARGARET WALKER. In more than 40 essays, each author provides autobiographical commentary on her own literary development and visions of the future, while a host of 20th-century critics, such as BARBARA CHRISTIAN, ADDISON GAYLE, JR., Eugenia Collier, DARWIN T. TURNER, and Jerry Ward, Jr., offer their critical perspectives.

Evans has coauthored works and made numerous contributions to leading anthologies published in the 1970s, such as *Dark Symphony: Negro Literature in America, Black Voices: An Anthology of Afro-American Literature, 3000 Years of Black Poetry: An Anthology, Afro-American Writing: An Anthology of Prose and Poetry, New Black Voices: An Anthology of Contemporary Afro-American Literature,* and *Black Out Loud: An Anthology of Modern Poems by Black Americans.*

Evans has received numerous awards: the John Hay Whitney Fellowship (1965–66), a Woodrow Wilson Foundation grant (1968), the Indiana University Writers' Conference Award, and the Black Academy of Arts and Letters first annual poetry award (both 1970) for *I Am a Black Woman,* as well as a MacDowell fellowship (1975), the Builders Award from the Third World Press in Chicago (1977), an Indiana Committee for the Humanities grant (1977), the Black Liberation Award from the Kuumba Theatre Workshop in Chicago (1978), an honorary doctorate of humane letters degree from Marian College (1979), a Copeland fellowship at Amherst College (1980), the Black Arts Celebration Poetry Award, Chicago (1981), the National Endowment for the Arts Creative Writing Award (1981), and the Yaddo Writers Colony fellowship (1984).

Noted as an award-winning writer with an authentic voice for the black community, Evans, who has produced creative works of unquestionable artistic excellence, has ensured herself a lasting place among her contemporaries who, during the 20th century, made innumerable contributions to African-American life and culture. According to Evans, "I write reaching for . . . what will nod Black heads over common denominators. The stones thrown that say how it has been/is/must be, for us. . . . I write according to the title of poet Margaret Walker's classic: 'for my people' . . . [and my] writing is pulsed by my understanding of contemporary realities" (Evans, 167–169).

BIBLIOGRAPHY

Dorsey, David. "The Art of Mari Evans." In *Black Women Writers 1950–1980: A Critical Evaluation,* edited by Mari Evans, 170–189. New York: Doubleday, 1983.

Edwards, Solomon. "Affirmation in the Works of Mari Evans." In *Black Women Writers 1950–1980: A Critical Evaluation,* edited by Mari Evans, 190–200. New York: Doubleday, 1983.

Evans, Mari. "My Father's Passage." In *Black Women Writers 1950–1980: A Critical Evaluation,* edited by Mari Evans, 165–169. New York: Doubleday, 1983.

Peppers, Wallace R. "Mari Evans." In *Dictionary of Literary Biography.* Vol. 41: *Afro-American Poets since 1955,* edited by Trudier Harris and Thadious M. Davis, 117–123. Detroit: Gale, 1985.

Loretta G. Woodard

Everett, Percival (1956–)

Born in Ft. Gordon, Georgia, Percival Everett grew up in Columbia, South Carolina, and was educated at the University of Miami, where he received a bachelor's degree in 1977, and Brown University, where he earned a master's degree in 1982. Everett has held a variety of jobs, ranging from jazz musician to ranch worker; since 1985, he has held a professorship in creative writing at various universities, including the University of Kentucky, the University of Notre Dame, and the University of California–Riverside. Currently, he directs the creative writing program at the University of Southern California. He and his wife divide their time between a ranch east of Los Angeles and a home on Vancouver Island.

A prolific writer of fiction, Everett has published 15 novels and short story collections. *Suder* (1983), his first novel, concerns the central character's attempts to make sense of a lifetime of absurdity. Traveling with his Charlie Parker record, a portable record player, a saxophone, an elephant named Renoir, an overweight Chinese homosexual, and a nine-year-old white girl named Jincy Jesse Jackson, failing baseball player Craig Suder wanders around the northwest trying to convince himself that he is not crazy. Suder tries to rid himself of the memory of his "crazy" mother, whose chief goal was to run around the city of Fayetteville, North Carolina, a distance of 23 miles, if for no other reason than to prove that she could. Suder later realizes that his mother possessed strength of character, and he resolves to live by conquering his own fear of flying.

Cutting Lisa (1986) and *Zulus* (1989) continue Everett's focus on bizarre and often improbable situations and outcomes. *Cutting Lisa* concerns the performing of an abortion to preserve a bloodline, while *Zulus* focuses on an overweight woman who is the last one on earth capable of childbearing. She becomes a highly prized commodity between warring factions because of her fertility.

In *For Her Dark Skin* (1990), Everett goes in another direction, retelling the myth of Jason and Medea with Medea cast as a black woman, and in *God's Country* (1994) he makes another foray into the western United States. Here he explores the dynamics between a racist white man, Curt Marder, who must, by necessity, rely on the services of Bubba, a black trapper and guide, to find his wife, who has been kidnapped by whites masquerading as Indians. In this novel, Everett adds to the volatility of his examination of race in America.

Two short story collections, *The Weather and the Women Treat Me Fair* (1989) and *Big Picture* (1996), present a number of complex characters who find themselves in bizarre and sometimes surreal circumstances, yet the best of the stories affirm that Everett is a competent craftsman of the short story. Later novels, including *Watershed* (1996), *Frenzy* (1997), and *Glyph* extend Everett's fascination with eclectic ideas, ranging from the modern-day dynamics between Native Americans and the U.S. government to the black experience in the West to the tenuous position of the genius in society. In *Frenzy,* Everett returns to his fascination with Greek mythology.

In *Erasure* (2001), Everett wades into the cauldron of gender and publishing politics, especially as they affect the careers of black male writers of serious literature. The main character, Thelonious "Monk" Ellison, frustrated over years of being ignored by major publishers for his serious reworkings of Greek myths, writes *My Pafology,* a novel of the most vapid sort, the kind preferred by an unimaginative reading public and a greedy press. It is immediately hailed as an important work. The fictional presentation is no doubt partly driven by Everett's own standing in the publishing world—the author of a number of works, none of which has been celebrated to the extent of other works of arguably lesser quality.

Everett is perhaps best described as a postmodern writer. Indeed, he employs many of the themes and approaches commonly associated with the postmodernists, especially the search for identity, the effects of alienation, and the frequent, bizarre mixtures of violence and comedy. And in *Erasure,* he joins fellow iconoclast ISHMAEL REED in taking the hard line against feminist politics in the publishing industry. While stylistically he is not a miniaturist, Everett tends to write concise, compact prose narratives.

Although Everett is a prolific writer, the critical appreciation of his work has been scant at best. There are the usual brief publication notices, reviews, and several interviews, but relatively few sustained inquiries have been made into his work. Yet Everett is still making his reputation, and there is little question that he is a significant writer of the contemporary period, occupying a transitional place between the older cadre of black postmodern writers, like RALPH ELLISON and CHARLES WRIGHT, and a younger generation of black comic writers who are now extending those boundaries.

Warren J. Carson

"Everybody's Protest Novel"
James Baldwin (1949)

The autobiographical information in JAMES BALDWIN's 1955 collection of essays, *Notes of a Native Son,* makes clear that *Uncle Tom's Cabin* (1852), by Harriet Beecher Stowe, is a text he read often, if not eagerly, while growing up. Stowe's novel became a fundamental part of his childhood memories and the resources he drew upon as a writer. However, in 1949, Baldwin's essay, "Everybody's Protest Novel," appeared in *Zero,* a European journal, and later that same year in *Partisan Review.* In this essay Baldwin revisits and candidly critiques Stowe's book with a resounding finality. Baldwin, the mature reader and thinker, was willing to take on this American classic text and critique it for what he now clearly saw as its greatest flaw, dishonesty. Baldwin concludes that *Uncle Tom's Cabin* denies, or at a minimum ignores, human complexity. However noble Stowe's abolitionist intentions

might have been, Baldwin argues, she reduced her characters to one-dimensional types, and thus she failed as "a novelist," becoming instead "an impassioned pamphleteer" (14). *Uncle Tom's Cabin* is, in the end, no more than protest fiction, which, in Baldwin's mind, is not art but propaganda.

In "Everybody's Protest Novel" Baldwin moves beyond critiquing *Uncle Tom's Cabin* as protest fiction to condemning outright RICHARD WRIGHT, the author of *NATIVE SON* (1940), for committing the same crime as Stowe. Like Stowe, Baldwin contends, Wright was merely a spokesperson for a political cause. Wright reduced Bigger Thomas, the protagonist of *Native Son,* to the same stereotyped flatness Stowe used in creating Uncle Tom (see SAMBO AND UNCLE TOM) and placed him in 20th-century Chicago. By placing Wright and Stowe in the same arena as writers, and by concluding that both *Uncle Tom's Cabin* and *Native Son* are flawed and failed novels, Baldwin provoked then, and continues to elicit now, much controversy and discussion through "Everybody's Protest Novel."

Whether it is a reasonable description or an overstatement, many biographical critics paint a picture of Wright as a mentor to the young Baldwin. Baldwin's condemnation, therefore, is often viewed as a betrayal of Wright personally and of the larger African-American community, since *Native Son* was such a landmark publication. Baldwin's now-classic essay is construed as "an oblique attack on Richard Wright—the first of several father-figures Baldwin was to symbolically slay" (Allen, 34). Regardless of how close the two male writers really were, "Everybody's Protest Novel" brought to an abrupt end any type of tutor or mentor relationship between Wright and Baldwin.

Despite the strained relationship between the two writers and the attention it has received over the years, the essence of Baldwin's essay must not be overlooked. The focus on "political and aesthetic maturity" (1025) that Geraldine Murphy alludes to in her reading of Baldwin is central to "Everybody's Protest Novel." According to Murphy, Baldwin is ready to grapple with the hegemony of white-dominated society when he unveils its ability "to convince those people to whom it has given inferior status of the reality" of the social hierarchy

(Baldwin, 20). Such an unveiling, such truthfulness is to Baldwin the real calling of the artist, for rather than composing untruthful political propaganda, "[i]t is the power of revelation which is the business of the novelist" (15). In 1949 Baldwin was an unabashed disciple of Henry James. It is not surprising, then, that in "Everybody's Protest Novel" he proffers artistry as of equal importance to political engagement—neither one supplants the other.

BIBLIOGRAPHY

Allen, Brooke. "The better [sic] James Baldwin." *The New Criterion* 16, no. 8 (1998): 29–36.

Baldwin, James. "Everybody's Protest Novel." In *Notes of a Native Son,* 13–23. Boston: Beacon, 1955.

Balfour, Lawrie. "Finding the Words: Baldwin, Race Consciousness, and Democratic Theory." In *James Baldwin Now,* edited by Dwight A. McBride, 79–99. New York: New York University Press, 1999.

Murphy, Geraldine. "Subversive Anti-Stalinism: Race and Sexuality in the Early Essays of James Baldwin." *ELH* 63, no. 4 (1996): 1021–1046.

Wright, Michelle M. "'Alas, Poor Richard!': Transatlantic Baldwin, the Politics of Forgetting, and the Project of Modernity." In *James Baldwin Now,* edited by Dwight A. McBride, 208–232. New York: New York University Press, 1999.

Timothy K. Nixon

Fabio, Sarah Webster (1928–1979)

Well known as a gifted teacher throughout northern California and specifically for her pioneering efforts to establish Black Studies Programs at Merritt Junior College, where her students included many founders of the Black Panther Party, including Huey P. Newton, and the University of California at Berkeley, winning her the title of "the Mother of the Black Studies," Sarah Webster Fabio was born January 20, 1928, in Nashville, Tennessee. A graduate of Fisk University, where she earned a B.A. degree in English and studied poetry with ARNA BONTEMPS, and San Francisco State University, where she earned an M.A. degree in language arts and creative writing, Webster Fabio was participating in the Iowa Writers Workshop and pursuing a doctorate degree in American studies and African-American studies at the University of Iowa, working with the distinguished scholar DARWIN T. TURNER, at the time of her death. Webster Fabio also taught African-American literature at Oakland College and Oberlin College. In 1966, she participated in the First World Festival of Negro Art in Dakar, Senegal, and in 1968 she participated in the Third Annual Writers Conference at her alma mater, Fisk University.

As a poet, Webster Fabio placed herself firmly in the camp of the BLACK ARTS MOVEMENT, declaring, like its architects, who were more often than not years her junior, that black was indeed beautiful. This is clearly the theme of "Evil Is No Black Thing," perhaps her best-known poem, in which the speaker declares,

> Evil is no black thing: black
> may be the undertaker's hearse
> and so many of the civil trappings
> of death, but not its essence:
> the ridersless horse, the armbands/ and
> veils of mourning, the grave shine
> darkly; but these are the rituals
> of the living.

Webster Fabio, who often read and performed with "Don't Fight the Feeling," a live jazz band, or to the music of John Coltrane or Equinox, wrapped in African traditional garb from head to toe, was fiercely committed to black culture, particularly its language, music, and traditional religion, mysticism, and magic—hoodoo or juju, as she called it. Through often intensely autobiographical poems, she sought to bear witness to the power of each. For example, invoking African traditional religious beliefs and mythology associated with New Orleans Voodoo queen Marie Laveaux, one of Webster Fabio's speakers declares:

> Jezuss
> you've forgotten

I'm of the order
of that bad New Orleans
sister, Marie.
And, I've been known
to have her power.

The speaker unabashedly signifies on conventional phallocentric Christian beliefs, while simultaneously empowering herself as high priestess-juju queen.

Equally important, black music—BLUES, jazz, rap—saturates Webster Fabio's work, forming its backdrop and heartbeat. In her poems she sets out not merely to invoke or intertextualize with song lyrics ("walk on by"), titles, and specific musicians but also to preserve their significance, meaning, sound, and language. She argues, through the vernacular speakers in many of her poems, that "the Black mother tongue is Soul language, / telling it like it is / socking it to you, letting it all hang out." Webster Fabio's self-identified role and task as poet is most evident in *Rainbow Signs* (1973), a seven-volume collection that she published and distributed. The collection is distinguished by Webster Fabio's symbolic use of a different color for each volume. Together she used the book colors ("turning from blue, mauve, to pink"), volume titles (*Soul Is: Soul Aint, Boss Soul, Black Back: Back Black, Juju / Alchemy of the Blues, My Own thing, Jujus & Jubilees* and *Together / to the Tune of Coltrane's Equinox*); and, above all, the poems themselves not only to celebrate all aspects of black culture but also to provide what she, as poet, saw as her task and legacy: the preservation of black culture through words, music, mythology, and language. Webster Fabio also produced albums that bore the titles of some of her books, for example, *Boss Soul,* on which she experiments with blues and rap forms.

Love as theme, particularly of culture and extended and immediate family, is sensitively written into all of Webster Fabio's poems. In the introduction to "My Own Thing," the volume with the red cover, perhaps to signify passion and love, Webster Fabio writes, "Love gives motion, if not direction; knowledge if not meaning. It is a move back toward the soul of self and forward toward quest for a future; a move toward an enlarged sphere of influence and, at the same time, a move toward the achievements of self control. This volume is about love—the reverie; memory; life force." The poems in this volume are candidly autobiographical, sensitive, moving, even painful. In it she speaks as former wife, mother, friend, and sister. For example, in "Estrangement," dedicated to her sisters, the poet writes,

At times,
you and I both
are strangers
when we meet
and not ourselves
at all.

But she resolves:

So,
we must remember
to pause in our
presences long enough
to let false shadows
fade and fall;
Then,
we must reach out
and touch whoever
we are, nakedly.

Comparing herself to "a bit of / driftwood— / sanded, beaten, / reshaped," Webster Fabio declares in "My Own Thing,"

but,
like it,
I have now
become
my own thing . . .
with a balanced,
graceful line—
hard, rough,
still radiating life—
I have, too
retained
the spark
the grain.

Webster Fabio also published several other collections of poetry, *Saga of a Black Man* (1968), *A Mirror: A Soul* (1969), *Black Is a Panther Caged* (1972), and *Black Talk: Soul, Shield, and Sword* (1973). She edited *Double Dozen: An Anthology of Poets from Sterling Brown to Kali* (1966). In 1972, she made two sound recordings for Folkways Records: "Boss Soul" and "Soul Ain't, Soul Is." Her poems often appeared in *Negro Digest/Black World, Journal of Black Arts Renaissance,* and *Phase II;* they were included in Addison Gayle's *Black Aesthetics* and Stephen Henderson's *Understanding the New Black Poetry.* Married to dentist Cyril L. Fabio, whom she later divorced, Webster Fabio was the mother of six children: Cheryl, Ronnie, Renee, Angela, Leslie, and Thomas.

BIBLIOGRAPHY

Henderson, Stephen, ed. *Understanding the New Black Poetry: Black Speech and Black Music as Poetic References.* New York: William Morrow and Company, 1973.

Wilfred D. Samuels

Fair, Ronald   (1932–   )

Novelist Ronald L. Fair was born in Chicago on October 27, 1932, to Herbert and Beulah Fair, whom Bernard Bell describes as transplanted Mississippi plantation "workers who were proud to be black" (301). After graduating from Chicago's public school system, Fair studied business at the Stenotype School of Chicago and enlisted in the U.S. Navy for three years, serving in the hospital corps. Returning to civilian life, Fair worked as a court reporter from 1955 to 1956, before embarking on a brief teaching career at Chicago's Columbia College; Northwestern University, where he was a visiting teacher; and Wesleyan University, where he was Visiting Professor of English from 1970 to 1971. He then moved to Europe, where he has lived for more than three decades.

Fair is known primarily as the author of two novels and three novellas: *Many Thousand Gone, An American Fable* (1965), *Hog Butcher* (1966), which was reprinted as *Cornbread, Earl and Me*

(1970), and *We Can't Breathe* (1972). In his fable *Many Thousands Gone,* whose title comes from black folklore, Fair revisits slavery and the slave narrative genre through the experiences of his major characters, Granny Jacobs and her great-grandson Jesse, who live in Jacobsville, Mississippi, where slavery is still a way of life. Jesse escapes with Granny Jacob's assistance and becomes a popular author. Granny Jacobs, with the assistance of Preacher Harris, the local black preacher, writes to the president, exposing the situation in Jacob County. In the end, however, the central theme, from slavery to freedom, encompasses the active role of the entire community in its quest for wholeness and meaning in the face of oppression and repression. Fair celebrates in the process the success and rise of militancy among young blacks, through which regeneration is possible.

Set in Chicago's South Side, *Hog Butcher* (1966) is written, to some degree, within the tradition of RICHARD WRIGHT's naturalistic novel *NATIVE SON.* Much like Bigger Thomas and his friends, who discuss the circumscription they know as urban dwellers, Wilford Robinson and his best friend Earl are aware that their life in Chicago, where there are no playgrounds, is not much better than the one their parents had left behind in Mississippi, where "[t]hem white bastards soon kill you as look at you" (8). The two friends witness the accidental shooting of their friend and hero, Nathaniel Hamilton (Cornbread), an 18-year-old high school basketball star, by two policemen, including a black officer. "Brave bastards come in here shootin' kids. . . . Yeah the bastards think they gods (25–26), responds the frustrated community before a small riot erupts and the policemen are beaten. During the inquest, in which Wilford and Earl are key witnesses, Wilford is pressured to change his testimony.

Fair explores resonant themes of the black community's search for meaning and wholeness in the suffocating urban environment in *World of Nothing* (1970), which contains two novellas, *Jerome* and *World of Nothing.* His somewhat autobiographical *We Can't Breathe* (1971) is the story of Ernie Johnson, who grows up in Chicago during the Great Depression and becomes a gang leader to survive, also transcending the impending limitation he faced to become a writer.

While self-exiled in Europe like JAMES BALDWIN and ALFRED B. CELESTINE, Fair also published two collections of poems, *Excerpts* (London, 1975) and *Rufus* (Germany, 1977). Fair also received a grant from the National Endowment for the Arts (1974) and a Guggenheim Fellowship (1975). Although his work has received mixed reviews overall, he received an award for *World of Nothing* from the National Endowment of Letters (1971) and a Best Book Award from the American Library Association for *We Can't Breathe* (1972).

BIBLIOGRAPHY

Baxter Miller, R. "Ronald L. Fair." In *Dictionary of Literary Biography,* vol. 33: *Afro-American Fiction Writers after 1955,* edited by Thadious Davis and Trudier Harris, 65–76. Detroit: Gale, 1984.

Bell, Bernard W. *The Afro-American Novel and Its Tradition.* Amherst: University of Massachusetts Press, 1987.

Fair, Ronald. *Hog Butcher.* New York: Bantam Books, 1966.

Rich Roberts

Fauset, Jessie Redmon   (1882–1961)

Jessie Redmon Fauset was born on April 27, 1882, the seventh child of Anna Seamon and Redmon Fauset, a Methodist Episcopal minister from Philadelphia. The family lived in Fredericksville, New Jersey. Her mother passed away when Jessie was still a child. Her father then married Bella Huff, a widow with three children of her own; together, Bella and Redmon had three children. In 1900, Fauset graduated with honors from the Philadelphia High School for Girls; she was probably the only African-American student in her high school. Fauset became the first African-American woman to attended Cornell University in Ithaca, New York, graduating in 1905. She was also the first African American to be elected to the honor society Phi Beta Kappa at Cornell University. She began her career as a teacher of Latin and French at Washington, D.C.'s M Street High School (later renamed Dunbar High School). Fauset received this post after a Philadelphia school had rejected her because of her race. Fauset also earned a master's degree in French from the University of Pennsylvania (1919) and studied in Paris at the Sorbonne. After her studies, Fauset went to live in New York City.

Often called "the Midwife of the HARLEM RENAISSANCE," Fauset, a prolific, economically secure writer and well-known editor, sought to mentor a younger generation of writers aiming to find voice and style. This group included LANGSTON HUGHES, JEAN TOOMER, GEORGE SCHUYLER, and COUNTEE CULLEN. Starting in 1919, Fauset was the literary editor of the NATIONAL ASSOCIATION FOR THE ADVANCEMENT OF COLORED PEOPLE (NAACP) publication *The CRISIS*; she became a contributing editor in 1926. Her work as an editor allowed her to collaborate closely with W. E. B. DUBOIS. From 1920 to 1921, she also worked on the NAACP's *The Brownies Book,* a publication modeled after *The Crisis* for African-American children. Her first novel, *THERE IS CONFUSION,* was honored at the 1924 March "Civic Club Dinner" in the presence of other Harlem Renaissance authors. In 1927 Fauset resigned as an editor of *The Crisis* and accepted a position as a teacher of French at New York City's De Witt Clinton High School. She taught in New York City until 1944. In 1929 Fauset married Herbert E. Harris; they moved to Montclair, New Jersey, in 1940. In 1945 Fauset's friend Laura Wheeler Waring painted her portrait. The painting is housed today in the National Portrait Gallery. Following her husband's death in 1958, Fauset returned to live in Philadelphia, where she died on April 30, 1961.

Fauset published several novels during the Harlem Renaissance, including *There Is Confusion* (1924), *Plum Bun: A Novel without a Moral* (1928), *The Chinaberry Tree: A Novel of American Life* (1931), and *Comedy, American Style* (1933). She also published a number of poems, essays, book reviews, children's stories, short stories, and translations. Fauset's creative work deals primarily with the situation of a highly educated black middle class. Her novels address topics like the situation of middle-class African-American women, racial passing, the psychological effects of racial injustice, race and the law, the accomplishments of middle-class African Americans, and romance plots.

Fauset's first novel, *There Is Confusion,* is set in Philadelphia and focuses on the challenges surrounding a highly motivated African-American middle class in a racist society. The plot centers on the lives of Joanna Marshall and Peter Bye, both of whom want to be socially respected. Their ambitious goals are set by their desire to make white society acknowledge, accept, and appreciate the strength of African-American professionals.

Plum Bun: A Novel without a Moral centers on the story of two African-American sisters. One sister, Angela, is light enough to pass for white and attempts to find fulfillment as an artist in New York City. Fauset's novel explores the legal, moral, and romantic effects of Angela's passing by portraying her altered relationship to her sister, her unsuspecting friends, and the men who are interested in her. The novel follows many artistic conventions of the novel of manners and resolves the tension by portraying Angela as a woman who finds her way back to her family and community.

The Chinaberry Tree: A Novel of American Life thematizes the history of two generations of middle-class African-American women. The story is set in Red Brook, New Jersey, and focuses on two cousins. One of them, Laurentine Strange, is the child of a black woman and a married white man. Laurentine's cousin, Melissa Paul, also has to confront issues of illegitimacy when she unwittingly almost marries her half-brother. In portraying the lives of the two women, Fauset again critiques the connections among racism, the law, and social conventions.

Fauset's last novel, *Comedy American Style,* returns to the idea of presenting a cautionary tale and thus motivating African Americans to take pride in their racial background. The protagonist, Olivia, is extremely driven by an internalized preference for whiteness. This fixation is so pronounced that Olivia chooses her husband because of his light skin color. To her disappointment, her son, Oliver, is born a dark child. As a result, Olivia rejects the son named after her and thus sabotages herself and her family.

BIBLIOGRAPHY

Christian, Barbara. *Black Women Novelists.* Westport, Conn.: Greenwood Press, 1980.

Johnson, Abby Arthur. "Literary Midwife: Jessie Redmon Fauset and the Harlem Renaissance." *Phylon: The Atlanta University Review of Race and Culture* 39 (1978): 143–145.

Nelson, Emmanuel S. "Jessie Redmon Fauset (1882–1961)." In *African American Authors, 1745–1945: A Bio-Bibliographical Critical Sourcebook,* edited by Emmanuel S. Nelson, 155–160. Westport, Conn.: Greenwood, 2000.

Sato, Hiroko. "Under the Harlem Shadow: A Study of Jessie Fauset." In *Remembering the Harlem Renaissance,* edited by Cary D. Wintz, 261–287. New York: Garland, 1996.

Sylvander, Carolyn Wedin. *Jessie Redmon Fauset: Black American Writer.* Troy, N.Y.: Whitston, 1981.

Wall, Cheryl A. *Women of the Harlem Renaissance.* Bloomington: Indiana University Press, 1995.

Éva Tettenborn

Fences   **August Wilson** (1985)

This drama is the second in AUGUST WILSON's 10-play cycle, each depicting a decade in 20th-century African-American life. First presented as a staged reading at the Eugene O'Neill Theater Center's 1983 National Playwrights Conference, *Fences* opened at the Yale Repertory Theatre in New Haven, Connecticut, on April 30, 1985, and on Broadway at the 46th Street Theatre on March 26, 1987. This critically acclaimed play won the 1987 Pulitzer Prize for Drama as well as a Tony Award and the New York Drama Critics Circle Award.

Although the final scene takes place in 1965, the central action of the play is set in 1957 Pittsburgh, Pennsylvania. *Fences* tells the story of Troy Maxson, a garbage collector, whose dreams of becoming a major league baseball player are shattered by the prohibition against integrated games that lasted until 1947—when Troy is past his prime. Embittered by the strictures placed on African Americans, Troy, in an attempt to protect his son, Cory, from also losing his dreams to racism, ironically thwarts Cory's ambition of playing college football. In trying to control his son, Troy alienates Cory; simultaneously, he is estranged from his wife, Rose, by his infidelity. While Troy asserts that life is a game that he can win and death is nothing but a "fast ball on the outside corner," he is overtaken by both, and he goes down swinging.

The central metaphors of the drama are baseball and the fence that Troy builds throughout the play. A rag ball, suspended from a string, hangs from a tree in the Maxsons' small dirt yard and serves as the focal point of the sparse setting. An unfinished fence frames the yard, and a sawhorse and a pile of lumber indicate Troy's building project. The fence has multiple meanings, representing Rose's desire to protect her family and Troy's need to shut out everything that threatens him. Additionally, it symbolizes the institutions that confine all of the major characters. Troy; Lyons, his oldest son; and Bono, his friend, have all been imprisoned. At the end, Cory joins the Marines, Rose seeks refuge in the church, and Troy's brother, Gabriel, is confined in a mental institution. Essentially, the fence represents the institutions that are the repositories of the characters' and, by extension, African Americans' dashed dreams.

Similarly, baseball, once considered the country's favorite pastime, symbolizes the American dream and represents Troy's hopes for an equal chance at life. It also signifies the bitterness that destroys his relationship with his son and, ultimately, is the instrument of his death. During an argument, Troy calls two strikes against Cory for his disobedience and warns him not to strike out. As they confront each other later in the play, Troy backs the young man against the tree, and Cory grabs the bat to strike his father. As a legacy, Troy leaves anger, failed dreams, and alienation. He dies alone in his backyard, while swinging his bat.

While Troy's death suggests that he is a tragic figure and the play is a pessimistic representation of black life, the story ends on a positive note, offering Troy redemption and the surviving characters hope. Gabriel serves as a mystical figure in *Fences*. Although severely wounded in World War II and left mentally deficient, believing that he is the archangel, Gabriel is the play's spiritual force. He forewarns Troy of his death and after Troy's fu-

neral performs a "life-giving" dance as he blows his trumpet and opens the gates of heaven. Through this flawed figure as well as the women Troy leaves behind, Wilson gestures toward hope and a life free of fences.

BIBLIOGRAPHY

Blumental, Anna. "'More Stories Than the Devil Got Sinners': Troy's Stories in August Wilson's *Fences.*" *American Drama* 9, no. 2 (Spring 2000): 74–96.

Gates, Henry Louis, and Alan Nadel, eds. *May All Your Fences Have Gates: Essays on the Drama of August Wilson.* Iowa City: University of Iowa Press, 1994.

Pereira, Kim. *August Wilson and the African-American Odyssey.* Urbana: University of Illinois Press, 1995.

Plum, Jay. "Blues, History, and the Dramaturgy of August Wilson." *African American Review* 27, no. 4 (Winter 1993): 561–567.

Shannon, Sandra G. *The Dramatic Vision of August Wilson.* Washington, D.C.: Howard Univerity Press, 1996.

Wang, Qun. *An In-Depth Study of the Major Plays of African American Playwright August Wilson: Vernacularizing the Blues on Stage.* Lewiston, N.Y.: Mellen, 1999.

Barbara Wilcots

Finney, Nikky (1957–)

Author, visionary, teacher, and poet Nikky Finney was born by the sea in Conway, South Carolina, to Frances Finney, a teacher, and Ernest Finney, a civil rights lawyer who is currently a Supreme Court justice for the state of South Carolina. The proud Finneys crowned their daughter with her Gullah legacy, out of which she continues to write. Finney recalls that when her grandmother died she participated in the Gullah ritual of placing newly minted coins over the eyelids: "I kissed the pennies then closed down the eyes of the woman who had taught me to see" (2003, 48). Finney is a graduate of Talladega College in Alabama, from which she received a B.A. degree in English literature. She pursued graduate studies at Atlanta University.

Finney, who started writing poetry at age 10 and was later influenced and encouraged by BLACK ARTS MOVEMENT writers NIKKI GIOVANNI, LUCILLE CLIFTON, TONI CADE BAMBARA, and JOHN O. KILLENS, is the author of two collections of poems: *On Wings Made of Gauze* (1985) and *The World Is Round* (2003). *Rice* (1995), her collection of poems, stories, and photographs, won the PEN American Open Book Award in 1999. Finney has also published a collection of short stories, *Heartwood* (1998).

A visionary whose life has been that of bearing witness to the human condition, Finney seeks to "anchor her words" in one central idea throughout her work, whether she writes about her parents, family, childhood memory, slavery, or lesbianism: "I truly believe, as James Baldwin said, that in the New Jerusalem, we really can be better as a people and a society" (Preston, 1E). "It is not my job to make people feel comfortable," Finney has said, "but to keep the human race aware of what it is doing to itself" (Johnson, 1C). She successfully calls attention to the continuation of oppression in America after the emancipation in the title and images of "The Running of the Bulls":

> After slavery there were other chains.
> The South still rounded up Black men
> who wouldn't look the other way,
> drop eyes or chin,
> pass or step aside,
> or be cheated. (*The World Is Round*)

In "Fishing among the Learned," Finney, an associate professor of creative writing at the University of Kentucky, digs deep within her family treasure and takes a page from the important lessons she learned from her grandmother, who fished with no more than a "five and dime pole in her hand," to explore and define her own challenges and commitment in the academic world:

> A poet needs to flyfish
> in order to catch glimpses of privileged information
> that there are too many meetings
> and not enough conversations going on

> I stand before the listening eyes
> of those who pay their hard earned money
> to wonder if i am teaching anything
> that the world will later ask of them.

In 1994, Finney won the Publisher's Marketing Association's Benjamin Franklin Award for *The World Is Round*. The award honors "the finest title within the independent publishing world." Phil Hall, one of the judges, wrote that *The World is Round* "was not only the best of the competition, but it is easily among the best poetry books in recent years" (39). He called the collection "an astonishing meditation on the severity of and occasional epiphanies that mark the human experience" (39).

BIBLIOGRAPHY

Finney, Nikky. "Fishing among the Learned." University of Kentucky, August 31, 1994.
———. *The World Is Round*. Atlanta: Innerlight Publishing, 2003.
Hall, Phil. "Spin the World." *New York Resident,* 21 June 2003, p. 39.
Johnson, Erika. "A Woman of Great Pluck." *The ITEM,* 5 September 1993, pp. 1C–2C.
Preston, Rohan. "Nikky Finney." *The Star Tribune.*

Wilfred D. Samuels

Fire!! (1926)

During the summer of 1926, while still affiliated with *The* MESSENGER, WALLACE THURMAN, along with ZORA NEALE HURSTON, Aaron Douglas, John P. Davis, BRUCE NUGENT, Gwendolyn Bennett, and LANGSTON HUGHES, established a new black publication for the arts called *Fire!!*. This name, they thought, was appropriate for a "quarterly dedicated to the younger Negro artists," for it was the intention of these young artists to "burn up a lot of the old, dead conventional Negro-white ideas of the past, *epater le bourgeois* into a realization of the existence of the younger Negro writers and artists while providing them with an outlet for publication" (Hughes, 233–234). This journal was intended, in many ways, to offer an alternative view to the cultural blossoming that was taking place in

Harlem during the 1920s that differed significantly from the perspective ALAIN LOCKE had presented in his New Negro anthology and essay with the same title.

The journal's tone and intention were established in its provocative "Foreword," which read in part:

> FIRE . . . *weaving vivid, hot designs upon*
> *an ebony bordered loom and satisfying*
> *pagan*
> *thirst for beauty unadorned. . . . the*
> *flesh is sweet and real. . . . the soul an*
> *inward flush of fire. . . . Beauty? . . . flesh*
> *on fire—on fire in the furnace of life*
> *blazing. . . .*

Each of the seven founders agreed to pay $50.00 to finance the first issue, and responsibilities were assigned to each. Thurman was to edit it, Davis to handle the business end, and Nugent to take charge of distribution. The others were to serve as an editorial board, contribute their own work, and serve wherever needed (Hughes, 236). But it was Thurman, not the editorial board, who was largely responsible for the production of *Fire!!* Unfortunately, the publication was begun with more optimism than sound financial backing; *Fire!!* survived only one issue.

The brash young editors expected *Fire!!* to create strong discussion among the reading public, but it attracted little attention. The reaction from black critics was mixed, perhaps less explosive than expected, while the white press hardly took notice of its publication. Benjamin Brawley angrily suggested that "if ever Uncle Sam finds out about [*Fire!!*], it will be debarred from the mails" (183), because of the base life that constituted the subject matter of the poems and stories, the profane language, and the journal's general disregard for the use of controversial literary language. Brawley also objected to the resistance to a work ethic that he discerned in some of the contributions. While generally castigating *Fire!!*'s contributors, Brawley said that Thurman's "Cordelia the Crude" should never have been written or published (178–179, 183). The *Baltimore Afro-American* critic, Rean

Graves, expressed the sentiments of other black journalists by opening his review, "I have just tossed the first issue of *Fire!!* into the fire" (quoted in Hughes, 237).

But *Fire!!* received favorable treatment from the pens of two of its own contributors in OPPORTUNITY. COUNTEE CULLEN suggested that only the unsophisticated would take offense at *Fire!!* because "there seems to have been a wish to shock in this first issue, and, though shock-proof ourselves, we imagine that the wish will be well realized among the readers of *Fire!!*." Cullen expressed optimism for the journal's future as an instrument in the development of black artists (" Dark Tower," *Opportunity* 25). In the same issue, Gwendolyn Bennett expressed sentiments similar to Cullen's, failing to acknowledge her own contribution to *Fire!!*, and praised Thurman for his editorship of the first issue. A surprising response came from W. E. B. DuBois, who was expected to respond to *Fire!!* with shocked indignation because of its affront to black bourgeois sensibilities. Instead, DuBois wrote:

> We acknowledge the receipt of the first number of *Fire!!* devoted to "Younger Negro Artists." It is strikingly illustrated by Aaron Douglas and is a beautiful piece of printing. It is issued quarterly at one dollar a copy. We bespeak for its wide support. (158)

Alain Locke praised the group for the youthful self-confidence that led to the establishment of *Fire!!*, but he saw the journal as "a charging brigade to literary revolt, especially against the bulwarks of Puritanism." Locke's objection was that *Fire!!* went too far. He argued that if Negro life is to provide a healthy antidote to Puritanism and to become one of the effective instruments of sound artistic progress, its "strong sex radicalism" (Locke, 563) must more and more be expressed in the clean, original, primitive, but fundamental terms of the senses and not, as too often in this particular issue of *Fire!!*, in hectic imitation of the "naughty nineties" and in effete echoes of contemporary decadence (Locke, 563).

Thurman saw *Fire!!* as a pioneer effort that "flamed for one issue and caused a sensation the like of which had never been known in Negro journalism before" (Editorial). It was an experimental journal that was "not interested in sociological problems." It was purely artistic in intent and conception, its contributors choosing subjects and characters from the proletariat, persons who "still retained some individual race qualities and were not totally white American in every respect except skin color" (Thurman, "Negro Artists and the Negro," 196).

BIBLIOGRAPHY

Brawley, Benjamin. "The Negro Literary Renaissance." *Southern Workman* 56 (1927).

Cullen, Counteś. "Dark Tower." *Opportunity* 25.

DuBois, W. E. B. "The Looking Glass." *Crisis* 33 (1927).

Hughes, Langston. *The Big Sea: An Autobiography.* New York: Knopf, 1940.

———. "The Negro Artist and The Racial Mountain." In *the Portable Harlem Renaissance Reader,* edited by David Levering Lewis, 91–95. New York: Penguin Books, 1994.

Locke, Alain. "Review of Fire!!" *Survey Graphic* 58 (1927), 563.

"Review of Fire!!" *Bookman,* 64 (1926), 258–259.

Thurman, Wallace. Editorial. *Harlem* 1 (1928), 21–22.

———. "Fire Burns." *Fire!!* 1 (1926), 47–48.

———. "Negro Artist and the Negro." In *The Collected Writings of Wallace Thurman,* edited by Armitjit Singh and Daniel M. Scott, 195–200. New Brunswick, N.J.: Rutgers University Press, 2003.

———. "This Negro Literary Renaissance." Unpublished typed manuscript, Thurman Folder. Yale University Beinecke Library, New Haven, Conn.

Lawrence T. Potter, Jr.

Fisher, Rudolph   (1897–1934)

Novelist, short story writer, and essayist Rudolph Fisher was born Rudolph John Chauncey on May 9, 1897, in Washington, D.C. After graduating from Rhode Island's prestigious Classical High School in Providence, where his parents, Glenora Williamson Fisher and John Wesley Fisher, raised him, he attended Brown University, receiving degrees in English and biology with honors. Although he pursued a master's degree in English, the Phi Beta Kappa, Delta Sigma Rho, and Sigma Xi honoree graduated from Howard University Medical School with highest honors in 1924. Fisher began his professional career in medicine in 1925, when he joined the staff of the National Research Council at Columbia University's College of Physicians and Surgeons as a fellow studying bacteriology and pathology. He began his own practice as a roentgenologist (X-ray specialist) in 1927.

In 1925, Fisher caught the attention of HARLEM RENAISSANCE writers when his signature story, "The City of Refuge," was published by the mainstream *Atlantic Monthly.* ALAIN LOCKE showcased Fisher as a quintessential example of new black writers by including this story in his pioneering anthology, *The New Negro,* placing it alongside stories by JEAN TOOMER, BRUCE NUGENT, ERIC WALROND, and ZORA NEALE HURSTON.

In "The City of Refuge," King Solomon Gillis, a fugitive from the law in his small southern town, travels north via Washington, D.C., to Harlem, "the land of plenty" and "the city of refuge," where he is totally mesmerized by his initial experience. Harlem, he decides, is the opposite of his southern Jim Crow world. "In Harlem black was white. You had rights that could not be denied you; you had privileges, protected by law" (58). Gillis is most struck by the fact that Harlem "even got cullud policemans" (59). Soon after his arrival in Harlem, however, Gillis becomes the victim of a scam in which, unbeknownst to him, his newly made friends use him as a fence for their drug dealing business. Ironically, Gillis is arrested and taken to jail by a black policeman, the symbol of his arrival to the Promised Land, which, in the end, Harlem is not.

With his focus on the city, subway system ("the screeching onslaught of the fiery hosts of hell" [Fisher, 57]), turnstiles, and throngs of meandering bodies on the streets of Harlem, Fisher must be recognized as an early 20th-century American and African-American modernist. Much as Harlem threatens to suffocate CLAUDE MCKAY's Jake in *HOME TO HARLEM* and destroys Violet and Joe

Trace's dreams in TONI MORRISON's *JAZZ*, it also proves to be King Solomon Gillis's downfall. He lacks both the wisdom and the understanding to survive this almost naturalistic, crabs-in-a-barrel world in which only the fittest survive.

As one critic notes, "A particular concern of Fisher's is the transformation of people and culture that inevitably follows the move from the rural South to the urban Northeast" (Davis, *From the Dark Tower,* 100). Fisher's short stories were published in the best-known black journals during the 1920s, including *CRISIS* and *OPPORTUNITY,* but they were also published in such mainstream venues as *The Atlantic Monthly* and *Survey Graphic.*

Fisher also wrote two novels: *The Walls of Jericho* (1928) and *THE CONJURE MAN DIES: A MYSTERY TALE OF DARK HARLEM* (1932). Whereas *Walls* critiques the well-known obsession of whites, such as CARL VAN VECHTEN, with Harlem and intraracial issues of class and color among blacks, exposing, as Lewis notes, "the cleavages within the Afro-American world" (230), *The Conjure Man* holds the distinction of being the first African-American detective novel and, for some critics, psychological thriller. When Harvard-educated N'Gana Frimbo, an African conjure man who plies his trade in Harlem, turns up "dead," Harlem detective Perry Dart and John Archer, a physician who assists homicide detectives, are called in to help solve the case. In the end, however, Frimbo, who, it is discovered, is very much alive, helps solve the mystery and find his would-be killer. The novel's strengths are Fisher's complex characters, his exploration and presentation of the spectrum of Harlem's black community, and each character's committed quest for wholeness.

For the most part, *The Conjure Man* was well received. Sterling Brown described it as "a plot of classic suspense." ARNA BONTEMPS and COUNTEE CULLEN adapted it for the stage as a Federal Theatre Project. It is considered a forerunner to the detective novels of CHESTER HIMES. Fisher died in 1934 at age 37 from complications related to abdominal cancer. His stories were collected and published posthumously as *The City of Refuge: The Collected Stories* (1987) and *The Short Fiction of Rudolph Fisher* (1987).

BIBLIOGRAPHY

Davis, Arthur P. *From the Dark Tower, Afro American Writers 1900–1960.* Washington, D.C.: Howard University Press, 1974.

Fisher, Rudolph. "The City of Refuge." In *The New Negro,* edited by Alain Locke, 57–74. New York: Atheneum, 1968. First published by Albert & Charles Boni, 1925.

Lewis, David Levering. *When Harlem Was in Vogue.* New York: Oxford University Press, 1979.

Wilfred D. Samuels

Flowers, Arthur   (1950–)

Arthur Flowers was born on July 30, 1950, in Nashville, Tennessee; at the time, his father was enrolled in Meharry Medical School. However, Flowers calls Memphis, the city in which he was raised and educated, home. Memphis is also the place, along with the rest of the Mississippi Delta, Flowers has labeled as "African American holyground," a title he has given to the region that gave birth to new cultural forms, including BLUES and jazz, while redefining existing cultural practices, such as hoodoo.

Flowers honed his writing skills, his "literary hoodoo," as he calls it, under the tutelage of JOHN OLIVER KILLENS, cofounder of the Harlem Writers' Guild, a writer's workshop that also helped nurture NIKKI GIOVANNI and TERRY MCMILLAN. Although Killens earned two Pulitzer Prize nominations, Flowers bemoans the fact that Killens's literary talents are today largely "unprecedented and unsung" (Gilyard). But Flowers never fails to salute his mentor at the beginning of each new work. At the onset of *Another Good Loving Blues,* he writes, "I am Flowers of the Delta clan Flowers and the line of O. Killens." Beyond invoking his mentor's name, he also pays homage to Killens in celebrating black expressive culture within his work, as did Killens. According to Flowers, "Blues novels, jazz novels and hip-hop novels are all attempts to bring the African vernacular to literature" (Edelstein). On the dust jacket for the original hardcover edition of *Another Good Loving Blues,* Terry McMillan noted Flowers's skill with vernacular speech. She wrote, "[He] has captured the soul and sound of southern folk in the most melodic manner I've seen in ages. The journey is magical and funky. I applaud him."

In his novels *De Mojo Blues* (2002) and *Another Good Loving Blues* (1994) as well as his children's book *Cleveland Lee's Beale Street Band* 1996), Flowers presents the blues as major "characters" as well as a major entity within black culture. The blues shape Lucas Bodeen's perception of himself in *Another Good Loving Blues,* help him express the range of emotions he experiences in his love relationship with Melvira Dupree, and reflect the changes taking place within the black community at the end of the 20th century. In Flowers's children's story, only after young Cleveland Lee learns from an old bluesman how to play trumpet from his heart does he gain the skills required to catch the attention of the whole city of Memphis and perform in his sister's marching band.

Flowers also amplifies the writing magic, the "literary hoodoo" tradition, pioneered by ZORA NEALE HURSTON and ISHMAEL REED, a tradition that, he believes, is another way of shaping and empowering the black community. He describes himself as a modern-day literary hoodoo practitioner in his memoir *Mojo Rising: Confessions of a 21st Century Conjureman,* and his other works are populated by practitioners of these magical arts as well. In Flower's first novel, *De Mojo Blues,* protagonist Tucept High John trains as a "hoodoo" practitioner in a wilderness park in Memphis. With his new skills, he is able to save himself and his former Vietnam War comrades even as he tries to rescue the larger black community. Author Wesley Brown described the novel as "a meditation on tradition, destiny, and the exercise of mojo (power) as a healing force in a world poised for destruction."

Lucas Bodeen shares his love with conjure/hoodoo woman Melvira Dupree in *Another Good Loving Blues.* She, in turn, is encouraged by Hootowl, the older hoodoo, to adapt to the challenges facing black people in the big cities, such as Memphis, during the Great Migration and to use her powers to strengthen African Americans to perform the spiritwork needed no matter where they live. In one scene Flowers brings Melvira face to face with Zora Neale Hurston, the literary genius and trained anthropologist who studied and wrote about hoodoo and the roots worker/spiritual practitioner in *Mules and Men.* The two women size each other up and silently agree that each has the power necessary to shape the souls of a people.

A veteran of the war in Vietnam, Flowers is a blues singer and a performance artist who performs both his own work and classics from black culture, such as "Shine and the *Titanic.*" "Shine and the Titanic" is perhaps one of the best known toasts, a genre, like rapping, SIGNIFYING, and boast, that is central to African-American oral culture. It offers another (vernacular) version of the historical sinking of the *Titanic,* which took place in 1912, a historical period colored by Jim Crow laws of "separate but equal." Denied passage in the segregated world of this super luxury liner other than as a laborer, Shine, a stoker on the *Titanic,* becomes aware of the impending danger, the looming icebergs, and inevitable damage and loss of lives should the ship continue forward. Although he warns Captain Smith, who is drunk with the magnificence of the ship, its passengers, and its maiden voyage, the captain ignores Shine's warnings and, verbally at least, demands that Shine remember and remain in his subordinate status and place. Shine, who is a good swimmer, swims to safety as the *Titanic* sinks, turning a deaf ear to the privileged voyagers to whom he had been invisible. He was not, in the end, among the privileged passengers who, despite their wealth and status, lost their lives when the *Titanic* went down.

Flowers, a modern-day conjure man, teaches at Syracuse University and is a cofounder of the New Renaissance Writer's Guild. His weblog, called "Rootwork the Rootsblog: A Cyberhoodoo Webspace," can be found at http://rootsblog.typepad.com/rootsblog/2003/10/.

BIBLIOGRAPHY

Brown, Wesley. Quoted in Review of *De Mojo Blues, Chicken Bones. A Journal of Literary and Artistic African American Themes* (Fall 2002). Available online. URL: http://www.nathanielturner.com/demojoblues.htm. Accessed February 14, 2007.

Dance, Daryl Cumber, ed. *From My People: 400 Years of African-American Folklore.* New York: W. W. Norton & Co., 2002.

Edelstein, Elana. "Honors Program Distinguished Speaker Series: Arthur Flowers." *Inside Dominguez Hills* (December 2000/January 2001). Available online. URL: http://www.csudhiedw/univadv/IDH0I01/Honors_Speakers0101.html. Accessed February 14, 2007.

Flowers, Arthur. *Another Good Loving Blues.* New York: Ballantine Books, 1994.

Gilyard, Keith. Review of *Liberation Memories: The Rhetoric and Poetics of John Oliver Killens. Chicken Bones* (April 2003). Available online. URL: http://www.nathanielturner.com.liberationmemories.htm. Accessed December 23, 2006.

Jablon, Madelyn. "The Künstlerroman and the Blues Hero." In *Black Metafiction: Self-Consciousness in African American Literature,* 50–80. Iowa City: University of Iowa Press, 1997.

Pollard, Deborah Smith. "African American Holyground in *Another Good Loving Blues.*" *CLA Journal* 44, no. 1 (September 2000): 65–87.

Schroeder, Patricia R. "Rootwork: Arthur Flowers, Zora Neale Hurston, and the "Literary Hoodoo Tradition." *African American Review* 36 (Summer 2002): 263–272.

Deborah Smith Pollard

for colored girls who have considered suicide/when the rainbow is enuf
Ntozake Shange (1976)

Poet, novelist, and playwright NTOZAKE SHANGE originally read this "choreopoem," as she called it, as a series of narrative prose poems about the lives of seven women—"colored girls"—of African descent. Despite moments in the choreopoem when, faced with an abortion after an "accidental" pregnancy, faced with unfaithful or selfish male partners, faced with the death of young children at the hands of a male lover, the "colored girls" first consider suicide, by the end of the play, they "find god in themselves and love her fiercely." Theirs is not the external Christian God but rather a spirit of independence and self-awareness that allows them to experience the "rainbow" at the end of the storm. Modeled on Judy Grahn's seven-sequence poem about women whose experiences make them anything but "common," Shange's work conjoins dance and poetry to create a moment of public celebration wherein her characters, after admitting their vulnerabilities, fears, and disappointments, ultimately witness their own triumphs. Their individual and shared stories represented a milestone in American theater and in black women's writings.

While many critics and audiences applauded Shange's daring and unadorned truth about women's experiences, others complained that, as form, the choreopoem was a contrived convention that ultimately left readers confused and disappointed. In his review, John Simon concluded: "Is this poetry? Drama? Or simple tripe? Can you imagine this being published in a serious poetry journal? Would it have been staged if written by a white male?" Others accused Shange of blatant black male bashing in her representation of male characters who are infidels, physical and sexual abusers, and liars. The most disturbing moment in the play—when Beau Willie Brown kills his two children by dropping them from an apartment window—not only sent shock waves throughout the viewing and reading audiences but also became the focus for those who attacked Shange's representation of men. In subsequent works about African-American women, Shange shows that writing about men, irrespective of their behavior, is critical to her objective. However, she maintains, her main concern is the presentation of truth and possibility, not the negative representation of black men. In the end, Shange tries to challenge women in abusive relationships to accept responsibility for their own physical and spiritual well-being.

A curricular staple in African-American theater, American theater, and women's studies courses, *for colored girls* encourages discussions of racial and gender identities, racial and gender stereotypes, cultural allusions, communal and individual identities, narrative (non)linearity, spoken and written language and identities, and language and emotion. Self-identifying as "a poet in American theater," Shange comments on her goal as a writer, as a poet, and as a storyteller: "quite simply a poem shd fill you up with something/ cd make you swoon, stop in yr tracks, change yr mind, or make it up. a poem shd happen to you like cold water or a kiss" (72).

BIBLIOGRAPHY

Lester, Neal A. *Ntozake Shange: A Critical Study of the Plays.* New York: Garland, 1995.

————. "*Shange's Men: for colored girls* Revisited, and Movement Beyond." *African American Review* 26 (Summer 1992): 319–328.

Shange, Ntozake. "Ntozake Shange Interviews Herself." *Ms.,* December 1977, pp. 35, 70, 72.

Simon, John. "On Stage: *Enuf* Is Not Enuf." *New Leader* 59 (July 5, 1976): 21.

Neal A. Lester

Forrest, Leon   (1937–1997)

Leon Forrest was born on January 8, 1937, in Chicago, Illinois. His interest in writing emerged during his grade school years, and his formal work as a writer began in 1960 when he became a public information specialist while touring Germany in the U.S. Army. In the early 1970s, Forrest met RALPH ELLISON, whose support of the young novelist is detailed in *Conversations with Ralph Ellison.* Forrest also met TONI MORRISON, who was then an editor at Random House in search of new African-American writers. Under Morrison's editorship, Forrest published his early novels and established himself as a prodigious novelist.

Forrest's works are best understood when read as his attempts to transform African-American life and history—from everyday occurrences to life-explaining and life-sustaining events and achievements—into art. His success as a major novelist rests in his ability to reinvent narrative strategy by employing African-American vernacular traditions such as spirituals, folk speech, the BLUES, and sermonic texts that observe conventions of oral language, repetition, and orality. In each of his novels, cultural themes and themes of religion, flight, and family emerge and are presented with substantial genre modifications. The action of each novel is presented using multiple narrative conventions, including the eulogy, the folk sermon, epistles, poetic monologues, and stream-of-consciousness surreal episodes. Because his novels investigate the way contemporary African-American identity is informed by the past, they find a readership with

anyone interested in how racial identity is formed in the contemporary moment.

Forrest's first novel, *There Is a Tree More Ancient Than Eden,* was published in 1973. Endorsed by fellow Chicagoan Saul Bellow and introduced by Ellison, *There Is a Tree* introduces readers to Forrest's fictional Forest County (modeled largely after Chicago) and to Nathaniel Witherspoon, who reappears in his later novels *The Bloodworth Orphans* (1977) and *Two Wings to Veil My Face* (1984). Experiencing the agony of a motherless child, Nathaniel is the editor of his life and his family's history. His attempts to process fragments of biographical, sociological, and emotional information about his relatives, his ancestors, historical figures, and, finally, himself in order to cope with his mother's death serve as the nonconventional plot of the novel.

Forrest's second novel, *The Bloodworth Orphans,* continues the saga of the Witherspoon family. Nathaniel has reached age 33 and has moved away from his role of journeyman in *There Is a Tree* to the role of witness to the fate of the many members of the extended Bloodworth family, most of whom have been orphaned either by death or by miscegenation at the hands of the white Bloodworth clan. *The Bloodworth Orphans* is divided into two large sections, chapters 1–7 and chapters 8–12, and it is centered primarily around two events—the suicidal death of Abraham Dolphin and the death of Rachel Flowers, who succumbs to cancer.

As in *There Is a Tree,* where Nathaniel and his aunt Sweetie Reed first appear, the main action in *Two Wings to Veil My Face,* Forrest's third novel, has already taken place, but it is told through the process of (re)memory. Fourteen years prior to the story's opening, Sweetie has promised to tell Nathaniel why she refused to go to her husband's and to Nathaniel's grandfather's funerals. What Nathaniel comes to realize during the course of the novel is that her story is her father's story, her husband's story, Nathaniel's story, and in a more general sense, the African-American story.

Forrest's fourth novel, *Divine Days* (1992), returns to the liminal space between chaos and re-creation developed in the latter stage of *The Bloodworth Orphans.* Forrest introduces a new protagonist, Joubert Antoine Jones, who, like Nathaniel, experiences an epiphany that reveals the redemptive power of African-American cultural heritage and the necessity to re-create this force in his own life. *Divine Days* develops around the conflict between the hipster Sugar-Grove and the trickster W. A. D. Ford and Joubert's relationship to them. However, the novel involves far more episodes and themes than this. As a whole, the 1,135-page comic epic richly explores a wide range of African-American experiences, including spirituality, myth, culture, and music. Central to each of these themes is the quest for transcendence.

In Forrest's final work, a collection of novellas titled *Meteor in the Madhouse* (published posthumously in 2001), Joubert returns as the narrating voice and brings the fictional world of Forest County to a close. By engaging a variety of characters, all of whom struggle to define their identity in a post–Jim Crow world, *Meteor* moves across the full spectrum of post-1970s rhetoric. Perhaps more so than in the other novels, which tend to examine the agony of a highly racial existence caused by external forces, *Meteor* turns the critique to a more internal investigation and is critical of many cultural responses that have erroneously become widely accepted as worthy solutions to enduring and transcending racism.

As a major author in contemporary African-American literature, Leon Forrest and his body of fiction aggressively deal with the soul's condition and the contemporary African American's response to the soul in agony. In short, his narratives acknowledge that African Americans created and used cultural traditions to survive the past, and he, in turn, uses these traditions as springboards into his writing and transforms them to lyrical fiction.

BIBLIOGRAPHY

Byerman, Keith E. "Orphans and Circuses: The Literary Experiments of Leon Forrest and Clarence Major." In *Fingering the Jagged Grain: Tradition and Form in Recent Black Fiction*, 238–274. Athens: University of Georgia Press, 1985.

Cawelti, John. *Leon Forrest: Introductions and Interpretations.* Bowling Green, Ohio: Bowling Green State University Popular Press, 1997.

Rosenburg, Bruce A. "Forrest Spirits: Oral Echoes in Leon Forrest's Prose." *Oral Tradition* 9 (October 1994): 315–327.

Special Leon Forrest Issue. *Callaloo* 16 (Spring 1993).

Williams, Dana A. *"In the Light of Likeness—Transformed": The Literary Art of Leon Forrest.* Columbus: Ohio State University Press, 2005.

———. "Preachin' and Singin' Just to Make It Over: The Gospel Impulse as Survival Strategy in Leon Forrest's Bloodworth Trilogy." *African American Review* 36 (Fall 2002): 475–485.

Dana A. Williams

Foxes of Harrow, The
Frank Garvin Yerby (1946)

With the publication of his first novel, *The Foxes of Harrow* (1946), FRANK YERBY made an abrupt transition from writing black protest fiction (mostly short stories) to writing American popular fiction. Sales of *The Foxes of Harrow* skyrocketed, magazines reprinted condensed versions, Twentieth Century Fox purchased the screen rights, and by the end of 1946, more than a million copies had been sold. Although subsequently Yerby would publish an impressive list of best sellers, *The Foxes of Harrow* remains, in many ways, his most commercially defining novel. It catapulted him to national recognition as a writer, it established the costume romance formula he used in most of his successive novels, and it charted a course for him to gain singular distinction as the first African American to become a millionaire by writing fiction.

Set in the antebellum South, *The Foxes of Harrow* is a historical romance that chronicles the adventures of Stephen Fox, an Irish immigrant who rises from poverty to wealth in New Orleans society, between 1825 and 1865. The novel begins with Fox being thrown off a steamboat on the Mississippi River and ends with the destruction of his plantation, Harrow. Between these years, however, Fox amasses a fortune from gambling, wins recognition among New Orleans aristocrats, sells cotton, and marries into a prominent family. Remaining an outcast, however, Fox lives on the margins of southern culture, neither accepting nor adhering to its beliefs and traditions. Unlike many protagonists in antebellum southern fiction, Fox is less than magnanimous. He comes from a disreputable background, holds non-southern views, and succeeds by less than admirable means. Although *The Foxes of Harrow* compares favorably to such contemporary historical romances as *Gone with the Wind* (1935) and *Anthony Adverse* (1933), it is in actuality a throwback to the picaresque tradition. In addition to producing a popular novel, therefore, Yerby achieved success in *The Foxes of Harrow* in his skillful adaptation and manipulation of the picaresque genre to create a vehicle for him both to write entertaining fiction and to debunk the myths of the South.

James L. Hill

French, Albert (1943–)

Like his cousin, the novelist JOHN EDGAR WIDEMAN, Albert French captures the violence and despair that marks the lives of many African Americans as they struggle to survive in a racist society. Born in Pittsburgh, Pennsylvania, in 1943, French grew up in Pittsburgh's Homewood, written about so often in Wideman's books. French's life took a different route from his cousin's, however. Following high school graduation, French joined the marines. He was soon sent to Vietnam. He was discharged in 1967, but the effects of his experience stayed with him for many years after the war. He had been seriously wounded in combat, and by 1991 French realized that he was suffering from post-traumatic stress disorder. He began writing to come to terms with these painful events in his life. It was at this time that he started to draft the work *Patches: A Story of War and Redemption,* published in 1997. An autobiographical account of Vietnam, it is also a chronicle of the ability of creative expression to heal inner wounds. The work also considers America's inability to come to terms with its history and the blight of racism.

Before the publication of *Patches,* however, French produced two novels. While he worked

on revising his memoir, he wrote *Billy* (1993) and *Holly* (1995). Wideman's wife saw the manuscript of *Billy* and passed it along to Wideman's book agent. The debut work met with critical success and established French as a powerful emerging African-American voice, even though he was 50 years old at the time. *Billy* tells the story of Billy Lee Turner, a 10-year-old African-American boy growing up in Baines, Mississippi, in 1937. Tragedy erupts when Billy kills a young white girl, Lori. The older and larger girl starts to beat up Billy when she catches him swimming in her family's pond. Billy defends himself the only way he knows how—with a knife. He accidentally and mortally wounds the teenager. What follows is Billy's trial and eventual execution. Billy is an innocent child unable even to comprehend his crime. The legal system and the society fail to see the human child or his family. Like the slave child of the past, Billy is torn from his mother, and his family is destroyed—all to satisfy the will of white authority. Alluding to works like RICHARD WRIGHT's *NATIVE SON* and the story of EMMETT TILL, French exposes American racism through the emotional and heart-wrenching loss of children—both Billy and Lori. If America cannot heal the wounds of history and face its prejudices, its future is in danger.

Critics also admired French's next novel, *Holly.* The title character is a white woman who falls in love with an African-American World War II veteran, Elias. Elias lost his arm during the war and is unable to pursue the career in music of which he had dreamt. Holly eventually becomes pregnant and is later beaten nearly to death by her racist father. Elias is able to save her life but later dies in jail. The novel is a further indictment of American racism and its destruction of loving relationships.

French's novel *I Can't Wait on God* (1999) is set in Homewood in 1950. Unlike his other novels, *I Can't Wait on God* focuses solely on the African-American community. Nevertheless, the community suffers from violence, poverty, and despair: Its main characters seem unable to escape the limited possibilities offered them by American society. French has also recently written a new foreword to Harper Lee's *To a Kill a Mockingbird* at the request of the author. The appeal comes, no doubt, from

Lee's recognition that French's *Billy* is destined to be a classic novel, examining as hers did the South, childhood, and racism in a timely and emotionally moving manner.

BIBLIOGRAPHY

Berben-Masi, Jacqueline. "From *Billy* to *I Can't Wait on God:* Building the Case for Victimization vs. Self-Affirmation." *Cycnos* 19, no. 2 (2002): 241–251.

Tracie Church Guzzio

Fuller, Hoyt   (1923–1981)

Scholar, writer, and activist Hoyt Fuller was born in Detroit, Michigan; he attended Wayne State University, where he majored in literature and journalism. An ardent critic of the representation of African Americans in mainstream American literature and cultural production, Fuller inspired African-American writers to examine African and African-American art forms in all of their manifestations to produce an art that celebrated African-American culture. He served as a leader of the BLACK ARTS MOVEMENT and as mentor to a new generation of African-American writers.

Fuller served as executive editor of *Negro Digest,* one of the premier journals featuring creative and journalistic writing on African-American life. *Negro Digest* became BLACK WORLD during the Black Arts Movement, and Fuller remained the editor. The name change signaled Fuller's determination to illustrate connections among blacks across the diaspora, to develop and further explain the BLACK AESTHETIC, and to pay homage to African-American writers and the literature they produced.

Fuller dedicated his life to providing a venue for African-American writers and their works. He sought to keep African Americans informed about current social and political events affecting black people throughout the world. As one of the key figures in developing the Black Arts Movement, Fuller dedicated himself to mentoring African-American writers and exposing bias in education, publishing, and literary criticism. As part of his mission to empower and elevate the African-American artist and advance the fight for equality, Fuller shared his talents as a teacher and writer with other African Americans. He founded the Organization of Black American Culture, a Chicago-based writer's workshop.

Fuller was a controversial figure. Many people, especially mainstream academics with ideological perspectives that differed from his, as well as those who felt threatened by the Black Arts Movement, were disturbed by the seemingly militant tone and focus of *Black World.* They were equally bothered by Fuller's speeches and written works on the state of black America and his critique of American educational institutions and the bias found in the curriculum in most American schools, from kindergarten through college. As a result of this perception; the threats received by Johnson Publishers, where *Black World* was housed; and constant surveillance by the police and COINTELPRO, *Black World* was discontinued in the mid-1970s. Undeterred, Fuller founded *First World.* He left Cornell University and returned to Atlanta in 1977.

In addition to editing important journals associated with the Black Arts Movement, Fuller wrote *Journey to Africa,* an autobiographical narrative, book reviews; and essays on African-American literature. In *Journey to Africa* Fuller describes the Pan-African movement of the 1960s and 1970s, urges African Americans to study their history, and encourages them to develop a sense of identity in connection with their African roots.

As a critic, Fuller is best known for his effort, along with contemporaries ADDISON GAYLE, LeRoi Jones (AMIRI BARAKA), and others, to shape the Black Arts Movement. In his essay "Towards a Black Aesthetic," Fuller attempted to define an African-American aesthetic. In it he connects the Black Arts Movement with the BLACK POWER movement of the 1960s. He examines the conflict between the white critic and the black writer and discusses how this conflict is rooted in American racism and the perpetuation of stereotypical images of African Americans found in literature by white authors, book reviews by white critics reviewing black texts, and images in American media. Fuller asserted that "the revolutionary black writer, like the new breed of militant activist, has decided that white racism will no longer exercise its insidious control over his work" (Gayle, 4). In "Towards a Black Aesthetic," as well as in his other writings and speeches, Fuller argues that the black writer and critic must recognize the unique experience of African Americans and the way this uniqueness shapes the art African Americans produce. Fuller asserts that African-American writers and critics "have the responsibility of rebutting white critics and of putting things in the proper perspective" (Gayle, 11).

Hoyt Fuller died of a heart attack in Atlanta in 1981. In "A Tribute to Hoyt Fuller (1927–1981)," published in *Black American Literature Forum,* Chester J. Fontenot notes that Fuller's "life and work were emblematic of sacrificial love for Afro-Americans" (Fontenot, 47). Fuller demonstrated this "sacrificial love" through his commitment to fighting for social justice and equality for African Americans and his willingness to support and mentor African-American writers as they developed their craft.

BIBLIOGRAPHY

Fontenot, Chester, ed. "A Tribute to Hoyt W. Fuller (1927–1981)." *Black American Literature Forum* 15, no. 2 (1981): 47.

Gayle, Addison. *The Black Aesthetic.* New York: Doubleday, 1971.

Randall, Dudley. *Homage to Hoyt Fuller.* Detroit: Broadside Press, 1984.

Deirdre Raynor

G

Gaines, Ernest (1933–)

Most of Ernest Gaines's fiction is set in Louisiana, in a community not unlike the one where he was born on January 15, 1933. New Roads, Louisiana, had once been a plantation and did not really constitute a "town," but Gaines lived there until he was 15, attending school in a one-room building. The family moved to Vallejo, California, in Gaines's sophomore year. After high school graduation, he served in the army for two years. Following his discharge, he enrolled at San Francisco State College, where he majored in English. He graduated in 1957, the same year he won the Wallace Stegner Award for Fiction. His success as a writer encouraged him to continue his studies at Stanford University in its creative writing program.

Early in his career, Gaines attempted to write several novels, but he did not find his "voice" until he returned to Louisiana for research. His first novel, *Catherine Carmier* was published in 1964; *Of Love and Dust* followed in 1967. *Of Love and Dust* did gain some critical attention, though most reviewers considered the novel sentimental. Nevertheless, Gaines became known as a promising young writer. And though a collection of short stories, *Bloodlines,* appeared in 1968, Gaines's potential and promise was not quite met until the publication of *The Autobiography of Miss Jane Pittman* in 1971. Gaines received a Guggenheim Fellowship in 1973 and completed *In My Father's House* in 1978. Gaines published *A Gathering of Old Men* in 1983 but did not publish another major work until 1993. The novel *A Lesson Before Dying* drew critical acclaim and garnered Gaines a Book Critics' Circle Award. The same year, Gaines was presented with a MacArthur Foundation "Genius" Award.

Gaines's work continues to draw both critical and popular attention. Several of his novels have been made into successful television movies. His reception is the result of his ability to render faithfully the lives of genuine and memorable characters. He also captures the energy and spirit of the rural South, its voices and its people, as well as the land itself. Often compared to William Faulkner, Gaines also examines the darker themes of southern history. His first novel, *Catherine Carmier,* deals with color prejudice within the African-American community. Its protagonist, a light-skinned Creole woman, falls in love with a much darker African American, Jackson Bradley. Their love story is complicated by their families' disapproval of their relationship. She is "accidentally" killed for her infraction against the community and its values.

The impact of prejudice on love relationships is also a central theme in *Of Love and Dust.* Gaines investigates the nature of interracial relationships on a plantation in Louisiana. The main character, Marcus, falls in love with the fragile, white wife of Marshall Hebert, the plantation owner.

Clearly, their love is doomed from the start, but it transforms Marcus. His anger softens, and his affair reveals his tenderness. While the novel illustrates throughout the emasculation that African-American men suffer at the hands of white men, it is love that ultimately affirms Marcus's true strength, honor, and manhood. Juxtaposed with Marcus's and Louise's tragic love is the affair between black Pauline and the white overseer, Bonbon. Society condemns the truer love of Marcus and Louise but seems to condone the shallow sexual relationship shared between the white man and the African-American woman. Bonbon has also vowed to "tame" Marcus, and Hebert sets the two men at odds to fulfill his own agenda. Bonbon eventually kills Marcus, an event that drives Louise insane.

The tragic history of the South is also displayed in Gaines's best-known work, *The Autobiography of Miss Jane Pittman.* A neo–slave narrative, the novel follows the life of one of African-American literature's most famous characters, the 110-year-old Jane. Born a slave, Jane lives to see the beginning of the civil rights era. Her story is told in a frame narrative to a young history teacher intent on collecting slave autobiographies. Jane's story reverberates in the history of the American South. Though a fictional account, the novel and its title character are representatives of all the silent stories of real African Americans who survived but were never heard.

Some of those voices are heard in *The Gathering of Old Men.* The novel is framed by the multiple accounts of some of the "old men" in the title. The community of voices, of stories, not only structures the work but also acts as a metaphor for all the tales lost to history. Several of the narrators are white as well, showing the interrelatedness of race in the South. The multiple narrators each tell their version of the killing of Beau Boutan, a white man. Charlie Biggs, his African-American employee, is guilty of the crime, but several old black men and a young white woman, Candy Marshall, claim responsibility. Each stands up to the law to protect Biggs. Their resistance to the sheriff—and to white America's idea of justice when it comes to black America—emboldens the old men to stand up and be seen as men by the white citizens for the first time. Biggs refuses to let others take his place and is ultimately charged with the crime, but he is treated fairly. The men's act of solidarity has changed the minds of many white citizens of the town about what constitutes a good man and about racial prejudice.

A Lesson Before Dying also explores how African Americans find dignity within a racist society that tries to strip them of their humanity. Also set in rural Louisiana, the novel narrates the tragic circumstances in the life of a young man who has been wrongly accused of a crime. Jefferson, who was only in the wrong place at the wrong time, is sentenced to die. His grandmother asks Grant Wiggins, a teacher, to educate Jefferson and to help him come to terms with his impending death. Under Wiggins's guidance, Jefferson learns to write, and begins to express himself on paper. His ability to finally find his "voice," not only gives him dignity, it allows him to have some sense of control over his identity that white society has stripped from him and the African-American community. As he did in *The Gathering of Old Men,* Gaines shows in *A Lesson Before Dying* that the South is not populated only by white bigots. Candy Marshall in *The Gathering of Old Men* stood beside the old African-American males, willing to risk her life to change the ways of the South. The deputy in *A Lesson Before Dying,* Paul, also transcends his community to embrace Jefferson and Wiggins. Gaines suggests that if America is ever going to be able to overcome the burden of the past it will require both races joining together to change the course of the future.

BIBLIOGRAPHY

Babb, Valerie. *Ernest Gaines.* Boston: Twayne, 1991.

Estes, David C., ed. *Critical Reflections on the Fiction of Ernest Gaines.* Athens: University of Georgia Press, 1994.

Lowe, John, ed. *Conversations with Ernest Gaines.* Jackson: University Press of Mississippi, 1995.

Tracie Church Guzzio

Garnet, Henry Highland   (1815–1882)

A teacher, preacher, editor, and apostle of revolt, Maryland-born Henry Highland Garnet "held up a banner of uncompromising resistance" (Bennett, 149) to slavery and other forms of oppression. Born in slavery, he bore witness to "what the monster had done" (Bennett, 155). Thus, his unreserved conviction and motto was "resistance! resistance! RESISTANCE!": "No oppressed people have ever secured their liberty without resistance" (Garnet, 153).

As a child, Garnet, who had been born into a cohesive slave family that included his father George, his mother Elizabeth, and his sister Eliza, learned about and embraced with pride the history of his African past. The fact that he was the progeny of Mandingo warriors and rulers gave him a positive sense of self and security, despite his legal status. When Garnet was nine, his father escaped from his New Market plantation with the entire family to a life of temporary freedom in New York City, where the young Garnet briefly attended the Free African Schools, founded by the New York Manumission Society and supported by such leaders as Samuel Cornish and John Russwurm, the editors of *Freedom's Journal.* However, he dropped out and went to work as a hired hand on a sailing vessel because his education proved financially prohibitive for his parents.

Returning home from work one day, Garnet discovered that slave catchers had raided his family home, scattered his fugitive family, and returned Eliza to slavery. To protect him, friends sent Garnet to live on Long Island. Returning to New York City two years later, he pursued his education in a high school established for black youths; along with Alexander Crummell, he was among the black students who sought to integrate Noyes Academy in Canaan, New Hampshire. The students were placed in danger by a group of Canaan citizens who destroyed the building by pushing it into a creek to prevent the black students from integrating. Garnet, despite an injured leg that eventually had to be amputated, took the leadership role in protecting the group.

In 1840 Garnet graduated from Oneida Institute at Whitesboro and settled in Troy, New York, where he taught school, studied theology, and provided a station for travelers on the Underground Railroad. Garnet later became an ordained Presbyterian minister, an inspirational leader in the antislavery movement, and the editor of the *Clarion,* a black newspaper. In these many roles, Garnet "consistently took progressive stands on vital issues from labor to anti-imperialism" (Ofari, x). For example, Garnet strongly opposed the emigration program to Liberia established by the American Colonization Society.

Throughout his exemplary career as an intellectual, pioneer Black Nationalist, and creator of a black protest tradition in America, Garnet, a prolific writer, expressed his ideas in sermons, letters, essays, and newspaper articles published in such venues as the *Colored American,* a black newspaper. Also, Garnet, an eloquent orator, was a popular speaker on the antislavery circuit and at various conventions, including the American Anti-Slavery Society and the founding convention of the American and Foreign Anti-Slavery Society, which favored direct political action against slavery.

However, Garnet made his most significant contribution to this movement with "An Address to the Slaves of the United States," which he first read at the National Negro Convention in Buffalo, New York, in 1843. Convention delegates, particularly the "moral suassionists" and Garrisonianists (including FREDERICK DOUGLASS), rejected "An Address" on the grounds that it was "warlike and encouraged insurrection" (Ofari, 38) and out of fear for their lives; the motion to adopt was defeated by one vote. Five years later Garnet, as a result of requests from friends, supporters like John Brown, and convention delegates who had voted for it, published "An Address," along with DAVID WALKER's *Appeal,* "praying God that [it] may be borne on the four winds of heaven, until the principles it contains shall be understood and adopted by every slave in the Union" (preface to "An Address").

In "An Address," Garnet assured those in bondage that their brothers and sisters who are free fully sympathized with them. "We, therefore, write to you as being bound with you" (144), he informed them. Garnet also criticizes Christians and the Christian church for their complicity in the oppression and enslavement of blacks. Garnet states that "slavery had stretched its dark wings of death over the land, the Church stood silently by—the priests prophesied falsely, and the people loved to have it so" (146). He tells his readers that "the diabolical injustice by which your liberties are cloven down, *neither God, nor angels, or just men command you to suffer for a single moment. Therefore it is your solemn and imperative duty to use every means, both moral, intellectual, and physical, that promises success*" (148; italics in original). He militantly challenges the slaves: "You had far better all die—die immediately, than live slaves, and entail your wretchedness upon your posterity. . . . If you must bleed, let it all come at once—rather *die freemen than live to be the slaves*" (150; italics in original).

According to Richard Barksdale and Keneth Kinnamon, the editors of *Black Writers of America: A Comprehensive Anthology*, "Garnet's speech was a blueprint for a massive armed insurrection that the convention could not endorse" (174). Condemned for his incendiary address by abolitionist Maria W. Chapman in a *Liberator* article, Garnet fired back: "I was born in slavery, and have escaped to tell you, and others, what the monster has done, and is still doing. . . . If it has come to this, that I must think and act as you do, because you are an abolitionist, or be exterminated by your thunder, then I do not hesitate to say that your abolitionism is abject slavery" (Ofari, 153–154).

Although Garnet lived to see the end of slavery in the United States, and although he was invited to address the House of Representatives in Washington, D.C., in 1865, he also lived to see the failure of the various Reconstruction programs. Growing tired of the struggle, he returned to the African homeland of his ancestors and died there in 1882.

BIBLIOGRAPHY

Barksdale, Richard, and Keneth Kinnamon, eds. *Black Writers of America: A Comprehensive Anthology.* New York: MacMillan Company, 1972, 173–176.

Bennett, Lerone. *Pioneer in Protest.* Chicago: Johnson Publishing Company, 1968.

Garnet, Henry Highland. "An Address to the Slaves of the United States of America." In *"Let Your Motto Be Resistance": The Life and Thought of Henry Highland Garner,* edited by Earl Ofari. 144–153. Boston: Beacon Press, 1972.

Loggins, Vernon. *The Negro Author. His Development in America to 1900.* Port Washington, N.Y. Kennikat Press, 1931.

Ofari, Earl. *"Let Your Motto Be Resistance": The Life and Thought of Henry Highland Garner.* Boston: Beacon Press, 1972.

Lewis Chidziva

Garvey, Marcus M.   (1887–1940)

Born on August 17, 1887, in St. Ann's Bay, Jamaica, Garvey came to the United States in 1916; he settled in New York City (Harlem) and started a chapter of the Universal Negro Improvement Association (UNIA), which he had founded in Jamaica in 1914. Garvey had come to America because his message resonated with BOOKER T. WASHINGTON's racial uplift through economic self-reliance program, although Garvey had adopted a more global perspective.

Garvey successfully unified followers around his nationalist philosophy, Garveyism, whose fundamental goals were to promote global black economic, social, and cultural independence; to celebrate racial (black) pride, and to establish a free African continent—the homeland of all Africans and their descendants who wished to return to help develop a colonially oppressed and ravished Africa. At the height of the UNIA's popularity, Garvey boasted, 4 million persons of African ancestry had pledged allegiance to him and his mission. He succeeded in attracting and inspiring a noble and prideful group of followers among black lower- and middle-class workers, who formed the proud nucleus of the UNIA.

In 1922 Garvey's repatriation objective (considered separatist by many) led him to meet with the leadership of the Ku Klux Klan; understandably, many UNIA members and African-American leaders, particularly W. E. B. DuBois, had difficulty accepting this meeting. This added to the acrimony that developed between the UNIA and the indigenous sociopolitical groups, such as the NATIONAL ASSOCIATION FOR THE ADVANCEMENT OF COLORED PEOPLE and the Brotherhood of Sleeping Car Porters, causing Garvey to operate often in a controversial environment.

An integral part of Garvey's unifying power was his astute use of pageantry with such UNIA satellite groups as the Universal Black Cross Nurses, the Universal African Motor Corps, and the Black Eagle Flying Corps; he added to this his many costumes appropriate to his role as provisional president of Africa and president of the UNIA, including his academic gown and military uniform accented by a French chapeau adorned with red, green, and white feathers, which he wore during weekly meetings and parades and annual conferences and conventions.

In his "Declaration of the Rights of Negro Peoples of the World," Garvey noted that the current U.S. government fosters conditions under which black citizens were lynched, discriminated against, and subjected to unfair trials, lower wages, inferior medical care, education, and housing. Furthermore, Garvey was convinced that "nowhere in the world, with few exceptions, are black men accorded equal treatment with white men." He demanded: "Wake up Ethiopia! Wake up Africa Let us work towards the one glorious end of a free, redeemed and mighty nation" (*Philosophy*, 135–136). Garvey's nationalist agenda and economic self-sufficiency programs were meant to combat this oppression. In 1917, Garvey began purchasing property in Harlem, including Liberty Hall, an auditorium to host the UNIA's gatherings. Such acquisitions were meant to establish a separate social space that was also economically independent.

Central to Garvey's economic program was the UNIA's official weekly newspaper, *The Negro World*, which he began publishing in 1920 to serve as a cultural and political center for the organization's activities and missions. Through *The Negro World*, Garvey sought to construct a counternarrative to extant racist messages in American newspapers and other media and to enhance the survival of the black race. Thus, *The Negro World*

featured black beauty contests, advertisements for black-owned businesses, and consistent examples of black literature and art to reinforce a sense of racial pride in the black community. With a peak subscription of 200,000 weekly readers, *The Negro World* signaled Garvey's strength and the success of his political message. Central to his legacy is the celebration of racial pride, the acknowledgment that "Black is beautiful," and the demand for black national independence, which had important social and cultural effects.

Garvey's most ambitious commercial endeavor was the creation of *The Black Star Line*, a shipping company that was exclusively owned and operated by black men and women. However, the company never lived up to the success that Garvey had intended; he was indicted in 1922 on mail fraud charges, imprisoned for five years, and deported to Jamaica in November 1927. Although he never returned to the United States, he continued to travel and speak out against global oppression of black peoples. The UNIA, which is still in existence, never attained the same enthusiastic following it celebrated in Harlem at the height of the New Negro Manhood Movement and the HARLEM RENAISSANCE, in which it clearly played a major role. Ironically, Garvey died on June 10, 1940, in London, England, the colonial "motherland" of his beloved Jamaica and Africa, which he had sought to liberate.

Garvey's imprisonment and ultimate inability to free Africa and found an independent nation for Africans and their descendants did little to discredit his vision and cultural legacy in the eyes of his followers, including, for example, the BLACK POWER movement of the 1960s, the emergence of the Nation of Islam and leadership of MALCOLM X, and the BLACK ARTS MOVEMENT.

BIBLIOGRAPHY

Garvey, Marcus. *Philosophy and Opinions of Marcus Garvey, or Africa for the Africans.* Edited by Amy Jacques Garvey. Vol. 2. 1925. 2d ed. London: Frank Cass, 1967.

———. "Speech by Marcus Garvey: Liberty Hall, New York, January 20, 1924." In *The Marcus Garvey and Universal Negro Improvement Association*

Papers, edited by Robert A. Hill, vol. 5, 536–547. Berkeley: University of California Press, 1986.

Hill, Robert A. "Making Noise: Marcus Garvey *Dada,* August 1922." In *Picturing Us: African American Identity in Photography,* 181–205. New York: New Press, 1994.

Lewis, David Levering. *When Harlem Was in Vogue.* New York: Oxford University Press, 1979.

Martin, Tony. *Literary Garveyism: Garvey, Black Arts and the Harlem Renaissance.* Dover, Mass.: Majority Press, 1983.

———. *Race First: The Ideological and Organizational Struggles of Marcus Garvey and the Universal Negro Improvement Association.* Dover, Mass.: Majority Press, 1976.

Keely A. Byars-Nichols

Gates, Henry Louis, Jr. (1950–)

Henry Louis "Skip" Gates, Jr., was born in 1950 in Keyser, West Virginia, to working-class parents. His mother was a domestic worker, and his father was a loader at the mill and a janitor for the telephone company. Gates had a close relationship with his mother, caring deeply for her, especially as she confronted severe clinical depression. After high school, Gates attended Yale, where he continued to develop his interest in Africa. In his junior year, Gates traveled in Africa and worked in a Tanzanian hospital. After graduating summa cum laude in English language and literature, Gates went on to study at Clare College, Cambridge, in England. He worked as a staff correspondent for *Time* magazine until he returned to the United States in 1975. He earned a doctorate from Cambridge in 1979. Gates went on to teach at Yale but left after four years and became a full professor in Cornell's English and Africana studies departments. Then, in 1990, Gates moved to Duke. While there, Gates's testimony in the 2 Live Crew obscenity trial made him a target for conservative criticism. In 1991, Gates moved to Harvard to become the head of the Afro-American studies department. As a result of Gates's leadership Harvard's Afro-American studies department ranks as one of the best in the nation.

Gates has established a distinguished and extensive writing career. His work includes *Figures in Black: Words, Signs, and the Racial Self* (1987), *The Signifying Monkey: A Theory of Afro-American Literary Criticism* (1988), *Loose Canons: Notes on the Culture Wars* (1992), *A Memoir* (1994), *Colored People: The Future of the Race* (1996, written with Cornel West), *Thirteen Ways of Looking at a Black Man* (1997), *Wonders of the African World* (1999), *Africana: The Encyclopedia of the African and African American Experience* (1999), and *The African American Century: How Black Americans Have Shaped Our Century* (2000). In addition to his own writing, Gates has edited a substantial number of books, including the 10-year project *The Norton Anthology of African American Literature* (1996) and *Our Nig; or Sketches from the Life of a Free Black, In a Two Story White House, North. Showing That Slavery's Shadows Fall Even There* (1983), which he identified and brought to critical attention as the first African-American novel written and published in America.

Gates has also edited several magazines, from *Transition* magazine and the *Dictionary of Cultural and Critical Theory* to the *Journal of Urban and Cultural Studies.* A prolific essayist, Gates writes pieces ranging from introductions for literary editions of novels to articles for *The New York Times, The New Yorker,* and *Essence* magazine. Gates traveled through 12 African countries in one year, and the trip was filmed as a six-part documentary for PBS called *Wonders of the African World with Henry Louis Gates, Jr.* In 2002 Gates edited and published yet another find, Hannah Crafts's *The Bondwoman's Narrative by Hannah Craft, a Fugitive Slave, Recently Escaped from North Carolina,* a 300-page holograph manuscript that had never been published before.

Easily one of the foremost scholars in African-American studies, Gates is a celebrated, innovative, and respected thinker. One of Gates's primary scholarly contributions is the theory he set out in *Figures in Black.* Here Gates argues for discussing black texts on their "artistic merits" rather than their "extraliterary purposes" (Spikes, 45) or "the black experience" (43). Gates shifted the focus for critiquing black texts "to form, to style and structure" (43) so that black works received respect as a literature in contrast to being treated as cultural tourism or literary anthropology. Perhaps Gates's most famous work, *The Signifying Monkey: A Theory of African-American Literary Criticism* is considered a central theoretical and critical text. *Signifying Monkey* traces and analyzes the African notion of interpretation in the figure of Esu-Elegbara, a mythological trickster.

Gates has received honorary degrees from several universities, prestigious scholarships and fellowships, including a MacArthur Fellowship, and numerous awards for his writing, including the 1989 American Book Award for *Signifying Monkey,* the Lillian Smith Book Award (1994), the George Polk Award for Social Commentary (1993), the Golden Plate Achievement Award (1993), and the Ainsfield-Wolf Book Award for Race Relations (1989).

BIBLIOGRAPHY

Spikes, Michael P. "Henry Louis Gates Jr.: African American Studies." In *Understanding Contemporary American Literary Theory,* 44–68. Columbia: University of South Carolina Press, 2003.

Kim Hai Pearson
Brian Jennings

Gayle, Addison, Jr.   (1932–1991)

Born in Newport News, Virginia, Gayle, a literary scholar, critic, and biographer, is best known for his effort to define, in his writings and speeches, the BLACK AESTHETIC. After earning a B.A. in English from the City College of New York (1965), Gayle pursued an M.A. in English at the University of California, Los Angeles. He was an eclectic writer who published essays on various topics, from the role of the black writer and literary critic and the African-American literary tradition to education and the African-American struggle for human rights.

In 1972, Gayle's editing of *The Black Aesthetic* placed him in the vanguard of the effort by black writers, scholars, and critics to move away from a Eurocentric definition of art and litera-

ture and create a clearly defined black aesthetic. This groundbreaking text included essays by such leading scholars and writers as HOYT W. FULLER, MAULANA KARENGA, AMIRI BARAKA (LeRoi Jones), SARAH WEBSTER FABIO, LARRY NEAL, ISHMAEL REED, DARWIN T. TURNER, and many others who were engaged in constructive debates (not consensus) about the ideological basis for studying and producing African-American literature. In his introduction, Gayle argues that "The serious black artist of today is at war with the American society" (xvii). Unlike the writers of RICHARD WRIGHT's generation, who waged a war "against the societal laws and mores that barred them from equal membership," Gayle noted, the proponents of a black aesthetics were engaged in a war that "is a corrective—a means of helping black people out of the polluted mainstream of Americanism"; this war, he concluded, "will determine the future of black art" (xxii–xxiii).

Gayle's collected work includes the anthology *Black Expression: Essays by and about Black Americans in the Creative Arts* (1969), The *Way of the New World* (1975), *Oak and Ivy: A Biography of Paul Laurence Dunbar* (1971), *Claude McKay: The Black Poet at War* (1972), and *Richard Wright: Ordeal of a Native Son* (1980). He also published two autobiographical texts, *The Black Situation* (1970), which records his involvement in the CIVIL RIGHTS MOVEMENT, and *Wayward Child: A Personal Odyssey* (1977).

Equally significant is the lecture Gayle delivered, along with several other leading African-American literary critics, in August 1971, at Cazenovia College, in which he outlined the role of the African-American writer and critic. In it, he argued that, in their work, black critics and writers have an enormous responsibility to the masses of African Americans to reflect accurately the experience of blacks living in the United States. Stating that "objectivity in the area of literary criticism is impossibility," Gayle outlined some of the key concerns he would continue to address throughout his work, and he argued that literature is more than a mechanical form or a system of norms. The African-American critic who buys into the notion that universal norms shape great literature, Gayle maintained, places himself in a precarious position by viewing the writings of black authors as part of a larger integrationist project.

At the same time, Gayle recognized that critics, including himself, and writers, including Don Lee (HAKI MADHUBUTI) and AMIRI BARAKA, would be challenged for their views by mainstream academicians who quickly labeled them "racist, separatist, hate mongers and anti-intellectual." Gayle, who was not affected by such criticism, argued that "the consignment of black writers who dare to speak realistically about American society to the outer limits of Dante's hell is one of the most nefarious crimes perpetrated by American critics in this country." African-American critics, Gayle maintained, should develop and use a methodology for critiquing works by African-American writers that will evaluate the relevance or irrelevance of the art to black people. For him the most important purpose of African-American literature is social and political revolution. Gayle asserted that "the job of the black writer and black critic is to wage war against the American society unceasingly and eternally."

Gayle returned to New York, where he taught at the City University of New York in the English department. He died in 1991.

BIBLIOGRAPHY

Gayle, Addison. *The Black Aesthetic.* Garden City, N.Y.: Anchor Books, 1972.
———. Lecture. Cazenovia College, August 1971.
———. *Wayward Child: a Personal Odyssey.* New York: Doubleday, 1977.

Deirdre Raynor

George, Nelson   (1957–   )

The author of nine books of nonfiction books and five novels, George was born and raised in Brooklyn, New York, where, while attending St. John's University, he embarked on his career as a writer. After graduating from St. John's in 1979, George worked part time for the *Amsterdam News,* a black newspaper, as a film critic and sports reporter, while he freelanced for *Billboard* magazine. In 1981, he worked full time as a music editor for *Record World,* where his first assignment was an interview with Prince. In 1982, George joined *Billboard* as editor in charge of black music, a position he held until 1989. His assignment coincided with the rise of hip-hop music and culture, and George was instrumental in promoting the emerging and developing hip-hop scene. He has won the respect of critics who, according to *The New York Times Book Review,* consider him an "intelligent informed insider" (Reisig, 724).

In his role as a black music editor for *Billboard,* George promoted African-American culture to an audience that was not exclusively black, the crossover audience of "Generation X," and black teens and rappers through his *Billboard* essays and articles but also through several critical books about popular culture. In the 1980s George published *The Michael Jackson Story* (1984), *Where Did the Love Go: The Rise and Fall of the Motown Sound* (1985), and *The Death of Rhythm and Blues* (1988), the last of which won the ASCAP Deems Taylor Award and was nominated for a National Book Critics Circle award. He continued his critical look at African-American culture in the 1990s with *Elevating the Game: The History and Aesthetics of Black Men in Basketball* (1992), *Buppies, B-Boys, Baps & Bohos: Notes on Post-Soul Culture* (1992), *Blackface: Reflections on African-Americans and the Movies* (1994), and *Hip Hop America* (1999), which won rave reviews and an American Book Award and was nominated for a National Book Critics Circle Award.

Besides George's extensive critical work, he is also an accomplished fiction writer, publishing such titles as *Urban Romance* (1993), *Seduced: The Life and Times of a One Hit Wonder* (1996), *One Woman Short* (2000), *Show and Tell* (2001), *Night Work* (2003), and *The Accidental Hunter* (2004). In his attempts to mirror the unification of the African-American experience, George has used the same characters in all his novels. He allows his characters to sink to the background or be drawn to the foreground depending on the situation, creating a valid and complex narrative of Brooklyn.

Finally, George also advanced his reputation as a chronicler of American and African-American popular culture, specifically hip-hop culture, through his role as filmmaker, screenwriter, and producer. His neighbor Spike Lee first introduced him to the world of film. He has written scripts for several television programs and two feature films and was associate producer for the critically acclaimed "Just Another Girl on the IRT."

BIBLIOGRAPHY

Barrett, Lindon. "Dead Men Printed: Tupac Shakur, Biggie Small, and Hip-Hop Eulogy." *Callaloo* 22, no. 2 (1999): 306–332.

George, Nelson. *Death of Rhythm and Blues.* New York: Plume, 1988.

———. *Hip Hop America.* New York: Penguin, 1999.

Kun, Josh. "Two Turntables and a Social Movement: Writing Hip-Hop at Century's End." *American Literary History* 14, no. 3 (2002): 580–592.

Reisig, Robin. "Review of *Buppies, B. Boy, BAPS, & Bohos.*" *New York Times Book Review,* 14 March 1993, p. 724.

Ryan Dickson

Giovanni, Nikki   (1943–   )

Born Yolande Cornelia in Knoxville, Tennessee, Nikki Giovanni attended Fisk University, where she began to demonstrate her passion for social activism. Giovanni published *Black Feeling, Black Talk* and *Black Judgement* (both 1968), her first two collections of poetry, shortly after graduating from Fisk. To date, Giovanni, who emerged as a writer during the BLACK ARTS MOVEMENT in the 1960s, has published 24 books, including memoirs, collections of essays, and children's books. Giovanni remains one of the most prolific African-American writers of the 20th and 21st centuries.

Giovanni played a central role in the development of the Black Arts Movement. Although she considered the poets of this movement unique, she was convinced that they were a meaningful part of the African-American literary tradition. In her autobiographical work *Gemini,* she wrote:

> Poetry is the culture of our people. We are poets even when we don't write poetry; just look at our life, our rhythms, our tenderness, our signifying, our sermons and our songs. I could just as easily say we are all musicians. We are all preachers because we are one. . . . The new Black Poets, so called, are in line with this tradition. We rap a tale out. . . . The new Black poetry is in fact just a manifestation of our collective historical needs. (95–96)

The tone, language, and themes of *Black Feeling, Black Talk/Black Judgment* (published as one volume, 1970) are representative of works produced during the Black Arts Movement. Giovanni includes such themes as freedom, violence, black love, and black pride; moreover, she makes gender a central theme, especially through her examination of the role assigned to black women in the movement. Giovanni's *Black Feeling, Black Talk/Black Judgement,* similar to many of her other books, illustrates her strong desire for change in American society and in the status of African Americans within that society. Giovanni's work is prophetic, timeless, and filled with insights on American race relations and blackness/BLACK POWER.

Giovanni sounds a clarion cry for African Americans to initiate political and social changes. She is most concerned about the rift between the black middle class and the masses and the effects of white physical and psychological violence on the black community as a whole. For example, in "Poem (No Name No. 3)," Giovanni writes, "If the Black Revolution passes you by it's for damned / sure / the white reaction to it won't" (Giovanni, 25). Giovanni is equally critical of the methods used to control and silence charismatic African-Americans leaders. The speaker in "Poem (No Name No. 3)" notes:

> *They already got Malcolm*
> *They already got LeRoi*
> *They already strapped a harness on Rap*
> *They already pulled Stokely's teeth*
> *They already here if you can hear properly*
> *negroes. (Giovanni 24)*

The "negroes" Giovanni refers to here are African Americans who place, in her view, too much stock in a white-defined integration.

Giovanni further develops the themes of violence and revolution in "Adulthood (For Claudia)"; however, she also focuses on the role of African-American women in the revolution, a theme that still interests her today. For example, in *Quilting the Black Eyed Pea* (2002), Giovanni pays homage to African-American women, including her grandmother, her mother, Rosa Parks, and Mamie Till Bradley, the mother of EMMETT TILL, who was kidnapped and murdered by two white men in Money, Mississippi, in 1955. The place of the black woman and black intellectual in the Black Power movement is foregrounded in a number of her poems, for example, "Racism 101." In "Adulthood" Giovanni describes the choice a young black female had to make between becoming part of the "colored bourgeois," which is expected of her, or becoming involved in the social activism of the Black Power movement. She embraces the latter course and eventually rejects the former. However, Giovanni is careful not to dismiss the importance of the black intellectuals in the movement. She writes:

> for a while progress was being made along
> with a certain
> degree
> of happiness cause I wrote a book and
> found a love
> and organized a theater and even gave
> some lectures on
> Black history
> and began to believe all good people could
> get
> together and win without bloodshed.
> (Giovanni, 69)

Giovanni challenges the black intellectuals who seek solace in the academy to become more involved in the black liberation struggle.

Giovanni is currently the University Distinguished Professor of English at Virginia Tech in Blacksburg, Virginia. She does not separate her role as an activist from that of an academic, and this becomes clear in the writing she continues to produce and the talks she gives at universities across the country. She continues to chronicle Af-rican-American history, pay homage to African-American leaders, and celebrate African-American culture and tradition. She demonstrates great pride and love for human beings in her writing.

BIBLIOGRAPHY

Giovanni, Nikki. *Gemini: An Extended Autobiographical Statement on My First Twenty-five Years of Being a Black Poet.* New York: Penguin Books, 1971.
Hodges, John. *Furious Flower: Warriors.* Film. San Francisco: California Newsreel, 1998.

Deirdre Raynor

Glave, Thomas   (1964–   )

Born in Jamaica in 1964, Thomas Glave spent his childhood in Kingston as well as in the Bronx, New York. By his own account, he started writing at age four or five. Educated in private and Catholic schools in New York City, Glave majored in English and Latin American studies at Bowdoin College, graduating with honors in 1993. He received a master's of fine arts degree in fiction from Brown University in 1998. Glave then spent one year in Jamaica as a Fulbright scholar, researching the rich intellectual and literary heritage of Jamaica and the Caribbean. He is an assistant professor of English at Binghamton University, State University of New York, where he teaches courses on JAMES BALDWIN, Nadine Gordimer, PAULE MARSHALL, Maryse Condé, Simone Schwarz-Bart, JAMAICA KINCAID, African and African-American queer writers, 20th-century Caribbean and Latin-American queer writers, Jamaican literary historiography, and Jamaican maroon societies.

Glave's short stories, articles, and essays have been published in anthologies as well as in several periodicals, including *Black Renaissance/Renaissance Noire,* CALLALOO, *The Evergreen Chronicles, Gay Community News, The Jamaica Daily Observer, The Jamaica Sunday Herald, The James White Review, The Kenyon Review,* and *The Massachusetts Review.* In 1997, he received the coveted O'Henry Award for his story "The Final Inning," published in *The Kenyon Review.* His first collection of short stories, *Whose Song? and Other*

Stories (2000), brought him accolades, including recognition by the *Village Voice* (June 2000), which named Glave "Writer on the Verge." *Whose Song?* was also a finalist for the American Library Association's Best Gay/Lesbian Book of the Year Award, as well as for the Quality Paperback Book Club's Violet Quill Award for Best New Gay/Lesbian Fiction in 2001.

Glave's writing is informed by his multilingual and multicultural understanding of the black diaspora. His work is deeply influenced by Jamaican, Jamaican-American, Caribbean-American, African-American, and African cultures. *Whose Song?* primarily thematizes the destructive and lethal effects of contemporary heterosexist identity politics on the often fragile identity of African-American gay men. Told with an unflinching attention to detail, stories like "The Final Inning," "Committed," and "Whose Song?" focus on the mental and physical assaults black gay men are often forced to endure because they are not allowed to express their identity freely, in life and even in death. For example, in "The Final Inning," a family pretends, during a funeral, that their deceased son was not gay and that he did not die of AIDS but was, instead, the victim of cancer. "Committed" portrays the life-threatening situation a young gay man endures when his father forces him to get married and abandon his male partner. "Whose Song?," perhaps the most shocking story in the collection, narrates how three sexually confused young men rape a black lesbian girl to prove they do not harbor homoerotic desires. In *Whose Song?* Glave explores the potential danger of a socially compulsory heterosexuality and warns of its detrimental effects, as does RANDALL KENAN in *A VISITATION OF SPIRITS*. In his short stories, Glave frequently constructs a link between compulsory heterosexuality and misogynist violence. Unable to fight the social pressures they often face, several of his unfulfilled black gay characters physically abuse women.

Glave is a founding member of the Jamaica Forum of Lesbians, All-Sexuals, and Gays (J-FLAG); he is a member of the Artist's Advisory Committee of the New York Foundation for the Arts, the Southern Poverty Law Center, the Center for Lesbian and Gay Studies of the City University of New York, Gay Men of African Descent, and the Fulbright Association.

BIBLIOGRAPHY

Jarret, Gene. "'Couldn't Find Them Anywhere': Thomas Glave's *Whose Song?* (Post)Modernist Literary Queerings, and the Trauma of Witnessing, Memory, and Testimony." *Callaloo* 23, no. 4 (2000): 1241–1258.

———. "A Song to Pass On: An Interview with Thomas Glave." *Callaloo* 23, no. 4 (2000): 1227–1240.

———. "Thomas Glave: Fiction Writer." *Callaloo* 23, no. 4 (2000): 1205–1272.

Éva Tettenborn

Goines, Donald   (1937–1974)

Self-confessed pimp, street hustler, heroin addict, and ex-convict, Donald Goines transformed his and others' life experiences into a 16-book canon between 1971 and 1974 with the speed and immediacy of the ghetto life he embraced. His fiction examines, exposes, and humanizes the black underworld as well as addresses the concerns of American ghettos. Born in Detroit, Michigan, Goines had an exceptionally comfortable upbringing as a result of his father's successful dry-cleaning business. The lure of the streets, however, was too strong for Goines to resist, and he succumbed to a life of criminality at an early age. His efforts to abandon his destructive path led him to falsify his age at 14 to enter the Air Force during the Korean War. After basic training, he was immediately stationed in Japan, where opiates were, though not legal, sanctioned by disregard. By the time he returned from Asia, he was battling a raging addiction to heroin. To finance his addiction, Goines participated in various criminal activities, from pimping to operating an illegal whiskey still, and served four prison terms totaling almost seven years. Though he developed an interest in writing during his third prison term, it was not until his fourth and final term that he found his voice.

A fellow inmate loaned him Robert Beck's *Pimp, the Story of My Life* (1967), whose protagonist details his life from childhood to his days as the notorious pimp, ICEBERG SLIM. Soon after, Goines penned *Whoreson* (1972), which also examines the life of a black pimp in America. His protagonist, however, is the son of a prostitute, who educates her son on various aspects of the black underworld and fosters a sense of destiny in his becoming a successful pimp. He submitted the manuscript to Robert Beck's publisher, Holloway House Publishing Company; they enthusiastically accepted. He followed with *Dopefiend* (1971), which publishers found so compelling and sincere that it preceded *Whoreson* in publication. Goines finally realized that he could utilize his knowledge of and lessons learned on the streets as material for his writing. He only veered away from this subject matter in *Swamp Man* (1974), the story of a southern black man's revenge on the white men who rape his sister and the least successful of his novels.

As Goines became more successful, he became more socially conscious about the power he held as a writer and conveyer of the urban, underworld black experience. His third novel, *White Man's Justice, Black Man's Grief* (1973) examines the economic and racial inequities of the criminal justice system. Goines, then, provides a voice for not only the black underworld but also the black masses of the urban ghettos. While he continues to focus on various aspects of the black underworld and the myriad issues facing blacks in a larger context, perhaps the most impressive works of his canon are the four novels originally published under the pseudonym Al C. Clark, which he used to avoid overexposure. This series, often referred to as the Kenyatta novels, consists of *Crime Partners* (1974), *Death List* (1974), *Kenyatta's Escape* (1974), and *Kenyatta's Last Hit* (1975) and revolves around Kenyatta's plan for the political and social liberation of the black community from an oppressive American status quo. These novels examine black militancy and racism and even propose theories about a government-sanctioned genocide of blacks through the international drug trade.

Depicting the lives of pimps, prostitutes, street hustlers, and drug addicts in their impoverished milieu is a fundamental aspect of Goines's work. He eradicates the intangible but distinct boundaries between the black and white communities by holding a mirror to both communities, demonstrating that no difference exists between the hierarchies of the underworld and of mainstream society. His work departs from the hackneyed trope of American racism and social protest to focus on the real, tangible underbelly of American society and the black community. What is immediately noticeable about Goines's work is its self-sufficiency; it is not a constant lament of social and political inequity but rather the manifestation of these inequities and the claiming of personal agency.

Goines, then, becoming a griot of the underworld, acknowledges the force and function of his work to give his readers agency, understanding, and voice. Through his characters and plot development, he allows readers to face their own immediate realities but also forces them to face the projected results of their realities. Goines does not just construct characters of an experience but rather collects these characters for the page. In essence, they are not the products of his literary imagination but its inspiration. Though he sometimes depicts gratuitous violence and masochistic characters, Goines still grasps the ultimate nuances of the black underworld and inner-city communities in America through the verisimilitude of his stories, which enables him, as a writer, to examine, insightfully and from within, the social tribulations of these communities.

The condemnations Goines makes are introspective, focusing on black autonomy and the sometimes destructive choices blacks make about their lives. Other authors have portrayed the impoverished conditions of the ghetto and its criminality as embattled against the white community. Goines's work is the result of his experiences in the ghetto and as a criminal, and his novels are primarily told from the vantage point of a criminal. Other authors deconstruct the black experience in America and focus overwhelmingly on poverty and racism; if criminality does surface, the black criminal is posited as the greater victim of economic and social inequities. In Goines's work, black criminals possess more personal agency about their choices. While it does not ignore the impact of the white community on the black community, it demonstrates that blacks share some culpability for the devastation of their bodies and their communities.

Throughout his canon, Donald Goines forces readers to live in the American ghettos, smell the stench of drug houses, feel the heroin seep into a character's veins, and experience the horrors of drug withdrawal. Goines has never been out of print, selling in excess of 5 million books since his first novel appeared in 1971, because his work continues to resonate with readers. Two of his novels have been optioned for cinematic development. *Black Gangster* was the first novel developed for film and soundtrack, and *Never Die Alone* was a major cinematic release starring rapper DMX in 2004.

Donald Goines and his girlfriend, Shirley Sailor, were murdered in their home in 1974. Their murders remain unsolved.

Candace Jackson

Golden, Marita (1950–)

A novelist, memoirist, essayist, literary cultural activist, poet, educator, and lecturer, Marita Golden was born on April 28, 1950, in Washington, D.C. Her parents, Francis Sherman Golden, a taxi driver, and Beatrice Lee Reid Golden, a property owner, were her first literary mentors. She credits her father for giving her the gift of storytelling and her mother for giving her the charge to write. An avid reader as a child and teenager, Golden attended Western High School (now Duke Ellington High School). Affected by the assassination of MARTIN LUTHER KING, JR., during her senior year, a shaken Golden became a civil rights activist the summer of 1968. Her activism was to play a major role in her early life and in her work.

In the fall of 1968 Golden attended American University on a Frederick Douglass scholarship. She became a contributing editor for the campus newspaper, the *Eagle*. While there, she was introduced to the works of black American, African, and women writers, all of whom shaped her cultural awareness and identity as a young black woman coming of age during the CIVIL RIGHTS MOVEMENT. After receiving her B.A. in journalism in 1972 and earning an M.S. in journalism from Columbia University in New York a year later, Golden worked as an editorial assistant in a publishing company for a year, wrote articles for the *Amsterdam News* and ESSENCE magazine, and was associate producer of WNET-Channel 13 from 1974 to 1975. She met and married Femi Ajayi, a Nigerian architect, and moved with him from New York to Nigeria, where Golden taught English at the Lagos Comprehensive Girls' School and journalism at the University of Lagos. After four years in Nigeria, Golden returned to the United States; she divorced Ajayi in 1989.

Golden found her niche as a creative writer in the 1980s, writing both fiction and nonfiction. She states: "For me autobiographical writing becomes a way of resisting the continuing aggression against my identity inflicted by the culture in nearly all its forms . . . [so] I write about my life to rescue it from those to whom it means nothing and who casually destroy it because they think they own it" (Golden). In 1983 Golden published her classic memoir, *Migrations of the Heart: A Personal Odyssey,* introducing many of the themes that recur throughout her works, particularly the heroine's quest for self-discovery and fulfillment. During this productive period, she wrote *A Woman's Place* (1986), and her best-selling novel *Long Distance Life* (1989). *Long Distance Life* depicts, through flashbacks, the life of 80-year-old Naomi Reeves Johnson, who escapes a sharecropper's farm in North Carolina and fights her way into Washington, D.C.'s black middle class in the 1920s, becoming in the process a self-made woman. Golden's *And Do Remember Me* (1992) was followed by *The Edge of Heaven* (1998) and her memoir *Don't Play in the Sun: One Woman's Journey through the Color Complex* (2004).

In her anthologies and collections of essays, Golden also addresses the issues of growing up black, either male or female, in a racist, sexist society. The anthologies include *Wild Women Don't Wear No Blues: Black Women Writers on Love, Men, and Sex* (1993), which, according to one reviewer, "leaves virtually no aspect of womanist issues unturned" (James, 19); *Skin Deep: Black Women and White Women Write about Race* (1995), with Susan Shreve; and *Gumbo: Stories by Black Writers,* with E. LYNN HARRIS (2002). Golden's first collection of essays, *Saving Our Sons: Raising Black Children in a Turbulent World* (1995), is based on the high death rate among young black men and is a personal narrative about Golden's son, Michael, who grew up in the "crime-ridden" streets of Washington, D.C. In it, Golden raises questions about why the collective nurturing of family and community is not enough to save young black males. Her collection *A Miracle Everyday: Triumph and Transformation in the Lives of Single Mothers* (1999) candidly documents and celebrates the successful sons and daughters of single mothers who are not counted in extant negative statistics.

Golden has received a number of awards recognizing her writing and her work as a literary cultural activist, including the 1992 Mayor's Arts Award for Excellence in an Artistic Discipline, an honorary doctorate from the University of Richmond, induction into the International Hall of Fame for Writers of African Descent at the Gwendolyn Brooks Center at Chicago State University, Woman of the Year Award from Zeta Phi Beta, a Distinguished Alumni Award from American University, the Barnes and Noble 2001 Writers for Writers Award presented by Poets and Writers, and the 2002 Authors Guild Award for Distinguished Service to the Literary Community.

Writing over two decades and representing a wide range of disciplines, Golden has established herself as a distinct voice among contemporary black women writers. Her works have been widely anthologized, and her articles and essays have appeared in *The New York Times, The Washington Post, ESSENCE, Africa Woman,* and the *Daily Times.* Lecturing nationally and internationally, Golden has held writer-in-residence positions at many schools, including Wayne State University, Brandeis University, Spelman College, Hampton

University, Antioch College, Simmons College, Columbia College, the College of William and Mary, Old Dominion University, and Howard University. She is the founder of the Washington, D.C.–based African-American Writers Guild and the cofounder and president/CEO of the Zora Neale Hurston/Richard Wright Foundation, which presents two national fiction awards to black college writers each spring.

Golden has taught at Roxbury Community College, Emerson College, American University, and George Mason University in Fairfax, Virginia. Currently, she is senior writer in the graduate M.F.A. creative writing program at Virginia Commonwealth University in Richmond, Virginia. She is married to Joe Murray, a high school educator, and has one son, Michael.

BIBLIOGRAPHY
Golden, Marita. "Autobiography as Mirror and Shadow: The Seductions of the Self." Thoughts on an Unruly and Surprising Literary Genre. Symposium, Columbia University, October 1999.

Jackson, Edward. "The African Male-Black American Female Relationship in Lorraine Hansberry's *A Raisin in the Sun* and Marita Golden's *Migrations of the Heart.*" In *Images of Black Men in Black Women Writers 1950–1990,* 33–41. Bristol, Ind.: Wyndham Hall, 1992.

James, Jennifer. "Something to Say—and the Means to Say It." (Review of *Wild Women Don't Wear No Blues: Black Women Writers on Love, Men and Sex,* edited by Marita Golden) *Belles Lettres* 9 (Winter 1993–94): 19–22.

Warren, Nagueyalti. Review of *Long Distance Life,* by Marita Golden. *Black American Literature Forum* 24, no. 4 (Winter 1990): 803–808.

Loretta G. Woodard

Gomez, Jewelle (1948–)
Born in Boston and now living in San Francisco, novelist, poet, and activist Jewelle Gomez holds a master's degree from the Columbia School of Journalism. Among her various university teaching and

administrative positions, she directed the literature program and the New York State Council on the Arts as well as the Poetry Center and American Poetry Archives at San Francisco State University.

Gomez's best-known work, the double Lambda Award–winning *The Gilda Stories: A Novel* (1991), is a rich and complex gumbo of science fiction, historical romance, vampire story, and picaresque novel. In the years spanning 1850 to 2050, Gilda, a young woman fleeing slavery in Louisiana, lives through 200 years of significant historical moments, including the internalized colorism that privileges "creamy-colored quadroons" over their darker sisters in antebellum New Orleans and the prison rebellion in Attica ("she'd seen the pictures of inmates killing and being killed, lined up in the prison yard, and the image was always the same as her memories of the slave quarters: dark men with eyes full of submission and rage"), as well as an apocalyptic 21st-century ecological tragedy. This remarkable genre-stretching work explores the notion of profound spiritual reciprocity; friendship and love across gender, generation, class, and race; the power of female sexual desire, and the liberating possibilities of transgressing sexual taboos. Most of all, it imaginatively reconstructs the way "one takes on others as family and continually reshapes that meaning" through the lesbian/gay ethos of chosen family and the idea of African-American community as family that is implicit in the vampire family that Gilda embraces. Asked by Gilda if Anthony believes that he and Sorel will "be together forever," Anthony replies, "Of course. Either in each other's company, as we are now, or separate and in each other's world. One takes on others as family and continually reshapes that meaning—family—but you do not break blood ties. We may not wish to live together at all times, but we will always be with each other." In contrast to patriarchal conventions of passing on the family name through birth of sons, in *The Gilda Stories,* the original Gilda passes on her name as well as her legacy to the young woman whom she embraces as chosen family.

Gomez recasts the popular culture genre of a vampire novel into a vehicle for serious, culturally significant literature. Structurally, the frame of the novel is a story inside a story, as if Gomez, like her character Gilda, were writing in a foreign language (in this case, in the language of science fiction and vampires) in order to conceal the historical and spiritual importance of her tale. Gilda remembers when Bird gave her a journal and encouraged her to "write in one of the other languages in the event someone should stumble upon the book," adding that she "sometimes even wrote as though it were a fiction." The novel is filled with extraordinary incidents, such as the moment when Gilda, tenderly holding the body of a girl from whom she is taking blood and reciprocating by infusing the girl with dreams of passion and possibilities, looks at the leaking blood and is reminded "of the wounds she and her sisters suffered on their tiny hands as they wrenched the cotton from its stiff branches."

Editor of two anthologies, *Swords of the Rainbow* (1996) and *The Best Lesbian Erotica of 1997,* Gomez is also the author of *Don't Explain: Short Fiction* (1998), whose title story borrows from a Billie Holiday song to celebrate Letty, an isolated waitress in 1959 Boston who finds both solace and lesbian community and who identifies with the famous BLUES singer whose "big hungers, and some secret that she couldn't tell anyone" resemble her own.

Gomez is also the author of three collections of poetry, including *The Lipstick Papers* (1980) and *Flamingoes and Bears* (1986), whose title poem celebrates (in a meter that seems like a delightful riff on Dr. Seuss) the rightness of the odd coupling of flamingo and bear, who

> *sleep forever entwined*
> *in all sorts of climes*
> *be it rainy or sunny,*
> *happy to know*
> *there's room in this world*
> *for a bear who likes palm trees*
> *and a bird who loves honey.*

The title poem of her collection *Oral Tradition: Selected Poems Old and New* (1995) is not only a tribute to African-American literature and culture but also a delicious pun on lesbian lovemaking. Some of the most moving poems in this collection are subtle, beautiful performance pieces from Gomez's play *Bones and Ash: A Gilda Story* (2001), which was performed by the Urban Bush Women company in 13 U.S. cities. Gilda's "Songs" in this poetry collection interrogate the experience of slavery ("Rest, which is for them. / Sleep, which is for us"), sexuality ("when my mouth is open to let ideas out and you in, / that is desire"), and female power ("I am not a woman ripe for splitting open / but a tightly wrapped package of everything we need to know").

Gomez's poem "El Beso" interrogates the unpublished poems and letters of Angelina Weld Grimke, the "evidence of unruly passion and wild sadness," that hints at her love for other women, while the poet draws analogies between the abolition of slavery and another kind of necessary abolition: the censure and denial of lesbian relationships.

Like her poetry and fiction, Gomez's essays are marked by lyricism and insight. Both the Middle Passage–evoking "A Swimming Lesson" and "I Lost It at the Movies" (Gomez's "coming out" story) are included in *Forty-Three Septembers: Essays* (1993). Infusing the personal essay with an acute political awareness, she describes coming out as "a reinterpretation of the traditional coming-of-age story," adding that for black lesbians and gay men, it not only is a "reconciliation of gay lifestyles with Black identity" but also has striking parallels with slave narratives, in that it is "usually a tale of triumph over repressive conditions in which the narrator emerges with a stronger, more positive identity." In "A Swimming Lesson" Grandmother Lydia passed on to the young Jewelle "a skill she herself had not quite mastered":

> The sea has been a fearful place for us. It swallowed us whole when there was no other escape from the holds of slave ships, and did so again more recently with the flimsy refugee flotillas from Haiti. To me, for whom the dark recesses of a tenement hallway were the most unknowable things encountered in my first

nine years, the ocean was a mystery of terrifying proportions. In teaching me to swim, Lydia took away that fear.

Gomez's other works include a comic novel about 1960s black activists facing middle age and a collaborative performance piece based on the life of JAMES BALDWIN.

BIBLIOGRAPHY

Hall, Lynda. "Lorde and Gomez Queer(y)ing Boundaries and Acting in Passion(ate) Plays 'Wherever We Found Space.'" *Callaloo* 23, no. 1 (2000): 394–421.

Gomez, Jewelle. "A Cultural Legacy Denied and Discovered: Black Lesbians in Fiction by Women." In *Home Girls: A Black Feminist Anthology,* edited by Barbara Smith, 110–123. New York: Kitchen Table Press, 1983.

Howard, John. "Selected Strands of Identity." (Review of *Forty-Three Septembers*) *Callaloo* 17, no. 4 (Autumn 1994): 1276–1278.

Lynda Koolish

Gordone, Charles (1925–1995)

A playwright, director, actor, film producer, and educator, Charles Gordone was born Charles Edward Fleming in Cleveland, Ohio. His father, William Fleming, was a garage mechanic; his mother, Camille Morgan Fleming, was a former dancer in Harlem's Cotton Club during the Duke Ellington era. Before his parents became dedicated Seventh Day Adventists and before she became a speech teacher in Cleveland, Ohio, Gordone's mother, who was light enough to pass for white, worked as a circus acrobat. Gordone described himself as being of "Negro, French, Italian, Irish and American-Indian descent" (Oliver and Sills, 383). He changed his name to Gordone as a result of his mother's marriage to William J. Gordon. Educated in the Elkhart public school system where he grew up, after graduating from high school Gordone relocated to Los Angeles, California, where, off and on, he attended University of California–Los

Angeles, California State University at Los Angeles and Los Angeles City College and served in the U.S. Air Force. Records show that, he received a B.A. degree from California State University in 1952.

By 1952, at age 27, Gordone relocated again, this time to New York, where he worked as a waiter and as an actor. He married Juanita Barton and fathered two children, Stephen and Judy Ann. After appearing in the original production of Jean Genet's *The Blacks,* Gordone won the Best Actor of the Year Award for his role in Luther James's all-black off-Broadway production of *Of Mice and Men;* he played the title role in Wole Soyinka's *The Trials of Brother Jero.* He was the associate producer of the film *Nothing but a Man.* Also in New York, Gordone became an activist, cofounding the Committee for the Employment of Negro Performance with Godfrey Cambridge and working with the Ensemble Studio Theatres, the Actors Studio, and the Commission of Civil Disorders. He also became an instructor for the New School for Social Research in New York from 1978 to 1979. He married Jeanne Warner, with whom he fathered a daughter, Leach-Carla.

In 1970, Gordone won the Pulitzer Prize for drama for his first produced play, *No Place to Be Somebody, a Black Comedy in Three Acts* (1969). This was the first time the award was given to an off-Broadway play, and Gordone was the first African-American playwright to win this award in this category. (GWENDOLYN BROOKS had won the Pulitzer for poetry in 1952.) Set in Johnnie's Bar, a West Village bar operated by Johnny Williams, a hustler and crook, *No Place to Be Somebody* focuses on the lives of several club regulars—prostitutes, gangsters, ex-cons, civil rights workers, and crooked politicians—but primarily on the ruthless and violent Williams, whose goal is to take over the neighborhood's racketeering underground life from the local syndicate. Equally important is biracial Gabe Gabriel, a playwright and actor whose difficulty getting parts is directly related to the color of his skin: He is too white for black roles. Gabriel seems to be the raconteur and the raisonneur of the play, the spokesperson for the author. *No Place to Be Somebody* is, fundamentally, Gabriel's play within a play.

Gabriel's recitative, "There's mo' to being black than meets the eye," remains among the classic lines in African-American letters:

> Bein' black is like the way yea walk an'
> Talk!
> It's the way'a lookin' at life!
> Being' black is like saying', "What's hap-
> penin',
> Babee!"
> An' bein' understood! (No Place to Be
> Somebody 432–433)

Ironically, over the years black playwrights, actors, and scholars made Gordone persona non grata for his declaration, at the height of the BLACK ARTS MOVEMENT, that "there has never been such a thing as 'black theatre'" (Gordone). Gordone is said to have declared: "There's no such thing as black culture" (quoted in Costa, 1). Gordone was more interested in a "multiracial American theatre"; he wanted a "truly American Theatre" (Costa, 2).

No Place to Be Somebody, whose original cast included Ron O'Neil (of "Super Fly" fame) as Gabe Gabriel, was a tremendous success. Although a few critics had problems with some identifiable dramaturgical flaws, most compared *No Place to Be Somebody* to the works of Eugene O'Neill and called Gordone the best playwright since Edward Albee. In addition to the Pulitzer Prize, Gordone received several awards for his professional achievements, including an Obie Award for best actor (1953), a Los Angeles Critics Circle Award (1970), a Drama Desk Award (1970), and the Vernon Rice Award (1970). Gordone died from cancer in College Station, Texas, where he was on the faculty of Texas A&M University for almost a decade.

BIBLIOGRAPHY

Costa, Richard H. "The Short Happy Afterlife of Charles Gordone." Available online. URL: http://www.rtis.com/Reg/bcs/pol/touchstone/February96/costa.htm. Accessed October 16, 2006.

Gordone, Charles. *No Place to Be Somebody.* In *Contemporary Black Drama from* A Raisin in the Sun *to* No Place to Be Somebody, edited by Clinton F.

Oliver and Stephanie Sills, 394–451. New York: Charles Scribner's Sons, 1971.

———. "Yes, I Am a Black Playwright, But . . ." *New York Times,* 25 January 1970, Sec. D, p. 1, 11.

Oliver, Clinton F., and Stephanie Sills, eds. *Contemporary Black Drama from* A Raisin in the Sun *to* No Place to Be Somebody. New York: Charles Scribner's Sons, 1971.

Wilfred D. Samuels

Go Tell It on the Mountain
James Baldwin (1953)

Although critics have provided numerous interpretations of *Go Tell It on the Mountain,* JAMES BALDWIN's first and most celebrated novel, it is essentially the coming of age narrative of John Grimes, the protagonist. The stepson of Gabriel Grimes, a Pentecostal preacher (like Baldwin's father), whom he believes to be his real father, John struggles to escape the life he feels he is destined to live as both an African-American male and the son of one of "God's Anointed." Divided into three sections, the main action of the narrative takes place during a Saturday night prayer meeting at the Temple of the Fire Baptized, where one by one the lives of the adults—Gabriel, his wife Elizabeth, and his sister Florence—are revealed through flashbacks as each approaches the altar to pray. Through these exposed memories, readers learn about the personal struggle each has undergone and its role in shaping their personalities and current behavior.

The second part, "Prayers of the Saints," unmasks the backgrounds of the adults who influence John's life. During "Florence's Prayer," the narrator reveals that Florence had abandoned the South and her insensible mother for Harlem, where she met and married Frank, a BLUES singer who "drank too much." Ultimately rejecting Frank, Florence seeks refuge in the church. Attempting to impede Gabriel's abuse of his family, Florence exposes his past as a "prancing tomcat." "Gabriel's Prayer" reveals that Gabriel's desire to force both his religious beliefs and his sense of damnation on John are directly related to his own tumultu-

ous and shameful past, in which he married the defiled and barren Deborah, the victim of a brutal rape, out of pity, and committed adultery with "the harlot" Esther, producing an illegitimate son, Royal, out of lust. Seeking redemption, Gabriel marries Elizabeth and commits to raising John, her son. However, wracked with guilt for his past sins and anxious to receive a sign of God's forgiveness, to be embodied in the conversion of his biological son, Roy, the true heir, Gabriel transfers his self-hatred to John, who, instead of Roy, stands at the threshold of conversion. Finally, as "Elizabeth's Prayer" begins, Elizabeth reveals that, raised by a religious aunt whom she despised, she had fled to New York with her lover, Richard, who later committed suicide in response to his overwhelming struggles against oppression and racism. Elizabeth is forced to raise John, their love child, alone after Richard's death. As a means of redemption, Elizabeth marries Gabriel, whose commitment to God she admires and whose professed love and promise to raise John as his own son offers her the security and assistance she needs.

The third section, "The Threshing Floor," relates the battle for John's soul and spiritual rebirth. Through surrealistic images and dizzying dreamlike sequences, Baldwin takes John through the Pentecostal rites of passage necessary to accept God. In the midst of this ritual, John hears two voices—one that condemns him and the other that urges him toward redemption. John, who at 14 had begun to develop homosexual interest, struggles to reconcile his sexuality with his faith. Baldwin highlights the eroticism and sensuality of the black worship service and locates both sexuality and spirituality in the body of teenage Elisha, John's love interest, whose voice is the second voice he hears during his struggle to find salvation.

BIBLIOGRAPHY

Baldwin, James. "Everybody's Protest Novel." In *The Price of the Ticket: Collected Nonfiction, 1948–1985,* 27–33. New York: St. Martin's, 1985.

———. *Go Tell It on the Mountain.* New York: Knopf, 1953.

Johnson, E. Patrick. "Feeling the Spirit of the Dark: Expanding Notions of the Sacred in the African

American Gay Community." *Callaloo* 21 (1998): 399–416.

David Shane Wallace

Go the Way Your Blood Beats: An Anthology of Lesbian and Gay Fiction by African-American Writers
Shawn Stewart Ruff, ed. (1996)

Go the Way Your Blood Beats chronicles four decades of fiction by African-American gays and lesbians and distinguishes the work as a major contribution to the contemporary African-American literary canon. As he notes in his introduction, editor Shawn Stewart Ruff juxtaposes the work of earlier African-American writers with the work of notable present-day authors to weave a common thread that represents the lives of gay and lesbian African Americans. Although the collection is organized thematically to direct gay or straight, black or white readers toward a compassioned understanding of the fears and intolerance that same-gender–loving (SGL) people often face, historically the overriding themes of the stories and novel excerpts remain the same.

Go the Way is divided into five sections. The first section, "Wet behind the Ears," includes stories on self-discovery amid adversity and isolation. "Bad Blood" opens with AMIRI BARAKA's "The Alternative." African erotica is explored in "Behind Closed Doors," a section written by true imagists. According to Ruff, the section "Blood, Sweat, and Tears" concentrates on stories of sexual ambiguity. He includes RICHARD WRIGHT's, "Man of All Work," which features a "desperate cross-dresser" (xxii), in this section. "Heartache" introduces "Just Friends," a series of journal entries written by Brooke M. Stephens that documents the spiritual and life journeys of two friends. "Hemorrhaging" opens with Orian Hyde Weeks's "Dissimulations" and continues with "Afro Jew Fro," a story by Catherine C. McKinley. All of the stories feature forms of self-abuse triggered by denial of sexual orientation.

Go the Way's strength lies in the variety, complexity, and candid and credible voices that speak in each entry. For example, in "The Women," Gayl Jones's 11-year old Winnie Flynn recounts her journey toward understanding that her mother is a lesbian. In SAPPHIRE's "There's a Window," a truly touching image appears through nonsensual sex. Two female prisoners engage in aggressive, latex-protected sex. The sex is cold and callous and as distant as the perverse imagistic wild West terrain that the role-playing activities generate. Slowly, though, sex is shown to be an escapist form of coping in prison. RICHARD BRUCE NUGENT's stream-of-conscious story "SMOKE, LILIES, AND JADE" paints a portrait of the African-American writer, artist, poet, and philosopher en route to discovering the meaning of beauty. Wright's story could easily be read as a radio play. Every detail of the story, every action, reaction, and emotion, is delivered in crisp, vibrant dialogue. There is a constant sense of entrapment to the chores and expectations, as if Carl's impersonation of his wife is truly awkward and uncomfortable. When Carl is finally allowed home, he is glad to be there as a man, as himself.

"To go the way your blood beats," according to Ruff, is to "live life instinctively, intuitively, with integrity and an awareness of consequences" (xxiii). In other words, Ruff suggests that there are no overriding themes in life, no general terms to guide us. Contributors to *Go the Way Your Blood Beats* offer generous insights into the mysteries that make all of us individual and whole.

BIBLIOGRAPHY
Ruff, Shawn Stewart, ed. *Go the Way Your Blood Beats: An Anthology of Lesbian and Gay Fiction by African-American Writers.* New York: Henry Holt and Company, 1996.

Lawrence T. Potter, Jr.

Greatest Taboo: Homosexuality in Black Communities, The   **Delroy Constantine-Simms** (2001)

Delroy Constantine-Simms, the editor of *Greatest Taboo,* was born and educated in England. He holds degrees in English, sociology, education, and occupational psychology. He identifies as heterosexual. *The Greatest Taboo: Homosexuality in Black Communities* is one of the most comprehensive attempts yet to document and culturally situate homosexuality, bisexuality, and transgender identities as regular and "normal" components of life throughout the African diaspora. Published by Alyson Press, the world's largest gay and lesbian press, *Taboo* won the Lambda Literary Award for best nonfiction anthology in 2001.

Taboo's 28 selections are spread over seven sections titled "Negotiating the Racial Politics of Black Sexual Identity," "Sexuality and the Black Church," "Homosexuality in Africa," "Homosexuality and Heterosexist Dress Codes," "Iconic Signifiers of the Gay Harlem Renaissance," "Heterosexism and Homophobia in Popular Black Music," "Homosexuality in Popular Black Literature," and "The Silent Mythology Surrounding AIDS and Public Icons." The selections systematically explore the discursive and performative strategies that have been used by and against transgendered and nonheterosexual blacks transhistorically and worldwide.

Mixing essays by well-known figures in black cultural studies such as HENRY LOUIS GATES, JR. (who contributes a foreword), BELL HOOKS, and Philip Brian Harper with work from emerging writers from a range of academic disciplines and public locations, the anthology functions as an activist document. All of the articles straightforwardly attempt to legitimate transgendered, homosexual, and bisexual identities on the diasporic stage. This activism is not presented, however, as a given.

According to the editor of the volume, "The notable absence of [antagonistic] views in this anthology indicates . . . an unwillingness to be recognized on a wider, and possibly global platform, as being homophobic" (xx). This sense that homophobia is becoming discursively untenable thanks no doubt to the kind of counterevidence marshaled in this anthology is articulated in the cri de coeur by Conrad Pegues that touchingly, although perhaps too blithely, closes the book. According to Pegues, "When the African American community comes to the expanded consciousness that same-gender-loving African Americans are not the enemy, then our 'other sexual' truth may set us all free" (454).

BIBLIOGRAPHY
"Delroy Constantine-Simms and *The Greatest Taboo*." Interview by Raj Ayyar. Gay Today: A Global Site for Daily Gay News. Available online. URL: http://gaytoday.com/garchive/interview/O60102in.htm. Accessed October 16, 2006.

Terry Rowden

Greenlee, Sam (1930–)

Chicago-born Sam Greenlee studied at the University of Chicago (1954–1957) and the University of Thesaloniki, Greece (1963–1964), after receiving his B.S. degree from the University of Wisconsin, Madison, in 1952. According to Greenlee, he was born to a "refugee family," "a second generation immigrant from the deep South." His father was a chauffeur, his mother a singer and dancer in the chorus line of the Chicago's Regal Theater. Joining the military with his undergraduate degree in hand, Greenlee served as a U.S. information officer for more than eight years in Asia, Europe, and the Middle East.

Greenlee is best known for his only successfully received novel, *The Spook Who Sat by the Door,* which was published in 1969 amidst the CIVIL RIGHTS MOVEMENT and the hovering discontent that became the Black Revolt. He almost immediately became a cult hero and celebrity for candidly revealing in his fiction the pervasiveness of racism within branches of the federal government; in the end, he satirizes and critiques the government for being more interested in window dressing than for its true commitment to integrating its most sacred institutions, particularly the FBI and CIA.

When U.S. senator Gilbert Hennington blackmails the CIA into hiring its first black agent, in order to appease the black vote and win reelection, protagonist Sam Freeman, a social worker from Chicago's South Side who works with street gangs, wins the token spot by outsmarting his middle-class black competitors. During training, Freeman, a former marine, isolates himself from the other blacks, perfects his genuflections, and simultaneously displays his skills in martial arts when he beats and shames his white trainer during a competition.

Despite his stellar performance on the test (he scores 480 points out of 500) and impeccable military experience, Freeman, deemed incapable of working in the field, where, because of his assumed intellectual inferiority, he might jeopardize his white colleagues, was assigned to the main office where he could be watched. When the general asks the director of the training school to describe Freeman, the director responds, "Well, slow-witted, a plodder. . . . Only in athletics does he seem to do things naturally. Physically, he could be expected to react instantly and efficiently, but in a mental crisis, I don't know" (29). Freeman is made the chief of the top-secret reproduction section—the operator of the mimeograph (ditto) machine: "being the only man in the section, he was little more than the highest paid reproduction clerk in Washington. Nevertheless, he was the Only Negro officer in the CIA" (40).

A year later Freeman is promoted to special assistant to the director of the CIA, given a glass suite within the director's office, and assigned the role of the "black and conspicuous . . . integrated Negro of the Central Intelligence Agency of the United States of American" (47). Freeman, who successfully assumes a dual identity as Washington's Uncle Tom (see SAMBO AND UNCLE TOM) during the week and as an urban hipster and playboy with an apartment and lover in Harlem on the weekends, uses this role as window dressing to his advantage, endearing himself to the general, who uses him as an administrative assistant and global travel partner. Remaining vigilant, Freeman devours the secret reports to which he has access.

Unbeknownst to the general, Freeman carefully observes and studies the global warfare in which the CIA plays a major role. Consequently, Freeman becomes a master of guerrilla warfare and eventually leaves the CIA; returns to Chicago; takes over and organizes the gangs, particularly the Cobras; trains them to become freedom fighters; and leads them into urban revolt.

Greenlee's protagonist, Dan Freeman, is the literary opposite of RALPH ELLISON's protagonist in *INVISIBLE MAN*. In his duplicitous role at the CIA, he masters and plays well Ellison's grandfather's advice to the naive protagonist: "our life is a war. . . . Live with your head in the lion's mouth. I want you to overcome 'em with yeses, undermine 'em with grins, agree 'em to death and destruction" (Ellison, 16). Freeman seems to accept this advice as a given, and, though some merely saw his invisibility as the equivalent of his identity as a ghost, no more than a "spook," a racial slur in black vernacular, he is anything but naive. He is a warrior who, though viewed as an apparition, not only is committed to the destruction of oppressive white society but also works to ensure it. In the end, no one, not even blacks, would believe a black man was capable of such an elaborate scheme, which, in the novel, the FBI calls "the most sophisticated underground in the Western Hemisphere, the creation of an expert" (242).

Greenlee is also the author of *Blues for an African Princess,* a collection of poems; *Baghdad Blues,* a novel; and *Ammunition: Poetry and Other Raps.* First published in London, perhaps because of the sensitive themes, *The Spook Who Sat by the Door* won the *London Sunday Times* Book of the Year Award in 1969. Ivan Dixon produced the movie version of it in 1973.

BIBLIOGRAPHY

Ellison, Ralph. *Invisible Man.* New York: Vintage Books, 1989.
Greenlee, Sam. *The Spook Who Sat by the Door.* New York: Bantam Books, 1969.

Wilfred D. Samuels

Griggs, Sutton E.   (1872–1933)

Novelist, essayist, orator, and Baptist pastor, Sutton Elbert Griggs was the first of five children of Allen, a prominent Baptist minister in the South, and Emma Griggs in Chatfield, Texas, on June 19, 1872. Profoundly influenced by his Baptist father, Griggs was baptized in 1885. He studied at Bishop College at Houston, Texas, and later earned his doctor of divinity degree at Richmond Theological Institute in 1893. While serving as a deacon at the First Baptist Church of Berkley, Virginia, he married Emma J. Williams in 1897, who became his lifelong companion, and began to write fiction.

His first novel, *Imperio in Imperio* (1899), was published by his own Editor Publishing Company. Influenced by BOOKER T. WASHINGTON's and W. E. B. DuBois's arguments on "the Negro problem," in the novel Griggs presents and mediates their perceptions through two protagonists, Belton and Bernard. He was the first African-American novelist to introduce the reader to the concept of the New Negro: "The cringing, fawning, sniffing, cowardly Negro which slavery left, had disappeared, and a new Negro, self-respecting, fearless, and determined in the assertion of his rights was at hand" (62). Although the sales of the novel were low (it was sold mostly at black churches and Christian conventions), Griggs continued to write, publishing two more novels, *Overshadowed* (1901) and *Unfettered with Dorlan's Plan* (1902).

Disappointed with the overall low book sales, after *Unfettered,* Griggs hesitated to write more novels but did so after the National Baptist Convention (St. Louis, Missouri) asked him to write one to respond to Thomas Dixon, Jr.'s racist novel *The Leopard's Spots* (1902). The convention pledged to provide financial support to Griggs for this project; however, when he completed *The Hindered Hand* in 1905, he was on his own again. Although this book sold more copies than his previous novels, the sales were still low. Turning to writing critical essays instead, he published *The One Great Question,* on the race problem, in 1907. The following year, he wrote his last novel, *Pointing the Way* (1908). Realizing that his essay collection was more popular than his novels, Griggs decided not to write any more fiction.

In his novels, Griggs borrows from the sentimental romance, with its major motifs of love and exaggeration, in order to present his thoughts on current race issues. While he ambitiously attempts to accommodate too many racial and sociopolitical issues, such as Jim Crowism, Black Nationalism, Garveyism, New Negroism, and miscegenation, his novels often include lengthy rhetorical discussion and argument among characters. Consequently they lack realistic plots and character development, which has led some critics to describe his fiction as "primitive." Viewed within the context of American modernism, however, Griggs's fiction might be considered fashionable; it could be described as what Robert Scholes calls "fabulation": "a return to a more verbal kind of fiction . . . a less realistic and more artistic kind of narrative; more shapely, more evocative; more concerned with ideas and ideals, less concerned with things" (quoted in Bell, 284). However, focusing more on social realism in Griggs's work, many critics have failed to place him within a modernist context.

Griggs also published his autobiography, *The Story of My Struggles* (1914); a biography, *Triumph of the Simple Virtue, or, The Life Story of John L. Webb* (1926); and more than 20 collections of essays and pamphlets on the issue of race, including *Wisdom's Call* (1911), *Life's Demands* (1916), *Guide to Racial Greatness* (1923), and *Friction between the Races: Causes and Cure* (1930). In these works, Griggs suggested conservatism, collective efficiency, and Christlike love as resolutions to the American race problem. In addition to publishing, Griggs was involved in DuBois's Niagara Movement as a member of the black literati; DuBois was pleased with Griggs's interest in the movement. Griggs served as pastor at the First Baptist Church of Berkley (Va., 1900–1901), First Baptist Church (East Nashville, Tenn., 1901–1908), Tabernacle Baptist Church (Memphis, Tenn., 1913–1922 and 1926–1931), and Hopewell Baptist Church (Denison, Tex., 1922–1924 and 1931–1932) and as the first president of American Baptist Theological Seminary (Nashville, Tenn., 1925–1926). Griggs moved from Denison to Houston in the winter of 1932. He died suddenly on January 3, 1933.

BIBLIOGRAPHY

Bell, Bernard. *The Afro-American Novel and Its Tradition.* Amherst: University of Massachusetts Press, 1987.

Elder, Arlene A. "Sutton Griggs: The Dilemma of the Black Bourgeoisie." In *The "Hindered Hand": Cultural Implications of Early African-American Fiction,* 69–103. Westport, Cincinnati, and London: Greenwood, 1978.

Frazier, Larry. "Sutton E. Griggs's *Imperium in Imperio* as Evidence of Black Baptist Radicalism." *Baptist History and Heritage* 30 (Spring 2000): 72–91.

Moses, Wilson Jeremiah. "The Novels of Sutton Griggs and Literary Black Nationalism." In *The Golden Age of Black Nationalism 1850–1925*, 170–193. Hamden, Conn.: Archon, 1978.

Jai Young Park

Grimké, Angelina Weld (1880–1958)

As a writer of plays, fiction, and poetry, Grimké devoted much of her art to examining the effects of racism on the African-American family. Born into a celebrated family herself, she seems to have always been interested in the dynamics of the parent-child bond within the context of African-American history. Grimké was biracial. Her mother, Sarah Stanley, was white, and her father, Archibald Grimké, was a prominent African-American writer and scholar who had been born a slave. Archibald's mother was also a slave, owned by his white father, Henry Grimké. Henry was the brother of the prominent abolitionists Sarah and Angelina Grimké (Weld), who fled their southern home for Massachusetts before the Civil War in protest of their family's slaveholding. Archibald's aunts later acknowledged him as their nephew and supported him during his years at Harvard Law School. Named after her great-aunt, Angelina grew up with her family's passionate commitment to civil and women's rights. She did not, however, grow up with her mother. A victim of mental health problems, Angelina's mother left the family shortly after her daughter was born. Archibald was a doting and involved father, and his love of learning and writing flourished in his daughter as well.

Employed for most of her life as a teacher, Grimké wrote poetry from a young age. Her first published writing was fiction and drama, however. The play *Rachel,* like most of Grimké's prose, exposed the roots of American racism and its detrimental effect on the hallowed ideals of the American family. The threat of lynching and rape deter the healthy interaction of the African-American family and the growth of love relationships. Produced in Washington, D.C., in 1916, *Rachel* was the first play written by and wholly performed by African Americans. The work was published in 1920. Grimké's other play, "Mara," was never published and did not meet with the same critical success as her first. Most scholars agree that the play is too sentimental—a criticism leveled at most of her short fiction as well. Grimké's target audience for her prose was white, middle-class women—notorious fans of sentimental novels of the time—and Grimké may have structured her writing too much to that taste. Nevertheless, all of her work examines how the most simple and natural human relationships, especially those between mother and children, are tragically altered by the effect of racial prejudice.

Grimké is best known for her poetry. Published in such hallmark anthologies as ALAIN LOCKE's *The NEW NEGRO* (1927) and COUNTEE CULLEN's *Caroling Dusk* (1927), Grimké's poetry is redolent with images of nature and the pain of lost love. "When the Green Lies over the Earth" is exemplary:

> . . . *when the wind all day is sweet*
> *With the breath of growing things,*
> . . . . .
> *Then oh! My dear, when the youth's in the year,*
> *Yours is the face that I long to have near*
> *Yours is the face, my dear.*
> *(Caroling Dusk 41–42)*

Recent feminist scholars suggest that Grimké's love poetry reflects her repressed lesbianism. Most of these poems are written through the voice of a white male persona to a female lover (often African American), and the choice to construct the poems in such a manner with an emphasis on forbidden racial love may indicate Grimké's displacement of her own desires in a world that would have not accepted her sexuality. Though she is often included in contemporary anthologies of HARLEM RENAISSANCE poets, she was not widely published with other members of the movement, nor was she known to meet or correspond with them. The themes found in her fiction and drama are not as present in her lyrics. The poetry represents something more private and personal for Grimké, while her prose more directly explores the social climate of her time.

BIBLIOGRAPHY

Cullen, Countee, ed. *Caroling Dusk.* New York: Citadel Press Book, 1927.

Hirsch, David. "Speaking Silences in Angelina Weld Grimké's 'The Closing Door' and 'Blackness.'" *African American Review* 26, no. 3 (1992): 459–474.

Hull, Gloria. *Color, Sex, and Poetry.* Bloomington: Indiana University Press, 1987.

Miller, Jeanne-Marie. "Angelina Weld Grimké: Playwright and Poet." *College Language Association Journal* 21 (1978): 513–524.

Tracie Church Guzzio

Grooms, Anthony (1955–)

Born in Charlottesville, Virginia, on January 15, 1955, Grooms received a bachelor's degree from the College of William and Mary in 1978 and an M.F.A. from George Mason in 1984. He has taught at various universities in Georgia, including the University of Georgia, Clark Atlanta University, Emory University, and Morehouse College. He has also taught at the University of Cape Coast in Ghana, West Africa, and has been on the faculty at Kennesaw State University since 1994.

While a theater major at William and Mary, Grooms had two of his plays, "Accidents" and "Dr. Madlove," produced. His stories and poems have been published in such journals as CALLALOO, AFRICAN AMERICAN REVIEW, *Crab Orchard Review,* and *George Washington Review.* Although he has published a collection of poems, *Ice Poems* (1988), Grooms found his most eloquent voice in his fiction, particularly on the subject of the CIVIL RIGHTS MOVEMENT. Grooms has given this context to his subject matter in a public interview:

I consider myself privileged to have come of age at the time of great social change in this country. I feel that in many ways my experiences straddle social and historical lines. Whereas I have vague memories of "Colored Only" signs, and of riding in the back of buses, my more vivid memories are of being "first" or "only" or "one of a few" as the various social barriers fell. In retrospect, it is

these latter memories that give me the sense of privilege and have contributed to the texture of *Trouble No More.* The events of the stories come from various origins—family, hearsay, and history.

Taking his title from a song by BLUES legend Muddy Waters, Grooms does his best work in "Negro Progress," a story in which a young man is caught in downtown Birmingham on the day that Bull Connor has ordered city fire fighters to bring out the hoses to attack civil rights marchers. Using the facts of history and the names of historical figures (MARTIN LUTHER KING, Walter Cronkite, and Bull Connor) and Birmingham neighborhoods (Mountain Brook and Titusville), Grooms blends in fictional characters who could have been caught in the fray. The story begins: "The water hunted the boy. It chipped bark from the oaks as he darted behind the trees. It caught him in the back. His lanky legs buckled. Then, as if the fireman who directed the hose were playing a game, the boy's legs were cut from under him, and he was rolled over and over in the mud" (26). Grooms captures in words the power of the disturbing photographs of the day.

In his first novel, *Bombingham* (2001), Grooms returns to the city of Birmingham of 1963. He begins with Walter Burke, a Vietnam foot soldier, who labors at writing a letter to the parents of his comrade who has been killed. Burke struggles with his words, unable to stop reflecting on his youth in Alabama. When he was 11, his mother died of cancer on the day the 16th Street Baptist Church was bombed, and his best friend, Lamar, died as well. Historically, on that day, two white 16-year-old boys shot a young boy named Virgil Lamar Ware while he was riding on the handlebars of a bicycle pedaled by his brother; he fell to the ground and died. Grooms's fictional Lamar's death matches the known details of young Ware's death, a tragedy that was lost in the more dramatic news of this infamous day. Grooms's novel calls attention to this oversight: the tragic death of a youth and the profound impact such loss has on the ordinary people who know firsthand what it feels like to grieve for the young.

For both *Trouble No More* and *Bombingham,* Grooms won the Lillian Smith Prize for Fiction (1996, 2002). He has received Wesleyan College's Lamar Lectureship and an Arts Administration Fellowship from the National Endowment for the Arts.

BIBLIOGRAPHY

Grooms, Anthony. *Bombingham.* New York: Free Press, 2001.
———. *Trouble No More.* Palo Alto, Calif.: LaQuesta Press, 1995.

Margaret Whitt

Gunn, William (Bill) Harrison
(1934–1989)

Playwright, actor, filmmaker, screenwriter, and novelist William (Bill) Harrison Gunn became a respected, admired, and versatile artist and broke new ground in the area of black independent film. He was born on July 15, 1934, in Philadelphia, Pennsylvania, where he grew up in a middle-class environment with creative parents and attended integrated public schools. His father, William Harrison, also known as Bill Gunn, was a songwriter, musician, comedian, and unpublished poet. Louise Alexander Gunn, his mother, was an actress and a beauty contest winner who ran her own theater group, where Gunn got an early taste for drama. He served for a short time in the U.S. Navy and then moved to New York, where he became an actor.

Gunn's career in the performing arts began in the 1950s. He appeared in *Member of the Wedding* (1950), *The Immoralist* (1954), *Take a Giant Step* (1954), *Sign of Winter* (1958), *The Sound and the Fury* (1959), *Moon on a Rainbow Shawl* (1962), *The Interns* (1962), *Anthony and Cleopatra, The Winter's Tale* (1963), *The Spy with My Face* (1966), and later in *Losing Ground* (1982). During this time, he also appeared in such popular television series and films as *American Parade, Danger, The Fugitive, Dr. Kildare, The Interns, Outer Limits, Route 66, Stoney Burke, Tarzan,* and *The Cosby Show.*

After Gunn saved up enough money as a Broadway and off-Broadway performer, he began a parallel career as a playwright and a writer; this provided him with the opportunity to steadily develop a degree of racial consciousness and explore issues of racial identity in his plays and novels. Devoid of racial overtones or issues, Gunn's first stage play, *Marcus in the High Grass* (1958), featured two white actors in the leading roles; consequently, some critics believed he was a white playwright. *Marcus* was followed by his 1972 Emmy Award–winning one-act play, *Johnnas* (1968), which focuses on the role of the black artist in a crass world. Gunn next wrote two musicals, *Black Picture Show* (1975), for which he received two AUDELCO awards for best playwright and best play of the year, and *Rhinestone Sharecropping* (1982); both were adapted from his novels with the same titles. Three years later, his *Family Employment* (1985) was produced, and he was cast in the leading role in his *The Forbidden City* (1989), produced by the New York Shakespeare Festival.

Gunn launched his career as a novelist in the mid-1960s, largely to supplement his income as an actor. Like his stage plays and several screenplays, his semiautobiographical novels address such broader themes as personal development and self-discovery, especially of the artist in conflict with society. Rooted in the French existentialist philosophies of Jean-Paul Sartre and Albert Camus, Gunn's first novel, the bildungsroman *All the Rest Have Died* (1964), chronicles a young man's quest for a successful, meaningful life; *Black Picture Show* (1975) depicts an artist whose standards are compromised, and *Rhinestone Sharecropping* (1981) portrays the black artist at odds with racism, greed, and commercialism.

Although many companies and studios resisted serious films about black culture, confining themselves, during the late 1960s and 1970s, to exploitation movies, Gunn wrote for movies and television. He was, according to film critic Melvin Donalson, among the handful of filmmakers and actors who moved beyond Hollywood's "formulaic predictability" to offer alternative black images and create "'art' outside the Hollywood system" (6).

Gunn acted in several of his screenplays, including *Fame Game* and *Friends* (1968) and *Stop* (1969). In 1970 he released three screenplays: *Angel Levine,* based on Bernard Malamud's "The Angel Levine"; *Don't the Moon Look Lonesome,* adapted from Don Asher's novel; and *The Landlord,* based on Kristin Hunter's novel. Gunn's screen biography, *Bessie* (1972), was adapted from Chris Albertson's novel. In 1973, *Ganja and Hess,* reedited as *Blood Couple,* was selected as one of the 10 best American films of the decade at the Cannes Film Festival in France. Gunn directed *Ganja and Hess* and appeared in it as George Meda. Gunn also wrote *The Greatest: The Muhammad Ali Story* (1976), starring Muhammad Ali, Ernest Borgnine, James Earl Jones, Roger E. Mosely, Paul Winfield, Lloyd Haynes, and Dina Merrill; he also wrote *Men of Bronze* (1988).

On April 5, 1989, one day before *The Forbidden City* opened at the Public Theater, Gunn died of encephalitis in Nyack Hospital in New York. In the spring of 1989, *Black Film Review* dedicated a special issue to him. In 1991 Phyllis Klotman co-dedicated *Screenplays of the African American Experience* to Gunn and to his friend Kathleen Collins Prettyman.

BIBLIOGRAPHY

Donalson, Melvin. *Black Directors in Hollywood.* Austin: University of Texas Press, 2003.

Monaco, James. *American Film Now.* New York: Oxford University Press, 1979.

Schraufnagel, Noel. *From Apology to Protest: The Black American Novel.* Deland, Fla.: Everett/Edwards, 1973.

Loretta Gilchrist Woodard

Guy, Rosa Cuthbert   (1925 or 1928–   )

A playwright, short story writer, and author of young-adult fiction, Rosa Cuthbert Guy was born in Diego Martin, Trinidad, to Henry and Audrey Cuthbert, who migrated to New York in the 1930s. Their daughters, Rosa and Ameze, followed later in 1932. By 1934 the girls had become orphans who lived with a cousin—a political radical with ties to MARCUS GARVEY's UNIA who taught Guy to be socially aware. By the time she was 14, Guy had to leave school to help take care of her older sister. She married Warren Guy, Sr., and gave birth to a son, Warren Jr. They divorced in 1950. During World War II, while her husband was in the service, Guy worked with the American Negro Theatre. Along with novelist JOHN KILLENS, Guy cofounded the Harlem Writers Guild, a workshop whose participants included MAYA ANGELOU, LONNE ELDER, and fellow Caribbean-born African-American writer PAULE MARSHALL. The guild provided a venue for Guy's further educational development, which she had also pursued at New York University. Guy, who became friends with MALCOLM X, became actively involved in the CIVIL RIGHTS MOVEMENT.

The author of more than 15 novels, Guy published her first novel, *Bird at My Window,* in 1966. Set in Harlem, as is much of Guy's fiction, during the period of the BLACK ARTS MOVEMENT, *Bird at My Window* is a painful examination of a mother-son relationship. Coffee House Press republished it in 2001. Guy's next book, *Children of Longing* (1950), a collection of essays, was followed by her trilogy, *The Friends* (1973), *Ruby* (1978), and *Edith Jackson* (1979). Guy, who lived in Haiti and New York during the 1980s, was prolific during that time, publishing *A Measure of Time* (1983), *New Guys around the Block* (1983), *Paris, Pee Wee and Big Dog* (1984), *My Love, My Love: or The Peasant Girl* (1985) *And I Heard a Bird Sing* (1987), and *The Ups and Downs of Carl David III* (1989), among other works. She published an adult novel, *The Sun, the Sea, a Touch of Wind,* in 1985. *My Love, My Love* became the basis of an award-winning musical.

However, among her young-adult fiction, Guy's award-winning, somewhat autobiographical novel *The Friends* remains her best known. Set in Harlem during the Great Depression, *The Friends* tells the story of the Cathy family, West Indian immigrants, and particularly the experiences of their daughters, Phyllisia and Ruby, who come of age in a new culture and educational system. Finding herself alone in her new environment, Phyllisia is desperate to make new friends and simultaneously keep the value system the family brings with them from "back home." Deemed ugly, even by her father, Calvin, Phyllisia is desperate to have a friend and fit in. Her classmates tease her and even beat her up because of her accent and intelligence. Phyllisia knows all the answers to the teacher's questions.

In the end Phyllisia chooses Edith Jackson, the class misfit. Motherless and surrogate mother to her siblings, Edith is often absent and, when she comes to school, she is disheveled. Clearly, Edith comes from the opposite end of the economic spectrum from Phyllisia. Edith, who cares deeply for Phyllisia, protects and defends her when the others tease and attempt to attack her. When Phyllisia finally invites Edith to meet her family, Calvin does not welcome her. Considering her poor, jinxed, and a "picky-headed ragamuffin," Calvin chases defenseless Edith from the family home, fracturing the friendship between the two girls. Phyllisia later admits that she was complicit; like her father, she, too, held elitist views and, consequently, had thought she was better than Edith.

By the time the two friends reunite and recommit to their friendship, their family lives have changed dramatically. Following their mother's death, Phyllisia and Ruby have to learn to accept their father for who and what he is. Although they consider him a strict disciplinarian who imprisons them in their home—they are not allowed to have boyfriends although they are in high school—they come to see him as hardworking and responsible. Following Edith's younger sister's death from measles and poverty (they are too poor to secure the medical care she needs), the welfare system breaks up the family, placing them, including Edith, in different foster homes. Despite these hardships, however, Phyllisia and Edith recommit to their friendships and love, promising to stay in touch and be there for each other. Guy examines the lives of Ruby and Edith in novels that bear their names.

The central themes of the trilogy are the problems that young black adolescents faced growing up in the 1960s, conflicts within families, friendship, quest for identity, prejudice and racism (inter and intraracial issues of race), conflict between African Americans and West Indians in the inner city,

violence, riots, and police profiling, among many others. Critics almost universally describe the trilogy as powerful and memorable. The trilogy received an American Library Association citation, and *The Friends* is required reading in many secondary school systems.

Guy has received the Coretta Scott King Award, the *New York Times* Outstanding Book of the Year citation, and the American Library Association Best Book Award. Guy continues to live in New York City.

Wilfred D. Samuels

Guy-Shetfall, Beverly   (1946–   )

Born in Memphis, Tennessee, Guy-Sheftall received her B.A. at Spelman College, an M.A. at Atlanta University (now Clark Atlanta University), and her Ph.D. in 1977 at Emory College. Guy-Sheftall has been a professor at Spelman since 1971, where she founded, in 1981, the Women's Research and Resource Center. Guy-Sheftall coedited *Sturdy Black Bridges: Visions of Black Women in Literature* (1979), a benchmark anthology of African-American women literature. In addition, she coedited *Double Stitch: Black Women Write about Mothers and Daughters* (1992), a collection of prose, poetry, and scholarship by 47 black women writers who explore the bond between black mothers and daughters.

Her most recent nonfiction works, *Words of Fire: An Anthology of African American Feminist Thought* (1995) and *Gender Talk* (2003), written with Johnnetta B. Cole, former president of Spelman College, are her most notable and enduring texts. In the preface to *Words of Fire*, Guy-Sheftall writes that the anthology "documents the presence of a continuous feminist intellectual tradition in the nonfictional prose of African-American women going back to the early nineteenth century when abolition and suffrage were urgent political issues. It is a rewriting of the familiar narrative of American feminism and a retelling of African American intellectual history." The anthology has seven chapters and includes the works of such notable feminists of the early 19th century as

Maria Stewart, Sojourner Truth, and FRANCES W. E. HARPER and the contemporary feminist writings of Barbara Smith, BELL HOOKS, Angela Davis, and Patricia Hill Collins.

In the preface to *Gender Talk,* Guy-Sheftall explains the book's genesis:

[It] was born while we [Cole and Guy-Sheftall] were coteaching; engaging in heated discussions outside the classroom about the state of the race; witnessing and debating a number of gender-related issues on and off campus—such as the founding of a new lesbian/bisexual student organization at Spelman, and Anita Hill's visit to the campus in the aftermath of the Clarence Thomas Supreme Court hearings.

The book explores a number of key issues surrounding gender politics within the African-American community: black women's liberation, the black church, hip-hop music and videos, and domestic abuse. In the book's critique of black men and women's gender relationships, many key questions are asked: Were the achievements of black women diminished by black men during the CIVIL RIGHTS and BLACK POWER movements? Has the black community ignored domestic abuse? Do hip-hop lyrics demean black women? Have black men aligned themselves with white patriarchal ideology?

Guy-Sheftall is the Anna Julia Cooper Professor of English at Spelman College, a coeditor of *Sage: A Scholarly Journal on Black Women,* and a frequent speaker on women's studies and feminist issues.

Beverly A. Tate

Hamer, Forrest (1956–)

Prize-winning poet, literary critic, and practicing psychologist Forrest Hamer was born on August 31, 1956, in Goldsboro, North Carolina, to Forrest T. Hamer (U.S. Army) and Bertha Barnes Hamer, an elementary school teacher. Raised in North Carolina, Hamer graduated from Yale with honors and received a doctorate in psychology from the University of California, Berkeley. The author of two volumes of poems, twice a nominee for the Pushcart Prize, and a semifinalist for the 1995 Yale Younger Poets Series, Hamer is also the author of essays and reviews on A. R. Ammons, George Higgins, Marilyn Nelson, and REGINALD SHEPHERD. An advanced candidate at the San Francisco Psychoanalytic Institute, Hamer is a lecturer in psychology and social welfare at the University of California, Berkeley.

Forrest Hamer's poetic voice is confessional, unsentimental, delicate, crystalline, and intensely autobiographical; it coheres around memories of his childhood and adolescence in the South. His syntax of affective association is brought on by such repeated injunctions as *Say* ("Middle Ear"), *Consider* ("Sign"), and *Suppose* ("13 Suppositions about the Ubiquitous"). He uses the quiet, spare elegance of contemporary free verse—the language of ROBERT HAYDEN and MICHAEL HARPER—not only to convey his own melancholy, as a gay man alone in the wake of loss (the specter of AIDS unspoken but present in poems like "With-out John") but also to describe his black kin and brethren with powerful precision. "Down by the Riverside" illuminates one intersection of personal and public history as Hamer guides the reader through a child's evolving consciousness of war as his father fights in Vietnam. "Choir Practice" explores Hamer's conscious reconnection, after long silence and alienation, to his family, heritage, and history from a multiplicity of angles, including his encounters with his hectoring muse, a slave woman calling him to authenticity. "Why/have you come here if not to sing?" she asks.

His first volume, *Call and Response* (1995), charting ". . . the story / about how ways change over time according / to an urgency the young feel to insist themselves / in history" ("The Fit of Old Customs"), won the 1995 Beatrice Hawley Award. Structured as a baptism, the volume's poems are trellised along the secular ramifications of black religious tradition, as the cadences of church music, the Bible, and sermons infuse the poems. The church organist, a "man who kept company with men," brings the assembled to confirmation, to deeper knowing: "Our family is here with us, even the dead and the not-born; / We are journeying to the source of all wonder, / We journey by dance. Amen" ("Goldsboro narrative #24: Second benediction").

Freer, less formally tied to meaning and traditional syntax, Hamer's second volume, *Middle Ear* (2000), winner of the Bay Area Book

Reviewers Association Award, makes of its title multiple metaphors, among them the ear as the organ of sentience ("a man goes deaf because he isn't listening') and the meaning of middle age: "I could be wrong, but I think my life is half over." But it is only with age—perhaps, in Hamer's case, with a necessary, painful silence occasioned by racial complexity and an initially shaming sexuality—that wisdom comes: ". . . change happens with small sights / Which accrete and feather. We see, we become" ("Arrival"). "The Tuning" reflects the ear as the body's music, Hamer's willingness to be as attuned to his body as to the poem: with deep presence, astonishing vulnerability, anguished beauty. "The Last Leg," the opening poem of *Middle Ear,* is an ambitious, mysterious, beautifully written, dreamlike poem about (among other things) the untethered imagination of poetry:

> When I approach the horse hued the bluing moon,
> It leans into the ground and will not be mounted.
> The whinny is laughter;
> I have been tricked. I can never go back.
> It rains gallops the rest of that night.

In "Grace," the vivid memory of a boy's love for his mother collapses the space between past and present. "When she would fall into her thoughts, we'd look for what distracted her from us," the poet recalls, gentle with himself in remembering the self-absorption of that first, fierce, love.

"Crossroads," a poem borrowing early BLUES rhythms and based on the legend of blues musician Robert Johnson's bargain with the devil, is a lyric meditation on a young man's coming to terms with his selfhood, his wholeness, his homosexuality: "A man give his hand and he pulled me to the shore / Man give his hand, pulled me over to the shore / Told me if I come I wouldn't drown no more." In "The Different Strokes Bar, San Francisco," the speaker in the poem wants to remember wonder, to stay alive to the thrill of discovering a body that begins to claim not only desire, but joy, "the dancing going on all about / your new and hungry body," while the specter of

absence, of loss—a precognition of AIDS, perhaps—haunts the poem: "Maybe I could see men dancing themselves invisible / one by handsome one, that year before they began to go." Even the poem titles in this volume are evocative, among them "13 Suppositions about the Ubiquitous," "Annual Visit of the Quiet, Unmarried Son," and "Charlene-N-Booker 4Ever."

"Cinder Cone," a poem from Hamer's third volume, *Rift: Poems,* imagines the violent military and political angers that separate land masses, continents, countries, and tribes, as painfully, familiarly familial: "The continents still ache for each other, / but before they find their ways back, they will go farther, / deny us."

Hamer's work has appeared in such journals as *CALLALOO, Kenyon Review, Ploughshares, TriQuarterly,* and *ZYZZYVA* and in the anthologies *Best American Poetry 1994* and *2000, The Geography of Home* (1999), and *Word of Mouth: An Anthology of Gay American Poetry,* as well as in Robert Hass's *Poet's Choice: Poems for Everyday Life* (1998) and in Billy Collins's *Poetry 180: A Turning Back to Poetry* (2003).

BIBLIOGRAPHY

Hamer, Forrest. "Poet and Psychoanalyst: Listening More Deeply." *American Psychoanalyst* 34, no. 3 (2000).

———. "The Visitor." In *Lucky Break: How I Became a Writer,* edited by Howard Junker, 47–51. Portsmouth, N.H.: Heinemann, 1999.

Koolish, Lynda. "Forrest Hamer." *African American Writers: Portraits and Visions.* Jackson: University Press of Mississippi, 2001.

Lynda Koolish

Hamilton, Virginia (1936–2002)

Growing up on a small farm near Yellow Springs, Ohio, in the 1940s, Virginia Hamilton was surrounded by the sights, sounds, and smells of rural America and by her large extended family of cousins, uncles, and aunts. All these things and people come into play in the children's stories Hamilton wrote as an adult. She was influenced by her parents and other family members, who were also storytellers. As a child, Hamilton's maternal grandfather, Levi Perry, escaped from slavery in Virginia, by crossing the Ohio River to freedom. He often recounted his tale of flight to the young Virginia, who was named for her grandfather's home state.

Hamilton majored in writing at Antioch College in Ohio and was a literature major at Ohio State University. She also attended the New School for Social Research in New York and New York University, studying novel writing. Hamilton began writing her own tales when MALCOLM X and the BLACK POWER movement were shifting the face of the CIVIL RIGHTS MOVEMENT. Growing up during a time of turbulent social activity inspired Hamilton to focus on themes of age, gender, and race in her writing. She acknowledged that maturing at the time of "Black is beautiful" increased her awareness of the centrality of African-American culture to American history. Her books resonate with issues of the social effects people face when excluded or included.

Hamilton wrote more than 20 books, including *Zeely* (1967), *The Time-Ago Tales of Jadhu* (1968), *Paul Robeson: The Life and Times of a Free Black Man* (1975), *The Magical Adventures of Pretty Pearl* (1983), *Plain City* (1993), and *Bluish, a Novel* (1999). She has written children's stories, biographies, and memoirs, as well as collections of poetry and folktales. Her first book, *Zeely* (1967), tells of Elizabeth, a young girl who isolates herself from other people so that she can tell herself her own stories. She becomes enamored of Zeely, a six-foot-tall local pig farmer. The relationship between these two women reaches its peak when Zeely, through the telling of a creation myth, advises Elizabeth to recognize her place in the world. After this exchange, Elizabeth acknowledges that the Night Walker stories she had been using to terrify her brother are really memories from tales her uncle told her about the Underground Railroad. Elizabeth ultimately embraces her own community while celebrating her own creativity.

Hamilton weaves the tale of a young girl discovering her cultural heritage together with her discovery of her own unique identity. The themes of age and the wisdom that comes with age are essential to Hamilton's work. She explores the confusions and inconsistencies that face young adults coming of age in a world full of difference, whether it is gender, ethnicity, or age. Hamilton's explorations ultimately celebrate the joy of youth and the importance of rich cultural traditions.

In 1974, Hamilton was the first African American to win the coveted John Newberry Medal for "the most distinguished contribution to literature for children" for *M. C. Higgins, the Great* (1974). Hamilton was also the winner of the prestigious Hans Christian Andersen Medal presented by the International Board on Books for Young People in Switzerland, an award equivalent to the Nobel Prize in literature. Hamilton was the first and only author of young-adult literature to receive a John D. and Catherine T. MacArthur Fellowship (1995), and she received the Coretta Scott King Award for *The People Could Fly: American Black Folktales* (1985), *Sweet Whispers, Brother Rush* (1982), and *A Little Love*.

BIBLIOGRAPHY

Carney Smith, Jessie, ed. *Notable Black American Women.* Detroit: Gale Research, 1992.

Metzger, Linda, et al., eds. *Black Writers: A Selection of Sketches from Contemporary Authors.* Detroit: Gale Research, 1989.

Trites, Rebecca Seelinger. "'I double never ever lie to my chil'ren': Inside People in Virginia Hamilton's Narratives." *African American Review* 32, no. 1 (1998): 147–156.

Kindra Briggs

Hammon, Jupiter   (1711–1806?)

The distinction of being the first black slave poet to write and publish a poem belongs to Jupiter Hammon, who published "An Evening Thought: Salvation by Christ with Penitential Cries: Composed by Jupiter Hammon, A Negro belonging to Mr. Lloyd of Queen's Village, on Long Island, the 25th of December, 1760." Hammon was born the property of Henry Lloyd, a wealthy merchant on Long Island, New York. From all indications and available records, he remained the property of several generations of Lloyds. According to Vincent Carretta, Hammon served his master as clerk and bookkeeper and was taken to Hartford, Connecticut, by one of Lloyd's son when the British captured Long Island in 1776. However, over the years, most scholars have labeled Hammon "an obedient, conservative minded servant, caught up in the fervor of Methodist preached piety and Christianity." Hammon "may well have been a minister of sorts, as there were black and Indian churches on Long Island" (Robinson, 5).

In his well-known published works, Hammon did not comment directly on slavery. For example, in his poem dedicated to his neighbor to the north, "Address to Miss Phillis Wheatly [sic], Ethiopian Poetess, in Boston, who came from Africa at eight years of age, and soon became acquainted with the gospel of Jesus Christ," Hammon seems more interested in the shackles of sin and the poetess's salvation than in critiquing the hypocrisy of her Christian enslavers (as she seems to do in "On Being Brought from Africa to America") or in abhorring their physical bondage as slaves and legally owned property. Instead, filling his poem with Methodist discourse, tropes, and pronouncements on the fall, redemption, and salvation of mankind, Hammon reminds Wheatley only that "God's tender mercy [had] set thee free." In fact, Hammon seems to celebrate what he might have viewed as the beneficence of slavery, as it served as the venue through which Wheatley, taken from her "dark abode" to learn about the Christian God, was able to seek and receive salvation and redemption from her fallen state. Hammon admonishes Wheatley to "adore / The wisdom of thy God," who had brought her "from distant shore, / To learn His holy word" (Robinson, 9). Had God not done this, Hammon reminds Wheatley, "Thou mightst been left behind, / Amidst a dark abode; / God's tender mercy still combines, / Thou has the holy word" (Robinson, 9).

Hammon's sermonic, pioneering poem "An Evening Thought," which is clearly influenced by Wesleyan hymns with its stanzaic pattern, meter, rime, diction, and imagery, identifies the definitive source of humanity's salvation as "Christ Alone, /

The only Son of God." Hammon's speaker pleads; "Lord, hear our penitential Cry: / Salvation from above; / It is the Lord that doth supply, / With his Redeeming Love" (Robinson, 7). Hammon, in his "An Address to the Negroes in the State of New York" (1789), encourages his fellow bondsmen and bondswomen to bear patiently their condition of servitude. This led editors RICHARD BARKSDALE and Keneth Kinnamon to level a harsh critical note against him in the anthology BLACK WRITERS OF AMERICA: "In the final analysis, Jupiter Hammon's religion was an opiate, that dulled him to the world's evil ways. Instead of giving him a revolutionary social vision, it filled him with penitential cries. And his poetry is aesthetically anemic and almost stifling in its repetitive religiosity" (46).

However, other critics argue that in Hammon's "A Dialogue Entitled the Kind Master and the Dutiful Slave," one finds "element of resistance, and, even more, elements of human equality" because it is "the servant who asserts the ultimate sovereignty of Christ" (Bruce, 51–52). Similarly, Hammon's emphasis on a more inclusive Christianity in "An Evening Thought"—one that does not limit redemption and salvation to the elect chosen few—can be seen as a radical rhetorical strategy, an indirect rebellion against the slave economy, which had reduced blacks to mere chattel, making their salvation null and void. Hammon's speaker supplicates Jesus: "Dear Jesus, give thy Spirit now, / Thy grace to every Nation" (7), "Dear Jesus, by thy precious Blood, / The World Redemption have," and "Dear Jesus, let the Nations cry, / And all the People say, / Salvation comes from Christ on high, / Haste on Tribunal Day" (7). Hammon's use of "every nation," "World," and "all people" clearly reveals his conviction of free and universal grace, allowing him to claim and ensure a place for blacks in God's heavenly kingdom. In the end, however, Hammon's reflection on the condition of man—his "evening thought"—might merely reflect the fundamental teachings of John Wesley, who willingly proselytized among the poor and downtrodden, unlike the Calvinist Puritan settlers of Massachusetts Bay, who claimed to have entered into covenant with God to establish God's "city upon a hill," a heavenly city on earth that excluded the likes of Jupiter Hammon and Phillis Wheatley. "An Evening Thought" can be seen as "a demonstration of Jupiter Hammon's religious capacity at a time when such capacity remained in open question" (Bruce, 38).

BIBLIOGRAPHY

Barksdale, Richard, and Keneth Kinnamon, eds. *Black Writers of America: A Comprehensive Anthology.* New York: Macmillan Company, 1972.

Bruce, Dickson D., Jr. *The Origins of African American Literature, 1680–1865.* Charlottesville: University Press of Virginia, 2001.

Carretta, Vincent, ed. *Unchained Voices: An Anthology of Black Authors in the English-Speaking World of the Eighteenth Century.* Lexington: University Press of Kentucky, 1999.

Robinson, William H., ed. *Early Black American Poets.* Dubuque, Iowa: Wm. C. Brown Company, 1969.

Wilfred D. Samuels

Hansberry, Lorraine   (1930–1965)

Despite the brevity of playwright, activist, and feminist Lorraine Vivian Hansberry's theatrical life, and although only two of her plays were produced during her lifetime, she remains one of the most celebrated black playwrights in America. Breaking the color barrier in the theater, protesting and validating the unfortunate circumstances of blacks in the United States, Hansberry became the voice of the people during the most critical era of racial segregation and the fight for civil rights in America. She used the stage as her platform to ignite the social and political consciousness of her audiences, both black and white.

The youngest of four children, Carl Jr., Perry, and Mamie, Hansberry was born on May 19, 1930, in Chicago, Illinois. Her father, Carl A. Hansberry, Sr., was a prominent real estate broker and the founder of one of Chicago's first black banks; her mother, Nannie Perry Hansberry, was a schoolteacher. Both were activists and natives of the South. In 1938, when Hansberry was eight years old, her family purchased a home in one of Chicago's restricted white, middle-class neighborhoods, where they were subjected to racial segregation and discrimination. Challenging Chicago's Jim Crow housing laws, her father won an antisegregation case before the Illinois Supreme Court. These injustices later influenced Hansberry's plays, especially *A RAISIN IN THE SUN,* making her a renowned pioneer in protest theater.

The Hansberrys sent their children to public schools to protest against segregation laws. Young Lorraine attended Betsy Ross Grammar School and graduated, in 1947, from Englewood High School, where she excelled in English and history and was elected president of the debating society. Upon seeing productions of Howard Richardson and William Berney's folk musical, *Dark of the Moon,* and William Shakespeare's *The Tempest* and *Othello,* starring Paul Robeson, she was captivated by the theater. Also, during her high school years Hansberry's creative imagination was sparked by such eminent black luminaries as W. E. B. DuBois, Paul Robeson, LANGSTON HUGHES, Jesse Owens, and Duke Ellington, who frequented her home. Hansberry was impressed with Hughes's poetry and specifically its reflection and celebration of black people's complex lives and their deferred dreams that sometimes dried up like "a raisin in the sun." She would borrow this line for the title of her first play, *A Raisin in the Sun.*

Hansberry attended the University of Wisconsin at Madison, where she spent two years studying English, drama, art, and stage design, and was active in the Henry Wallace campaign; she was elected president of the Young Progressives of America and the Labor Youth League. During a rehearsal of Sean O'Casey's *Juno and the Paycock* (1924), she was fascinated by the manner in which the Irish playwright portrayed the oppressed. In the summer of 1949, Hansberry attended the University of Guadalajara's art workshop in Ajijic, Mexico, before moving to New York City in 1950, where she began studying at the New School for Social Research. A year later, she launched her career as a writer and worked full time as a reporter for Paul Robeson's *Freedom,* a radical black magazine that provided her with numerous opportunities to broaden her understanding of the existing domestic and world problems. In 1952 she became an associate editor, taught classes at the Frederick Douglass School, and traveled extensively. That same year, she met Robert B. Nemiroff, a Jewish writer and activist, while covering a picket line at New York University, where he was a graduate student. They were married on June 20, 1953, in Chicago, and moved to Greenwich Village.

Hansberry left the *Freedom* staff in 1953 and devoted herself to her personal writing, working odd jobs, studying African history with DuBois and teaching black literature at the Marxist-oriented Jefferson School for Social Sciences. These experiences further heightened her awareness of social injustice. In 1956 she began writing *A Raisin in the Sun,* which was published in 1959 by her music publisher and friend Philip Rose. Debuting at the Ethel Barrymore Theatre and running for 530 performances, the emotionally charged play chronicles the plight of the poor, black Younger family, who, though trapped in Chicago's South Side, find spiritual and social ways to overcome their personal weaknesses and the barriers erected by the dominant culture.

A Raisin in the Sun was named best play of the year (1959). Hansberry received the New York Drama Critics' Circle Award and was hailed as the youngest playwright, the fifth woman, and the first black to win such a prestigious drama award. The 1961 film version of the play, starring Sidney Poitier, Claudia McNeil, Ruby Dee, and Diana Sands, brought Hansberry a special award at the Cannes Film Festival and a nomination for a Screen Writer's Guild Award for her screenplay. Now an American classic, *A Raisin in the Sun* has also been adapted for television. One adaptation starred Danny Glover, Esther Rolle, and Kim Yancey.

After completing the screenplay of *A Raisin* and *Drinking Gourd,* Hansberry began work on several plays in the early 1960s, including *Les Blancs;* she completed *What Use Are Flowers?* in 1962. Although she became ill in April 1963, Hansberry continued to write and to be politically active. Although Nemiroff and Hansberry were quietly divorced in Mexico on March 10, 1964, they continued to collaborate on projects. She completed her second staged "play of ideas," *The Sign in Sidney Brustein's Window* (1964). Recognized as a play that was ahead of its time, it examines family relationships, marriage, prostitution, homosexuality, politics, dramatic absurdity, abstract art, anti-Semitism, and racism (Cheney, 72). The show closed on the evening of her death.

At the time of her death from cancer of the pancreas on January 12, 1965, Hansberry left behind several unfinished works. After her death, Nemiroff, the executor of her estate, adapted from Hansberry's writings and posthumously published *To Be Young, Gifted and Black* (1969), which appeared in book form a year later. Also, he completed *Les Blancs* (1970) and *Les Blancs: The Collected Last Plays of Lorraine Hansberry* (1972). In 1973, *A Raisin in the Sun* was adapted into a musical titled *Raisin* (1973) by Nemiroff and Charlotte Zaltzberg. This Tony Award–winning musical was revived in 1981.

Hansberry's life and significance as a major 20th-century African-American dramatist, social and political activist, and pioneer of the woman's movement have been well documented, for example, in "Lorraine Hansberry," a 1976 documentary written and produced by Ralph J. Tangney, and also in a special *Freedomways* magazine retrospective issue, *Lorraine Hansberry: Art of Thunder, Vision of Light* (1979). Two plays based on Hansberry's life and works have appeared on stage: *Lovingly Yours, Langston and Lorraine* (1994) and *Love to All, Lorraine* (1995). Today, Hansberry is still considered a phenomenal contemporary playwright who paved the way for other African-American performers and dramatists, including JAMES BALDWIN, CHARLES GORDONE, AMIRI BARAKA, ED BULLINS, and AUGUST WILSON.

BIBLIOGRAPHY

Adler, Thomas P., ed. *American Drama, 1940–1960: A Critical History.* New York: Twayne, 1994.

Brown-Guillory, Elizabeth. "Alice Childress, Lorraine Hansberry, Ntozake Shange: Carving a Place for Themselves on the American Stage." In *Their Place on the Stage: Black Women Playwrights in America,* edited by Elizabeth Brown-Guillory, 25–49. Westport, Conn.: Greenwood, 1988.

Carter, Steven R., and Helen Maclam. "Inter-ethnic Issues in Lorraine Hansberry's *The Sign in Sidney Brunstein's Window.*" *Explorations in Ethnic Studies* 11 (July 1988): 1–13.

Cheney, Anne. *Lorraine Hansberry.* Boston: Twayne, 1984.

Gavin, Christy, ed. *African American Women Playwrights: A Research Guide.* New York: Garland, 1999.

Loretta G. Woodard

Hardy, James Earl   (1970–)

A prolific freelance journalist, entertainment critic, and author, born and raised in Bedford-Stuyvesant, Brooklyn, New York, James Earl Hardy graduated with honors from St. John's University and the Columbia University Graduate School of Journalism. Hardy distinguished himself by introducing American readers to the plight of black gay men living in the hip-hop community with his first novel, *B-Boy Blues* (1994), a journey into the complexities of being black, male, homosexual, and a "home-boy" in late 20th-century America. The post–civil rights hip-hop generation was the first to attend nonsegregated schools, live outside the realities of Jim Crow laws, be truly middle class, and witness and benefit from their parents' flight to the suburbs. This generation's urban language and music is a historical record of its self-defined disassociation with the previous generation. The hip-hop generation was the first free teenage rebellion expressed by African Americans.

B-Boy Blues received high critical acclaim and gained Hardy a solid readership for his accurate portrayal of an Afrocentric gay love story. The success led Hardy to create a series in which he further develops the central characters, Mitchell "Little Bit" Crawford and Raheim "Pooquie" Rivers, and explore their love story and duplicitous roles within the African-American community. In his second novel, *2nd Time Around* (1996), Hardy chronicles a tougher black gay street scene. Hip-hop culture reigns supreme in a community that proves ideal for a black homosexual to "come out." Hardy's characters are placed amid street mores

and music youthful enough to define, redefine, and rediscover itself. Although broader conflicts, such as cultural differences and layers of acceptance between black and white homosexuals, are explored in *2nd Time Around*, Hardy delivers a more intimate, honest struggle of what it means to be black and gay through Pooquie's role as a father.

Hip-hop culture also dominates Hardy's third novel, *If Only for One Nite* (1997), in which, by coupling well-known song lyrics with strong reminiscences, he explores the discrepancies between romantic fantasies and love. Attending his 10-year high school reunion, Mitchell, the protagonist, becomes reacquainted with his first lover; through a series of flashbacks intensified by Hardy's narratives on the AIDS crisis in the 1980s, the novel fosters confident notions of black-on-black homosexual love in America. As the final segment in the *B-Boy Blues* series, *If Only for One Nite* appropriately instills concern in his readers over his characters' possible infidelities.

Hardy's novels address the depths of friendship and love that are shared between same-gender–loving (SGL) men, breaking the contemporary canon of literature written by black heterosexual and white gay male authors. The hip-hop language of Hardy's dramatic narratives draws real characters who challenge the stereotypical attributes mainstream America often affixes to black men, gay or straight. Furthermore, Hardy disrupts the expected traditional costumes (representations) of homosexuality. His characters never look, act, talk, dress, or walk in an effeminate manner. Instead, Hardy pens a new realism that is informed by a truer, gruffer language cultured on the streets of hip-hop.

The AIDS crisis of the 20th century filters through Hardy's series, most powerfully in *The Day Eazy-E Died* (2001). In this novel, Hardy explores and discusses, thematically and through characterization, such issues as HIV prevention, safe sex, infidelity, and sexual engagement with multiple partners. Hardy seems aware that these are issues facing young people of all sexual persuasions, particularly young black men, who are disproportionately infected and affected by AIDS. However, Hardy omits from his true, often graphic and torrid depictions of gay street life the use of crack cocaine, a profound, irreversible influence on hip-hop culture. Hardy has chosen to grapple with the issues that can best serve and inform his readers directly. In his novel *Love the One You're With* (2002), Hardy tackles issues of infidelity and monogamy between gay men. He also returns to Mitchell "Little Bit" Crawford and Raheim "Pooquie" Rivers. Hardy suggests in the acknowledgments of *A House Is Not a Home* (2003) that he was writing the final chapter on these familiar characters.

Hardy's novels render true characters and representations of the ordinary daily struggles most black gay men face. He explores the intricacies of sexual orientations within the 1980s hip-hop culture, a period of uncertainty, purposefully to destroy black male stereotypes that are still too often perpetrated by the media. Economic discrepancies between black homosexual lovers, homosexuality and fatherhood, the complexity of being straight and turning gay, AIDS, and family are other strong Hardy themes. His characters are immersed in family, though, which shows that the fundamental concerns of gay black men are not really different from other men. Further, Hardy introduces his readers to acronyms like SGL (same-gender loving, used by African Americans instead of LGBT) and DL (on the down low, or men who live dual as gay and heterosexual men), deepening his reader's knowledge of gay black life.

Hardy has been showered with accolades for his work. He has earned grants from the E. Y. Harburg Arts Foundation and the American Association of Sunday and Feature Editors, two Educational Press Association Writing Awards, a Columbia Press Association Feature Writing Citation, a *Village Voice* writing fellowship, and scholarships from the Paul Rapoport Memorial Foundation and the national and New York chapters of the Association of Black Journalists. His byline appears in *Entertainment Weekly, Newsweek, The Advocate,* and *The Washington Post.*

BIBLIOGRAPHY

Greene, Beverly, ed. *Ethnic and Cultural Diversity among Lesbians and Gay Men: Psychological Per-*spectives on Lesbian and Gay Issues.* Vol. 3. Thousand Oaks, Calif.: Sage Publications, 1997.

Hawkeswood, William G. *One of the Children: Gay Men in Black Harlem.* Berkeley: University of California Press, 1996.

Reid-Pharr, Robert F., ed. *Black Gay Man: Essays.* New York: New York University Press, 2001.

Lawrence T. Potter

Harlem Renaissance
(New Negro Renaissance, New Negro Movement, or Negro Renaissance)

Although scholars and critics often disagree on whether the so-called Harlem Renaissance was a formal movement, most agree that from post–World War I America to the beginning of the Great Depression, African-American culture blossomed like never before, imprinting the mainstream with its music, particularly blues and jazz; nightlife in the cabarets of its black mecca, Harlem; and, above all, the proliferation of its artistic, visual, critical, and literary voices, major and minor, including MARITA BONNER, ARNA BONTEMPS, COUNTEE CULLEN, W. E. B. DUBOIS, ALICE DUNBAR-NELSON, JESSIE REDMON FAUSET, LANGSTON HUGHES, ZORA NEALE HURSTON, AARON DOUGLAS, GEORGIA DOUGLAS JOHNSON, NELLA LARSEN, ALAIN LOCKE, CLAUDE MCKAY, BRUCE NUGENT, GEORGE SCHUYLER, WALLACE THURMAN, JEAN TOOMER, ERIC WALROND, DOROTHY WEST, WALTER WHITE, and many others.

Given the renaissance's celebration of racial consciousness and black culture, many scholars consider Harvard graduate DuBois's *The* SOULS OF BLACK FOLK (1903) its genesis; in *Souls* DuBois not only delineated the complexity of African-Americans' experience—from slavery to freedom—but also declared their undeniable gifts to American culture. He wrote, "And so by faithful chance the Negro folk song—the rhythmic cry of the slave—stands to-day not simply as the sole American music, but as the most beautiful expression of human experience born this side the seas . . . [I]t still remains as the singular spiritual heritage of the nation and the greatest gift of the Negro people" (378). DuBois, who also advanced a theory of the "Talented Tenth," members of the black aristocracy who would, through their leadership and vision, move the black race and masses further up the ladder of social progress, had referred to "The New Negro" in an essay he submitted to *Century Magazine* before the turn of the 20th century.

More specifically, Rhodes scholar ALAIN LOCKE, in the lead essay, "The New Negro," of his special *Survey Graphics* issue on Harlem, which he also included in his anthology, *The NEW NEGRO* (Albert & Charles Boni, 1925), offered a general explanation for the emergence of the New Negro and the accompanying cultural movement, which Locke attributed to black migration and urbanization, the emergence of Harlem as a black mecca, a deepening racial pride, a new generation of determined and self-reliant writers, and the founding of sociopolitical organizations such as JAMES WELDON JOHNSON and DuBois's NATIONAL ASSOCIATION FOR THE ADVANCEMENT OF COLORED PEOPLE (NAACP) and MARCUS GARVEY's black nationalist Universal Negro Improvement Association (UNIA). Garvey motivated and multiplied the membership of his mass movement with his motto: "Up you mighty race! You can accomplish what you will!" Equally important was black participation in World War I, the founding of the Association for the Study of Negro Life and History by historian Carter G. Woodson and its journal *The Journal of Negro Life and History,* and the founding of such publishing organs as the NAACP's *The CRISIS* (edited by DuBois), the National Urban League's *OPPORTUNITY* (edited by CHARLES JOHNSON), and the UNIA's *The Negro World* (edited by Garvey), all of which published and promoted (through annual contests) the work of emerging black writers. Many renaissance writers first published in these venues or won literary contests sponsored by them.

Many of the emerging writers, including Hughes, Hurston, and Thurman, who stood in the vanguard of this cultural blossoming, saw it as the cultural harvest of the spirit of the black masses rather than merely the progress being made by black intellectuals, the "thinking Negro," and sociopolitical leaders, as DuBois and Locke maintained and celebrated. Locke, in defining the New Negro, wrote, almost with uncertainty, that the objectives of the New Negro's "inner life are yet in the process of formation, for the new psychology at present is more of a consensus of feeling than of opinion, of attitude rather than of program" (10). In contrast, Hughes almost chauvinistically declared in his signature essay, "The Negro Artist and the Racial Mountain,"

> Let the blare of Negro jazz bands and the bellowing voice of Bessie Smith singing Blues penetrate the closed ears of the colored near intellectual until they listen and perhaps understand. Let Paul Robeson singing "Water Boy" and Rudolph Fisher writing about the streets of Harlem, and Jean Toomer holding the heart of Georgia in his hands, and Aaron Douglas drawing strange black fantasies cause the smug Negro Middle class to turn from their white, respectable, ordinary books and papers to catch a glimmer of their own beauty. We younger Negro artists who create now intend to express our individual dark-skinned selves without fear or shame. (95)

As an alternative to Locke and DuBois, Hughes, Hurston, Nugent, Douglas, Thurman, and others published the short-lived *FIRE!!* (1926), a journal for the younger generation of writers who wished to "burn up a lot of the old, dead conventional Negro-white ideas of the past" (Hughes, 233–234).

Significant, too, as Cheryl A. Wall argues in *Women of the Harlem Renaissance* (1995), "The Harlem Renaissance was not a male phenomenon. A substantial number of literary women played significant roles" (9). As Wall carefully points out, this group includes not only the better-known writers, Hurston, Fauset, and Larsen, but also "a host of lesser-known poets" (9), MARITA BONNER, ALICE DUNBAR-NELSON, GEORGIA DOUGLAS JOHNSON, and Anne Spencer, to name a few, who published in extant journals and magazine. Johnson's weekend parlor gatherings in Washington, D.C., provided a central venue for introduction and exposure for many of the renaissance's luminaries.

Equally important, as George Hutchinson points out in *The Harlem Renaissance in Black and White,* were the "interracial dynamics" (15) of this racial renaissance, particularly the support and patronage provided by white philanthropists and "interlopers," specifically CARL VAN VECHTEN and Charlotte Osgood Mason. Despite criticism from black scholars like Nathan Huggins, who argues that, under the influence of these interlopers, renaissance writers emphasized black exoticism, and Chidi Ikonné, who concludes that whites, particularly Van Vechten, author of the best seller *NIGGER HEAVEN,* were a corrupting influence on this movement, Hutchinson maintains, "there were many different white positions (as well as black positions) on African American literature, and these positions tended to correlate with positions on the nature of American culture and the meaning of culture in the modern age" (20). White participation played a critical role in opening the doors of mainstream publishers, including Knopf, Macmillan, and Harcourt, Brace, to African-American writers, including Hughes, McKay, Cullen, and Toomer.

Various scholars consider the beginning of the Harlem Renaissance to be 1903, the date of the publication of DuBois's *Souls of Black Folk;* 1910, the date associated with the formation of the NAACP; and 1916, the beginning of World War I; similarly, whereas some scholars consider the end of the renaissance to be 1929, at the start of the Great Depression, others place it in 1940, the date associated with Richard Wright's emergence as a major American writer following the publication of his naturalistic novel, *Native Son* (1940). Regardless of the exact time line, during the first quarter of the 20th century, African-American culture was ebulliently celebrated from one end of the color spectrum to the next. Popular culture scholars often refer to this period as "the jazz age." Renaissance or not, as Huggins points out,

> the experience of Harlem in the 1920s was not for naught. It left its mark as a symbol and a point of reference for everyone to recall. . . . The very name continued to connote a special spirit, new vitality, black urbanity, and black

militancy. Through the activities of the writings, the promotion of Negroes in the 1920s, Harlem had become a racial focal point for knowledgeable black men the world over. (303)

BIBLIOGRAPHY

DuBois, W. E. B. *The Souls of Black Folk.* In *Three Negro Classics,* 207–389. New York: Avon Books, 1965.

Huggins, Nathan Irvin. *Harlem Renaissance.* New York: Oxford University Press, 1971.

Hughes, Langston. *The Big Sea: An Autobiography.* New York: Knopf, 1940.

———. "The Negro Artist and The Racial Mountain." In *The Portable Harlem Renaissance,* edited by David Levering Lewis, 91–95. New York: Penguin Books, 1994.

Hutchinson, George. *The Harlem Renaissance in Black and White.* Cambridge: Harvard University Press, 1995.

Lewis, David Levering. *W. E. B. DuBois: Biography of a Race, 1868–1919.* New York: Henry Holt and Company, 1993.

Locke, Alain. "The New Negro." In *The New Negro,* edited by Alain Locke, 3–16. New York: Albert & Charles Boni, 1925.

Wall, Cheryl A. *Women of the Harlem Renaissance.* Bloomington: Indiana University Press, 1999.

Wilfred D. Samuels

Harlem Shadows **Claude McKay** (1922)
Published by Jamaican-born poet and novelist CLAUDE MCKAY. *Harlem Shadows* is among the major works produced by luminaries of the HARLEM RENAISSANCE. In fact, *Harlem Shadows* was the first collection of poems published by a Harlem Renaissance writer. Although McKay spent more than 10 years during the time the renaissance was in full bloom living and traveling throughout Europe, he is considered a major voice of this historical juncture in African-American history and culture.

Preceded by *Song of Jamaica* (1912) and *Constab Ballads* (1912), which McKay published before migrating to the United States in 1912 to study agriculture at Booker T. Washington's Tuskegee Institute, and by *Spring in New Hampshire and Other Poems* (1920), which was published in London, *Harlem Shadows* is, for the most part, a collection of many of the poems McKay had published in such journals and newspapers as *Liberator, Negro World, Seven Arts, Pearson's Magazine, Cambridge Magazine,* and *Worker's Dreadnought* and had included in *Spring in New Hampshire.*

Among the 70 poems in *Harlem Shadows,* McKay included his signature poem, "If We Must Die," which had been published in *Liberator* in 1919 but was not included in *Spring in New Hampshire.* "If We Must Die" is among McKay's more militant poems in the collection. In this now-classic sonnet, McKay's speaker adamantly and militantly announces his determination to actively and fearlessly assume total existential responsibility for his life. He demands that racism must be met head on: "And for their thousand blows, deal one death-blow! / What though before us lies the open grave." The intrepid speaker exhorts in the ending couplet, "Like men we'll face the murderous, cowardly pack, / Pressed to the wall, dying but fighting back" (McKay, 43).

McKay begins *Harlem Shadows* with "America," another equally militant sonnet in which his speaker not only acknowledges his love/hate relationship with America but also prophesies America's inevitable doom under the weight of racism and modernity:

> Darkly I gaze into the days ahead,
> And see her might and granite wonders there,
> Beneath the touch of Time's unerring hand,
> Like priceless treasures sinking in the sand.
> (Selected Poems, 30)

However, McKay also included such poems as the title poem, "Flame Heart," "The Tropics in New York," and "When Dawn Comes to the City," which explore the major themes that came to dominate his oeuvre throughout his career as a poet and which feature more sensitive, gentle, idealistic and romantic speakers. Whereas "Flame Heart" ("So much have I forgotten in ten short years") and "Tropics" ("A wave of longing through my body swept") romantically recall lost childhood and innocence in a more Edenic setting, "Harlem Shadows" ("I see the shapes of girls who pass / To bend and barter at desire's call") and "When Dawn Comes" ("Out of the tenements, cold as stone, / Dark figures start for work") decry the consequences of modernity, a world in which, McKay's speakers maintain, humanity is inevitably commodified and marginalized.

Reviewing *Harlem Shadows* in major venues like *The New York Times, New Republic,* and Marcus Garvey's *Negro World,* black and white critics identified McKay as the best black poet since Paul Laurence Dunbar. Walter White wrote that McKay "is not a great Negro poet—he is a great poet" (quoted in Cooper, 164–165). Celebrating McKay's accomplishments as a new poetic voice, Robert Littel, the reviewer for *New Republic,* wrote that McKay strikes "hard and pierce[s] deep. It is not merely poetic emotion [he] express[es], but something fierce and constant, and icy cold, and white hot" (quoted in Cooper, 164).

BIBLIOGRAPHY

Cooper, Wayne F. *Claude McKay: Rebel Sojourner in the Harlem Renaissance.* New York: Schocken Books, 1987.

McKay, Claude. *Selected Poems.* Edited by Joan R. Sherman. Mineola, N.Y.: Dover Publications, 1999.

Wilfred D. Samuels

Harper, Frances Ellen Watkins
(1825–1911)

Novelist, poet, short story writer, essayist, journalist, orator, and activist Frances Ellen Watkins Harper was one of the most dynamic orators and best-known poets of the 19th century and gained public attention in the time between poets Phillis Wheatley and Paul Laurence Dunbar. She was also a pioneer of the short story and the author of *Iola Leroy: Or, Shadows Uplifted* (1892), the best-selling novel written by an African-American before the 20th century. Born the only child to free parents in Baltimore, Maryland, on September 24, 1825, and orphaned before the age of three, Harper was placed in the care of her aunt and uncle, Mr. and Mrs. William Watkins. She attended the William Watkins Academy for Negro Youth, founded by her uncle, where he taught her the classics, Bible, rhetoric, and antislavery writings. At age 14, Harper hired herself out as a seamstress and a housekeeper to the Armstrong family. Using books she borrowed from their bookstore, Harper advanced her education and enhanced her intellectual growth. In 1839, she published her first poems in local newspapers and abolitionist periodicals. She published her first collection of verse and prose, *Forest Leaves,* in 1845.

In 1850 Harper became the first woman to teach at Union Seminary, a vocational school near Columbus, Ohio, which later became Wilberforce University. She later accepted a teaching position in Little York, Pennsylvania, where she witnessed the suffering of African Americans bound in legal slavery. In 1853, Harper moved to Philadelphia to devote herself exclusively to the anti-slavery movement and the Underground Railroad. In 1854, she served as a full-time lecturer and poetic orator for the Maine Anti-Slavery Society, touring the northeastern United States, Canada, Michigan, and Ohio. Between 1865 and 1870, she toured the southern states. Harper, who lectured without notes, became known for her fiery oratory on the issues of racism, feminism, and classism. She also became a prominent speaker for and member of several leading women's organizations, including the American Woman Suffrage Association, the National Association of Colored Women (NACW), the National Council of Women of the United States, the American Equal Rights Association, and the Women's Christian Temperance Union. She often incorporated her own original prose and poetry in her fiery addresses.

Simultaneously with her work in the antislavery and women's movements, Harper launched her literary career as a poet, publishing the collection of poems and essays *Poems on Miscellaneous Subjects* in 1854, which pioneered the tradition of African-American protest poetry. Her best-known volume of poems, *Poems on Miscellaneous Subjects* centers on slavery and its horrors, religion, heroism, racial pride, women's rights, and temperance. In it she included "Bury Me in a Free Land" and "The Slave Mother," which address the separation of families and the devastating pain that mothers, in particular, suffered in bondage. Both poems are still anthologized and highly regarded today. Harper's other volumes include the long blank-verse allegory, *Moses, A Story of the Nile* (1868); *Sketches of Southern Life* (1872), a series of six dialect poems narrated by Aunt Chloe, who exemplifies feminist thought and womanly strength; and *The Martyr of Alabama and Other Poems* (1894). Critics note that most of Harper's poems are "crafted with great care" and that she was unafraid to experiment with form and technique.

Over the years, Harper continued to be a prolific writer, publishing poetry, letters, and essays in national and international abolitionist journals such as *the Liberator, Provincial Freeman, Frederick Douglass's Monthly,* and the *National Anti-Slavery Standard.* Her works also appeared in African-American periodicals. Along with FREDERICK DOUGLASS and several others, Harper coedited and contributed to the *Weekly Anglo-African Magazine,* the earliest African-American literary journal. In 1859, Harper published "Two Offers," generally considered the first short story by an African American. In it Harper explores two central themes, temperance and a woman's right to choose not to marry. The story charts the lives of two cousins—Laura, who believes she will become an old maid if she does not marry, and Janette, who wishes to remain independent and pursue a career in writing. Harper juxtaposes the women's class differences—one is the product of privilege, while the other comes from poverty—and reveals how, ultimately, the contrast in the lives of the two women represents the true choices found in the two offers: independence, autonomy, and life versus oppression, depression, and death.

During her career, Harper published several novels designed for political and religious advocacy, concentrating specifically on racial identity and commitment to social change. Three of her serialized novellas, *Sowing and Reaping: A Temperance Story* (1867), *Minnie's Sacrifice* (1867–1868), and

Trial and Triumph (1888–1889), were published in the *Christian Recorder*. Her *Iola Leroy: Or, Shadows Uplifted* (1892) is one of the first novels published by a black woman in the United States. Considered a classic among African-American novels today, Harper's most popular full-length novel focuses on the issues of race, gender, and class and embodies a number of themes and techniques.

Set during the Civil War and Reconstruction periods, *Iola Leroy* weaves the melodramatic tale of the beautiful mulatto slave Iota Leroy, who initially passes for white, but when her true "black" identity is discovered, she is sold into slavery. When she later becomes an army nurse in a Union camp, Iola meets Dr. Gresham, the wealthy white hospital physician who falls in love with her, but she refuses to marry Gresham because he is white. Later, she meets and marries Dr. Latimer, a black physician who shares her devotion to social reform and racial uplift. Throughout the novel, Harper brings together many of the themes found in her poetry and oratory presentations, including the themes of temperance and education. In addition, she illustrates the complexity of African-American life during the post–Civil War period, particular the search for family members through various religious organizations.

Hailed as one of the most gifted writers among her contemporaries, Harper, like FREDERICK DOUGLASS, WILLIAM WELLS BROWN, HARRIET JACOBS, and IDA B. WELLS-BARNET, changed the course of American history with her activism and oratory. Combining pragmatic idealism, courageous action, and lyrical words, she continued to argue for freedom, equality and reforms in all of her works until her demise from heart disease on February 22, 1911. Harper's legacy as a writer has lived on well into the 20th century through the works of such literary descendants as SONIA SANCHEZ, NIKKI GIOVANNI, AUDRE LORDE, ALICE WALKER, GLORIA NAYLOR, MARGARET WALKER, RITA DOVE, Patrice Gaines, and JILL NELSON.

BIBLIOGRAPHY

Boyd, Melba Joyce. *Discarded Legacy: Politics and Poetics in the Life of Francis E. W. Harper, 1825–1911.* Detroit: Wayne State University Press, 1994.

Foster, Frances Smith. ed. *A Brighter Coming Day: A Frances Ellen Watkins Harper Reader.* New York: Feminist Press, 1990.

Still, William. *The Underground Railroad.* Chicago: Ebony Classics, 1970.

Loretta G. Woodard

Harper, Michael S. (1938–)

When he was 13, Brooklyn-born Michael Harper's family moved to a predominantly white neighborhood in Los Angeles, California. The move, Harper would recall later, along with the latent postwar racial tensions bubbling in this West Coast metropolis, were distressing enough to make Harper, who would later be called "Chief" by his friends and students, devote his life to writing poetry. After graduating from a local public high school, Harper first attended Los Angeles City College and later Los Angeles State College, where he graduated in 1961 with both bachelor's and master's degrees. While in Los Angeles, he took a job as a postal worker, a position central to Harper's development as a poet of the American experience. The system of the postal service would "play against your dreams, where you came from and where you wanted to go" (Rowell, 786). In the many long and monotonous hours, socializing with "nonstop talkers and monosyllabic wits" (Rowell, 786) taught Harper "the silences inherent in speech, and how to pace, by duration, a given story" (Rowell, 786). Such lessons have become manifest in much of the conversational musicality of Harper's poetry. The jazz that would inflect so much of Harper's poetry might have found its impetus in Billie Holliday, playing piano for the Harper household, or in Charles Mingus's sister, who worked long shifts alongside Harper at the post office.

In 1961, Harper moved east to attend the prestigious Iowa Writer's Workshop at the University of Iowa, where he was the only black student in both his poetry and fiction classes. He received an M.F.A. in 1962. After completing his work at Iowa, Harper went on to teach writing at various universities, including Pasadena City College (1962), Contra Costa College (1964–1968), and California

State College (1968–1969). In 1970, Harper took a position in the creative writing program at Brown University, where he is a university professor and professor of English. Harper has received many distinctions, including the Melville-Cane Award from the Poetry Society of Americas and the Robert Haydn Poetry Award from the United Negro College Fund. He has been recognized by grants and awards from the National Institute of Arts and Letters, the Black Academy of Arts and Letters, the National Endowment of the Arts, the Guggenheim Foundation, the Library of Congress, and other institutions. He also served as Rhode Island's first poet laureate from 1988 to 1933.

While Harper's credentials mark him as a preeminent academic working in a university setting today, he is primarily identified as a prolific and productive poet. He has published more than 10 books of poetry, including *Dear John, Dear Coltrane* (1970), nominated for the National Book Award; *History Is Your Heartbeat* (1971); *Nightmare Begins Responsibility* (1975); *Images of Kin* (1977), also nominated for the National Book Award; *Healing Song for the Inner Ear* (1985); *Honorable Amendments* (1995); and *Songlines in Michaeltree* (2000). He has edited *Collected Poems of Sterling A. Brown* (1980) and coedited, with Robert Steptlo, *Chant of Saints: A Gathering of Afro-American Literature, Art, and Scholarship* (1979) and, with Anthony Walton, *Every Shut Eye Ain't Asleep: An Anthology of Poetry by African Americans since 1945* (1994).

Harper's work continually wrestles with concepts of history and mythology. For Harper, these two notions, usually divided in American society between what is fact and what is fiction in an either/or fashion, have an important kinship: Neither is a completely whole version of human experience. Poetry is a medium through which a new notion of history and myth, one in which a more holistic, both/and, sense of the human experience of the universal can be accurately and compellingly depicted. In the compact and complex phrasings of Harper's poetic architectonics, personal history and national history are merged, often in the space of a single metaphor. In this way, Harper states, "the microcosm and the cosmos are united." He incorporates this notion of poetry into

a sense of what he has called "redefinitions and refinements of 'an American self . . . the American of nightmare, and waking up.'"

In *Dear John, Dear Coltrane,* the American self is reconceptualized as one through which a figure like John Coltrane might prevail as an exemplary American citizen. "He stands as a banner for an attitude, a stance against the world," Harper says of the prolific jazz saxophonist. This first collection of poetry, as well as his later works, reshape 19th-century meter with a quintessentially jazz-inflected rhythm. The language is syncopated; words and phrases are repeated, often multiple times; and just as jazz improvisation often quotes, or, to use a term coined by Henry Louis Gates, Jr., "signifies on," other material, so too does Harper's verse. Historical moments, as well as the actions and experience of Harper's friends, family members, colleagues, and artistic role models are all relevant material for the jazz poet to signify on.

Nightmare Begins Responsibility expands on the stylistics in *Dear John* by furthering an explicit notion of kinship. Often considered Harper's richest volume, the poetry here addresses the central responsibility of the American individual to notions of empathy, to an awareness of one's location within a particular history, as well as in the larger scene of a holistic universe. The network of relationships that grows out of this volume encompasses the kinship between Harper and a diversity of other "responsible" African-American literary and historical figures, including Ralph Albert Dickey and Jackie Robinson.

Key to *Dear John, Dear Coltrane, Nightmare Begins Responsibility,* and other, more recent works is a concept Harper calls "modality," which "describes an environment larger than most words can contain" (O'Brien, 97–98). It is a technique that a poet at work can enter and exit from depending on the context of the work itself. Just as a musician can improvise a multitude of melodies in a single scale or mode, so too can the poet. In this way, historical information, folk knowledges, and multiple vocalities can be voiced in the same poem.

While Harper's enduring legacy will most likely be his vast and intensive poetical reexamination of the experience of what it means to be American in the contemporary moment, one should also note the importance of his pedagogy to African-American studies. He has been a central and influential teacher to a generation of critics and poets, including Robert Dale Parker, Anthony Walton, Herman Beavers, and Suzanne Keen. Walton states that one of the key insights about books he learned in Harper's classroom is that they "could be *weapons*, against ignorance, against forgetfulness, against revisionism" (808). Such a statement deeply resonates with Harper's poetic output as well.

BIBLIOGRAPHY

Antonucci, Michael. "The Map and the Territory: An Interview with Michael S. Harper." *African American Review* 34, no. 3 (Fall 2000): 501–508.

Cooke, Michael G. *Afro-American Literature in the Twentieth Century: The Achievement of Intimacy.* New Haven: Yale University Press, 1985.

Dodd, Elizabeth. "The Great Rainbowed Swamp: History as Moral Ecology in the Poetry of Michael S. Harper." *Isle* 7, no. 1 (Winter 2000): 131–145.

———. "Michael S. Harper: American Poet." *Callaloo* 13, no. 4 (Fall 1990): 749–829.

Lenz, Gunter H. "Black Poetry and Black Music: History and Tradition: Michael Harper and John Coltrane." In *History and Tradition in Afro-American Culture,* edited by Gunter H. Lenz, 277–319. Frankfurt: Campus, 1984.

O'Brien, John. "Michael Harper." In *Interviews with Black Writers,* 95–107: New York: Liveright, 1973.

Rowell, Charles H. "'Down Don't Worry Me.' An Interview with Michael S. Harper." *Callaloo* 13, no. 4 (Autumn, 1990): 780–800.

Stepto, Robert B. "After Modernism, After Hibernation: Michael Harper, Robert Hayden and Jay Wright." In *Chant of Saints: A Gathering of Afro-American Literature, Art, and Scholarship,* edited by Michael S. Harper et al., 470–486. Urbana: University of Illinois Press, 1979.

———. "Michael S. Harper, Poet as Kinsman: The Family Sequences." *Massachusetts Review* 17 (Autumn 1976): 477–502.

Walton, Anthony. "The Chief." *Callaloo* 13, no. 4 (Fall 1990): 807–809.

Keith Feldman

Harris, E. Lynn   (1957–   )

One of black America's most prolific contemporary novelists and social activists, E. Lynn Harris is a member of the board of trustees of the Hurston/Wright Foundation and the Evidence Dance Company and is the founder of the E. Lynn Harris Better Days Literary Foundation. Harris was born in Flint, Michigan, and reared by his mother. When Harris was four, his family moved to Little Rock, Arkansas, where he began working odd jobs to help meet the family's financial needs. Determined and motivated to better his situation, Harris attended the University of Arkansas, Fayetteville, from which he graduated with a bachelor's degree in journalism in 1977.

In 1983, Harris met author-poet MAYA ANGELOU, an Arkansas native, who encouraged him to write, "even if it's just one word a day." Inspired by Angelou's *I KNOW WHY THE CAGED BIRD SINGS* (1970) and JAMES BALDWIN's *GO TELL IT ON THE MOUNTAIN* (1953), Harris began to write full time in 1990, leaving behind a secure, well-paying computer sales position at IBM. He invested $25,000 from his savings to self-publish his first novel, *INVISIBLE LIFE* (1991), and traveled door-to-door to black-owned businesses—from bookstores to hair salons—to promote it. Word of mouth led to greater fortunes. As customers (mostly women) began to request *Invisible Life,* sales reached more than 10,000 copies. *ESSENCE* magazine named *Invisible Life* one of 1992's best novels. This recognition secured Harris a contract with Doubleday Books, led to a reprint of *Invisible Life,* and placed the novel in national mainstream bookstores beyond the parameters of the black community, inevitably increasing Harris's readership and sales.

Although Harris has been criticized for his novels' lack of substance, as well as for creating characters that lack depth, Harris is a strong, consistent stylist who adheres to a linear, plot-driven narrative, which attracted, from the beginning, a powerful female constituency. As a result of an early life shared with sisters and a determined single mother who had left an abusive relationship to improve the quality of her children's lives, Harris draws on his own familial experiences to render what for him are honest depictions of black women. This commitment to realism, which became Harris's niche, allowed him to credibly introduce, in a non-threatening manner, the spectrum of homosexuality found in the black community and to create what is now a familiar cast of characters, voices, and circumstances in his successive novels.

Just as I Am (1994) a sequel, reintroduces Raymond Winston Tyler, Jr., who is on a quest to define and discover his true sexual orientation amidst rising confusion about the AIDS epidemic and media-hyped stereotypes of black Americans. Narrated by Nicole, Tyler's girlfriend from *Invisible Life,* the novel establishes Harris as a competent author capable of creating a credible "black" woman's voice. Harris is equally successful in boldly exploring the theme of homosexuality among professional athletes, faith in God, and commitment to the truth, central themes of *And This Too Shall Pass* (1996). Emphasis on these themes is, perhaps, Harris's way of convincing his readers that black gay men often lead ordinary but complex lives.

However, Harris is not always as successful with the general treatment of his male characters. He sometimes employs elements of escape or fantasy that prevent his characters from confronting real dilemmas and otherwise life-altering experiences head-on. For example, in *Not a Day Goes By* (2000), although an incestuous experience between John Basil Henderson and his uncle is mentioned in passing, readers are left to ponder how 'sexual molestation by a much beloved uncle' (7) helped shape Basil's life and character. This unaddressed and unanswered question leads readers to wonder why this sexual violation is mentioned in the first place. Further, the novel opens with Basil cowardly backing out of marriage during a telephone conversation. Although this might be a good hook to get readers to turn the page, Basil's fickle behavior extends throughout the novel, preventing readers from seeing him, in the end, as a well-rounded, complex character.

Despite Harris's commitment to realism, fantasy seems to dominate his works on many levels. In this sense, Harris's novels provide an escape for his readers, not unlike many romance potboilers. A majority of Harris's readers do not live as extravagantly as do his characters. Hypothetically, however, Harris may be exploring, through rich details, particularly those of wealth and success, how detached or invisible individuals like Basil, an NFL player living a double life, are. On the one hand, Basil lives as a heterosexual male who is engaged to be married; on the other hand, he is a closeted homosexual male trying to find his identity.

Harris understands that diversity is the fabric of American life. His fiction, written with love and compassion, renders honest, if not always totally complex, black male homosexual and female heterosexual characters to a broad readership. Yet Harris is dedicated to strengthening the gay and lesbian literary pallet, as is shown by his four novels written between 1997 and 2001: *If This World Were Mine* (1997), *Abide with Me* (1998), *Not a Day Goes By* (2000), and *Any Way the Wind Blows* (2001). In 2002, he published his eighth novel, *A Love of My Own,* in which he seems determined to remind readers that, despite the escapism found in his work, he remains committed to creating credibly lived lives—not ones that are merely shrouded in fantasy. In *Say A Little Prayer* (2006), a humorous novel, Harris explores the experiences of black gays and lesbians in the black church.

With just two novels to his credit, Harris became the first black male author to reach the top of *Blackboard,* the best-seller list for African-American writers. Harris received a NATIONAL ASSOCIATION FOR THE ADVANCEMENT OF COLORED PEOPLE Image Award nomination and a James Baldwin Award for Literary Excellence in 1997 for *If This World Were Mine.* In 1999 he was awarded the Distinguished Alumni Award from the University of Arkansas, Fayetteville. In 2002 Harris received the Writers for Writers Award from Barnes & Noble for his E. Lynn Harris Better Days Literary Foundation, whose goal is "to provide new writers with guidance and assistance in publishing their works so that society is exposed to and enriched by the works of these authors."

BIBLIOGRAPHY

Greene, Beverly. *Ethnic and Cultural Diversity among Lesbians and Gay Men: Psychological Perspectives on Lesbian and Gay Issues.* Vol. 3. Thousand Oaks, Calif.: Sage Publications, 1997.

Hawkeswood, William G. *One of the Children: Gay Men in Black Harlem.* Berkeley: University of California Press, 1996.

Reid-Pharr, Robert F., ed. *Black Gay Man: Essays.* New York: New York University Press, 2001.

Lawrence T. Potter

Hayden, Robert Earl   (1913–1980)

Born Asa Bundy Sheffey in Paradise Valley, a neighborhood of Detroit, Michigan, to parents Asa and Ruth Sheffey, Robert E. Hayden was renamed and reared by adoptive parents, William and Sue Hayden, who were family friends. Four loving but quarrelsome and impoverished parents made childhood difficult for the young Robert. Nevertheless, he persisted against difficult circumstances to become a renowned poet. From 1931, when he published his first poem, to 1982, when the final version of his *American Journal* appeared posthumously, Hayden's poetry changed dramatically. While Hayden's early poems imitate revered precursors, including Countee Cullen and Langston Hughes, his dense, experimental, and groundbreaking poems on African-American history define his middle period. Characterized by its spare diction and precise symbolist imagery, Hayden's later poetry makes a singular contribution to the African-American poetic tradition. But Hayden's life and work also display continuities: sensitivity to poetry's liberating force, a commitment to wrestle poetic art's difficulties, and a defiant championing of the poet's duty to be first and foremost a poet.

With eyes that were damaged at birth, Hayden suffered from poor vision, but the precocious teenage Hayden committed himself to poetry. He avidly read the HARLEM RENAISSANCE poets, the British romantics, and Hart Crane. After a social worker arranged tuition, Hayden attended Detroit City College. During the depression, he worked for the WPA Federal Writers' Project researching the antislavery movement's history. A John Reed Club participant, Hayden absorbed Marxist notions of the writer's role in the class struggle and

gave a reading at a Detroit United Auto Workers rally. These activities and his didactic verse resulted in Hayden being tagged "'The People's Poet' of Detroit" (Fetrow, 7). In 1940 Hayden married Erma Inez Morris. The couple converted to the Bahá'í faith. Attending the University of Michigan, Hayden studied with W. H. Auden and attained an M.A. in English; in 1946, he was appointed to assistant professor of English at Fisk University. In 1969 he became professor of English at the University of Michigan, his final academic appointment.

Perhaps judging too harshly, Hayden eventually dismissed his first book, *Heart-Shape in the Dust* (1940), as apprentice work. The collection includes poems derivative of Harlem Renaissance themes, imitations of British romantic poetry, and antiracist, proworker protest poems (Hatcher, 64–66). Bearing titles such as "Poem in Time of War" and "The Negro to America," the protest poems achieve little more than leftist political statements. For example, with the refrain "Hear me, black brothers, / White brothers, hear me," "Speech" calls for proletarian solidarity against the capitalists (12–13). Hayden ensured that *Heart-Shape*'s poems would not appear in his *Collected Poems* (1985), which includes poems, many significantly revised, from all his other books.

During the 1940s, Hayden struggled to write poems adequate to his ambition. Eschewing didacticism, Hayden wrote poems, including "Runagate Runagate" and "Fredrick Douglas," that dismantle stereotypes about African-American history to recover the heroism of the African-American struggle for liberation. These poems utilize the historical knowledge Hayden accrued from his Federal Writers Project research and subsequent study. One such poem, "Middle Passage," deals with the 1839 rebellion of enslaved Africans on the *Amistad.* Complexly weaving the authorial voice with those of slave owners and slave ships' officers and crew members, the poem's climactic lines herald the revolt's leader:

> *The deep immortal human wish,*
> *the timeless will:*

Cinquez its deathless primaveral image,
life that transfigures many lives.
Voyage through death
to life upon these shores. (172–77)

Cinquez images the human drive for life that, however perversely and contradictorily, the poem's characters exercise in refusing to recognize the Africans' "human wish" and oppressing the Africans' "timeless will." Cinquez acts in concert with the humanity the slave owners necessarily embody yet deny in themselves and in others. Despite the genocidal cruelty the poem evokes, Cinquez constitutes an "image" of the human will that may precipitate renewal and change. Repudiating T. S. Eliot's pessimism in "The Wasteland," "Middle Passage" joins Hart Crane's *The Bridge* as a major poetic statement concerning America's past and potential future.

In the 1940s Hayden also experimented to establish his own poetic voice and to shed *Heart-Shape in the Dust*'s compulsory fixed rhyme and meter. Hayden described these years as his "Baroque period" (Fetrow, 18). Deploying esoteric diction and surreal imagery, poems such as "A Ballad of Remembrance" and "Homage to the Empress of the Blues" require careful reading and attention to nuance. Hayden gathered these poems and others in *The Lion and the Archer* (1948), co-authored by Myron O'Higgins and published as the Counterpoise Series's first volume. Hayden and a few Fisk colleagues had established the Counterpoise Series and distributed a manifesto announcing its guiding principles. The manifesto asserts the poet's freedom to write unconstrained by extrapoetic concerns and demands that critics judge African-American and non–African-American poets by the same standards (*Collected Prose*, 41–42). Hayden's *Figure of Time* (1955) was the third Counterpoise volume.

Collecting new poems with Hayden's best previous work, *A BALLAD OF REMEMBRANCE* appeared in 1962. One poem, "Theme and Variation," employs a favorite Hayden character, the outcast or outsider, and captures Hayden's exaltation of the poetic imagination. The poem features a persona called "the stranger" (4): "There is, there is, he said, an immanence / that turns to curiosa all I know" (13–14). The imagination discloses a sublime "immanence" that, in evading conceptualization, shows the world how our conceptions organize to be an oddly pornographic ("curiosa") spectacle. This "immanence" subtly awakens a will to resistance by changing that drearily alienated world's "light" to a "rainbow darkness / wherein God waylays us and empowers" (15–16).

A Ballad of Remembrance won the Grand Prize for Poetry awarded by the First World Festival of Negro Arts held in Dakar, Senegal, in 1966—the same year Hayden's *Selected Poems* was published. But 1966 also saw the beginning of a polemic between Hayden and more militant writers of the BLACK ARTS MOVEMENT, who were concerned with art as propaganda and political weapon and identified racial identity as the overriding concern of the African-American poet. Describing poetry as "the art of saying the impossible" (Hatcher, 37), Hayden insisted that authentic poetry is universal.

Hayden's *Words in Mourning Time* (1970) meditates on America's imperial violence in Southeast Asia and on the tragic assassinations of the 1960s. "El-Hajj Malik El-Shabazz" mourns MALCOLM X, tracing his pilgrimage from a "false dawn of vision" disclosing "a racist Allah" to his final vision of "Allah the raceless in whose blazing Oneness all / were one" (22, 24, 53–54). "Words in Mourning Time" links the assassinations of MARTIN LUTHER KING, JR., and Robert Kennedy to the cold hatred implicit in America's conduct of the Vietnam War and concludes that "We must go on struggling to be human" and to "renew the vision of / a human world" (112, 115–116).

Hayden became more introspective in *The Night-Blooming Cereus* (1972). While "The Night-Blooming Cereus" celebrates itself as exemplifying what the "focused / energy" of the poetic "will" can achieve, "The Peacock Room" and "Traveling through Fog" contemplate poetry's human and cognitive limits (39–40), confirming Hayden's belief that, in its universal appeal, poetry is "the art of saying the impossible."

Although it contains some new poems, *Angle of Ascent* (1975) gathers Hayden's best work from previous volumes.

American Journal (1978, 1982), Hayden's last book, evidences Hayden's desire that his readers enter the worlds of the marginalized. "The Rag Man" treats a homeless person's existence, and "The Prisoners" recounts Hayden's visit to a penitentiary to give a reading. "A Letter from Phillis Wheatley" and "John Brown" continue Hayden's interest in portraying historical figures. The persona of "the stranger" finds its apotheosis in "American Journal," a movingly hopeful yet tough-minded assessment of the United States. A visitor from outer space, the speaker uses disguises, including the earthlings' "varied pigmentations," secretly to observe "the americans," whom the visitor describes as "this baffling / multi people" (7, 1–2). Though the visitor's "skill in mimicry is impeccable," he concludes that among America's diverse individuals "some constant" remains that "defies analysis and imitation" and that the visitor "cannot penetrate or name" (94, 96, 97, 115).

Besides the Dakar prize, Hayden won two Hopwood Awards (1938, 1942), the Detroit Mayor's Bronze Medal (1969), and the Russell Loines Award (1970); he was inducted into the American Academy (1979). Hayden served as the Library of Congress's Consultant in Poetry (1976–78). Perhaps best known for his poems on African-American history, Hayden also contributed fine poems reflecting on poetic art and on universal themes of spirituality, mortality, and human destiny. His work deeply influenced two important African-American poets in particular: MICHAEL S. HARPER and JAY WRIGHT.

BIBLIOGRAPHY

Fetrow, Fred M. *Robert Hayden*. Boston: Twayne Publishers, 1984.
Friedlander, Benjamin. "Robert Hayden's Epic of Community." *MELUS* 23, no. 3 (1998): 129–143.
Goldstein, Laurence, and Robert Chrisman, eds. *Robert Hayden: Essays on the Poetry*. Ann Arbor: University of Michigan Press, 2001.
Hatcher, John. *From the Auroral Darkness: The Life and Poetry of Robert Hayden*. Oxford: George Ronald, 1984.

Robert S. Oventile

Hemphill, Essex C.   (1957–1995)

Renowned poet, essayist, editor, and activist Essex C. Hemphill was born in Chicago, Illinois, in 1957; he grew up in Anderson, Indiana; Columbia, South Carolina; and southeast Washington, D.C. The second of five children, Hemphill began writing at age 14. After graduating from Washington, D.C.'s Ballou High School, Hemphill studied English and journalism at the University of Maryland before completing a degree in English at the University of the District of Columbia. Soon thereafter, Hemphill became involved in various writing collectives on the East Coast. In 1980, he publicly proclaimed his gay identity during a poetry reading at the Founders Library at Howard University. From the mid-1980s until his death, Hemphill became perhaps the most well-known black gay male writer in the United States since JAMES BALDWIN.

Although initially influenced by the BLACK NATIONALIST ideology of the BLACK ARTS MOVEMENT, Hemphill eventually distanced himself from what he came to see as its narrow political perspective and spectrum. In the end, this ideology did not address issues that concerned him, specifically the black gay man's exclusion from the collective African-American community. Hemphill was most interested in exploring in his poetry such difficult subjects as estrangement, racism, isolation, homophobia, denial, and fear. For example, in his poem "Commitments," Hemphill says poignantly of his family photos,

> *My arms are empty . . .*
> *so empty they would break*
> *around a lover . . .*
> *I am the invisible son . . .*
> *I smile as I serve my duty. (Brother to Brother, 58)*

Hemphill's poetry often struggled against this complacency on the part of black gay men within the larger context of black American politics and community.

The cofounder of the *Nethula Journal of Contemporary Literature*, Hemphill's poetry appeared in *Obsidian, Black Scholar, CALLALOO,* and *ESSENCE.* He wrote numerous essays for gay publications and taught a course on black gay identity at the Institute for Policy Studies in Washington, D.C. Hemphill's first collections of poems, *Earth Life* (1985) and *Conditions* (1986), were self-published chapbooks. He gained national attention, however, after his work appeared in *In the Life* (1986), the first contemporary anthology of writings by black gay men, edited by Hemphill's friend Joseph Beam. He also contributed to *Tongues Untied* (1987), a British collection that also included the work of Dirg Aaab-Richards, Craig G. Harris, Isaac Jackson, and ASOTTO SAINT.

After Joseph Beam's death from AIDS in 1988, Hemphill compiled and edited BROTHER TO BROTHER: NEW WRITINGS BY BLACK GAY MEN (1991), a follow-up collection to *In the Life. Brother to Brother* won a Lambda Literary Award. Hemphill, who received a National Endowment for the Arts Fellowship in poetry in 1986, later published *Ceremonies: Prose and Poetry* (1992), the only complete collection of his works. In it he offers provocative commentary on such topics as Robert Mapplethorpe's photographs of African-American men, feminism among men, and AIDS in the black community. *Ceremonies* was awarded the National Library Association's Gay, Lesbian, and Bisexual New Author Award in 1993.

Hemphill's bold, assertive poems were often written to be performed aloud, as he believed strongly that poetry was not solely intended for the page but was meant to be heard. He performed readings and lectured at Harvard University, University of Pennsylvania, Massachusetts Institute of Technology, University of California at Los Angeles, the Folger Shakespeare Library, the National Black Arts Festival at the Whitney Museum, and many other institutions. He received four grants from the District of Columbia Commission for the Arts and was a visiting scholar at the Getty Center for the History of Art and the Humanities in Santa Monica in 1993.

Hemphill, with Larry Duckett and later Wayson Jones, created Cinque, a Washington, D.C.–based performance trio that first performed at the Enik Alley Coffeehouse. The trio also worked with Emmy- and Peabody Award–winning filmmaker MARLON RIGGS on his final film, *Black Is . . . Black Ain't,* which deals with the explosive conflicts over African-American identity. Hemphill's work was also featured in two other award-winning films: Isaac Julien's *Looking for Langston* (1989) and Riggs's documentary *Tongues Untied* (1991), in which he also performs his poetry.

At his death, Hemphill left three projects uncompleted: *Standing in the Gap,* a novel in which a mother challenges a preacher's condemnation of her gay son who is suffering from AIDS; *Bedside Companions,* a collection of short stories by black gay men; and *The Evidence of Being,* narratives of older black gay men, which he had been working on since the early 1990s in order to satisfy his curiosity about cultural and social history before the term "gay" entered popular usage. Unlike some gay activists, Hemphill was greatly concerned that black gay men recognize the entire range of possibilities that exists in their lives and that they not disconnect from primary institutions like family and community. He saw gay life as only a part of the greater African-American family and experience. Hemphill died in Philadelphia, Pennsylvania, on November 4, 1995, from complications related to AIDS.

BIBLIOGRAPHY

Abbott, Franklin, ed. *Men and Intimacy: Personal Accounts Exploring the Dilemmas of Modern Male Sexuality.* Freedom, Calif.: Crossing Press, 1990.

Avena, Thomas, ed. *Life Sentences: Writers, Artists and AIDS.* San Francisco: Mercury House, 1994.

Bean, Joseph, ed. *In the Life: A Black Gay Anthology.* Los Angeles: Alyson Publications, 1986.

Hemphill, Essex, ed. *Brother to Brother: New Writings by Black Gay Men.* Los Angeles: Alyson Publications, 1991.

———. *Ceremonies: Prose and Poetry.* New York: Plume, 1992.

Larkin, Joan, and Carl Morse, eds. *Gay and Lesbian Poetry in Our Time.* New York: St. Martin's, 1988.

G. Winston James

Henderson, David   (1942–   )

David Henderson, born and reared in Harlem, attended Hunter College and the New School for Social Research. Henderson became a poet, labor organizer, and political activist during the explosive 1960s, which were dominated by BLACK NATIONALISM and the functionally prescribed BLACK ARTS MOVEMENT. He also taught at City College, where he was poet resident. Henderson was married to the scholar and black feminist critic BARBARA CHRISTIAN; together they had a daughter, Najuma.

Henderson was among the founding members of the Society of Umbra, a critical component of the Black Arts Movement housed in the Lower East Side. Its members were committed to providing an arena for the discussion and exploration of the complex meanings of black art tenets related to artist and community. Umbra workshop participants included Tom Dent, CALVIN HERNTON, ISHMAEL REED, and Rolland Snelling (ASKIA MUHAMMAD TOURÉ). The inaugural issue of its journal, *Umbra,* of which Henderson was editor, outlined its purpose:

> *Umbra* exists to provide a vehicle for those outspoken and youthful writers who present aspects of social and racial reality which may be called "uncommercial" but cannot with any honesty be considered non-essential to a whole and healthy society. . . . We will not print trash, no matter how relevantly it deals with race, social issues, or anything else. (Redmond, 321)

That there was not consensus within the group is clearly indicated by its early breakup and the formation, under the leadership of AMIRI BARAKA, of the Black Arts Repertory Theatre/School (BART/S).

Henderson is the author of several collections of poems, including *Felix of the Silent Forest* (1967), *De Mayor of Harlem* (1970), *Forest the East Side* (1980), and *'Scuse Me While I Kiss the Sky: Life of Jimi Hendrix* (1983). His work appeared in the *Paris Review, 7th Street Quarterly, Evergreen Review,* and *Journal of Black Poetry,* and it was anthologized in *New Negro Poets: U.S.A.,* Stephen Henderson's *Understanding the New Black Poetry,* Baraka and Neal's *BLACK FIRE,* and Jerry Ward's *Trouble the Water.*

BIBLIOGRAPHY

Breman, Paul. "Poetry into the Sixties." In *The Black American Writers,* Vol. 2, edited by C. W. Bigsby, 99–109. Baltimore: Penguin Books, 1971.

Henderson, Stephen, ed. *Understanding the New Black Poetry.* New York: William Morrow & Company, 1973.

Redmond, Eugene. *Drumvoices, The Mission of Afro-American Poetry: A Critical History.* Garden City, N.Y.: Anchor Books, 1976.

Michael Poindexter

Henderson, George Wylie   (1904–   )

Novelist, short story writer, and journalist George W. Henderson was born in Warrior's Stand, Alabama. He was educated at Tuskegee Institute, where he also served as a printer's apprentice before moving to New York, where he wrote for the *New York Daily News.* Henderson authored several short stories and two novels, *Ollie Miss* (1935) and *Jule* (1946), a sequel.

In *Ollie Miss,* Henderson, like many of his contemporaries in the 1930s, turned to the rural South for the settings, character types, and dramatic situations in his work, demonstrating his familiarity with black folk life of this region. At the beginning of the novel, Ollie embarks on a journey to visit her lover, Jule, who lives on a neighboring farm. There, she is physically assaulted by one of Jule's girlfriends; however, she fulfills her intense desire to become pregnant with Jule's child. In the closing section of the novel, Ollie vows to have the child without marrying Jule and to work 10 acres for herself in order to live independently and care for her child.

Jule continues the story by focusing on Jule, Ollie's son, whom she named for his father and raised alone. During his youth, Jule moves to Hannon, Alabama, where he has an altercation with a white man who has made sexual advances to his girlfriend, Bertha. In the aftermath of this attack, Jule flees to New York to escape the inevitable white retaliation. In New York, Jule grows into adulthood, eventually becoming a printer's apprentice. In the novel's conclusion, Jule returns to Alabama to attend his mother's funeral. Also, he plans to marry Bertha and return with her to New York.

Although *Ollie Miss* is clearly the stronger of the two, the novels share the realistic setting and unromanticized portraits of the South that are hallmarks of Henderson's writing. In addition, *Ollie Miss* presents a strong, uncompromising, attractive, black female who decides what is right for her; she accepts responsibility for the choices she makes without apology. In this regard, Ollie compares favorably with other fictional black heroines of the period, particularly ZORA NEALE HURSTON's JANIE CRAWFORD and RICHARD WRIGHT's Aunt Sue. Although it contains much of the same sensitive portrayal of the South found in *Ollie Miss, Jule* suffers from superficial characterization and several structural flaws. However, there are suggestions of social and racial protest in *Jule* that are not as discernible in *Ollie Miss.* In addition, there is a strong sense of autobiography at work in *Jule,* much more so than in *Ollie Miss.*

Henderson's reputation as a writer rests on these two novels and, while neither was a major critical or commercial success, Henderson occupies a place of importance in the African-American literary canon in that these works help constitute the transition from the best-foot-forward fiction of the Harlem Renaissance to the more pronounced and strident protest works of the 1940s.

BIBLIOGRAPHY

Carson, Warren J. "Four Black American Novelists, 1935–1941," M.A. thesis, Atlanta University, 1975.

Kane, Patricia, and Doris Y. Wilkinson. "Survival Strategies: Black Women in *Ollie Miss* and *Cotton Comes to Harlem." Critique* 16 (1974): 103.

Warren J. Carson

Henderson, Stephen Evangelist
(1925–1997)

An administrator, teacher, scholar, and champion of BLACK AESTHETIC, Henderson was born and reared in Key West, Florida; his family ties extended to the Bahamas, Cuba, and the West Indies. He studied English and sociology at Morehouse College and completed an M.A. in English at the University of Wisconsin. He taught at Virginia Union while simultaneously completing his Ph.D. degree in English and art history at Wisconsin, finishing in 1959. In 1962, he returned to Morehouse to join the English faculty; he eventually became department chair. After the 1968 assassination of MARTIN LUTHER KING, JR., Henderson and Vincent Harding, the civil rights historian and professor of religion, were engaged in discussions that led to the creation of *The Institute of the Black World* in Atlanta. Henderson was a senior research fellow with the institute until 1971, when he was hired by Howard University to teach in the Afro-American studies department. From 1973 to 1987, Henderson ran Howard's Institute of Arts and Humanities; when funding was cancelled, he returned to teaching full time.

Henderson's administrative prowess was evident again in his direction of the Institute of Arts and Humanities. Designed to be a creative scholarly center as well as a bridge between the academy and the black community, the institute offered programs, workshops, and action-centered seminars, research fellowships, and internships, as well as public lectures and performances. Henderson worked with STERLING BROWN, JOHN OLIVER KILLENS, HAKI MADHUBUTI, and other notable figures to sustain the institute. In addition to bringing distinguished faculty, community activists, artists, writers, and musicians together with young people, the institute honored local faculty, staff, and artists whose work enhanced black life. Guests included GWENDOLYN BROOKS, AMIRI BARAKA, Harry Belafonte, Bernice Reagon, ED BULLINS, and Richard Wesley. The institute sponsored several publications, as well as the National Conference of Afro-American Writers and the first Ascension Poetry Reading. Henderson ensured that key events were recorded and major figures were interviewed on video or audiotape; these records are currently housed in the African American Resource Center and in the Moorland-Spingarn Library at Howard University.

Henderson's contributions to literature are best interpreted within the milieu of the CIVIL RIGHTS, BLACK POWER, and BLACK ARTS movements. People respected him across the political spectrum, especially black nationalists. Henderson's fellow critics included George Kent, LARRY NEAL, and ADDISON GAYLE, JR. As a literary critic, Henderson documented the interdisciplinary influence of all the arts on black poetry; defined several African-American specific key terms, including "soul"; and created new ones, such as "saturation," to develop and promote African-American literary theory. In "'Survival Motion,' A Study of the Black Writer and the Black Revolution in America," Henderson describes "soul" as a primal spiritual and physical energy that taps into the black collective unconscious and is deeply existential. He asserts the militancy inherent in any person's statement of Black Pride. He calls creative expression an act of survival and regeneration, as well as a means to self-knowledge and self-celebration (65).

In his groundbreaking anthology, *Understanding the New Black Poetry,* Henderson uses his introduction to further explain the innovations and continuity between writers in the 1960s and previous generations of African-American poets. He refers to the cumulative element of black experience contained by a black poem as "saturation" and insists that black poetry can only obtain validity from the black community. Henderson's selections of poetry include both the rural and urban black oral traditions and music. He moves from the beginnings in the 18th century through the HARLEM RENAISSANCE toward the BLUES, the ballad, and jazz as the links to the major section featuring black poetry of

the 1960s, arranged in order of publication. That the names he selected are widely known today is evidence of his astute judgment. As a critic, a professor, an administrator, and a leader inspired to document the contributions of blacks, Henderson's legacy rests in the generations of students and colleagues whom he inspired to continue to celebrate black life through scholarship and the arts, and in the unfinished business of documenting the black contribution to arts and letters.

BIBLIOGRAPHY

Henderson, Stephen E. "Inside the Funk Shop: A Word on Black Words." *Black Books Bulletin* 1 (Summer/Fall 1973): 9–12.
———. "Saturation: Progress Report on a Theory of Black Poetry." *Black World* 24 (1975): 4–17.
———. "'Survival Motion,' A Study of the Black Writer and the Black Revolution in America." In *The Militant Black Writer in Africa and the United States,* edited by Mercer Cook, 65–129. Madison: University of Wisconsin Press, 1969.
———. *Understanding the New Black Poetry, Black Speech & Black Music as Poetic References.* New York: Morrow, 1973.
Miller, E. Ethelbert. "A Conversation with a Literary Critic." *New Directions: The Howard University Magazine* 13, no. 2 (1986): 20–27.
Salaam, Kalamu Ya. "A Deeper Understanding—Stephen E. Henderson: A Profile of a Critical Thinker." In *Fertile Ground: Memories and Visions,* edited by Kalamu Ya Salaam and Kysha N. Brown, 126–129. New Orleans, La.: Runagate Press, 1996.

Julia A. Galbus

Heritage Series of Black Poetry

One of the most important publishing outlets for African-American poetry of the 1960s and 1970s was an improbable venture run by a Dutchman in London. In the late 1940s, a young BLUES aficionado from Amsterdam named Paul Breman (b. 1931) "theorized" the existence of African-American poetry before ever encountering it. Breman reasoned that the poetic discipline that underlies the blues would eventually have led to more "formal" poetry. He began searching for African-American poetry while still a student at Amsterdam University. After meeting Rosey Pool, who was lecturing on black poetry in Amsterdam, and discovering poetry by COUNTEE CULLEN, CLAUDE MCKAY, LANGSTON HUGHES and others, Breman's interest was solidified.

In 1959, Breman moved to London. In May of that year, he wrote to Waring Cuney, "For some time I have been thinking of issuing a series of smallish well-printed books of poetry by U.S. Negro authors. I want to print ROBERT HAYDEN's latest verse, STERLING BROWN's second book, reprint the GEORGE MOSES HORTON broadsides, and make an anthology of the younger poets." That year, Hayden sent Breman A BALLAD OF REMEMBRANCE, which launched the Heritage Series in 1962 and four years later won Hayden the poetry prize at the first black arts festival, in Dakar.

The series eventually resulted in 27 numbered volumes published between 1962 and 1975. Breman chose the name Heritage because "the poet is a bridge between past and present, and also between present and future—he uses a heritage, and leaves one." In that spirit of linking past with present, Breman determined that the series would focus on HARLEM RENAISSANCE poets who never had published a book and on new poets, to "give them a platform from which to take off." Some of the important forerunners in the series were ARNA BONTEMPS, Waring Cuney, and Frank Horne. The exciting newcomers included ISHMAEL REED, whose first poetry collection, *catechism of d neoamerican hoodoo church,* was the 11th volume in the series. Other significant Heritage authors included Lloyd Addison, Samuel Allen, Russell Atkins, Sebastian Clarke, OWEN DODSON, Ray Durem, MARI EVANS, Frank John, Dolores Kendrick, AUDRE LORDE, CLARENCE MAJOR, DUDLEY RANDALL, Ellease Southerland, James W. Thompson, and many other newcomers in the influential Heritage anthology *Sixes and Sevens,* edited by Breman.

The Heritage Series held an important place in the development of many African-American poets who later went on to establish significant literary careers. Many poets whose work was published in the series credited the books' uniformity of presentation in quality and style and the publisher's lack of editorial interference with the poets' vision for their work.

The legacy of the Heritage Series will be its preservation of African-American poetry of excellence by fine poets, some of whom are still underrepresented in print. It enabled some established figures to publish a book of their writing. Finally, the Heritage Series offered an important breakthrough into the realm of professionalism for many poets who look back on this series as providing them with the opportunity that launched their careers.

BIBLIOGRAPHY

Bontemps, Arna. *Personals.* Heritage Series. Vol. 4. London: Paul Breman, 1963.

Hayden, Robert Earl. *The Night-Blooming Cereus.* Heritage Series. Vol. 20. London: Paul Breman, 1972.

Lorde, Audre. *Cables to Rage.* Heritage Series. Vol. 9. London: Paul Breman, 1970.

Major, Clarence. *Private Line.* Heritage Series. Vol. 15. London: Paul Breman, 1971.

Randall, Dudley. *Love You.* Heritage Series. Vol. 10. London: Paul Breman, 1970.

Lauri Ramey

Hernton, Calvin Coolidge   (1932–2001)

Calvin Coolidge Hernton was a writer and social scientist for whom these two roles were seamlessly connected. Hernton was born to Magnolia Jackson in Chattanooga, Tennessee, and was raised there primarily by his grandmother, Ella Estell. A vivid portrait of his childhood, showing his grandmother's influence and his awakening race consciousness, appears in his autobiographical essay "Chattanooga Black Boy" (1996). Hernton attended Talladega College, earning the nickname "Socrates" for his intellectual and philosophical bent, and received a B.A. in sociology (1954). In college, Hernton first exhibited his talent and passion for writing and began to think of himself as a poet. He attended graduate school at Fisk University, receiving an M.A. in sociology (1956). His M.A. thesis, "A Thematic Analysis of Editorials and

Letters to the Editors Regarding the Montgomery Bus Protest Movement," presages his lifelong interest in social conditions affecting African Americans. He married Mildred Webster in 1958, with whom he had one son, Antone. In 1975, the marriage ended in divorce. Hernton taught social science at four historically black colleges and universities: Benedict College (1957–58), Alabama A&M (1958–59), Edward Waters College (1959–60), and Southern University and A&M (1960–61). He moved to New York in 1961 for further study in sociology at Columbia University and worked for the New York Department of Welfare (1961–62) and the National Opinion Research Center (1963–64).

Moving to the Lower East Side of Manhattan brought Hernton in contact with other African-American poets, including Raymond Patterson, Tom Dent, and DAVID HENDERSON. Hernton became cofounder of a collective of writers, artists, and musicians called the Society of Umbra (1961), whose participants included Dent, Henderson, ISHMAEL REED, LORENZO THOMAS, Norman Pritchard, Brenda Walcott, and ASKIA M. TOURÉ. This experience is described in his essay "Umbra: A Personal Recounting" (1993). The society met to critique each other's work and hold poetry readings, and it published a literary magazine, Umbra. Umbra was an important force in developing the BLACK ARTS MOVEMENT by combining art with politics, stressing performance, providing a community-based forum for African-American voices, and joining art, music, and literature. Hernton received a fellowship to study in London at the Institute of Phenomenological Studies directed by R. D. Laing (1965–69). From 1970 until he retired in 1999, he was professor of African-American studies and creative writing at Oberlin College. Hernton's second marriage to Mary O'Callaghan (1998) lasted until his death.

Hernton published three poetry collections: The Coming of Chronos to the House of Nightsong (1964), Medicine Man (1976), and The Red Crab Gang and Black River Poems (1999). Reflecting Black Arts Movement values, Hernton's poetry highlights performative features such as rhythm and repetition and makes references to African-

American culture. Ballads and BLUES poems in Medicine Man echo STERLING BROWN and LANGSTON HUGHES in using a folk-based aesthetic (including musical idioms, especially blues, jazz and spirituals) to create sophisticated African-American cultural portraits. Hernton's most famous poem is "The Distant Drum," a clarion call to his primary identity as a poet. His poems sometimes display dry wit, as in "Low Down and Sweet," where he plays the dozens with Ishmael Reed. His extended lyrics, such as "Medicine Man," show the influence of modernists such as MELVIN B. TOLSON. The Red Crab Gang reflects his final battle with cancer. The Coming of Chronos to the House of Nightsong, subtitled An Epical Narrative of the South, is an illustrated chapbook-length tone poem. Hernton also wrote scripts for the television series "A Man Called Hawk," which starred his former Oberlin College student, Avery Brooks.

Hernton published one novel, Scarecrow (1974), about travelers to Europe on board the Castel Felice. Its central theme is the focus of his writing: the psychological and sexual ramifications of racism. Hernton published many essays on literature, psychology, and social conditions. His most important work of literary criticism is The Sexual Mountain and Black Women Writers: Adventures in Sex, Literature, and Real Life (1987). The title of this groundbreaking essay collection alludes to Hughes's essay on African-American artists and race pride, "The Negro Artist and the Racial Mountain" (1926). (Hughes was a mentor to Hernton, who, when young and hungry in New York, regularly appeared at Hughes's door on Sundays at suppertime, where he was assured of being invited for dinner, perhaps his one solid meal of the week.) The Sexual Mountain is one of the earliest examinations of the accomplishments and obstacles of African-American female writers. It controversially cites negative images of African-American women by male novelists, notably RICHARD WRIGHT and RALPH ELLISON, in contrast with more positive images by JAMES BALDWIN. Hernton received acclaim from African-American women for courage in articulating his pro-female stance. The book contains an influential opening chapter in which Hernton interprets ALICE WALKER's *The Color Purple* (1982) as a slave narrative. Another chapter is one of the first serious assessments of ANN PETRY's novel *The STREET* (1946), which Hernton considers a pivotal work of African-American women's fiction.

Although lauded as a feminist by female literary critics and readers, Hernton preferred to think of himself as a "non-sexist male" for refusing to tolerate bias based on race, class, or gender. This point of view appears in his most famous book, *Sex and Racism in America* (1965), a "social study" that places black women in the "lowest status group" in American society, designating them "an oppressed class." The book's central premise is that "[A]ll race relations tend to be, however subtle, sex relations" (6). This statement echoes JAMES WELDON JOHNSON's idea that "in the core of the heart of the American race problem the sex factor is rooted," a quotation from *Along This Way* that serves as the epigraph to *Sex and Racism in America*. Hernton made a major contribution to African-American literary and cultural studies as an early advocate of the womanist movement, a developer of the Black Arts Movement, an innovative teacher and researcher, a prescient commentator on the connections between sex and racism, and a creative writer.

BIBLIOGRAPHY

Hernton, Calvin C. "Chattanooga Black Boy: Identity and Racism." In *Names We Call Home: Autobiography on Racial Identity,* edited by Becky Thompson and Sangeeta Tyagi, 139–154. New York: Routledge, 1995.

———. *The Coming of Chronos to the House of Nightsong: An Epical Narrative of the South.* New York: Interim Books, 1964.

———. *Coming Together: Black Power, White Hatred, and Sexual Hang-Ups.* New York: Random House, 1971.

———. *The Red Crab Gang and Black River Poems.* Berkeley, Calif.: Ishmael Reed Publishing Co., 1999.

———. *Scarecrow.* Garden City, N.Y.: Doubleday, 1974.

———. *Sex and Racism in America.* New York: Grove Press, 1965.

———. *The Sexual Mountain and Black Women Writers: Adventures in Sex, Literature, and Real Life.* New York: Anchor Press, 1987.

———. "Umbra: A Personal Recounting." *African American Review* 27, no. 4 (1993): 579–584.

Lauri Ramey

Himes, Chester   (1909–1984)

One of the most prolific writers among the generation of black authors to emerge from the 1940s fascination with the "protest novel," Chester Himes is best known today as the inventor of black noir fiction. Born in 1909, the "third generation" out of slavery, Himes was reared in the South and migrated north with his family to Cleveland, where he spent his adolescence. Learning his way on the city streets, he gravitated to the Scovil District, a haven for gangsters and speakeasies during Prohibition. It was here that he would earn his moniker, "Little Katzi," beginning as a gambler and pimp and soon graduating to armed robbery, a crime for which he was sent to the Ohio State Penitentiary for 20 to 25 years.

In prison Himes passed the time reading *Black Mask,* the slick magazine where the noir stories of Dashiell Hammett and Raymond Chandler first appeared. Certain that he could write his own crime stories, since he was surrounded by criminals, Himes began writing prison stories that he sold to the nationally circulated *Esquire* magazine. One of these, "To What Red Hell," was about the Easter Sunday fire at the Ohio State Penitentiary that killed 330 prisoners and fueled the public outcry that moved legislators to reduce long-term sentencing. Himes was eventually paroled from prison after seven and a half years, and he reentered society with the hopes of publishing his prison novel and becoming a writer.

In 1936, he returned to Cleveland as the industrial city was in the throes of the depression. For a black ex-con, finding work was nearly impossible. He soon received a Works Project Administration

(WPA) job, working for the federal government first as a laborer, then as a librarian, and later as a writer recording a history of Cleveland. When his public assistance ran out, he began working for the Congress of Industrial Organizations (CIO), writing histories about the newly formed union that, for the first time, recruited black workers. At the Karamu House, a community arts center in Cleveland, he met LANGSTON HUGHES, who served as a role model for the aspiring Himes. Periodically in the 1940s he would visit Hughes in New York and attend "rent" parties among the Harlem crowd, where he met RICHARD WRIGHT, CARL VAN VECHTEN, RALPH ELLISON, Roy Ottley, OWEN DODSON, STERLING BROWN, and others. Many of these parties were hosted by Himes's cousin Henry Lee Moon, prominent in the NATIONAL ASSOCIATION OF THE ADVANCEMENT OF COLORED PEOPLE, and his gracious wife Mollie Lewis, the subjects of Himes's farcical novella *Pinktoes* (1961). With the help of Hughes, Pulitzer Prize–winning novelist Louis Bromfield, and other contacts in the labor left, Himes moved to the West Coast hoping to find work in the movie industry.

When Himes moved to Los Angeles, the city was undergoing a major boom from laborers migrating to work in the war plants, causing the city's population to double in size during the wartime 1940s. He was promptly rejected by Hollywood (Jack Warner had ordered, "I don't want no niggers on this lot") and joined the pool of workers flooding into Los Angeles. After the passage of Roosevelt's Executive Order #8802 prohibiting discrimination in the war industries, he was one of the Negro "firsts" to be promoted into skilled industrial jobs. In these years, he was closely associated with the Communist Party, which sent him to many segregated war factories to test the antidiscrimination policy. Himes's interest in communism was reflected in short stories that featured proletarian themes and several fiery essays in which he expressed his hatred for capitalist oppression, hope for blacks within the union movement, and support for the Soviet Union. A few of these writings appeared in leftist journals such as *New Masses, Common Ground* and *War Worker,* but the majority of them appeared in the black periodi-

cals, which climbed in circulation during the war, such as OPPORTUNITY, CRISIS, and *Negro Story.*

The blockbuster success of Wright's *Native Son* in 1940 generated a flurry of interest in the "protest novel" during the 1940s, what some even called a renaissance, and America looked to black writers for a solution to the "race problem." While their novels were often compared to Wright's, black writers such as Himes benefited most from a more willing white publishing industry that had been closed to them. Himes's black noir aesthetic was apparent in his debut novel *IF HE HOLLERS LET HIM GO* (1945), which took readers on a drive down Central Avenue, the jazz and BLUES district of Los Angeles, and depicted the wartime racial tensions that were "as thick in the street as gas fumes." The main character, Bob Jones, is a black shipyard worker who witnessed the internment of the Japanese and the attacks on Mexican "zoot-suiters," all the while fearing that he might be the next scapegoat of white racial xenophobia. A second Los Angeles novel, *Lonely Crusade* (1947), deals more directly with the ongoing chasm between black and white workers that divided the labor left from within and foreshadows the Cold War repression that would crush the movement from the outside. Excoriated by the left and the right, hated by black and white reviewers alike, Himes attributed the book's failure to an act of sabotage and descended into a five-year writer's block.

Moving to Paris in 1953, Himes was both looking for a place to restore his writing energies and to flee from the communist witch hunt. He joined other black exiles, many of whom were also former leftists, on the "black bank" in Paris. He, Richard Wright, and Ollie Harrington formed a close friendship (which he satirically portrays in another novella, *A Case of Rape* [1963]) and left a distinct mark on the line of American literary modernists abroad. In Paris, Himes reinvented himself, writing what he believed was the masterpiece of his career, *The End of Primitive* (1956). In this book he announced the end of the "protest novel" and his realization of the "absurdity" of American racism. This absurd vision is repeated in nine detective novels set in Harlem: *A Rage in Harlem* (1957), *The Real Cool Killers* (1959), *The*

Crazy Kill (1959), *The Big Gold Dream* (1960), *All Shot Up* (1960), *Cotton Comes to Harlem* (1965), *Blind Man with a Pistol* (1969), and *Plan B* (posthumously published in 1993). His two detectives, Coffin Ed Johnson and Grave Digger Jones, were a hit on the big screen when the movie adaptation of *Cotton Comes to Harlem* (1970) became the prototype for a flood of blaxploitation films during the early 1970s. He was also recognized as a forefather of the BLACK ARTS MOVEMENT by burgeoning black talents ISHMAEL REED and JOHN A. WILLIAMS.

Bringing his prolific career to an end, Himes wrote two autobiographies, *The Quality of Hurt* (1972) and *My Life of Absurdity* (1976). Today, the legacy of Himes's black noir vision lives on in WALTER MOSLEY's Easy Rawlins books. Still, Himes's life and his art demand greater recognition as one of the most perceptive records of the race, class, and gender conflicts of 20th-century American literature.

BIBLIOGRAPHY

Fabre, Michel. *From Harlem to Paris: Black American Writers in France, 1840–1980.* Urbana: University Illinois Press, 1993.

Margolies, Edward, and Michel Fabre. *The Several Lives of Chester Himes.* Jackson: University Press of Mississippi, 1997.

Milliken, Stephen F. *Chester Himes: A Critical Appraisal.* Columbia: University of Missouri Press, 1976.

Muller, Gilbert H. *Chester Himes.* Boston: Twayne, 1989.

Reed, Ishmael. "Chester Himes: Writer." *Black World* (March 1972): 23–38, 83–86.

Sallis, James. *Chester Himes: A Life.* New York: Walker and Company, 2000.

Soitos, Stephen. *The Blues Detective.* Amherst: University of Massachusetts Press, 1996.

Brian Dolinar

historically black colleges and universities (HBCUs)

The Higher Education Act of 1965 defines historically black colleges and universities (HBCUs) as "any historically black college or university that was established prior to 1964, whose principle mission was, and is, the education of black Americans." From the establishment of the first HBCU in 1837, the Institute for Colored Youth (the present-day Cheyney University of Pennsylvania), these institutions of higher learning provided training for African Americans when none was to be found in the American university system. Before the Supreme Court's decision in *Brown v. Board of Education* (1954) overruled its *Plessy v. Ferguson* (1896) "separate but equal" decision, HBCUs were virtually the only viable choice for higher education accessible to most African Americans.

State governments, philanthropic and religious societies, African-American organizations, and individuals founded many HBCUs just after the Civil War. At the turn of the 20th century, BOOKER T. WASHINGTON and W. E. B. DUBOIS debated what the mission of these universities should be: vocational or professional. Irrespective of their identified mission and curriculum, these institutions, some built on former slave plantations, offered and continue to offer culturally and historically rich links to past struggles as well as connections to a legacy of African-American intellectual pursuits. They have produced a vast number of African-American professionals who would have been denied opportunities elsewhere. Today, HBCUs stand as "reservoirs of culture, tradition, and opportunity" for many minority, and an increasing number of nonminority, students. The 107 HBCUs currently in existence are located mostly in the southeastern United States.

Although historically most HBCUs have not established formal creative writing programs, they continue to produce and nurture African-American writers. For example, in 1966, JOHN O. KILLENS organized, at Fisk University, the first National Black Writers Conference, which brought together artists such as AMIRI BARAKA, NELLA LARSON, and HAKI R. MADHUBUTI for a series of workshops. Contact with these artists influenced NIKKI GIOVANNI, then a student at Fisk. Other notable literary personalities who are the products of HBCUs include DuBois, ALAIN LOCKE, LANGSTON HUGHES,

ZORA NEAL HURSTON, TONI MORRISON, and ALICE WALKER. Significantly, many of the early literary scholars, critics, and anthologists of this literary tradition, including Nick Aaron Ford. RICHARD BARKSDALE, Arthur P. Davis, STERLING BROWN, and SAUNDERS REDDING, served on the faculty of these institutions.

BIBLIOGRAPHY

Ashley, Dwayne, and Juan Williams. *I'll Find a Way or Make One: A Tribute to Historically Black Colleges and Universities.* New York: Amistad/Harper Collins, 2004.

U.S. Department of Education, Office of Civil Rights. "Historically Black Colleges and Universities and Higher Education Desegregation." Available online. URL: http://www.ed.gov/about/offices/list-locr/docslhq9511.html. Accessed October 17, 2006.

Derrick R. Spires

Home to Harlem Claude McKay (1928)

Home to Harlem, CLAUDE MCKAY's first published and most successful novel, tells the story of Jake, a black World War I veteran, who returns to Harlem after deserting because of the racism he encounters in the military, England, and Europe. It depicts what McKay called the "underworld" of Harlem life, a social spectrum that includes everyone from pimps, day-laborers, gamblers, and prostitutes to exotic cabaret partiers, jazz musicians, members of the black intelligentsia, and others. However, much of the novel centers on Jake's adventures with sex, alcohol, and gambling as he searches for his "little brown girl," a part-time prostitute with whom he has become smitten at a cabaret his first night back but cannot find again.

McKay also addresses labor issues, particularly the exploitation of the common worker (the Marxist proletariat) through Jake's experience as a waiter on the railroad. Not only are the workers referred to as animals, as mules, but also, in their overnight run between New York City and Pittsburgh, the workers are forced to sleep in a bug-in-fested "hell of a dump" (146). Equally significant, through Jake and Ray, McKay questions the arbitrariness and validity of racial designation and categories. Ray declares, "Races and nations were like skunks, whose smell poisoned the air of life" (153–154).

McKay's frank portrayal of the Harlem masses was key to the book's success; until RICHARD WRIGHT's *NATIVE SON* (1940), *Home to Harlem* was the best-selling book by a black author. Black intellectuals' response was more mixed. W. E. B. DUBOIS, who emphasized an educated "talented tenth" of blacks, was upset at the novel's description of less respectable black life; he famously wrote that after reading *Home to Harlem,* he wanted to bathe. Younger writers, such as LANGSTON HUGHES, were more enthusiastic. At the same time, unlike "proletarian" novels by other leftist authors (such as Mike Gold, with whom McKay had worked on the socialist *Liberator*), *Home to Harlem* is not a political novel per se and does not turn Jake into a working-class hero; rather, it uses politics to imbue Jake with a sense of dignity and worth. Thus, while Jake displays class-consciousness—most strikingly, when he refuses to help break a strike by white dockers—he also has real human foibles. And while he refuses to scab, he also refuses the union's offer to join. In part, this reflects the fact that by 1928, McKay had already become disillusioned with the communist movement. Another theme woven throughout the novel is the question of "home": Despite the novel's title and the Jake's yearning to return to Harlem, none of the main characters are actually from Harlem. Instead, the novel is inhabited by various rootless cosmopolitans, especially migrants from the South (such as Jake) or the Caribbean (such as Jake's alter ego, Ray). Further, many of the characters have jobs that involve traveling, such as dockers, railway employees, and sailors. Instead of being a literal "home," McKay suggests, Harlem is instead the figurative home of the black diaspora. In the end, Jake leaves Harlem in search of a more fulfilling life. Harlem proves not to be the black mecca he envisioned at the beginning of the novel.

BIBLIOGRAPHY

McKay, Claude. *Home to Harlem.* New York: Harper & Bros., 1928. Rpt. Boston: Northeastern University Press, 1987.

J. A. Zumoff

hooks, bell   (1952–   )

bell hooks (née Gloria Jean Watkins) was born in 1952 in Hopkinsville, Kentucky, the daughter of Rosa Bell and Veodis Watkins. She went to all-black public schools before attending Stanford to earn a bachelor's degree. [h]ooks went on to earn a master's degree from the University of Wisconsin and a doctorate from the University of California, Santa Cruz. Although she had extensive schooling, hooks began writing one of her major works, *Ain't I a Woman?* when she was only 19 years old. She went on to teach as an associate professor in the Yale African-American studies department. She has also taught in the English and women's studies department at Oberlin College, the African studies program at City College of New York, and women's and African-American studies in the English department at City College of New York. hooks, who changed her name when she published her first book, uses a pseudonym to pay tribute to her mother and grandmother. She avoids capital letters as a way to direct the reader's attention to the contents of her work rather than to her as the author.

hooks has authored numerous books and scholarly articles in addition to being an accomplished and popular public speaker. Her first work, *Ain't I a Woman?,* appeared in 1981. She has also written *Talking Back: Thinking Feminist, Thinking Black* (1989), *Breaking Bread: Insurgent Black Intellectual Life* (1991) with Cornel West, *Black Looks: Race and Representation* (1992), *Sisters of the Yam: Black Women and Self-Recovery* (1993), *Outlaw Culture: Resisting Representations* (1994), *Killing Rage: Ending Racism* (1995), *Art on My Mind: Visual Politics* (1995), *Reel to Real: Race, Sex, and Class at the Movies* (1996), *Bone Black: Memories of Girlhood* (1996), *Remembered Rapture: The Writer at Work* (1999), *Happy to Be Nappy* (1999), *Feminist Theory: From Margin to Center* (2000), *Feminism Is for Everybody: Passionate Politics* (2000), *All about Love: New Visions* (2000), *Salvation: Black People and Love* (2001), *Homemade Love* (2002), *Communion: The Female Search for Love* (2002), *Be Boy Buzz* (2002), and *Rock My Soul: Black People and Self-Esteem* (2003), *We Real Cool* (2003), and *The Will to Change* (2004).

hooks's writings are concerned, as the various titles reveal, with the issues of race, gender, and class as they intersect on black women's bodies. She seeks an end to the exploitation and oppression of black women in society as a way to undo white supremacy. hooks is also concerned with the apathy apparent in learning situations due to systematic racist, sexist, and classist attitudes in education. To counter apathy and reenergize learning environments, hooks's "engaged pedagogy" aims to rethink the "knowledge base," empowering students to participate in more meaningful education. As her career has developed, hooks has moved to cultural and social critique. She entered the political arena to present innovative challenges that are normally found only in elite scholarly settings. hooks "demonstrates [individuals'] complicity in structures that oppress" because of choices informed by personal beliefs. Another facet of dealing with race, gender, and class issues is the extreme loneliness of marginalization. Several of her works are infused with a sense of painful isolation. Even though there is a sense of loneliness, hooks refuses to "settle down" and be "politically correct." Her voice is frank and confrontational; she is unafraid to critique rather than court social, political, or economic groups. Nonetheless, she maintains humanist and spiritual ideals with an interest in self-renewal, community, love, forgiveness, and care. These ideals form the centerpiece of her most recent works: *Salvation, Communion,* and *All about Love.*

BIBLIOGRAPHY

Florence, Namulundah. *bell hooks' Engaged Pedagogy: A Transgressive Education for Critical Consciousness.* Westport, Conn.: Bergin and Garvey, 1998.

Hua, Julia. "bell hooks." *Voices from the Gaps.* February 12, 1998. Department of English, University of Minnesota, Minneapolis. Available online. URL: http://voices.cla.umn.edu/vg/Bios/entries/hooks_bell.html. Accessed October 17, 2006.

Kim Hai Pearson
Brian Jennings

Hopkins, Pauline Elizabeth   (1859–1930)

The most prolific African-American woman writer of her generation, Pauline Elizabeth Hopkins, a contemporary of FRANCES ELLEN WATKINS HARPER, CHARLES W CHESNUTT, PAUL LAURENCE DUNBAR, BOOKER T. WASHINGTON, and W. E. B. DUBOIS, was born in Portland, Maine, but spent most of her life in Boston. The daughter of William [Northrop?] and Sarah Allen Hopkins, she first gained recognition as a writer at age 15 when she won a 10-dollar prize for her essay "The Evils of Intemperance and Their Remedy" from the Congregational Publishing Society of Boston. When the distinguished African-American writer WILLIAM WELLS BROWN presented her with this award, neither could have known they would both someday be hailed as forerunners of the diverse, innovative African-American literary tradition.

Soon after graduating from Boston's Girls High School, Hopkins pursued a career in theater and writing and wrote musical dramas, including *The Colored Aristocracy* and *Slaves' Escape; or The Underground Railroad.* A gifted singer, she became known as "Boston's Favorite Soprano." Her love for the theater and for music probably stemmed from her participation in her family's theatrical group, the Hopkins Colored Troubadors, as both an actor and a playwright. Despite her many talents, however, Hopkins found she could not support herself with her writing and put her artistic aspirations on hold, spending more than a decade working as a stenographer.

In 1900, Hopkins returned to writing. During this year she published her first novel, *Contending Forces: A Romance Illustrative of Negro Life North and South,* and began pouring her intellectual and creative energies into the newly created periodical *Colored American Magazine.* First published in May 1900, the journal, according to its founders, was meant to provide "the colored people of the United States a medium through which they can demonstrate their ability and tastes, in fiction, poetry, and art, as well as in the arena of historical, social and economic literature." Hopkins played a major role in seeing this goal come to fruition, serving as an editor and as one of its major contributors. She published three serial novels, seven short stories, numerous biographical essays about famous black men and women, and several editorials about political and social issues during the four years she spent at the *Colored American Magazine.* Her belief in the power of the written word, especially fiction, to bring about social change no doubt fueled her remarkable productivity during this period.

Hopkins dedicated her literary career to racial uplift. As she states in her preface to *Contending Forces,* "In giving this little romance expression in print, I am not actuated by a desire for profit, but to do all that I can in an humble way to raise the degradation of my race." She goes on to say that

> Fiction is of great value to any people as a preserver of manners and customs—religious, political and social. It is a record of growth and development from generation to generation. No one will do this for us; we must ourselves develop the men and women who will faithfully portray the inmost thoughts and feelings of the Negro with all the fire and romance which lie dormant in our history, and, as yet, unrecognized by writers of the Anglo-Saxon race.

Her novels and short stories may strike many readers as flawed because she often relies on the stereotypes, contrived plots, sentimentality, and melodrama found in 19th-century popular fiction. Hopkins, however, understood the entertainment value of popular fiction. She employed its narrative strategies and their ability to entertain as a means for reaching a wide audience in order to teach her readers about history, philosophy, morality, political issues, race, and gender. By delighting and instructing her audience, she hoped to inspire them to take political action.

The plot of *Contending Forces,* for example, revolves around a series of highly improbable connections among its characters, including the eventual reunion of African-American and white descendants of the same family. The novel also includes a tragic mulatto character forced into prostitution by a villainous uncle. This woman finally overcomes the shame of her past and marries a good-hearted African-American man dedicated to civil rights. The contrived plot and familiar character types might have consigned *Contending Forces,* to the large body of largely forgettable 19th- and 20th-century works designed primarily to titillate and entertain. But in it and in her other fiction, Hopkins raises sentimental, domestic, and melodramatic fiction to a higher level by skillfully weaving history and political and social commentary into the narrative.

Divided into two parts, *Contending Forces* begins in the 1790s and ends about 100 years later. Consequently, Hopkins uses these unlikely events and seemingly stereotypical characters to explore the struggle of African Americans during slavery and Reconstruction. The characters, although sometimes one-dimensional, reflect the ongoing struggle of African Americans to overcome the effects of racism. The deeply ingrained attitudes that made slavery possible remained part of the postbellum culture. Nor was racial oppression confined to the southern United States. Hopkins also uses one of melodrama's stock character types, the villain, to jar her African-American readers into examining their own complicity in perpetuating racism, forcing them to grapple with the complexity of American culture and human nature in general. Greed, jealousy, love, a desire for power, and lust drive both whites and blacks within the pages of *Contending Forces.* In addition, Hopkins creates a character who expresses ideas similar to those of Washington and one whose thinking parallels that of DuBois. Because both of these characters have positive character traits and present their ideas well, readers cannot draw facile conclusions about the Washington-DuBois debate. Likewise, Hopkins offers several strong, intelligent, independent female characters, making *Contending Forces* a prototype of African-American feminist literature.

In her magazine novels and short fiction, Hopkins also experimented with the conventions of popular fiction. *Hagar's Daughter,* for example, although sentimental in many regards, resists closing with a happy ending and resolving all conflicts. Its plot centers on the relationship between a white man and a light-skinned black woman who fall in love before they know the woman's racial heritage. Throughout most of the novel, the man embodies the noble characteristics of the typical sentimental hero. But once he realizes he has fallen in love with and married an African-American woman, he cannot accept her. Instead, he gives in to his own prejudice, despite his northern upbringing and his family's long-standing involvement in the cause of African-American freedom and racial progress. Through this character, Hopkins addresses a larger issue: the deeply embedded racial prejudice abolitionism and philanthropy often mask. Her third magazine novel, *Of One Blood,* may be her most innovative literary effort. This work explores the notion of Pan-Africanism, and some critics consider it an early example of African-American science fiction.

Hopkins left the *Colored American Magazine* in 1904, possibly because of her political disagreements with Washington, who had taken control of the journal. Nonetheless, she continued to write. In 1905 she published a book titled *A Primer of Facts Pertaining to the Early Greatness of the African Race and the Possibility of Restoration by Its Descendants—with Epilogue* and started another journal, *New Era,* in 1916. However, her financial situation led her to take a position as a stenographer at Massachusetts Institute of Technology. Although a well-known figure for many years, by the time she died in a fire in 1930, Hopkins had faded into obscurity. Fortunately, literary critics have now begun to recognize the vital place she holds in the development of African-American literature.

Candis LaPrade

Hopkinson, Nalo (1960–)

Nalo Hopkinson was born in Kingston, Jamaica, on December 20, 1960. Her father, a journalist, teacher, actor, and poet-playwright, and her mother, a library technician, belonged to a Caribbean arts group. The family lived in the Caribbean (Jamaica, Trinidad, Guyana). For a time the family also lived in the United States, while her father attended Yale, until they moved to Toronto in 1977. Hopkinson graduated from the University of York in 1982 with combined honors in Russian and French; she received her M.A. in writing popular fiction in 2002 from Seton Hill College in Pennsylvania.

Hopkinson, a science fiction author, began to write and publish in 1993, the year her father passed away. Like that of her literary foremother, OCTAVIA BUTLER, Hopkinson's vision is a strong, feminist one that subverts the speculative fiction genre, which, as Hopkinson puts it, "speaks so much about the experience of being alienated, but contains so little written by alienated peoples themselves." Suddenly becoming the member of a minority in Canada resulted in an awareness of life on the margins that often appears in Hopkinson's writing. Hopkinson also conveys a strong sense of the uniqueness of people and place through setting, Jamaican and Trinidadian creole, and Caribbean myth, folklore, and literature.

Taking her title from a Caribbean singing game, Hopkinson's *Brown Girl in the Ring* (1998) won Warner Aspect's First Novel Competition, the Locus Award for Best First Novel, and the John W. Campbell Award for Best New Writer. Rich with Afro-Caribbean culture and language, this dystopia is set in the near future in Toronto. The rich have fled, leaving the poor to a dangerous predatory environment in which old ways—farming, barter, and folk medicine—become essential for survival. When Ontario's premier needs a transplant and a boost in her approval ratings, the protagonist's drug-addicted boyfriend is enlisted to find a human heart. The young new mother, Ti-Jeanne, convinces her grandmother, a Voudoun priestess, to help. Caught up in a battle to the death, Ti-Jeanne discovers her own power as she comes to understand the ancient spirits.

Hopkinson's second novel, *Midnight Robber* (2000), another coming-of-age story, was a *New York Times* Notable Book of the Year; it received honorable mention for the Casa de las Americas Prize. Initially set during Carnival on a Caribbean-settled planet, the young protagonist accompanies her corrupt father into exile in a brutal parallel existence. Incest and murder force her into yet another layer of banishment where folkloric predecessors and her own nonhierarchic and postcolonial sensibility allow her to survive and begin to carve out a new social order. Technologies of African diasporic culture in this novel include communication devices known as "four-eyes" (a Jamaican word for "seers") and home operating systems called "eshus," from the omnipresent, omniscient West African trickster deity Eshu Elegbara.

In her novel *The Salt Roads* (2003), Hopkinson explores women's relationships with lovers, each other, the community, and the divine. When three Caribbean slave women gather one night to bury a stillborn baby, their collective mourning calls up the deity Ezili, the Afro-Caribbean goddess of sex and love. The spirit goes on to make a global journey, inhabiting the minds of living women through history.

Hopkinson has two short fiction collections. Caribbean lore informs most of the tales in *Skin Folk* (2001), which won the World Fantasy Award for Best Collection and the Sunburst Award for Canadian Literature of the Fantastic and was a *New York Times* Notable Book of the Year. While some of the stories celebrate life, others are more ominous. In "Greedy Choke Puppy," a woman discards her skin at night and kills children for their life force. In *Mojo: Conjure Stories* (2003), supernatural powers obtain justice for Africans in the diaspora. Mojo, a West African term for a cloth bag with magical contents, today refers to magic itself and the powerful inheritance of African cultures.

Hopkinson's work in drama includes a radio play, *Indicator Species* (CBC Radio, 2000) and three monologues. She has taught creative writing and science fiction literature courses in Toronto and elsewhere, including a stint as writer-in-residence at Seattle's Clarion West. Anthologies edited by Hopkinson include *Whispers from* the Cotton Tree Root: Caribbean Fabulist Fiction (2000), which showcases distinguished writers and many newcomers, and the global *So Long Been Dreaming: Postcolonial Science Fiction and Fantasy* (2004). Hopkinson has also coedited *TESSERACTS NINE: New Canadian Speculative Fiction* (2005), an anthology of Canadian science fiction and fantasy with Geoff Ryman; developed a graphic novel, *Mr. Fox,* in collaboration with David Findlay; and written two novels, *Egungun* and *The Old Moon's Arms.*

BIBLIOGRAPHY

Hopkinson, Nalo. *Brown Girl in the Ring.* New York: Warner Aspect, 1998.

———. *Midnight Robber.* New York: Warner Aspect, 2000.

———. *Mojo: Conjure Stories.* Introduction by Luisah Teish. New York: Warner Aspect, 2003.

———. *The Salt Roads.* New York: Warner Books, 2003.

———. *Skin Folk.* New York: Warner Aspect, 2001.

———, ed. *Whispers from the Cotton Tree Root: Caribbean Fabulist Fiction.* Montpelier, Vt.: Invisible Cities Press, 2000.

Hopkinson, Nalo, and Uppinder Mehan, eds. *So Long Been Dreaming: Postcolonial Science Fiction and Fantasy.* Vancouver, B.C.: Arsenal Pulp Press, 2004.

Elizabeth McNeil

Horton, George Moses   (1797–1883)

Born a slave in Northampton County, North Carolina, Horton, according to William H. Robinson, was "America's first professional black poet" (18). He was well known by the male students of the University of North Carolina at Chapel Hill (UNC). According to DARWIN T. TURNER, who calls Horton "a black Cyrano," students "commissioned him to write love lyrics to their sweethearts" (17). He earned anywhere from 25 to 75 cents for each of his poems. Given his popularity with UNC's students, Horton arranged with his master to rent himself out, which allowed him to move closer to the campus, where he "began something like full time support of himself by dictating until he could

write and then by writing occasional verses, some of which found their way into the local newspaper" (Robinson, 18), the *Raleigh Register.* Horton found favor not only with the students who helped him and paid him to write his poems but also with the college president, Joseph D. Caldwell. The black abolitionists and anticolonizationists also embraced him. For example, SAMUELS CORNISH and John B. Russwurm published Horton's poems in *Freedom's Journal,* "the first black edited, black controlled periodical in the United States" (Bruce, 165), placing Horton and his work in the vanguard of the antislavery movement for many years. William Lloyd Garrison, the leader of the American Abolitionist Movement, published Horton's poem "Slavery" in his abolitionist newspaper, *The Liberator,* in March 1834.

However, it was Horton's friendship with the New England–born poet and novelist Caroline Lee Hentz that enhanced his career as a poet and led to the publication of his first collection of poems, *Hope of Liberty* (1829), in Raleigh, North Carolina, with which he hoped to earn enough money to purchase his freedom and, some believe, to sail to Liberia, the American colony in West Africa. He accomplished neither of these goals. Although he republished his collection of poems under a new name, *Poems by a Slave* (1837), Horton did not acquire the sum necessary to purchase his freedom. He remained a slave until the Civil War brought an end to slavery in 1865. Horton published his last collection of poems, *Naked Genius,* the same year. *Poetical Works of George M. Horton, the Colored Bard of North Carolina* (1845), which includes a prefatory autobiography, "The Life of George M. Horton, the Colored Bard of North Carolina," preceded *Naked Genius.*

Horton wrote on a variety of topics, including love, Christianity, slavery, and liberty. His work shows the clear influence of Byron and Wesleyan hymns. "The Lover's Farewell" and "To Eliza" are exemplary of the love poems he wrote for UNC students. In the former, the lover pines because of unrequited love: "I strove, but could not hold thee fast, / My heart flies off with thee at last. . . . I leave my parents here behind, / And all my friends—to love resigned— / 'Tis grief to go, but death to stay:

Farewell—I'm gone with love away!" (Robinson, 20). In the latter, the speaker confronts his unfaithful lover while confessing his undying love for her:

> *Eliza, tell thy lover why*
> *Or what induced thee to deceive me?*
> *Fare thee well—away I fly—*
> *I shun the lass who thus will grieve me*
> *. . . Eliza, pause and think awhile—*
> *Sweet lass! I shall forget thee never:*
> *Fare thee well although I smile,*
> *I grieve to give thee up forever. (Robinson, 20)*

Unlike these overly sentimental and almost pedestrian lines and rhyme, however, Horton's discourses on freedom and slavery strike a deeper note. In fact, he, unlike Wheatley and Hammon, was the first black (written) versifier who addressed more candidly the direct relationship between race and slavery. For example, in "Slavery," the speaker almost militantly asks,

> *Is it because my skin is black,*
> *That thou should'st be so dull and slack,*
> *And scorn to set me free?*
> *Then let me hasten to the grave,*
> *The only refuge for the slave,*
> *Who mourns for liberty. (Robinson, 21)*

In "The Slave's complaint," the speaker demands, "Leave me not a wretch confined, / Altogether lame and blind— / Unto gross despair consigned, / Forever" (Robinson, 22).

According to Robinson, Horton seemed "always aware of his unique role as an early black American poet in a world of white unbelievers" (19). That Horton took his role or calling as poet quite seriously is recorded in his poem, "The Art of a Poet," in which his speaker declares:

> *A bard must traverse o'er the world,*
> *Where things concealed must rise unfurled,*
> *And tread the feet of yore;*
> *Tho' he may sweetly harp and sing,*
> *But strictly prune the mental wind,*
> *Before the mind can soar. (Robinson, 25)*

BIBLIOGRAPHY

Bruce, Dickson D., Jr. *The Origins of African American Literature, 1680–1865.* Charlottesville: University Press of Virginia, 2001.

Robinson, William H., ed. *Early Black American Poets.* Dubuque, Iowa: Wm. C. Brown Company Publishers, 1969.

Turner, Darwin T., ed. *Black American Literature: Poetry.* Columbus, Ohio: Charles E. Merrill Publishing Company, 1969.

Wilfred D. Samuels

Hughes, Langston James Mercer
(1902–1963)

One of the outstanding American authors of the 20th century, Langston Hughes wrote poetry, novels, nonfiction, drama, and short stories. Born James Mercer Langston Hughes in Joplin, Missouri, in February 1902, he spent his early years living with his mother in the household of his grandmother in Lawrence, Kansas. It was from his grandmother's background that Hughes had ties to political activists from the past. The grandmother, Mary Langston, was an abolitionist herself and the wife of Lewis Leary, who was killed as one of John Brown's army at Harper's Ferry. Mary's second husband, Charles Langston, who was Hughes's grandfather, was also an abolitionist, and Charles's brother, John Mercer Langston, was an abolitionist who, in the 1890s, became a United States congressman from the state of Virginia.

Despite that distinguished history, Hughes's parents were unable to maintain a stable environment for their son. His father had moved to Mexico, leaving his mother a single parent who worked various jobs to support Hughes and the grandmother. In this poor environment, Hughes found escape in books, which led to an interest in writing. Moving from Kansas to Lincoln, Illinois, and then to Cleveland, Ohio, where he attended high school, Hughes began publishing poetry and short fiction in the school magazine. In 1921 he went to Mexico to live with his father, but the stay was emotionally disturbing. While there, Hughes taught English and had his poem "The Negro Speaks of Rivers" accepted for publication in CRISIS magazine, the literary voice of the NATIONAL ASSOCIATION FOR THE ADVANCEMENT OF COLORED PEOPLE (NAACP).

Returning to the United States, Hughes attended Columbia University in New York for one year but found it unsatisfying and was thus motivated to work various jobs and to travel abroad. He traveled to countries in West Africa and then to Paris before returning to the United States around 1924 to live in Washington, D.C., finding odd jobs to support himself. During his travels he wrote and published his poetry, which "was often written in free verse or loosely rhymed verse, reflecting the poet's admiration for Walt Whitman and Carl Sandburg" (Hatch and Strickland, 177). These publications helped him get his first book, *The Weary Blues,* published in 1926. The volume received praise, and Hughes was acclaimed as one of the significant new black voices emanating from the HARLEM RENAISSANCE of the 1920s. In a chapter titled "Harlem Literati" in his first autobiography, Hughes commented on the favorable and disappointing aspects of the Harlem Renaissance, noting:

> During the summer of 1926, Wallace Thurman, Zora Neale Hurston, Aaron Douglas, John P. Davis, Bruce Nugent, Gwendolyn Bennett, and I decided to publish 'a Negro quarterly of the arts' to be called *Fire!!*—the idea being that it would burn up a lot of the old, dead conventional Negro-white ideas of the past . . . into a realization of the existence of the younger Negro writers and artists, and provide us with an outlet for publication. (Barksdale and Kinnamon, 525)

Expressing both a generational and racial gap, Hughes goes on to recount the negative reception to *Fire!!,* including disparaging assessments of his poetry. However, Hughes continued to write about black cultural themes. His next volume, *Fine Clothes to the Jew* (1927), showed him

writing blues poems without either apology or framing devices from the traditional world of poetry . . . delving into the basic subject mat-

ter of the blues—love and raw sexuality, deep sorrow and sudden violence, poverty and heartbreak . . . treated with sympathy for the poor and dispossessed, and without false piety, [making] him easily the most controversial black poet of his time. (Rampersad, 370)

In 1926, Hughes became a student at Lincoln University in Pennsylvania, graduating in 1929. His first novel, *Not Without Laughter,* was published that next year, winning the Harmon Prize for literature and convincing him to write professionally. Using the prize money, he traveled to and lived in Cuba and Haiti, and when he returned to New York, he became associated with the political left and members of the John Reed Society, the literary arm of the Communist Party. His writings began to reflect his more political consciousness, as he published essays in the *New Masses* and wrote a poetic drama, *Scottsboro Limited* (1931), about the controversial trial of nine black men accused of raping two white women. In 1932, he traveled with a group of 22 young blacks who were invited to the Soviet Union to participate in a film being made about racism in America. Although the film was never completed, Hughes lived in the country for a year, publishing poetry, which would later be controversial for its anti-American perspectives. After traveling to Japan and China, Hughes returned to America in the early 1930s, living in Carmel, California, while writing a collection of stories published as *The Ways of White Folks* (1934). The book contained stories that emphasized hypocrisy and racism within white society, setting the tone for his play *Mulatto* (1935), which opened on Broadway in New York.

Mulatto follows the tragedy of a young black man parented by a white father and his black mistress. The biracial son confronts his father, seeking acknowledgment and an accountability for his father's rejection. The play became a commercial success, leading to numerous other plays by Hughes during the decade, including *Little Ham* (1936), *Joy to My Soul* (1936), *When the Jack Hollers* (1936; with ARNA BONTEMPS), *Soul Gone Home* (1937), *Front Porch* (1938), and *Don't You Want to Be Free?* (1938). Hughes was not widely revered by critics as a playwright despite the popular success of *Mulatto;* however, one critic surmised, "The dramatic world of Langston Hughes is a quite different world from that of any other playwright, and the discovery of that world is, in itself, an entertaining, wonderful, and enlightening experience" (Smalley, 269).

In 1940, Hughes published *The BIG SEA,* an autobiography that covered his first 30 years, assessing the strained relationship with his father and the impact of the Harlem Renaissance. His later autobiographical volume, *I Wonder as I Wander* (1956), covers his years lived abroad, detailing the Soviet Union experience and his support of socialist principles at the time.

By the 1940s, Hughes had moved away from his leftist perspectives, publishing another volume of poetry, *Shakespeare in Harlem* (1942), and in that same year taking on a role as a columnist for the *Chicago Defender,* a weekly black newspaper. For the column, Hughes created a memorable character, Jesse B. Semple, who spoke on various issues and concerns of the day. This character, who became known as "Simple," possessed

> the right blend of qualities to be Black America's new spokesman—just enough urban humor, cynicism, and sardonic levity and just enough down-home simplicity, mother-wit, innocence, and naiveté. . . . At times, Simple is full of pain; at times, he is full of wise tolerance; at times, he is vocally indignant to the black man's lot; but he is never consumed by anger or overwhelmed by fear or paralyzed by racial paranoia. (Barksdale and Kinnamon, 516).

Hughes wrote this column for more than 20 years, placing selected pieces into five books, including *Simple Speaks His Mind* (1951), *Simple Takes a Wife* (1953), *Simple Stakes a Claim* (1957), *The Best of Simple* (1961), and *Simple's Uncle Sam* (1965). Additionally, the stage production of the musical play *Simply Heaven* (1957) enjoyed a popular Broadway run.

During the 1940s Hughes also produced more verse, including the poetry volume *Jim Crow's Last Stand* (1943) and a book of poems titled *Fields of Wonder* (1947). But Hughes found a related success during this decade in writing song lyrics, as he collaborated on the musical play *Street Scene* (1947), which brought still further attention to his creativity during its five-month Broadway appearance.

In 1953, Hughes was required to answer questions at Senator Joseph McCarthy's anti-Communist committee hearings. Because of his activities and writings in the Soviet Union, Hughes's politics were publicly examined, but he denied ever having been a member of the Communist Party. His responses and willingness to divorce himself from his political writings of the 1930s apparently provided an acceptable contrition for McCarthy and his followers. Hughes published two more collections of short fiction in his impressive career: *Laughing to Keep from Crying* (1952) and *Something in Common* (1963). In addition, he completed two more collections of poetry in the 1960s, *Ask Your Mama* (1961) and *The Panther and the Lash: Poems of Our Times* (1967).

It is worth noting that Hughes wrote books for children, most of which provided cultural and historical lessons as well as entertainment. Those cultural and historical concerns prevailed also when he joined his nonfiction to photos by Milton Meltzer in two collaborations: *A Pictorial History of the Negro in America* (1956) and *Black Magic: The Pictorial History of the Negro in American Entertainment* (1967). In conjunction with the NAACP, he wrote the history and development of the organization in the book *Fight for Freedom* (1962). Likewise, as an editor, he contributed to the recognition and celebration of black literary and cultural expressions in numerous books: *The Poetry of the Negro, 1746–1949* (1949), coauthored with Bontemps; *The Book of Negro Folklore* (1958), also with Bontemps; *New Negro Poets USA* (1964); *The Book of Negro Humor* (1966); and *The Best Short Stories by Negro Writers* (1967).

When Langston Hughes died in 1967 in New York, he had firmly positioned himself as a literary giant and an internationally known voice in American letters. And perhaps more significant to Hughes, he had confirmed his role as a spokesperson for generations of blacks who were continually kept invisible because of their race, class, and gender. He was a keeper of black culture and a talent not limited by the boundaries of genre.

In his 1926 essay "The Negro Artist and the Racial Mountain," Hughes wrote proudly about the "common" black folk:

> These common people are not afraid of spirituals . . . and jazz is their child. They furnish a wealth of colorful, distinctive material for any artist because they still hold their own individuality in the face of American standardizations. And perhaps these common people will give to the world its truly great Negro artist, the one who is not afraid to be himself. (quoted in Gates and McKay, 1268)

That artist did appear in Langston Hughes, a truly individual and prodigious talent.

BIBLIOGRAPHY

Barksdale, Richard, and Keneth Kinnamon, eds. *Black Writers of America.* New York: Macmillan, 1972.

Donalson, Melvin. *Cornerstones: An Anthology of African American Literature.* New York: St. Martin's Press, 1996.

Gates, Henry Louis, and Nellie Y. McKay, eds. *The Norton Anthology of African American Literature.* New York: Norton, 1997.

Rampersad, Arnold. "Langston Hughes." In *African American Writers,* 2d ed., Vol. 1, edited by Valerie Smith, 367–378. New York: Scribners, 2001.

Smalley, Webster. "Langston Hughes." Quoted In *Five Plays* In *Drama Criticism,* Vol. 3, edited by Laurence J. Trudeau, 268–269. Detroit: Gale, 1993.

Melvin Donalson

Hurston, Zora Neale   (1891–1960)

Born in Notasulga, Alabama, to John Hurston, a sharecropper, carpenter, and preacher, and Lucy Potts Hurston, a schoolteacher, Zora Neale Hurston spent her childhood in Eatonville, Florida. When in 1904 the family broke up after her mother's death, Zora was without a home. Educated at Baltimore's Morgan Academy (1918), Howard Prep School (1918–19), and Howard University

(1919–24), Hurston arrived in New York City in 1925 at the height of the HARLEM RENAISSANCE. She studied anthropology at Barnard College (1925–1927), did field work for Franz Boas, and briefly married Herbert Sheen. In 1935 she studied anthropology under Franz Boas and worked with Alan Lomax on a Library of Congress folk music recording project, and in 1936 she received a Guggenheim Fellowship to study African traditional religions, specifically Obeah and Vodun, in the West Indies. During the 1930s Hurston collected valuable folklore for the Works Project Administration (WPA) Federal Writers Project in Florida. She briefly married Albert Price III in 1939 and thereafter worked intermittently all through her life as a beautician, maid, secretary, teacher, performer, producer, playwright, folklorist, librarian, and substitute teacher.

When her last novel, *The Seraph on the Suwanee* (1949), was published, Hurston was falsely accused of molesting a retarded 10-year-old boy. Though her passport proved she was in the West Indies at the time, the scandal destroyed her reputation and spelled the end of her publishing career. Desperately poor, she worked as a maid in Miami in the 1950s, published her famous reactionary position against desegregation in 1954, and in 1956 moved one last time to Fort Pierce, Florida. She had a major stroke early in 1959, entered the St. Lucie Welfare Home in Fort Pierce in October, and died there on January 28, 1960. She was buried in an unmarked pauper's grave in the Garden of Heavenly Rest, having apparently died of starvation and neglect. Though THEIR EYES WERE WATCHING GOD remains her most beloved book, Hurston's first passion was as a collector and preserver of black oral culture and folk speech. Hurston wrote constantly, traveled endlessly, and was often fired. However, in the popular imagination she is a sassy young black woman driving a Model T; toting a gun; passing as a bootlegger; and woofin' (lying or joking) in the turpentine camps and juke joints of rural Florida, Alabama, and Georgia; and studying African traditional religions.

Hurston produced an impressive body of work. Her first novel, *Jonah's Gourd Vine* (1934), which was originally conceived as a tribute to black preachers, documents the psychological wounds she and her mother sustained from John Hurston's constant infidelities and abandonment of the family. A gifted black man, John Pearson (based on John Hurston), married to Lucy Pearson (read Lucy Hurston), becomes a renowned preacher who loses all when his repeated adulteries finally kill his wife, alienate his children, outrage his parishioners, and end in his own violent death. Its folk religious practices reveal the linguistic richness of the black church and the pain of women and children held hostage by flawed preacher-poets. MULES AND MEN (1935) is a collection of 70 tales arranged in two parts, "Folk Tales" and "Voodoo." A narrator unifies the collection. Her contextualizing, largely absent from the modern "scientific" ethnography, transformed the discipline. *Their Eyes Were Watching God* (1937) Hurston's *Künstlerroman* and most beloved novel, stages the spiritual and artistic coming of age of an African-American woman griot. A classic "speakerly" text with its free and indirect African-American rhetorical strategies, this novel features signifying, front porch storytelling, baiting, boasting, and lying. *Tell My Horse: Voodoo and Life in Haiti and Jamaica* (1938), Hurston's three-part account of the voodoo cults of Jamaica and Haiti, contains sections on Haitian culture, politics, personalities, and voodoo practices.

Moses, Man of the Mountain (1939) is a creative black vernacular telling of the purported back story of the biblical Moses, whom Hurston blames for Judeo-Christianity's racism, sexism, anti-Semitism, fascism, and nationalism. It is never specified whether Moses is Egyptian or Jewish, black or white. *Moses* is a fascinating minor work that reveals a black female perspective on Western racial and gender injustices. *DUST TRACKS ON A ROAD: An Autobiography* (1942), written under severe financial pressure, was seriously distorted when her white editors removed many of the 12 prophetic dream visions that structured the book. The most problematic of all Hurston's works, *Dust Tracks* is now finally available in the form she intended. In it Hurston styles herself as folk character, performer, narrator, and trickster. Critics black and white have dismissed the book as "lying," make-believe, or a propagandistic act of appeasement to the white readership. Hurston's problem was her own racial anguish, her audience, her white editors, and her times. *The Seraph on the Suwanee: A Novel* (1948) also deals with femininity, marriage, and religion, this time within the sphere of poor white Southern womanhood. Reviewers were provoked by Hurston's departure from her usual colorful "Negro subjects."

The Sanctified Church: The Folklore Writings of Zora Neale Hurston (1984) written 60 years before its publication, contains some material recently shown not to be Hurston's. It contains innovative essays on the folklore, legend, popular mythology, and spiritual configurations of the Black Southern Baptist Church. Section I, "Herbs and Herb Doctors," contains pieces on cures and beliefs and figures like Mother Catherine and Uncle Monday. Mother Catherine and Uncle Monday taken together suggest the intersection of Afrocentric voodoo culture and Christianity. Section II, "Characteristics of Negro Expression," contains pieces on the tricksters, shamans or conjurers, High John the Conqueror, and Daddy Mention. Section III, "The Sanctified Church," is rich in contextualized folk material about the spirituals, neospirituals, conversions, visions, shouting, sermons, and the sanctified church service itself. It is a valuable source of information about the Holiness-Pentecostal movements of the late 19th and early 20th centuries and about how religious forms from Africa were subsequently grafted onto Christianity.

Mule Bone: A Comedy of Negro Life (1991) was discovered in 1991, 60 years after Hurston and LANGSTON HUGHES wrote it. A black dialect folk comedy, it was thought by some Harlem Renaissance writers to reflect poorly on the black community. If this play had appeared in the 1930s it might have influenced the development of black vernacular theater. In 1991, when the Lincoln Center Theater staged *Mule Bone*, many wondered if the producer had tried to resuscitate a hokey, lost, unfinished work. *The Complete Stories* (1995) containing 19 previously published and seven previously unpublished stories, reflects modernist themes of love, betrayal, and death. A newly discovered short story entitled "Under the Bridge" will be published in *American Visions.* This collection firmly demonstrates Hurston's command of narrative voice, plot, themes of human injustice, and the Southern black vernacular voice. *Every Tongue Got to Confess* (2001) a large collection of more than 500 folktales collected in the Gulf States, was compiled in the late 1920s. It constitutes a major part of Hurston's folkloric literary legacy, which has lain forgotten in the Library of Congress since 1927. In December 1996 a short story titled "Under the Bridge" was found, as well as the text of another play, "Spear." "The Woman of Gaul," a short story, was finally printed in 1995. Scribner's rejected *The Golden Bench of God,* a novel based on the life of Madame C. J. Walker, in 1951. From 1953 to 1960 Hurston worked on a major novel on the life of Herod the Great, hoping Cecil B. DeMille would make a major epic motion picture of it. What she came to refer to as her "great obsession" is now an incomplete, charred, water-stained manuscript.

Zora Neale Hurston's literary reputation waxed briefly and waned quickly. In 1960 she was little more than a footnote in American literary history. Her literary resurrection in the early 1980s had much to do with the rise of feminist and womanist studies, African-American studies, multiculturalism, and the search by young black and white women writers like ALICE WALKER for a literary matrilineage. In 1973 Walker located and marked the possible site of Hurston's grave, and in 1975 Walker published her famous *Ms.* magazine essay chiding those who had neglected one so talented. Alice Walker's powerful account of finding Hurston's gravesite published in *Ms.* magazine greatly spurred the revival of her reputation. The post-1970s boom in interest in Hurston's career has resulted in the emergence of a vigorous critical and biographical reexamination of her life and writings. In 1996 Hurston became the fourth African-American and the fifth woman to be published in the prestigious Library of America series. Hurston, who always presented herself as a performance artist, folk character and writer with deep roots in black oral and print culture traditions, significantly helped establish the foundations of a BLACK AESTHETIC. Celebrated as griot, actress, preacher, signifying ethnographer, BLUES singer, trickster, and literary artist, she is seen by many as the literary foremother of the 20th-century African-American and women's literary traditions.

Gloria L. Cronin

Iceberg Slim (Robert Beck) (1918–1992)

Born in Chicago in 1918, Iceberg Slim spent 30 years as one of Chicago's most successful pimps. In his 1969 autobiography, *Pimp: The Story of My Life,* Slim describes his decision to turn to writing while serving his fourth jail term. This decision resulted in a flurry of texts, all of which were commercial successes. Slim's most famous texts, *Trick Baby, The Naked Soul of Iceberg Slim,* and *Pimp,* were all published between 1967 and 1969. Indeed, Slim is one of the best-selling African-American writers of all time, having published five novels, one collection of essays, an autobiographical work, and a collection of short writings. More than this commercial success, however, Slim's texts achieved cult status; ICE-T writes that Slim's books, often dog-eared and coverless, were eagerly sought after as they circulated around his high school.

For his readers, Slim's work is a voice speaking from ghetto streets that are often spoken for but seldom spoken from. In his introduction to Slim's novel *Trick Baby* (1967), Ice-T writes that Slim "shows you the unglamorous dark side to the hustling life, the side that leaves you strung out, messed up and dying inside" (v). Slim memorably captures the historical permanence of the oppression of ghetto residents as a stench, a physical reminder of the ways in which the lives of generations have been crushed; their sweat, blood and suffering have seeped into the fabric of the buildings themselves.

Slim's texts inhabit a cynical world where sensual imagery of the text creates memorable visions of racial, sexual, and class violence and the claustrophobia of economically, politically, and socially marginalized lives. He walks a borderline of sensationalizing and exploiting, while also critiquing and bearing witness. The unapologetic, uncompromising bleakness of Slim's vision is paralleled with a refusal to idealize himself or the world of his past.

Iceberg Slim presents *Pimp* as a brutal cautionary tale that will provoke the revulsion of its readership. He claims that his aim is to save young men and women from making the mistakes he did. Under the pretense of presenting himself as a penitent sinner, Slim is allowed to revel at length in a narrative of his decades of success as a pimp. Moreover, Slim seeks to maintain his credibility as the ghetto self-made man, who made his money from the streets while distancing himself as a successful writer from his past self.

Slim's work is difficult to read, as it is unclear whether the violence is critiqued, glorified, or simply exploited for shock value; his writings are certainly tainted by misogynistic and homophobic views. In Slim's refusal to write triumphant narratives, however, the audience can read an unflinching honesty, a willingness to write of the nihilism that drove the autobiographical character Iceberg Slim to self-destructive excess in *Pimp.* As Ice-T writes, "If the role of an artist is to tell you what he sees, then Iceberg Slim is a true artist" (v).

BIBLIOGRAPHY

Ice-T. Introduction. In *Trick Baby: The Story of a White Negro* (1967), by Iceberg Slim. Edinburgh: Payback-Canongate, 1996.

Scott Bunyan

Ice-T (1959–)

Ice-T (née Tracy Morrow), who was born in Newark, New Jersey, has been one of the most enduring icons of hip-hop culture. His career has spanned music, movies, and television for two decades. After the death of his parents in an automobile accident, Ice-T went to California to be raised by family members. He was attracted to hip-hop while attending Los Angeles's Crenshaw High School. As a teen he danced with break dancers and pop lockers. Additionally, the gangs and pimps in the Los Angeles area influenced him. He eventually adopted the name Ice-T, which he took from the name of one of his favorite novelists, ICEBERG SLIM.

Ice-T's early career featured several 12-inch singles and movie appearances in *Rappin', Breakin',* and *Breakin' II.* In 1987 he signed a record deal with Sire Records (a subsidiary of Time-Warner) and released *Rhyme Pays.* He followed up his debut album with *Power* in 1988, released under Ice-T's own label, Rhyme Syndicate. A year later Ice-T exposed his fans to his political critique and analysis on his third album *The Iceberg/Freedom of Speech . . . Just Watch What You Say.*

New Jack City, a film by Mario Van Peebles, would be Ice-T's first role in a major film. Ice-T portrayed a police officer who was determined to take down drug kingpin Nino Brown. The movie's theme song "New Jack Hustler," in which he unabashedly made known his political ideology, with such lyrics as "In my brain I got a capitalist migraine," earned Ice-T a Grammy nomination. The following year he released his most successful album, *O.G. Original Gangster.*

In 1992 Ice-T began performing with his rock band Body Count. Body Count became the focal point of political controversy around its song "Cop Killer," which narrated the frustration of an African American who seeks revenge for police brutality. Numerous law enforcement agencies, the National Rifle Association, and politicians protested the song, eventually prompting Time-Warner to remove the song from the album. In the aftermath of this experience, Ice-T lectured at several major universities on freedom of speech.

Ice-T would release several more albums throughout the 1990s, but none were as successful as his first four releases. More recently Ice-T's musical career has been overshadowed by his successes in the movie and television industry. He has appeared in a number of films, including *Ricochet* (1991), in which he starred with Denzel Washington; *Surviving the Game* (1994); *Johnny Mnemonic* (1995); and others. He has appeared on numerous television shows including the hip-hop crime drama series *New York Undercover.* Ice-T currently stars on NBC's award-winning series *Law and Order.* He has also hosted a documentary titled *Pimpin' 101* (2003) that introduces the viewer to the "science of pimping." Ice-T's impact, appeal, and success as rapper-actor has helped define hip-hop culture as a major sociopolitical voice of 20th-century America.

BIBLIOGRAPHY

Erlewine, S. T. "Ice-T." Available online. URL: http://www.vh1.com/artists/az/ice_t/bio.jhtml. Accessed October 17, 2006.

Higa, B. "Early Los Angeles Hip Hop." In *The Vibe History of Hip Hop,* 111–119. New York: Random House, 1997.

Kamau Rashid

If He Hollers Let Him Go
Chester Himes (1945)

CHESTER HIMES uses Robert Jones, the protagonist of his first novel, *If He Hollers Let Him Go,* to expose the impact of racism on America and American lives in the mid-20th century. In this novel, Himes begins an exploration of his premise and conviction that American racism is, at its core, absurd, as he explains in his autobiography, *My Life of Absurdity.* Himes wrote:

Racism introduces absurdity into the human condition. Not only does racism express the absurdity of the racist, but it generates absurdity in the victims. And the absurdity of the victims intensifies the absurdity of the racist, ad infinitum. If one lives in a country where racism is held valid and proactive in all ways of life, eventually, no matter whether one is a racist or a victim, one comes to feel the absurdity of life. (1)

Although he would conduct a more in-depth exploration of this existential premise in his postmodern novel *The Primitive* (1955), Himes—through his treatment and characterization of Jones; Alice Harrison, Jones's middle-class girlfriend; and Madge Perkins, his middle-aged southern white coworker—choreographs relationships that can be described as absurd at best and dysfunctional at worst. The setting is four days in Jones's life in the San Pedro area of Los Angeles, California, at the height of World War II. Jones, a college-educated black male, works as the crew leader of a segregated group of black workers in the Atlas Shipyard. Despite his intellect and expertise, Jones is demoted when Texas-born Madge, who refuses to take instruction from a black man—a "Nigger!"—complains to her white supervisor that Jones has called her a "slut."

Jones's attempts to regain self-respect, a sense of agency, and subjectivity prove fruitless. For example, his effort to integrate an all-white, luxury restaurant with light-skinned Alice fails when, although they are seated, they are placed near the kitchen. Equally disastrous are Jones's attempts to get even with, to kill, Johnny Stoddard, a white coworker who, during a fight, embarrassed him in front of his crew, and his plot to visit Marge in her apartment pretending to be sexually interested in her, only to reject her. Jones abandons his plans when, during their encounter, Marge becomes the aggressor as she advances and demands that he "rape" her. Shortly thereafter, when Marge accuses Jones of rape and entraps him, her white coworkers—committed to protecting white womanhood at any cost, even the truth—beat Jones. Although the charges are eventually dropped when Marge's

nefarious plot is revealed, Jones, though innocent, is forced to join the army and go off to war to fight for and ensure the democracy he is denied at home—the ultimate absurdity.

Living "between anger and void, nightmare and consciousness" (Lee, 68), Jones, as character, bears witness to the experience and contentions of RICHARD WRIGHT's Bigger Thomas in *NATIVE SON*, feeling similarly trapped. Even after he concedes to Alice that perhaps he needed to adjust his ways of thinking "to the actual condition of his life" (157) and resolves to live within the sociopolitical constraints of American life, Jones is forced to conclude that, as a black man living in America, his destiny (Bigger's fate) is in the hands of whites. Jones's reflections echo Bigger's personal convictions: "Sometimes I get the feeling that I don't have anything at all to say about what's happening to me. I'm just like some sort of machine being run by white people pushing buttons. Every white person that comes along pushes some button or other on me and I react accordingly" (156). Jones confesses, "all I ever wanted was just a little thing—just to be a man" (190). However, as Roger Rosenblatt notes, "As for the potential for violence in each hero, it becomes a question of how they deal with their fears. When Bigger is afraid, he acts to cover his fears. When Bob is afraid, he thinks" (167). Thus, although both Bigger and Bob respond with existential responsibility to the condition of their lives, Bigger, who ends up in the electric chair, is more destructive, while Bob, despite being shipped off to the war, is more creative.

Significantly, yet another evidence of the absurd, the setting of *If He Hollers* is not the American South, where racism and segregation were legally practiced and enforced through Jim Crow law, but the West, Southern California, which, by definition, was a more open society. Himes moves his literary lens across a culturally diverse California to reveal the spectrum of an American racism that was to be found, from the segregated Asian community of Little Tokyo, located in the very heartbeat of Los Angeles, to the black ghetto of South Central Los Angeles. During a discussion about "the race problem," Himes reveals through one of his characters his conviction that race is one of several variables. Cleo states, "But this isn't just a problem of race. . . . It is a ghetto problem involving a class of people with different cultures and traditions at a different level of education" (80). Also significant, Himes unabashedly points out that this class, culture, and educational difference exists as well between middle- and lower-class blacks.

However, *If He Hollers Let Him Go* is not merely a political diatribe or pseudosociological report. It is filled with rich literary allusions and integration of African-American folklore—music and tales. For example, in the novel Himes creates scenes of storytelling and signifying games among his crew members (who have such interesting names as Peaches, Zula Mae, Arkansas, and Pigmeat) that resonate with ZORA NEALE HURSTON's porch scenes in *MULES AND MEN* and *THEIR EYES WERE WATCHING! GOD*.

As JAMES BALDWIN noted in discussing Himes's accomplishments, *If He Hollers Let Him Go* is "one of those books for which it is difficult to find any satisfactory classification: not a good novel but more than a tract, relentlessly honest, and carried by the fury and the pain of the man who wrote it" (3).

BIBLIOGRAPHY

Baldwin, James. "History as Nightmare." In *The Critical Response to Chester Himes,* edited by Charles L. P. Silet, 3–5. Westport, Conn.: Greenwood Press, 1999.

Himes, Chester. *My Life of Absurdity: The Autobiography of Chester Himes,* vol. II. New York: Doubleday & Company, 1976.

———. *The Quality of Hurt: The Autobiography of Chester Himes,* vol. I. New York: Doubleday & Company, 1972.

Lee, Robert, A. "Violence Real and Imagined: The Novels of Chester Himes." In *The Critical Response to Chester Himes,* edited by Charles L. P. Silet, 65–81. Westport, Conn.: Greenwood Press, 1999.

Rosenblatt, Roger. *Black Fiction.* Cambridge, Mass.: Harvard University Press, 1974.

Wilfred D. Samuels

I Know Why the Caged Bird Sings
Maya Angelou (1970)

I Know Why the Caged Bird Sings (1970) is the first of a series of six books through which poet, actress, and dancer MAYA ANGELOU records her life. When Robert Loomis, her eventual Random House editor, challenged her to write her autobiography as literature, Angelou took him seriously. This first book covers 16 years of Angelou's life, focusing largely on her early life in segregated, poverty-ridden Stamps, Arkansas, and her teenage years in San Francisco and San Diego. When her parents' marriage ends, Maya and Bailey, her slightly older brother, are sent, address-tagged and alone, across the country by train from Long Beach, California, to their paternal grandmother, Annie Henderson, in Stamps, Arkansas. Within a few years of being taken in by Henderson, Angelou and Bailey are then reclaimed by their mother, Vivienne Baxter, and sent back to St. Louis. When raped at age eight by her mother's boyfriend, Angelou, who was warned not to tell, subsequently confides in Bailey, who quickly informs the family. After spending only one day in jail, the molester was released and was found dead in a nearby parking lot the next day; he apparently had been kicked to death. The traumatized Angelou believes that her voice, and perhaps her relatives, caused her victimizer to lose his life. Thereafter, she chooses not to speak to anyone other than Bailey for many years to come.

Returning to live with her grandmother, Annie Henderson, and Uncle Willie in Stamps, Angelou begins to read prodigiously, memorizes large amounts of poetry, and is eventually encouraged to speak with the help of her dedicated teacher, Mrs. Flowers. After graduating from Lafayette Country Training School at age 14, Angelou and Bailey rejoin their mother in San Francisco. Soon after, Maya spends her summer in Southern California with her father and his lover, Dolores. However, after being stabbed during a jaunt into Mexico, she avoids her father's wrath by going to live in a car junkyard with a tight-knit band of Mexican, Negro, and white runaways. There, accepted and protected by this racially mixed group, she begins to understand the concept of universal brotherhood. Returning to San Francisco, she attends high school, becomes pregnant, gives birth to her son, Guy, and subsequently agitates to be hired as San Francisco's first black female streetcar conductor.

I Know Why the Caged Bird Sings is a story of the racial tragedy of black childhood in the South, the Ku Klux Klan, segregation, betrayal, wandering, sexual molestation, and rootlessness. It is also the story of Angelou's grandmother's Puritan world of racial pride, the southern black church, the fast saloon life of Vivienne Baxter, and the theme of segregation outside the South, particularly on the West Coast.

Following the journey pattern of the journey out, the quest, the achievement, and the transition to the next home, *I Know Why the Caged Bird Sings* is an affirmative narrative. The prose is rich in brilliant social portraiture, self-irony, memorable anecdotes, poignant metaphor, and the sharply evoked ethos of various places. Its values of healing, growth, courage, and the achievement of personal voice and spiritual wholeness are foregrounded against a background of precariousness, racial tragedy, and ever-present death. Angelou records the beginnings of her personal self-constructions from idolizing her brother to being overwhelmed by her mother's beauty to her rejection of her selfish father along with her sexual naiveté, her southern religious heritage, her numerous self-deceptions, and her premature emergence into motherhood at age 16. Angelou's narrative stages the development of personal mythos; racial self-hatred; fear, love, and rage toward her parents; moments of great humor; willful self-destructiveness; and the desire to transcend social death.

In the five volumes that follow this one, Angelou makes American literary history through the development of the new genre of a serial authoethnography. In *I Know Why the Caged Bird Sings* she writes both her individual self and her collective and communal black female self as she discovers language, voice, and her longing for "home." As a métis, or cultural translator, Angelou reclaims a series of multiple cultural and racial traditions, which she then ethnographs into a coherent identity. It is out of her deliberate work as a cultural translator that she manages to create a sense of place, people, and "tribe," unified out of both per-

sonal and collective fragmentations. Eschewing the typically tragic mode of such writing, Angelou's work turns to the ironic and comic mode, staging a narrative of transcendence forged through linking herself to the long tradition of African-American first-person autobiographical literature found in such classic works as OLAUDAH EQUIANO's *The Interesting Narrative of the Life of Olaudah Equiano*, FREDERICK DOUGLASS's *The NARRATIVE OF THE LIFE OF FREDERICK DOUGLASS*, and HARRIET JACOBS's *INCIDENTS IN THE LIFE OF A SLAVE GIRL*. *I Know Why the Caged Bird Sings* is one of America's most beloved autobiographic works.

Gloria Cronin

Incidents in the Life of a Slave Girl
Harriet Jacobs (1861)

Written by HARRIET JACOBS (under the pseudonym Linda Brent), *Incidents in the Life of a Slave Girl* was the first published narrative written by a former female slave. Lydia Maria Child, the white abolitionist, edited the work, and for many years critics and historians believed that Child was the author. It was not until the 1970s, when scholar Jean Fagan Yellin verified the authenticity of the narrative and the life of Harriet Jacobs, that proof was provided that *Incidents in the Life of a Slave Girl* was not a work of fiction. In this narrative, Jacobs, a former slave in North Carolina, recounts her experiences in slavery, her growing awareness of her true condition of bondage, her painful quest for freedom, her determination to protect her children at any cost, her flight to freedom, and her life as a freeperson.

Significantly, Jacobs adopts the tone of the sentimental novel, a genre popular with 19th-century middle-class white women, to frame her story. She uses the formula to critique the domestic slavery of women as well as the slavery of millions of African Americans. Moreover, this genre allowed Jacobs to gain a wider audience; like her fictional counterpart, Linda Brent, trapped by her poverty and beauty, Jacobs fell prey to an unscrupulous, older man. In Jacobs's case, the sexual predator is also her white slave owner, Dr. Flint—a man nearly old enough to be her grandfather. But, as Jacobs points out at the end of her narrative, the story does not end in the traditional manner of the sentimental story with marriage, "but with freedom." Jacobs takes control of the narrative form in a way that she was never fully allowed to take control of her own life because of her race and gender. At the same time, she critiques the extant "cult of true womanhood" that condemned the morality of a slave girl caught in the situation in which she had found herself.

Orphaned at an early age, "Linda Brent" grows up under the watchful eye of her grandmother, but she soon draws the interest of Dr. Flint and the ire of his wife. Mrs. Flint, driven by jealousy, is a notorious abuser of slaves, especially young, pretty women. Linda finally decides to become involved with another man, Mr. Sands, hoping that Dr. Flint will lose interest. Instead, Flint, who responds with jealousy, threatens Linda's family. After she gives birth to children fathered by Sands, Linda becomes more vulnerable to Flint's demands. Threatened by Dr. Flint, who promises to sell her children if she does not give in to him, Linda flees to the North. In reality, however, she takes residence in the crawlspace of her grandmother's shed, and for the next seven years watches, in a prone position that leaves her crippled, her children through a knothole.

Harriet Jacobs's contributions to the development of the slave narrative and to the female tradition in the African-American novel is outlined in Joanne Braxton's work on these genres. Jacobs's focus on both women's rights and the abolition of slavery foreshadows the intersection of the politics of race and gender in the works by contemporary writers such as Toni Morrison, Paule Marshall, and Alice Walker. The emphasis on black women's sexuality and its commodification by American culture, the special problems of African-American mothers, and the antagonism between white and black women—all themes and topics addressed in Jacobs's narrative—continue to be relevant in African-American women's novels today. Jacobs's strength, her dedication to her children, and her sense of self helped define a well-known type of heroic figure in the women's

literary tradition. Unlike many of the narratives of slave men, Jacobs's story reminds readers how slavery destroys the most natural of human communities, the family. Today, writers still echo Jacobs's sentiment when they illustrate the impact of racism on children, mothers, and the contemporary African-American household.

BIBLIOGRAPHY

Braxton, Joanne. "Harriet Jacobs' *Incidents in the Life of a Slave Girl:* The Re-definition of the Slave Narrative Genre." *Massachusetts Review* 27, no. 2 (1986): 379–387.

Foreman, P. Gabrielle. "The Spoken and the Silenced Narrative in *Incidents in the Life of a Slave Girl.*" *Callaloo* 13, no. 2 (1990): 313–324.

Stover, Johnnie M. "Nineteenth-Century African-American Woman's Discourse: The Example of Harriet Ann Jacobs." *College English* 66, no. 2 (2003): 133–154.

Yellin, Jean Fagan, ed. *Incidents in the Life of a Slave Girl.* Cambridge: Harvard University Press, 1987.

Tracie Church Guzzio

Invisible Life   E. Lynn Harris (1994)

E. Lynn Harris's *Invisible Life* chronicles the early adult life of Raymond Winston Tyler, Jr., and his struggle to discern his sexual identity in the midst of concurrent heterosexual and homosexual relationships. Ray, a college senior who is in love with his high school sweetheart, Sela, develops a previously unfelt homosexual desire for Kelvin Ellis, a new man on campus. Ray is attracted to Kelvin at first glance at a frat party; he becomes aroused again when the two meet in the university locker room. Leaving the gym, they purchase beer and return to Ray's apartment, where Kelvin, somewhat assertively, seduces Ray, providing him with his first homosexual experience. Although he is at first disturbed that he thoroughly enjoyed this new experience, Ray continues to date both Sela and Kelvin until he graduates and moves to New York City to attend law school at Columbia University.

The novel begins six years after Ray has left Alabama and moved to New York, where he is able to accept and freely establish his gay identity. Successfully employed in a prestigious, predominantly white law firm, Ray frequents the gay bar scene and engages in a gay lifestyle outside of work. Ray develops close platonic friendships with Kyle, an openly gay fashion designer, and JJ, with whom he initially had a one-night sexual interlude. They form a "family" and look out for each other. However, Ray must still keep his gay lifestyle invisible to family and coworkers.

When Ray coincidentally encounters Kelvin six years later, Kelvin introduces him to his fiancé, Candance; they exchange phone numbers. Ray is not only shocked to see Kelvin (the reader does not know how their relationship ended), but also to learn that he is in a committed heterosexual relationship. Shortly thereafter, Ray enters a committed relationship with Quinn, a married man and simultaneously a heterosexual relationship with Nicole, Candance's friend, whom he had met on a blind date set up by Candance and Kelvin. When he tells Quinn that he wants "to go back to the other side exclusively" (216), Quinn responds: "Your desire for me and other men isn't going away because you think you're in love with some woman. . . . I know because I live that lie everyday" (218).

In addition to his bisexual desires, Ray struggles with keeping his invisible life from his parents who, during his visit home to Alabama for a Christmas holiday, query him about his marriage plans. While there, he also reunites with his former girlfriend and, although she is engaged, attempts to seduce her. His fear of having unprotected sex with her and passing on to her any sexually transmittable disease he might unknowingly have introduces HIV/AIDS as a theme in the novel. Before Ray leaves for New York, his father tells him, "your mother and I didn't raise you to be no sissy" (116), compounding the issues he faces.

Although he eventually comes out to Nicole, Ray's problems are compounded when Nicole tells him that Candance, Kelvin's fiancé, has been diagnosed with AIDS. Becoming despondent, Ray falls into deep depression and isolates himself in his apartment. Concerned, his father visits him. After an all night face-to-face talk, Ray reflects, "We realized that things and feelings were not going to be changed in one night, but we started to break down the barriers" (248). Ray writes a letter to Nicole asking for her forgiveness and prepares to return to Alabama to sort things out with his parents. Before he leaves New York, he attends Candance and Kelvin's wedding, which occurs in her hospital room the day before she dies. Ray gives Nicole the letter and asks her to reply. When Nicole asks him why Candance had to die from AIDS, he replies, "I don't know the answer to that, Nicole. The only way you can be certain is to have someone love you enough to tell the truth about who and what they are" (253). Ray takes a leave of absence from work and returns home to prevent any possible fragmentation of his relationship with his parents. While he is there, his parents accept his past and commit to supporting him as he tries to walk away from his invisible life with the hope that his relationship with Nicole can be salvaged. Ray is heartened when he receives a call from Nicole to wish him a happy birthday and to tell him that their AIDS tests came back negative.

Invisible Life is a novel that conveys the social realism of a black man searching for his true identity amidst passion and desire for members of both sexes. Although he is also concerned with race, Harris chooses to deemphasize issues of race to keep the focus on the issues that concerned him: that the black community has homosexual members among its ranks, that many of those members engage in bisexual behavior to mask their homosexual tendencies and relationships, and the harm inflicted on the community because of its reluctance to acknowledge homosexuals and bisexuals and the proliferation of AIDS among its ranks.

The novel appears incomplete because it ends without any resolution for the protagonist. Though Nicole calls Ray in the last chapter to wish him a happy birthday, the reader has no idea if the two will ever marry. Ray's relationship with Quinn, though cooled sexually, has also not been resolved or redefined. However, because of the author's final statement, THE END FOR NOW, the reader can assume that the story is going to pick up where it is left off in a future novel—and it does.

BIBLIOGRAPHY
Harris, E. Lynn. *Invisible Life.* New York: Doubleday, 1994.

Lawrence T. Potter, Jr.

Invisible Man Ralph Ellison (1952)

Greeted by controversial reviews when it was first published in 1952, RALPH ELLISON's *Invisible Man* continues to stand the test of time. The main character journeys through the United States at a crucial moment in history—a moment that promised freedom and infinite possibilities but kept that for a privileged few. The main character, however, does not know this and optimistically moves from one disappointment to the next, believing that this time he will be allowed to succeed; in the words of Dr. Bledsoe, the president of the African-American college to which the protagonist wins a scholarship in a circus-like contest, he is kept running.

The inspiration for the novel was a book and a concept: Lord Raglan's *The Hero* and the problem of white-picked black leaders. Ellison's craft is so careful and precise that much of the long, tightly woven novel was mapped from the beginning. According to Ellison,

> I began it with a chart of the three-part division. It was a conceptual frame with most of the ideas and some incidents indicated. The three parts represent the narrative's movement from, using Kenneth Burke's terms, purpose to passion to perception. These three major sections are built up to smaller units of three which mark the course of the action and which depend for their development upon what I hoped was a consistent and developing motivation. However, you'll note that the maximum insight on the hero's part isn't reached until the final section. After all, it's a novel about innocence and human error, a struggle through illusion to reality.

Ellison's invisible and unnamed protagonist attends college until he makes the mistake of allowing a white board member to see beneath the layers of blackness created by the college president; he is sent to New York, with what he believes are letters of recommendation, to keep him from ever returning to the school. In New York he encounters and survives one harrowing experience after another. A large portion of the book examines the Communist Party in the United States. By the end, the novel follows the main character's journey from childhood to adulthood, from naiveté to self-realization, and demonstrates the paradox that is the United States: a country founded on ideals where the lived reality, for many, is a betrayal of these ideals.

Though the book was awarded the National Book Award in 1953, most contemporary reviewers hedged when it came to Ellison's creative prowess, exalting the book's theme or character or subject but qualifying the praise with "but he's not perfect," "the book is not flawless." Additionally, many pointed the finger at Ellison for not overtly participating in African-American literary movements. And Ernest Kaiser, in a 1970 review of the novel and of its reviews, argues,

> With a Niagara of words, with innuendoes and rationalizations aplenty, he tries to justify his nightmarish, escapist, surreal, nonsocial protest, existential novel. But it is to no avail. That a white critic has to ask him about the lack of protest against Black oppression in his novel embarrasses us all. Ellison tries to destroy Wright and his social view in fiction. But here again Ellison is speaking for the somewhat insulated, educated Black middle class in the South. He says he fears the Left more than he fears the murdering state of Mississippi. He says that Blacks are not pressuring him to join the Freedom Movement and that his inane reply to Howe is action in the struggle for Black freedom! (Kaiser, 92–93).

In his own work and interviews, Ellison responded with an unpopular position for the times. When confronted with Irving Howe's critique of his work he remarked that Howe and others like him want to designate the role which Negro writers are to play more rigidly than any Southern politician—and for the best of reasons. We must express 'black' anger and 'clenched militancy;' most of all we should not become too interested in the problems of the art of literature, even though it is through these that we seek our individual identities. And between writing well and being ideologically militant, we must choose militancy. Well, it all sounds quite familiar and I fear the social order which it forecasts more than I do that of Mississippi (Ellison, 120).

Perhaps the strongest testament to the value of Ellison's novel is twofold: first, the book spawned conversation about art, black art, and representation among authors, critics, and students; second, its theme of invisibility, overlooked for several decades, speaks to a new and growing body of readers and scholars. *Invisible Man,* now hailed as one of the great American novels, has a lasting place in literature.

BIBLIOGRAPHY

Benston, Kimberly. *Speaking for You: The Vision of Ralph Ellison.* Washington, D.C.: Howard University Press, 1987.

Busby, Mark. *Ralph Ellison.* Boston: Twayne Publishers, 1991.

Callahan, John C. "Frequencies of Eloquence: The Performance and Composition of Invisible Man." In *The Craft of Ralph Ellison,* edited by Robert O'Meally, 55–94. Cambridge: Harvard University Press, 1980.

Ellison, Ralph. "The World and the Jug." In *Shadow and Act,* edited by Ralph Ellison, 107–143. New York: Vintage Books, 1972.

Foley, Barbara. "The Rhetoric of Anticommunism in Ralph Ellison's *Invisible Man. College English* 59 (September 1997): 530–547.

Kaiser, Ernest. "A Critical Look at Ellison's Fiction and at Social Literary Criticism by and about the Author." *Black World,* December 1970, pp. 53–97.

O'Meally, Robert. *The Craft of Ralph Ellison.* Cambridge: Harvard University Press, 1980.

Sundquist, Eric. *Cultural Contexts for Ralph Ellison's Invisible Man.* Boston: Bedford Books, St. Martin's Press, 1995.

Shauna Lee Eddy-Sanders

Jackson, Major (1968–)

The product of urban North Philadelphia, where he was born in 1968, Major Jackson is a graduate of Temple University. From the appearance of his first book, *Leaving Saturn* (2001), to the present, Jackson has been lauded for his poetic genius. He was immediately showered with accolades. CALLALOO included him in its emerging writers issue. He won the 2000 Cave Canem Poetry Prize and the Whitting Writer's Award, which is given annually to "emerging writers of exceptional talent and promise." His many other fellowships and awards include inclusion in the Bread Loaf Writers' Conference, a Pew Fellowship in the Arts, a Library of Congress Witter Bynner Fellowship, and a National Book Critics Circle Award in poetry. Jackson also earned an M.F.A. from the University of Oregon. His work has been published in *American Poetry Review, Boulevard,* and *The New Yorker.*

Much in the way that JOHN EDGAR WIDEMAN, in his *Homewood Trilogy,* gives voice to the urban Pittsburgh community in which he grew up, Jackson brings to life the world he knew intimately growing up in North Philadelphia. From the outside, this world might look like the bombed-out residue of war and urban renewal. However, like GWENDOLYN BROOKS, who created the fictional world Bronzeville, where real people live real, complex, credible lives, Jackson lifts the veil cast over his seldom entered North Philadelphia world to reveal a pulsating world of pain and joy, lives destroyed and lives fulfilled, and lives of despair and lives of hope. In his work Jackson not only pays attention to the lives of the people he grew up knowing but also teaches us "How to Listen," the title of one of his poems:

> I am going to cock my head tonight like a
> dog
> in front of McGlinchys Tavern on Locust;
> I am going to pay attention to our lives.

From 1992 to 1999, Jackson was the literary arts curator of the Painted Bride Art Center in Philadelphia. He is an associate professor of English at the University of Vermont and a member of the low-residency M.F.A. creative writing program at Queens College in Charlotte, North Carolina.

BIBLIOGRAPHY

Gabbin, Joanne V., ed. *Furious Flower: African American Poetry from the Black Arts Movement to the Present.* Charlottesville: University of Virginia Press, 2004.

Wilfred D. Samuels

Jacobs, Harriet   (Linda Brent) (1813–1897)

Considered a "literary foremother," Harriet Jacobs continues to engage scholars, critics, and storytellers. Her life as a former slave, devoted mother, writer, and activist inspires readers with her humble tales of the experiences she had to endure as a young, vulnerable African-American slave girl. Born in 1813 in North Carolina, Jacobs was left an orphan during her young adulthood after the death of both parents. Although slavery as an institution often compromised strong familial bonds—through slave auctions, the removal of children from their parents, and the practice of forbidding marriage among slaves—Jacobs had a close relationship with her family, particularly her grandmother. However, in the end, her family could not protect her from the advances of her slave owner, Dr. James Norcom. Educated and light-skinned (one of her grandfathers was white), Jacobs admits that she led an easier life than many slaves; nevertheless, she illustrates that the constant threat of rape and of losing her children was psychologically as damaging as some of the most horrific stories of slavery and torture.

Unable to protect herself completely from either Norcom's advances or his wife's anger, Jacobs decided to take a lover, Samuel Tredwell Sawyer. Hoping that her relationship with another man would dissuade Dr. Norcom from his "seduction," Jacobs continued the relationship with Sawyer for years, ultimately producing two children. The relationship offended her pious grandmother, which devastated Jacobs. Deciding finally that Dr. Norcom would not let her go or leave her alone, she pretended to run away and lived in hiding for seven years in the crawlspace of her grandmother's shed. By the time she was finally able to escape, Jacobs was physically weakened. Heading north, she was ultimately reunited with one of her children (who had been purchased by Sawyer from Norcom). While a fugitive she found sanctuary among and received assistance from white abolitionists.

Later, after meeting Harriet Beecher Stowe, author of the best-selling 19th-century novel *Uncle Tom's Cabin,* Jacobs decided to write her own narrative. INCIDENTS IN THE LIFE OF A SLAVE GIRL (1861), which was edited by Lydia Maria Child (1802–

1880), a writer of historical novels, abolitionist, and editor of the *National Antislavery Standard.* Using the pseudonym Linda Brent and changing the names and locales to further hide her identity and location, Jacobs declared in the preface to her narrative: "Reader, be assured this narrative is not fiction. . . . I have not exaggerated the wrongs inflicted by Slavery; on the contrary, my descriptions fall far short of the facts" (xiii). Jacobs was able to elude Norcom, his family, and the slave catchers after the narrative was published. Later in her life, Cornelia Willis, her employer, purchased Jacobs's freedom.

For many years, historians erroneously believed Child had written Jacobs's narrative. It was not until the 1970s, when Jean Fagan Yellin was able to prove that "Linda Brent" did exist, that critics and readers could fully appreciate the life of Harriet Jacobs. Jacobs was a tireless abolitionist and later a crusader for the rights of African Americans and women. She started a free school in the South during the Civil War (under the guard of the Union Army) and tended the wounded. She was later actively involved with the NATIONAL ASSOCIATION FOR THE ADVANCEMENT OF COLORED PEOPLE, and with her daughter she continued teaching and fighting for women's rights in Washington, D.C., where she died in 1897. Her work as a writer and as an activist complemented each other. Her family, her dream of their togetherness in a warm home, was the vision of ideal freedom and a dream that should be open to all Americans.

BIBLIOGRAPHY

Beardslee, Karen E. "Through Slave Culture's Lens Comes the Abundant Source: Harriet A. Jacobs's *Incidents in the Life of a Slave Girl.*" *MELUS* 24, no. 1 (1999): 37–58.

Yellin, Jean Fagan. *Harriet Jacobs: A Life.* New York: Basic Civitas, 2004.

Tracie Church Guzzio

James, Glenroy Winston   (1967–)

Born in Kingston, Jamaica, Glenroy Winston James immigrated with his family to New Jersey in 1971 at age four. He grew up in Paterson, New Jersey. After graduating from Paterson Catholic Regional High School, he received a B.A. degree in Latin American/Iberian Studies from Columbia College, Columbia University. He earned an M.F.A. degree in fiction from Brooklyn College in 2004 and completed an M.B.A. in computer information systems and marketing at Zicklin School of Business at Baruch College in New York in 2005. Also an avid student of anthropology, James is an international traveler who has lived in Brazil, Spain, and Mexico, where he studied Spanish and Portuguese and learned about the distinctive and multifaceted cultures in each of these geographical locations by immersing himself in the daily lives of the people.

Over the past decade, James has emerged as an important activist voice in the black gay and lesbian movement. He currently serves as a Craig G. Harris Fellow for the New York State Black Gay Network's Fluid Bodies project, addressing the quality-of-life issues of New York City's same-sex-desiring Caribbean community. He was the chairman and executive director of Other Countries: Black Gay Expression; the coprogrammer for Bromfield Street Educational Foundation, with responsibilities for the OutWrite 1999 national lesbian and gay writers' conference, and the development officer for the Lesbian and Gay Community Service Center of New York City. James was one of the organizers of the first Fire & Ink: A Writers Festival for Black GLBT Writers, which was held at the University of Illinois at Chicago in September 2002.

James's prose and essays have been published in *Think Again, Brooklyn Review,* CALLALOO: *A Journal of African American and African Arts and Letters, Fighting Words: Personal Essays by Black Gay Men, The Mammoth Book of Gay Erotica, His 2: Brilliant New Fiction by Gay Men of African Descent,* and *Waves: An Anthology of New Gay Fiction.* James, who is also a former coeditor of *Kuumba,* an African-American gay and lesbian journal, has published his poetry in *Freedom in This Village: Twenty-five Years of Black Gay Men's Writing, Bloom: Queer Fiction, Art, Poetry and More, The Nubian Gallery: A Poetry Anthology, Black Ivy: A Literary and Visual Arts Magazine, Role Call: A Generational Anthol-* ogy of *Social and Political Black Art and Literature, Milking Black Bull: 11 Gay Black Poets,* and two Lambda Literary Award–winning anthologies: *Sojourner: Black Gay Voices in the Age of AIDS,* and *The Road before Us: 100 Gay Black Poets. Spirited, Affirming the Soul of Black / Gay Lesbian Identity,* which he edited with Lisa C. Moore, was published by Red Bone Press in 2006.

The recipient of a 1997 fellowship from the Lillay Colony for the Arts, James published his first collection of poetry, *Lyric: Poems along a Broken Road* in 1999. It was a finalist in the 1999 Lambda Literary Awards competition for poetry. James's activist commitment is often heard in his speaker's voice, as in "Uprising":

> I want to start a campaign
> One that gets homosexuals
> To recall
> What it means to be gay.

James's other projects include *The Damaged Good* (2006), his second collection of poetry, which was published in November 2006, and *Shaming the Devil,* a collection of short fiction, which is scheduled to be published in 2007.

BIBLIOGRAPHY

James, G. Winston. "Storm." *Callaloo* 22, no. 4 (Fall 1999): 893–894.

Wilfred D. Samuels

Jazz Toni Morrison (1992)

Jazz, the middle novel of TONI MORRISON's trilogy, which includes BELOVED (1987) and *Paradise* (1998), weighs the human costs of the Great Migration of World War I on African Americans. Set in 1920s Harlem with numerous flashbacks to 19th-century rural Virginia, *Jazz* brings together all genres of African-American culture: black speech, BLUES aesthetics, slave narrative elements, call and response, multivocality, and jazz ensemble structure. In short, it is an entirely new kind of novel with its refusal of the usual numbered chapter divisions, its blank pages, riffs, motifs, transitional slurs, bridges, cuts, departures, returns, and head tunes. Characters sidestep and evade their narrator/composer in redemptive solo digressions and revise their lives in their own ways.

Like Palmer Hayden, in his paintings of Harlem scenes, Morrison provides impressionistic images of hairdresser's salons, speakeasies, jazz clubs, funeral parlors, corpse dressers, fried chicken joints, baby buggies, and rooftop jazzmen, in contrast to F. Scott Fitzgerald's images of the same era—white, upper-class, Long Island mansions, and flapper-era parties. Morrison's inspiration for the figure of Dorcas, the emblematic lost black daughter whose story lies at the heart of this novel, came from James Van der Zee's famous picture of a dead girl in his *The Harlem Book of the Dead.* Her name recalls the biblical Dorcas, whom the apostle Peter raised from the dead, and in like manner Morrison textually "raises up" Dorcas and all the lost young black women she represents. As *Jazz* opens Joe has shot the 18-year-old Dorcas, his lover, who then allows herself to bleed slowly to death. Violet, Joe's middle-aged and childless wife, is now haunted by this dead girl whose face she has mutilated in a fit of jealous rage and who gazes back at both of them from the photograph Violet keeps on their mantelpiece.

Throughout the novel Joe, Violet, and Dorcas's aunt, Alice Manfred, seek to redeem Dorcas's memory by tracing and healing their own histories of family dysfunction. The characters' individual and collective emotional wounds and disfiguring substitutions begin in 1855, the year white Vera Louise Gray becomes pregnant by black Henry Lestory (or LesTroy), and flees to Baltimore with her black maid, True Belle, Violet's grandmother. True Belle leaves behind two very dark-skinned children, May and Rose, who in later years are confused by their mother's enthusiastic stories of a glorious white-skinned mulatto boy for whom, it seems, she has abandoned them.

Abandonment of orphans marks every generation. When the angry Golden Gray returns to Virginia to enact revenge on his absentee black father, he reluctantly helps Wild give birth to a black male child, probably Joe Trace, whom she then abandons. In 1893 the adult Joe Trace, a hunter, literally

tracks his mother to an earthy warren in the same Virginia woods in which Golden Gray has sought to destroy Henry LesTroy. He finds only her evocative scent. Violet is abandoned by her unmothered mother, Rose, a suicide who flings herself down a well in 1892. Dorcas is orphaned when her parents, along with 200 others, are murdered in a deadly fire during the 1917 East St. Louis race riots and then is emotionally denied by her embittered aunt, Alice Manfred.

Morrison's plot uncovers a generationally compounding series of losses, all of which explode in 1925–26. Joe, now middle-aged, tracks, seduces, and eventually shoots the unloved black orphan, Dorcas, who in turn allows herself to bleed slowly to death. Violet literally sits down in the street one day unable to go on with her life's journey. She has experienced serial abortions, sleeps with dolls, nearly abducts a baby, stabs the dead Dorcas in the face, and then releases her caged parrot to its sure death.

Morrison's script for reversing this series of downward spirals involves a historical and emotional accounting. Joe comes to understand that his misplaced desire for a young black woman has to do with his search for his mother. Alice Manfred admits her failure to love Dorcas because of her lifelong murderous rage over marital abandonment. Culpability, understanding, love, and sister friendship bring all three to awareness of the long history of the lost black daughters. Alice regains the ability to love, and Violet and Joe once again whisper nightly under their quilt. When the young Felice arrives all alone in New York, she finds a surrogate family waiting to nurture her. Unlike Joe, however, she finds more than the trace of the lost African parents.

In *Jazz* Morrison once more mourns the absence of the African mother and motherland. But as she mourns the scattered children, she also attests to both the spiritual presence of the African mother and to her physical incarnation in contemporary black parents. Violet will nurture Felice, and Joe will teach her to dance. Van der Zee's dead girl is brought to life in the figures of both Dorcas and Felice, while Morrison's jazz composition suggests a potent redemptive grammar for the endless improvisational possibilities of African-American identity and survival.

Selected Bibliography

Barnes, D. H. "Movin' On Up: The Madness of Migration in Toni Morison's *Jazz.* In *Toni Morrison's Fiction: Contemporary Criticism,* edited by D. Middleton, 283–296. New York: Garland, 1997.

Leonard, J. Review of *Jazz.* In *Toni Morrison: Critical Perspectives Past and Present,* edited by Henry Louis Gates, Jr., and K. A. Appiah, 36–49. New York: Amistad Press, 1993.

Mbalia, D. D. "Women Who Run with Wild: The Need for Sisterhoods in *Jazz.*" *Modern Fiction Studies* 39, no. 3 and 4 (1993): 623–646.

Rodrigues, Ralph. "Experiencing *Jazz.*" *Modern Fiction Studies* 39, no. 3 and 4 (Fall/Winter 1993): 733–753.

Gloria L. Cronin

Jeffers, Lance   (1919–1985)

Born in Fremont, Nebraska, in 1919, Lance Jeffers was raised by his grandfather in Stromberg, Nebraska. When he was 10 years old, he moved to San Francisco, California, to live with his mother and stepfather. During World War II, Jeffers served in the U.S. Army in Europe. After the war, Jeffers attended Columbia University, where he earned his bachelor of arts (cum laude) and master of arts degrees. He taught at California State University, Long Beach; Bowie State University; and Howard University, where he was a part of the Howard Poets and was associated with *Dasein: A Quarterly Journal in the Arts.* From 1947 until his death in 1985, Jeffers taught at North Carolina State University.

Jeffers's collections of poetry include *My Blackness Is the Beauty of This Land* (1970), *When I Know the Power of My Black Hand* (1975), *O Africa, Where I Baked My Bread: Poems* (1977), and *Grandsire: Poems* (1979). The title poem of his first published collection, which AMIRI BARAKA included in *BLACK FIRE,* celebrates blackness in the tradition of the writers of the BLACK ARTS MOVEMENT, although it was written more than a decade before

this movement began. In a pride-filled voice resonant of such Black Arts writers as SARAH WEBSTER FABIO, NIKKI GIOVANNI, and ETHERIDGE KNIGHT, Jeffers's speaker declares:

> *My blackness is the beauty of this land,*
> *my blackness,*
> *Tender and strong, wounded and wise,*
> *my blackness*
> *. . . (Jones and Neal, 272)*

Although he also wrote fiction and criticism, Jeffers saw poetry as a way of reclaiming a racial self-knowledge. By combining "history and protest and demand and rage" (King, 78) and celebrating the black experience, writers and poets would discover the nature of African Americans. Jeffers believed that America was the birthplace for the "ultimate grandeur in black poetry" (78). Jeffers's only novel, *Witherspoon* (1983), focuses on the effort of a black minister to save the life of a condemned convict. Jeffers was interested in social issues like the Holocaust, the Vietnam War, and everyday racial injustices in America. Although he was concerned with social and political issues, Jeffers also wrote personal poems, some dedicated to his wife, Trellie.

BIBLIOGRAPHY

Jones, LeRoi, and Larry Neal, eds. *Black Fire: An Anthology of Afro-American Writing.* New York: William Morrow & Company, 1968.

King, Woodie, Jr., ed. *The Forerunners: Black Poets in America.* Washington, D.C.: Howard University Press, 1975.

Kim Hai Pearson
Brian Jennings

Joans, Ted   (1928–2003)

Born to riverboat entertainers in Cairo, Illinois (though, despite the well-known myth, not on a riverboat), on July 4, 1928, Joans, a poet, painter, jazz musician, surrealist, griot, and self-proclaimed nomad who has lived throughout Africa, Europe, and Asia, was described by STEPHEN HENDERSON in

Understanding the New Black Poetry as "one of the most inventive of contemporary poets.... [H]is work is on the growing edge of the poetry/Jazz synthesis" (388). Joans earned a degree in painting from Indiana University in 1951. Moving to New York to pursue studies at the New School for Social Research, he became involved, like BOB KAUFMAN and AMIRI BARAKA (LeRoi Jones) with the Greenwich Village beat movement and its founders Jack Kerouac and Allen Ginsberg, although he remains the least known of the group.

His well-known claim that "Jazz is my religion" and "surrealism is my point of view" is readily confirmed in his more than 35 books of poems, published mostly by small American and European presses. The most recent ones include drawings by his wife, Laura Corsiglia. His collected work includes *Beat Poems* (1957), *Funky Jazz Poems, Beat* (1961), *All of Ted Joans* (1961), *The Hipsters* (1961), *The Truth* (1970), *Afrodisia: New Poems by Ted Jones* (1970), *Double Trouble* (1992), *Black Pow Wow: Jazz Poems* (1969), *A Black Pow Wow of Jazz Poem* (1974), *Okapi Passion* (1999), *Teducation: Selected Poems 1949–1999* (1999), and *Our Thang: Selected Poems by Ted Joans with Drawings by Laura Corsiglia* (2001). Associating himself with Baraka and the BLACK ARTS MOVEMENT, his richly surrealistic, jazz-driven poems are often nationalistic, offering social and political critiques of what it means to be black in white America, but they are also filled with humor, wit, sensuality (he is pictured in the nude on the back of *Afrodisia*), creative wordplay (evident in the spelling of his last name, "Joans" for Jones), and a jazzlike, improvisational sensibility.

He explained that he "developed a method of reading his pomes [*sic*] that was similar to the way [he] blew trumpet." Joans is most interested in validating with his work the role of the poet as speaker of the truth, as he does in "The Truth":

> If you should see
> a man walking
> down a crowded street
> talking aloud
> to himself
> don't run

> in the opposite direction
> but run toward him
> for he is a POET!
> . . . You have NOTHING to fear
> from the poet
> but the TRUTH. (Black Pow Wow, 1)

It is not surprising that he would identify and celebrate MALCOLM X in his poem "MY ACE OF SPADES" as a truth teller: "Malcolm X freed me and frightened you / Malcolm X told it like it damn shor is! / He said I gotta fight to be really FREE / Malcolm X told both of us / the truth, now didn't he?" Thus, although a beat poet, Joans also placed himself firmly in the philosophical camp of the Black Arts Movement and its artists who emphasized the revolutionary and functional character of art, as in "LETS GET VIOLENT":

> LETS GET
> . . . VIOLENT . . . AND . . . ATTACH THE
> WHITESASH
> . . . ICING CAKED . . .
> ON OUR BLACK MINDS
> . . . LETS GET SO VIOLENT
> . . . THAT WE LEAVE that white way
> of thinking
> . . . IN THE TOILET BENEATH OUR . . .
> BLACK BEHINDS . . .
> LETS/ GET VIOLENT! (Black Pow Wow,
> 13)

Black music, particularly jazz and BLUES, remain for Joans the embodiment of life, in fact, as the speaker says in "JAZZ ANATOMY": ". . . and my souls is where the music lies" (*Afrodisia*, 131). His signature poem, "JAZZ IS MY RELIGION," begins with this mantra: "JAZZ is my religion . . . and it alone do I dig . . . the jazz clubs are my houses of worship," where jazz greats preside:

> I know and feel the message [jazz] brings
> like Reverend Dizzy Gillespie
> Brother . . . Bird and Basie
> Uncle Armstrong
> Minister Monk
> and Deacon Miles Davis

Rector Rollins
Priest Ellington
His Funkiness Horace Silver
and the great Pope JohnJohn Coltrane . . .
They preach a sermon that always swing.
(Black Pow Wow, 71)

Joans began scrawling "Bird Lives" with chalk all over Manhattan after his former roommate, Charlie Parker, died in 1955.

However, Joans remained ever mindful and thankful that, in his poetry, his mentor, LANGSTON HUGHES, "the greatest black poet," had introduced him to all there is to celebrate in African-American culture, particularly its music.

the sonata of Harlem
the concerto to shoulder bones/pinto beans/
hamhocks IN THE DARK
the slow good bouncing grooves
That was the world of Langston Hughes.
("Homage to a Poet," Black Pow Wow, 2)

Two years before his death in Vancouver, Joans, who left the United States after hearing the court decision in the Rodney King case and vowing never to return, won the Columbus Foundation's American Book Award for Lifetime Achievement. According to Robin D. Kelley, "all of [Joan's] writing, like his life, was a relentless revolt." In his unfinished memoir, however, Joans wrote: "I find myself filled too the beautiful brim with love and with this shared love I continue to live my poem-life."

BIBLIOGRAPHY

Foley, Jack. "Goodbye, Ted Joans." *The Alsop Review.* Available online. URL: http://www.alsopreview. com/columns/foley/jfjoans.html/. Accessed October 17, 2006.

Henderson, Stephen. *Understanding the New Black Poetry: Black Speech & Black Music As Poetic Reference.* New York: William Morrow & Company, Inc. 1973.

Kelley, Robin G. "Ted Joans, 1928–2003." *The Village Voice,* May 16, 2003.

Wilfred D. Samuels

Johnson, Angela   (1961–)

Author of children's books, picture books, and young-adult fiction Angela Johnson was born in Tuskegee, Alabama. She recalls sitting in school and listening to stories being read and being able to feel the characters sitting right next to her. Her love of storytelling and the spoken word extended into her family life as well. Johnson describes herself as a shy person who is inspired by her own childhood memories and the stories that her father and grandfather told her. During high school, Johnson wrote free-form poetry, which eventually led her to write children's books. After graduating high school, Johnson attended Kent State University. She also worked with Volunteers in Service to America (VISTA), in Ravenna, Ohio, as a child development worker from 1981 to 1982.

Johnson has written more than 23 books, including *Bird* (2004), *Looking for Red* (2003), *The First Part Last* (2003), *Heaven* (1998), *The Wedding* (1999), *Gone from Home: Short Tales* (1998), *Shoes like Miss Alice's* (1995), *Julius* (1993), *The Girl Who Wore Snakes* (1993), and *Toning the Sweep* (1993). In these works Johnson generally depicts experiences that are common to young children in a way that expresses the joys of everyday life and personal relationships. Her stories, which feature black characters usually in the same age group as her readers, explore both sibling and intergenerational family relationships, highlighting the value of close and affectionate family ties. Johnson celebrates the uniqueness of African-American families while addressing themes that could be experienced by any ethnic group.

Johnson's stories depict familiar scenes of friendship and family regardless of ethnicity. For example, in *Tell Me a Story, Mama* (1992), a picture book, the mother talks to her preschool-aged daughter as the mother prepares the child for bed. Mama's childhood memories, as related by her daughter, are slices of life from a previous generation. The story is so familiar that the daughter becomes the primary teller, while the mother simply fills in comments as needed. *One of Three* (1995) relates a story about three sisters. The story is written through the eyes of the youngest as she and her sisters do almost everything together.

But sometimes the big sisters leave and, with her parents, the narrator becomes one of three in the story she is telling. This particular story, like many of her other works, highlights Johnson's celebratory tone that reflects the rich cultural traditions of African-American oral heritage.

The First Part Last is a companion novel to Johnson's *Heaven* (1998), the story of a young girl, Marley, discovering her true family identity. Johnson narrates just how Bobby, the single father for whom Marley babysits in *Heaven,* landed in that small Ohio town. Beginning his story when his daughter, Feather, is just 11 days old, 16-year-old Bobby tells his story in chapters that alternate between the present and the bittersweet past that has brought him to the point of single parenthood. This father-daughter tale skillfully relates the need for hope in the midst of pain. Johnson continually addresses themes that traverse gender barriers, age, and ethnic differences while maintaining an understanding and reflection of African-American heritage.

Reviewers have praised Johnson for her engaging, first-person narration and simple texts while commending the emotional depth and sensitivity of her stories. She has received numerous awards, including the Coretta Scott King Award for her book *When I Am Old with You* and the 2004 Coretta Scott King Award in Writing and the 2004 Michael L. Printz Award for Excellence in Young Adult Literature for *The First Part Last.* Johnson lives and writes in Cleveland Heights, Ohio.

BIBLIOGRAPHY

Dewind, Anna. "Angela Johnson." *African American Literature Book Club.* Available online. URL: http://aalbc.com/authors/angela.htm. Accessed October 17, 2006.

Kindra Briggs

Johnson, Charles   (1948–   )

Charles Richard Johnson was born at the all-black Community Hospital of Evanston, Illinois, to Benny Lee and Ruby Elizabeth Johnson. Johnson attended Southern Illinois University at Carbondale, where he began a literary apprenticeship with the novelist John Gardner. During a summer in which Johnson worked in Chicago, he met his future wife Joan New, to whom Johnson has been married since 1970; they have two children. While at Southern Illinois, Johnson began the intensely productive working schedule that has characterized his whole writing life. Working as a satirical cartoonist, Johnson produced his first two books, *Black Humor* (1970) and *Half-Past Nation Time* (1972). Before Gardner taught him to slow down, and while he was working toward a Ph.D. at the State University of New York at Stony Brook's philosophy department, Johnson rapidly composed six novels and numerous short stories. His graduate training and research focused on Marxism and phenomenology. Johnson left Stony Brook before submitting his thesis, and in 1998 he was awarded a Ph.D. for the publication of *Being and Race* (1988).

Johnson has published four novels, beginning with *Faith and the Good Thing* (1974). The comically rendered spiritual quest of the eponymous heroine Faith was well reviewed, but it was Johnson's second novel, *Oxherding Tale* (1982), that really captured the attention of readers and received glowing reviews. As a result, Grove Press republished the novel, and Johnson became an established writer. *Oxherding Tale* is, like Johnson's first novel and like MIDDLE PASSAGE (1990), a picaresque quest for freedom. The journey of protagonist Andrew Hawkins is explicitly modeled on the life of FREDERICK DOUGLASS, though Johnson's neo–slave narrative is a (sometimes shockingly) postmodern variation of well-known themes. This playful treatment of even the direst situations, like Brecht's alienation effect, aims at "liberation of perception." Johnson won the National Book Award for *Middle Passage* before turning his attention to MARTIN LUTHER KING, JR., in his next novel, *Dreamer* (1997). Arguing in essays such as "The King We Left Behind" that Americans have settled for a hagiographic version of King in place of the political volatility of the actual King, Johnson refreshes this perception through a fictional reimagination of King as he took his antipoverty campaign into Chicago in the last months of his life. Johnson posits an exact look-alike to King, a man named Chaym Smith who was born on exactly the same day. Unlike King, Smith is a ne'er-do-well and has studied Buddhism in the Far East. Smith begins the novel as a failed man who is extremely envious of the black middle class as typified by King, which Johnson clearly intends as a comment on racial politics in contemporary America. Narrator Matthew Bishop, commenting on the death of King, says, "Exalting the ethnic ego proved far less challenging than King's belief in the beloved community." *Dreamer* is largely the story of Smith's journey from Cain-like envy, but it is also about Bishop's decision to take up the work of reeducating America about the way to beloved community.

Johnson has published three collections of short stories. Stories from *The Sorcerer's Apprentice: Tales and Conjurations* (1986) have received the most critical comment. "Exchange Value" investigates the ways in which the hunger to acquire material goods feeds itself and grows through the acquisition of material goods until the possessor becomes himself the possession of the so-called possessions. This philosophical parable is comically dramatized by the plight of two thieves who break into the wrong apartment and end up acquiring not only the owner's valuables but also her hunger for them. Other stories in this volume extend the dimensions of the imaginary African tribe, the Allmuseri, that Johnson describes most fully in *Middle Passage.* Johnson's second collection, *Soulcatcher and Other Stories* (2001) brings together stories Johnson wrote for a WGBH public television series that has been published in book form as *Africans in America: America's Journey through Slavery* (1998). Frederick Douglass, Martha Washington, and numerous fictional characters animate these stories. *Dr. King's Refrigerator and Other Bedtime Stories* (2005) includes occasional stories connected by the bedtime theme.

Johnson's two most important nonfiction books are *Being and Race* and *Turning the Wheel: Essays on Buddhism and Writing* (2003). The first develops Johnson's interests in the philosophical context of fictional form and technique as apprehended from a phenomenological viewpoint.

This book is at once a philosophical argument, a literary history of black American fiction, and a writer's manual of sorts. *Turning the Wheel* collects essays on Buddhism, cultural politics, and literary art. The phrase "turning the wheel" signifies teaching in Buddhist traditions, and this book is at once Johnson's most explicit declaration of his religious beliefs and his most public, engaged book.

Johnson has also written numerous introductions, reviews, and uncollected essays. For his screenplay *Booker,* he won the Writers Guild award (1985) and the Prix Jeunesse Award in 1987. In addition to National Endowment for the Arts, Rockefeller, and Guggenheim awards, he has won the National Book Award (1990) and the MacArthur Genius Fellowship (1998). He is currently the Pollock Professor of English at University of Washington.

BIBLIOGRAPHY

Byrd, Rudolph P. *I Call Myself an Artist: Writings by and about Charles Johnson.* Bloomington: University of Indiana Press, 1999.

Nash, Will R. *Charles Johnson's Fiction.* Urbana: University of Illinois Press, 2002.

Selzer, Linda Furgerson. "Charles Johnson's 'Exchange Value': Signifyin(g) on Marx." *Massachusetts Review* 42, no. 2 (1995): 253–268.

John Whalen-Bridge

Johnson, Georgia Douglas   (1880–1966)

Georgia Douglas Johnson, renowned HARLEM RENAISSANCE poet, playwright, and mentor, was born in Atlanta, Georgia. In 1896 she graduated from Atlanta University, and in 1906 she married Henry Lincoln Johnson, an attorney. Johnson published her first poem in 1916. She divided her time between writing, being a homemaker, teaching, and serving as a civil service clerk; she even worked as commissioner of conciliation for the Department of Labor. She also acted as a mentor for other African-American writers and encouraged a dialogue between writers by hosting a literary salon in her home. Many African-American artists referred to Douglas Johnson's home as the "Halfway-House" because she allowed them to stay there when visiting the Washington, D.C., area.

Despite her busy schedule, Johnson felt passionate about her writing. She wrote across genres, producing four volumes of poetry: *The Heart of a Woman* (1918), *Bronze* (1922), *An Autumn Love Cycle* (1928), and *Share My World* (1962). Johnson also wrote at least 28 plays, of which her antilynching plays remain most well known. These include *A Sunday Morning in the South* (1925), *Blue Blood* (1926), *Safe* (1929), and *Blue Eyed Black Boy* (1930). Although many of her plays were lost by the time of her death—along with her manuscript about the famous literary salons she hosted in her D.C. home, numerous short stories, and a novel— many of her works have been found, including three short stories, two of which were published in *Challenge* (1936 and 1937).

Between 1926 and 1932, Johnson wrote a weekly newspaper column titled "Homely Philosophy" that appeared in 20 newspapers. Her other newspaper columns include "Wise Saying" and "Beauty Hints"; she also wrote a column for the *New York Amsterdam News*. A trained musician, Johnson used her talent in collaboration with Lillian Evanti in the 1940s.

Thematically, Johnson wrote about justice, love, displacement, power, isolation, and violence. In developing these themes, she called attention to the connections among race, class, and gender. Overall, in her collections of poems *The Heart of a Woman* and *Autumn Love Cycle,* Johnson explores the tension between Victorian notions of womanhood and the emerging definition of womanhood associated with the New Woman. She emphasizes female sexuality and sensuality in some of her poems. Johnson explores female desire and passion in poems such as "Afterglow," "To a Young Wife," and the famous "I Want to Die While You Love Me."

In "The Heart of a Woman," Johnson describes the stifling effect of patriarchal society. "The heart of a woman falls back with the night / And enters some alien cage in its plight / And tries to forget it has dreamed of the stars / While it breaks, breaks, breaks, on the sheltering bars" (Honey, 66). Although the speaker focuses on gender-specific

themes, many critics have drawn comparisons between this poem and Paul Laurence Dunbar's "Sympathy," in which he uses the metaphor of the caged bird to describe the experiences of African Americans in general. As Claudia Tate, editor of a collection of Johnson's work, notes, Johnson "refused to subscribe to a patriarchal sexuality that designated women as male property" (Tate, 1997).

Although Johnson continues to show the intersections of race, gender, and class in *Bronze,* she foregrounds racial themes as well as the themes of protest and violence. *Bronze* includes 65 poems in which Johnson explores life as an African-American in a racist society that denies blacks their humanity. In some of the poems in this collection as well as those that appeared in *The Crisis* and Countee Cullen's *Caroling Dusk* (1927), Johnson overtly calls for resistance to such treatment. She calls attention to the history and ludicrous nature of American racism in poems such as "Common Dust," "Your World," and "The True American."

In her antilynching plays, Douglas Johnson further develops the theme of violence and protest along with other racial themes, including miscegenation, racial passing, and race-based oppression. Moreover, she exposes the myth of the black male rapist described earlier by Ida B. Wells (see Ida B. Wells-Barnet) in *A Red Record* (1895). In *A Sunday Morning in the South,* Johnson shows how easily innocent African-American men were often accused of rape in order to justify white mob violence and lynching prevalent at the time she was writing her antilynching plays. She illustrates the impact of lynching on the African-American family and community as a whole, in *A Sunday Morning in the South* and *Safe,* by demonstrating how the virulent racism and socially and politically condoned violence directed at African Americans rendered them powerless. Johnson used her work to expose these heinous crimes and call for justice.

Johnson also examines the plight of the black maternal figure in these plays. First, she explores the effects of rape on African-American women; she looks specifically at the rape of African-American women by white men. She develops themes of rape, miscegenation, and prejudice in *Blue Eyed Black Boy* and *Blue Blood,* emphasizing the experience of the African-American mother in illustrating these themes. In "Motherhood" she exposes how the right to motherhood is compromised for African-American women. The female speaker in this poem chooses to remain childless rather than bring a child into the world where he or she will inevitably be victimized by racism.

Georgia Douglas Johnson died in 1966. By the time of her death she had contributed a vast amount of writing to the American and African-American literary traditions honoring and celebrating the lives and experiences of African Americans.

BIBLIOGRAPHY

Honey, Maureen. *Shadowed Dreams: Poetry of Women of the Harlem Renaissance*, New Brunswick, N.J.: Rutgers University Press, 1989.

Hull, Gloria. *Color Sex, and Poetry: Three Women Writers of the Harlem Renaissance*. Bloomington: Indiana University Press, 1987.

Perkins, Kathy A., and Judith L. Stephens, eds. *Strange Fruit: Plays on Lynching by American Women*. Bloomington: Indiana University Press, 1997.

Tate, Claudia, ed. *The Selected Works of Georgia Douglas Johnson*. New York: G. K. Hall, 1997.

Deirdre Raynor

Johnson, Helene   (1906–1995)

Although Helene Johnson properly belongs in the group Cheryl A. Wall calls the women of the HARLEM RENAISSANCE, including DOROTHY WEST, ZORA NEALE HURSTON, NELLA LARSEN, JESSIE REDMOND FAUSET, and ANNE PETRY, she remains a forgotten voice of this movement. According to Wall, Johnson was "a poet of great promise, who wrote only a handful of poems and who, like several other mysterious women, disappeared from the Harlem Renaissance leaving barely a trace" ("Chromatic Words," x–xi).

Johnson was born in July 1906 in Boston, the only child of George William Johnson and Ella Benson Johnson. Johnson grew up with her maternal first cousin, Dorothy West, with whom she spent her summers in the village of Oak Bluffs on Martha's Vineyard Island. After being educated in Boston's public school system, including the prestigious Boston Girls' Latin School, Johnson took courses at Boston Clerical School and Boston University. In 1926, Johnson, who together with West had joined the Saturday Evening Quill Club, an organization of aspiring black Boston writers, gained national attention when her poem "Trees at Night" was published in OPPORTUNITY magazine. That year both Johnson and West attended *Opportunity*'s second annual Literary Award Dinner, where three of Johnson's poems received honorable mentions. West and Hurston shared the second place prize for fiction.

In 1927, after Johnson and West made New York City their home, Johnson's poem "Bottled" was published in *Vanity Fair*. Johnson, who was introduced to Harlem and its celebrated writers by Hurston, maintained a close friendship with many of the luminaries, including LANGSTON HUGHES and WALLACE THURMAN. She married William Warner Hubbell III, a New York City motorman, and had one child, Abigail Calachaly Hubbell. Johnson, unlike West, did not return to her native Boston. She remained in New York City, where she died in 1995 at 89 years of age, three years before West died in Boston at age 92.

In 1931, JAMES WELDON JOHNSON wrote that Johnson "possesses true lyric talent. . . . She is one of the younger group who has . . . the 'racial bull by the horns" (quoted in Mitchell, 9) In "My Race" Johnson alludes to W. E. B. DUBOIS's *The SOULS OF BLACK FOLK* and specifically to its first chapter, "Of Our Spiritual Strivings," as well as to declarations by Hughes in several of his poems:

> *Ah my race,*
> *Hungry race,*
> *Throbbing and young—*
> *Ah, my race,*
> *Wonder race,*
> *Sobbing with song—*
> *Ah, my race,*
> *Laughing race, Careless in Mirth—*
> *Ah, my veiled race*
> *Unformed race,*
> *Rumbling in birth. (24)*

In "The Road," Johnson merges nature, a central recurring theme in her work, with her concern about the oppression and struggles blacks face. Although the road becomes a metaphor for the oppression blacks had suffered, the speaker demands a proud response that registers action, determination, and even militancy, much like the speaker in CLAUDE MCKAY's "If We Must Die."

> Ah little road, brown as my race is brown,
> Your trodden beauty like our trodden pride,
> Dust of the dust, they must not bruise you down.
> Rise to one brimming golden, spilling cry! (25)

Johnson's "A Southern Road" offers a more stark and indicting image—that of a lynched black body:

> A blue-fruited black gum,. . .
> Bears a dangling figure—. . .
> Swinging alone,
> A solemn, tortured shadow in the air. (35)

"What do I care for Morning" is representative of Johnson's nature poems. "What do I care for morning, / For the glare of the rising sun, / For a sparrow's noisy prating, / For another day begun" (42). In describing her mother, in "A Daughter Reminisces," the afterword of *This Waiting for Love,* Abigail McGrath wrote, "Let us say that my mother, the poet, was extremely eccentric. Even though she had stopped writing poetry on a professional level before I was born, she continued to live life with the soul of a poet until she died" (125).

BIBLIOGRAPHY

Mitchell, Verner D., ed. *This Waiting for Love: Helene Johnson, Poet of the Harlem Renaissance.* Amherst: University of Massachusetts Press, 2000.

Wall, Cheryl A. "'Chromatic Words': The Poetry of Helene Johnson." In *This Waiting for Love: Helene Johnson, Poet of the Harlem Renaissance,* edited by Verner D. Mitchell, ix–xii. Amherst: University of Massachusetts Press, 2000.

Wilfred D. Samuels

Johnson, James Weldon (1871–1871)

Born in Jacksonville, Florida, in 1871, James Weldon Johnson was an educator, lawyer, diplomat, writer, and activist. He is perhaps best known as an exemplar of African-American professional competency, artistic innovation, and political leadership. His most widely read works include the novel *The AUTOBIOGRAPHY OF AN EX-COLORED MAN* (1912); two major anthologies, *The Book of American Negro Poetry* (1922) and *The Books of American Negro Spirituals* (1925, 1926); a volume of poetry, *God's Trombones: Seven Negro Sermons in Verse* (1927); a history, *Black Manhattan* (1930); and an autobiography, *Along This Way: The Autobiography of James Weldon Johnson* (1933). He additionally published many poems and authored a range of articles, books, and reviews critiquing the prevalent issues of his times. In his collaborations with his brother, J. Rosamond Johnson, and Bob Cole, the trio composed more than 200 popular songs, librettos, and light operas, including the hits "Nobody's Lookin' but de Owl and de Moon" (1901) and "Under the Bamboo Tree" (1902). James and Rosamond together composed the Negro national anthem "Lift Every Voice and Sing" in 1900. Johnson, who dedicated his life to advancing the status of African Americans, was a key designer of the New Negro Renaissance of the 1920s. Along with W. E. B. DuBOIS, he was one of the period's most articulate spokespersons, arguing the interconnectedness between black art and black politics.

Johnson was raised in Jacksonville, Florida, one of the period's most progressive cities. Johnson's mother, Helen Louise Johnson, a schoolteacher, was originally from Nassau, Bahamas. His father James, a Virginian, was the headwaiter at the St. James hotel in Jacksonville. Helen and James senior, both freeborn blacks, sheltered the young James from the complications of racial identity in the United States. When James was nine years old, a preacher asked him what he wished to be when he grew up, to which James confidently replied, "I am going to be governor of Florida" (quoted in Williams, ix). However, when working as a schoolteacher in the "backwoods of Georgia" he grasped the divisive nature of American race relations.

He later wrote in his autobiography, "in all of my experience it was this period that marked . . . the beginning of my knowledge of my own people as a 'race'" (119). After graduating from Atlanta University, a HISTORICALLY BLACK COLLEGE, Johnson accepted a position as principal of the Stanton School in Jacksonville and established it as the first black high school in Florida. In 1898, he passed the Florida state bar exam—the first African American to do so—but rather than practice law or continue his administrative position at Stanton, he moved to New York City and began collaborations with his brother and Bob Cole. Together they formed the popular Broadway songwriting team Cole and the Johnson Brothers, which catered to Broadway audiences in innovative ways; they prospered for four years. Professionalism is an unremitting theme in Johnson's writing, and the success of Cole and the Johnson Brothers symbolized the team's deliberate project to raise the "status of the Negro as a writer, composer, and performer in the New York theater and world of music" (*Along This Way* 172–173).

In 1905, Johnson toured Europe, and after a year there he decided to pursue a career in diplomatic service. He received his first post in 1906 as a United States consul in Puerto Cabello, Venezuela. Three years later he was commissioned to head the United States Consulate in Corinto, Nicaragua. While in Nicaragua, he began writing poetry, which he published in *The Century Magazine* and *The Independent.* In 1910, he married Grace Nail, who had grown up in a traditional, middle-class black neighborhood in Brooklyn. Continuing to write poetry through this period, Johnson revisited the manuscript of a novel he had begun years earlier while studying literature at Columbia University with Brander Matthews, who had read the first two chapters of the manuscript and encouraged Johnson to keep writing.

In 1912, Johnson anonymously published the novel under the title *The Autobiography of an Ex-Colored Man.* In this novel, Johnson's anonymous narrator, a musician and composer, comes to grips with his biracial identity by eventually passing for white. Though poorly received in its first printing, when scant attention was paid to African-American novels, some critics today consider it the finest American novel of the 1910s. Alfred Knopf, whose imprint published many HARLEM RENAISSANCE texts in the 1920s, republished the novel in 1927 at the height of the New Negro Renaissance. By then the public was eager for African-American writing, and the novel was an enormous success. In this later edition, Johnson's name appeared prominently on the dust jacket, and he received numerous letters from a confused public inquiring about various periods of his life. "That is, probably," he admits in his autobiography, *Along This Way,* "one of the reasons why I am writing the present book" (239).

Johnson quit the Foreign Service in 1913 and became a columnist for the *New York Age,* a black-run newspaper that supported BOOKER T. WASHINGTON over DuBois in the famous debate over the two politicians' disparate methods of activism. Johnson chose the finer points from each side in an attempt to reconcile seemingly irreconcilable differences. In 1916 he became the national organizer of the NATIONAL ASSOCIATION FOR THE ADVANCEMENT OF COLORED PEOPLE (NAACP) and within four years transformed that organization from one with three full-time staff members and a membership of less than 9,000 to one that boasted 165 branches and 44,000 members nationwide. In 1920, he became the first African American to head the NAACP.

During the 1920s, the decade of the Harlem Renaissance, then called the New Negro Renaissance, Johnson took a pragmatic look back in African-American history to find a usable past upon which to buttress the authority and legitimacy of African-American art forms in his own time. Many of his findings are collected in *The Book of American Negro Poetry* (1922) and *The Books of American Negro Spirituals* (1925, 1926). His preface to *The Book of American Negro Poetry* is foremost a pronouncement that African-American poetry and music are "the only things artistic that have yet sprung from American soil and been universally acknowledged as distinctive American products" (quoted in Andrews, xiv). African-American culture, he maintained, was the only singularly American culture uncompromised by European influences. The preface charts

the course of African-American cultural production, citing dance steps, such as the "cakewalk" and
the "shimmy"; music, like spirituals, ragtime, and
the BLUES; and poetry, from the 18th-century slave
poet Phillis Wheatley to writers of his own time—
PAUL LAURENCE DUNBAR, CLAUDE MCKAY, John W.
Holloway, and JESSIE FAUSET, to name a few. He
emphasized the artistic quality of the work, as
"nothing will do more to change that mental attitude [racism] and raise [the Negro's] status than a
demonstration of intellectual parity by the Negro
through the production of literature and art" (vii).
He argued that "dialect" poetry was no longer a
viable poetic form; it had, for too long, been associated with weak-minded sentimental tales and
racist propaganda. "*Traditional* Negro dialect as a
form for Aframerican poets," he wrote later, "is absolutely dead" (*God's Trombones*, 8). His preface to
The Book of American Negro Poetry contains a passage that outlines his vision of African-American
poetry, which can be applied to other artistic and
social forms as well:

> What the colored poet in the United States
> needs to do is something like what Synge did
> for the Irish; he needs to find a form that will
> express the racial spirit by symbols from within
> rather than by symbols from without—such as
> the mere mutilation of English spelling and
> pronunciation. He needs a form that is freer
> and larger than dialect, but which will still hold
> the racial flavor; a form expressing the imagery,
> the idioms, the peculiar turns of thought and
> the distinctive humor and pathos, too, of the
> Negro, but which will also be capable of voic-
> ing the deepest and highest emotions and aspi-
> rations and allow the widest range of subjects
> and the widest scope of treatment. (xl–xli)

Along with these collections, he produced *God's
Trombones: Seven Negro Sermons in Verse* (1927), a
book of poetry inspired by black preachers he had
heard over the years. Despite his secular beliefs,
Johnson found in Negro sermons a folk tradition
that rivaled the already well-documented African-
American traditions, such as spirituals, plantation
tales, and dance steps. One evening in Kansas City,
he witnessed a powerful preacher move his audience with a voice "not of an organ or a trumpet,
but rather of a trombone, the instrument possessing above all others the power to express the wide
and varied range of emotions encompassed by the
human voice" (*God's Trombones*, 7). Before the
preacher concluded his sermon, Johnson had already begun to compose his poem, "The Creation,"
which was later included in *God's Trombones*. This
volume succeeds in capturing the cadence and
rhetorical flourish of Negro preaching, though he
admits his poetry leaves out the most important
elements of the experience—namely, the reactions
of the congregation and the preachers' irresistible
intonations (*God's Trombones*, 10).

In 1930, Johnson published a history of blacks
in New York from the colonial period to the Harlem Renaissance titled *Black Manhattan*, which
remains a nearly definitive reference guide on the
subject. The same year that *Black Manhattan* appeared, he was awarded the Adam K. Spence Chair
of Creative Literature and Writing at Fisk University in Nashville, Tennessee, a position that was
created specifically for him and that he held until
his death in 1938. His last great book, *Along This
Way: The Autobiography of James Weldon Johnson*,
is not only a major autobiographical achievement
but also an important resource for understanding
American cultural history from 1870 to 1930. The
frantic pace of his career was punctuated by enormous artistic and political successes. Johnson's
last words in *Along This Way* reflect the breadth
and depth of his life's work, from his experiences
as an educator, diplomat, intellectual, and artist,
to his pragmatic approach to spirituality: "each
day, if [man] would not be lost, he must with renewed courage take a fresh hold on life and face
with fortitude the turns of circumstance. To do
this, he needs to be able at times to touch God;
let the idea of God mean to him whatever it may"
(414). The James Weldon Johnson Memorial Collection of Negro Arts and Letters, a vital collection
of letters, manuscripts, and memorabilia pertaining to African-American life, now resides at Yale
University.

BIBLIOGRAPHY

Andrews, William L. Introduction. In *The Autobiography of an Ex-Colored Man,* by James Weldon Johnson (1912). New York: Penguin Books, 1990.

Baker, Houston A., Jr. *Singers of Daybreak: Studies in Black American Literature.* Washington, D.C.: Howard University Press, 1974.

Bell, Bernard. *The Afro-American Novel and Its Tradition.* Amherst: University of Massachusetts Press, 1987.

Collier, Eugenia. "James Weldon Johnson: Mirror of Change." *Phylon* 21 (Winter 1960): 351–359.

Fleming, Robert E. *James Weldon Johnson.* Boston: Twayne, 1987.

Dowling, Robert M. "A Marginal Man in Black Bohemia: James Weldon Johnson in the New York Tenderloin." In *Post-bellum, Pre-Harlem: The Achievement of African-American Writers, Artists, and Thinkers, 1880–1914,* edited by Caroline Gebhard and Barbara McCaskill, 216–246. New York: New York University Press, 2006.

Gates, Henry Louis, Jr. Introduction. In *The Autobiography of an Ex-Colored Man* (1912). New York: Vintage Press, 1990.

Skerrett, Joseph T., Jr. "Irony and Symbolic Action in James Weldon Johnson's *The Autobiography of an Ex-Colored Man.*" *American Quarterly* 32 (1980): 540–558.

Sondra Kathryn Wilson. Introduction. In *Along This Way: The Autobiography of James Weldon Johnson,* by James Weldon Johnson (1933). New York: Da Capo Press, 2000.

Robert M. Dowling

Jones, Edward P.   (1951–   )

Pulitzer Prize–winning novelist and short fiction writer Edward P. Jones was born in Washington, D.C. His illiterate mother, Jeanette S. M. Jones, a native of North Carolina, supported the family, Jones, his sister, and his disabled brother, by washing dishes and scrubbing floors. Although Jones earned an English degree at Holy Cross College, a Jesuit school in Massachusetts, he was briefly homeless after he graduated. In 1979, at the invitation of John Casey and JAMES ALAN McPHERSON, Jones attended the University of Virginia, where he received his M.F.A. in 1981. For the next two decades, he worked with *Tax Notes,* a financial magazine, and wrote fiction at night. He has taught fiction at Princeton University, George Mason University, the University of Maryland, and University of Virginia.

Although Jones admits he is addicted to watching television, thinking, and writing, he also acknowledges that reading has honed his craft. He states:

> I always loved reading. When I started reading black writers, I discovered two books that had a great impact on me: Ethel Waters's *His Eye Is on the Sparrow* and RICHARD WRIGHT's *NATIVE SON.* I felt as if they were talking to me, since both books had people in them that I knew in my own life. I was shocked to learn black people could write such things. A memorable moment for me occurred when I finished Ellison's *INVISIBLE MAN,* turned it over and saw the picture of the author. I was amazed that a black man had written something like this. (Fleming 254)

Jones was influenced by a number of favorite writers, including ANN PETRY, PAUL LAURENCE DUNBAR, GWENDOLYN BROOKS, William Faulkner, and Anton Chekhov; however, he confesses that James Joyce's *Dubliners* is the primary inspiration for his collection of stories *Lost in the City* (1992). Winner of the PEN/Hemingway Award and finalist for the National Book Award. The 14 stories are set in the poverty-ridden neighborhoods of Washington, D.C., in the 1960s and 1970s. Jones, in this collection, juxtaposes a variety of themes through a wide range of characters, young and old, who struggle daily for spiritual survival in a cold, cruel world. In such stories as "The Girl Who Raised Pigeons," "The Night Rhonda Ferguson Was Killed," "The Store," "His Mother's House," "Gospel," "A New Man," and "Marie." Jones brilliantly captures the heartbeat of the "lost city" and depicts how it is still possible for people to preserve fragile bonds of family and community in the midst of endless adversity.

Jones won the Pulitzer Prize for his first novel, *The Known World* (2003), which critics describe as an "exceptional," "powerful," "fascinating" debut novel of epic proportions that ranks with the works of Faulkner, TONI MORRISON, and Gabriel Garcia Marquez. *The Known World* is set in Manchester County, Virginia, in 1855, and centers around the life and death of black Virginia farmer and former slave Henry Townsend, who gains his freedom, acquires 50 acres of farmland, and becomes a slave master to 33 slaves, whom he treats as a white master would. After Townsend dies, the "known world" that centers on his Virginia plantation gradually disintegrates: Freedmen are reenslaved, slaves run away to freedom, his mistress consorts with servants, and white men get away with murder. According to St. John, "By focusing on an African American slaveholder, Jones forcefully demonstrates how institutionalized slavery jeopardized all levels of civilized society so that no one was really free" (131).

Commenting on the writing of his carefully researched book, which was also selected for the Today Show Book Club, Jones stated during an interview:

> I was trying to find out how these people survived in these horrifying conditions. I think one way the slaves survived was through the strength of their families. In many ways, we are facing the same problem: the unraveling and destruction of our families and the consequences of that. Families indicate we have a love for something beyond ourselves and that is the key to our survival. (Fleming 254)

Jones is the recipient of the Lannan Foundation Grant (1994, 2003), the Cleveland Foundation Anisfield Wolf Book Award (2004), and a National Endowment for the Arts fellowship. His stories and articles have been published in numerous journals and magazines, including *ESSENCE, CALLALOO, Ploughshares, Paris Review,* and *The New Yorker.*

Jones continues to build his oeuvre, capturing the attention of American readers across racial and educational lines. Heralded as a new talent, Jones takes his writing seriously. When asked about the current popular trends of African-American literature, Jones answered: "I refuse to write about ignorance, despair and weakness, [or] about people going to clubs and doing dumb things. I don't want to write about 'you go, girl' people. I want to write about the things which helped us to survive: the love, grace, intelligence and strength of us as a people" (Fleming, 254).

BIBLIOGRAPHY

Fleming, Robert. "Just Stating the Case Is 'More than Enough'" (Interview with Edward P. Jones). *Publishers Weekly* 250, no. 32 (August 11, 2003): 254.

Grossman, Lev. "On Top of the World." *Time,* 19 April 2004, p. 74.

Jackson, Lawrence P. Interview with Edward P. Jones. *African American Review* (Spring 2000): 95.

Review of *Lost in the City. Publishers Weekly* 239, no. 15 (March 23, 1992): 59.

Review of *The Known World. Kirkus Review* 71, no. 14 (July 15, 2003): 928.

St. John, Edward. Interview with Edward P. Jones. *Library Journal* 128, no. 13 (August 2003): 131.

Loretta G. Woodard

Jones, Gayl   (1949–   )

Although Gayl Jones has only recently received critical and public attention, she has distinguished herself over the last 25 years as a teller of intense psychological tales. Early in her career she wrote of violence and madness in the lives of African Americans, especially women, in vivid detail. She did so by allowing the victims to speak for themselves. In her early work, the stories focus on physical and sexual abuse and its psychological effects; the later poetic narratives present the historical experience of slavery, especially in Brazil. More recently, her novels have emphasized the possibility of healing within the context of personal and social problems. In all the work, the voices of the speakers follow the black oral tradition.

Both the oral tradition and the desire to tell stories emerged from Jones's childhood in Lexington, Kentucky. She found the languages of both everyday experience and of storytelling to be rich with possibility when she began her career. Writing narratives was also a part of her family heritage. Her grandmother wrote plays for the church, and Jones's mother, Lucille, began writing when she was in fifth grade and later created stories to entertain her children. Jones herself began writing stories when she was seven or eight.

In addition to this personal education, she received training in the public schools of Lexington, which were segregated until she was in 10th grade. From Lexington, she went to Connecticut College, where she majored in English and received prizes for her poetry. After graduating in 1971, she undertook graduate studies in creative writing at Brown University under the direction of William Meredith and MICHAEL S. HARPER. While still at Brown, she published her first novel. After receiving her B.A. in 1976, she went on to teach at the University of Michigan. Since then, she has lived and taught in France and the United States.

In her fiction, Jones creates worlds radically different from those of "normal" experience and of conventional storytelling. Though the narrators of her early novels and short stories are close to if not over the edge of sanity, the experiences they record reveal clearly that society acts out of its own obsessions, often violently. The authority of these depictions of the world is enhanced by Jones's refusal to intrude on or judge her narrators. She remains outside the story, leaving the readers with none of the usual markers of a narrator's reliability. She gives these characters the speech of their region, which, by locating them in time and space, makes it more difficult to dismiss them; the way they speak has authenticity that carries over to the stories they tell. The results are profoundly disturbing tales of repression, manipulation, and suffering.

CORREGIDORA (1975), Jones's first novel, is what she calls BLUES narrative, in the sense that it deals with both the pains and pleasures of human relationships. As Ursa tells the story of her female ancestors suffering in slavery under the title character and then the story of her own abuse at the hands of her husband, she shapes experience into a song in which forgiveness for both herself and her husband becomes possible.

Eva's Man (1976), Jones's second novel, is much more radical than Corregidora in plot, theme, and narrative structure. Refusing to accept the tension of men and women, love and hate, that Ursa accepts in her last scene, Eva commits an act of violence—sexual dismemberment—that lands her in a hospital for the criminally insane. Through her obsessive narration, she articulates the experiences that led her to rebel against male domination in such an extreme way. But her story cannot be dismissed simply as the ravings of a psychotic woman, since the tale she tells is, in exaggerated form, the tale of all women in a male-dominated society. By pushing common events beyond their usual limits, the novel forces the reader to reconsider the "normality" of such events.

The stories in White Rat (1977) continue to address concerns with sexuality, violence, madness, and race. "Asylum," for example, is in some ways an abbreviated version of Eva's Man. The narrator is a young woman committed to a mental hospital for her irrational behavior. She will not allow the doctor to examine her genital area, even though she was admitted for deliberately urinating in the living room when her nephew's teacher visited their home. Her madness is apparent in her obsession with acts of violation and in her graphic expression of resistance to such acts.

Song for Anninho (1981), a long narrative poem, addresses similar themes but in the very different context of 17th-century, slave-holding Brazil. Though a poem, this book began as a novel titled "Palmares," and it retains much of the storytelling force of fictional narrative. It is the story of the love between Anninho and his wife Almeyda, the narrator, residents of the maroon community of Palmares. They are separated when Portuguese soldiers overrun the camp, and Almeyda attempts through memory to recapture their lives together. In the process of coming to terms with past and present, she demonstrates, as did Ursa Corregidora, the impact of history and society on the human psyche, but also the power of love to transcend degradation.

Jones's books of poetry that follow Song for Anninho can be seen as developing this notion of women's songs of love and trouble. Euclida,

Almeyda's granddaughter, narrates the title piece of *Xarque and Other Poems.* She remembers the stories of her grandmother, as told by her mother, who has become a healer and a cook for the master. The world has become more complex, and the pure heroism of Almeyda and Anninho is no longer possible.

Orality is also important in the poems that make up *The Hermit Woman* (1983). Most of the poems are narrated by black women of Brazil. "Wild Figs and Secret Places," for example, describes the interaction between a woman of vast local knowledge and a mapmaker sent by the colonizers. The text mingles her comments to and about him, her memory of a trial of a woman for consorting with the devil, and his later comments about the narrator to other Europeans. What this blend suggests is the dangerous nature of free women, their resistance to being "mapped," and the Western impulse to control the world by naming it.

The relationship of storytelling to resistance and freedom is also the theme of Jones's book of criticism, *Liberating Voices.* In it she explores the consequences for 20th-century African-American writing of the choice to incorporate aspects of the oral tradition into written literature.

In two more recent novels, *The Healing* (1998) and *Mosquito* (1999), Jones continues the positive direction evident in her poetry. Harlan Jane Eagleton, a beautician turned faith healer, narrates *The Healing.* Her restorative powers are a gift that she neither understands nor exploits. In many ways she seeks to be seen as an ordinary person, dealing with love, loneliness, and human conflict. Her normality in seen as well in her southern black speech, which reinforces the importance to Jones of the oral tradition. The first novel to ever be published by Beacon Press, *The Healing* was nominated for a National Book Award and as a *New York Times* Notable Book for 1998. Jill Nelson of *The Nation* (May 25, 1998) called *The Healing* "a haunting story, beautifully written."

Mosquito is, in some ways, the most radical of Jones's works. Its title character violates all expectations of black narrative in that she is a truck driver working in the Southwest who becomes involved in the sanctuary movement, bringing in Latin American refugees. Her best friend is a Chicana bartender-novelist-detective, and their conversations, as well as Mosquito's narrative, conflate the discourses of black English, "Spanglish," and literary theory. Through the characters and their stories, the author challenges virtually all the stereotypes associated with race and gender in American culture.

Jones's achievement is in her testing of the boundaries of violence, sanity, sexuality, and storytelling as these subjects are represented in both fiction and poetry. She raises profound questions about the dynamics of race and gender and does so in texts that themselves defy conventional classification. Yet, as her criticism suggests, she sees such experimentation in the tradition of African-American literature.

BIBLIOGRAPHY

Byerman, Keith E. *Fingering the Jagged Grain: Tradition and Form in Recent Black Fiction.* Athens: University of Georgia Press, 1985.

Gottfried, Amy S. "Angry Arts: Silence, Speech, and Song in Gayl Jones's *Corregidora.*" *African American Review* 28, no. 4 (1994): 559–570.

Harris, Trudier. "A Spiritual Journey: Gayl Jones's Song for Anninho." *Callaloo* 5 (1982): 105–111.

Lionnet, Francoise. "Geographies of Pain: Captive Bodies and Violent Acts in the Fictions of Myriam Warner-Vieyra, Gayl Jones, and Bessie Head." *Callaloo* 16, no. 1 (1993): 132–152.

Nelson, Jill. "Hiding from Salvation." *Nation,* (25 May 1998), pp. 30–32.

Tate, Claudia C. "*Corregidora:* Ursa's Blues Medley." *Black American Literature Forum* 13 (1979): 139–141.

Keith Byerman

Jordan, June   (1936–1999)

A prolific writer and poetic genius, June Jordan was born on July 9, 1936, in Harlem to Jamaican and Panamanian immigrant parents, Granville Ivanhoe and Mildred Jordan, and raised in the Bedford Stuyvesant section of Brooklyn. She began writing poetry at age seven. Educated at Barnard College and the University of Chicago (and earlier in a virtually all-white environment at Milwood High School and Northfield School for girls), Jordan married Michael Meyer, a student, in 1955; in 1958 they had a son, Christopher David Meyer, and eight years later they divorced. Her poem "Let Me Live with Marriage" records that marriage's unraveling, ending with a heartbreaking Shakespearean couplet: "if this be baffling then the error's proved / To live so long and leave my love unmoved." Jordan taught at City University of New York, Connecticut College, Sarah Lawrence College, State University New York at Stony Brook, and Yale University before accepting her final academic position as a deeply committed professor of African-American studies and director of Poetry for the People at the University of California at Berkeley.

Jordan's early childhood affected her work in remarkable ways. Her father, who was determined to make June a "soldier" because "there was a war on against colored people," instructed her in the survival skills he felt were necessary for her to have, demanding that she memorize and recite—before she was five—Shakespeare's plays, the Bible, and the poetry of PAUL LAURENCE DUNBAR and Edgar Allan Poe.

Jordan is the author of 28 books, including *Some of Us Did Not Die: New and Selected Essays of June Jordan* (2002); *Soldier: A Poet's Childhood* (2000), a bittersweet, unsettling memoir of the first 12 years of June Jordan's life; and *Kissing God Goodbye: Poems, 1991–1997* (1997). Jordan's poems are a singular howl against the relentless laughter of evil. When she is angry, that anger is purposeful. Her voice is decisive, and empowered and it expresses her love for those she has reason to claim in community and sisterhood.

Her determination to fight for social justice is apparent in *Soldier,* which describes her father's misguided frustration, anger, protectiveness, and love emerging in violence: "Like a growling beast, the roll-away mahogany doors rumble open, and the light snaps on and a fist smashes into the side of my head and I am screaming awake: 'Daddy! What did I do?!'" Filled with lyrical recounting of harrowing moments in the Jordan family home, *Soldier* describes her father treating June like the

son he was determined to have, "This child him my son," Granville insisted to his wife: "What you mean by Black? You want that she stay in the pits where they t'row us down here?" Carried by her mother to the Universal Truth Center on 125th Street in Harlem on Sundays, Jordan observed that by the age of two or three, "the distinctive belief of that congregation began to make sense to me: that 'by declaring the truth, you create the truth.'" Despite despair and disappointment at what she saw as her mother's self-abnegation, her mother's influence on her is apparent in her essay "Many Rivers to Cross" and in poems like "Ah Momma," "Gettin Down to Get Over," or "Ghaflah" (its title a reference to the Islamic term for the sin of forgetfulness, the poem itself an acknowledgement of Jordan's mother's suffering in those years before her suicide).

Jordan's poetry includes *Passion* (1980), *Living Room: New Poems 1980–1984* (1985), *Naming Our Destiny: New and Selected Poems* (1989), and *Haruko/Love Poems* (1994). She is the author of a children's biography, *Fannie Lou Hamer* (1972); several plays, one of which, *The Issue,* was directed by NTOZAKE SHANGE at the New York Shakespeare Festival; and two librettos, *Bang Bang Uber Alles* (1985) and *I Was Looking at the Ceiling and Then I Saw the Sky* (1995). Her young adult novel *His Own Where* (1971), nominated for a National Book Award, was the first novel ever published in the United States written entirely in black vernacular.

The author as well of six collections of political essays, Jordan encouraged readers to explore the power, beauty, and linguistic integrity of Black English. In *Civil Wars* (1981), Jordan made an impassioned and eloquent plea for the survival of Black English as a cultural and poetic necessity: "If we lose our fluency in our language, we may irreversibly forsake elements of the spirit that have provided for our survival." In *On Call* (1985), she described translating, with a group of her students, a part of ALICE WALKER's *The Color Purple* into white English so that they could see how much gets lost, how much poetry is turned to prose, in that translation. Among the essays in *Technical Difficulties: African-American Notes on the State of the Union* (1992), the collection that followed *Moving*

Towards Home (1989), three especially resonate: an essay on MARTIN LUTHER KING, JR., "The Man Who Was Not God," which refuses to mistake this great man for a hypocrite; an equally compassionate essay, "Requiem for the Champ," that deconstructs and excoriates the spiritual and economic poverty of Mike Tyson's childhood, a world in which violence and contempt for women were a badge of masculinity; and "The Dance of Revolution," which describes a kind of choreography between "the lone Chinese man who stood in front of the advancing line of tanks at Tiananmen Square" and the tank driver who attempts but fails in his efforts to evade crushing him.

In "Besting a Worse Case Scenario" (*Affirmative Action: Political Essays* 1998), Jordan wrote about her own breast cancer, linking, as she often did, her individual experience with a necessary wider struggle: "I want my story to help to raise red flags, public temperatures, holy hell, public consciousness, blood pressure, and morale—activist/research/victim/morale so that this soft-spoken emergency becomes the number-one-of-the-tip-of-the-tongue issue all kinds of people join to eradicate, this afternoon/tonight /Monday morning."

June Jordan has written poems that demand deepest apprehension, that resist stripping things of their complexity. Her work is a cartography of resistance against racism, against political and cultural and economic colonialism and misogyny. She insisted on the necessity of taking action against injustice, instead of passively—or hopelessly—waiting for things to change, because, as she has so wryly observed, no one will do it for us—"God is vague and he don't take no sides." Her poems take place in Chile, Managua, Soweto, and Lebanon, as well as on the streets of America.

In "The Rationale, or 'She Drove Me Crazy'"—at turns ironic, witty, and savagely funny, Jordan deconstructs, and then withers, a man's excuse for sexual violence. The title poem of Jordan's first book, *Who Look at Me* (1969), repudiates the white stare, one that refuses to notice the beauty of blackness, "the turning glory / of a spine." Jordan's poem celebrates a black self that remains intact, alive, growing: "black face black body black mind/ beyond obliterating. . . . / We grew despite the crazy killing scorn / that broke the brightness to be born." "Poem about my Rights" decried the violation of apartheid and Jordan's actual and psychic rape, insisting "I am not wrong: Wrong is not my name / My name is my own my own my own."

Her poems often allude to historical incidents while omitting certain details, so that the poems are experienced first in an almost surreal imagined way, before the reader comes to realize, as in the poem "Greensboro: North Carolina" that the horrifying cruelty she conjures is factually based on such details of the American past (or present) as a white man's acquittal for murder because his black victim dared to say out loud "death to the Klan." In "Richard Wright Was Wrong," she demolishes the racist myth of the black rapist/murderer and describes the "real Bigger Thomas" as "a whiteman," as a figure of power who uses that power to demolish the lives of others, as one who "allocates this/appropriates that, incinerates, assassinates / he hates he hates he hates." "Poem about Police Violence," one of her best-known poems, savages "the diction of the powerful," the "justifiable accident" in which 18 cops "subdue" and "scuffle" one black man to death:

> *What you think would happen if*
> *everytime they kill a black boy*
> *then we kill a cop. . . . .*
> *you think the accident rate would lower*
> *subsequently?*

But June Jordan's love poetry—vulnerable, genuine, principled, and full both of complexity and longing—is also central to her canon, as in the untitled *Haruko/Love Poem:* "I do not forget / the beauty of one braid / black silk that fell / as loose as it fell long." or the final lines from "On a New Year's Eve," in the voice of the speaker watching a lover sleep:

> *and*
> *as I watch your arm*
> *your*
> *brown arm*
> *just*
> *before it moves*

I know
all things are dear
that disappear
all things are dear
that disappear.

Like Whitman, she put her queer shoulder to the wheel to write not only of eros in its widest sense but of a passionate, familial love of humanity. Like GWENDOLYN BROOKS—who, when asked, "Race?" answered "Human," and when asked "Religion?" replied "Kindness"—Jordan claimed her African-American identity most intensely by the political convictions that accompanied her profound sense of moral responsibility to the entire human race. After the 1982 massacre of refugees in Beirut, Jordan declared in "Moving Towards Home," "I was born a Black woman / and now / I am become a Palestinian."

The winner of numerous prizes and honors, among them, Rockefeller and National Endowment fors the Arts grants and the Prix de Rome in Environmental Design for a project originating from a plan for the architectural redesign of Harlem (a collaboration with Buckminster Fuller) in 1998, she received both the American Institute of Architecture's Award as one of the coauthors of a proposal for a design for the African Burial Ground in New York City and a lifetime achievement award from the National Black Writers' Conference.

During a decade long struggle with breast cancer (she died on June 14, 2002), June continued to teach and to write until almost her last breath. Jordan's commitment and love lives on in Poetry for the People, the enormously successful program created in her name at University of California at Berkeley. With outreach to local high schools, church congregations, and correctional facilities as well as to university students from all disciplines, Poetry for the People introduces students to poetry as culture, history, criticism, politics, and practice, requiring students to learn both the technical structure of various forms of poetry and the worldviews that inform specific poetic traditions.

Summoning America in the aftermath of September 11 to honor the dead by fighting for the living, by fighting for justice, not for vengeance,

June yoked the image of cultural survival to her own courageous struggle. *Some of Us Did Not Die* contains a poem in which June imagines a predatory hawk circling above her own dying body:

"He makes that dive
to savage
me
. . . I roll away
I speak
I laugh out loud
Not yet
big bird of prey
not yet."

BIBLIOGRAPHY

Ards, Angela. "The Faithful, Fighting, Writing Life of Poet-Activist June Jordan, 1936–2002." *Black Issues Book Review* 4, no. 5 (September/October 2002): 63–64.

DeVeaux, Alexis. "A Conversation with June Jordan." *Essence,* September 2000.

Erickson, Peter, "June Jordan." In *Dictionary of Literary Biography.* Vol. 38, *Afro-American Writers after 1955: Dramatists and Prose Writers,* 146–162. Detroit: Gale Research Co., 1985.

———. "The Love Poetry of June Jordan." *Callaloo* (Winter 1986): 221–234.

MacPhail, Scott. "June Jordan and the New Black Intellectuals." *African American Review,* 33, no. 1 (Spring 1999): 57–71.

Lynda Koolish

Jubilee   **Margaret Walker Alexander** (1966)
Preceding such award-winning novels as Alex Haley's *Roots* (1976), TONI MORRISON's *BELOVED* (1987), and SHERLEY ANNE WILLIAMS's *DESSA ROSE* (1986), MARGARET WALKER's *Jubilee* in many ways initiated the neo–slave narrative genre in 20th century African-American literature. In it Walker chronicles Vyry Johnson's movement from slavery to freedom. Submitted as part of her work toward a Ph.D. degree at the University of Iowa, *Jubilee* is based on the oral stories Walker's grandparents,

former slaves, told her as bedtime stories during her childhood. In her dedication, Walker wrote that *Jubilee* was dedicated "to the memory of my grandmothers: my maternal great-grandmother Margaret Duggans Ware Brown, whose story this is; my maternal grandmother, Elvira Ware Dozier, who told me this story; and my paternal grandmother, Margaret Walker."

Jubilee follows Vyry's life from her childhood during the antebellum years to the early Reconstruction period. Vyry, the daughter of a white plantation owner, John Dutton, and his black slave mistress, Sis Hatte, is two years old when the novel begins. Her mother, on her deathbed, asks to see her last child. After Hatte's death, Mrs. Dutton summons the child to the Big House to serve as chambermaid for her white half sister and playmate, Lillian, who looks like Vyry's identical twin, as retribution for her husband's infidelity. (Hatte produced 15 slave children for Mr. Dutton.) Vyry's rite of passage into her role as slave comes early in her experience, when Mrs. Dutton throws the contents of Lillian's chamber pot into her face because Vyry forgot to empty it one morning. Following the death of her mother and surrogate mothers and the sale of Aunt Sally, a grieving Vyry becomes the head cook in the Big House by default. Although she attempts to run away with her children and Randall Ware, her husband, a free black, on the Underground Railroad, Vyry is caught, punished, and returned to slavery.

Emancipation means freedom, but Vyry, a woman of commitment and the highest morals, remains on the plantation to be near Lillian, whose failing physical and mental health require her continued support. Vyry also stays because she is convinced Randall Ware will return for the family he left behind when Vyry was captured and returned to slavery. Although she remains faithful and waits to reunite with Ware, Vyry, who, like the heroine Clotel in William Wells Brown's novel *Clotel, Or the President's Daughter* (1854), is white enough to pass but does not choose to do so, marries Innis Brown, "a maroon"; moves with him and the children to Alabama; and builds a new life in freedom together as a family and as farmers. "And in their

joy to be building a home of their own, everything seemed possible" (267).

Walker draws Vyry's and Innis's lives against the history of blacks in America during the historical period she covers. She provides credible insights into life on the plantation, the separation of black families during slavery, the Civil War, and black quests for meaning, political freedom, education, and economic stability during this period. The strength of the novel, most critics agree, is Walker's treatment and characterization of Vyry who, according to Bernard Bell, is one of "the most memorable women in contemporary Afro-American fiction" (287). Further describing her as a "pillar of Christian faith and human dignity," Bell concludes that Vyry "commands our respect first as an individual and then as a symbol of the nineteenth century black womanhood" (287).

BIBLIOGRAPHY

Bell, Bernard. *The Afro-American Novel and Its Tradition.* Amherst: University of Massachusetts Press, 1987.
Walker, Margaret. *Jubilee.* New York: Bantam Books, 1966.

Wilfred D. Samuels

Juneteenth   Ralph Ellison (1999)

Although Ralph Ellison had been working on *Juneteenth*, his second novel, since the completion of *Invisible Man* (1952), it was published posthumously, in 1999. In 1967, the original manuscript of *Juneteenth*—then more than 300 pages in length with several of the chapters already published as short stories or excerpts—was destroyed in a house fire. By the time of Ellison's death in 1994, eight chapters had appeared in print. Although in the work Ellison emphasizes many of the same themes found in his monumental, classic first novel, he was not satisfied with *Juneteenth*'s development during the many years he spent working on it. However, the executor of his estate, critic and scholar John Callahan, finally published the work as a novel. Editing the existing sections and reconstructing the remainder of the novel from Ellison's notes, Callahan presented *Juneteenth,* the finished product, in 1999. For the most part critics have been generally receptive of Callahan's attempt and Ellison's legacy.

While *Juneteenth* suffers by comparison to *Invisible Man,* it clearly illustrates Ellison's stylistic genius and his continuing exploration of African-American history. The novel follows the interactions of two characters, Reverend Hickman and Senator Sunraider (known as Bliss when he was a child). Although the senator is a racist southern politician, when Reverend Hickman learns about a plot to assassinate him, he tries to warn the senator but is too late. Wounded in the attempted assassination, the senator calls the reverend to his bedside and, in a series of dream-like flashbacks, their family relationship is unveiled. Sunraider, who has been "passing" for white, is a victim of his own self-hatred. As a child, Sunraider, who was called Bliss, was placed in the care of his uncle, Hickman, a former jazz musician who became a traveling preacher. During his travels, Hickman took Bliss along with him as a performer and child preacher. Aided by memory and Hickman's storytelling, Sunraider recovers his past and his identity to find psychological, though not physical, healing.

Ellison uses Sunraider's healing process as a metaphor for the importance of historiography and storytelling—the need to remember the past in healthy ways. In those spaces where Sunraider's memory fails him, the audience is invited to tell their own stories of the African-American past in order to confront the negative portrait of African-American life, embodied by Sunraider's choice to pass as white rather than embrace his black identity. As Ellison suggests, this process will finally guarantee that all African Americans will know the freedom and the possession of self promised by the Union troops on "Juneteenth," the unofficial holiday celebrating black emancipation.

BIBLIOGRAPHY

Butler, Robert J. "The Structure of Ralph Ellison's *Juneteenth.*" *College Language Association Journal* 46, no. 3 (March 2003): 291–311.

Johnson, Loretta. "History in Ellison's *Juneteenth.*" *Studies in American Fiction* 32, no. 1 (Spring 2004): 81–99.

Yukins, Elizabeth. "An 'Artful Juxtaposition on the Page': Memory, Perception, and Cubist Technique in Ralph Ellison's *Juneteenth.*" *PMLA* 119, no. 5 (October 2004): 1247–1263.

Tracie Church Guzzio

K

Karenga, Maulana (Ron N. Everett)
(1941–)

Born on July 14, 1941, in Parsonsburg, Maryland, the son of a Baptist minister, the activist, scholar, educator, and creator of the "Seven Principles of Blackness," Maulana Karenga received his B.A. degree from City College of Los Angeles. He continued his education at the United States International University and at the University of Southern California, where he earned two doctoral degrees, in political science and social ethics. During the early 1960s, at the height of the CIVIL RIGHTS MOVEMENT, Karenga met MALCOLM X, with whom he debated and discussed the value of BLACK POWER and imperatives of social change.

In 1965 Karenga, who would later add the title "maulana" to his name, which in Swahili means "master teacher," founded Us (for "just us black folks"), through which he promoted cultural nationalism and separatism. Following a dispute with members of the Black Panther Party, which resulted in the death of two students at the University of California, Los Angeles, and charged on two counts of felonious assault and one count of wrongful imprisonment, Karenga was sentenced to the California State Prison system for 10 years. Upon his release he restructured and reestablished his organization—now called US, United Slaves Organization (US Organization)—and formu-lated a new philosophy, Kawaida, which in Swahili means reason and tradition. He founded a Pan-African holiday, Kwanzaa, a cultural holiday of seven days of observation, and his doctrine of *Nguzu Saba*, the "Seven Principles of Blackness," to guide Kwanzaa celebration, which takes place from December 26 to January 1 after Christmas.

Kwanzaa was first celebrated in California in 1967. Each day coincides with one of the principles of Nguzo Saba, which formulate the fundamental values of Kwanzaa. These principles are

1. *Umoja,* meaning unity: the principle of unity of family, community, nation, and the Pan-African world.
2. *Kujichagulia,* meaning self-determination; espouses self-definition, self-defense, the creation of self, and speaking for oneself.
3. *Ujima,* meaning collective work and responsibility: the commitment to active and informed collectivity on common issues and interests.
4. *Ujamaa,* meaning cooperative economics: the principle of shared resources and shared wealth.
5. *Nia,* meaning purpose: the principle of a collective vocation of building, defending, and developing the black national community.

6. *Kuumba*, meaning creativity: the principle of building as opposed to destroying and of being proactive as opposed to reactive or fluid.

7. *Imani*, meaning faith: the principle of being committed to the collective as well as the self.

From 1967 to 1968 Karenga worked with Congressman Adam Clayton Powell, Jr., to hold the historic 1967 Black Power conference in Newark, New Jersey. This conference called for a partitioning of America into two separate states. One state was to be the homeland of black people, the second to be the homeland of white people.

Karenga, through his scholarship, helped shape the BLACK ARTS MOVEMENT and concepts of Afrocentricity, which were popularized by Molefi Asante in *Afrocentricity* (1989). In 1978 Karenga authored *Introduction to Black Studies,* a comprehensive and perhaps the most widely used introductory text in black studies curricula.

In 1979 Karenga took the post of chair of the black studies department at California State University at Long Beach. His contemporaries have recognized Karenga's career as an activist scholar and awarded him with the National Leadership Award for Outstanding Scholarly Achievements in Black Studies from the National Council for Black Studies, the Diop Exemplary Leadership Award from the department of African-American studies of Temple University, among numerous other awards for scholarship, community service, and leadership.

BIBLIOGRAPHY

Franklin, John Hope, and Alfred A. Moss. *From Slavery to Freedom: A History of African Americans.* 8th ed. Vol. 2. New York: McGraw-Hill, 2000.

Karenga, Maulana. *Introduction to Black Studies.* 3d ed. Los Angeles: University of Sankore Press, 2002.

———. *Kawaida Theory: An African Communitarian Philosophy.* Inglewood, Calif.: Kawaida Publications, 1966.

Gwinyai P. Muzorewa

Kaufman, Bob (1925–1986)

Committed, as biographer Mel Clay notes in *Jazz, Jail and God,* "to a lifestyle where all behavior was directed to fulfillment of his art and muse" (x), poet Bob Kaufman was born in New Orleans, the son of a black mother and a Jewish father. Choosing the sea over a classroom during his early teens, he became a merchant marine, using the nine times he traveled around the world and the many cultures he experienced during his travels as living textbooks and simultaneously exploring the creative worlds of F. García Lorca, Hart Crane, T. S. Eliot, Walt Whitman, Vladimir Lenin, and Karl Marx. Abandoning the sea after 20 years, Kaufman embraced the political left and became a union organizer in post–World War II America, a role that left him with lifelong psychological and physical scars. Kaufman, according to Clay, "learned the dreams and fears of his fellow men first hand in prisons, in meeting halls, and in hospital wards" (x), environments that reflect Kaufman's eclectic and, given his unconventional and anarchistic behavior, troubled life.

Kaufman's life as poet formally began in the 1950s when he traveled to New York, where he met Allen Ginsberg and William S. Burroughs and became, like LeRoi Jones (AMIRI BARAKA) and TED JOANS, a meaningful player in Greenwich Village's "experimentation and heresy" (Clay, x) in art, the Beat movement. Kaufman, together with Ginsberg, Bill Margolis, and John Kelley, became one of the movements leading architects in San Francisco's North Beach when they founded and published *Beatitude* magazine in 1959. Although a contemporary of such black poets as MARGARET WALKER, GWENDOLYN BROOKS, ROBERT HAYDEN, and MELVIN TOLSON, and although "a caustic critic of American culture" (214), according to Hayden, like many of the writers of the BLACK ARTS MOVEMENT Kaufman was seldom associated with them, although he identified himself as black. Writing to the editors of the *San Francisco Chronicle* (October 5, 1983), Kaufman declared, "One thing is certain I am not white. Thank God for that. It makes everything else bearable" (quoted in Henderson, 206).

In addition to three broadsides published by City Lights Books: *Second April* (1959), *Abominist Manifesto* (1959), and *Does the Secret Mind Whisper* (1960), Kaufman published three collections of poems: *Solitudes Crowded with Loneliness* (1965), *The Golden Sardine* (1967), and *The Ancient Rain* (1981). In addition, his work has appeared in several journals, including *Swank, Nugget,* and *Jazz Hot.* Published also in French, *Solitude* brought Kaufman immediate international attention, making him better known in France than in America, even among black poets.

Stylistically and thematically, Kaufman's poetry is often imprinted with the sound and beat of African-American music, specifically BLUES and jazz, the heartbeat of his New Orleans birthplace, as one finds, for example, in "Walking Parker Home," in which a roll call of jazz masters is improvisingly sounded:

> *Sweet beats of jazz impaled on slivers of wind*
> *Kansas Black Morning/First Horn Eyes/*
> *Historical sound pictures on New Bird wings*
> *Lurking Hawkins/shadow of Lester/*
> *realization.*

His speaker in "Blues Notes," dedicated to Ray Charles on his birthday, is equally celebratory: "He bursts from Bessie's crushed black skull / One cold night outside of Nashville, shouting, / And grows bluer from memory, glowing bluer, still."

Kaufman's surrealistic prose poems and free verse are not only the centerpieces of his oeuvre but also, more important, tropes of his life. Like many of the musicians he invokes, Kaufman, a nominee for England's coveted Guinness Poetry Award and the recipient of a grant from the National Endowment for the Arts, also descended into a devastating world of drugs and alcohol, engulfed by a darkness of self-imposed silence and insanity. He describes his internal turmoil in his autobiographical poem, "I Wish" with biting irony and humor:

> *I wish that whoever it is inside of me,*
> *Would stop all that moving around.*
> *& go to sleep, another sleepless year*

> *like the last one will drive me sane. (Golden Sardines 66)*

Kaufman died in his sleep in January 1986. His life fulfilled his proclaimed commitment to his first love: "This is the end, / Which art, that proves my glory has brought me / I would die for Poetry" (*Golden Sardines* 24).

BIBLIOGRAPHY

Clay, Mel. *Jazz, Jail and God: Bob Kaufman, an Impressionistic Biography.* San Francisco: Androgyny Books, 1987.

Hayden, Robert, ed. *Kaleidoscope: Poems by American Negro Poets.* New York: Harcourt, Brace & World, 1967.

Henderson, Stephen. *Understanding the New Black Poetry. Black Speech and Black Music as Poetic References.* New York: William Morrow & Company, 1973.

James Celestino

Kelley, William Melvin   (1937–)

William Melvin Kelley, who was born in the Bronx to William Kelley, an editor, and Narcissa Agatha Kelley, grew up the only black child in his Italian neighborhood. He was president of the student council of Fieldston School, a private, mostly white high school. He attended Harvard University, where he studied creative writing with Archibald MacLeish. Kelley delighted readers with five books before 1970: the novel *A DIFFERENT DRUMMER* (1962); his collection of short stories, *Dancers on the Shore* (1964); and the novels *A Drop of Patience* (1965), *dem* (1967), and *Dunsfords Travels Everywheres* (1970). His short story "Carlyle Tries Polygamy" was published in the August 4, 1997, issue of *The New Yorker.* Though Kelley's stories from *Dancers on the Shore* were frequently anthologized through the early 1970s, and though *A Different Drummer* was the subject of more than two dozen critical articles and book chapters, Kelley stopped either writing or publishing in 1970.

Most critical attention on Kelley's work has focused on the rebellion of a Negro farmer named Tucker Caliban who salts his fields, slaughters his cattle, and marches out of state. As every other Negro in the fictional, unnamed state follows him, the novel is a magic-realist parable of boycotts and black pride: a resolution of the MALCOLM X/MARTIN LUTHER KING, JR. binary. Like much of Kelley's work, *Drummer* expresses the urgent appeal for social justice and black pride of the BLACK ARTS MOVEMENT through modernist (and specifically Faulknerian) fictional techniques. The novel *dem* has been reissued by Coffee House Press's Black Arts Movement series. It is dedicated to "The black people in (not of) America" and marshals satirical modes associated with Nathanael West, John Hawkes, and ISHMAEL REED in its treatment of "dem" white people. Mitchell Pierce is a white man in a Madison Avenue advertising agency whose home life falls apart in a phantasmagoric and irrealistic mixture of dream, parody, and reality. His wife gives birth to twins, one white and one black—suggesting one of many infidelities: His wife may or may not have had an affair with the maid's boyfriend. Pierce watches his life change from the definition of success to something altogether more confusing.

A Drop of Patience tells the coming-of-age story of Ludlow Washington, a jazz musician who is blind since birth and grows up in a state home. Washington struggles and prevails; he eventually becomes a visionary leader within the New York jazz world. As in *A Different Drummer* and *dem,* Kelley's main theme is moral blindness, and in this work he literalizes and deepens the metaphor.

Like many other African-American writers who were celebrated as African-American writers, Kelley often expressed annoyance at being read as a black American first and as an artist second. He develops artistic experimentalism to a peak in *Dunsfords Travels Everywheres,* a three-part novel that reflects the artistic freedom of Joyce's *Finnigans Wake.* This novel does not abandon race as a theme—it demands a "unmisereaducation" and follows two characters, one a Harlem black and one a Harvard black, through a grand tour—but

the Joycean language accomplishes a displacement of sorts, and race is effectively de-emphasized. Kelley lives in Harlem and teaches in the creative writing program at Sarah Lawrence College and at the Taos Institute of Art.

BIBLIOGRAPHY

Gayle, Addison. *The Way of the New World: The Black Novel in America.* New York: Anchor, 1975.

Klotman, Phyllis. "Examination of the Black Confidence Man in Two Black Novels: *The Man Who Cried I Am* and *dem.*" *American Literature* 44 (January 1973): 596–611.

John Whalen-Bridge

Kenan, Randall Garrett   (1963–   )

As part of a new generation of African-American writers, Randall Kenan combines realistic detail with surreal narrative to create a southern fictional world. In his fiction, he depicts Tims Creek, North Carolina, as a space occupied by demons and ghosts as well as the ordinary lives of its residents. Through this portrayal, he reveals the difficult and sometimes tragic experiences of homosexual young men. At the same time, his stories do not fit the conventional modes of either racial or gay fiction.

Though born in Brooklyn, at the age of six weeks Kenan was taken by his paternal grandfather to Wallace, North Carolina, and then to Chinquapin in rural Duplin County, to be raised by his father's relatives. The name "Kenan" has long been associated with the area, specifically with a white immigrant slave owner. Some of his slaves were apparently the ancestors of the author. The black Kenans were prosperous farmers with a staunchly conservative religious faith. Formal schooling came at a segregated kindergarten and then at integrated public schools. Kenan's interest in science led him to major in physics when he enrolled at the University of North Carolina. In addition to science courses, he took classes in African-American studies and, in his sophomore year, signed up for a creative writing class. This combination led him away from physics and into an English major. The summer after his junior year, he went to Oxford University to study British literature. He graduated with a B.A. in English and a minor in physics in December 1985.

The following February Kenan landed a job at Random House as a receptionist. Within a year, he had been promoted, first to assistant to the vice president and then to assistant editor at Knopf. During this time, he continued to work on a novel, *A VISITATION OF SPIRITS* (1989), which was published by Grove Press. The novel is set in Tims Creek, a rural Carolina community. Its central family is the Crosses, similar to the Kenans in being prominent, having white and black branches, and having a town named after them. In creating this world, which he continues to use in later fiction, Kenan was influenced by William Faulkner's Yoknapatawpha County in inventing for it a history, a culture, and a set of recurring characters. It is also possible to see, as he has acknowledged, the importance of Katharine Anne Porter, Gabriel Garcia Márquez, Yukio Mishima, and JAMES BALDWIN in his writing.

The publication of *A Visitation of Spirits* opened new career possibilities for Kenan. He left the publishing world in 1989 to begin teaching at Sarah Lawrence and Columbia University. Since 1994 he has held various visiting writer positions and is currently professor of creative writing at the University of Memphis. During this time, he pulled together some of the stories he began earlier with material originally intended as part of *A Visitation of Spirits.* This collection was published as *Let the Dead Bury the Dead* (1992). It was nominated for the Los Angeles Times Award, was a finalist for the National Book Critics Circle Award, and was named a Notable Book for 1992 by *The New York Times.*

Let the Dead Bury the Dead is a series of short fiction about Tims Creek and a long oral history. As in the novel, the central themes are death and desire, in the context of the supernatural. The stories that focus on desire are much more conventionally realistic, though their subject matter has generally been considered taboo, especially among African-American writers. "The Foundations of the Earth," for example, tells of Maggie MacGowan Williams's developing friendship with the white gay lover of her grandson, Edward. The final story, or more properly novella, is also the most radical in terms of structure. "Let the Dead Bury the Dead" is set up as a book put together by James Malachai Greene, found and edited by Reginald Gregory Kain (who has the same initials as Kenan). It is composed of an oral history, diary entries, letters, and passages of academic discourse on a variety of subjects, complete with footnotes. The story told, primarily by Zeke (from *A Visitation of Spirits*), is the history of Tims Creek, a narrative of magic, racial violence, and a maroon community created by escaped slaves, which eventually becomes the town.

Kenan's two books since the short stories find him turning away from fiction, though they still involve narrative. In 1994, he published a short biography of James Baldwin as part of the Lives of Notable Gay Men and Women series, designed for young adult readers. *Walking on Water: Black American Lives at the Turn of the Twenty-first Century* addresses the question of what it means to be black in America through interviews with dozens of people from Martha's Vineyard, Massachusetts, to Anchorage, Alaska, and from all walks of life. Here, as elsewhere, Kenan focuses on the diversity within black life as much as the difference it makes in the nation. As he makes clear in the introduction, he does not believe that race is a fixed biological category but that it is a product of history and culture. Early in his career, Randall Kenan has displayed versatility not often found in writers of any age. In long and short fiction, he has successfully combined the realistic and the fantastic, traditional storytelling with experimentation, and the spiritual with the mundane.

BIBLIOGRAPHY

Betts, Doris. "Randall Garrett Kenan: Myth and Reality in Tims Creek." In *Southern Writers at Century's End,* edited by Jeffrey J. Folks and James A. Perkins, 9–20. Lexington: University Press of Kentucky, 1997.

Harris, Trudier. *The Power of the Porch: The Storyteller's Craft in Zora Neale Hurston, Gloria Naylor, and Randall Kenan.* Athens: University of Georgia Press, 1996.

Holland, Sharon Patricia. "(Pro) Creating Imaginative Spaces and Other Queer Acts: Randall Kenan's *A Visitation of Spirits* and Its Revival of James Baldwin's Absent Black Gay Man in *Giovanni's Room.*" In *James Baldwin Now,* edited by Dwight A. McBride, 265–288. New York: New York University Press, 1999.

McRuer, Robert. "A Visitation of Difference: Randall Kenan and Black Queer Theory." *Journal of Homosexuality* 26, no. 2–3 (1993): 221–232.

Keith E. Byerman

Kennedy, Adrienne (1931–)

Adrienne Kennedy was born Adrienne Lita Hawkins to Cornell and Etta Haugabook Hawkins in Pittsburgh on September 13, 1931. Her father was a social worker and executive officer of the YMCA; her mother was a teacher. Kennedy attended Ohio State University, where she began writing fiction while taking a course in 20th-century literature. She received a bachelor's degree in education in 1953 and, soon thereafter, married Joseph Kennedy; they had two sons, Joseph C. and Adam. The Kennedy family moved to New York City, where Adrienne studied creative writing at Columbia University while her husband taught at Hunter College.

The Kennedys traveled to Europe and Africa in 1960. Kennedy's writing was influenced while she was living in West Africa. She states, "I couldn't cling to what I had been writing—it [Africa] changed me so. . . . I think the main thing was that I discovered a strength in being a black person and a connection to West Africa" (qtd. in Draper, 1149). Elements of the new geographical spaces appear in Kennedy's *Funnyhouse of a Negro.* Selected by Edward Albee for the Edward Albee Playwrights' Workshop, this play had a successful off-Broadway run; it won a *Village Voice* Obie Award in 1964. She was also awarded a CBS Fellowship at the School of Drama in 1973, a Creative Artists public service grant in 1974, a Yale Fellowship in 1974, and an American Book Award in 1990. Kennedy has served as a lecturer at Yale University and the University of California at Berkeley; she has taught playwriting at Princeton and Brown Universities.

Kennedy's autobiographical writing includes characters who are psychologically linked to her and are in search of identity and agency in American society. She explains, "I see my writing as being an outlet for inner psychological confusion and questions stemming from childhood. . . . It's really figuring out the 'why' of things—that is, if that is even possible" (quoted in Draper, 1149).

In *Funnyhouse of a Negro* and *The Owl Answers,* Kennedy uses African and English images to display the fragmentation of her biracial protagonists. Her contemporary characters seek subjectivity and agency while having conversations with William Shakespeare, William the Conqueror, and Patrice Lumumba. Kennedy wrote these biracial, women-driven plays at a time when other African-American dramatists were concerned with black pride and power.

In Kennedy's *A Lesson in Dead Language,* a teacher dressed as a white dog leads menstruating, white-clad students on a philosophical journey toward adulthood. *A Rat's Mass* depicts an incestuous relationship between hybrid siblings with rat and human features who regress to a state of animal-like existence. In her mystery novel and journal *Deadly Triplets,* she includes "An Evening with Dead Essex," which was inspired by a sniper incident in Vietnam. In "A Movie Star Has to Star in Black and White," Kennedy shares her fascination with Hollywood stars Bette Davis, Marlon Brando, and Montgomery Clift.

Kennedy's play *Sleep Deprivation Chamber,* written with her son Adam, captures his real-life experience of being abused by corrupt police officers. *The Ohio State Murders* includes Kennedy's *The Alexander Plays,* in which character Suzanne Alexander chronicles Kennedy's real-life experiences as a student at Ohio State. The other three plays of this volume are *She Talks to Beethoven, The Film Club,* and *The Dramatic Circle.*

Kennedy's multifaceted talents can also be found in such works as *A Beast's Story,* which describes the unkind treatment of animals by humans; *The Lennon Play: In His Own Write,* cowritten with John

Lennon; *Sun;* "A Poem for Malcolm X Inspired by His Assassination"; *A Lancashire Lad,* based on the childhood of Charlie Chaplin; and *Orestes* and *Electra,* adaptations of the plays by Euripides.

In 1993, Kennedy published "Letter to My Students" in the *Kenyon Review,* which reintroduces her audience to the Suzanne Alexander character, who chronicles events from past Kennedy literary works. This essay, along with many of Kennedy's previous and more recent work, can be found in *The Adrienne Kennedy Reader* (2001), which also includes *June and Jean in Concert (Concert of Their Lives), A Letter to Flowers, Sisters Etta and Ella (Excerpt from a Narrative),* and *Grendel and Grendel's Mother.* Kennedy won an Obie for *June and Jean in Concert* in 1996.

BIBLIOGRAPHY

Draper, James P., ed. *Black Literature Criticism: Excerpts from Criticism of the Most Significant Works of Black Authors over the Past 200 Years.* Detroit: Gale Research, 1992.

Kennedy, Adrienne. *The Adrienne Kennedy Reader.* Minneapolis: University of Minnesota Press, 2001.

Weaver, Angela E. "Women of Color: Women of Words." School of Communication, Rutgers University. Available online. URL: http://www.scils.rutgers.edu/~cybers/Kennedy.html. Accessed October 17, 2006.

Daintee Glover Jones

Killens, John Oliver   (1916–1987)

John Oliver Killens, an accomplished novelist, editor, essayist, activist, and critic, was born in Macon, Georgia, on January 14, 1916. He challenged racial issues directly, writing about segregation and racism in the South and the military. From 1936 to 1942, Killens attended college at night while working during the day for the National Labor Relations Board. He attended various colleges and universities, including Morris Brown College and Howard, Columbia, and New York universities, and he taught at two HISTORICALLY BLACK COLLEGES AND UNIVERSITIES, Fisk and Howard universities. Killens served in the Pacific during World War II. For the last seven years of his life, Killens was the writer-in-residence at New York's Medgar Evers College. During this time, his Brooklyn home served as a meeting place for various artists and activists.

Killens traced the desire to become a writer back to his childhood, when he listened to his great-grandmother's stories of her childhood experiences in slavery. In the late 1940s, Killens began meeting with young writers John Henrik Clarke, ROSA GUY, and Walter Christmas in a Harlem storefront. This group, which became the Harlem Writers Guild in 1950, continues to meet to this day. Some of the more notable participants have included OSSIE DAVIS, MAYA ANGELOU, TERRY MCMILLAN, AUDRE LORDE, ALICE CHILDRESS, and WALTER MOSLEY. Killens, Clarke, Guy, and Christmas banded together as the guild in order to critique each other's stories, united as writers with a nationalistic outlook and commitment to social change. A decade later, the guild became identified with the BLACK ARTS MOVEMENT. Killens is thought of as one spiritual father who inspired a genre of African-American protest novels.

Killens's 1954 novel *Youngblood* was the first work to be published by a member of the guild. Set in Crossroads, Georgia, *Youngblood* follows Joe Youngblood and family in their struggle to define and maintain their dignity in the Jim Crow South. Unlike many of Killens' contemporaries, including RICHARD WRIGHT, RALPH ELLISON, and JAMES BALDWIN, who, in their work focus on a similar theme and consequently, more often than not, on the Great Migration, southern blacks moving and adjusting to the urban North, Killens does not allow the Youngblood family to migrate. Instead they remain in their southern home and struggle with dignity to survive. Killens highlights this struggle through Joe Youngblood's relationship with Richard Myles, a teacher from the North who has come to the South to identify with the families' and workers' efforts for fairness. Myles is considered a member of the Youngblood family after Joe Youngblood's martyrdom.

Killens's second novel, *And Then We Heard the Thunder* (1962), details the experiences of a soldier, Solly Saunders, in the segregated military. Killens traces Saunders's route from basic training in Georgia to battlefields throughout the South Pacific. The novel is also notable in recording a three-day race riot among American soldiers in Sydney, Australia. Killens's third novel, *'Sippi* (1967), begins with the Supreme Court 1954 decision in *Brown v. Board of Education* to outlaw segregation in education. The central character, Jesse Chaney, a jubilant black sharecropper, is enamored with this landmark decision. Wanting to enact his own end to segregation, Chaney confronts his employer, Charles Wakefield, a rich, white Mississippi plantation owner and so-called "friend of the Negro," wishing to address him as Charles, in place of the prescribed "Mister Charlie." Rather than an embracing response of equality, Wakefield calls Chaney "nigger," directly informing Chaney that the Court's decision is irrelevant, as far as he is concerned. Thus, *'Sippi* is a realistic exploration of the struggle to change the traditional class relationships of a South steeped in the social hierarchy that retained the legacy of slavery.

Killens's fourth novel, *The Cotillion, or One Good Bull Is Half the Herd* (1971), which is set in the North, explores and critiques intraracial issues and satirizes the black middle class and class division within the black community. *The Cotillion* follows the efforts of the young and beautiful Yoruba of Harlem to bring her 1960s Black Power sensibilities to her black middle-class family. The novel reaches an eventful and humorous climax when Yoruba and friends arrive at her debutante ball wearing a militant afro and African Dashiki instead of the coiffure and formal style of the old South. Killens wrote two screenplays, *Odds against Tomorrow* (1959) and *Slaves* (1969), the latter of which was also published as a novel.

Killens contributed to the debate over black aesthetics, publishing major essays in such journals as *The Black Scholar, Negro Digest,* and BLACK WORLD on this central movement. He published a collection of essays, *Black Man's Burden* (1965), and an exploration of the working class in *Black Labor and the Black Liberation Movement* (1970). His essay "The Black Writer vis-à-vis His Country" appeared in ADDISON GAYLE, JR.'s *The Black Aesthetic* (1971),

and "Rappin' with Myself" appeared in *Amistad 2: Writings On Black History And Culture* (1971); In the latter essay he interviews himself on topics concerning black leaders Paul Robeson, MARTIN LUTHER KING, JR., and MALCOLM X. He also wrote two biographical novels: *Great Gittin' Up Mornin': The Story of Denmark Vesey* (1972), based on *The Trial Record of Denmark Vesey* (1970), which he edited, and the posthumously published *Great Black Russian: A Novel on the Life and Times of Alexander Pushkin, African American Life* (1989). Many scholars consider Pushkin "the father of Russian literature"; however, Killens argued that Pushkin's African ancestry should also be viewed as central to his identity. Killens also wrote a book for young adults, *A Man Ain't Nothin' but a Man: The Adventures of John Henry* (1975). Killens worked with Jerry Ward to compile *Black Southern Voices: An Anthology of Fiction, Poetry, Drama, Nonfiction, and Critical Essays* (1992). This collection featured 56 famous and less-known southern African-American authors. His last novel, *The Minister Primarily,* remains unpublished.

Killens, who served as vice president of the Black Academy of Arts and Letters from the 1977 foundation of the Junior Black Academy of Arts and Letters, received Pulitzer Prize nominations for *Youngblood* (1954), *And Then We Heard* (1964), and *The Cotillion* (1971). However, during the years his works were nominated, prizes for the novel were not awarded. Killens shares this distinction with Richard Wright, whose NATIVE SON (1940) was nominated in a year (1941) when no award for the novel was given.

Although firmly entrenched in the school of social realism, Killens's work has not been included in contemporary canonical anthologies. Killens's exclusion partially stemmed from his political affiliation and embrace of leftist politics. But criticism also came from blacks who did not take kindly to his criticism of Ellison's INVISIBLE MAN (1952). In a review printed in *Freedom,* a journal edited by Paul Robeson, Killens derided Ellison's novel for promoting stereotypes, the "Uncle Toms, pimps, sex perverts [and] guilt ridden traitors," regarding it as a mainstream publisher's dream of a black novel.

Although out of print for the most part, Killens's work has been translated into Italian, Spanish, French, Chinese, Russian, and German. His body of work, influence as a teacher and mentor, and communal political focus make Killens a vital, if underappreciated, proponent of African-American culture. Killens died of cancer on October 27, 1987, in Brooklyn, New York.

BIBLIOGRAPHY

Gilyard, Keith. *Liberation Memories: The Rhetoric and Poetics of John Oliver Killens.* Detroit: Wayne State University Press, 2003.

Rivera, Louis Reyes. "John Oliver Killens: Lest We Forget." In *New Rain.* Vol. 9: *Our Fathers/Ourselves.* Bronx: Blind Beggar Press, 1999.

Ray Black

Kincaid, Jamaica (1949–   )

Recognized as one of the most innovative and provocative Caribbean-American writers of the late 20th century, Jamaica Kincaid was born Elaine Potter Richardson on May 25, 1949, in Antigua, British West Indies. For the first nine years of her life, Kincaid lived in Saint John's, the capital of her Caribbean homeland, with her aging father and his young wife, Annie Richards. Kincaid left Antigua for New York when she was 16 years old to work as an au pair and study nursing—an experience that is the basis of her second novel, *Lucy* (1990). Rather than pursuing nursing, though, Kincaid studied photography and wrote for various magazines, including a breakthrough interview with Gloria Steinem for the magazine *Ingénue.* Eventually Kincaid graduated to writing for *The New Yorker,* where she published sections of *At the Bottom of the River* and *Annie John.* Kincaid changed her name when she began publishing her work in America.

Kincaid immediately won recognition as an important new voice in American fiction when she published *At the Bottom of the River* (1983), a collection of short stories, dreams, and reflections. It won the Morton Dauwen Zabel Award from the American Academy and Institute of Letters and Arts in 1983. Although critics found the book obscure, others praised its poetic explorations of the themes of mother-daughter relationships and ordinary life. These two themes are also chronicled in Kincaid's first novel, *Annie John,* which recounts the struggles of a young girl who becomes progressively estranged from her mother and is often assumed to be autobiographical. When asked in a 1985 interview about the similarities between her own life and that of the protagonist in *Annie John,* Kincaid responded, "The feelings are autobiographical, yes. I didn't want to say it was autobiographical because I felt that would be somehow admitting something about myself, but it is, and so that's that" (quoted in Smith, 806).

In books about Antigua, her Caribbean island homeland, Kincaid employs a highly poetic literary style. Her work is celebrated for its rhythms and imagery, as well as its elliptical narration and strong characterizations. Kincaid's work explores issues both grand and personal: the nature of individual consciousness, the pain of family relationships, the nearness of history and the devastation of cultural domination. CALL AND RESPONSE, an anthology of African-American literary tradition, identifies Jamaica Kincaid as one of the major emerging voices of the new wave of black literary culture.

Kincaid's third published book, *A Small Place,* is perhaps her most critical work. An essay addressed to a tourist from North America or Europe traveling in Antigua, *A Small Place* examines Antigua's postcolonial culture. It employs stark prose throughout that exposes the destructive effects of colonialism. Kincaid's narration is doubtlessly informed by her own status as an exile. While some reviewers were upset by its rage, others, especially in Europe, praised its powerful critique of imperialism.

Kincaid followed up *A Small Place* with her fourth novel, *Lucy* (1990). This tale, in many ways, is complementary to her first novel. *Lucy* is a young Antiguan woman who comes to New York to work as an au pair for a young white couple and feels estranged from the mother she left behind. *The Autobiography of My Mother* is another text that centers on the theme of motherhood. Kincaid's narrators often seem alienated from those around them, seeking both control over and freedom from these human connections known as relationships. Kincaid's tight, lyrical prose guides the reader through her tortured recollections of her mother. Her books depict the relationships that take on the dual gravity of mother-daughter association as well as of the hegemonic interactions between motherland/country (England) and daughter island (Antigua). Stacking these parallel visions on top of each other and infusing them with her own feelings of anger and suffocation, Kincaid draws the reader through the struggle for personal development not only of her narrators but also of the writer herself.

My Brother (1997) is a searing account of her brother, Devon, who died of AIDS in 1996. The narrative relentlessly attacks the postcolonial Antiguan culture that imprisoned Devon. Kincaid's voice reveals an alienating detachment from her brother's death and her former life in Antigua yet maintains a frank recounting of family life on the island.

All of Kincaid's work engages in a serious reflection on what it means to live in a world fraught with postcolonial politics of identity and tense intergenerational conflict implicit in the mother-daughter relationship. Kincaid remains a prominent figure in African-American literature, acknowledged as a talented and unique writer. She lives in Vermont with her husband and their two children.

BIBLIOGRAPHY

Guzzio, Tracy Church. "The Kincaid File." *Literary Cavalcade* 53, no. 5 (2001): 27.

Hill, Patricia Liggins, et al., eds. *Call and Response: The Anthology of the African American Literary Tradition.* Boston: Houghton Mifflin Company, 1998.

Lichtenstein, David P. "A Brief Biography of Jamaica Kincaid." Caribbean Web. Available online. URL: http://www.postcolonialweb.org/caribbean/kincaid/bio.html. Accessed October 17, 2006.

McLarin, Kim. "BIBR Talks with Jamaica Kincaid." *Black Issues Book Review* 4, no. 4 (2002): 34.

Smith, Ian. "Misusing Canonical Intents: Jamaica Kincaid, Wordsworth, and Colonialism's 'Absent Thing'" *Callaloo* 25, no. 3 (2002): 801–820.

Kindra Briggs

Kindred Octavia Butler (1979)

OCTAVIA BUTLER's novel *Kindred* explores the history of slavery within the genre of science fiction. Like TONI MORRISON's *BELOVED* and SHERLEY ANNE WILLIAMS's *DESSA ROSE,* the work also belongs to the category of the neo–slave narrative, illustrating the link between past and the present racist attitudes in America. While *Kindred* might be considered an example of "speculative" fiction, its portrait of antebellum Maryland and the horrors of plantation slavery are profoundly realistic.

The novel opens in the bicentennial year (1976) in California. Dana and Kevin Franklin are in the process of moving when suddenly Dana is transported back in time to the 19th-century, where she saves the life of a drowning boy named Rufus Weylin. Rufus, the son of a slave owner, is Dana's white great-grandfather, who will at some point in his future rape Dana's great-grandmother, Alice, one of his slaves. Dana moves back and forth across time periods several times in the work, reinforcing Butler's theme that the past and the present are inexorably bound. In the midst of her transportations, Dana decides to educate Rufus about the evils of slavery, knowing that this might prevent her own birth in the future. Despite Rufus's dependence on and even trust in Dana, he develops into the violent sexist and racist that he was destined to become. The fault lies not in Dana's ability as a teacher but in America's indoctrination of its citizens in the ideology of white male supremacy.

Dana's experience presents her with a visceral history of slavery that provides her with strength and a renewed sense of her racial identity in ways that are healthy and even celebratory. Her life is endangered when Rufus threatens to rape her as well, and it is only by sacrificing a part herself that she is able to extract herself from the past. Her last return from the 19th century occurs on July 4, 1976—a symbolic marker of Dana's freedom from slavery and from the burden of history. The significance of the date and Dana's escape also remind us that the inception of America as a free land was dependent on enslaving men and women of color. Like other science-fiction writers, Butler uses the genre to comment on the problems of the present in a manner that forces its readers to confront their society's attitudes to race, identity, and history.

BIBLIOGRAPHY

Brooks-Devita, Novella. "Beloved and Betrayed: Survival and Authority in *Kindred.*" *Griot* 22, no. 1 (Spring 2003): 16–20.

Reed, Brain. "Behold the Woman: the Imaginary Wife in Octavia Butler's *Kindred.*" *College Language Association Journal* 47, no. 1 (2003): 66–74.

Steinberg, Marc. "Inverting History in Octavia Butler's Postmodern Slave Narrative." *African American Review* 38, no. 3 (2004): 467–476.

Tracie Church Guzzio

King, Martin Luther, Jr.   (1929–1968)

Martin Luther King, Jr., was born on January 15, 1929, in Atlanta, Georgia; he was the first son of Reverend Martin Luther King, Sr., and Alberta Williams King. At his birth, his father named him Michael King, but in 1934, he changed the name to Martin Luther King, Jr. King excelled in the segregated public schools of Atlanta and graduated with honors from Booker T. Washington High School, earned a degree in sociology from Morehouse College (1948) at the age of 15, graduated with honors from Pennsylvania's Crozer Theological Seminary (1951), and earned a Ph.D. degree in systematic theology from Boston University (1955). King married his lifelong wife, Coretta Scott King, in 1953, and they had four children, Yolanda, Martin III, Dexter, and Bernice. King's first job as pastor was at the Dexter Avenue Baptist Church of Montgomery, Alabama. In 1960, he returned to Atlanta

to copastor with his father the Ebenezer Baptist Church. He was the author of several works, including *Stride toward Freedom: The Montgomery Story* (1958), *Why We Can't Wait* (1963), and *Strength to Love* 1963), a collection of sermons.

King is best known as the charismatic leader of the modern CIVIL RIGHTS MOVEMENT, a role he was propelled into in Montgomery, Alabama, in December 1955, after Rosa Parks refused to give up her bus seat to a white man and was jailed. The 26-year-old King was elected by blacks to head the Montgomery Improvement Association, which successfully boycotted Montgomery's segregated public transportation system for more than a year. King used a nonviolent, civil disobedience strategy and encouraged his followers to love their enemies. Harassment, threats, and the bombing of King's house drew media attention on Montgomery, eventually forcing the federal government to confront the injustice and racism created by more than a half century of Jim Crow laws. On a visit to India in 1959, King studied the teachings of Mohandas Gandhi and refined his nonviolent, civil disobedience strategy.

In 1957, King and a cadre of black ministers organized the Southern Christian Leadership Conference (SCLC), a movement that would become international, making King's influence felt as far as independence-seeking Africa. However, the movement achieved its greatest success in 1963 with demonstrations in Birmingham, out of which came King's "Letter from a Birmingham Jail" and the March on Washington, during which King shared the hopes of the Civil Rights movement in his "I Have A Dream" speech, concluding with the words of the old Negro spiritual: "Free at last, free at last, thank God almighty, we are free at last." Feeling the momentum of King's leadership and the Civil Rights movement, Congress passed the 1964 Civil Rights Act, prohibiting segregation and discrimination. For his strong moral stance and his civil rights efforts, King received the 1964 Nobel Peace Prize.

In 1965, King led a voting rights protest march starting in Selma, Alabama, with some 300 participants and growing to some 20,000 by the time marchers arrived in Montgomery. As a result of their effort, President Lyndon B. Johnson signed the Voting Rights Act of 1965, in August, which suspended and later banned literacy and other voter qualification tests.

Near the end of his life King sought to cast a wider political net with his public criticism of American foreign policy in the Vietnam conflict, his concern with broader economic issues through the Poor People's Campaign on Washington, and his support for striking black garbage workers in Memphis, Tennessee, during the spring of 1968, where he delivered his last speech, "I've Been to the Mountaintop," at Mason Temple the night before he was assassinated, on April 4, 1968, while standing on the balcony of the Lorraine Motel. James Earl Ray, an escaped white convict, pleaded guilty to the shooting in 1969 and spent the rest of his life in prison, where he died in 1998. King is entombed at the Martin Luther King, Jr., National Historic Site in Atlanta, Georgia.

The son and grandson of black preachers, King exemplified the power of black orality, represented best in the black sermon as literary art form, taking the style of the black preacher to its highest dramatic and oratorical forms. This was not surprising, given that, by his third year at Crozer Theological Seminary, King, who was ordained a Baptist minister at age 18, was recognized as a powerful speaker. He not only employed but mastered the rhythms and antiphonal (call-response) patterns of the African-American oral tradition. The black church and its music provided the hotbed of King's spiritual fervor, his organizational structure, and his base of operation for the Civil Rights movement.

King, who grew out of strong family roots, demonstrated great courage, practiced high moral leadership, and, gave his life for the cause of justice and righteousness. Guided by his wife, Coretta Scott King, the Martin Luther King, Jr., Center for Social Justice was developed in 1969 and is part of the National Historic Site of his birthplace and the Ebenezer Baptist Church. In 1983, Congress set aside the third Monday in January as a legal public holiday in honor of King's birthday.

BIBLIOGRAPHY

Branch, Taylor. *Parting the Waters: America in the King Years 1954–63.* New York: Simon & Schuster, 1988.

Carson, Clayborne, and Peter Halloran, eds. *A Knock at Midnight.* New York: Warner Books, 1998.

Garrow, David. "King the March the Man the Dream." *American History* 38 (August 2003): 26.

Erskine, Noel Leo. *King among the Theologians.* Cleveland: Pilgrim Press, 1994.

Mays, Benjamin E. *Born to Rebel.* Athens: University of Georgia Press, 1987.

France A. Davis

Knight, Etheridge   (1931–1991)

In "The Idea of Ancestry" in which he catalogues his family tree, Knight writes that his only uncle had disappeared when he was 15: "just took / off and caught a freight (they say) . . . he causes uneasiness in / the clan, he is an empty space." Ironically, Knight could have written this about himself, for although he knew family, and in fact attended family reunions from which his uncle, "whereabout unknown," was physically absent, Knight, though physically present at such clan gatherings, could not find total contentment—could, given his drug addiction, only "almost" catch up with himself.

Knight was born in the brown hills and red gullies of the still-segregated society of Corinth, Mississippi, in 1931, where he soon found himself snared by racism and oppression. A school dropout by age 14, he would use the underworld of juke joints, pool halls, and poker games as his classrooms before joining the army from 1947 to 1951. He served in Korea, returning to the United States with shrapnel wounds and a drug addiction for medals. He would later write: "I died in Korea from a shrapnel wound and narcotics resurrected me" (Rowell, 973). Turning to robbery to support his heroin addiction, Knight was arrested while meandering across the United States and sentenced to eight years in the Indiana State Prison.

In prison, as he explained, "poetry brought me back to life." *Poems from Prison* (1968), Knight's first book of poems, was published one year before he was released. In her preface to the collection, GWENDOLYN BROOKS celebrated Knight's poetry as "a major announcement . . . certainly male—with formidable austerities, dry grins, and a dignity that is scrupulous even when lenient." Knight's reputation grew rapidly as his poems, essays, and short stories began to appear in *Negro World* (BLACK WORLD), *Journal of Black Poetry, Prison Magazine, Cardinal Poetry Quarterly, Music Journal,* and other periodicals.

Poems from Prison was a critical success. "Vital. Vital," wrote Brooks. Eugene Redmond wrote: "Knight roams the deep crevices of black spiritual and psychic world as he combines the language of the prison subculture with the rhythms of black American street speech" (*Drumvoices,* 385). Between 1969 and 1973 Knight's work was included in many of the new anthologies of African-American literature, including DUDLEY RANDALL's *Black Poetry* (1969), Adam David Miller's *Dices and Black Bones* (1971), Randall's *The Black Poet* (1971), Brooks's *A Broadside Treasury* (1971), Bernard Bell's *Afro-American Poetry* (1972), RICHARD BARKSDALE and Keneth Kinnamon's BLACK WRITERS OF AMERICA (1972), and STEPHEN HENDERSON's *Understanding the New Black Poetry* (1973).

Knight began his literary career as the BLACK ARTS MOVEMENT was emerging in America, and like poets AMIRI BARAKA, SONIA SANCHEZ (to whom Knight was briefly married), and HAKI R. MADHUBUTI, he embraced its spiritual goals. Thus, like LARRY NEAL, Knight called for the development of a black aesthetic:

> Unless the black artist established a "Black aesthetic," he will have no future at all. To accept the white aesthetic is to accept and validate a society that will not allow him to live. The Black artist must create new forms and new values, sing new songs (or purify old ones); and along with other Black authorities, he must create a new history, new symbols, myths, legends (and purify old ones by fire). And the Black artist, in creating his own aesthetic, must

be accountable for it only to the Black people. (Neal, 258–259)

Knight, an active advocate of poetry as an oral art, sang new songs and mastered the art of "saying poems," as he described his delivery. He was a poet-performer.

In 1970 Knight edited *Black Voices from Prison,* an anthology of prison writing. His vision and style inspired other black prisoners to express themselves creatively and to strive toward a collective celebration of a new black nationalism. He also published three volumes of his own poetry: *Belly Song* (1973), *Born of a Woman* (1980), and *The Essential Etheridge Knight* (1986), which won the American Book Award. Knight, who held teaching positions at University of Pittsburgh, the University of Hartford, and Lincoln University, was recognized with grants and honors from the Guggenheim Foundation, the National Endowment for the Arts, and the Poetry Society of America. Married to May Ann McAnally, with whom he fathered two sons, Knight, before his death in 1991, successfully completed a B.A. degree in American poetry and criminal justice from Martin Center University in Indianapolis.

BIBLIOGRAPHY

Henderson, Stephen. *Understanding the New Black Poetry.* New York: William Morrow & Company, 1973.

Neal, Larry. *Visions of a Liberated Future.* St. Paul: Thunder's Mouth Press, 1989.

Redmond, Eugene B. *Drumvoices, The Mission of Afro-American Poetry, A Critical History.* Garden City, N.Y.: Anchor Books, 1976.

Rowell, Charles H. "An Interview with Etheridge Knight." *Callaloo,* 19, no. 4 (1966): 967–980.

George Barlow

Komunyakaa, Yusef (1947–)

The oldest of five children, Komunyakaa was born in Bogalusa, Louisiana. His family life was tumultuous, mostly because of his father's abuse and extramarital relationships. However, his mother introduced him to books at an early age by purchasing a set of encyclopedias. During his teenage years, Komunyakaa was also influenced to write by JAMES BALDWIN's *Nobody Knows My Name.* During the late 1960s Komunyakaa served in the military in the Vietnam War, where he edited a military newspaper and won a bronze star. Returning home, he enrolled at the University of Colorado, where he earned his bachelor's degree and began writing poetry. Komunyakaa continued with graduate work at both the University of Colorado, where he earned an M.A. degree, and the University of California at Irvine, where he earned an M.F.A. degree. He has taught creative writing for a number of universities, including Princeton University, where he served as professor of humanities and creative writing and was elected chancellor of the Academy of American Poets, and the University of New Orleans, where he met and married Australian writer Mandy Sayer.

A prolific poet, writer, and editor, Komunyakaa has produced a large and impressive body of work, beginning with his first collection of poetry, *Dedications and Other Dark Horses* (1977), *Lost in the Bonewheel Factory* (1979), *Copacetic* (1984), *I Apologize for the Eyes in My Head* (1986), *Toys in a Field* (1986), *Dien Cai Dau* (1988), and *February in Sydney* (1989). During the 1990s, he published *Magic City* (1992), *Neon Vernacular: New and Selected Poems* (1993), and *Thieves of Paradise* (1998) and edited the *Jazz Poetry Anthology* with Sascha Feinstein (1991). He also wrote *Blue Notes: Essays, Interview and Commentaries* (1995). His most recent works include *Talking Dirty to the Gods: Poems* (2000), *Pleasure Dome: New and Selected Poems* (2001), and *Taboo* (2004).

Even though Komunyakaa's poetic style has been characterized as "firmly rooted in the stylistic innovations of early-twentieth century American modernists," his reflection that the black experience should not "particularize the presentation of art" (Komunyakaa 2000, vii) appears in his poetry. Komunyakaa's early poems deal with violence, especially as informed by his experiences in Vietnam and the pain of going home after the war.

The "it" in "Facing It" refers to the Vietnam Veterans Memorial in Washington, D.C. Komunyakaa's speaker declares:

> *I'm inside*
> *the Vietnam Veterans Memorial*
> *again, depending on the light to make a*
> *difference.*
> *I go down the 58,022 names, half expecting*
> *to find*
> *my own in letters like smoke.*
> *I touch the name Andrew Johnson;*
> *I see the booby trap's white flash.*

Another speaker declares:

> *The monsoon uncovers troubled*
> *seasons we tried to forget.*
> *Dead men slip through bad weather,*
> *stamping their muddy boots to wake us*
> *their curses coming easier. ("Monsoon*
> *Season")*

Komunyakaa's use of childhood memories and his experiences in Vietnam connect abstract expressions and images into an improvisational, jazzlike method of pulling readers into the poetry, as is clearly seen in "Tu Do Street";

> *Music divides the evening.*
> *I close my eyes & can see*
> *men drawing lines in the dust.*
> *American pushes through the membrane*
> *of mist & smoke, & I am a small boy*
> *again in Bogalusa. White Only*
> *signs and Hank now.*

Like fellow Louisianan poet KALAMU YA SALAAM, Komunyakaa uses both BLUES and jazz as a backdrop and underpinning for many of his poems.

Komunyakaa's awards for poetry include the Creative Writing Fellowship from the National Endowment for the Arts in 1981 and 1987. He won the San Francisco Poetry Center Award in 1986. In 1994 Komunyakaa was awarded the Pulitzer Prize for *Neon Vernacular,* a collection of poems from his other books along with new poems. From 1989 to 1990, Komunyakaa held the Lilly Professorship of Poetry at Indiana University in Bloomington and the Kingsley-Tufts Poetry Award from Claremont Graduate School.

BIBLIOGRAPHY

Komunyakaa, Yusef. *Blue Notes: Essays, Interviews, and Commentaries.* Edited by Radiclani Clytus. Ann Arbor: University of Michigan Press, 2000.

———. *Neon Vernacular: New and Selected Poems.* Middletown, Conn.: Wesleyan University Press, 1993.
———. *Pleasure Dome: New and Collected Poems.* Middletown, Conn.: Wesleyan University Press, 2001.

Kim Hai Pearson
Brian Jennings

Larsen, Nella (1891–1964).

Nella Larsen, one of the luminaries of the HARLEM RENAISSANCE, has been praised for her treatment, particularly in her major works, of the theme of marginality—the concern with the limits placed on people's lives in America because of race and gender. According to biographer Thadeous Davis, Larsen's preoccupation with this theme has more than a passing connection to her life. Born in Chicago, Illinois, on April 13, 1891, Larsen was the child of a Danish mother and a West Indian father. In spite of her international heritage, however, Larsen was considered legally black. Clearly a victim of the constraints of being female and of mixed heritage in early 20th-century America, Larsen often thematizes these issues in her work.

With a superior education and a marriage of some prominence, Larsen moved within the upper echelons of black society for many years. She entered Fisk University in Nashville, Tennessee, in 1907, studying in a three-year certificate program in the normal department. She continued her studies at the University of Copenhagen, where she audited classes from 1910 to 1912, before returning to New York City to study nursing at Lincoln Hospital. She completed these studies in 1915 and, for a time, worked as a nurse at Lincoln Hospital. Her marriage to the prominent physicist Elmer Samuels Imes in 1919 afforded her access to intellectual and high social circles, but it was apparently unstable throughout its 14 years and ended in a very public divorce in 1933. During these troubled years, Larsen took refuge in books and in the company of a wide circle of Harlem literary associates, including JAMES WELDON JOHNSON, LANGSTON HUGHES, JEAN TOOMER, and JESSIE REDMON FAUSET. She enjoyed the friendship and patronage of WALTER WHITE and CARL VAN VECHTEN as well.

Larsen's commitment to a career as a writer seems to have fermented between 1922 and 1926, when she worked as a librarian with the New York Public Library. Although she had published two "Playtime" articles for children for *Brownies' Book* in 1920, Larsen generated critical attention when her short story "Correspondence" was published in *OPPORTUNITY* magazine in September 1926. However, her major works remain *Quicksand* (1928) and *Passing* (1929), which critics generally agree are largely autobiographical. The central theme of both works is the intersection of race and gender.

Although Larsen's short story "Sanctuary" (1930) led to her becoming the first woman of African-American descent to receive a Guggenheim Fellowship, she was charged with plagiarizing the story. She responded forthrightly to the charge in an essay published in *Forum* in April 1930. Although cleared of the charge, Larsen's career as a writer, if not her writer's "heart," seemed irreparably damaged. She returned to nursing for a livelihood, withdrawing from her former social and intellectual friendships until 1964, when she was found dead in her New York apartment.

Larsen's best known novels, *Quicksand* and *Passing,* focus on the complex lives of her biracial heroines. In *Quicksand,* she relates the story of Helga Crane, who, like the author, is the child of mixed parentage. Helga's mother is also Danish, while her biracial father is of West Indian heritage. Helga, by profession a teacher at a HISTORICALLY BLACK COLLEGE in Naxos, Mississippi, wearies of the hypocrisy of her colleagues. She rejects their notion of racial "uplift." Feeling stifled by their conservative attitudes and behavior, she isolates herself in the oasis of her apartment. To escape and ultimately embark on a quest for personal identity, freedom, and self-actualization, Helga travels to Chicago, Harlem, and Copenhagen before ending up trapped in rural Alabama in an oppressive marriage to a Christian minister. The novel ends with Helga in a prone position, preparing to deliver her sixth child.

Passing, perhaps the more popular of the two novels, is the story of two biracial women and former friends, Clare Kendry and Irene Redfield, who encounter each other while engaged in racial passing in a tea room at a fashionable Chicago hotel. Although black-identified Irene, who is married to a black Harlem physician, periodically engages in this practice, Clare, who is married to a white racist, Jack Bellew, has totally assumed a white identity and lifestyle. Despite her initial reluctance, Irene agrees to meet Clare again. Envious of Irene's comfortable lifestyle, the fact that she does not have to live in fear of being outed, and her social status, Clare begins to visit Harlem, where she is once again able to experience the life she left behind. The story ends tragically as the separate lifestyles created by each of them eventually collide. At the end of the novel, Bellew follows his wife to Harlem, where he discovers her true identity. In the ensuing confusion, Clare either accidentally falls (or Irene pushes her) from a window on the sixth floor of a Harlem residence.

Despite her relatively small literary productivity, Larsen's work has received much critical attention. Critics have primarily focused on details of her near-tragic life and the demise of her promising career as a writer. But critics have also focused on Larsen's vision, recorded primarily through her heroines, which extends beyond the autobiographical to a theme more ancient and universal: the human compulsion to strive for self-actualization in an unfriendly and impersonal environment. This vision, critics argue, links Larsen to American realism. In the end, Larsen's heroines pursue illusory and unrealistic goals of personal freedom and security because they strive for absolutes in a realm of moral relativity. They pursue self-actualization on their own terms, but their efforts are thwarted by the imposition of factors over which they have no control. When Larsen wrote *Quicksand* and *Passing,* she was most probably grappling with difficulties in her own life, but her plots also suggest that she was concerned about the higher moral questions that have, since the beginning of time, engaged the human mind. In returning to nursing, she possibly found some sense of inner peace through service, after grappling, both personally and artistically, with the irreconcilable moral issues posed by a life of striving.

BIBLIOGRAPHY

Brown-Guillory, Elizabeth. "Nella Larsen (1891–1964)." In *Black Women and America: An Historical Encyclopedia,* vol. 1, 695–697. Brooklyn: Carlson Publishing, 1993.

Carby, Hazel. "The Quicksands of Representation." In *Reconstructing Womanhood,* 163–175. New York: Oxford University Press, 1995.

Clemmen, Yves W. A. "Nella Larsen's *Quicksand:* A Narrative of Difference," *College Language Association Journal* 40, no. 4 (June 1997): 458–467.

Davis, Thadious M. *Nella Larsen, Novelist of the Harlem Renaissance: A Woman's Life Unveiled.* Baton Rouge: Louisiana State University Press, 1994.

Hostetler, Ann E. "The Aesthetics of Race and gender in Nella Larsen's *Quicksand.*" *PMLA* 105, no. 1 (January 1990): 35–46.

McLendon, Jacquelyn Y. *The Politics of Color in the Fiction of Jessie Fauset and Nella Larsen.* Charlottesville, Va.: University Press of Virginia, 1995.

Wall, Cheryl. "Passing for What? Aspects of Identity in Nella Larsen's Novels." *Black American Literature Forum* 20 (Spring/Summer 1986): 114–120.

Washington, Mary H. *Invented Lives.* New York: Doubleday, 1987.

Joyce L. Cherry

Lee, Spike (Sheldon Lee)   (1957–)

Born in Atlanta, Georgia, as Sheldon Lee, the future independent filmmaker was nicknamed Spike when he and his family moved to Brooklyn, New York. Only a few years old at the time of the move, Lee would later use the ethnically diverse urban environment as a cinematic canvas for a number of his films. The most productive and well-known African-American director at the beginning of the 21st century, Lee studied filmmaking at New York University, where his student film, *Joe's Bed-Stuy Barbershop: We Cut Heads* (1983), won him praise and an agent. Through release of his first three feature films, Lee commanded the attention of mainstream audiences, critics, and film scholars.

Lee's first independent feature film, *She's Gotta Have It* (1986), moved him into a national spotlight that would shine on him for the next 20 years. A stylized and controversial film, *She's Gotta Have It* follows a contemporary African-American woman, Nola Darling, who leads a life of professional success and sexual independence. Critics often compared her independent spirit to ZORA NEALE HURSTON's JANIE CRAWFORD in *THEIR EYES WERE WATCHING GOD.*

Just as controversial was his second film, *School Daze* (1988), a studio-backed project, which presents the issues of colorism and class within the black community. In a more intense manner, Lee's third film, *Do the Right Thing* (1989) examines more than 15 characters who intersect and clash on a hot summer day in New York's Bedford-Stuyvesant neighborhood. Under the cautionary rap of Public Enemy's "Fight the Power," the movie forces a look into the manner in which race and class erupt into biased attitudes and violent behavior. These latter two films announced a topic that would drive many of Lee's projects—namely, the politics of race in the United States.

An inextricable component of several films was Lee's effort to demystify the filmmaking process, using companion books to encourage aspiring film and video enthusiasts to understand the challenging steps in completing feature-length projects. Lee published *Spike Lee's Gotta Have It: Inside Guerrilla Filmmaking* (1987) and then co-wrote and coedited, with Lisa Jones, the book *Uplift the Race: The Construction of School Daze* (1988). Lee ends that book by observing: "There's a market for black films, it's proven. . . . [A]ll I want to do is make films where my creative integrity is respected and preserved. Where I'm in control" (329). The book *Do the Right Thing: The New Spike Lee Joint* (1989) added to the printing of viewpoints and personal testimonials about the filmmaking process, while the text *By Any Means Necessary: The Trials and Tribulations of the Making of Malcolm X* (1992), written and edited with Ralph Wiley, shared the complications and rewards of completing that film.

Lee followed the movie *Do the Right Thing* with noteworthy films that showed his own particularly visual style and his commitment to exploring African-American experiences. His impressive list of productions includes *Mo'Better Blues* (1990), *Jungle Fever* (1991), *Malcolm X* (1992), *Crooklyn* (1994), *Clockers* (1995), *Girl 6* (1996), *Get on the Bus* (1996), the documentary *4 Little Girls* (1997), *He Got Game* (1998), *Summer of Sam* (1999), *Bamboozled* (2000), the concert film *The Original Kings of Comedy* (2000), *The 25th Hour* (2002), *She Hate Me* (2004), *Inside Man* (2006) and *When the Levees Broke: A Requiem in Four Acts* (2006).

His most ambitious and expensive film, *Malcolm X,* was funded through a combination of studio and private investors. More than three hours in length, the film depicts the life of the celebrated black human rights leader who rose to power both within his Black Muslim religion and within the black community, as recorded in his autobiography, *The AUTOBIOGRAPHY OF MALCOLM X,* written with the assistance of Alex Haley. The film, which starred Denzel Washington in the title role, chronicled the protagonist's criminal past, his prison time and religious conversion, and his political activism and assassination. Lee viewed MALCOLM X as a "hero" and "wanted to send young black youth the message . . . that education and personal growth were the real point of the life of Malcolm X" (Haskins, 87–88). Lee's *Malcolm X,* particularly his emphasis on the full spectrum of the black experience and urban culture, represent well the direct relationship between film and literature. Lee's textual depictions correspond to the written texts of RICHARD WRIGHT and JOHN EDGAR WIDEMAN.

Spike Lee has achieved a distinct significance in African-American culture and American cinema. His advocacy for more black filmmakers and black representation on screen has made him a consistent and demanding voice for inclusion within the Hollywood system and American society in general. Much more than just a filmmaker, Spike Lee has been an activist whose work has been a weapon for transforming old racial politics and celebrating African-American experiences.

BIBLIOGRAPHY

Donalson, Melvin. *Black Directors in Hollywood.* Austin: University of Texas Press, 2003.
Jim Haskins, *Spike Lee: By Any Means Necessary.* New York: Walker and Company, 1997.
Lee, Spike, and Lisa Jones. *Uplift the Race: the Construction of School Daze.* New York: Fireside Books, 1988.

Mel Donalson

Lester, Julius   (1939–   )

A columnist, political activist, author, folk singer, radio personality, and photographer and the son of a Methodist minister who later converted to Judaism, Lester was born in St. Louis, Missouri. He grew up in Nashville, Tennessee, and on his grandmother's farm in Arkansas in the segregated South, where he came to know firsthand the struggles, challenges, achievements, and victories of black life recorded by RICHARD WRIGHT, MAYA ANGELOU, and ERNEST GAINES in their fiction and nonfiction. After graduating from Fisk University with a degree in music and literature in 1960, Lester became actively involved in the CIVIL RIGHTS MOVEMENT, joining the Student Non-violent Coordinating Committee (SNCC) and serving as the head of its photo department from 1966 to 1968.

Before embarking on a career in literature, folklore, and history, Lester was a folk singer; he performed with Pete Seeger, Phil Ochs, and Judy Collins and recorded two albums.

While working for SNCC, Lester wrote and published his first political text, *Look Out Whitey! Black Power Is Gon' Get Your Mama!* (1969), in which he attempts to use his voice and eyes as vehicles of the BLACK POWER movement that burgeoned at the end of the 1960s. He sets out to explain to a primarily white reading audience the political transformation, indeed revolution, taking place in America during this decade, simultaneously recording his own political activism and reflecting his radicalism and ideology, which he also vociferously made known through his weekly radio program for the Pacifica Foundation on New York's WBAI-FM, his live television show on New York's WNET, the black history courses on cultural revolution he taught at the New School for Social Research, and articles he published in *The Guardian* and *Liberation.* Many of his essays were collected and published in *Revolutionary Notes* (1969). As someone who did not merely experience the turbulent 1960s but tried to shape them through political activities, Lester attempted to give insights into this most troubled time in American history in *Search for the New Land* (1969).

Lester gained attention for his award-winning juvenile literature, particularly *To Be a Slave* (1968)—the 1968 Newbery Medal runner-up—and *Black Folktales* (1969). Lester's interest in his personal history as the descendant of slaves led him to collect and write the memories of former slaves in *To Be a Slave,* allowing readers to imagine what it was like to be a slave—to be chattel—though a human being. *To Be a Slave,* which runs the gamut of experiences from being captured in traditional Africa to life on the plantation and life after emancipation, has been a touchstone children's book for more than three decades. Lester also engages the topic of slavery in *Long Journey Home* (1972), *This Strange New Feeling* (1982), and *From Slave Ships to Freedom Road* (1998).

Lester's *Black Folktales* is a powerful record of black orality and its central place in the African-American literary tradition. He tells a variety of tales that run the gamut in the function of folklore. He provides explanation tales in "How God Made the Butterflies," "Why Men Have to Work" and "How the Snake Got His Rattles." He offers an African love story in "The Son of Kim-Ana-u-eze and the Daughter of the Sun and the Moon." Above all, he tells tales of black heroic figures such as High John the Conqueror of slavery days and Stagolee, an urban bad man, and he records black resistance to slavery in "Keep On Stepping" and "People Who Could Fly," a tale that is central to TONI MORRISON's award-winning novel *Song of Solomon*. In the introduction to *Black Folktales,* Lester explains, "Each person who tells a story molds the story to his tongue and to his mouth, and each listener molds the story to his ear. Thus, the same story, told over and over, is never quite the same" (viii). Lester has a well-established reputation as a master storyteller with a powerful, stentorian voice.

Equally well known are Lester's novels, particularly *And All Our Wounds Forgiven* (1994), his fictional account of his Civil Rights and SNCC experience. Lester uses his central characters, John Calvin Marshall (a famous assassinated civil rights leader) and Bobby Card, Marshall's field lieutenant in Mississippi, to provide insights into the physical and psychological complexity of the movement and its impact on participants. Lester uses Marshall's widow, Andrea (whose impending death reunites the characters), and his white mistress, Lisa Adams, to reveal the human frailty and tangled web of Marshall's private, domestic life. Through Card, Marshall's assistant who is tortured by a white southern sheriff, Lester demonstrates the level of emasculation often experienced by black male civil rights workers who practiced Marshall's nonviolent civil disobedience.

Lester's treatment of the Civil Rights movement in *And All Our Wounds Forgiven* was both lauded and criticized for its historical accuracy. Although Lester's credibility in presenting the historical facts about the Civil Rights movement is not questioned (he uses flashbacks with actual discussion and debates that took place during the movement), and although his presentation of such important political leaders as the Kennedys, MALCOLM X, J. Edgar Hoover, and President Lyndon B. Johnson

is generally considered accurate, Lester's treatment of MARTIN LUTHER KING, JR., fictionalized in Marshall, is considered controversial, insensitive, and even denigrating. Particularly problematic for many critics is Lester's emphasis on the private relationship Marshall maintains with Lisa Adams, his personal secretary, travel partner, and hotel bedroom mate at the expense of his devoted wife, the mother of his children. Although there is a sense of healing at the end of the novel, Lester seems to ask if the wounds, particularly the psychological ones, suffered by all participants of the Civil Rights movement were worth it in the end.

Lester, the author of more than 25 books of fiction, nonfiction, children's stories, and poetry, has received or been a finalist for several awards, including the Newbery Honor Award, the American Library Association Notable Book, the National Jewish Book Award (finalist), *The New York Times* Outstanding Book, the National Book Critics Circle (finalist), and the National Book Award (finalist).

In 1971, Lester joined the faculty of the University of Massachusetts, Amherst, where he is a full professor of the Judaic and Near Eastern studies department and adjunct professor in the English and history departments.

BIBLIOGRAPHY

Lester, Julius. *Black Folktales.* New York: Grove Press, 1969.

Wilfred D. Samuels

"Letter from Birmingham Jail"
Martin Luther King, Jr. (1963)

As president of the Southern Christian Leadership Conference (SCLC), MARTIN LUTHER KING, JR., in 1963 identified Birmingham, Alabama, as "probably the most thoroughly segregated city in the United States" (King, 85). His decision to make Birmingham the next battlefield on which to implement his nonviolent civil disobedience strategy brought him condemnation and criticism from fellow clergymen, friends and enemies, black and white. Alabama, they argued, under the leadership of the new governor, Albert Boutwell, would be taking giant steps forward away from the racist and segregationist past promoted and maintained by former governor George Wallace. The prominent evangelist Bill Graham encouraged King to patiently wait, "to put the brakes on" (Miller, 150).

Indirectly identifying King and his supporters as outsiders, ignorant of Alabama's true internal affairs and new promise of progress, eight local fellow clergymen, convinced that the courts, not demonstrations, were the appropriate venues through which to effect change, made their convictions known; and the *Birmingham News* published their views and sentiments in a 13-paragraph article titled "White Clergymen Urge Local Negroes to Withdraw from Demonstrations," on April 13, 1963. The men challenged King, rebuking the Birmingham demonstration as "unwise and untimely" (Miller, 150). Perhaps more important, "the clergymen invoked their religious authority against civil disobedience," the very heartbeat of King's strategy, concluding, "We do not believe that these days of new hope are days when extreme measures are justified in Birmingham" (Branch, 738)

Angered by this rebuke, King, who did not make a habit of addressing his critics, responded by writing an open letter, "Letter from a Birmingham Jail," from his prison cell on April 16, 1963, literally in the margins of the *Birmingham News*, on scraps of paper and on paper borrowed from his assistant, Clarence Jones, who then smuggled it out of the jail. Later published in King's collection of essays *Why We Can't Wait* (1963), "Letter from a Birmingham Jail" represents his most effective and convincing argument on the importance and moral justification of his nonviolent civil disobedience program and pronouncements during the CIVIL RIGHTS MOVEMENT of the 1960s. In it King argues from the fundamental premise that "injustice anywhere was a threat to justice everywhere" (King, 85), making "Letter from a Birmingham Jail," in the end, perhaps the finest apologetic for the modern Civil Rights movement.

Addressing his response to "My Dear Fellow Clergymen," King debunked their argument of the poor timing of his Birmingham demonstrations, arguing, "we must use time creatively, and forever realize that the time is always ripe to do right" (King, 88). In fact, he noted that blacks, who had been waiting more than 300 years for the changes he was working to effect, had "many pent-up resentments and latent frustration. . . . So let [them] march sometime, let [them] have [their] prayer pilgrimages." Time is critical, King concluded, if gains toward freedom were to be made. Blacks had learned that "wait" has almost always meant "never" (88).

Responding to his critics' denouncement of him as an "outside agitator," King responded that when it came to nonviolent civil disobedience and direct action, all are invited members of the community who, in their desire to be accountable, must respond to injustice. Dr. King sought to teach his fellow clergymen, asking, "How does one determine when a law is just or unjust / . . . To put it in the terms of Saint Thomas Aquinas, an unjust law is a human law that is not rooted in eternal and natural law" (King, 89). And he implored, "All segregation statutes are unjust because segregation distorts the soul and damages the personality." (King, 89). Consequently, the clergy, King concluded, had the responsibility to not hide behind traditional church polity but instead to pursue the fulfillment of God's law of love. King insisted that organized religion must leave the comforts of congregational facilities to walk the streets as a partner in the nonviolent struggle for freedom. He reminded them of the four basic steps of a nonviolent campaign: (1) collection of the facts, (2) negotiation, (3) self-purification, and (4) direct action (King, 85). He then informs them, "We have gone through all of these steps in Birmingham. There can be no gainsaying of the fact that racial injustice engulfs this community" (85).

King's "Letter from a Birmingham Jail" had "an instant and astonishing response; it was published in full in *Liberation* and *The Christian Century* as well as in *Gandhi Marg*. . . . At least two separate editions had been published in pamphlet form for the FOR, the American Friends Service Committee, and the American Baptist Convention" (Miller, 180). "Letter from a Birmingham Jail" appeals to young and old, rich and poor, black and white, by citing authorities such as Reinhold Niebuhr and Saint Augustine, by telling stories, with sensitive argument, by comparison to biblical characters, quoting songs, and using visual images.

King closes "Letter" with echoes of hope and expectations of fulfillment from "Yours for the cause of Peace and Brotherhood, Martin Luther King Jr. April 16 1963." As a result, King "established a kind of universal voice, beyond time, beyond race. As both humble prisoner and mighty prophet, as father, harried traveler, and cornered participant, he projected a character of nearly unassailable breadth" (Branch, 740).

BIBLIOGRAPHY

Branch, Taylor. *Parting the Waters: America in the King Years, 1954–63.* New York: Simon and Schuster, 1988.

King, Martin Luther, Jr. "Letter from a Birmingham Jail." In *Martin Luther King, Jr.: I Have A Dream, Writings and Speeches That Changed the World,* edited by James M. Washington, 83–100. San Francisco: Harper Collins Publishers, 1986.

Miller, William Robert. *Martin Luther King, Jr.: His Life, Martyrdom and Meaning for the World.* New York: Avon Books 1968.

France A. Davis

Lewis, William Henry (Hank) (1967–)

Although born in his family's hometown of Denver, Colorado, Hank Lewis, poet and short story writer, grew up in Chattanooga, Tennessee. He received a B.A. degree in literature and literary writing from Trinity College (1989) in Hartford, Connecticut, and an M.F.A. in fiction from the University of Virginia (1994). In addition to serving as Allan K. Smith Assistant Professor of Creative Writing, Fiction, an endowed chair at Trinity College, Lewis has taught at the Greater Hartford Academy of Arts, University of Virginia, Mary Washington College, Denison University, and the Hurston/Wright Summer Writing Workshops. After teaching at the College of the Bahamas and Centre College for several years, Lewis currently teaches at Colgate College in New York.

Lewis, whose poetry is included in the anthology *Beyond the Frontier: African American Poetry for the 21st Century,* has also won accolades for his short stories, which have been published in *Ploughshares, Callaloo,* and *African American Review.* Lewis's award-winning short story, "Shades," was included in *Best American Short Stories of 1996.* Narrated from the point of view of a 14-year-old boy, "Shades" is a bildungsroman. The nameless protagonist sees his father for the first time, at age 14, during a neighborhood festival, when his mother points him out. "There is your father," she said. Wishing to know his "real" father, in place of the one he had imagined, the protagonist approaches his father, briefly getting his attention, gesturing to shake his hand. "I arched my hand out to slide across his palm, but he pulled his hand back, smiling, a jokester, like he was too slick for my eagerness." Though close enough to engage a conversation, the protagonist's father fails to recognize the son he conceived and left behind more than 14 years before, after making love to the protagonist's mother in the midst of the summer heat. In the end, watching his father walk out of his life once again, the protagonist is left to imagine the conversation they might have shared and to complete his rites of passage into manhood without the guidance of his father.

In the Arms of Our Elders (Carolina Wren Press, 1994), Lewis's first collection of stories, won the 1993 Sonja S. Stone Fiction Contest and earned rave reviews. Lewis's one-act play, *Peeling Potato,* has been produced at Waldorf College and was anthologized with *Road to the Black Mesa,* another one-act play, in *Strawberries, Potatoes and Other Fantasies* (Trinity College, 1988). Lewis's second collection of short stories, *I Got Somebody in Staunton* (2005) registers his commitment to exploring the complex lives of and giving voice to African-American males. *I Got Somebody* received the Black Caucus of the American Library Association (BCALA) Honor Book Award (2006).

Rosemarie Mundy Shephard

Living Is Easy, The   Dorothy West (1948)

DOROTHY WEST's critically acclaimed novel, *The Living Is Easy,* takes its title from the hit song,

"Summertime," which comes from Du Bose Heyward's Broadway play *Porgy*. An autobiographical novel, *The Living Is Easy* satirizes the snobbery, shallowness, racism, sexism, and elitism of middle-class blacks in Boston around 1914, who pursue the false values of white society and connive to obtain positions of power. Although she does not love him, 19-year-old, light-skinned Cleo Jericho Judson, the eldest of several sisters, marries the wealthy Bart Judson, a much older southern gentleman. Situating herself in a space for female power, the self-serving and domineering Cleo manipulates and deceives her three sisters into living with her and eventually breaks up their marriages. Then her own world is shattered when her husband's banana business goes bankrupt and he leaves Boston to find other means of income; her three sisters are forced to work at the menial jobs she despises.

Although on the surface Cleo appears to get what she desires, West depicts Cleo's ultimate defeat by her own selfish needs, as well as by prevailing economic and gender issues. For example, Cleo forgets that Bart is her helpmate and sole means of financial support, so when the money runs out, she finds herself caught between her own pride and the racism of the rest of the world. She forgets, too, that she occupies only a small space in the community. Resisting her mother's control, Judy, Cleo's daughter, observes that her mother "was the boss of nothing but the young, the weak, the frightened. She ruled a pygmy kingdom" (308).

Skillfully and brilliantly written, *The Living Is Easy* is considered West's most successful book. One critic stated in the October 1948 issue of CRISIS, "Miss West has enlarged the canvas of Negro fiction and has treated a phase of Boston life which the popular novels of that city have neglected" (Moon, 308). In 1982, the Feminist Press reprinted *The Living Is Easy*, with an afterword by Adelaide Cromwell Gulliver. The novel has since been widely recognized as a major text in African-American women's literature.

BIBLIOGRAPHY

Guinier, Genii. "Interview with Dorothy West." May 6, 1978. *Black Women Oral History Project.* Cambridge, Mass.: Schlesinger Library, Radcliffe College, 1981. 1–75.
Moon, Henry L. "Proper Bostonian Black." *Crisis* 55 (1948): 308.
Rodgers, Lawrence R. "Dorothy West's *The Living Is Easy* and the Ideal of Southern Folk Community." *African American Review* 26 (1992): 161–172.

Loretta G. Woodard

Locke, Alain Leroy   (1885–1954)

Philosopher, educator, and cultural critic Alain Leroy Locke, the only son of Plimy Ishmael Locke and Mary Hawkins Locke, was born in Philadelphia, Pennsylvania. Locke's parents came from distinguished free black families. For example, his paternal grandfather, Ishmael Locke, was a New Jersey schoolteacher who, during the 19th century, had attracted the attention of the Society of Friends, which eventually sponsored his education at Cambridge, England, before he was sent to Liberia, the American colony in West Africa, where he established several schools. Returning to the United States, Ishmael Locke became headmaster of a school in Providence, Rhode Island; was principal of the Institute for Colored Youth in Philadelphia; and graduated from Howard University's law department before serving as an accountant for the Freedman's Bureau and becoming a clerk for the U.S. Post Office.

Young Locke, who was six when his father died, grew up with this genteel privilege as his legacy. His mother, a teacher, saw to it that her son attended one of Philadelphia's pioneer Ethical Culture schools advocated by Felix Alder. Restricted to his home as a result of a bout with rheumatic fever, young Locke took refuge in "the cloistered world of books, and in his study of the piano and the violin." Despite his illness and restrictions, Locke was able to attend Philadelphia Central High School, from which he received a B.A. degree and graduated with honors. He received a second B.A. degree from the Philadelphia School of Pedagogy before enrolling at Harvard College, where he completed its four-year undergraduate program in three years, won the Bowdoin Prize in English (1907), was elected to Phi Beta Kappa, and graduated magna cum laude. Locke became the first African-American Rhodes Scholar. Rejected by five Oxford colleges, he studied Greek, philosophy, and literature at Hertford College and spent a year at the University of Berlin.

Although towered over by the more senior black intellectual of the early 20th century, Dr. W. E. B. DuBois, with whom he shared educational paths and the sociocultural concerns outlined in DuBois's *The Souls of Black Folk* (1905), Locke, too, was clearly a member of this privileged group. Locke made his mark as a faculty member of Howard College's Teachers College and then as dean of the College of Arts and Sciences, where he taught courses in philosophy, literature, education, and English. He also infused new life into African-American drama by cofounding the Howard Players, one of the earliest black little theater groups. Equally important was his initial work with *Survey Graphic;* a special issue edited by him in March 1925, "Harlem, Mecca of the New Negro," was devoted to describing the emergence of what he called "the New Negro" and the transformation of Harlem, New York, into an international black mecca. Contributors included CHARLES S. JOHNSON, editor of the Urban League's *OPPORTUNITY* magazine, DuBois, editor of the NATIONAL ASSOCIATION FOR THE ADVANCEMENT OF COLORED PEOPLE's *CRISIS* magazine, JAMES WELDON JOHNSON, and Arthur Schomburg. By December 1925, Albert and Charles Boni published *The NEW NEGRO: AN INTERPRETATION,* an expanded book-length work of the original *Survey Graphics,* now a handsome anthology with graphics by Winold Reiss and Aaron Douglas that included poetry, fiction, and scholarly essays by HARLEM RENAISSANCE luminaries, including LANGSTON HUGHES, CLAUDE MCKAY, JEAN TOOMER, ZORA NEALE HURSTON, DuBois, Schomburg, and Kelly Miller.

Including five of Locke's own essays on African-American art, literature, and music, *The New Negro,* an instant success, made Locke a spokesperson for the "New Negro Movement." Locke explained in the foreword: "This volume aims to document the New Negro culturally and socially,—to register the transformation of the inner and outer life of the Negro in America that have so significantly taken place in the last few years." In his introductory essay, "The New Negro," he boldly announced the death of the "Old Negro." "The day of the 'aunties,' 'uncles' and 'mammies' is equally gone. Uncle Tom and Sambo have passed on. . . . The popular melodrama has about played itself out, and it is time to scrap the fictions, garret the bogeys and settle down to a realistic facing of facts" (5). Locke reiterates DuBois's premise from *The Souls of Black Folks* that the Negro is a cultural bearer—a contributor to and definer of American art and literature.

Throughout his life Locke remained in the vanguard of the best-known scholars of African-American culture. After his death in 1954, his full-length work-in-progress, *The Negro in American Culture,* was eventually completed by Margaret Just Butcher.

BIBLIOGRAPHY

Davis, Arthur P. *From the Dark Towers: Afro-American Writers, 1900–1960.* Washington, D.C.: Howard University Press, 1974.

Locke, Alain L., ed. *The New Negro: An Interpretation.* New York: Albert and Charles Boni, 1925. Reprint with preface by Robert Hayden. New York: Atheneum, 1968.

Winston, Michael R. "Alain Locke." In *Dictionary of American Negro Biography,* edited by Rayford Logan and Michael R. Winston, 398–404. New York: W. W. Norton & Company, 1982.

Wilfred D. Samuels

Lorde, Audre Geraldine   (1934–1992)

Self-described "Black lesbian, mother, warrior, poet," Audre Geraldine Lorde was born on February 18, 1934, in New York City to West Indian parents Frederic Byron and Linda Belmar Lorde. A beloved teacher and committed social activist, Lorde wrote the Carriacou biomythography *ZAMI: A NEW SPELLING OF MY NAME* (1982), as well as 12 volumes of poetry, including *The First*

Cities (1968), *Cables to Rage* (1970), *From the Land Where Other People Live* (1973); nominated for the 1974 National Book Award; *The New York Head Shop and Museum* (1974); *Between Our Selves* (1976), *Our Dead behind Us* (1986), and a posthumous volume, *The Collected Poems of Audre Lorde,* (1997). Lorde was also a brilliant essayist. New York State's poet laureate in 1991, Lorde received, among her many awards, honorary doctorates from Haverford College (1989), Oberlin College (1990), and Hunter College (1991).

Fiercely and incisively exposing racism, tokenism, exclusion, invisibility, silencing, and the erasure of difference, Lorde's feminist vision is more than subversive; it is incendiary. In poetry and prose that is as compelling for its ethical vision as for its language, Lorde dares to imagine a changed world, insisting, "for women . . . poetry is not a luxury. It is a vital necessity of our existence. It forms the quality of light within which we predicate our hopes and dreams towards survival and change, first made into language, then into idea, then into more tangible action" (Lorde, 37–38). Reversing the racist stereotypes equating darkness with fear, hatred, and death, her poems associate darkness with strength, integrity, beauty, vision, and magic.

The title poem from *Coal* (1976) invokes a powerful and joyous recognition of self, and of the beauty of blackness: "I am Black because I come from the earth's inside / now take my word for jewel in the open light." The love poems from *The Black Unicorn* (1978) are sensuous, tender, fiercely passionate. Dreaming in "Woman" of a time when "the commonest rock / is moonstone and ebony opal," Lorde envisions racial healing between white and black women. In "Fog Report," the poet describes the powerful force of sexuality, its potential to throw a person off balance, as well as its ability to be centering and empowering—a place to "solve [one's] own equations." In "Meet," Lorde borrows from the legend of Mawulisa as a prophecy, vowing to resist the lies uttered against loving and the censure and denial of lesbian relationships. "Coniagui Women" premises itself on the necessity for black women to teach black men to care for themselves. The woman who feeds her sons "yam soup / and

silence" refuses the persistent, seductive entreaties of her young. In "Power," she warns that real power is not the simple possession of the means of violence but a means to individual transformation, insisting that the appropriate use of this power will engender the muscular, cohesive vision that makes social revolution possible. Poems such as "Power" or the later "Need: A Choral of Black Women's Voices" and "Afterimages" (a brilliant choral echo of GWENDOLYN BROOKS's poem about the murder of EMMETT TILL)—both from *Chosen Poems Old and New* (1982)—are as visceral and devastating as the actual events they describe, avoiding any semblance of conventional poetic diction or syntax.

Our Dead behind Us (1986) opens with the poem "Sisters in Arms," the tragedy of "six-year-olds imprisoned for threatening the state." The stench of death, of apartheid, of "the seeping Transvaal cold"—metaphoric and actual—remains in the lovers' bed. In Germany for cancer treatment during the period she was writing this volume, Lorde wrote of Ravensbruck and other Nazi atrocities. The poems here and in *The Marvelous Arithmetics of Distance* (1993), nominated for the National Book Critics Circle Award, speak of Sharpeville, Soweto, Shatila, and lowercase alabama—sites of anguish and resistance. The final poem of Lorde's last individual volume evokes quiet despair, a more personal confrontation with death, of "How hard it is to sleep / in the middle of life."

In their unflinching gaze into much that is nightmare in American culture, many of these are not comforting poems. But because Lorde's work imagines what poet Adrienne Rich has called "the possibilities of truth between us," they are poems that chart a new, essential geography, one whose terrain we ignore only at our own peril.

Lorde's speeches and essays share a common cause with her poetry. Her best-known speech, "The Master's Tools Will Never Dismantle the Master's House" (*Sister Outsider,* 1984), delivered in 1979 at the Second Sex Conference, condemns predominantly white, middle-class, and heterosexual feminists, who, while speaking against their own oppression, fail to listen to, support, and include as equals speakers representing communities disadvantaged by color, class, and sexual identity.

In "Feminism and Black Liberation: The Great American Disease," Lorde writes of the danger of black women's sacrificial love: "If society ascribes roles to black men which they are not allowed to fulfill, is it black women who must bend and alter our lives to compensate, or is it society that needs changing?" And in "The Erotic as Power," Lorde explores how "our erotic knowledge empowers us, becomes a lens through which we scrutinize all aspects of our existence . . . [providing] a grave responsibility . . , not to settle for the convenient, the shoddy, the conventionally expected, nor the merely safe." Audre Lorde's courageous struggle with cancer, described in both *The Cancer Journals* (1980) and *Burst of Light* (1988), she regarded as "only another face of that continuing battle for self-determination and survival that black women fight daily, often in triumph." *The Cancer Journals,* which received the Critics' Choice Award, 1995–1996, while deeply personal, focused attention on the politics of women's health care and the mistreatment of women by the medical establishment. One passage describes the political consciousness behind Lorde's refusal to wear a prosthesis: "Prosthesis offers the empty comfort of 'Nobody will know the difference.' But it is that very difference which I wish to affirm, because I have lived it and survived it, and wish to share that strength with other women." Another passage celebrates community in the same breath as it acknowledges difference: "I am defined as other in every group I'm a part of. . . . Yet without community there is certainly no liberation, no future, only the most vulnerable and temporary armistice between me and my oppression."

Gloria T. Hull has described the complex and profoundly ethical positionality Lorde represents in her life and her work by noting that "[w]hen Lorde names herself 'sister outsider,' she is claiming the extremes of a difficult identity. . . . Lorde has placed herself on that line between the either/ or and both/and of 'sister outsider'—and then erased her chance for rest or mediation."

Other collections of Lorde's essays include: *Apartheid U.S.A. and Our Common Enemy, Our Common Cause: Freedom Organizing in the Eighties* (with Merle Woo; 1986), and *I Am Your Sister:* *Black Women Organizing across Sexualities* (1986). Among her many activist endeavors, Lorde cofounded Kitchen Table: Women of Color Press (1981), helped establish Sisterhood in Support of Sisters in South Africa (SISA) (1985), and, in 1989, was instrumental in raising U.S contributions toward relief efforts for the island of Saint Croix after the devastation caused by Hurricane Hugo.

Audre Lorde received a B.A. from Hunter College (1959) and an M.A. in library science from Columbia University in 1961. A librarian until 1968, when she published her first book of poems and became poet-in-residence at Tougaloo College (Mississippi), she later became professor of English at John Jay College of Criminal Justice, teaching poetry, race relations, and urban studies, and held the Thomas Hunter chair in the English department at Hunter College.

Married in 1962 to attorney Edwin Ashley Rollins, from whom she was subsequently divorced, Lorde had two children, Jonathan and Elizabeth, whom she raised with Frances Clayton, her partner of 17 years. The final years of her life were spent with her partner Gloria Joseph on the island of St. Croix, where, after a 14-year battle with cancer, she died on November 17, 1992.

In a ceremony not long before her death, Audre Lorde was given the African name Gamba Adisa, meaning "Warrior: She Who Makes Her Meaning Clear." Like the shimmering robe she was given at the 1990 "I Am Your Sister" conference held in Boston to celebrate her work and the values it reflects and encourages, Lorde's African name was a singularly fitting honor—for words drenched in clarifying truth are Audre Lorde's greatest legacy.

BIBLIOGRAPHY

Alexander, Elizabeth. "'Coming out Blackened and Whole': Fragmentation and Reintegration in Audre Lorde's *Zami* and *The Cancer Journals.*" *American Literary History* 6, no. 4 (1994): 695–715.

Avi-Ram, Amitai F. "Apo Koinou in Audre Lorde and the Moderns: Defining the Differences." *Callaloo* 9, no. 1 (1986): 193–208.

Hall, Lynda. "Lorde and Gomez Queer(y)ing boundaries and Acting in Passion(ate) Plays 'Wherever

We Found Space.'" *Callaloo* 23, no. 1 (2000): 394–421.

Hull, Gloria T. "Living on the Line: Audre Lorde and *Our Dead Behind Us.*" In *Changing Our Own Words: Essays on Criticisms, Theory, and Writing by Black Women,* edited by Cheryl A. Wall, 150—172. New Brunswick, N.J.: Rutgers University Press, 1989.

Lorde, Audre. "Poetry I: Not a Luxury." In *Sister outsider: Essays and Speeches,* 37–38. Berkeley, Calif.: Crossing Press, 1984.

Morris, Margaret Kissam. "Audre Lorde: Textual Authority and the Embodied Self." *Frontiers: A Journal of Women Studies* 23, no. 1 (2002): 168–188.

Rudnitsky, Lexi. "The 'Power' and 'Sequelae' of Audre Lorde's Syntactical Strategies." *Callaloo* 26, no. 2 (2003): 473–485.

Lynda Koolish

Lyrics of Lowly Life
Paul Laurence Dunbar (1896)

When he published *Lyrics of Lowly Life,* a collection of poems with New York's Dodd, Mead & Company, in 1896, the then 23-year-old PAUL LAURENCE DUNBAR, America's first professional black poet, had already privately printed by patronage two volumes of his work: *Oak and Ivy* (1892) and *Majors and Minors* (1895). During his short life (he died at age 33), Dunbar, the Ohio-born son of former slaves and an elevator operator by profession, would publish five more volumes, including *Lyrics of the Hearthside* (1899), *Lyrics of Love and Laughter* (1903), *Lyrics of Sunshine and Shadow* (1905), and *Complete Poems* (1913). Influenced by the British romantic poets, particularly Alfred Tennyson and Percy Bysshe Shelley, and American poet Russell Lowell, Dunbar gained recognition as an American literary phenomenon when the dean of American letters and father of American realism, William Dean Howells, favorably reviewed *Majors and Minors* in *Harper's Weekly,* noting, "So far as I could remember, Paul Dunbar was the only man of pure African blood and of American civilization to feel the negro [sic] life aesthetically and express it lyrically." (quoted in Dunbar, xvi)

As a result of Howell's endorsement, Dunbar gained international attention; he traveled to England in 1897 to give poetry readings, and he became "the most famous African American poet and one of the most famous American poets of his time." (Robinson, 639). Although Dunbar wrote in both standard English and black dialect, Howells chose to celebrate his accomplishment as a dialect poet. Eugene Redmond, in his critical history of African-American poetry, notes that "Howell's praise was a curse in disguise," for Dunbar "struggled for the rest of his life to remove the dialect stigma" (121). Dunbar laments this apparent marginalization in "The Poet": "He sang of love when earth was young, / And love, itself, was in his lays. / But ah, the world, it turned to praise / A jingle in a broken tongue."

Lyrics of Lowly Life, which Howells arranged to have published by a mainstream press, includes poems that first appeared in *Oak and Ivy* and *Majors and Minors.* As a whole, they clearly reveal not only Dunbar's range but also his masterful competence as a poet. He begins the collection with "Ere Sleep Comes Down to Soothe the Weary Eyes" and ends it with "The Party." Many of the poems have become often-anthologized classics, including "Frederick Douglass," "A Negro Love Song," "When the Co'n Pone's Hot," "We Wear the Mask," and "When Malindy Sings." Most of them, as critics have pointed out over the decades, lack "racial fire." Dunbar preferred to think of blacks as human beings rather than as Africans—hence the celebration of and emphasis on black humanity and sensitivity, as found in "When Malindy Sings," than on racially specific themes. Malindy is memorialized by the speaker for her gift as a talented musician: "But fu' real melojous music, / Dat jes' strikes yo' hea't and clings / Jes' you stan' an' listen wif me / When Malindy sings" (196). Similarly, the speaker in "Sympathy" contrasts freedom and destructive oppression in any form, racial or aesthetic. The speaker, whose purpose is to bear witness—"I know"—at the beginning of each stanza, could be an artist, a male or female former slave, or a black South African who experienced dehumanizing apartheid.

However, this does not mean Dunbar was unaware of or wished to distance himself from detrimental white racism. "Sympathy" (which is not included in *Lyrics*), clearly denotes Dunbar's painful awareness:

> I know why the caged bird beats his wing
> Til its blood is red on the cruel bars;
> For he must fly back to his perch and cling
> When he fain would be on the bough a-swing;
> And a pain still throbs in the old, old scars
> And they pulse again with a keener sting—
> I know why he beats his wing!

Near the end of the 20th century, critics became more forgiving of Dunbar's overall lack of attention to racial issues in his work. For example, DARWIN T. TURNER argued that Dunbar should be remembered for his conscious artistry and experimentation with meter and rhyme and his tributes to African-American heroes and for writing more poetry in standard English than in dialect. However, Turner also argued that Dunbar's dialect poems are his major contribution to American literature.

BIBLIOGRAPHY

Brawley, Benjamin. *Paul Laurence Dunbar, Poet of His People.* Port Washington, N.Y.: Kennikat Press, 1936.

Dunbar, Paul L. *Lyrics of Lowly Life.* Introduction by William D. Howells. New York: Dodd, Mead & Co., 1896.

Redmond, Eugene B. *Drumvoices: The Mission of Afro-American Poetry: A Critical History.* Garden City, N.Y.: Anchor Books, 1976.

Robinson, Lisa Clayton. "Paul Laurence Dunbar." In *Africana: The Encyclopedia of the African and African American Experience,* edited by Kwame Anthony Appiah and Henry Louis Gates, Jr., 639–640. New York: Basic Civitas Books, 1999.

Turner, Darwin T. "Paul Laurence Dunbar: The Poet and the Myths." In *A Singer in the Dawn, Reinterpretations of Paul Laurence Dunbar,* edited by Jay Martin, 59–74. New York: Dodd, Mead and Company, 1975.

Wilfred D. Samuels

Mackey, Nathaniel (1947–)

Born in Miami and raised in Southern California, Mackey attended Princeton, then Stanford, where he earned a Ph.D. in literature. He then taught briefly at the University of Wisconsin–Madison and the University of Southern California, before he found a teaching position at the University of California at Santa Cruz. During his tenure as a student, Mackey was introduced not only to the poets of the BLACK ARTS MOVEMENT, such as AMIRI BARAKA, but also to the Black Mountain poets, such as Charles Olson and Robert Creeley. Pulling on these different sources has allowed Mackey to continue to draw from a wide array of influences to create a writing style and form that reflects the postmodern and global culture he seems to know so well and embrace. The themes expressed in his work are taken from African and Caribbean folklore, European poetics, and African-American music, particularly jazz. In summary, Mackey's work defies the notion that an African American should only be interested in African-American literature and culture.

Mackey's versatility is reflected in his body of work. He is a poet, novelist, writer of cultural and literary criticism, and accomplished editor. His first publications were poetry chapbooks, all of which were eventually collected in *Eroding Witness* (1985). In this collection, Mackey introduces two poetic series that he has since continued to expand: "Song of the Andoumboulou" and "mu" (a title taken from trumpeter Don Cherry's same-named series). *School of Udhra* (1993) and *What-said Serif* (1998) are further offerings of Mackey's poetry and continue the two series.

Attempting to move beyond the written word, Mackey has released *Strick: Song of the Andoumboulou 16–25* (1995), a compact disc recording of poems read with musical accompaniment by Royal Hartigan and Hafez Modiradeh. He is also the author of an ongoing prose composition, *From a Broken Bottle Traces of Perfume Still Emanate,* of which three volumes have been published: *Bedoin Hornbook* (1986), *Djbot Baghostus's Run* (1993), and *Atet A.D.* (2001). Beyond his career in poetry and fiction, he has published two books of literary criticism, *Gassire's Lute: Robert Duncan's Vietnam War Poems* (published in five installments from 1990 to 1992) and *Discrepant Engagement: Dissonance, Cross-Culturality, and Experimental Writing* (1993). He edited, with Art Lange, the anthology *Moment's Notice: Jazz in Poetry and Prose* (1993) and founded the literary magazine *Hambone.*

This variation of work represents Mackey's effort to communicate the slippage between these forms and, consequently, to explore their interconnectedness. Mackey believes that the lore and history he draws from is not fixed. Instead, he sees lore and history as "active and unfinished" traditions receiving further transformation when combined with new traditions. For example, "Song of the Andoumboulou" is literally a funeral song of the Dogon, a West African people. Later, while reading an anthropology text, Mackey discovered that according to Dogon mythology, the Andoumboulou are an earlier form of human beings that were flawed and that failed to sustain themselves. This latter part of the puzzle is what gives Mackey the context within which to compose his series of poems that focus on not only fallen comrades but the fallen ways of life, too, like the Mistress erzulie, the Haitian voudoun goddess of love:

> One hand on her hip, one hand
> arranging her hair,
> blue heaven's
> bride. Her beaded hat she hangs
> from a nail on the danceroom
> wall. . . .

In this poem, number 8 in the series, Mackey explicitly uses Haitian lore to invoke images of female debauchery but still holds onto the goddess portion of the tradition. Mackey's erzulie embodies womanhood, someone to honor and adore. He continues, "*From whatever glimpse / of her I get I take heart, I hear them / say / By whatever bit of her I touch / I take / hold.*" This poem is emblematic of Mackey's interest in rethinking myth, folklore, and language.

BIBLIOGRAPHY

Mackey, Nathaniel. *Discrepant Engagement: Dissonance, Cross-Culturality, and Experimental Writing.* Cambridge: Cambridge University Press, 1993.

———. *Djbot Baghostus's Run.* Los Angeles: Sun & Moon Press, 1993.

———. *Eroding Witness.* Urbana and Chicago: University of Illinois Press, 1985.

———. "Gassire's Lute: Robert Duncan's Vietnam War Poems, I–V" *Talisman* 5–9 (Fall 1990–Fall 1992).

———. *School of Udhra.* San Francisco: City Lights Books, 1993.

Naylor, Paul. "The 'Mired Sublime' of Nathaniel Mackey's 'Song of the Andoumboulou.'" *Postmodern Culture* 5, no. 3 (May 1995): n.p.

———, ed. *Nathaniel Mackey.* Special issue of *Callaloo* 23, no. 2 (Spring 2000).

O'Leary, Peter. "An Interview with Nathaniel Mackey." *Chicago Review* 43, no. 1 (1997): 30–46.

Ryan Dickson

Madgett, Naomi Long   (1923–   )

The poet laureate of Detroit and a cofounder of Detroit's Lotus Press, Naomi Long Madgett is considered one of America's leading editors and publishers. She has advanced the literary career of a generation of black and other minority poets, has celebrated the experiences of black Americans in her writings, and has encouraged a generation of writers and students in her work. A poet since childhood, she was born Naomi Cornelia Long on July 5, 1923, in Norfolk, Virginia. Her father, Clarence Marcellus Long, Sr., was a Baptist minister; her mother, Maude Hilton Long, was an educator. She spent her early childhood in East Orange, New Jersey; in 1937 her family moved to St. Louis, Missouri, where she was encouraged to write while attending the all-black Sumner High School. At age 17, she published her first volume of poetry, *Songs to a Phantom Nightingale* (1941), mostly nature poems, which show the influence of the British romantic poets John Keats, William Wordsworth, and Alfred Tennyson.

In 1945 Madgett earned a B.A. from Virginia State College (now Virginia State University). She married Julian F. Witherspoon, the first of her three husbands, and moved to Detroit in 1946, where she worked for the *Michigan Chronicle* before giving birth to her daughter, Jill, in 1947. When her marriage ended in 1948, she worked for Michigan Bell Telephone Company until 1954, at which time she married William H. Madgett, whose name she continued to use after their divorce in 1960. She completed her M.Ed. in English at Wayne State University and taught in the Detroit public schools (1955–1968) and at Eastern Michigan University

(1968–1984) and was artist-in-residence at Western Michigan University (1998).

An award-winning poet, Madgett has published eight collections of poetry since 1941. Her second volume, *One and the Many* (1956), records her life through the mid-1950s. Through her narrator, Madgett reveals the personal conflict she experienced as a poet who was considering shifting from the lyricism found in such poems as "The Ivory Tower" to the social and racial concerns found in "Not I Alone," where she speaks with a strong, protesting voice against racism. In her next volume, *Star by Star* (1965), Madgett, through her speakers, explores the complexity of the black experience in such poems as "For a Child," "Violet," "Alabama Centennial," "Pavlov," and her most popular 1959 poem, "Midway," in which her black speaker embodies the voice of all Americans who were seeking peace during a time of civil unrest. During this period, Madgett, along with DUDLEY RANDALL, ROBERT HAYDEN, OWEN DODSON, RONALD MILNER, and HOYT FULLER, was a member of Margaret Danner's writer's workshop at Boone House in Detroit from 1962 1964.

In 1972 Madgett, three friends, and Leonard Patton Andrews, her third husband, founded Lotus Press in Detroit. In 1974 she and Andrews assumed total responsibility for Lotus Press, and Madgett was the publisher and editor for nearly two decades. Madgett published the works of such poets as Samuel Allen, James A. Emanuel, May Miller, Dudley Randall, LANCE JEFFERS, HAKI R. MADHUBUTI, GAYL JONES, JUNE JORDAN, MARGARET WALKER, Pinkie Gordon Lane, E. ETHELBERT MILLER, TOI DERRICOTTE, PAULETTE CHILDRESS WHITE, Ojaide Tanure, and Selene DeMedeiros. Since 1993, Michigan State University Press has distributed books for Lotus Press, which has remained in Detroit. Madgett has served as senior editor of its new Lotus Poetry Series.

Lotus Press published Madgett's *Pink Ladies in the Afternoon: New Poems, 1965–1971*, (1972), which describes her life from the late 1960s and early 1970s and addresses her dedication to her career in the midst of civil disorder and the Vietnam War, her approaching middle age, and her deep-seated awareness of her heritage and identity in such poems as "Black Woman"; "Glimpses to Africa," based on her trip to Africa with Operation Crossroads; and "Newblack," where the poet argues against the senseless attacks on distinguished black leaders from BOOKER T. WASHINGTON to MARTIN LUTHER KING, JR.

Madgett's fifth poetry collection, *Exits and Entrances: New Poems* (1978), another Lotus Press publication, continues and enlarges the autobiographical focus of *Pink Ladies,* reemphasizes the poet's interest in Afro-American themes, and contains her most recent lyrics in poems such as "Family Portrait," "The Silver Cord," "Fifth Street Exit, Richmond," "City Night," "Monday Morning Blues," and "The Old Women." Her next volume, *Phantom Nightingale: Juvenilia* (1981), includes poems that reflect her formal classroom education, her informal education, and her contemporary life, with titles like "Threnody," "Sonnet," "Pianissimo," "Democracy," and "Market Street."

By the 1970s and 1980s, Madgett's work shifted from a political stance to more personal, major social concerns with black women and their relationships with their families. *Octavia and Other Poems* (1988), a national cowinner of the College Language Association Creative Achievement Award, re-creates black family life in Oklahoma and Kansas in the early 20th century and centers on Madgett's great-aunt, Octavia Cornelia Long, and several other members of her family, depicting the personal responsibility of women for the welfare of the community. *Remembrances of Spring: Collected Early Poems* (1993) commemorates Midgett's work as an editor and publisher and provides a retrospective examination of a powerful poetic voice and social conscience that has touched her readers' imaginations. Madgett's latest collection is *Connected Islands: New and Selected Poems* (2004).

Madgett, like Dudley Randall, founder of Broadside Press, has been a champion in the struggle to promote the creation, distribution, and preservation of African-American poetry over three decades. For her commitment, and for her own love of self-expression, which she hopes "will continue to have meaning to others after [her] voice is still," Madgett's work has earned her many awards. She was inducted into the Literary Hall of

Fame for Writers of African Descent and the Michigan Women's Hall of Fame and received lifetime achievement awards from the Furious Flower Poetry Center and the Gwendolyn Brooks Center for Black Literature. Other awards include an American Book Award, a Michigan Artist Award, an Alain Locke Award, a George Kent Award, a Creative Achievement Award, and the *Black Scholar Magazine* Award of Excellence; in 1993 the Hilton-Long Poetry Foundation offered its first annual Naomi Long Madgett Poetry Award for excellence in a manuscript by an African-American poet. In September 2000 she became Detroit's poet laureate. She published her autobiography *Pilgrim Journey* in 2006.

BIBLIOGRAPHY

Bailey, Leaonead Pack. *Broadside Authors and Artists: An Illustrated Biographical Directory.* Detroit: Broadside Press, 1974.

Redmond, Eugene B. *Drumvoices: The Mission of Afro-American Poetry.* New York: Anchor/Doubleday, 1976.

Thompson, Julius E. *Dudley Randall, Broadside Press, and the Black Arts Movement in Detroit, 1960–1965.* Jefferson, N.C.: McFarland, 1999.

Loretta G. Woodard

Madhubuti, Haki (Don Luther Lee) (1942–   )

Haki Madhubuti (born Don L. Lee) is, as GWENDOLYN BROOKS described him, an artist, pioneer, and "loyalist." His active loyalty to black awareness and community became influential during the late 1960s and has driven a prolific career since. Born Don Luther Lee in Little Rock, Arkansas, on February 23, 1942, he was raised poor in Detroit by his mother, Maxine. Her early death from a drug overdose forged an independent survivor in Lee, who was adamant about racial solidarity and self-help. He is the founder of Third World Press, a million-dollar enterprise that publishes about 25 titles annually.

Madhubuti's systematic and tireless study of black literature began in high school, after he read RICHARD WRIGHT'S *BLACK BOY*. He recalls his reading of the book as a generative moment, as having "introduced me to myself." Madhubuti carried his burgeoning awareness and black conservatism into the U.S. Army (1960–1963), which informed much of his early interest and posture in the BLACK ARTS MOVEMENT. He began writing poetry in the military to articulate his experiences and eventually carried his works to Crane Junior College in 1963, where he continued to produce poetry for his first collections, *Think Black!* (1967) and *Black Pride* (1968). While at Crane, Madhubuti became apprentice to Margaret Burroughs at the DuSable Museum of African History. His four years with Burroughs, a Pan-African scholar, introduced him to many prominent members of the African-American arts community, including Gwendolyn Brooks, who encouraged him to publish his own work. *Think Black* and *Black Pride* result from this period, both self-published and independently distributed. Madhubuti sold his first 600 copies of *Think Black* in one week, standing on the corner of 63rd Street and Cottage Grove Avenue on Chicago's South Side. After such wide reception and positive response, he resolved to become a full-time writer and independent publisher. Seeking freedom to write critically without containment, Madhubuti founded Third World Press with his partner, Johari Amini, in a basement apartment on Chicago's southwest side. Formed to help nascent writers receive literary recognition, the press is now the nation's oldest and most prolific independent black book publisher. Third World Press authors include Gwendolyn Brooks, SONIA SANCHEZ, AMIRI BARAKA, Derrick Bell, and Chancellor Williams. With more than 22 books of essays and poetry to his own name, Madhubuti has proved himself a prominent and potent poet in American letters, fully independent of major publishing houses.

With his wife, Safisha, Madhubuti founded and continues to direct the Institute of Positive Education/New Concept Development Center (NCDC), which, in its grade school, promotes an Afrocentric curriculum. Children in preschool to third grade recite the school's pledge each morning: "We are African people struggling for national liberation. We are preparing leaders and workers to bring about positive change for our people. We stress the development of our bodies, minds, souls, and consciousness. Our commitment is to self-determination, self-defense, and self-respect for our race."

From 1970 to 1978 Madhubuti was a writer-in-residence at Howard University. There he produced *We Walk the Way of the New World* (1970) and *Directionscore* (1971); in 1971 he sold more books of poetry than any black poet who came before him. He actively invested his efforts and influence into the Student Nonviolent Coordinating Committee (SNCC), the Congress of Racial Equality (CORE), and the Southern Christian Leadership Conference (SCLC). During this formative period, in 1973, he renamed himself and began writing as Madhubuti, Swahili for "justice, awakening, strong." His 1973 collection, *Book of Life,* bears this new name (Mwalimu Haki R. Madhubuti).

Madhubuti is hailed as one of the leading Black Nation builders. His political, field, and academic work mingles him with many profound artists and authors, including LARRY NEAL, with whom he created a forum for book reviews for the work of African-American writers. This effort produced *The Black Books Bulletin,* published quarterly for eight years as an important resource for reviews on Black Arts authors. Madhubuti published *Book of Life* (1973), followed by *Earthquakes and Sunrise Missions* (1984), and *Killing Memory, Seeking Ancestors* (1987). In the interim, he continued to publish political essays and received an M.F.A. from the University of Iowa. Madhubuti returned to Chicago in 1984 to become a faculty member at Chicago State University, where he is a professor of English and director of the Gwendolyn Brooks Center.

In the record of Madhubuti's life, one sees the drive behind his poetry. Brooks described his work as "a razor; it's sharp and will cut deep, not out to wound but to kill the inactive Black mind" ("Haki Madhubuti"). Liz Gant observed, "his lines rumble like a street gang on the page, . . . his startling metaphor, variations of refrain, unexpected turns-of-phrases, wordplay, and staccato repetitions combine to produce an impact that keeps audiences spellbound" ("Haki Madhubuti"). Per-

haps best known for his poem "But He Was Cool or: he even stopped for green lights" (from *Don't Cry, Scream*), Madhubuti is ever concerned with the evolution of black souls, especially those of black men. His recent *Tough Notes: A Healing Call* (2002) responds, he says, "to the hundreds of letters, notes and telephone calls I have received over the years from prisoners and students—mainly young black men (many without caring or existing fathers), seeking guidance and a kind word" (preface). *Tough Notes* responds intimately to the readership he addresses with paternal admonition and sensitive scolding in *Black Men: Obsolete, Single, Dangerous?* (1990). These widely read books (*Black Men* has sold in excess of 750,000 copies) attempt, says one critic, "to give all Blacks a sense of unity, purpose, and direction, so that they may finally finish their 'history' on a successful note" ("Haki Madhubuti"). His street-style vernacular, staccato rhythms, and rough truth demand attention and speak to whiteness, while charting an evolution for black Americans into more conscious, self-determined activity.

As an independent black publisher, Madhubuti addresses the constant problems of access afforded to white privilege in America, especially in business, and sends a call to the African-American community to increase support.

Madhubuti has received the Distinguished Writers Award from the Middle Atlantic Writers Association in 1984 and the Paul Robeson Award from the African-American Arts Alliance. He has received fellowships from both the National Endowment for the Arts and the National Endowment for the Humanities.

BIBLIOGRAPHY

Gladney, Marvin J. "The Black Arts Movement and Hip-Hop." *African-American Review* 29, no. 2 (1995): 291–301.

Golden, Lizzie Thomas. "Change and Duality: Black Poetry and the 1960s." *Journal of Black Studies* 12, no. 1 (1981): 91–106.

"Haki Madhubuti." Available online. URL: http://www.coas.howard.edu/english/legends=Madhubuti.html. Accessed February 14, 2007.

Henderson, Errol A. "Black Nationalism and Rap Music." *Journal of Black Studies* 26, no. 3 (1996): 308–339.

Johnson, Lemuel A. "'Ain'ts,' 'Us'ens,' and 'Mother-Dear': Issues in the Language of Madhubuti, Jones, and Reed." *Journal of Black Studies* 10, no. 2 (1979): 139–166.

"Third World Press: Thirty Years of Book Publishing." *The Journal of Blacks in Higher Education* 18 (1997–98): 66–67.

Madhubuti, Haki. *Tough Notes: A Healing Call for Creating Exceptional Black Men.* Chicago: Third World Press, 2002.

Kevin Morgan

Major, Clarence   (1936–)

Clarence Major is a poet, novelist, short fiction writer, visual artist, essayist, lexicographer, editor, and anthologist. Although known best for his experimental novels, he has long demonstrated his versatility in both the artistic forms he uses and the subject matter he selects. He tests boundaries, asserting and enacting the freedom of the artist to explore the full range of human experience. One source of his versatility was his early exposure to both the North and the South. Though born in Atlanta, he moved, at age 10, to Chicago with his mother after his parents were divorced. A key Chicago experience for him was exposure to modern art, especially the impressionists. He studied briefly at the Chicago Art Institute when he was 17. Although he decided to focus his artistic efforts primarily in writing, he has used his painting and photography in his fiction, especially *Reflex and Bone Structure* (1975) and *Emergency Exit* (1979).

Much of Major's work, especially fiction, has been experimental in that it has broken down conventional assumptions about character, plot, and narrative voice. His early texts in particular tend to be fragmentary rather than unified in structure; likewise, their principal theme is the impossibility of a coherent identity in contemporary society. This pattern holds in the two novels mentioned above, as well as *All-Night Visitors* (1969), *No*

(1973), *My Amputations* (1986), and some of the stories in *Fun and Games* (1988). In these works, Major joins Donald Barthelme, Thomas Pynchon, and ISHMAEL REED in challenging the view that fiction either reflects or constructs a meaningful reality. But like Reed, Major also sees cultural significance in metafictional storytelling. His fragmented characters are rootless and often paranoid, in quest of a meaning that forever eludes them.

In two novels that are more realistic, he examines the same issue. *Such Was the Season* (1987) uses a southern folklike narrative voice that echoes ERNEST GAINES's *The AUTOBIOGRAPHY OF MISS JANE PITTMAN* and GLORIA NAYLOR's *MAMA DAY* in its down-home wisdom as well as its position as a moral center by which to judge others. But Major complicates the narrative by having the character Annie Eliza draw much of her knowledge not from traditional black experience but from television talk shows and soap operas. Similarly, *Painted Turtle: Woman with Guitar* (1988) tells the experiences of a Zuni woman who has been forced out of the tribe because she has worked as a prostitute and because she questions the traditional ways. She makes her living as an itinerant folk singer whose songs become her means of trying to claim an identity for herself as Zuni. A man who is himself Hopi-Navajo and thus outside of her experience, as well as uncertain about his own identity, narrates the novel. *Dirty Bird Blues* (1996), with its focus on the odyssey of a BLUES musician, Manfred Banks, finds Major returning to his southern roots. Set in the 1950s, it focuses on the migration of southern blacks to the North and Midwest and the culture they brought with them to this new environment. It also plays out the rootlessness of modern life as a version of the blues.

Another of the early influences on Major's writing was the work of French artists such as Raymond Radiguet and Arthur Rimbaud; his interest in white European and American literature is reflected in many allusions in both his fiction and poetry. The importance of the Western tradition is clear in a recent book of poetry, *Surfaces and Masks* (1988), which is entirely about the experiences of Americans in Venice, with literary references to

Benjamin Disraeli, Charles Dickens, Percy Bysshe Shelley, and Thomas Mann. His exploration of Native American issues is continued in a collection of poems titled *Some Observations of a Stranger at Zuni in the Latter Part of the Century* (1989).

Major's range of forms and subjects reflects his commitment to artistic freedom made explicit in his essays and interviews, many of which are collected in *The Dark and Feeling* (1974). He insists that it is the quality of the work rather than its ideology that determines its importance. Even in his 1967 manifesto, "Black Criteria," which calls for greater use of African-American materials and a rejection of much of Western tradition, he still concludes that the integrity of the artistic vision is the essential criterion. With this perspective, he has insisted on his difference from the BLACK AESTHETIC artists of the 1960s and 1970s and from the more recent variation associated with Afrocentrism. He has consistently argued that, while the African-American artist should make use of black cultural materials as part of the environment, the primary obligation is to the work itself and not to political and social ideas.

Major's work as editor and lexicographer has demonstrated his commitment to language and to literary freedom. His *Dictionary of Afro American Slang* (1970), expanded and updated in *Juba to Jive* (1994), provides a major resource for discussions of African-American language use. His anthologies, *The New Black Poetry* (1969), *The Garden Thrives: Twentieth-Century African-American Poetry* (1996), and *Calling the Wind: Twentieth-Century African-American Short Stories* (1993), offer a wide range of literary expression within the African-American tradition. He is professor of English at the University of California, Davis, where he teaches American literature and creative writing. With his wife, Pamela Ritter Major, he lives in Davis, where he continues to write and paint.

BIBLIOGRAPHY

Bell, Bernard W. *Clarence Major and His Art: Portraits of an African American Postmodernist.* Chapel Hill: University of North Carolina Press, 2001.

Byerman, Keith Eldon. *Fingering the Jagged Grain: Tradition and Form in Recent Black Fiction.* Athens: University of Georgia Press, 1985.

Klinkowitz, Jerome. "The Self-Apparent Word: Clarence Major's Innovative Fiction." In *Black American Prose Theory,* edited by Joe Weixlmann and Chester J. Fontenot, 199–214. Greenwood, Fla.: Penkevill, 1984.

Special issue, *Black American Literature Forum* 13 (Summer 1979).

Special issue, *African American Review* 28 (Spring 1994).

Keith Byerman

Major, Marcus   (1975–   )

Marcus Major was born at Fort Bragg, North Carolina, into a military family. During his childhood, he lived on military bases in Maryland, Alabama, Wisconsin, Kentucky, and New Jersey, while his father pursued his career in the army. Major is a graduate of Richard Stockton College, in Pomona, New Jersey, where he received a degree in literature and a teaching certificate in African-American studies. Although he began a career in education, teaching elementary and middle school in Newark, New Jersey, he turned to his real joy, writing, in 1998 at the encouragement of a former classmate.

Major is the author of three novels: *Good Peoples* (2001), *A Man Most Worthy* (2002), and *Four Guys and Trouble* (2001). Properly described as romance novels, the central theme in Major's novels is developing and maintaining fidelity, respect, and reciprocity in monogamous relationships. This is not often easy to do, given the urban "players" who people Major's fiction as well as the seductress female player who knows what she wants and goes after it, no matter what. In *Good People,* when Myles Moore meets and falls in love with Marisa Marrero, a successful Latina attorney and talk show host, he is happy finally to be in a meaningful relationship with the woman of his dreams. However, monogamy is not among Myles's character strengths, and when Marisa discovers his infidelity, she leaves him, testing in the end the true strength of his love for her.

A Man Most Worthy revisits *The Great Gatsby's* theme. Like Gatsby, John Sebastian is a successful businessman who has realized all his dreams, except one: a lasting relationship with Josephine Flowers, the love of his life. Although he has a new girlfriend, Scent, and Josephine, after seven years, has married and has gone on with her life, John is determined to win a second chance to prove himself worthy of her love.

Hot and passionate love and complex relationships are also central to *Four Guys and Trouble*. Four friends, Ibn, Colin, Michael, and Dexter, encounter "trouble" in the form of Erika, the sister of their deceased fraternity brother whom they promised to care for and protect. However, when they are called upon to protect Erika, now a 24-year-old, very attractive medical student, from one of their own, Michael, who has developed more than familial love for her, the bonds and friendship among the four men are challenged; they must come to grips with issues of loyalty and friendship and reinforce and strengthen their relationship if possible.

Major's novella "Kenya and Amir" was published in the best-selling *Got to Be Real* (2001), which also includes works by E. LYNN HARRIS, ERIC JEROME DICKEY, and COLIN CHANNER, some of the most critically acclaimed male writers of African-American fiction. Fidelity and friendship are also major themes in "Kenya and Amir." Although Amir spends the most glorious year of his life in a relationship with Kenya, he is unable to resist the bait set for him by two women, Hope and Kenya's good friend Raquel, who want to spend a memorable night having sex with him in a motel while Kenya is out of town. Amir falls for the trap, losing Kenya in the process, although, as he tries to justify to Kenya, he did not have sex with the women. The story ends on a positive note when the two former lovers begin to discuss what went wrong in their relationship.

In his collected work, Major, like Harris, revisits the lives of his characters and their families. This sequence ensures him an audience that will want to know more about the memorable characters Major continues to create in his fictional world.

Carlos Perez

Malcolm X (Malcolm Little, El Hajj Malik El Shabazz)   (1925–1965)

Born in Omaha, Nebraska, on May 19, 1925, Malcolm Little was the third son of Earl and Louise Little. His parents were both active members in MARCUS GARVEY's Universal Negro Improvement Association—a fact that ultimately helped shape Malcolm's Pan-African perspective on culture, human rights, political struggle, and world history. After having their house burned to the ground by the Ku Klux Klan in Omaha, Earl and Louise Little moved their family to Lansing, Michigan. As in Omaha, the Littles' expressions of black pride, economic independence, and cultural integrity riled the social sensibilities of Lansing's white citizenry. Earl Little died after being run over by a streetcar in downtown Lansing, in 1931.

After the death of his father, Malcolm's childhood and adolescence took a drastic turn for the worse. The family's economic self-sufficiency disappeared as Louise Little found herself depending on state aid for her family's subsistence. As social workers made repeated visits to the Little household, her psychological health finally declined. Eventually, the state declared her mentally unfit to rear her children and committed her to the state mental hospital at Kalamazoo. The court then placed Malcolm and his siblings into different orphanages. Although Malcolm had been among the top students in his class, his performance in school weakened during this time. After completing the eighth grade, he dropped out of school and moved to Boston to live with his half sister Ella. Malcolm traveled between Boston and New York, taking jobs as a shoeshine boy and porter before settling on the vices offered in Harlem's street life at age 16. His rapid descent into the moral abyss of Harlem's underworld was countered only by the notoriety he gained as one of the most successful and flamboyant drug-dealing pimps in the city. A professional con artist and numbers runner, Malcolm quickly began abusing the drugs and alcohol that he sold to members of Harlem's political and social elite. In time, Malcolm's lifestyle caught up with him, and he went to prison on burglary charges in 1946.

While serving his time in prison, Malcolm found solace and wisdom in the teachings of Elijah Muhammad and the Nation of Islam (NOI). Elijah Muhammad's instruction on the importance of family life, black pride, economic independence, literacy, thrift, self-discipline, and self-knowledge resonated with Malcolm's life experiences. In the course of a year, Malcolm experienced a spiritual transformation, became a member of the NOI, and changed his name to Malcolm X. He began to participate on prison debate teams and to study the philosophy and writings of Herodotus, Socrates, Shakespeare, and Gandhi. Most important, Malcolm regained his cultural awareness while mastering the English language by memorizing the English dictionary.

Paroled in 1952, Malcolm committed himself to serving the NOI, earning the attention of prophet and founder Elijah Muhammad, who made Malcolm minister of Temple No. 12 in Philadelphia. Malcolm's skills as a prolific orator, master scholar, and brilliant organizer were further rewarded when Muhammad made Malcolm minister of Temple No. 7 in Harlem and NOI National Spokesperson in 1961. From 1954 to 1960 Malcolm continued to spread the teachings of Elijah Muhammad nationally and internationally. Throughout the 1950s, he traversed the country, organizing 49 NOI temples. Membership in the NOI increased to 40,000 during this period. In 1960 Malcolm X created the newspaper *Muhammad Speaks* in the basement of his home in New York to communicate further the teachings and philosophy of Elijah Muhammad. *Muhammad Speaks* became the largest circulating weekly in the history of the African-American press.

In 1963 Malcolm X confronted Elijah Muhammad after learning of Muhammad's marital infidelities with members of the NOI. Muhammad's inability to admit his humanness to the body of the NOI led Malcolm to question the divine nature of Muhammad's mission to Afro-Asiatic people. In the process of questioning his own ethics, Malcolm committed his first act of rebellion against Muhammad by making critical remarks about the assassination of President John F. Kennedy. Although Muhammad placed Malcolm on indefinite suspension for his remarks, Malcolm broke all ties with the NOI on March 8, 1964. He created the Muslim Mosque Incorporated (MMI) as a way for Muslims in America to practice Sunni Islam in a communal environment. In April 1964, he fulfilled the Islamic requirement to make hajj, an experience that forever altered his perception of the possibilities of humanity.

Both during and after his affiliation with the NOI, Malcolm X presented a critical challenge for the other major African-American leader of his time, MARTIN LUTHER KING, JR. He disagreed with King's use of nonviolence as a strategy to gain social, political, or economic justice and in its place offered a philosophy of human unity based on mutual human respect. Likewise, Malcolm X and King disagreed on the basic definition of freedom. While Malcolm X did not believe that African Americans could achieve freedom through integrating diners, public accommodations, or transportation, he considered freedom to be the absence of police brutality and of economic and political exploitation.

Furthermore, as a Pan-Africanist, Malcolm understood the African-American struggle for social and political equality in America within the context of the worldwide liberation movements taking place among other African peoples in the world at the time. He created the Organization for African American Unity (OAAU) in the spirit of the Organization for African Unity (OAU) for the purpose of organizing African peoples in the Western Hemisphere. With this in mind, he traveled throughout Africa and the Middle East attempting to garner international support of the OAAU's effort to have the United States of America brought before the United Nations on charges of violating the human rights of African Americans. Before he moved forward with these plans, Malcolm X was murdered at the Audubon Ballroom in Harlem, on February 21, 1965. Malcolm X's insistence on the dignity of African culture and heritage and the centrality of Africa in the African-American struggle for human rights was perhaps his greatest philosophical influence on the literature produced during the BLACK ARTS MOVEMENT.

Malcolm X delineated and dispersed his powerful and at times strident ideas ("revolution by any means necessary") and ideology in his writings, The AUTOBIOGRAPHY OF MALCOLM X (1965; written with Alex Haley) and several of his now-classic speeches and lectures. He added his voice to those of such important literary forerunners as *DAVID WALKER, FREDERICK DOUGLASS, HENRY HIGHLAND GARNETT,* and *MARCUS GARVEY.* The best-known speeches/essays include "Message from the Grass Roots" (1964), "The Ballot or the Bullet" (1964), "The Oxford Debate" (1964), and "The Last Message" (1965). The recurring theme in these essays, as in *The Autobiography,* is the need for black people to unite to defeat white racism and black oppression wherever they are found. For example, in "Message to the Grass Roots" he admonishes, "We have a common enemy. We have this in common: We have a common oppressor, a common exploiter, and a common discriminator. But once we all realize that we have this common enemy, then we unite on the basis of what we have in common." Malcolm's speeches and essays also record his development and ideological metamorphosis to a more global perspective and an emphasis on human rights.

BIBLIOGRAPHY

Malcolm X. *The Autobiography of Malcolm X.* New York: Grove Press, 1965.

Sales, William W. *From Civil Rights to Black Liberation: Malcolm X and the Organization of Afro-American Unity.* Boston: South End Press, 1994.

Turner, Richard Brent. *Islam in the African American Experience.* Bloomington: Indiana University Press, 1997.

Malachai Crawford

Mama Day   Gloria Naylor (1992)

GLORIA NAYLOR's postmodern neo–slave narrative *Mama Day* is set in Willow Springs, a politically liminal space reminiscent of St. Helena's Island. Naylor's narrative style is much influenced by ZORA NEALE HURSTON's celebration of communal oral narrative as the true key to black history. The oral tale telling is split between three local voices. A chatty local insider offers a cautionary tale about Reema's boy, who went away to college and came back with a tape recorder in order to write a scholarly account of the historical truth of 1823. Sadly, by trusting academic methods and scientific deduction, he has missed the real clues embedded in oral tradition, local history, and the legacy of slavery written large on the landscape, on the tongue, and on literal black bodies. The local guide gradually reveals Sapphira Wade's and Mama Day's stories and then goes to the graveyard to overhear George and Cocoa, who offer each other their life stories while she sits by his grave. George is a northerner, the son of a teenage black prostitute who abandoned him to a New York orphanage where he learned to rely only on himself and the present moment.

Ophelia is a provincial southerner who, after widening her cultural experiences in New York City, comes only slowly to appreciate her island heritage and her special powers. In Willow Springs, a sacred ritual ground and lush mythic ecotone, the local Gullahs relish their geographic isolation, negotiate storms, tease nosy anthropologists, play tricks, tell tales, honor their ancestors, preserve their folk culture, and evade the developers. Day family history, we discover, begins in 1823, when African conjure woman Sapphira Wade murdered Bascombe Wade, her white slave owner and lover. She first secured freedom for herself and her seven sons, plus the deeds to the plantation, and then rested on the seventh day and accordingly re-named her family Day. However, despite such gifts of freedom and African conjure power, tragedy ensued for her generations. Sapphira lived only a thousand days after this.

Mama Day, Sapphira's descendant and a power-ful local practitioner, must now teach Cocoa what it means to be the lineal descendant of the seventh son of this African conjure woman. First, a fitting consort, a truly greathearted black man, must be found for her. She begins a stormy love relationship with George, a black New York professional man conjured by Mama Day's special powders whom she subsequently takes home on the annual August pilgrimage to Willow Springs. These two special lovers, on whom the future rests, fall quickly into Mama Day's conjuring designs until Ruby, a jeal-ous rival practitioner, curses Cocoa with a deadly infestation of worms. When George fails to believe in Mama Day's African conjure powers and relies only on his love and physical strength to save her, he dies needlessly of a heart attack. However nec-essary and effective his sacrifice for love, it need not have resulted in his death.

In the context of this cautionary tale, Naylor deconstructs disabling oppositions between Africa and America, North and South, science and reli-gion, pragmatism and faith, print and oral culture, Afromysticism and Christianity. Out of a mixture of Sea Island Afromystical and Christian rituals, Gullah folkways, the Bible, Shakespeare, and the contemporary urban black experience, Naylor's text bridges contemporary African-American hy-bridities and transformations in an effort to knit back together the traditions and generations of the Great Migration. From her sea island stage emerge voices from beyond the grave; beneficent, bogus, and evil conjurers; a gigantic storm; an old grave-yard; a haunted house; a tragic family saga; true lovers; plantation history; and the whole North-ern urban experience. Cocoa and George must bridge them all by growing into the potent legacy of Sapphira's black matrilineage, by healing the rift between black men and women, and by claiming their shared African-American history. Theirs is the cosmic sexual union of god and goddess that will realign the tilted cosmos of the African di-aspora. As textual conjurer, Naylor builds on the foundation of their love a brave new black world that will transcend colonial history. Together George and Ophelia span Africa, the Middle Pas-sage, and the Great Migration.

BIBLIOGRAPHY

Awkward, Michael. "A Circle of Sisters." *Dissertation Abstracts International*. Diss. Michigan University, 1987.

———. *Inspiriting Influences: Tradition, Revision, and Afro-American Women's Novels*. New York: Columbia University Press, 1991.

Felton, Sharon, and Michelle Loris, eds. *The Criti-cal Response to Gloria Naylor*. Westport, Conn.: Greenwood Press, 1997.

Gates, Henry Louis, Jr., and K. A. Appiah, eds. *Gloria Naylor: Critical Perspectives Past and Present*. New York: Amistad Press, 1993.

Gloria Cronin

Mammy

Mammy is a fictional character created in slavery and perpetuated in the present day. Her founda-tion is in the mythical world of the "Old South." African-American female slaves who took care of the plantation owner's white children were referred to as "Mammies." Mammy as a job title became a mask that could be placed on African-American women. This mask erased their individ-uality and objectified them. They could be made into the image of perfect slaves: genuinely loving their oppressors, thus justifying slavery. As type, Mammy is depicted as a large, black, head-ragged, African-American woman. She made her first ap-pearance in American art—often depicted in the background of a white family's portrait. Her ap-pearance in art has been used as proof of the genu-ine Americanism of the work.

One of Mammy's earliest appearances in litera-ture was in James Paulding's *The Dutchman's Fire-side* (1831). She also made early appearances in children's literature such as Louise-Clarke Pynelle's

Diddie, Dumps, and Tot (1882). Mammy is always ready and willing to help her white folks. She is Mark Twain's "nigger woman" in *The Adventures of Huckleberry Finn* (1884), Laura Lee Hope's Dinah in the Bobbsey Twins series (1904), Fannie Hurst's Delilah in *Imitation of Life* (1904), and Margaret Mitchell's Mammy in *Gone with the Wind* (1936). She even appears in the contemporary romance novels like Nora Hess's *Wildfire* (1994).

While Mammy continues to be a well-known and well used figure in literature, her most famous exposure began in 1890, when R. T. Davis created Aunt Jemima and put her smiling face on pancake boxes. This image has been used to sell numerous items, including syrup, flour, kitchen appliances, and cleaning products.

Mammy's career in film has remained stable. She made her early screen appearance in America's first epic film, *The Birth of a Nation,* where a white male actor in blackface played her role. She sometimes changed out of her head-rag and put on a maid's uniform, as in Mae West's classic 1933 film *I'm No Angel.* In the Shirley Temple 1935 film *The Little Colonel,* she was back in her familiar slave garb. In contemporary films, she is not as fat or as black, but she is still Mammy in regard to her stereotypical qualities.

No matter the genre or the name given her, this type is identified by certain characteristics: She is an African-American female who is usually isolated or separated from the African-American community. She is usually loving and yet not loved. She is mothering but is rarely shown with children of her own or connected to African-American children. She has little or no past and little or no indication of a future; she exists in the here and now. Though she is not usually successful, she can and does help her white family succeed. She is always able and willing to help without any justifiable prodding.

Mammy is well entrenched in American history, literature, and popular culture. The mere mention of her name can evoke strong emotional responses. Mammy's soothing touch has been used to ease the conscience of a nation ravaged by the guilt of slavery. She has been used to placate and subjugate. She is a ready mask that can be placed on the body of any African-American woman. She is powerful and powerless. She is an American icon.

BIBLIOGRAPHY

Collins, Patricia Hill. *Black Feminist Thought.* New York: Routledge, 1991.

Manring, M. M. *Slave in a Box: The Strange Career of Aunt Jemima.* Charlottesville: University Press of Virginia, 1998.

Morton, Patricia. *Disfigured Images.* Westport, Conn.: Greenwood Publishing, 1991.

Roberts, Diane. *The Myth of Aunt Jemima: Representations of Race and Region.* New York: Routledge, 1994.

White, Deborah Gray. *Ar'n't I A Woman?* New York: Norton, 1987.

Yvonne Atkinson

Manchild in the Promised Land
Claude Brown (1968)

Like RICHARD WRIGHT's *BLACK BOY,* MALCOLM X's *AUTOBIOGRAPHY OF MALCOLM X,* and NATHAN McCALL's *Makes Me Wanna Holler,* CLAUDE BROWN's *Manchild in the Promised Land* offers a firsthand view of what the author, a native of New York's Harlem, experienced as he moved from boyhood to young adulthood during the post–World War II era. Cumulatively, these autobiographies by black men suggest that growing up in America during the 20th century was similar for many African males, no matter their geographical location. None of these writers was granted the luxury of enjoying a childhood of innocence, much less a young adulthood filled with dreams and expectations. According to them, the black male is often forced to be simultaneously a child and a man, given his socioeconomic and political status. Like Richard, Malcolm, and Nathan, Sonny Boy, the young novice of this now-classic autobiographical novel, is forced to grow up within "the veil," to borrow from W. E. B. DuBois, within the marginalized world he is assigned to whether in Georgia, North or South Carolina, or "the promised land," Harlem. The black mecca created dream-filled migrating black southerners, like Sonny's grandparents, during the periods after World War I and the Great Depression.

Brown lays out his purpose and fundamental premise in the preface: "I want to talk about the experiences of a misplaced generation, of a misplaced people in an extremely complex, confused society. . . . These characters are sons and daughters of former Southern sharecroppers. These were the poorest people of the South, who poured into New York City during the decade following the Great Depression. . . . To them this was the promised land" (vii). What "these descendants of Ham" found was not an ideal "city upon a hill," as did the Puritans immigrants who settled New England, but, instead, a "slum ghetto" (vii–viii). "There were too many people full of hate and bitterness crowded into a dirty, stinky, uncared-for closet-size section of a great city" (viii). This is the mythical world, full of curses, anger, and disappointment, Sonny and the other children of "these disillusioned colored pioneers" (viii) inherited. Calling attention to the thematic resonance of Brown's *Manchild* with the slave narrative, Sidone Smith points out, "What previously were the harsh realities of the plantation are transferred to the larger more deadly plantation, the ghetto. There are no direct overseers: instead, the overseer is now the greater society surrounding the ghetto, forcing it into self-destructive patterns of existence." (156–157).

Brown captures the violence found in this idealist world of dream deferred in the opening scene of his text when 13-year-old Sonny Boy, a street gang member since age 11, is shot during a robbery. The first word of the text, "Run," sets the pace and tone for the remainder of the narrative; like the fugitive slave, Sonny Boy is in flight, seeking sanctuary in a community where "there is no hiding place" to be found. Sonny has been, since age eight, a ward of New York's juvenile system, having been institutionalized in every agency from Warwick, a mental institution, to Wiltwyck School for Boys, which was founded by Eleanor Roosevelt, to whom Brown dedicates his autobiography, where he spent two and a half years. In these institutions, Sonny finds the wholeness and meaning not available to him at home, given his father's verbal and physical abuse and his mother's passivity, or in the public school system, from which he and his friends, feeling imprisoned, are truant. Driven by fear, he adopts the criminality that governs the code of the streets, despite knowing firsthand the dead-end life that lies ahead, having witnessed the death and imprisonment of his friends and the eventual devastation of his brother, Pimp, a hustler and drug abuser. "It was fighting and stealing that made me somebody" (61), Brown writes; "My friends were all daring like me, tough like me, dirty like me, ragged like me, cursed like me, and had a great love for trouble like me. . . . Although none of my sidekicks was over twelve years of age, we didn't think of ourselves as kids" (21–22).

Deeply influenced by Mr. Papenek, an administrator at Wiltwyck who provided him with a different perspective on life, Sonny Boy, feeling alienated upon his return from Wiltwyck, eventually leaves Harlem and enters the white world of Greenwich Village, where he becomes gainfully and legally employed, pursues his education, becomes interested in his spirituality, and begins to find value in music, particularly jazz. However, although "Greenwich Village frees him physically from Harlem, it does not free him spiritually" (Smith, 165); he is driven back home to Harlem by the racism he encounters in the village, especially while he is in an interracial romantic affair. Upon his return, Sonny Boy (Brown) accepts existential responsibility for himself—for his own life and the choices he makes—despite the inevitable struggles he knows he still has to face. This decision, Sonny Boy confesses at the end, was "a move way from fear, toward challenges, toward the positive anger that I think every young man should have" (413).

BIBLIOGRAPHY

Brown, Claude. *Manchild in the Promised Land.* New York: Macmillan Company, 1965.
Smith, Sidone. *Where I'm Bound: Patterns of Slavery and Freedom in Black American Autobiography.* Westport, Conn.: Greenwood Press, 1974.

Wilfred D. Samuels

Marrow of Tradition, The
Charles W. Chesnutt (1901)

The Marrow of Tradition is one of CHARLES W. CHESNUTT's most controversial books. Following the success of his two short story collections, *The Conjure Woman* and *The Wife of His Youth and Other Stories of the Color Line* (1899), Chesnutt worked on *The House behind the Cedars* (1900). Chesnutt was certain that his next work, an epic account of the Wilmington, North Carolina, race riots, would signal his arrival as a serious novelist. However, *The Marrow of Tradition* (1901), now considered one of most important works in African-American literature, met with little critical acclaim. William Dean Howells, Chesnutt's editor, called the novel "bitter." Most readers found its unflinching portrait of Jim Crow segregation, white supremacy, and lynching too realistic, though by today's standards the novel would be considered tame.

Set in the fictional town of Wellington, North Carolina, *The Marrow of Tradition* traces the lives of the Miller and Carteret families. The Millers (he is a medical doctor) represent rising middle-class black families of the post-Reconstruction South, while the Carterets represent the old guard, southern plantation aristocracy. Janet Miller, as the result of a prevailing plantation concubine system, is Olivia Carteret's half sister. Throughout the novel, Chesnutt emphasizes doubles—each major character has a counterpart illustrating the interrelatedness of the American community—white and black alike. Chesnutt also uses the metaphor of the double to highlight one of his prevalent themes, "second slavery," a term used to suggest that the problems of race in the post-Reconstruction South were as violent and dehumanizing—if not worse—than in the antebellum period.

Chesnutt uses his principal characters, Dr. William Miller, Janet (his wife), Major Carteret, and Olivia, to explore the complicated foundations of blood relationships that obscure the path to healing for the South and the nation. Unable to forget the largely mythologized "glorious" past of the South and accept the changes occurring in the present, the Carterets deny kinship rites and participate in both legal and unlawful measures to secure their status as powerful whites. Carteret, who considers blacks "an inferior and servile race" (25), "believed in the divine rights of white men and gentlemen as his ancestors had believed" (34). To ensure that Janet and her black mother, Julia, who was legally married to Olivia and Janet's father, William Merkell, at the time of his death, will not be recognized as legitimate heirs, Polly Ochiltree, Olivia's aunt, chases Julia and Janet away and hides the documents that confirm Janet's legal right to half the estate.

Whites' fear of "Negro domination" forms a threat to the community and leads to a near-lynching and the riot that results in the death of numerous African Americans. Miller, a doctor light enough to "pass," resists the urge to violence but ultimately cannot forgive his white neighbors for the tragedy that befalls his family when his infant son is killed by a stray bullet during the riot. Significantly, although Chesnutt peoples his novels with the familiar literary black stereotypes popularized by plantation local color fiction, he imbues the characters, for the most part, with admirable moral qualities. Jude Green, a dark-skinned African American and the epitome of the "Negro beast," becomes the quintessential warrior and champion of equal rights. During the riots, he intrepidly declares, "we ain' gwine ter stan' up an' be shot downward like dogs. We're gwine ter defen' ou' lives, an' we ain' gwine ter run away f'm no place where we've got a right ter be" (281).

Chesnutt's moral voice of the tale is Janet Miller, who is able to overcome her grief and anger and offer compassion and forgiveness to those who have wronged her and her family. In the end, the reader is not certain if Chesnutt's tone is optimistic or cautious: "there's time but none to spare." If America cannot find honest, healthy, and open means to deal with its troubled past, its children and its future will be irrevocably lost.

BIBLIOGRAPHY
Chesnutt, Charles W. *The Marrow of Tradition.* New York: Penguin, 1993.

Roe, Jae H. "Keeping an 'Old Wound' Alive: *The Marrow of Tradition* and the Legacy of Wilmington." *African American Review* 33, no. 2 (1999): 231–243.

Sundquist, Eric. Introduction. *The Marrow of Tradition.* New York: Penguin, 1993.

Wilson, Matthew. *Whiteness in the Novels of Charles W. Chesnutt.* Jackson: University Press of Mississippi, 2004.

Tracie Church Guzzio

Marshall, Paule   (1929–)

Paule Marshall, née Valenza Pauline Burke, was born April 9, 1929, in Brooklyn, New York, to Samuel and Ada Burke, who had emigrated separately from Barbados after World War I. At 18, Marshall's mother paid her passage with "Panama money" inherited from an older brother who had died, like thousands of other West Indian migrant laborers, digging the Panama Canal. Growing up during the Depression in a close-knit West Indian community in Brooklyn, Marshall vividly experienced Barbadian—or Bajan—culture through her mother's friends' conversations around the kitchen table. Prominent in Marshall's writing are the language patterns, figures of speech, and relentless character analyses she overheard. Marshall visited Barbados for the first time when she was nine. Although the trip inspired a series of poems, she would reject her West Indian heritage for a time later in her youth.

Also during her youth, Marshall suffered a painful period when her father left home to become a devotee of cult leader Father Divine. As a teenager, the consistent neglect or distortion of African-American culture disturbed Marshall. An avid reader, Marshall spent countless hours at the public library, though no literary representations of black people—African, African-American, or African-Caribbean—were readily available to her. When she finally had the opportunity to read the great black male writers, such as PAUL LAURENCE DUNBAR and RICHARD WRIGHT, Marshall realized that black women's voices were largely missing from the impressive body of material she had found. Over her 50-year career, she has worked to fill this void, and in the process also paved the way for other important writers, among them TONI MORRISON, JAMAICA KINCAID, ALICE WALKER, NTOZAKE SHANGE, EDWIDGE DANTICAT, and NALO HOPKINSON.

Marshall's inspiration to write came after an illness forced her to leave Hunter College, where she was majoring in social work, to spend a year at a sanatorium in upstate New York. There, in a tranquil lake setting, she wrote letters so vividly describing her surroundings that a friend encouraged her to think of a career in writing. Upon her release from the sanatorium, she transferred to Brooklyn College, changed her major to English literature, and graduated cum laude and Phi Beta Kappa in 1953. She then took courses toward a master's degree at Hunter College. Unable to find a job with a major publishing company in New York, Marshall was employed briefly as a librarian and then became food and fashion editor for the small, popular African-American magazine *Our World,* where she worked until 1956.

Despite the sexism she encountered as the only woman on the staff, she was eventually given features, and some of those writing assignments took her to the West Indies and Latin America. Marshall wrote fiction in her free time, publishing her first short story, "The Valley Between," in 1954. In 1957, she married psychologist Kenneth Marshall, with whom she had a son, Evan Keith, a year later. Over her husband's strong protests, Marshall hired a babysitter so that she could finish her first and best-known novel, *Brown Girl, Brownstones* (1959), which is regarded by many scholars as the beginning of contemporary African-American women's writing. Marshall divorced in 1963 and began teaching part-time at several universities. In 1970, she wed Haitian businessman Nourry Ménard and began dividing her time between New York and Haiti.

Marshall has produced five novels and two collections of short fiction: BROWN GIRL BROWNSTONES (1959), *Soul Clap Hands and Sing* (1961), *The Chosen Place the Timeless People* (1969), *Reena* (1983), and *Praisesong for the Widow* (1983). In her earliest work, Marshall broke new literary ground with her exploration and celebration of black immigrant communities, the African diaspora, and black women's experience. Marshall interrogates the past as a vital step toward constructing the future—one that is rich with a unifying, timeless Pan-African mythos. One result of this historical, spiritual, and feminist revisionist agenda is that Marshall's work has sometimes been critiqued as idealistic. What seems to be most important to Marshall is posing questions about the diaspora while offering narrative pathways that help readers realize strengthening continuities of African culture, as BARBARA CHRISTIAN and other critics have shown. Her childhood identification with Africa through the MARCUS GARVEY movement was intensified after visits in 1977 and 1980 to Africa, where she was welcomed by the people of Nigeria, Kenya, and Uganda as a long-lost daughter returning home.

In her first novel, BROWN GIRL, BROWNSTONES (1959), which is somewhat autobiographical, Marshall portrays a Caribbean immigrant family. Set in Brooklyn, the story chronicles the coming of age of Selina Boyce. Selina's mother, a hardworking, cruelly honest woman, is fiercely pursuing the American Dream, while her father alternately fantasizes about instant American success and returning home to the Caribbean. Over the course of the novel, Selina and the reader are educated about love, sacrifice, and African-American history. Marshall's focus on a black girl as protagonist and her exploration of gender dynamics within the black community were new to American and African-American literature. Although *Brown Girl, Brownstones* was initially well received, it did not become a commercial success until interest in black women writers heightened in the early 1970s; it gained widespread recognition when it was reprinted in 1981.

Marshall wrote *Soul Clap Hands and Sing* (1961) while on a Guggenheim Fellowship in 1960. She takes the title of this collection of four novellas from William Butler Yeats's poem "Sailing to Byzantium." In this book, each story depicts an elderly man of African descent living in a different part of the black diaspora who has lost himself to Western materialism. Each man, in his need to develop meaningful human relationships, reaches

out to a young woman. In the end, each finds he has waited too long. This collection earned Marshall the National Institute of Arts and Letters Rosenthal Award. A Ford Foundation grant (1964–65) and National Endowment for the Arts award (1967–68) followed.

In her second full-length work of fiction, *The Chosen Place, The Timeless People* (1969), Marshall presents the memorable West Indian heroine Merle Kinbona. In the novel, set on the fictional Caribbean island of Bourne, Marshall, through Merle, the daughter of a white planter and black servant, explores the troubled West Indian psyche. Merle is an educated woman who has been abused by the perverted ideals of British white supremacy. Merle's lack of self-awareness has ultimately led to the end of her marriage with her African husband and her return to her homeland. When the novel's other main character, the Jewish-American anthropologist Saul Amron, comes to the island to conduct a preliminary survey that aims to better the life of the inhabitants, he and Merle develop a romantic affair that eventually results in the cancellation of Saul's project, his wife's suicide, and Merle's decision to move to Africa to find her husband and daughter. In this novel, Marshall's Pan-Africanist focus, exceptional characterizations (black and white, male and female), and subtle handling of homosexuality, race, and culture were pioneering.

Though there was a lull in her major fiction works over the following decade, Marshall received a second grant from the National Endowment for the Arts (1978–79), which led, in 1983, to the publication of two books: her third novel, *Praisesong for the Widow*, which won the Before Columbus Foundation American Book Award (1984), and *Reena and Other Short Stories*, which includes the often-anthologized autobiographical "To Da-duh, In Memoriam" and "The Making of a Writer: From the Poets in the Kitchen." In the latter, Marshall expresses her gratitude to her mother and other Barbadian women for having taught her the power of the word as an instrument of communication and survival. Not only have these two short pieces been key to our understanding Marshall's oeuvre, but they, along with Marshall's fiction, also have offered an intimate glance into an Afro-Caribbean

American sensibility that has helped create a receptive readership for more recent writers.

In *Praisesong for the Widow* (1983), Avatara "Avey" Johnson, a recent widow, is on a Caribbean cruise when her materialistic existence is disrupted by a dream of her dead aunt. So begins for Avey the traditional pattern of the Gullah Praise House initiate's liminal "seeking" journey and subsequent ritual entrance into full community membership. In the novel, Marshall's metaphor for spiritual resistance to psychic colonization is the famous Gullah folktale of Ibo Landing that tells of a group of captured Ibo who, upon reaching the Sea Islands in chains, simply walk into the ocean to return to Africa. Beginning to confront and occupy the previously vacuous silence of the Middle Passage in oral and literary traditions, Marshall insists that the future of U.S. society is possible only if Americans first embrace slavery's terrible past, as TONI MORRISON similarly emphasized four years later in BELOVED (1987). Liberation of self and the greater community can come only with the visceral experience of history, myth, and ritual of the African diaspora, which is the mission of individual storytellers, like Avey Johnson and Marshall herself, to tell.

After winning the Tribute to Black Womanhood Award from Smith College (1983), the Langston Hughes Medallion Award (1986), the New York State Governor's Arts Award (1987), and the John Dos Passos Award for Literature (1989), Marshall experienced, during the 1990s, another fruitful decade. She received the PEN/Faulkner Award (1990); published her fourth novel, *Daughters* (1991); was awarded a MacArthur Fellowship (1992); and was designated a Literary Lion by the New York Public Library (1994).

Daughters is set in New York City, the home of 34-year-old freelance consumer researcher Ursa Mackenzie, and on the fictional island of Triunion, Ursa's birthplace and the home of her politician father, Primus Mackenzie, her American-born mother, Estelle; and Primus's mistress, Astral Forde. When the story opens, Ursa, who has just had an abortion, is about to end a stagnant relationship with her long-time boyfriend. On her job, she is studying black empowerment in a New

Jersey city where the black mayor is selling out to the white establishment. She is also thinking about her long-delayed thesis project on the Triunion slavery legend of freedom fighters and lovers Congo Jane and Will Cudjoe. Estelle summons Ursa to Triunion, where her formerly incorruptible father is cooperating with white developers in plans that will despoil the environment and endanger the poverty-stricken residents. Marshall's interest in individual responsibility to community, the resurrection of history, gender relations, and female empowerment are again emphasized in this book.

A framed snapshot in Marshall's grandmother's house of a cousin she never met was the inspiration for her fifth novel, *The Fisher King* (2000), a story that echoes JAMES BALDWIN's "SONNY'S BLUES" (1957). Against family and community pressures, this cousin had aspired to be a jazz musician but was drafted into the Army during World War II and died soon thereafter. In the novel, disowned by his family for his choice of career, Sonny-Rett Payne, a jazz pianist, had fled New York for Paris in 1949 to escape family disapproval and U.S. racism. His success in Europe and subsequent death there form the background of the story. Decades after Sonny-Rett left, his eight-year-old Parisian grandson is brought to his old Brooklyn neighborhood to attend a memorial concert in Payne's honor and ends up a pawn in the adults' family feud and inability to settle past grievances. The family begins to reevaluate their ideas about themselves during the course of the novel, but the text is open-ended, by which Marshall may be suggesting that life is short and that examining oneself, repairing lost relationships, and creating a stronger community is up to the reader. As she does in *Daughters*, in *The Fisher King* Marshall poses certain questions for which she does not provide answers. In both texts, the ambiguous endings have been frustrating for some readers and reviewers.

Marshall's many honors include a Guggenheim Fellowship, a Ford Foundation grant, and two National Endowment for the Arts awards. The recipient of five honorary doctorates, Marshall has taught at numerous universities in the United

States and abroad, including Yale, Columbia, Cornell, Oxford, Virginia Commonwealth University, the University of California at Berkeley, and the Iowa Writers Workshop. Since 1997 she has been on the faculty of New York University's graduate creative writing program, where she holds the Helen Gould Sheppard Chair of Literature and Culture. Through careful research into historical events and figures that is followed by painstaking writing, Marshall has done justice to the past in order to affect positively her readers' present and future. Marshall reminds us of the solace and joy to be found in embracing one's past and heritage, a universal message that, through her vivid characterizations, transcends culture.

BIBLIOGRAPHY

Christian, Barbara. "Ritualistic Process and the Structure of Paule Marshall's *Praisesong for the Widow.*" *Callaloo* 18 (Spring–Summer 1983): 74–84.

———. "Trajectories of Self-Definition: Placing Contemporary Afro-American Women's Fiction." In *Conjuring: Black Women, Fiction and the Literary Tradition,* edited by Marjorie Pryse and Hortense Spillers, 233–248. Bloomington: Indiana University Press, 1985.

DeLamotte, Eugenia C. *Places of Silence, Journeys of Freedom: The Fiction of Paule Marshall.* Penn Studies in Contemporary American Fiction, edited by Emory Elliott. Philadelphia: University of Pennsylvania Press, 1998.

Denniston, Dorothy Hamer. *The Fiction of Paule Marshall: Reconstructions of History, Culture, and Gender.* Knoxville: University of Tennessee Press, 1995.

Hathaway, Heather. *Caribbean Waves: Relocating Claude McKay and Paule Marshall.* Bloomington: Indiana University Press, 1999.

Marshall, Paule. "Characterizations of Black Women in the American Novel." In *In the Memory and Spirit of Frances, Zora, and Lorraine: Essays and Interviews on Black Women and Writing,* edited by Juliette Bowles, 76–79. Washington, D.C.: Institute for the Arts and the Humanities, Howard University, 1979.

———. "The Negro Woman in Literature." *Freedomways* 6 (1966): 21–25.

———. "Shaping the World of My Art." *New Letters* 40, no. 1 (Autumn 1973): 97–112.

Elizabeth McNeil

Maud Martha   Gwendolyn Brooks (1953)

Maud Martha reveals the developing consciousness of a young girl living in a northern city before, during, and after World War II. Composed of 34 very poetic sketches, the novel expands DuBoisian double consciousness—the almost schizophrenic identity African Americans must assume of being both black and American—to include matters of gender, caste, and color. For most of the story, Maud Martha Brown is overly preoccupied with the way others (a domineering mother, a chauvinistic husband, boys who prefer light-skinned girls with good hair, people of wealth, and white society in general) see her. GWENDOLYN BROOKS renders the loosely autobiographical narrative from the third-person limited omniscient perspective.

The novel opens with a description of preschool-aged Maud Martha and introduces the metaphor of the dandelion (a common thing of undervalued beauty) to which Maud compares herself. Desire is the overwhelming emotion depicted in this opening sketch, which introduces the protagonist's longing. Brooks uses the second sketch to provide detail about a spring landscape and to depict children at play in the schoolyard in the morning. The day is cool and blustery, and the overwhelming mood is one of anticipation and possibility. The third vignette provides insight into Maud's parents' relationship and Maud's paradoxical relationship with her mother. The death of Maud's grandmother is the focus of the fourth vignette, which evokes feelings of vulnerability and disgust. In the fifth sketch, Maud's feelings of racial inferiority surface as she anticipates a visit from a white classmate. From Maud's perspective, he is the entire white race sitting in judgment of her, the entire black race. The dominant emotion is self-loathing. In the 13th vignette, titled "Low Yellow," Brooks explores the definition of "pretty" and how it is defined in terms of skin color and hair texture. Dark-skinned, coarse-haired Maud realizes she does not fit the prevailing definition of "pretty."

The remaining vignettes take us through Maud's somewhat uneventful adolescence, her marriage, and the birth of her daughter Paulette. Always the driving force is desire, but Brooks uses each vignette to highlight other moods, attitudes, and emotions, including intrigue, anxiety, shame, resolve, despair, resignation, and optimism. Especially poignant is the vignette "kitchenette folks," which describes the people who live in the building where Maud and Paul's disappointing kitchenette apartment is located.

Several experiences eventually help Maud Martha toward a sense of self that is not based on others' perceptions. A stint as a domestic worker helps her better understand her husband's attitudes, but a major turning point comes when she gives birth and realizes that she is responsible for the life of another human being. She stands up to her mother for the first time; she realizes that she need not envy her "prettier," more desirable sister Helen; and she even musters up enough self-confidence to confront both a pushy salesperson and a white Santa Claus who tries to snub her child. Thus, Brooks ties motherhood to the protagonist's self-development. The novel ends on a note of optimism as Maud looks forward to the birth of her second child. The reader is left with the feeling that Maud Martha is finally in touch with her own creative power, her natural love of life, and her capacity for self-definition.

Though *Maud Martha* received scant attention when it was first published, black feminist critics resurrected the novel in the 1980s. It represents the multiplied effects of both the perception and the reality of being on the bottom rung of society's race, class, gender, caste, and color hierarchies. Initially published by Harper and Row, *Maud Martha* was reissued in 1993 by Chicago's THIRD WORLD PRESS. Students should read the novel with Brooks's poetry, particularly *Annie Allen*. This story of self-discovery (bildungsroman) also fits in well among texts such as HARRIET JACOBS's INCIDENTS IN THE LIFE OF A SLAVE GIRL (1861), ZORA NEALE HURSTON's THEIR EYES WERE WATCHING GOD, PAULE MARSHALL's BROWN GIRL,

BROWNSTONES (1959), TONI MORRISON's *The Bluest Eye* (1970), AUDRE LORDE's ZAMI (1982), and Alice Randall's *The WIND DONE GONE* (2001). Comparable to RALPH ELLISON's INVISIBLE MAN, Brooks's *Maud Martha* represents a pending break with the naturalistic and deterministic tone set by RICHARD WRIGHT in NATIVE SON (1940) and ANN PETRY in *The STREET* (1946). In some ways *Maud Martha* is more akin to the realism of *Their Eyes Were Watching God* with its focus on a woman's journey of self-discovery and her growing awareness of her own agency. Certainly *Maud Martha* and Paule Marshall's *Brown Girl, Brownstones* help connect the relatively few previously published quest narratives with black female protagonists to the proliferation of women-centered texts that would appear in subsequent decades.

BIBLIOGRAPHY
Bryant, Jacqueline K. *Gwendolyn Brooks' Maud Martha: A Critical Collection.* Chicago: Third World Press, 2002.

Lovalerie King

Mayfield, Julian   (1928–1984)

Journalist, essayist, dramatist, and novelist Julian Mayfield was born in 1928 in Greer, South Carolina, but was raised by his parents, Hudson and Annie Mae Prince Mayfield, in Washington, D.C. After graduating from Dunbar High School, Mayfield joined the U.S. Army, serving a stint in the Pacific before returning home to continue his education at Lincoln University in Pennsylvania. He lived in New York working as an actor, producer, playwright, and director. His play *417* was produced off-Broadway. As a journalist, he wrote for the *Puerto Rico World Journal.* He was briefly involved in the CIVIL RIGHTS MOVEMENT and the Marxist organizations Jefferson School for Social Research and the Committee for the Negro in the Arts.

In 1961 Mayfield left the United States for Ghana, where he served as a communications adviser to the Nkrumah government and worked as a journalist and editor for the *African Review.* Returning home in 1966, he appeared in his cowritten film *Up Tight* (1968), which starred Raymond St. Jacques. He served as a government adviser again from 1971 to 1974 in Guyana. A Fulbright scholar in Turkey, Algeria, Austria, Denmark, and Germany, Mayfield published his essays in the *Nation, Commentary, Negro Digest* (*Black World*), and many other journals.

Mayfield published three novels: *The Hit* (1957), *The Long Night* (1958), and *The Grand Parade* (1961), which was reissued as *Nowhere Street* in 1963. His plays include *417, A World Full of Men,* and *Fount of the Nation.* He published *Ten Times Black: Stories from the Black Experience* in 1972. Set in Harlem, *The Hit* focuses on the Cooley family, Hubert, Gertrude, and son James Lee, and specifically on Hubert's effort to make enough money to support his family by playing the numbers. However, when his number, 417, finally hits, the numbers man does not pay off. Ironically, Hubert's faith in God ensures him an inevitable victory over his impoverished condition through gambling.

Also set in Harlem, *The Long Night* develops, among many themes, an exploration of a father-son relationship. Abandoned by his father, Steely Brown is forced to grow up fatherless in the ghetto. When his mother hits the numbers and sends him to collect her prize, his own gang members rob Steely. Although he turns to several sources in an effort to replace the money, he is turned away and fails to do so. At the end of the night, he tries to roll a drunken man asleep in a doorway. The drunk turns out to be his father, Paul Brown. At daybreak, after a long talk, father and son walk home together: "they turn their steps homeward and seem to face the day and the days to come with at least a modicum of hope" (Paris, 201).

Mayfield's early novels explored the "cruel paradox" (Richards, vi) of the 1950s, when personal opportunities were plentiful but blacks were denied those opportunities. He posited that black people should find their places within their neighborhoods, in the margin, rather than fight for an unattainable goal. Although Mayfield's Harlem is not the best environment, particularly for young boys, "it is by no means hopeless" (Davis, 201). Mayfield's novels are partially autobiographical,

based on his experiences living in the margin and being denied an opportunity to excel in mainstream America. Mayfield continued to explore the nexus between art and politics in his career, which spanned the black experience. In his signature essay, "Into the Mainstream," delivered as a paper at the First Conference of Negro Writers (March 1959), Mayfield urged black writers to stay away from the mainstream: "The likelihood is that the Negro people will continue for several years to occupy, to a diminishing degree, the position of the unwanted child who, having been brought for a visit, must remain for the rest of his life." For the black writer, he concluded, this means, "the façade of the American way of life is always transparent" (560–561).

BIBLIOGRAPHY

Davis, Arthur P. *From the Dark Tower.* Washington, D.C.: Howard University Press, 1974.

Mayfield, Julian. "Into the Mainstream." In *Dark Symphony: Negro Literature in America,* edited by James A. Emanuel and Theodore Gross, 557–561. New York: Free Press, 1968.

———. *The Hit* and *The Long Night.* Boston: Northeastern University Press, 1989.

Rodney, Ruby V. "Julian Mayfield." In *The Oxford Companion to African American Literature,* 486–487. New York: Oxford University Press, 1997.

Kim Hai Pearson
Brian Jennings

McCall, Nathan   (1955–)

Journalist, lecturer, and writer-autobiographer Nathan McCall was born and reared by his mother and stepfather in Key West, Florida. He chronicles his youth and early adult life in his award-winning autobiography, *Makes Me Wanna Holler: A Young Black Man in America* (1994).

Like RICHARD WRIGHT's *BLACK BOY* and MALCOLM X's *The AUTOBIOGRAPHY OF MALCOLM X,* McCall's *Makes Me Wanna Holler* records the effort of an African-American male to find meaning, self-respect, and wholeness in white, phallocentric, patriarchal America. When he was 10, McCall's parents moved from Florida to Cavalier Manor, an African-American middle-class neighborhood in Portsmouth, Virginia. This was the family's first real house, a symbol of their fulfillment of the American dream. Surrounded by his extended family, which included his grandmother, McCall and his brothers lived relatively normal lives as mischievous boys who played hooky from their Presbyterian Sunday school, played cowboys and Indians, held paper routes, and went skinny-dipping in Crystal Lake. Security and community extended beyond the walls of the family home, for Cavalier Manor was a neighborhood filled with surrogate parents, "people who would punish you like your mama and daddy if they caught you doing wrong." McCall adds, "School was also part of that surrogate system. . . . Those teachers spanked us like we were their own when we acted up in class" (8).

McCall experienced a damaging rite of passage into southern social stratification when his stepfather took him to work with him for the first time in Sterling Point, "the most affluent neighborhood in Portsmouth," located on the other side of the bridge. Here, in this "ghostly antiseptic place," McCall sees only near-invisible black domestic workers and witnesses his stepfather's degradation, not only by his wealthy clients, who address him by his first name (Bonnie, a name not even Nate's mother used), but also by their disrespectful children, who failed to acknowledge his presence as an adult, the way southern black children are taught to do. Embarrassed by his stepfather's obsequious behavior, McCall rejects outright this prescribed legacy. He would not be like the "downtrodden sharecroppers and field slaves [he'd] seen in books" (17). McCall's association of his stepfather's behavior with subjugation and slavery recalls the impetus that drove both FREDERICK DOUGLASS and Richard Wright to take flight.

In 1966, the first year Virginia integrated its public schools, McCall was in the sixth grade; he was transferred to Alford J. Mapp, "a white school across town," where he was devalued by both students and teachers. A year later, he was transferred to W. E. Waters Middle School, a predominantly black school, which provided not only a sanctuary for the psychologically damaged youth but above all membership in his age group, a "set" (gang) that eventually provided him with "the standard for manliness," including styling or dressing, putting waves in his hair, dancing, and strutting or pimping, which provided the identity that shaped his youth (27). Membership in this gang, he explains, "was a confidence booster, a steady support for my fragile self-esteem. Alone I was afraid of the world and insecure. But I felt cockier and surer of myself when hanging with my boys" (33).

McCall's effort to overcome his fears, define his own masculinity (including through the sexual abuse of black women), and gain respect as a black man through gang criminal activities (breaking and entering and armed robbery) eventually led him, at age 20, to prison for robbing a McDonald's restaurant. Ironically, he had served only 30 days in jail previously for shooting and nearly killing another black man. Prison was a wake-up call for McCall. After reading Malcolm X's works and Wright's NATIVE SON and abandoning Christianity and embracing Islam while in prison, McCall returned rehabilitated to society when he was released early for good behavior after serving three years. Like Douglass, Wright, and Malcolm X, McCall found in self-education a meaningful avenue to the quality of life he desired. Returning to Norfolk State University, he completed a degree in journalism and later found work with several major newspapers, including the *Virginia Pilot-Ledger Star*, the *Atlanta Journal Constitution*, and *The Washington Post*.

Makes Me Wanna Holler: A Young Black Man in America "shows that there are no simple explanations or pat solutions to the problems of racism and street violence. It answers questions only about its author, who wonders 'I was not special. How did I endure when so many others were crushed'" (Gadler, 45). The book was a *New York Times* best seller and was named Blackboard Book of the Year (1995). McCall published a collection of personal essays, *What's Going On*, in 1997. In 1998 he joined the journalism faculty at Emory University, where he also taught classes in creative writing and African-American studies.

BIBLIOGRAPHY

Cauchon, Dennis. "On the Streets and in School: Two Views of Growing Up Black." *USA Today,* 10 March 1994, p. 6D.

Gadler, Erica. "The Culture of Street Violence, by a Survivor." *At Random* 3, no. 1 (Winter 1994): 44–49.

Wilfred D. Samuels

McDonald, Janet (1953–)

A writer of young adult fiction and an international attorney who lives in Paris, Janet McDonald grew up in the Farragut Houses public housing project of Brooklyn, New York. She is one of seven children born to William McDonald, a World War II veteran who moved to New York to escape southern racism, and Florence McDonald, a domestic engineer. She briefly attended Erasmus in Brooklyn and the Harlem Prep School before receiving a scholarship to Vassar in 1973 to major in French. While there she was not prepared for the vast differences from her world in the Brooklyn projects, and she began using heroin. After dropping out of Vassar she returned and spent her junior year in Paris, France, and it was there that Janet felt free and like "just another American." She later earned a master's degree in journalism at Columbia University and a law degree at New York University.

Writing since the age of nine or 10, McDonald admits she likes to write mostly about teenage girls because not enough books have been written to address their problems. McDonald is the author of the award-winning memoir *Project Girl* (1999), a powerful, brutally honest, and troubling account of her personal struggle of trials, failures, and comebacks after coming to terms with her bouts of depression, drug abuse, arrest for arson, rape, and a nervous breakdown. With its realistic street dialogue and raps, McDonald's book, according to Sara Ivory of the *New York Times,* shows "the strength of her perseverance and her spirit in her willingness to relive her traumas by writing about them" (17). *Time'*s Romesh Ratnesar remarks that McDonald "writes with lucid-

ity and drama" but noted that "her cynicism . . . become[s] toxic" (81).

Following *Project Girl,* McDonald turned to a younger audience, addressing the themes of determination, courage, loyalty, familial love, and friendship. She published the first of her award-winning urban trilogy, *Spellbound* (2001), which was praised for the authenticity and credibility of her character and their voices, as well as the presentation of the house in which they live. Centering on 16-year-old Raven Jefferson and her best girlfriend, Aisha Ingram, both high school dropouts, unwed mothers, and virtually unemployable teens, the novel offers hope. Raven, unlike Aisha, is not content to rely on "the system" for support and is motivated to enter a spelling bee that will afford her an opportunity to enter a college preparatory program and to attend college on a full scholarship.

The second novel, *Chill Wind* (2001), the winner of the 2003 Coretta Scott King-John Steptoe New Talent Award, traces the life of the bullish yet naive 19-year-old high school dropout, Aisha Ingram, who, unlike in the first novel, tries to figure out ways to support herself and her two young children in New York once her welfare has ended and she must enter the workplace or "get kicked to the curb." Determined not to accept any of the "slave jobs" she has been offered, she stops at nothing to succeed. Among McDonald's successes in this novel is the way she presents Aisha's authentic voice and unique perspective. Janet Gillen, in a review in *School Library Journal,* also notes that McDonald's "language is real and believable and invokes life in an urban setting" (173).

Twists and Turns (2003), the third novel in the trilogy, examines the lives of two Brooklyn teenagers, Keeba and Teesha Washington. The recent high school graduates learn with the assistance of family and friends a number of life's important lessons, including that anything is possible if a person believes in herself. Reviewer Sharon Morrison notes that the main characters "exhibit both strengths and considerable vulnerability" (217). Even though McDonald's latest novel, *Brother Hood* (2004), does not have a young girl as its central character, it also focuses on an urban teen who must face and overcome major obstacles in his lives. *Brother Hood* captures the dilemma of the 16-year-old protagonist, Nathaniel Whitely, who grows up in Harlem and earns a scholarship to attend a prestigious boarding school in upstate New York. Although he is made to straddle two different worlds as a result—the wealth and privilege at the school and the danger and bleak prospects in his Harlem neighborhood—Nathaniel must still try to carve a niche for himself without losing his soul. According to reviewer Hazel Rochman, "With all the laughter and trouble, [*Brother Hood*] is a stirring celebration of Harlem, its roots, diversity, and change" (108).

In a short time, McDonald's works, with their upbeat messages and gritty, urban realism, have found a following among many new young readers. Targeting especially black girls and challenging them to "deal with the real," McDonald believes that there is hope for young adults—even those who live in some of the toughest environments, like the one she survived. McDonald's works, which demonstrate her wit and talent, are a welcome new addition to African-American young adult literature written since the 1970s by her contemporaries Kristen Hunter, Louise Meriwether, Sharon Bell Mathis, ROSA GUY, and Virginia Hamilton.

BIBLIOGRAPHY

Gillen, Janet. Review of *Chill Wind*. *School Library Journal* (November 2002): 173.

Ivory, Sara. Review of *Project Girl*. *New York Times Book Review*, 7 February 1999, p. 17.

Kennedy, Thomas E. "Up from Brooklyn: An Interview with Janet McDonald." *Literary Review* 44, no. 4 (Summer 2001): 704–720.

Morrison, Sharon. Review of *Twists and Turns*. *School Library Journal* 49, no. 9 (2003): 217.

Ratnesar, Romesh. Review of *Project Girl*. *Time*, 1 March 1999, p. 81.

Review of *Spellbound*. *Publishers Weekly* 250, no. 48 (December 1, 2003): 59.

Rochman, Hazel. Review of *Brother Hood*. *Booklist* (January 1, 2004): 108.

Loretta G. Woodard

McElroy, Colleen Johnson   (1935–   )

In her own account of the genesis of her writing career, Colleen McElroy writes, "I was educated in a school system that led me to believe all writers were male, white, and dead—three conditions I had no wish to assume. There. I've said it. What I consider tradition does not fall within that formula. Those literature courses I could endure presented poems as exacting, technical snippets of obscurity and abstraction. Those courses neglected my world and the people in it, all the women in my family—my grandmother, mother and her sisters—women who wove wonderful tales of truth and love, life and death. Yet it is because of those women that I have become a poet, or more precisely, a storyteller" (McElroy, 125).

A gifted poet, writer of fiction and nonfiction, and folklorist, McElroy is a native of St. Louis, Missouri. She was born on October 30, 1935, to Percia Purcell and Ruth Celeste Rawls. She grew up on Kennerly Avenue in the home of her grandmother, Anna Belle Long, or "Mama," as she was affectionately called. As a young girl, Colleen often eavesdropped on her mother and her aunts spinning stories. Learning early the rudiments of storytelling, she developed what she has called her "romance with language." McElroy attended the segregated Public School of St. Louis, graduating from the all-black Charles Sumner High School in 1953. A decade earlier, however, her mother had remarried, this time to Jesse Dalton Johnson, a native of Columbus, Georgia; McElroy moved often with her family, beginning her lifelong fascination with travel. By age 21 she had lived in St. Louis, Wyoming, Kansas, Frankfurt, and Munich, Germany, where she attended college from 1953 to 1955.

After graduating from Kansas State University in 1956, McElroy entered the University of Pittsburgh to become a speech therapist. While there, she met and married Burl Wilkinson, with whom she had two children; subsequently, she returned to Kansas State University, where, in 1963, she completed her master's degree. Her multiple careers as mother, student, and speech therapist, however, apparently took their toll, and in 1964, her marriage to Wilkinson ended. In 1966 McElroy migrated to the Pacific Northwest to become the director of speech and hearing services at Western Washington State University (WWS), Bellingham. Seduced by academic life, she enrolled in courses at WWS and subsequently entered the doctoral program at the University of Washington (UW), where she completed her degree in 1973; she joined UW's faculty the same year. After relocating to Washington, she married poet David McElroy, who adopted her children.

"A late bloomer," by her own admission, McElroy was in her 30s when she began writing seriously. While she was an emerging writer living in the Pacific Northwest, other writers in the region, including Richard Hugo, John Logan, Knute Skinner, Robert Huff, and Denise Levertov, encouraged her. During this time, she also discovered and devoured the works of African-American writers such as Langston Hughes, Joseph S. Cotter, Ann Spencer, Robert Hayden, Margaret Walker, and Gwendolyn Brooks. Later, when she moved to Seattle, she met other African-American writers and, through the United Black Artists Guild, she formed relationships with Ishmael Reed, Al Young, and John Edgar Wideman. Her early experiences in the Pacific Northwest influenced her first chapbook, *The Mules Done Long Since Been Gone* (1973). Three years later, she published *Music from Home: Selected Poems* (1976), a collection of poems in which McElroy, as she often does, focuses on the locales and people of St. Louis. In a subsequent volume, *Winters without Snow* (1979), she details the pain of her divorce from her second husband, David McElroy.

During the next two decades, McElroy emerged as an acclaimed African-American writer, demonstrating her poetic skill and productivity and publishing six more volumes of poetry and another chapbook. Uniquely, however, her writings transcend the long-standing but often oversimplified black versus universal dichotomy: While she embraces the African-American literary tradition in all of its complexities, she often extends beyond it, exploring new subjects and links in the human continuum.

Like many African-American writers, McElroy is intensely autobiographical, drawing liberally on her life experiences. In such poems as "Caledonia" in *Lie and Say You Love Me* and "Tapestries" in *Queen of the Ebony Isles,* for example, she focuses on the potency of a caring black family life and the strength of black people, two major themes in her writing. In *Bone Flames* and *What Madness Brought Me Here,* such masterful poems as "Years That Teach What Days Don't Even Know, "Foul Line—1987," "Webs and Weeds," and "Amen Sister" reveal her skillful use of African-American history and folk traditions to anchor her narratives. In *Traveling Music,* she extends the ethos of her early years in St. Louis to other locales.

As she developed her poetic craft, McElroy also broadened her interests as a writer. In 1976 she participated in a Breadloaf Writers' Workshop led by John Gardner, expanding her interest to fiction. During this period, she also became an accomplished writer of television scripts and plays, earning membership in both the Writers Guild and the Dramatists Guild. In 1982 she collaborated with Ishmael Reed on a Choreopoem play, *The Wild Gardens of the Loup Garou,* and in 1987 she wrote *Follow the Drinking Gourd,* a play about Harriet Tubman. That same year, capitalizing on her Breadloaf Workshop experience, McElroy published her first collection of short stories, *Jesus and Fat Tuesday and Other Stories,* and in 1990 she published her second volume of stories, *Driving under the Cardboard Pines.*

Though primarily a poet, McElroy incorporates her characteristic poetic sensibility, lyrical prose, humor, and deft description into her fiction. In the 29 stories included in *Jesus and Fat Tuesday and Other Stories* and *Driving under the Cardboard Pines,* she presents a panorama of characters— outlaws, pimps, prostitutes, strippers, lesbians, family matrons, undertakers, gang members, and futuristic lab technicians. McElroy's stories transcend time and geographical boundaries. Within her fictional borders, however, McElroy focuses on the psychological and social divides—conflicts between black and white, young and old, female and male, and traditional and contemporary. Set mostly in the Midwest in the early 20th century, the stories in *Jesus and Fat Tuesday* illustrate McElroy's treatment of psychological and social issues that divide individuals and communities. "A Brief Spell by the River," for example, portrays Cressy Pruit, who is raped by Sam Packer, one of Jesse James's henchmen; unable to negotiate the great racial divide, she reconciles her life and moves on. In the story "Jesus and Fat Tuesday," Toulouse seeks refuge in an alcohol ward because he is unable to reconcile his estrangements from his family. Similarly, in "The Return of the Apeman" in *Diving under the Cardboard Pines,* Franklin Washington cannot escape the gang life of St. Louis, while racial injustice lures Alleeda Grace Sykes back into a life of crime in "Amazing Grace and Floating Opportunity." No matter what her subject matter or theme in her stories, however, McElroy interweaves the potency of African-American culture.

Established as a poet long before she began writing fiction, McElroy has received many accolades for her writing. Widely anthologized, she is often recognized for her lyricism, humor, rich narrative style, sense of place, and transcendence of geography. Additionally, McElroy is highly praised for the dialogue and mythic dimensions of her short fiction. Among her numerous awards and honors are the National Endowment for the Arts Creative Writing Award, the Pushcart Prize, the Matrix Women Achievement Award, the Before Columbus American Book Award for *Queen of the Ebony Isles,* and the Catalyst Black Women in Education Award. In recent years, too, McElroy's nonfiction books, *A Long Way from St. Louie: Travel Memoirs* and *Over the Lip of the World: Among the Storytellers of Madagascar,* have attracted interest.

BIBLIOGRAPHY

"Colleen McElroy." In *The Writer's Mind: Interviews with American Authors,* edited by Irv Broughton, 39–67. Fayetteville: University of Arkansas Press, 1990.

McElroy, Colleen J. "If We Look for Them by Moonlight." In *Where We Stand: Women Poets on Literary Tradition,* edited by Sharon Bryan, 125–138. New York: W.W. Norton and Company, 1993.

Sherman, Charlotte W. "Walking across the Floor: A Conversation with Colleen J. McElroy." *American Visions* 10 (April/May 1998): 30.

James L. Hill

McGruder, Aaron (1974–)

Groundbreaking comic strip writer, artist, social commentator, and satirist Aaron McGruder was born in Chicago, Illinois. When he was six years old, his parents moved to Columbia, Maryland, where he grew up. McGruder attended the University of Maryland, where he earned a bachelor of arts degree in Afro-American studies with a concentration in social and cultural analysis. McGruder is the creator and writer of the poignant, award-winning, nationally syndicated newspaper comic strip *The Boondocks.*

The Boondocks, which debuted in *The Diamondback,* the University of Maryland's student newspaper, in 1996, is developed around the lives of two brothers, Huey and Riley Freeman, and their grandfather, who move from the inner city of Chicago into Woodcrest, a suburban neighborhood. Other characters include rambunctious Caesar, a Brooklynite and Huey's best friend, and Jazmine DuBois, a young biracial girl struggling to find her identity. Receiving rave reviews, after its debut it was later published by *The Source* magazine; by 1999 Universal Press Syndicate began syndicating the strip nationally to newspapers.

The Boondocks follows the Freemans' cultural shock, transition, and attempts to acculturate in their new environment. Throughout the strip Huey, the older brother, is characterized as militant scholar; he is a representative of and role model for the underrepresented in modern America. Riley, the younger brother, typifies contemporary urban popular culture. As the product of his time and representative of his generation, he is obsessed with gangsters, violence, rap music, and hip-hop culture in general. Despite their radically different personalities and generations, the characters are empowered through their voices. They speak with humorous but sharp, thought-provoking voices saturated with political satire and social commentary. Through humor, McGruder candidly and unapologetically addresses topics and issues related to politics, popular culture, race, elected and appointed political officials, black public personalities and entertainers, and all aspects of hip-hop culture. Although the comic strip sometimes creates controversy (intentionally and unintentionally) over its content, it has managed to weather the storm and stay in print with outstanding success.

McGruder has published some of *The Boondocks* comic strips in book form, including *The Boondocks: Because I Know You Don't Read the Newspaper* (2000), *Fresh for '01 . . . You Suckas: Boondocks Collection* (2001), and *A Right to Be Hostile: The Boondocks Treasury* (2003). McGruder has also worked as a coauthor for the graphic novel *Birth of a Nation.* McGruder and *The Boondocks* have received national and international media attention from such mainstream venues as *Time, Newsweek, People, National Journal, The Washington Post,* and London's *The Guardian,* as well as many newspapers and magazines. McGruder was awarded the "Chairman's Award" at the NATIONAL ASSOCIATION FOR THE ADVANCEMENT OF COLORED PEOPLE Image Awards.

McGruder represents an astounding voice of the hip-hop generation. His thought-provoking work challenges established stereotypes and familiar and widely accepted negative images of African Americans. McGruder lives and works in Los Angeles, California.

BIBLIOGRAPHY

McGruder, Aaron. *The Boondocks: Because I Know You Don't Read the Newspaper.* Kansas City: Andrew McMeel Publishing, 2000.
———. *A Right to Be Hostile: The Boondocks Treasury.* New York: Three Rivers Press, 2003.

Carlos Perez

McKay, Claude (Festus Claudius McKay) (1889–1948)

Festus Claudius McKay (Claude, as friends called him) was born on September 15, 1889, in Sunny Ville, in the Clarendon hills of Jamaica, to peasant farmers. His mother, Hannah Ann Elizabeth Edwards, was said to have come from Madagascar; his father, Thomas Frank McKay, from the Ashanti nations in West Africa. As a wealthy propertied man, McKay's father was able to provide his children with the education requisite to garner a place in Jamaica's rising black middle class. For young Claude, this meant being tutored—between ages seven and 14—by his elder schoolmaster brother, Uriah Theodore (U. Theo), who introduced Claude, an "omnivorous read [er]" (McKay 1937, 12), to a library dominated by the ideas of the great free thinkers, particularly Thomas Huxley and Herbert Spencer.

While working in Kingston as a constable, McKay became the protégé of Walter Jekyll, a British gentleman and anthropologist who also placed his personal library at McKay's disposal. Encouraged by Jekyll to record and validate the voice and folk culture of the Jamaican peasantry he had known as a boy, McKay published *Songs of Jamaica* (1912) and *Constab Ballads* (1912), his first two volumes of poetry, written in the island's rich dialect, before he migrated to America to study agronomy at BOOKER T. WASHINGTON's Tuskegee Institute in Alabama and the University of Kansas. "Hard Times" is representative of the poems in these collections, in which speakers champion the cause of the peasantry—the proletariat—as McKay's later socialist leanings would lead him to identify members of the working class: "De mo' me wuk, de mo'time hard, / I don't know what fe do; / I ben' me knew an' pray to Gahd, / Yet t'ing same as before" (McKay 1972, 53).

McKay's *Spring in New Hampshire* (1920) and *Harlem Shadows* (1922) were published during the height of the HARLEM RENAISSANCE. Although he would spend most of the period associated with this "movement" outside the United States, specifically in Russia, England, France, and Morocco, McKay is often identified as one of its significant writers. While for some scholars, McKay's very formal English sonnets "Harlem Shadows" and "Innovations," published in 1917 in the *Liberator,* place him among Renaissance harbingers, for most his more militant sonnets, "If We Must Die," "The White House," and "America," first published in 1919, epitomize the voice of the "New Negro movement."

The empowered "New Negro" is evident in the martial and militant "If We Must Die" and "America." In the former, the speaker calls upon his "kinsmen" to meet their "common foe":

*Though far outnumbered let us show us
brace.
And for their thousand blows deal one
deathblow!
What though before us lies the open grave?
Like men we'll face the murderous cowardly
pack,
Pressed to the wall, dying but fighting back.*

The speaker in "America" resolves to face the hate he experiences in America strong and erect, "as a rebel fronts a king in state": "And I am sharp as steel with discontent; / But I possess the courage and the grace / To bear my anger proudly and unbent."

Though he was associated with the radical political left, specifically the Communist Party, McKay remained an incurable romantic, infected by the pastoral legacies of agrarian Jamaica. This is clearly the theme in "Home Thought":

*Amid the city's noises, I must think
Of mangoes leaning to the river's brink,
And dexterous Davie climbing high above,
The gold fruits ebon-speckled to remove.*

For McKay, modernity's greatest crime is the loss of memory, the disorientation and fragmentation it creates. He poignantly records this sense of loss in his autobiographical poem "Flame Heart," in which more than lost childhood and youth are lamented; also lamented is a modern world that inhibits an intimate relationship between humans and Nature: "I have forgotten much, but still remember / The poinsettia's red, blood-red, in warm December." One finds in McKay's speaker's recollection clear resonance and allusion to the British romantic poets, particularly William Wordsworth, in its tendency to celebrate feeling, imagination, and intuition over analysis and reason: the emotive over the rational, the romantic over the modern.

In addition to poetry, McKay is the author of three novels, HOME TO HARLEM (1929), *Banjo* (1929), and *Banana Bottom* (1932), and *Gingertown* (1932), a collection of short stories. *Home to Harlem* is the story of Jake Brown, a World War I soldier who goes AWOL in Europe to return home to Harlem, which he recalls in idyllic terms, to find a more rewarding life. Caught up in the rhythms of the Jazz Age found in Harlem cabaret, exposed to the exploitation known by the common laborer through his job as a waiter on the railroad, and frustrated by his efforts to find his lover, Jake comes to see Harlem from a different perspective. At the end of the novel, Jake and his girlfriend, appropriately named Felice ("Happy/Happiness") leave Harlem in search of a more meaningful wholeness and fulfillment. With its daily struggle for survival, rampant exploitation and violence, and disappointments, Harlem, the black mecca, had come to epitomize the modern world.

Written during an era that, as one critic notes, "pandered to the stereotypes of the primitive exotic" (McDowell, 80), *Home to Harlem* pulsates with the requisite controversial stereotypes: cabaret scenes, exotics, primitives, boozers, jazzers, and dancers, popularized by CARL VAN VECHTEN in his best seller, *NIGGER HEAVEN* (1925), in which, many readers and scholars have argued, blacks are essentialized as racially, culturally, and sexually different. Ironically, Van Vechten had set out to validate the complexity of Harlem—to "reject definitions of the Negro as a type," as Nathan Huggins argues in *Harlem Renaissance.* In the end, however, Huggins concludes, "the reader was expected to accept the Negro as a natural primitive, [who] when he was true to himself … was saved from civilized artificiality" (102–103).

Reviewers hotly debated whether McKay had done the same in *Home to Harlem.* LANGSTON HUGHES praised it as "Undoubtedly the finest thing we've done yet. … Everyone is talking about the book, and even those who dislike it say it's well written." However, W. E. B. DU BOIS of the NATIONAL ASSOCIATION FOR THE ADVANCEMENT OF COLORED PEOPLE and in general the black middle class found little or no merit in *Home to Harlem.* In his *CRISIS* review, DuBois wrote that he felt "unclean and in need of a bath," after reading the novel.

A more objective reading of *Home to Harlem* reveals ways in which McKay did more than merely appropriate Van Vechten's themes, discourse, and paradigm. For example, read as a naturalistic novel, in the tradition of Theodore Dreiser and

Frank Norris, *Home to Harlem* gives insights into the self-affirming lives of working-class blacks who inhabit a modern world in which they are trapped, pessimistically determined in the classical naturalist sense by heredity and environment.

In contrast to *Home to Harlem,* neither *Banjo* nor *Banana Bottom* was a financial success, although reviewers were generally kind. Set in Marseille, *Banjo* focuses on more Pan-African political issues, including colonization, although the protagonist, Agrippa Daily (Banjo), like Jake, is also involved in a quest for spiritual wholeness. McKay uses Ray, his intellectual alter ego who is introduced in *Home to Harlem,* as his spokesman in *Banjo.*

Considered by many critics to be McKay's best novel, *Banana Bottom,* a romantic tale, is set in the pastoral world of Jamaica, for which McKay seemed ever to yearn. Although its heroine, Bita Plant, is formally educated and "refined" in England, she returns to her Jamaican roots, embraces Jamaica's folk culture, and marries her father's drayman, resolving the conflicts she had encountered between her cultural roots and colonizing experience.

McKay's nonfiction works include two autobiographies, *A Long Way from Home* (1937) and *My Green Hills of Jamaica* (published posthumously in 1979), and a collection of essays, *Harlem: Negro Metropolis* (1940). *Selected Poems of Claude McKay* (1953) was published posthumously. Ironically, ever the freethinker and political radical, McKay converted to Catholicism in 1944. He died in Chicago, on May 22, 1948, a long way from home.

BIBLIOGRAPHY

Cooper, Wayne. *Claude McKay: Rebel Sojourner in the Harlem Renaissance.* New York: Schocken, 1987.

———, ed. *The Passion of Claude McKay.* New York: Schocken, 1973.

Huggins, Nathan I. *Harlem Renaissance.* New York: Oxford University Press, 1971.

McDowell, E. Deborah. *The Changing Same: Black Women's Literature, Criticism, and Theory.* Bloomington: Indiana University Press, 1995.

McKay, Claude. *Home to Harlem.* Boston: Northeastern University Press, 1987.

———. *A Long Way from Home: An Autobiography.* New York: Harvest Books, 1937.

———. *Selected Poems of Claude McKay.* New York: Bookman Associates, 1953.

———. *Songs of Jamaica. The Dialect Poetry of Claude McKay.* New York: Books for Libraries Press, 1972, 53–54.

Samuels, Wilfred D. *Five Afro-Caribbean Voices in American Culture, 1917–1929.* Boulder, Colo.: Belmont, 1977.

Van Vechten, Carl. *Nigger Heaven.* New York: Harper & Row, 1971.

Wilfred D. Samuels

McKinney-Whetstone, Diane (1955–)

Diane McKinney-Whetstone grew up in Philadelphia, where she attended public schools with her five sisters and one brother. She graduated from the University of Pennsylvania in 1975 with a bachelor's degree in English. Her father served two terms as a state senator; later, McKinney-Whetstone worked for several years at the Philadelphia City Council and then at the Forest Service. She lives in Philadelphia with her husband, with whom she has twins.

Hailed as a writer who participates in writing and recording "a sort of urban microhistory of the revival of Philadelphia neighborhoods" (Ganim, 374), McKinney-Whetstone writes novels of relationships and tradition rooted in the neighborhoods of South Philadelphia. However, McKinney-Whetstone is interested in reaching a wide audience. She accomplishes this by focusing on family relationships (defined loosely and by necessity) and domestic issues.

In her first novel, *Tumbling* (1996), a period novel that explores the physical and emotional landscape of a declining neighborhood in the 1940s and 1950s, McKinney-Whetstone explores questions about two women who live together and are as close as sisters. The loving couple, Noon and Herbie, are devoted to each other. Noon's traumatic past, told in indirect and haunting fragments, prevents them from consummating their marriage. They become parents quite by accident when two girls are left on their doorstep. When urban progress threatens to destroy their neighborhood, Noon comes to grips with her past, assuming a leadership role in her neighborhood and congregation, healing herself and her family. Also a period novel, *Tempest Rising* (1998), McKinney-Whetstone's second novel, returns to themes related to the city, declining neighborhoods, and families that are not biologically linked. Three children, all girls, are born to the middle-class privilege few African Americans enjoyed in the 1960s. Their father, Finch, is economically successful, and their mother, Clarise, is a beautiful homemaker. When Finch's lucrative catering business begins to fail, Clarise has a nervous breakdown. Placed in the foster care system, the girls are sent to live with Mae and her beautiful but spiteful daughter, Ramona, who neglect and emotionally abuse them. When the girls disappear, Mae and Ramona are left to figure out the reasons. In the process, they become aware of the complexity of their own relationship, which is driven by a brutal secret they must confront. Told in a simultaneously folksy and poetic style, *Tempest Rising* examines the effects of brutality, honesty, and secrets on a family.

Blues Dancing (1999), McKinney-Whetstone's third novel, explores new regions. Like the first two novels, *Blues Dancing* is set in Philadelphia, but unlike them it confronts more directly such gritty urban issues as drug addiction. The main character, Verdi, a pampered preacher's daughter, moves from the South to Philadelphia, where she attends college and demonstrates tremendous promise at first. However, when she meets Johnson, a student activist leader, Verdi becomes involved with drugs and eventually becomes addicted to heroin. Rowe, a former professor, eventually rescues Verdi from total disaster. In this novel McKinney-Whetstone brings herself and her readers closer to the present; Rowe and Verdi become life partners for 20 years until Johnson reenters Verdi's life. McKinney-Whetstone's characters are complex and credible. Thematically, the novel explores the nature of relationships and love within the political reality of South Philadelphia during the past 60-plus years.

McKinney-Whetstone began writing because she had a burning passion to write something other than government documents. She got up every morning around 4:30 A.M. to write so that she could continue working full time as well as be a full-time mother. She found herself negotiating with her children: "I would bargain with them for Saturday mornings, would let them stay up late Friday, and would make all kinds of deals with them, like be quiet in the morning and then I'll do something special in the afternoon with you. I'd get a lot of writing done on Saturday mornings, which was a big help. I meshed the roles of mother and writer by continuing to write early in the morning" (Dellasega). By participating in the Rittenhouse Writing Group, McKinney-Whetstone found a venue for publishing her work. Like a number of other major African-American women authors, McKinney-Whetstone started to write late in life and managed to balance several lives in the process. Her writing is enriched because of this.

BIBLIOGRAPHY

Dellasega, Cheryl. "Mothers Who Write: Diane McKinney-Whetstone." *Writers Write: The Internet Writing Journal.* Available online. URL: http://www.writerswrite.com/journal/oct00/whetstone.htm. Accessed October 18, 2006.
Ganim, John M. "Cities of Words: Recent Studies on Urbanism and Literature." *MLQ: Modern Language Quarterly* (September 2002): 365–382.

Shauna Lee Eddy-Sanders

McMillan, Terry (1951–)

In her groundbreaking anthology *Breaking Ice: An Anthology of Contemporary African-American Fiction* (1990), Terry McMillan writes:

Not once, throughout my entire four years as an undergraduate, did it occur to me that I might one day be a writer. I mean, these folks had genuine knowledge and insight. They also had a fascination with the truth. They had something to write about. Their work was bold, not flamboyant. They learned how to exploit the language so that readers would be affected by what they said and how they said it. And they had talent. (xvi)

Born in 1951 in Port Huron, Michigan, Mc-Millan is the daughter of Edward McMillan and Madeline Washington Tilman. Her father worked as a sanitation worker. Her mother held numerous jobs after her parents divorced. As the eldest of five children, McMillan worked, while in high school, to help her single mother raise her siblings. One of her jobs was in the public library, where she discovered a love of reading:

As a child, I didn't know that African-American people wrote books. I grew up in a small town in northern Michigan where the only books I came across were the Bible and required reading for school. I did not read for pleasure, and it wasn't until I was sixteen when I got a job shelving books at the public library that I got lost in a book. It was a biography of Louisa May Alcott. (xv)

McMillan took a course in Afro-American literature when she enrolled at the University of California, Berkeley, in 1973, discovering the works of such prominent black writers as COUNTEE CULLEN, LANGSTON HUGHES, ANN PETRY, ZORA NEALE HURSTON, RALPH ELLISON, JEAN TOOMER, and RICHARD WRIGHT. She recalls, "I signed up and couldn't wait for the first day of class. I remember the textbook was called *Dark Symphony: Negro Literature in America* because I still have it. I couldn't believe the rush I felt" (xvi).

While teaching at the University of Wyoming in 1987, McMillan discovered that very few contemporary anthologies included works of fiction by African-American writers: "What became apparent almost immediately was that I couldn't recall any recent anthologies in which contemporary African-American fiction writers—who'd been published from the early seventies to now—had been published. . . . I learned very quickly that there hadn't been an anthology comprised of fiction in

over seventeen years" (xix). That insight became the genesis for *Breaking Ice: An Anthology of Contemporary African-American Fiction* (1990). This anthology includes a plethora of black literary intellectuals: AMIRI BARAKA, RITA DOVE, ISHMAEL REED, CLARENCE MAJOR, PAULE MARSHALL, and ALICE WALKER, to name a few. In the preface, novelist and essayist JOHN EDGAR WIDEMAN acknowledges the marginality of black writers and the way this position in American society "refined our awareness, our proficiency in nonliterary modes of storytelling."

After editing *Breaking Ice,* McMillan published her first novel, *Mama* (1987), whose protagonist, Mildred Peacock, is a strong black mother similar to McMillan's mother. In the novel, the mother triumphs over poverty, domestic abuse, and rape. After *Mama,* McMillan published her second novel, *Disappearing Acts* (1989), a novel about the relationship between a young woman, Zora Banks, a teacher and aspiring singer who hangs her hope on becoming a successful star, and Franklin Swift, an out-of-work construction worker and not-quite-divorced father of two. Franklin dreams of starting his own business. Like most of McMillan's characters, although as lovers the two are involved in a stormy relationship, they eventually learn to overcome individual weaknesses. In 2000, *Disappearing Acts,* directed by the African-American woman director Gina Prince-Blythewood, was made into a cable television movie, starring Sanaa Lathan and Wesley Snipes.

In 1992, after the success of *Disappearing Acts,* McMillan published *Waiting to Exhale,* her most controversial novel. The story follows the lives of four middle-class African-American women, Savannah Jackson, Bernadine Harris, Gloria Matthews, and Robin Stokes, as they struggle through and overcome familial, romantic, and career relationships and issues. A best seller, the novel continues to garner attention because of its portrayal of the complications and hardships between black men and women.

Although well received by the majority of African-American women, many African-American men felt, at the time of its publication, that the novel and the subsequent film, directed by Forest Whitaker and starring Whitney Houston and Angela Bassett, denigrated black men. Black men compared it to Alice Walker's *The COLOR PURPLE*, condemning what they saw as the novels' and authors' unrelenting bashing and stereotyping of black men in general. Despite this negative controversy within the African-American community, however, *Waiting to Exhale* remains a significant novel in the publishing world. With its overwhelming financial success (it sold more than 4 million copies), this novel opened the door for future African-American romance novelists.

In 1996, McMillan published her fourth novel, *How Stella Got Her Groove Back,* whose protagonist, Stella, is a highly successful, 40-something San Francisco stockbroker. During a vacation to Jamaica with her girlfriend, Delilah, Stella encounters a young islander, Winston Shakespeare, who pursues her, forcing her to examine her life and dreams. As in McMillan's previous novels, through a steamy yet stormy relationship, Stella and Winston discover their own weaknesses as well as the meaning of true love. The overwhelming financial success of *Waiting to Exhale* allowed McMillan to option *How Stella Got Her Grove Back* to film studios. Starring Angela Bassett and Taye Diggs, it was directed by John Deming.

Published in 2001, McMillan's novel *A Day Late and A Dollar Short* focuses on Viola and Cecil Price and their loving but dysfunctional family. The novel is different from McMillan's other novels. Married, Viola and Cecil argue and face many dilemmas within their family; however, they do not struggle with issues related to single parenthood, nor is Viola concerned about finding "Mr. Right," as are most of McMillan's other female protagonists.

Terry McMillan's novels continue to give mainstream America a glimpse into the complex lives of middle-class black women as they struggle and triumph over adversities in their familial and romantic relationships. Some critics have argued that the issues McMillan addresses are not intellectually challenging or demanding. Others, however, argue that McMillan has touched and exposed a significant core within the community of middle-class African-American women who are successful professionally but consider themselves failures in their personal lives. McMillan's works may not address the long-standing history of racial politics in America, but she expertly exposes the deep fissures of sexual politics within the African-American community.

Historically, few African-American writers have experienced the financial success Terry McMillan has known. Three of her novels have been on the *New York Times* best seller list and have been optioned for films. In addition, the novels and films appeal to a crossover audience. This financial success has generated a range of conversations about McMillan's works. African-American literary critics will continue to revisit McMillan and the significance of her works in years to come.

BIBLIOGRAPHY

McMillan, Terry. *Breaking Ice: An Anthology of Contemporary African-American Fiction.* New York: Penguin Books, 1990.

Beverly Tate

McPherson, James Alan   (1943–   )

James Alan McPherson was born in 1943 in Savannah, Georgia, to James and Mabel McPherson. His mother was a domestic worker; his father was Georgia's first licensed black master electrician. After earning a bachelor of arts degree at Morris Brown College, McPherson went to Harvard Law School in 1965. That year, his short story "Gold Coast" won first prize in a writing competition sponsored by the United Negro College Fund and *Reader's Digest.* Choosing creative writing over law, he went to the University of Iowa, where he received a master of fine arts from Iowa's writing workshop in 1969. Simultaneously he won a grant from the *Atlanta Monthly* to publish his first collection of short stories, *Hue and Cry.*

McPherson is the author of several works, including *Hue and Cry: Short Stories* (1969), *Elbow Room: Short Stories* (1977), *Crabcakes* (1998), and

Region Not Home: Reflections from Exile (2000). In them McPherson focuses on the connection between geography and identity, the posturing found in regional identity. This emphasis allows McPherson to develop his characters more completely, as he is able to unravel their psychological and emotional states, which are reflected in the landscape. McPherson also uses the oral tradition as a core for his writings, often featuring a character telling stories. Most important, McPherson's vision is that all Americans have basic common values, regardless of racial identity. He supported the CIVIL RIGHTS MOVEMENT rather than the BLACK POWER movement.

"Solo Song: For Doc," McPherson's signature short story, is exemplary. When a college student joins the regular crew of waiters on board a railroad during the summer, he encounters the narrator, an employee who sees him as an opportunist and the railroad managers as exploiters. He tells the youth, "The man uses you but he does not need you. But me he needs for the winter, when you are gone" (1676). Ultimately, the narrator wishes to celebrate members of the Old School, like Doc Craft (Leroy Johnson), a waiter's waiter, a passing breed. The narrator tells the novice, "He [Doc] danced down these aisles with us and swung his tray with the roll of the train, never spilling in all his trips a single cup of coffee" (1674). In the end, however, McPherson, who had spent his summers working on the railroad, much like the young apprentice in the story, not only celebrates a dying class of railroad workers—porters and waiters, their economic plight as members of the working class whose cause is championed by the union—but also of the death of the railroad itself.

Hue and Cry: Short Stories won the National Institute of Arts and Letters Grant (1970), a Rockefeller Grant (1970), and a Guggenheim Fellowship (1972). In 1981, McPherson won the MacArthur Foundation Grant and in 1978 the Pulitzer Prize for *Elbow Room*. Throughout his career, McPherson has taught African-American literature and creative writing at the University of Iowa; the University of California, Santa Cruz; Morgan State University; and the University of Virginia.

BIBLIOGRAPHY

Beavers, Herman. *Wrestling Angels into Song: The Fictions of Ernest J. Gaines and James Alan McPherson.* Philadelphia: University of Pennsylvania Press, 1995.

Kim Hai Pearson
Brian Jennings

Messenger, The   (1917–1928)

World War I, the Great Migration, African-American participation in the war, and the formation of such civil rights organizations as the NATIONAL ASSOCIATION FOR THE ADVANCEMENT OF COLORED PEOPLE (NAACP), the National Urban League, and MARCUS GARVEY's Universal Negro Improvement Association (UNIA) are often identified as the impetus for the cultural blossoming known as the HARLEM RENAISSANCE and the more militant, defiant, and self-reliant African American who presented himself in America during the postwar era. These major organizations and their leaders, W. E. B. DuBOIS, CHARLES S. JOHNSON, and Garvey, strategically founded publishing organs—*The CRISIS, OPPORTUNITY,* and *The Negro World,* respectively—to promulgate their ideological and political platforms and agendas, and, in the case of Garvey, his economic program managed through the *Black Star Line.*

Although it was not connected to any of these sociopolitical and economic organs, *The Messenger,* "the only magazine of scientific radicalism in the world published by Negroes," was an equally important venue that sought to champion the voice of the New Negro and spearhead the Renaissance movement. It, too, served, according to editor Sondra Kathryn Wilson, as "an intellectual and cultural outlet for black artists" (xx) during the 1920s.

The ardent socialists A. Philip Randolph and Chandler Owens founded *The Messenger.* Opponents of World War I and supporters of the economic program of the Industrial Workers of the World, Randolph and Owens were included by the FBI's J. Edgar Hoover among the most dangerous radicals in America. This classification led the postmaster general to ban *The Messenger.* Significantly, however, the coeditors of *The Messenger* were equally critical of the extant black leadership, including DuBois, R. R. Moton (who succeeded BOOKER T. WASHINGTON at Tuskegee), and Garvey, and satirized them and their organizations in *Messenger* articles. Its circulation reached 26,000 at its height of success.

The Messenger's editorial staff included the well-known Renaissance writers WALLACE THURMAN and GEORGE S. SCHUYLER and the less-known drama critic Theophilus Lewis, who together promoted the work of the younger Renaissance writers, including LANGSTON HUGHES, who published his first short story in *The Messenger.* The editors also published the poetry of ARNA BONTEMPS, COUNTEE CULLEN, ANGELINA GRIMKE, GEORGIA DOUGLASS JOHNSON, and CLAUDE MCKAY. They also published the short stories of ZORA NEALE HURSTON, DOROTHY WEST, and ERIC WALROND.

The Messenger ceased publication in 1928, by which time Owens had left the editorial board and Randolph had become the leader of the Brotherhood of Sleeping Car Porters. It lacked an audience for its socialist message, and its treasury had been exhausted. (In 1921 Randolph had run for the office of New York's secretary of state on the Socialist ticket.) As Wilson concludes, "In spite of its turbulent history, *The Messenger* proffered an essential radical dimension of African American social and political thought" (xxii).

BIBLIOGRAPHY

Lewis, David Levering. *When Harlem Was in Vogue.* New York: Oxford University Press, 1989.
Wilson, Kathryn Sondra, ed. *The Messenger Reader.* New York: Random House, 2000.

Wilfred D. Samuels

Micheaux, Oscar   (1884–1951)

In the comprehensive study of Oscar Micheaux's life and creative works, *Writing Himself into History: Oscar Micheaux,* authors Pearl Bowser and Louise Spence provide an insightful assessment:

Oscar Micheaux used his life as a catalyst for his imagination, dramatizing his experiences and envisioning himself as a model for other African Americans. His self-image as a pioneer, on the land, in his novels, and in his filmmaking, was a charmed space.... This space embodied his dreams and ambitions as he struggled within the limits he set for himself and in defiance of those imposed by others. (222)

A novelist, filmmaker, and entrepreneur, Micheaux was born in January 1884 near Metropolis, Illinois, gaining a formal education in the public schools before going to Chicago. Once there, he worked shining shoes and then as a Pullman car porter on the railroad. Working the trains allowed him to travel and see the country, and as he began to write about those travels he gravitated to the form of the novel. Some scholars consider Micheaux's novels to be fictional replications of his life. One writes, "Micheaux's first novel, published in 1913, is a good guide to his first three decades, because it is thinly disguised biography.... [T]he biographical and historical accuracy of the book should not be underemphasized.... Micheaux's subsequent novels are also rich in autobiographical material" (Green, xii). Micheaux's first novel, *The Conquest,* focuses upon the black protagonist, named Oscar Devereaux, who works in the Chicago area as a Pullman car porter before pursuing life in the South Dakota frontier.

The Conquest is a book written after Micheaux's efforts at farming as well as his short, troubled marriage, failed. Micheaux published the novel himself, traveling to promote and sell it in the Midwest and the South. While traveling, he organized a network of contacts and developed his second novel, *The Forged Note,* which continued the exploits of the protagonist, Devereaux, as he becomes a farmer and landowner. His third novel, *The Homesteader* (1917), was completed during the aftermath of the feature film *The Birth of a Nation* (1915), whose negative depiction of black Americans prompted the formation of numerous black independent film companies. One of those companies, Lincoln Motion Picture, entered negotiations with Micheaux to adapt *The Homesteader* into a film. Unable to reach an agreement on Micheaux's desire to direct the film, Micheaux formed his own film business in 1918, the Oscar Micheaux Corporation, which began making short movies and then feature films.

Having learned how to network his novels, Micheaux followed the same strategy for his films. Using his renowned charm, he managed to convince theater owners, including southern whites, that there was an existing, eager black audience ready to pay to see an all-black cast on screen. His boasting proved prophetic, and from 1919 to 1948 he made and released more than 40 films, though only a few survive today. Some of the better-known movies included *The Homesteader* (1919), *Body and Soul* (1925), *The Exile* (1931), *God's Stepchildren* (1937), *Lying Lips* (1939), and *Betrayal* (1948).

The marketing of his movies has been a point of praise as much as the movies themselves. According to one plan, Micheaux would go to venues to talk up his most recently completed movie, asking for an advance payment to book the film, and then he would return to New York, where he lived and worked, to shoot the film on a budget from the advance money. His other notable strategy was to publicize his black actors by associating them with popular Hollywood personalities. For example, he billed black actor Lorenzo Tucker as the "black Valentino" and black actress Bee Freeman as the "sepia Mae West" (Bogle, 114).

Although his early films examined politically charged topics such as interracial dating, lynching, and Ku Klux Klan terrorism, Micheaux was both lauded and berated because many of his films focused on middle-class aspirations and the black characters who lived within those "cultured" environments. Committed to using his movie images to counter the racial stereotypes in Hollywood features, Micheaux's recurring emphasis on educated, professional blacks often excluded the black working class. However, even while presenting the accomplished black milieu, Micheaux's films criticized the flaws and hypocrisies he perceived in that group, as in his film *Body and Soul*. In that piece, black legend Paul Robeson played a dual role—an immoral black minister and his hardworking, conscientious twin brother. The movie condemns both the minister's exploitive behavior and a congregation's willingness to permit his actions just because he is church leader.

By the 1940s, Hollywood decided to capitalize on the proven black and white audience for all-black cast films, and, unable to compete with studio budgets and distribution power, black-owned film companies, including Micheaux's, began to disappear. During this decade, Micheaux began writing novels again, including *The Winds from Nowhere* (1941), another autobiographical novel that reworked the material in his first novel; *The Case of Mrs. Wingate* (1944, a detective novel); *The Story of Dorothy Stanfield* (1946), about an insurance con; and *The Masquerade* (1947), which owes much to CHARLES CHESNUTT's *The House behind the Cedars* (Bolden, 254).

Micheaux died in 1951 of a heart attack, but he became an inspiration for many independent and black filmmakers who followed him. In 1974, the Black Filmmakers Hall of Fame began presenting the annual Oscar Micheaux Award to deserving black filmmakers who exemplified pioneering creativity, and in 1987, Micheaux received a star on the Hollywood Walk of Fame to acknowledge his contributions to American cinema.

BIBLIOGRAPHY

Bogle, Donald. *Toms, Coons, Mulattoes, Mammies, and Bucks.* New York: Continuum, 1990.

Bolden, Tanya. "Oscar Micheaux." In *African American Writers: A Dictionary,* edited by Sharon Dorante Hatch and Michael Strickland, 253–254. Santa Barbara, Calif.: ABC-CLIO, 2000.

Bowser, Pearl, and Louise Spence. *Writing Himself into History: Oscar Micheaux, His Silent Films, and His Audiences.* New Brunswick, N.J.: Rutgers University Press, 2000.

Green, J. Ronald. *Straight Lick: The Cinema of Oscar Micheaux.* Bloomington: Indiana University Press, 2000.

Reid, Mark A. *Redefining Black Film.* Berkeley: University of California Press, 1993.

Mel Donalson

Middle Passage　Charles Johnson (1990)

Middle Passage is, among other things, a burlesque and a rich parody of African-American freedom and neo–freedom narratives. The story is set in 1830 in New Orleans, Africa, and aboard a ship on the Atlantic Ocean. Primarily comprising a ship's log entries, the linear narrative charts the radical transformation of Rutherford Calhoun, the central character. Though he is physically free when the narrative begins, Rutherford is still bound by the predestination clause of his former master's narrative, a clause that links his literary destiny to that of Richard Wright's socially overdetermined thief and murderer, Bigger Thomas (*Native Son*, 1940). Stealing what others own and value brings Rutherford material property and the experiences associated with owning it, but it leaves him in a perpetual state of desire.

Rutherford believes he possesses no capital, cultural or otherwise. Charles Johnson captures his protagonist's mindset with the question, "for was I not, as a Negro in the New world, born to be a thief?" (47). In such a state of perceptual blindness, Rutherford can see himself only as the reader sees him—as a thief, a deceiver, and an opportunist who engages in human interaction for the sole purpose of self-gratification. By casting Rutherford as someone who is physically free but nevertheless limited by perceptual blindness, Johnson tackles the very definition of freedom as it is understood in Western culture, as a state or quality associated with property ownership.

Rutherford's transformation takes place during a reverse journey through Middle Passage, after he stows away on the *Republic,* a slave ship. (The Middle Passage is the path slave ships traveled through the Atlantic Ocean with their human cargo, where African-American identity is said to have begun.) Rutherford is attempting to escape the obligation of marriage to the schoolteacher who has paid his debts to Papa Zeringue, a major figure in the New Orleans underworld. Soon discovered by the ship's staff, Rutherford is aided by a group of captive African Allmuseri wizards and their god, who are among the *Republic*'s cargo. After coming face to face with the Allmuseri god and witnessing extraordinary examples of self-sacrifice during the ship's doomed return voyage, Rutherford sees with new eyes. This liberated perception begins his real freedom; it allows him to restructure a faulty syllogism that has driven his thieving behavior: Freedom is property; I have property; therefore, I am free. Transformed, he embraces his obligations and opens up the possibility for the love that will displace his unfulfillable desire.

Richly complex and deeply philosophical, *Middle Passage* intertextualizes with Plato's *The Republic,* Herman Melville's *Moby-Dick* and *Benito Cereno,* Dante's *Inferno,* Ralph Ellison's *Invisible Man,* Toni Morrison's *Beloved,* *The Odyssey,* and *Native Son.* More important, Johnson's protagonist owes his existence as a fictional character to the existence of real-life freedom narratives, records of the experience of New World slavery. Moreover, *Middle Passage* is a fitting contribution to the tradition of the African-American male quest narrative. Johnson's best-known novel and most critiqued work, *Middle Passage* won a National Book Award in 1990, although Johnson has claimed that *Oxherding Tale* (1982) is a better effort. Several critics have compared the novel to Toni Morrison's *Beloved* for its treatment of slavery, property, and desire.

BIBLIOGRAPHY

Boccia, Michael. "An Interview with Charles Johnson." *African American Review* 30, no. 4 (Winter 1996): 611–618.

Byrd, Rudolph, ed. *I Call Myself an Artist: Writings By and About Charles Johnson.* Bloomington: Indiana University Press, 1999.

Fagel, Brian. "Passages from the Middle: Coloniality and Postcoloniality in Charles Johnson's *Middle Passage.*" *African American Review* 30, no. 4 (Winter 1996): 625–634.

Goudie, S. X. "Leavin' a Mark on the Wor(l)d: Marksman and Marked Men in *Middle Passage.*" *African American Review* 29, no. 1 (1995): 109–112.

Johnson, Charles. *Being and Race.* Bloomington and Indianapolis: Indiana University Press, 1988.

———. "Philosophy and Black Fiction." *Obsidian* 6, no. 1–2 (1980): 55–61.

Little, Jonathan. "An Interview with Charles Johnson." In *I Call Myself an Artist: Writings by and about Charles Johnson,* edited by Rudolph Byrd, 225–243. Bloomington: Indiana University Press, 1999.

O'Keefe, Vincent A. "Reading Rigor Mortis: Offstage Violence and Excluded Middles in Johnson's *Middle Passage* and Morrison's *Beloved.*" *African American Review* 30, no. 4 (1996): 635–647.

Parrish, Timothy. "Imagining Slavery: Toni Morrison and Charles Johnson." *Studies in American Fiction* 24, no. 1 (Spring 1997): 81–100.

Scott, Daniel M., III. "Interrogating Identity: Appropriation and Transformation in *Middle Passage.*" *African American Review* 29, no. 4 (Winter 1995): 645–655.

Travis, Molly Abel. "*Beloved* and *Middle Passage:* Race, Narrative, and the Critic's Essentialism." *Narratives* 2, no. 3 (October 1994): 179–200.

Walby, Celestin. "The African Sacrificial Kingship Ritual and Johnson's *Middle Passage.*" *African American Review* 29, no. 4 (1995): 657–669.

Lovalerie King

Miller, Eugene Ethelbert   (1950–   )

E. ETHELBERT MILLER is an African-American poet born to a Panamanian father and a mother with paternal West Indian heritage in the Bronx, New York. Growing up in an ethnically diverse neighborhood, he lived with his parents, Egberto and Enid, and his older siblings, Marie and Richard, in New York, until he left to attend college at Howard University in 1968. After graduating with a degree in Afro-American Studies in 1972, he worked at the African American Resource Center at Howard, which he has directed since 1974. He currently teaches in the Bennington Writing Seminars but has also held visiting positions at Emory and Henry, George Mason University, American University, and the University of Nevada, Las Vegas.

Miller entered college at the height of the BLACK POWER and BLACK ARTS movements. HAKI MADHUBUTI, AMIRI BARAKA, JOHN KILLENS, and SONIA SANCHEZ were popular when Miller began writing. On the Howard campus, he came under the influence of critic STEPHEN HENDERSON and literary elders STERLING A. BROWN and Leon Damas.

Miller was drawn in the 1980s toward the aesthetic and political ties between black America and oppression in other countries. His understanding of global issues evokes empathy and understanding across cultures. Friendships with writers like JUNE JORDAN and Ariel Dorfman have augmented his political vision. Defining himself as a literary activist as well as a writer, he is an indefatigable networker, sharing information about publishing and personal contacts. He began the Ascension Poetry Reading Series in Washington to make up for the lack of publishers for African-American writers. The series lasted from 1974 to 2000, organizing more than 100 readings, and it included Puerto Rican, Asian-American, and Arab-American writers.

Miller has published nine books of poetry: *Andromeda* (1974), *The Land of Smiles and The Land of No Smiles* (1974), *The Migrant Worker* (1978), *Season of Hunger / Cry of Rain* (1982), *Where Are the Love Poems for Dictators?* (1986), *First Light: New and Selected Poems* (1994), *Whispers, Secrets and Promises* (1998), *Buddha Weeping in Winter* (2001), and *How We Sleep on the Nights We Don't Make Love* (2004). Responding to the lack of published anthologies of African-American poetry when he was growing up, he collected poems for *In Search of Color Everywhere,* which won the 1994 PEN Oakland Josephine Miles Award. He also edited three other anthologies, *Synergy: An Anthology of Washington, D.C. Poetry* (1975), *Women Surviving Massacres and Men: Nine Women Poets* (1977), and *Beyond the Frontier* (2002). His most recent edited anthology, *Beyond the Frontier: African American Poetry for the 21st Century* (2002), features the next generation of emerging African-American poets. In addition, his first memoir, *Fathering Words: The Making of an African-American Writer* (2000), chronicles his career and pays tribute to the lives of his brother and his father, who died prematurely when Miller was in his 30s. That book was chosen for the second annual Washington, D.C., We Read program.

Miller's work contains the voices of characters surviving and grieving during revolutions in Latin America by responding to antidemocratic regimes in Chile, Nicaragua, and El Salvador. He has traveled to Nicaragua, as well as to Yemen, the Soviet Union, England, Iraq, Saudi Arabia, and Bahrain. By drawing on international incidents as well as commonplace events happening to ordinary citizens, Miller's testimonies demand that readers work against complacency and forgetfulness and remember to love their neighbors. His poetry, which can be poignant and comedic, covers a range of topics including baseball, jazz, politics, love, and family. In his "Omar" poems, in *Whispers, Secrets and Promises,* and in *How We Sleep on the Nights We Don't Make Love,* he addresses with sensitivity and warmth the influence of Islam within the black community through the friendship of two boys. "Rebecca" employs a female voice to consider the implications of losing a breast to cancer. In a move typical of Miller's style, the character wonders whether she will hate mirrors after surgery, but then she thinks:

> this is my body
> this is not south africa or nicaragua
> this is my body
> losing a war against cancer
> and there are no demonstrators outside
> the hospital to scream stop. (174)

His latest volume, *How We Sleep on the Nights We Don't Make Love,* traverses the familiar territory of love, loneliness, and desire but also breaks new ground. The recent influence of teaching the craft of poetry to advanced graduate students is demonstrated in the precision of "Alexander Calder," which verbally draws an artist's mobile, and in "All That Could Go Wrong," where tercets stall time as the speaker realizes melancholy parallels between his father's life and his own.

Miller's background in ubiquitous studies rather than literature has served him well. Having learned to operate video cameras documenting African-American culture in his early days at Howard, he has hosted two radio shows, *Maiden Voyage* (WDCU) and *Vertigo on the Air* (WPFW), and is often heard on National Public Radio. He currently hosts *Humanities Profiled,* a television program sponsored by the Humanities Council of Washington, D.C. Understanding the infrastructure that supports the arts, Miller has served on a number of boards, including the Associated Writing Programs, the PEN/Faulkner Foundation, the Arts Commission for the City of Washington, D.C., the National Writer's Union, and the Institute for Policy Studies. He also contributes to the editorial boards of AFRICAN AMERICAN REVIEW, CALLALOO, *Washington Review,* BLACK ISSUES BOOK REVIEW, *Poet Lore,* and *Arts & Letters.* Through these traditional academic and scholarly venues as well as programs in schools, prisons, and libraries, he ensures that poetry reaches beyond academic boundaries.

Ethelbert Miller was honored with the Columbia Merit Award (1975), the O. B. Hardison Jr. Poetry Prize (1995), the Mayor's Art Award for Literature (1982), and the Public Humanities Award from the District of Columbia Community Council (1988). He was the second recipient of the Stephen Henderson Poetry Award for Outstanding Achievement by the African American Literature and Culture Society (1995). Miller was also one of the American authors selected and honored by Laura Bush and the White House at the National Book Festivals in 2001 and 2003. He lives in Washington, D.C., with his wife, Reverend Denise King-Miller, and his two children, Jasmine-Simone and Nyere-Gibran.

BIBLIOGRAPHY

Galbus, Julia. "*Fathering Words* and Honoring Family: E. Ethelbert Miller's First Memoir." *Re-Markings* 2, no. 2 (September 2003): 7–19.

Pettis, Joyce. "E. Ethelbert Miller." In *African American Poets: Lives, Works and Sources,* 249–254. Westport, Conn.: Greenwood, 2003.

Julia A. Galbus

Miller, May   (1899–1995)

The most widely published woman playwright of the HARLEM RENAISSANCE, publishing plays and poems in 29 periodicals and magazines and more than 20 anthologies, May Miller was born on January 26, 1899, in Washington, D.C., to Annie May

Butler and Kelly Miller, a distinguished professor of sociology at Howard University. Professor Miller counted among his friends and colleagues a circle of intellectuals that included W. E. B. DU-BOIS, BOOKER T. WASHINGTON, Carter G. Woodson, and ALAIN LOCKE, who left an indelible impression on the young May Miller. At Paul Laurence Dunbar High School, Miller studied with the prominent African-American dramatist Mary Burrill and poet ANGELINA WELD GRIMKÉ, subsequently studying drama at Howard University, where she received her B.A. in 1920, directing, acting, and producing plays and collaborating with Alain Locke and Montgomery Gregory in the founding of a black drama movement. She did postgraduate work at Columbia University and American University; taught speech, theater, and dance at Frederick Douglass High School, in Baltimore, Maryland; and later was a lecturer and poet at Monmouth College, the University of Wisconsin–Milwaukee, and the Philips Exeter Academy. Most of her plays were written between 1920 and 1945. In 1942, Miller married former jazz musician Bud Sullivan, a Washington, D.C., school principal, and retired the following year from teaching in order to concentrate on her writing.

A number of Miller's early plays won drama prizes, including *Within the Shadows* (which earned an award while Miller was still an undergraduate at Howard), *Bog Guide,* and *The Cuss'd Thing.* Four of her plays were published in the anthology she edited with Willis Richardson in 1935, *Negro History in Thirteen Plays,* a collection that established firmly Miller's national reputation. Of these, *Sojourner Truth* is notable for its inclusion of white characters who are changed by their contact with a black character, but this play seems somewhat wooden compared with the powerful *Harriet Tubman,* about a spurned mulatto suitor named Sandy who attempts to betray other slaves in order to obtain money with which to buy his own freedom. The plays, whose settings are in the African Sudan (*Samory*) and Haiti (*Christophe's Daughters*), lack the verisimilitude of her other work. Miller's *Ridin' the Goat,* included in Willis Richardson's *Plays and Pageants from the Life of the Negro* (1930), subversively employs humor to challenge the values of the black middle class and to suggest the importance of community rituals and cultural practices. In the play, Miller's Aunt Hetty speaks in the least educated vernacular of any character in her text, yet she most represents an Afrocentric perspective of wisdom, clarity, and strength. Other plays include *Scratches* (1929), which, like the fiction of FRANCES E. W. HARPER before her and of ZORA NEALE HURSTON after her, courageously tackled the taboo subject of internalized colorism and class bias within the African-American community; *Stragglers in the Dust* (1930), about African Americans in the military; and *Nails and Thorns* (1933) an antilynching play published in Lee Hamalian and James V. Hatch's anthology *The Roots of African American Drama* (1991). Radical for their time, her plays sometimes seem dated to more recent critics and readers such as DARWIN TURNER, perhaps because of their problematic didacticism and somewhat formal style. Nevertheless, they continue to be included in contemporary collections of early black theater, such as Kathy A. Perkins's *Black Female Playwrights* (1989), Elizabeth Brown-Guillory's *Wines in the Wilderness* (1990), and Hatch and Hamalian's anthology, as well as in Arthur P. Davis and J. SAUNDERS REDDING's highly regarded 1971 anthology, CAVALCADE. Brown-Guillory claims that May Miller's "contribution to black drama is almost inestimable."

The author of an uncompleted novel, *Fine Market,* as well as several short stories on themes of violence, death, sexuality, substance abuse, and war, Miller, by the mid 1940s, devoted most of her attention to poetry. Fairly traditional in their form and language, Miller's volumes of poetry include *Into the Clearing* (1959), *Poems* (1962), *Lyrics of Three Women: Katie Lyle, Maude Rubin, and May Miller* (1964), *Not That Far* (1973), *The Clearing and Beyond* (1974), *Dust of Uncertain Journey* (1975), *The Ransomed Wait* (1983), and *Collected Poems* (1989). The editor of *Green Wind* (1978) and *My World* (1979), she also authored a book of children's poems, *Halfway to the Sun* (1981). Her poems, which were influenced by the work of Archibald MacLeish and the Chicago Imagists, frequently engage in significant spiritual and ethical questions. "Late Conjecture," for instance, questions the meaning of Christ's sacrifice, while Miller's "The Dream of Wheat" envisions "unnumbered rows of ripened wheat" that "March to greedy ovens." The poem ends by demanding starkly, "Who will eat? / Who go hungry?" With cool-eyed realism, Miller explores in "Weatherwise" the inability of poetry to effect material change: "Not one wind dies down / Because poets rage / Against cold out of season." "Blazing Accusation" (*The Ransomed Wait*) includes a poem about the murder of four young schoolgirls in the 1963 Birmingham, Alabama, church bombing; the poem quietly evokes the locus of Christ's crucifixion to suggest the magnitude of this tragedy.

Miller has been praised by GWENDOLYN BROOKS as "excellent and long-celebrated" and by ROBERT HAYDEN, who has said that Miller "writes with quiet strength, lyric intensity" (Stoeling, 242). Miller is the author of poems that have been published in *Phylon, The Antioch Review, The CRISIS, The Nation, The New York Times,* and *Poetry.* She has read her poetry at the Washington, D.C., bicentennials of 1973 and 1974, as well as at the inauguration of President Jimmy Carter, and she was included in a 1972 Library of Congress Collection of Poets Reading Their Own Works. Living well into her 90s, May Miller must have rejoiced to know of the African-American historical plays by AUGUST WILSON, envisioning them, perhaps, as an outgrowth of her own prediction of the importance of the movement she encouraged. May Miller died on February 8, 1995, in Washington, D.C.

BIBLIOGRAPHY

Harris, Will. "Early Black Women Playwrights and the Dual Liberation Motif." Black Women's Culture Issue. *African American Review* 28, no. 2 (Summer 1994), 205–221.

Meier, Joyce. "The Refusal of Motherhood in African American Women's Theater." Revising Traditions Double Issue. *MELUS,* 25, no. 3/4 (Autumn–Winter 2000): 117–139.

Stephens, Judith L. "Anti-Lynch Plays by African American Women: Race, Gender, and Social Pro-

test in American Drama." Poetry and Theatre Issue. *African American Review* 26, no. 2 (Summer 1992): 329–339.

Stoeling, Winifred L. "May Miller." In *Dictionary of Literary Biography,* vol. 41: *Afro-American Poets since 1955,* edited by Trudier Harris and Thadious Davis, 241–247. Detroit, Mich.: Gale Research Group, 1985.

Lynda Koolish

Milner, Ronald (Ron) (1938–2004)

An award-winning playwright, director, author, editor, critic, and activist, Ron Milner was one of the finest craftsmen to emerge from the BLACK ARTS MOVEMENT. Born on May 29, 1938, in Detroit, Michigan, he grew up on Hastings Street, known as Black Bottom, with his parents Edward Roscoe "Cappy" Milner and Thelma Allen Milner. He graduated from Northeastern High School, where he juggled basketball and writing, and attended Highland Park Junior College, the Detroit Institute of Technology, and Columbia University in New York. He was a writer-in-residence at Margaret Danner's Boone House Writers, 1962–64, where he became acquainted with DUDLEY RANDALL, NAOMI LONG MADGETT, and ROBERT HAYDEN, and at Lincoln University in Pennsylvania, 1966–67, where he met LANGSTON HUGHES, who encouraged him to use a more personal voice in his writing. He taught at Michigan State University, 1971–72, and the University of Southern California, 1979–81. Later he and Shahida Mausi created the Michigan Theatre Center at the Paul Robeson Center in Detroit. More recently, Milner worked with Inside Out, a creative writing project associated with the Detroit public schools.

Milner's plays were first staged at the independent Concepts East Theatre, founded in Detroit in 1962, with Woodie King, Jr., David Rambeau, Clifford Frazier, and Dick Smith. In 1964, Milner went to New York with Woodie King, who collaborated with him for 44 years, and joined the American Place Theatre, which produced his plays. By the end of the 1960s, Milner had established himself as a skillful craftsman and a compelling dramatist as well as a forceful spokesman on behalf of the aesthetic and economic independence of the black playwright. In the 1970s, Milner chose to return to live and work in his native Detroit, where he organized his own theater company, The Spirit of Shango, a community-based black theater. Milner opened his Langston Hughes Theatre in 1975.

Milner's many plays are characterized by their attention to African-American social and psychological culture. As critic Beunyce Rayford Cunningham notes, "Ron Milner's is essentially a theater of intense, often lyrical, retrospection devoted primarily to illuminating the past events, personalities, and values which have shaped his struggling people." In 1967 his first major play, *Who's Got His Own* (1966), a furious fever-pitch drama inspired by Billie Holiday's song "God Bless the Child," premiered in Harlem. In 1974, Milner's *What the Wine-Sellers Buy,* which won the Audeloc Award and earned more than $1 million, became the first play by an African-American to be produced by Joseph Papp at the New York Shakespeare Festival at Lincoln Center. Set in the 1950s and 1960s Hastings Street of Detroit, *What the Wine-Sellers Buy* examines the conflict between the lure of the streets and a mother's teachings. Milner's tribute to jazz, the highly innovative *Jazz-Set,* was one of Drama Circle's Ten Best Plays for 1979. Produced in 2000 by Plowshares of Detroit, *Jazz* works like a jazz composition, where the music and musicians are one and characters' life experiences and memories are "played" as music. *Checkmate* (1987), the recipient of the 1998 NATIONAL ASSOCIATION FOR THE ADVANCEMENT OF COLORED PEOPLE Image Award, which ran on Broadway and starred Denzel Washington, Paul Winfield, Ruby Dee, and Marsha Jackson, is a comedy about the relationships of two black couples who are generations apart in age and attitudes. *Urban Transition: Loose Blossoms* (1996) picks up on themes introduced in *What the Wine-Sellers Buy* to examine how the drug subculture has made its way into current mainstream culture. In 1997, Milner wrote *Inner City Miracle,* a musical, about then 36th District Court Judge Greg Mathis's rise from young crim-

inal to respected jurist—before Mathis got his own television show. The play was produced at the Scottish Rite theatre at the Masonic Temple in Detroit.

Milner's other plays include *The Monster* (1968), *M(ego) and the Green Ball of Freedom* (1968), *The Warning—A Theme for Linda* (1969), *These Three* (1974), *Season's Reason's: Just a Natural Change* (1976), *Work: Don't Let Your Attitude Intrude* (1978), *Crack Steppin'* (1984), *Roads of the Mountain Top* (A Tribute to Dr. Martin Luther King, Jr.; 1986), *Don't Get God Started* (1987; with music by Marvin Winans), *Life Agony* (1965), *The Greatest Gift,* and *Looking for Ronnie Savoy.*

Milner also expressed his vision of the world in mediums other than plays. His novels include *The Life of the Brothers Brown* (1965), and *Don't Get God Started* (1988). His screenplays include *The James Brown Story.* His articles and plays have appeared in *Negro Digest, Drama Review,* and BLACK WORLD. Also, in 1972, Milner, in association with Woodie King, Jr., edited the seminal *Black Drama Anthology.*

Over the years, Milner has received several other awards and honors. He is the recipient of the John Hay Whitney Award (1962), a Rockefeller Grant (1965), and a National Endowment for the Arts playwright grant (1985). He received an honorary doctorate from Wayne State University (2001) and was honored for his contributions to the theater at the Charles H. Wright Museum of African American History (2004).

Known affectionately as the "people's playwright," Milner was considered a pioneering force in African-American theater for more than four decades, ranking with playwrights such as AUGUST WILSON, AMIRI BARAKA, LOFTEN MITCHELL, and Pulitzer Prize winner SUZAN-LORI PARKS. Since the 1960s his plays have been produced at African-American theaters around the country. Ron Milner died from liver cancer at Harper Hospital in Detroit on July 9, 2004.

BIBLIOGRAPHY

Cunningham, Beunyce Rayford. "Ron Milner." In *Dictionary of Literary Biography.* Vol. 38: *Afro-American Writers after 1955: Dramatists and Prose*

Writers, edited by Thadious Davis and Trudier Harris, 201–207. Detroit: Gale, 1985.

King, Jr., Woodie. "Directing *Winesellers.*" *Black World* 25 (April 1976): 20–26.

"Playwright Ron Milner Dies." News Briefs. *Michigan Chronicle* 67, no. 43 (July 14–20, 2004): A1.

Smitherman, Geneva. "'We Are the Music': Ron Milner, People's Playwright." *Black World* 25, no. 6 (April 1976): 4–19.

Loreta G. Woodard

Mitchell, Loften   (1919–2001)

A playwright, actor, theater historian, novelist, and teacher, Loften Mitchell was an eminent early leader of the black theater movement in America. Born in Columbus, North Carolina, on April 15, 1919, to parents who migrated to Harlem, Mitchell attended Cooper Junior High and graduated with honors from DeWitt Clinton High School in 1937. A year before graduation, he launched his theatrical career in New York City as an actor, performing with the Salem Community Dramatizers, the Pioneer Drama Group, and the Rose McClendon Players.

After high school, Mitchell studied playwriting for a year at City College of the City University of New York before accepting a scholarship to Talladega College in Alabama, where he received a B.A. in sociology and a minor in creative writing in 1943. While there, he wrote the musical *Prelude to the Blues* (1940) with the late Wallace Prickett, which, in 1941, won the Delta Sorority's Jabberwock Prize for the best play written by a student. Additionally, Mitchell studied at Union Theological Seminary and General Theological Seminary before serving in the U.S. Navy from 1944 to 1945. Three years later he returned to Harlem and married Helen Marsh, with whom he had two sons, Thomas and Melvin. He studied playwriting with John Gassner and earned an M.A. degree from Columbia University in 1951.

Although he began his acting career in New York City during the 1930s, Mitchell also worked as a social worker and social publicity director for the Jewish Federation of Welfare Services. From 1946 to 1952, he was an actor, stage manager, and press agent at People's Theatre and Harlem Showcase. From 1950 to 1962 he worked as a writer for the New York City WNYC-Radio weekly program "The Later Years" and for the New York City WWRL-Radio daily program "Friendly Adviser." As a professor of theatre arts, Mitchell taught at Long Island University, New York University, and State University of New York at Binghamton, where he taught drama and reactivated the Playwright's Program. He retired in 1985.

Inspired to become a playwright from his visits to the old Lafayette, Lincoln, and Alhambra vaudeville houses in Harlem, Mitchell has contributed generously to the black American stage, revealing his remarkable shifts among dramatic concerns, music, and history. His earlier plays include *Shattered Dreams* (1938), *Blood in the Night* (1946), *The Bancroft Dynasty* (1948), *The Cellar* (1952), *A Land beyond the River* (1957), *Ballad for Bimshire* (1963), *Ballad of the Winter Soldiers* (1964), *Star of the Morning* (1965), *Tell Pharaoh* (1967), *The Phonograph* (1969), and *The Final Solution to the Black Problem in the United States; or, The Fall of the American Empire* (1970). His later plays include one of his best-known theatrical works, *Bubbling Brown Sugar* (1975), *And the Walls Came Tumbling Down* (1976), *Cartoons for a Lunch Hour* (1978), *A Gypsy Girl* (1982), and *Miss Ethel Waters* (1983).

Most critics agree that A *Land beyond the River* (1957), which focuses on the efforts of blacks to integrate American southern public schools, is Mitchell's most important dramatic work. The main character, the Reverend Dr. DeLaine of South Carolina, commits himself to championing the cause of rural black students to achieve equal education, including bus transportation to school. Although the blacks initially lose their case, they appeal to the Supreme Court and win, echoing the issues and outcome of the history-making Supreme Court decision in *Brown v. Board of Education of Topeka, Kansas.*

Mitchell's screenplays include *Young Man of Williamsburg* (1954), *Integration-Report One*

(1960), *I'm Sorry* (1962), and *The Vampires of Harlem* (1972). His books include *Black Drama: The Story of the American Negro in the Theatre* (1967), *The Stubborn Old Lady Who Resisted Change* (1973), and *Voices of the Black Theatre* (1975).

Mitchell was the recipient of numerous awards, including a Guggenheim fellowship for creative writing in drama (1958), a Rockefeller Foundation grant (1961), the Harlem Cultural Council special award for writing (1969), a playwriting award from the Research Foundation of the State University of New York (1974). He received a Tony Award nomination for *Bubbling Brown Sugar* (1976), Best Musical of the Year in London for *Bubbling Brown Sugar* (1977), and the Outstanding Theatrical Pioneer Award, Audience Development Committee (AUDELCO) in 1979.

On May 14, 2001, Mitchell died in Queens, New York. His manuscript collections are housed at State University of New York at Binghamton, the New York City Library Schomburg Collection, Talladega College in Alabama, and Boston University.

Loretta Gilchrist Woodard

Mitchell, Margaree King   (1953–)

Margaree King Mitchell was born July 23, 1953, in Holly Springs, Mississippi, to Joe and Susie Mae King, Jr. She grew up on the family farm and attended Brandeis University, where she earned a B.S. degree in education.

Although she has written and published short stories and numerous television scripts, Mitchell is best known for her two award-winning children's books: *Uncle Jed's Barbershop* (1993) and *Granddaddy's Gift* (1996). Set in the segregated South, where hospital occupants were separated according to race, *Uncle Jed's Barbershop* is a heartwarming story about unselfish giving and returning to give up one's dreams. Uncle Jed, an itinerant barber who services black sharecroppers and their families, who pay him with farm goods and food, dreams of one day owning his own barbershop. But when Sara Jean, the narrator, becomes sick and needs money for surgery, Uncle Jed willingly

provides the money he had been saving, deferring his dream. The Great Depression compounds Jed's financial situation, as his entire savings are lost in the crash. Jed holds onto his dream, nevertheless, fulfilling it at age 79 when he opens his own barbershop, encouraged by the dignity, pride, and joy of all his family members, including Sara Jean.

In *Granddaddy's Gift* Mitchell addresses directly southern black life under Jim Crow laws, specifically, African Americans' struggle to get the right to vote. Called Little Joe because she follows her grandfather, Joe Morgan, a Mississippi farmer, everywhere he goes, Mitchell's main character learns about the world she lives in and how it denies blacks access to their rights and responsibilities as citizens when she decides she no longer needs to attend school because she already knows how to read and write. To illustrate the alternative to an education, her grandfather (who affectionately calls her "Daughter") drives Little Joe to school, passing by cotton fields filled with workers, including some her age. Her grandfather insists that her education will be a great investment.

When her grandfather, who never had the opportunity to go to school but learned to read nevertheless, is selected to test the laws that prohibit blacks from voting, Little Joe is called upon to bear witness to the way he and the black community are harassed simply for trying to exercise their rights as American citizens. When her grandfather studies Mississippi's state constitution, takes the test, and passes it to demonstrate he is literate, Little Joe celebrates his and the community's determination and victory. As a result of her grandfather's effort and victory, Little Joe is able to register to vote on her 18th birthday without having to endure the harassment her grandfather had known. Her grandfather has paved the way. By standing up for his rights, he has given her the greatest gift he can.

Margaree King Mitchell is the winner of several awards and honors for her sensitively written and beautifully illustrated children stories, including a Best of 1993 citation from the Society of School Librarians, a Coretta Scott King Honor Award, a Notable Children's Trade Book citation from the

National Council for the Social Studies, the Notable Children's Book citation from the American Library Association, and the "Living the Dream" Award (1995).

Michael Samuels

Moody, Anne (1940–)

Like RICHARD WRIGHT in BLACK BOY (1945) and MAYA ANGELOU in I KNOW WHY THE CAGED BIRD SINGS (1970), Anne Moody, who was given the name Essie Mae at birth, chronicles, in Coming of Age in Mississippi, her experience of growing up black in America when segregation, maintained through Jim Crow laws of "separate but equal" practices sanctioned by the Supreme Court in its Plessy v. Ferguson decision (1896), was the way of life in the American South. Published in 1968, Moody's autobiography is a powerful bildungsroman, an account of the educational process to selfhood of a black girl born in 1940 and raised in poverty in the rural segregated landscape of Mississippi during the postwar 1940s and 1950s. This educational process told young Moody who she was and the choices open to her, given the color of her skin, or at least her sociopolitical identity as the daughter of Mississippi sharecroppers, Fred and Elmira Moody. This extraordinary, candid, honest, riveting, and at times heart-wrenching personal account ends in 1964 with an account of her involvement in the CIVIL RIGHTS MOVEMENT.

Moody begins her personal narrative with the domestic issues her parents encountered when she was four years old. Like many southern black males of his generation, her father experienced great difficulty providing for the family. Fred Moody left his wife and three children when economic difficulties exacerbated by gambling and an extramarital affair strained his domestic relationship. Moody's mother sought employment in domestic service and restaurant work while the family struggled and was frequently forced to move. At one point, the family briefly lived in a white residential area in a small house on the property of her mother's employer. Although Moody and her

brother Junior frequently played with neighborhood white children, she became aware of the material advantages their white playmates enjoyed and wished her mother could provide her children with a bicycle or a pair of skates.

One of the first turning points in her life took place when Moody and her family arrived at the local movie theater at the same time as her white playmates. Naively, the Moody siblings joined their playmates in the "white-only" lobby before their mother became aware of the infraction they had committed. Immediately, to protect them and teach them a vital lesson about the world they lived in and the expected behavior, their mother quickly admonished them, telling them they had to go to the side door entrance that led to the colored-only balcony. The incident opened Moody's eyes and confirmed what she had begun to surmise: Whites enjoyed advantages over blacks simply because they were white. This, Moody learned, was even true for her two maternal uncles who, to her, looked as white as her playmates but were not white according to her mother, who refused to explain why. Moody knew one thing: Racial segregation was more than skin deep.

By the time she was in the fourth grade, Moody had to begin working, given the family's financial needs. Working as a domestic in the homes of several white families, Moody, over an extended period, observed the differences between her white employers who either looked at her with contempt or, impressed with her intelligence, encouraged her to do well in school. In school, Moody worked hard to achieve academic success; she received outstanding grades at both the elementary and secondary levels. Assertive and competitive, she also was a good athlete and would go on to win an athletic scholarship to Natchez Junior College after graduating from high school.

In 1955, the newly renamed Anne Moody (Essie May was replaced by Anne May on a replacement birth certificate after a fire destroyed their family home) experienced yet another major turning point, as this was also the infamous year that 14-year-old Emmett Till, a Chicago resident who was spending the summer with relatives in Mississippi, was kidnapped and brutally murdered. Till's murder symbolized to her the mean sickness, the cancer ravishing the body of white Mississippians and other white southerners. Equally appalling, however, was her mother's seeming lack of interest and that of other black residents of her community, and in particular her white employer's indifference to Till's murder as well as her contempt for the NATIONAL ASSOCIATION FOR THE ADVANCEMENT OF COLORED PEOPLE (NAACP).

In the fall of 1959, Moody was awarded a basketball scholarship to Natchez Junior College (NJC). Upon her arrival she immediately found herself on the wrong side of the staff and administration, a result of clashes with the women's basketball coach and the dean of the college. Remarkably strong willed, Moody had refused to submit to perceived injustices. She found herself in trouble once again with NJC staff when she led a boycott to protest the discovery of maggots in the grits served to students. Called in to face NJC's President Grant, Moody calmly pointed to the source of the problem: a leaking shower above the kitchen pantry. Impressed, President Grant not only had the repair done but encouraged Moody to apply for available full-paying tuition at four-year institutions. Moody's outstanding grades at NJC and high exam scores resulted in her receiving a full-tuition scholarship to Tougaloo College, reportedly the best black college in Mississippi.

At Tougaloo, the 21-year-old became actively involved with the campus chapter of the NAACP, although she was worried about the harm that might come to her or members of her family. Moody also developed a close friendship with Joan Trumpauer, a white student who was a secretary for the Student Non-violent Coordinating Committee (SNCC). Moody became actively involved in the voter registration drive in the Greenwood and Greenville areas of the Mississippi Delta. Moody wrote, "That summer I could feel myself beginning to change. For the first time I began to think that something would be done about whites killing, beating and misusing Negroes. I knew I was going to be a part of whatever happened" (254). She enthusiastically attended the 1962 State

NAACP convention in Jackson, although, out of fear of retaliation, her participation was discouraged and strongly rebuked by her mother and other family members.

When NJC delayed the approval of transfer credits to Tougaloo College, Moody's graduation plans for spring 1963 were delayed; however, she saw this as an opportunity to be further involved the Civil Rights movement. She wrote, "It no longer seemed important to prove anything. I had found something outside of myself that gave meaning to my life." Moody immersed herself in sit-in demonstrations and mass meetings, and she conducted nonviolent defensive workshops for potential demonstrators, primarily high school- and college-age students. Moody and her associates persisted, although they were verbally and physically abused by rowdy white youth and on one occasion attacked by dogs under the direction of local law enforcement officers, who later arrested them.

On June 12, 1963, black Mississippians and black Americans in general were shocked by the news of the brutal murder of Medgar Evers, a veteran and the Mississippi NAACP field secretary, in the driveway of his home. Driven by the despair and internal schisms in Jackson's black community, Moody volunteered to help the Congress of Racial Equality (CORE) open a voter registration office in Canton, Mississippi, in Madison County, which had a reputation for violence against blacks although blacks outnumbered whites three to one. However, fear of white retribution subsided among blacks as more internal support came from black church leaders and businesspeople for nightly registration workshops.

A final major turning point in her life came when Moody was deeply affected by the September 1963 bombing of a black church in Birmingham in which four black girls were killed. She questioned the fairness of a god who would allow this to happen and, in a moment of rhetorical blasphemy, declared, "I will be my own God." She also concluded that nonviolence was dead. Depression, stress, and weight loss led Moody to take a leave of absence from her political activities. Her physical and emotional condition was further exacerbated by the news of the assassination of President John Kennedy on November 22, 1963. For Moody and millions of black Americans, Kennedy had represented a glimmer of hope.

In May 1964 Moody returned to Mississippi from her hiatus in Louisiana to participate in Tougaloo College's graduation exercises. Before the graduation she met with old friends from the movement and decided to join them in a planned demonstration in Canton. Local law enforcement officers resorted to violence in attempting to force the demonstrators to turn around. Moody and her fellow protestors turned their attention to the FBI agents who watched and, as usual, did nothing to intervene.

On Sunday May 31, 1964, Moody was awarded her college degree. She was alone, without any family to share the occasion. When she returned to New Orleans, Moody learned that, to save money to buy her a graduation present, Adeline, her younger sister, had not attended the graduation services.

Moody returned to Canton, where she worked with CORE's Summer Project. She was invited to join SNCC's Bob Moses and others for the Mississippi Council of Federated Organizations (COFO) hearings that were to be held in Washington, D.C. COFO was a statewide organization that incorporated all national, state, and local protest groups operating in Mississippi. As the bus sped down the highway, the civil rights activists repeatedly sang verses of "We Shall Overcome," while Moody quietly thought: "I wonder. I really wonder" (384).

BIBLIOGRAPHY

Moody, Anne. *Coming of Age in Mississippi.* New York: Dell Publishing, 1968.

Ronald G. Coleman

Morrison, Toni (Chloe Anthony Wofford) (1931–)

Morrison was born in 1931 in Lorain, Ohio. Her parents, George and Ramah Wofford, migrants from the South, were hardworking members of the working class. Family life featured storytelling and music. At age 12, Chloe converted to Catholicism and adopted the name Anthony, after St. Anthony, which became shorted to Toni. After graduating with honors from Lorain High School in 1949, she went to Howard University. She left Howard in 1953, with a major in English and a minor in classics, to attend Cornell University, where, in 1955, she received an M.A. in English. She wrote her thesis on the fiction of William Faulkner and Virginia Woolf.

Between 1955 and 1965, she married and was divorced from Harold Morrison; had two sons, Harold Ford and Slade Kevin; and taught English at Howard University and Texas Southern University. After her divorce, she began work as an editor at L.W. Singer Publishing Company, a textbook division of Random House. In 1967 she became a fiction editor at Random House, a position she held until 1984. As editor, Morrison nurtured the literary careers of many contemporary African-American writers, and she edited *The Black Book,* a compilation of photographs and primary texts documenting African-American history. From 1984 to 1989, she taught at the State University of New York at Albany as the Albert Schweitzer Chair in humanities and fine arts, and since 1989 she has been the Robert H. Goheen Professor in humanities at Princeton University.

In the early 1960s, while participating in an informal writers' group, she jotted down a short story about an African-American girl who longed for blue eyes. Encouraged by the group's response, she expanded the story into *The Bluest Eye* (1970), an astonishing first novel, although the little critical attention it received was mixed. It relates not only the tragedy of Pecola Breedlove's fantasy but also the stories of her angry and dispossessed father, Cholly; of her self-righteous mother, Pauline; of her friend Claudia, who tries desperately to make sense of what happens; and by extension of the African-American community in Lorain, Ohio.

Morrison followed *The Bluest Eye* with SULA (1973), which, widely praised, was nominated for the National Book Award. It tells the story of two friends, Sula Peace and Nel Wright. Growing up in the African-American section of a southern Ohio town, their intimate friendship as girls is severed when Sula, like her grandmother and mother, chooses a nonconforming life, while Nel, like her mother, opts for respectability and conformity. As their lives span the middle decades of the 20th century, Morrison delineates many of the economic, social, and psychological issues that confront African-Americans.

Song of Solomon (1977), winner of the National Book Critics' Circle Award, is more ambitious, and with it Morrison's status as one of the leading contemporary fiction writers in America was firmly established. In Part I, its central character, Milkman Dead, struggles to attain a meaningful identity amidst familial and societal tensions, much like Pecola, Claudia, Sula, and Nel. In Part II, he travels from the North to the South, at first in search of a cache of gold, but his search becomes a heroic quest for his ancestral past, his cultural heritage, and his rightful identity. The two protagonists, of Morrison's fourth novel, *Tar Baby* (1981), Jadine Childs and Son, attempt unsuccessfully to pair up. Neither the Caribbean mansion of Jadine's white patron nor Son's hometown in rural Florida nor the glitz of New York City provides a hospitable setting for them. Compared with Morrison's other novels, this one received less praise and less critical attention.

Morrison's best-known novel, BELOVED (1987), won the Pulitzer Prize. The central character is Sethe Garner, who in 1855 escapes slavery to freedom in Cincinnati. When her former owner comes to reclaim her and her four children, she kills one of them, Beloved, and tries to kill the others rather than see them returned to slavery. Most of the novel occurs in 1873, when Sethe; her surviving daughter, Denver; and another former slave, PAUL D, try painfully to live with the nearly fatal effects of the slave past, including the mysterious presence of a young woman who claims to be named Beloved.

Beloved was followed by *Jazz* in 1992. The main plot of this novel is the story of Joe and Violet Trace, who migrate from Virginia to New York in the 1920s. Thrilled by the excitement and relative prosperity of their life there, they nevertheless endure debilitating identity problems, centered on Violet's lack of a child and on Joe's ignorance about his mother. In 1993 Morrison won the Nobel Prize in literature, and her acceptance speech was published that year. *Paradise* (1998), Morrison's third novel in what she has called a trilogy on the subject of love, recounts the history of an all-black town in rural Oklahoma and the tragic confrontation between some of the male leaders of that town and a group of socially outcast women living nearby. In 2003, Morrison's eighth novel, *Love,* was published.

In addition to her novels, Morrison has published a play, *Dreaming Emmett* (1985); a short story, "Recitativ" (1982); a book of literary criticism, *Playing in the Dark: Whiteness and the Literary Imagination* (1992); several essays on African-American and American culture; and several children's books coauthored with her son Slade. She has also edited two volumes of essays: *Racing Justice and Engendering Power* (1992) on the Anita Hill/Clarence Thomas hearings and *Birth of a Nation'hood* (1997) on the O. J. Simpson trial.

As indicated by the prizes and honors Morrison has accumulated, she has achieved phenomenal literary success—both popular and critical. Critics have examined her works, especially *Song of Solomon* and *Beloved,* from a multitude of perspectives and have enthusiastically praised her fiction and her role as a public intellectual. She regularly gives readings of her own works and insightful lectures throughout the country and the world. She has also collaborated with renowned musicians, such as Kathleen Battle, Jessye Norman, and Andre Previn, in various compositions, including a new opera based on Margaret Garner, the historical prototype for Sethe.

In the broadest terms, Morrison's novels have propelled her to the heights of her profession because they unflinchingly address issues that are close to the heart, not only of African Americans' experience or all Americans' experience but also, more broadly, of human experience. They deeply satisfy readers in their bold examinations of the difficulties and the possibilities of finding viable identities and meaningful living spaces. That means coming to terms with the racialized conditions of American society and with the effects of that racialized past on African-American identities, families, and communities. Morrison places her characters in the margins between historical, geographical, and cultural forces, where they must negotiate past and present, North and South, black and white.

Morrison's fiction also resonates with readers because it is simultaneously realistic and mythical. The novels depict the historical realities of African-American and American experience from the Middle Passage, through slavery and Reconstruction, to life in the rural South, migration to the West and the urban North, and the CIVIL RIGHTS MOVEMENT and beyond. Yet magic and myth exist alongside realism, as in Milkman's heroic leap at the end of *Song of Solomon,* Son's headlong flight into the swamps at the end of *Tar Baby,* and Beloved's very presence. By requiring readers to engage in both historical and mythical dimensions, Morrison lifts her fiction, and her readers, into multiple planes of consciousness.

That pluralism is enriched by the intriguing open-endedness of Morrison's fiction. For example, she uses multiple modes of narration, including numerous flashbacks and flash-forwards that suggest that time is more circular than linear. She also insists on constructive ambiguity, leaving space for readers' imaginations to participate in the fiction, for example, in the uncertainty surrounding Beloved's existence and the unresolved question of which girl is white in *Paradise.* In their openness, Morrison's novels articulate both an African-American perspective that privileges double-consciousness and a postmodern perspective that privileges multiplicity, polyvocalism, and process. In her vision, the cultural and human conditions that the novels reflect and re-create can only be voiced, not resolved, and yet must be voiced and revoiced. Solution and resolution are illusory, because African-American life is always at least double, because American culture is always already multiple and fragmented and because the human condition is caught in the endless play of alternatives.

BIBLIOGRAPHY

Bouson, J. Brooks. *Quiet as It's Kept: Shame, Trauma, and Race in the Novels of Toni Morrison.* Albany: State University of New York Press, 2000.

Conner, Marc C., ed. *The Aesthetics of Toni Morrison: Speaking the Unspeakable.* Jackson: University of Mississippi Press, 2000.

Duvall, John. *The Identifying Fictions of Toni Morrison: Modernist Authenticity and Postmodern Blackness.* New York: Palgrave Macmillan, 2000.

Middleton, David, ed. *Toni Morrison's Fiction: Contemporary Criticism.* New York: Garland, 2000.

Page, Philip. *Dangerous Freedom: Fusion and Fragmentation in Toni Morrison's Novels.* Jackson: University of Mississippi Press, 1995.

Peach, Linden. *Toni Morrison: Historical Perspectives and Literary Contexts.* New York: St. Martin's, 2000.

Rigney, Barbara Hill. *The Voices of Toni Morrison.* Columbus: Ohio State University Press, 1991.

Philip Page

Mos Def (1973–)

Born Dante Terrell (Beze) Smith on December 11, 1973, in Brooklyn, New York, Mos Def (a name taken from the slang term for "Most Definitely") is widely regarded as one of the most introspective, socially conscious, and talented artists of his time. Rising to prominence as a hip-hop M.C. in the 1990s, Mos Def appeared on tracks for several well-known rap musicians, including De La Soul and da Bush Babees. In 1997 he released his first solo project, the single "Universal Magnetic." His first full-length album was a collaborative project; he partnered with fellow artist and activist Talib Kweli and D.J. Hi-Tek to form the group Black Star. Their self-titled album was released in 1998.

In 1999 Mos Def released his first solo album *Black on Both Sides,* which is widely regarded as one of the most important albums in contemporary hip-hop history. He won acclaim for his unique flow, his range of subject matter, and, most notably, his willingness to address key social, political, and economic challenges facing the African-American community and oppressed peoples around the world. Album tracks address topics ranging from the appropriation of rock music ("Rock N Roll") to capitalism and environmental degradation ("New World Water"); "Four carbons and monoxide / Push the water table lopside / Used to be free now it cost you a fee / Cause all things fully loaded they roam cross the sea." In 2004 Mos released his second solo project, *The New Danger.* The widely anticipated release quickly garnered critical acclaim.

Mos Def, along with his partner Talib Kweli and contemporary Common, are widely credited for the revival of "message rap," which had been overtaken in the early 1990s by "gansta rap." Influenced by pioneers of the genre, including AFRIKA BAMBATAA AASIM, Rakim, and De La Soul, Mos believes that music can and should be used as a vehicle for collective empowerment. He also recognizes the potential held by a range of musical forms. In 2000 he partnered with four rhythm-and-blues and rock music legends, keyboardist Bernie Worrell (Parliament/Funkadelic), guitarist Dr. Know (Bad Brains), drummer Will Calhoun (Living Colour), and bassist Doug Wimbush (the Sugar Hill Gang, Grandmaster Flash and the Furious Five, and Living Colour), to form the rap rock hybrid the Black Jack Johnson project, aimed at reclaiming the black roots of rock music.

Mos Def began his career as a television actor in the late 1980s. He had all but abandoned this career track until 2001, when he appeared in *Bamboozled,* a SPIKE LEE film bringing to light ways in which contemporary media continue to advance stereotypical views of black people. Since his film debut, he has appeared in *The Italian Job,* MTV's *Carmen: A Hip Hopera, Monster's Ball, Brown Sugar,* HBO's *Something the Lord Made,* and *The Woodsman.* In addition to his work in film, he has worked as a stage actor in the Tony-nominated *Top Dog/ Underdog* and the off-Broadway play *Fucking A.*

A longtime believer in the poetic value of hip-hop, Mos Def, whose lyrics often read like poetry,

has been influenced by recognized poets and writers, including PAUL LAURENCE DUNBAR, CHESTER HIMES, WALTER MOSLEY, JOHN EDGAR WIDEMAN, and SONIA SANCHEZ, as well as hip-hop artists. In 2002, Mos Def joined Russell Simmons to launch an original series on HBO, *Def Poetry Jam.* Mos served as co-executive producer, host and music supervisor. The series—a televised poetry slam—showcases urban contemporary poets as well as highlights established works and writers, sparking a revival in the urban poetry movement.

BIBLIOGRAPHY
Cook, Dara. "The Aesthetics of Rap," *Black Issues Book Review* 2, no. 2 (March/April 2002).

Melina Abdullah

Mosley, Walter   (1952–)
Born and raised in Los Angeles, California, Walter Mosley traveled to the East to complete his college education. In Vermont, he studied at Goddard College before receiving his B.A., in 1977, from Johnson State College. While pursuing a doctorate at the University of Massachusetts in Amherst, he supported himself by working as a computer programmer. As a way of passing time on the job one day, Mosley typed several creative lines, which hooked him to the writing process. In 1985 he decided to study in the graduate-level creative writing program at the City College of New York, eventually winning the college's fiction award. From there, with the assistance of his writing professor, he secured an agent and entered the publishing world.

Through seven novels, Mosley develops a protagonist, Ezekiel "Easy" Rawlins, who coalesces traditional notions of the hard-boiled detective and the cultural aspects of the black hero. In doing so, Mosley asks readers to ponder various meanings of masculinity in America even as they consume the escapist elements of the detective genre. Covering a time frame from the late 1930s to the late 1960s, Mosley's detective novels collectively chronicle the eventful and challenging experiences of Easy Rawlins, while exploring the dynamics of economical, political, and ethical issues facing an urban black community. Another crucial dimension of the seven-novel series is the friendship between Easy and his best friend, Raymond "Mouse" Alexander. Easy and Mouse maintain a volatile relationship, the latter viewing the world as a hostile place where a violent response guarantees survival and manhood. The tension between the friends represents the anxiety among black men, who constantly walk a line of adherence to or confrontation with America's status quo.

The titles in the Easy Rawlins series appear to be linked by references to colors, though the author insists that the colors hold no hidden symbolic value: *Devil in a Blue Dress* (1990), *A Red Death* (1991), *White Butterfly* (1992), *Black Betty* (1994), *A Little Yellow Dog* (1996), *Gone Fishin'* (1997), and *Bad Boy Brawly Brown* (2002). *Gone Fishin'*, though published later in the series, sits chronologically at the beginning of the easy Rawlins saga, as it presents Easy and Mouse in their late teens in Texas, while the remaining stories are set in Los Angeles. *Devil in the Blue Dress*, published first, won public accolades from then-president Bill Clinton, who identified Mosley as his favorite writer; it was the only novel in the series to be made into a feature film, in 1995.

Well-suited for the detective genre, Mosley introduces a different black hero in the form of *Fearless Jones* (2001), the title character of a novel set in Los Angeles in the 1950s. Jones is a gutsy, intuitive man who can navigate city streets and hidden dangers. In his quest to locate missing Swiss bonds, Fearless unites with his friend Paris Minton, a bookstore owner and intellectual who also serves as the narrator for the novel. A reflective everyman, Minton's cautious nature complements Jones's fierceness and acuity for survival.

Although financially successful with his detective novels, Mosley has ventured beyond the niche of the detective genre. In 1995, he published *RL's Dream*, a novel that highlighted the character Soupspoon Wise, a black musician from Mississippi. Soupspoon makes his way to Manhattan, where he attempts to survive cancer, economic hardships, and an unusual interracial relationship and to nurture his passion for his music.

In another journey from the detective world, Mosley tackles science fiction in *Blue Light* (1998) and *Futureland* (2001). *Blue Light* is a novel in which a mysterious light beam streaks across the universe, transforming the humans touched by its energy. Anointing those humans with the abilities of prophecy and knowledge, the result is a minority of humans with extraterrestrial powers who become targeted by those without them. In *Futureland*, Mosley presents nine short stories that are linked by the environment of accelerated technology. Although the critical and popular response to Mosley's science fiction has not equaled the praise for his detective fiction, he has nonetheless demonstrated his skills at crafting works that are not limited to one particular category.

This proficiency at writing popular fiction across genre lines is further demonstrated with two other books—*Always Outnumbered, Always Outgunned* (1997) and *Walkin the Dog* (1999). In these two collections of short stories, Mosley returns to the streets of Los Angeles with a protagonist who might be best called an antihero. Both collections focus on Socrates Fortlow, a black ex-con in his 50s who, returning to the community of Watts, attempts to reconstruct a material and spiritual life. In the first book of stories, Socrates discovers that after 27 years in prison, his life experience has given him a wisdom that he can pass along as he chisels out a home and new friendships. In the latter collection of stories, Socrates finds that the brutality and hardships of the environment chip away at his moral resolve. He once again confronts his violent nature as the best means of enduring the jungle of a world he did not create. In 1998, the first collection of stories was turned into an HBO movie of the same title with Laurence Fishburne portraying Socrates Fortlow.

In addition to his diverse publications, Mosley has been an outspoken critic of the publishing practices that contribute to the limitations placed on established authors and the exclusion of new writers. In 1997 he made a bold statement by deliberately placing his novel, *Gone Fishin*, with the black publishing house Black Classic Press, rather than a larger firm with more marketing dollars.

Likewise, he has been critical of the ongoing exploitation that resonates in the capitalistic system toward people of color and the underclass. In 1996, while working with the African Studies Institute at New York University, Mosley organized a lecture series of various black figures, including Angela Davis, Randall Robinson, and BELL HOOKS, called "Black Genius." That series led to his coediting of the book *Black Genius: African-American Solutions to African-American Problems* (1999), in which Mosley writes an introduction and a reflective essay. In 2000 he published *Workin' on the Chain Gang: Shaking Off the Dead Hand of History*, a nonfiction book that assesses the American economic and political system and the responsibilities of readers to reject dehumanizing practices and to consider alternative approaches when choosing leadership.

In less than 15 years, Walter Mosley has carved out a significant position in American popular literature and established himself as a formidable presence in the African-American literary tradition. He provides an example of a black writer finding international fame and financial success, but more important, he serves as a model of a black author who merges a passion for creativity with a commitment to his community.

BIBLIOGRAPHY

Berger, Roger A. "'The Black Dick': Race, Sexuality, and Discourse in the L.A. Novels of Walter Mosley." *African American Review* (Summer 1997): 281–294.

Crooks, Robert. "From the Far Side of the Urban Frontier: The Detective Fiction of Chester Himes and Walter Mosley." *College Literature* (October 1995): 68–90.

Fine, David, ed. *Los Angeles in Fiction: A Collection of Essays: From James M. Cain to Walter Mosley.* Albuquerque: University of New Mexico Press, 1995.

Frumkes, Lewis Burke. "A Conversation with Walter Mosley." *Writer* (December 1999): 20.

Mason, Theodore O., Jr. "Walter Mosley's Easy Rawlins: The Detective and Afro-American Fiction." *Kenyon Review* (Fall 1992): 173–183.

Woods, Paula L. *Spooks, Spies, and Private Eyes: Black Mystery, Crime, and Suspense Fiction.* New York: Doubleday, 1996.

Mel Donalson

Motley, Willard Francis   (1909–1965)

Motley, the son of a Pullman porter, was born into a middle-class black Chicago family on July 14, 1912. The Great Depression prevented Motley from attending college after graduating from Englewood High School in 1929. Motley, who grew up in a predominantly white neighborhood on Chicago's South Side, worked at various low-paying jobs during his youth and young adulthood, including as a farm worker, waiter, shipping clerk, and cook. To know intricately the living and working conditions of the American poor of his day, Motley secured an apartment in the Bowery section of Chicago. Motley, whose first published short story appeared in the *Chicago Defender* when he was 13, eventually wrote for the socialist journal *Commonweal* and worked for the Federal Writers Project to learn more about economic and living conditions in Chicago's impoverished black community.

Although writing during the post–World War II period meant that he was inevitably associated with the school of literary naturalism, dominated by RICHARD WRIGHT, Motley was among a cadre of black writers who broadened their perspectives to include nonracial themes and white protagonists (Bell, 189), including FRANK YERBY, CHESTER HIMES, WILLIAM DEMBY, ANN PETRY, JAMES BALDWIN, and even Wright himself. Thus, although *Knock on Any Door*, Motley's 1947 best-selling novel, focuses on the experience of a character like Wright's Bigger Thomas, Motley's protagonist, Nick Romano, a former Catholic altar boy, is the son of Italian immigrants. After he is sent to reform school for a crime he did not commit, Nick returns home a converted criminal.

Although his family moves from Denver to Chicago to provide new opportunities for their son, Nick cannot change. *Knock on Any Door* ends with Nick being tried and executed for murdering a Chicago police officer. Nick, the product of his environment, like Bigger, cannot escape his fate. But Motley is equally careful to critique Chicago's judiciary and penal system. In 1949, Columbia Pictures converted Motley's well-researched novel into a movie, with Humphrey Bogart playing the part of Nick's attorney.

In his other works, *We Fished All Night* (191), *Let No Man Write My Epitaph* (1958), and *Let Noon be Fair* (1966), Motley continued to use an array of ethnic characters, emphasizing his concern with more than race and the African-American experience. For example, *We Fished All Night* explores the physical and psychological impact of war on its three central characters, while *Let No Man Write My Epitaph* returns to the Romano family and examines the devastating effect of drugs on Nick Jr. and his mother, who are drug addicts. In the end, however, Nick Jr. takes control of his life after completing a detoxification program. Columbia Pictures also made a movie of this novel.

Motley, who received high critical acclaim for his first novel, died of gangrene in Mexico City on March 4, 1965. His last novel, *Let Noon Be Fair* (1966), was published posthumously.

BIBLIOGRAPHY

Bell, Bernard. *The Afro-American Novel and Its Tradition.* Amherst: The University of Massachusetts Press, 1987.

Wilfred D. Samuels

Mules and Men
Zora Neale Hurston (1935)

ZORA NEALE HURSTON's anthropological study *Mules and Men* is one of her most significant contributions to African-American culture. Generally regarded as the first authentic collection of African-American folklore, *Mules and Men* is drawn mainly from Hurston's hometown culture in Eatonville, Florida, an all-black community. Assisted by a research fellowship from the Association for the Study of Negro Life and History (ASNLH), Hurston became immersed in the culture, collecting and documenting the folktales, spirituals, work songs, sermons, blues, children's games, and "hoodoo," traditional African religious practices and beliefs among southern blacks throughout Florida, Alabama, and Louisiana from 1927 to 1932. *Mules and Men,* which includes an introduction by Hurston's professor, the anthropologist Franz Boas, is the result of this research. It was followed by *Tell My Horse,* Hurston's second volume of ethnography, which grew out of her research in Haiti and Jamaica, where she studied Vodun (Voodoo) practices.

Divided into two parts, *Mules and Men,* which is narrated in the first person, employs fictional techniques to re-create and shape the work. In Part I, Hurston records folklore gathered in her own hometown of Eatonville, reported usually in "lying sessions" created as setting by Hurston on store porches, backwoods churches, and turpentine camps or during contests among lumberjacks. Although most of the tales throughout Part I are told for the sake of storytelling, a number of other stories are adaptations of the popular Brer Rabbit stories known in the South and the tales of High John de Conqueror, the black folk hero who is the embodiment of the strong, even bad, black man. In the glossary, which Hurston includes at the end of her collection, she describes John as "the wish fulfillment hero of the race. The one who nevertheless, or in spite of laughter, usually defeats Ole Massa, God and the Devil. Even when Massa seems to have him in a hopeless dilemma he wins out by a trick" (305). Also, while Hurston makes little or no effort to classify or analyze her simple tales in Part I, they all provide a better glimpse into a way of life that Hurston considered "priceless art."

Some of the stories include "The Talking Mule," "John Henry," "How Jack Beat De Devil," "The Fortune Teller," "Why the Sister in Black Works Hardest," "How the Negroes Got Their Freedom," "How Brer 'Gator Got His Tongue Warn Out," "Card Game," "Why They Always Use Rawhide on a Mule," "How the Church Came to Be Split Up," and "Sermon by Traveling Preacher."

In Part II of *Mules and Men* Hurston presents the origin of hoodoo and recounts not only her experiences but also her fascination with a number of Voodoo doctors. One of her most memorable and lengthy initiation rites was with the popular New Orleans hoodoo doctor Luke Turner, during which she was completely naked and, after fasting for 69 hours, was crowned with a consecrated snakeskin. Hurston provided initiation ceremonies by hoodoo practitioners, including Marie Leveau, Eulalia, Anatol Pierre, Father Watson, Dr. Samuel Jenkins, Dr. Duke, and Kitty Brown, that ranged from how to put a curse on someone to how to keep a husband true, and from how to keep a person down to how to make love stronger. Though Part II presents Hurston's personal experiences, it mirrors the religious and spiritual beliefs of a larger black community, derived African beliefs that survived the Middle Passage to take root in America, that she discovered during her research in Louisiana.

Despite its omissions and also despite its complexity and controversy, which critics have noted, *Mules and Men* still offers valuable insight into a class of people and a way of life rich in history and culture. More important, Hurston's "interesting and entertaining" collection has made the public aware of the African American's innumerable contributions to American folk tradition.

BIBLIOGRAPHY

Faulkner, Howard J. "*Mules and Men:* Fiction as Folklore." *CLA Journal* 34 (1991): 331–339.

Ford, Nick Aaron. "A Study in Race Relations: A Meeting with Zora Hurston." In *Zora Neale Hurston,* edited by Harold Bloom, 7–10. New York: Chelsea House Publishers, 1986.

Hurston, Zora Neale. *Mules and Men.* Philadelphia: J. B. Lippincott, 1935. Reprinted with an introduction by Darwin T. Turner, New York: Harper and Row, 1970.

Preece, Harold. "The Negro Folk Cult." *Crisis* 43 (1936): 364, 374.

Loretta G. Woodard

Mullen, Harryette Romell   (1960–   )

An associate professor of English and African-American studies at the University of California at Los Angeles, Harryette Mullen was born in Alabama, grew up in Fort Worth, Texas, the daughter of teachers and the granddaughter and the great-granddaughter of Baptist ministers, amidst a varied racial and cultural setting. Mullen's work reflects the tensions engendered by those multiple influences that form what critic Elisabeth Frost calls the "miscegenated culture" of her poetry. A strong scholarly voice as well, Mullen completed her undergraduate work at the University of Texas at Austin, where she received a B.A. in English in 1975. She received a Ph.D. in literature from the University of California at Santa Cruz in 1990. Mullen's poetic career began, she recounts, after she won a poetry contest while she was a high school student in Texas. Over the years, she has continued to develop the impressive and exciting poetic voice that readers have come to expect and appreciate.

Mullen's poetry interrogates the intersection of race and gender within the structure and structuring forces of language. She combines elements of Oulipo's intriguing wordplay game "N+7" (a technique that replaces each noun [N] with the seventh [7] noun that follows it in the dictionary) with the literary techniques of parody, pun, hyperbole, and metonymy into her lyrical poems—or, as Mullen calls them, "mongrel" lyric poetry. Through this specific lens, Mullen explores how the borders of language, culture, and race have been undeniably blurred and opens new spaces for interpretation of the processes of writing. Additionally, Mullen's work, particularly *Tall Tree Woman* (1981), has strong connections to that of earlier African-American writers and poets, specifically JAMES WELDON JOHNSON, HARLEM RENAISSANCE poet LANGSTON HUGHES, and MELVIN B. TOLSON. She values as well the literary voices and struggles expressed in the literature of the BLACK ARTS MOVEMENT, which sought to deconstruct the hegemonic structure of the status quo while positing and celebrating a viable and important black life and world. In *Trimmings* (1991) and *S*PeRM**K*T* [Supermarket] (1992),

Mullen further examines language and questions subjectivity and audience. In *S*PeRM**K*T* Mullen employs the lens of the consumer marketing strategies of major supermarkets, where language in advertisements and store displays reinscribe the language of gender differences in American culture. Puns, parodies, and metaphors abound in metonymic play in lines such as "Iron maidens make docile martyrs. / Their bodies on the rack stretched taut." However, all of Mullen's poetic work—*Tall Tree Woman* (1981), *Trimmings, S*PeRM**K*T* [Supermarket], *Muse and Drudge* (1995), *Sleeping with the Dictionary* (2002), and *Blues Baby: Early Poems* (2002), a collection of previously uncollected poems and a reprint of *Tall Tree Woman*—seem to resonate not only through these cultural, political, and social elements but also through important elements of Mullen's personal milieu.

According to Mullen, her award-winning collection *Sleeping with the Dictionary,* literally was started when she fell asleep with a dictionary in her bed and was awakened by pain caused by the dictionary poking her in her back. Several poems in the collection find Mullen's intricately "nudging" her readers, awakening them to language and its various uses. For example, in "Resistance Is Fertile," Mullen weaves cultural symbols into stinging parodies of social moralists, punning on words and phrases associated with various familiar expressions and combining them with a play on the body's consumption, conversion, and expulsion of fecal matter. Here, Mullen reminds us of the waste we daily spew out of our bodies and asks, "Did you need to read the label on Olean to know that the SOS goes out when the ship's going down?"

In "European Folktale Variation" Mullen becomes trickster-storyteller, reenvisioning the classic tale of *Goldilocks and the Three Bears.* Her central character, a young "platinum blond" lacking in "proper socialization," perpetrates a "B and E" and breaks and enters into the house of some surprisingly humanlike "bruins" (bears) residing in a cottage outside of town. The humorous play moves the reader from the rustic European countryside to suburban Anytown USA, or even to an American college campus (perhaps to the University of California at Los Angeles—the "bruins"), where young, restless youths destroy and deface with disregard for order and rules, glad to be away from the watchful gaze of their parents. The poem's complexity allows multiple interpretations.

"We Are Not Responsible" responds to the state of a litigious society, manifested as the overly pretentious world of the airline industry, in which everything has a disclaimer for liability. The voice of an airline attendant spews company policy and regulations, explaining why bags have been lost, reservations have been canceled, and people of a certain color, "gang color," as Mullen aptly calls it, who fit a racial profile, seem to be prone to search and seizure. With this reference, Mullen draws directly from the contemporary political climate of America—a model that is readily identifiable.

Mullen was a finalist in the 2002 National Book Award and Book Circle Critics Awards competitions in poetry for *Sleeping with the Dictionary,* and recent recognition of Mullen's poetry reflects a growing awareness in both the scholarly and popular worlds of her impressive poetic craft and art. However, Mullen is also an important scholarly voice in the formation and discussion of African-American literature. She has published an impressive collection of critical musings on a variety of topics, including critical studies on gender, race, and subjectivity in the slave narrative and her introduction to *Oreo* (2000), Fran Ross's poignant book exploring black and Jewish relations. Mullen's voice is an important new presence in African-American literature, not only because of its self-reflexive attention to earlier traditions in African-American literature but also because of the new developments in African-American literature—fiction and poetry—that her work represents. In particular, her poetry is a rejoining of the audiences of the past and a promise to audiences of the future—illuminating the power and promise of the word in each poetic work of art she creates.

BIBLIOGRAPHY

Bedient, Calvin. "The Solo Mysterioso Blues: An Interview with Harryette Mullen." *Callaloo* 19, no. 3 (1996): 651–669.

Frost, Elisabeth A. "Ruses of the Lunatic Muse: Harryette Mullen and Lyric Hybridity." *Women's Studies* 27, no. 5 (September 1998): 466.

Hogue, Cynthia. "An Interview with Harryette Mullen." *Postmodern Culture* 9, no. 2 (January 1999): 1.

Sullivan, Meg. "Spotlight: Harryette Mullen, Poet." *UCLA Today* February 2003. Available online. URL: http://www.ucla.edu/spotlight/archive/html_2002_2003/fac0203_mullen.html. Accessed October 18, 2006.

Gena Elise Chandler

Mumbo Jumbo   Ishmael Reed (1972)

Typically considered Ishmael Reed's most important work, *Mumbo Jumbo,* his third novel, is an experimental tour de force, containing equal parts detective novel, comedy, literary criticism, history book, and critique of Western monocultural domination. It examines the suppression and erasure of African influences from "official" American culture. Set during the 1920s in New York City (when the Jazz Age and the Harlem Renaissance were thriving), the Jes Grew Carriers (the JGCs), members of the African diaspora, threaten the cultural domination of the Atonists, the Eurocentric cultivators of Western civilization, by infecting them with Jes Grew, an "anti-plague" "characterized by ebullience and ecstacy" (6), that enlivens its host with jazzy rhythms, vibrant colors, jive talk, crooked lines, and expressive dance. Jes Grew is seeking its "text," and the sterile, geometric, uptight Atonists wish to intercept it in order to stop its promulgation.

The Voodoo-practicing "astrodetective" PaPa LaBas (a variation on Papa Legba, the loa, or spirit, closest to humankind in the Voodoo tradition) is the novel's protagonist. He is searching for the murderers of Abdul Sufi Hamid, who had the Jes Grew text (known as "The Book of Thoth"). A trail of dead bodies and mysterious newspaper headlines lead LaBas to Hinckle Von Vampton, who is a member of the Knights Templar (a group banished from the Atonist Path). He claims to have the ability to anthologize "The Book of Thoth," which has been separated into 14 sections and sent to JGCs in Harlem. Once anthologized, he will "be in charge of the anti-Jes Grew serum" (69) and therefore will be able to restore the legacy of the Knights.

Now considered a hallmark of postmodernist fiction, *Mumbo Jumbo* often disrupts the regimented format of the mass-produced novel. The first chapter appears before the title page, pertinent illustrations are peppered throughout (including a handwritten letter written by character Abdul Sufi Hamid), and features a "Partial Bibliography." PaPa LaBas's theory that this "struggle between secret societies" extends back to the ancient Egyptian figures Osiris (Jes Grew) and Set (the Atonists) is meant to be taken with the utmost seriousness by Reed's audience.

The novel's reputation has been continually strong since it first appeared in 1972. In a *Village Voice* review, Lorenzo Thomas writes that *Mumbo Jumbo* is about "the crisis of a culture that refuses to acknowledge itself," adding that "it goes beyond assault to re-definition" (38–39). More critically, Henry Louis Gates, Jr., states in *The Signifying Monkey* that *Mumbo Jumbo* "is both a definition of Afro-American culture and its deflation. . . . [It is] rife with hardened convention and presupposition as is the rest of the Western tradition" (220). *Mumbo Jumbo* was nominated for the National Book Award in 1973. The most ironic acclaim given to this novel appeared when Harold Bloom included it in his list of masterpieces of the Western canon in 1994.

BIBLIOGRAPHY
Fox, Robert Elliot. *Conscientious Sorcerers: The Black Postmodernist Fiction of Leroi Jones/Amiri Baraka, Ishmael Reed, and Samuel R. Delany.* Westport, Conn.: Greenwood, 1987.

Gates, Henry Louis. *The Signifying Monkey: A Theory of African-American Literary Criticism.* New York: Oxford University Press, 1988.

Ludwig, Sami. *Concrete Language: Intercultural Communication in Maxine Hong Kingston's* The Woman Warrior *and Ishmael Reed's* Mumbo Jumbo. Frankfurt, Germany: Peter Lang, 1996.

Martin, Reginald. *Ishmael Reed and the New Black Aesthetic Critics.* New York: St. Martin's, 1988.

Thomas, Lorenzo. "The Black Roots Are Back." Review of *Mumbo Jumbo,* by Ishmael Reed. In *The Critical Response to Ishmael Reed,* edited by Bruce Allen Dick, 38–41. Westport, Conn.: Greenwood, 1999.

Brian Flota

Murray, Albert　(1916–)

Born in Nokomis, Alabama, the novelist, cultural critic, essayist, and poet Albert Murray graduated from Tuskegee Institute in 1939. He undertook graduate work at the University of Michigan and at New York University, where he completed a master's degree in English in 1948. At Tuskegee, he met RALPH ELLISON, author of *INVISIBLE MAN,* and the two would later seal a lifelong friendship during Murray's New York sojourn. Though he was at work on a novel during the early 1950s, the same time that Ellison was completing his masterpiece, Murray would not publish his first book until 1970, almost 20 years later.

Murray's oeuvre may be characterized as an effort at first defining and then putting into practice the idea of the "BLUES idiom," which he introduces in *The Omni-Americans* (1970) and continues to develop in such subsequent nonfiction titles as *The Hero and the Blues* (1973), *Stomping the Blues* (1985), *The Blue Devils of Nada: A Contemporary American Approach to Aesthetic Statement* (1996), and most recently *From the Briarpatch File: On Context, Procedure, and American Identity* (2001). A key phrase, the blues idiom signifies, at base, a "definitive statement" that echoes the intent of a song such as Duke Ellington's dance tune "It Don't Mean a Thing If It Ain't Got That Swing." For Murray, the blues, a musical form distinguishable from the affective condition known as "having the blues," constitutes "an affirmative and hence exemplary heroic response to that which André Malraux describes as *la condition humaine*" (*The Omni-Americans,* 89). Such heroic action generally takes place in the face of chaos or irruption, which are themselves characteristic of life's flow. Life is, Murray concludes, a "lowdown dirty shame" and is best met with a sense of acceptance of its vicissitudes and a determination to overcome its obstacles through improvisation.

Such a principle for living is wholly consistent with the blues, which translates and refines the hardships and particularities of everyday life into an art form. When Murray talks of "refining," he means "ragging, jazzing, and riffing and even jamming the idiomatic into fine art" (*Blue Devils,* 93). The art of the blues thus assumes an agency of sorts, and the dance hall—necessary to the swinging, physical movement that allows one actively to employ the body in stomping the blues away—becomes a "temple" (*Stomping,* 17). Likewise, the dance becomes ritual, and the lyrics and music (together constitutive of a blues idiom) become sacred lingua. Is the blues musician then priest or oracle? Murray's concept is, he admits, Dionysian: a fabulous invocation that leads us to regard the blues performance as participatory theatre and as a syncopated expressive performance act that recalls the catharsis of tragic drama. The blues also acts as a purgative ritual that cleanses the participants of the negative affects of the blues, but cleanses them only to a certain extent. Murray insists that some trace of the blues remains to remind the supplicant that life itself is a never-ending struggle and that one should not only expect but also thrive on and within adversity (*Stomping,* 17).

The Blue Devils of Nada and *From the Briarpatch File* serve as elaborations on this theme. The aim of *Blue Devils* is "to suggest (as does *The Hero and the Blues*) that the affirmative disposition toward the harsh actualities of human existence that is characteristic of the fully orchestrated blues statement can be used as a basis upon which (and/or frame of reference within which) a contemporary storybook heroism may be defined" (7). Art—literary, visual, and musical—"is the ultimate extension, elaboration, and refinement of the rituals that reenact the primary survival techniques (and hence reinforce the basic orientation toward experience) of a given people in a given time, place, and circumstance" (13). The blues hero relates a "representative anecdote" (a phrase borrowed from Kenneth Burke) because he is, Murray maintains, a "representative man":

He tells his own story, which Murray idealizes as being mythical and epic in proportion. The blues hero rises from the singularity of his own narrative to tell a tale that is concerned with the state of the human condition. Singing of life itself, of its loves and joys alongside its abysmal pains, the blues hero purports to speak for everyone.

Such universalism is not ethereal, but earthy, Murray insists: "All of this is nothing if not down-home stuff. Which brings us to our chorus: it is precisely such southern 'roots' that will dispose and also condition my protagonist to function in terms of the rootlessness that is the basic predicament of all humankind in the contemporary world at large" (17). And, he concludes in *From the Briarpatch File*, the blues hero narrates his or her story from a "frame of acceptance" of life's hardships rather than from a "frame of rejection." This latter, which he deems to be reflective of so much black "protest literature," gives voice to a discourse of victimhood.

A return to his southern roots, which is also, paradoxically, recognition of the "rootless" nature of human existence, forms the occasion for Murray's second book, *South to a Very Old Place* (1971). This memoir-cum-travelogue, fictionalized in some instances, serves as a portal through which we might read Murray's approach to the writing of fiction. Murray has composed a trilogy of autobiographical novels: *Train Whistle Guitar* (1974), *The Spyglass Tree* (1991), and *The Seven League Boots* (1995).

In *South*, where Murray's oft-used stream-of-consciousness technique, which he inherited from Ernest Hemingway and James Joyce, two of his strongest influences (Thomas Mann, Kenneth Burke, and William Faulkner are three more), sometimes lapses into a bluesy, down-home idiom that is nothing short of eloquent. Here he identifies himself with Hank Aaron, a Mobile homeboy whom Murray spies coming out of the Alibi Lounge in Atlanta:

I see you, Mobile; I see you man, and me, I just happen to be the kind of homeboy that can smell glove leather, red mound clay, and infield grass all the way back to the days of Bo Peyton and

Bancy and Tanny, who, as Chick Hamilton must have told you, was without a doubt the fanciest first baseman who ever did it. I see you, Mobile and I don't even have to mention old Satchel Paige, who is not only still around but right here in Alana to boot. I see you, Hank. Three hundred and seventy-five miles from Mobile by way of Boston and Milwaukee plus the time it took Atlanta to make it out of the bushes. What say, home? (94–95, italics in original).

This passage fairly sings with the vernacular rhythms of home—warm, earthy, relaxed, and easy.

Murray's project is the illustration of the omni-American ideal: that America (itself a composite culture—Murray calls it "mulatto") is the home of those who have walked its soil and worked its land through the generations, and this is especially true of African-Americans. He reiterates this image, fraught as it is with a subtle nationalism that Murray himself might deny, in his first novel, *Train Whistle Guitar*. Here, he introduces the character Luzana Cholly, a blues-playing Charlie from Louisiana who is adored by Scooter, Murray's alter-ego protagonist:

Because the also and also of all of that was also the also plus also of so many of the twelve-bar twelve-string guitar riddles you got whether in idiomatic iambics or otherwise mostly from Luzana Cholly who was the one who used to walk his trochaic-sporty stomping-ground limp-walk picking and plucking and knuckle knocking and strumming (like an anapestic locomotive) while singsongsaying Anywhere I hang my hat anywhere I prop my feet. Who could drink muddy water who could sleep in a hollow log. (4–5)

The beauty of *Train's* prose arguably marks it as Murray's strongest fictional effort. Scooter's story continues in *The Spyglass Tree*, which depicts his college years, and *The Seven League Boots*, as he joins a jazz band. Each sequel retells portions of the novels preceding it, but with markedly less intensity.

Murray made his initial foray into poetry with *Conjugations and Reiterations* (2001), a slim volume of poems, sometimes written in a syncopated Kansas City 4/4 time, that contains reflections on jazz, the blues, and another enduring theme of Murray's, "the folklore of white supremacy" and "the fakelore of black pathology." He also cowrote *Good Morning Blues: The Autobiography of Count Basie (As Told to Albert Murray)* (1985) and contributed to Ken Burns's acclaimed documentary, *Jazz* (2000).

Murray has received numerous awards and honors, including the Ivan Sandorf Award for lifetime achievement from the National Book Critics Circle (1997). He is a member of the American Academy of Arts and Letters and holds honorary doctorates from Colgate University and Hamilton College. He currently serves on the board of directors of Jazz at Lincoln Center and is at work on a fourth novel, tentatively titled *The Magic Keys*.

BIBLIOGRAPHY

Jones, Carolyn M. "Race and Intimacy: Albert Murray's *South to a Very Old Place.*" In *South to a New Place: Region, Literature, Culture*, 58–75. Baton Rouge: Louisiana State University Press, 2002.

Kerrer, Wolfgang. "Nostalgia, Amnesia, and Grandmothers: The Uses of Memory in Albert Murray, Sabine Ulibarri, Paula Gunn Allen, and Alice Walker." In *Memory, Narrative, and Identity: New Essays in Ethnic American Literatures*, 128–144. Boston: Northeastern University Press, 1994.

Maguire, Roberta S., ed. *Conversations with Albert Murray.* Jackson: University Press of Mississippi, 1997.

———. "Walker Percy and Albert Murray: The Story of Two 'Part Anglo-Saxon Alabamians.'" *Southern Quarterly: A Journal of Arts in the South* 41, no. 1 (2002): 10–28.

Pinsker, Sanford. "Albert Murray: The Black Intellectuals' Maverick Patriarch." *Virginia Quarterly Review: A National Journal of Literature and Discussion* 72, no. 4 (1996): 678–684.

Rowell, Charles H. "'An All-Purpose, All-American Literary Intellectual': An Interview with Albert Murray." *Callaloo* 20, no. 2 (1997): 399–414.

Wideman, John. "Stomping the Blues: Ritual in Black Music and Speech." *American Poetry Review* 7, no. 4 (1978): 42–45.

Rebecka R. Rutledge

Murray, Pauli (Anna Pauline Murray) (1910–1985)

An activist, feminist, attorney, teacher, priest, and poet, Pauli Murray was born in Baltimore to William Henry, a public school teacher, and Agnes Murray, a nurse. Pauli is the maternal granddaughter of grandparents whose past was rooted in slavery. Her grandfather worked with the Freedmen's Bureau and was the founder of the first school system for free blacks of Virginia and North Carolina. After attending the public schools in Durham, North Carolina, where she grew up, Murray finished her secondary education at Richmond Hill School in New York, where she lived with relatives. She received a B.A. degree in English from Hunter College, which she attended when Harlem was still in vogue. Murray received an LL.B. degree (*cum laude*) from Howard University School of Law and an LL.M. degree from the University of California at Berkeley's School of Jurisprudence. She later earned a J.D.S. at Yale University Law School. Murray accomplished these goals and objectives during a time when racial and gender lines blocked the path of even biracial African-Americans who, should they claim to do so, could point to their "blue blood" ancestry, as Murray could.

After passing the state bar examinations of both California and New York, Murray became a deputy attorney general for the state of California, served as a staff member of the Commission on Law and Social Action of the American Jewish Congress, and taught at Ghana School of Law and Brandeis University before being ordained an Episcopal priest. To accomplish these goals, Murray had to face tremendous adversity and, in the end, not merely knock on but also knock down many doors. Murray served on John F. Kennedy's Commission on the Status of Women, 1962–1963, and became a founding member of the National Organization for Women in 1966. As Eleanor Holmes Norton notes in the introduction to Murray's award-winning autobiography, *Song in a Weary Throat* (1987; republished as *Pauli Murray: The Autobiography of a Black Activist, Feminist, Lawyer, Priest, and Poet* [1989]); "If Pauli did not become everything she wanted to be, she surely became everything it was possible for her to be" (ix).

Personal history was always a priority for Murray, who was orphaned by age four. She was adopted and raised by a loving aunt, Aunt Pauline, who "had the unerring intuition of a great teacher and a master artisan" (Murray, 16). Aunt Pauline kept the family genealogy ever present before the young Pauline, and *Proud Shoes: The Story of an American Family* (1956), Murray's first published text, chronicles the story of the slave past of her maternal grandfather, Robert G. Fitzgerald, a veteran of the Civil War, a teacher, and an administrator. Murray's wealthy great granduncle, Richard Fitzgerald was a successful businessman who was instrumental in helping to organize Durham, North Carolina's first black-owned bank, the Mechanics and Farmers Bank (29).

Although she knew firsthand what it meant to ride in a Jim Crow railroad car, attend segregated public schools, be defined as "colored" or Negro, and be made to feel invisible by teachers who intentionally erased her history as an African-American from their lectures, Murray, who later became a Gandhian nonviolent civil rights activist and developed a special friendship with Eleanor Roosevelt, never relinquished the pride she inherited from Aunt Pauline and her family. This is clearly registered in the title, *Proud Shoes,* of the book that details her family history.

While attending Hunter College, Murray, who had grown up reading and being deeply influenced by the poetry of PAUL LAURENCE DUNBAR, was introduced to the works of HARLEM RENAISSANCE writers CLAUDE MCKAY, COUNTEE CULLEN, and LANGSTON HUGHES. She would later meet Hughes, Cullen, DOROTHY WEST, WALLACE THURMAN, STERLING BROWN, and ROBERT HAYDEN. Murray, who had spent a year working as a field representative

for *OPPORTUNITY* magazine, published her first poem, "Song of the Highway," in Nancy Cunard's anthology *Color* (1934). Describing her as "an occasional poet," ARNA BONTEMPS included two of Murray's poems in his anthology *American Negro Poetry* (1963), as did Arnold Adoff in his *Poetry of Black America* (1973). In 1970 Murray published her only collection of poetry, *Dark Testament and Other Poems,* including poems composed between 1933 and 1969.

The title poem, "Dark Testament," which Stephen Vincent Benét encouraged her to write, resounds with the determination of Hughes's speaker in "I, Too," and the militancy of McKay's speaker in "If We Must Die."

> *Of us who darkly stand*
> *Bared to the spittle of every curse,*
> *Nor left the dignity of beast,*
> *Let none say,*
> *"Those were not men but cowards all"*
> *(Bontemps, 107)*

Murray's commitment to political activism and social change is registered in "Mr. Roosevelt Regrets," in which she critiques President Franklin Delano Roosevelt's failure to actively and aggressively speak out against racism after several major race riots broke out in 1943, particularly in Detroit. To President Roosevelt's response, "I am sure that every true American regrets this [national fragmentation]," Murray wrote in a militant tone:

> *What do you get, black boy*
> *When they knocked you down in the gutter . . .*
> *What'd the top Man say, black boy?*
> *"Mr. Roosevelt regrets. . . ."*
> *(Pauli Murray 212)*

The CRISIS magazine published this poem in its August 1943 issue. Eleanor Roosevelt quickly responded, upon receiving a copy of the poem that Murray had sent her, "I am sorry but I understand" (Murray, 212). Although, as poet, Murray sang in a minor key throughout the 20th century, her refrain championing race, gender, and class issues, through her sociopolitical and literary contributions, was anything but minor.

BIBLIOGRAPHY

Bontemps, Arna, ed. *American Negro Poetry.* New York: Hill & Wang, 1963.

Murray, Pauli. *Pauli Murray: The Autobiography of a Black Activist, Feminist, Lawyer, Priest, and Poet.* (Originally published as *Song in a Weary Throat.*) Knoxville: University of Tennessee Press, 1989.

Wilfred D. Samuels

N

Narrative of the Life of Frederick Douglass, An American Slave, Written by Himself   Frederick Douglass (1845)

Although FREDERICK DOUGLASS wrote three autobiographies—*Narrative of the Life of Frederick Douglass, An American Slave* (1845), *My Bondage and My Freedom* (1855), and *Life and Times of Frederick Douglass* (1893)—*Narrative*, which James Olney calls "the greatest of the slave narratives" (3), became the classic.

Structurally, *Narrative* is divided into two parts. In the first part, approximately the first nine chapters, Douglass describes his birth into slavery in Tuckahoe, Talbot County, Maryland, as Frederick Bailey (noting that he had no certification of the date of his birth); his vicarious awareness of his status as a slave through the brutal treatment of his Aunt Hester by their owner, Captain Anthony; his lack of knowledge of his father's identity (more than likely his father was his slave master); his lack of communication with his mother, Harriet Bailey, and his deep love for his surrogate mother, his grandmother, Betsey Bailey, who reared him through age six; the violence of chattel slavery, as practiced by overseers like Mr. Severe, "a cruel man" (Douglass, 29); and the imaginative tactics slaves created to deal on a daily basis with their bondage, particularly their sorrow songs. Douglass wrote, "They would sometimes sing the most pathetic sentiment in the most rapturous tone, and the most rapturous sentiment in the most

pathetic tone" (31). The second part of *Narrative*, the last two chapters, describes Douglass's escape from "the jaws of slavery" (24), in which he had been both "witness and participant" (25), and his rebirth symbolized by his naming himself Frederick Douglass.

Narrative represents Douglass's early effort of self-identification and authentification. Finding that whenever he mounted the antislavery platform to bear witness to and speak out against the atrocities of slavery, his credibility was questioned because he was deemed too polished, too articulate, and too intelligent to be a fugitive slave, Douglass, encouraged by the major white abolitionists, particularly William Lloyd Garrison, decided to write his own story. Garrison, who wrote the preface to the *Narrative*, attests, "Mr. Douglass has very properly chosen to write his own Narrative, in his own style, and according to the best of his ability, rather than to employ some one else. It is, therefore, entirely his own production" (ix).

So that readers would not mistakenly conclude that an amanuensis had produced his text, Douglass included the phrase "Written by Himself" in the title of his narrative. This was not mere egocentrism on Douglass's part but an act of self-authorship:

> an act of linguistic assertion and aggression, in the language and literary mode of the oppressor. . . . [I]t is explicitly an act of assertion and

aggression against the slaveholder who tried to prevent the slave's ever learning to read and write; and it is implicitly an act of assertion and aggression against abolitionists who were too often inclined to confuse sponsorship with authorship. (Olney, 5)

Equally significant is Douglass's self-identification as an American and a slave also mentioned in the title, simultaneously calling attention to the hypocrisy being practiced in the birthplace of the Declaration of Independence, where human beings were held as chattel, and to his identity and rights as an American citizen. Douglass's very act of writing was revolutionary. It represents "the most radical, the most aggressive, the most thoroughgoing challenge imaginable to the very idea of the American nation . . . that proclaimed and summoned into existence the 'United States of America'" (Olney, 6).

In the end, Douglass wanted to do more than merely indict the American system of chattel slavery with his *Narrative.* At the core of his *Narrative* he records the story of a self-made man—a man who, though converted into a brute once again became a man, for the most part on his own accord, despite "the bitterest dregs of slavery" (Douglass, 75) he was made to drink. Douglass, in providing a text that became the paradigm for the slave narrative genre, identifies three significant turning points in his personal movement from slavery to freedom. First, he was sent to live in Baltimore, which, he explains, "laid the foundation and opened the gateway, to all my subsequent prosperity" (46–47). Second, his new slave owner, Mrs. Auld, initiated his formal education before her husband forbade her to do so, warning her that an educated slave would be "unfit" to be a slave, leading Douglass to conclude that, indeed, education was "the pathway from slavery to freedom" (49) and to find ways to become self educated.

Douglass's final turning point was the two-hour fight he had with Robert Covey, "an odd but vicious overseer" (Stepto, 21) whose primary task was to teach the previously almost benevolently treated Douglass what it really meant to be a slave

by attempting to whip him into shape. Douglass confesses that, at first, Covey succeeded in breaking him physically and spiritually: "the dark night of slavery closed in upon me" (75). However, by resolving to fight back physically, Douglass was able to rise from "the tomb of slavery to the heaven of freedom" (83), overthrowing his oppressor and enslaver. He resolved, "however long I might remain a slave in form, the day has passed forever when I could be a slave in fact" (83).

With *Narrative of Frederick Douglass, An American Slave, Written by Himself,* Douglass made at least two unmatchable contributions to the African-American literary tradition. In his introduction to *Great Slave Narratives,* ARNA BONTEMPS notes that, on the one hand, Douglass added his voice to the ongoing 19th-century debate about the "condition of man on earth" (vii), which Douglass's personal history seemed to epitomize; on the other hand, Douglass provided the genesis of "the spirit and the vitality and the angle of vision responsible for the most effective prose writing by black American writers from WILLIAM WELLS BROWN to CHARLES CHESNUTT, from W. E. B. DUBOIS to RICHARD WRIGHT, RALPH ELLISON, and JAMES BALDWIN" (Bontemps, x). To Bontemps's list can be added TONI MORRISON, PAULE MARSHALL, SHERLEY ANNE WILLIAMS, CHARLES JOHNSON, and many others.

BIBLIOGRAPHY

Bontemps, Arna, ed. *Great Slave Narratives.* Boston: Beacon Press, 1969.

Douglass, Frederick. *Narrative of the Life of Frederick Douglass, An American Slave, Written by Himself.* New York: New American Library, 1968.

Olney, James. "The Founding Fathers—Frederick Douglass and Booker T. Washington." In *Slavery and the Literary Imagination,* edited by Deborah E. McDowell and Arnold Rampersad, 1–24. Baltimore: Johns Hopkins University Press, 1989.

Stepto, Robert. *From Behind the Veil: A Study of Afro-American Narratives.* Urbana: University of Illinois Press, 1979.

Wilfred D. Samuels

National Association for the Advancement of Colored People   (NAACP)

On February 12, 1909, men and women of various religions and races met in New York for a conference on the 100th birthday of Abraham Lincoln. They organized the National Association for the Advancement of Colored People in response to the lynching and intimidation accompanying "separate-but-equal" Jim Crow practices. They sought to achieve equal rights and to remove racial discrimination in housing, employment, the courts, education, transportation, recreation, prisons, voting, and business. They would approach the issues through education, legislation, and litigation. They pledged to agitate and take legal action against racial discrimination. The phrase "colored people" was used intentionally in the title to indicate the broad concerns of the group.

W. E. B. DuBois and William M. Trotter, along with several other black intellectuals who came together to express their opposition to Booker T. Washington's accommodation strategy, played leading roles in the formation of this new civil rights organization. Joining them were William Walling, Mary Ovington, Henry Moskowitz, and other whites who wanted to assist blacks in the fight for equal rights and racial justice. The organization conducted press campaigns, published pamphlets, conducted in-depth studies, and educated the community. DuBois became the early director of research and publications. In 1910, the magazine The Crisis became the principal philosophical organ.

With the help of James Weldon Johnson, the NAACP spread slowly, branch by branch, across the country into places like Boston, Tacoma, Kansas City, Topeka, Atlanta, Baltimore, Detroit, and Salt Lake City, resulting in 310 branches by the end of 1919. The independence of the local branches made it possible for a wide range of actions to be implemented. Furthermore, as early as 1912, the NAACP inspired the formation of South Africa's African National Congress. After challenging D. W. Griffith's film The Birth of a Nation for assassinating the character of black America, creating damaging stereotypes of blacks as illiterate and immoral, and of the 1916 death of Washington, events around World War I set the NAACP on its two-pronged legal and political course.

During the 1920s, critics such as A. Philip Randolph emerged and complained about the excessive legalism of the group. Marcus Garvey added his objections to the interracial notions about integration and the predominantly light-skinned, middle-class leadership of the organization. However, both Walter White and Roy Wilkins led the organization in forming effective coalitions, carrying out mass demonstrations, and lobbying legislators.

When the American economy collapsed in 1929, initiating the Great Depression, the NAACP was urged to pay more attention to the needs of and disproportionate hardship on the masses of black America. Some of the younger members pushed for more focus on racial pride and solidarity of the working class. The membership grew, and the communities were mobilized to eliminate all legally imposed discrimination.

The most significant achievement of the organization started with the legal work of Charles Hamilton Houston. Houston, along with his law students, including Thurgood Marshall, brought precedent cases on equal pay and public access that led to the 1954 Brown v. Board of Education Supreme Court decision. That ruling settled several cases concluding that "separate but equal" was inherently unequal, and it eliminated legal segregation in public education. Having challenged the acts of violence toward blacks, the NAACP killed and laid to rest legalized Jim Crow.

In addition to its vanguard role in championing the social, educational and civil rights of African-Americans, the National Association for the Advancement of Colored People played a major role in promoting, celebrating and validating the African-American literary tradition. Its journal, The Crisis, and its founding editor, W. E. B. DuBois, the author of Souls of Black Folk, were not only instrumental in introducing and promoting the idea of a Harlem Renaissance but also its major writers, including Langston Hughes, Zora Neale Hurston, and Jessie Redmon Fauset, its literary editor. *The Crisis* first published Hughes's signature poem, "The Negro Speaks of Rivers." Other well-established and prominent writers, including JAMES WELDON JOHNSON, the author of *THE AUTOBIOGRAPHY OF AN EX-COLORED MAN*, and WALTER WHITE, the author of *Fire and Flint* (1924) and *Flight* (1926), served on its editorial board. Both Johnson and White served as executive secretaries of the National Association for the Advancement of Colored People.

Equally important, in 1924 *The Crisis* established the Amy Spingarn Prizes in Literature and Art. While judges of this award included the novelist CHARLES CHESNUTT, author of *THE MARROW OF TRADITIONS* and *House behind the Cedar*, recipients included Hughes, ARNA BONTEMPS and RUDOLPH FISHER. Renaissance writers and poets Hughes, COUNTEE CULLEN, Georgia Douglass, JEAN TOOMER, Johnson, Jessie Fauset, and many others published their early works in *The Crisis*. Finally, the leaders of the National Association for the Advancement of Colored People provided a venue for young black writers to meet important New Yorkers with influence in the publishing world, including Carl Van Vechten and Sinclair Lewis, by hosting social events and parties in their fashionable Harlem apartment. In sum, early on in the 20th century, the National Association for the Advancement of Colored People, paved the way, particularly through *The Crisis*, for African-American literature and culture to gain respectability, viability and value in the American mainstream.

Some renewal for the NAACP as the oldest civil rights organization for equality came with the passage of the 1964 Civil Rights Act. In the years that followed, the NAACP confronted systemic discrimination, media stereotypes, and the unfair application of the death penalty in particular. The NAACP continues its search for revitalization, new direction, and effective leadership to resolve the problems of black America.

BIBLIOGRAPHY

Harlan, Louis T., and Raymond W. Smock, ed. *The Booker T. Washington Papers.* Vol. 12: *1912–14.* Urbana: University of Illinois Press, 1982.

Mandela, Nelson. *Long Walk to Freedom.* New York: Little, Brown, 1994.

Salzman, Jack, ed. "National Association for the Advancement of Colored People." In *The African-American Experience,* 479–493. New York: MacMillan, 1993.

Smith, Jessie C., and Joseph M. Palmisanoe, eds. *The African-American Almanac.* 8th ed. Detroit: Gale Group, 2000.

France A. Davis

Native Son Richard Wright (1940)

Richard Wright's first and greatest novel features Bigger Thomas, an intelligent, courageous, and defiant African-American youth living in the tenements of Chicago's South Side in the 1930s. Bigger Thomas is not only the best-known black male protagonist of the African-American literary tradition but also its most villainous. A black boy born in the South, in Mississippi, and reared during his teenage years on Chicago's South Side, the literary symbol of the urban ghetto during and after the Great Depression, Bigger cannot escape his fate. This remains true even though Bigger's name suggests that he will never be as obsequious as his predecessor, the passive Uncle Tom (see SAMBO AND UNCLE TOM) created by Harriet B. Stowe in her American classic *Uncle Tom's Cabin* (1854).

The novel's three sections, "Fear," "Flight," and "Fate," encompass Bigger's life and experiences. Marginalized in the segregated world of the rat-infested urban slum where he shares a one-bedroom apartment with his mother, brother, and sister, Bigger lives in fear of crossing the visible and invisible social lines in the larger world in which he lives. Stepping out of his apartment building, he is prophetically reminded of his assigned status and place by a billboard featuring the penetrating gaze of the local attorney general who, inevitably, will indict Bigger for murder, sending him to his fate: the electric chair:

The poster showed one of those faces that looked straight at you when you looked at it and all the while you were walking and turning your head to look at it it kept looking unblinkingly back at you until you got far from it you had to take your eyes away, and then it stopped, like a moving blackout. Above the top of the poster were tall red letters: "IF YOU BREAK THE LAW, YOU CAN'T WIN!" (11)

Bigger can only vicariously escape this world through the games of empowerment he plays with his friends, in which he is a pilot, the president of the United States, and the wealthy financier J. P. Morgan at the movies, where he wastes his blighted manhood in masturbatory rituals with his friends to further confirm their stunted status as perpetual "black boys."

When the Daltons, wealthy slumlords and philanthropists, hire Bigger as a chauffer, his first assignment is to drive their daughter, Mary, to a lecture at the University of Chicago. Mary, rather than attending the lecture, instructs Bigger to drive her and Jan, her communist boyfriend, to a Marxist lecture followed by dinner in a restaurant in the black community. When Mary becomes drunk and passes out, Bigger, aware of his responsibility to guard Mary's welfare, is forced to deliver her safely to her bedroom. Afraid he will lose his job not only if her parents discover Mary in a drunken stupor but especially if he is found breaking well-known southern racial taboos if he is caught in Mary's bedroom by her blind meandering mother, Bigger instinctively attempts to protect himself. He covers Mary's face with a pillow when Mrs. Dalton enters Mary's bedroom. When he removes the pillow after Mrs. Dalton leaves, Bigger discovers he has accidentally smothered Mary to death. He dismembers and burns her body in the basement furnace to erase, he thinks, any trace of his heinous crime.

Ultimately, however, Bigger is forced to take flight when his crime is discovered. Like the trapped rat he kills at the beginning of the novel, Bigger attempts to escape. Running into the cold Chicago winter night, through labyrinthine corridors and atop ghetto roofs, Bigger is flushed out of hiding with a water hose, caught, and dragged to the street level. Bigger's capturers

started down the stairs with him, his head bumping along the steps. He folded his wet arms about his head to save himself, but soon the steps had pounded his elbows and arms

so hard that all his strength left. He relaxed, feeling his head bounding painfully down the steps. He shut his eyes and tried to lose consciousness. . . . He was in the street now being dragged over snow. His feet were up in the air, grasped by strong hands. (228–229)

Bigger is tried for the rape and murder of white Mary Dalton. Although he killed his black girlfriend, Betsy, during his flight, he is not tried for that crime.

Bigger is defended by Max, a Jewish Marxist. The Library of America 1991 edition of *Native Son* highlights Max's role, whereas the censored 1940 edition deletes, among other things, all the references to Max's being Jewish. Himself a victim of racial prejudice, Max is painfully aware of the racist tone of the press against Bigger and of "the silence of the church." Max asks, "Were Negroes liked yesterday and hated today because of what he [Bigger] has done?" Max's objective vision contrasts sharply with the racist attitude in the prosecutor's probing. However, it is equally important not to overlook Max's socialist perspective. He asks, "Your Honor, is this boy alone in feeling deprived and baffled? Is he an exception? Or are there others?" He answers himself: "There are others, Your Honor, millions of others, Negro and white, and that is what makes our future seem a looming image of violence" (468–469). Both Bigger's race and his class matter in the end.

True to strains of literary naturalism that dominate Wright's style in this novel, Bigger is trapped and pessimistically determined by his heredity and socioeconomic environment. In his introduction to the novel, Arnold Rampersad notes that Wright "had been studying Bigger Thomases all his life. Wright's essential Bigger Thomas was not so much a particular character caught in a specific episode of criminal activity as a crime waiting to happen; all the elements to create Bigger's mentality were historically in place in America, stocked by the criminal racial situation that was America" (xvii–xix). Wright himself wrote in "How 'Bigger' Was Born," "there was not just one Bigger, but many of them, more than I could count, and more than you suspect" (506).

Ironically, however, at the end of *Native Son* Bigger seems to experience an existential epiphany, as his final declaration to his attorney suggests:

> Sounds funny, Mr. Max, but when I think about what you say I kind of feel what I wanted. It makes me feel I was kind of right. . . . Maybe it ain't fair to kill, and I reckon I really didn't want to kill. But when I think of why all the killings was, I begin to feel what I wanted, what I am. . . . I didn't want to kill! . . . But what I killed for, I am! (358)

To exist in a world bent on suffocating him, Bigger concludes, he had to kill—to re-create himself—not merely to think, as the Cartesian *cogito* suggests.

Native Son was universally reviewed, receiving both praise and condemnation. In his *Atlantic Monthly* review, David Cohn declared, "Richard Wright, a Mississippi-born Negro, has written a blinding and corrosive study in hate. . . . The race hatred of his hero, Bigger Thomas, is directed with equal malevolence and demoniac intensity toward *all* whites" (77). Writing for the *New York Times,* Charles Poore noted, "It is a long time since we've read a new novelist who had such command of the technique and resources of the novel. Mr. Wright's method is generally Dreiserian; but he has written his American tragedy in a notably firm prose" (42). Clifton Fadiman, in *The New Yorker,* called *Native Son* "the most powerful American novel to appear since *The Grapes of Wrath*" (45). Ralph Ellison, writing for *New Masses,* declared *Native Son* to be "the first philosophical novel by an American Negro. This work possesses an artistry, penetration of thought, and sheer emotional power that places it into the front rank of American fiction" (12).

As a Book-of-the-Month Club selection for March 1940, the novel became a best seller overnight, earning popularity accorded to no previous African-American work. Irving Howe declared in 1963,

> The day *Native Son* appeared, American culture was changed forever. No matter how much qualifying the book might later need, it made impossible a repetition of the old lies. In all its crudeness, melodrama and claustrophobia of vision, Richard Wright's novel brought out into the open, as no one ever had before, the hatred, fear and violence that have crippled and may yet destroy our culture. (137)

Today, *Native Son* remains among the most important cultural and literary documents in America.

BIBLIOGRAPHY

Abcarian, Richard, ed. *Richard Wright's* Native Son: *A Critical Handbook.* Belmont, Calif.: Wadsworth, 1970.

Cohn, David. *"Atlantic Monthly* Review of *Native Son."* In *Richard Wright's* Native Son: *A Critical Handbook,* edited by Richard Abcarian, 77–80. Belmont, Calif.: Wadsworth, 1970.

Ellison, Ralph. "Review of *Native Son.*" In *Richard Wright,* edited by Henry Louis Gates and K. A. Appiah, 11–19. New York: Amistad Publishers, 1993.

Fadiman, Clifton. *"New Yorker* Review of *Native Son."* In *Richard Wright's* Native Son: *A Critical Handbook,* edited by Richard Abcarian, 45–47. Belmont, Calif.: Wadsworth, 1970.

Howe, Irving. "Black Boys and Native Sons." In *Richard Wright's Native Son: A Critical Handbook,* edited by Richard Abcarian, 135–143. Belmont, Calif.: Wadsworth, 1970.

Poore, Charles. *"New York Times* Review of *Native Son."* In *Richard Wright's* Native Son: *A Critical Handbook,* edited by Richard Abcarian, 41–43. Belmont, Calif.: Wadsworth, 1970.

Rampersad, Arnold. Introduction. In *Native Son,* New York: Harper Perennial, 1987.

Wright, Richard. "How 'Bigger' Was Born." In *Native Son,* 505–540. New York: Harper Perennial, 1987.

———. *Native Son.* New York: Harper and Brothers, 1940.

Yoshinobu Hakutani

Naylor, Gloria   (1950–)

A novelist, essayist, screenplay writer, columnist, and educator, Gloria Naylor was born in New York

City on January 25, 1950. Her parents, Roosevelt and Alberta McAlpin Naylor, were former sharecroppers who migrated north from Robinsonville, Mississippi. The eldest of three sisters, Naylor, who was a shy child, graduated high school in 1968. That same year, she became a Jehovah's Witness like her mother. She worked as a missionary for seven years in New York, North Carolina, and Florida before deciding to make a career change. Returning to New York City, she worked full time as a switchboard operator in several hotels from 1975 to 1981. For a short time she studied nursing at Medgar Evers College before transferring to Brooklyn College of the City University of New York system, where she received a B.A. in English in 1981. She earned an M.A. in Afro-American studies from Yale in 1983.

While working and pursing her degrees, Naylor also launched her writing career, discovered feminism, and immersed herself in African-American literature. Together, each experience provided her with the foundation she needed to define herself as a black woman. In 1979 Naylor began writing fiction; she submitted a story to ESSENCE magazine, whose editor, impressed by what she had read, advised Naylor to continue writing. Before reading TONI MORRISON's *The Bluest Eye* Naylor did not consider herself a writer. Naylor recalls, "The writers I had been taught to love were either male or white," but Morrison's novel "said to a young black woman, struggling to find a mirror of her worth in this society, not only is your story worth telling but it can be told in words so painfully eloquent that it becomes a song" (Naylor, 567).

Each of Naylor's novels, which she deliberately links together, details the experiences of black men and women struggling to survive and succeed in a racist world. By creating her own distinct literary landscapes, replete with a wealth of complex characters; by remodeling classical writers; and by drawing extensively on the Bible, Naylor creates her unique vision of modern African-American society and its complex experiences. Her works reflect the literary influence of such writers as ZORA NEALE HURSTON, Morrison, and NTOZAKE SHANGE.

Naylor is the author of five novels. Her popular first novel, *The WOMEN OF BREWSTER PLACE* (1982),

winner of the National Book Award for first fiction in 1983, centers on seven women from diverse backgrounds who manage to blossom and bloom, despite their location in an impoverished neighborhood on a dead-end urban street, by bonding and finding solace in one another. Their experiences run the gamut from those of Mattie Johnson, a single, doting mother, and Sophie, the neighborhood gossip, to Black Nationalist Kiswana Browne and lesbian lovers Lorraine and Theresa. *The Women of Brewster Place* was made into a popular television miniseries in 1989, produced by Oprah Winfrey and Carole Isenberg.

Naylor's second novel, *Linden Hills* (1985), which was her master's thesis at Yale, is a story of resistance and rebirth; it portrays a world in which middle-class blacks achieve status and some measure of power, but at an expensive price, for in the interim they lose their hearts and souls. In her ambitious third novel, *MAMA DAY* (1988), Naylor uses alternating narrators who examine, deconstruct, and redefine the past. Naylor's fourth novel, *Bailey's Cafe* (1992), explores female sexuality, female sexual identity, and male sexual identity. In 1994 the stage adaptation of *Bailey's Cafe* was produced by Hartford Stage Company. Like *The Women of Brewster Place, The Men of Brewster Place* (1998) presents the experiences on Brewster Place from the perspective of the men, who struggle to survive the numerous obstacles they encounter as they attempt to live meaningful lives in a decaying urban housing project.

Naylor has received several prestigious awards, fellowships, and honors. She was a writer-in-residence at Cummington Community of the Arts (1981) and the University of Pennsylvania (1986). She was a visiting professor and lecturer at George Washington University (1981), New York University (1986), Princeton University, (1986), Boston University (1987), and Brandeis University (1988), and a senior fellow in the Society for Humanities, Cornell University (1988), Marygrove College (1989), the University of Kent in Canterbury, England (1992), and in India. She also received the Distinguished Writer Award from the Mid-Atlantic Writers Association (1983), a National Endowment for the Arts Fellowship for her novels (1985), the New York Foundation for the Arts Fellowship for screenwriting (1985), the Candace Award of the National Coalition of One Hundred Black Women (1986), a Guggenheim fellowship (1988), the Lillian Smith Book Award (1989), and the President's Medal from Brooklyn College.

Calling herself a wordsmith and a storyteller, Naylor, along with other talented writers, has helped shape the course of African-American literature within the last two decades. Naylor is working on a fifth novel, *Sapphira Wade,* and runs her own multimedia production company, One Way Productions, established in 1990.

BIBLIOGRAPHY

Andrews, Larry. "Black Sisterhood in Gloria Naylor's Novels." *CLA Journal* 33 (1989): 1–25.

Awkward, Michael. *Inspiring Influences: Tradition, Revision, and Afro-American Women's Novels.* New York: Columbia University Press, 1991.

Fowler, Virginia. *Gloria Naylor: In Search of Sanctuary.* New York: Twayne, 1996.

Gates, Henry Louis, Jr., and K. A. Appiah, eds. *Gloria Naylor: Critical Perspectives Past and Present.* New York: Amistad, 1993.

Kelley, Margot Anne, ed. *Gloria Naylor's Early Novels.* Gainesville: University Press of Florida, 1999.

Naylor, Gloria. "A Conversation between Gloria Naylor and Toni Morrison." *Southern Review* 21, no. 3 (Summer 1985): 567–593.

Tucker, Lindsey. "Recovering the Conjure Woman: Texts and Contexts in Gloria Naylor's Mama Day." *African-American Review* 28, no. 2 (1994): 173–188.

Wheliss, Sarah, and Emmanuel S. Nelson. "Gloria Naylor." In *Contemporary African-American Novelists,* edited by Emmanuel S. Nelson, 366–376. Westport, Conn.: Greenwood, 1999.

Loretta G. Woodard

Neal, Larry   (1937–1981)

A poet, literary critic, essayist, editor, playwright, folklorist, filmmaker, and noted figure of the BLACK ARTS MOVEMENT, Lawrence Paul Neal, who preferred to be known as Larry Neal, was born on September 5, 1937, the son of Woodie and Maggie Neal, in Atlanta, Georgia. He spent his formative years in Philadelphia, where he completed his early education. Neal earned his B.A. at Lincoln University in 1961 and an M.A. degree at the University of Pennsylvania in 1963. He moved to New York City in 1964. He married Evelyn Rodgers, a chemist, in 1965, and they adopted a son, Avatar, in 1971.

Between 1964 and 1966, Neal wrote articles on cultural events and conducted interviews with artists for *Liberator* magazine. He also wrote articles on the arts and social issues for *Negro Digest/Black World, Essence,* and *Drama Review.* In New York, where he spent the majority of his adult life, Neal befriended AMIRI BARAKA, with whom he collaborated on several projects about the Black Arts Movement. Neal and Baraka were among the founders of the Black Arts Repertory Theater in Harlem in 1964. Later they coedited *BLACK FIRE: AN ANTHOLOGY OF AFRO-AMERICAN WRITING* (1968), an important collection of works by several key figures of the Black Arts Movement. Throughout the Black Arts Movement, Baraka and Neal covered overlapping topics and promoted each other's artistic endeavors as well as the works of several other writers and jazz musicians who emerged during the 1960s and 1970s.

As an essayist, Neal explained the value and validity of the Black Arts Movement. His "And Shine Swam On," published as the afterword in *Black Fire,* and his now-classic essay "The Black Arts Movement," first published in *Drama Review,* reveal Neal's talents as an essayist and theorist of the BLACK AESTHETIC. Neal's interest in African-American musical traditions is apparent in his personal work as well as in his interviews with jazz musicians. In retrospect, Neal's preoccupation with black music's importance to the black aesthetic locates him among several well-known black writers such as RALPH ELLISON, Baraka, and ALBERT MURRAY.

Journal of Black Poetry Press, a small, independent African American–owned press, published Neal's first book of poetry, *Black Boogaloo: Notes on Black Liberation* (1969), which reveals Neal's interest in African mythology, memory, black American history, and jazz. In 1974 Howard University

Press published Neal's second volume of poetry, *Hoodoo Hollerin Bebop Ghosts,* which includes works that extend Neal's interest and presentation of topics related to African-American culture, especially folklore and jazz. Although in general his works received relatively little critical attention, Neal's poetry was frequently published in literary magazines and edited collections during the Black Arts Movement.

In addition to writing poetry and essays, Neal wrote two plays, *A Glorious Monster in the Bell of the Horn* and *In an Upstate Motel.* He also wrote short stories, including "Sinner Man Where You Gonna Run To?," which appeared in *Black Fire.* Neal cowrote and helped produce television scripts as well, including *Lenox Avenue Sunday* and *Deep River,* which aired in 1966 and 1967, respectively. Also, between 1963 and 1976, Neal taught at or served as a writer-in-residence at several universities, including City College of New York, Wesleyan University, and Yale University; he served as executive director of the Commission on the Arts and Humanities in Washington, D.C., from 1976 to 1979.

Larry Neal died of a heart attack in 1981. His selected works, *Visions of a Liberated Future: Black Arts Movement Writings,* were published posthumously in 1989. Neal's writings have been anthologized in several recent collections, including *The Norton Anthology of African American Literature, Trouble the Water: 250 Years of African-American Poetry,* and *African American Literary Criticism.* By the time of his death, Neal had revised some of his earlier positions on art and artists and critiqued the shortcomings of the Black Aesthetic as he continually sought to develop "new spaces" for interpreting African-American expressive culture. Ultimately, however, Larry Neal's critical and creative works testify to the vitality of the Black Arts Movement and to the promise of multigenre African-American writers.

BIBLIOGRAPHY

Larry Neal: A Special Issue Callaloo, 23 (Winter 1985).

Howard Rambsy II

Neely, Barbara (BarbaraNeely)
(1941–   )

Born in Lebanon, Pennsylvania, BarbaraNeely (who spells her name as one word) has crafted a career of literary achievement and community activism. Since earning a master's degree in urban and regional planning from the University of Pittsburgh in 1971, she has been active in causes promoting social justice. Among these activities, she has organized shelters for formerly incarcerated women; served as director for Women for Economic Justice, a nonprofit advocacy organization for low-income women; helped found Women of Color for Reproductive Freedom; and worked on behalf of the YWCA and Head Start. For her activism Neely has received the Community Works Social Action Award for Leadership and Activism for Women's Rights and Economic Justice, the Fighting for Women's Voices Award from the Coalition for Basic Human Needs, and the Woman of Courage and Conviction Award for Literature. Additionally, she has worked as a radio producer for African News Service and as a staff member of *Southern Exposure Magazine.* She is also host of *Commonwealth Journal,* a radio interview program in Massachusetts.

Neely grew up loving the works of writers like TONI CADE BAMBARA and ZORA NEALE HURSTON, who offered tales of assertive black women. She explains that her writing career began in earnest after she encountered an old woman dancing in San Francisco. The dancing woman "started pointing to people, and when she turned and pointed to me, it seemed to me that she was saying, 'Do it today, because today is all you have'" (McNaron and Miller). That charge seems to be the motto of the main character of Neely's best-known detective novels.

In the four volumes of her Blanche White mystery series, BarbaraNeely presents a working-class hero who is as unconventional in her personal life as she is in her approach to solving crimes. In Blanche's fictive world, race is primary. So too are her own distinctive African-American and feminist ways of knowing, which she uses to uncover the racial and gender hypocrisies of both blacks and whites, as well as the scarring pretensions of wealth. Her position as "other" subverts racial, gender, and genre stereotypes in ways that suggest the positive power of life in the margin as theorized by critics like BELL HOOKS, Patricia Hill Collins, and Molefi Assante.

Much of Blanche's unique epistemic approach arises from her status as outsider and her defiance of expectations. When the reader first meets Blanche she is presented as a large, dark, middle-aged black domestic worker fleeing a courtroom following her conviction for passing bad checks (*Blanchy on the Lam* 5–6). She hardly fits the stereotypical aristocratic or genteel detective heroes of Arthur Conan Doyle or Agatha Christie, nor does she, or her rural North Carolina background, suggest the misogynistic, booze-soaked, gritty urban "noir" of Dashiell Hammett's, Rex Stout's, or Mickey Spillane's tough guys. Instead, "Blanche defies the dominant culture's expectations for women of color and domestic workers both" (Mar, 2). Within the genre, then, Blanche arrives as an outsider protagonist. This outsider position is one of many that force Blanche to employ a distinctively African-American epistemology to solve crimes.

One of the clearest expressions of Blanche's sleuthing life on the margin comes from her ability to play with and against stereotypes. As a large, black woman working as a domestic in white households, Blanche physically conjures the stereotypical MAMMY character of the antebellum South, a fact of which she seems well aware. At the beginning of the second novel, Blanche slips into a pair of size 16 shorts and wonders at her foolishness as a young woman in believing that "she needed to be a woman-in-a-boy's-body to be attractive, even though big butts were never out of style in her world" (*Talented Tenth,* 1). Her size and color also lead whites in the text to read her as a Mammy. Early in the first novel, Grace, her wealthy white employer for the moment, bursts into tears and glances up at Blanche with "Mammy-save-me eyes" (*Lam,* 39). Blanche follows this display with a wearied surprise at how many white people still "longed for Aunt Jemima" and how often it led black people to contract "Darkies Disease" (39–40, 48). To Blanche, this tendency of some blacks to defend whites for or with whom they work leads

those blacks into foolishly believing that "their" whites return the affection. To believe such nonsense requires that "you had to pretend that obvious facts—facts that were like fences around your relationship—were not true" (48–49). In such lines Blanche reveals an astute awareness of white privilege and black powerlessness that denies any mammy-like consciousness.

Blanche also disrupts gender and class scripts. She refuses to marry or let a man dominate her life and put her in a position in which he and their children will assume that "her labor was their due" (*Talented Tenth,* 11). Her affection is reserved for her mother, Miz Cora; her best friend Ardell; and her dead sister's children, Malik and Taifa, children she was at first reluctant to raise but comes to love completely. In place of the nuclear family, Blanche relies on a complex network of women, a community of "bloodmothers and other-mothers" to provide a sense of family and to help her create a space as mother that suits her (179). This community of women, including her female ancestors, helps her nurture the children and herself (*Lam* 9–10; *Talented Tenth,* 2–3, 8). In *Blanche among the Talented Tenth,* Blanche directly confronts attitudes of racial and class deference by agreeing to join the children and their friends at the tony all-black Maine Resort of Amber Cove. She is not there merely to luxuriate; she is there to fight Taifa's desire to straighten her hair and the girls' "dumb ideas about a lawyer or a doctor being a better person than someone who hauls garbage" (*Talented Tenth,* 7–8, 99, 150–152). Her relation to the extended community of women highlights the folk orientation of the novels and suggests her own subversive epistemic approach.

BIBLIOGRAPHY

Bailey, Frankie Y. "*Blanche on the Lam,* or the Invisible Woman Speaks." In *Diversity and Detective Fiction,* edited by Kathleen Gregory Klein, 186–204. Bowling Green, Ohio: Bowling Green University Popular Press, 1999.

Mar, M. Elaine. "Guilty Pleasures: Barbara Neely, *Blanche on the Lam, Blanche among the Talented Tenth, and Blanche Cleans Up.*" *Peacework.* July/August 2000. Available online. URL: http://www.

peaceworkmagazine.org/pwork/0700/072k20htm. Accessed October 18, 2006.

McNaron, Toni, and Miller, Carol. "Barbara Neely." *Voices from the Gaps: Women Writers of Color.* University of Minnesota. 2002. Available online. URL: http://voices.cla.umn.edu/vg/Bios/entries/neely_barbara.html. Accessed October 18, 2006.

Neely, Barbara. *Blanche among the Talented Tenth.* New York: Penguin, 1994.

———. *Blanche Cleans Up.* New York: Penguin, 1998.

———. *Blanche on the Lam.* New York: Penguin, 1992.

———. *Blanche Passes Go.* New York: Penguin, 2000.

Witt, Doris. "Detecting Bodies: Barbara Neely's Domestic Sleuth and the Trope of the (In)Visible Woman." In *Recovering the Black Female Body: Self Representations by African-American Women,* edited by Michael Bennett and Vanessa D. Dickerson, 165–194. New Brunswick, N.J.: Rutgers University Press, 2000.

Jay Hart

Neely, Letta (1976–)

Born and raised in Indianapolis, Letta Neely walked onto the literary stage at the end of the 20th century as a popular New England slam poet, playwright, and civil rights activist who seeks to confront homophobia, emerging as an important voice of the gay and lesbian movements, along with poets ESSEX HEMPHILL and ASSOTTO SAINT. Like the members of the BLACK ARTS MOVEMENT, Neely, who admits to having an obsession with history, uses her works to address political issues; however, her focus adds sexuality and sexual orientation as yet another important aspect of voice that should not be ignored or denied. Neely writes, "it is important to say i am a black lesbian (dyke) because when I first started looking for our relatives (to know i am wasn't alone) i smiled the first time i read Audrey Lorde's bio" (Neely, 440).

Neely's best-known play, *Hamartia Blues,* explores the lesbian relationship between Jay/San and her lover Neferdia and their interaction with Jay/San's brother, Afir, who will soon be released from prison. Another one of Neely's plays is about breast cancer, basketball, and lesbianism. Neely has published two collections of poetry, *juba* and *Here.* In her poetry, Neely unabashedly celebrates lesbian love: "girl / when you / come / I swear I / feel god / squeezing / my hand" ("3 Movements"). Neely, who was named Best Local Author 2001 by a Boston *Phoenix* reader's poll, was twice a finalist for Lambda Literary Awards for lesbian poetry.

BIBLIOGRAPHY
Neely, Letta. "3 Movements." In *Step into a World: A Global Anthology of the New Black Literature,* edited by Kevin Powell, 347. New York: John Wiley and Sons, 2000.

Wilfred D. Samuels

Negritude (*la négritude*)

As a literary movement, Negritude, scholars argue, preceded the HARLEM RENAISSANCE and the New Negro movement. It is often associated with the Pan-African movement of the early 20th century, in which W. E. B. DuBois played a major role, although it blossomed as a movement during the 1930s and 1940s and was clearly influenced by the major Renaissance writers, particularly LANGSTON HUGHES and CLAUDE MCKAY. Critics agree that the Negritude movement was begun by three Francophone writers: the Martinican poet Aimé Césaire, who is credited with coining the term *négritude*; the Senegalese intellectual and political leader Lèopold Sèdar Senghor; and French Guyanese poet Leon Damas. Also central to the movement was Haitian novelist Jacques Roumain. Equally important, however, was the interest Europeans took in African culture, particularly art, during the 1920s and through the art of Pablo Picasso; the writings of Jean Cocteau, Blaise Cendrars, and André Gide; and the music of Darius Milhaud.

As political leaders, intellectuals, philosophers, and writers, Césaire, Senghor, and Damas, French colonial subjects, sought, in their respective homelands and their Paris-based intellectual venues, to valorize black African culture and experience over that of the colonial rulers. Specifically, they sought to affirm a more positive use of the term *nègre* and objected to the assimilation of blacks into French culture. Collectively, they were interested in identifying, defining, celebrating, and instituting a black African aesthetic that spoke to the needs of blacks and reflected a unique and distinctive black African culture, rather than blindly embracing the culture of their colonial rulers. The three men founded several journals, including *La Revue du monde noir* (The journal of the black world), *L'Étudiant noir* (The black student), and *Présence African,* to provide an arena for open intellectual debate about the significance of this movement. In 1947 Damas published an anthology of poetry from the French colonies, and in the following year Senghor published a similar collection, *Anthologie de la nouvelle poesie Negre et malgache.*

During the First International Conference on Negro Artists and Writers, held in Paris in 1956, the Senegalese intellectual Alioune Diop confirmed the continued emphasis on the central mission of this movement:

> to liberate or de-Westernize the African music and art

Through this conference and other literary venues, the leading architects of the Negritude movement often engaged in open debate with African-American writers, including RICHARD WRIGHT, JAMES BALDWIN, and RALPH ELLISON. By the late 1960s it was possible to identify the BLACK ARTS MOVEMENT led by AMIRI BARAKA and HAKI MADHUBUTI as the spiritual sister not only of the BLACK POWER movement but also of the Negritude movement.

BIBLIOGRAPHY

Chapman, Abraham. "Concepts of the Black Aesthetics in Contemporary Black Literature." In *The Black Writer in Africa and the Americas,* edited by Lloyd Brown, 11–44. Los Angeles: Hennessey & Ingalls, 1973.

Ikonné, Chidi. *From DuBois to VanVechten, The Early New Negro Literature, 1903–1926.* Westport, Conn.: Greenwood, 1981.

Nesbitt, Nick. "Negritude." African Writers Index. Available online. URL: www.geocities.com/africanwriters/Negritude.html. Accessed October 18, 2006.

Jeffrey Ratcliffe

Negro Caravan: Writings by Negro Writers, The   Sterling A. Brown, Arthur P. Davis, and Ulysses Lee, eds. (1941)

Along with *The NEW NEGRO: AN INTERPRETATION* (1925), edited by ALAIN LOCKE, *The Negro Caravan* and its editors stand in the vanguard of pioneering works and scholars that sought not merely to call attention to the existence of respectable and valuable works by African-American writers but also to validate, in the process, the voices of African-American writers who had successfully established a credible African-American literary tradition that is a fundamental part of American literature.

Noting the continued popularity of African-American subjects and characters in the works of white writers, from Harriet Beecher Stowe and Thomas Page to Margaret Mitchell, Edward Shelton, and Vernon Duke, the editors wrote, "White authors, basing their interpretations [of African Americans] on necessarily limited knowledge derived from an outside view, run the risk of stereotyping [them]." Respectfully disagreeing with publishers who maintained that white authors "know the Negro best," the editors expressed their belief that the "inside view" of black writers and critics "is more likely to make possible the essential truth [about black life] than the 'outside view.'" The editors argued, "When the Negro artist has expressed his own people, he has almost always refuted, or differed from, or at least complicated the simpler patterns of white interpretation."

Claiming that "The record of the Negro author extends well over a century and a half," the editors objected to having these works placed under the simple rubric of "Negro literature." Black writers, they wrote, ask that their works be judged "without sentimental allowances"; they concluded, "Literature by Negro authors about Negro experience is a literature in process and like all such literature (including American literature) must be considered as significant, not only because of the body of established masterpieces, but also because of the illumination it sheds upon social reality."

The editors divided their anthology into eight categories or genres, plus an appendix, including short stories, novels, poetry, folk literature, drama, biography, and essays. Consequently, *Negro Writing* provided the paradigm for successive anthologies that continued to value and validate the African-American literary tradition through the end of the 20th century, including DARWIN T. TURNER's *BLACK AMERICAN LITERATURE: ESSAYS, POETRY, FICTION, DRAMA* (1970), Arthur P. Davis and SAUNDERS REDDING's *CAVALCADE: NEGRO AMERICAN WRITING FROM 1760 TO THE PRESENT* (1971), RICHARD BARKSDALE and Keneth Kinnamon's *BLACK WRITERS OF AMERICA: A COMPREHENSIVE ANTHOLOGY* (1972), Patricia Liggins Hill's *CALL AND RESPONSE: THE RIVERSIDE ANTHOLOGY OF THE AFRICAN AMERICAN LITERARY TRADITION* (1998) and HENRY L. GATES, JR. and NELLIE Y. MCKAY's *The Norton Anthology of African-American Literature* (1997).

Wilfred D. Samuels

Nelson, Jill   (1952–   )

Freelance journalist, novelist, and lecturer Jill Nelson was born June 14, 1952, in New York City to Stanley Earl Nelson, a dentist, and A'Lelia Ransom Nelson, a librarian. She received a B.A. from the City College of the City University of New York in 1977 and an M.S. degree from the Columbia School of Journalism in 1980. In 1986, Nelson became the first black woman to write for *The Washington Post's Sunday Magazine* and was named Washington, D.C., Journalist of the Year for her work there. She was an adjunct lecturer at City College of New York (1982) and Hunter College at City University of New York (1983) and a professor of journalism at the City College of New York (1998–2003).

After over two decades of writing journalism and nonfiction, Nelson began writing fiction. Reflecting on her experience, she states, "it was a true pleasure to simply be able to let my imagination take my words as far out as I wanted to go" (Nel-

son). Citing as her literary mentors JAMES BALDWIN, TONI MORRISON, Barbara Kingsolver, Leslie Marmon Silko, Gore Vidal, JOHN A. WILLIAMS, PEARL CLEAGE, and Ian McEwan, Nelson has written two memoirs and a novel and edited an anthology.

Nelson's best-selling memoir, *Volunteer Slavery: My Authentic Negro Experience* (1993), won an American Book Award. Reminiscent of NATHAN J. MCCALL's *Makes Me Wanna Holler: A Young Black Man in America* (1994) and GWENDOLYN M. PARKER's *Trespassing: My Sojourn in the Halls of Privilege* (1997), *Volunteer Slavery* chronicles Nelson's four years of experiences in the white, male-dominated world of corporate politics at *The Washington Post*. It further details her journey from a middle-class childhood to near poverty, divorce and single motherhood, a few bad love affairs, and a nervous breakdown.

Straight, No Chaser (1997), Nelson's second book of nonfiction, combines autobiography, political analysis, and self-help to state boldly what seems to be the problem with the African-American community at the turn of the new century. Writing for the *New York Times Book Review*, BEVERLY GUY-SHETFALL noted that Nelson does a superb job "melding together . . . hard-hitting, in-your-face writing that says in no uncertain terms: Here's my truth; deal with it."

In her debut novel, *Sexual Healing* (2003), Nelson, through her characters, candidly discusses sex, politics, race, religion, and writing. Though humorous, it is "a compelling narrative," with biting social commentary about middle- and upper-class black America. Set in Reno, Nevada, where prostitution thrives, Lydia Beaucoup and Acey Allen, two clever, feisty, financially independent professional black women in their 40s, decide to open a discreet brothel called "Sisters' Spa" where women can have their sexual needs met. The result is a solid friendship between women who eventually take control of their own sexuality and their lives in a world where they have been exploited and oppressed.

Nelson is also the editor of the anthology *Police Brutality* (1999), a pioneer work fueled by the shooting of unarmed and innocent Amadou Diallo at the hands of New York City police officers. Most critics agree it is a work of immense social importance on an issue that can no longer be ignored. In the 12 essays, the contributors—prominent academicians, activists, social critics, a congressman, writers, and a former New York City police detective, all of whom have suffered at the hands of police or personally know others who have been maimed or killed by police—attempt to trace the roots of police brutality in African-American communities and to determine its profound influence in shaping American identity.

Nelson's work has appeared in numerous publications, including *The New York Times, ESSENCE, The Washington Post, The Nation, Ms., The Chicago Tribune, Village Voice, New York Review of Books, USA Today,* MSNBC.com, and NiaOnline.com. She also writes a twice-monthly column titled "On the Verge," lectures extensively throughout the country, and is active in the Harlem community.

Though Nelson is more established as a journalist than as a memoirist or novelist, her small body of work has attracted the attention of such writers as ISHMAEL REED, PEARL CLEAGE, TERRY MCMILLAN, and E. LYNN HARRIS. Together, they agree that Nelson is one of the boldest, most honest writers in contemporary African-American literature, who puts her message in a much-needed historical and intellectual context.

BIBLIOGRAPHY

Review of Jill Nelson's *Sexual Healing. Publishers Weekly* (May 12, 2003): 44.

Nelson, Jill. "Serpent's Tail Interviews: Jill Nelson." Available online. http://www.serpentstail.com. Accessed May 10, 2007.

"Volunteer Slavery: My Authentic Negro Experience. An Excerpt from *Washington Post* Writer Jill Nelson's New Book." *Essence* 24, no. 2 (June 1993): 82.

Loretta G. Woodard

New Negro, The: An Interpretation
Alain Locke, ed. (1925)

Edited by ALAIN LOCKE, a Harvard graduate and dean of the College of Humanities at Howard University, *The New Negro: An Interpretation,* was originally published in 1925; it was reissued in 1968 with a preface by ROBERT HAYDEN. The anthology, which grew out of a special edition of *Survey Graphic* magazine, also edited by Locke, became, as Hayden noted, "the definitive presentation of the artistic and social goals of the New Negro movement" (ix)—its manifesto. In his now-classic introductory essay, "The New Negro," Locke boldly demanded that "the Negro of today be seen through other than the dusty spectacles of past controversy" (5). He further maintained that "the mind of the Negro seems suddenly to have slipped from under the tyranny of social intimidation and to be shaking off the psychology of imitation and implied inferiority" (4).

Locke believed that the younger contributing writers and artists would guide the HARLEM RENAISSANCE by rediscovering and reimagining African arts and music, particularly jazz and the Negro spirituals. Locke's vision is integrationist; it is driven by an effort to show the black community the value of their contributions and thereby encourage black people to participate in white society and culture as equals. Simultaneously, however, Locke emphasized the need for blacks to embrace their African roots for inspiration in music and art, creating a black aesthetic that would be a valuable addition to American identity rather than a separating force. This is the argument and perspective found in several essays, including Arthur A. Schomburg's "The Negro Digs Up His Past" and Locke's "The Legacy of the Ancestral Art" and "The Negro Spirituals."

The New Negro is divided into two major parts. Part One focuses on the Harlem Renaissance, and Part Two on the future of the New Negro. Locke contributes five essays, including the introductory essay. The Harlem Renaissance section contains essays, fiction, poetry, drama, music, and folk stories written by writers who became the luminaries of the period, including JEAN TOOMER, ZORA NEALE HURSTON, COUNTEE CULLEN, CLAUDE MCKAY, W. E. B. DUBOIS, ARNA BONTEMPS, GEORGIA DOUGLAS JOHNSON, and LANGSTON HUGHES. The poems range in tone from McKay's radical "The White House"

(Locke changed the title to "White Houses" in order not to offend his audience) to the more celebratory "The Negro Speaks of Rivers" by Hughes and "The Creation" by JAMES WELDON JOHNSON. The second section is devoted to nonfiction essays that look forward with optimism and excitement for the future. Both the general positive tone and the tension provided by McKay and DuBois's piece "The Negro Mind Reaches Out," from the second section, rounds out the anthology, which ends with a diverse bibliography listing important works in literature and music.

BIBLIOGRAPHY

"Alain LeRoy Locke." *The Black Renaissance in Washington.* District of Columbia Public Library. Available online. URL: http://www.dclibrary.org/blkren/bios/lockea.html. Accessed October 18, 2006.

Hayden, Robert. "Preface to the Atheneum Edition." In *The New Negro,* edited by Alain Locke New York: Atheneum, 1968.

Locke, Alain. "The New Negro." In *The New Negro,* edited by Alain Locke, 3–16. New York: Macmillan, 1925.

Kim Hai Pearson Brian Jennings

Nigger Heaven   Carl Van Vechten (1926)

At its publication, CARL VAN VECHTEN's *Nigger Heaven* proved both a central text of the HARLEM RENAISSANCE and a lightning rod for controversy. Despite some positive reviews from both white and black writers, it was seen very quickly as "bad form" among blacks to be caught reading the novel, and both Van Vechten and his text received blistering receptions in Harlem and elsewhere within the black community. W. E. B. DUBOIS wrote that it was "a blow in the face . . . an affront to the hospitality of black folk and to the intelligence of white. . . . It is not a true picture of Harlem life. . . . It is caricature . . . an astonishing and wearisome hodgepodge of laboriously stated facts, quotations, and expressions, illuminated here and there with something that comes near to being noth-

ing but cheap melodrama" (vii). Likewise, ALAIN LOCKE and COUNTEE CULLEN despised the novel, though neither said so publicly (Lewis, 181). Petitions were circulated to ban the book in New York, especially in public libraries. The Pittsburgh *Courier* instituted a moratorium on ads for the book, which was lifted only after the direct intervention of the NATIONAL ASSOCIATION FOR THE ADVANCEMENT OF COLORED PEOPLE's WALTER WHITE. Others were less reticent. In December 1926 pages of the novel were burned by Professor S. R. Williams at a Harlem meeting to protest recent lynchings (Worth, 466).

The novel that occasioned this vitriol was divided into two books and a prologue introducing highly exoticized Harlem characters. Byron Kasson, oozing with literary ambitions and precious little actual effort, finds himself unable to obtain work as a writer and fails equally when forced to take what he sees as a demeaning job as an elevator operator. Byron ignites the passion of Mary Love, an overly refined and repressed librarian, who finds herself passed over for promotion by less qualified white peers. Mary spends her time worrying if she is sufficiently black. Byron eventually abandons the virtuous Mary for the notorious Harlem heiress Lasca Sartoris, who dallies with him and then tosses him aside. The novel ends where it began, in a nightclub populated by pimps, prostitutes, and bootleggers, but with the final twist of a crime of passion, for which Byron is framed.

For this grossly primitive and exotic depiction, Van Vechten was denounced as a voyeur of Harlem's rich black culture, though a few praised him for his brave foregrounding of black themes and characters. Referring to himself as a "Nordic struggling with Ethiopian psychology," Van Vechten did offer one of the first novels set in urban America peopled with African-American characters, as well as the complicating reality of a white author writing as a champion for blacks. Yet he seemed ambiguous about his own motivation, and his ambivalence may help explain why the novel is, as charged, saturated in the exotic and the primitive.

While the primitive dominates, anything seen as lower class and black is brutally rejected. Adora exclaims, "Sometimes I hate Niggers" (26). Snobbish Mrs. Albright and her daughter, Hester, decry the African art Mary is trying to champion and anything else "low" associated with their race. While readers learn that blacks are by nature tardy to meetings, Byron detests the working-class blacks with whom he briefly works for their dress, dialect, and lack of education. Intellectuals are, one critic notes, stifled by "black snobbery on the one side and white bigotry on the other" (Worth, 464).

Herein, however, lies the irony. Within this overwhelming tumble of primitive images, readers also find debates about racism, the New Negro, and the future of race relations. Characters debate the merits and costs of passing, the absurdity of white supremacism, the trap of black "exceptionalism," the economic exploitation of Harlem, and the racism of U.S. foreign policy. Mary also praises the race for producing the beauty of its spirituals. Though they are set piece debates, they are put in the mouths of sympathetic characters. Van Vechten seems to be acting as the ally of African Americans in these sections. He shows white readers the indignities faced by educated blacks, yet the text's narrative framing device of Anatole Longfellow, the Scarlet Creeper, suggests that Van Vechten ultimately defaulted to a more primitive depiction of Harlem and blacks than the inclusion of New Negro characters can overcome. The Creeper is a womanizing cabaret folk hero who slinks through speakeasies in which "Hottentots and Bantus" sway to the music, and even the waiters Charleston on the tables. Ultimately he guns down a rival who has stolen "his woman" and inadvertently frames Byron for the murder.

The stereotypes and primitive imagery seem puzzling coming from Van Vechten, who tried to help blacks. They clearly increased sales and acceptance from white readers, who would be the target audience. The title itself arises from an image of racism, "linking the life of blacks in Harlem to the segregated balcony section of theatres" (Worth, 464). Van Vechten was exercising privileges denied black writers, who, above all, did not enjoy the access to publishing that he did. Beyond that, any more authentic depiction of Harlem and

black culture offered by a black author would not find a market.

The self-referential nature of the text reinforces this conclusion. Van Vechten never tired of telling his black friends that the Great White Market awaited the proper portrayal of Harlem and black culture. He proved his point, when he became that white author and *Nigger Heaven* became a best seller, going through nine printings in its first four months, eventually selling better than all books written by black authors in the Harlem Renaissance. At several points in the text, Van Vechten seems to critique his own enterprise, while illustrating his own power. Van Vechten seems to have understood, even if he could not resist.

BIBLIOGRAPHY

DuBois, W. E. B. Review of *Nigger Heaven.* 1926. In *Nigger Heaven,* vii–x. New York: Harper & Row, 1971.

Kellner, Bruce. *Carl Van Vechten and the Irreverent Decades.* Norman: University of Oklahoma Press, 1968.

Lewis, David Levering. *When Harlem Was in Vogue.* New York: Penguin, 1997.

Worth, Robert F. "*Nigger Heaven* and the Harlem Renaissance." *African American Review* 29, no. 3 (Fall 1995): 461–473.

Jay Hart

Nugent, Richard Bruce   (1906–1987)

An artist, writer, actor, dancer, dilettante and bohemian, Bruce Nugent was born Richard Bruce Nugent to middle-class, light-skinned Washington, D.C., socialites Richard Henry Nugent and Pauline Minerva Bruce Nugent. His father was a Pullman porter, his mother a biracial product of African and French blood. According to David Levering Lewis, Nugent "bore a striking resemblance to Langston Hughes—a handsomer, more bohemian, Hughes" (196). Nugent attended Washington, D.C.'s Dunbar High School. After his father's death, Nugent's mother moved the family to New York, where Nugent, then 13 years old, worked at various odd jobs through age 18.

A year after arriving in New York City, he discovered Harlem.

When Nugent told his mother he had decided to become a writer, she sent him back to Washington, D.C., to live with his grandmother (who had connections with ALAIN LOCKE). Nugent began to frequent the Saturday salons for writers hosted by GEORGIA DOUGLAS JOHNSON. On one occasion Johnson introduced Nugent to Hughes, a meeting that changed the faltering direction of Nugent's life forever. Nugent wrote that Hughes "was a made-to-order Hero" for him (Watson, 91). Nugent followed Hughes back to Harlem shortly thereafter.

Despite his ubiquitous presence in Harlem and intimate friendship with the black luminaries who inhabited "Niggerati Manor," a term Nugent coined and WALLACE THURMAN (his roommate) popularized in *Infants of the Spring* (1932), a satire of the "New Negro," Nugent remains a minor player among the giants of the HARLEM RENAISSANCE. Nevertheless, Nugent carved a historical place for himself on the wall of fame of renaissance stars: He was, with Hughes, ZORA NEALE HURSTON, and Thurman, one of the coeditors of *Fire!!!,* the avant-garde journal they hoped would represent the true voice of the younger generation of African-American writers, unlike Locke's edited anthology *The NEW NEGRO,* in which, ironically, they had all published their works. Along with his drawing of Nordic figures, Nugent also published "SMOKE, LILIES, AND JADE," now his signature short story, in the first and only issue of *Fire!!,* which appeared in November 1926.

The homosexual theme in "Smoke, Lilies, and Jade" is currently celebrated as a historical first. Like Nugent, Alex, the protagonist in this story, proudly embraces his homosexual orientation and lifestyle. Duke University has recently published *Gay Rebel of the Harlem Renaissance: Selections from the Work of Bruce Nugent* (2002), edited by Thomas Wirth.

BIBLIOGRAPHY

Cullen, Countee, ed. *Caroling Dusk: An Anthology of Verse by Black Poets.* New York: Citadel Press, 1927, 1993.

Lewis, David Levering. *When Harlem Was in Vogue.* New York: Oxford University Press, 1979.

Watson, Stephen. *The Harlem Renaissance: Hub of African American Culture, 1920–1930.* New York: Pantheon Books, 1995.

Wilfred D. Samuels

Nuñez, Elizabeth   (1944–)

A native of Trinidad, Elizabeth Nuñez immigrated to America after she completed secondary school. She received her bachelor's degree in English from Marian College in Wisconsin and her master's and Ph.D. degrees in English from New York University. She is presently a City University of New York distinguished professor of English at Medgar Evers College, where she designed and implemented many of the colleges' first major academic programs. Along with JOHN OLIVER KILLENS, she founded the National Black Writers Conference, sponsored by the National Endowment for the Humanities. Nuñez was also the director of the conference from 1986 to 2000.

Nuñez is the author of four novels: *When Rocks Dance* (1986), *Beyond the Limbo Silence* (1998), *Bruised Hibiscus* (2000), and *Grace* (2003). Nuñez's debut novel, *When Rocks Dance,* is about one woman's desire to own a plot of land. *Bruised Hibiscus* presents a smoldering tale of two Trinidadian women and the escalating psychological abuse each endures after a fisherman discovers the mutilated corpse of a white woman floating in Freeman's Bay. For research, Nuñez returned to her Trinidadian birthplace to read newspaper accounts of the 1954 Dalip Singh case, which was the basis of her novel. For the author, this case epitomizes a troubled era in her native country, a time, she remembers, when women felt "very vulnerable, very at risk." Although *Grace,* an urban love story, seems to be the quietest of Nuñez's novels, a closer look reveals that it is presented in real time. The slow pace of the work is true to the domestic setting and the everyday challenges that couples face in their work and other relationships.

Nuñez's *Defining Ourselves: Black Writers in the 90*s (1999) represents her perspective on black literature. This anthology contains works by 29 black writers and critics, including PAULE MARSHALL, AMIRI BARAKA, JOHN A. WILLIAMS, ISHMAEL REED, MARITA GOLDEN, JILL NELSON, TERRY MCMILLAN, and HOUSTON A. BAKER, Jr., among others. Nuñez applies the same ideological reflections on gender equality and racial difference in each of her novels and critical works. She explores the question whether black literature is experiencing another renaissance during the 1990s. In addition to these topics, Nuñez investigates the concerns of black readers, the universality of black literature, and the politics of publishing as is reflected not only in her literature but in her lifelong career as a champion for African-American writers.

Nuñez is the current chair of the PEN American Open Book Committee, which provides access for minorities to various aspects of the publishing industry. She has served in the United States as an evaluator for national and local programs in the arts and education. In addition to her distinguished career, Nuñez has received the Vera Rubin Residency Fellowship Award for the Yaddo Artist Colony, the YWCA Woman of Distinction Award, the Sojourner Truth Award from the National Association of Black Business and Professional Women's Clubs, and the Carter G. Woodson Outstanding Teacher of the Year Award.

BIBLIOGRAPHY

Carroll, Denolyn. "Grace." *Black Issues Book Review* 5, no. 2 (2003): 34.

"Elizabeth Nuñez." *African American Literature Book Club.* Available online. URL: http://www.aalbc.com/authors/elizabet.htm. Accessed October 18, 2006.

Peterson, V. R. "Elizabeth Nuñez." *Essence* 25, no. 7 (1994): 70.

Kindra Briggs

Opportunity: A Journal of Negro Life

Begun January 1923 as the official organ of the National Urban League, the journal *Opportunity* continued until 1949. The title of the journal came from the league's slogan: "Not alms, but opportunity." The role of *Opportunity,* according to Eugene Kinckle Jones, the first executive secretary of the league, in his first-issue editorial, was to try to set down interestingly but without sugar-coating or generalization the findings of careful scientific surveys and the facts gathered from research, undertaken not to prove pre-conceived notions but to lay bare Negro life as it is" (5).

Unlike *The Crisis, Opportunity* never became self-sustaining, and its circulation peaked in its early years at around 11,000. Like *The Crisis,* however, *Opportunity* had a strong editor, Charles S. Johnson, who was capable of attracting unknown African-American literary talent to its pages. Under the editorship of Johnson, *Opportunity* made a significant contribution to the birth of the Harlem Renaissance. He was among those, including James Weldon Johnson, W. E. B. DuBois, and Alain Locke, who understood that a race capable of boasting its own literary and artistic lights would be able to break existing barriers—for those who would come later and for those whose talent at the time might have gone unsung.

Opportunity did not seriously challenge *The Crisis,* nor was it intended that it should. What Johnson offered, however, that was creative and fresh were dinners that brought together in a social setting talented young writers with more established ones who had wealthy white patrons and well-connected white publishers. Johnson was the host of the New York Civic Club's dinner on March 21, 1924, which most critics consider the formal launching of the New Negro movement. Among those present were Jesse Redmon Fauset, Countee Cullen, Gwendolyn Bennett, Langston Hughes, and Alain Locke.

Johnson's next idea was to establish the *Opportunity* literary awards contests. He sought distinguished judges, such as Fannie Hurst, James Weldon Johnson, Carl Van Vechten, Eugene O'Neill, and Robert Benchley, who readily agreed to participate. First, second, and third prizes were awarded in the following categories: short stories, poetry, plays, essays, and personal experience sketches. The top prize was $100 and the least was $5. To fund all the awards in the first year, $440 was needed, a considerable sum in the 1920s. In subsequent years, Johnson found a patron in Casper Holstein, a kingpin mobster from the West Indies who controlled the numbers racket in Harlem. The response was overwhelming: 723 entries the first year and more than 1200 the following year.

For three years (1925–1927), Johnson hosted dinners to announce and award the contest winners. Johnson, using *Opportunity* as his means, significantly increased the socializing between the races and launched new African-American writings for a wider reading public. The magazine monthly, from 1923 to 1942 and thereafter a quarterly until its demise in 1949, contained poetry, plays, fiction, reviews, and assorted essays. Contributors who filled its pages included ZORA NEALE HURSTON, Hughes, CLAUDE MCKAY, ALICE DUNBAR-NELSON, Paul Robeson, Adam Clayton Powell, Sr., and Mary Bethune.

BIBLIOGRAPHY

Jones, Eugene Kinckle. "Co-operation and Opportunity." *Opportunity* 1 (January 1923): 4–5.
Wilson, Sondra Kathryn, ed. *The* Opportunity *Reader*. New York: Modern Library, 1999.

Margaret Whitt

Our Nig   **Harriet Wilson** (1859)

Written in 1859, HARRIET WILSON's *Our Nig* continues to generate critical interest and discussion. Identified by HENRY LOUIS GATES, JR., in 1984 as the first African-American novel published in America by a woman of color, the novel went for years with very little notice or attention. The novel was assumed to be the work of a white author initially, and it does not seem to have been either a popular or a critical success when it first appeared. There are several reasons for this, including its controversial portrait of the North and especially of Mrs. Bellmont, a white, middle-class northerner "imbued with Southern principles" who resembles a jealous plantation mistress. The book's full title, *Our Nig, or the Sketches of a Free Black in a Two Story White House, North, Showing that Slavery's Shadows Fall Even Here,* clearly suggested the hypocrisy of well-meaning, religious white northerners. The novel also included the two interracial marriages of Mag Smith, a white woman discarded by her lover. Left with no friends, she marries Jim, a black man. The two have a daughter, Frado, the title character of the novel. When Jim dies, Mag marries again—also to a black man. Wilson's sympathetic portrayal of Mag would have been unsettling to white female readers accustomed to the sentimental novel tradition. It would also have confronted their racial prejudices about the possible romantic relationships that might exist between white women and black men.

Our Nig is also stylistically a conundrum. It is a mixture of fiction and autobiography. While this is not an unusual characteristic of works of the time, Wilson switches between first- and third-person voice frequently. The introduction states that the novel developed out of Wilson's need to make money to take care of her son, so some editorial lapses might be due to the state of emergency in which the author found herself, without the luxury of time to take care of such matters. The work also tries to balance the genres of the slave narrative and sentimental novel, which could also account for the problematic shifts.

However, Frado is clearly based on Wilson, as their life stories are nearly identical. After Mag remarries, she abandons Frado at the Bellmonts'. Mr. Bellmont; the two sons, Jack and James; and Aunt Abby treat her kindly, but Mrs. Bellmont and her daughter, Mary, beat and abuse Frado in a manner common in slave households. Frado's life as an indentured servant is as cruel as any story found in slave narratives. No family member is able to convince Mrs. Bellmont to stop mistreating poor, sickly Frado. James and Abby are devoutly religious but buckle under Mrs. Bellmont's control of the home. The novel thus illustrates the religious (Christian) hypocrisy that allowed the horrible treatment of women and slavery in 19th-century America. Both James and Jack befriend Frado in scenes reminiscent of the typical sentimental romance, but neither man is able to rescue Frado from their mother's temper. Ultimately, Frado stands up to Mrs. Bellmont; after nearly 12 years, she leaves the "two-story white house."

Frado marries a man pretending to be an escaped slave, who later leaves her and their young son. After years of beatings, Frado is not physically able to work. To support herself and her very sick son, she sits down to write her story. The novel is a testament of the abuse of women, the indigent, and the African American—whether free or slave—in the domestic sphere. Such treatment, the novel indicates, is condoned by society. Wilson's novel set the stage for the work of contemporary African-American women writers and feminist theorists and scholars. Perhaps more important, *Our Nig,* together with WILLIAM WELLS BROWN's *Clotel, or The President's Daughter* (1853), Frank Webb's *The Garies and Their Friends* (1857), and Martin R. Delany's *Blake, or The Huts of America* (1859), initiates the African-American novelistic tradition: a blend of personal narrative, history, protest, and fiction.

BIBLIOGRAPHY

Bell, Bernard W. *The Afro-American Novel and Its Tradition.* Amherst: University of Massachusetts Press, 1987.

Ernest, John. "Economics of Identity: Harriet Wilson's *Our Nig.*" *PMLA* 109, no. 3 (1994): 424–438.

Leveen, Lois. "Dwelling in the House of Oppression: The Spatial, Racial, and Textual Dynamics of Harriet Wilson's *Our Nig.*" *African American Review* 35, no. 4 (2001): 561–576.

West, Elizabeth J. "Reworking the Conversion Narrative: Race and Christianity in *Our Nig.*" *MELUS* 24, no. 2 (1999): 3–27.

Tracie Church Guzzio

P

Parable of the Sower
Octavia Butler (1993)

Parable of the Sower is the tale of an apocalyptic world that gives birth to a spiritual leader, Lauren Olamina. In the year 2024, the violence in the United States has escalated to the point that people cannot venture outside of their barricaded communities without weapons and people constantly live with the threats of robbery, rape, assault, and murder. Fifteen-year-old Lauren lives with her family and neighbors in a small, walled society, where they struggle to gather what few natural resources are available and guard against violent transients. A victim of "hyperempathy" syndrome—a delusional disorder that allows her to feel the pleasure and pain she witnesses—Lauren is especially sensitized to the horrors of her environment. She turns away from a Christian God toward a "God-is-Change belief system" that she calls Earthseed, a spiritual practice designed to teach people to survive the daily horror she witnesses. When her family is decimated and her world is destroyed, Lauren teaches both spiritual and material survival skills to a group of people she meets as she travels north; she establishes a community based on Earthseed's principles. In the sequel, *Parable of the Talents* (1998), Octavia Butler continues Lauren's story through the voices of Lauren and her daughter. These texts artfully blend tragedy and hope, focusing on a flawed prophet whose life work rarely manages to benefit those who are closest to her.

Now a classic among scholars of feminist utopian and dystopian fiction, *Parable of the Sower* ranks with Joanna Russ's *The Female Man,* Marge Piercy's *Woman on the Edge of Time,* and Margaret Atwood's *The Handmaid's Tale.* These novels experiment with what feminist power structures might look like and critique 20th-century conservative movements, which thrive on regulating the bodies of the poor, women, and people of color. Butler, the most prominent African-American woman science fiction writer, has always placed poor and working-class black women at the center of her fiction, challenging standards in science fiction, which either ignore race or explore racial issues only allegorically. Butler's novel productively explores what possibilities for agency exist under oppressive conditions and gestures toward slave history. Lauren's journey north mimics the history of slaves escaping to Canada, and Earthseed evokes an African-American tradition of transforming Western Christianity so that it speaks to black culture and politics. *Parable*'s place in feminist, science fiction, and African-American literary canons should ensure its study for years to come.

BIBLIOGRAPHY

Baccolini, Raffaella. "Gender and Genre in the Feminist Critical Dystopias of Katharine Burdekin, Margaret Atwood, and Octavia Butler." In *Future Females, The Next Generation: New Voices and Velocities in Feminist Science Fiction Criticism,* edited by Marleen S. Barr, 13–34. Lanham, Md.: Rowman & Littlefield, 2000.

Dubey, Madhu. "Folk and Urban Communities in African-American Women's Fiction: Octavia Butler's *Parable of the Sower*." *Studies in American Fiction* 27, no. 1 (Spring 1999): 103–28.

Rebecca Wanzo

Parker, Gwendolyn M.   (1950–)

Gwendolyn Parker was born into a middle-class family on June 9, 1950, in Durham, North Carolina. Her father, "Yip" Judson Garrett Parker, a pharmacist, owned a drugstore. Her mother, Arona Moore McDougald Parker, a mathematician, taught at North Carolina Central. Aaron McDuffie Moore, her great-grandfather, was cofounder of the North Carolina Mutual Life Insurance Company; he was also the founder of the Mechanics and Farmers Bank and North Carolina Central University. Feeling confined in the South, her father relocated the family to Mount Vernon, New York, in the late 1950s. In an interview with Susan McHenry, a former Radcliffe classmate, Parker disclosed that "her father wanted his children to be part of the whole world," a place where they would have more "options than that of a college president of a historically black college or a black-owned business" (McHenry, 34). Taught by her parents and grandparents that education and achievement were the pinnacles of success, Parker attended Kent Prep School, Radcliffe College, and New York University School of Law before going to work in corporate America for 10 years as an international tax attorney and a marketing manager at the American Express Company. Later, while working in the Office of Strategic Planning, she received the Black Achiever in Industry Award.

In 1986, after 10 years of battling stereotypes on Wall Street, and after adhering to her family's message: "work hard at something that will bring you assured success" (Carroll, 197), Parker left the corporate world to pursue her first love, a career in writing. According to Parker, from the time she was five writing was her passion, though "Writing for a living was a dream that I had, but . . .

[it] never seemed a realistic option as I was growing up" (Carroll, 197). However, she confesses, "Once I started writing, the happiness I felt was overwhelming . . . [as writing] allow[ed] me to follow my own natural rhythms" (Carroll, 201). Influenced by such writers as Willa Cather, Fyodor Dostoyevsky, and TONI MORRISON, and following her "natural rhythms," Parker published her first novel, *These Same Long Bones* (1994).

Rich in striking metaphors, *These Same Long Bones* is set in the Durham of Parker's childhood, on the eve of integration. It captures the experiences of a middle-class couple, Sirus and Aileen McDougald, as they struggle to come to terms with the tragic death of their daughter Mattie and with their own fears and suspicions about how she died. While critics praise the novel's "vivid multiplicity of detail . . . [and] exquisitely drawn characters" (Johnson, 102), Parker's forte in this novel is her ability to dramatize the growing tensions between the black and white communities during an era when the segregated South was poised for change. While detailing several injustices in a racist South, Parker explores the dehumanizing consequences of historical slavery on a "close-knit, thriving, and nurturing" black community, and offers a new literary landscape for its survival. In the *New York Times Book Review,* Josephine Humphreys observes that the novel "shows a life 'both blessed and hard,' sustained by human resilience" (19).

In her ambitious first novel, Parker introduces and develops a vast terrain of themes, including fear, hatred, racism, loss, grief and reconciliation, friendship, the coming of grace, materialism, loneliness and community, community failure, community responsibility, and a loss of community. Like many of her contemporaries, such as MARITA GOLDEN, she probes each theme and often challenges her characters and her readers to test their own resilience.

Three years after publishing her first novel, Parker published her memoir, *Trespassing: My Sojourn in the Halls of Privilege* (1997), chronicling her childhood in Durham, her personal journey in corporate America, and her decision to leave it and become a writer. More specifically, as the title implies, it depicts the growing tensions Parker experienced as a black female "intruder" in corporate America and offers a scathing indictment of the triple oppressions of racism, sexism, and classism that she experienced in white America. Throughout *Trespassing*, Parker boldly articulates her anger and frustration at a society that rejects her as an equal. The last three sections, "Climbing the Ivy," "The Letter of the Law," and "Uppity Buppie," are painful testimonies about the racial discrimination and gender bias experienced by blacks with wealth and education. Parker states that her continued challenge was "to prove that you had what it took, in a system that was convinced it was impossible that you did" (161). In the *New York Times Book Review*, Deborah McDowell praises the work for its "frank[ness], humor and compassion" and claims that it "pleads a worthy case for the privileged few, who should not be expected to barter their dignity and self-respect for the pottage of wealth and position" (22–23).

Although Gwendolyn Parker has written only two literary works, along with two screenplays, she has already made a powerful contribution to the existing body of contemporary African-American literature. She joins such new and emerging voices as Davida Adejouma, TINA MCELROY ANSA, BEBE MOORE CAMPBELL, Patrice Gaines, MARITA GOLDEN, JANET MCDONALD, JILL NELSON, JEWELL PARKER RHODES, and CHARLOTTE WATSON SHERMAN, to name a few, who were also born during the late 1940s and early 1950s and share a spectrum of experiences known to African-American women during the CIVIL RIGHTS MOVEMENT and Black Revolution. Parker lives in Connecticut where she enjoys her life as a writer.

BIBLIOGRAPHY

Carroll, Rebecca. *I Know What the Red Clay Looks Like: The Voices and Visions of Black Women Writers.* New York: Carol Southern, 1994.

Humphreys, Josephine. "The Thing about White People." Review of *These Same Long Bones. New York Times Book Review,* 17 July 1994, pp. 12–19.

Johnson, Cynthia. Review of *These Same Long Bones. Library Journal* 119, no. 5 (15 March 1994): 102–107.

McDowell, Deborah E. "My Life as a Token." Review of *Trespassing: My Sojourn in the Halls of Privilege. New York Times Book Review,* 19 October 1997, pp. 22–23.

McHenry, Susan. "The Making of an 'Uppity' African-American: An Interview with Gwendolyn Parker '72." *Radcliffe Quarterly* (Fall/Winter 1997): 34.

Loretta Gilchrist Woodard

Parker, Pat   (1944–1989)

Blunt, courageous, uncompromising, humorous, willing us with her words to defeat within ourselves the things that divide us, Pat Parker, born in Houston, Texas, has been above all a poet of community. Unlike many of her literary and political contemporaries, in the early 1970s Parker, the youngest of four daughters, claimed solidarity with gay men, in defiance of lesbian separatists, and with white women, in defiance of black separatists. Her absolute openness about being a lesbian when that was an especially transgressive acknowledgment within the African-American community and the writers of the BLACK ARTS MOVEMENT was coupled with absolute respect for that community. Determinedly a poet for the people, when she used an even faintly advanced word, like *protocols,* in a poem, she asterisked it and provided a definition.

Writing out of an oral tradition, in ordinary language, Parker demanded accountability:

> *Brother*
> *I don't want to hear*
> *about*
> *how my real enemy*
> *is the system.*
> *i'm no genius,*
> *but i do know*
> *that system*
> *you hit me with*
> *is called*
> *a fist.*

Among her best-known poems are two whose titles suggest her stripped-down style: "For the white person who wants to know how to be my friend" and "For The Straight Folks Who Don't Mind Gays But Wish They Weren't So BLATANT."

She celebrated and valorized black women's lives, working-class lives, and lesbian lives. She wrote unabashedly autobiographical poetry, and with her words she invited those who had been taught that their lives were not the stuff of poetry to love themselves. In the process, she also encouraged many readers to love poetry, too.

The archetypal image of a woman as midwife at her own birth finds its representation in the opening poem of Parker's *Child of Myself* (1972), which blasts the Genesis myth of Eve being taken from Adam's rib. In no longer claiming "a mother of flesh / a father of marrow," Parker metaphorically gives birth to herself, becomes a poet, a truthteller. Such an image repudiates the biblical denial of women's procreative powers and heals the schism between artistic and procreative conception. Writing about the murders of black children in Atlanta, she titled a poem with the bitterest irony, "georgia, georgia, georgia on my mind." In the title poem of *Womanslaughter* (1978), the poet describes the murder of her sister, Shirley, at the hands of Shirley's ex-husband. Parker calls this a communal act of male violence and announces her allegiance to all women, warning that if one of her "sisters" is hurt or killed:

> I will come with my many sisters
> and decorate the streets
> with the innards of those
> brothers in womanslaughter.

Parker's love, however, was as legendary as her anger, as witnessed by the evocative poem about her first meeting with poet AUDRE LORDE: "My muse sang of you— / watch the sky for / an ebony meteorite." Lorde's foreword to Parker's *Movement in Black* (1978) describes with admiration the precision of Parker's images, the plain accuracy of her visions, and calls her words "womanly and uncompromising."

Parker was the author of five volumes of poetry, including *Pit Stop* (1974) and *Jonestown and Other Madness* (1985). She was married in the early 1960s to playwright ED BULLINS but by the late 1960s had embraced lesbian feminism. Her collaborations with poet Judy Grahn, especially the Olivia record albums *Where Would I Be without You? The Poetry of Pat Parker and Judy Grahn* (1976) and *Lesbian Concentrate* (1977), introduced both poets to wider audiences. Parker's political activism nourished her poetry and took numerous forms, including involvement with the Black Panther Party, the Black Women's Revolutionary Council, and the Women's Press Collective and a nine-year tenure as medical coordinator at the Oakland Feminist Women's Health Center. Pat Parker died at age 45 from breast cancer, survived by her partner of many years, Marty Dunham, and two daughters, Cassidy Brown and Anastasia Dunham Parker.

BIBLIOGRAPHY

Annas, Pamela. "A Poetry of Survival: Unnaming and Renaming in the Poetry of Audre Lorde, Pat Parker, Sylvia Plath and Adrienne Rich." *Colby Library Quarterly* 18 (March 1982): 9–25.

Callaghan, Dympna. "Pat Parker: Feminism in Postmodernity." In *Contemporary Poetry Meets Modern Theory*, edited by Antony Easthope and John O. Thompson, 128–138. Toronto: University of Toronto Press, 1981.

Clarke, Cheryl. "Review of Movement in Black." *Conditions Six* 2 (Summer 1980): 217–225.

Garber, Linda. "Lesbian Identity Poetics: Judy Grahn, Pat Parker, and the Rise of Queer Theory." Dissertation, Stanford University, 1995.

Smith, Barbara. "Naming the Unnamable: The Poetry of Pat Parker." *Conditions Three* 1 (Spring 1978): 99–103.

Lynda Koolish

Parks, Gordon   (1912–2006)

Gordon Parks distinguished himself in numerous artistic fields, winning an international acclaim and stature. Parks has been an accomplished photographer, composer, and film director. His literary achievements have been equally outstanding, as he published autobiographies, poetry, and novels.

Born in Fort Scott, Kansas, in 1912, Park's family and farm background provided him with a work ethic and self-esteem that would be crucial in facing the economic and racist challenges in his life. At 16, following his mother's death, he traveled to stay with a sister and her husband in Minnesota, but it was an uneasy relationship, forcing Parks to leave and survive on his own by working various jobs. By the mid-1930s, while working as a waiter on a train, he was inspired by the beauty of magazine photographs he found in discarded periodicals. He taught himself to use a camera and began to photograph the many people he observed. Bluffing his way into a job as a fashion photographer, Parks began to make a name for himself in Chicago, and he won a position with the Farm Security Administration in 1942 to photograph working-class people. The first black photographer for *Glamour* and *Vogue* magazines, he earned a staff position at *Life* magazine in 1948. His first assignment was to cover gang confrontations in Harlem, and over the next two decades Parks's photographs won him accolades and brought him in contact with numerous celebrities and politicians.

His visual talent translated effectively to motion pictures, and in 1968 Parks completed *The Learning Tree,* the first Hollywood feature film by a black director. On that film, based on his novel of the same title, Parks also served as screenwriter, music composer, and producer. His next film, *Shaft* (1971), introduced one of the black male cinematic icons of the decade, ushering in the attitudes, language, sexuality, and styles of the superheroes of the black urban action genre. Parks followed with a number of additional films, including *Shaft's Big Score* (1972), *The Super Cops* (1974), *Leadbelly* (1976), and, for television's American Playhouse series, *Solomon Northup's Odyssey* (1985).

As he made history in still photography and motion pictures, Parks also nurtured his writing talents. He gained perhaps his largest readership with his three autobiographical books. The first, *A Choice of Weapons* (1966), recounts his struggles at age 16 to be self-sufficient and to survive on his own, while presenting his early love for photography. *To Smile in Autumn: A Memoir* (1979) covers his life from the early 1940s to the late 1970s, as-

sessing his professional success and aspects of being a black celebrity in arenas dominated by whites. The third volume, *Voices in the Mirror: An Autobiography* (1990), touches on his earlier years but provided a more detailed look at his marriages and children, as well as his experiences during the civil rights era, the BLACK POWER movement, the Hollywood studio years, and travels abroad. Toward the end of the book, Parks reflects, "I have learned a few things along the way. The lesson I value most is to take human beings as they are, to take the measure of them; to accept or reject them, regardless of wealth, impoverishment or color" (327).

Parks also went on to complete other nonfiction works, in which he combined essays and photographs to tell his thoughts. *Born Black* (1971) contains essays on black civil rights fighters and highlights a struggling black family in Harlem. *Flavio* (1978) tells the story of a young Brazilian boy named Flavio da Silva, whom Parks met and befriended while photographing the slums of Rio de Janeiro for *Life* magazine. At the same time, in three volumes, Parks complemented his poetry with photographs to explore a range of themes and topics: *Gordon Parks: A Poet and His Camera* (1968), *In Love* (1971), and *Moments without Proper Names* (1975).

Of his fiction, two novels were published: *The Learning Tree* (1963) and *Shannon* (1981). The first novel, inspired by the author's younger years in Kansas, has been the better known of the two and served as the foundation for the 1968 film bearing the same title. The novel follows the coming of age of the black protagonist, Newt Winger, who finds that happiness and tragedy are inextricably connected in his racially divided town. At a pivotal point in the novel, Newt has to choose between his integrity and racial allegiance when he confesses to witnessing a black man murder a white farmer, thereby freeing the accused white man with his testimony. *Shannon*, set in New York City, from World War I to the Great Depression, explores the complexity of American life across racial and class backgrounds and boundaries.

Gordon Parks not only worked in numerous fields but was outstanding in all of them. Over his lifetime, he has been awarded 24 honorary degrees, the NATIONAL ASSOCIATION FOR THE AD-VANCEMENT OF COLORED PEOPLE's Spingarn Medal in 1972, and the national Medal of Arts at the White House in 1988. In *Voices in the Mirror,* he evaluates his purpose as a photographer: "I have, for a long time, worked under the premise that everyone is worth something; that every life is valuable to our own existence. Consequently, I've felt it was my camera's responsibility to shed light on any condition that hinders human growth or warps the spirit . . . whether its victims are black or white" (179–180).

BIBLIOGRAPHY

Donalson, Mel. *Above the Line: Black Directors in Hollywood.* Austin: University of Texas Press, 2004.
Parks, Gordon. *Voices in the Mirror: An Autobiography.* New York: Anchor Books, 1990.

Melvin Donalson

Parks, Suzan-Lori   (1964–   )

Pulitzer Prize–winning playwright, screenwriter, songwriter, novelist, essayist, lecturer, and educator Suzan-Lori Parks was born in Fort Knox, Kentucky, on May 10, 1964. The daughter of an army colonel and educator, Parks lived in several states before her family was transferred to Germany, where she attended high school and learned to speak German. In 1985 she graduated Phi Beta Kappa and cum laude from Mount Holyoke College with a B.A. in English and German literature before pursuing an acting career at the Drama Studio in London for a year. Parks has taught creative writing at a number of institutions, including the Yale School of Drama, the Pratt Institute for the Arts, the New School for Social Research, and the Dramatic Writing Program at California Institute for the Arts (CalArts), where she was the director of the new A.S.K. Theater Projects Writing for Performance program (2000–2004). She is currently a distinguished writing fellow at CalArts and lives in California with her husband, blues musician Paul Oscher.

Parks began her writing career during her sophomore year at Mount Holyoke College, where she studied creative writing with her mentor JAMES BALDWIN, who encouraged her to write plays after hearing her read her works aloud. There is a strong emphasis on historical events, characters, and language throughout her works. Parks's early short plays include *The Sinners' Place* (1984), produced while she was in college, *Betting on the Dust Commander* (1987), *Pickling* (1989), and *Fishes* (1989).

Parks's full-length plays include the Obie Award–winning *Imperceptible Mutabilities in the Third Kingdom* (1989), which is set on the day in 1865 that slaves in America were freed; *The Death of the Last Black Man in the Whole Entire World* (1990), a historical dreamscape of death and nonreligious resurrection; *Devotees in the Garden of Love* (1992), a tragicomedy of courtly ritual; and *The America Play* (1993), which features the protagonist the "Foundling Father," who is obsessed with Abraham Lincoln.

Parks's other full-length plays include Obie Award–winner *Venus* (1996), which traces the life of a young woman who travels from South Africa to Europe with high hopes of becoming successful; a 2000 Pulitzer nominee, *In the Blood* (1999), about the tough life of an inner-city homeless single mother who has given birth to five children by five fathers; and *Fucking A* (2000), based on Nathaniel Hawthorne's *The Scarlet Letter.* In *Fucking A,* set in an indeterminate future where people speak different languages, it is a crime to procreate out of wedlock. Her play *365 Days/365 Plays* (2003) is a 30-hour play with varying lengths. Written for each day over a year, *365 Days* takes note of actual historical events and the passing of celebrities such as Johnny Cash and George Plimpton.

Parks wrote her Pulitzer Prize–winning play, *Topdog/Underdog* (2001), the idea for which came from *The America Play* (1993), in three days. In 2002 it became the first play by an African-American woman to win the Pulitzer. Premiering on Broadway at the Ambassador Theatre in New York, starring Jeffrey Wright as Lincoln and Don Cheadle as Booth and featuring as well hip-hop artist MOS DEF, who later filled the role of Booth, *Topdog/Underdog* depicts the plight of two brothers—Lincoln, a card shark and Abraham Lincoln impersonator, and Booth, a master shoplifter obsessed with becoming adept with the three-card monte con game. With meager family ties, little education, and limited employment opportunities, the brothers act out their misfortunes, each searching for ways to succeed. Performed to great critical acclaim on Broadway and in theaters throughout the United States and Europe, Parks's comic drama was acknowledged by critics as "profoundly moving." It was an extraordinary new departure for Parks, whose work more closely resembles RALPH ELLISON's *INVISIBLE MAN* in its generally more integrationist perspective.

Parks has also written screenplays. Her credits include *Anemone Me* (1990); *Girl 6* (1996), directed by SPIKE LEE; *Gal,* for Universal Pictures; *God's Country,* for Jodie Foster and Egg Pictures; and *THEIR EYES WERE WATCHING GOD* (2005), an Oprah Winfrey Harpo Production of ZORA NEALE HURSTON's classic novel.

Parks received widespread acclaim for her debut novel, *Getting Mother's Body* (2003). Told from a series of first-person narratives and drawing comparisons to ZORA NEALE HURSTON and William Faulkner, two of Parks's literary influences, the novel traces the survivors of Willa Mae Beade as they travel to Arizona to exhume her body to find the jewels that were supposedly buried in her coffin. However, pursued by Willa Mae's former lover, who is committed to having the jewels remain with the body as he had promised, they are unsuccessful.

Parks has received numerous grants and awards from such organizations as the National Endowment for the Arts (1990, 1991), the Rockefeller Foundation, the Ford Foundation, the New York State Council on the Arts, the New York Foundation for the Arts, the TCG-PEW Charitable Trusts, and the Guggenheim Foundation; she also won the PEN-Laura Pels Award. She was twice awarded the Obie for Best New American Play, for *Imperceptible Mutabilities in the Third Kingdom* (1990) and *Venus* (1996). Additional awards include the Whiting Writers' Award (1992), the W. Alton Jones Grant Kennedy Center Fund for New American Plays, the Kennedy Center Fund for New American Plays (1994), Lila-Wallace Reader's Digest

Award (1995), a CalArts/Alpert Award in the Arts (Drama) (1996), a MacArthur Foundation "Genius" Award (2001), and a Pulitzer Prize for Drama for *Topdog/Underdog* (2002). Parks holds honorary doctor of fine arts degrees from Mount Holyoke College (2001) and Spelman College (2005).

Hailed by *The New York Times* as the "year's most promising playwright" in 1989, Parks has become one of America's leading, most innovative and provocative theater artists. Like such contemporaries as LORRAINE HANSBERRY, Anna Deavere Smith, NTOZAKE SHANGE, ADRIENNE KENNEDY, PEARL CLEAGE, Kia Corthron, Cassandra Medley, Lynn Nottage, Karen Jones-Meadows, Marian X (Marian Washington), and Cheryl L. West, she brings a powerful African-American female perspective to contemporary avant-garde theater, reinventing it as a site of "transformation, healing, and regeneration" (Mahone, 11).

BIBLIOGRAPHY

Mahone, Sydné. "The Sista Masses (1970s–1990s): African American Women Playwrights." In *Women Playwrights of Diversity,* edited by Jane T. Peterson and Suzanne Bennett, 11. Westport, Conn.: Greenwood Press, 1997.

Solomon, Alisa. "Signifying on the Signifyin': The Plays of Suzan-Lori Parks." *Theater* 21, no. 3 (1990): 73–80.

Loretta G. Woodard

Paul D

Paul D, "the last of the Sweet Home men" and the youngest of three brothers, is a protagonist in TONI MORRISON's *BELOVED* (1987). *Beloved* is equally the story of his life in bondage and in freedom as it is SETHE's, the heroine's. Readers follow their different efforts to beat back the ever-present and painful past that, despite their every effort to "disremember," seems to dominate their lives as they search for meaning and wholeness through their shared history, stories, (re)memory, and love.

Although Mr. Garner, a somewhat benevolent master, had treated Paul D and his other male slaves kindly, Schoolteacher, who replaced Mr. Garner at Sweet Home plantation after Mr. Garner's death, was determined to emasculate Paul D, whose interaction with a plantation rooster named "Mister" reminded Paul D that, as slave, he was anything but a man. Paul D becomes a fugitive in response to Schoolteacher's determination to break him and make him aware of his status as chattel. However, Paul D is captured and returned to Sweet Home. Shackled to a buckboard with a bit in his mouth that causes his fiery red tongue to hang out, Paul D resembles, in form if not in fact, the wild man Schoolteacher defines him to be. Paul D is left with the painful memory of his experiences, which he sometimes sings in the BLUES that are central to his legacy. Until he is reunited with Sethe, however, he never talks about them. He keeps his pain locked in a "tobacco tin buried in his chest where a red heart used to be. Its lid rusted shut" (Morrison, 71–72), much like Sethe, who symbolically carries the scars of her pain in the form of a chokecherry tree inscribed on her back.

When Paul D attempts to kill Brandywine, his new owner, he is again shackled; however, this time he is placed on a chain gang with 46 men in Alfred, Georgia, where he spends 86 days. At the end of each day Paul D and his fellow prisoners are symbolically entombed in a wooden prison in a ditch. During a torrential rain that converts their prison into a muddy grave as the ditch caves in, the men escape, "simply duck[ing] down and push[ing] out, fighting up, reaching for air" (110).

Paul D, who desperately yearns for a family and personal history, spends the next 25 years searching for the only surrogate family he had known at Sweet Home, which included Sethe, her husband Halle, and his mother-in-law, Baby SUGGS. When he finally finds Sethe, he immediately embraces the opportunity to fulfill his dream, which is immediately affected and deferred by Sethe's ghost child, Beloved. Wanting no interference with her effort to seek revenge on her mother for murdering her, Beloved aggressively confronts Paul D and tries to drive him away. When her efforts fail, Beloved attempts to seduce him sexually. Determined to be patriarch, provider, and protector, Paul D remains relentless in his territorial battle to drive Beloved from the family home at 124 Bluestone Road, only to be rebuffed by Sethe, for whom motherhood and children are priorities.

However, Paul D leaves on his own after Stamp Paid reveals Sethe's heinous crime to him as a way of explaining Beloved's spiteful and venomous behavior. Paul D is unsympathetic and unforgiving. After verbally abusing Sethe—"You got two feet, Sethe, not four" (163)—Paul D, who was known for his sensitivity and compassion, walks out. He finds temporary sanctuary in the cellar of the local church, which, in the end, he comes to view as oppressive as was slavery and his experience on the chain gang in Georgia. In conversations with Stamp Paid, Paul D discovers the path to his own rebirth and redemption and returns to Sethe and Bluestone Road. He gives the "good news" Sethe needed to hear—that she is her own "best thing"—and, in a gesture of humility, offers to wash Sethe's feet. With Paul D, Morrison creates a Christ-like character who, as a result of his own symbolic death and rebirth, is able to suggest that, ultimately, each individual is responsible for his or her own salvation.

BIBLIOGRAPHY
Morrison, Toni. *Beloved.* New York: A. Knopf, 1987.

Wilfred D. Samuels

Pawley, Thomas W., Jr.   (1917–   )
Although his reputation remained primarily within the HISTORICALLY BLACK COLLEGE AND UNIVERSITY circuit, Thomas Pawley was also a successful dramatist. Born in Jackson, Mississippi, Pawley was educated at Virginia State College and Iowa State University. He began his career as the director of drama at Prairie View State University in Texas. He served on the staff of the Atlanta University Summer Theatre before becoming director of drama at Lincoln University (Missouri). Pawley's many one-act plays include *Jedgement Day* (1938), *Smokey* (1938), and *Freedom in My Soul* (1938). *Son of Liberty* (1938) is among his better-known longer works.

Jedgement Day is exemplary among Pawley's one-act plays. Zeke Porter does not share the religious zeal of his wife, Minerva, who is concerned about his salvation. Whereas Minerva attends church every Sunday, Zeke goes solely on communion Sunday, when free wine is served. Moreover, Zeke untiringly argues, the Bible sets aside Sunday as a day of rest. "An' dat's jus' what I'm gonna do!" In a dream, Zeke finds himself after death standing before Gabriel and Mephistopheles on Judgment Day. The two emissaries gamble for his soul, but neither comes out a winner. They decide to divide his body between them. Zeke awakens as the devil's agent comes after him with a knife. Hearing the singing and worshipping across the street from his home, Zeke decides he still has time to be saved. However, he also decides he still has time for a nap and goes back to sleep.

Jedgement Day is filled with humor. Pawley's use of black dialect is reminiscent of the folk characters and culture in ZORA NEALE HURSTON's short stories, such as "Sweat." In many ways, Pawley uses his play as folklore to satirize the black church and churchgoers, who may laugh upon seeing the play but simultaneously recognize themselves in Zeke's behavior, Minerva's commitment to Zeke, and Preacher Brown's fire and brimstone preaching style. In the end, *Jedgement Day* represents well black orality, which is central to the African-American literary tradition.

Wilfred D. Samuels

Perry, Richard H.   (1944–   )

A New York native who was born in the Bronx and raised in Monticello, Perry, a product of the local school system, is a graduate of City College of New York. He holds an M.F.A. degree from Columbia University. For nearly 40 years, Perry has been on the faculty of the department of English at Pratt Institute in Brooklyn, where he is currently the dean of liberal arts and sciences.

Perry has authored three novels: *Changes* (1974), *Montgomery's Children* (1984), and *No Other Tale to Tell* (1994). *Montgomery's Children*, which was reissued in 1998, won the Quality Paperback Books' "New Voices" Award in 1985. Like TONI MORRISON in her novels, particularly *Sula, Song of Solomon,* and *Paradise,* Perry, in *Montgomery's Children,* is concerned with the transformation of an American small town, Montgomery, New York, into an urban, crime-ridden space and its impact on the lives of the affluent, committed Christian black community of freedom seekers who were isolated in the woodlands of central New York before the metamorphosis.

Montgomery's Children might be described as an "ecological novel," given Perry's central theme of deforestation. At the beginning of the novel the narrator explains, "In 1948, people in Montgomery, New York, did not understand that natural resources are limited. So although the opposition to the racetrack was vocal and well organized, none of its energy was directed to the preservation of trees" (3). Soon a four-lane highway connects the formerly undeveloped land between the town and the track, accompanied with restaurants, gasoline stations, motels with waterbeds, and X-rated movies. Even the dope dealer finds a market in this American town to ply his trade. By 1980, when the novel ends, more than the town has been transformed, for equally visibly defective are the now-polluted lives of Montgomery's residents, whose secret lives include murder, infidelity, infanticide, and corruption of every sort. Like Theodore Dreiser and Sinclair Lewis, who wrote at the beginning of the 20th century, Perry, writing at its end, reminds readers that provincialism associated with small-town America remains more fiction than fact. It is only an imagined Garden of Eden.

The recipient of a National Endowment for the Arts award, Perry is also a three-time winner of the New Jersey State Council on the Arts Award for Fiction.

BIBLIOGRAPHY

Perry, Richard. *Montgomery's Children: A Novel.* 2d ed. Columbus, Miss.: Genesis Press, 1998.

Kaye Richards

Peterson, Louis Stamford, Jr.

(1922–1998)

A pioneer in the film industry, Louis Peterson was a playwright, screenwriter, actor, and educator. Born June 17, 1922, in Hartford, Connecticut, he was the son of Louis Peterson, Sr., and Ruth Conover Peterson, bank employees who stressed the importance of a college education. Although, initially, Peterson planned to pursue a degree in music, he graduated from Morehouse College with a B.A. in English in 1944. While at Morehouse, he participated in the Little Theatre and acted in several plays. Peterson attended Yale University from 1944 to 1945; he received an M.A., degree in drama from New York University in 1947.

As an actor, Peterson performed in Edwin Bronner's *A Young American* (1946), Theodore Ward's *Our Lan'* (1947), and *Justice* (1947). For a year, he studied acting with Stanford Meisner at the Neighborhood Playhouse School of the Theatre and the Actors Studio in New York City. While pursuing playwriting, he worked closely with Clifford Odets and Lee Strasberg's Actors' Studio. He wrote his debut play, *Take a Giant Step,* while touring as an actor and stage manager in a production of Carson McCullers's *The Member of the Wedding* and acting with Lee Strasberg. In 1952 he married Margaret Mary Feury; they had two sons before the marriage dissolved in 1961.

Peterson's career reached a turning point in 1953 when his first two-act semiautobiographical play, *Take a Giant Step,* a coming-of-age story, opened on Broadway, earning him critical acclaim in American theater for writing a pioneering work that shattered the race barrier. *Take a Giant Step* did so by focusing on the psychological problems of a black youth reared in a predominantly white neighborhood. Louis Gossett, Jr., then a high school senior, made his stage debut as the sensitive Spencer "Spence" Scott in the initial Broadway production. According to DARWIN T. TURNER, "Afro-American drama came of age professionally with Louis Peterson's *Take a Giant Step*" (12). However, although it received favorable reviews, it ran for only eight weeks and 76 performances at the Lyceum Theater in New York. It was later revived off-Broadway in 1954, where it ran for 246 performances, starring Bill Gunn as Spencer in a production by the New York Theatre Company. Following the tremendous success of *Take a Giant Step,* Peterson wrote scripts for film and television. "Padlocks" on the CBS series *Danger* and *Class of '58,* which was considered a sequel to *Take a Giant Step,* with an all-white cast, were produced in 1954. These were followed by *Joey,* starring Anthony Perkins and Kim Stanley (1956), "The Emily Rossiter Story," produced on the series *Wagon Train* (1957), and "Hit and Run" on the series *Dr. Kildare* (1961).

In addition, Peterson wrote film screenplays, including an adaptation of Shakespeare's *The Tempest* (1957) with Alberto Lattuada, which was produced in Italy. He adapted his own production of *Take a Giant Step* (1960) with Julius J. Epstein, starring Johnny Nash and featuring Ruby Dee. Although he was the first African-American screenwriter in Hollywood, Peterson, finding himself subjected to its instability, left Hollywood in the 1960s. He continued to write, especially plays, but seemed unable to meet the expectations of East Coast theatergoers, who were always awaiting another *Take a Giant Step*. Nevertheless, in April 1962, almost a decade after the debut of his first play, Peterson's *Entertain a Ghost* opened at the Actors Playhouse to poor reviews. His audience was not prepared for the intricate plot, a style he continued in other plays over the next 20 years.

In 1972, Peterson joined the faculty at State University of New York at Stony Brook, where he taught in the department of theater arts. While there, he wrote the screenplay *The Confessions of Nat Turner* in the 1970s and *Crazy Horse,* another semiautobiographical play, staged for a brief stint at the Henry Street Settlement's New Federal Theatre in November 1979. His student production of *Another Show,* concerning the suicide of an adolescent young male, was produced at Stony Brook in February 1983; it captured the attention of Broadway critics during its two-week world premiere.

Peterson was the recipient of the Benjamin Brawley Award for Excellence in English at Morehouse College (1944). *Take a Giant Step was* named as one of the best plays of 1953–54 by the Burns

Mantle Yearbook. He also received an Emmy nomination for *Joey* (1956) and the Black Filmmakers Hall of Fame Award, as a pioneer in the film industry (1975). In 1993, Peterson retired from Stony Brook; he continued writing for the next five years, cowriting a musical with musician and composer Ken Lauber. He died of lung cancer on April 27, 1998, in New York.

BIBLIOGRAPHY

Abramson, Doris E. *Negro Playwrights in the American Theatre, 1925–1959.* New York: Columbia University Press, 1969.

"Peterson, Louis." In *Contemporary Black American Playwrights and Their Plays,* edited by Bernard L. Peterson, Jr., 381–382. Westport, Conn.: Greenwood, 1988.

Turner, Darwin T., ed. *Black Drama in America.* Greenwich, Conn: Fawcett Publication, 1971.

Loretta Gilchrist Woodard

Petry, Ann   (1908–1997)

A novelist, short story writer, essayist, poet, and author of children's and young adult works, Ann Petry was born on October 12, 1908, in Old Saybrook, Connecticut, to Peter and Bertha Lane, the only African-American family in this white New England town at the turn of the 20th century. Her father, Peter Clark Lane, was a pharmacist who owned drugstores in Old Saybrook and in the nearby town of Old Lyme. Her mother, Bertha James Lane, was a chiropodist and the founder and owner of a linen and embroidery business. For their two daughters, the Lanes provided what Ann, their youngest, called a "warm, rich, and life-sustaining environment," filled with books, music, storytelling, travel, and festive celebrations of birthdays and holidays. Like her father, Ann became a pharmacist and worked in the family-owned drugstore in Old Saybrook. Privately, however, Ann, who began reading at age four, desired also to write and publish short stories.

In 1938, Ann married George Petry of New Iberia, Louisiana. They moved to Harlem, where she abandoned her inherited profession and pursued her dream to become a writer. To prepare herself, between 1938 and 1942, Petry studied creative writing with Mabel Louise Robinson, professor of English at Columbia University, who suggested that she study plays. Petry also studied paintings of landscapes. To gain further experience, Petry worked as a reporter and editor for various newspapers from 1938 to 1944, including the *Amsterdam News* and *People's Voice,* where she edited the woman's page, and contributed weekly to her column, "The Lighter Side." Petry published her first short story, "Marie of the Cabin Club" (1939), under the pseudonym Arnold Petri, in Baltimore's *Afro-American.* Set in Harlem, this suspense-romance is often eclipsed by "On Saturday the Siren Sounds at Noon" (1943), which was published in *The Crisis* under her real name. Petry was invited to apply to the 10th annual Houghton Mifflin Literary Contest by an editor who had read the *Crisis* short story. She entered five chapters of her work-in-progress and won in the fiction category, receiving an award of $2,400 and the chance to publish her first novel, *The Street* (1946).

A prolific writer, Petry is the author of three novels: *The Street,* a classic of urban American realism; *Country Place* (1947), a novel of manners that examines class and gender within an all-white New England community; and *The Narrows* (1953), a complex novel of psychological realism. Of Petry's 16 short stories, 13 were published in *Miss Muriel and Other Stories* (1971). She is also the author of *The Drugstore Cat* (1949), a children's story; she created convincing human depictions of well-known slaves in *Harriet Tubman; Conductor on the Underground Railroad* (1955) and *Tituba of Salem Village* (1964), and of less-known saints in *Legends of the Saints* (1970) for juvenile readers. Petry's works have been translated into at least 12 languages. She also wrote essays and poetry, including the essays "The Novel as Social Criticism" (1950) and "The Common Ground" (1965) and the poems "Noo York City 1," "Noo York City 2," and "Noo York City 3" (1976); however, these works were often anthologized under titles that do not bear Petry's name.

Although in the 1950s Petry gained some critical attention, following seminal essays by African-American feminist critics such as Mary Helen Washington, BARBARA CHRISTIAN, and Barbara Smith in the later 20th century, Petry's work received renewed serious critical attention, including such book-length works as Hazel Arnett Ervin's *Ann Petry: A Bio-Bibliography* (1993) and Hilary Holladay's *Ann Petry* (1996). Generally, critics call attention to Petry's style, which they describe as controlled yet electrifying, swift yet absorbing, gripping yet simplistic, detailed yet lyrical. Because of her sensitivity to landscape and to personalities, Petry is said to create narratives that allow readers to see and to feel.

Petry was recognized for her craftsmanship with citations, lectureships, and honorary degrees. In 1946 Martha Foley, the editor of *The Best American Short Stories 1946,* included Petry's "Like a Winding Sheet" in the collection, which she also dedicated to the writer. Petry also received citations from the Greater Women in Connecticut History and from the United Nations Association. She lectured at Miami University at Ohio and was visiting professor at the University of Hawaii. Petry holds honorary degrees from Suffolk University (1983), the University of Connecticut (1988), and Mount Holyoke College (1989). The largest collection of Petry's manuscripts, letters, first editions, and translations are in a special collection at Boston University. Smaller collections are at Yale University, the Woodruff Library at the Atlanta University Center, and Emory University. Although Petry's most celebrated works, *The Street* and "Like a Winding Sheet," remain masterpieces of the African-American fiction of Harlem, in one of her last interviews she asked to be remembered not just for those but for all she had written.

BIBLIOGRAPHY

Bell, Bernard. *The Afro-American Novel and Its Tradition.* Amherst: University of Massachusetts Press, 1987.

Christian, Barbara. "Images of Black Women in Afro-American Literature: From Stereotype to Character." In *Black Feminist Criticism: Perspectives on Black Women Writers,* 1–30. New York: Pergamon, 1985.

Clark, Keith. "A Distaff Dream Deferred? Ann Petry and the Art of Subversion." *African American Review* 26 (1992): 495–505.

Drake, Kimberly. "Women on the Go: Blues, Conjure and Other Alternatives to Domesticity in Ann Petry's The Street and The Narrows." *Arizona Quarterly: A Journal of American Literature, Culture and Theory* 54, no. 1 (Spring 1999): 65–90.

Ervin, Hazel Arnett. *Ann Petry: A Bio-Bibliography.* New York: G. K. Hall, 1993.

Holladay, Hilary. *Ann Petry.* New York: Twayne, 1996.

Hazel Arnett Ervin

Pharr, Robert Deane   (1916–1989)

Novelist and essayist Robert Dean Pharr was born in Richmond, Virginia, in 1916; he grew up in New Haven, Connecticut. Pharr returned south in 1933 to Lawrenceville, Virginia, to attend St. Paul's Normal and Industrial School (currently St. Paul's College). In 1934, he attended Lincoln University (Pennsylvania) and completed his undergraduate degree at Virginia Union in 1939. He continued graduate studies at Fisk, Columbia, and New York universities. Pharr did not have an uninterrupted or easy transition into a writing career; instead, Pharr confronted problems with poverty, alcoholism, and illness. He worked most of his life as a waiter, traveling along the East Coast for employment in resorts and private clubs and living in a single-room occupancy hotel while completing *The Book of Numbers* (Epps). A mentally deranged woman destroyed the only copy of the completed manuscript. After having a nervous breakdown, triggered perhaps by the loss of his manuscript, Pharr recovered and rewrote the manuscript from memory. While waiting tables at the Columbia University Faculty Club, Pharr asked Lewis Leary, chair of the English department at Columbia, to read his manuscript. Leary turned the script over to a friend at Doubleday, which finally published it as *The Book of Numbers* in 1969. It depicts urban landscapes and the lives of black men and women who play and control the numbers and who are heroin dealers and addicts trying to kick their habits.

In his novels, *The Book of Numbers, S.R.O.* (acronym for single-room occupancy [1971]), *The Soul Murder Case* (1975), and *Giveadamn Brown* (1978), Pharr is an ethnographer, revealing and exploring the underworld cultures of black cities like Harlem and Chicago and offering a participating narrator's view of the seemingly limitless talents of the numbers operator, the physical challenges of the recovering addict, and the tenuous lifestyle of the addict determined to keep the drug habit.

In *The Book of Numbers,* Pharr does not omit the southern city, thereby suggesting in all of his novels that major American cities have evolved into black microcosms. The city of El Dorado, Arkansas, in *The Book of Numbers* is an example of such a microcosm. The central characters, Dave and Blueboy, are numbers dealers out to make a fortune from the game. However, when they become wealthy, they catch the attention of white officials, who determine to wrest the numbers business away and crush Dave and Blueboy's power. Reminiscent of RICHARD WRIGHT's *The Long Dream,* in which the black male figure must defend with his life his power in his community, *The Book of Numbers* both celebrates and mourns the struggle to survive against racial bigotry.

Just as he uses aspects of the life of a traveling waiter in *The Book of Numbers,* Pharr also uses elements of his own experiences as a struggling writer in *S.R.O.* With *S.R.O.,* Pharr journeys further into the lives of addicts, drug dealers, prostitutes, lesbians, homosexuals, and the mentally ill, all of whom live in a welfare, single-room occupancy hotel in New York City. While *The Soul Murder Case* focuses on one family's efforts to cope with drugs, *S.R.O.* is more than 500 pages of psychological, social, and interracial study of the tenants in Hotel Logan, which can be seen as a trope for inner-city life. The novel is structured with italicized, inner chapters, which Pharr called "insights" into the events at the Logan. As an alcoholic and part-time waiter with dwindling funds, Sid Bailey, the central character, narrates the lives and interrelationships of the tenants and engages

in extended philosophical discussions about the intersections of drug life, race, and politics. Bailey's co-discussants, residents of the Logan, are the Sinman, a wealthy white drug dealer and addict who believes God is dead, and Sinman's friend, Blind Charlie, a fearsomely large black man with an unpredictable temper. While Pharr romanticizes life at the Logan, his main character, Sid, must nevertheless try to find a means to stabilize his life amid the violence and self-indulgence of the Logan experience.

The Soul Murder Case: A Confession of the Victim adopts the violence of *S.R.O.,* but the violence in Pharr's third novel opens the locked door that encloses the addict fighting to shake drug dependency. Having recovered from being a heroin addict, Bobby Dee, the main character, acknowledges his experience as a former addict in helping Marion, his 15-year-old adopted daughter, shake heroin. Pharr does not spare the reader in reporting the harrowing details of Marion's withdrawal: her violent attack on Bobby to get more drugs, her delirium, diarrhea, nightmares, and sweats. Sex and passion between Candace, Marion's mother, and Bobby match the intensity of the effort to cure Marion.

Pharr's last novel, *Giveadamn Brown,* is a picaresque, comedic adventure set in Harlem and its underworld of drugs. The theme of the outsider moving into an underworld urban community is one that Pharr employed in his first two novels, but in *Giveadamn Brown,* the effect of the naive, small-town southerner outwitting big-time drug dealers is raucous. Except for *The Book of Numbers,* Pharr's novels are out of print. They deserve renewed attention for their incisive study of survival in the black urban underworld.

BIBLIOGRAPHY

Clarke, Graham. "Beyond Realism: Recent Black Fiction and the Language of 'The Real Thing.'" In *Black Fiction: New studies in the Afro-American Novel Since 1945,* edited by A. Robert Lee, 204–221. New York: Barnes & Noble, 1980.

Epps, Garrett. "To Know the Truth: The Novels of Robert Deane Pharr." *Hollins Critic.* 13, no. 5 (December 1976): 1–10.

O'Brien, John, and Raman K. Singh. "Interview with Robert Deane Pharr." *Negro American Literature Forum* 8 (Fall 1974): 244–246.

Schraufnagel, Noel. *From Apology to Protest.* De Land, Fla.: Everett/Edwards, 1973.

Whitlow, Roger. *Black American Literature.* Chicago: Nelson-Hall, 1973.

Australia Tarver

Philadelphia Fire
John Edgar Wideman (1990)

JOHN EDGAR WIDEMAN's novel about the bombing of the house of the political group MOVE by the Philadelphia police department in 1987 garnered him his second PEN/Faulkner award. At the center of the novel are the writer, Cudjoe, and his search for a survivor—a little boy named Simba. The postmodern work is structured by three voices and identities, including that of Wideman. Wideman's metafictional narrative mirrors that of Cudjoe in many ways, and in the text, Cudjoe's search for Simba becomes Wideman's metaphorical quest to understand the tragic life of his own son. The novel's nonlinear presentation, as well as its weaving of multiple rhetorics (rap, Greek tragedy, journalism, etc.), question the nature of "true" stories, of realistic narrative, memory, and history.

The novel not only alludes to Shakespeare's *The Tempest* but signifies on it, implying that it is the play in Western culture that Cudjoe believes needs to be rewritten in order for African-Americans to control perceptions of their collective identity. The play takes place at "the birth of the nation's blues," where Caliban is forced to see himself only through Prospero's eyes, to tell his story only through Prospero's tongue. Wideman uses silence as a controlling image not only to reflect Caliban's inability to construct his own tale but also to suggest that African-American history and culture is still relegated to stereotypes ("de tail within the tale") within the American consciousness.

Cudjoe's investigation of the MOVE bombing and the search for Simba are ultimately fruitless efforts, and Wideman, in the novel, is unable to aid his son. The loss of children, and thus of the fu-ture, permeates the work. Standing at a memorial service for the victims of the bombing, Cudjoe is reminded of a mob that attacked African-Americans in 1850 in Philadelphia. The conflation of the past and the future in the novel's closing sections motivates its readers to consider the still-unresolved and still-violent impact of slavery and racism in America. Wideman returns to this theme in *Two Cities* (1998), using the MOVE incident to explore the black-on-black violence within the urban community.

BIBLIOGRAPHY

Mbalia, Dorothea. *John Edgar Wideman: Reclaiming the African Personality.* London: Susquehanna Press, 1995.

Tracie Church Guzzio

Phillips, Carl (1959–)

Carl Phillips was born in 1959 in Boston, Massachusetts. He was born into an air force family and moved almost every year of his life until he was 10 years old. His father was stationed as a master sergeant in Germany, where Phillips studied German. Phillips wrote poems in high school but went on to study Greek and Latin at Harvard, graduating with a bachelor of arts degree in 1981. He earned a master of arts degree in Latin and classical humanities in 1983 from the University of Massachusetts–Amherst. He also earned a master's degree in creative writing in 1993 from Boston University. Phillips taught Greek and Latin to high school students for eight years. After that, he entered a doctorate program in philology at Harvard. He took time off to write and left the doctorate program after the publication of *In the Blood,* his first collection of poetry, in 1992. He went on to publish *Cortege* (1995), *From the Devotions* (1998), *Pastoral* (2000), *The Tether* (2001), *Rock Harbor* (2002), and *The Rest of Love: Poems* (2004).

About passion, homoerotics, relationships, and dreams, Phillips's poetry is characterized as innovative, bold, and explosive. Critics warmly received Phillips's homoerotic poetry, which harks back to classical Greek and Roman texts, providing a new African-American voice in gay and lesbian writing. Phillips goes beyond his classical roots to address gender, race, and moral issues, avoiding polemic and writing the unexpected. His collection *In the Blood* is marked by reticence and control underscored passion and dreamlike lyrics in a delicate balance.

Before Phillips began publishing, he was awarded the George Starbuck Fellowship from Boston University (given to the graduate student considered the best writer) and a cash award from the Massachusetts Artist Foundation. In 1992 he won the Samuel French Morse Poetry Prize for his first work, *In the Blood.* In 2000 he won the Lambda Literary Award for Pastoral, and in 2001 the Kingsley Tufts Poetry Award for *The Tether.* He has also received an Award in Literature from the American Academy of Arts and Letters, a Guggenheim Fellowship, the Witter Bynner Foundation Fellowship from the Library of Congress, two Pushcart Prizes, and an Academy of American Poets prize. Phillips directs the creative writing program at Washington University in St. Louis.

BIBLIOGRAPHY

"Carl Phillips." *Washington University News and Information.* February 2004. Washington University, St. Louis. Available online. URL: http://news-info.wustl.edu/sb/page/normal/143.html. Accessed May 11, 2007.

Georges, Cynthia. "Phillips' career is poetry in motion." *Record.* May 1, 1997. Washington University, St. Louis. Available online. URL: http://wupa.wustl.edu/record/archive/1997/05-01-1997/3416.html. Accessed May 11, 2007.

Phillips, Carl. *In the Blood.* Boston: Northeastern University Press, 1992.

Kim Hai Pearson
Brian Jennings

Plumpp, Sterling (1940–   )

Legendary as a poet, teacher, and scholar, Sterling Plumpp worked in the cotton fields and cornfields of rural Mississippi, where his maternal grandfather was a sharecropper, during his early youth until an aunt sponsored his education, allowing him to attend Holy Ghost High School in Jackson, Mississippi. With a small scholarship to St. Benedict's College in Atchinson, Kansas, Plumpp began his college education but left two years later for Chicago, where he worked in the post office and briefly, served in the U.S. Army. Plumpp eventually earned his B.A. (1968) and M.A. (1971) degrees in psychology from Chicago's Roosevelt University.

Plumpp, who served on the editorial staff of HAKI MADHUBUTI's *Black Books Bulleting* and published his first poems in HOYT FULLER's *The Negro Digest* (BLACK WORLD), is the author of 14 books of poetry. Plumpp is internationally known for his use of BLUES and jazz, which contextually and structurally center his collected work, including *Portable Soul* (1969), *Half Black, Half Blacker* (1970), *Black Rituals* (1972), *The Mojo Hands Call* (1982), *Ornate with Smoke* (1988), *Blues: The Story Always Untold* (1989), *Johannesburg and Other Poems* (1993), *Hornman* (1995), and *Blues Narratives* (1999). Staccato, fractured lines and discursive, interrupted narratives in his poems parallel the form and rhythm of the blues, suggesting the socially constructed obstacles to wholeness that the blues often explore. In other words, for this Mississippi native son, the blues are defiantly personal. "When a bluesman sings," Plumpp announces, " It / is my history and / it / is my autobiography," since the blues is "Celebration from / denial's mouth."

Plumpp has received several awards, including the Richard Wright Literacy Excellence Award, the Carl Sandburg Literary Award for poetry, and three Illinois Arts Council Awards. In 2001 Plumpp retired from the University of Illinois at Chicago, where he had taught in the English and African-American studies departments for nearly three decades.

BIBLIOGRAPPHY

Collins, Michael. "Sterling Plumpp." In *The Oxford Companion to African-American Literature,* edited by William Andrews, Frances Smith Foster, and Trudier Harris, 583–584. New York: Oxford University Press, 1997.

Lynda Koolish

Polite, Carlene Hatcher   (1932–   )

One of the most original and, until recently, least-read major writers of her generation, Carlene Hatcher Polite was born on August 28, 1932, in Detroit, Michigan. She attended Sarah Lawrence College in New York and later studied at the Martha Graham School of Contemporary Dance before embarking on a successful career as a dancer. In the early 1960s Polite became extremely active in the burgeoning black CIVIL RIGHTS MOVEMENT, eventually organizing the Northern Negro Leadership conference in 1963. In 1964 Polite moved to Paris, where she stayed until 1971. During her time in France, Polite's primary interest shifted from dance to literature, and she began work on her first novel, *The Flagellants,* which was originally published in French in 1966; it was published in English by Farrar, Straus & Giroux in 1967. Polite's second novel, *Sister X and the Victims of Foul Play,* appeared in 1975. In 1971 Polite accepted a position as associate professor of English at the State University of New York at Buffalo, where she would later be promoted to full professor.

Of the African-American novelists who began publishing in the late 1960s, Polite is second only to ISHMAEL REED in her seemingly total commitment to formal experimentation and her willingness to work outside of and contest the essentially realist conventions to which most black novelists of the time adhered. Unlike Reed, however, Polite's political agenda and convictions are always manifest. Each of Polite's novels uses avant-garde techniques to explore the cultural and emotional politics of American and international racism and the difficult particulars of African-American life and gender relations.

The Flagellants unfolds as an intensively extended presentation of the discursive battles of the heroine, the tellingly named Ideal, and her lover, Jimson, as they attempt to find some common ground on which they can build the kind of loving and mutually satisfying relationship that they seem to both desire and dread. Deploying long and often disorienting theatrical monologues, as well as internal musings that serve as corrective counterpoints to their ravings, the couple lacerate each other with historically inflected accounts of the damage that they and, by implication, all African-American men and women, do to each other. Polite's point seems to be that, by refusing to attend to the reality of their similarities and differences and the necessity of a united front in their struggle against a white world committed to the eradication of black humanity and self-respect, black men and women can meet only as "flagellants."

Sister X and the Victims of Foul Play offers a more emotionally measured and playful consideration of many of the same issues. With an almost burlesque linguistic exuberance and formal daring, the novel presents a day in the life of the expatriate black American Abyssinia and her friend and sometime lover Willis B. Black (Black Will) as, over a breakfast of grits in her Paris apartment, they remember the life and attempt to piece together the truth of the death of their friend, the celebrated black dancer Arista Prolo, or Sister X.

In part because of the critical attention that has been accorded African-American women's fiction over the last two decades and the republication of *The Flagellants* by Beacon Press in 1987, in recent years there has been a resurgence of interest in Polite's work. This renewed attention will no doubt be greatly bolstered by the appearance of the two novels that she is purported to have been working on since the publication of her last novel in 1975.

BIBLIOGRAPHY

Coles, Robert. *Black Writers Abroad: A Study of Black American Writers in Europe and Africa.* New York: Garland Publishing, 1999.

Dubey, Madhu. *Black Women Novelists and the Nationalist Aesthetic.* Bloomington: Indiana University Press, 1994.

Reid, Margaret A. "The Diversity of Influences on Carlene Hatcher Polite's *The Flagellants and Sister X and the Victims of Foul Play.*" *Connecticut Review* 18 (Spring 1966): 39–50

Terry Rowden

Powell, Kevin   (1970–   )

Considered one of the most prolific voices of the hip-hop generation, Kevin Powell has produced and inspired a new genre of literature and determined how mainstream America views hip-hop culture. A journalist, poet, hip-hop historian, and political activist, Powell was also one of the original cast members on the first season of MTV's *Real World* in New York. Hailed as "one of America's most brilliant young cultural critics," Powell's writing range includes several collections of poetry as well as edited volumes that explore the politicization of race, class, and gender in popular culture.

The only child of a single mother, Powell was born in Jersey City, New Jersey in 1970. As a child he possessed an intense passion for knowledge and reading. Overcoming obstacles of poverty, he attended Rutgers University, where he studied political science and English. An avid reader and passionate writer, Powell has published at least four books that examine the post–BLACK AESTHETIC period in African-American culture.

His first volume of poetry, *Recognize* (1995), demonstrates how music, hip-hop, and global events shaped his life. Passionately expressing a new flavor of African-American literature, *Recognize* exposes the fears and hopes of urban black America. Powell next coedited with Ras Baraka *In the Tradition: An Anthology of Young Black Writers.* His next work, *Keeping It Real: Post-MTV Reflections on Race, Sex, and Politics* (1997), a collection of four conversational essays that examines America's political and social landscape through personal experiences.

The current hip-hop generation resonates with the generation that produced the HARLEM RENAISSANCE and such writers as LANGSTON HUGHES, CLAUDE MCKAY, and ZORA NEALE HURSTON. Powell and his contemporaries, including Jessica Care More and Zadie Smith, are pioneering the Word Movement. In *Step into a World: A Global Anthology of the New Black Literature* (2000), Powell demonstrates the continuity of the Harlem Renaissance and the Word Movement, yet at the same time he shows the evolution and transformation of newer writing styles and emphasis. *Step into a World* serves as a venue for some of the most profound underground and mainstream observers of black culture, the hip-hop generation, and society. The anthology offers a collection of essays and poems that examine the nature and changing dynamics of

hip-hop, its growing influence on white America, and its minimal respect among mainstream media and music critics.

Capturing the voice of young Americans, Powell's insightful critique offers the traditional literary world a different view of life, popular culture, and politics. His works continue the rich legacy of black literature because they carry a sense of optimism and hope for black America while reflecting the truth and pain of African-Americans, who continue to endure the politics of race, gender, and class in 21st-century America.

BIBLIOGRAPHY

George, Nelson. *Hip Hop America.* New York: Penguin Group, 1998.

Powell, Kevin, ed. *Step into a World: A Global Anthology of the New Black Literature.* New York: Wiley & Sons, 2000.

LaShawn D. Harris

Powell, Patricia (1966–)

Born in Spanish Town, Jamaica, where she was raised by a great-aunt, and educated in England and the United States, where she emigrated with her family in 1982, Patricia Powell holds a bachelor's degree from Wellesley College and an M.F.A. in creative writing from Brown University. Powell continues a well-established tradition of black Caribbean writers who have made significant contributions within the African-American literary tradition. CLAUDE MCKAY (Jamaica), PAULE MARSHALL (Barbados), JAMAICA KINCAID (Antigua), and COLIN CHANNER (Jamaica) are among the award-winning and best-selling black writers who fit this complex category. Powell, whose themes in her novels center around issues of race, gender identity, sexuality, colonialism, and class, formally entered the literary scene with the publication of her first three novels: *Me Dying Trial* (1993), *A Small Gathering of Bones* (1994), and her best-known and well-received novel, *The Pagoda* (1998). All three are set in Jamaica.

In her debut novel, *Me Dying Trial,* Powell focuses on the experiences of Gwennie Agusta Blaspole, a schoolteacher who, caught in a loveless and physically and psychologically abusive marriage, commits adultery and gives birth to Peppy, a love child. Afraid her husband, Walter, will discover her infidelity, Gwennie eventually leaves Peppy, who favors Gwennie's lover, Luther, with her aunt and relocates to Connecticut to achieve independence. *A Small Gathering of Bones,* Powell's second novel, is a bold discussion, through her main characters, Dale, Ian, and Nevin, of two unspeakable and unspoken subjects in Jamaica's patriarchal and homophobic society: homosexual love and the HIV/AIDS epidemic.

In *The Pagoda,* protagonist Mr. Lowe, a Chinese shopkeeper, lives in an arranged marriage with Miss Sylvie, a biracial woman who gave up her dark-skinned children for adoption. They never fully consummate their marriage, however, although they engage in passionate foreplay and fantasy. Mr. Lowe, it is revealed, is a woman who has cross-dressed to pass as a man for more than 30 years because it was illegal for Chinese women to emigrate. Lowe's complex past involves his horrific journey from China to Jamaica, an unwanted pregnancy and the destruction of his business. The novel is about more than cross-dressing, lesbianism, 19th-century colonialism in Jamaica, sexism, or racism. The central metaphor of the novel, found in its title, *The Pagoda,* represents the personal healing and wholeness each character, particularly Lowe, seeks.

Powell was a finalist for the Granta/Best of Young American Novelists Award (1993) and, since 1997, has been the Briggs-Copeland Fellow in Fiction at Harvard. She is the recipient of the Lila-Wallace Readers Digest Writers Award.

Wilfred D. Samuels

Public Enemy

A well-known, influential rap group that had its beginnings at Adelphi University in Long Island in the early 1980s, Public Enemy's members included Chuck D, Flavor Flav, Professor Griff, and DJ Terminator X. With producers Hank Shocklee and the legendary Bomb Squad, Public Enemy revolutionized rap music, helping define hip-hop culture while garnering a place as a major social and political voice. Before 2000 Public Enemy, which was under contract with Russell Simmons's Def Jam records since 1987, had released eight records known for strong political messages. The first album, *Yo! Bum Rush the Show,* contained the important tracks "Rightstarter (Message to a Black Man)" and "My Uzi Weighs a Ton." Both tracks exemplified an early version of Chuck D's sociopolitical style of rap, which would make him famous.

Although 1987 was certainly a monumental year for the group, 1988 was the year Public Enemy ensured a place for itself in hip-hop history by releasing two radical singles that have become hip-hop classics as well as antiestablishment themes. "Bring the Noise" paid homage to Lewis Farrakhan, whom they called a prophet, while assailing black radio stations that refused to play the group's records. According to Bakari Kitwana, "The Nation of Islam . . . [was] largely responsible for politicizing many hip-hop generationers in some shape, form or fashion," including Public Enemy (167). The now-classic "Don't Believe the Hype," which Alan Light called "PE's manifesto of skepticism," followed "Bring the Noise." With Flav and the scratching of Terminator on the hooks, Chuck D responded to criticism directed at the group and himself, declaring: "Suckers, liars, give me a shovel / Some writers I know are damn devils." Chuck D used the lyrics of both songs to promote his emphatic message that the system must be changed and that hip-hop was the means to produce such change. Chuck's message was so impactful that by the end of the year, the heavyweight champion of the world, Mike Tyson, had a leather jacket custom-made with the words "Don't Believe the Hype" stitched into the back.

Later that year, Public Enemy released the classic album *It Takes a Nation of Millions to Hold Us Back,* which, despite the on-stage anti-Semitic and homophobic ravings of Professor Griff, made politically conscious rap acceptable. By tackling such issues as drugs, black-on-black crime, BLACK NATIONALISM, and poverty, Chuck D contributed greatly to building a critical consciousness among a generation. In doing so, he seems to support those critics who argue that "the Hip Hop Nation is the true voice of the black lumpenproletariat whose descriptions of street life are the real thing"

(Kelley, 37). Chuck D promised to deliver 5,000 new, young black leaders, while calling rap the black CNN.

In 1989, at the height of their popularity and of a movement toward youth consciousness, Public Enemy released the single "Fight the Power" for Spike Lee's film *Do the Right Thing*. However, in May 1989, in a *Washington Times* interview, Professor Griff's anti-Semitic comment that Jews caused the evils of the world marked the end for Public Enemy. Chuck D dismissed Griff from the group, reinstated him, and then disbanded the group, though it soon reformed. Public Enemy went on to release singles and albums, including *Fear of a Black Planet* and *Apocalypse '91 . . . The Enemy Strikes Black*. Both albums were filled with more astute political attacks on racism than ever, but Public Enemy never fully recovered from accusations of being anti-Semitic until it was too late. Much like poets AMIRI BARAKA, HAKI MA-DHUBUTI, GIL SCOTT-HERON, and NIKKI GIOVANNI, who sought to use the BLACK ARTS MOVEMENT as a vehicle for black consciousness and liberation, Public Enemy sought to empower their generation and the black community through rap lyrics and hip-hop sounds.

BIBLIOGRAPHY

Kelley, Robin D. G. *Yo Mama's DisFUNKtional!* Boston: Beacon Press, 1997.

Kitwana, Bakari. *The Hip Hop Generation: Young Blacks and the Crisis in African-American Culture.* New York: Basic Ovitas Books, 2002.

Light Alan. "Public Enemy." In *The Vibe History of Hip Hop.* New York: Three Rivers Press, 1999: 165–169.

Matthew Birkhold

Purlie Victorious   Ossie Davis (1961)

Purlie Victorious, OSSIE DAVIS's most lauded theatrical work, is a three-act satire examining traditional southern race relations during the early days of the CIVIL RIGHTS MOVEMENT. With irony-laden humor, *Purlie Victorious* addresses the perpetuation of slavery through the sharecropping system, white liberalism, and the ongoing battle between segregationists and integrationists for control of the South's consciousness and conscience. The play also focuses equally on the interpersonal relationships among African Americans as well as the making and ultimate deification of African-American leaders.

Purlie Victorious Judson, the title character, is an autodidact and preacher who has returned to the South to purchase a church, which will become the first integrated church in Georgia's Cotchipee County. (A Georgia native, Davis patterns the fictional setting after his birthplace, Cogdell, Georgia.) Judson plans to purchase the church, Big Bethel, with a $500 inheritance bequeathed to deceased relatives by the wife of Ol' Cap'n Cotchipee, the plantation owner. With him is Lutiebelle Gussiemae Jenkins, who will pretend to be his cousin Bee, one of the original inheritors. Bee, however, was a college student at the time of her death, and Lutiebelle is not only uneducated but also overly obsequious, idolizing her former white employer to the point of deification. Her character is Purlie's polar opposite, and while Purlie possesses a singular, uncompromising focus toward the purchase of Big Bethel and the duping of Ol' Cap'n Cotchipee, Lutiebelle only wants to please Purlie and eventually become his wife.

Davis rounds out the play with representative characters, Gitlow and Missy Judson, Purlie's cousins. These characters not only represent both the Old Negroes of the South but also speak to the continued plantation system in the South in their roles as sharecroppers, or field hands. Although Gitlow and Missy also want Big Bethel, they are emotionally and psychologically unable to request the money from Ol' Cap'n Cotchipee until Purlie returns, which allows Davis to comment on African-American leaders and leadership as well as the masses who follow them. Ol' Cap'n Cotchipee, a die-hard segregationist and supremacist, has maintained his plantation in much the same manner as existed during slavery. Yet, his son, Charlie, is an integrationist and liberal who challenges his father's system of shares and southern racism and fights, figuratively and literally, for the equality of African Americans, much to his father's chagrin.

Charlie's attitude toward blacks is largely shaped by his relationship with Idella Landy, a house servant who became a surrogate mother to him and represents the mammy figure prominent in the culture and history of the American South. Ossie Davis's *Purlie Victorius* deftly navigates through the South's traditions and mores, forcing the audience to confront certain issues but allowing them to laugh at themselves and each other in the process.

The cinematic adaptation of *Purlie Victorious* appeared in 1963 as *Gone Are the Days*.

Candace Love Jackson

Queen Latifah (Dana Owens) (1970–)

From living in the urban projects to attending the Academy Awards ceremony, Queen Latifah has enjoyed a professional career that has extended from hip-hop to mainstream celebrity status. Born Dana Owens in Newark, New Jersey, she experienced a close family life with both her parents and a brother, nicknamed Winki. At age 8, she followed her brother and other friends in taking a Muslim name, choosing "Latifah" because it meant "sensitive, kind, and delicate." During that same year, her parents separated, transforming her life into a series of difficult, inner-city experiences as she and Winki lived with their mother, Rita. Observing her mother's strength and commitment for a better life, young Latifah discovered her own capabilities. Latifah won popularity during high school by singing in talent shows, performing in school plays, and participating on the girls' basketball team. At the same time, during those high school years, Latifah, like her peers, gravitated toward hip-hop.

Latifah organized her own girls' rap trio, called Ladies Fresh, and began socializing and creating rhymes with a group of male rappers, who called themselves the "Flavor Unit." She soon became the only girl in the Flavor Unit, becoming known as the "Princess of the Posse." Together, the crew of teens wrote lyrics, composed beats, frequented hip-hop clubs, and encouraged one another. Then, at age 18, as she aspired to become known in the local area as a rapper, she added "Queen" to her professional name. By age 19, Queen Latifah signed with Tommy Boy Records, releasing her first album, *All Hail the Queen*, which went on to sell 1 million copies. (Ruth 57)

By 1989, the world of the MC or rapper was male dominated, and other than a short list of well-known women rappers, such as ROXANNE SHANTE, Salt-N-Pepa, JJFad, MC Lyte, and Yo-Yo, Queen Latifah jumped into a highly competitive business, which was on the brink of moving into gangsta rap. However, Queen Latifah took the challenge head-on, using her lyrics to address gender issues. The first album contained the song, "Ladies First," which was a tribute to black women as freedom fighters (Tracy 18). Additionally, other songs on the album presented the lives and viewpoints of black women, including "Latifah's Law" and "Mama Gave Birth to the Soul Children" (Ruth 58).

With her bold expression of a woman's perspective and her African-influenced attire, Queen Latifah developed an image as a dynamic MC who could get the listener on the dance floor or could challenge the listener to think about social, racial, and/or gender messages. Her second album, *Nature of a Sista* (1991), included the song "Fly Girl," which was about men showing respect to women. Her third album, *Black Reign* (1993), was dedicated to her late brother, and it garnered three Grammy Award nominations, with a win for the Best Solo Rap performance for the song, "U.N.I.T.Y." The song received praise for its lyrics which denounced physical violence and sexist language against women. The next album, *Order in the Court* (1998), featured songs that reflected on the deaths of her brother, TUPAC SHAKUR, and the Notorious B.I.G., as well as the self-explanatory tune titled "Black on Black Love" (Ruth 93–94). Her fifth album, *The Dana Owens Album* (2004), was a collection of songs that moved away from hip-hop and featured her vocals with jazz, R & B, and popular tunes.

In addition to her recordings, Queen Latifah composed the inspirational autobiography, *Ladies First: Revelations of a Strong Woman* (1999). Written to motivate women readers toward positive thinking, she states in the text: "The power to be who I wanted to be was—and is—with me the whole time. We all have the power to be the person we set our sights on being." (Latifah 170–171) Her ambitions achieved successful results as Queen Latifah earned a wider fan base with television and film appearances. Her situation comedy, *Living Single* (1993–1998), presented the lives of four African-American professional women, and *The Queen Latifah Show* (1999–2000), a talk show, featured celebrity guests and live music. Then, from 1991 to 2006, she appeared in 17 movies, winning critical praise for her roles in *Set It Off* (1996), *Living Out Loud* (1998), *Chicago* (2002, gaining an Oscar nomination for Supporting Actress), *Beauty Shop* (2005), and *Last Holiday* (2006).

BIBLIOGRAPHY

Donalson, Melvin. *Hip Hop in American Cinema.* Peter Lang Publishing, 2007.

Latifah, Queen. *Ladies First: Revelations of a Strong Woman.* New York: William Morrow and Company, 1999.

Ruth, Amy. *Queen Latifah.* Minneapolis, Minn.: Lerner Publications Company, 2001.

Tracy, Kathleen. *Queen Latifah.* Hockessin, Del.: Mitchell Lane Publishers, 2005.

Mel Donalson

Quest of the Silver Fleece, The
W. E. B. DuBois (1911)

Set in rural Alabama and urban Washington, D.C., *Quest of the Silver Fleece,* W. E. B. DuBois's first novel, examines the racial, cultural, and political tensions of the North and South. While ADDISON GAYLE, JR., identifies *Quest* as the first African-American bildungsroman, Nellie McKay argues that DuBois depicts the first "black" heroine within a sea of near-white female protagonists in early African-American literature. DuBois himself referred to the novel as "an economic study of some merit," depicting the larger social and economic forces acting on the African-American community as the nation moved through swift changes and suggesting a socialist model for change. DuBois uses cotton as a thread that unifies all the characters and critiques the manipulation of poor southern workers through a sharecropping system that was no less than a revised form of slavery. Equally important, in *Quest* DuBois, during a time still dominated by ideas BOOKER T. WASHINGTON set forth in his "Atlanta Exposition Address," also questions racial uplift as a viable strategy for African-American success, promotes the effectiveness of his view of the New Negro and the concept of the Talented Tenth leadership, and argues for black men to value black womanhood.

Blessed Alwyn and Zora Cresswell are the central characters. Their rise from slavery to political empowerment and agency through education and high moral character symbolizes the history of their larger African-American community. On the one hand, Blessed represents the part of the community with available (though limited) opportunities; he is willing to believe in the possibilities of inclusion in the nation. On the other hand, Zora comes from the most humble beginnings; she is a child of the swamp. Although she has suffered almost every baseness imaginable, she finds joy apart from the dominant society. Blessed and Zora are drawn to each other because of their different backgrounds and upbringing, each complementing the skills and talents lacking in the other. Together they dream, plan, and plant a magical crop of cotton harvested from mystical African seeds. DuBois intertextualizes his novel with the familiar western myth of Jason and the Golden Fleece as a reference; *Quest* has corresponding characters, such as Elspeth, Zora's mother, as Medea the witch.

Blessed, a gifted public speaker, quickly makes a name for himself and is given the opportunity to become U.S. treasurer (a titled but mostly honorary appointment) through the assistance of Caroline Wynn, a polished but unscrupulous black woman. He loses the position through his refusal to silence his criticism of the Republican Party's (his own party) treatment of racial issues. He returns to the swamp and recommits himself to community uplift. Zora's time in the North, as a personal assistant to a wealthy white woman,

transforms her into the polished, educated woman Blessed always desired her to become. She also returns home and becomes a great grassroots leader, organizing the sharecroppers to achieve financial independence. Through their commitment to the community, Blessed and Zora are reunited.

BIBLIOGRAPHY

Bell, Bernard W. *The Afro-American Novel and Its Tradition.* Amherst: University of Massachusetts Press, 1987.

Gayle, Addison. *The Way of the New World: The Black Novel in America.* Garden City, N.Y.: Doubleday, Anchor Books, 1980.

Adenike Marie Davidson

Rachel   Angelina Weld Grimké (1916)

ANGELINA WELD GRIMKÉ's *Rachel* was the first full-length drama written in the 20th century by a black female playwright to be performed by black actors for a white audience. Sponsored by the Drama Committee of the NATIONAL ASSOCIATION FOR THE ADVANCEMENT OF COLORED PEOPLE (NAACP) at the Myrtilla Miner Normal School in Washington, D.C. (March 3–4, 1916), Grimké's groundbreaking first production was intended to raise the white audience's awareness of racial inequality. In describing her own play, Grimké stated, "This is the first attempt to use the stage for race propaganda in order to enlighten the American people relating to the lamentable condition of ten millions of Colored citizens in this free republic" (Jones, 134).

A social protest play, Grimké's *Rachel,* like GEORGIA DOUGLASS JOHNSON's *A Sunday Morning in the South* (1925) and Mary Burrill's *Aftermath* (1919), makes a scathing indictment against lynching and the terrible consequences of living in a racist society. Set in New York, *Rachel* focuses on the aftermath of Mrs. Loving's revelation to her children, Rachel and Tom, of the horrible truth that their father, Mr. Loving, the editor of a small southern Negro newspaper, and their stepbrother, Tom Loving, had been lynched by a mob a decade earlier. Following this painful revelation, both Rachel, a graduate in domestic science, and Tom, trained as an electrical engineer, experience racism in the North, where they are unable to obtain permanent employment. Moreover, Rachel, named for her biblical namesake, learns that the children in the neighborhood and her own adopted son, Jimmy, are tormented and called names at school. Overwhelmed by the injustices of white oppression, Rachel rejects a proposal of marriage from John Strong, who also has a college degree but works as a waiter. She vows to spend the rest of her life taking care of black children rather than bringing them into such an insensitive, cruel, cold world.

While some scholars have criticized *Rachel's* sentimentality, melodrama, and awkwardness, others have praised it for its dramaturgical skills, honesty, intensity, and historical significance. Still others have observed how Grimké explores the problems of institutionalized racism, unemployment, poverty, and various issues centering on love, marriage, and motherhood, rendering her play as timely as those of 20th-century playwrights ALICE CHILDRESS, LORRAINE HANSBERRY, and NTOZAKE SHANGE. Although *Rachel* was published in 1920 and later performed in New York City and Cambridge, Massachusetts, subsequent productions have been limited to college campuses, including the 1990 production at Spelman College in Atlanta, Georgia, after more than five decades of neglect.

Although Grimké was not as prolific and visible as some of her contemporaries during the HARLEM RENAISSANCE, she, along with MARITA BONNER, Mary Burrill, May Miller, Eulalie Spence, ALICE DUNBAR-NELSON, and Georgia Douglas Johnson, made an important contribution to a wealth of existing protest literature, which offers a unique vision into the black experience.

BIBLIOGRAPHY

Brown-Guillory, Elizabeth, ed. *Their Place on Stage: Black Women Playwrights in America.* Westport, Conn.: Greenwood Press, 1988.

Jones, Tisch. "Rachel." In *Black Theatre USA: Plays by African Americans 1847 to Today,* rev. ed., edited by James V. Hatch and Ted Shine, 133–135. New York: The Free Press, 1996.

Stephens, Judith L. "Anti-Lynch Plays by African-American Women: Race, Gender, and Social Protest in American Drama." *African American Review* 26, no. 2 (Summer 1992): 329–339.

Loretta G. Woodard

Raisin in the Sun, A
Lorraine Hansberry (1959)

A Raisin in the Sun, which opened on Broadway in 1959, was LORRAINE HANSBERRY's first play to appear on the national stage. An immediate critical and popular success, *Raisin,* which was compared to the masterpieces of Arthur Miller and Eugene O'Neill, won the New York Drama Critics Circle Award in that year. The original production included actors Ruby Dee, Claudia McNeil, and the already celebrated Sidney Poitier and director Lloyd Richards, who went on to work with another major American playwright, AUGUST WILSON. Like Wilson, Hansberry examined the problems of racism in America through the African-American family and through history.

Set in Chicago, *A Raisin in the Sun* follows the Younger family, whose patriarch, Walter Lee Younger, Sr. (Big Walter), has died, leaving a life insurance death benefit of $10,000 as inheritance. As the play opens, Lena Younger (Mama), his widow and legally the sole beneficiary, considers the ways the family as a whole could invest the money to honor the memory of her late husband. Walter Jr. continuously argues with Mama over whether the money should be given solely to him, as he is now the male head of the family, to invest in a liquor store, a source, he is convinced, he will need to provide financial security for the family. As a devout Christian, Lena will not allow herself (or her husband's legacy) to be involved in such a sinful project. Instead, Lena wants to invest in a home in the currently all-white suburbs, where the family can live in the comfort and safety not available to them in the tenements of Chicago's South Side. Mama wants a garden and she wants Travis, her grandson (Walter and Ruth's son), to experience a positive and salubrious childhood as he grows up in a secure place. Lena also plans to invest in the education of her daughter, Beneatha, who is determined to attend medical school.

For the most part, the conflict of the play centers on Lena and Walter Jr.'s different expectations and sense of what is best for the family. However, the play fundamentally is about the family members' various ways of achieving the American dream. Hansberry takes the title of her play from "Harlem," a poem by LANGSTON HUGHES, in which the speaker asks, "What happens to a dream deferred? / Does it dry up / like a raisin in the sun? . . . Maybe it just sags / like a heavy load. / *Or does it explode?*" In this poem, the speaker suggests that dreams that are deferred for too long can result in devastation, even violence.

Also, the generational antagonism Hansberry explores in *Raisin* suggests that as African Americans move through the social classes, their desires and definitions of "equality" change. Hansberry uses the family's dilemmas as an indictment of American society and the often-unattainable dreams that it proffers to its people of color and underclass. The play foreshadowed the political upheavals of the African-American community in the 1960s: on the one hand, the CIVIL RIGHTS MOVEMENT led by MARTIN LUTHER KING, JR., and its rhetoric of the "American dream" valued by Lena; on the other hand, the BLACK NATIONALISM and Pan-Africanism advocated by MALCOLM X, the leaders of the BLACK POWER movement, and writers of the BLACK ARTS MOVEMENT, which are valued by afro-wearing Beneatha, who is interested in exploring her African roots.

When Lena accuses Walter Jr. of not being a "man" like his father, Hansberry also expresses the necessity of African Americans to discuss notions of masculine identity. Walter Jr.'s need to establish his "manhood" is one of the primary concerns of the play. He accuses the women of trying to "keep him down," and whites of treating him like a "boy." In the final act, when he refuses to accept the offer made by the white neighborhood association that would keep the Younger family from moving to the suburbs, Walter Jr. enacts his own dream and creates his own identity.

Finally, in *A Raisin in the Sun* Hansberry makes a definitive statement about the importance of making choices. Her characters are forced to make choices that allow them to control their personal future. Hansberry makes this point most poignantly in her treatment and characterization of the three women characters, Mama (Lena), Ruth (Walter's wife), and Beneatha. Whereas Lena clearly represents the traditional prescribed domestic role assigned to the women of her generation, Ruth, who represents a generation in transition, debates with herself and her mother-in-law whether she has the right to have an abortion, which is something Lena would never have considered. Not only is Beneatha not interested in getting married and being cared for by a man, but also she is fiercely intent on becoming a doctor, a profession generally set aside for men. Beneatha insists on exercising total agency over her life. Interested in experimenting "with different forms of expressions" (53), Beneatha is convinced that she alone—not her mother's Christian God, her brother, her sister-in-law, or anyone else—can choose the direction and outcome of her life. As she tells her mother; "There simply is no blasted God—there is only man, and it is he who makes miracles" (55).

A pioneering work that explored issues of race, class, and gender in the middle of the 20th century, literally decades before it became vogue to do so in the academy, *A Raisin in the Sun* is now a classic of American realistic drama. It continues to be one of America's most widely performed plays.

BIBLIOGRAPHY

Bernstein, Robin. "Inventing a Fishbowl: White Supremacy and the Critical Reception of Lorraine Hansberry's *A Raisin in the Sun.*" *Modern Drama* 42, no. 1 (Spring 1999): 16–27.

Hansberry, Lorraine. "A Raisin in the Sun." In *Contemporary Black Drama, From A Raisin in the Sun to No Place to Be Somebody,* edited by Clinton F. Oliver and Stephanie Sills, 27–120. New York: Charles Scribner's Sons.

Keppel, Tim. "Interpreting Legacies: Echoes of Hansberry's *A Raisin in the Sun* in Wilson's *The Piano Lesson.*" *Griot* 19, no. 2 (Fall 2000): 55–61.

Washington, J. Charles. "A Raisin in the Sun Revisited." *Black American Literature Forum* 22, no. 1 (Spring 1988): 109–124.

Tracie Church Guzzio

Randall, Dudley   (1914–2000)

Dudley Randall was born in Washington, D.C., on January 14, 1914; while he was still a child, his family moved to Detroit, where he spent most of his life. He graduated from Wayne State University in 1949; in 1951, he received a master's degree in library science from the University of Michigan. Randall worked in the foundry at Ford and served in the Signal Corps in the South Pacific during World War II before embarking on his college education. During his college days he worked as a clerk and delivered mail for the postal service. After receiving the library of science degree, he served as a librarian at Lincoln University in Missouri, Morgan State College in Maryland, and Wayne County Public Library in Detroit. He ended his librarian career at the University of Detroit, where he was also poet-in-residence. Married to Vivian Barnett Spencer for 43 years, Randall was father to one daughter. He died at age 86, in Detroit, on August 5, 2000.

In 1965, Randall founded and became the first publisher of Detroit's Broadside Press, through which he succeeded in bringing established poets, such as GWENDOLYN BROOKS and AUDRE LORDE, to a new audience; he also introduced fresh voices, such as NIKKI GIOVANNI and SONIA SANCHEZ, who became major poets of a new generation. Under Randall's leadership, Broadside Press, in its glory days from 1965 to 1976, published more than 400 poets in more than 100 broadsides, books, and recordings. Broadside Press, which continues to publish today, was among the most important and influential presses of the BLACK ARTS MOVEMENT.

As a poet, Randall is best known for his most frequently anthologized poem, "Ballad of Birmingham," which he wrote in response to the Klu Klux Klan's bombing of the 16th Street Baptist Church in Birmingham, in which four young black girls were killed. Set to music by songwriter Jerry Moore, this poem was first published as a broadside; Randall launched the press simultaneously. In this poem, he employs the conventions of the ballad, in which the naive questioner addresses the older, supposedly wiser respondent. In this case, a child asks her mother for permission to participate in a freedom march in Birmingham's streets. Wanting the child to be safe, the mother suggests instead that her baby go to church, fearing the "clubs and hoses, guns and jails," all allusions to Bull Connor's reign of terror in the spring days of 1963 Birmingham. Confident that she is in a "sacred place," the mother's smile freezes when she hears the explosion and races "through the streets of Birmingham / calling for her child" but finding only "the shoe [her] baby wore." As a broadside, the first edition of the ballad recalled the elegiac broadsides of earlier centuries and suggested the possibilities and choices that were available in graphic formatting to beginning poets who wished to be published.

In his poetry, Randall made frequent use of autobiographical incidents for subject matter. His travels to Russia in the summer of 1966 ignited his interest in translating and publishing such Russian poets as Pushkin; his study in Ghana in 1970 allowed him to connect his poetry with his African reflections. When Detroit, among other cities, burst into flames and rioting in the summer of 1967, Randall responded with *Cities Burning* (1968), a collection of poems that reflected the turbulence of the era. When MALCOLM X was assassinated in 1965, Randall and Margaret Burroughs coedited the first book by Broadside Press,

For Malcolm: Poems on the Life and the Death of Malcolm X, a collection that honored a political figure as poetic inspiration: "What they admire in Malcolm is that he didn't bite his tongue, but spelled out the evil done by the white man and told him to go to hell" (xxi). In addition to his work for Broadside, Randall edited *The Black Poets: A New Anthology* (1971), which contributed more new voices, helping define a black poetry that was "turning away from white models and returning to its roots" (xxvi).

Randall was named poet laureate of Detroit in 1981, but his crowning compliment was a Lifetime Achievement Award in 1996 from the National Endowment for the Arts.

BIBLIOGRAPHY
Randall, Dudley. *Cities Burning.* Detroit: Broadside, 1968.

———, ed. *The Black Poets: A New Anthology.* New York: Bantam, 1971.

Randall, Dudley, and Margaret Burroughs, eds. *For Malcolm: Poems on the Life and the Death of Malcolm X.* Detroit: Broadside, 1967.

Margaret Whitt

Reading Black, Reading Feminist: A Critical Anthology
Henry Louis Gates, Jr., ed. (1990)

In his introduction to *Reading Black, Reading Feminist* (1990), editor HENRY LOUIS GATES, JR., explains the importance of an anthology focused on black feminist theory:

> In reading these texts, we overhear a black woman *testifying* about what the twin scourges of sexism and racism, merged into one oppressive entity, actually *do* to a human being, how the combination confines the imagination, perplexes the will, and delimits free choice. What unites these texts, what makes them cohere into that imaginary metatext we call a tradition, is their shared structures and common themes. (7)

To that end, *Reading Black, Reading Feminist* represents what Gates calls "an embracive politics of inclusion" that characterizes the conversation that black women writers have been engaged in through their works (8). He asserts that the anthology is a useful tool not only for reading black women's writing, but for understanding any writing that requires readers to consider their own position in society.

Reading Black, Reading Feminist features such theorists and writers as ZORA NEALE HURSTON, Mary Helen Washington, Michele Wallace, Hazel Carby, HOUSTON BAKER, JR., and JAMAICA KINCAID. It is divided into three subheadings: "Constructing a Tradition," "Reading Black, Reading Feminist," and "Interviews." "Constructing a Tradition" presents various essays that attempt to establish the tenets of black feminist theory. Although there is no one set theory, each essay presupposes the existence of a black woman's literary tradition and thus explicit ways to approach works from that tradition. For example, in "Speaking in Tongues: Dialogics, Dialectics, and the Black Woman Writer's Literary Tradition," Mae Gwendolyn Henderson proposes that black feminist criticism should be a "model that seeks to account for racial difference within gender identity and gender difference within racial identity" (117). Theory is put into practice in the section "Reading Black, Reading Feminist," where critics offer black feminist readings of such works as ALICE WALKER's *The COLOR PURPLE,* HARRIET JACOBS's *INCIDENTS IN THE LIFE OF A SLAVE GIRL,* and GLORIA NAYLOR's *The WOMEN OF BREWSTER PLACE.* Most of the essays feature an author's take on how to read the writings of black women; however, some essays, like Nellie Y. McKay's "The Souls of Black Women Folk in the Writings of W. E. B. DuBois," delve into the larger implications of black feminist theory for African-American literature in general, whether by black women or by black men. The anthology concludes with two interviews, one with RITA DOVE and the other with Jamaica Kincaid. In these conversations, the authors discuss their art as well as the traditions that may have influenced their artistic visions. *Reading Black, Reading Feminist* contin-

ued the trend toward black female literary theory started in the late 1970s in response to the proliferation of published works by African-American women writers.

BIBLIOGRAPHY

Wall, Cheryl, ed. *Changing Our Words: Essays on Criticism, Theory, and Writing by Black Women.* New Brunswick: Rutgers University Press, 1989.

Stephanie Powell Hankerson

Redding, Jay Saunders   (1906–1988)

Literary critic, social historian, educator, and author Jay Saunders Redding was, like W. E. B. DU-BOIS, one of the leading African-American pioneers of the study of race relations in America. Redding was born in 1906 in Wilmington, Delaware, to Lewis Alfred and Mary Ann Holmes Redding, both graduates of Howard University. He grew up in a predominantly white middle-class neighborhood and was home-schooled through the third grade by his parents, who introduced him to the works of poet PAUL LAURENCE DUNBAR. Redding spent his formative years at Howard High School, where he excelled in journalism, debate, basketball, drama, and speech. Redding's English teacher at Howard High School was ALICE DUNBAR-NELSON, Dunbar's former wife and a family friend.

Redding, who began his college career at Lincoln University in Pennsylvania from 1923 to 1924, received a B.A. in English from Brown University in 1928 and an M.A. in 1932. He also attended Columbia University from 1933 to 1934. Choosing a career in education, Redding taught at Morehouse College (1928–31) and Louisville Municipal College (1934–36), and served as chair of the English department at Southern University in Baton Rouge (1936–38) and Elizabeth City State Teachers College (1938–43). He was the first Johnson Professor of English literature and creative writing at Hampton Institute, 1943 to 1966. Toward the end of his teaching career, he taught at Cornell University, where he was Ernest I. White Professor of American Studies and Humane Letters, 1970 to

1975, before becoming professor emeritus, 1975 to 1988. Redding was also a visiting professor at Brown University, 1949 to 1950, and the first black appointed to the faculty. He was a lecturer at several universities and colleges abroad, including in India, Africa, and South America.

A prolific writer, Redding wrote several scholarly works on the black experience in America. DARWIN T. TURNER calls Redding's groundbreaking volume of literary criticism, *To Make a Poet Black* (1939)—which was preceded by the pioneering scholarly contributions of such major 20th-century scholars as Benjamin Brawley's *The Negro in Literature and Art* (1910), Vernon Loggins's *The Negro Author* (1931), Nick Aaron Ford's *The Contemporary Negro Novel* (1936), and STERLING BROWN's *The NEGRO CARAVAN* (1941)—the "best single volume of criticism by a black" (69). Redding divides his book into categories such as "The Forerunners," "Let Freedom Ring," "Adjustment," and his final chapter, "Emergence of the New Negro." In the last, he offers both praise and ridicule of the writers of the HARLEM RENAISSANCE and the period itself. In his introduction to a more recent edition of *To Make a Poet Black,* critic HENRY LOUIS GATES, JR., notes that Saunders attempted "to bring together certain factual material and critical opinion[s] on American Negro literature in a sort of history of Negro thought in America" (xxix) through the 1930s.

Redding followed his first book of criticism with social histories and personal narratives, chronicling the story of black literature in America from its beginnings to the contemporary period. Redding's works address the dominant themes of courage, achievement, and at times betrayal. They include the autobiographical *No Day of Triumph* (1942), his first novel, *Stranger and Alone* (1950), and social histories and observations: *They Came in Chains: Americans from Africa* (1950; revised 1973), *On Being Negro in America* (1951), *An American in India: A Personal Report on the Indian Dilemma and the Nature of Her Conflicts* (1954), *The Lonesome Road: The Story of the Negro's Part in America* (1958), *The Negro* (1967), *Of Men and the Writing of Books* (1969), and *Negro Writing and the Political Climate* (1970).

Redding received numerous awards, including the Rockefeller Foundation Fellowship (1939–40), the Mayflower Award for *No Day of Triumph* (1942), two Guggenheim Fellowships (1944–45 and 1959–60), the New York Public Library citation for outstanding contribution to interracial understanding (1945 and 1946), the National Urban League citation for outstanding achievement (1950), and a Ford Foundation fellowship (1964–65). He also received honorary degrees from Virginia State College, Hobart College, the University of Portland, Wittenberg University, Dickinson College, Brown University, and the University of Delaware. Redding's scholarly articles have appeared in such journals as *North American Review, American Mercury, Atlantic Monthly, Antioch Review, Publishers' Weekly, American Scholar, Phylon, Saturday Review, The Nation, Survey Graphic, American Heritage, New Leader, COLLEGE LANGUAGE ASSOCIATION JOURNAL, Massachusetts Review, Negro Digest, African Forum, William and Mary Review, Contemporary Literature, Boston University Journal,* and *American Studies.*

Hailed as one of the first serious and influential black critics to contribute to his race, Redding, whose literary career spanned the Harlem Renaissance, the Great Depression, the two world wars, and the CIVIL RIGHTS MOVEMENT, championed African-American literature as a subject for serious academic study in the context of American literature. Although he criticized much of African-American literature for its artistic shortcomings, and although he spent the latter part of his life revising and refining his views, he, like Darwin T. Turner, STEPHEN HENDERSON, HOUSTON A. BAKER, JR., and Henry Louis Gates, Jr., set the bar high. He valued specific criteria by which to judge writers and their work. Redding died of heart failure on March 2, 1988, in Ithaca, New York.

BIBLIOGRAPHY

Davis, Arthur P. *From the Dark Tower: Afro-American Writers, 1900–1960.* Washington, D.C.: Howard University Press, 1974.

Gates, Henry Louis, Jr. Introduction. In *To Make a Poet Black,* edited by J. Saunders Redding, vii–xxiv. Ithaca, N.Y.: Cornell University Press, 1988.

Turner, Darwin. "Afro-American Literary Critics: An Introduction." In *The Black Aesthetic,* edited by Addison Gayle, Jr., 57–74. Garden City: Doubleday, 1971.

Loretta G. Woodard

Redmond, Eugene B.   (1937–   )

A poet, playwright, editor, literary historian, educator, and photographer, Eugene Benjamin Redmond is a multitalented writer whose literary art celebrates and embodies the dynamic spectrum of black culture. His skills as an organizer have led him to found or cofound cultural institutions that provide publishing opportunities for a wide range of writers. Redmond was born December 1, 1937, in St. Louis, Missouri. Soon after his birth, Redmond's family moved across the Mississippi River to East Saint Louis, Illinois, where he spent his formative years. Throughout his career as a poet and cultural worker, Redmond has found in East St. Louis a constant source of inspiration and site of presentation for his artistic productivity.

After serving in the U.S. Marines from 1958 to 1961, Redmond began a career as a journalist while pursuing a college education. From 1961 to 1962 he served as an associate editor for *The East St. Louis Beacon.* In 1963, after assisting in founding *The Monitor,* a weekly East St. Louis newspaper, Redmond became one of its editors and writers. In 1964, he earned his bachelor's degree in English literature from Southern Illinois University Edwardsville (SIUE), where he had served as the editor of the student newspaper. Two years later, he completed graduate studies in literature at Washington University in St. Louis.

During the mid-1960s, Redmond, who had begun to publish his poetry on a regular basis, played an active role in the emerging BLACK ARTS MOVEMENT. He published numerous volumes of poetry, including *A Tale of Two Toms: Tom-Tom (Uncle Toms of East St. Louis & St. Louis)* (1968), *Sentry of the Four Golden Pillars* (1970), *Songs from an Afro/Phone: New Poems* (1972), *In a Time of Rain and Desire: New Love Poems* (1973), and *The Eye in the Ceiling: Selected Poems* (1991). In 1973

Redmond released *Bloodlinks and Sacred Places,* a recording that features him reading his poems to music. Overall, his writings focus on black relationships, culture, African heritage, and politics, and he utilizes the stylistics of black speech and music to convey his messages. In 1976, Redmond became poet laureate of East St. Louis; he was inducted into the National Literary Hall of Fame for Writers of African Descent in 1999.

In addition, Redmond is an accomplished literary critic and historian. *Drumvoices: The Mission of Afro-American Poetry, A Critical History* (1976) stands as his most noted contribution to the study of African-American poetry. Covering the years 1746 to 1976, *Drumvoices* illustrates the development of the African-American poetic tradition. Redmond's book serves as a valuable resource for students and scholars of black literary history, as he identifies dozens of lesser-known poets and makes connections among various modes of black expressive culture and poetry.

Combining his interests in literary arts with activism and community development, Redmond has taught writing courses and assisted in the development of cultural events. From 1967 to 1969 he served as a consultant to dancer Katherine Dunham at Southern Illinois University's Performing Arts Training Center. During this time, he also served as a director of language workshops at SIUE's East St. Louis educational initiative, the Experiment in Higher Education. He has taught English and creative writing at Oberlin, California State University, Sacramento, Southern University in Louisiana, and Southern Illinois University Edwardsville.

While he continues to have a distinguished career as a writer and educator, Redmond's services as a mentor to emerging writers and his contributions as an editor are particularly impressive. After the death of his friend HENRY DUMAS in 1968, Redmond became the writer's literary executor, playing a decisive role in bringing Dumas's work into print. He served as editor for Dumas's posthumously published works, including *Play Ebony, Play Ivory* (1974), *"Ark of Bones" and Other Short Stories* (1974), *Knees of a Natural Man: The Selected Poetry of Henry Dumas* (1989), and *Echo Tree: The Collected Short Fiction of Henry Dumas*

(2003). In 1986, Redmond cofounded the Eugene B. Redmond Writers Club, which is based in East St. Louis. For nearly two decades, the group has met regularly for writing workshops and organized community arts programs. In 1991 Redmond founded the literary magazine *Drumvoices Revue: A Confluence of Literary, Cultural and Visions Arts,* which has published the works of several established poets and hundreds of emerging writers.

Finally, blending his skills as a reporter with his interests in literary history, Redmond began taking photographs of fellow writers and cultural workers in the 1970s. Over the past three decades, this practice has resulted in a collection of more than 60,000 photographs, primarily of African-American writers, creative intellectuals, and political figures. His collection includes in-depth pictorial narrative of AMIRI BARAKA, MAYA ANGELOU, SONIA SANCHEZ, and HAKI MADHUBUTI, to name a few. An exhibit, *Visualizing Black Writers: An Extra-literary Exhibit from the Eugene B. Redmond Collection,* focusing on Redmond's photographs was mounted at Southern Illinois Edwardsville and later at the University of Ibadan in Nigeria in 2004. His poems that represent the features of African-American life, his editorial and critical projects that document black literary history, and his extensive collection of photographs place Eugene Redmond as the chronicler extraordinaire.

BIBLIOGRAPHY

Burton, Jennifer, "Redmond, Eugene." In *The Oxford Companion to African American Literature,* edited by William L. Andrews, Frances Smith Foster, and Trudier Harris, 623–624. New York: Oxford University Press, 1997.

Onwueme, Tess, "Another African Artist's Wayward Thoughts on Eugene Redmond's Poetry." In *Dreams Deferred, Dead or Alive: African Perspectives on African-American Writers,* edited by Femi Ojo-Ade, 83–95. Westport, Conn.: Greenwood Press, 1986, 1996.

Pettis, Joyce, "Eugene B. Redmond," in *Dictionary of Literary Biography.* Vol. 41, *Afro-American Poets since 1955,* edited by Trudier Harris and Thadious M. Davis, 274–281. Detroit, Mich.: Gayle Research, 1985.

Howard Rambsy II

Reed, Ishmael   (1938–)

Ishmael Reed has written nine novels, four collections of essays, five plays, and five collections of poetry. He has also recorded an album of his work, written a libretto, and cofounded several journals, foundations, and a publishing company. The life of this prolific artist began in humble surroundings. Born in Chattanooga, Tennessee, on February 22, 1938, Reed cultivated a love of art and expression at an early age. He moved to Buffalo, New York, with his mother, Thelma Coleman, and his stepfather, Bennie Reed in 1942. As a young child he wrote stories and performed them at school. By age 14 he was writing a regular jazz column for the African-American community newspaper, *Empire Star Weekly.* Reed graduated from high school in 1956 and started attending Millard Filmore College before transferring to the University at Buffalo. Though he never completed a degree, Reed has since received an honorary doctorate from the State University of New York at Buffalo.

By 1960, Reed had dropped out of college and married Priscilla Thompson, with whom he had a daughter, Timothy Brett, who was born in the same year. During the early 1960s, Reed developed his craft, worked for *Umbra* magazine, and interviewed thinkers and artists, among them MALCOLM X. Reed's involvement with *Umbra* exposed him to some of the most influential writers of the BLACK ARTS MOVEMENT, a group he would later criticize in his fiction and essays. In 1963 Reed separated from his wife. They divorced in 1970, and Reed later married dancer and choreographer Carla Blank. By 1967 Reed had moved on to Berkeley, California, and published his first novel, *Free-Lance Pallbearers.* Reed began teaching at the University of California, Berkeley. He was denied tenure there in 1977 (the same year his daughter, Tennessee, was born). He has since taught at Yale, Harvard, Dartmouth, Columbia, University of Washington, and State University of New York–Buffalo.

During his career, Reed has both garnered praise and courted controversy. One of the few African-American satirists, Reed's postmodern, complex style and uncompromising dedication to literary, political, and cultural freedom, has earned him as many detractors as fans. He has steadfastly fought to speak his mind in the manner that suits him best. An outspoken advocate of individuality and iconoclasm, he is also, perhaps somewhat paradoxically, deeply devoted to the community of artists. He co-created the Before Columbus Foundation, which celebrates the work of multicultural writers. He also edited the poetry and fiction anthologies of the foundation and helped establish its American Book Awards. He was also the cofounder of a publishing company and several journals (including *Yardbird*), all committed to presenting and nurturing writers.

Reed's project as a writer and editor is to satirize and parody Western tradition, ideologues, public figures, and historiography—whatever stands in the way of the freedom of expression, of telling one's own story. Reed consistently works to dismantle African-American stereotypes, the "fictions" that others have created. This is diversity and multiculturalism as practiced by Reed. No one story should take precedence over another, and all stories and styles are valid as long as they take other voices into account. Reed's vision of America is a truly multicultural one, which seeks to illuminate the interwoven complexity of our national and cultural identity. No one story defines us all.

In 1970 Reed formally presented the blueprints of his aesthetic: "The Neo HooDoo Manifesto," published as a prose poem in Reed's poetry collection *catechism of d neoamerican hoodoo church*. The poem defines and celebrates what Reed calls "neo hoodooism." A "neo hoodoo" writer or text is possessed of the spirit, a voice emanating in the African diaspora. The quality is jazzlike in style and content. In an often-quoted remark, the jazz musician Max Roach called Reed the "Charlie Parker of American fiction." The multiple stories and styles, the textual hybridity, the rebellion against tradition, the playful, soulful voice in Reed's work is reminiscent of jazz, or what Reed himself has called "gumbo." Neo hoodoo embraces rhythm, magic, nature, intuition, music, the past, openness, and creativity.

Even his first novel echoes this ideal. The hero of the novel is Bukka Doopeyduk, a man who lives in the country called HARRY SAM. Doopeyduk has had little success surviving in this oppressive society until he is asked by the "dictator" to be a mouthpiece for his government. At first, Doopey-

duk agrees, but after undergoing significant changes (including at one point turning into a werewolf) he decides to plan a revolt. This early novel presents many of Reed's major themes. The cartoon-like names illustrate the simplistic stereotypes that others force on African-Americans. Doopeyduk's ability to shape-shift suggests that the only way African-Americans can escape this racism is by "shaping" and redefining their own identities.

This idea is expressed in Reed's second novel, *Yellow Back Radio Broke Down* (1969), as well. A parody of the American western, the work satirizes not only dime-store novels but also the canons of 'Western (i.e., European) literature.' The main character, a cowboy named "the Loop Garoo Kid," also suggests shape-shifting and multiple identities and perspectives. A "garou," etymologically connected to the character's name, is a werewolf. The "kid" symbolizes a new generation of African-American artists, who are attempting battle with literary standards and history. His antagonist, Drag Gibson, represents the white, Anglo-Saxon tradition, while Loop Garoo's other enemy, Bo Shmo, is the leader of a "neo-social realist gang," a description of the Black Arts Movement. Garoo fights for the right to tell his story his way ("what if I write circuses?"), and he is able to achieve this because of his celebration of the neo-hoodoo aesthetic.

Reed's most acclaimed work is *MUMBO JUMBO,* a novel with a multilayered, open-ended plot. Published in 1972, the novel was nominated for the National Book Award. Reed's collection of poetry, *Conjure,* also published in 1972, received a National Book Award nomination as well. It was the first time in the history of the award that a single author had been nominated in two categories in the same year. *Mumbo Jumbo* appears on the surface to be a detective story, but it is really an "anti-detective" story. Reed's purpose is not to unravel the mystery but to celebrate it. The "mystery" surrounds "JES GREW" (JAMES WELDON JOHNSON's term for jazz) and the "Jes Grew" text, a representation in this novel of neo hoodooism.

HENRY LOUIS GATES, JR., calls the novel the "black intertext" and Reed's parodying an "extended commentary on the history of the black novel" (217). The novel is a montage of texts, photos, flyers, music, and so forth. The novel, like American culture, is a composite of multiple voices and traditions. Whites and blacks alike are interested in stealing or destroying the jes grew text. While PaPa LaBas, the "hoodoo detective," searches for jes grew, he uses magic and intuition to help him. Reed criticizes here the genre of the detective novel and its reliance on reason. As in Western tradition, only logic and rational thought can supposedly discover truth. This denies that there are multiple truths or ways to find truth. The lack of closure at the end of the novel reinforces this notion. PaPa LaBas returns as the detective in Reed's next novel, *The Last Days of Louisiana Red.* LaBas tries to solve the murder of a "gumbo works" owner whose gumbo has been found to cure the illness brought on when people forget history. The gumbo (or what Reed has said is a symbol of neo hoodooism) is the way to connect back to the spirit of the African past.

Reed's next novel, *Flight to Canada* (1976), also gained a reputation as an important African-American literary work. A parody of the slave narrative (as well as just about everything else), the novel follows the escape and return of Raven Quickskill, a slave and writer. The novel's numerous anachronisms (a common technique in Reed's fiction) criticize the lack of progress in America's cultural and historical definition of race. The anachronisms and neo–slave narrative structure also argue that little has changed in the ways that African-American expression and history are controlled by white power. Both Quickskill and Uncle Robin (a critical response to Harriet Beecher Stowe's character Uncle Tom [see SAMBO AND UNCLE TOM]) are writers, and in their creative act they can experience some manner of control of their identity and their past. When Quickskill returns to the plantation, he finds that Robin has rewritten his master's will so that Robin is now the owner of the land. He transforms it into a writer's community, which reminds the reader of the power of art to shape the world. As in Reed's other works, writing is neo hoodoo; it is a way to change the stories that have confined African-American freedom and expression.

Reed's remaining novels, *Reckless Eyeballing* (1986), *Japanese by Spring* (1993), *The Terrible Twos* (1982), and *The Terrible Threes* (1989) satirize political correctness, feminism, the Reagan era, the 19th-century novel, the African-American middle class, and academia. The collections of essays *Shrovetide in Old New Orleans* (1978), *God Made Alaska for the Indians* (1982), *Writin' Is Fightin'* (1988), and *Airing Dirty Laundry* (1993) all provide scholars with further examples of Reed's intellect, creativity, and cultural examinations. While there has not been much scholarly consideration of Reed's poetry, it has been critically successful. *The New and Collected Poems* were published in 1988. Reed's three plays, *Mother Hubbard, Savage Wilds,* and *Hubba City,* have not been published, though they have had notable readings.

Reed's significant contributions to African-American literature are evidenced by the longevity and productivity of his career and by the numerous awards he has won. Besides the nominations for the National Book Awards, *Conjure* was also nominated for the Pulitzer Prize. In 1979, Reed won the Pushcart Prize for poetry. He has also won the Poetry in Public Places Award and the American Civil Liberties Award. He has been honored with a National Institute of Arts and Letters Award and a Guggenheim Foundation Award for fiction in 1974. However, his influential place in the African American Literary tradition was solidified by two awards in the 1990s: the Langston Hughes Medal for Lifetime Achievement in 1994 and the prestigious MacArthur Fellowship (the "Genius" award) in 1998. A truer testament to Reed's place in American letters may be that his work never ceases to inflame, inspire, or educate.

BIBLIOGRAPHY

Davis, Matthew R. "'Strange, History, Complicated, Too': Ishmael Reed's Use of African-American History in *Flight to Canada.*" *Mississippi Quarterly* 49, no. 4 (Fall 1996): 734–744.

Dick, Bruce, and Amritjit Singh, eds. *Conversations with Ishmael Reed.* Jackson: University Press of Mississippi, 1995.

Fabre, Michel. "Postmodernist Rhetoric in Ishmael Reed's *Yellow Back Radio Broke Down.*" In *The Afro-American Novel Since 1960,* edited by Peter

Bruck and Wolfgang Karrer, 167–189. Amsterdam: Gruner, 1982.

Fox, Robert Elliot. *Conscientious Sorcerers: The Black Postmodernist Fiction of LeRoi Jones (Amiri Baraka), Ishmael Reed, and Samuel R. Delaney.* Westport, Conn.: Greenwood Press, 1987.

Martin, Reginald. *Ishmael Reed and the New Black Aesthetic Critics.* New York: St. Martin's Press, 1988.

McGee, Patrick. *Ishmael Reed and the Ends of Race.* New York: St. Martin's Press, 1997.

Weixlmann, Joe. "African-American Deconstruction of the Novel in the Work of Ishmael Reed and Clarence Major." *MELUS* 17, no. 4 (Winter 1991): 57–79.

Tracie Church Guzzio

Rhodes, Jewell Parker (1954–)

Novelist, short fiction writer, and essayist Jewell Parker Rhodes was born in Pittsburgh, where she lived through grade three before moving to California. At age 15 Rhodes returned to Pittsburgh, where she lived with her grandmother, since her mother had abandoned the family when Rhodes was very young. Rhodes, who was addicted to watching television during her youth, dreamed of becoming an actress. However, after receiving a bachelor of arts in drama criticism, a master of arts in English, and a doctor of arts in English (creative writing) from Carnegie-Mellon University, she was inspired to become a writer. Although she had written short stories in her youth, Rhodes was first influenced to become a writer after reading GAYL JONES's first novel, *CORREGIDORA*. Rhodes's other literary influences include ZORA NEALE HURSTON, TONI MORRISON, and Charles Dickens.

Like Hurston, Morrison, ISHMAEL REED, and JOHN EDGAR WIDEMAN, Rhodes was inspired to create and weave into her work her own folk magic, as is seen in her first historical novel, *Voodoo Dreams: A Novel of Marie Laveau* (1993). This novel is based on the life of voodoo priestess Marie Laveau of 19th-century New Orleans. Rhodes admits that in the novel Marie Laveau's quest for self-rediscovery becomes "a metaphor for a larger process of rediscovery of lost [African] traditions and lost vision" that African Americans have experienced (Mvuyekure, 402). Spiraling outward from its center, *Voodoo Dreams* also focuses on such themes as sexuality and power, voodoo and Catholicism, South and North, black and white, and three generations of folk heroes and heroines, including Marie and High John de Conqueror. Noting the novel's "splendid and deft narrative style," HOUSTON A. BAKER, JR., asserts that Rhodes "ably demonstrates that she possesses as much conjuring literary ability as some of the most outstanding (and more frequently reviewed) writers in the United States" (158).

Rhodes's *Magic City* (1997), reminiscent of Wideman's *PHILADELPHIA FIRE*, examines the 1920 Tulsa, Oklahoma, riot that took place after the National Guard bombed Greenwood, a thriving black neighborhood, from the air. Though a fictitious account, Rhodes's underlying themes are woven into an even larger context of themes of magic, dream, escape, and survival, as she probes why blacks migrated to Oklahoma and why whites allowed a black community to establish itself but disallowed its economic success and empowerment (Mvuyekure, 404).

The winner of several awards, including Urban Spectrum's #1 Historical Fiction of the Year, Rhodes's finest novel to date, *Douglass' Women* (2002), reinvents the lives of one of the greatest American heroes and orators of the 19th century, FREDERICK DOUGLASS, and the two women in his life—his first wife, Anna Douglass, of 44 years, a free woman of color who bore him five children, and his mistress, Ottilie Assing, a German-Jewish intellectual who simultaneously provided Douglass with the mental companionship he needed. Rhodes resurrects these two extraordinary historical women to imagine the life they led together under the same roof of the Douglass home. Throughout the novel, passion, jealousy, and resentment intertwine as the women negotiate their shared love for this exceptional and powerful man. Like other historical novels, such as BARBARA CHASE-RIBOUD's *Sally Hemings* (1979), Rhodes's

Douglass' Women fills the many gaps and silences that history has left unchanged or unchallenged.

Rhodes, who had difficulty getting her creative work published, has written several guide books, including *Free within Ourselves: Fiction Lessons for Black Authors* (1999), *Celebrating Ourselves: Lessons in Autobiography, Memoir, and Personal Essays for the Black Writer* (2001), and *The African-American Guide to Writing and Publishing Non-fiction* (2002). In them, Rhodes invokes the works of such writers as JAMES BALDWIN, Hurston, BEBE MOORE CAMPBELL, RITA DOVE, HENRY LOUIS GATES, Wideman, E. LYNN HARRIS, CHARLES JOHNSON, Yolanda Joe, and EDWIDGE DANTICAT, among others, to offer inspirational advice and guidance to prospective writers, visionaries and artists.

Rhodes's numerous awards and honors include the Yaddo Creative Writing Fellowship, the National Endowment of the Arts Award in Fiction, the Creative Writing Delegate for the Modern Language Association, an appointment as writer-in-residence for the National Writer's Voice Project, and a Distinguished Teaching Award at California State University and Arizona State University. For *Douglass' Women,* she also received the Pen Oakland Josephine Miles Award, the Before Columbus Foundation American Book Award, and the Black Caucus of the American Library Association Award.

Rhodes is a master of oral traditions, storytelling, and history, and like her contemporaries, MARGARET WALKER, SHERLEY ANNE WILLIAMS, and Chase-Riboud, she has made a valuable contribution to the African-American literary tradition. Now, as she continues to write, she can say with ease: "I am living my best dream. I am a writer . . . a mythic storyteller. . . . I tell stories that I need to believe in, stories that help me through life. . . . That's the nature of myth, I think: to inspire, to awe, to promote belief in miracles in our own lives" ("How I Came to Write"). Rhodes is a professor of creative writing and American literature, the former director of the master of fine arts program in creative writing at Arizona State University (1996–99), and an affiliate faculty of Arizona State's women's studies program.

BIBLIOGRAPHY

Baker, Houston A., Jr. Review of *Voodoo Dreams: A Novel of Marie Laveau. African American Review* 29, no. 1 (Spring 1995): 157–160.

Handman, Fran. Review of *Voodoo Dreams: A Novel of Marie Laveau. The New York Review of Books,* 30 January 1994, p. 24.

Mvuyekure, Pierre-Damien. "Jewell Parker Rhodes." In *Contemporary American Novelists,* edited by Emmanuel S. Nelson, 401–406. Westport, Conn.: Greenwood Press, 1999.

Rhodes, Barbara, and Allen Ramsey. "An Interview with Jewell Parker Rhodes." *African American Review* 29, no. 4 (Winter 1995): 593–603.

Rhodes, Jewell Parker. "How I Came to Write." March 2, 2005. Formerly available online. URL: http://www.pageturner.net/JewellParkerRhodes/voodoo.html.

Loretta G. Woodard

Riggs, Marlon (1957–1994)

Journalist, independent film and documentary producer, and political activist Marlon Riggs was born in 1957 in Fort Worth, Texas. He earned a bachelor of arts degree from Harvard, graduating magna cum laude, and a master of arts degree from University of California, Berkeley, where he also became a tenured professor in the School of Journalism. He participated in activism for a more democratic television, testifying before a U.S. Senate Committee in 1988 to create a public television service that would support independent, nonmainstream voices.

Although Riggs is an accomplished writer, his documentaries earned him the most praise and controversy. Riggs's filmography includes *Ethnic Notions* (1986), *Affirmations* (1990), *Anthem* (1991), *Color Adjustment* (1991), *Tongues Untied* (1991), *No Regret* (1992), *Boys' Shorts: The New Queer Cinema* (1993), and *Black Is . . . Black Ain't* (1994). Beginning with *Ethnic Notions,* Riggs shows how American history is infused with racial stereotypes. *Ethnic Notions* won critical acclaim and has become a standard text in classrooms.

Tongues Untied, on the other hand, generated controversy about public funding for the arts. Riggs, a recipient of a number of grants for the arts, used grant money to create the first documentary about gay, black issues for public television. Even though critics warmly received *Tongues Untied,* like *Ethnic Notions,* the conservative public was angry over a perceived misuse of public funding. *Tongues Untied* is an important exploration of racism and homophobia, positing that gays and lesbians can gain a better appreciation and understanding of their community by celebrating their histories, stories, and sexuality.

Riggs's work is also important because of his experimental, jazzlike method of storytelling. His narrative voices fuse poetry, history, documentary, and autobiography. Because he draws from multiple storytelling methods, Riggs creates a new kind of documentary that is neither wholly documentary nor wholly fiction, while addressing deeply divisive issues like race and sexuality. His most poignant film, *Black Is . . . Black Ain't* explores the complexities of blackness as defined and perceived in the black community, particularly as it relates to the community's multifaceted perspective on racism, sexism, and homophobia. *Black Is . . . Black Ain't* was filmed while Riggs was sick and dying. In the film he speaks from his hospital bed: "As long as I have work then I'm not going to die, 'cause work is a living spirit in me—that which wants to connect with other people and pass on something to them which they can use in their own lives and grow from."

Riggs received the National Emmy Award in 1987 for *Ethnic Notions,* an award for Best Documentary at Berlin for *Tongues Untied* in 1989, and the Maya Daren Lifetime Achievement Award for *Color Adjustment.* He produced films until he died from AIDS in 1994.

BIBLIOGRAPHY

"Biography of Marlon Riggs." *Gravity.* Formerly available online. URL: http://www.newsavanna.com/gravity/BlackIs/biographyofMarl_419.html.
Holmlund, Chris, and Cynthia Fuchs, eds. *Between the Sheets, in the Streets: Queer, Lesbian, Gay Doc-umentary.* Minneapolis: University of Minnesota Press, 1997.

Kim Hai Pearson
Brian Jennings

Ringgold, Faith   (1930–)

Visual artist, storyteller, and feminist activist Faith Ringgold was born on October 8, 1930, at Harlem Hospital in New York City to Andrew Louis Jones, Sr., and Willie Edell Jones (Willi Posey), a fashion designer and dressmaker. An arts graduate from City College in New York City and professor of art at San Diego State University until her retirement in 2003, Ringgold divided her residence between her New York and New Jersey home and studios and Southern California. Her 17 honorary doctorates reflect the art world's broad appreciation of her extensive traveling shows and appearances on university campuses. Ringgold's versatile expression includes paintings, Tibetan-style tankas, performance art, masks, freestanding sculptures, and painted quilts in U.S. museums and international collections. Her publications, primarily children's books, complete this impressive catalogue. *Tar Beach,* the Caldecott Award winner for 1992, is acknowledged by many as a children's classic.

African-American identity and its history motivate her writing, her 14 publications, and her visual art creations. Images expressing struggle and transformation, freedom, and overcoming adversity illuminate this heritage. For instance, Ringgold's picture stories for children, *Tar Beach* and *Aunt Harriet's Underground Railroad in the Sky* (1992), denote freedom through their flying characters. The pathways of "The Coming to Jones Road" an exhibit of a series of prints and paintings that opened at the ACA Gallery in January 2002, are likewise metaphors of freedom. A second focus in Ringgold's work displays historic struggles that promoted societal change and transformation. Although her work is sometimes bloody, such as "The Flag Is Bleeding," a powerful 1960s painting, "peaceful" change and transformation are highlighted in two illustrated children's books, *My Dream of Martin Luther King* (1998) and *If a Bus Could Talk* (1999). The latter is the story of the Rosa Parks sit-in, including biographical material of Parks's frightening childhood in rural Alabama. At that time, the Ku Klux Klan and the nightriders terrified African Americans. Also, Rosa walked to school while her white peers rode buses. The climax of the story is Rosa's courageous sit-in, an example that awakens the world. A parallel to this theme is the MARTIN LUTHER KING story, which embraces a peaceful fight for civil rights. Young readers are dared to fulfill King's dreams. A third theme, finding and surmounting difficulties, underpins Ringgold's engaging autobiographical work *Talking to Faith Ringgold,* coauthored by Linda Freeman and Nancy Roucher. Illustrations of Ringgold's works from the 1980s and 1990s enliven the text, which is appropriate for both young and older adults. The same concept of courage, freedom, and peace resonate in *The Invisible Princes* (1998). Presented in fable-like context with colorful imagery, the book tells of a young girl who leads her oppressed people from slavery to freedom. *Dancing at the Louvre: Faith Ringgold's French Collection and Other Quilt Stories* presents a selected overview of her famed story quilts (paintings with texts) and reflects Ringgold's insight, wit, and joyful take on art world icons. The New Museum of Contemporary Art in New York City and The University of California Press publish it.

Ringgold draws from personal and community histories, from confrontational yet peaceful struggles within and beyond the art world. She presents and explores transformation through paintings, painted story quilts, performance, and writings. In recognition of her vision and creative contributions, she has received more than 75 awards, fellowships, citations, and honors, including the Solomon R. Guggenheim Fellowship and two National Endowment for the Arts awards.

BIBLIOGRAPHY

Cameron, Dan, ed. *Dancing at the Louvre: Faith Ringgold's French Collection and Other Story Quilts.* New York: Simon and Schuster, 1999.

Ringgold, Faith. *Aunt Harriet's Underground Railroad in the Sky.* New York: Random House, 1992.
———. *If a Bus Could Talk.* New York: Simon and Schuster, 1999.
———. *The Invisible Princes.* New York: Crown, 1998.
———. *My Dream of Martin Luther King.* New York: Random House, 1998.
———. *Talking to Faith Ringgold.* New York: Crown, 1996.
———. *Tar Beach.* New York: Crown, 1992.

Donnette Hatch Atiyah

Rodgers, Carolyn M.   (1945–   )

Poet, short story writer, and literary critic Carolyn Marie Rodgers was born in Chicago on December 14, 1945, the daughter of Clarence and Bazella Rodgers. Rogers attended public schools in Chicago and she enrolled at the University of Illinois in 1960. A year later, she enrolled at Roosevelt University in Chicago, where she received her bachelor's degree in 1965. During the mid-1960s, while working as a social worker at the YMCA and with a poverty program, Rodgers began meeting writers associated with the Chicago-based writer's group Organization of Black African Culture (OBAC).

During the BLACK ARTS MOVEMENT, Rodgers emerged as an important writer and member of OBAC, which included HOYT FULLER, then the editor of *Negro Digest/BLACK WORLD;* HAKI MADHUBUTI; Johari Amini; and GWENDOLYN BROOKS. *Paper Soul* (1968), Rodgers's first volume of poetry, was published by THIRD WORLD PRESS, which she cofounded with Madhubuti and Amini. Thematically, *Paper Soul* address cultural identity, religion, black liberation, and a woman's considerations of love. Two of her later volumes of poetry, *Songs of a Black Bird* (1969) and *2 Love Raps* (1969), also published by Third World Press, extend Rodgers's considerations of themes relating to black cultural identity, her role as a black woman poet, street life, and the possibilities of black revolution. In 1975 Anchor/Doubleday published Rodgers's *how i got ovah: New and Selected Poems;* in 1978 it published

The Heart as Ever Green. In these two volumes of poems, which are autobiographical, Rodgers is less concerned with the overt BLACK NATIONALIST ideas that served as a major thrust of the Black Arts Movement. The poems focus on issues pertaining to God, religion, and feminism. Rodgers published two more volumes of poetry, *Translation* (1980) and *Other Poems* (1983).

The central issues Rodgers raises in several of her poems continue to resonate in discussions of African-American literature and culture. For example, "It Is Deep" is concerned with generational conflicts. Recognizing the differences between her own perspectives and those of an older generation of blacks, the young speaker eventually acknowledges the older generation as a "sturdy Black bridge that I / crossed over, on." Similarly, Rodgers's "The Last M.F." is concerned with complex struggles, specifically those of an African-American woman poet working within the context of a Black Nationalist movement that promotes traditional and restrictive views of women. In this poem, Rodgers humorously explains that, within the context of "the new Black Womanhood," "Black Men" encourage women to become or remain reserved and respectful. Ironically and purposefully, throughout the poem Rodgers's speaker uses the word "muthafuckas," proclaiming she will not use this term anymore. Finally, in "Poems for Malcolm," which memorializes MALCOLM X, Rodgers contributes to the larger body of commemoration and "call" poems, making repeated calls for the production and publication of more black poems.

In addition to her poetry, Rodgers published short stories and essays. A series of her writings on black poetry and poetics appeared in *Negro Digest/Black World* between 1969 and 1971. Rodgers's essays, especially "Black Poetry—Where It's At," describes the methods and practices that characterized the poetry of the Black Arts Movement. Utilizing African-American vernacular–based terms to explain the shape and function of 1960s and 1970s black poetry, Rodgers's essays provide an example of African-American literary criticism that is both intellectual and accessible. Moreover, as literary critic Jerry Ward has explained, Carolyn Rodgers's articles provide "prototypes for the thinking" in more recent and well-known African-American literary scholarship, including works by HENRY LOUIS GATES, JR., and HOUSTON A. BAKER, JR. Indeed, Rodgers offered innovative yet grounded models for pursing black literary criticism.

Although she continued to write after the 1970s, reprints and discussions of Rodgers's poetry in anthologies and critical studies suggest that her best-known contributions were made during the Black Arts Movement. Her poetic descriptions of African-Americans and women's experiences, as well as her creative approaches to literary criticism, offer promising ideas about the vitality of BLACK AESTHETIC theories and the new black poetry. Rodgers's focus on topics such as black liberation, culture, women, music, and religion allowed her to address ideas and issues firmly rooted within the tradition of African-American literature.

BIBLIOGRAPHY

Parker-Smith, Bettye J. "Running Wild in her Soul: The Poetry of Carolyn Rodgers." In *Black Women Writers (1950–1980): A Critical Evaluation,* edited by Mari Evans, 393–410. Garden City, N.Y.: Anchor/Doubleday, 1984.

Ward, Jerry W. "Literacy and Criticism: The Example of Carolyn Rodgers." *Drumvoices Revue* 4, no. 1–2 (Fall–Winter 1994–95): 62–65.

Howard Rambsy II

Ross, Frances Delores (1935–1985)

The only daughter of Gerald Ross, a welder from Littleton, North Carolina, and Bernetta Bass Ross, a store clerk from Petersburg, Virginia, Ross was born in Philadelphia, Pennsylvania, where she grew up on Pearl Street in a loving and religious family that included her two younger brothers, Gerald Ross, Jr., and Richard Ross, as well as her maternal grandmother, Lena Bass Nelson. During her teens, Ross accompanied her grandmother to the home of her wealthy employer where her grandmother worked as a domestic. During the summers, she also spent time with her grandmother on Lake Winnipesaukee in New Hampshire in her employer's summer home. By age 16, "Frosty," as she was called, had graduated with honors from Overbrook High School, whose student body was predominantly white and Jewish. Ross received a full scholarship to Temple University, where she earned a B.S. degree in communication, journalism, and theater in 1956.

After working briefly for Curtis Publishing Company, which housed *Saturday Evening Post,* Ross moved to New York in 1960, where she worked as a proofreader and copy editor at McGraw-Hill and Simon & Schuster, as well as a freelance writer. Over the years her articles were published in such magazines as ESSENCE, *Titters,* and *Playboy.* Ross was also was part owner of a mail-order company that produced educational media. Moving to Los Angeles, California, in 1977, Ross worked as a comedy writer for the short-lived *Richard Pryor Show* before returning to New York. According to poet HARRYETTE MULLEN, who wrote the introduction to the reissued edition of Ross's only novel, *Oreo* (Greyfalcon House, 1974), Ross "discovered that she was even more of an anomaly as a black comedy writer in Los Angeles than she had been an editor and author in New York" (xvi).

Oreo is the story of bicultural Christine Clark, who although nicknamed Oriole was called Oreo, after the cookie. Shortly after Oreo's brother, Moishe (Jimmie C), was born, her African-American mother, Helen, and Jewish father, Shmuel Schwartz, separated and then divorced. Helen returned briefly to her parents' home in Philadelphia before joining a touring theatrical group, leaving Oreo and Jimmie C to grow up in an African-American home and environment dominated by their southern grandparents, James and Louise Clark. However, before separating from the family, Shmuel had provided Helen with a piece of paper on which he had written clues that Oreo, when she was old enough to do so, could use to learn and understand "the secret of her birth" (Ross, 9). Before her 18th birthday, Oreo, who had been privately tutored and had grown into an intelligent and perceptive teenager, embarked on her journey to New York to find her father, using the list of

clues he had provided. Her hilarious picaresque quest, grounded in Ross's take on African-American–Jewish relations, resounds with the narrative of the Greek mythological character Theseus, who also searches for his paternal history and identity. By the end of the novel, Oreo successfully finds her father and solves the riddle of her personal history. As Mullen notes, "Oreo claims no cookie cutter identity; rather, she is a character whose cultural hybridity has given her an intimate view of two of the diverse subcultures that made significant contributions to the production of American culture" (xxvi).

Although *Oreo* was published during the height of the BLACK ARTS MOVEMENT, Ross, like JOHN EDGAR WIDEMAN, did not make the demands of the movement's architects or BLACK AESTHETIC prophets relevant to her focus or her definition of herself as a writer. In fact, imaginatively and creatively, Ross seems to move in a counterdirection to the Black Arts Movement in *Oreo.* She debuts as a satirist, adding to this her talent as a writer of comedy, her interest in cartoons, and her love for Jewish culture, particularly Yiddish, which she had heard spoken in school and in the larger Philadelphia community. The result is not only an idiosyncratic novel in which Ross combines ghettoized vernacular (African-American and Yiddish), graffiti, palmistry, cooking recipes, dream books, jokes, and cartoons, but also her creation of what might be called post-realist or "innovative fiction." This fiction moves beyond postmodern fiction to "Super Fiction," in which writers such as Ronald Sukenick, Donald Barthelme, Kurt Vonnegut, Jr., ISHMAEL REED, and CLARENCE MAJOR, to name a few, intentionally set out to reconfigure the language/reality ratio associated with a more traditional, Western art form (Klinkowitz, 3).

Ross makes form and language central issues in *Oreo.* On the one hand, Helen, Oreo's mother, not only speaks standard English but also peppers her sentences with Yiddish, the language she learned from her father, James, who managed a mail-order business that catered exclusively to Jews. Ironically, James had suffered a stroke and stopped talking when he learned of his daughter's plans to marry a "Jew boy" (Ross, 3). On the other hand, Oreo's brother, Moishe (Jimmie C), has his own secret musical language, "cha-key-key-wah . . . a radical second language" (42). Jimmie C's language and character represents Ross's reconfiguration of language and reality. According to Mullen, "Ross aims her satire at the commercialization of culture that tends to produce reductive and often degrading caricature, while it deprives many Americans of a richer, livelier linguistic heritage" (xxiv).

BIBLIOGRAPHY

Klinkowitz, Jerome. *The Life of Fiction*. Urbana: University of Illinois Press, 1977.
Ross, Fran. *Oreo*. Introduction by Harryette Mullen. Boston: Northwestern University Press, 2000.

Wilfred D. Samuels

S

Saint, Assotto (Yves-François Lubin)
(1957–1994)

Writer, performer, editor, and AIDS activist Assotto Saint was born Yves-François Lubin in Port-au-Prince, Haiti, where he was reared. He moved to New York City in 1970, where he attended Queens College as a premedicine major. He also danced with the Martha Graham Dance Company. As his interests broadened to include theater and writing, Lubin chose the pseudonym Assotto Saint. *Assotto* is the Haitian Creole pronunciation of one of the drums used in Vodun (Voodoo) rituals and ceremonies, and Lubin took the name *Saint* from one of his heroes, Toussaint Louverture. Although Lubin initially spelled *Assotto* with only one *t*, he added the second *t* when his CD4 T-cell count fell to only nine.

An outspoken member of the gay and lesbian community, Lubin was committed to speaking the "truth at all costs." He encouraged HIV-infected gay men to be open about their seropositivity (HIV status). As editor of the history-making anthology *The Road before Us* (Galiens Press, 1991), a compilation of the works of 100 black gay writers, Lubin urged contributors not to hide their HIV status, particularly if they were infected. In the introduction Lubin writes, "there is nothing that those of us in this predicament could reveal in our bios that is more urgent and deserving of mention than our seropositivity or diagnosis" (*The Road before Us*, xxi).

Lubin's actions spoke as loudly as did his words. Well known is Lubin's interruption of the funeral service for gay black poet Donald Woods in order to "out" and affirm Woods's life, so Woods would not be buried in secrecy and shame. In his poem "going Home Celebration," Lubin writes, "Donald / the spectacle of your funeral / was a wake-up call from the dead . . . in lunatic denial of an epidemic that decimates us / gay black men" (*Spells of a Voodoo Doll*, 135). This event is the subject of Thomas Glave's short story "The Final Inning," which received the O. Henry Award for Fiction in 1997. Lubin appears in Emmy and Peabody Award–winning filmmaker Marlon Riggs's film *Non, je ne regrette rien*, in which five sero-positive black gay men speak of their individual confrontations with AIDS.

Lubin was founder and artistic director of Metamorphosis Theater, through which, in collaboration with his life partner, Jaan Urban Holmgren, he created and staged theatrical works that focused on the complexity of the lives of black gay men. His works include *Risin' to the Love We Need*, his first play, which was awarded second prize in the 1980 Jane Chambers Award for gay and lesbian playwriting; *New Love Song; Black Fag;* and

Nuclear Lovers. A contemporary, friend, and colleague of such writers as Joseph Beam, Donald Woods, MELVIN DIXON, ESSEX HEMPHILL, David Warren Frechette, Redvers Jeanmarie, and RANDALL KENAN, Lubin was a part of New York's Blackheart Collective, formed in 1981 by a group of artists and writers. During the 1980s and early 1990s, a period that witnessed the death of many black and gay writers, Lubin served as literary executor of the work of several writers who died of HIV/AIDS-related complications.

Lubin was also a charter member of Other Countries: Black Gay Expression, the New York-based black gay writers' collective, which, when it was founded in 1985, helped mark the beginning of what many scholars and critics now consider a renaissance in black gay writing and literature. Lubin served as the poetry editor of the distinguished journal *Other Countries: Black Gay Voices* (Other Countries Press, 1988); he later independently edited and published two anthologies through Galiens Press, which he founded in 1989: the Lambda Literary Award–winning *The Road before Us: 100 Gay Black Poets* (1991) and *Here to Dare* (1992). A third anthology, *Milking Black Bull,* which he conceived and edited, was ultimately published posthumously by Vega Press (1995), one of the few black gay presses in existence at the time.

Lubin's chapbook *Triple Trouble* was published in *Tongues Untied* (GMP, 1987), a British collection that also included the work of Dirg Aaab-Richards, Craig G. Harris, Essex Hemphill, and Isaac Jackson. Galiens Press published two collections of his poetry: *Stations* (1989) and *Wishing for Wings,* which was published in November of 1994, five months after his death. In 1990 Lubin was awarded a Fellowship in Poetry from the New York Foundation for the Arts and recieved the James Baldwin Award from the Black Gay and Lesbian Leadership Forum. A compendium of Lubin's writings, *Spells of a Voodoo Doll: The Poems, Fictions, Essays and Plays of Assotto Saint* (Richard Kasak, 1996), was collected posthumously by his publicist and long-time friend, Michelle Karlsberg.

Considering the realities of the period during which he matured as a writer, Lubin's work, particularly his poems written in the early 1990s, often dealt with AIDS, the politics of AIDS, race, and identity. Much of his work was created "at the mercy of an age where horrific images hang / in an oblivious silence that draws poetry / which must be written / with blood" (*Wishing for Wings,* 1). Succumbing to AIDS-related complications, Lubin died on June 29, 1994, in New York City.

BIBLIOGRAPHY

Hemphill, Essex, ed. *Brother to Brother: New Writings by Black Gay Men.* Los Angeles: Alyson Publications, 1991.

Hunter, Michael B, ed. *Sojourner: Black Gay Voices in the Age of AIDS.* New York: Other Countries Press, 1993.

Jugular Defenses: An AIDS Anthology. London: Oscars Press, 1994.

Larkin, Joan, and Carl Morse, eds. *Gay and Lesbian Poetry in Our Time.* New York: St. Martin's, 1988.

Lassell, Michael. *The Name of Love: Classic Gay Love Poems.* New York: St. Martin's, 1995.

Other Countries: Black Gay Voices. New York: Other Countries Press, 1988.

Saint, Assotto, ed. *Here to Dare: 10 Gay Black Poets.* New York: Galiens, 1992.

———, ed. *Milking Black Bull: 11 Gay Black Poets.* Sicklerville, N.J.: Vega, 1995.

———, ed. *The Road before Us: 100 Gay Black Poets.* New York: Galiens, 1991.

———. *Spells of a Voodoo Doll: The Poems, Fiction, Essays and Plays of Assotto Saint.* New York: Richard Kasak, 1996.

———. *Stations.* New York: Galiens Press, 1989.

———. *Wishing for Wings.* New York: Galiens Press, 1994.

Steward, Douglass. "Saint's Progeny: Assotto Saint, Gay Black Poets, and Poetic Agency in the Field of the Queer Symbolic." *African American Review* (Fall 1999): 507–518.

G. Winston James

Saint James, Synthia (1949–)

Born in Los Angeles, California, self-taught artist Synthia Saint James, who sold her first commissioned painting at age 19, is today recognized internationally as a major African-American artist. In addition to being the first African American to be commissioned to design a holiday stamp, the Kwanzaa stamp, by the U.S. Postal Service, Saint James is also an illustrator of children's books, an author, and a songwriter. She has been commissioned to provide original artwork by Ontario International Airport, Coca-Cola USA, the Girl Scouts of the USA, and ESSENCE magazine, among many others. Her work has decorated the covers of more than 50 books, including works by Iyanla Vanzant, Julia Boyd, ALICE WALKER, and TERRY MCMILLAN.

Although Saint James has published original collections of her prose and poetry, *Girlfriends* (1997) and *Can I Touch You: Love Poems and Affirmations* (1997), she is best known for the 13 children's books she has written or illustrated. Among her best-known illustrated works are *Tukama Tootles the Flute* (1994); *Snow on Snow on Snow* (1994); *How Mr. Monkey Saw the Whole World* (1996); *Neeny Coming . . . Neeny Going* (1996); *Greetings, Sun* (1998); *No Mirrors in My Nana's House* (1998); *Girls Together* (1999); written by SHERLEY ANNE WILLIAMS; *To Dinner, To Dinner* (2000); *Hallelujah: A Christmas Celebration* (2000); and *Enduring Wisdom* (2002), her first Native American book. Her best-known single-authored children's works are *The Gifts of Kwanzaa* (1995), *Sunday* (1996), and *It's Kwanzaa Time* (2001). Saint James is often praised for her solid blocks of color and for her success in introducing the concepts of Kwanzaa to young readers.

Saint James, whom MAYA ANGELOU has lauded for her "heart and art," is the recipient of several major awards and honors, including the Coretta Scott King Honor Award for Illustration, an Oppenheim Gold Award, a National Parenting Publications Gold Award, a Parent's Choice Silver Honor, and the History Maker Award.

Michael Alain Fikes-Samuels

Salaam, Kalamu ya (1947–)

A poet, fiction writer, dramatist, activist, essayist, music and literary critic, journalist, and producer, Kalamu ya Salaam is a dynamic cultural worker whose literary art addresses politics, love, music, and the wide spectrum of black life and history in general. His abilities to blend various expressive forms and work in several mediums allow him to create multifaceted artistic productions. Kalamu ya Salaam was born Vallery Ferdinand III on March 24, 1947, in New Orleans, Louisiana. He attended Carleton College in Minnesota, Southern University in Louisiana, and Delgado Junior College and served in the U.S. Army from 1965 to 1968.

During the late 1960s, Salaam became active in a number of community-based political and cultural organizations, including the World Black and African Festival of Arts and Culture, Free Southern Theater (which changed its name to BLKART-SOUTH in 1969), and Ahidiana (a Pan-African Nationalist Organization). He was a founding editor of the *Black Collegian* and worked for the publication from its inception in 1970 until 1983. Salaam was also an active participant in the BLACK ARTS MOVEMENT of the 1960s and 1970s, his writings appearing in several publications associated with the movement. Over the years, Salaam has organized cultural events and artistic productions and collaborated with veteran writers. In addition, he has led writers' workshops and is the founder of the NOMMO literary society, serving as a mentor to developing writers.

Although Salaam traveled extensively over the course of his career, the South has remained his main base of operation. In an exhaustive bibliography of Salaam's publications, literary critic Jerry Ward wrote, "The breadth of his work marks him as the most prolific African-American writer and thinker of his generation in the South" (106). Salaam's writings address a range of issues, including family, interpersonal relationships, music, the South, African-American liberation, history, and black culture in general. Salaam's literary art consistently addresses what he envisions as social and political imperatives for black people. As he once wrote, "I believe in Black literature socially committed &/or culturally grounded."

Like his fellow poets AMIRI BARAKA, SONIA SANCHEZ, and Jayne Cortez, Salaam frequently incorporates a deep sense of black musicality into his poetry. He often performs his public readings accompanied by a group of musicians known as the "Wordband." A typical Salaam reading might include singing, shouts, nonverbal phrasings, and call and response between the poet and his audience. In short, he blends several black expressive forms into his readings.

Salaam has authored numerous books, including *The Blues Merchant* (1969), *Hofu Ni Kwenu* (1973), *Revolutionary Love* (1978), *What Is Life? Reclaiming the Black Blues Self* (1994), and *A Nation of Poets* (1989). He coedited *360 Degrees: A Revolution of Black Poets* (1998) and *Fertile Ground 1996: Memories and Visions* (1996). He has also produced an audio recording, *My Story, My Song* (1996).

In recent years, Salaam has applied his artistic visions and mixed-media understanding of black expressive culture to new technologies. As a result, he has directed and produced short films focusing on poetry and the arts. He has led seminars for students and cultural workers on how to utilize video as another medium to create artistic productions. His interests in organizing and technology also led him to found CyberDrum, a listserv of black writers and cultural workers. As the moderator of the group, Salaam facilitates the circulation of reports on cultural events and announcements on publishing opportunities to the listserv, which totals more than 1,000 members. Salaam's tireless efforts as an organizer, his dynamic artistic productions, and his focus on issues pertaining to black liberation enable him to create multidimensional and far-reaching cultural work.

BIBLIOGRAPHY

Tombs, Charles P. "Kalamu ya Salaam." In *The Oxford Companion to African American Literature,* edited by William L. Andrews, Frances Smith Foster, and Trudier Harris, 640–641. New York: Oxford, 1997.

Ward, Jerry W., Jr. "Kalamu ya Salaam: A Primary Bibliography (in Progress)." *Mississippi Quarterly* 51, no. 1 (Winter 1997–1998): 105–148.

Howard Rambsy II

Sambo and Uncle Tom

Created during the 18th century, primarily by white writers and dramatists, Sambo and Uncle Tom were among the stereotypes used to maintain the slave economy in the American South. As stereotypes, they were meant to deride African-American males.

Sambo, who can be traced back to the late 17th century, was more than likely an offshoot of the European medieval jester, who, ironically, was accorded knowledge and wisdom. In America, Sambo became the embodiment of follies and foolishness in the plays and popular literature in which he appeared. For example, a 1795 play featured the main character Sambo, a singing and dancing servant who seeks to be the equal of his white owner. Freed in the latter half of the play, Sambo, who is unable to function as an equal, becomes a drunk. By the early 19th century, Sambo characters were represented as either purely comical buffoons or romanticized noble savages. Clearly, such undignified individuals were neither capable nor deserving of freedom. Although the War of 1812 brought a rejection of European ways and a call for a distinctly American form of entertainment, Sambo buffoonery crystallized alongside the more positive images of the emerging American everyman: the Yankee and "Mose," the urban volunteer fireman.

Sambo's popularity continued with the emergence of delineators and minstrels, white actors who performed in blackface and exaggerated attire. In 1822 Charles Matthews, an Englishman, attended a performance of the African Theater Company, a black theatrical troupe in New York City, where he studied the scraps and malaprops of black speech. Matthews also transcribed songs, speeches, and sermons that he used in his own minstrel act. By 1827 minstrelsy introduced the soon-to-be-stock characters of the plantation darky, a slave who moved and thought slowly, and the city dandy, a freed black who comically imitated upper-class whites.

In 1843, the Virginia Minstrels, four white delineators with experience in the circus, introduced to New York City's theatrical stages an act that became the model for the minstrel show (rather than a show with minstrels) when they performed, for the first time ever, an entire evening of comedy from the "Sable Genus of Humanity." Their success led to many large and small, traveling and resident minstrel troupes that performed a variety of stock routines. One sketch that became popular was "Old Uncle Ned," which showed the paternal kindness of slave owners. Ned, a kind old black man, was nursed by his owner through a long illness and painful death. The tears of the master in the first incarnations became the tears of the slave as this minstrel act passed through the century. The slave could no longer live without the master.

Sambo, Ned, and other black stereotypes were turned into a positive force for abolition in Harriet Beecher Stowe's sentimental novel, *Uncle Tom's Cabin or, Life among the Lowly* (1854), based loosely on the story of Josiah Henson, a fugitive slave. Capitalizing on the success of slave narratives like FREDERICK DOUGLASS's *NARRATIVE OF THE LIFE OF FREDERICK DOUGLASS, AN AMERICAN SLAVE, WRITTEN BY HIMSELF* (1843), Stowe countered the image of the black nonhuman other, popularized by those who wished to justify slavery, with her sensitive treatment and characterization of Tom, a devoutly pious and obsequious slave. Ironically, Stowe's novel also codified other black stereotypes, including the ghoulish Topsy, who "jes grew" rather than was born; the assertive black MAMMY, Tom's wife, Aunt Chloe; and the wild, unruly woolly-headed slave children, the picaninnies. The book's popularity led to its immediate and widespread adaptation into minstrel shows, replete with the brave frozen river escape of biracial Eliza with her prized child and the egalitarian sentiments of her noble octoroon husband, George Harris, complementing the sacrificing Uncle Tom, whose bond with his new master's child, Evangeline, helped create an American classic.

The minstrel images and sentimental stereotypes survived the Civil War and boldly reappeared in the latter part of the 19th century—for example, in the historical collection of black folklore published as the *Uncle Remus* stories in the plantation literature of Joel Chandler Harris. African-American writer CHARLES CHESNUTT, in his *CONJURE WOMAN* and *The House behind the Cedars,* sought to challenge these images, directly or indirectly. However, his resolute effort and those of FRANCES ELLEN WATKINS HARPER, BOOKER T. WASHINGTON, W. E. B. DuBois, and others were not enough to overcome the popularity of minstrelsy in 19th-century America. Sambo emerged in the 20th-century motion picture industry, specifically its first epic, *The Birth of a Nation,* and also in a toned-down version with the arrival of talkies like *The Jazz Singer.* During the depression of the 1930s, the Federal Theatre Project of the Works Progress Administration (WPA) promoted the national production of minstrel shows and distributed minstrel scripts. Stowe's *Uncle Tom's Cabin,* rivaled in popularity only by the King James Bible, is still produced as serious drama or parody today.

Much in the way that HARLEM RENAISSANCE authors challenged various forms of literary representations steeped in racist perceptions of African Americans, post–World War II black writers also challenged them head on. RICHARD WRIGHT stands in the vanguard, as the title of his collection of short stories *Uncle Tom's Children* (1938) suggests. Similarly, in *INVISIBLE MAN* (1952), RALPH ELLISON tackles both Owens's presentation of Uncle Remus's Brer Rabbit and the image of the puppetlike dancing Sambo.

However, the most direct criticism came from JAMES BALDWIN in "EVERYBODY'S PROTEST NOVEL." While identifying *Uncle Tom's Cabin* as the "cornerstone of American social protest fiction," Baldwin indicts Stowe and her novel for ultimately giving more hindrance than benefit. Its stereotypes, Baldwin argues, confined rather than liberated, separated blacks from society, and sanitized them for saintly existence with superior whites, as it forgot the enduring bond and mutual bind she (and white society) had with blacks. Baldwin derides Stowe's Uncle Tom for his willingness to endure, solely on the basis of the promise of a metaphysical reward in his future life, as well as Stowe and her descendants for presenting a "lie more palatable than the truth" (16).

Baldwin's attack heralded the rise of social protest of the 1960s CIVIL RIGHTS MOVEMENT and the popular effective resistance to the Sambo image. For example, bowing to this pressure from civil rights groups and adverse publicity, the Philadelphia Shriners New Year's Day Annual Mummers Parade's customary blackface was discarded in favor of goldface. The Sambo pancake restaurant chain, one of the last overt markers, succumbed to protest and pressure in the 1970s. The 1970s also saw copies of the popular 1899 children's book *Little Black Sambo* removed from most public libraries. However, the book is still in print and readily available today.

One of the last challenges to these images of America's antebellum origin in the 20th century is black filmmaker Spike Lee's *Bamboozled*. The film's protagonist believes Sambo to be so repulsive to the American psyche that he instantly rejects his "New Millennium Minstrel Show," a sketch comedy show set on a cotton plantation with black actors in blackface. The show, nevertheless, is a huge success; the film satirizes the television industry at the end of the 20th century as still promoting minstrel images. The dancing Sambo and pious Uncle Tom continue to undergird American popular media into the 21st century.

BIBLIOGRAPHY

Baldwin, James. "Everybody's Protest Novel." In *Notes of a Native Son*, 13–23. Boston: Beacon Press, 1990.

Bogle, Donald. *Toms, Coons, Mulattoes, Mammies, and Bucks: An Interpretive History of Blacks in American Films.* New York: Viking Press, 1973.

Boskin, Joseph. *Sambo: The Rise and Demise of an American Jester.* New York: Oxford University Press, 1986.

Lott, Eric. *Love and Theft: Blackface Minstrelsy and the American Working Class.* New York: Oxford University Press, 1993.

Mahar, William J. *Behind the Burnt Cork Mask: Early Blackface Minstrelsy and Antebellum American Popular Culture.* Urbana: University of Illinois Press, 1999.

Ray Black

Sanchez, Sonia (Benita Driver) (1934–)

With more than 20 books to her name, poet, playwright, essayist, and educator Sonia Sanchez was born Benita Driver in Birmingham, Alabama. Her father, Wilson L. Driver, was a musician and teacher; her mother, Lena (Jones) Driver, died when Sanchez was a baby. By the time Sanchez was six, her grandmother, who had become her surrogate mother, also died. The consequences of these painful losses included stuttering, which Sanchez developed at an early age. At age nine Sanchez moved with her father to Harlem, New York, where she completed secondary school. She graduated from Hunter College with a bachelor of science degree in political science, after which she studied poetry with Louise Bogan at New York University. Writing poetry became a form of healing and a venue to address her speech impediment. At the height of the BLACK ARTS MOVEMENT, Sanchez added her self-empowered though often maudlin and haunting voice to that of male architects AMIRI BARAKA and LARRY NEAL, becoming a central player, along with NIKKI GIOVANNI, MARI EVANS, SARA WEBSTER FABIO, and CAROLYN RODGERS, in its formation and definition. Her voice matched Baraka's in his militant "Black Art." One of her speakers declares, "us blk / niggers / are out to lunch / and the main course / is gonna be … white meat."

Initially committing herself to the fundamental goals of the CIVIL RIGHTS MOVEMENT, although later growing skeptical of mainstream culture, Sanchez joined the Congress of Racial Equality (CORE). However, blacks, she concluded, were required to pay too high a price for integration; she uses as an example the Supremes, Motown's singing divas led by Diana Ross, who, Sanchez noted in her poem "Memorial," had to "bleach out their blackness." After teaching at New York's Community College, Sanchez moved to California, taught at San Francisco State College and became heavily involved in efforts to make black studies an acceptable discipline at University of California at Berkeley. She would also teach at University of Pittsburgh, Rutgers University, City College of the City of New York, and the University of Massachusetts.

Joining another radical poetic voice of the Black Arts Movement, Don L. Lee (HAKI MADHUBUTI), Sanchez began her publishing career at Broadside Press with DUDLEY RANDALL, who, in his introduction to Sanchez's *We A BaddDDD People* (1970), called her a revolutionary and wrote, "This tiny woman with the infant's face attacks the demons of this world with the fury of a sparrow defending her fledglings in the nest. She hurls obscenities at things that are obscene" (9). To confirm this, Randall chooses an image by artist Emory for the cover of Sanchez's *Home Coming* (1971), featuring the silhouette of a young black female warrior, spear in hand, poised to let her weapon fly. And let her weapon—her raw and piercing words—fly is exactly what Sanchez does on each of the 32 pages of her second collection of her poems. In "definition for blk / children," Sanchez's speaker teaches,

> *a policeman*
> *is a pig*
> *and he shd be in*
> *a zoo*
> *with all the other pigs*
> *. . . .*
> *until he stops*
> *killing blk people. (19)*

Singularly important are lessons that celebrate and preserve black culture—black myths. In "now poem. for us," her speaker warns:

> *don't let them die out*
> *all these old / blk / people*
> *don't let them cop out*
> *with their memories*
> *of slavery // survival. (We a BaddDDD 67)*

Equally raw and unadulterated are the former black nationalist and member of the Nation of Islam's celebratory poems, whose central purpose throughout her work is to abandon destructive

white Western values that promote black self-hate, to critique black self-destructive behavior, embrace blackness as a positive signifier, and ultimately celebrate all aspects of black culture. These themes recur in Sanchez's many works, which include *Homecoming* (1969), *A Blue Book for a Blue Black Magical Woman* (1974), *I've Been a Woman: New and Selected Poems* (1980), *Homegirls and Handgrenades* (1984), *Under a Soprano Sky* (1987), and *Wounded in the House of a Friend* (1995). Her poem "nigger" embodies many of these themes:

> *nigger. . . .*
> *that word don't turn*
> *me on man.*
> *i know i am*
> *black.*
> *beautiful.*
> *with meaning. (Homecoming 12)*

Sanchez's racial and cultural affirmative is evident in her very abandonment of the more formal (written/readerly) Western language. She not only validates black vernacular (rap) but creates a musical, jazzlike sound and rhythm in the alphabet she inscribes. Her speech sings; the urban experience is reflected in its language.

Sanchez's critique of Western culture was strongest when she was a member of the Nation of Islam. She directed pronouncements to black women promote the teachings of Elijah Mohammad and the black Muslims in *A Blue Book for Blue Black Magical Women.*

> *Black wooooomen of today must under-*
> *stand*
> *is that looooove /*
> *peace /*
> *contentment will never*
> *be ours for this crackerized country has*
> *dealt*
> *on us and colonized us body and soul. (12)*

Sanchez calls for the preservation and celebration of black heroes and heroines, such as JAMES BALDWIN, TONI MORRISON, Johnnetta Cole, John

Coltrane, Sterling Brown, Martin Luther King, Jr., and Malcolm X, as central to her agenda of black survival.

Sanchez has received many awards, including the American Book Award for *Homegirls and Handgrenades,* her most acclaimed work; the PEN Writing Award; the NA Award; the Lucretia Mott Award; and the Oni Award from the International Black Women's Congress. Sanchez is the Laura Carnell Professor of English and Women's Studies at Temple University in Philadelphia.

BIBLIOGRAPHY

Koolish, Lynda. *African American Writers, Portraits and Vision.* Jackson: University Press of Mississippi, 2001.

Sanchez, Sonia. *A Blue Book for Blue Black Magical Women.* Detroit: Broadside Press, 1974.

———. *Home Coming.* Detroit: Broadside Press, 1969.

———. *We a BaddDDD People.* Detroit: Broadside Press, 1970.

Wilfred D. Samuels

Sapphire (Ramona Lofton) (1950–)

Born in Fort Orr, California, Ramona Lofton, who uses the pen name Sapphire, spent most of her life in and around military bases. Her father was an army sergeant, and her mother was a member of the Women's Army Corps. Because of the military, her family moved many times throughout her young life, from California to Texas to Philadelphia to Germany. These numerous relocations were difficult for the family and were complicated by her mother's alcoholism. In 1983 two major tragedies struck Sapphire's life. Her mother passed away, and her brother, who was then homeless, was killed. Although Sapphire attended San Francisco City College during the 1970s, majoring in dance, she dropped out of school and moved to New York City, where, in 1993, she received a degree in modern dance.

After finishing her degree, Sapphire taught reading to students in the Bronx and Harlem. Her literary works, fiction and poetry, emerged from the complex life stories of those she knew personally. While living in Harlem from 1983 to 1993, she observed the hardships faced by many of the young people in the building. In a 1996 interview, she comments:

> I saw a complete generation grow up while I was living in Harlem. The children who were seven and eight when I moved in were seventeen and eighteen when I moved out. I saw girls who had their first babies at fourteen. I listened to someone I had gone over a little primer with talking about their friend who got shot. I wasn't someone who came in for a year or two and then went on. I saw the way things get repeated.

These experiences became the grist for her first published book, *American Dreams* (1994), a combination of poetry and prose about the violent realities of inner-city life. The speaker in the somewhat autobiographical title poem, "American Dream," embodies the achievement of agency through voice that characterizes many, if not most, of Sapphire's characters, particularly her women, who are anything but silenced, one-dimensional beings:

> *The woman looked at me & hissed,*
> *"Stand up for the general!"*
> *I said, "My father's in the army not me."*
> *& I remained seated.*
> *& throughout 38 years . . .*
> *there has been a quiet*
> *10 year old in me*
> *who has remained seated.*
> *She perhaps is the real American Dream.*
> *(American Dreams, 21)*

Equally self-empowered is the mother, Willa Mae Justice, a domestic, in the short story "A New Day for Willa Mae." When Willa Mae finds her boyfriend locked in a passionate sexual embrace with Jadine, her 26-year-old daughter, a dancer who lives with her, Willa Mae chases them both from her house. Feeling betrayed by her only child, whom she supports, Willa Mae follows up by discarding her daughter's few belongings, clinically cleaning her bedroom, painting the room a new color of her choice. Willa Mae concludes, "what's past is past, can't change the past. And tomorrow ain promised. But I got today, yeah. I got today and life to live. I am" (72). Critics praised *American Dreams,* and in 1994 Sapphire won the MacArthur Scholarship in Poetry. In that same year, she was awarded *Downtown Magazine*'s Year of the Poet III Award.

However, *Push* (1996), Sapphire's debut novel, garnered her the most critical recognition. *Push* recounts the life of Clarice Precious Jones, an illiterate, HIV-positive teenager who has been sexually and physically abused by her father and her mother. At the beginning of the novel Precious, raped continuously by her father since she was an infant, is pregnant for the second time. Still in junior high school at age 16, she is sent as the client of Advancement House to Each One Teach One, an alternative school. There, Precious meets Ms. Rain, who sees her as more than a "client"; she teaches Precious to read and write by encouraging her to write and talk about herself. Above all, Ms. Rain helps Precious come to grips with her identity and negative self-concept.

When told as part of her therapy to write a fantasy about herself, Precious reveals a deeply held self-hatred that resonates with that of TONI MORRISON's Pecola in *The Bluest Eye.* For her life to be perfect, Precious notes,

> I would be light skinned, thereby treated right and loved by boyz. Light even more important than being skinny; you see them light-skinned girls that's big an' fat, they got boyfriends. Boyz overlook a lot to be wif a white girl or yellow girl, especially if it's a boy that's dark skin wif big lips or note, he will go APE over yellow girl. So that's my first fantasy, is get light. Then I get hair. Swing job, you know like I do with my extensions. (*Push,* 113–114)

Asked to present an in-class reading of a poem, Precious appropriately selects and reads LANGSTON HUGHES's "Mother to Son." At the end of the novel, it is clear that Precious will fulfill her many dreams for herself and her son, despite her life-threatening disease. She will not only get her GED but also go on to college. In an interview by Lisa Miller for *Urban Desires* in 1996, Sapphire comments; "As a political writer I was really trying to paint a picture of a person who I feel is the object of almost genocidal neglect and genocidal assault in terms of the removal of services that someone like Precious would need." *Push* was praised for its raw portrayal of life. In 1997 Sapphire won the Black Caucus of the American Library Association's First Novelist Award and the Book-of-the Month Stephen Crane Award for First Fiction. Sapphire's book *Black Wings and Blind Angels* (1999) addresses a plurality of topics: abusive parents, sexual identity, and police brutality.

In an interview Sapphire identified BLACK ARTS MOVEMENT poets HAKI MADHUBUTI, SONIA SANCHEZ, NIKKI GIOVANNI, and NTOZAKE SHANGE as writers who have influenced her. Her three critically acclaimed literary works identify her as a strong contemporary African-American literary voice.

BIBLIOGRAPHY

Sapphire. *American Dreams.* New York: Vintage Books, 1994.

———. *Push.* New York: Vintage Books, 1997.

Beverly Tate

Schuyler, George Samuel   (1895–1977)

The most prolific African-American journalist of his day, Schuyler is best remembered now for his essay "The Negro-Art Hokum" (1926), his satirical novel *Black No More* (1931), and his conservative political views. These aspects of Schuyler's career reveal only part of a complex man who was variously a cultural assimilationist and a Pan-Africanist, a socialist and a vitriolic anticommunist, a NATIONAL ASSOCIATION FOR THE ADVANCEMENT OF COLORED PEOPLE (NAACP) activist and a critic of MARTIN LUTHER KING, JR. Such contradictions characterized his role in the HARLEM RENAISSANCE, his fiction, and his five decades as a journalist.

Born in Providence, Rhode Island, Schuyler soon moved to Syracuse, New York, where he grew up in a middle-class family largely secluded from the harshest forms of American racism. Schuyler served in the army and worked various odd jobs before turning to journalism in New York City, where he would live and work for the bulk of his life. He began his career in 1923 as a columnist for *The MESSENGER,* a publication reflecting his socialist leanings at the time. He soon joined *The Pittsburgh Courier,* however, where he served as correspondent and editor over the next four decades. During this period he also wrote for numerous other publications, including *The Nation, American Mercury, CRISIS, The Washington Post, The New York Evening News,* and *Reader's Digest.* Schuyler brought his scathing satirical wit to bear on a variety of subjects, but most significantly he addressed racism, literature, imperialism, and communism. His writing grew increasingly anticommunist over the years, and he eventually left *The Pittsburgh Courier* to write for more conservative publications. His articles criticizing Martin Luther King, Jr., and MALCOLM X earned him a reputation as an Uncle Tom (see SAMBO AND UNCLE TOM) and even as a race traitor. This characterization has tended to overshadow his earlier work with the NAACP, his articles attacking racism, and his fiction.

Even early in his career, Schuyler emerged as a controversial figure during the Harlem Renaissance. In his essay "The Negro-Art Hokum," he argues that African Americans and African-American culture are essentially the same as white Americans and white American culture. For Schuyler the American belief in racial difference was an obstacle to racial progress; authors, he argued, should not take mistaken concepts of racial difference as the basis for their art. This faith in cultural assimilation, however, was not a popular doctrine with many artists of the Harlem Renaissance who were engaged in establishing an African-American cultural identity distinct from white America. Schuyler's description of the African American as "merely a lampblacked Anglo-Saxon" and his dismissal of BLUES, jazz, and spirituals brought a quick response from LANGSTON HUGHES in his famous artistic manifesto, "The Negro Artist and the Racial Mountain" (1926). Hughes criticized Schuyler and others for their desire "to be as little Negro and as much American as possible" (1311). Throughout his career, however, Schuyler defined his position differently than Hughes had done. In his essay, "Do Negroes Want to Be White?" (1956), for example, he asserts that the "goal is not to be white but to be free in a white world" (72). Schuyler expended his satirical energy attacking elements of both white and black society that he saw as obstructing this objective.

BLACK NO MORE: Being an Account of the Strange and Wonderful Workings of Science in the Land of the Free, A. D. 1933–1940 stands as Schuyler's most significant literary achievement. Critics commonly cite the book as both the first satirical novel and the first science fiction novel in the African-American tradition. Schuyler assaults American racism by exploring what happens when a scientific invention allows African Americans to turn themselves into Caucasians. More and more people avail themselves of this "chromatic emancipation" (87) and pass with ease into white society. It becomes clear that wealthy white economic interests and skin color are the only things preventing black participation in mainstream America. Schuyler lambastes concepts of racial purity when a genealogist reveals that the majority of Americans—including the leading white supremacists—have black ancestry. As a further irony, America reverses its color obsession, and darker skin becomes the desired norm. Even as Schuyler indicts America's preoccupation with skin color and the economic causes of racism, he satirizes African-American leaders such as MARCUS GARVEY, W. E. B. DUBOIS, and JAMES WELDON JOHNSON as self-interested agitators of the race problem. This willingness to criticize race leaders as well as racism was characteristic throughout Schuyler's career. *Black No More* remains an essential novel of the Harlem Renaissance, and its satirical edge influenced later writers such as RALPH ELLISON, ED BULLINS, and ISHMAEL REED.

Schuyler's second novel appeared in the same year as *Black No More*. He traveled to Liberia in the first half of 1931, secretly investigated rumors of slavery, and drew on this experience for *Slaves Today: A Story of Liberia*. The novel explores the tensions between native Liberians and the Liberian descendants of former American slaves whom Schuyler implicated in a contemporary slave trade of their own. *Slaves Today* was the last complete novel Schuyler published. He continued to write short stories, novellas, and novels, but these works appeared serially and often under Schuyler's various pen names. Four African novellas have been collected and published posthumously in *Black Empire* (1991) and *Ethiopian Stories* (1994). These pan-Africanist works highlight Schuyler's anticolonial sentiments and further complicate any tendency to dismiss him as a mere Uncle Tom. Schuyler's autobiography *Black and Conservative* (1966) provides valuable recollections of the Harlem Renaissance and its major figures, but the book drew the ire of critics who took offense at Schuyler's dismissal of the CIVIL RIGHTS MOVEMENT as a communist plot. *Rac[e]ing to the Right* (2001), a recently published collection of essays, offers a valuable selection of Schuyler's writing. The process of recovering and reconsidering Schuyler's work appears likely to continue as more scholars and students engage one of the most controversial figures of African-American literature.

BIBLIOGRAPHY

Hughes, Langston. "The Negro Artist and the Racial Mountain." In *The Norton Anthology of African American Literature*, edited by Henry Louis Gates, Jr., and Nellie Y. McKay, 1311–14. New York: W. W. Norton, 1997.

Hutchinson, George. *The Harlem Renaissance in Black and White*. Cambridge: Harvard University Press, 1995.

Leak, Jeffrey B. Introduction. In *Rac[e]ing to the Right: Selected Essays of George S. Schuyler*, by George S. Schuyler. Knoxville: University of Tennessee Press, 2001.

Peplow, Michael W. *George S. Schuyler*. Twayne's United States Author Series, 349. Boston: Twayne, 1980.

Schuyler, George S. "Do Negroes Want to Be White?" In *Rac[e]ing to the Right: Selected Essays of George S. Schuyler*, edited by Jeffrey B. Leak, 68–72. Knoxville: University of Tennessee Press, 2001.

———. "The Negro-Art Hokum." In *The Norton Anthology of African American Literature*, edited by Henry Louis Gates, Jr., and Nellie Y. McKay, 1171–1174. New York: W. W. Norton, 1997.

Andrew Leiter

Scott-Heron, Gil   (1949–   )

Often referred to as a modern griot and still best known for his classic poem and rap song "The Revolution Will Not Be Televised" (1974), the poet, novelist, musician, and songwriter Gil Scott-Heron has forged, over the last 30 years, one of the most influential, varied, and critically underconsidered bodies of work in modern African-American cultural production.

Scott-Heron was born in Chicago, Illinois on April 1, 1949, to a mother who was a college-educated librarian and a father who was a Jamaican professional soccer player. After his parents' divorce, the young Scott-Heron was taken to Lincoln, Tennessee to live with his maternal grandmother. While in Lincoln, he became one of three black students chosen to integrate the elementary school system in the adjoining city of Jackson. Shaken and, to some extent, politicized by this experience, Scott-Heron was later reunited with his mother in the Bronx, where he would experience and critically observe the northern and urban manifestations of the types of racism that he had experienced in the South.

Having begun writing poetry in his early teens, Scott-Heron left New York to attend the historically black Lincoln University in Pennsylvania. Although he left after a year, at Lincoln he met the musician Brian Jackson, who, over the course of a series of groundbreaking albums, became Scott-Heron's most significant musical collaborator.

Scott-Heron's experience at Lincoln University would also lay the groundwork for the depiction of a troubled black college that he would later offer in his novel *The Nigger Factory*. After leaving Lincoln, Scott-Heron attended and received an M.A. in creative writing from Johns Hopkins University. Following a stint teaching creative writing in Washington D.C., he committed himself fully to his musical and literary vocations and quickly achieved popular and critical success on both fronts. As recognition of the importance of his contribution to contemporary African-American popular music has grown, Scott-Heron's two published novels have been accorded renewed attention.

Organized as a murder mystery, his first novel, *The Vulture* (1968), offers a portrait of urban drug culture and of the ways in which the increasing availability and ease of production of illegal and unprecedentedly addictive drugs in the late 1960s and 1970s devastated black urban communities. Set in lower Manhattan, this complex and surprisingly self-assured novel depicts the lives and evolving social awareness of a group of young black men as they respond with varying degrees of satisfaction, self-interestedness, and regret to the question "Who killed John Lee," a childhood friend who, before his mysterious death, had become the most prominent local drug dealer. In this novel Scott-Heron suggests that the economy of exploitation and systematic immiseration that the drug culture produced existed in ironic counterpoint to the narratives of upward mobility and "black capitalism" that prominent political conservatives of the time were fashioning.

Despite its provocative title, Scott-Heron's second novel *The Nigger Factory* (1972) takes a politically evenhanded approach to its depiction of the power struggle between the students at the fictional black college Sutton University and the institution's conservative president as the students attempt to replace the school's traditional Eurocentric focus with a "blacker" curriculum and social mission. By way of its depiction of the black radical group MJUMBE (Members of Justice United for Meaningful Black Education) and their contentious relationship with the more moderate black student leader Earl Thomas, the novel offers a surprisingly critical portrait of black radicalism and Afrocentric pretensions and suggests that these ideas can have disastrous consequences when they are not placed in the context of a well-thought-out plan for social change.

Despite his early success as a poet and novelist, Scott-Heron is still almost exclusively known by popular audiences as a musical performer. Although unfortunate, this is understandable given the magnitude of his achievement as a singer and songwriter and the relative paucity of his literary output. Over the past 30 years, Scott-Heron has released more than 15 albums of original material. These include the landmark collections *Pieces of a Man* (1971), *Free Will* (1972), and *Winter in America* (1974), as well as now-classic songs like "Johannesburg," "The Bottle" "Lady Day and John Coltrane," "Whitey on the Moon," and "Home Is Where the Hatred Is." With the possible exception of Nina Simone, no other African-American musical performer has more consistently deployed the idioms of black popular music as a means of offering so thoroughgoing a critique of American and global social injustices.

As a reflection of the emerging dialogue between black poetry and popular music then taking place, the first of Scott-Heron's albums, *Small Talk at 125th and Lenox Avenue* (1970), was concurrently published as a poetry volume of the same name. The 30 poems in this collection are fully informed by and reflect the aesthetic that had been developed by the most significant radical black poets of the period—LeRoi Jones (AMIRI BARAKA), Don Lee (HAKI MADHUBUTI), NIKKI GIOVANNI, and especially JAYNE CORTEZ, who, like Scott-Heron, would become one of the most important and adept practitioners of rap/jazz/poetry. Scott-Heron's contribution to this art form has been increasingly acknowledged by recent critics of rap and hip-hop, whose examination of his reissued albums from the 1970s represents a corrective to the pronouncement of early critics who considered his essentially jazz-based work to be either irrelevant or lateral to the evolution of hip-hop culture. More and more Scott-Heron's music and performing style, like that of the group The Last Poet, is recognized as having set the stage for the emergence of contemporary rap, especially in its earlier and more politically charged manifestations. Reflecting this reevaluation, after a 12-year hiatus, Scott-Heron reemerged as a recording artist with the much-praised album *Spirits* in 1994.

BIBLIOGRAPHY

Erlich, Dimitri. "Gil Scott-Heron." *Rolling Stone,* 25 August 1994, p. 46.
Bordowitz, Hank. "Music Notes: Gil Scott-Heron." *American Visions* 13, no. 3 (June 1998): 40.

Terry Rowden

Senna, Danzy   (1970–   )

Writer Danzy Senna was born in Boston, the daughter of two writers active in the CIVIL RIGHTS MOVEMENT—Carl Senna, a journalist, and Fanny Howe, a poet and novelist. During the 1970s and 1980s Boston was convulsed over court-directed mandatory school desegregation through busing. Senna, the biracial daughter of a black-Mexican father and white mother, came of age in this racially charged environment. A graduate of Stanford University, Senna received an M.F.A. from the University of California at Irvine. She holds the William H. Jenks Chair in Contemporary English Letters in the department of English at the College of the Holy Cross in Worcester, Massachusetts.

Drawing on her own experiences, Senna explored the complexities and paradoxes of race in the United States in her debut novel, *Caucasia* (1997). Birdie, the heroine, is the biracial daughter of a black father and white mother who is raised with her sister, Cole, in 1970s Boston. The tortured racial politics of the day finally rip the young family apart. Birdie's father leaves the United States for Brazil, where he hopes to find a multiracial paradise. He takes Cole, the darker of the siblings, with him. On the run from Boston and from an imagined pursuit by the feds, Birdie and her mother, Sandy, change their identities. They camouflage Birdie's black identity by self-identifying as the wife and daughter of a deceased Jewish professor.

Birdie, now Jesse Goldman, struggles to figure out her identity as a biracial child who looks white and is forced to "pass" as white.

Boosted by critical acclaim, *Caucasia* became popular with the general reading public. Within educational institutions, where it is also popular, it is studied for its arresting treatment of the intersections of issues of gender, race, and class. Like RALPH ELLISON's *INVISIBLE MAN* and NELLA LARSEN's *Passing, Caucasia* focuses on the manner in which race and class challenge and define American culture. Rather than offering a strident polemic or resorting to the pedantries of the melting pot, the novel foregrounds the paradox of race in America in the 20th century.

BIBLIOGRAPHY

Boudreau, Brenda. "Letting the Body Speak: 'Becoming' White in *Caucasia.*" *Modern Language Studies* 32, no. 1 (Spring 2002): 59–70.
Hunter, Michele. "Revisiting the Third Space: Reading Danzy Senna's *Caucasia.*" In *Literature and Racial Ambiguity,* edited by Teresa Hubel and Neil Brooks, 297–316. Amsterdam: Rodopi Press, 2002.
Milian Arias, Claudia. "An Interview with Danzy Senna." *Callaloo* 25, no. 2 (Spring 2002): 447–452.

Nicolé N. Aljoe

Sethe

Few fictional characters of the African-American literary tradition have the indelible impact on readers of Sethe, the infanticide-committing heroine of TONI MORRISON's award-winning novel *BELOVED* (1987). In order to protect her "already crawling baby girl" from the atrocities of the slave economy, including the inevitable desecration of her body, Sethe, a fugitive slave who runs from the Kentucky Sweet Home Plantation of her slave owners, the Garners, to 28 days of freedom in Cincinnati, Ohio, before she is found by slave catchers, decides to kill her children. She succeeds in killing only her infant daughter, whom she eventually names Beloved. Sethe is sent to prison for her crime; however, once released, she is haunted by the ghost of her dead child, who returns as a living person seeking retribution for Sethe's heinous crime.

Sethe, the child of a slave mother who chose to carry her to full term rather than abort her as she had done several other pregnancies in revolt against the system of slavery, theoretically commits the most dangerous crime a slave mother could commit: She not only loved but also claimed rights to her own children, who were, in most cases, the legal property of the slave owner. In Sethe's case, as she tells PAUL D, also a Sweet Home slave, Beloved is "my best thing" (*Beloved* 272). In attempting to explain her actions to Paul D, who cannot understand how she could knowingly make such a costly mistake, Sethe claims ownership of her children and the right to act as their agent and protector: "I took and put my babies where they'd be safe" (164). Paul D concludes that Sethe, who in his mind clearly did not understand her status and role in the slave economy, "talked about love like any other woman; talked about baby clothes like any other woman. . . . Sethe didn't know where the world stopped and she began" (164). He accuses Sethe of having a love that was too thick. She responds, "Love is or it ain't. Thin love ain't love at all" (164).

As fictional character, Sethe is a complex woman, mother, friend, wife, and lover. As a fugitive, her goal is to reach her destination in order to nurse her infant daughter. She indulges and dotes on her daughters, Beloved and Denver; she is saddened by the news of the tragic end of her husband, Halle, and commits herself to caring for his mother, BABY SUGGS, whose freedom her husband had bought while he was still in slavery. She enjoys the intimacy she shares with Paul D, who searches for her to form a family for 25 years after they were separated. She is nurtured by the community of women she enters in Cincinnati who help her mend, particularly Baby Suggs. Sethe is eventually pardoned and rescued by the women in the larger community, whom she had offended with her murderous act. En route to freedom, Sethe had initiated a friendship with Amy, a young runaway indentured white girl, revealing, in the end, the similarities of their oppression as women, despite their racial differences. Significantly, Amy, like Ella and the women who rescue Sethe at the end of the novel and like Baby Suggs and her spiritual sermons in The Clearing, also becomes central to Sethe's healing and restoration. By the end of the novel, Sethe comes to the realization, with encouragement from Paul D, that she, not her children, is her own "best thing"—that she has not merely yesterdays but "some kind of tomorrow" (273) ahead of her.

BIBLIOGRAPHY

Morrison, Toni. *Beloved.* New York: Knopf, 1987.

Wilfred D. Samuels

Shade: An Anthology of Fiction by Gay Men of African Descent Bruce Morrow and Charles H. Rowell, eds. (1996)

With GO THE WAY YOUR BLOOD BEATS, BROTHER TO BROTHER, *and In the Life, Shade* is part of the "national, public black gay and lesbian cultural apparatus," which, according to W. Lawrence Hogue, was created to enhance an "Africentric gay and lesbian community building" (201). *Shade's* contributors and stories cross multiple borders to explore the lives of black homosexuals who live in Columbian, Creole, West Indian, and Puerto Rican communities and settings. Veterans, lawyers, travelers, and young men getting by populate its global landscape. Its stories spin a delicate tapestry of truths that transcend geography to reveal the universal isolation, escapist mentality, and overall quest for sexual openness and freedom of the central characters.

Introduced by SAMUEL DELANY, *Shade* represents globally the texture of ordinary lives of black gay men. Common histories unfold in Larry Duplechan's "Zazoo," Robert E. Penn's "Uncle Eugene," and Brian Keith Jackson's "The View from Here." Commercial urban settings and persuasions cloak L. Phillip Richardson's protagonist, George, in "Powers That Be," as he embarks on a routine life of homosexual peep shows, a diet of French fries, and unemployment. The exotic dominates Jaime Manrique's surrealistic "Twilight at the Equator," in which homosexuality as taboo in Colombia is the central theme. Racial and class conflicts are explored in Reginald Shepherd's "Summertime, and the Living Is Easy"; their juxtaposition allows Shepard to reveal their insidious impact on a friendship that lacks historical connection. Readers inevitably conclude that in certain cultures, race, like homosexuality, must be concealed. A few stories explore the domestic boundaries of tradition, which are often grounded in myth. For example, "Spice," by A. Cinqué Hicks, challenges the mild flavors of acceptance, while "Nobody Gets Hurt," by Bennett Capers, juxtaposes lifelong, homosexual friendship against the conventions of marriage.

Perhaps the most powerful story is Delany's "Citre et Trans," which, set in Athens, submits readers to a brutal homosexual rape, the consequence of the protagonist's attempt to transplant his American–based socialization, relative to general free association, to Greece, whose citizens can be equally as uncomfortable with dogs as they are with Negroes (309). In the end, Delany's American black male protagonist, whose travel from Athens to Munich to London is dominated by thought of the rape, can only make his experiences his own, singular, individual: "But I used my waking up with a sailor beside me, his leg against my arm, his hand between his legs. I did it first with fear, then with a committed anger, determined to take something from them, to retrieve some pleasure from what, otherwise, had been just painful, just ugly" (330). Delany never openly addresses the rape, yet the silence speaks to the experience of a black man who, unable to conceal his race, is further oppressed by the dominant class in an international setting. However, Delany's closing address on barbarism and torture, generalized according to race, creed, or type, incorporates deeper notions of the difficulties individuals face in a world ignorant of love.

BIBLIOGRAPHY

Hogue, Lawrence W. *The African American Male, Writing and Difference: A Polycentric Approach to African American Literature, Criticism and History*. Albany: State University of New York Press, 2003.

Morrow, Bruce, and Charles H. Rowell, eds. *Shade: An Anthology of Fiction by Gay Men of African Descent*. New York: Avon Books, 1996.

Lawrence T. Potter, Jr.

Shakur, Tupac (2PAC)   (1971–1996)

Although born Lesane Parish Crooks in Brooklyn, New York, on June 16, 1971, his mother and stepfather raised him as Tupac Shakur. He never knew his biological father. Members of the Black Panther Party, his parents nurtured him on a strong dosage of social consciousness, political radicalism, Marxist ideology, and black pride. By the time he was a young adult, Tupac displayed the degree to which he had learned his lessons by rebelling against society, the music industry, and anything and everything that attempted to box him in, even the hip-hop culture in which he was becoming a major icon and player. He made it clear that no one could dictate to him, define him, or marginalize him. Tupac defined himself with his own words. Rap music, particularly the lyrics of his songs, was his conduit for this personal celebration.

Although Tupac began his career as a dancer and guest rapper for the rap group Digital Underground, he released his first solo album, *2Pacalypse Now*, in November 1991. This album immediately placed him on the charts as an emerging rapper. Two years later, his second album, *Strictly 4 My N.I.G.G.A.Z*, which included the hit singles "Keep Ya Head Up," an inspirational song for the black community, and "I Get Around," a track in which he celebrates his promiscuity, became his first platinum album.

Tupac's turbulent and "thuggish" lifestyle, which was, for him at least, an integral part of hip-hop culture and the music industry he was helping shape, direct, and define, caught up with him in 1994, when he was shot five times in a recording studio lobby. Soon after, he was sentenced to prison for sexual abuse. However, Tupac became the first artist to release a platinum album while incarcerated when sales of his third LP, *Me against the World,* soared through the roof. After being released from prison, Tupac once again made hip-hop history when he released hip-hop's first double-CD album, *All Eyez on Me.*

Tupac's meteoric career and his life in a dog-eat-dog world that views killing as necessary for survival inevitably crashed when, on September 13, 1996, he died from multiple gunshot wounds. He was 25 years old. He had been the victim of a drive-by shooting, in which Suge Knight, chief executive officer of Death Row Record Company was also shot. They were riding in a car after watching a Mike Tyson fight in Las Vegas, Nevada, when the incident took place. Tupac was the violent shooting's only fatality. Although many believe his death was the result of a brutal battle between East Coast and West Coast rappers, his killer was never apprehended. After his death, Tupac's work in progress *Makaveli: The Don Killuminati,* named after Niccolo Machiavelli, was released.

Tupac's influence continues to be felt not only in the numerous tribute songs, DVDs, and movies that give insight into his life but also through the lyrics of his songs, which, for many social and literary critics, resonate with the language and objectives of the BLACK ARTS MOVEMENT and many of its poets: LeRoi Jones (AMIRI BARAKA), HAKI MADHUBUTI, and NIKKI GIOVANNI. Some critics even argue that Tupac and hip-hop culture ushered in yet another black renaissance movement, despite the misogyny that is endemic in rap lyrics. Tupac's posthumously published collection of poetry and lyrics, appropriately titled *X* (published with the help of his mother), made him the first and only hip-hop artist to date to publish his work in book form. Courses in which his poetry is studied are offered on campuses from University of California at Berkeley to State University of New York at Binghamton.

Tupac's rap lyrics and poems are raw, personal, and autobiographical. Their themes run the gamut from life, death, hatred, sex, women, relationships, and single parents to politics and religion. True to the contradictions in his own life and in hip-hop culture, Tupac's lyrics and poems are often also filled with love. Tupac had an uncanny desire to give the world an all-inclusive picture into his life. "Dear Mama," an ode to his mother, is exemplary. He writes; "But even as CRACK FIEND, mama / You always was a BLACK QUEEN, mama." Here, the son embraces and elevates his drug-addicted mother to status of royalty while indirectly critiquing a postmodern world that made her a crack fiend.

His political awareness and critical voice are found in most of his lyrics. He is not afraid to indict the white world while celebrating his black identity and critiquing the black community, as he does in "White Man's World": "Proud to be black, but why we act like we don't love ourselves / Don't look around, check yourselves. Know what it means to be black, whether man or GIRL / We still strugglin', in this white man's world."

Many critics could not understand how the same person who, at times, glorified a promiscuous and thuggish lifestyle could also write lyrics with such strong political insight and raw cynicism, apparent in the following lines: "Should we cry, when the Pope die, my REQUEST / We should cry if they cried when we buried Malcolm" or "You know it's funny when it rains it POORS / They got money for WARS, but can't feed the POOR." However, many people, especially those of the hip-hop generation, identified with, admired, and understood Tupac's mentality, pain, suffering, internal struggle, and seemingly contradictory lifestyle in his public battle to define himself in a world that had mislabeled him. Tupac was his own yin and yang who never sought to justify his nature to the public. Much of who he was can be summed up by his words in *Life of an Outlaw;* he is known to "Make TRACKS burst whenever I RAP / ATTACK / Words bein' known to explode on CONTACT / Extreme at times, blinded by my passion and fury."

BIBLIOGRAPHY

Ardis, Angela. *Inside a Thug's Heart, with Original Poems and Letters by Tupac Shakur.* New York: Dafina Books, 2004.

hooks, bell. *Outlaw Culture: Resisting Representations.* New York: Routledge, 1994.

Kitwana, Bakari. *The Hip Hop Generation: Young Blacks and the Crisis in African American Culture.* New York: Civitas Books, 2002.

Rose, Tricia. *Black Noise: Rap Music and Black Culture in Contemporary America.* Middletown, Conn.: Wesleyan University Press, 1994.

Detavio Ricardo Samuels

Shange, Ntozake   (1948–   )

Ntozake Shange is known the world over as the fiercely articulate author of the "choreopoem" FOR COLORED GIRLS WHO HAVE CONSIDERED SUICIDE/WHEN THE RAINBOW IS ENUF (1974). Shange has written and published prodigiously in the quarter of a century since *for colored girls* premiered on Broadway, but her name and image will forever be linked to this play, which explores the rites and rituals of modern black womanhood. Shange's description of her work in the preface of the published play could characterize her entire oeuvre: "our struggle [is to] become all that is forbidden by our environment, all that is forfeited by our gender, all that we have forgotten."

Ntozake Shange was born Paulette Linda Williams in Trenton, New Jersey. The oldest of four children of Paul and Eloise Williams, Shange was reared in a socially and intellectually stimulating environment. Her father, a surgeon, and her mother, a psychiatric social worker and educator, instilled in their children a strong sense of their cultural heritage as politically engaged people of color in the African diaspora. The Williams counted among their friends and acquaintances such artists, performers, and social activists as Josephine Baker, Dizzy Gillespie, Chuck Berry, Charlie Parker, Miles Davis, and W. E. B. DuBois. The Williams family tells the story of Shange as an infant being carried up to bed by DuBois, who was visiting at the time. Looking back, it seems appropriate that she should be linked with one of her intellectual models so early on.

When Shange was eight, she moved with her family to a then racially segregated St. Louis, where she was among the first students to integrate a German-American school, an event she recounts in *colored girls* and in the semiautobiographical novel *Betsey Brown* (1985). The family moved back to Trenton when Shange was 13, and it was there that she began in earnest to broaden her intellectual horizons, reading a wide variety of books, including the works of Dostoevsky, Melville, Carson McCullers, Edna St. Vincent Millay, Simone de Beauvoir, and Jean Genet. Her parents supported and encouraged her artistic predilections by providing music lessons (she played the violin), dance lessons, an introduction to the opera, and even crafts such as knitting.

In 1966, Shange enrolled in Barnard College in New York City, where she graduated with honors in 1970. During her years at Barnard, Shange became personally aware of social, political, and gender inequities in society. Her parents had instilled in their children a strong social and political conscience, especially with regard to people of color. Her undergraduate years were a time of discovery and emotional turmoil. Shange attempted suicide after a separation from her husband, then a student in law school. However, she soon turned her considerable creative energies toward life and spirit-sustaining endeavors. She eventually used her experiences and the experiences of her women friends and colleagues to create art that spoke to and for a generation on issues of race and gender.

In 1971, while studying for a master's degree in African-American studies at the University of Southern California, Shange, then Paulette Williams, decided to take an African name: In the Zulu dialect Zhosa, *Ntozake* means "she who comes with her own things," and *Shange* means "who walks like a lion." Shange's name change signaled her embrace of the tenets of BLACK NATIONALISM, an intellectual movement among black youth that shaped the BLACK ARTS MOVEMENT and the BLACK POWER movement. In the years since that time, Shange has come to play a significant role in shaping and defining the black aesthetic.

From 1972 to 1975, Shange taught women's studies and Afro-American studies at Sonoma State College, Mills College, and University of California Extension. During the same period, she was dancing and reciting poetry with the Third

World Collective, Raymond Sawyer's Afro-American Dance Company, West Coast Dance Works, and her own company, which was then called For Colored Girls Who Have Considered Suicide. In 1975, Shange moved to New York, where Joseph Papp's Public Theater produced *for colored girls who have considered suicide/when the rainbow is enuf.* The play achieved phenomenal success and was only the second play by an African-American woman to reach Broadway (the first being Lorraine Hansberry's *Raisin in the Sun*, which opened on Broadway in 1958). Shange's play won an Obie and the Outer Critics Circle award and was nominated for Emmy, Grammy, and Tony awards.

The success of *for colored girls* is due in part to Shange's innovated combination of poetry, music, and dance and to its deliberately minimalist stage setting. The play is structured as a series of 20 monologues performed by seven women dressed in Shange's personal interpretation of the colors of the rainbow, with the addition of brown to symbolize the earth. This groundbreaking choreopoem explores the personal and political implications of race and gender in the late 20th century. Central to the play's movement is the poet/playwright's insistence on the inextricability of body/voice/spirit. Part of her project is to redeem stigmatized femininity, to subvert patriarchal values.

In his analysis of Shange's invention and treatment of the choreopoem, Kimberly Benston asserts the primary features of Shange's ethnic and gendered approach to theater and modern dance:

> Most distinctive in relation to the canons of modernist dance is Shange's sensuous, cerebral, and political amalgamations of word, movement, gesture, and music, which insists on a modal relation between private and public expression. Shange insists not merely on dancing the ethnic body but on 'strutting' it in a social arena that is rife with multiple vernacular habits, attitudes and sonorities. (87)

Shange's own statement of her orientation to a vernacular aesthetic echoes John Coltrane's modal approach to jazz:

> The freedom to move in space, to demand of my own sweat a perfection that continually be approached, though never known, waz poem to me . . . [D]ance . . . insisted that everything African, everything halfway colloquial, a grimace, a strut, an arched back over a yawn, waz mine. I moved what waz my unconscious knowledge of being in a colored woman's body to my known everydayness. (*for colored girls*, xi)

Shange's preface to *for colored girls* simultaneously traces the play's production history and expands upon Shange's poetics of the shape, direction, and philosophical trajectory of African-American theater. Like Paul Carter Harrison and a host of others associated with theater in the black vernacular, Shange is concerned always with a crystallization of *nommo*, the sacred word. Benston likens her poetics to a manifesto and argues that "Shange's Preface emerges as one of the most textured theater manifestos of the era, surely its most dazzling synthesis of historical, political, affective, and pragmatic criteria for a revolutionary mode of African-American dramatic performance" (83).

Since the premiere of *colored girls,* Shange has gone on to publish poetry, fiction, and essays. *Nappy Edges* (1978), Shange's second poetry collection, continues the poet's idiosyncratic approach to sound and sense, delineating something of her autobiography but also, and perhaps more important, the spiritual autobiography of the black nation. In the preface, which shares the spirit of Langston Hughes's "The Negro Artist and the Racial Mountain" and Paul Carter Harrison's "Black Theatre in the African Continuum: Word/Song as Method," Shange provides an explanation of her poetics, of the performative affinities as well as the distinctions between contemporary African-American poets and musicians, particularly modern and contemporary musicians of all musical genres. In the tradition of her African-American literary forebears, Shange is not afraid to re-create Western forms and traditions.

Shange's most recent adult fiction is the novel *Liliane: Resurrection of the Daughter* (1994) and a collection of essays on Third World cuisine and culture, *If I Can Cook, You Know God Can* (1999).

However, in recent years, Shange has aimed her work at the youth of the nation. In 2002 she published the picture-book biography of Muhammad Ali, *Float Like a Butterfly,* with pastel and gouache illustrations by Edel Rodriguez, and in 2003 she published a novel aimed at adolescents, *Daddy Says.* In 2004, she published a lavishly illustrated children's book, *Ellington Is Not a Street.*

These recent works define in simple but beautiful language what a hero is. However, in keeping with her poetics, her recent works also reiterate the author's insistence on the voice's singularity and her commitment to social and political activism. They characteristically celebrate cultural and gendered identity: what it means to be a daughter, mother, sister in the 21st century. Her works retain their wit, their lyricism, and a sense of urgency in their message. Shange's influence is evident in the works of contemporary novelists, playwrights, and spoken-word artists, including Elizabeth Alexander, Hottentot Venus, and SUZAN-LORI PARKS, who won the Pulitzer Prize in 2002 for her play *Topdog/Underdog.* Shange's influence will be evident for generations to come.

BIBLIOGRAPHY

Benston, Kimberly. *Performing Blackness: Enactments of African-American Modernism.* New York: Routledge Press, 2000.

Betsko, Kathleen, and Rachel Koenig, eds. *Interviews with Contemporary Women Playwrights.* New York: Beech Tree Books, 1987.

Lester, Neal A. *Ntozake Shange: A Critical Study of the Plays.* New York: Garland, 1995.

Hermine Pinson

Shante, Roxanne (Lolita Shante) (1969–   )

Widely hailed as the "foremother" of feminist/womanist rap, Roxanne Shante is credited with launching the infamous "Roxanne" battles with "Roxanne's Revenge," her response to UTFO's "Roxanne, Roxanne." Born Lolita Shante Gooden in Queens, New York, on November 9, 1969, she began her career in hip-hop at age 14. Partnering with old-school rap's producer, Marly Marl, Roxanne Shante's witty reply track challenged the male rappers of UTFO and affirmed the sexual autonomy of women. To the advances of the Kangol Kid, Dr. Ice, and The Educated Rapper—the M.C.s of UTFO—she retorts, "Me the Rox give up the box? / So you can brag about it for the next six blocks / Where's the beef you guys can't deal it / I need a man that can make me feel it." Her release sold more than 250,000 copies and spawned more than 100 answerback records. Working closely with lyricist and solo artist Big Daddy Kane, Shante followed up "Roxanne's Revenge" with the hit singles "Have a Nice Day" and "Go On Girl." Her first album further affirmed her feminist / womanist identity with the track "Independent Woman."

At age 25 Gooden left the music world to return to school, earning a degree in psychology. Roxanne Shante launched a new career, opening a thriving clinical practice in New York City. She also emerged as a public speaker and hip-hop icon, often making public appearances to discuss what she terms "hip-hop herstory."

BIBLIOGRAPHY

Abdullah, Melina. "Hip Hop as Political Expression: Potentialities for the Power of Voice in Urban America." In *From Dusk Til Dawn: Black Urban America,* edited by Lewis Randolph and Gayle Tate, 465–474. New York: St. Martin's Press, 2005.

Melina Abdullah

Shepherd, Reginald   (1963–   )

Born in New York City, the son of Goldburn Shepherd and Blanche Althea Berry, Shepherd was raised in tenements and housing projects in the Bronx in extreme poverty. After his mother's death when he was 15, Shepherd was sent to live with relatives in Macon, Georgia. This experience proved devastating to the teenage Shepherd, who, by age 13, was fully aware of his developing gay identity, which made him liminal in the Bronx, as opposed to his new southern black community, where he was "probed and stared at and taunted," like a Martian ("This Place/Displace"). Shepherd, who attended several private primary and secondary schools in the Bronx and Manhattan as a gifted student before being sent to Macon, received his B.A. degree from Bennington College in 1988 and M.F.A. degrees from Brown University (1991) and the University of Iowa (1993). He described his youth and young adulthood as a time when he "wandered from place to place, from school to school, a deeply unheroic Odysseus less in search of a home . . . than fleeing a place . . . in which he feared being trapped" ("This Place/Displace").

To escape his world of alienation, Shepherd found sanctuary in literature, at first Greek mythology and then poetry, particularly T. S. Eliot's "The Waste Land." In an interview with Charles Rowell, the editor of CALLALOO, Shepherd explained, "I had a sense from a very early age that literature was a world to which I aspired, something preferable to the circumstance in which I grew up. I believed that language would save me from the housing projects and tenements of the Bronx, would save me from myself, even, if only I could get to it" (290). Through poetry, Shepherd continues to inhabit and find legitimacy in the world of language that attracts and eludes him, simultaneously allowing him to define himself as an artist rather than as a black or gay artist. He told Rowell, "I've never had an interest in being a 'black writer . . . in speaking 'for' or 'as' a black person" (291). "I prefer to call myself a writer who is gay and black or a writer who is black and gay than to call myself a gay black writer" (294), Shepherd said, distinguishing himself from ESSEX HEMPHILL and ASSOTTO SAINT.

As a writer whose primary interest is in literature, language, and art, Shepherd unabashedly proclaims and embraces his subscription to an aesthetic that is fundamentally Western, in the tradition of Plato, Francis Bacon, T. S. Eliot, Wallace Stevens, and Harold Bloom. In his work he reveals his obsession with desire and beauty. In his essay "Notes Toward Beauty" he explains:

> I decided I wanted to be a poet (an asymptote, approached but never truly reached, in that regard like beauty itself) because I was so overwhelmed by the ambivalent, contradic-

tory beauty of Eliot's "Love Song of J. Alfred Prufrock" (the first poem I ever read: I was fourteen) that it seemed not simply to speak to and of my life but to replace it, if only fleetingly, with something better because more meaningful and patterned. Amorphous misery had been made form, suffering transformed to shape. I hated the poem for eluding me, for not surrendering itself immediately to my understanding; I loved it for the enthrallment it induced, the power of its fascination. I sought by becoming a poet a share in that power, to be, if not a thing of beauty in myself, then perhaps at least a source of beauty.

Ultimately, for Shepherd this "source of beauty" is rooted in whiteness and, in respect to his sexual orientation, white men, a fact that has caused some black critics to level charges of black self-hate against him. Shepherd has candidly written about this desire in his essay "On Not Being White," in which he asks: "Is my desire for a beautiful man a desire to possess that ultimately validating prize, the white man; or is my desire for white men a desire to possess that ultimate validating prize, the beautiful man? How can I separate them when whiteness and beauty are equated in my society and in my mind, when my definition of one inevitably encompasses that of the other?" In attempting to explain his perspective to Rowell, Shepherd stated, "obviously to be a black person who desires white people is to desire something one is not. A lot has to do with a completeness I imagine the other to have which I lack" (298).

Shepherd's use and exploration of form, language, and themes related to race and sexuality dominate his four published collections of poems: *Some Are Drowning* (1994) *Angel, Interrupted* (1996), *Wrong* (1999), and *Otherhood* (2003). All point to his continued quest for a better understanding of the muddled difference between beauty and desire. His speaker in "Paradise" admits, "I don't trust beauty anymore / when will I stop believing it" (*Some Are Drowning,* 10). As if to address his dilemma, his speaker in "Popular Beauty" candidly admits: "In Plato's cave I still can't come / to a decision."

Critics generally focus on Shepherd's "forays into the classical world" (Henry, 59). Title after title confirms this journey: "Eros in His Striped Blue Shirt," "Narcissus at the Adonis Theater," "Tantalus in May," and "A Man Name Troy"; however, Shepherd is not merely interested in simplistic allusions but instead wishes to explore the deep, complex signification of language. "Narcissus Loved Rivers Best," in which the speaker is the title mythological figure, suggests the complexity of Shepherd's allusion and invocations—his engagement with language's multifaceted signification: "Those foaming horses never change, their manes / white billows in the current, pillows to rest / my head" (*Some Are Drowning*, 59). Similarly, he uses language in "Bacchus" as paintbrush strokes on his word-dominated personal canvas: "Like something out of Carravaggio: / the young god leans over the banquet board / to offer up the grapes like small red flames, yellow apples / piled like summer waves" (*Some Are Drowning*, 28).

Shepherd seems well aware that, despite his mastery of language and form within the confines of "Western tradition," he lives in a world that stands poised at all time to marginalize him, label him black, and even erase his significance as poet. His speaker says in "Art and illusion":

> You wanted the classic white on white,
> unbounded
> expanse of snow or sand.
> . . .
> I scribbled my name
> in charcoal and you erased it. My fingers
> tried to leave prints on your world." (*Angel Interrupted*, 58–59)

Despite his desire for whiteness, Shepherd seems to say, through his speaker in "Desire and the Slave Trade," that by no means should this personal quest indicate either ignorance or denial on his part. He is well aware of his history and legacy as a black American male which, if only through textual excursions, he knows well.

> I dreamed a walk with docents, gusts, damp
> dead leaves of sepia dioramas. We walked past
> depots . . . Wandered the hold of

> The first American slave ship, the Desire.
> (*Angel Interrupted*, 9–10)

Through his speaker, Shepherd correlates this legacy of oppression with events in today's world: "In Florida / they doused a black man from Detroit / with gasoline, kindling to put out the dark" (*Angel Interrupted* 10). His speaker calls attention to a similar event that took place in New York in 1723, when the leader of a slave revolt "was slow roasted for eight hours as / a warning beacon."

Shepherd has received a Discovery/The Nation award (1993), a Paumanok Poetry Award (1993), the 1994 George Kent Prize from *Poetry* magazine, the Amy Lowell Poetry Traveling Scholarship (1994–1995), and grants from the NEA, the Illinois Arts Council, and the Constance Saltonstall Foundation, among other awards and honors. His second collection, *Angel Interrupted*, was a finalist for the 1997 Lambda Literary Award. He has taught at Northern Illinois University and Cornell University and currently lives and writes in Pensacola, Florida.

BIBLIOGRAPHY

Boxwell, David A. "Reginald Shepherd." In *Contemporary Gay American Poets and Playwrights: An A–Z Guide*, edited by Emmanuel S. Nelson, 398–406. Westport, Conn.: Greenwood Press, 2003.

Henry, Brian. Review of *Wrong. Boston Review* 25, no. 3 (Summer 2000): 59–60.

Rowell, Charles H. "An Interview with Reginald Shepherd." *Callaloo* 21, no. 2 (1998): 290–307.

Shepherd, Reginald. *Angel Interrupted*. Pittsburgh: University of Pittsburgh Press, 1996.

———. "Notes Toward Beauty." Available online. URL: http://www.poetrysociety.org/journal/articles/beauty.html. Accessed October 26, 2006.

———. "On Not Being White." In *In the Life: A Black Gay Anthology*, edited by Joseph Beam. Boston: Alyson Publications, 1986: 46–57.

———. *Some Are Drowning*. Pittsburgh: University of Pittsburgh Press, 1994.

———. "This Place/Displaced." In *The Place of the Self*, edited by Mark Doty, St. Paul, Minn.: Graywolf Press, 2002.

Wilfred D. Samuels

Sherman, Charlotte Watson   (1958–   )

Novelist, short story writer, and editor Charlotte Watson Sherman was born and raised in Seattle, Washington, to working-class parents from the South. A voracious reader, Sherman, along with her brothers, attended the public schools of Seattle, where they were among the few people of color. In 1980, she received her B.A. in social sciences from Seattle University. Sherman has worked as a jail screener, sexual and domestic abuse counselor, creative writing workshop facilitator, and child welfare caseworker.

While in college, Sherman wrote poetry; she began writing fiction in 1988. Although she claims not to have had a model early on, Sherman identifies JAMES BALDWIN as one of the first black authors she read in high school. However, like GLORIA NAYLOR and others, Sherman came to believe she could become a writer after being introduced to the works of ZORA NEALE HURSTON, ALICE WALKER, and MAYA ANGELOU in college.

In 1992, Sherman published *Killing Color,* a collection of short stories. Set in Mississippi and Seattle, the stories are told by women narrators who speak in black dialect. Sherman provides glimpses into their fears, dreams, desires, and expectations, exploring themes relating to their past and the present. Reviewers highly commended *Killing Color* for its "originality, in the use of metaphors, dreams, mystery, and myth" (Clair, 3). In 1993, *Killing Color* won the Great Lakes College Association Fiction Award and the Governor's Writers Award.

Sherman wrote her first novel, *One Dark Body,* in 1993. Using one of the novel's strongest features, magical realism, Sherman juxtaposes personal stories with ancient cultural tales and legends to explore relationships between descendants and ancestors, like TONI MORRISON, AUGUST WILSON, and Sandra Jackson-Opoku. As many critics note, Sherman masterfully captures the sense of loss and longing and the true essence of W. E. B. DUBOIS's now-classic double-consciousness metaphor: "One ever feels his twoness—an American, a negro; two souls two thoughts, . . . in one dark body," which she invokes (364–365) in the title of her novel. Sherman's novel *Touch* (1995) is a heart-wrenching work that explores the consequences and emotions of a black woman who is HIV-positive. The

title of the novel refers to the way those who have AIDS or HIV are often deprived of human contact. Most reviewers of the novel find the work moving, timely, and relevant.

Sherman also writes nonfiction and juvenile literature. She edited the groundbreaking anthology *Sisterfire: Black Womanist Fiction and Poetry* (1994). Her two children's books are *Nia and the Golden Stool* (1988) and *Eli and the Swamp Man* (1995). Her work has also been published in *Black Scholar* and *Obsidian.*

Sherman has received several other honors and distinctions. She was granted the Seattle Arts Commission Individual Artist Award (1989), the Fiction Publication Award from the Kings County Commission (1989), a Seattle Artists grant (1991), and a literary fellowship from the Washington State Arts Commission (1993); *Granta* named Sherman to its "Fabulous 52" (1995).

Although her output thus far is small, Sherman has made a valuable contribution to contemporary African-American literature, and she plans to continue. She states, "The strength to keep on publishing comes from knowing that Toni Morrison is doing it too, that Ntozake Shange is doing it. That we are all doing it" (Carroll, 221). Presently, Sherman is completing *The Blues Ain't Nothing but a Good Woman Feeling Bad,* a work of nonfiction on black women and depression.

BIBLIOGRAPHY

Bahar, Saba. Review of *One Dark Body. Race and Class* 36, no. 1 (1994): 104–105.

Clair, Maxine, "Sleight of Voice." Review of *Killing Color. Belles Lettres* (Summer 1992): 3.

Carroll, Rebecca. *I Know What the Red Clay Looks Like: The Vision of Black Women Writers.* New York: Crowne Trade, 1994.

DuBois, W. E. B. *The Souls of Black Folk.* In *W. E. B. DuBois Writings.* New York: The Library of America, 1996: 359–547.

DuCille, Anne. "Haunts of History." Review of *One Dark Body. Women's Review of Books* 10, no. 10–11 (July 1993): 23.

Malieckal, Bindu. "Charlotte Watson Sherman." In *Contemporary African American Authors,* edited by Emmanuel S. Nelson, 426–432. Westport, Conn.: Greenwood, 1999.

Petty, Jill. "The Human Touch." Review of *Touch. Ms.* 6, no. 2 (September 1965): 78–79.

Loretta G. Woodard

Signifying Monkey, The: A Theory of African-American Literary Criticism
Henry Louis Gates, Jr. (1988)

The Signifying Monkey is a seminal text in African-American literary theory. In it HENRY LOUIS GATES, JR., argues that there is a discrete and distinct black vernacular voice located simultaneously within early African-American folk traditions and in indigenously derived West African cultural origins. Specifically, Gates maintains, black signifying (signifyin') unites the figures of Esu Elegbara, a West African Yoruban god of indeterminacy, and the Signifying Monkey, a TRICKSTER who is the central figure of the African-American signifying monkey tales that date back to slavery, to create a theory of African-American literary criticism. To derive meaning from a black text, Gates theorizes, it is necessary to analyze or interpret it through structures that came from black and African cultures.

The Signifying Monkey points out "signal" differences between black speech and white speech or language. According to Gates, the critical focus is on the way in which words are used or signified, rather than on the actual meaning assigned by words. As in the signifying monkey tales, in which three animals (monkey, lion, and elephant) are involved in a conversation in which meaning is "comically" confused, black signifyin' relies on misinterpretations to supply true meaning. In the tales, the monkey is said to be signifyin' on or mocking the lion through an indirect reference to the elephant as the carrier of the tale about the lion. An insult is misunderstood by the lion to have come directly from the elephant through the monkey—as in the monkey's claim that "I heard the elephant said you were too small to be king of the jungle." While these African-American folktales are told in a variety of ways, with similar results—a thrashed lion, after foolishly confronting the elephant, returns to find the monkey sitting safely in a tree laughing at him. In a similar fash-

ion, this text uses Esu, the "Pan-African cousin," as the African trickster figure who also obscures meaning in order to convey.

Key points have emerged in African-American literature and criticism as a result of *The Signifying Monkey*. Specifically, meaning in black literature is based on an understanding of black language as double-voiced and indirect. To interpret black literature properly one must look for meaning not only in what is directly stated but also, and more important, in what is not said, what is implied, and what is repeated. Consequently, a reader must pay close attention to the way in which words are presented rather than in their literal meaning. Further, signification in the African-American literary tradition is as much about the mode and manner of the text's signifying upon itself and other texts as it is about the content (what is being signified about). Formal aspects, such as indirection, double-voicedness, pastiche (or motivated signification), parody (unmotivated signification), self-reflexiveness and referentiality, hidden polemic, and "narrative parody and critical signification" also constitute formal aspects of signifying.

A key concept in this system of writing and making meaning out of words and wordplay is the relationship between identity and difference. Words signal difference and difference constitutes identity. In this case, black difference (blackness, Africanness) is located in the black vernacular—black identity is located in black speech. White and black critics have overwhelmingly questioned this tenet of Gates's theory of signifying. The strongest opponents have been African-centered critics who argue that Gates fails to sufficiently analyze underlying indigenously derived African knowledge bases and therefore misrepresents African ontology and epistemologies that are foundational to African language and subjectivity and inform the cultural and linguistic fusion incorporated in the theory of signifyin'. Rowland Abiodum suggests the following remedy: "we must look beyond what is easily observed if we are to understand something . . . an artwork in its cultural depth as the expression of the local thought or belief system, lest we unwittingly remove the 'African' in African Art" (qtd. in Badego, 47).

BIBLIOGRAPHY

Badejo, Diedre. *Osun Seegesi: The Elegant Deity of Wealth, Power, and Femininity.* Trenton, N.J.: Africa World Press, 1996.

Gates, Henry L. *The Signifying Monkey: A Theory of African-American Literary Criticism.* New York: Oxford University Press, 1988.

Ogundipe, Ayodele. "Esu Elegbara, The Yoruba God of Chance and Uncertainty: A Study in Yoruba Mythology." Vols. I and II. Ph.D. diss. Indiana University, 1978.

Olupona, Jacob K. "The Study of Yoruba Religious Tradition in Historical Perspective." *Numen* 40 (September 1993).

Peters, Erskine A. "Afrocentricity: Problems of Logic, Method and Nomenclature." *Twenty-first Century Afro Review* 2 (Winter 1996): 1–44.

April Langley

Simmons, Judy Dothard   (1944–   )

A poet, essayist, feature writer, editor, reviewer, and broadcaster, Judy Dothard Simmons was born in Westerly, Rhode Island, on August 29, 1944, the daughter of Amanda Catherine Dothard and Edward Everett Simmons, Jr., who divorced when she was five. Simmons attended public schools in Connecticut, Rhode Island, New York, and Alabama and finished at Allen High, a Methodist boarding school, in 1960. After a year at venerable Talladega College, she graduated California State University–Sacramento with a B.A. in psychology in 1967. Coming of age during the height of the BLACK POWER movement, Simmons was moved by her social conscience to teach disadvantaged youths in the newly created Job Corps at Rodman Center, in New Bedford, Massachusetts. In 1968 she was among the first black female college hires at AT&T; she spent six years in corporate management.

During the BLACK ARTS MOVEMENT Simmons performed with AMIRI BARAKA (Le Roi Jones) in San Francisco and Oakland. DUDLEY RANDALL published her first poetry collection, *Judith's Blues* (1973), with historic BROADSIDE PRESS in Detroit. Her second collection, *A Light in the Dark,* containing poems and writings commissioned by Literacy Volunteers of America, was published in 1983. In 1984 Blind Beggar Press published *Decent Intentions,* her third collection of poems. In *Drumvoices,* EUGENE REDMOND identified her as one of New York's up-and-coming poets.

Widely anthologized, Simmons's poems appeared in Redmond's *Drumvoices,* Amiri and Amina Baraka's *Confirmation,* QUINCY TROUPE's *Giant Talk,* and STEPHEN HENDERSON's *Understanding the New Black Poetry.* For example, Simmons's "The Answer" placed her squarely in the ideological camp of Baraka, NIKKI GIOVANNI, and SARAH WEBSTER FABIO:

> *Ask me why I don't write joyous verses*
> *On childhood rambles; odes to tenderness*
> *Politely touched with bearable nostalgia*
> *For little loves and little pains and freight trains*
> *. . . All of which are proper in their place*
> *. . . As guns and deadly poems are*
> *For my race.*

"It's Comforting" crafts a compelling continuity between autobiography and the social histories in caste and class. Thematically, Simmons's work is a fierce welding of personal accomplishment with social responsibility as exampled by her father's great-great-grandfather, the civil rights leader George T. Downing (1819–1903), an associate of SOJOURNER TRUTH and FREDERICK DOUGLASS, and her maternal grandmother, educator Mary Julia Ross (1890–1991), who was the first of three college-educated generations—a rarity for most American families in the first half of the 20th century.

As a gifted communicator based in New York, Simmons has been a respected editor with *Essence, Ms.,* and *Emerge* as well as for authors AUDRE LORDE, Baraka, Wesley Brown, and George Davis, among others. Simmons's writing has been featured in *American Legacy, BLACK ISSUES BOOK REVIEW, 33 Things Every Girl Should Know about Women's Lib* (Random House), *Wild Women Don't Wear No Blues* (Doubleday), *The Black Woman's Health Book* (Seal Press), *The Psychopathology of Everyday Racism and Sexism* (Harrington Press), *QBR, The Village Voice,* and *The New York Daily News.* Simmons was an early talk-radio host (1978–1984), first on Pacifica's WBAI-FM and then winning numerous awards for *The Judy Simmons Show* on Inner City Broadcasting's WLIB-AM. Based in Alabama after mid-1991, Simmons was managing editor of the NATIONAL ASSOCIATION FOR THE ADVANCEMENT OF COLORED PEOPLE's magazine *The CRISIS,* editor-at-large with AOL-Time Warner's webzine *Africana. com* (founded by HENRY LOUIS GATES, JR.), and an award-winning columnist for *The Anniston* (Alabama) *Star.*

BIBLIOGRAPHY

Henderson, Stephen. *Understanding the New Black Poetry: Black Speech and Black Music as Poetic References.* New York: William Morrow & Company, 1973.

Redmond, Eugene B. *Drumvoices: The Mission of Afro-American Poetry, a Critical History.* Garden City, N.Y.: Anchor Books, 1976.

Rich Roberts

Sinclair, April (1954–   )

Born in Illinois, Sinclair was raised on Chicago's South Side. After graduating from Western Illinois University, she moved to San Francisco and later to Oakland, California, where, as a community activist, she served as the director of the Emergency Food Coalition and taught at Oakland's Read-a-Lot Program. In the interim, Sinclair wrote essays for small womanist and feminist publications and took graduate courses in film at San Francisco State University. Discouraged from pursuing a career in film, Sinclair, who wrote poetry at age 10, began working on her first novel, *Coffee Will Make You Black* (1994), which, after she had written the first 20 pages, she began promoting through public readings. As a result of her self-promotion and the positive response and feedback she received, Sinclair was able to secure an agent and a contract for her novel.

Coffee Will Make You Black, like ROSA GUY's *The Friends* and PAULE MARSHALL's *BROWN GIRL, BROWNSTONES,* is a bildungsroman. It chronicles the coming of age of its protagonist, Jean "Stevie" Ste-

venson, who grows into young womanhood during the CIVIL RIGHTS MOVEMENT and BLACK POWER movement of the 1960s and 1970s. Sinclair followed *Coffee Will Make You Black* with *Ain't Gonna Be the Same Fool Twice* (1997), in which the main character, Stevie, discovers and explores her lesbianism while living in San Francisco's Castro District, and *I Left My Backdoor Open* (1999), in which the main character, Dee Dee, a deejay, yearns for a more mature, successful romantic experience.

Coffee Will Make You Black is, to some degree, reminiscent of LORRAINE HANSBERRY's *A RAISIN IN THE SUN* and RICHARD WRIGHT's *NATIVE SON,* which are also set in the South Side of Chicago. Jean, like Bigger and Beneatha, grows up in a working-class family that has migrated from the South in search of a better life. However, thematically, Sinclair is concerned with Jean's sexuality and emotion, family relationships, political awareness, friendships, and, above all, ultimate existential responsibility for herself. As a domestic, Jean's grandmother had to work on holidays, while her own family had to wait until the following day to celebrate. However, as Jean's grandmother explains to her daughter Evelyn: "Chile, when I would be cooking them dinner, I'd be thinking about how good the leftovers was gonna taste. We might not have ate good on Thanksgiving, but, chile, we sho greased the next day" (33). From the exchange between her mother and grandmother, Jean learns that, like her parents (her father is a janitor), her grandmother, too, "had to do whatever [she] could to make a honest dollar" (33). Like Ruth, Lena, and Beneatha of *A Raisin in the Sun,* Jean, her grandmother, and her mother form a community of women who mentor and guide Jean to maturity and womanhood. Life for Jean, unlike for Bigger, is filled with love, despite the family's economic status.

Equally important are the friendships Jean develops, particularly with Nurse Horn and her best friend, Carla. When Jean, who plays basketball as well as anyone around her, male or female, tells Carla she was unable to lose her virginity to her boyfriend, Sean, and that she thinks one reason for her emotional fear was the possibility that she might be "funny," a lesbian, Carla tells Jean she will never have a freak for a best friend. Jean, who remains uncertain about her possible sexual orientation and identity, responds, "Carla, if you can't accept me for who I am, no matter what, then our friendship is really tired" (224).

Jean's sexual identity is further confused by the fact that she has strong emotional ties to (and perhaps even secret desires for some form of intimacy with) Nurse Horn, the white nurse at her high school, for whom she works as a work-study student. When the Afro-Club meets to determine whether to oust Nurse Horn and replace her with a black nurse, Jean feels obligated to defend her mentor and friend before her peers, even if she is the only one to do so. When Carla confronts Jean about her friendship with Nurse Horn, Jean simply responds, "good people come in all colors and types, just the same as bad people" (224). At the end of the novel, Jean comes to the realization and accepts the fact that she, like Nurse Horn, may well "march to the beat of a different drummer" (238). When Jean seeks Nurse Horn's advice about her thoughts, Nurse Horn tells her, "because you have a schoolgirl crush on me doesn't make you a homosexual" (234), while encouraging, "shine by becoming more who you already are" (238).

Simultaneously, throughout *Coffee Will Make You Black,* Sinclair reverses some of the issues Hansberry explored in *A Raisin in the Sun* by turning the camera inward, providing insights into intraracial issues of color and exploring how, during an important historical period of black empowerment, blacks were still color struck. Like her grandmother's and mother's generations, which looked askance at blackness as a symbol of ugliness (hence the relevance of the novel's title) Jean's generation still values beauty if it is closer to white. Jean's brother, David, is attracted to Shantelle, a militant member of the Afro Club that is seeking to replace Nurse Horn, because she is light skinned with green eyes.

Coffee Will Make You Black was received with mixed reviews. The American Library Association named *Coffee Will Make You Black* Book of the Year (young adult fiction) for 1994, and the Friends of the Chicago Public Library awarded Sinclair the Carl Sandburg Award for her debut novel. Sinclair lives in Berkeley, California.

BIBLIOGRAPHY

Baxter, Nicky. "A Second Cup of Coffee for April Sinclair." Review of *Ain't Gonna Be the Same Twice.* Available online. URL: http://www.metroactive.com/papers/metro/04.25.96/sinclair-9617.html. Accessed October 26, 2006.

Sinclair, April. *Coffee Will Make You Black.* New York: Hyperion, 1994.

Wilfred D. Samuels

Slade, Leonard, Jr.   (1942–   )

Born in Conway, North Carolina, Leonard Slade, Jr., is the oldest son of the nine children of Elizabeth and Leonard Slade, Sr. He grew up on the family's 75-acre farm, where siblings and parents worked side by side, harvesting peanuts, cotton, and corn. For the young Slade, gathering peanuts was not as burdensome as picking cotton, which cut his fingers.

Slade attended W. S. Creecy High School in segregated Rich Square, North Carolina. Like all of his siblings, Leonard attended college, earning a B.A. degree in English from North Carolina's Elizabeth City State University, an M.A. degree in English from Virginia State University, and a Ph.D. degree in English from the University of Illinois at Urbana-Champaign. He taught for 22 years at Kentucky State University, where he was also chair of the division of literature, languages, and philosophy and dean of the College of Arts and Sciences.

Slade developed his love for literature, specifically such poets as William Shakespeare and the British romantic poets William Wordsworth and John Keats, while an undergraduate. He did not become interested in such major black writers as Langston Hughes, Gwendolyn Brooks, Richard Wright, and Ralph Ellison until he was engaged in his Ph.D. work. To date, he has published 15 books, including 11 books of poetry: *Another Black Voice: A Different Drummer* (1988), *The Beauty of Blackness* (1989), *I Fly like a Bird* (1992), *The Whipping Song* (1993), *Vintage* (1995), *Fire Burning* (1995), *Pure Light* (1996), *Neglecting the Flowers* (1997), *Lilacs in Spring* (1998), *Elisabeth and Other Poems* (1999), and *For the Love of Freedom* (2000).

Dedicated to his mother, Slade's "Black Madonna" combines the various themes found in his poems: deep love for his humble but Christian southern roots, parents, family, God, and nature, as well as the influence of the British romantic poets:

> She crawled on her knees
> until the sun bowed
> to her. Eight children
> planted beneath the stars
> The earth felt good to her. (Black Voice, 47)

Reliance on God provides balm in Gilead and strength to continue. However, Slade does not romantically embrace all memories of his past, as in the clearly indicting "For My Forefathers":

> For my forefathers
> Whose fingers pierced cotton bolls
> Beneath the sun roasting human flesh
> And darkness told master
> To rape black women
> for labor and profit

The titles of Slade's works (for example, *Black Voice: A Different Drummer*) suggest that he sets out to offer a different agenda and perspective from that of the poets of the BLACK ARTS MOVEMENT, for whom revolution, as MALCOLM X promoted, "by any means necessary" was an alternative. In "We Love" Slade's speaker lucidly presents his agenda:

> I
> teach
> love
> first self
> then
> burn
> the universe—our inner selves
> cleansed
> unashamed of blackness. Redeemed. We
> learn
> love. (Beauty of Blackness, 7)

Throughout his work Slade remains hopeful. He makes his quintessential dream clear in "My Dream," in which each stanza defines each quality of his dream: "My dream is real . . ., My dream is romantic . . ., My dream is sacred . . ., My dream is aesthetic." The poem ends: "My dream continues."

A writer-in-residence at Bennington College, Vermont; at The Bread Loaf Writers' Conference, Middlebury College, Vermont; and at The Ragdale Artists' Colony, Lake Forest, Illinois, Slade has published his work in ESSENCE magazine, *The COLLEGE LANGUAGE ASSOCIATION JOURNAL, The American Poetry Review, The Zora Neale Hurston Forum, The Journal of Southern History, The Black Scholar,* and *The Griot: Journal of the Southern Conference on Afro-American Studies,* to name a few. He is also the author of two books of literary criticism, including *Symbolism in Herman Melville's Moby Dick: From the Satanic to the Divine* (1998). He has received several teaching awards, grants, and fellowships, including the Kentucky Humanities Grant, the Northeast Modern Language Association Fellowship, and the Ford Foundation Fellowship. In May 1989 Elizabeth City State University awarded Leonard a doctor of humane letters degree. Slade is professor of Africana studies, adjunct professor of English, chair of the department of Africana studies, interim director of the Humanistic Studies Program, and director of the Master of Arts in the Liberal Studies Program at the State University of New York at Albany.

BIBLIOGRAPHY

"Poetry Flows from the Heart of Black Experience." University at Albany, State University of New York. Available online. URL: http://www.albany.edu/feature97/slade/. Accessed October 26, 2006.

Slade, Leonard A., Jr. *The Beauty of Blackness.* Nashville, Tenn.: Winston-Derek Publishers, Inc., 1988.

———. *Black Voice: A Different Drummer.* Nashville, Tenn.: Winston-Derek Publishers, 1988.

———. "The Days before Brown." Available online. URL: http://www.hoover.org/publications/ednext/3260641.html. Accessed October 26, 2006.

Wilfred D. Samuels

Smith, William Gardner (1927–1974)

Journalist, novelist, and expatriate William Gardner Smith was born and raised in south Philadelphia. He attended the mostly white Barratt Junior High School and graduated from Benjamin Franklin High School, where he was editor of the school newspaper. He began his career as a writer at age 18 with the *Pittsburgh Courier*. After being drafted into the U.S. Army in 1946, he served eight months in Berlin, Germany, as a clerk typist. Upon returning to the United States, Smith, who had refused scholarships to both Howard and Lincoln Universities, historically black universities, briefly attended Temple University with his new wife, Mary Sewell Smith. In 1951, perhaps desirous of escaping the bourgeois life he had inherited with his marriage, he returned to Europe to live in Paris, like RICHARD WRIGHT, FRANK YERBY, and CHESTER HIMES.

Despite his primarily northern and urban experience, Smith became an adult in a segregated America, unable to escape ubiquitous racism. He came to know, during his youth in "the city of brotherly love," what James Baldwin calls attention to in "Notes of a Native Son": Racism was as present "up South" in New Jersey as it was "down South" in Mississippi. While stationed in Europe during World War II, however, Smith found what he thought was a greater sense of acceptance, respect, and freedom; these, along with his familiarity with and love of French culture, his appreciation of the works of the French realists from Balzac to Zola, and the impact he saw Wright having on the intellectual and artistic communities in France, became central factors in his decision to return to Europe to live.

Smith's published work is almost entirely autobiographical; like him, his central characters search for wholeness and meaning in a world that is not polluted by racial or ethnic domination and hatred. Smith published four novels between 1947 and 1963. At age 21, he published his first novel, *Last of the Conquerors* (1947). Set in Germany, *Last of the Conquerors* thematically celebrates, through interracial love, the freedom black soldiers enjoyed outside the United States, the country whose ideals they had gone to Germany to uphold and defend with their lives if necessary. *Last of the Conquerors* was followed by *Anger and Innocence* (1950), a novel in which the main characters, like the characters in Wright's *Savage Holiday* (1954) and Himes's *Cast the First Stone* (1952), are white. It was translated into French. *South Street* (1954), Smith's third novel, treats life in south Philadelphia and the racial issues blacks encountered there. Michel Fabre calls *South Street* "an angry book" (243). Smith's fourth novel, *The STONE FACE* (1963), widely considered his best, is about the new "lost generation" that meandered in Paris after World War II, four decades after Gertrude Stein coined the label to identify post–World War I American writers, including Ernest Hemingway, whom Smith admired.

Smith emphasized race and racial issues, but unlike his contemporary Richard Wright, he had no desire to use his work as a political tool. He remained committed to aesthetics. He wrote, "I don't want to write out of anger. I don't want a book to be a cry of anguish. I want it to shed light [that] will come from the friction of the characters . . . and the characters will be part of me" (Fabre, 244).

Although the prestigious Club Français du Livre recognized *Anger and Innocence*, Smith remained in the shadow of Wright, who, during his sojourn in Paris, received all the attention. Fabre claims that "*The Stone Face* never really attracted the attention it deserved" (245) because it was published in 1963, when attention had switched from the French Algerian War to the CIVIL RIGHTS MOVEMENT in America. Smith returned to America in 1967 to cover the extant race riots for the Agence France Presse. He later worked in Accra, Ghana, with MAYA ANGELOU, at the invitation of Shirley Graham DuBois, as the assistant editor-in-chief of the Ghana Television Network, the director of the School of Journalism, and the developer of the African News Service.

Following his divorce from his African-American wife, who returned to America to live, Smith married Solange, a Frenchwoman, and fathered two children. This marriage would also end in divorce before his death from cancer in 1974.

BIBLIOGRAPHY

Baldwin, James. "Notes of a Native Son." In *Notes of A Native Son* [1955], 85–114. Boston: Beacon Press, 1990.

Fabre, Michel. *From Harlem to Paris: Black American Writers in France, 1840–1980.* Urbana: University of Illinois Press, 1991.

Wilfred D. Samuels

"Smoke, Lilies and Jade"
Bruce Nugent (1926)

Included in the short-lived, single-issue literary magazine *FIRE!! Devoted to Younger Negro Artists,* RICHARD BRUCE NUGENT's story "Smoke, Lilies and Jade" explores the complexities of the life of an artist. Less about what happens than how narrative details are presented, the story embodies a modernist consciousness of psychological interiority and emotional ambivalence and ambiguity. As the central character, Alex, looks at his life, both past and present, Nugent challenges common assumptions about the relationship between society and the artist and about the relationship between art and the artist. In a consumerist Western culture that uses capitalist gain and materialism as measures of self-worth and social value, the story examines the extent to which the artist is socially and self-defined by product or by process. It equally questions the extent to which social conformity and blind submission to an ideal about production lead ultimately to spiritual and social death. Such issues are couched within complicated racial, gender, and sexual identity politics.

Nugent's attention to the centrality of thought, thinking, and creative process is evident in the format of "Smoke, Lilies and Jade." Considered a prose poem by some, the story uses ellipses throughout to punctuate and re-create Alex's seemingly fragmented and often spiraling ideas about his father's death, his family's response to his father's death, his past and present male (Beauty) and female (Melva) love interests, his focus on himself, and his strained relationships with his mother and father. Unwilling to restrict his desires to social constructions of heterosexuality and homosexuality, Alex accepts at the story's end the power of his unboundaried attractions, boldly declaring, "one *can* love two at the same time" (39). This admission in both thought and action represents the artist as one whose ultimate responsibility and challenge is to be true to himself. In the face of social suspicion and the perception of the artist as "lazy and shiftless" (Nugent, 34), Alex basks in his own self-acknowledged decadence: "*He wanted to do something . . . to write or draw . . . or something . . . but it was so comfortable just to lay there on the bed . . . his shoes off . . . and think . . . think of everything . . .*" (Nugent, 33).

Within the context of *FIRE!!,* whose editors included LANGSTON HUGHES and WALLACE THURMAN, as a literary experiment expressly created to disrupt the aesthetic and social sensibilities of conservative African-American middle-class intellectuals who fit ALAIN LOCKE's model of "The New Negro" (Huggins, 47–56), "Smoke, Lilies and Jade" was the first published story to acknowledge and celebrate publicly African-American homosexuality and to announce that presence without shame or apology. Other participants in the *FIRE!!* project included ZORA NEALE HURSTON, whose short play "Colorstruck" considers the tragic results of skin color discrimination among African Americans; Wallace Thurman, who contributed a story suggestive of prostitution, and Langston Hughes, who offered the volume's lead poem about "flaming, burning, searing, and penetrating far beneath the superficial items of the flesh to boil the sluggish blood" (foreword to *FIRE!!*). Blurring lines between the sacred and the sexual, Hughes simultaneously teases, flaunts, dares, and warns. Indeed, the slender 48-page volume represented a diversity of voices and experiences even among those artists and writers expected to limit their public celebrations solely to racial identity politics.

While Alex's story resembles Nugent's own personal life—some details are outlined in Charles Michael Smith's "Bruce Nugent: Bohemian of the Harlem Renaissance"—the story's multiple symbolisms foreground its complexity. Cigarette smoke and smoking, the ornate cigarette holder, lilies, color imagery, and names underscore themes of memory and what TONI MORRISON calls rememory, death and dying literally and figuratively, definitions of beauty, black and white interracial intimacies, conflicts between spiritualism and materialism, contradictions, the definition of the artist, and the fluidity of truth. Even as the narrative's surface alleges no action on Alex's part to "do anything," the story itself demonstrates quite the opposite: Alex wishes, wants, wonders, goes out. In fact, Alex is spiritually content just to "walk and think and wonder . . . think and remember and smoke" (36).

That the story, signed only "Richard Bruce," ends with ellipses and with what appears to be Nugent's pledge to say or write more—"To Be Continued . . ." (39)—embodies the artist's unwillingness to be controlled either by social or reader expectations. The story was never continued—at least on the page, further suggesting that the artist committed to self and the craft can indeed be "hungry and comfortable" (33) in the same moment.

BIBLIOGRAPHY

Glick, Elisa F. "Harlem's Queer Dandy: African-American Modernism and the Artifice of Blackness." *MFS Modern Fiction Studies* 49, no. 3 (2003): 414–442.

Nugent, Richard Bruce. "Drawings for Mulattoes" [1927]. In *Gay Rebel of the Harlem Renaissance,* edited by Thomas H. Wirth, 67–70. Durham, N.C.: Duke University Press, 2002.

———. "Smoke, Lilies and Jade." *FIRE!! Devoted to Younger Negro Artists* 1, no. 1 (1926): 33–39.

Silberman, Seth Clark. "Looking for Richard Bruce Nugent and Wallace Henry Thurman: Reclaiming Black Male Same-Sexualities in the New Negro Movement." *In Process: A Graduate Student Journal of African American and African Diasporan Literature and Culture* [College Park, Md.] 1 (Fall 1996): 53–73.

Smith, Charles Michael. "Bruce Nugent: Bohemian of the Harlem Renaissance." In *In the Life: A Black Gay Anthology,* edited by Joseph Beam, 209–220. Boston: Alyson Publications, 1986.

Neal A. Lester

"Sonny's Blues" James Baldwin (1965)

First published in *Partisan Review* (Summer 1957) and later included in his only collection of stories, *Going to Meet the Man* (1965), "Sonny's Blues" is JAMES BALDWIN's best-known and most often anthologized short story. It is about Sonny and his relationship with his brother, the nameless narrator. Although they were reared during the Great Depression in the tumultuous and even violent reality of their urban environment, Harlem, Sonny and his brother took different paths in life after the death of their parents. While Sonny had become a jazz musician and drug abuser, his brother, seven years Sonny's senior, had become a high school math teacher. Distanced from Sonny by a generation and by their life choices and lifestyle, the narrator, at the beginning of the story, learns from the morning newspaper that Sonny has been arrested the previous night for using and selling heroin. On his way to the subway station at the end of his workday, the narrator is met by one of Sonny's nameless friends, a drug addict who, more than likely, first turned Sonny on to drugs. He brings the news of Sonny's arrest and inevitable imprisonment. Ironically, in listening to Sonny's friend, the narrator comes to the realization that, over the years, he failed to listen to his younger brother. Acknowledging their alienation, the elder brother is forced to conclude that, perhaps, "Sonny had had a story of his own" (106) to which he did not listen.

Upon his release from prison, Sonny goes to Harlem, where his brother still lives, to stay with his brother, who recently lost his baby daughter, Gracie, to polio. Not only is Sonny's brother anxious to reunite with him; he also feels guilty for having reneged on the promise he made to their mother before her death always to look out for Sonny. On their taxi drive uptown to Harlem, Sonny asks the driver to drive along the park on the West side, in order that he might revisit what the narrator calls "the vivid, killing streets of [their] childhood" (112). Through the brothers' vicarious journey back to their youth, Baldwin unveils the utter entrapment, destructiveness, and suffocation of their urban, modern ghetto experience. Like RICHARD WRIGHT's Bigger Thomas, Sonny and his brother grew up in a naturalistic world dominated by pessimistic determinism—trapped like animals by the streets and tenement buildings that formed labyrinthine paths around them:

These streets hadn't changed, though housing projects jutted up out of them now like rocks in the middle of a boiling sea. Most of the houses in which we had grown up had vanished, as had the stores from which we had stolen, the basements in which we had first tried sex, the rooftops from which we had hurled tin cans and bricks. But houses like the houses of our past yet dominated the landscape, boys exactly like the boys we once had been found themselves smothering in these houses, came down into the streets for light and air and found themselves encircled by disaster. Some escaped the trap, most didn't. Those who get out left something of themselves behind, as some animals amputate a leg and leave it in the trap. . . . Yet, as the cab moved uptown through streets which seemed, with a rush, to darken with dark people, and as I covertly studied Sonny's face, it came to me that what we both were seeking through our separate cab windows was that part of ourselves which had been left behind. (112)

Unlike before, however, by living together and revisiting their past through a never before broached conversation about their parents, particularly their father, Sonny's brother, who admits Sonny had disappointed him by choosing to become a jazz musician like Charlie Parker rather than a classical pianist, finds time not merely to talk but also to listen to his younger brother. He learns, above all, the degree to which music had become a vehicle for Sonny, who had privately suffered in silence as he attempted to deal with his painful life. Sonny tells his brother, "It's terrible sometimes, inside . . . that's what's the trouble. You walk these streets, black and funky and cold, and there's not really a living ass to talk to, and there's nothing shaking and there's no way of getting it out—that storm inside" (133). Suffering, Sonny tells his brother, is fundamental to life. The brother asks Sonny, "But there's no way not to suffer—is there, Sonny?" Sonny replies, "No, there's no way not to suffer. But you try all kinds of ways to keep from drowning in it, to keep on top of it" (132).

At the end of the story, Sonny invites his brother to go with him to a nightclub to hear him play. While listening to Sonny, his brother becomes aware of the transformative power of music in Sonny's life. Listening to Sonny play "Am I Blue," witnessing his catharsis and transformation, the narrator concludes, "Freedom lurked around us and I understood, at last, that [Sonny] could help us to be free if we would listen, that he would never be free until we did" (140). By listening, Sonny's brother gains unprecedented access and insight into Sonny's life, his own, and ultimately, the human condition.

Although Baldwin explores issues of race and racism, modernity's destructive impact on the human spirit, and African-American culture, particularly music—BLUES and jazz—and its salubrious power in "Sonny's Blues," the overarching theme is the centrality of suffering to the human experience. Everyone must suffer, the narrator concludes, yet everyone must simultaneously respond responsibly to his personal experience—his personal blues. Whereas heroin is, for Sonny, a destructive escape, music is a creative energy and life force; through his music Sonny faces his Sisyphean quest for freedom—face his blues, choose life, re-create himself, and find freedom and wholeness, albeit for a brief moment.

BIBLIOGRAPHY

Baldwin, James. "Sonny's Blues." In *Going to Meet the Man*, 101–141. New York: The Dial Press, 1965.

Wilfred D. Samuels

Souljah, Sister   (1964–)

Rapper, author, lecturer, and social activist Sister Souljah was born Lisa Williamson in the Bronx, New York, in 1964. Raised by a single mother who was often forced to resort to the welfare system to survive, Souljah committed herself to avoiding the traps into which she felt her mother had fallen. In high school the highly motivated Souljah won the American Legion's Constitutional Oratory Contest and was offered a scholarship to attend a summer program at Cornell University. Souljah then attended Rutgers University, where she became a prominent campus activist and writer and came to the attention of members of the rap group PUBLIC ENEMY, who encouraged her musical aspirations. This association led to her debut rap album, *360 Degrees of Power* (1992), which featured guest appearances by such prominent hip-hop figures as Chuck D. and Ice Cube.

Upon the release of this record, Souljah came to widespread public prominence when, on June 13, 1992, then presidential candidate Bill Clinton criticized Jesse Jackson for including Souljah on a Rainbow Coalition panel. Clinton was responding to Souljah's *Washington Post* interview in which she had stated, "If black people kill black people every day, why not have a week and kill white people." Although Souljah later claimed she was simply paraphrasing the mindset of a gang member, she did not significantly distance herself from the remarks. This controversy failed to ignite sales of her album, but it did gain her popular recognition that she has sustained with the publication of her autobiography *No Disrespect* (1995) and her best-selling novel *The Coldest Winter Ever* (1999).

No Disrespect uses accounts of Souljah's turbulent romantic history to document her transformation from apolitical ghetto girl to self-conscious social activist. Each chapter is devoted to a particularly significant figure in her life, and Souljah offers both castigation and advice to black women about how to negotiate the shoals of black male-female relationships and achieve emotional stability. The novel is characterized by and has been criticized for the almost egotistical self-regard that is one of the most commented-on aspects of Souljah's public persona.

This self-regard is given an even more complex deployment in Souljah's first novel. *The Coldest Winter Ever* tells the story of Winter Santiago, the beautiful and amoral daughter of a Brooklyn drug dealer, as she falls from the heights of privilege to the depths of the prison system. This breathlessly fast-paced novel, which mixes Souljah's hectoring seriousness, by way of strategic cameo appearances by the author herself, with an essentially soap opera–like narrative of sex and deceit among the bad and the beautiful of the New York City drug

underworld, has become one of the best-selling works of African-American popular fiction.

BIBLIOGRAPHY

De Lancey, Frenzella Elaine. "Sonia Sanchez's *Blues Book for Blue Black Magical Women* and Sister Souljah's *The Coldest Winter Ever:* Progressive Phases amid Modernist Shadows and Postmodernist Acts." *BMA: The Sonia Sanchez Literary Review* 6, no. 1 (Fall 2000) 147–179.

Terry Rowden

Soul on Ice Eldridge Cleaver (1968)

When ELDRIDGE CLEAVER, a major figure in the BLACK POWER movement of the 1960s and one of the founders of the Black Panther Party and its minister of information, wrote this critically acclaimed collection of biographical essays, he was in prison for rape. With this volume, he joined a well-established tradition of black male writers who embark on a personal, spiritual, cultural, social, and political quest for identity and specifically for a sense of manhood. Such writers include W. E. B. DuBois (*The SOULS OF BLACK FOLK* [1903]), RICHARD WRIGHT (*12 Million Black Voices* [1941]), JAMES BALDWIN (*The Fire Next Time* [1963]), and JOHN EDGAR WIDEMAN (*BROTHERS AND KEEPERS* [1984]). Cleaver divides his collection into four general subject areas—"*Letters from Prison*," "*Blood of the Beast*," "*Prelude to Love*," and "*White Woman, Black Man*"—and he includes 15 essays on a variety of subjects, from race and gender issues to religion and the war in Vietnam, with such titles as "'The Christ' and His Teachings," "A Day in Folsom Prison," "The White Race and Its Heroes," "The Black Man's Take in Vietnam," and "To All Black Women, from All Black Men."

In each essay he speaks ferociously, unabashedly, and militantly to white America, in the tradition of James Baldwin, whose anger critics often noted. For example, in "The White Race and Its Heroes," Cleaver, a former follower, like MALCOLM X, of the teaching of Elijah Muhammad and member of the Nation of Islam (NOI), examines what he claims to be the psychological behavior of young whites during the 1960s, "a time of fundamental social change" (66). "The new generation of whites," Cleaver writes, "are rejecting the panoply of white heroes, whose heroism consisted in erecting the inglorious edifice of colonialism and imperialism; heroes whose careers rested on a system of foreign and domestic exploitation, rooted in the myth of white supremacy and the manifest destiny of the white race" (68). Similarly, in "The Black Man's Stake in Vietnam," Cleaver warns, "What the black man in America must keep in mind is that the doctrine of white supremacy . . . lets the black man in for the greatest portion of the suffering and hate which white supremacy has dished out to the non-white people of the world for hundreds of years" (122). He writes with passion on his response to the news that Malcolm X had been assassinated: "I existed in a dazed state, wandering in a trance around Folsom, drifting through the working hours in the prison bakery" (53). In "Lazarus, Come Forth," he attacks MARTIN LUTHER KING, JR., for his "inflated image [after receiving the Nobel Prize] to that of an international hero," concluding "the only Negro Americans allowed to attain national or international fame have been the puppets and lackeys of the white power structure—and entertainers and athletes" (87). In "Notes on a Native Son," he takes James Baldwin to task for the "quirk" in his "vision which corresponds to his relationship to black people and to masculinity" (105).

Cleaver wears on his sleeves his concern with issues of manhood and masculinity, which he makes a recurring theme in the entire collection. It remains the central theme of what many critics consider the key essay in the collection, "On Becoming," in which Cleaver confesses that in order to retaliate against his white male oppressors—to trample "upon the white man's law, upon his system" (14)—he committed the ultimate "insurrectionary act": He "crossed the tracks and sought out white prey" (14). He began raping white women. Before doing so, however, he empowered himself and boosted his sense of masculinity by "practicing on black girls in the ghetto" (14). This statement led BELL HOOKS to write that by praising violence Cleaver had told the world "that he

had consciously chosen to become the brutal black beast of white racist imagination" (52). For hooks, a feminist critic, Cleaver's work is sexist, misogynist, and homophobic; while calling his claimed "revolutionary act" "reactionary," Sidonie Smith notes that rape, for Cleaver is really "false freedom, another more self-destructive form of oppression that catapults him back to literal imprisonment" (107).

BIBLIOGRAPHY

Cleaver, Eldridge. *Soul on Ice.* New York: Dell Publishers, 1968.

hooks, bell. *We Real Cool: Black Men and Masculinity.* New York: Routledge, 2004.

Smith, Sidone. *Where I Am Bound: Patterns of Slavery and Freedom in Black American Autobiography.* Westport, Conn.: Greenwood Press, 1974.

Wilfred D. Samuels

Souls of Black Folk, The
W. E. B. DuBois (1903)

W. E. B. DuBois published his now-classic collection of essays, *The Souls of Black Folk,* more than a century ago. Made up of 14 essays, some of which had been previously published, *Souls* articulates several key concepts that have continued to shape discussions of African-American experience. It includes, in addition to historical and sociological pieces, personal essays, biography, short fiction, music criticism, polemic, and moral inquiry. The first essay, "Of Our Spiritual Strivings," connects two of these ideas, but in a totally new way. It opens with a restatement of what was at the time commonly referred as "the Negro problem." Distancing himself from others commenting on this issue, DuBois claims that whites cannot understand blacks in terms other than race, that they cannot understand them in straightforward human terms. He attempts to portray the true source of the "Negro problem" as residing in white attitudes and behaviors.

He argues that the ability of whites, who strategically have shut blacks out from their world by placing them behind a "vast veil" (DuBois's trope for legal segregation), imposing definitions on blacks from a position of dominance, creates a psychological problem for blacks. He labels this condition "double-consciousness," a term that continues to resonate in discussions of the significance of race in America. "Double-consciousness" had various connotations during the late 19th and early 20th centuries. It implies a situation of self-alienation that borders on the pathological. DuBois's usage carries some of this implication:

> After the Egyptian and Indian, the Greek and Roman, the Teuton and Mongolian, the Negro is a sort of seventh son, born with a veil, and gifted with second-sight in this American world—a world which yields him no true self-consciousness, but only lets him see himself through the revelation of the other world. It is a peculiar sensation, this double-consciousness, this sense of always looking at one's self through the eyes of others, of measuring one's soul by the tape of a world that looks on in amused contempt and pity. One ever feels his twoness,—an American, a Negro; two souls, two thoughts, two unreconciled strivings; two warring ideals in one dark body, whose dogged strength alone keeps it from being torn asunder. (364)

This passage opens in the realm of magic, of seventh sons, veils, and second sight—qualities that, in the African-influenced Haitian folk religion of voudoun, are associated with powers beyond ordinary humanity. However, in the case of African Americans, DuBois wants us to believe, these qualities result from marginalization and oppression inasmuch as they create a situation in which blacks are not permitted "true self-consciousness" and thus are forced to see themselves second-hand. Survival requires being able to see oneself as the oppressor sees and being willing to submit to that gaze. But accepting that negative view as the whole self is to sacrifice all personal identity and integrity. DuBois argues that it is essential to maintain a "second-sight" that reveals the truth of the self. The tension between these two images is the black condition in America, and DuBois considers living within this tension to be a heroic act. He asks at the end of "Of Our Spiritual Strivings" that readers of *Souls* "listen to the strivings in the souls of black folk" (371).

DuBois intentionally asks readers to "listen to the strivings" because, in the end, he argues, blacks made their greatest contribution to American culture through their music, their "sorrow songs." DuBois writes in chapter 14, "The Sorrow Songs":

> And so by faithful chance the Negro folk-song—the rhythmic cry of the slave—stands today not simply as the sole American music, but as the most beautiful expression of human experience born this side the seas.... [I]t still remains as the singular spiritual heritage of the nation and the greatest gift of the Negro people. (536–537)

BIBLIOGRAPHY

DuBois, W. E. B. *The Souls of Black Folks.* In *W. E. B. DuBois Writing*, 357–547. New York: Penguin Books, 1986.

Keith Byerman

Southern Road   Sterling Allen Brown   (1932)

Southern Road was STERLING ALLEN BROWN's first collection of poems. Many of the pieces here reflect Brown's love of black folk culture, speech, and music, especially the blues. Sterling Stuckey notes in his introduction to *Southern Road* that Brown's use of "the great body of Negro music . . . extend[s] rather than reflect[s] meaning" (9). Stuckey also notes that "Brown realized the need to explore the life of the Southern Negro below the surface in order to reveal unseen aspects of his being, his strength and fortitude, his healing humor, and his way of confronting tragedy" (9).

"Ruminations of Luke Johnson" confirms Stuckey's premise. Luke Johnson watches each morning as Mandy Jane goes to work "wid a great big basket" on her head. "She swings it moughty easy, / An' 'pears to me at such times / It ain't no awful load." However, he also notices that on her return home each evening, Mandy Jane's basket "seems a burden," but she does not ask for help. Although Luke is certain the load is food Mandy takes from her employer to distribute to her less fortunate neighbors (she takes the darkest path home and is followed by hungry dogs), Luke refuses to pass judgment on her, for "tain't my business noway." Moreover, Luke rationalizes, Mandy's employer lives on money "comes from niggers pick / cotton, / Ebbery dollar dat she squander / Nearly bust a nigger's back" (30). Concluding that Mandy Jane's action is justified, Luke remarks:

> So I'm glad dat in the evenin's
> Mandy Jane seems extra happy,
> An' de lady at the big house
> Got no kick at all, I say;—
> Cause what huh "dear grandfawthaw"
> Took from Mandy Jane's grandpappy—
> Ain' no basket in de world'
> What kin tote all that away. (36–37)

Here, Brown expertly manipulates language not only to signify race and class with his use of "grandfawthaw" and "grandpappy" but also, with his use of "kin" as metonymy, to burrow deep beneath the surface of the poem's meaning to expose the exploitation of southern black laborers and the potential tragedy of their blues life, had it not been for their fortitude, dogged strength, and propensity to transcend, to fight back through indirection, to signify on their would-be oppressors, disarming them in the end. The Lady in the Big House "Got no kick at all."

A similar kind of dogged strength is found in "Southern Road," in which the prisoner working on the chain gang defiantly and proudly declares that he has no need to be told what his condition is:

> White man tells me—hunh—
> Damn yo'soul;
> White man tells me—hunh—
> Damn yo'soul;

> Got no need, bebby,
> To be tole. (52)

As MICHAEL HARPER writes in the preface to *The Collected Poems,* Brown's

poetry teaches in the sense that it illustrates a clarity and precision of form as the skeletal structure of the expressive design of language, and that language has a purity of diction because the poet's selectivity is the voice of authority—he controls the atmosphere, the cadence, and pace of utterance, activating the landscape and voicing of the poem, while disarming his reader, his hearer. (xiii)

Brown's equally masterful use of blues forms to denote a trope of black life and, indeed, of the human condition is readily seen in such poems as "Memphis Blues" and "Ma Rainey." In "Memphis Blues" the refrain "What you gonna do when Memphis on fire" recalls not only an old Negro spiritual and Old Testament narratives about man's inevitable destruction, as recorded in the story of Sodom and Gomorrah, but also the biblical prophesy of the fire next time when God, Christians believe, will destroy the world by fire not water as he did in Noah's days. Yet in "Ma Rainey" Brown also focuses on destruction by water, by including the song Ma Rainey sings, "Backwater Blues," which deals with a more immediate and relevant experience of the members of her audience, a song about "de hard luck / Round' our do'" and about "de lonesome road / mus' go."

However, Brown's use of a flood, of a natural disaster: *Thundered an' lightened an' the storm begin to roll / Thousan's of people ain't got no place to go,"* speaks to a more global experience than a racially specific incident. In fact, as a trope for human tragedy, the flood in "Backwater Blues" moves readers and hearers beyond the boundaries of race, class, or gender. No one ("thousan's of people") escaped the disaster; all are made victims who, like Sisyphus, are left to climb an "ol' lonesome hill" where they are left alone to helplessly contemplate their existential fate. Aware of the ultimate condition of all humankind, those who had come to hear Ma Rainey sing "natchally bowed dey heads an' cried" as they return to their river settlements, black bottom cornrows, and lumber camps. Tears, tangible evidence of their experienced catharsis, replace the superficial laughter with which they had entered the music hall.

This perspective extends rather than merely reflects the meaning of the black experience, the blues, and black folk culture in general. It further confirms Gates and West's claim that Brown "was the first major intellectual to discern and defend a democratic mode of the tragicomic" (121) through the blues. Significantly, however, if, as Stuckey points out, Brown speaks of tragedy, "he also holds out the ultimate hope of triumph" (12). This is the theme of one of Brown's signature poems "Strong Man," in which, after chronicling the atrocities heaped upon blacks in American society, Brown's speaker sings this refrain: "The strong men keep a-comin' on / The strong men git stronger."

BIBLIOGRAPHY

Brown, Sterling A. *The Collected Poems of Sterling Brown* (selected by Michael Harper). With an introduction by Sterling Stuckey. Evanston, Ill.: Tri-Quarterly Books, 1989.

Gates, Henry Louis, Jr., and Cornel West. *The African American Century. How Black Americans Have Shaped Our Country*, 119–121. New York: The Free Press, 2000.

Wilfred D. Samuels

Sport of the Gods, The
Paul Laurence Dunbar (1902)

Although he is best known for his poetry, particularly his dialect poetry, and for his six collections of short fiction, PAUL LAURENCE DUNBAR authored four novels: *The Uncalled* (1898), *The Love of Landry* (1900), *The Fanatics* (1901), and *The Sport of the Gods* (1902). Dunbar's first two novels are primarily about whites and do not treat race as a theme; however, *The Sport of the Gods* is considered by many scholars the first African-American

protest novel and the first novel about black life in Harlem.

Dunbar sets out in *The Sport of the Gods* to debunk and critique the well-established plantation tradition created by such white southern local colorists as Thomas Page and Thomas Dixon. Even during the post-Reconstruction period, as he illustrates through his main characters, a form of master/slave relationship was maintained by southern gentility that, on the surface, appeared complementary and congenial. Dunbar's Hamilton family is a middle-class black family who enjoy a comfortable lifestyle as a result of their employment by the Oakleys, to whom they have remained loyal for more than 20 years after the Civil War. In the tradition of the Faithful Friday, Berry Hamilton continues to serve as Maurice Oakley's butler, while his wife, Fannie, continues the tradition of the MAMMY by serving in the role of the family's housekeeper. Their children, Joe and Kitty, also provide domestic services for whites. Like Uncle Tom and Aunt Chloe of Harriet Beecher Stowe's *Uncle Tom's Cabin* (1854), who live on the master's property, the Hamiltons occupy a neat little cottage—"a bower of peace and comfort" (19)—in the Oakleys' backyard.

After a total of 40 years of faithful service, Berry Hamilton, despite his innocence, is accused of, found guilty, and imprisoned for theft when a large sum of money is missing from the Oakley home. Disgraced by Berry's imprisonment, evicted by the employers to whom they have committed their entire lives, unable to gain meaningful employment, and shunned even by the members of the black community, Mrs. Hamilton, Kit, and Joe migrate north to New York: "They had heard of New York as a place vague and far away, a city that like Heaven, to them had existed in faith alone" (68). New York is anything but the expected paradise. The Banner Club, "an institution for the lower education of Negro youth," as the Hamilton children find out, symbolizes the reality of New York life; it is "a social cesspool, generating a poisonous miasma and reeking with the stench of decayed and rotten moralities" (94–95). The city proves to be "cruel and cold and unfeeling"

(70–71). In the end, the agrarian Hamiltons are corrupted by city life and, eventually, morally destroyed. Joe becomes a drunk and murderer, Kitty a nightclub stage performer on a chorus line, and Mrs. Hamilton the victim of physical abuse at the hands of her new husband.

Released from the penitentiary after serving five years, Berry, whose innocence is proved (the real thief is Oakley's playboy brother—a member of southern gentility), travels to New York to search for his family. Upon learning what has happened to each member of his family, he returns home to the South with Fannie, whose abusive husband has been killed in a brawl. At the end of the novel, husband and wife are living once again in their cottage behind the Oakleys' mansion. In summary, Dunbar suggests through his characters that, although the postbellum South is not a virtual paradise, neither is the North. In the end, Dunbar's premise is made clear by his narrator, who states that "the South has its faults—no one condones them—and its disadvantages, but that even what [blacks] suffered from these was better than what awaited them in the great alleys of New York" (160).

The Sport of the Gods is also a modernist text that explores, and in fact didactically reveals, the "pernicious influence of the city" (159), its demoralization and degradation of those who fall prey to its gilded attractions and qualities. The city is a "whirlpool" that, after its victims "enjoyed the sensation for a moment," sweeps them "dizzily down" (159). Consequently, as Charles Nilon points out in his introduction to the novel, *The Sport of the Gods* is also "contemporary in that it provides an example of the problems of social and psychological adjustment that face the black family in the large city" (12). It is a forerunner not only to JAMES WELDON JOHNSON's *The AUTOBIOGRAPHY OF AN EX-COLORED MAN* and CLAUDE McKAY's *HOME TO HARLEM*, but also to RICHARD WRIGHT's *NATIVE SON* and CLAUDE BROWN's *MANCHILD IN THE PROMISED LAND*.

Similarly, published at a time when literary naturalism, promoted particularly in the works of Theodore Dreiser (*Sister Carrie*), Jack London (*Call of the Wild*), and Upton Sinclair (*The Jungle*), was popular, Dunbar also infuses *The Sport of the Gods* with strains of naturalistic thought. Despite the heavy dose of sentimentalism in the novel, the Hamiltons are the victims of circumstances over which they have no control. "Whom the Gods wish to destroy," the narrator tells the reader, "they first make mad" (74). The Hamiltons are, fundamentally, defeated by cruel destiny. According to Bernard Bell, "*The Sport of the Gods* signals both a break with the plantation tradition and the culmination of a constantly shifting but discernible movement of black novelists toward a less simple form of realism that is more compatible with their distinctive experiences and aesthetic vision" (74).

BIBLIOGRAPHY

Bell, Bernard W. *The Afro-American Novel and Its Tradition.* Amherst: University of Massachusetts Press, 1987.
Dunbar, Paul Laurence. *The Sport of the Gods.* Introduction by Charles Nilon. New York: Collier Books, 1970.

Wilfred D. Samuels

"Spunk"   Zora Neale Hurston (1925)

"Spunk" won second prize in the Urban League's literary contest and was published both in OPPORTUNITY and *The NEW NEGRO*, an anthology edited by ALAIN LOCKE.

"Spunk" is quintessential ZORA NEALE HURSTON: a combination of traditional African-American folk traditions and culture. Hurston has taken tropes from African-American oral traditions and transferred them to written discourse. The narrative becomes a storytelling event. Known for his bravado and raw strength, Spunk Banks is admired and envied by his sawmill coworkers. His fearless feats convince them that he "ain't scared of nothing on God's green foot stool" (26). Spunk's narcissism and intrepidness are manifested in the love affair he develops with Lena, Joe Kanty's wife, whom Spunk masterly controls. He boasts, "A woman knows her boss an' she answers when he calls" (28). When Joe confronts Spunk in an effort to defend his honor and masculinity, Spunk shoots and kills him. Spunk, who is haunted by a huge black cat that he believes is Joe's spirit come back from hell, is killed in a violent accident when he falls on the circle saw at the sawmill.

In "Spunk," Hurston celebrates the life of rural blacks, who "inhabit a world dominated by stringent morality," according to Wilfred Samuels (246). This story, Samuels also argues, demonstrates Hurston's interest in "exploring and filtering the rich and complex dynamic of a patriarchal 'villa,' male sexuality, and heterosexual relationships," which she developed in her other short stories and novels, particularly THEIR EYES WERE WATCHING GOD (246). Most important, however, "Spunk" itself is a "signifying" moment. According to Geneva Smitherman, "*Signification* refers to the act of talking negatively about somebody through stunning and clever verbal put downs. In the black vernacular, it is more commonly referred to as . . . *signifyin*" (82). The signification of "Spunk" encompasses individuals in the narrative, Spunk Banks, Joe, 'Lige, as well as the community within the story. However, the story also signifies on the reader, for signifyin, while always a put-down, is also teacherly, instructive. There are lessons to be learned from the event. In "Spunk," the characters, community, and readers are reminded of lessons from African-American culture: "What goes around comes around" and "God don't like ugly," to name two.

Other aspects of the story are also taken from African-American folk traditions and culture: The black English language of the characters, references to folk beliefs such as the anecdote of the "black bob-cat," beliefs of "h'ant[s]" and haunting, burial and death rituals ("We laid him on the sawdust pile with his face to the east so's he could die easy"), and the idea that death is not a end. Spunk says as he is dying, "Ah'll git the son-of-a-wood louse soon's Ah get there an' make Hell too hot for him" (31).

"Spunk" is one of the few narratives of the HARLEM RENAISSANCE that focuses on rural African Americans, their culture and their folk traditions.

BIBLIOGRAPHY

Cronin, Gloria, ed. *Critical Essays on Zora Neale Hurston.* New York: G. K. Hall, 1998.

Hurston, Zora Neale. "Spunk." In *Zora Neale Hurston. The Complete Stories,* 26–32. New York: Harper Collins, 1995.

Samuels, Wilfred D. "The Light at Daybreak: Heterosexual Relationships in Hurston's Short Stories." In *Critical Essays on Zora Neale Hurston,* edited by Gloria Cronin, 239–256. New York: G. K. Hall, 1998.

Smitherman, Geneva. *Talking and Testifying, The Language of Black America.* Detroit: Wayne State University Press, 1977.

Yvonne Atkinson

Staples, Brent   (1951–)

Journalist, advocate for children, and author Brent Staples was born in Chester, Pennsylvania, in 1951, to parents Melvin Staples, a truck driver, and Geneva Staples. His father's alcoholism and his mother's depression paralyzed the family. The eldest of nine children, Staples had an unstable childhood. His family moved from one home to another, always staying one step ahead of the next eviction. Fortunately, Staples was chosen to attend a special program for nontraditional students at the Philadelphia Military College and Penn Morton College. He earned a B.A. with honors in behavioral science from Widener University in Chester (1973), an M.A. in psychology from the University of Chicago (1976), and a Ph.D. in psychology on a Danforth Fellowship from the University of Chicago (1982). Staples began his journalistic career as a freelance reporter and jazz and literature critic. His first newspaper appointment was as a staff reporter with the *Chicago Sun-Times* (1983–85). In 1985 he moved to the *New York Times* and became editor of *The New York Times Book Review* (1985–87) and assistant metropolitan editor (1987–90). Since 1990 Staples has served on the editorial board of *The New York Times,* writing on politics and culture. In recognition of his articles on reading and literacy, the New York Branch of the International Dyslexia Association awarded Staples the Priscilla Vail Award (2004).

Before Staples wrote his autobiography, he began to explore his voice as a writer during his early 20s by carrying a journal with him everywhere he went. He writes,

> I wrote on buses and on the Jackson Park el ... traveled to distant neighborhoods, sat on their curbs, and sketched what I saw in words. I went to a nightclub in The Loop and spied on the patrons, copied their conversations and speculated about their lives. The journal was more than 'a record of my inner transactions.' It was a collection of stolen souls from which I would one day construct a book. (Staples, 221)

In 1994, Staples published his highly personal memoir, *Parallel Time: Growing Up in Black and White,* winner of the Anisfield Wolff Book Award, which had been won previously by such writers as JAMES BALDWIN, RALPH ELLISON, and ZORA NEALE HURSTON. Addressing such themes as family, leaving home, and the quest for identity, Staples records his childhood experience in Chester, Pennsylvania, a racially mixed, crime-ridden, working-class town; his young adult years during which he earned academic degrees in places where he was a distinct minority; his final year at the University of Chicago; and the tragic plight of his younger brother, Blake, a drug dealer, who was killed in the streets at age 22 and whose funeral Brent did not attend. One reviewer notes that the parallels Staples draws between himself and his brother "add a sadness that permeates the text even when we would want to celebrate Staples's successes" (Donohue, 334). However, critic Verlyn Klinkenborg points out that Staples is a careful observer of several other parallels and pairs of subjects: those between black and white, between black Chester and white Polish and Ukrainian Chester, and between Chester and Chicago.

Although some critics may argue that Staples's memoir is not as powerful as the now-classic works of such 20th-century black writers as RICHARD WRIGHT, MALCOLM X, CHESTER HIMES, ELDRIDGE CLEAVER, CLAUDE BROWN, and NATHAN MCCALL, *Parallel Time: Growing Up in Black and White* made a valuable contribution to a genre that reaches all the way back to FREDERICK DOUGLASS and BOOKER T. WASHINGTON, earning Staples a place as a gifted writer in the African-American literary tradition. Staples continues to work as journalist, contributing to such periodicals as *Ms.* and *Harper's.*

BIBLIOGRAPHY

Donohue, Stacey L. "Brent Staples." In *African American Autobiographers,* edited by Emmanuel S. Nelson, 333–337. Westport, Conn.: Greenwood Press, 2002.

Klinkenborg, Verlyn. "An American Story." Review of *Parallel Time: Growing Up in Black and White. New York Times Book Review,* 20 February 1994, pp. 1, 26.

Nelson, Jill. "Hiding in Plain Sight." Review of *Parallel Time: Growing Up in Black and White. Nation* 258 (1994): 562.

Staples, Brent. *Parallel Time: Growing Up in Black and White.* New York: Random House, 1994.

White, Jack E. "Between Two Worlds." Review of *Parallel Time: Growing Up in Black and White. Time,* 7 March 1994, p. 68.

Loretta G. Woodard

Steptoe, John Lewis   (1950–1989)

An award-winning author of children's books, illustrator, and artist, John Lewis Steptoe was the first and still is the youngest African-American artist to publish a mainstream children's book that dealt with the realities and interactions of black Americans. He used language reflecting the black experience and painted pictures that celebrated all aspects of black American life. John used his tools—crayons, pencils, inks, watercolors, brushes, and paints—to lead the children who read his books on adventures exploring imaginative terrains, from urban neighborhoods to ancient Zimbabwe.

Steptoe was born to Elesteen and John Oliver Steptoe September 14, 1950, at Unity Hospital in Brooklyn, New York. He was the oldest of four children, having two brothers, Freddie and Charles, and one sister, Marcia. They grew up in a small one-family home in the Bedford-Stuyvesant section of Brooklyn. As a youth he attended grade school at P.S. 309 and later went to Art and Design High School. From an early age, John, affectionately called John Lewis by his family, displayed a strong independence of spirit and strength of character. Like most other boys in his neighborhood, he spent time playing sports and getting into mischief, but he was also quite sensitive to his surroundings. Sitting in his bedroom watching how light made different shapes and patterns on the walls was just as important to him as roughhousing.

While receiving his formal art training at the High School of Art and Design in Manhattan and participating in the Haryou Act arts program in Harlem, John embarked on his professional artistic career at age 16 when he won a contest by submitting a children's book. Although John developed a love for books early on in life, he was saddened by the absence of stories about and for black children. When his contest entry was published in *Life* magazine in 1969, it received national attention as "a new kind of book for black children" and brought him attention for being one of the pioneers this genre. One of the Haryou Act arts program teachers introduced Steptoe to an editor at Lothroop Lee and Shepard, which published the story as *Stevie* in book form. Steptoe was 19 at the time. *Stevie* is about the love/hate relationship between the main character, Robie, and a little boy named Steve his mother is babysitting.

To publish "Stevie" in a mainstream magazine like *Life* was a tremendous accomplishment for a 16-year-old, and the timing of Steptoe's achievement also became a catalyst for reshaping the landscape of children's books. Steptoe's books created an avenue for black artists and writers as well as for other ethnic and cultural groups to decide how they would be represented by the mainstream publishing world and received by their reading audience. Steptoe was a pioneer in other ways. In *Stevie* he proudly used authentic Bedford-Stuyvesant slang instead of "proper" English.

In *My Special Best Words* he unabashedly revealed the private parts of the main characters Bweela and Javaka while Bweela potty trains Javaka. In *Marcia* he broached the then unspeakable subject of teenage pregnancy.

In his 20-year career, Steptoe published 16 books, 11 of which he wrote and illustrated: *Stevie* (1969), *Uptown* (1970), *Train Ride* (1971), *Birth day* (1972), *My Special Best Words* (1974), *Marcia* (1976), *Daddy Is a Monster . . . Sometimes* (1980), *Jeffrey Bear Cleans Up His Act* (1983), *The Story of Jumping Mouse: A Native American Legend* (1984), *Mufaro's Beautiful Daughters* (1987), and *Baby Says* (1988). In addition he illustrated five stories: *All Us Come Cross the Water* (1973), *She Come Bringing Me That Little Baby* (1974), *Mother Crocodile* (1981), *Outside/Inside Poems* (1981), and *All the Colors of the Race* (1982). These works reflect Steptoe's evolving style as an artist and colorist (the influence of his Haryou Act art teacher, the African-American oil painter Norman Lewis), his interest in the relationship between light and dark, and his realism.

However, Steptoe's childhood memories were the inspiration for many of his early books. His first book, *Stevie* (1969), was based on his experience of having to babysit his younger brother, Charles. *Uptown* (1970) was based on the day he and his friends sneaked off and went to 125th street in Harlem. *Marcia,* a young adult novel, is based on the teenage pregnancy of his younger sister. These themes of family and community were always instrumental to Steptoe's creative process. In fact, Steptoe often used people in his neighborhood and members of his family as models for his work. In *Mufaro's Beautiful Daughter* (1987), Steptoe used his mother for the queen mother, his nephew Antoine as the little boy in the forest, and his daughter Bweela as the model for both sisters. Javaka, the main character in *Birthday* (1972), is named after Steptoe's son.

Steptoe received numerous citations and awards for his work, including the Child Study Association Book of the Year (1969), the School Library Journal Best Books award (1969), the Society of Illustrators Gold Medal (1970), the *New*

York Times Outstanding Book award (1971), the National Council for the Social Studies/Children's Book Council, Joint Committee, Notable Children's Book in the Field of Social Studies (1972), the Brooklyn Museum and Brooklyn Public Library Art Books for Children Citation (1973), the Lewis Carroll Shelf Award (1978), an ALA Booklist award (1981), and the Reading Rainbow Book award (1983).

Steptoe created his work with the hope of providing children with the encouragement "to love themselves enough to accomplish the dreams I know are in their hearts." Steptoe died of AIDS on August 28, 1989, at Saint Luke's Hospital in Manhattan. He was 38 years old and lived in Brooklyn.

Javaka Steptoe

Stone Face, The   William Gardner Smith
(1963)

Literary critics concur that the finest and most mature work of expatriate writer WILLIAM GARDNER SMITH is his novel *The Stone Face*. Set in Paris, *The Stone Face* is divided into three parts: "The Fugitive," "The White Man," and "The Brother." Smith's protagonist, black artist Simeon Brown, seeks to escape American racism and oppression by fleeing to France. While there Brown continues to be haunted by the ever-present face "of discord, of disharmony with the universe" of the white racist who intentionally and brutally put out one of his eyes during his youth. Throughout the novel this stone face functions as a symbolic embodiment of universal destructive racism.

In Paris, Brown finds community with a group of American expatriates, journalists, artists, bohemians, and philosophers, and enjoys the respect and universal camaraderie denied him in America solely on the basis of his race. The Arabs living in Paris label Brown a political "white man," because they consider him to have no less political influence than white French citizens. Involved in an interracial romantic affair with Jewish Marie, accorded respect by all around him, and participating in debate and discussion about current social and political issues in daily meanderings from café to café, Brown initially believes he has found the rewarding and fulfilling freedom he so desperately sought.

However, by objectively viewing the way his Algerian friends are oppressed and treated as second-class citizens—in fact, as less than human, particularly by the French police—listening to their stories of brutality and violence, by witnessing the social oppression they encounter, and by observing their fight for freedom and civil rights through protest and war in Algeria and in France, Brown comes to the realization that he had not escaped racism after all but has merely come to a place where different people, the Arabs, are defined as the other and marginalized. Following a bloody riot in which his Algerian friend is killed and during which he, too, is arrested, Brown decides to leave France and return to the United States. Before he is released from his temporary imprisonment, Brown is warned not to get involved with the Algerians by the police officer in charge: "You understand, we like Negroes here, we don't practice racism in France. It's not like the United States."

BIBLIOGRAPHY

Baldwin, James. "Notes of a Native Son." In *Notes of a Native Son [1955],* 85–114. Boston: Beacon Press, 1990.
Fabre, Michel. *From Harlem to Paris: Black American Writers in France, 1840–1980.* Urbana: University of Illinois Press, 1991.

Wilfred D. Samuels

Street, The   Ann Petry   (1946)

Written at the height of RICHARD WRIGHT's dominance of the African-American literary landscape following the publication of his autobiography *Black Boy* (1945) and his now-classic novel *NATIVE SON* (1940), ANN PETRY's *The Street* is almost always placed within the context of a Wrightian school of literary naturalism and protest tradition. Arthur P. Davis argues that *The Street* is "perhaps the best novel to come from the followers of Wright" (193). Like Wright's infamous protagonist, Bigger Thomas, Lutie Johnson, Petry's heroine, is pessimistically determined. She is the victim of her heredity, environment, and gender: She is black, poor, and female.

A resident of New York's Harlem, Lutie finds that she is economically trapped despite her sense of independence and self-reliance. Although she is a committed mother and wife and a hard worker who believes in the American dream, Lutie is doomed to fail, in spite of her strong Puritan work ethic and admiration of Ben Franklin, a self-made man whose values of bettering oneself she shares. Forced to become a single parent and head of household by her philandering husband, Lutie must work to support herself and her son, Bub, who turns to crime during his youth. Their lives become a struggle for survival in their depressed environment and circumscribing apartment, where the possibility of being raped is one of the realities Lutie must face.

The novel opens with not only a powerful scene and commentary on American modernity, symbolized by the street and meandering urban bodies, but also the ultimate symbol of Lutie's entrapment, the engulfing wind that tosses her about and the filth that threatens to suffocate her as she searches for an apartment for herself and her son:

There was a cold November wind blowing through 116th Street. It rattled the tops of garbage cans, sucked window shades out through the top of opened windows and set them flapping back against the windows; and it drove most of the people off the street in the block between Seventh and Eighth Avenues except a few hurried pedestrians who bent double in an effort to offer the least possible exposed surface to its violent assault. . . . It found all the dirt and dust and grime on the sidewalk and lifted it up so that the dirt got into their noses, making it difficult to breathe. . . . The wind lifted Lutie Johnson's hair away from the back of her neck so that she felt suddenly naked and bald. (1–2)

By the end of the novel, Lutie, who commits murder in self-defense, flees like a fugitive slave in the night to escape imprisonment. Her pursuit of the American dream is left in shambles, her innocence lost.

The Street was received with rousing acclaims at its publication. After its resurrection at the end of the 20th century, critics continue to debate its value. Bernard Bell argues that its strength lies in the fact that "Lutie Johnson is neither psychologically tormented nor driven by fear of white people" (179), like Wright's Bigger. In contrast, Mary Helen Washington argues that despite the importance of social protest fiction, "hidden beneath the surface of deterministic fiction is an ideology that is mainly concerned with men." Such fiction "threatens to marginalize and repress women in particular" (298).

BIBLIOGRAPHY

Bell, Bernard. *The Afro-American Novel and Its Tradition.* Amherst: University of Massachusetts Press, 1987.
Davis, Arthur P. *From the Dark Tower: Afro-American Writers 1900 to 1960.* Washington, D.C.: Howard University Press, 1974.
Petry. Ann. *The Street.* Boston: Beacon Press, 1946.
Washington, Mary Helen, ed. *Invented Lives: Narratives of Black Women 1860–1960.* Garden City, N.Y.: Anchor Books, 1987.

Wilfred D. Samuels

Suggs, Baby

In TONI MORRISON's Pulitzer Prize–winning novel *BELOVED,* Baby Suggs is an ancestor figure, a wise elder who conveys the spiritual and philosophical theses of the work. The mother-in-law of the protagonist, Sethe, Baby Suggs is a folk preacher who holds "church" in the clearing in the woods beyond 124 Bluestone Road. She preaches self-love, not only through her sermons but also through the act of self-naming. In both instances, Baby Suggs demonstrates that self-love brings the capacity for loving others more deeply and spiritually.

During her manumission from slavery on Sweet Home plantation, Baby Suggs learns that her bill of sale bears the name "Jenny Whitlow." When the master of Sweet Home, Mr. Garner, informs Baby of her official name, he asks why she does not refer to herself as "Jenny" but prefers the more unusual name "Baby Suggs." She responds that her husband called her Baby and his name was Suggs. How would he find her in freedom, she wonders, if she used her bill-of-sale name? Baby Suggs's choice to claim her husband's surname and embrace the affectionate name he gave her not only illustrates her rejection of her slave identity but also demonstrates the power of choosing a name given out of love. Baby Suggs declares her love for her husband by maintaining the name they shared to ensure that he can find her after emancipation.

Baby Suggs extends her lesson of love to the African-American community in Cincinnati, Ohio, through her sermons in the clearing. She encourages them to embrace their emotions and celebrate their bodies. Laugh, cry, dance, she tells them. She urges them to love their necks, hands, feet, and most important their hearts. Love all of the parts that the slave masters despised and would maim or mutilate, she intones. The language and message of Baby Suggs's sermon invokes Romans 12:1–2, in which Saint Paul appeals to the people to present their bodies "holy and acceptable to God," to be "transformed by the renewal of [their] minds," and to know that their bodies are "good and acceptable and perfect." Similarly, Baby Suggs reminds the African-American community that despite the abuses they suffered in slavery, their bodies—their lives—are holy and worthy of love.

Baby Suggs faces a crisis of faith when the slave masters enter her yard to reenslave Sethe and her children. Feeling defeated and fearing that love is a lie, Baby Suggs takes to her bed to "ponder color" and in doing so raises the central philosophical question of the novel. Through her contemplation of color, Baby Suggs asks how skin color can be more important than humanity. How could slave masters fail to see beyond skin color to their shared humanity with the slave? As a folk philosopher and "unchurched" preacher in the novel, Baby Suggs suggests that love should matter more than race.

BIBLIOGRAPHY

Morrison, Toni. *Beloved.* New York: Alfred A. Knopf, 1987.

Barbara Wilcox

Sula   Toni Morrison   (1974)

Sula is principally about the history of a black midwestern community called the Bottom, and the people who live there, particularly Eva Peace and her son, Plum; her daughter, Hannah; and her granddaughter, Sula; Sula's best friend, Nel Wright; and Shadrack, the Bottom's misfit. Through careful emphasis on setting, history, memory, and characterization, TONI MORRISON provides valuable insights into and understanding of the complex lives of each character, all of whom are trying to become the sole agent of their lives, to achieve total subjectivity, no matter the cost.

To indicate the community's importance, Morrison's narrator calls attention to the significance of place at the beginning of *Sula:*

> In that place, where they tore the nightshade and black berry patches from their roots to make room for the Medallion City Golf Course, there was once a neighborhood. It stood in the hills above the valley town of Medallion and spread all the way to the river. It is called the suburb now, but when black people lived there it was called the Bottom. (3)

The community's name is filled with irony, for although it is located at the top of the hill, it is called the Bottom. This inversion was the result of a "nigger joke," the narrator explains, "The kind white folks tell when the mill closes down and they're looking for a little comfort somewhere. The kind colored folks tell on themselves when the rain doesn't come, or comes for weeks, and they are looking for a little comfort" (5). The white farmer, who bargained with his slaves to give them their freedom and a piece of rich and fertile bottom land after they performed certain chores, reneged on his promise after emancipating them. Explaining his reasons for giving them the land at the top (the worse land) instead of at the bottom, the farmer said that although the land was high up from the center of town, "when God looks down, it's the bottom. . . . It's the bottom of heaven—best land there is" (5).

In *Sula* Morrison is concerned, argues BARBARA CHRISTIAN, with the community's "philosophy of survival" as much as she is with that of her main characters. Confirming this, Morrison told Robert Stepto in an interview that when she wrote *Sula* she "was interested in making the town, the community, the neighborhood, as strong a character as [she] could" (214). The members of the community are killed when, instead of adhering to their own convictions, they follow Shadrack to a construction site, ignore the "do not enter" sign, and are killed when a faulty bridge collapses. In the end, the Bottom also collapses when urban renewal demands its relocation, leaving only its history as place.

During the Bottom's heyday, three independent-minded women who comprise the Peace family, who refuse to relinquish their subjectivity to the community or its values, challenge the Bottom. Driven to provide economic sustenance for her family, Eva, the community gossip, kicks out her husband and goes in search of work. She returns with crutches and a missing leg that she lost in an accident with an oncoming train, intentionally placed there, it is further rumored, to collect insurance. Eva builds a family home on Carpenter Street and, from her thronelike bedroom at the top, attempts to run the life of each member of her family. When Plum returns from World War I addicted to heroin, which he uses to numb the psychologically damaging experience of war, Eva burns him to death to release him from his suffering. Eva's action suggests her empowerment as the giver of life and death, as her name also implies.

Eva and Hannah model for free-spirited Sula, whose friendship with Nel, her alter ego, comple-

ments and balances Sula after she overhears her mother, Hannah, telling her friends that, although she loves Sula, she does not like her. Throughout her adolescence, during which Sula grows to view and treat sex with casual disregard and develops a more self-reliant life, she also develops an intrepid personality and her life becomes experimental. Inevitably, she has become the more compliant community's scapegoat—a pariah. As a young adult, Nel settles for the prescribed domestic role of mother and wife, and Sula goes off to college. When she returns from college, Eva asks Sula why she does not conform, marry, and raise a family. Sula responds, "I don't want to make somebody else. I want to make myself" (92).

Two men, Shadrack and Ajax, affect Sula's life to some degree, however. When she falls in love with gift-bearing Ajax, Sula confuses love with possession, becoming totally willing to sacrifice the sanctity of herself for him, although he never asks her to do so. Sula realizes how dangerously foolish her behavior has been when she realizes she did not even know Ajax's real name, Albert Jacks. Shadrack teaches Sula about permanence and change. When she stumbles into Shadrack's cabin in the woods, Sula discovers that, unlike the insanity and inappropriate behavior he displays publicly, Shadrack, a veteran like Plum, has successfully ordered his private civilian life, although he had been injured in a life-threatening conflagration. Upon returning home to the Bottom, he founded National Suicide Day to address once a year his greatest fear, death, freeing himself to exercise complete agency over his life.

Ultimately, however, *Sula* is about the sanctity of true friendship between women. After Sula dies, Nel comes to the realization that she treasured their friendship and that Sula's death has left a void in her life, one that is greater than the one left by her husband, who, after sleeping with Sula, left her. Aware of her sense of loss, Nel cries out at the end of the novel: "We was girls together . . . O Lord Sula . . . girl, girl, girlgirlgirl" (174).

Despite reviews that suggested that the novel fell short in some respects, *Sula* garnered accolades for Morrison, who was, critics agreed, an emerging contender for a meaningful place in American letters.

BIBLIOGRAPHY

Christian, Barbara. "Communities and Nature: The Novels of Toni Morrison." In *Black Feminist Criticism: Perspective on Black Women Writers,* edited by Barbara Christian, 47–64. Elmsford, N.Y.: Pergamon Press, 1985.

Stepto, Robert. "'Intimate Things in Place': A Conversation with Toni Morrison." In *Chant of Saints,* edited by Michael S. Harper and Robert Stepto, 213–229. Urbana: University of Illinois Press, 1978.

Wilfred D. Samuels

Tademy, Lalita (1940–)

Lalita Tademy was born and reared in Castro Valley, California. Her life story is embedded in her debut historical novel, *Cane River* (2001). Tademy was a former vice-president of Sun Microsystems when she began to trace her family's history. The two-year project began when Tademy found a bill of sale for her great-great-great-great-grandmother, Elisabeth, who in 1850 was sold away from a Louisiana plantation in Cane River for $800. This bill of sale became the genesis of Tademy's search for facts about Elisabeth, as well as about her great-grandmother, Emily. Tademy went back to Louisiana and absorbed herself in researching her family's lineage. *Cane River* covers 137 years of her family's history, written as fiction but rooted in historical fact and family lore.

In *Cane River* Tademy focuses on four generations of African-American women. The first generation is Tademy's ancestor, Elisabeth, who is born in slavery. The second generation is Elisabeth's youngest daughter, Suzette, who discovers freedom. The third generation of women explored in the novel is Suzette's strong-willed daughter, Philomene, who uses determination to reunite her family and gain economic independence. The last generation is Emily, Philomene's daughter, who fights to preserve her children's freedom against all obstacles. In an interview with Jamie Engle of Bookreporter.com, Tademy comments on her interest in her great-grandmother, Emily:

> Among the many stories I heard about my roots in Louisiana, the stories about my great grandmother, Emily, especially fascinated me, but puzzled me more and more as I got older. There was such a contradiction between the "elegant lady" that my mother and her brothers described and the image I began to piece together of a snuff-dipping, homemade wine drinking, fun-seeking dancing diva of a woman from the backwoods of Louisiana. I found myself wanting to know which one of these memories was true, what made her the way she was, and how she was raised.

In addition to its grand historical scope, the novel explores a number of complex issues Tademy's family had to face: slavery, war, freedom, injustice, color and class bias, interracial relationships, and loss.

Tademy's novel, which includes photographs and other documents of authentication, was selected by Oprah's Book Club.

BIBLIOGRAPHY

Engle, Jamie. Interview with Lalita Tademy. Bookreporter.com. Available online. URL: http://www.

bookreporter.com/authors/au-tademy-lalita.asp.
Accessed May 18, 2006.

Beverly Tate

Tea Cake   (Vergible Woods)

In Chapter 10 of ZORA NEALE HURSTON's *THEIR
EYES WERE WATCHING GOD,* Tea Cake saunters into
the store and Janie's life. He banters with Janie as
though they have always known each other. They
make small talk before they do business; they compete in a checkers game before she learns his name.
Perhaps most important, before he compliments
her looks, he compliments her brain: "Folks is
playin' [checkers] wid sense and folks is playin' it
without. But you got good meat on yo' head. You'll
learn" (96). Tea Cake reverses the expected role
and order of male-female relationship; he backs
into the relationship with Janie, assuming a depth
of connection that Janie surprisingly discovers she
shares: "Tea Cake wasn't strange. Seemed as if she
had known him all her life" (99).

Consequently, Tea Cake, who is younger than
Janie, quickly becomes the antithesis of Janie's
former husbands, Logan Killicks and Joe (Jody)
Starks, who were much older than Janie. Whereas
they wanted to think for Janie, Tea Cake encourages Janie to think for herself. They praised her
youth and beauty; he adores her brains and companionship. Logan and Jody thought of how Janie
could work for them; he thinks of how Janie can
play with him. They liked how she enhanced their
lives; he seeks to enhance hers. In her treatment
and characterization of Tea Cake, Hurston offers
a more intriguing depiction of a complex African-American male as a man maturing, a man of
surprises. Until his death in chapter 19, Tea Cake
constantly evolves, emerging and transforming so
that his presence after his death appears to Janie to
be as powerful as during his life.

During their courting, Tea Cake lives and loves
in the present. He has no savings, no life plan, and
no dream to pursue. When Janie comes into his
life, though, he knows without question that, for
him, she "got de keys to de kingdom" (109). Early
in their marriage, Tea Cake makes a declaration to

Janie: Whatever he eats, she will eat. The money
they live on will be his, and where they can best
do this will be on the Everglades muck. Here, he
knows the score: Arrive early, get hired by the best
boss, secure convenient housing, and prepare to
laugh, play, and work hard. He accepts Janie as his
full partner. He wants her by his side during the
day in the fields and at night in their home.

During the hurricane that takes place near the
end of the novel, Tea Cake comes into full maturity. When he sees that a rabid dog is about to attack Janie, he sacrifices his life for hers. He takes
the rabid bite and, consequently, goes insane. Ironically and sadly, in order to save her own life, Janie
has to kill him, in "the meanest moment of eter-
nity" (184). Despite this tragic end, Tea Cake manages to live his entire life in laughter. His whole
life is lived in the present where he finds love, one
great enough to die for.

BIBLIOGRAPHY

Hurston, Zora Neale. *Their Eyes Were Watching God.*
New York: Perennial Classics, 1998.

Margaret Whitt

Tervalon, Jervey   (1958–   )

Poet, screenwriter, editor, and fiction writer Jervey
Tervalon has received both popular and critical
praise for his work. Born in New Orleans, Louisiana, in 1958, the author moved with his family
to Los Angeles, where he was raised in the inner
city before moving to the small coastal city of
Santa Barbara for his college education. Receiving
his B.A. in 1980 from the University of California–Santa Barbara, Tervalon then returned to Los
Angeles to teach at Locke High School. The experience of being an educator in the disadvantaged
environment inspired Tervalon to write about the
people and events in his first novel, *Understand
This* (1994). In particular, he was touched by the
murder of one of his promising students.

Tervalon wrote that first novel while working
on his master's degree in creative writing at the
University of California–Irvine. *Understand This*
won the 1994 New Voices Award from the Qual-

ity Paperback Club and received critical praise. In the novel, the author constructs a story with eight narrators, including a teacher, who reflect and comment on the murder of a popular high school student.

Tervalon followed his impressive debut with *Living for the City* (1998), a book that was again set in South Los Angeles, containing numerous interlinked stories about black teens confronting gang-infested and oppressive neighborhoods. The author continued to win readers and accolades for his novels *Dead Above Ground* (2000) and *All the Trouble You Need* (2002). In 2001, he received the PEN Oakland/Josephine Miles National Literacy Award for Excellence in Multicultural Literature, and in 2005, he coedited with Gary Phillips an anthology of original short stories titled *The Cocaine Chronicles.*

BIBLIOGRAPHY

Powells.com. *Understand This.* Available online. http://www.powells.com/biblio/17-9780385478243-1. Accessed May 11, 2007.

Melvin Donalson

testifying

As African Americans have been witnesses to the best and worst of American culture, "testifying" has come to have a variety of meanings and functions in the African-American experience and folk life. Spiritually speaking, testifying to the personal revelation of God in one's daily life is a consistent feature of African-American religion. Whether in work songs or the highly religious dance ceremonies called ring shouts—which trace their origin back to the early 19th century—African Americans' testimony to the day-to-day presence of God in their lives usually occurred in a communal environment. Within these environments, the culturally centered communicative form of call and response was critical to the process of testifying. In early African-American history, the autobiography, a form of historical testifying, served to inform humanity of the brutal nature of slavery in America. FREDERICK DOUGLASS's *NARRATIVE OF THE LIFE OF FREDERICK DOUGLASS, AN AMERICAN SLAVE, WRITTEN BY HIMSELF* (1845) and *My Bondage and My Freedom* (1855) are among many classic narratives in this tradition that assisted in ending American slavery. Yet freedom as well as slavery provides a dominant theme in African-American testimony. In a political sense, African-American testifying offered a means of securing freedom by helping Union soldiers determine the loyalties of whites in border states such as Kentucky, Maryland, and Missouri during the Civil War. In the mid- to late 1930s, the Federal Writers' Project, a program under the Works Progress Administration (WPA), collected a large body of oral histories of formerly enslaved African Americans and their families in the American South. Historical, political, or spiritual testifying is always an active process in African-American culture and tradition.

Malachai Crawford

Their Eyes Were Watching God
Zora Neale Hurston (1937)

Their Eyes Were Watching God, ZORA NEALE HURSTON's most beloved book, stages the spiritual and artistic coming of age of an African-American woman griot. A classic "speakerly" text with its free and indirect African-American rhetorical strategies, this novel features signifying, woofing (lying/joking and making excuses), front porch storytelling, baiting, boasting, and lying. Janie, the protagonist, the child of a raped mother is raised by her ex-slave grandmother, who prematurely marries her off to Logan Killicks, a crude older man with 60 acres and a mule. Failing to find love, Janie remembers the magnificent and prophetic pear tree vision of higher sexual and spiritual fulfillment and soon leaves Killicks for Joe Starks. An ambitious black man, Starks is determined to become "the big voice" in his own black township. It appears that Janie has escaped being Killicks's "mule of the world" only to become Mayor Starks's silenced and socially isolated trophy wife. As love flees this marriage bed, Janie discovers her own signifying voice, an event that sends Joe into a shocked physical decline at the assault on his male ego. When he dies two years later, Janie is courted by Vergible "TEA CAKE" Woods, a gambler and wandering BLUES man. As an Afromystical god of the woods and mythic figure of springtime regeneration, he loves Janie and leads her back into axial relation to Nature, the folk community, and her own body. Within this spiritually enlivening folk life of love, hunting, shooting, fishing, wearing overalls, freeing her hair, dancing, singing, and juke jointing on the fertile ecotone of the Muck, Janie completes this phase of her regenerative process. However, her initiation rites involve learning not just the revitalizing powers of love and nature but its destructive potential as well. Now she must negotiate a devastating flood, mass deaths, shooting the rabid Tea Cake, community betrayals, and trial for Tea Cake's murder. Her final rites of passage, therefore, involve transcending society and nature. Having "been to the far horizon" of human testing, Janie returns as a priestly wisdom giver, a powerful female griot capable of spiritually initiating other women.

In 1936, while in Haiti on a Guggenheim fellowship to study Obeah practices, Afromysticism, and medicine, Hurston instead wrote *Their Eyes Were Watching God*. This love story took its impetus from her extensive study of voodoo in both New Orleans and Haiti and from her love affair with a West Indian whom she had first met in New York in 1931. Written in just seven weeks, the book underwent little revision before its publication in 1937. Critics, black and white, were unprepared for it, calling it unfashionable, anachronistic, a minstrel performance, folksy, romantic, and socially irrelevant to struggling urban blacks. Virtually ignored from 1947 until ALICE WALKER's rediscovery of it in the 1970s, *Their Eyes* is now hailed as one of the great women's texts in American literature and has generated an avalanche of critical response. It has been called a vital precursor to RALPH ELLISON's *THE INVISIBLE MAN*, a pivotal female *Künstlerroman*, an icon of the HARLEM RENAISSANCE, a critique of African-American women's psychic history from slavery to the present, a critique of the emerging black middle class, an aesthetic and political "rupture" in American literary history, a precursor

womanist text, and a parable of race and gender relations. By 1990 more than 200,000 copies of *Their Eyes Were Watching God* had been sold. It has been hailed as a typically modernist novel about alienation from one's ancestral roots and celebrated as the key text in the development of a genuine black literary aesthetic. Some see it as the watershed female *Künstlerroman* that enabled contemporary black female literary careers such as those of Alice Walker and TONI MORRISON. The immense popularity of this book in the 1980s and 1990s has been attributed to support from the Modern Language Association, the book trade, women's studies programs, and the burgeoning of African-American cultural studies. As the most widely taught black gateway novel in America's schools, it is of concern to many black critics that white readers may find it entirely too assuring of black well-being in the troubled contemporary African-American moment.

Gloria L. Cronin

There Is Confusion
Jessie Redmon Fauset (1924)

The first of four novels by JESSIE REDMON FAUSET (1882–1961), *There Is Confusion*, along with the three novels that follow it—*Plum Bun: A Novel without a Moral* (1929), *The Chinaberry Tree: A Novel of American Life* (1931), and *Comedy, American Style* (1933)—positions Fauset as the most prolific woman novelist of the HARLEM RENAISSANCE and adds to her renown as an editor and a sharp judge of literary talent. The novel was written as a corrective to the negative portrayal of the black middle class in T. S. Stribling's *Birthright* (1922) and unfolds in the urban settings of Philadelphia and New York. These cities, while indispensable to the action that takes place in the novel, seem simply to serve as a background to this hurried but lengthy narrative of the lives of a number of black bourgeois residents. Fauset sets up a triangle of young lovers—Joanna Marshall (the main character), Peter Bye, and Maggie Ellersley—whose lives and stories become entangled. *There Is Confusion* also constructs spaces of dreams and realities reflected partly in Joanna's longing for achievement and fame in spite of her dark color and partly in the contradictory forces of racist and patriarchal ideologies, which eventually force Joanna into a different set of personal and social constraints. The central irony of the text is that although Joanna initially struggles to define herself as an independent black woman in a world dominated by white men, she ends by willingly relinquishing her autonomy in order that she might be fully accepted by the black patriarchs of her community.

This abrupt reversal of Joanna's ideals might be at the heart of much criticism of the novel. Eric Walrond reviewed Fauset's novel in the July 9, 1924, issue of *The New Republic.* He noted that the book was important because it had been penned by a black woman but disparaged it because it was not a "younger generation Negro" work like Jean Toomer's *Cane* (1923). Walrond unsympathetically labeled the narrative "a work of puny, painstaking labor." Later 20th-century critics such as Barbara Christian (*Black Women Novelists,* 1980) and Hazel Carby (*Reconstructing Womanhood,* 1987) have criticized Fauset's style, form, and subject matter. There is, however, much to be gained in further considering this text, which paints a portrait of the psychology of racism and its impact on modern society. Claudia Tate, in *Domestic Allegories of Political Desire* (1992), points out that Fauset's novel contains certain strategies aimed at not only promoting middle-class values but also "swelling the ranks of the black middle class and middle-class aspirants" (113). Fauset biographer Carolyn Sylvander calls the romantic story plot "deceptive." Indeed, while Fauset undertakes a traditional, almost Victorian style deemed to be outside the realms of modernist thought, she presents a critique of race, class, and gender that demonstrates clearly her modernist sensibilities.

BIBLIOGRAPHY

Allen, Carol. *Black Women Intellectuals: Strategies of Nation, Family, and Neighborhood in the Works of Pauline Hopkins, Jessie Fauset, and Marita Bonner.* New York: Garland Publishing, 1998.

Calloway, Licia Morrow. *Black Family (Dys)function in Novels by Jessie Fauset, Nella Larsen, and Fannie Hurst.* New York: Peter Lang, 2003.

Jones, Sharon L. *Rereading the Harlem Renaissance: Race, Class, and Gender in the Fiction of Jessie Fauset, Zora Neale Hurston, and Dorothy West.* Westport, Conn.: Greenwood Press, 2002.

Levison, Susan. "Performance and the 'Strange Place' of Jessie Redmon Fauset's *There Is Confusion.*" *Modern Fiction Studies* 46, no. 4 (2000): 825–848.

McDowell, Deborah. "The Neglected Dimension of Jessie Fauset." In *Conjuring: Black Women, Fiction and Literary Tradition,* edited by Marjorie Pryse and Hortense Spillers, 86–104. Bloomington: Indiana University Press, 1985.

Sylvander, Carolyn Wedin. *Jessie Redmon Fauset: Black American Writer.* Troy, N.Y.: Whitson, 1981.

Tate, Claudia. *Domestic Allegories of Political Desire: The Black Heroine's Text at the Turn of the Century.* New York: Oxford University Press, 1996.

Rebecka R. Rutledge

Third Life of Grange Copeland, The
Alice Walker (1970)

Although often overlooked by critics and readers, Alice Walker's first novel, *The Third Life of Grange Copeland,* is a searing look at cycles of violence, racism, and despair. The story takes place in Georgia and spans three generations of the Copeland family. The main character, Grange Copeland, has an abusive relationship with his wife. In despair over grinding poverty and racism, Grange leaves his wife, son, and tenant farm for the North. His wife commits suicide. His son, Brownfield, while searching for his father, ends up in a sexual relationship with Grange's former mistress, Josie, and her daughter, Lorene. Brownfield ends up marrying Josie's niece, Mem, whom he later shoots to death in one of the most violent scenes in the African-American literary tradition. When Grange returns to Georgia, he discovers Brownfield in jail for Mem's murder. Grange marries Josie and takes custody of Ruth, Mem and Brownfield's daughter. In an attempt to break the cycle of violence, Grange faces his own mistakes by loving and caring for Ruth. Josie becomes distanced by Grange and Ruth's relationship and seeks solace with Brownfield. Brownfield regains custody of Ruth. Grange, knowing that Ruth will be destroyed if placed in Brownfield's care, kills Brownfield. Grange is then killed for Brownfield's murder.

Grange's first life takes place in Georgia, where he works as a sharecropper. He believes that white people are inherently better than black people. When Grange leaves for a better life in the North, his second life, he discovers that whites are no better than blacks. He sees a reflection of his own actions toward his family in Georgia and starts to understand the human suffering that follows selfishness. When he returns to Georgia, he begins his third life. His new understanding and hope is manifested in the sacrifice he makes for his granddaughter, Ruth.

Walker was criticized for employing stereotypes of violent, debased black characters in *The Third Life of Grange Copeland*. However, the examination of powerlessness in desperate situations and Grange's personal transformative journey represent the theme that by confronting past mistakes, taking responsibility, and being willing to love and sacrifice, one can find grace. Grange's ultimate sacrifice for Ruth transcends stereotypical representations of black characters because Grange transforms himself throughout the novel rather than remaining a one-dimensional character.

BIBLIOGRAPHY

Gates, Henry Louis, Jr., and K. A. Appiah, eds. *Alice Walker*. New York: Amistad, 1998.
Walker, Alice. *The Third Life of Grange Copeland.* New York: Washington Square Press, 2000.

Kim Hai Pearson
Brian Jennings

Third World Press

Along with Detroit's Broadside Press, founded by poet DUDLEY RANDALL, and New Jersey's Jihad Press, founded by poet AMIRI BARAKA, Chicago's Third World Press, founded by poet Don L. Lee/

HAKI MADHUBUTI in his basement, remains among the more important independent black publishers of the 20th century. He was joined in his effort by fellow poets Johari Amini and CAROLYN RODGERS, whose works were the press's first offerings. Third World Press was instrumental in promoting and advancing the poets and fundamental tenets of the BLACK ARTS MOVEMENT, given its emphasis on fostering "a healthy development and sociopolitical activity" within the black diaspora.

For more than three decades, Third World Press has provided a venue for young talented poets and writers, fundamentally those with a more BLACK AESTHETIC perspective, to publish and gain recognition. It has also published the work of such well-known writers and scholars as Pulitzer Prize winner GWENDOLYN BROOKS, who joined the Black Arts camp in the 1970s; SONIA SANCHEZ, Amiri Baraka, MARI EVANS; Dudley Randall, MARGARET WALKER; John H. Clarke; STERLING PLUMPP; KALAMU YA SALAAM; PEARL CLEAGE; and Derrick Bell. Its perennial favorites include the radical best sellers *The Isis Papers: The Keys to the Colors,* by Frances Cress Welsing, and *The Destruction of Black Civilization: Great Issues of a Race,* by Chancellor Williams.

It is possible that Lee's interest in the publishing business grew out of his relationship with Dudley Randall, the editor of Broadside Press. According to Melba Joyce Boyd, "Lee's popularity drew attention to Broadside while Randall's credentials brought credibility to Third World Press" (234). Lee supported the merger of the two presses, but Randall was not interested. Nevertheless, the longevity of Third World Press, the global work it continues to do, and the impact it continues to have attest to its importance beyond the Black Arts Movement. Today, it serves as adviser for the publishing branch of the Institute of Positive Education, which runs the fully accredited preschool, the Bethune Teacher's Training Program, and the Betty Shabazz International Charter School.

BIBLIOGRAPHY

Boyd, Melba Joyce. *Wrestling with the Muse: Dudley Randall and the Broadside Press.* New York: Columbia University Press, 2003.

Wilfred D. Samuels

This Bridge Called My Back: Writings by Radical Women of Color Cherríe Moraga and Gloria Anzaldúa, eds. (1981)

This Bridge Called My Back: Writings by Radical Women of Color is a groundbreaking collection of essays, poems, journal entries, and academic articles addressing the central concerns of what has become known as Third World feminism. Persephone Press originally published *This Bridge* at a time when divisions in feminism fell deeply along racial and ethnic lines. Contributors voiced two central critiques of mainstream feminist practices: The social, political, and cultural gains were being felt only by middle-class white women, and mainstream feminists were making major unfounded claims about the experiences and political concerns of African-American, Asian-American, Chicana, Latina, Native American, and lesbian women. In their introductory essay, editors Cherríe Moraga and Gloria Anzaldúa assert that the book's intention is to "reflect an uncompromised definition of feminism by women of color in the U.S." In the original foreword, TONI CADE BAMBARA notes that *This Bridge* "lays down the planks to cross over on to a new place where stooped labor cramped quartered down pressed and caged up combatants can straighten the spine and expand the lungs and make the vision manifest."

Moraga urges, after AUDRE LORDE, that each woman of color "reach down into that deep place of knowledge inside herself and touch that terror and loathing of any difference that lives there." The writing of Norma Alarcón, hattie gossett, Naomi Littlebear, Genny Lim, Lorde, Nellie Wong, Mitsuye Yamada, and many others does just that. Alarcón, for example, explores the possibilities of a matrilinear pantheon of mythical cultural images, starting with Malintzin, the Aztec noblewoman presented to Cortes upon his 1519 "discovery" of Mexico. Gossett imagines the possibilities of learning to give voice to African-American cultural difference in the beauty of a Billie Holliday vocal. Wong attempts to relocate the cultural vibrancy of Chinese-American women in the "confetti of voices" that carry tradition and history through the works of Maxine Hong Kingston, Jessica Hagedorn, Hisaye Yamamoto, and others. Rosario Morales stresses

the importance of living with a difference within, addressing the connections between Puerto Rico and the United States, the working and the middle classes, the "housewife and intellectual, feminist, Marxist, and anti-imperialist."

This Bridge has had at least two profound and lasting effects since its publication. First, it has inspired feminists to publish other collections of marginalized literature, including *Home Girls,* a collection of black women's writing; *Making Waves,* by Asian-American women; *Food for Our Grandmothers,* by Arab-American women; and the Native American *A Gathering of Spirit.* Also, the loud call in *This Bridge* for an ethic of antiracism and specificity in the practices and scholarship of feminism has influenced feminist studies to focus resources on issues of prejudice on the basis of class, race, and sexuality. While the specific political concerns addressed in *This Bridge* are a part of history, the exuberant power of its language loudly resonates in the present moment.

Keith Feldman

Thomas, Joyce Carol (1938–)

After spending her early childhood through age 10 in Ponca City, Oklahoma, where she was born, Thomas grew up in Tracy, a city in northern California. She received a bachelor of arts degree from California State University, San Jose, and a masters of arts degree in education from Stanford University. Although she has taught at the middle and high school levels, Thomas has spent most of her career teaching at the university levels, including at the University of California, Santa Cruz, San Jose State College, St. Mary's College, and the University of Tennessee, Knoxville, where, as a full professor, she taught creative writing from 1989 to 1994.

Thomas is an award-winning poet, novelist, short story writer, playwright, and author of children's books. Thomas's first collection of poetry, *Bittersweet* (1973), was followed by *Crystal Breeze* (1974), *Blessing* (1975), *Black Child* (1981), *Inside the Rainbow* (1982), *Brown Honey in Broomwheat Tea* (1993), *The Blacker the Berry* (1997), *A Mother's*

Heart, a Daughter's Love: Poems for Us to Share (2001), and *Crowning Glory* (2002).

Although several of her collections of poems were written for children and young adults, for example, *Brown Honey in Broomwheat Tea*, Thomas's early poems, many of which first appeared in *Yardbird Reader II*, a journal edited by ISHMAEL REED, with themes of love, the black church, and black women, were clearly directed at a more adult audience. "Rain" is exemplary:

> Rain
> Background music
> for a dream
> in C minor
> tap dancing
> off beat, on beat
> tiny drums
> tickling
> glass lookouts
> spilling
> wetted balls
> in evanescent designs
> on waiting
> window panes. (Bittersweet, 16)

Similarly, "Did You Know Tomorrow" echoes the texture in Thomas's language that, as Eugene Redmond describes, "economize[s] without displaying abruptness or undecipherable code" (411).

Memories of preparation for going to church on Sunday are celebrated in "Church Poem":

> The smell of sage
> mingles with burnt hair
> and mama prepares
> Sunday dinner
> on Saturday night.

"Blessing" reveals the deep influence of Thomas's fundamentalist Christian upbringing, particularly its central lessons of forgiveness and compassion, as well as the bittersweet humor and emphasis on the positive that pervades many of her poems.

From 1982 to 2003, Thomas published almost 20 collections of stories and fiction for young adults, including *Marked by Fire* (1982), *Journey* (1988), *I Have Heard of a Land* (1998), and *The Gospel of Cinderella* (2000). Thomas is the editor of two anthologies: *A Gathering of Flowers: Stories about Being Young in America* and *Linda Brown, You Are Not Alone: The Brown v. Board of Education Decision* (2003), a collection of stories, poems, and personal reflections by prominent writers and individuals, including Reed and QUINCY TROUPE, commemorating the 50th anniversary of the 1954 landmark Supreme Court decision in *Brown v. Board of Education*, which tore down the walls of legal segregation in American public schools in the South. Curtis James beautifully illustrates the text. Thomas also published adult fiction, including *House of Light: A Novel.*

Thomas has received a plethora of awards and recognition for her work. Her first novel, *Marked by Fire* (1982), won the National Book Award, the American Book Award, the Outstanding Book of the Year from *The New York Times*, and Best Book for Young Adults from the American Library Association. She has won several Coretta Scott King Author Honor Book awards and the Notable Children's Book from the National Council of Teachers of English. Thomas currently lives in Berkeley, California.

BIBLIOGRAPHY

Redmond, Eugene B. *Drumvoices: The Mission of Afro-American Poetry: A Critical Mission.* Garden City, N.Y.: Anchor Books, 1976.

Tomas, Joyce Carol. *Bittersweet.* San Jose, Calif.: Firesign Press, 1973.

———. *Blessing.* Berkeley, Calif.: Jocato Press, 1975.

Wilfred D. Samuels

Thomas, Lorenzo (1944–2005)

A native of the Republic of Panama, Thomas, the son of Herbert Hamilton Thomas and Luzmilda Gilling Thomas, grew up in New York City, to which his parents migrated in 1948 when he was four years of age. Thomas attended Queens College. A music historian and veteran of the Vietnam War, Thomas, during the height of the BLACK ARTS

MOVEMENT, was a member of the Umbra workshop, which included DAVID HENDERSON. He was on the editorial staff of *Roots,* a journal published by Texas Southern University, where he worked as a visiting writer. His work is anthologized in AMIRI BARAKA and LARRY NEAL's *BLACK FIRE* (1968), Chapman's *New Black Voices* (1972), and Ward's *Trouble the Water: 250 Years of African-American Poetry* (1997).

Thomas published six collections of poems: *Chances Are Few* (1972), *The Bathers* (1981), *Fit Music* (1972), *Dracula* (1973), *Framing the Sunrise: Selected Poems* (1975), and *Dancing on Main Street* (2004). Also, his essays and poetry have been published in *AFRICAN AMERICAN REVIEW, Ploughshares* and *Popular Music and Society*. Often filled with musical references and metaphors, Thomas's poetry is honest, his language precise, and his voice direct and even uncompromising. For example, Thomas is almost didactic in "L'Argent":

> *I know you don't know what*
> *Love is it isn't*
> *Dagwood kisses on the way to work*
> *It's going to work.*
> *. . .*
> *Love could be but it's not*
> *A 50/50 partnership. (Furious Flower, 148)*

Thomas begins "The Marvelous Land of Indefinitions" with a quotation from Ricardo Miro, "the poet's business is telling the truth," and continues with a speaker whose purpose is to do just that:

> *How nice! How convenient!*
> *We have all gathered to read & listen to*
> *poems*
> *As if everyone were actually equal*
> *Laborers in the corn fields. . .*
> *But poeting with poor people doesn't end*
> *poverty.*
> *(Chances are Few, 78)*

His speaker in "Historiography" speaks as if to set the record straight about the real, not the mythic, Charlie Parker (Bird). He was not the "god of good graciousness" as TED JOANS would have

us to believe, Thomas writes. In fact, in real life, Thomas's speaker reminds us, Bird was a junkie— a drug abuser: "Those who loved music made his memory live / And made the young ones never forget Bird / Was a junkie." (*Trouble the Water* 429)

Thomas worked with the national Poetry in the Schools Program and taught American literature and creative writing at the University of Houston, Downtown and was a long time contributor to the *HOUSTON CHRONICLE*. Thomas died of emphysema on July 4, 2005.

BIBLIOGRAPHY

Gabbin, Joanne V., ed. *Furious Flower: African American Poetry from the Black Arts Movement to the Present.* Charlottesville: University of Virginia Press, 2004.

Ward, Jerry W., Jr., ed. *Trouble the Water: 250 Years of African American Poetry.* New York: Mentor Book, 1997.

Wilfred D. Samuels

Thomas, Trisha R.   (1964–)

San Diego–born Trisha R. Thomas attended the University of Southern California (USC) in Los Angeles after graduating from Morse High School. She left USC and returned to San Diego to attend the University of California at San Diego, where she was discouraged from pursuing a career in creative writing. Taking her counselor's advice to do whatever she loved doing best, Thomas started her own business, designing unique painted clothing. Despite her modest success, Thomas abandoned her business to continue her education. She enrolled at California State University, Los Angeles, and pursued a degree in marketing, which she completed in 1989. While assisting her husband, who was writing his memoir, Thomas, rediscovered her love for writing. The result was the publication of her debut novel, *Nappily Ever After* (2000), with which she began the story of Venus Johnston, a successful young black businesswoman.

On the one hand, as the title suggests, Thomas's central theme in *Nappily Ever After* is a ritual most black women have painfully faced throughout their lives: straightening their hair to rid themselves of the coarse (nappy) hair associated with basic African-American identity, to approximate the more culturally acceptable silken hair validated by Western aesthetics. For many years, fair-complexioned Venus (and those around her) had been rather proud of her straight hair, the symbol, as it is for Janie in ZORA NEALE HURSTON's *THEIR EYES WERE WATCHING GOD* (1937), of her beauty and female identity.

To maintain this more acceptable appearance, Venus had spent years and thousands of dollars shackled to her beautician's chair having her hair chemically treated:

> This was my ball and chain, aka my hair and about 360 relaxers. What was the sense of going through the ritual, the wash, the conditioner, and combing it out ever so gently so as not to raise the grain? I counted back to the age of four, the tender age of my introduction to the lye. Averaging out to fifty bucks a pop, it could've been a nice little padding for my retirement fund, to the sum of eighteen thousand dollars, not including interest" (7)

Much to the displeasure of all around her, Venus cuts her hair and wears it in a short, curly afro.

On the other hand, *Nappily Ever After* is about Venus's relationship with her live-in noncommittal boyfriend, Clint, a doctor with whom she has spent three years without being married. To liberate herself and achieve the freedom needed for true rebirth and self-empowerment, Venus has to let Clint go, and she does. Thomas followed her debut novel with a sequel, *Would I Lie to You: A Novel* (2004), in which readers find a more mature Venus Johnston, living and working in Washington, D.C., as the director of a marketing firm and also in Los Angeles, where she becomes part of the business world of hip-hop fashion and culture.

Wilfred D. Samuels

Thurman, Wallace (1902–1934)

During the HARLEM RENAISSANCE Wallace Thurman had an impressive influence on such contemporaries as LANGSTON HUGHES, DOROTHY WEST, and BRUCE NUGENT. His influence has lasted, at least indirectly, and is evidenced in the works of JAMES BALDWIN, TONI MORRISON, MARLON RIGGS, and E. LYNN HARRIS. In his brief life, Thurman experimented with many genres in hopes of finding a niche that would propel him to be a great American writer. Thurman's nine-year hegira in Harlem was preceded by a middle-class, provincial life that began with his birth in Salt Lake City, Utah, on August 6, 1902, where his parents (Oscar and Beulah Thurman) and grandparents, Western pioneers, had settled. His grandparents, after his parents' marriage ended early, raised Thurman; he describes in a 1929 letter his poignant first meeting with his father. The family's gypsy-like existence, which took them from Boise, Idaho, to Chicago, Illinois, to Omaha, Nebraska, and back to Salt Lake City, resulted in Thurman's attending school in a succession of midwestern cities while continually combating illnesses. In Salt Lake City, Thurman not only managed to complete high school, in 1918, but also he spent two years as a pre-medical student at the University of Utah.

During the next three years, 1922–25, Thurman decided to dedicate his life to writing. He moved to Los Angeles, worked as a postal clerk, and, simultaneously studied for two years at the University of Southern California. Through coincidence, Thurman and ARNA BONTEMPS, another renaissance literary artist, worked for several months as night clerks for the same post office. In Los Angeles, Thurman published and edited his own magazine, *Outlet,* which grew out of his unsuccessful efforts to establish a West Coast–based "New Negro" movement. In addition, Thurman also wrote a column titled "Inklings" for a black Los Angeles newspaper. Thurman traveled to Harlem in 1925, during the heightened black literary activity and, as he told a friend, began "to live."

In Harlem, the Thurman best known to scholars began to emerge. He worked as a reporter and editor at *The Looking Glass* and became managing editor of the MESSENGER, where his editorial expertise earned him renown. He published works by Hughes and ZORA NEALE HURSTON. He left in the autumn of 1926 to join the staff of a white-owned periodical, *World Tomorrow.* In summer 1926, Thurman, along with Hughes, edited *FIRE!!.* Two years later, Thurman published *Harlem: A Forum of Negro Life,* a more moderate, broadly focused magazine that was devoted to displaying works by younger writers. Both *Fire!!!* and *Harlem* failed after their premier issues.

Although considered a minor literary figure, Thurman was lauded as a satirist. Thurman rejected the idea that the Harlem Renaissance was a substantial literary movement, claiming that the 1920s produced no outstanding writers and that those who were famous exploited whites and allowed themselves to be patronized by them. He claimed, as did a number of authors of the decade, that white critics judged black works by lower standards than they judged white efforts.

Written in collaboration with Jourdan Rapp, Thurman's first play, *Harlem: A Melodrama of Negro Life,* opened on Broadway on February 20, 1929, at the Apollo Theater, bringing Thurman immediate success. *Harlem* centers on the Williams family, who relocate in New York City to escape economic difficulties at the time of the Great Migration of southerners to the North during the first two decades of the 20th century. But instead of finding the city a promised land, they encounter many of the problems that often plagued the families of the migration: unemployment and tensions between generations heightened by difficulties in adjusting to city life.

Thurman's best-known work is his first novel, *The Blacker the Berry* (1929). Taken from the folk saying "the blacker the berry, the sweeter the juice," the title is ironic, for the novel is an attack on prejudice within the race. Emma Lou, the protagonist, is a dark-skinned girl from Boise who is looked down on by her fairer family members and friends. When she attends the University of Southern California, she again is scorned; she travels to Harlem, believing she will not be snubbed because of her dark color. However, like the Williamses in *Harlem* and like Thurman in his own life, Emma Lou is disillusioned by the city. She becomes unhappy with her work, her love affairs, and the pronounced discrimination she experiences in the nightclubs, where lighter-skinned females star in extravagant productions while darker-skinned performers are forced to sing offstage. She uses hair straighteners and skin bleachers and takes on the appearance and attitudes of the fairer-skinned people who degrade her, and ironically she snubs darker men, whom she considers inferior. She dates light-skinned Alva, who is cruel and verbally abusive, but when she accidentally catches him in a homosexual embrace, Emma Lou awakens to her life of contradiction and hypocrisy.

Although critics praised Thurman for devoting a novel to the plight of a dark-skinned heroine, they criticized him for being too objective. Thurman, they argued, had failed to judge critically the world in which Emma Lou lived. They also criticized Thurman for trying to do too much with *The Blacker the Berry,* accusing him of crafting a choppy and occasionally incoherent narrative by touching on too many themes.

Also set in Harlem, Thurman's second novel, *Infants of the Spring* (1932), revolves around Raymond Taylor, a young black author who is trying to write a weighty novel in a decadent, race-oriented atmosphere. Taylor resides in a boardinghouse, nicknamed "Niggerati Manor," with a number of young blacks who pretend to be aspiring authors. Thurman makes these pretenders the major victims of his satire, suggesting that they have destroyed their creativity by leading decadent lives.

Critics considered *Infants of the Spring* one of the first books written expressly for black audiences and not white critics and contended that Thurman based his characters on well-known figures of the Harlem Renaissance, including Hughes, Locke, Hurston, COUNTEE CULLEN, Nugent, and Aaron Douglas. As they did with *The Blacker the Berry,* reviewers objected to Thurman's examining too many issues. Unlike his first novel, which was considered too objective, critics thought *Infants* was overly subjective and Thurman overly argumentative. Yet critics also praised Thurman for his frank discussion of black society. Martha Gruening wrote in the *Saturday Review of Literature,* "No other Negro writer has so unflinchingly told the truth about color snobbery within the color line, the ins and outs of 'passing' and other vagaries of prejudice. [*Infants of the Spring's*] quota of truth is just that which Negro writers, under the stress of propaganda and counter propaganda, have generally and quite understandably omitted from their picture."

Thurman's third novel, *The Interne* (1934), was a collaboration with Abraham L. Furman, whom he had met while working at Macaulay's Publishing Company. The novel portrays medical life at an urban hospital as seen through the eyes of a young white doctor, Carl Armstrong. In his first three months at the hospital, during which he witnesses staff members' corrupt behavior and comes in contact with bureaucratic red tape, Armstrong's ideals are shattered. Although he participates in the prevailing vices, he soon realizes his own loss of ethics and saves himself by taking his practice to the country. Critics could not agree whether Thurman's accounts of medical wrongdoing were based in fact; many claimed that the novel had no semblance of reality, while others stressed that incidents were actual, if unusual. Wallace Thurman died on December 21, 1934, at age 32.

BIBLIOGRAPHY

Blackmore, David. "'Something ... Too Preposterous and Complex to Be Recognized or Considered': Same-Sex Desire and Race in *Infants of the Spring.*" *Soundings* 80, no. 4 (1997): 519–29.

Gaither, Renoir W. "The Moment of Revision: A Reappraisal of Wallace Thurman's Aesthetics in *The Blacker the Berry* and *Infants of the Spring.*" *College Language Association Journal* 37, no. 1 (1993): 81–93.

Ganter, Granville. "Decadence, Sexuality, and the Bohemian Vision of Wallace Thurman." MELUS 28, no. 2 (2003): 83–104.

Glick, Elisa F. "Harlem's Queer Dandy: African-American Modernism and the Artifice of Blackness." *Modern Fiction Studies* 49, no. 3 (2003): 414–442.

Henderson, Mae Gwendolyn. "Portrait of Wallace Thurman." In *Remembering the Harlem Renaissance,* edited by Cary D. Wintz, 289–312. New York: Garland, 1996.

Hughes, Langston. "Harlem Literati in the Twenties." In *Remembering the Harlem Renaissance,* edited by Cary D. Wintz, 393–394. New York: Garland, 1996.

Silberman, Seth Clark. "Looking for Richard Bruce Nugent and Wallace Henry Thurman: Reclaiming Black Male Same-Sexualities in the New Negro Movement." *In Process* 1 (1996): 53–73.

Lawrence T. Potter, Jr.

Till, Emmett   (1941–1955)

The story of Emmett Louis "Bobo" Till is the tragic story of a 14-year-old black Chicago youth who was brutally lynched in Money, Mississippi, on August 28, 1955. His so-called crime was to whistle at Carolyn Bryant, a 22-year-old white woman, the night before. Her husband, Roy Bryant, and his stepbrother, J. W. Milam, sought revenge for the youth's naive act of indiscretion. Till's naiveté lay in the fact that, as a young northern boy, he did not understand southern etiquette, which demanded that white women must be protected from any and all infractions or violations by black males, whom southerners stereotypically perceived as black brutes. Till and his innocent whistling act fit the profile. What makes Till's murder so poignant is the victimization of a youth who brought to the scenario his innocence as a child and the naiveté of a northerner.

Throughout the last half of the 20th century, many black writers made Till's murder a central theme in their works. Writers often used the grotesque image of his bloated face and body lying in an open coffin as demanded by his mother as the frontispiece for works produced during the CIVIL RIGHTS MOVEMENT of the 1950s and the 1960s. In such works, Till's plight evoked both empathy for the murdered child and commitment from black adults, who collectively vowed never to allow such an atrocity to happen again. Black literary texts—short stories, poetry, autobiography, and drama—have made the Till case a familiar one and made the painful lessons to be learned much easier to grasp. Examples abound, including Arthenia Bates Milligan's "Lost Note," a short story; GWENDOLYN BROOKS's "The Last Quatrain of the Ballad of Emmett Till," a 10-line poem rendering the response of Till's mother to the news of her son's death; ANNE MOODY's autobiographical novel, *Coming of Age in Mississippi,* which contains two powerful chapters on Till's lynching; and two plays that dramatically render the lynching and its significance: Endesha Ida Mae Holland's *From the Mississippi Delta* and JAMES BALDWIN's *Blues for Mr. Charlie.* Whereas Holland's work opens with a rendition of the Till incident, focusing on the setting and the victimization of blacks in the South and particularly blacks in Mississippi, which had become a symbol of brutal American racism, Baldwin's play dramatizes the murder to emphasize the insidious arrogance of a culture that refused to see itself as accountable for such crimes. In the state of Mississippi, blacks had no rights that whites were bound to respect.

In many of the black literary texts of the second half of the 20th century, Emmett Till's lynching became a living testimony. These texts provide the true legacy of Emmett Till, a catalyst of the Civil Rights movement.

BIBLIOGRAPHY

Hudson-Weems, Clenora. "Emmett Till: The Impetus of the Modern Civil Rights Movement." Dissertation. University of Iowa. 1988.
———. *Emmett Till: The Sacrificial Lamb of the Civil Rights Movement.* Columbia: University of Missouri Press, 1994.

Clenora Hudson-Weems

Tolson, Melvin B.   (1898–1966)

Politician, professor, and poet Melvin Beaunorus Tolson was born on February 6, 1898, in Moberly, Missouri. Labeled a black modernist in part for his complex poetic constructions and allusions, Tolson infused the modernist project with African-American issues and images, declaring at one point that he would "visit a land unvisited by Mr. Eliot" (quoted in Nelson, "*Harlem Gallery.*" xl).

After attending Fisk University, Tolson transferred to Lincoln University, where he graduated with honors in 1922. That same year he married Ruth Southall. For a time he taught and coached at Wiley College in Marshall, Texas, but left in 1931 to attend Columbia University on a Rockefeller Foundation scholarship. This sojourn at Columbia brought him to New York City near the end of the HARLEM RENAISSANCE; he conducted interviews for his thesis that brought him introductions to many of the leading lights of that movement, especially LANGSTON HUGHES. His research and immersion in this artistic swirl led to his first published poetic efforts. He returned to Wiley College to teach and remained there until 1947. He was named poet laureate of Liberia that year and was commissioned to write a poem in celebration of the former American colony's centennial. In 1947 Tolson left Wiley College to teach at Langston University in Langston, Oklahoma. He also served as Langston's mayor from 1954 to 1960. Tolson, who continued working as a poet and cultural critic at the onset of the BLACK ARTS MOVEMENT of the 1960s, won the Arts and Letters Award for Literature from the American Academy and Institute of Arts and Letters in 1966, just before his death on August 29, 1966.

Though Tolson published a few poems that originated in his year at Columbia, most of his early efforts remained unpublished until Robert Farnsworth compiled and published *A Gallery of Harlem Portraits* (1979). "Dark Symphony," which was first published in *Atlantic Monthly* in September 1941, was among the most important poems in this collection. In it Tolson uses six stanzas to explore the New Negro's experience and journey through American history. Assigning each stanza a musical signature, Tolson moves the Negro from the moderately quick pace of the *allegro moderato* of Crispus Attucks, who "taught / Us how to die / Before white Patrick Henry's bugle breath" uttered his famous cry for liberty or death, to the powerfully hopeful marching pace of the *tempo di marcia* in which "We advance!" Between the two, as RITA

Dove has noted, Tolson confronts the horror of slavery, soothed only by the faith embodied in sorrow songs.

Throughout much of his career, Tolson's work was assessed on the reception of *A Gallery of Harlem Portraits*. His use of numerous and often obscure references placed him in the modernist company of Ezra Pound and Eliot and gained him praise for his radical experimentation, yet white commentators often criticized Tolson's layering of classical allusions atop the references to the history and culture of Africans and African Americans they considered more credible. In his preface to the *Libretto for the Republic of Liberia,* Allen Tate hinted that the long work was derivative and "breaks down into Whitmanesque prose-paragraphs into which Mr. Tolson evidently felt that he could toss all the loose ends of history, objurgation, and prophecy" (142).

In contrast, black critics, especially those in the Black Arts Movement of the 1960s, occasionally complained that his art relied too heavily on classical allusion and too little on black culture and history. His work, they claimed, did not reflect the experience of African Americans but was intended, instead, to impress a white literary audience. He was warned that such complicated verse would outrage the readers of *Black Gazette, Ebony,* and *The Negro World.* Michael Berube especially notes that Robert Davis, a black critic for the *Chicago Sunday Bee,* praised *Libretto* as a whole, but lamented its "use of well worn allusions" (169) and its uneven images. Tolson in this case agreed, for he revised one stanza highlighted by Davis. However, legend has long held that Tolson undertook the revision at the behest of Tate and not Davis.

Tolson, however, is best known for three major poetic works: *Rendezvous with America* (1944), *Libretto for the Republic of Liberia* (1953), and *Harlem Gallery* (1965). Robert Farnsworth cites the claim that in the *Libretto* "Tolson's integrity would not allow him to retreat into the folksiness of Langston Hughes—making things 'simple'—nor would it allow him to lose his own voice in mere imitation. He gives us folk-wisdom

and out-Pounds Pound to show what is involved in a country that is profoundly both African and American" (173). The poem reflects Tolson's long study of Africa and his belief that, as he noted in "The Negro Scholar" (1948):

> *The ground the Negro scholar stands upon*
> *Is fecund with the challenge and tradition*
> *The Ghana knew, and Melle, and Ethiopia,*
> *And Songhai.... (178)*

Libretto traces the history of Liberia, but in doing so poetically resurrects the power of the Songhai Empire and ends in hope at the end of World War II.

However, it is the 150 epic pages of *Harlem Gallery* that are most often cited as Tolson's magnum opus, a work that was intended to be the first of five parts. In 24 sections, each corresponding to a letter of the Greek alphabet and subtitled "The Curator," he offers what Raymond Nelson claims is a poem full of "extensive and precise learnedness and uncompromising obscurities, . . . syncopation of puns, neologisms, double negatives, labyrinthine syntax, and acrobatic prosody" ("Harlem Gallery"). The need for annotation, in fact, spawned Robert Huot's 1971 dissertation and Raymond Nelson's more recent annotated rendering. The reception at publication was far less ambiguous. Black critics tended to decry its "vast, bizarre, pseudo-literary diction" which was certainly "not 'Negro' to any significant degree." These comments allude to Karl Shapiro's claim in the foreword that "Tolson writes and thinks in Negro" (Nelson, "Harlem Gallery"). Even at the end of his life, Tolson's poetry proved controversial, though in the controversies over the poems, too few bothered to read them.

BIBLIOGRAPHY

Berube, Michael. *Marginal Forces/Cultural Centers: Tolson, Pynchon, and the Politics of the Canon.* Ithaca, N.Y.: Cornell University Press, 1992.

Farnsworth, Robert M. *Melvin B. Tolson, 1898–1966: Plain Talk and Poetic Prophecy.* Columbia: University of Missouri Press, 1984.

Huot, Robert Julian. "Melvin B. Tolson's *Harlem Gallery:* A Critical Edition with Introduction and Explanatory Notes." Dissertations: University of Utah, 1971.

Lenhart, Gary. "'Caviar and Cabbage': The Voracious Appetite of Melvin Tolson." *The American Poetry Review.* March 2000. Available online. URL: http://www.aprweb.org/issues/mar00/lenhart.html. Accessed October 26, 2006.

Nelson, Raymond. "Harlem Gallery: An Advertisement and User's Manual." *Virginia Quarterly* (Summer 1999). Available online. URL: http://www.vqronline.org/articles/1999/summer/nelson-harlem-gallery. Accessed February 14, 2007.

———, ed. *"Harlem Gallery" and Other Poems of Melvin B. Tolson.* Introduction by Rita Dove. Charlottesville: University Press of Virginia, 1999.

Nielsen, Aldon L. "Melvin B. Tolson and the Deterioration of Modernism." *African American Review* 26, no. 2 (Summer 1992): 241–256.

Russell, Mariann. *Melvin B. Tolson's "Harlem Gallery": A Literary Analysis.* Columbia: University of Missouri Press, 1980.

Jay Hart

Toomer, Jean (1894–1967)

Jean Toomer came of age as an artist in an era on the verge of great cultural change. Influenced by trends in European modernism, but deeply impressed by the loss of the natural beauty and African-American community in the rural American South, Toomer composed one of the most unique and enduring works of American literature, *Cane.* The work itself is as enigmatic as its writer. As a biracial man in early 20th-century America, Toomer struggled with his identity most of his life, at various times even denying his African-American heritage. Born in 1894 as Nathan Eugene Pinchback Toomer in Washington, D.C., he spent even his earliest years in turmoil. His father, Nathan Toomer, left the family when Toomer was only a year old. His maternal grandfather took Toomer and his mother, Nina, into his home but was apparently a difficult surrogate father. P. B.

S. Pinchback, Toomer's grandfather, once an acting lieutenant governor in the state of Louisiana during Reconstruction, at different times lived as an African American or passed as a white man. The racial and cultural confusion of this situation helped forge Toomer's own ambivalent identity.

In 1905 Toomer's mother remarried. The family moved to Brooklyn, but four years later, after his mother's death, Toomer was back in Washington, D.C., with his grandparents. Toomer also lived for a time with his uncle, who was a scholar. Toomer, who had always excelled in school, was later influenced by his uncle when he began to consider a career as a writer. However, he first enrolled in college at the University of Wisconsin–Madison to study agriculture. Toomer's father had been a farmer and perhaps inspired this choice of study. But the next year, in 1915, Toomer dropped out of school to pursue other interests. His college career was marked by diverse studies and indecision. At various times he studied at the University of Chicago, the American College of Physical Training, New York University, and City College of New York. He took courses in biology, philosophy, psychology, history, pre-law, and sociology, at various points desiring to become a medical doctor and a physical education instructor. By 1918, he was studying music and literature on his own in Wisconsin. He finally returned to New York to continue his interest in music at the behest of his frustrated grandfather.

In New York City Toomer began to seriously consider writing as a vocation. Surrounded by modernist intellectuals and artists, he finally found his niche. Between 1920 and 1922, Toomer read the important writers of the time, including Sigmund Freud, James Joyce, Sherwood Anderson, and Theodore Dreiser. In 1920 Toomer returned to Washington when his grandfather became ill. Toomer cared for his grandparents until he was forced to look for a job to ease the family's financial burden. He accepted a position as the head of an agricultural school in Sparta, Georgia. This trip to the South would profoundly affect Toomer and lead to the composition of *Cane.*

Though *Cane* is often highlighted as one of the great works of the HARLEM RENAISSANCE, Toomer was not often associated with either the writers or artists of the period, nor was he directly engaged with them. Nevertheless, the work is a reflection of the themes and style of the Renaissance, as well as being indicative of the modernist period. The work is an expressionistic montage of sketches, poems, short stories, and songs and includes a closet drama. Reminiscent of a jazz piece, it echoes the communal voices of the African-American community. *Cane* inaugurated a new form and, as many critics suggest, it laid the foundations for contemporary African-American literature.

Cane was published in 1923 after Toomer's return north. It garnered critical accolades for its inventive style, and ALAIN LOCKE included two sketches from the work in *The New Negro* (1925). A half century later, ALICE WALKER noted that the work, especially its portrayal of women, had exerted a powerful influence on her own writing. Toomer admitted in a letter to Sherwood Anderson that *Cane* was indebted to *Winesburg, Ohio.* Like Anderson's collection of vignettes, *Cane* attempts to paint the life of the African-American poor in the rural South and their dispossessed counterparts in the North. The work also focuses its attention on the troubled relationships between men and women at a time when gender roles were being challenged and readjusted.

Toomer's own uncertainty about his racial identity can also be felt in the work. A double-consciousness pervades its themes, characters, and style. Most of the female characters are biracial and suffer for their marginal position in society. But these BLUES women also embody an earthy sexuality connected to the South, to the past, and to their African heritage. The South itself also possesses a dual identity: It is both frightening and beautiful. At once, it is the site of the horrors of slavery and lynching but also a place of African-American folk history and culture, where people maintained a discernible connection to nature. Toomer called the work a "swan song," a lament for the past. Concerned that the modern era that brought with it an end to agrarian life would also signal the death of the vibrancy of African-American culture, Toomer set out to capture the tone of the land and the people.

While the cane and its "roots" symbolize the history and the people of the community (as well as their connectedness to nature) of the South, the sketches that are set in the North are marked by images that suggest alienation. Here characters are trapped in their urban environment by boxes, houses, metal, and anything that cuts them off from nature, their past, and themselves. Male and female relationships are even more dislocated than in the South. Human relationships in general signify a growing isolation from the world of the North. The stories of the first and second sections of the work—those set in the South and then the North, respectively—respond to each other, emphasizing again the duality of *Cane* and of African-American life. The work closes with "Kabnis," a drama set in the South. Its lead character is a northerner, however, haunted by the fear of being lynched. The circular narrative pattern of *Cane*—from the South to the North and back again—illustrates Toomer's belief that African Americans must remain connected to the South and to their past, even in light of the horrors of their history, if they want to be free from the psychological burdens of slavery and racism.

Toomer never matched the success of *Cane*, but he continued to write and experiment with form and style. In 1931, he published *Essentials: Definitions and Aphorisms.* The same year he married Margery Latimer, a white woman, who died the following year while giving birth to their daughter, Margery. Two years later, he married again, this time to Marjorie Content. The couple studied many different forms of religion and spirituality, even for a time joining a Quaker congregation. The poem "Blue Meridian" was published in 1936 and reflects Toomer's interest in Eastern philosophy and modernist style, but he never had a major publication again even though he lived another 30 years, dying in 1967.

BIBLIOGRAPHY

Baker, Houston A., Jr. "A Journey toward Black Art: Jean Toomer's *Cane*." In *Afro-American Poetics: Revisions of Harlem and the Black Aesthetic,* 11–44. Madison: University of Wisconsin Press, 1988.

Benson, Brian, and Mabel Dillard. *Jean Toomer.* Boston: Twayne, 1980.

Fabre, Genevieve, and Michel Fabre. *Jean Toomer and the Harlem Renaissance: Dream-Fluted* Cane. New Brunswick, N.J.: Rutgers University Press, 2000.

Hutchinson, George. "Jean Toomer and American Racial Discourse." *Texas Studies in Literature and Language* 35, no. 2 (1993): 226–250.

MacKethan, Lucinda H. "Jean Toomer's *Cane:* A Pastoral Problem." *Mississippi Quarterly* 35, no. 4 (1975): 423–434.

McKay, Nellie. *Jean Toomer, Artist: A Study of His Literary Life and Work, 1894–1936.* Chapel Hill: University of North Carolina Press, 1984.

O'Daniel, Therman B. *Jean Toomer: A Critical Evaluation.* Washington, D.C.: Howard University Press, 1988.

Turner, Darwin. T. *In a Minor Chord: Three Afro-American Writers and Their Search for Identity.* Carbondale: Southern Illinois University Press, 1971.

Tracie Church Guzzio

Touré, Askia Muhammad (Roland Snellings) (1938–)

Born in Raleigh, North Carolina, poet, musician, educator, and community activist-artist Askia Touré, along with AMIRI BARAKA and LARRY NEAL, was one of the architects of the BLACK ARTS MOVEMENT. A participant in the Umbra workshop founded by DAVID HENDERSON, Touré, a former air force enlistee, coauthored the Student Non-Violent Coordinating Committee (SNCC) Black Power "Position Paper." With SONIA SANCHEZ and Baraka, Touré helped build one of the first black studies programs in the country at San Francisco State University. His political vision, sense of community, and Afrocentric perspective are reflected in the name he has claimed for his own: Askia Touré is the name of a 16th-century African king who united the entire central region of the Western Sudan.

The author of five books of poetry, including *Earth* (1968), *Juju: Magic Songs for the Black Nation* (with Ben Caldwell, 1970), *Songhai!* (1972), the American Book Award-winning *From the Pyra-* mids to the Projects (1990), and *Dawnsong!* (1999), Touré writes with revolutionary fervor of "the dawn of Socialism's promise" in *"CUBA: A LOVE-SONG!"* and celebrates exiled Black Panther activist Assata Shakur as an "African freedom fighter, a warrior-spirit in the mold of Harriet Tubman in Palenque Queen by Habana's Shores." But, as he does in "The Frontier of Rage," Touré also calls attention to the destructive consequence of racism on black male/female relationships:

> The frontier of rage that exists
> between Black men and women
> is an open wound slowly
> dripping through the years
> causing us to miss each other, dismembered
> by our needs and self-righteous vindications
> of our egos.

Among his more recent works, *Dawnsong!* engages Egyptian myths of birth, death, and rebirth, particularly the myths of Isis and Osiris. The tonality and phrasing of his poetry is often grounded in African-American music, especially gospel, rhythm & blues and jazz. He was deeply influenced by John Coltrane. In summary, Touré's first love, African-American music, continues to center his life and work. When combined with his black nationalism, cosmic perspective, and Islamic faith, the result, like "Extensions," is a demand for black spiritual renewal, transformation and transcendence: "BROTHERS: Fools, you can't beat the Devil at his game. / You are men of the Spirit—earth-gods; reclaim your thrones!" (*Understanding a New Black Poetry* 304–306)

THIRD WORLD Press published Touré's poetry, which also appeared in *Negro Digest/BLACK WORLD, Black Scholar, Liberator,* and *Freedomways.*

BIBLIOGRAPHY

Henderson, Stephen. *Understanding the New Black Poetry.* New York: William Morrow & Company, 1973.

Miller, E. Ethelbert, ed. *In Search of Color Everywhere: A Collection of African American Poetry.* New York: Stewart, Tabori and Chang, 1994.

Redmond, Eugene B. *Drumvoices: The Mission of Afro-American Poetry.* Garden City, N.Y.: Anchor Books, 1976.

Wilfred D. Samuels

Train Whistle Guitar   Albert Murray (1974)

In 1974 ALBERT MURRAY introduced readers to Scooter, his sidekick Little Buddy Marshall, and Gasoline Point, Alabama, in his novel *Train Whistle Guitar,* which, published to wide acclaim, won the Lillian Smith Award for Southern Fiction. Departing from the traditional bildungsroman, *Train Whistle Guitar* successfully combines the novel form with the aesthetics of BLUES and jazz as a way to look at African-American life of the 1920s. Murray created the fictional world of Gasoline Point to address what he identified as the "folklore of white supremacy and the fakelore of black pathology." Absent in this novel are the explicit stresses and dilemmas of racial oppression and its impact on black life. Instead Murray masterfully creates a world that, much like ZORA NEALE HURSTON's Eatonville in THEIR EYES WERE WATCHING GOD, celebrates the richness of the black folk community and the power of the black vernacular tradition.

Throughout the novel, the celebration of the blues aesthetic is apparent in the way that the story weaves music into the lives and individual stories of the supporting characters, such as Stagolee Dupas, Claiborne Williams, Miss Blue Eula Bacote, sisters Lucinda Wiggins and Miss Libby Lee Taylor, and most notably blues man Luzana Cholly. It is in the moments of the "also and also" of the novel, where words just are not enough to capture the meaning and the message, that the narrator uses music to convey meaning. Deeply rooted in the storyteller tradition, the novel progresses in episodic sequences that follow Scooter and Little Buddy through a variety of adventures as they pretend to explore deep into the realm of boyhood imagination, through which they travel into the swamp where they discover a dead body, try train hopping with Luzana Cholly, and even experience adolescent love.

Considered a classic of contemporary literature, *Train Whistle Guitar,* Murray maintains, is not a story solely for African Americans but a story that speaks to anyone who can sit back and appreciate the experience of the journey and the magical sound of a train whistle being played out on a guitar and the stories that could be told from those memories. It is a story about seeking individual identity within a communal spirit.

BIBLIOGRAPHY

Carson, Warren. "Albert Murray: Literary Reconstruction of the Vernacular Community." *African American Review* 27, no. 2 (1993): 287–295.

Murray, Albert, and Roberta S. Maguire. *Conversations with Albert Murray.* Jackson: University Press of Mississippi, 1997.

Schultz, Elizabeth. "Albert L. Murray." In *Dictionary of Literary Biography.* Vol. 38: *Afro-American Writers after 1955: Dramatists and Prose Writers,* edited by Thadious M. Davis and Trudier Harris, 214–224, Detroit: Gale, 1985.

Terry Bozeman

trickster

"Eshu, the Trickster, will meet you at the Threshold. He stands there in the crossroads between power and fear" (Nalo Hopkinson, *Mojo*). The term *trickster,* which first appeared in print in 1711 to refer to someone who practices trickery (a rogue, cheat, knave), had its literary debut in Samuel Richardson's *Pamela* (1741). The term was later applied to figures from oral tradition by anthropologist Daniel Brinton in his 1868 study of Native American mythology (161–162) and is today used by anthropologists in reference to similar ethnological phenomena from cultures worldwide, as well as by critics in regard to characters in literature. Religious historians, anthropologists, folklorists, and psychologists have been keenly interested in trickster figures (Carroll, 105). Mythic trickster stories have traditionally explained phenomena such as the human acquisition of fire and the earth's creation or re-creation after the flood, and are linked to the origin of human beings and language. Worldwide, for perhaps thousands of years, humans have told and retold tales of tricksters. Both culture-hero and buffoon, the trickster is usually comical and often randy or scatological. Tricksters "cause laughter . . . as they profane nearly every central belief, but at the same time they focus attention precisely on the nature of such beliefs" (Hynes and Doty, 2).

Out of the context of slavery in the New World emerged ancient and new trickster figures and syncretisms (blendings) of figures from more than one culture. Myths of the West African "ur-trickster" Eshu Elegbara have been "as influential in West Africa and its New World diaspora as Greek mythology has been in Europe" and European America (Cosentino, 261). Slavery and freedom produced retellings of familiar trickster tales as well as new stories and categories of tales told in response to the much harsher environment of the colonial multicultural Americas.

In the United States, African-American trickster stories began to be collected in the mid-19th century. In her 1892 volume, A. M. H. Christensen notes that she had published some Gullah trickster tales before Joel Chandler Harris's Uncle Remus stories began to appear in newspapers (x). Harris is, however, the author known for having popularized Brer Rabbit tales to a wide audience. Both Christensen's and Harris's texts exemplify how early European-American collectors failed to capture the intellectual complexity and sociopolitical contexts of the tales, though the original storytellers had something to do with this. In slavery, blacks did not intend whites to understand all of the survival humor or the double entendres that bespoke black intellectual autonomy and critiqued whites; such was the case with the Brer Rabbit category of tales that whites heard and enjoyed. Developed and told in U.S. slavery (and not collected until the 20th century), High John the Conqueror trickster tales were even more obviously cautionary and revolutionary; as such, they were told exclusively in black community circles. John Roberts traces the evolution of African-American tricksters from the original West African animal trickster figures and John tales in slavery through to the "Badman" character in African-American post–Civil War folklore.

For hundreds of years, trickster figures, tales, and discourse strategies have helped those of African descent in the Americas negotiate brutally delineated cultural boundaries. The comic adaptive and transformative qualities of trickster figures and tales have proved attractive to 20th-century postmodernist American ethnic writers generally. As a cross-cultural mediation tool, comedy reaches across boundaries to provoke participation in the parallel ongoing processes of reconstructing history, recognizing U.S. cultural pluralism, and demanding social justice.

Toward these literary and social aims, tricksters and trickster discourse appear in works by established and emerging African-American and Caribbean authors. ISHMAEL REED's parody of the detective novel *MUMBO JUMBO* features detective Papa LaBas, Louisiana Hoodoo's refraction of the West African Eshu/Legba figure. Set in the crossroads of the Caribbean, TONI MORRISON's *Tar Baby* is an obvious rearticulation of the best-known Brer Rabbit tale. In Part Two of Morrison's *BELOVED*, Sixo's argument that he stole and ate a pig simply to improve the master's "property" is a classic High John tale. In PAULE MARSHALL's *Praisesong for the Widow*, the protagonist is guided through a ritual of spiritual rebirth by Lebert Joseph, a literary rearticulation of New World Voodoo's divine mediator, old Papa Legba.

Award-winning Caribbean-Canadian science fiction writer NALO HOPKINSON employs multiple tricksters. In her novel *Midnight Robber*, each citizen is injected with nanomites at birth that develop into a receiver linking the individual to "Granny Nansi's Web," a data-gathering and -disseminating system that protects, guides, and guards the people. The Caribbean and U.S. Nanny/Nansi evolved from the West African spider trickster, Anansi. The young protagonist in *Midnight Robber* also has her own personal Eshu as guardian, just as all adults have their "personal Legba" in Old and New World Voodoo traditions. Rearticulations of Eshu Elegbara/Legba have appeared in European-American literature as well; Russell Banks's novel *Continental Drift* (New York: Harper and Row, 1985), for example, contains a Legba figure.

HENRY LOUIS GATES, JR.'s *The SIGNIFYING MONKEY: A Theory of African-American Literary Criticism* (1988) is the best-known work on trickster discourse in African-American literature. In contrast to Gates's careful study, many other critics who have used anthropology to study contemporary trickster literature have tended to apply information about particular tricksters uncritically and across cultures, with too little regard for the literature's specific cultural contexts. Tricksters share qualities and can be cautiously compared; however, scholars must remember that "the trickster is not an archetypal idea, but a symbolic pattern that . . . includes a wide range of individual figures" and the trickster's many roles within a given culture (Pelton, 3).

Omnipotent and omnipresent, embodying everything human and everything necessary for life, traditional tricksters mediate inclusivity within a society. Tricksters embody "both the spiritual past and cultural future in the guise of personal responsibility and responses" (Spinks, 184), and trickster mediation discloses "the underlying connection between the transcendent center of reality and the human matrix of life, the family" (Pelton, 73). In contemporary cross-cultural American ethnic literary trickster texts, which serve a much less conservative social role than their older counterparts in oral tradition, the purposeful concomitant breakdowns of imaginative boundaries and social constructs remind readers of our essential interrelatedness, past, present, and future.

BIBLIOGRAPHY

Brinton, Daniel G. *The Myths of the New World: A Treatise on the Symbolism and Mythology of the Red Race of America.* New York: Leypoldt & Holt, 1868.

Carroll, Michael P. "The Trickster as Selfish-Buffoon and Culture Hero." *Ethos* 12, no. 2 (1984): 105–231.

Christensen, A. M. H. *Afro-American Folk Lore, Told Round Cabin Fires on the Sea Islands of South Carolina.* Boston: J. G. Cupples, 1892. New York: Negro Universities Press, 1969.

Cosentino, Donald. "Who Is That Fellow in the Many-Colored Cap?: Transformations of Eshu in Old and New World Mythologies." *Journal of American Folklore* 100, no. 397 (July–September 1987): 261–275.

Gates, Henry Louis, Jr. *The Signifying Monkey: A Theory of African-American Literary Criticism.* New York and Oxford: Oxford University Press, 1988.

Hynes, William J. "Inconclusive Conclusions: Tricksters—Metaplayers and Revealers." In *Mythical Trickster Figures: Contours, Contexts, and Criticisms,* edited by William J. Hynes and William G. Doty, 202–217. Tuscaloosa: University of Alabama Press, 1993.

——— and William G. Doty. "Introducing the Fascinating and Perplexing Trickster Figure." In *Mythical Trickster Figures: Contours, Contexts, and Criticisms,* edited by William J. Hynes and William G. Doty, 1–12. Tuscaloosa: University of Alabama Press, 1993.

Pelton, Robert D. *The Trickster in West Africa: A Study of Mythic Irony and Sacred Delight.* Hermeneutics Studies in the History of Religions 8. Gen. ed. Kees W. Bolle. Berkeley, Los Angeles, London: University of California Press, 1980.

Roberts, John W. *From Trickster to Badman: The Black Folk Hero in Slavery and Freedom.* Philadelphia: University of Pennsylvania Press, 1989.

Spinks, C. W., Jr. *Semiosis, Marginal Signs and Trickster: A Dagger of the Mind.* Houndmills, Basingstoke, Hampshire, London: Macmillan, 1991.

Elizabeth McNeil

Tropic Death   Eric Walrond   (1926)

Harlem Renaissance writer ERIC WALROND was best known for his short stories, particularly his collection *Tropic Death* (1926), in which he looks through international lenses at the black experience. His emphasis on racism, oppression, segregation, economic deprivation, and inevitably ignorance, often manifested in his underclass characters' blind obedience to and dependence on religion as an opiate or false source of empowerment, reveals not only the often autobiographical emphasis in his work but, perhaps more important, his concern, similar to CLAUDE McKAY's, with the working class.

The finest story is "The Wharf Rats," which on the surface is about unrequited love, revenge, and voodoo. The main character, Phillip, despite his father's objection, spends his days as a wharf rat, diving for coins to entertain tourists who toss them into the ocean from their luxury liners cruising the Panama Canal. When Maffi, a peasant girl who frequents his home to assist his mother, falls in love with Phillip, she wrongfully assumes he is in love with Marua, whose beauty causes people to turn and stare. Driven by her sense of rejection and jealousy, Maffi visits the obeah (Voodoo) priest to have him perform the proper ritual of revenge. The next day, when Phillip dives for coins, a shark attacks him and takes him to his death at the depths of the ocean. At the end of the story, Maffi takes comfort in knowing that at least Phillip is no longer pursuing Marua rather than her.

"The Wharf Rats" is filled with action, danger, and suspense. Through Walrond's vivid descriptive language, readers hold their breath as Phillip and Ernest dive into the ocean deep, swim "like a garfish," and are chased by a shark the first day. But "The Wharf Rats" is more than a love story, for Walrond uses the setting to give insights into the plight of common Latin American workers whose colonized lives revolve around the Panama Canal and the European and English cruise ships that pass through it. Phillip's family and the other laborers—blacks, Hindu, Chinese, Maroons—live in "Silver City" a segregated community in Coco Té. "At the Atlantic end of the canal, the blacks are herded in box car huts buried in the jungles of 'Silver City'; in the murky tenements. . . . The 'Silver Quarter' harbored the inky ones, their wives and pickaninnies" (549). In this labor camp, dominated by race and class stratification, ignorance and economic oppression, hopeless residents are also psychologically enslaved by their religious practices and belief in witchcraft (brujeria), obeah, and coombia. Their community, like the ocean,

forms a whirlpool of marginalization, alienation, and inevitable destruction in an almost scientific naturalistic manner. The story also reflects Walrond's interest in the gothic.

Generally, *Tropic Death* was well received. Waldrond's efforts and style were often compared to JEAN TOOMER and *Cane,* although most critics conceded that Toomer was the more talented and gifted of the two writers. Robert Bone writes that "*Tropic Death* was a remarkable achievement for a man of twenty-eight" (202). David Levering Lewis concludes that in *Tropic Death* Walrond "captured the premodern, polyglot culture of men and women battered by the global backwash of capitalism, in order to present one of the Renaissance's most haunting allegorical reflections about vitality and innocence being toyed with and fatally sucked under by the despoiling forces of modernity" (548).

BIBLIOGRAPHY

Bone, Robert. *Down Home: A History of Afro-American Short Fiction from Its Beginnings to the End of the Harlem Renaissance.* New York: Capricorn Books, 1975.

Lewis, David Levering. *When Harlem Was in Vogue.* New York: Oxford University Press, 1979.

Walrond, Eric. "The Wharf Rats." In *The Portable Harlem Renaissance Reader,* edited by David Levering Lewis, 549–568. New York: Penguin Books, 1995.

Wilfred D. Samuels

Troupe, Quincy Thomas, Jr. (1943–)

Troupe has a history as elusive as a line of his own poetry. He was born in St. Louis, Missouri, on July 23, 1943, to Thomas Quincy Troupe, Sr., and Dorothy Marshall Smith. Troupe attended but did not graduate from Grambling College (now Grambling State University). However, he graduated with an A.A. degree in journalism from Los Angeles City College (1967). Troupe joined the army and played on the All-Army basketball team until he was permanently sidelined by injuries.

The injury led to Troupe's discovery and love of writing. Troupe is married to Margaret Porter, has four children—Antoinette, Tymme, Quincy, and Porter—and lives in La Jolla, California.

Troupe got his poetic start in the late 1960s during the height of the BLACK ARTS MOVEMENT, a period when black artists began to focus on the spiritual and cultural needs of black America. In Los Angeles Troupe was active as a member of the Watts Writers' Workshop, whose members touted the slogan "arm yourself or harm yourself" to respond to America's racial injustice. Troupe edited *Shrewd* magazine in 1968; in 1972 he published his first collection of poems, *Embryo Poems 1967–71* (New York: Barlenmir, 1972), in which he revealed his concern with the division between black America and white America. This concern reverberates throughout "White Weekend: April 5th to the 9th, 1968," in which the author laments the death of Martin Luther King—"& the bearer of peace / lying still in Atlanta"—while indicting white America for its blindness, represented by Wall Street, where the significance of King's death was registered by an increasing stock market: "but in new york, on wall street / the stock market went up 18 points."

In his second publication, *Snake-Back Solos: Selected Poems 1969–1977* (1978), which won the American Book Award in 1979, as well as in *Weather Reports: New and Selected Poems* (1991) and *Avalanche* (1996), Troupe clearly demonstrates the talent that made him one of the master poets of the late 20th century. Through his singular ability to integrate jazz, poetry, and gospel, Troupe develops a transcendental form of communication that engages the reader at multiple levels of consciousness.

Troupe's "New York City Beggar," in which the narrator conjures up an image of the urban panhandler as an addict enslaved by his addiction and the cycle of begging, is most representative. After the narrator refuses to give the panhandler a dime,

> *he put a Halloween leer on me & said:*
> *"thank you boss"*

> *gave the V for victory/peace sign, cursed*
> *under his breath*
> *& left, like an apparition*
> *flapping his raggedy black coat*
> *like giant crow wings in the wind.*

By refusing to contribute to the panhandler's welfare, the narrator, whom the beggar first addresses as brother, "brother can you spare a dime," seems to establish a master/slave relationship in which he (the narrator) represents freedom, while the beggar represents the enslaved. The narrator's refusal to "spare a dime" serves as a potential avenue for unlocking the beggar's shackles—to eliminate the beggar's potential dependency. However, the beggar "gave the V for victory/peace sign, [and] cursed under his breath." By transforming the beggar into a crowlike apparition, Troupe's narrator makes him an easily recognizable trickster figure, whose strength comes by disrupting the status quo. Consequently, the reader is forced to recognize that it is the master, not the slave, who is responsible for unsettling the institution of slavery.

Throughout his oeuvre, Troupe rigs the Black Arts Movement's themes, making them accessible to white America while still keeping them real—as evidenced by his appearance on Bill Moyer's Emmy Award–winning series, *The Power of the Word* (1989). Troupe's ability to talk in two tongues, to communicate simultaneously to both black and white America, is aided by his knack for freezing moments of humankind caught being human—as is the case in the authentic and sometimes narcissistic Miles Davis that emerges in the musician's autobiography, *Miles: The Autobiography of Miles Davis with Quincy Troupe* (1990), which Troupe coauthored. This authenticity allows Troupe's subjects to remain real to the black experience and at the same time approachable to a broader reading audience. His subjects are often the strong who, though caught in the avalanche of life, become heroic role models for betterment rather than victimized role models for embitterment.

This message is driven home in "A Poem For 'Magic'" (*Avalanche*, 1996), in which the narrator conjures a "magic" Johnson who achieves at a singular level, but the narrator is also aware that the famous basketball player's achievements have been momentarily overshadowed by his announcement that he is HIV positive and his retirement from the NBA. The narrator's voice seems to echo Troupe's own experience, which led him to leave the game he loved and mastered:

> in victory, we suddenly sense your glorious
> uplift
> your urgent need to be champion
> & so we cheer with you, rejoice with you
> quicksilver moment of fame
> so put the ball on the floor again, "magic"

Refusing to let "magic" be victimized by his circumstances and recognizing Johnson's new "urgent need to be champion"—to champion over HIV, the narrator invokes a ritualistic incantation designed to bring "magic" Johnson out of retirement: ". . . deal the roundball like the juju man that you am / like the sho-nuff shaman that you am, / 'magic.'" While the incantation restores "magic" with each repetition, the "you am" declares his agency, subjectivity, and being. In the end the audience finds reassurance of infinite possibilities in their own lives and can rejoice with the athlete.

Troupe has taught at the University of California at Los Angeles, University of Southern California, Ohio University, Richmond College, University of California Berkeley, California State at Sacramento, University of Ghana at Legon, College of Staten Island, the City University of New York, and the University of California at San Diego. His publications include *Snake-Back Solos: Selected Poems, 1969–1977* (*I. Reed Books,* 1978), *Weather Reports: New and Selected Poems* (Writers and Readers, 1991), *Avalanche: Poems* (Coffee House Press, 1996), *Choruses: Poems* (Coffee House Press, 1999), *Transcircularities: New and Selected Poems* (Coffee House Press, 2002), *Miles and Me* (2000), and *Take It to the Hoop, Magic Johnson* (with Shane W. Evans, illustrator, Hyperion Press, 2000). Among his honors, he was California's first poet laureate, he won two American Book Awards,

and he is the two-time winner of the Heavyweight Championship of Poetry at the World Poetry Bout in Taos, New Mexico.

Troupe's work as poet, biographer, critic, community activist, teacher, and sometimes shaman has continued the Black Arts Movement into the 21st century by giving mainstream America a space for dialogue with the black experience. Through a tireless effort, his message reaches his audience where they are, whether in prison, a jazz club, or the academy. Keeping true to the shaman persona he has developed, Troupe is continually changing, changing his poetry, finding new voices to publish, and creating imaginative and relevant ways to influence a literary scene that is inspired by his past work and looks forward to his latest.

BIBLIOGRAPHY
Pettis, Joyce Owens. *African American Poets: Lives, Works, and Sources.* Westport, Conn.: Greenwood Press, 2002.

Erik B. Ludwig

Truth, Sojourner   (1797?–1883)
Born a slave between 1797 and 1800 in Hurley, Ulster County, New York, Sojourner Truth became an iconic figure of strength and courage for her relentless work in abolition, feminism, and activism. Named Isabella, Truth was the second youngest of 12 or 13 children of James and Elizabeth, all owned by Johannes Hardenbergh, Jr., a Dutch planter and heir to the Hardenbergh patent, and then to his brother Charles. Charles died when Truth was "near nine years old," and Truth and her family were sent to auction and sold. Within four years, she was sold twice more, eventually becoming the slave of John Dumont in New Paltz, New York. After Dumont reneged on his promise to free her, Truth "walked to freedom" in the fall of 1826 with her youngest infant child.

Following her self-emancipation, Truth adopted the last name van Wagenen, in recognition of the family who provided her with sanctuary and purchased her from Dumont and made her legally free. After hearing "voices" that proclaimed she would become an "instrument of God," she changed her name to Sojourner Truth. Proclaiming her mission to "sojourn" the land, speaking God's "truth," she began a life as a traveling preacher. From this turning point to her death in November 1883, Truth traveled the country. Before the Civil War she became an abolitionist. During the war she recruited Union forces and taught, counseled, and helped resettle freed slaves. Following the war she promoted equal rights and full suffrage. During her travels, Truth met with Presidents Lincoln and Grant, was brutally beaten and attacked on several occasions, and succeeded in filing an 1865 lawsuit that resulted in the desegregation of Washington, D.C.'s streetcars.

Truth related many of the details of her early life in slavery to Olive Gilbert, who transcribed them in *The Narrative of Sojourner Truth: A Bondswoman of Olden Time,* which Truth first published in Boston in 1950. The narrative begins when young Isabella is separated from her parents and ends with Dumont's confession that slavery was "the greatest curse the earth had ever felt." Truth's *Narrative* offers a unique view of slavery outside the southern context and of African Americans' efforts to maintain family bonds despite slavery's destructive effects. It is a spiritual autobiography, which, like OLAUDAH EQUIANO's *Interesting Narrative of the Life,* records Truth's conversion to Christianity and spiritual visions. In it she also combines elements of Dutch Pentecostal and African festival traditions.

Missing from Truth's *Narrative,* however, are the accounts of sexual abuse and the focus on literacy found in narratives of HARRIET JACOBS or FREDERICK DOUGLASS. Instead, as a traveling preacher, Truth stressed spiritual literacy, often saying, "You read books, I talk to God." Although she does not provide explicit references to sexuality in her *Narrative,* Truth does offer clear insights into the dangers of slave life for women between each line. Truth also speaks freely and vehemently about African-American womanhood.

The Narrative of Sojourner Truth went through seven editions. In the 1870s Frances Titus, Truth's neighbor and manager, added Truth's "Book of Life," her scrapbook that includes letters and newspaper clippings. After her death in 1883, Titus added obituaries and eulogies. The most reprinted version (1878) includes Harriet Beecher Stowes's 1863 essay, "Sojourner Truth, the Libyan Sibyl" and Dana Gage's version of Truth's speech, "Ar'n't I a Woman?," which Truth gave, extemporaneously, in Akron, Ohio, at the Women's Rights Convention in 1851. In this now-classic speech, Truth proclaims that women's rights should be equal to those enjoyed by men; she contends, "I have heard the bible and learned that Eve caused man to sin. Well, if woman upset the world, do give her a chance to set it right side up again." Gage, the chair of the meeting, wrote the most widely read version of Truth's speech in 1863, adding the famous "ar'n't I a woman?" refrain. Several other versions of the speech are available, including one recorded in *Anti-Slavery Bugle* during the 1851 meeting.

Sojourner Truth is one of the foundational figures of African-American feminist, WOMANIST, and Africana womanist activism. She represents the power of the oral tradition and spirituality that continues to permeate African-American writing and that provided power to both the CIVIL RIGHTS MOVEMENT of the 1960s and the BLACK ARTS MOVEMENT of the 1970s.

BIBLIOGRAPHY

Mabee, Carleton, and Susan Mabee Newhouse. *Sojourner Truth: Slave, Prophet, Legend.* New York: New York University Press, 1995.

Olive, Gilbert. *Narrative of Sojourner Truth: A Bondswoman of Olden Time, with a History of Her Labors and Correspondence Drawn from Her "Book of Life."* New York: Oxford University Press, 1991.

Samra, Matthew K. "Shadow and Substance: The Two Narratives of Sojourner Truth." *Midwest Quarterly: A Journal of Contemporary Thought* 38, no. 2 (Winter 1997): 158–171.

Washington, Margaret, ed. *Narrative of the Life of Sojourner Truth.* New York: Vintage, 1993.

Derrick R. Spires

Turner, Darwin T. (1931–1989)

An educator, humanitarian, literary scholar, editor, and critic, Darwin T. Turner was born in Cincinnati, Ohio. A child prodigy, he received a B.A. degree at age 16 from the University of Cincinnati in 1947 and an M.A. from the same institution two years later, in 1949. He achieved a Ph.D. degree from the University of Chicago in 1956, by age 25. His degrees were in English and American dramatic literature. Turner began his teaching career at Clark College in Atlanta, Morgan State College in Maryland, and Florida A&M, all HISTORICALLY BLACK COLLEGES AND UNIVERSITIES (HBCUs). At yet another HBCU, North Carolina A&T University, Turner became the first chair of the department of English and subsequently the dean of the graduate school. He ended his academic career at the University of Iowa, where, as professor of English and director of African-American studies for almost two decades, he led one of the first seriously committed and academically sound and respected programs in African-American studies in the United States, mentoring graduate students who were successfully placed as beginning junior professors at major mainstream institutions. Turner was at the helm of this program when it morphed into the African-African American World Studies Program, a graduate degree–granting program associated with the University of Iowa's American Studies Program.

At the beginning and throughout most of his career as a scholar and critic of African-American literature, Turner voiced his concerns about the paucity of black literary scholars directly involved in creating a cadre of scholarship on black literature. He did so, for example, in his now-classic essay "Afro-American Literary Critics: An Introduction," in which he wrote, "even in this decade of discovery of black culture, Afro-American critics remain blackly invisible" (59). Ironically, the role had been left, for the most part, to white critics such as Robert Bone, whose *The Negro Novel in America* (1952) many considered the definitive text on this subject for several decades, despite the pioneering work of Benjamin Brawley, ALAIN LOCKE, Hugh Gloster, and SAUNDERS REDDINGS.

Turner further lamented, "The fact is ironic and regrettable, since black American critics can offer insights into the language, styles and meanings intended by black writers, insights infrequently denied to those who have not shared the experience of living as black people in the United States of America" (60).

A prolific scholar, editor and compiler, Turner did his part to change the critical landscape. *In a Minor Chord: Three African American Writers and Their Search for Identity* (1971), a study of the lives and works of ZORA NEALE HURSTON, JEAN TOOMER, and COUNTEE CULLEN, is Turner's best-known and somewhat controversial text. He edited the Norton authoritative edition of Toomer's *Cane* and compiled *The Wayward and the Seeking: Collection of Writings by Jean Toomer* (1980). He compiled his three separately published anthologies—*Black American Literature: Essays* (1969), *Black American Literature: Poetry* (1969) and *Black American Literature: Fiction* (1969)—into a single anthology, BLACK AMERICAN LITERATURE: *Essays, Poetry, Fiction, Drama* (1970), which became central to the study of African-American literature on college campuses across the United States during the 1970s and 1980s. In 1971, the editors of *Blacks in America, Bibliographic Essays* noted that Turner's *Afro-American Writers* (1970) was "the best and most comprehensive bibliography listing works by and about Black American writers" (McPherson et al., 6). Similar accolades were heaped on his anthology of African-American plays, *Black Drama in America* (1971).

By the time of his death in 1991, Turner had witnessed the emergence of a new generation of young African-American scholars, including BARBARA CHRISTIAN, Hortense Spillers, Trudier Harris, Karla F. C. Holloway, Bernard Bell, Deborah McDowell, HOUSTON A. BAKER, JR., and HENRY L. GATES JR., who set out to verify the complexity of the African-American literary tradition and define new directions in African-American literary criticism, fulfilling Turner's dreams and wishes by the end of the 20th century.

In 1976 the University of Cincinnati established the Darwin T. Turner Scholars Program and

Services (formerly the Minority Scholars Program) for its youngest graduate ever. It remains one of the oldest ethnic scholarship programs in America and has graduated hundreds of students.

BIBLIOGRAPHY

McPherson, James M., and Laurence B. Holland, et al., eds. *Blacks in America: Bibliographical Essays.* Garden City, N.Y.: Doubleday, 1971.

Turner, Darwin T. "Afro American Literary Critics: An Introduction." In *The Black Aesthetics,* edited by Addison Gayle, 59–81. Garden City, N.Y.: Doubleday, 1971.

———. *In a Minor Chord: Three Afro-American Writers and Their Search for Identity.* Carbondale: Southern Illinois University Press, 1971.

Wilfred D. Samuels

Turner, Nat   (1800–1831)

Nat Turner, prophet and revolutionary, was single-handedly responsible for the bloodiest slave revolt in American history, which he led in Southampton County, Virginia, in 1831. Setting out to strike a fatal blow against America's inhumane chattel slavery, Turner and his insurgent army of fellow slaves—between 60 and 80 in number—succeeded in killing between 55 and 65 whites within 48 hours, beginning with his own master, Joseph Travis, and his family. Lerone Bennett describes Turner as "A mystic with blood on his mind, a preacher with vengeance on his lips, a dreamer, a fanatic, a terrorist . . . a fantastic mixture of gentleness, ruthlessness and piety" (88).

Born the slave of Southampton County's Benjamin Turner, Nat, a precocious child whose intelligence was identified early in his youth, was taught to read and write, probably by his parents. His strong religious convictions and Christian faith led him to believe, from early youth, that God had called him, in the way he had called Moses of the Old Testament, to accomplish a special mission, which he came to identify with the deliverance of blacks from bondage. Blacks and whites alike, he claims in *The Confessions of Nat Turner* (1831),

knew God had ordained him for "some great purpose" (166). So convinced was Turner of this mission that he, who escaped as fugitive to freedom, returned himself to bondage and his former slave master, who sold him to Joseph Travis. In preparation for what he saw as his destiny, Turner practiced a life of asceticism, often isolating himself from others.

Turner details his sense of mission and gives an account of the revolt in *The Confessions of Nat Turner.* While providing an account of his birth, education, and religious upbringing, Turner emphasizes his conviction that, from age four or five, the spirit of God had appeared to him and, in several visions, instructed him to prepare himself for his mission. In perhaps what is the most important vision of them all, Turner explains that one day while he was in the woods, he discovered blood on the corn and hieroglyphic characters and numbers on the leaves. Experiencing what he took to be yet another vision and revelation from God, Turner concluded, "it was plain to me that the Savior was about to lay down the yoke he had borne for the sins of men, and the great day of judgment was at hand" (167). He knew, "the time was fast approaching when the first should be last and the last should be first" (167). The symbols in his visions meant he "should arise and prepare [himself], and slay [his] enemies with their own weapon" (167). With his trusted warriors, Turner originally decided to initiate the revolt on July 4, 1831, but his illness from the stress of his monumental task caused them to postpone their plans until August 20. As William Andrews points out, "Nat Turner evidently wanted his confession to be read as a spiritual testament of his faithfulness to his mission in life" (72).

Despite his literacy, Turner did not write *The Confessions of Nat Turner* but instead dictated it to Thomas R. Gray, the court-appointed white attorney who also served as his amanuensis while Turner was in prison waiting to be hanged for his crime. In his preface to *The Confessions,* Gray wrote that Turner "frankly acknowledges his full participation in all the guilt of transaction. He was not only the contriver of the conspiracy, but gave the first blow towards the execution" (Barksdale, 164). Gray, who Andrews tells us "takes control of the narrative from the outset" (Andrews, 73), "was determined that the narrative be read as a terrible tale of religious dementia" (Andrews, 72), and this leads to questions of authenticity.

Although he and his followers were caught and hanged, Turner became and remains a hero for African Americans. As Richard Barksdale and Keneth Kinnamon point out, despite the fact that Turner's revolt brought

a wave of repression from slaveholders, it also energized Black and white abolitionists. The resulting polarization between the North and South was necessary . . . to force the crisis that culminated in the Civil War and the end of chattel slavery. As a martyr to Black freedom . . . Turner set an example that has inspired his own and succeeding generations (162–163).

Bennett, who calls Turner the "prototype of twentieth century revolutionaries," writes, "Nat Turner reminds us that oppression is a kind of violence which pays in coins of its own minting" (84).

White novelist William Styron denigrated and spurned Turner's character through his treatment and characterization of this historical icon in his "historical" novel *The Confessions of Nat Turner,* earning the ire of African-American scholars, writers, and historians, who responded in *William Styron's Nat Turner; Ten Black Writers Respond* (Beacon Press, 1968). Nevertheless, Turner is often viewed by black writers and critics as the embodiment of DAVID WALKER's *An Appeal* and, like FREDERICK DOUGLASS and MALCOLM X, he is lionized and celebrated in fiction, poetry, and drama.

BIBLIOGRAPHY

Andrews, William L. *To Tell a Free Story: The First Century of Afro-American Autobiography, 1760–1865.* Urbana: University of Illinois Press, 1986.
Barksdale, Richard, and Keneth Kinnamon, eds. *Black Writers of America: A Comprehensive Anthology.* New York: Macmillan, 1972.
Bennett, Lerone. *Pioneers in Protest.* Chicago: Johnson Publishing Company, 1968.
Clarke, John H., ed. *William Styron's Nat Turner: Ten Black Writers Respond.* Boston: Beacon Press, 1968.
Loggins, Vernon. *The Negro Author: His Development in America to 1900.* Port Washington, N.Y.: Kennikat Press, 1931.
Turner, Nat. *The Confessions of Nat Turner.* In *Black Writers of America, A Comprehensive Anthology,* edited by Richard Barksdale and Keneth Kinnamon, 163–172. New York: Macmillan, 1972.

Rondell Nelson Richard

Turpin, Waters E.   (1910–1968)

Novelist, critic, and academician Waters E. Turpin was born in Oxford, on Maryland's Eastern Shore, April 9, 1910, to Simon and Rebecca Waters Turpin. He earned a bachelor's degree from Morgan College in Baltimore and M.A. and Ed.D. degrees from Columbia University. Turpin devoted himself to college teaching at several historically black colleges, the last years of which he spent at his alma mater, now Morgan State University, where he remained until his death in 1968.

As a novelist, Turpin is best remembered for two sweeping family chronicles, *These Low Grounds* (1937) and *O Canaan!* (1939). He is also the author of a historical novel, *The Rootless* (1957), a play on the life of FREDERICK DOUGLASS, and *St. Michael's Dawn* (1956). *These Low Grounds* follows a black family from pre–Civil War days through four successive generations, ending just after the Great Depression. *O Canaan!* concerns the migration of a black family from rural Mississippi to Chicago in 1916. In the middle of *O Canaan!,* Turpin incorporates a continuation of the plot from *These Low Grounds,* extending the chronicle to the latter part of the 1930s. Taken together, these novels explore Turpin's idea that the social tragedy of African Americans is both cumulative and intertwined, and the complexity of this situation is underscored by the complexity of the novels. These works explore myriad aspects of the black experience, including both inter- and intra-familial dynamics, life during and in the aftermath of the Great Migration and the Great Depression, and rural versus urban lifestyles for African Americans during the first part of the 20th century. Philosophically, Turpin explores many attitudes toward life held by African Americans from before the Civil War through the Great Depression. Perhaps the most important of these is the attitude toward education as a panacea for the social and economic ills African Americans faced.

The Rootless, Turpin's last published fictional work, focused on slave practices on Maryland's Eastern Shore. Considered with his two previous works, *The Rootless* completes an interesting trilogy that probes the incapacitating effects of history on the black man in America.

Turpin's works remain obscure for the most part, garnering little critical attention during the time of their publication and in subsequent reexaminations of the period or the African-American canon. Even so, these works contribute to the diversity of the African-American literary canon and offer yet another view of black life in America.

BIBLIOGRAPHY

Carson, Warren J. "Four Black American Novelists, 1935–1941." Master's thesis. Atlanta University, 1975.

Ford, Nick Aaron. "Tribute to Waters Turpin." *College Language Association Journal* 12 (March 1969): 281–83.

Reid, Margaret Ann. "Water Turpin." In *The Oxford Companion to African American Literature,* edited by William Andres, et al., 739–740. New York: Oxford University Press, 1997.

Warren J. Carson

Tyree, Omar (1969–)

Novelist, performance poet, and publisher, Philadelphia-born Tyree graduated from prestigious Central High School there in 1987. Although he began his undergraduate studies pursuing a career in pharmacy at the University of Pittsburgh, he discovered his talents as a writer and, at the end of his freshman year, transferred to Howard University, where he majored in journalism. By the end of his senior year, Tyree had gained recognition as a columnist for the school's award-winning newspaper, *The Hilltop,* for which he became the first student in the paper's history to have a featured column, "Food for Thought."

Tyree began his professional career as a journalist and editor with Washington, D.C.'s *The Capitol Spotlight,* a weekly newspaper. He continued in journalism by working for *News Dimension* and *Washington View Magazine* before founding his own publishing company, MARS Production, and turning to a career as a novelist and publisher. He self-published his first novel, *Colored, On (a) White Campus* (1992), with funds borrowed from family members and friends. Tyree used the royalties to publish *Flyy Girl* (1993); he had written both novels by his senior year at Howard University. His initial publishing success caught the attention of and won him a formal contract with mainstream publisher Simon & Schuster, which republished his best-selling *Flyy Girl* in 1996 in hardcover. Today, Tyree, who is often described as a man on a mission given his goal of publishing a Tyree classics series, is included in the ranks of such popular African-American best sellers as E. LYNN HARRIS, ERIC JEROME DICKEY, CARL WEBER, TERRY MCMILLAN, and ZANE, whose works fill display shelves and windows in popular bookstores.

Tyree's novels include *Capitol City: The Diary of a D.C. Underworld* (1993); *Battlezone* (1994); *Flyy Girl* (1996); *Capital City* (1997); *A Do Right Man* (1997); *Single Mom* (1998); *For the Love of Money* (2000), which made the *New York Times* Bestseller List one week after publication; *Sweet St. Louis* (2000); *Just Say No* (2001); *Leslie* (2002); *College Boy* (2002); and *The Boss Lady* (2005). Tyree has also published novels under the pseudonym The Urban Griot, including *The Underground* (2001), *College Boy* (2003), and *One Crazy Ass Night* (2003).

Set in a Philadelphia that beat to the rhythm of hip-hop culture during the ostentatious 1980s, *Flyy Girl* is a coming-of-age story of Tracy Ellison, who grows up in a middle-class family that lives in Germantown. Although her parents are separated, Tracy has a fairly stable family life, which is ensured by her hardworking parents. Found attractive, favored and doted on by family and friends primarily because of her light skin and almond-shaped hazel eyes, Tracy, during her teens and high school years, is, fundamentally selfish and rambunctious. She is willing to do almost anything to lure the most popular boys in the neighborhood, only to exploit and intimidate them. By the time she is 16, her identity is wrapped up in the designer clothing, jewelry, behavior, and the fast-paced lifestyle that earns her the enviable title of "flyy girl" (which means an attractive and beautiful girl in hip-hop culture), like her former neighbor and friend, Mercedes. Mercedes's philosophy is shown in her advice to Tracy on how she should treat her boyfriends: "don't give tem *nothin'* unless they got something to give you. . . . get a nice-looking nut dude with some money and romance his ass. If you can get somethin' without doing anything with him, then do it. But if you can't, then make sure you play with his mind real good before you do" (212–213). However, by age 17, seeing the shallowness and ephemerality of such advice, Tracy resolves to embrace a more responsible, quality-filled lifestyle as she moves toward true womanhood. In both *For the Love of Money* (2000) and *Boss Lady,* sequels to *Flyy Girl,* Tyree revisits Tracy's growth, development, and success as a professional, movie star, producer, and astute businesswoman.

In *Flyy Girl* Tyree offers deft insight into urban life and teen hip-hop culture in America during the 1980s. Although Tracy and her friends lack the sophistication of CLAUDE BROWN's protagonist in *MANCHILD IN THE PROMISED LAND,* they, too, are African-American teens who, to a large degree, grow up prematurely in a drug-infested world. They seem irresponsible as they nonchalantly experience traditional adolescent rites of passage and rituals, particularly those related to their sexual identities as young men and women, with abandon. Adolescent girls readily lose their virginity to handsome but totally irresponsible young boys merely to be identified as their conquerors' girlfriends. However, Tyree's sexually active, aggressive teenage girls do not seem to worry about getting pregnant or contracting sexually transmitted diseases. The exception is Raheema, Tracy's neighbor and off-and-on friend.

In *Flyy Girl,* Tyree successfully captures the urban, hip-hop language of his characters. At teen parties, boys wearing gold-framed Neostyle glasses (which cost more than $150) attend expecting to "rack up" or collect many phone numbers. Their dialogue and exchange is almost monosyllabic: "I'on know" (I don't know), "Aw'ight" (all right), "What 'chew think?" (What do you think?). They do "The Wop" and dance to The Boogie Boys's hit rap song "Flyy Girl," "The Show" by Slick Rick and Doug E. Fresh, "Computer Love" by Zapp, and "Do Me Baby" by Mel'isa Morgan.

From the outset, Tyree has been identified as a talented new voice. He was particularly lauded for his use of dialogue. According to Shirley Gibson Coleman, "Tyree has a way [of] making each phrase of every conversation true to life, whether spoken by a child or an adult" (98). Writing as The Urban Griot, under his new line of "hard core novels," Tyree contributed "Human Heat" to *Dark Thirst: An Anthology,* a collection of original vampire stories by African-American writers published by Simon & Schuster Adult Publishing Group in 2004. He has also released a spoken-word album, *Rising Up* (2003), and he added *Cold Blooded* (2004), a novel, to his Urban Griot series featuring Big Bronze. His novel *What They Want* was published in 2006. The recipient of the 2001 NATIONAL ASSOCIATION FOR THE ADVANCEMENT OF COLORED PEOPLE Image Award for Outstanding Literary Work in Fiction, Tyree lives in Charlotte, North Carolina, with his wife, Karintha, and two sons, Ameer and Canoy.

BIBLIOGRAPHY

Coleman, Shirley Gibson. Review, *Library Journal.* September 1996, p. 98.

Review, *Publishers Weekly,* October 1996.

Tyree, Omar. *Flyy Girl.* New York: Simon & Schuster, 1996.

Wilfred D. Samuels

Up from Slavery
Booker T. Washington (1901)

BOOKER T. WASHINGTON's autobiography, *Up from Slavery,* records one of the most remarkable success stories in American literature and history. At the beginning of the 20th century, Washington's ascendance to power, as W. E. B. DUBOIS noted in *The SOULS OF BLACK FOLK* (1903), was "easily the most striking thing in the history of the American Negro since 1876" (240). Although Washington had achieved relative success as the founder of Tuskegee Normal School in Alabama in 1881, he did not gain national fame until 1895 when he delivered his now-infamous "Atlanta Exposition Address" to a mixed audience of blacks and southern and northern whites attending the opening of the 1895 Atlanta Exposition in Georgia. Washington's national fame and prominence were enhanced by the publication of *Up from Slavery* (1901), which grew out of a serialized narrative of his life published in *The Outlook,* a popular magazine.

Washington had published an earlier autobiography, *The Story of My Life and Work* (1900), which, although it had sold well, was generally criticized in some quarters as being incomplete. His supporters and friends suggested he write a new autobiography—one that would portray him more successfully and provide greater insights into his philosophy and goals. Washington hired Max Bennett Thrasher, a white New Englander with outstanding journalistic talent, for the project. He also received advice on the most effective way to organize the new project from his friend Lyman Abbott, the editor of *The Outlook.* The result was the widely read best-selling autobiography *Up from Slavery,* which was considered extraordinary. It had a major impact on MARCUS GARVEY, the Jamaican founder and leader of the Universal Negro Improvement Association (UNIA), who was living in London when he read it. Garvey came to America to discuss his own economic and political plans with Washington. After reading the autobiography some readers were so impressed with Washington that they donated money for his work at Tuskegee.

In the opening chapters of *Up from Slavery,* Washington revisits his boyhood in slavery in Franklin County, Virginia; discusses his recollections of his family; and records his life following emancipation. Although Washington's account of slavery coincides, for the most part, with those of other former slaves, such as FREDERICK DOUGLASS, his personal life was far better than that of most. Besides the wooden shoes he was given to wear, the "most trying ordeal" he "was forced to endure as a slave boy . . . was the wearing of a flax shirt" (34). In *Up from Slavery,* Washington's record of the slave/master relationship contradicts those of other major slave narrators, for, according to Washington, the detrimental aspects of slavery were greater for the master. On the whole, Washington wrote, slaves were devoted to their masters. He overlooked, for example, the possibility that the perceived willingness of former slaves to remain on the plantations was not one of blind loyalty to former owners but a calculated assessment of how to survive in an oppressive environment.

Washington wrote, "we must acknowledge that, notwithstanding the cruelty and moral wrong of slavery, the ten million Negroes inhabiting this country . . . are in a stronger and more hopeful condition, materially, intellectually, morally, and religiously, than is true of an equal number of black people in any other portion of the globe" (37). Thus, in *Up from Slavery,* Washington presented an account of the slave experience that, for the most part, glosses over its dehumanizing and abusive aspects. Some historians believe Washington engaged in much speculation when presenting his memories of slavery. Washington placed his slave days within the traditional plantation setting, mentioning an overseer and the "Big House." Washington actually lived on a farm, and his owner did not employ an overseer. Some of Washington's claimed experiences were probably those of his older brother, John.

Washington also devoted a portion of *Up from Slavery* to his view of the Reconstruction, an era during which southern whites, and Washington himself, believed that the priorities of African Americans were misdirected. Washington not only argued that blacks were too dependent on the federal government for support but also believed their focus on politics and the study of Greek and Latin were misdirected. Instead, he argued, the newly freed blacks should have concentrated on agricultural cultivation and industrial education. Washington failed to discuss the powerlessness of southern blacks to protect themselves from the former Confederates, nor does he mention the restrictions and limitations placed on them by Black Codes or the inability of the majority of former slaves to acquire land.

In *Up from Slavery,* Washington also discusses his thirst for and valuing of education, which eventually led him to Hampton Institute. So driven was he to gain an education that, when he ran out of funds on his travels from Malden to Hampton (a distance of 500 miles), Washington walked the remaining distance, sleeping under sidewalks at night for safety in Richmond, an unfamiliar urban environment. Arriving at Hampton, Washington, to gain admission and pay for boarding, demonstrated his determination and commitment by cleaning a classroom with precision, using the lessons he had learned from Mrs. Viola Ruffner, a former New England schoolteacher who had employed Booker as a servant in her family home in Virginia and taught him the value of hard work. Washington wrote, "I had the feeling that in a large measure my future depended upon the impression I made upon the teacher in the cleaning of that room" (56). He was given work as a janitor, which allowed him to meet his financial responsibilities. "The work was hard and taxing, but I stuck it out" (57), Washington proudly admitted. At Hampton, Washington came under the direct influence of General Samuel Chapman Armstrong, the founder, who, Washington writes, "made an impression upon me of being a perfect man. . . . [T]here was something about him that was superhuman" (58). Like Mrs. Ruffner, Armstrong taught Washington to value hard work and the fundamental principles of the Puritan work ethic. Armstrong, who believed that the Reconstruction had failed because the former slaves were misguided, undoubtedly shaped Washington's negative portrayal of southern blacks.

Approximately two years after graduating from Hampton Institute, Washington enrolled at Wayland Seminary in Washington, D.C. This was his first experience with urban living and higher education, and he rejected them both. As a result of his urban experience, Washington condemned the moral values of urban living and expressed a belief that industrial education was more valuable than a liberal college education.

Washington spends much of the second half of *Up from Slavery* discussing the preparation, delivery, and significance of his "Atlanta Exposition Address"; he includes the text in its entirety in his autobiography. "When I arose to speak," he candidly explains, "the thing that was uppermost in my mind was the desire to say something that would cement the friendship of the races" (146). As a result, he urged the cultivation of a new friendship between blacks and southern white leaders. The basis for such a relationship was black accommodation and acceptance of white dominance, including the separation of the races. Washington declared, "In all things that are purely social we can be as separate as the fingers, yet one as the hands in all things essential to mutual progress" (148).

In addition to embracing segregation, which would be legalized by the Supreme Court in its *Plessy v. Ferguson* decision in 1896, Washington encouraged both black and white southerners to "cast down their buckets" where they were to establish and cement a complementary and expedient relationship. He reminded blacks that "it is in the South that the Negro is given a man's chance in the commercial world" (147). He reminded whites that blacks not only had remained faithful to them but also had "without strikes and labour wars, tilled your fields, clear your forests, builded [sic] your railroads and cities, and brought forth treasures from the bowels of the earth" (147).

According to HOUSTON BAKER, who compares Washington's rhetorical posture with that of minstrel actors, Washington, in his "Atlanta Exposition Address," emerges as an astute speaker and politician who mastered the form of the minstrel's mask to accomplish his objective. Baker concludes, "Washington's work becomes a *how to* manual, setting forth strategies of address (ways of talking black and back) designed for Afro-American empowerment" (31).

Washington's *Up from Slavery* continues to be described as a rags-to-riches story, a particular American genre popularized by the stories of Horatio Alger and Andrew Carnegie's *Gospel of Wealth* (1889). Its popularity is verified by efforts, shortly before his death, to make a motion picture based on the autobiography. *Up from Slavery* remains a valuable source of information to scholars interested in the life of this former slave and significant 20th-century African-American leader. As autobiography, it illustrates the skills employed by Washington in handling specific areas of his experience and how this handling reflects his subjective and personal intent.

BIBLIOGRAPHY

Baker, Houston A., Jr. *Modernism and the Harlem Renaissance.* Chicago: University of Chicago Press, 1987.

DuBois, William E. B. *The Souls of Black Folk.* In *Three Negro Classics*, 207–389. New York: Avon Books, 1965.

Harlan, Louis R. *Booker T. Washington: The Making of a Black Leader, 1856–1901.* New York: Oxford University Press, 1972.

Harlan, Louis R. *Booker T. Washington: The Wizard of Tuskegee 1901–1915.* New York: Oxford University Press, 1983.

Washington, Booker T. *Up from Slavery.* Doubleday, Page and Company, 1909. Reprinted in *Three Negro Classics*, 23–205. New York: Avon Books, 1965.

Ronald. G. Coleman

Van Peebles, Melvin (1932–)

Melvin Van Peebles exemplified independent film-making in the late 1960s, and by the early 1970s he became a pioneer in making the kind of black-oriented films that revitalized Hollywood studios. Outspoken and determined, he has assumed a legendary status among filmmakers and has con-nected with audiences across age and racial lines. But from the critics, Van Peebles has often been a target of harsh commentary for his film styliza-tions and content, particularly for his second film, *Sweet Sweetback's Baadasssss Song* (1971).

Born in Chicago in 1932, Van Peebles received a B.A. in English literature at Ohio Weslyan Univer-sity. By the time he went into the air force in the late 1950s, he was in an interracial marriage with three children, including his son Mario. After three years in the service, he settled his family in San Fran-cisco, where he began to make short films, namely *Sunlight* (1958) and *Three Pickup Men for Herrick* (1958), hoping to earn a ticket into Hollywood. However, the only jobs offered him at one studio were attending the parking lot and running the el-evator. Leaving the country, he studied science at the University of Amsterdam and took acting les-sons, but faced with marriage problems, he finally settled in Paris, drawn once more to filmmaking. Realizing that he could get financial support from the government as a filmmaker, Van Peebles taught himself French and wrote several novels to make a

name for himself. One of the works was titled *Story of a Three Day Pass,* which he made into a film in 1968. The focus of the fictional work was the inter-racial love affair between a black American service-man and a white Parisian woman, emphasizing the racial consciousness of the black soldier and the racism of his fellow white soldiers.

The film garnered critical attention at film festi-vals, providing Van Peebles access to Hollywood for his first American film, *Watermelon Man* (1970), a satire about a conservative white man who awak-ens one morning to find that he is suddenly black. However, it was the controversial images in Van Peebles' next film, *Sweet Sweetback's Baadasssss Song,* that prompted conflicting critiques.

Highlighting graphic sexual scenes and violence, *Sweet Sweetback* follows the odyssey of the title character, a black man who works as a performer at an underground sex theater and who becomes a fugitive after beating white police officers who were attacking a black radical. Van Peebles claimed the film was revolutionary, depicting the triumph of a black man who confronts and escapes the oppres-sive white system. Others, however, saw the movie as a celebration of racial stereotypes, specifically the alleged sexual obsession and prowess of blacks. In addition to what some perceived as negative content, other critics also dismissed the film for its awkward and elliptical cinematic techniques. Regardless, on a $500,000 budget that he raised,

Van Peebles acted, wrote, produced, directed, and created the musical score for the film, which eventually had a box office return of $10 million.

When Van Peebles returned to writing, the responses to his work were still mixed. His musical play *Ain't Suppose to Die a Natural Death* (1971) examined the interaction among black Harlem dwellers caught within the oppressive limitations of their lives. One critic concluded, "With a combination of music, dialogue, dance, beautiful acting. . . . Van Peebles' characters come alive and make us deal with them on their own terms" (Riley and Harte, 447). In a more abrasive vein, another critic stated, "the whole thing is rather like a splendid mansion built on sand. . . . The most important elements of drama are totally absent. . . . [T]hese characters are far from tragic. They are pathetic clowns . . . [The] whole show was overloaded with filth" (Riley and Harte, 447).

Undaunted by his hostile critics, Van Peebles went on to write another musical play, *Don't Play Us Cheap* (1972), which fared no better in its reception than its predecessor had. A musical comedy, the play was "a fantasy wherein two demons (a cockroach and a rat) assume human form and attempt to wreck the festivities" of a Harlem party (Woll, 54). In 1973 he made a movie version of the play bearing the same title, but the film never found an audience or box office success. Three years later, he moved to the small screen, writing *Just an Old Sweet Song* (1976), a teleplay for the CBS network.

Into the next decade, Van Peebles worked in theater as a director, including the off-Broadway productions, *No Commercial Value* (1981), *Body Bags* (1981), *Waltz of the Stork* (1982), and *Champeeen!* (1983). That same year, he also combined his acting and writing for a television miniseries for NBC, *Sophisticated Gents*—adapted from *The Junior Bachelor Society* by JOHN A. WILLIAMS. In 1989 he directed the film *Identity Crisis*, based on the script by his son Mario, who also portrayed the film's dual protagonists. The movie focuses on a gay French fashion designer who, under a spell, moves in and out of the body of a black rap performer.

Van Peebles worked again with his son on two projects that the latter directed. First, the elder Van Peebles acted in a small role in the film *Posse* (1993), a story about black soldiers of the Spanish-American War who made their way west into the American frontier. Melvin Van Peebles served as a screenwriter on the second project, *Panther* (1995), based on his novel of the same title about the rise and fall of the Black Panther Party.

Throughout his decades of work as a filmmaker, Van Peebles continued to write in various genres. His novel *A Bear for the FBI* (1968) was a study of middle-class black life; eight years later, he completed the novel *The True American: A Folk Fable*, which followed a black prisoner who died and went to hell, where blacks were privileged while whites, the majority, were not. In 1977 he was a co-screenwriter on the film *Greased Lightning*, a vehicle for comedian Richard Pryor. Two additional nonfiction books followed in the next two decades: *Bold Money: A New Way to Play the Options Market* (1987) and *No Identity Crisis: A Father and Son's Own Story of Working Together* (1990), the latter written with Mario.

Melvin Van Peebles has proved himself a creative survivor, expressing himself on his own terms as a fiction writer, playwright, music composer, and film and stage director. For most, he will forever be connected to his 1971 film that, despite the stormy debates surrounding it, ushered in a new wave of black urban action films that provided more primary roles for blacks in Hollywood productions. Film critic Ed Guerrero wrote that "Melvin Van Peebles . . . demonstrated . . . that there is a critical mass of black people eager to see heroic images of themselves rendered from a black point of view and that through a series of hustles, maneuvers, and creative financing, independent money can be raised to make such films" (146). Van Peebles was elected to the Black Filmmakers Hall of Fame in 1976.

BIBLIOGRAPHY

Bogle, Donald. *Toms, Coons, Mulattoes, Mammies, and Bucks: An Interpretive History of Blacks in American Films*. New York: Continuum, 1990.

Donalson, Melvin. *Black Directors in Hollywood.* Austin: University of Texas Press, 2003.

Guerrero, Ed. *Framing Blackness: The African American Image in Film.* Philadelphia: Temple University Press, 1993.

Riley, Carolyn, and Barbara Harte, eds. "Melvin Van Peebles." In *Contemporary Literary Criticism,* vol. 2, 447–448. Detroit: Gale, 1979.

Woll, Allen. *Dictionary of the Black Theatre.* Westport, Conn.: Greenwood Press, 1983.

Melvin Donalson

Van Vechten, Carl   (1880–1964)

Carl Van Vechten was a writer, critic, and photographer best known as a white promoter of African-American cultural expression. Van Vechten initiated his career as an arts critic for such periodicals as the *New York Times,* the *New York Press,* and the *New Music Review.* After tiring of criticism in the early 1920s, Van Vechten authored a number of popular novels offering satirical explorations of the decadent lifestyle of his "modern" social circle; the most notable of these are *Peter Whiffle* (1922), *The Blind Bow-Boy* (1923), *Firecrackers* (1925), *Spider Boy* (1928), and *Parties* (1930). His most widely read work both then and now, however, is his popular Harlem novel *NIGGER HEAVEN* (1926), a highly controversial though sympathetic and candid account of the burgeoning New Negro Renaissance.

Van Vechten was born into a progressive Victorian household in Cedar Rapids, Iowa. Both parents taught him to respect individuals regardless of race or socioeconomic standing. He was deeply influenced by his father, Charles Duane Van Vechten, a founder of the Piney Woods School for African-American children in Mississippi, who had an unorthodox concern for African Americans. Carl, or "Carlo" as he was later called by friends, learned to treat local black laborers in the same manner he treated middle-class whites (Bernard, xviii). While attending the University of Chicago, Van Vechten explored black neighborhoods and spent time at churches and nightclubs run by

Chicago blacks. During this period he adopted an idealistic image of African Americans as a whole and later admitted that his early experiences may have made him more sympathetic to blacks than any social grouping deserves. Writing to CHESTER HIMES, Van Vechten, at age 76, explained that his youthful sympathy toward the black race, benign as it may have been, vanished after a revelation that, in fact, not all African Americans were the same: "one day I came home shouting, 'I HATE a Negro! I HATE a Negro!' It was my salvation and since then I've had no trouble at all. From that point on I understood that they were like everybody else that is they were thieves and cut-throats, generous and pious, witty and wise, dumb and foolish" (*Letters* 259).

In 1924, Van Vechten met writer and civil rights activist WALTER WHITE at a party hosted by their publisher Alfred Knopf (Knopf had published White's novel *The Fire in the Flint* that year); they instantly became friends. Within weeks White introduced Van Vechten to life in Harlem, where he met and befriended many black intellectuals and celebrities, including LANGSTON HUGHES, JAMES WELDON JOHNSON, JESSIE FAUSET, Paul Robeson, and WALLACE THURMAN. The relationships became mutually beneficial: The writers provided Van Vechten with access to black Manhattan, and in return, he promoted their works to the "great white" publishing market. Within three weeks of meeting Langston Hughes, for example, Van Vechten convinced Knopf to publish the 23-year-old's first book of poetry, *The Weary Blues* (1926).

Van Vechten was, in Ann Douglas's words, "a liaison and PR man extraordinaire between Harlem and white New York" (81). He was instrumental in securing publication for many key Harlem Renaissance texts, including a new edition of James Weldon Johnson's *The AUTOBIOGRAPHY OF AN EX-COLORED MAN* (1912, 1927), NELLA LARSEN's novels *Quicksand* (1928) and *Passing* (1929), and poetry by Langston Hughes and COUNTEE CULLEN. Van Vechten, who was older than many of the youthful talents he supported, assumed a paternal role in their career. After Paul Robeson's wife, Essie, referred to him as "godfather," the *Herald Tribune* adopted this appellation, reporting in 1925 that Carlo was "the beneficent godfather of all sophisticated Harlem" (quoted in Douglas, 288).

Van Vechten's explorations of Harlem life were widely publicized; he hosted many salon parties for New York's cultural elite in his Fifth Avenue apartment, singularly inviting both black and white guests. One Van Vechten soirée in June of 1925 was kicked off by George Gershwin playing show tunes at the piano; Paul Robeson then sang a number of Negro spirituals, and the evening concluded with James Weldon Johnson reciting "Go Down, Death" (Kellner, 200–201). When his novel *Nigger Heaven* appeared in 1926, it sold more copies than all of the books by African-American writers during the Harlem Renaissance combined (Worth, 466). Hughes confirms this, noting, "more Negroes bought [*Nigger Heaven*] than ever purchased a book by a Negro author" (quoted in Worth, 466). The original 16,000 copies sold out immediately, and it went through nine printings in its first four months.

A social novel more than a romance, *Nigger Heaven* revolves around two central characters, Mary Love and Byron Kasson, both of whom are doing their part for the New Negro movement, as they engage each other in discussions about culture and middle-class values and the place of the "race" as a criterion for assessing the aesthetic value of a work of art. Although scenes are set in Harlem cabarets, where jazz and gin flow and dancers lindy hop to African rhythmic drum sounds, *Nigger Heaven* contains few scandalous scenes, a fact that adds an ironic punch to the sensationalist title. Van Vechten had merely borrowed a popular term for the title of his novel: "Nigger Heaven" was most commonly used to refer to the balcony seats to which African Americans were confined in segregated theaters and movie palaces. Van Vechten used the expression metaphorically to connote both Harlem's location at the northern end of Manhattan and the irony of its application: Readers are meant to see that Negro society in Harlem transcends racial stereotyping, transcendence even a white man could accomplish.

Regardless, the novel, particularly its title, predictably stirred up enormous controversy in the black press. The most violent response came from W. E. B. DuBois, who hated it utterly; he began his review in *The Crisis* magazine with: "Carl Van Vechten's 'Nigger Heaven' is a blow in the face. . . . It is an affront to the hospitality of black folk and to the intelligence of the white" (81). The most benign response came from James Weldon Johnson, who vigorously defended it. The scenes Du Bois identified as "wildly barbaric drunken orgy," Johnson argued, "set off in sharper relief the decent, cultured, intellectual life of Negro Harlem" (393). Whether in the cabaret or in the intellectual salon, Johnson argues, "It is all life. It is all reality" (393).

Criticism was not limited to the black press. Van Vechten's father, who died seven months before *Nigger Heaven* appeared, was one of the first of the notorious title's long line of critics. In a letter to Carl he wrote, "Your 'Nigger Heaven' is a title I don't like. . . . I have myself never spoken of a colored man as a 'nigger.' If you are trying to help the race, as I am assured you are, I think every word you write should be a respectable one towards the black" (quoted in Kellner, 210–11).

If there is any consensus about Van Vechten, it is that he was not a racist. Perhaps his worst transgression of *Nigger Heaven* and his Harlem exploits was that he betrayed, as Emily Bernard describes it, "a combination of naiveté and arrogance [that] led him to believe he was unique, a white man who had transcended his whiteness" (xix). The defining contradiction of his race writing, and a cause for critical tension, is that his belief in collapsing racial boundaries is never reconciled with his celebration of Negro exceptionalism. This issue alone, with all of its relevant applications today, will ensure that Van Vechten criticism will continue to flourish. Van Vechten's final, pragmatic legacy to the African-American literary tradition was his donation of the James Weldon Johnson Memorial Collection of Negro Arts and Letters to Yale University. The collection, named in his friend's honor, holds writings, letters, and memorabilia pertaining to African-American life that Van Vechten had compulsively amassed over the years. It remains one of the richest scholarly collections for American literary study. Van Vechten died in New York City on December 21, 1964.

BIBLIOGRAPHY

Bernard, Emily, ed. and introd. *Remember Me to Harlem: The Letters of Langston Hughes and Carl Van Vechten, 1925–1964.* New York: Alfred A. Knopf, 2001.

Douglas, Ann. *Terrible Honesty: Mongrel Manhattan in the 1920s.* 1995. New York: Papermac, 1997.

Helbling, Mark. "Carl Van Vechten and the Harlem Renaissance." *Negro American Literature Forum* 10 (Summer 1976): 39–47.

Kellner, Bruce. *Carl Van Vechten and the Irreverent Decades.* Norman: University of Oklahoma Press, 1968.

Lueders, Edward. *Carl Van Vechten and the Twenties.* Albuquerque: University of New Mexico Press, 1955.

———. *Letters of Carl Van Vechten.* Edited by Bruce Kellner. New Haven: Yale University Press, 1987.

Worth, Robert F. "*Nigger Heaven* and the Harlem Renaissance." *African American Review.* 29, no. 3 (Fall 1995): 461–473.

Robert M. Dowling

Visitation of Spirits, A
Randall Kenan (1989)

Published by Grove Press, RANDALL KENAN's first novel, *A Visitation of Spirits,* immediately established him as one of America's most promising and challenging new writers. Similar to J. CALIFORNIA COOPER's *Family* and TONI MORRISON's *BELOVED, Visitation* uses a complex mix of realism, dramatic dialogue, and fantasy to render a provocative image of African-American sexual and cultural alienation and of the inescapable imbrications of history in manifestly personal experiences of trauma.

The story takes place in Tims Creek, North Carolina, a thinly disguised version of the town of Chinquapin, North Carolina, to which the New York–born Kenan moved while still a young child. Tims Creek is also the setting for many of the stories in Kenan's acclaimed collection *Let the Dead Bury Their Dead* (1992). Through a complex narrative that details the lives of four generations of the Cross family, most notably those of Horace Cross and his cousin James Malachi Green, or Jimmy, this compact but dramatically dense work intensively explores issues of homosexuality, familial responsibility, historical memory, and the cultural dynamics of interracial contact and class mobility.

A Visitation of Spirits is divided into five sections titled "White Sorcery," "Black Necromancy," "Holy Science," "Old Demonology," and "Old Gods, New Demons." These titles refer to the polarized notions of race and history by which the members of the Cross family will be, often literally, bedeviled. The destructive force of these binaries is experienced most dramatically by the 16-year-old Horace, who attempts and fails to deploy sorcery as a strategy for transcending the complications and guilt attending his struggles with his homosexuality and his longing to achieve what he imagines to be the utopian state of emotional coherence and physical ease signified by a red-tailed hawk.

The grounding narrative in *A Visitation of Spirits* consists of a recounting of the hellish night on which, while cradling a shotgun, a naked and mud-begrimed Horace travels through Tim's Creek in search of death and salvation after the failure of his attempt at physical transformation. Simultaneously, in another temporal mode, the heterosexual Jimmy tries to come to terms emotionally with the failures of his unrewarding life as a minister, high school principal, and widowed husband of an unfaithful wife. The novel's masterly web of stories and flashbacks leads to a final confrontation that leaves Horace dead and Jimmy even more culturally and emotionally bereft.

BIBLIOGRAPHY

Holland, Sharon Patricia. "(Pro)creating Imaginative Spaces and Other Queer Acts: Randall Kenan's

A Visitation of Spirits and Its Revival of James Baldwin's Absent Black Gay Man in *Giovanni's Room*." In *James Baldwin Now,* edited by Dwight McBride, 265–306. New York: New York University Press, 1999.

McKoy, Sheila Smith. "Rescuing the Black Homosexual Lambs: Randall Kenan and the Reconstruction of Southern Gay Masculinity." In *Contemporary Black Men's Fiction and Drama,* edited by Keith Clark, 15–36. Urbana: University of Illinois Press, 2001.

McRuer, Robert. "A Visitation of Difference: Randall Kenan and Black Queer Theory." *Journal of Homosexuality* 26, no. 2 and 3 (1993): 227–228.

Terry Rowden

Walker, Alice M. (1944–)

Alice Malsenior Walker was born the eighth child of sharecroppers Willie Lee and Minnie Lou Grant Walker, on February 9, 1944, in Eatonton, Georgia. Following the physically and emotionally scarring experience of being blinded in her right eye when her brother shot her with his BB gun, Walker turned inward and began recording her emotions. In 1961 she graduated at the top of her high school class, and for the next two years she attended Spelman College in Atlanta on a Georgia Rehabilitation scholarship. In 1963 she transferred to Sarah Lawrence College and, after receiving her B.A., moved to New York City. In 1967 she married Melvyn Roseman Leventhal, a civil rights attorney, whom she divorced in 1977; the couple had moved to Mississippi, where Walker became active in the CIVIL RIGHTS MOVEMENT. Their only child, Rebecca Grant, was born in 1969. Like her mother, Rebecca is also a writer; she considers herself part of the third wave of black feminism. In Mississippi, Walker taught as writer-in-residence, first at Jackson State College and later at Tougaloo College. At Wellesley College, Walker would also create and teach the first course in the country devoted to black women writers. She has also taught at the University of Massachusetts–Boston, University of California–Berkeley, and Brandeis University.

A prolific writer, Walker has published several volumes of poetry, including *Once* (1968), *Revolutionary Petunias* (1973), *Good Night, Willie Lee, I'll See You in the Morning* (1979), *Horses Make a Landscape Look More Beautiful* (1986), and *Her Blue Body Everything We Know* (1991). She is the author of such well-known novels as *The THIRD LIFE OF GRANGE COPELAND* (1970), *Meridian* (1976), *The COLOR PURPLE* (1982), *The Temple of My Familiar* (1989), *Possessing the Secret of Joy* (1992), and *By the Light of My Father's Smile* (1998). Walker's short stories are collected in *In Love and Trouble: Stories of Black Women* (1973) and *You Can't Keep a Good Woman Down* (1981); her children's books include *Langston Hughes, American Poet* (1974), *The Life of Thomas Hodge* (1974), *To Hell with Dying* (1988), and *Finding the Green Stone* (1991). Her nonfiction prose includes *Living by the Word* (1988), *The Same River Twice* (1996), and *The Way Forward Is with a Broken Heart* (2000). In 1993 and 1994, Walker and Pratibha Parmar produced the documentary film *Warrior Marks* and published the accompanying book of the same title.

Walker's *In Search of Our Mother's Gardens* (1983) is a collection of "WOMANIST prose," prefaced by her four-part womanist aesthetic, which is meant to identify the nuances between white feminism and what she identified as womanism based on the popular black vernacular trope "womanish." Walker's womanist aesthetics took shape in the late 1970s and early 1980s while she was searching for a relevant vehicle with which to assess and evaluate the literary and artistic contributions of African-American women. She had become particularly aware of the need for such tools during her successful literary recovery of foremother ZORA NEALE HURSTON. Ultimately, however, Walker's model is less a means for judging the value of black women's art than it is a framework for imagining the black female subject in the process of achieving wholeness. The womanist model is exhibited through Walker's fiction, particularly in her novels from the award-winning *The Color Purple* forward. Walker and other black women artists have had to confront the "racial and gender mountain," and in her 30-plus years of writing for publication, Walker has often been plagued by criticism for the manner in which she has chosen to explore the social and cultural roots of women's oppression.

Walker has received numerous awards, grants, and fellowships. These include a Pulitzer Prize (the first by an African American for fiction) and an American Book Award for *The Color Purple,* the Lillian Smith Award for her poetry, the Richard and Hinda Rosenthal Award for her short stories, a Langston Hughes Award, a National Endowment for the Arts grant, a Radcliffe Institute fellowship, a PEN West Freedom to Write award, a Guggenheim grant, and several others. Walker is also cofounder of Wild Trees Press (1984 and 1988). Walker continues her social and political activism to this day—though it has taken on a more international scope that parallels her personal spiritual development and her belief in the oneness of the universe.

BIBLIOGRAPHY

Dieke, Ikenna, ed. *Critical Essays on Alice Walker.* Westport, Conn.: Greenwood Press, 1999.

Gates, Henry Louis, Jr., and Kwame Anthony Appiah, eds. *Alice Walker: Critical Perspectives Past and Present.* Amistad Literary Series. New York: Amistad, 1993.

Lauret, Maria. *Alice Walker.* New York: St. Martin's Press, 2000.

Winchell, Donna Haisty. *Alice Walker.* New York: Twayne, 1992.

Lovalerie King

Walker, David   (1785–1830)

Born in Wilmington, North Carolina, Walker was the son of a slave father, who died before Walker was born, and a free mother; at birth, he inherited the free status of his mother, who reared him. Abhorring slavery, the slave-holding South, and its "hypocritical slaveholders," Walker relocated to Boston, "where the previously illiterate and soon-to-become key figure in the abolitionist movement" (Aptheker 1965, 33) learned to read and write, became a clothing merchant, and married. As a leader in Boston's black community, Walker was a member of the Massachusetts General Colored Association and an agent of and contributor to *Freedom's Journal,* the first black newspaper, edited by John B. Russwurm and Samuel E. Cornish, which was first published on March 16, 1727. Walker was also a subscriber to a freedom fund for poet GEORGE MOSES HORTON.

Walker wrote, according to RICHARD BARKSDALE and Keneth Kinnamon, "the most radical of the early written protests against the Black man's condition in America" (151), *Walker's Appeal in Four Articles, together with a Preamble, to the Coloured Citizens of the World, but in Particular and Very Expressly to Those of the United States of America, Written in Boston, State of Massachusetts, September 28, 1829,* which, as the title reveals, he structured after the Constitution of the United States. By the time of Walker's death, he had overseen the publication of the second and third editions of his *Appeal,* in which his voice became progressively more militant and radical. The preamble and four articles confirm Lerone Bennett's contention that Walker was a "firebell that wouldn't stop ringing" (69).

Walker, in the preamble, developed his fundamental thesis around his "unshaken conviction" that blacks were "the most degraded, wretched, and abject set of beings that ever lived since the world began" (1). Therefore, his purpose in writing his *Appeal* was "to awaken in the hearts of my afflicted, degraded, and slumbering brethren, a spirit of inquiry and investigation respecting our miseries and wretchedness in this *Republican Land of Liberty!*" (2). Walker identified four main sources, "Our Wretchedness in Consequence of Slavery," "Our Wretchedness in Consequence of

Ignorance," "Our Wretchedness in Consequence of the Preachers of the Religion of Jesus Christ," and "Our Wretchedness in Consequence of the Colonizing Plan," for the inhumane treatment and wretched condition of blacks. Walker argued that racism stood at the core of all four categories. According to Aptheker, Walker was "among the pioneer antagonists of racism" (1965, 55).

Walker directs his most scathing and acrimonious language and attack at white Christian slave owners—"pretenders to Christianity"—who treated blacks "more cruel than . . . devils themselves ever treated a set of men, women and children on earth" (Barksdale, 153). He warns:

> I tell you Americans! That unless you speedily alter your course, you and your Country are gone!!!!!! For God Almighty will tear up the very face of the earth!!! Will not that very remarkable passage of Scripture be fulfilled on Christians? . . . 'He that is unjust, let him be unjust still:—and he which is filthy let him be filthy still: and he that is righteous, let him be righteous still.' (*Appeal* 39–40)

Walker's militancy is most evident in "Article II: Our Wretchedness in Consequence of Ignorance," in which he admonished the oppressed slaves to strike a physical blow against slavery, rather than remain in bondage. He wrote, "they want us for their slaves, and think nothing of murdering us in order to subject us to that wretched condition—therefore, if there is an attempt made by us, kill or be killed" (24). His words would be echoed by MALCOLM X, AMIRI BARAKA, and other black militant leaders and writers of the BLACK POWER and BLACK ARTS MOVEMENTS who advocated "revolution by any means necessary" more than a century and a half later. According to Barksdale and Kinnamon, Walker was "the first black writer to speak out without fear or restraint" (153) against slavery.

Significantly, however, Walker also directed his *Appeal* "particularly" to freed and educated "men of colour," whom he admonished to work actively and aggressively to gain the freedom and improve the condition of enslaved brethren. Walker wrote, "I call upon you . . . to cast your eye upon the

wretchedness of your brethren and to do your utmost to enlighten them and yourselves from degradation" (28). He further wrote:

> "There is a great work for you to do, as trifling as some of you may think of it. You have to prove to the Americans and the world, that we are MEN and not *brutes,* as we have been represented, and by millions treated. Remember, to let the aim of your labours among your brethren, and particularly the youths, be the dissemination of education and religion." (30)

Walker was also vociferous in his objection to the colonization program, which he saw as a plan by slaveholders "to get those of the coloured people, who are said to be free, away from among those of our brethren whom they unjustly hold in bondage, so that they may be enabled to keep them the more secure in ignorance and wretchedness, to support them and their children, and consequently they would have more obedient slaves" (47). Adamantly rejecting any such plans, Walker boldly declared, "This country is as much ours as it is the whites, whether they will admit it now or not" (54).

While many blacks "warmly and unequivocally" endorsed Walker's *Appeal* for its "undeniable power and genuine moral fervor" (Barksdale and Kinnamon, 152–153), leaders in the slave-holding South were shocked and alarmed. Aptheker reports that in response to Walker's *Appeal,* "a firebrand [which] was hurled into the charged American air" "the slave holder's newspapers were thrown into paroxysms of rage . . . at what the *Richmond Enquire* called this 'monstrous slander'" (Aptheker, 1965, 1). State governments met to consider what actions should be taken against Walker: "draconian laws were enacted; editorials were published; armories were replenished" (Aptheker, 1965, 1). Southern slaveholders placed a reward on his head. The *Appeal* was even critiqued and condemned by supporters of emancipation and such white abolitionists as Benjamin Lundy and William Lloyd Garrison, who referred to the *Appeal* as a "most injudicious publication," although he also described Walker as intelligent and brave.

Walker was found dead in his place of business shortly after the publication of the third edition of his *Appeal*. Although long believed to have been killed by the composite hand of the agents of slavery, more than likely Walker died from natural causes, perhaps a heart attack.

BIBLIOGRAPHY

Aptheker, Herbert. *The Negro in the Abolitionist Movement.* New York: International Press, 1941.

———. *"One Continual Cry": David Walker's Appeal to the Colored Citizens of the World (1829–1830), Its Sting and Its Meaning.* New York: Humanities Press, 1965.

Barksdale, Richard, and Keneth Kinnamon, eds. *Black Writers of America.* New York: Macmillan Company, 1972.

Bennett, Lerone. *Pioneers in Protest.* Chicago: Johnson Publishing Company, 1968.

Loggins, Vernon. *The Negro Author; His Development in America to 1900.* Port Washington, N.Y.: Kennikat Press, 1931.

Walker, David. *Appeal in Four Articles Together with a Preamble, to the Coloured Citizens of the World but in particular and very expressly to those in the United States of America.* Edited by Charles M. Wiltse. New York: Hill and Wang, 1965.

Wilfred D. Samuels

Walker Alexander, Margaret Abigail
(1915–1998)

Poet, author, essayist, lecturer, and educator Margaret Abigail Walker dedicated more than seven decades of her life to writing about the black experience in America, which she chronicled in poetry and prose, centering on such themes as time, racial equality, love, and freedom. She was born on July 7, 1915, in Birmingham, Alabama, to Sigismund C. Walker, a Methodist minister, and Marion Dozier Walker, a music teacher who played ragtime. At age 14, Walker earned her high school diploma from New Orleans Gilbert Academy, and upon completion attended New Orleans University (now Dillard University) for two years. She received a B.A. in English from Northwestern University (1935)

and worked with the Works Progress Administration (WPA) (1936–39) before earning both her M.A. in creative writing (1940) and her Ph.D. (1965) from the University of Iowa. She taught at Livingstone College (1941–42), West Virginia State College (1942–43), and Jackson State University (1946–79) and was a visiting professor at Northwestern University (1968–69). She was the founder and director of the Institute for the Study of History, Life, and Culture of Black People (now the Margaret Walker Alexander National Research Center) (1968–79) and professor emerita of Jackson State University (1979–98).

In Walker's *This Is My Century,* she credits her parents for inspiring her to write early in her life. She writes, "My father was . . . my first teacher of poetics. . . . My mother's music, vocal and instrumental, gave me my only sense of rhythm" (xi–xii). Her mother also introduced her to the poetry of PAUL LAURENCE DUNBAR, John Greenleaf Whittier, William Shakespeare, LANGSTON HUGHES, and COUNTEE CULLEN. In 1931 she met family friend, literary mentor, and poet Hughes, who read her poetry, recognized her talent, suggested she strive for musicality in verse, and encouraged her parents and her teacher, Miss Fluke, to provide the necessary climate for an aspiring writer outside of the South. During her undergraduate work, she met editor, scholar, and author W. E. B. DU BOIS, who was influential in publishing her poetry in *The CRISIS* magazine in 1934. Her creative writing teacher, Edward Buell Hungerford, admitted her to the Northwestern chapter of the Poetry Society of America. While living in Chicago for four years, working as a social worker and later as a member of the WPA, Walker honed her craft. In Chicago she was a member of the South Side Writer's Group, initiated by RICHARD WRIGHT, between 1936 and 1939; she associated with such artists and scholars as Nelson Algren, FRANK YERBY, GWENDOLYN BROOKS, ARNA BONTEMPS, Frank Marshall Davis, Katherine Dunham, Margaret Taylor Goss Burroughs, and Theodore Ward. Of these artists and scholars, her most valuable literary experience was with Wright, who broadened her vision of how literature, in particular, could be a vital part of political action, but her friendship and mentorship with Wright ended rather abruptly and painfully. Walker writes about her experience with Wright in her detailed biography *Richard Wright: Daemonic Genius* (1988).

Walker completed her master's degree thesis, *For My People,* in 1942. It became her first collection of poems. Walker became one of America's youngest black writers to have a volume of poetry published in the 20th century. Through rhythmic verses and strong imagery, the work affirms the proud heritage and integrity of black Americans. Generally, critics, reviewers, and her peers praised the work.

In 1966, Walker published JUBILEE, which was the basis for her doctoral dissertation begun at Northwestern many years earlier. A neo–slave narrative that incorporates actual and historical events from slavery to Reconstruction, the novel chronicles the life of the daughter of a slave, Walker's great-grandmother, Margaret Duggans Ware Brown, on whom the character Vyry is based, and a white plantation owner. When the novel was first published, it had a mixed reception, but over the years the novel has garnered more favorable criticism, focusing specifically on Walker's status as an important historian, her characterization, and her use of music.

After she published *Jubilee,* Walker returned to writing poetry. She wrote the highly critically acclaimed *Prophets for a New Day* (1970), which depicts "a people striking back at oppression and emerging triumph" (Collier). This slim volume, unlike *For My People,* reveals an even more expansive political consciousness, which includes her civil rights poems influenced by the turmoil of the 1960s. Walker published *October Journey* (1973), followed by two books: *A Poetic Equation: Conversations between Nikki Giovanni and Margaret Walker* (1974) and the definitive biography *Richard Wright: Daemonic Genius* (1988). *This Is My Century: New and Collected Poems* (1989), her last volume of poetry, is a culmination of her collective political vision. A few years before Walker died, she published, with editorial assistance from Maryemma Graham, *How I Wrote Jubilee and Other Essays on Life and Literature* (1990). Her final published work was *On Being Female, Black,*

and Free: Essays by Margaret Walker, 1932–1992 (1997).

Walker's numerous awards and honors include the Yale Younger Poets Award (1942), the Rosenwald Fellowship for Creative Writing (1944), Ford Fellowship at Yale (1954), a University of Iowa fellowship (1963), a Houghton Mifflin literature fellowship (1966), a Fulbright Fellowship to Norway (1971), senior fellowship from the National Endowment for the Humanities (1972), doctor of literature, Northwestern University (1974), doctor of letters, Rust College (1974), doctor of fine arts, Dennison University (1974), doctor of humane letters, Morgan State University (1976), the Living Legacy Award, the Lifetime Achievement Award of the College Language Association (1992), the Lifetime Achievement Award for Excellence in the Arts (1992), and the White House Award for Distinguished Senior Citizen. She was inducted into the African American Literary Hall of Fame (October 1998), and Jackson, Mississippi, designated July 12 Margaret Walker Day.

Walker was one of the most formidable, gifted literary voices of the 20th century, whose encouraging works gave hope to the masses. She bridged the generations of the HARLEM RENAISSANCE of the 1920s and the BLACK ARTS MOVEMENT of the 1960s and became one of America's foremost poetic historians for a race. Indeed, Walker will be remembered for her legacy, which spanned almost an entire century. Walker died of breast cancer in Chicago on November 30, 1998.

BIBLIOGRAPHY

Barksdale, Richard K. "Margaret Walker: Folk Orature and Historical Prophecy." In *Black American Poets between Worlds, 1940–1960,* edited by R. Baxter Miller, Knoxville: University of Tennessee Press, 1986.

Bell, Bernard W. *The Afro-American Novel and Its Tradition.* Amherst: University of Massachusetts Press, 1987.

Collier, Eugenia. "Fields Watered with Blood: Myth and Ritual in the Poetry of Margaret Walker." In *Black Women Writers (1950–1980): A Critical Evaluation,* edited by Mari Evans, Garden City, N.Y.: Anchor Doubleday, 1984.

Gibson, Donald B., ed. *Modern Black Poets: A Collection of Critical Essays.* New York: Prentice Hall, 1983.

Pettis, Joyce. "Margaret Walker: Black Woman Writer of the South." In *Southern Women Writers: The New Generation,* edited by Tonette Bond Inge, 9–19. Tuscaloosa: University of Alabama Press, 1990.

Ward, Jerry W., Jr. "A Writer for Her People: An Interview with Dr. Margaret Walker Alexander." *Mississippi Quarterly* 41, no. 4 (Fall 1988).

Loretta G. Woodard

Walrond, Eric (1898–1966)

An important voice of the Harlem Renaissance, journalist, essayist, and short story writer, Eric Walrond, in his personal life, exemplified the complex immigration patterns of blacks during the first two decades of the 20th century. His life perhaps also reveals how these patterns might have been instrumental in fashioning and defining the dynamic spectrum of experiences of what Alain Locke called the "New Negro." A British subject, like poet Claude McKay, Walrond was born in Georgetown, British Guiana (presently Guyana); he grew up in Barbados and Colón, Panama, where his father, who deserted the family, worked on the Panama Canal. Walrond completed his secondary education, becoming bilingual and "thoroughly exposed to Spanish culture" (Bone, 175). Before migrating to New York at age 20, Walrond had worked as a secretary and stenographer and launched a successful career in journalism working as a reporter and sportswriter for the Panama *Star Herald.*

In the United States, Walrond attended City College of New York and Columbia University, where he studied creative writing. His strong antipathy for the racism and oppression he came to perceive as global problems led Walrond to align himself with Marcus Garvey's Universal Negro Improvement Association (UNIA), serving as the editor of Garvey's newspaper, *The Negro World,* as well as the editor of the National Urban League's journal, Opportunity. In his article "The Negro Faces America" (*Current History,* 1923), Walrond, who had also owned and edited the *Brooklyn and Long Island Informer,* voiced his ideological differences with Booker T. Washington, W. E. B. DuBois, and the National Association for the Advancement of Colored People. He concluded that Garvey was the only extant black leader who could lead the New Negro movement. For Walrond, the New Negro was above all "race conscious. He does not want to be like the white man." In the end he would become dissatisfied with Garvey and separate himself from the UNIA movement.

A Guggenheim grant took Walrond back to Panama and to the West Indies to study and write about the experience of black immigrants and workers in these areas. Thus, like McKay, Walrond spent many of the years associated with the Harlem Renaissance traveling and living abroad, although, as many critics note, he helped foster this important black cultural and literary moment in African-American history through his reviews, stories, and essays.

Walrond was best known for his short stories, many of which were published in *Opportunity.* Many of these stories, such as "On Being a Domestic," focused on working-class blacks and the racism they often encountered in America. His most important book was his collection of 10 stories, *Tropic Death* (1926), in which he looks through international lenses at the black experience.

Generally, *Tropic Death* was well received. Walrond's efforts and style were often compared to Jean Toomer and *Cane,* although most critics conceded that Toomer was the more talented and gifted of the two writers. At the height of his literary career, Walrond left the United States to travel throughout Europe. He settled in England, where he died in 1966.

BIBLIOGRAPHY

Bone, Robert. *Down Home: A History of Afro-American Short Fiction from Its Beginnings to the End of the Harlem Renaissance.* New York: Capricorn Books, 1975.

Lewis, David Levering. *When Harlem Was in Vogue.* New York: Oxford University Press, 1979.

Walrond, Eric. "The Wharf Rats." In *The Portable Harlem Renaissance Reader,* edited by David Levering Lewis, 549–568. New York: Penguin Books, 1995.

Wilfred D. Samuels

Ward, Douglas Turner (1930–)

An acclaimed dramatist, actor, and producer and the cofounder and artistic director of the famed Negro Ensemble Company, Douglas Turner Ward is a major figure in American theater. Born on May 5, 1930, to Roosevelt and Dorothy Short Ward, in Burnside, Louisiana, a rural town near New Orleans, Ward grew up on a plantation with his parents and his mother's three sisters. Later, he was sent to New Orleans to live with a relative and attended public school there; he developed a passion for reading and graduated from high school at age 15. In 1946 he enrolled in Wilberforce University in Xenia, Ohio, and in fall 1947 he transferred to the University of Michigan, where he briefly studied journalism before suffering a knee injury on the junior varsity football squad. At the end of the 1947–1948 academic year, he left college for New York City.

Before leaving college, Ward was actively involved in left-wing political activism, which he continued after arriving in New York, where he wrote for the *Daily Worker.* His participation in politics further advanced his interest in the theater. At age 19 he became a playwright, though his career was put on hold after his arrest and conviction on a draft evasion charge. Cleared of the charge, he returned from Louisiana to New York and began to train as an actor at Paul Mann's Actor's Workshop. During the 1950s and 1960s, Ward was featured in *The Iceman Cometh* (1956); *A Land beyond the River* (1957); *Lost in the Stars* (1957), and understudied Sidney Poitier in *A Raisin in the Sun*, eventually playing the leading role; *One Flew over the Cuckoo's Nest* (1963); *Rich Little Rich Girl, The Blacks* (1964); *Blood Knot* (1963); and *Coriolanus* (1965).

In 1965 Ward, along with actor-director Robert Hooks and off-Broadway producer Gerald S. Krone, formed the Tony Award–winning Negro Ensemble Company (NEC), a repertory group that focuses on African-American themes. As artistic director, Ward both acted and directed for the company, which was initially located at the St. Marks Playhouse on the Lower East Side of Manhattan. Also in 1965 Hooks produced Ward's two most controversial one-act plays, *Happy Ending* and *Day of Absence,* which opened at St. Marks Playhouse on November 15. Among the first plays to approach theater from a modern black perspective using humor, both comedies examine black/white relations, showing a different perspective on the interdependence between the races. Audiences were not prepared for Ward's biting satire and extended jokes at their expense. Receiving mixed reviews, the plays were dismissed by critics. Despite this, the plays ran for 504 performances, and Ward won a Vernon Rice Drama Desk Award and an Obie Award in 1966, one for his performance as the mayor and one for writing the plays.

After the success of these two plays and the publication of his most influential essay, "American Theatre: For Whites Only?," Ward published several other plays. *The Reckoning* (1969), a play about black rap, features a battle of words between two smooth-talking antagonists. Ward both wrote and acted in this play, which was presented by Hooks Productions in cooperation with the Negro Ensemble Company on September 4. Ward's *Brotherhood,* a one-act fantasy that examines the social relations between suburban whites and blacks, debuted on March 17, 1970—presented by the Negro Ensemble Company. Ward's *The Redeemer* (1979) uses six stereotypical characters—an old Christian woman, a rabbi, a black woman, a young white feminist, a black militant, and a white revolutionary—to explore each character's attitudes and clashes between them at the specific juncture when they hear that the Redeemer is going to appear.

Since the 1970s, Ward, who has remained committed to black dramatic literature, has supported many black writers and staged a number of the best black plays, including LONNE ELDER's *Ceremonies in Dark Old Men* (1969), Joseph Walker's *The River Niger* (1973), Leslie Lee's *The First Breeze of Summer* (1975), Charles Fuller's *The Brownsville*

Raid (1976), Steve Carter's *Nevis Mountain Dew* (1978), Samm-Art Williams's *Home* (1979), and Charles Fuller's *A Soldier's Play,* which won a Pulitzer Prize in 1982.

Known for his "great force" and "dedication," Ward made an invaluable contribution to the black theater explosion of the 1960s. His vision of a theater by and for promising actors, playwrights, directors, technicians, and administrators was highly influential in the African-American literary community. Although he has been unable to write much since the late 1970s, his short, satiric plays, along with his publications in the *New York Times* and the *Negro Digest,* helped widen the range and depth of understanding of the black experience through the theater.

BIBLIOGRAPHY

Beauford, Fred. "The Negro Ensemble Company: Five Years against the Wall." *Black Creation* 3 (Winter 1972): 16–18.

Floyd, Gaffney. "Ward, Douglas Turner." In *The Oxford Companion to African American Literature,* edited by William L. Andrews, Frances Smith Foster, and Trudier Harris, 756–757. New York: Oxford University Press, 1997.

Peavy, Charles D. "Satire and Contemporary Black Drama." *Satire Newsletter* 7, no. 1: 40–48.

Peterson, Maurice. "Douglas Turner Ward." *Essence,* June 1973, pp. 44–45, 75.

Ribowsky, Mark. "'Father' of the Black Theatre Boom." *Sepia* 25 (November 1976): 67–78.

Vallillo, Stephen M. "Douglas Turner Ward." In *Dictionary of Literary Biography.* Vol. 38: *Afro-American Writers after 1955: Dramatists and Prose Writers,* edited by Thadious M. Davis and Trudier Harris, 264–270. Detroit: Gale, 1985.

Loretta G. Woodard

Washington, Booker T.   (1856–1915)

Although born a slave—the son of a white slave-holding father and a black mother—educator, administrator, political leader, and autobiographer Booker T. Washington was, by the turn of the 20th century, not only the principal of Tuskegee Normal and Industrial Institute, which he and his students built with bricks they had made, but also readily identified, according to W. E. B. DuBois, Washington's contemporary and nemesis, as one of the "most notable figures in a nation of seventy million." This was in part because, DuBois further argued, Washington's economic program and public contention that demands for black political and social privileges were secondary—particularly his willingness to disenfranchise blacks—"practically accept[ed] the alleged natural inferiority of the Negro races" (246). Despite his popularity among blacks and whites, critics including IDA B. WELLS-BARNETT and Monroe Trotter maintained that Washington's program of accommodation was an acceptance of white domination.

Although Washington is generally credited with producing two autobiographies, *The Story of My Life and Work* (1900) and *UP FROM SLAVERY* (1901), both were written with the assistance of various ghostwriters. Of the two, *Up From Slavery,* written with the assistance of Max Bennett Thrasher, in which Washington describes his life in slavery, emancipation, quest for education, validation of manual labor and Puritan work ethic, and rise to power, is the better known. First published serially in *The Outlook* magazine with advice from Lyman Abbott, its editor, *Up From Slavery,* a best seller, resonated with the Horatio Alger rags-to-riches stories popular at the beginning of the 20th century. Reporting that the "the most trying ordeal of slavery" for him was "the wearing of a flax shirt" (34), Washington concluded that, in the end, the "school of American slavery" fortified blacks, leaving them "in a stronger, more hopeful condition, materially, intellectually, morally, and religiously" than blacks anywhere in the world. In fact, Washington concluded, "notwithstanding the cruel wrongs inflicted upon us, the black man got nearly as much out of slavery as the white man did" (37).

Working in the Virginia coal mines during a brief hiatus from employment in the home of the Ruffners, young Booker learned about Hampton Institute, a school for blacks where financially disadvantaged students could work in lieu of paying their board. Wishing to gain admission to Hampton, Washington traveled at first by coach to Hampton, then walked after he ran out of funds, sleeping under wooden sidewalks in Richmond. Undiscouraged, he arrived at Hampton dirty and disheveled. To gain admission, he cleaned a classroom, immaculately, the way Mrs. Ruffner, a strict taskmistress, had taught him to do. This experience, which Washington described as his first test, as well as the lessons he learned while at Hampton from his mentor, General Samuels C. Armstrong, the founder who had dedicated his life to "lifting up [the black] race" (59), convinced Washington of the value of discipline, hygiene, and industrial education. These are the principles and values Washington employed in his critical role as the architect of the Tuskegee experiment in Alabama.

By the beginning of the 20th century, many Americans came to view Washington as the leading black expert on what was frequently referred to as the "Negro Problem," largely because of the program for black economic self-reliance he outlined in his infamous "Atlanta Exposition Address" (1895). Beginning with the premise that the South was the only place that would give blacks "a man's chance for economic growth," Washington discouraged black migration to the North and admonished them, instead, to "cast down your buckets where you are" (147). Simultaneously declaring the ostensible faithfulness and docility of the former slaves, Washington encouraged southern whites to cast down their buckets "among the eight millions of Negroes whose habits you know, whose fidelity and love you have tested." He further assured them, "As we have proved our loyalty to you in the past . . . so in the future, in our humble way, we shall stand by you with a devotion that no foreigner can approach" (148). To illustrate his commitment to work within well-established post-Reconstruction southern boundaries of "separate but equal," Washington promised, "In all things that are purely social we can be separate as the fingers, yet one as the hand in all things essential to mutual progress."

With this stance, Washington was recognized by whites as the most important black leader—

indeed as one of the founding fathers of the nation, like Benjamin Franklin, whose name Washington indirectly invokes from the beginning of *Up from Slavery.* President Grover Cleveland, to whom Washington sent a copy of his speech, wrote to offer his congratulations, confirming Washington's accomplished goal. "Your words cannot fail to delight and encourage all who wish well for you and your race, and if our coloured fellow-citizens do not from your utterances gather new hope and form new determinations to gain every valuable advantage offered them by their citizenship, it will be strange indeed" (151).

Calling Washington's "Atlanta Exposition Address" the "Atlanta Compromise," DuBois wrote, "His doctrine has tended to make the whites, North and South, shift the burden of the Negro problem to the Negro's shoulder and stand aside as critical and rather pessimistic spectators; when in fact the burden belongs to the nation" (251). According to biographer Louis R. Harlan, with this speech, Washington "stood on its head the whole theory of abolition and Reconstruction" (219). Recent critics such as HOUSTON A. BAKER, JR., identify Washington—preeminently a southern spokesperson—as an accomplished speaker, deft in his ability to manipulate and master the minstrel's mask. According to Baker, "Washington's narrator not only plays the role of the judiciously southern, post-Reconstruction racist but also supplies a preposterous character direct from minstrelsy to play the darky role in this condemnatory drama" (28).

BIBLIOGRAPHY

Baker, Houston A., Jr. *Modernism and the Harlem Renaissance.* Chicago: University of Chicago Press, 1987.

DuBois, William E. B. *The Souls of Black Folk.* In *Three Negro Classics,* edited by John H. Franklin, 213–289. New York: Avon Books, 1965.

Harlan, Louis R. *Booker T. Washington: The Making of a Black Leader, 1856–1901.* New York: Oxford University Press, 1971.

Olney, James. "The Founding Fathers—Frederick Douglass and Booker T. Washington." In *Slavery and the Literary Imagination,* edited by Deborah E. McDowell and Arnold Rampersad, 1–24. Baltimore: The Johns Hopkins University Press, 1987.

Washington, Booker T. *Up From Slavery.* In *Three Negro Classics,* edited by John H. Franklin, 1–205. New York: Avon Books, 1965.

Ronald G. Coleman

Watts Writers Workshop   (1965–1973)

In 1965 award-winning scriptwriter and biographer Budd (Wilson) Schulberg of Beverly Hills founded the Douglass House Watts Writers Workshop, a multimillion-dollar cultural center and writers' development program, in response to the Watts Rebellion. After touring postrebellion Watts, while it "still smoked," Schulberg posted a note at the Westminster Neighborhood Association announcing a creative writing workshop. Three months later, CHARLES JOHNSON became the first recruit; others, including Johnnie Scott and John Eric Priestley, would follow.

The workshop was initially located on 103rd Street in the Watts area of Los Angeles, California, down the street from what is now Mafundi Institute and not far from Simon Rodia's Watts Towers. According to Watts native Anthony "Amde" Hamilton, cofounder and member of the spoken-word trio The Watts Prophets, the workshop was "a cultural laboratory for black ideology created as a positive gesture in reaction to the 1965 Watts riots" (quoted in Jackson). From 1965 to 1973, the workshop functioned as a fine arts development haven for writing, critiquing, honing, performing, and publishing poetry, essays, and stories based in the life experiences of the writers. Other programs, such as drama, martial arts, studio recordings, and first-run movie screenings, extended the workshop's core writing program and earned it the status of a multidisciplinary cultural arts and education complex. Within a year after it was founded, the workshop outgrew the Westminster building and relocated to Watts Happening Coffee House, an abandoned furniture store converted by neighborhood youths into an art center that is now part of Mafundi Institute.

On August 16, 1966, NBC aired "The Angry Voices of Watts." The one-hour, prime-time network news documentary that featured workshop writers sparked press attention and support from prominent academic, literary, entertainment, and political figures from across the country, including writers JAMES BALDWIN and John Steinbeck, television writer Digby Wolfe, actors Richard Burton and Steve Allen, singer Abbey Lincoln, composer Ira Gershwin, and Senator Robert F. Kennedy.

By 1971 Schulberg and Fred Hudson founded the Frederick Douglass Creative Arts Center in New York, an offshoot of the workshop in Watts, adding about 40 to 50 writers to the original membership list. Writers who developed and presented their skills in the workshop and who lectured and taught there included Fannie Mae Brown, Jayne Cortez, Kamau Daàood, Marla Gibbs, Edna Gibson, Juanita Brittain Gist, Charmaine Grant, Odie Hawkins, James Thomas Jackson, Charles Johnson, Yaphet Kotto, Ted Lange, K. Curtis Lyle, Sunora McKeller, Dee Dee McNeil, Louise Meriwether, Birdell Chew Moore, Roger Mosley, Ojenke, Blossom Powell, J. Eric Priestley, Johnnie H. Scott, Ymmas Sirrah (aka Sammy Harris), Nola Richardson Satcher, Jimmie Sherman; The Watts Prophets—Anthony "Amde" Hamilton, Otis O'Solomon, and Richard Anthony Dedeaux—and QUINCY TROUPE. The Westminster building was vandalized and destroyed by fire in 1973.

BIBLIOGRAPHY

Carter, Curtis L. "Watts: The Hub of the Universe, Art and Social Change." Watts: Art and Social Change in Los Angeles, 1965–2002. Marquette University Haggerty Museum of Art. Available online. URL: http://www.marquette.edu/haggerty/exhibitions/past/watts/watts.html. Accessed October 26, 2006.

Jackson, Major. "The Watts Prophets." *earSHOT,* April 1997. Available online. URL: http://www.citypaper.net/earshot 0497/zoom.wattsprophets.shtml. Accessed February 15, 2007.

The Watts Prophets. *Change Is Overdue.* With Don Cherry. London: New World Rhythm, 1992.

Merilene M. Murphy

Ways of White Folks, The
Langston Hughes (1933)

LANGSTON HUGHES begins his first collection of short fiction, released during the Great Depression, by quoting Millberry Jones: "The ways of white folks, I mean some white folks . . ." The collection's title, a nod to W. E. B. DuBois's *The Souls of Black Folk,* reflects Hughes's intent to continue the exploration of racism in American nearly 70 years after emancipation. Many of the stories included in the collection were previously published in *Esquire, Abbot's Monthly,* and other magazines. Hughes's characters struggle to coexist in a racially charged atmosphere where the white characters often become confused, frustrated, and sometimes violent when the black characters refuse to fit into their prescribed subservient roles. Hughes begins with a powerful story, "Cora Unashamed," in which Cora, a servant for a white family, speaks bluntly and honestly at a funeral for the family's 19-year-old daughter, whose death was the result of an abortion forced upon the daughter by a mother trying to save face. From there, the collection gives readers a black author's view of the various relationships between the races, a perspective unique at the time.

"Slave on the Block" encapsulates a white couple's infatuation with their black "boy" whom they want to turn into a piece of art. In "Home," a jazz musician comes home from Paris to see his mother, only to be lynched for speaking to a white music teacher in public, as his time in Europe made him forget the "way things were" in the South. Hughes also deals with art in "The Blues I'm Playing," where a white patron cannot understand why her young black female protégé insists on keeping ties with her black culture, culminating in a wonderful description of the BLUES from Oceola: "This is mine. . . . Listen! . . . How sad and gay it is. Blue and happy—laughing and crying. . . . How white like you and black like me. . . . How much like a man. . . . And how like a woman" (119). Oceola's description could easily be applied to Hughes's entire collection.

Hughes deals with interracial relationships in "Passing," "Red-Headed Baby," "Poor Little Black Fellow," "Little Dog" (cited by many reviewers at the time of publication as the best story), "Mother and Child," and "Father and Son"—a 48-page novella that Hughes eventually rewrote into the play *Mulatto* (Tracy, 45). Within each story, Hughes finds a different perspective from which to explore the realities of interracial identities in early 20th-century America, some invariably ending in lynching. In "A Good Job Done," "Berry," and "One Christmas Eve," Hughes explores the implications of blacks finding themselves in the employment of whites and the subsequent tenuous nature of their position.

Hughes's collection stands apart from his contemporary Richard Wright's portraits of race relations after Reconstruction, in that he presents "numerous black and white women characters, demonstrating the integral role white women play in propagating social and moral racial codes that affect the lives of both black women and men" (Joyce, 100). Women are the protagonists of 11 of 14 stories, leading Joyce Ann Joyce to note: "*The Ways of White Folks* reveals a profound mind artistically capable of identifying with the intricacies of female consciousness and of censuring female participation in the cultural behavioral patterns that stifle their humanity" (101). Hughes does the same with his male characters; in fact, the sheer breadth of the work led David Michael Nifong to note, "the collection offers a unique opportunity for the study of numerous different points of view in a single volume" (93).

Initial reaction to *The Ways of White Folks* varied in 1934. Mason Roberson wrote, "It will make you think, although what you think will not always be pleasant" (187). Lewis Gannet noted, "these stories cut deep" (189). The *Pasadena Star-News* concluded, "If Langston Hughes never wrote another short story, he would have to be reckoned with for what this volume contains" (189). However, some reviewers could not get past Hughes's portrayal of his white characters. George Schuyler believed that Hughes "twisted his material to fit the pattern of Negro propaganda" (201), and H. Bond Bliss wrote of the "pathetic and tragic bitterness which characterizes most of these . . . tales" (220). Today,

The Ways of White Folk still finds itself in print, in homes, and in the classrooms; its themes continue to resonate with an American culture still in a state of recognition and healing.

BIBLIOGRAPHY

Anonymous. "'White Folks' Ways: Relations of Races Interpreted by Negro Poet Hughes. *Pasadena Star-News,* 23 June 1934, p. 6." In *Langston Hughes: The Contemporary Reviews,* edited by Tish Dace, 189. Cambridge: Cambridge University Press, 1997.

Bliss, H. Bond. "Bitter Stories of Negro Race. *Miami Herald,* 15 July 1934, p. 16." In *Langston Hughes: The Contemporary Reviews,* edited by Tish Dace, 220–221. Cambridge: Cambridge University Press, 1997.

Gannet, Lewis. "Books and Things. *New York Herald Tribune Books,* 27 June 1934, p. 15." In *Langston Hughes: The Contemporary Reviews,* edited by Tish Dace, 189–190. Cambridge: Cambridge University Press, 1997.

Hughes, Langston. *The Ways of White Folks.* New York: Alfred A. Knopf, 1969.

Joyce, Joyce Ann. "Race, Culture, and Gender in Langston Hughes's *The Ways of White Folks.*" In *Langston Hughes: The Man, His Art, and His Continuing Influence,* edited by C. James Trotman, 99–107. New York: Garland Publishing, 1995.

Nifong, David Michael. "Narrative Technique and Theory in *The Ways of White Folks.*" *Black America Culture Forum.* 15, no. 3 (Autumn 1981): 93–96.

Roberson, Mason. "Hughes Talks on Tragedy of Race. *Spokesman,* 7 June 1934, p. 6." In *Langston Hughes: The Contemporary Reviews,* edited by Tish Dace, 187. Cambridge: Cambridge University Press, 1997.

Schuyler, George. "Views and Reviews *Pittsburg Courier,* 30 June 1934, p. 10." In *Langston Hughes: The Contemporary Reviews,* edited by Tish Dace, 200–201. Cambridge: Cambridge University Press, 1997.

Tracy, Steven C. *A Historical Guide to Langston Hughes.* Oxford: Oxford University Press, 2004.

Michael Perry

Weaver, Afaa Michael (Michael S. Weaver) (1951–)

A poet, playwright, fiction writer, and freelance journalist, Weaver spent 15 years working in the factories of Baltimore, Maryland, his birthplace, where he was educated in the local public schools. Although he began his college education at the University of Maryland in College Park at age 16, he attended for only two years before going to work in the factory. After leaving the factory, Weaver attended Regents College, where he earned a B.A. degree before attending Brown University on a University Fellowship. While at Brown, he worked with MICHAEL HARPER and earned an M.F.A. in creative writing.

Weaver published his first collection of poems, *Water Song* (1985), while he was working in the factory. He published two other collections of poems: *My Father's Geography* (1992) and *Timber and Prayer: The Indian Poems* (1995), under the name Michael S. Weaver. His most recent collections (appearing after the name change) include *Talisman* (1998), *The Lights of God* (1999), and *Multitudes: Poems Selected and New* (2000). A faculty member of Cave Canem, Weaver, who acknowledges being influenced by Pablo Neruda, is a traditionalist in many ways, but he has also been influenced by black popular culture, particularly gangsta rap and progressive hip-hop music. He employs a diverse array of cultural references from African, Asian, and European history in his work. The title poem from *My Father's Geography* illustrates this:

> I was parading the Côte d'Azur,
> hopping the short trains from Nice to Cannes,
> At a phone looking to Africa over the Mediterranean,
> I called my father, and, missing me, he said,
> "You almost home boy. Go on cross the sea."

The positive father-son relationship Weaver celebrates in this poem is echoed in "Afternoon Train." Upon seeing hip-hoppers clad in baggy pants

board a Philadelphia commuter train, intruding
their black proud selves in a space where they are
obviously being gazed on as outsiders, Weaver's
speaker celebrates their pride, determination, and
refusal to be erased or merely denoted as "other."
Perhaps more important, they remind him of his
own youth, causing him to identify with them:
"Into the train come the smooth faces / of young
black men with too big pants / and too little time.
They bring a din / with the bravado of wearing
dark skin."

The founder of a small press and the literary
magazine *Blind Alleys,* as well as the editor of
Obsidian II, Weaver has received several awards,
including an NEA Fellowship, a Pew Fellowship,
a National Endowment for the Arts award, the
Pennsylvania Council on the Arts award, and a
PDI Award for his play *Elvira and the Lost Prince.*
His short story "By the Way of Morning Fire" was
included in GLORIA NAYLOR's *Children of the Night.*
Weaver is currently on the faculty of Simmons
College in Boston, Massachusetts.

BIBLIOGRAPHY
Gabbin, Joanne V., ed. *Furious Flower, African Ameri-
can Poetry from the Black Arts Movement to the
Present.* Charlottesville: University of Virginia
Press, 2004.

Wilfred D. Samuels

Weber, Carl (1970–)
Together with ERIC JEROME DICKEY, MARCUS MAJOR,
E. LYNN HARRIS, ZANE, and COLIN CHANNER, Carl
Weber tops the list of a new group of African-
American best-selling authors whose propensity
"to tell it like it is" has made them appealing to
popular and hip-hop cultures. His inner-city love/
erotica novels satisfy the taste of readers who want
to read but, rather than undergo the rigorous engagement demanded by novelists like TONI MOR-
RISON, prefer to laugh, be entertained, eavesdrop
on the couple next door, circulate gossip about the
pastor, and get the inside scoop on the real life of

a player. As he told Leah Mullen in an interview,
Weber caters to readers who want books with
"page after page of pure, unadulterated drama."
The titles of his first three novels—*Lookin' for Luv*
(2000), *Married Men* (2001), and *Baby Momma
Drama* (2003)—confirm that he is intent on meeting their needs.

After receiving his B.S. degree from Virginia
State University in accounting and an M.B.A. degree from the University of Virginia in marketing,
Weber opened his own bookstore, African American Bookstore, initially as a mail order business,
after an assignment related to starting a business
he had given his Riker's Island students proved
to be filled with lots of possibilities. In fact, the
idea to write his first novels came from customers
who described the kinds of books they wanted to
read—books that were more relevant to their daily
experiences.

Weber's first novel, *Lookin' for Luv,* a modern
romance, was his immediate response. *Lookin'
for Luv* addresses the pros and cons of dating in
the 21st century through a 1–900 number. Four
friends with different tastes in women—23-year-
old Kevin (a physical education teacher who blew
his chances with the NBA), Antoine (the intellectual in the group), Tyrone (a security guard and
former drug addict), and Maurice (a married man
who needs more than one woman in his life)—decide to find the right partner through a phone service, "1–900 Black Luv." Each man's search for a
soul mate further complicates his life in humorous
ways. This novel is filled with drama.

Married Men, his second novel, explores the experiences of Kyle, Allen, Wil, and Jay, four fairly
successful married men and the various women
(mothers, lovers, girlfriends, and wives) who play
dominant roles in their lives, demanding commitment and fidelity, which the four friends seem
incapable of providing. *Baby Momma Drama* revolves around the lives and loves of two sisters—
Jasmine, the older and more focused sister, and
Stephanie, who is more interested in having a good
time and maintaining various relationships. While
the older sister's search for true love and long-term

commitment ends in an exploitative relationship (her partner, a hustler, has already fathered a child with another woman), her younger sister seems unable to make up her mind about the two men in her life, Travis and Malek, her high school sweetheart and the father of her son. The experienced and loving Big Momma keeps the two sisters from personal destruction and helps them sort out their lives. Weber was named the Blackboard Bookseller of the Year in 2000.

BIBLIOGRPAHY

Mullen, Leah. "Carl Weber Gives 'Best Selling' Author a New Meaning." Available online. URL: http://authors.aalbc.com/carlweber.htm. Accessed October 26, 2006.

Wilfred D. Samuels

Wells-Barnett, Ida B.   (1861–1931)

Born a slave on July 16, 1862, in Holly Springs, Mississippi, Ida B. Wells-Barnett came of age during the Reconstruction and Southern Redemption and became one of the most important African-American activist leaders at the end of the 19th and the beginning of the 20th century. Her countless articles, pamphlets, and editorials against lynching, discrimination, and other forms of racism, along with her journals, lectures, and autobiography, made her one of the most prolific journalists, male or female, of her time. Her grassroots, community-based work ethic represented a high degree of accessibility and set precedents for the work of such organizations as the Southern Christian Leadership Conference (SCLC), the Student Non-Violent Coordinating Committee (SNCC), and the Black Panther Party, major players in the CIVIL RIGHTS MOVEMENT and BLACK POWER movement of the 1960s and 1970s.

Wells-Barnett was the first of eight children born to Jim and Elizabeth Barnett. She attended Shaw University (present-day Rust College) in Holly Springs until her parents and youngest brother died during the Mississippi yellow fever epidemic of 1878. At age 16, she left Shaw to become a county schoolteacher to provide for her younger brothers and sisters. By 1884 she had moved to Memphis, Tennessee, where she taught in the public schools and attended Fisk University and the Lemoyne Institute.

In 1884 Wells-Barnett sued the Chesapeake, Ohio & Southwestern Railroad Company after being forcibly removed from the first-class coach to the already crowded smoking car. As she relates in her autobiography, *Crusade for Justice*, Wells-Barnett literally fought the conductor all the way to the smoker. Wells-Barnett's suit came almost 12 years before the Supreme Court's 1896 decision in *Plessy v. Ferguson*. The circuit court ruled in her favor in December of that year; however, the Tennessee Supreme Court overturned the decision three years later. Though she lost the legal battle, Wells-Barnett began her lifelong journalistic barrage against racism, writing letters and articles for African-American and Christian newspapers such as the *New York Freeman*. Two years after her suit, Wells-Barnett became the editor of the *Evening Star* and wrote editorials under the pen name Iola for the *Living Way*, a religious paper. Wells-Barnett also kept a two-year diary from 1885 to 1887 detailing her economic and political journey through her lawsuit and racial violence, as well as the links between gender and racial discrimination.

In 1891 Wells-Barnett began writing full time after her "militant" editorials cost her the teaching position in Memphis. She bought an interest in *Free Speech and Headlight*, owned by Reverend R. Nightingale, whose congregation helped make the newspaper flourish. A year later she used its pages and others across the nation to draw attention to the mob lynching of three African-American grocers in Memphis on March 9, 1892. Her burning commentary urged the Memphis African-American community to leave the city in protest, and her analysis of the lynch mob mentality placed blame squarely on racist fears of an economically independent Negro community. As a result of the uncompromising language of Wells-Barnett's editorials, whites destroyed the newspaper office and dared her to return to Memphis.

Undaunted by these threats, Wells-Barnett continued her campaign, writing continuously over the next 10 years and buying an interest in the *New York Age*. Some of her best-known publications included *Southern Horrors: Lynching in All Its Phases* (1892), *A Red Record: Tabulated Statistics and Alleged Causes of Lynching in the United States, 1892, 1893, and 1895* (1895), and *Mob Rule in New Orleans* (1900). In all of her writings and speeches, Wells-Barnett resists the tradition of claiming the rape of white women by African-American men as a justification for lynching. Instead, she focused her arguments on lynching as a form of terrorism perpetrated by whites against African Americans, particularly African-American men.

Wells-Barnett collaborated with FREDERICK DOUGLASS, J. Garland Penn, and F. L. Barnett, who protested the exclusion of African Americans from the 1893 World's Columbian Exposition by contributing a chapter to *The Reason Why the Colored American Is Not in the World's Columbian Exposition—the Afro-American's Contribution to Columbia Literature* (1893). Her essay is indicative of her methodical style; her relentless use of concrete evidence in the form of firsthand accounts, letters, and statistics; and her frank, vivid description of lynching scenes. In all of her accounts, Wells-Barnett linked racial oppression with gender and economic oppression. Also in 1893, Wells-Barnett went on the first of two lecture tours of Great Britain; she kept a journal that was later published in her autobiography, *Crusade for Justice*. She returned a year later, writing a series of articles for the Chicago *Inter-Ocean* titled "Ida B. Wells-Barnett Abroad."

After marrying F. L. Barnett on June 27, 1895, Wells-Barnett bought the *Chicago Conservator* and settled into a short "retirement." However, she continued to write blistering essays critiquing the government's continued denial of lynching as terrorism and the disconnect she saw between African-American public intellectuals, such as BOOKER T. WASHINGTON and W. E. B. DUBOIS, and the community at large. Broadening her activism to include women's suffrage, Wells-Barnett became one of the founding members of the National Association of Colored Women in 1896. She played major roles both in the Niagara Movement and in the National Afro-American Council's evolution into the NATIONAL ASSOCIATION FOR THE ADVANCEMENT OF COLORED PEOPLE) in 1909. In 1910 she founded the Negro Fellowship League to help southern migrants gain solid footing in Chicago.

Throughout her later years, Wells-Barnett continued her community-based fight against racism, founding a kindergarten for black children, leading community campaigns against police harassment, and conducting voter registration drives. Seeing a less than satisfactory ballot of candidates for the 1930 Illinois state legislature, she even ran for office, becoming one of the first African-American women to do so. Her writing from this period included coverage of the East St. Louis, Illinois, race riots of 1918 in *The Arkansas Race Riot* (1922), an investigative report on the murder of 12 Arkansas farmers, and the beginnings of her autobiography, *Crusade for Justice: The Autobiography of Ida B. Wells-Barnett*. Though she did not live to finish her autobiography, begun in 1928, it was published posthumously by her daughter, Alfreda Duster.

BIBLIOGRAPHY

Bogues, Anthony. "The Radical Praxis of Ida B. Wells-Barnett: Telling the Truth Freely." In *Black Heretics, Black Prophets: Radical Political Intellectuals*, 47–67. New York: Routledge, 2003.

Duster, Alfreda, ed. *Crusade for Justice: The Autobiography of Ida B. Wells-Barnett*. Chicago: University of Chicago Press, 1972.

Harris, Trudier, ed. *Selected Works of Ida B. Wells-Barnett*. New York: Oxford University Press, 1991.

Miller, Ericka M. *The Other Reconstruction: Where Violence and Womanhood Meet in the Writings of Wells-Barnett, Grimké, and Larsen*. New York: Garland, 2000.

Royster, Jacqueline Jones, ed. *Southern Horrors and Other Writings: The Anti-lynching Campaign of Ida B. Wells-Barnett, 1892–1900*. Boston: Bedford Books, 1997.

Rydell, Robert W., ed. *Why the Colored American Is Not in the World's Columbian Exposition: The*

Afro-American's Contribution to Columbian Literature. 1893. Urbana: University of Illinois Press, 1999.

Schechter, Patricia A. *Ida B. Wells-Barnett and American Reform, 1890–1930.* Chapel Hill: University of North Carolina Press, 2001.

Derrick Spires

West, Cornel (1953–)

Cornel West was born in 1953 in Tulsa, Oklahoma. His mother worked as an elementary school teacher and principal; his father was in the U.S. Air Force, which meant the family moved frequently; they eventually settled in California. As a young man, West was influenced by stories he heard about slavery and religious faith. He learned about community political action from members of the Black Panther Party who had an office next to his church. West attended Harvard, graduating in Near Eastern languages and literature. He earned a master of arts and doctorate in philosophy at Princeton University. West has taught at prestigious schools, chairing the department of Afro-American studies at Yale and at Harvard University as the Alphonse Fletcher, Jr., Professor. He was also appointed the Class of 1943 University Professor of Religion at Princeton University. West moved to Harvard in 1994 but left in 2002 after a dispute with Harvard's president, Lawrence Summers. He returned to Princeton. West has stayed true to his interest in community political action, working with efforts like the Million Man March, national youth gang summits, and conversations about music and culture; he has been the co-chair of the Democratic Socialists of America.

West's works are varied, consisting of writing, speaking, music, film, and political efforts. West published *Prophesy Deliverance!: An Afro-American Revolutionary Christianity* in 1982, *Prophetic Fragments* in 1988, and *American Evasion of Philosophy: A Genealogy of Pragmatism* in 1989. He wrote *Ethical Dimensions of Marxist Thought* (1991). In the same year, he wrote *Breaking Bread: Insurgent Black Intellectual Life* with BELL HOOKS. *Race Matters,* one of West's most important works,

appeared in 1993, as did *Beyond Eurocentrism and Multiculturalism.* He wrote *Keeping Faith: Philosophy and Race in America* in 1994. He coauthored *Jews and Blacks: Let the Healing Begin* (1995) and *Jews and Blacks: A Dialogue on Race, Religion, and Culture in America* (1996) with Michael Lerner. In 1997 West wrote *Restoring Hope: Conversations on the Future of Black America* and coauthored, with HENRY LOUIS GATES, JR., *Future of the Race.* In 1998 he worked with Roberto Mangabeira Unger to write *Future of American Progressivism: An Initiative for Political and Economic Reform* and with Sylvia Ann Hewlett to write *War against Parents: What We Can Do for America's Beleaguered Moms and Dads. The Cornel West Reader* appeared in 1999. He published *Democracy Matters: Winning the Fight against Imperialism* in 2004. West has created a rap album, *Sketches of My Culture,* featuring music in praise of past African-American leaders. He has also appeared in the films *Black Is . . . Black ain't* (1995), *Give a Damn Again* (1995), *All God's Children* (2001), *The Matrix Reloaded* (2003), and *The Matrix Revolutions* (2003). His political affiliations and work have included associations with Louis Farrakhan of the Nation of Islam and Benjamin Chavis Muhammad, a former executive officer of the NATIONAL ASSOCIATION FOR THE ADVANCEMENT OF COLORED PEOPLE.

As demonstrated by his work, West's interests range from theology and politics to existentialism and gritty urban reality, always with an interest in synthesizing disparate elements in new ways. West combines life experience with theory and politics, asking his students and readers to face complex issues. His style is outspoken and performative, combining oral and musical elements that stem from jazz, rap, and call and response. West is concerned with class and race issues exemplified by the nihilism in black communities resulting from capitalism and poor black leadership. He encourages such community-based solutions as activism and insurgency and a "universal love ethic" as a way to combat nihilism. Working to organize and build coalitions is addressed in *Race Matters,* but the collection of essays is most notable for its close examination of culture—focusing on race issues that white America does not wish to face.

West's statement "If you love black folks, you hate white supremacy. If you love human beings, you love justice. If you love the life of the mind, then you hate all forms of dogmatism and parochialism" exemplifies his passionate drive to inspire communities to confront and solve divisive issues. West has aligned himself with dissident elements rather than the usual forms of academic activism, being unafraid to dispute publicly Harvard's commitment to diversity and the investigation into the validity of his scholarship.

West has been awarded the American Book Award. He worked on Al Sharpton's presidential exploratory committee and President Bill Clinton's National Conversation on Race. More than 20 honorary degrees have been conferred on West.

BIBLIOGRAPHY

"Cornel West." *This Far by Faith.* PBS. 2003. Available online. URL: http://www.pbs.org/thisfarbyfaith/witnesses/cornel_west.html. Accessed October 26, 2006.

Engelhardt, Elizabeth Sanders Delwiche. "Cornel West." In *The Oxford Companion to African American Literature,* edited by William L. Andrews, et al., 765–766. New York: Oxford University Press, 1997.

Lott, Eric. "Cornel West in the Hour of Chaos: Culture and Politics in *Race Matters.*" *Social Text* 40 (Autumn 1994): 39–50.

West, Cornel. *Race Matters.* Boston: Beacon Press, 1993.

"Who Is Cornel West?" CNN.com January 10, 2002. Available online. URL: http://www.archives.cnn.com/2002/fyi/teachers.ednews/01/10/west.harvard.ap/. Accessed October 26, 2006.

Kim Hai Pearson
Brian Jennings

West, Dorothy   (1907–1998)

A novelist, short fiction writer, journal founder, publisher, editor, and columnist, Dorothy West was the youngest and the longest-surviving member of the HARLEM RENAISSANCE. She was born an only child on June 2, 1907, in Boston, Massachu-setts, to Isaac Christopher West, an entrepreneur, eventually known as the "Black Banana King" of Boston, and Rachel Pease Benson, a native of Camden, South Carolina. A precocious child, West, at age four, attended the Farragut School and completed her elementary education at the Martin School Mission Hill District in Boston. In 1923 she graduated from the Girls' Latin School and studied journalism and philosophy at Boston University and Columbia University.

West began her literary career at age seven with her first story, "Promise and Fulfillment," published in the *Boston Globe.* After her 18th birthday, she wrote several short stories over the next couple of decades for OPPORTUNITY, *The MESSENGER,* and *The Saturday Evening Quill,* including the award-winning "The Typewriter" (1926), which launched her, along with ZORA NEALE HURSTON, as a serious and talented writer; "Hannah Byde" (1926); "An Unimportant Man" (1928); "Prologue to a Life" (1929); "The Black Dress" (1934); and "Mammy" (1940). What most critics note about these stories is the Dostoyevskian influence that dominates these works, especially in one of West's best pieces of fiction, "The Typewriter," which portrays a frustrated, spiritually and economically wasted black father named J. L. Jones, who uses his daughter's typewriting lessons to gain a modicum of personal worth. Each time he pretends to be her boss and dictates a letter, he imagines himself the successful businessman that a racist culture prevents him from becoming. According to critic Deborah McDowell, West's short stories "are the most perfect literary form" (281).

For several decades, West was a consistent and spirited contributor to the black American literary canon. She was founder during the 1930s of two important magazines: *Challenge* (1934) and *New Challenge* (1937), in which she sought to crystallize the dominant black literary attitudes of the day and to nurture new, post-Renaissance literary talent. Featured were the works of West's colleagues and friends, such as LANGSTON HUGHES, CLAUDE MCKAY, ZORA NEALE HURSTON, COUNTEE CULLEN, ARNA BONTEMPS, WALLACE THURMAN, FRANK YERBY, RICHARD WRIGHT, MARGARET WALKER, and RALPH ELLISON. After the magazine folded, West worked as a welfare investigator and then participated in the Federal Writers' Project (WPA) until it ended in the mid-1940s. From the 1940s to the 1960s, she wrote more than 26 short stories for the *New York Daily News.* After World War II, West left New York permanently to live on Martha's Vineyard, where she contributed intermittently to the *Vineyard Gazette* from the 1960s until the early 1990s, including her weekly column on the year-round social activities of the residents of Oak Bluffs on the island.

As a novelist, West's work was sparse. Her first and only known novel for several decades was *The Living Is Easy* (1948), which satirizes affluent black Bostonians for allowing class differences to create gaps between them and the working-class community. Published in 1995, *The Wedding,* her second novel, was developed and adapted for television by Oprah Winfrey. Enthusiastically received by critics and the public, *The Wedding* chronicles the life of the main character, a 90-year-old near-white woman, who, forced by her economic condition, moved in with her fair-skinned daughter and her hated dark-skinned son-in-law. Also in 1995, West published her collection of short stories and essays *The Richer, The Poorer: Stories, Sketches, and Reminiscences,* some of which were published in periodicals from the 1960s to the 1990s.

Though Dorothy West's literary career spanned more than 70 years, she has not received the critical attention her contributions to black American literature deserve. However, since her publications in the 1990s, critics have reexamined her works in the context of her contemporaries and have found that West's writings exemplify the wealth of artistic talent prevalent during and after the Harlem Renaissance. Among the first to explore the ironic possibilities of the black urban lifestyle for literature, West, who demonstrated great energy and creativity until the end of her productive career, has become a highly regarded writer. West died on August 16, 1998, in Boston.

BIBLIOGRAPHY

Clark, Dorothy A. "Rediscovering Dorothy West." *American Visions* 8 (1993): 46–47.

Ferguson, Sally A. "Dorothy West." *Dictionary of Literary Biography.* Vol. 76: *Afro-American Writers, 1940–1955,* edited by Trudier Harris, 187–195. Detroit: Gale, 1988.

McDowell, Deborah E. "Conversation with Dorothy West." In *The Harlem Renaissance Re-Examined,* edited by Victor A. Kramer, 265–282. New York: AMS Press, 1987.

Steinberg, Sybil. "Dorothy West: Her Own Renaissance." *Publishers Weekly* 242 (July 3, 1995): 34–35.

Loretta G. Woodard

What You Owe Me
Bebe Moore Campbell (2001)

What You Owe Me is a novel of epic proportions. It addresses a host of 20th-century race and class dilemmas, particularly the similar histories yet strained relations and unequal opportunities of African Americans and Jews, the achievement of reparations for Jews and the stalled debate over reparations for African Americans, the complications of interracial friendships, the obligations of economically successful upper-class Americans toward poor and working-class Americans, and the enduring racial discrimination deeply entrenched in America's free-enterprise system. The novel's overarching theme, to which all these subplots adhere, illustrates that restoration from theft and betrayal requires contrition and restitution. To narrativize this grand theme, Bebe Moore Campbell creates a multigenerational landscape and a multiplicity of characters and subplots, all drawn lucidly but connected with varying degrees of success.

Campbell's modern epic is most successful in creating and connecting the protagonists—Hosanna Clark, an African-American migrant to post–World War II Los Angeles from a racially hostile town in Inez, Texas, and Gilda Rosenstein, a Holocaust survivor and immigrant to Los Angeles from Poland. However, these characters must move to the margins of the narrative to demonstrate the intergenerational legacy that Gilda and Hosanna's friendship sets in motion and to demonstrate the difficulties of personal and social restoration when those who incur "debts" do not acknowledge them.

Hosanna and Gilda open a business and learn the ways that racism functions in commercial establishments. Although Hosanna is the engine behind the business and makes all the sales, Gilda's white skin gives her access to the ladder of economic advancement. Their business venture prospers as long as suppliers and bankers do not "see" Hosanna. The business venture folds, however, when Gilda's uncle discovers it and discovers that Hosanna is black.

For the rest of Hosanna's life, she sells cosmetics out of her car, never able to achieve her dream of owning a prosperous cosmetic business that builds black women's self-esteem. As a result of Gilda's betrayal, Hosanna harbors a tenacious bitterness, which she instills in her daughter, Matriece. Hosanna's stressful life causes her untimely death, but she returns repeatedly in ghostly visits, insisting that her daughter claim the business that Hosanna was denied.

Determined to reclaim what was stolen from her mother, Matriece's entire life is also consumed with work to the exclusion of all else, including the loving husband and family that her older sister, Vonette, enjoys. Matriece's compulsion, hatred for her father, and uneasiness with intimacy underscore the intergenerational personal damage caused by Gilda's betrayal. Gilda's betrayal also overshadows her own life. Although she now owns a multimillion-dollar enterprise, Gilda Cosmetics, her relationships with her own children are strained and she has been married four times.

Hosanna's peace, Matriece's release from bitterness, and Gilda's release from guilt and evasion become possible when Matriece reveals to Gilda who her mother is and when Gilda acknowledges Hosanna's contribution to her success. From her place beyond the grave, Hosanna rejoices. But the Clark family still must contend with the knowledge that they were defrauded of 200 acres in Inez, Texas. Behind the Clarks' claim and behind every act of betrayal in the novel, there is another unspoken and unsettled but highly visible betrayal—the claim still owed to African Americans for generations of dispossession as slaves and decades of unequal treatment as second-class citizens in America.

BIBLIOGRAPHY

Campbell, Jane. "An Interview with Bebe Moore Campbell." *Callaloo: A Journal of African American Arts and Letters* 22 (Fall 1999): 954–972.
Russell-Robinson, Joyce. "Bebe Moore Campbell." In *Contemporary African American Novelists: A Bio-Bibliographic Critical Sourcebook.* Edited by Emmanuel S. Nelson, 76–81. Westport, Conn.: Greenwood Press, 1999.

Veta S. Tucker

Wheatley, Phillis   (1753?–1784)

Phillis Wheatley, slave, poet, teenage celebrity, pioneer, and one of the founders of the African-American literary tradition, was a unique, talented, assertive, controversial, and respected writer who, from her early teens, earned and won her way into the literary world of 18th-century Boston and, to a degree, London. Wheatley's accomplishments are even more astonishing considering that, in 1761, at age seven, she was bought "for a trifle" (Gates, 17) at a Boston slave auction. At the time a "frail female child" (16), Wheatley had been kidnapped from Senegal, West Africa. The slave child was named Phillis, after the ship that deposited her in New England, by Susanna Wheatley, the wife of a prosperous tailor and merchant, who bought her to serve as a domestic in their fashionable mansion on Kings Street, in the very shadows of the site of the Boston Massacre, where black Crispus Attucks would be the first to die during the initial battle between the colonialists and British soldiers for American independence.

Fascinated by her new playmate, Mary, the Wheatley's daughter, began to educate Phillis. The inquisitive, precocious, and intellectually alert Phillis learned to read and write English within 16 months of her arrival. She was tutored as well in the Bible and Latin and introduced to the classics and to British literature, particularly the poetry of Alexander Pope. Phillis, who began writing her own poetry, imitating the style of the neoclassic poets, published her first poem in 1767 with the assistance of her mentor and teacher, Mary. She was 13 years old. Another early effort, "On the Affray in King Street, On the Evening of the 5th of March, 1770," written when Wheatley was 17, memorializes the Boston Massacre and her fellow black Bostonian, Crispus Attucks, preserving his role and place in this significant moment in colonial America's fight for freedom and independence in the following lines:

> Long in Freedom's Cause the wise contend,
> Dear to your unity shall Fame extend;
> While to the World the letter's Stone shall
> tell,
> How Caldwell, Attucks, Gray, and
> Mav'rick fell.
> (Gates, The Trials, 21)

These verses illustrate the rhetorical strategy Wheatley often took in her poetry. Without mounting an abolitionist podium to claim or declare it vociferously, she records, like FREDERICK DOUGLASS, the African American's love of freedom, to the degree that he was willing to give his life to obtain it. Thus, though not as directly or as radically, Wheatley uses her pen as a powerful weapon against oppression.

Wheatley gained celebrity status when her elegy "On the Death of the Rev. Mr. George Whitefield 1770," memorializing the popular 18th-century British evangelist, was published as a broadside in Boston and, later, throughout the northeastern colonies. A large number of Wheatley's poems were elegies, "commemorating the deaths of fellow Bostonians, and apparently written at the request of families" (Bruce, 41). "On the Death of the Rev. Mr. George Whitefield 1770" offers an excellent example of her use of this genre. In it Wheatley celebrates Whitefield, the historical personality, and his reputation as a superb and unequalled rhetorician and preacher of the gospel:

> HAIL, happy saint, on thine immortal
> throne,

> Possessed of glory, life and bliss unknown;
> We hear no more the music of thy tongue,
> Thy wonted auditories cease to throng,
> Thy sermons in unequalled accents flowed;
> And every bosom with devotion glowed;
> Thou didst in strains of eloquence refined
> Inflame the heart, and captivate the mind.
> (The Poems 15)

Wheatley celebrates and records as well Whitefield's more inclusive stance—his willingness to convert everyone, irrespective of race or class, which, might also indicate her indirect critique of the racism that surrounded her.

> "Take him, my dear Americans," he said,
> "Be your complaints on his kind boson laid:
> "Take him, ye Africans, he longs for you;
> "Impartial Savior is his title due;
> "Washed in the fountain of redeeming
> blood,
> "You shall be sons, and kings, and priest to
> God."
> (The Poems 16)

Similarly, Wheatley celebrates the chivalry of intrepid General George Washington in "To His Excellency General Washington," encouraging him: "Proceed, great chief, with virtue on thy side, / Thy every action let the goddess guide. / A crown, a mansion, and a throne that shine, / With gold unfading, Washington be thine" (Robinson, 109). With seeming humility yet authoritative voice, Wheatley writes in "To the University of Cambridge, in New England" to the students of Harvard, calling their attention to the consequences of living a sinful life.

> Let sin, that baneful evil to the soul,
> By you be shunned, nor once remit your
> guard;
> Suppress the deadly serpent in its egg.
> Ye blooming plants of human race divine,
> An Ethiope tells you 'tis your greatest foe;
> Its transient sweetness turns to endless pain,
> And in immense perdition sinks the soul.
> (The Poems 11)

The rich irony recorded here offers another example of her rhetorical strategy; it is the unpolished and formally uneducated slave teenager—who as woman and black slave could never have gained access to Harvard—who chides these "sons of science" members of the ostensibly superior race, sex, and class.

In this and several poems Wheatley readily seems to embrace her African identity. Despite this, however, she also seems to have accepted the common notion of her day that Africa was a "Pagan land," a dark continent, "The land of errors, and Egyptian gloom." Consequently, early scholars criticized Wheatley for her failure to speak out directly against slavery, failing to her see that her simple but not simplistic language and muffled voice conveyed her biting critique of slavery as well as an attack on the hypocrisy of nominal Christians.

This is clearly the case in "On Being Brought from Africa to America," in which her speaker declares, "Remember, *Christians, Negroes,* black as *Cain,* / May be refined, and join the' angelic trains" (*The Poems* 12). Dickson Bruce provides insight into current evaluations of her perspective and work when he writes:

> Her lines are at once simple and fairly complex, given Wheatley's position. At one level asserting her own identity, they assert her perceptiveness and her ability to comment on the world around her. Somewhat more deeply, and ironically, they allowed her, from her own marginal position, to see the failure in others that others failed to see in themselves. (44)

In 1773, in London, where she had gone to recuperate from illness, Wheatley, no longer a slave, published her first collection of poems, *Poems on Various Subjects, Religious and Moral,* which contained 38 verses. Not surprisingly, given the 18th-century enlightened world's discourse on race, in which blacks were deemed incapable of intellectual development, Wheatley was called on to prove, during what HENRY LOUIS GATES, JR., calls an "oral examination," that she had penned the verses in this, the first collection of published poems written in English by a former slave, before her work could be validated in America. Gates argues, "If she had indeed written her poems, then this would demonstrate that Africans were human beings and should be liberated from slavery" (26–27).

In the end, Wheatley and her work received attestations and authentication from some of "the most respectable characters in Boston" (Gates, 5), including Thomas Hutchinson, the governor of Massachusetts; his lieutenant governor, Andrew Oliver; Reverend Mather Byles, the grandson of Increase Mather and nephew of Cotton Matter; the Reverend Samuel Mather, son of Cotton Matter; and John Hancock. Washington wrote thanking Wheatley for her flattering verse, commenting on her genius and noting, "the style and manner exhibit a striking proof of [her] poetic talents" (Gates, 38). To show his appreciation, Washington invited Wheatley to visit him at his Cambridge headquarters.

A notable exception was the reception Wheatley received from the distinguished statesman and author of the Declaration of Independence, Thomas Jefferson, who found it impossible to accept as credible Wheatley's intelligence and, by extension, her humanity. Jefferson, who was convinced that blacks, "in imagination . . . are dull, tasteless, and anomalous," wrote in his infamous *Notes on the State of Virginia* that "the compositions published under [Wheatley's] name are below the dignity of criticism. (Gates, 42–43). History, in the end, has proved him wrong.

Wheatley, who married John Peters and lost three children in their infancy, died in 1784. She has taken her rightful place next to the Founding Fathers as an important colonial voice who cherished freedom and as one of the founders of the African-American literary tradition.

BIBLIOGRAPHY

Bruce, Dickson D., Jr. *The Origins of African American Literature, 1680–1865.* Charlottesville: University Press of Virginia, 2001.

Gates, Henry Louis, Jr. *The Trials of Phillis Wheatley: American's First Black Poet and Her Encounter with the Founding Fathers.* New York: Basic Civitas Books, 2003.

Robinson, William H., ed. *Early Black American Poets.* Dubuque, Iowa: W. C. Brown Company Publishers, 1969.

Wheatley, Phillis. *The Poems.* Philadelphia: R. R. and C. C. Wright, 1909.

Zafar, Rafia. *We Wear the Mask: African Americans Write American Literature, 1760–1870.* New York: Columbia University Press, 1997.

Wilfred D. Samuels

White, Paulette Childress   (1948–   )

Although Paulette Childress White's dream was to become an artist, she attended art school for only one year and later became a poet, short fiction writer, and educator instead. A native of Detroit, Michigan, White was born on December 1, 1948, to Norris and Effie Storey Childress. After high school, she married Bennie White, Jr., a postal employee and artist, with whom she had five boys: Pierre, Oronde, Kojo, Kala, and Paul. In 1986, she earned a B.A. in English from Wayne State University, where she also received a Ph.D. in 1998. White has been a visiting writer in several arts programs, including the Creative Writers in the Schools Program for the Michigan Council of the Arts (1980–90), the Detroit Council of the Arts Summer Youth Program (1986–90), the Broadside Press Writers in Residence Program (1993), and the Saginaw Valley State University (1994). White has taught at Wayne State University (1987–97) and Henry Ford Community College in Dearborn, Michigan, where she developed its first African-American literature course.

Although responsibilities related to raising a family and attending graduate school hindered her opportunities to publish, White, in 1972, at age 30, published her first poem in *Deep Rivers.* White's talents were "discovered" by NAOMI LONG MADGETT during one of her poetry workshops. At Madgett's encouragement, White published her first collection of poetry, *Love Poem to a Black Junkie* (1975), with Detroit's Lotus Press. Thematically, *Love Poem to a Black Junkie* addresses, in part, BLACK NATIONALISM and the poet's redis-

covery of Africa. Lotus Press also published *The Watermelon Dress: Portrait of a Woman* (1984), a highly autobiographical narrative poem in four parts: "Old Calico," "Being Fitted," "Days in the Dress," and "Beyond the Watermelon Dress: Notes on the Composition." With a compelling use of illustrations throughout the work, the poem traces White's development as a closeted artist and an unfulfilled woman, from adolescence through the most painful, difficult, and challenging times of a first marriage and motherhood to the eventual awareness of selfhood and discovery of "her own / green wonder." Speaking of why she writes and paints, White comments, "I write from a sense of irony, because I want to make sense of my experience of life. . . . I write and paint because I have a need to give substance to my ideas, feelings, and experiences, and because I believe it is good and important work" (White, 508).

White's short fiction has appeared in numerous anthologies, academic textbooks, and journals, including CALLALOO, *The Michigan Quarterly Review,* and *The Harbor Review.* Her first short story, "Alice," published in ESSENCE (January 1977), explores the need for reconciliation between women, and her second short story "The Bird Cage," which appeared in *Redbook* (June 1978), centers on the discontent women sometimes feel in their prescribed roles. Of her first two stories, critics have noted similarities to GWENDOLYN BROOKS's novel *MAUD MARTHA* (1953) (Washington, 37). Like Brooks, White's characters are superbly drawn, particularly her young black women of the inner city. Although these characters are all articulate, working-class housewives who dream of becoming artists, they often must face the constraints of their roles as wife and mother, which alienate them even further from their husbands and cause anger, which they often repress and deny. Madgett observes that White often writes of women who share a common bond, a sisterhood born out of a painful existence. This theme resounds through White's poem "Humbled Rocks," as well as in the short stories "Dear Aku" (*Harbor Review,* 1986) and "Getting the Facts of Life" (*Rites of Passage,* 1994). Overall, in her works, White's lyricism and metaphorical and alliterative use of language make her fiction almost indistinguishable from her poetry (Madgett, 773).

White has received several awards, including the African World Festival of Arts and Culture Lagos's Nigeria Creative Writing Award (1976); the Michigan Council for the Arts Creative Artists Award/Grant (1984), the State of Michigan 82nd Legislature Special Tribute Award (1984); the Black Women in Michigan Recognition Award, Resource/Study Guide, Detroit Historical Department (1985); and the Women's Recognition Award, sponsored by the Focus on Women Program at Henry Ford Community College (2000).

BIBLIOGRAPHY

Madgett, Naomi Long. "White, Paulette Childress." In *The Oxford Companion to African American Literature,* edited by William L. Andrews, Frances Smith Foster, and Trudier Harris, 772–773. New York: Oxford, 1997.

"Paulette Childress White." In *Black-Eyed Susans/ Midnight Birds,* edited by Mary Helen Washington, 35–53. New York: Anchor, 1990.

"White, Paulette Childress (1948–   )." In *Contemporary Authors.* Vol. 111, edited by Hal May, Diane L. Dupuis, Lillian S. Sims, and Susan M. Trosky, 508. Detroit: Gale, 1984.

Loretta G. Woodward

White, Walter Francis   (1893–1955)

As a blond-haired, blue-eyed, lightskinned man of African-American descent, the author and political activist Walter White could have lived within the white community; instead, he chose to identify himself as African-American. In his autobiography, *A Man Called White* (1948), he describes his moment of racial identification at 13, when a white mob threatened his home during the 1906 Atlanta race riot. "I knew then who I was," White explains; "I was a Negro, a human being with an invisible pigmentation which marked a person to be hunted, hanged, abused, discriminated against, kept in poverty and ignorance, in order that those whose skin was white would have readily at hand

a proof of their superiority" (11). White's family and house narrowly escaped the violence, but the memory of that night shaped White's lifelong commitment to racial justice.

White's work for the NATIONAL ASSOCIATION FOR THE ADVANCEMENT OF COLORED PEOPLE (NAACP) largely overshadows his literary reputation. His political activism began shortly after his graduation from Atlanta University, when he protested cuts in the funding of Atlanta's black public schools. The successful protest brought him to the attention of JAMES WELDON JOHNSON, field secretary of the NAACP, who convinced White to leave his job as an insurance salesman and join the fledgling organization's New York headquarters in 1918. White spent the rest of his life working for the NAACP, serving as executive secretary from 1931 until his death in 1955. During his tenure with the NAACP, White investigated dozens of lynchings and race riots. Relying on his light skin, he infiltrated white communities (narrowly escaping being lynched himself at least once) and collected and delivered evidence to newspapers and prosecutors in a tireless effort to shed light on the atrocities plaguing America. As executive secretary he advised generals, senators, and presidents on racial justice. White received the Spingarn Medal in 1937 for his civil rights work.

In the literary circle of the HARLEM RENAISSANCE, White had the reputation as a man who could get things published. If his activism overshadowed his literary career during his lifetime, his role as a facilitator for other African-American authors has tended, in retrospect, to overshadow his literary production as well. He established connections with some of the most influential white publishers, critics, authors, and patrons of his day, including Alfred A. Knopf, Horace Liveright, H. L. Mencken, Sinclair Lewis, and CARL VAN VECHTEN. White used these connections to aid many emerging authors of the Harlem Renaissance: LANGSTON HUGHES, CLAUDE MCKAY, COUNTEE CULLEN, GEORGIA DOUGLAS JOHNSON, NELLA LARSEN, RUDOLPH FISHER, and others.

White's own literary career began in 1922, when Mencken encouraged him to write a novel depicting black life. White took up the challenge, and in a writing frenzy of 12 days, he produced *The Fire in the Flint* (Knopf, 1924), which portrays the harsh opposition of a small southern town to any form of black progress. When Kenneth Harper, an African-American doctor, returns from the North, he finds himself relentlessly drawn into the racial strife he had hoped to avoid. Economic, social, and psychological factors within the white community ultimately boil over in violent acts that reassert white supremacy. The novel sold well and was warmly received. White described the work as "a modest best-seller, far beyond its literary merits" (White, 68).

Despite this comment, White was clearly pleased enough with the novel and its reception to write his second novel, *Flight* (1926). In this novel, White presents a light-skinned female protagonist, Mimi Daquin, who "passes" into white society after she gives birth to an illegitimate child. Driven by shame, she moves from Atlanta to Harlem. Disenchanted with the black community, she enters the white community, where she lives a successful but unsatisfying life. Realizing, after several encounters with African-American music, that the emptiness in her life results from her distance from the black community, Mimi reclaims her African-American identity. *Flight* offers a compelling portrait of troubled racial identification—a theme that intrigued numerous authors of the Harlem Renaissance—but this second novel sold poorly. Although critics labeled his fiction melodramatic, unpolished, and didactic, White offered, through his novels, a strong indictment of the racial injustice he saw in America; they earned him a Guggenheim Fellowship in 1926.

White used the fellowship to move to France, where he planned to write his third novel, which he never completed. Instead, he began a work of nonfiction: *Rope and Faggot: A Biography of Judge Lynch* (1929). For this invaluable work, White drew on his experience investigating lynching throughout the South to expose the economic, religious, sexual, and social causes of lynching in a systematic and compelling fashion. White never returned to fiction, devoting his literary energies

to essays, articles, and books that complemented his work with the NAACP. *A Man Called White: The Autobiography of Walter White* is his other major nonfiction contribution to African-American letters. This work is less White's autobiography (although there are some gripping personal details) than a history of the early NAACP. White offers extensive firsthand accounts of the investigative, legal, and political roles the NAACP played in battling segregation and racial violence. His other works include *The American Negro and His Problem* (1927), *The Negro's Contribution to American Culture* (1928), *What Caused the Detroit Riots?* (1943), *A Rising Wind: A Report on the Negro Soldier in the European Theater of War* (1945), *How Far the Promised Land?* (1955), and numerous articles and essays. In these works, as in his other writing and his politics, Walter White stressed a basic but unrealized truth: Shared humanity necessitates shared rights, opportunities, and respect.

BIBLIOGRAPHY

Brooks, Neil. "We Are Not Free! Free! Free!: *Flight* and the Unmapping of American Literary Studies." *College Language Association Journal* 41, no. 4 (1998): 371–386.

Scruggs, Charles W. "Alain Locke and Walter White: Their Struggle for Control of the Harlem Renaissance." *Black American Literature Forum* 14, no. 3 (1980): 91–99.

Waldron, Edward E. *Walter White and the Harlem Renaissance*. Port Washington, N.Y.: Kennikat Press, 1978.

White, Walter. *A Man Called White: The Autobiography of Walter White*. 1948. Bloomington: Indiana University Press, 1970.

Andrew Leiter

Whitehead, Colson   (1970–)

Novelist and essayist Colson Whitehead was born in New York City in 1970. During his adolescent years, he moved with his family to various locations within the city. In 1991 he earned a bachelor's degree from Harvard University, where he studied English and comparative literature. Upon graduating, Whitehead worked as a freelance journalist, publishing in *Newsday, Spin,* and *Vibe.* He eventually became a television editor for *The Village Voice,* writing a regular column on popular and contemporary shows. Whitehead published two novels, *The Intuitionist* (1999) and *John Henry Days* (2001). In 2002 he was awarded a MacArthur Genius Award.

In Whitehead's first novel, *The Intuitionist,* set in the pre–Civil Rights era and in a city reminiscent of New York, the main movers and shakers of the city are elevator inspectors. In the past-yet-futuristic world that Whitehead creates, elevator inspectors understand that "Whoever owns the elevator owns the new cities." They attend elevator inspector school; write theoretical articles for their influential publication, *Lift;* and take their membership in the powerful guild of elevator inspectors very seriously. The two groups of almost exclusively white men who are constantly jockeying for power and position to control the elevators identify themselves as either Empiricists or Intuitionists, depending on their traditional or sensory-based approach to repairing and building elevators.

The narrative also focuses on Lila Mae Watson, a highly intellectual black woman Intuitionist who is often used as a pawn in the men's struggles for power. Seeking to clear her name after being framed, Lila Mae begins to trace the mysterious histories of the "black box," a futuristic plan for elevator construction initially conceived by the deceased yet influential elevator theoretician James Fulton. Lila Mae discovers that Fulton, who had been "passing" for white, had included coded language about race and social progress in his treatises on elevators. The focus on "uplift" and "elevation" and the struggle to find answers concerning the mysterious "black box" resonate with racial and historical themes within African-American and American contexts. The complexity of Whitehead's first novel is found in its fragmented sentences, distinctively black conscious narrator, and fascinating treatment of the social implications of technology. A stylistically remarkable novel, *The*

Intuitionist earned Whitehead the Quality Paperback Book Club's New Voices Award in 1999 and the Whiting Writers' Award in 2000.

John Henry Days, Whitehead's second novel, reveals the novelist's keen insight into and critique of the functions of contemporary popular culture. Moreover, the numerous characters and large area of time-space that the novel presents provides evidence of Whitehead's capabilities and daring ambitions as a writer. Utilizing the 130-year-old legend of John Henry, the black railroad worker who defeated a steam-powered drill in a tunnel-drilling contest, Whitehead shows how his main character, J. Stutter, and several other minor yet vibrant characters live and work in a society dominated by money, power, technology, and publicity.

As a journalist, J. and his closest associates are aware of the shallowness and dangers of "the machine" known as popular culture. For the most part, they have learned how to survive, going along with the politics and demands of the computer and information age. During a trip to West Virginia for a publicity event to unveil a John Henry stamp, however, J. begins to reflect on his life and whether he wants to continue as he always has or take the John Henry route and go against the machine. As J. searches for answers, the narrative takes readers on twists and turns through the lives of characters such as John Henry, Paul Robeson (who once played John Henry in a Broadway production), various other contributors to the John Henry myths, and several modern-day figures who populate the novel. Whitehead's work is humorous, witty, and original. In 2002, Whitehead's *John Henry Days* received the Young Lions Fiction Award sponsored by the New York Public Library.

Overall, Whitehead's work represents continuity—with several added innovations—within the tradition of African-American literature. For instance, his work draws on black folklore, culture, and ways of knowing. At the same time, his writing styles, his insight regarding contemporary popular culture and new technologies, and his riffs on the past situate his prose on the cutting edges of American fiction. As evidenced by the characters in his two novels, Whitehead seeks to create new subject positions for African Americans to assume in the world.

BIBLIOGRAPHY

Larimer, Kevin. "Industrial Strength in the Information Age: A Profile of Colson Whitehead." *Poets and Writers* (July–August 2001): 21–25.

Howard Rambsy II

Wideman, John Edgar   (1941–   )

An intellectual, educator, novelist, essayist, biographer, short fiction writer, social critic, and commentator, Wideman was born in Washington, D.C., to John Edgar Lawson and Lizabeth French Wideman; he grew up at the foot of Bruston Hill in Pittsburgh, Pennsylvania's Homewood community. His maternal great-great-great-grandmother, Sybela Owens, a runaway slave, was among the original founders and settlers of this community. A Phi Beta Kappa graduate of the University of Pennsylvania, which he attended on a Benjamin Franklin Scholarship, Wideman was also the captain of the university's basketball team. He graduated with a B.A. degree in English in 1963. Wideman holds the distinction of being only the second African-American Rhodes Scholar. He graduated from Oxford University in 1966, where he studied philosophy. Before launching his teaching career at the University of Pennsylvania, where he also chaired the African American studies program, Wideman spent a year as a Kent Fellow at the University of Iowa's Writers' Workshop. He later relocated to the University of Wyoming in Laramie, where he spent more than a decade, and then to the University of Massachusetts at Amherst.

Wideman is considered one of the finest 20th-century American writers and is often compared to William Faulkner. In 1967, at age 26, Wideman published his first novel, *A Glance Away*. Although this first work appeared during the BLACK ARTS MOVEMENT, Wideman clearly wanted to distance himself from the black literary avant-garde, whose architects were championing a more BLACK AESTHETIC approach to African-American literature. Unlike his contemporaries LeRoi Jones (AMIRI BARAKA), LARRY NEAL, and ADDISON GAYLE, who were more interested in making African-American art the "spiritual sister" of the BLACK POWER concept, Wideman—as he writes in his autobiography, *BROTHERS AND KEEPERS* (1984), written with his brother Robert (Robby)—when he left Pittsburgh to attend University of Pennsylvania in Philadelphia was running toward freedom, which, for him, meant "running away from Pittsburgh, from poverty, from blackness" (26–27).

As Wideman explained to John O'Brien in a 1976 interview, classically trained, he was interested in experimenting with the form of the novel, as did the "experimentalist" 18th-century British writers who stand in the vanguard of the beginning of the novel, including "Defoe, Fielding, and particularly Laurence Sterne. If there is any single book I learned a hell of a lot from, it's *Tristram Shandy*" (O'Brien, 217). As he read more African-American writers, however, Wideman also became interested in the novels of RICHARD WRIGHT and RALPH ELLISON. He was particularly interested in JEAN TOOMER's *Cane* "because of its experimentation and open form and also because of Toomer's vision" (216).

Wideman, a former basketball star, is the author of eight novels, three collections of short stories, and three collections of social and autobiographical essays. Wideman's second and third novels, *Hurry Home* (1969) and *The Lynchers* (1973), confirmed his willingness to continue to move away from a validation and fuller exploration of the unique qualities of the African-American experience (particularly language and issues of race) as the serious and legitimate subject matter for art, although *The Lynchers* indicated a minor movement in that general direction. He peopled his fictional worlds with major white and black characters, establishing a more universal or basic human experience as his central concern. Nevertheless, Wideman could not escape the racial label "black" writer. In fact, critics continued to place him in the vanguard of contemporary black literature.

From 1975 to 1983, Wideman took an eight-year hiatus during which he tried "to learn to use a difference voice." During this period, he explains, "I was 'woodshedding,' as the musicians would say—catching up. . . . I was learning a new language to talk about my experience." With the publication of his Homewood Trilogy: *Damballah* (1981), *Hiding Place* (1981), and *Sent for You Yesterday* (1983), Wideman emerged from his personal exile to reclaim with pride his history and heritage as Sybela Owens's great-great-great-grandson. He concluded, "if you've read T. S. Eliot, James Joyce, or William Faulkner, . . . those are not the only 'keys to the kingdom.' If you have grown up Black, you also have some 'keys.'" (Samuels, 85).

In his more recent works, Wideman blurs the distinction between fiction, history, and autobiography to validate the intricate relationship between the past and the present. In *Damballah* (1981), *Hiding Place* (1981), and *Sent for You Yesterday* (1984), Wideman uses fiction to explore his family history by looking at the beginning of Homewood, where Sybela Owens settled with her children and her lover, the son of her slave master. However, to gain insights into the African past that is also his legacy, in *Damballah* Wideman tells the story of an uncontrollable African whose resistance leads to his lynching but whose only desire is to return spiritually to Africa after his physical death. The stories in *Damballah* bear the names of individual family members, "Tommy," "Rashad" and "The Song of Reba Love Jackson." "Tommy," for example, explores through fiction the incredible pain a family, particularly the mother, is made to suffer when her son, like Wideman's brother Robby, (sentenced to life in prison for murder) is incarcerated for robbery and murder. The title, *Damballah,* is the name of an African god who has the responsibility of restoring the family. Wideman begins each text in the trilogy with the image of his family tree, suggesting that, like Damballah, he, as writer, is able to restore his personal family and by extension all families that have known fragmentation.

Wideman's other collections of short stories, *Reuben* (1987), *Fever* (1989), and *All Stories Are True* (1992), as well as his later novels, *Philadelphia Fire* (1990), *The Cattle Killing* (1996), and *Two Cities* (1998), are grounded in historical events, namely, plague-ridden 18th-century Philadelphia, the brutal bombing of the MOVE members in Philadelphia in 1985, and the domination of black gang activities in Philadelphia during the 1990s. By taking on these themes and subjects in these works, Wideman seems to reconfirm his commitment to exploring cultural collapse, as a central theme in his work much in the way that Eliot did in *The Waste Land.* This focus is also found in Wideman's autobiographical text, *Brothers and Keepers* (1984), in *Father/Along* (1994), and in *Hoop Roots: Basketball, Race and Love* (2001).

In *Hoop Roots: Basketball, Race and Love,* Wideman compares his two loves: basketball and writing. He explains, "Though the writer seems to be in charge, he's more like a coach who can't insert himself in the lineup. The closest he can come to the action is sending in a substitutive for himself and reflecting the action from the sub's point of view. He can lend the sub his uniform, name, number, but the writer remains stuck on the pine" (11). Wideman concludes, "hoops frees you to play by putting you into a real cage, Writing cages the writer with the illusion of freedom. . . . Writing lets you imagine you're outside time, freely generating rules and choices" (12).

Thus, in his collected work, Wideman becomes a coach, a writer as seer prophet. He continues to use his work as a vehicle, a conduit through which the hauntingly human experience of African-American history and culture are accessed, assessed, recorded, restored and celebrated. Through them he attempts to "break out, to knock down the walls" (*Brothers and Keepers,* 18) of the imprisoning cages known by African Americans, whether the cage of self-hate—such as the one that led him to become fugitive from his own culture and identity in his first works—or the pervasive cage, the Panopticon of racism. In Wideman's works, the protagonists struggle with memory versus forgetting. They assiduously work to create spaces to redeem and (re)create their past. He continues this theme in *The Island: Martinique* (2003), a travel memoir.

Wideman has received two PEN/Faulkner Awards for Fiction and the American Book Award for Fiction. He received the Lannan Literary Fellowship for Fiction in 1991 and has been a finalist for both the National Book Critics Circle Award and the National Book Award. He won the REA Award for short story. In 1993, he received a MacArthur Prize Fellowship.

BIBLIOGRAPHY

Coleman, James W. *Blackness and Modernism: The Literary Career of John Edgar Wideman.* Jackson: University of Mississippi Press, 1989.

Mbalia, Doreatha Drummond. *John Edgar Wideman: Reclaiming the African Personality.* Selinsgrove: Susquehanna University Press, 1995.

O'Brien, John. *Interviews with Black Writers.* New York: Liveright, 1973.

Rowell, Charles H. "An Interview with John Edgar Wideman." *Callaloo* 13, no. 1 (Winter 1990): 47–60.

Rushdy, Ashraf H. A. "Fraternal Blues: John Edgar Wideman's Homewood Trilogy." *Contemporary Literature* 32, no. 3 (Fall 1991): 312–345.

Samuels, Wilfred D. "Going Home: An Interview with John Edgar Wideman." *Callaloo* 6, no. 1 (February 1983): 40–59.

TuSmith, Bonnie, ed. *Conversations with John Edgar Wideman.* Jackson: University Press of Mississippi, 1998.

Wideman, John E. *Brothers and Keepers.* New York: Penguin Books, 1984.

———. *Hoop Roots: Basketball, Race and Love.* Boston: Houghton Mifflin, 2001.

Wilfred D. Samuels

Williams, John Alfred (1925–)

Although born in segregated Hinds County, Mississippi, Williams grew up in Syracuse, New York's multiethnic Fifteenth Ward, where Jews, blacks, Italians, Irish, Poles, Indians, and others, as he fondly recalls in his autobiographical odyssey, *This Is My Country Too,* "shared conversation and other small joys" and "the religious holidays of all were greatly respected." In 1943 William disrupted his high school education to join the navy; he served in the Pacific during World War II. In the navy, he became disillusioned by the racism he encountered. Receiving an honorable discharge in 1946, Williams returned to Syracuse, completed high school, married, fathered two sons, and enrolled at Syracuse University, where, in 1950, he completed his B.A. degree in journalism and English. Although he sought to pursue a graduate degree in English immediately, family responsibilities demanded that he work full time. He returned to the foundry where he previously worked, but a back injury forced him to leave it for employment in various occupations, including as a life insurance salesman and a staff worker for CBS and NBC TV.

Williams is best known for his novel *The Man Who Cried I Am* (1967); however, he began writing poetry while in the Pacific and later was a freelance journalist writing for and publishing in such prestigious black newspapers and magazines as *The Chicago Defender, Jet,* and *Ebony.* In 1963 he traveled across the United States on a two-article assignment for *Holiday* magazine, and the following year he traveled extensively in Europe, Africa, and the United States for *Newsweek.* These personal experiences greatly influenced Williams's writing, including *This Is My Country Too,* which is an expansion of the *Holiday* assignment. He draws on his experiences as a civil rights activist and journalist for *Newsweek* for *Africa: Her History, Lands and People* (1963) and *The King God Did Not Save* (1970), a comprehensive indictment of the historical distortions of the life and death of MARTIN LUTHER KING, JR.

In *The Man Who Cried I Am,* Williams, grounding his protagonist's quest for meaning in fundamental existentialist tenets, explores issues related to existence, much in the manner that RICHARD WRIGHT does in *The Outsider.* Williams's protagonist, Max Reddick, is, like the author, a journalist and novelist. In the process of reflecting on his historical and racial identity before he dies (he is suffering from rectal cancer), Max must come to grips with what he has learned in 30 years of working and traveling about being black in 20th century America. While attending a funeral in Paris, Max gains access to the King Alfred Plan, which details the American government's plan to commit genocide against black Americans rather than grant them full citizenship. Despite the implied pessimism and bleakness of the novel, *The Man Who Cried I Am* is not a protest novel of the tradition associated with Wright. Max, realizing his condition, must act to give meaning to his existence; a failure to be responsible for his own existence would be to act falsely and in bad faith.

Williams authored several other novels, including *The Angry Ones* (1960). *Night Song* (1961), *Sissie* (1963), *Sons of Darkness, Sons of Light: A Novel of Some Probability* (1969), *Captain Blackman* (1972), *The Junior Bachelor Society* (1976), *Click Song* (1982), *The Berhama Account* (1985), and *Jacob's Ladder* (1987). He is also the editor (with Charles F. Harris) of *Amistad I* and *Amistad II* and McGraw-Hill's *Bridges: Literature across Culture* (1993).

Williams has received several awards and honors, including a National Institute of Arts and Letters award, a Linback Award from Rutgers University, and an American Book Award from the Before Columbus Foundation. He lives in New York with his second wife, Lorrain Isaac Williams.

BIBLIOGRAPHY

Muller, Gilbert. *John A. Williams.* Boston: Twayne, 1984.

George Barlow

Williams, Sherley Anne   (1944–1999)

Novelist, poet, playwright, professor, and critic Sherley Anne Williams was born on August 25, 1944, in Bakersfield, California, to Lena-Leila Marie Siler and Jesse Winson. The daughter of migrant workers, Williams described her upbringing as "the most deprived, provincial kind of existence you can think of." After her father's death when she was eight, the family was forced to go on welfare. When she was 16, her mother died, and Williams, cared for by her loving older sister Ruby, survived by working in the same dusty San Joaquin Valley fruit orchards and cotton fields where her parents had endured back-breaking work.

Williams relates how she discovered in the autobiographies of Eartha Kitt and Ethel Waters the stories of strong, successful black women who had endured childhood poverty, who "had had to cope with early and forced sex and sexuality, with mothers who could not express love in the terms that they desperately needed" (768), and how "it was largely through these autobiographies I was able to take heart in my life" (770). Her love of language

and literature was born from her determined search in libraries for the kinds of books she rarely found in her classes: "No book affected my life so much as reading LANGSTON HUGHES's *Montage on a Dream Deferred*, for here was my life and my language coming at me" (770).

Encouraged by teachers, Williams enrolled at California State University (CSU) Fresno, where she earned a bachelor's degree in English in 1966. A year later, her first short story, "Tell Martha Not to Moan" (1967), was published. She did graduate work at Fisk with ROBERT HAYDEN and with STERLING BROWN at Howard University, and completed a master's degree in American literature at Brown University in 1972, deciding to discontinue the Ph.D. program in which she was enrolled there in order to focus on being a writer rather than a critic. Williams taught briefly at CSU Fresno before becoming the first African-American literature professor at the University of California at San Diego in 1973, where she taught until her death at age 54. Williams was also a Senior Fulbright Lecturer at the University of Ghana in 1984.

While women's lives have been the focus of her creative work, her major critical text, *Give Birth to Brightness: A Thematic Study in Neo-Black Literature* (1972), focuses primarily on AMIRI BARAKA, JAMES BALDWIN, and ERNEST GAINES, exploring the ways in which black writers of the 1960s and 1970s were creating a new language—one quite different from earlier black writers—and devoting chapters to the black musician as hero/lawbreaker, "The Streetman" as hero and "Light Bearer," as well as a chapter on the limitations of middle-class literary heroes.

Unsuccessful at getting her first novel published (and unwilling to capitulate to the publisher's suggestions that she involve its protagonist, a domestic, in prostitution, Williams saw a nine-year hiatus occur between her writing of "Meditations on History" (a story written partly in repudiation of William Styron's *Confessions of Nat Turner*, which she later expanded into her novel *DESSA ROSE*) and the publication of the story in 1980.

Her earlier *Peacock Poems* (1975), nominated for both a Pulitzer Prize and a National Book Award, introduces Odessa, namesake and touchstone for her novel DESSA ROSE. In "I Sing This Song for Our Mothers," Williams takes on the persona of a newly freed black man who announces quietly, surely: "I was a man full growed / when the otha folks freedom come, had / a wife and sons o' my own / and wa'n't nary-a-one o' us / eva belongst to no one but us selves." Odessa's son, the narrator in this poem, knows that through his own resistance and love, and through the love and kinship of family and friends, he belongs to himself in the deepest sense. Following his admonition to black people to carry on the story of freedom by telling it "to yo daughters most especial / cause this where our line comes from," the poem shifts narrators from Odessa's son to Odessa. Forced to live in a world in which speech and naming is forbidden, even the right to name her own children, Odessa paradoxically claims the power of naming:

> I say yo name
> now and that be love. I say
> yo daddy name and that be
> how I know free. I say Harker
> name and that be how I
> keep loved and keep free.

The poem "Ruise" in *Peacock Poems* is filled with tenderness for Williams's older sister Ruby (Ruise) Birdson, "the girl / who took the womanme in."

Williams's *Some One Sweet Angel Chile* (1982), also nominated for a National Book Award, received an Emmy for a television performance of the poems. The collection opens with a series of epistolary poems, "Letters from a New England Negro," subsequently performed as a full-length, one-woman drama in the National Black Theatre Festival (1991) and the Chicago International Theatre Festival (1992). The poems are full of evocative, piercing small ironies: Reconstruction schoolteacher Hannah's quiet moments of resistance. Hannah's refusal to wear a headscarf or braid her hair is a refusal of a symbol of subservience and slavery, yet the plaiting—required by whites—becomes an emblem of tenderness between black mothers and daughters. In a wonderfully understated poem, Hannah refuses the implications of her slave name, Patience, and

"answer[s] roughly / some harmless question, My name is Hannah. Hannah. There is / no Patience to it." The collection's middle section, exuberant, boisterous, and sexy, skips 60 years to the 1930s to celebrate a similar spirit of rebelliousness in the persona of famed BLUES singer Bessie Smith. Refusing the terrible legacy of colorism—the belief that lighter is better, is more beautiful—Bessie bewitches even those black men who "bragged [they] didn't deal in coal," into her bed. In these poems, Bessie Smith, the "angel chile," the wild woman of the traditional blues song, is not mythologized but is remembered for the ways in which her spirit brought courage, hope, and humor into the lives of others. In the final sequence of poems, there are echoes of Hannah and Bessie in a profusion of contemporary voices. Although the poems in this section seem loosely autobiographical, the narrator of "WITNESS," the opening poem, sternly warns that she speaks not just for herself but for the generations that preceded her and the generations to come: "I give voice to the old stories. This is not romance, private fiction."

Williams is most famous for her novel *Dessa Rose*. She is also the author of two children's books, *Working Cotton* (1992), which won an American Library Association Caldecott Award and a Coretta Scott King Book Award, and *Girls Together* (1999), as well as several influential essays on the blues. In 1998, Williams was awarded the African American Literature and Culture Society's Stephen Henderson Award for Outstanding Achievement in Literature and Poetry, and a conference called "Black Women Writers and the 'High Art' of Afro-American Letters" was held in her honor at University of California at San Diego to mark the 12th anniversary of the publication of *Dessa Rose*.

Poet MICHAEL S. HARPER described Williams as "a musician whose blues, comedy and heartbreak are a testimony to autobiography/history where both oral and literary Afro-American traditions touch and fuse" (Henderson 1999, 763). At the time of her death, of cancer, on July 6, 1999, she was working on a sequel to *Dessa Rose* as well as a novel set in the 20th century. She is survived by a son, John Malcolm Stewart, and three grandchildren, as well as students, colleagues, and generations of readers.

BIBLIOGRAPHY

Davis, Mary Kemp. "Everybody Knows Her Name: The Recovery of the Past in Sherley Anne Williams's *Dessa Rose.*" *Callaloo* 40 (Summer 1989): 544–558.

Henderson, Gwendolyn. "In Memory of Sherley Anne Williams: 'Some One Sweet Angel Chile' 1944–1999." *Callaloo* 22, no. 4 (1999): 763–767.

———. "(W)riting the Work and Working the Rites." *Black American Literature Forum* 23, no. 4 (Winter 1989): 631–660.

McDowell, Deborah E. "Negotiating between Tenses: Witnessing Slavery after Freedom—*Dessa Rose.*" In *Slavery and the Literary Imagination,* edited by McDowell and Arnold Rampersad, 144–163. Baltimore: Johns Hopkins University Press, 1989.

McKible, Adam. "'These are the Facts of the Darky's History': Thinking History and Reading Names in Four African American Texts." *African American Review* 28, no. 2 (Summer 1994): 223–235.

Rushdy, Ashraf H. A. "Reading Mammy: The Subject of Relation in Sherley Anne Williams' *Dessa Rose.*" *African American Review* 27, no. 3 (Autumn 1993): 365–389.

Williams, Sherley A. "Meditation on History." *Callaloo* 22, no. 4 (1999): 768–770.

Lynda Koolish

Wilson, August   (1945–2005)

Although he began writing poetry in his youth, it is his playwriting that has made August Wilson a celebrated author. Born in 1945 in Pittsburgh, Pennsylvania, to Frederick and Daisy Kittel, Wilson struggled early with family and economic hardships that would later inform his art. His father was white and his mother was African-American, and life as a biracial child in 1940s America could certainly be troubled. His parents separated when August was quite young, and his mother struggled as a cleaning woman to take care of her six children. Wilson's stepfather, David Bedford, became a stronger presence in Wilson's life than his father had been. He moved the family to a predominantly white suburb when Wilson was in high school, where he was accused of plagiarizing a paper. Rather than submit to the charges, Wilson dropped out of school and never graduated.

Wilson worked odd jobs as he worked on his craft. He also spent a year in the army. When he began his writing career, he took his middle name, August, and his mother's maiden name, Wilson, to forge his new identity. In Pittsburgh in 1968, he cofounded the Black Horizons on the Hill Theater Company with Rob Penny. He also cofounded the Center Avenue Poets Theater Workshop. In 1969 he married Brenda Barton and in the following year became the father of Sakina Ansari. By the late 1970s, he focused most of his attention on playwriting and completed *The Homecoming* (based on the life of BLUES singer Blind Lemon Jefferson) and *The Coldest Day of the Year* in 1979. His marriage to Barton ended in 1972, and by 1981 Wilson had remarried a social worker named Judy Oliver. (Their marriage ended in 1990; he married Constanza Romero, a costume designer, in 1994.)

The first major play, *Jitney,* appeared in 1982 in the Allegheny Repertory Theater. A two-act play, the work was finished in 1979, and the performance established Wilson on the stage, but it was *Ma Rainey's Black Bottom* that brought Wilson's name and his work into the New York theaters. *Ma Rainey's Black Bottom* explores the world of music production in Chicago at the height of the popularity of swing and jazz. The white ownership of record companies and the use of underpaid, black musicians sets the racial and sociocultural backdrop for the play. The work also serves as an example of the type of exploitation of African-American art and talent that often was the benchmark of American capitalism. Influenced by the music of Bessie Smith, the work embraces Wilson's infectious love of music that is the cornerstone of all of his drama. First produced at the Yale Repertory Company in 1984, under the guidance of director, Lloyd Richards—who continued to collaborate with Wilson—the play appeared in New York City the same year. It won a Tony nomination and a New York Drama Critics Circle Award in 1985. Wilson began work on his next play, *Fences,* at the same time that *Ma Rainey's Black Bottom* was reaching the production stage.

Fences (1986) surpassed even *Ma Rainey's* success. The play about a former Negro Leagues ballplayer, Troy Maxson, and his family also first appeared at Yale. The work went on to garner the Tony for Best Drama, the New York Drama Critics Circle Award, and the Pulitzer Prize for Drama in 1987. The play featured the respected actor James Earl Jones as Troy. With *Fences* and *Ma Rainey's Black Bottom,* Wilson not only established himself as America's most significant playwright but initiated his historical cycle of plays meant to reflect African-American life in each decade of the 20th century. *Fences* captured the world of the 1950s, while *Ma Rainey's Black Bottom* explored the 1920s.

Often compared to *Death of a Salesman,* with Troy Maxson as its Willy Loman, *Fences* critiqued the American dream at its core: the game of baseball. Though Troy was once a star in the Negro Leagues, he could never play America's sport in the majors because of race discrimination and segregation. His son, Cory, now has an opportunity to win a football scholarship, which his father opposes. Still bitter about his own inability to break the color barriers, Troy is torn between wanting to protect his son from the pain he endured and envying his son's future promise. The two engage in bitter arguments, and throughout the play Wilson uses the building of a fence around the home as a symbolic testament to the social and historical forces that have "fenced" in Troy. By the play's final act, Troy has helped destroy his own son's dreams and estranged himself from Cory and his mother, Rose. The closing scene, Troy's funeral, signals the waste and anger that has controlled his life because of racism.

Joe Turner's Come and Gone (1988) continued the historical cycle. Set in 1911, the work won numerous nominations for its portrayal of African Americans in search of an African past in the midst of a changing America. The main character, Herald Loomis, is a former minister. Wrongfully taken and forced to work by the governor of Tennessee's brother, Joe Turner, on a chain gang, Loomis is psychically scarred by his experience and blames

Christianity. It is only by reconnecting to his African spiritual roots through the juba dance that he is healed.

Wilson won the Pulitzer Prize again for his next drama, *The Piano Lesson* (1990). Based on a Romare Bearden painting, the play follows the Charles family as they come to terms with their past. They represent a people who have forgotten their music and thus their heritage and history. Linked by a piano that was once owned by the family that held them as slaves, the Charleses must exorcise the "ghosts" of slavery and embrace their ancestral voices. Set in 1937, the play also characterizes the hardships that African Americans suffered during the Depression. The two principals, Boy Willie and Berniece—brother and sister—view the piano as a symbol of family values. For Boy Willie, the piano represents financial security. By selling it, he will be able to afford to buy land that was once worked by his ancestors. Berniece fights with him, refusing to let the piano ever leave their family's possession. For her it stands as a reminder of everything the family has lost. Both come to realize that the piano is far more valuable: Carved into its wood is the history of the Charles family. Their past—its pain and its joy—is meant to be remembered, cherished, and celebrated.

Two Trains Running (1993), set in the 1960s in a rundown diner, and *Seven Guitars* (1995) have also seen successful runs in New York. *Seven Guitars* follows the life of blues musician Floyd Barton and covers the decade of the 1940s in Wilson's cycle. *King Hedley II,* which premiered in Philadelphia in 2003, was followed by *Gem of the Ocean* (2004), which had a very brief run on Broadway. Wilson's final play, *Radio Golf* (2005), premiered by the Yale Repertory Theater, is scheduled to open on Broadway in 2007. *Radio Golf* deals with redevelopment in the black community as a venue for blacks to achieve the American dream. It completes Wilson's 10-play cycle. Wilson died of cancer in 2005.

Praised for his "musical language" and his blending of myth, memory, and history, Wilson has remained the most powerful American dramatic voice for almost the last 20 years. He received a Guggenheim for his achievements on the stage in 1992. Reaching the ranks of Tennessee Williams,

Eugene O'Neill, and Arthur Miller, Wilson found a way to bring an authentic African-American experience to the footlights of America, and in the process he educated generations already born and yet to come about the often silent histories of African Americans.

BIBLIOGRAPHY

Bogumil, Mary. *Understanding August Wilson.* Charleston: University of South Carolina Press, 1999.

Elkins, Marilyn. *August Wilson: A Casebook.* New York: Garland Press, 2000.

Herrington, Joan. *I Ain't Sorry for Nothin' I Done: August Wilson's Process of Playwriting.* New York: Limelight, 1998.

Nadel, Alan, ed. *May All of Your Fences Have Gates: Essays on the Drama of August Wilson.* Ames: University of Iowa Press, 1994.

Pereira, Kim. *August Wilson and the African-American Odyssey.* Chicago: University of Illinois Press, 1995.

Shannon, Sandra G. *The Dramatic Vision of August Wilson.* Washington, D.C.: Howard University Press, 1996.

Tracie Church Guzzio

Wilson, Harriet (1828?–)

Harriet Wilson, born Harriet Adams in Milford, New Hampshire, in 1828 (some sources indicate 1827), was the child of a white mother and an African-American father. Little is known about her, the author of *Our Nig* (1854), the first novel published by an African-American woman and the first African-American novel published in North America. At the time of its publication, *Our Nig* garnered Wilson little acclaim or attention. Even less is known about her whereabouts after the book's publication. However, it is known that at age six she was left with the Hayward family, whom she fictionalizes as the Bellmonts in the novel. Mistreated from the start, Wilson lived virtually as the Hayward's indentured servant until she turned 18.

In 1851 Harriet married Thomas Wilson, a con artist who made money selling his story as a fugitive slave (a story that later proved to be fabricated). Wilson abandoned Harriet and their son, George; when George became sick, Harriet was unable to care for him, so she placed him in a state hospital. As she explains in the introduction, her novel represents her attempt to make enough money to reclaim her son and nurse him back to health. Unfortunately, the novel did not provide Wilson with the financial stability she had hoped for; a few months after its publication, George died, after which Wilson seems to have disappeared without a trace.

It was not until the 1980s that Professor HENRY LOUIS GATES, JR., who recovered *Our Nig* in 1984 and identified it as an African-American novel, verified much of Wilson's life. Wilson's history and her novel highlight America's neglect and mistreatment of those marginalized by race, class, and gender. Home, family, marriage—all the promises of security offered to orphaned young women in the sentimental novels that *Our Nig* alludes to— could not save Wilson or her son. In the years since the book's rediscovery, readers have found a young mother and writer to admire. Her style and her examination and criticism of American families, religious attitudes, and labor issues have made her an important figure of the past who inspires contemporary African-American writers.

BIBLIOGRAPHY

Jones, Jill. "The Disappearing 'I' in *Our Nig*." *Legacy: A Journal of American Women Writers* 13, no. 1 (1996): 38–53.

White, Barbara. "'Our Nig' and the She-Devil: New Information about Harriet Wilson and the 'Bellmont' Family." *American Literature* 65, no. 1 (1993): 19–52.

Tracie Church Guzzio

Wind Done Gone, The
Alice Randall (2001)

In *The Wind Done Gone,* ALICE RANDALL sifts pieces of the antebellum American past into a richly textured narrative that contests the myths immortalized in the novel *Gone with the Wind.* Randall's work, invoking and signifying on Margaret Mitchell's *Gone with the Wind,* set off a firestorm of controversy. The Margaret Mitchell Trust sued to block publication of *The Wind Done Gone,* claiming it was plagiarism. The judge initially agreed with the Mitchell Trust and issued an injunction against publication but ultimately decided that Randall's novel was protected as a literary parody under "fair use" laws.

The work follows the conventions of neo–slave narratives. As the story of a black woman's emergence from patriarchal domination, it is situated at the intersection of race and gender ideologies. Its gender motifs give the text a privileged place in 20th-century black feminist fiction. Randall threads these discourses together into a masterwork of metafiction. Randall's self-conscious narrator, Cynara, a biracial plantation child, and Pallas, her slave mother, embody and undermine every plantation stereotype the myths of the Old South invented for them.

Cynara crosses the boundaries between races, appropriates the masters' discourse, and writes herself into Scarlett O'Hara's story. Through Cynara, Randall reimagines the antebellum plantation, rewrites the slaves' motives and desires, and recalibrates the scales of history, giving the house slaves the chance to tell their side of the plantation's story. Like historical slave narrators, Cynara makes her journey to literacy at great cost, and the knowledge literacy provides is cruel. With literacy, however, comes Cynara's voice. At unexpected moments in her narration, Cynara's slave vernacular displaces her literate voice, exposing a sensibility formed in the sorrows of slavery.

Much of Cynara's pain derives from her connection to her slave mother, Pallas. Cynara must revisit her past and discover the reasons her mother rejected her. In Cynara's memories, the reader confronts a dynamic usually absent from contemporary African-American women's fiction: a slave mother who has rejected her own daughter. Randall also uses Pallas to critique the stereotype of the "MAMMY" figure in traditional plantation fiction, who is typically represented as a loyal, self-repressing, asexual servant who dotes excessively on white children to the exclusion of her own. Pallas emerges as a far more complex and human mother.

In the spirit of Reconstruction and in the discovery of racial pride, Cynara is reconciled to her mother, her identity, and her past. Cynara no longer desires to erase her racial memory. Her earlier attempts at erasure through denial, isolation, and self-immolation did not enable her liberation. Until Cynara knew her past and embraced all that it bequeathed to her, she was not free to pursue her own vision for her future. Cynara's difficulties with her past reflect America's difficulties with its antebellum history and possibly suggest a pathway to America's liberation from that past, which, if the actions of the Margaret Mitchell Trust are any indication, still captivates public memory. Troubled by America's fascination with a mythic past inscribed in the novel *Gone with the Wind,* Randall revisited the myth and created another version—one that augments the deficient myth and embraces all of who we are: masters and slaves, saints and sinners, the loved and the rejected.

BIBLIOGRAPHY

Gillespie, Nick. "Tomorrow Is Another Day in Court." *Reason* 33, no. 3 (July 2001): 61–63.

Grossett, Jeffrey. "The Wind Done Gone: Transforming Tara into a Plantation Parody." *Case Western Reserve Law Review* 52, no. 4 (Summer 2002): 1–16.

Tucker, Veta S. "Scarlett Dethroned, or Hell Hath No Fury like *The Wind Done Gone:* Malicious Mammy and her Plucky Daughter." *Warpland: A Journal of Black Literature and Ideas* 7, no. 1 (2001): 178–193.

Veta S. Tucker

Wolfe, George   (1954–   )

Born in Frankfort, Kentucky, in 1954, George Wolfe became active in local theater at an early age and considered himself "obsessed" with theater by age six. He majored in acting and theater design at Pomona College and wrote plays, winning the

American College Theater Festival Award for his first play, *Up for Grabs.* By 1979 Wolfe headed to New York City, where he took a position teaching at City College and polishing his plays. He also worked as a musical director and a dramaturge. In 1983 he completed a masters of fine arts in musical theater at New York University.

Wolfe's first major work to receive critical acclaim was *The Colored Museum* in 1986. A sophisticated satire of the lies America tells itself, the play remains one of the most controversial examples of contemporary African-American drama. Composed of 11 vignettes, the play explores African-American attitudes toward sexual identity and the community's homophobia. The work mocks the African-American middle class and its hunger for mobility and, at turns, humorously and poignantly reminds its audience that the past is an inescapable burden. The sketch "Celebrity Slaveship" garnered some of the harshest criticism, yet it challenges African Americans to consider honestly where they have been historically as a race and what they will have to sacrifice to embrace the American dream. *The Colored Museum* was produced at the New York Public Theater in 1986. PBS televized a version in 1991.

Adapting the work of ZORA NEALE HURSTON, Wolfe wrote and directed the play *SPUNK* in 1989. Wolfe captured Hurston's African-American communal folk voice in the play's chorus. He won an Obie Award for directing the play the following year, and its success elevated Wolfe in the New York theater community. In 1990 he was appointed artistic associate of the New York Shakespeare Festival/Public Theater. The same year, he directed Thulani Davis's version of Bertolt Brecht's *The Caucasian Chalk Circle.*

Jelly's Last Jam, the story of pianist Jelly Roll Morton, was first performed in 1991. Wolfe brought the play to Broadway the following year. In the work, Wolfe examines African-American identity and culture within the context of the birth of jazz and the larger-than-life personality of Jelly Roll Morton. A musical sensation, the play drew critical and popular acclaim, winning three Tony Awards. In the same year, Wolfe was made artistic director of the New York Shakespeare Festival/ Joseph Papp Public Theater. As the artistic director, Wolfe produced and directed Tony Kushner's award-winning AIDS drama, *Angels in America,* and won a Tony Award for his directing. He also helmed Anna Deavere Smith's *Twilight: Los Angeles 1992.* In 1995 he directed a postcolonial reading of Shakespeare's *The Tempest* for the Public Theater. Emphasizing Afro-Caribbean dance, costumes, and masks in the production, Wolfe's version examined the cultural imperialism inherent in Prospero's "education" of Caliban. Wolfe also revised Caliban as an intelligent revolutionary unable to thwart the powerful "magic" of Prospero's control. In Wolfe's hands, this production illustrated the struggle of African-American cultural identity within the framework of Western ideology and civilization. The island embodies nature, orality, community, and kineticism, while Prospero symbolizes a world of books, ideas, and individualism—high humanism. The production has generated praise as one of the first successful multicultural presentations of Shakespeare's work.

The year after *The Tempest,* Wolfe wrote and directed *Bring in Da Noise, Bring in Da Funk,* a history of African-American dance. One of the most unique productions of the contemporary American stage, the play celebrates African-American heritage entirely through music and movement. Wolfe won another Tony for best director for the work and continues to direct and produce for the Public Theater. Averaging a production a year, he also continues to win numerous Drama Desk Awards from New York theater critics and to write original plays. His contributions to the New York stage make him one of the most prolific African-American playwrights and directors of the American theater.

BIBLIOGRAPHY

Elam, Harry. "Signifyin(g) on African-American Theater: *The Colored Museum* by George Wolfe." *Theater Journal* 44, no. 3 (1992): 291–303.

Rowell, Charles. "Interview with George Wolfe: Playwright, Director, and Producer." *Callaloo* 16, no. 3 (1993): 591–629.

Silverstein, Marc. "'Any Baggage You Don't Claim, We Trash': Living with (in) History in *The Colored Museum*." *American Drama* 8, no. 1 (1998): 95–121.

Tracie Church Guzzio

womanist/womanish

At the beginning of the collection of essays *In Search of Our Mothers' Gardens*, ALICE WALKER defines the term *womanist*. Derived from *womanish*, this term refers to "outrageous, audacious, courageous or willful behavior" (xi). It has roots in the "black folk expression of mothers to female children, 'You acting womanish,' i.e. like a woman" (xi). A womanist, therefore, refers to a responsible woman who is brave and has triumphed over obstacles to shape and define her own identity. She is mature, independent, and playful. Instead of being exclusively grounded in achieving freedom from male domination, as are some feminist theorists, a womanist critic is "committed to [the] survival and wholeness of [an] entire people, male and female. Not a separatist, except periodically, for health" (xi). Although she is not a separatist, she "appreciates and prefers women's culture, women's emotional flexibility (values tears as natural counterbalance of laughter), and women's strength" (xi). Walker defines the social and communal interests of a womanist, who gains her strength from her community and uses that strength to uplift her people, physically, spiritually, economically, and politically.

The term *womanist* can be used to describe many African-American women who have played important historical roles. According to Jacqueline Grant, this includes "Sojourner Truth, Jarena Lee, Amanda Berry Smith, Ida B. Wells, Mary Church Terrell, Mary McLeod Bethune, Fannie Lou Hamer and countless others not remembered in any historical study." (Grant, 205). Black women often strive to deconstruct the identity assigned to them by the dominant culture. Acting in the community, women have formed women's clubs, written literature, produced plays, established women's place in uplifting the community and the family, and participated in the struggle for equality.

Equally important is the role womanists have played in defining and developing an African-American literary tradition. Alice Walker is an ideal example; her award-winning novel *The Color Purple* is a womanist text. Walker develops female characters who are womanists; thematically, the novel goes beyond Celie's individual identity formation to explore the complexity and the importance of community. Similarly, in many of GLORIA NAYLOR's works—*The Women of Brewster Place, Mama Day*, and *Bailey's Café*—the women exhibit womanist behavior through their desire to empower themselves, their voices, and their communities. JANIE CRAWFORD, the protagonist in ZORA NEALE HURSTON's *Their Eyes Were Watching God*, exhibits womanist behavior in her interactions with her grandmother, Nanny; her friend Phoebe; and her husbands, Logan Killicks, Joe, and Tea Cake. AUGUST WILSON's Ma Rainey, the central female character in *Ma Rainey's Black Bottom*, is an example of a womanist created by a male author. Ma Rainey truly has control over her music and thus is able to empower her voice. Womanists work to create and define their own identities between oppressive forces and in the margins of the dominant culture.

BIBLIOGRAPHY

Allan, Tuzyline Jita. "Womanism Revisited: Women and the (Ab) Use of Power in *The Color Purple*." In *Feminist Nightmares*, edited by Jennifer Fleischner and Susan Ostrov, 88–105. New York: New York University Press, 1994.

———. *Womanist and Feminist Aesthetics: A Comparative Review*. Athens: Ohio University Press, 1995.

Grant, Jacquelyn. *White Women's Christ and Black Women's Jesus: Feminist Christology and Womanist Response*. American Academy of Religion Series 64. Atlanta: Scholars Press, 1989.

Jamison-Hall, Angelene. "She's Just Too Womanish for Them: Alice Walker and *The Color Purple*." In *Censored Books*, edited by Lee Burress, Nicholas J. Karolides, and John M. Kean, 191–200. Metuchen, N.J.: Scarecrow Press, 1993.

Kirk-Duggan, Cheryl A. "Justified, Sanctified, and Redeemed." In *Embracing the Spirit: Womanist*

Perspectives on Hope, Salvation, and Transformation, edited by Emilie M. Townes, 140–166. New York: Orbis Books, 1997.

Walker, Alice. *The Color Purple.* New York: Pocket Books, 1982.

———. *In Search of Our Mothers' Gardens.* New York: Harcourt Brace & Company, 1983.

LaJuan Simpson

Women of Brewster Place, The
Gloria Naylor (1982)

Initially a short story, GLORIA NAYLOR's novel centers on the lives of seven black women of diverse backgrounds and ages who struggle to survive the deplorable social conditions of their lives. They live on a dead-end street, trapped in an endless cycle of racism, poverty, and sexism. Nevertheless, Naylor's special community of women attempts to rise above their circumstances "like an ebony phoenix, each in her own time" (5). In the end, they find solace in their relationship with one another as mothers, daughters, sisters, friends, and lovers.

The Women of Brewster Place, a tapestry of African-American folk and historical traditions, tells separate but interlocking stories about each of the female protagonists: Etta Mae Johnson, Mattie's childhood friend and a good-time woman; Lucielia Louise Turner, Miss Eva's granddaughter who loses her young daughter, Serena; Kiswana (formerly Melanie) Browne, a naive, middle-class idealist; Cora Lee, the young unwed welfare mother with seven children; and Theresa and Lorraine, the lesbian couple known as "the two." Mattie Michael, the central character who connects the stories, is a middle-aged matriarch who unselfishly and unconditionally provides the other women with love, guidance, support, strength, and protection. According to Naylor, her "slice of life tales" are structured this way, "Because one character couldn't be the Black woman in America. So I had seven different women, all in different circumstances, encompassing the complexity of our lives, the richness of our diversity, from skin color on down to religious, political and sexual preference" (*Ebony,* 123). Together, Naylor's gallery of women

stands as "hard-edged, soft-centered, brutally demanding, and easily pleased women" (5) united to fight a hostile world.

The Women of Brewster Place is an impressive first novel, addressing such themes as motherhood, love, sex, birth, death, and grief, among others. However, although it was well received, and although Naylor had, in her own words, "bent over backwards not to have a negative message come through about the men" (Naylor, 579), the novel, along with ALICE WALKER's *The COLOR PURPLE* (1982), which was published the same year, was criticized nonetheless for its portrayal of black males as "Negro Beast stereotypes" (Johnson, 111). Despite such negative assessments, however, Naylor has been ranked with such literary giants as ZORA NEALE HURSTON, TONI MORRISON, and ALICE WALKER.

In 1983, *The Women of Brewster Place* won the American Book Award for First Fiction. During the 1985–86 television season, it was produced for PBS's American Playhouse; Naylor wrote the script. In 1989, Oprah Winfrey's firm, Harpo, Inc., produced it as an ABC television miniseries, starring Mary Alice, Olivia Cole, Robin Givens, Moses Gunn, Lonette McKee, Paula Kelly, Jackèe, Barbara Montgomery, Phyllis Yvonne Stickney, Cicely Tyson, Douglas Turner Ward, Lynn Whitfield, Paul Winfield, and Oprah Winfrey as Mattie Michael. In 1990, a spin-off of the miniseries titled *Brewster Place,* also produced by Harpo, Inc., aired for a few weeks on ABC but was canceled because of low ratings. Today, Naylor's "love letter to the Black women of America" (McDowell, 636) continues to be a mainstay in contemporary African-American literature and especially women's studies courses.

BIBLIOGRAPHY

Gottlieb, Annie. "Women Together." Review of *The Women of Brewster Place. New York Times Book Review,* 22 August 1982, pp. 11, 25.

Johnson, Charles. *Being and Race: Black Writing since 1970.* Bloomington: Indiana University Press, 1988.

McDowell, Margaret B. "Naylor, Gloria." In *Contemporary Novelists,* edited by D. L. Kirkpatrick, 636–637. New York: St. Martin's, 1986.

Naylor, Gloria. "A Conversation between Gloria Naylor and Toni Morrison." *Southern Review* 21, no. 3 (Summer 1985): 567–593.

"*The Women of Brewster Place.*" *Ebony,* March 1989, pp. 122–124, 126.

Loretta Gilchrist Woodard

Woods, Vergible   See TEA CAKE.

Woodson, Jacqueline Amanda
(1963–)

Born in Columbus, Ohio, on February 12, 1963, Woodson grew up in Greenville, South Carolina, and in Brooklyn, New York. Living in an ethnically and culturally diverse community enriched her life and served as a well from which she drew inspiration to craft characters from various ethnic groups and social classes. She received a bachelor's degree in English and worked as a children's drama therapist for runaways and homeless children in New York City before she became an author. Her writing summons readers to wrestle with myriad issues, including lesbian parenting, child abuse, and teenage pregnancy.

In 1990, Jacqueline Woodson published her first young adult novel, *Last Summer with Maizon.* Woodson's work includes *The House You Pass on the Way* (Puffin, 2003), *If You Come Softly* (Putnam, 1998), *I Hadn't Meant to Tell You This* (Delacorte, 1994), *From the Notebooks of Melanin Sun* (Scholastic, 1997), the Maizon trilogy—*Last Summer with Maizon* (Delacorte, 1990), *Maizon at Blue Hill* (Delacorte, 1992), and *Between Madison and Palmetto* (Delacorte, 1993), *Behind You* (Putnam Juvenile, 2004)—and *The Dear One* (Delacorte, 1991). Her picture books include *Coming On Home Soon, Sweet, Sweet Memory* (Jump at the Sun/Hyperion, 2000), *We Had a Picnic This Sunday Past* (Hyperion, 1998), and *The Other Side* (G. P. Putnam's Sons, 2001), which won the Texas Blue Bonnet Award and a Child Magazine Best Book Award. She edited *A Way Out of No Way: Writings about Growing Up Black in America* (Henry Holt, 1996), a collection of stories about children. Woodson's novels *Hush* (Putnam, 2002) and *Locomotion* (Putnam, 2003) were both finalists for the National Book Award for Young People's Literature.

In her work, Woodson adeptly transports readers into adolescent worlds, navigating with authentic emotions, observations, and insight communicated through her prose. "With each book, Woodson has taken a risk—confronting issues of race, class, teenage pregnancy and interracial and gay relationships—and her sympathetic characters make the big questions more accessible for teens to examine," says critic Jennifer Brown.

Woodson has been a fellow at the MacDowell Colony and the Fine Arts Work Center in Provincetown, Massachusetts. She has been a visiting writer in the Goddard College M.F.A. writing program and has taught creative writing in the graduate program at City College.

Woodson has received four Coretta Scott King Honors, a Coretta Scott King Award, the *Los Angeles Times* Book Award, two Jane Addams Peace Awards, three Lambda Literary Awards, a *Granta* Best Writer Under Forty Award, *Publisher's Weekly* Best Book of 1994, and a number of American Library Association Best Book Awards. *Miracle's Boys* (Putnam, 2000), a touching story about three parentless brothers, earned the author a Coretta Scott King Award for Fiction. It debuted in February 2005 as a miniseries directed by LeVar Burton. Woodson lives in Brooklyn with her partner and their daughter Toshi.

BIBLIOGRAPHY
Bashir, Samiya A. "Tough Issues, Tender Minds—Jacqueline Woodson—Critical Essay." *Black Issues Book Review* 3, no. 3 (May 2001): 78.

Brown, Jennifer. "From Outsider to Insider." *Publishers Weekly* (February 2002).

Jeannine F. Hunter

Wright, Charles Stevenson   (1932–)
Wright was born and reared in segregated New Franklin, a small midwestern town near Columbia, Missouri, to Stevenson and Dorothy Hughes Wright. By the time Wright was four years old, his

mother, who had separated from his father, a laborer, had died. His maternal grandparents, who showered him with unconditional love and taught him to love reading, raised Wright. Victimized by the inequalities of "separate but equal" education that denied access to the best and most up-to-date educational material, Wright turned to newspapers and magazines to enhance his commitment to personal development.

By age 10 Wright began writing stories, which he would read to disbelieving classmates who accused him of copying them from the *Reader's Digest.* Wright, who was drafted into the U.S. Army after graduating high school, never attended college. Although he meandered about from California to Missouri, he remained an avid reader and a committed writer, spending summers at the Lowney Handy Writers Colony in Marshall, Illinois. Although, as his work reflects, Wright was deeply influenced by Ernest Hemingway and F. Scott Fitzgerald, he also recalls the tremendous impact RICHARD WRIGHT had on him during his teens after he had read a *Life* magazine article on BLACK BOY. Richard Wright's story of southern life under Jim Crow ethics would be a life-changing experience for Charles Wright.

Although Charles Wright did not find a publisher for "No Regrets," the first novel he wrote, he did for his second, *The Messenger,* which, published in 1963 by Farrar, Straus, and Company, received rave reviews. Wright was showered with accolades by the leading African-American author JAMES BALDWIN. The fair-skinned protagonist of *The Messenger,* 29-year-old Charles Stevenson (the autobiographical resonance throughout the novel is by no means incidental), is a liminal character engaged, through his job as a New York City messenger in the Rockefeller Center, in a quest for meaning and knowledge. He continuously finds himself surrounded by the power denied him because of his race and class: He is a black laborer earning minimum wages, living in a room condemned by the Housing Authority, surrounded by members of the underclass: pimps, prostitutes, drug addicts, gypsies, and every imaginable type of hustler. He is surrounded by powerful individuals who have achieved the American dream that

is denied him. Stevenson declares, "This country has split open my head with a golden eagle's beak. Regardless of how I try, the parts won't come together" (*The Messenger,* 4).

Near the end of *The Messenger,* Stevenson returns to Missouri to visit his aging grandmother and reflect on his life. Recalling past memories and experiences while sitting in the courthouse square of the small midwestern town in which he grew up, Charles declares, "My life seemed like that of a tomcat who had slunk down too many alleys and had gotten nothing but a whore's bag of experience" (111–112). Back in his dark, cluttered room in Manhattan, Charles again contemplates the "Why of my life, the meaning" (116). Finding no green light at the end of the novel, Charles decides to leave New York to continue his Sisyphean journey. Lawrence Hogue argues that, given Charles's growing awareness of his loneliness, *The Messenger* is fundamentally an existentialist novel that moves beyond the black/white binary critical model often used to examine and assess the African-American literary text.

After the success of *The Messenger,* however, Wright's next novel, *The Wig* (1966), which he wrote in 29 days, was not well received. Lester Jefferson, the protagonist of *The Wig,* like Charles in *The Messenger,* is a black male questing after the American dream. In his attempt to better his condition in modern New York, he has unsuccessfully assumed every imaginable charlatan mask. Failing, he designs a master disguise to improve his chances by straightening (conking) his hair to end up with "good hair"—hair that approximates the straight hair of white Americans rather than "kinky" hair associated with African Americans.

With his new, smooth-haired identity, Lester was "reborn, purified, anointed, beautified" (*The Wig,* 141). His new wig (slang for hair), he is convinced, "is going to see me through these troubled times" (143). Although Lester temporarily succeeds in getting his all-American girl (a prostitute named the Deb who is in love with his "good hair"), and although he lands a high-paying job—his avenue to The Great Society although he has to don a chicken costume and crawl around on all fours shouting, "Cock-a-doodle-doo. . . .

Eat me. . . . All over town. Eat me at the King of Southern Fried Chicken!" (228)—Lester ends up castrated and alone at the end of the novel.

Perhaps one of the reasons (if not the central reason) *The Wig* did not succeed is its experimental form—its surrealistic bends, dips, and turns. Wright tells John O'Brien, "*The Wig* is not a plotted novel; it's in episodes and you might think of it in relation to vaudeville" (252). The novel received lukewarm reviews; however, some critics praised it highly. Ishmael Reed acknowledges being influenced by Wright's experimental fiction. *The Wig* is, he argued "one of the most underrated novels" written in the 20th century (Weixlmann, 1984, 291). Ironically, perhaps what caused reviewers to ignore *The Wig* is the very quality of the novel and the role Wright played in helping shape and direct African-American fiction at mid-20th century. Joe Weixlmann claims as much when he notes that Wright, as a member of the avant-garde, will be "remembered as an innovator in breaking with traditional fictional modes during the 1960s" (1997, 791–792).

Written during his widespread meanderings, Wright's final work, *Absolutely Nothing to Get Alarmed About,* a collection of his nonfictional pieces, sometimes celebrated for its journalistic and novelistic quality, was similarly received with mixed reviews. HarperPerennial published it as part of Wright's New York trilogy, together with *The Messenger* and *The Wig,* in 1999. Like his major characters, Wright has lived a life of meandering about from the United States to Mexico.

BIBLIOGRAPHY

Hogue, Lawrence. *The African American Male, Writing and Difference.* Albany: State University of New York, Press, 2003.

O'Brien, John, ed. "Charles Wright." In *Interviews with Black Writers,* 245–257. New York: Liveright, 1973.

Weixlmann, Joe. "Charles Stevenson Wright." In *Dictionary of Literary Biography,* Vol. 33: *Afro-American Fiction Writers after 1955,* edited by Thadious M. Davis and Trudier Harris, 288–293. Detroit: Gale Research Company, 1984.

———. "Charles Wright." In *The Oxford Companion to African American Literature,* edited by William L. Andrews, Frances Smith Foster, and Trudier Harris, 791–792. New York: Oxford University Press, 1997.

Wright, Charles. *Absolutely Nothing to Get Alarmed About.* In *Absolutely Nothing to Get Alarmed About: The Complete Novels of Charles Wright,* 255–387. New York: Harper Perennial, 1999.

———. *The Messenger.* In *Absolutely Nothing to Get Alarmed About: The Complete Novels of Charles Wright,* 1–131. New York: Harper Perennial, 1999.

———. *The Wig.* In *Absolutely Nothing to Get Alarmed About: The Complete Novels of Charles Wright,* 133–254. New York: Harper Perennial, 1999.

Wilfred D. Samuels

Wright, Jay   (1934–   )

Poet and dramatist Jay Wright was born in Albuquerque, New Mexico, to Leona Daily, a Virginian of African and Native American ancestry, and Mercer Murphy Wright (a.k.a. George Murphy), a native New Mexican of Irish, Cherokee, and African-American descent. Living mostly with foster parents in his younger years, Wright absorbed the Southwest's various cultures. As an adolescent, he moved with his birth father to San Pedro, California. While still in high school and for a short while after graduating in 1953, Wright played baseball in the minor leagues of Arizona, Texas, and California. While doing a stint in the U.S. Army (1954–57) and stationed in Germany, Wright traveled throughout Europe.

Wright earned a bachelor's degree in comparative literature, in 1961, from the University of California, Berkeley. Additionally, he won a Rockefeller Brothers Theological Fellowship, briefly attended New York's Union Theological Seminary, and, in 1962, began graduate study in comparative literature at Rutgers. He left graduate school in 1964 to teach medieval history and English in Guadalajara, Mexico, at the Butler Institute. Returning to

Rutgers, Wright lived in Harlem, where he developed acquaintances with BLACK ARTS MOVEMENT writers, including LeRoi Jones (AMIRI BARAKA). In 1966 Wright completed his Rutgers master's degree, writing a thesis on the 17th-century Spanish baroque poet and dramatist Pedro Calderón.

Wright became a nomadic poet-scholar. After another lengthy sojourn in Mexico, he moved to Scotland to serve at Dundee University as the fellow in creative writing (1971–73). Returning to the United States, he settled in New Hampshire and taught at Yale (1975–79), where his colleagues included the literary critic Harold Bloom, a champion of Wright's poetry. Wright has also taught or been writer-in-residence at Texas Southern University, Princeton, and Dartmouth.

Wright became a published author as early as 1964, when LANGSTON HUGHES included his poem "This Morning" in *New Negro Poets: USA*. In 1967 Wright published a poetry chapbook titled *Death as History*. His "The End of Ethnic Dream" and "The Frightened Lover's Sleep" appeared in the ideologically militant *BLACK FIRE: An Anthology of Afro-American Writing* (1968), edited by LeRoi Jones (Amiri Baraka) and LARRY NEAL. A prolific decade ensued for Wright, beginning in 1971 with the publication of *The Homecoming Singe,* his first novel, which was dedicated to black poet ROBERT HAYDEN and to Harold Bloom. *The Homecoming* was followed by *Soothsayers and Omens* (1976), *Explications and Interpretations* (published in 1984 but written in the 1970s), *Dimensions of History* (1976), and *The Double Invention of Komo* (1980). Wright's more recent publications are *Elaine's Book* (1988), *Boleros* (1991), and *Transfigurations: Collected Poems* (2000), which includes a compilation titled *Transformations* (1997). Wright's plays include *Balloons: A Comedy in One Act* (1968), *Love's Equations* (1983), and *The Delights of Memory, I: Lily* (1994).

Wright has several affinities with poet Robert Hayden. The Spanish language and Mexican culture inform both Hayden's and Wright's sensibility. As Hayden rejected what he took to be the Black Arts poets' artistically limiting and politically questionable nationalist aesthetic, so Wright

explores traditions of Africa, the Americas, and Europe to elaborate an African-American heritage that encompasses diverse historical antecedents and cultural references. But perhaps the crucial example Hayden set for Wright was Hayden's attempt in "Middle Passage" to imagine the path Africans journeyed through to become slaves, and so the history of the "New World," from a perspective outside Eurocentric and white supremacist frameworks. Wright redirects readers to think from such a perspective. Beyond referring to diverse cultures, Wright complexly bridges those cultures both to retrieve connections with Africa, especially West Africa's indigenous religions and rituals, and to create paths toward an unheard-of future.

Wright is avant-garde in his conceptually sophisticated yet intensely personal engagement with the Americas' cross-cultural past and global multicultural future. For example, in "The Anatomy of Resonance," from *Elaine's Book,* epigraphs from the German poets Friedrich Hölderlin and Paul Celan instigate a meditation that accesses Scottish, Christian, Aztec, Roman, and African mythologies to achieve a poetic sublimity intimating deliverance from the past's ethnocentric impasses. Confronting works such as "The Anatomy of Resonance," scholars realize that most existing critical paradigms are simply inadequate to Wright's poetry. Among scholars, perhaps Harold Bloom has given Wright the highest praise. For Bloom, Wright defines authentic multicultural authorship, displays the most accomplished skills as an African-American poet, is among the strongest American poets, and may yet emerge as an African-American Dante: an author of permanent importance to world literature.

Besides accolades from scholars, Wright has garnered literary honors and influenced other African-American poets, including NATHANIEL MACKEY and Cyrus Cassells. Wright's honors include a National Council of the Arts grant (1967), a Woodrow Wilson/National Endowment for the Arts Poets-in-Concert fellowship (1968), a Princeton Hodder fellowship (1970), an Ingram Merrill Foundation Award (1974), two Guggenheim Fellowships (1974 and 1975), a MacArthur Fellowship

(1986–91), a Fellow of the Academy of American Poets (1995), and a Lannan Literary Award for Poetry (2000).

BIBLIOGRAPHY

Bloom, Harold, ed. *Jay Wright*. Philadelphia: Chelsea House, 2004.

Manson, Michael Tomasek. "The Clarity of Being Strange: Jay Wright's *The Double Invention of Komo*." *Black American Literature Forum* 24, no. 3 (1990): 473–489.

Robert S. Oventile

Wright, Richard   (1908–1960)

A novelist, autobiographer, fiction writer, essayist, scriptwriter, dramatist, poet, and editor, Richard Wright was born in Natchez, Mississippi, in 1908. When Richard was six, his father abandoned the family, forcing his mother to work at low-paying jobs and often causing Richard and his brother, Leon, to go without food. When he was about eight and living in Elaine, Arkansas, where his mother had taken the family to live with her sister, they were forced to take flight in the middle of the night after learning that white men had killed his uncle because they had long envied his successful liquor business. Richard's family eventually returned to Mississippi, where, because of his mother's illness, they lived with his grandmother, forced to endure her religious fervor.

At age 15, Wright, who never completed his formal education because his family continually moved about, started reading widely, becoming influenced by such major writers as H. L. Mencken, Fyodor Dostoyevsky, Sinclair Lewis, Sherwood Anderson, and Theodore Dreiser. Convinced he could live a better life elsewhere, Wright left the South for Chicago in 1927, where, during the Great Depression, he worked at menial jobs and joined the Works Progress Administration's Federal Writers' Project and became an active member of the Communist Party, publishing fiction, articles, and poems in communist newspapers. However, coming to resent the narrow-mindedness of his fellow members, Wright resigned from the party in 1944.

In the interim Wright had published *Uncle Tom's Children* (1938), a collection of stories that addressed the racism and violence southern blacks were daily forced to endure. Dissatisfied with the general response to his work, which had won a prize offered by *Story* magazine, Wright decided to write a book that "would be so hard and deep that [readers] would have to face it without the consolation of tears." His next book was the much-acclaimed novel NATIVE SON (1940), which addresses the dire consequences of urban ghetto conditions in Chicago's South Side, where blacks lived oppressed lives much as they did in the rural South. Born, like Wright, in Mississippi, Bigger Thomas, the 20-year-old protagonist, lives in a one-bedroom, rat-infested apartment with his widowed mother, his sister Vera, and his brother Buddy. While working as a chauffeur for the Daltons, a wealthy white family, Bigger accidentally kills their daughter, Mary; driven by fear, he mutilates her body and stuffs it in the furnace. Although he tries to escape—and even to extort money from the Daltons—Bigger is caught, tried, and sentenced to die in the electric chair. Wright's protégé, JAMES BALDWIN, celebrated the novel as a forceful statement about "what it meant to be a Negro in America." However, Baldwin also dismissed Wright's characterization of Bigger as a mere stereotype, lacking lifelike representation with his strengths and weaknesses.

Wright next published his autobiography, BLACK BOY (1945), which centers on the experiences of a young black boy's quest for identity in the South, in a world governed by Jim Crow laws. Although Wright is interested in exposing and attacking white oppression, he is also interested in unveiling factors other than race in the daily lives of blacks that enslaved and oppressed them, particularly orthodox Christianity, such as the Seventh-Day Adventist faith his grandmother practiced, which, he was convinced, pacified black people into subjugation. He added to *Black Boy* a second autobiographical account of his years in Chicago, urban and modern America, and his experiences in the Communist Party, and published it under the title *American Hunger*. The racial intolerance in the South highlighted in *Black Boy* seems to reenact itself in different ways in the urban north and in the Communist Party as Wright presents it *American Hunger.*

After enjoying the success of *Native Son* and *Black Boy,* Wright moved with his second wife and daughter to Paris, France, in 1947, where the impact of French intellectuals, especially the existentialists Jean-Paul Sartre, Simone de Beauvoir, and Albert Camus, on his writing became evident in his novels *The Outsider* (1953), *Savage Holiday* (1954), and *The Long Dream* (1958). None of these novels matched the public acclaim his early works received, however.

Wright's *The Outsider* is one of the first existentialist novels written by an American author; it is also a "raceless" novel, for Wright is more concerned with the psychological behavior of his character, Cross Daemon, the embodiment of good and evil, than with race. Mistakenly reported killed in a train accident, Daemon assumes a new identity, joins the Communist Party, and kills in an attempt to navigate the meaning of life and of his individual identity. Similarly, *Savage Holiday* is a psychological thriller about a white retired insurance salesman, Erskine Fowler, who gradually becomes a criminal. When Fowler's neighbor's son sees him standing fully naked outside his apartment, after he has accidentally locked himself out, the youth, shocked, falls from the balcony to his death. When Mabel, the boy's mother, discovers who was responsible for her son's death, Fowler is forced to kill her. In *Savage Holiday,* Fowler represents the modern alienated man.

In *The Long Dream* Wright probes the psychological development of Fishbelly, a black southern youth who is forced into maturity by confronting his father's immoral business tactics and the racial power dynamics in the South. Fishbelly's father, a materialist whose wealth comes from his prostitution business, teaches his son that a rich black person is equal to whites. When the police chief arranges his father's murder, Fishbelly discovers that his father's dictum is a myth. When his girlfriend is killed in a fire and he is jailed falsely for raping a white woman, Fishbelly comes to grips with the reality of his true destiny, which seems to be in the hands of the police chief. After serving a two-year sentence for the alleged rape, Fishbelly leaves the

United States for France, where he hopes to start a new life. None of these expatriate novels received much favorable critique. Scholars argued that by becoming an expatriate Wright had washed his hands of the African-American experience in the United States. This view has been challenged and is generally no longer accepted.

Wright's collection of short stories, *Eight Men* (1961), was published posthumously. One of the stories, "The Man Who Lived Underground" was based on Dostoyevsky's *Notes from the Underground.* Rejected by publishers in the late 1930s but posthumously published in 1963, his novel *Lawd Today* did not receive positive public response until recently. In a racist urban environment, Jake Jackson and his three friends from the post office sink lower and lower into lust, a life of sexual obsession with white women. Another posthumously published work, a novella titled *Rite of Passage* (1994), which Wright completed in 1945 and later tried to include in *Eight Men* just before his death, unmasks whiteness as a mark of ideology and racial privilege. The story centers on the main character's rite of passage as he moves from being a prospective student to becoming a criminal. The 15-year-old black male protagonist, Johnny Gibbs, is a hardworking student, but his whole life is shattered when he learns that he is a foster child and city authorities demand that he move to live with another family. Unable to deal with the identity crisis, Johnny seeks solace in gang membership.

In addition to fiction, Wright wrote hundreds of haiku poems, which were published posthumously, in 2000. He seemed to turn to a deeper vision of life in haiku while ignoring the Western versions of haiku such as Ezra Pound had written.

Wright published nonfiction works as well, including *12 Million Black Voices: A Folk History of the Negro in the United States* (1941), a textual and photographic documentary about the racial discrimination in the rural South and in the urban North following the Great Migration. He also wrote travelogues, *Black Power* (1954), *The Color Curtain* (1956), *Pagan Spain* (1957), and *White Man, Listen!* (1957). *Black Power* details Kwame Nkrumah's anticolonial strategies in establishing the Gold Coast as an independent Ghana in 1953.

The Color Curtain records the Bandung Conference in Indonesia that united the leaders of decolonized nations. *Pagan Spain* explains how the fascist leadership of Franco oppressed religious groups (non-Catholics) and gender identities (women). Within the context of these travel narratives, *White Man, Listen!* emerges as a text shaped by Wright's attempt to dismantle the imperial discourse, writing the history of blacks inside the West, as he maps the territory of what constitutes a Western intellectual.

All in all, Wright's works stand out as a forceful statement on the ideology and racial violence of 20th-century America. In a racist world, Wright's works demand attention. His attacks are directed at white oppression while deconstructing the ideology of whiteness that assumes that racist oppression has produced minimal effects on the black mind. A prolific writer and intellectual, Wright died in Paris on November 28, 1960.

BIBLIOGRAPHY

Baldwin, James. *Notes of a Native Son.* 1955. New York: Bantam Books, 1979.

Fabre, Michel. *The Unfinished Quest of Richard Wright.* 1973. Translated by Isabel Barzun. Urbana: University of Illinois Press, 1993.

Joyce, Joyce Ann. *Richard Wright's Art of Tragedy.* Iowa City: University of Iowa Press, 1986.

Hakutani, Yoshinobu, ed. *Critical Essays on Richard Wright.* Boston: G. K. Hall, 1982.

Smith, Virginia Whatley, ed. *Richard Wright's Travel Writings: New Reflections.* Jackson: University Press of Mississippi, 2001.

E. Lâle Demirtürk

Wright, Sarah Elizabeth   (1928–   )

Novelist, poet, essayist, and activist, Sarah Elizabeth Wright was born December 9, 1928, in Wetipquin, part of the Eastern Shore of Maryland, to Willis Charles and Mary Amelia Moore Wright. As the third of nine children, Sarah witnessed her parents' effort to make a living in the uncompromising environment of Maryland's Eastern Shore. Willis Wright, a man of diverse talents, was an oysterman, farmer, pianist, and organist, and Mary Wright helped support the family by doing farm and factory work and serving as a barber. According to Guilford, Wright showed writing talent as a child. Her grade school teachers encouraged her, and the support resulted in Wright's attending Howard University from 1945 to 1949. While at Howard, she received support and guidance from STERLING BROWN and OWEN DODSON and began an acquaintance with LANGSTON HUGHES, who continued to be interested in her writing until the year before his death.

Still searching for an identity, Wright moved to the Philadelphia area and attended Cheyney State Teacher's College (now Cheyney State College) and the University of Pennsylvania. While in Philadelphia, Wright taught school, did bookkeeping, and became an office manager for a printing and publishing firm owned by the Krafts. She also helped found the Philadelphia Writer's Workshop, where she met poet Lucy Smith. With the help of Kraft Publishing, Wright and Smith published a collection of their poems, *Give Me a Child* (1955). In 1959 Wright's move to New York proved to be a vital step in her life. In addition to marrying Joseph Kaye, a man who supported her writing efforts, Wright joined the Harlem Writers Guild, a group guided by her mentor and friend, JOHN OLIVER KILLENS. Wright helped organize the first and second national conferences of black writers in 1959 and 1965; she was among other guild writers, such as PAULE MARSHALL and OSSIE DAVIS, who offered mutual support.

This cultural and artistic stimulation and the creative writing workshops helped Wright create *This Child's Gonna Live* (1969), the novel that has garnered her national attention. She has continued to write for varied audiences, including the biography for children *A. Phillip Randolph, Integration in the Workplace* (1990) and the introduction to *Missing in Action and Presumed Dead* (1992), a collection by African poet Rashidah Ismaili. Wright has also contributed her poetry to such volumes as *Poetry of the Negro, 1746–1970* (1970), edited by Langston Hughes and ARNA BONTEMPS, and *The Poetry of Black America* (1973), edited by Arnold Adoff.

In a published speech called "The Responsibility of the Writer as Participant in the World Community," Wright confirms the central ideas that drive her views as a writer and activist: The writer must be true to herself; this self-grounding will reflect the writer's determination to present the black experience realistically in all of its beauty and suffering. Thematically, Wright's work has reflected this pursuit of truth: The oppression of the black working class mirrors world poverty but does not prevent the emergence of a spirituality and courage that helps blacks transcend adversity and work toward unity, and black women, as writers and fictional characters, have borne the burden of racism just as black men, but black women have also struggled against the oppression of black men and have refused to be silenced.

Wright's coedited volume *Give Me a Child* reflects her interest in speaking for the voiceless and celebrating courage, as she does in A. Phillip Randolph's biography. In the poem based on a actual incident, "To Some Millions Who Survive Joseph Mander, Sr.," Guilford explains that Mander, a black man, drowned (in Philadelphia) while trying to save the life of a white youth. Wright universalizes Mander's experience and pleads that her readers remember the irony of his sacrifice for a white youth who later might join others in denying life to blacks like Mander.

The details of *This Child's Gonna Live* are startlingly real, resembling an earlier black novel, *These Low Grounds* (1937) by Waters Turpin, about black oyster pickers on Maryland's Eastern Shore. Wright immerses the reader in the grinding poverty, racism, sexism, and intraracial strife of the lives of blacks on Maryland's oyster-bearing Eastern Shore during the late 1920s. The driving force in the novel is Mariah Upshur, wife of Jacob and mother to three boys. Mariah's central motivation is to leave Tangierneck ("the Neck," in local dialect) with her children and save the life of her unborn child who, like her previous child, might not survive without sufficient food and clothing. Mariah and her family subsist on potatoes, molasses sandwiches (for the children's lunches), an occasional slab of fatback, and chicken (in rare instances for company). The time of the novel is significant because Wright implies a connection between the decline in the availability of oysters for blacks to pick and the 1929 stock market crash. The reader, then, is encouraged to compare the half-starved, scantily clad, worm-infested Tangierneck blacks who somehow manage to survive with some of the more privileged urban whites who commit suicide because of their lost fortunes.

The racial oppression of the Upshur family and other blacks is due to lost fertile land, a valuable source for farming when there are no oysters to bring in income. Wright combines the Neck's interracial history and violence with white greed, despite racially mixed bloodlines. At least two generations of Upshurs owned land before hard times fell on Jacob's father, Percy Upshur. To relieve himself of debt, Percy borrowed money from Bannie Dudley, a white neighbor, who eventually took the land when Percy could not pay her. Blacks who pay higher rents to live on the Upshurs' less fertile ground are bitter and resentful toward Bannie, who is supported by other whites, and Percy, who is powerless to retrieve the land, although he and Bannie have a son and share one white ancestor. Against this backdrop of communal strife, Wright implies that it is Mariah's spirituality—even with its many shortcomings—that encourages Jacob to keep the family together.

Wright, like Mariah, continues to work by sharing her creative talents; now in her 70s, she is a licensed poetry therapist and teaches creative writing.

BIBLIOGRAPHY

Campbell, Jennifer. "'It's a Time in the Land': Gendering Black Power and Sarah E. Wright's Place in the Tradition of Black Women's Writing." *African American Review* 31 (Summer 1997): 211–223.

Guilford, Virginia. "Sarah Elizabeth Wright." *Dictionary of Literary Biography*. Vol. 33, 293–300. Detroit: Gale, 1984.

Wright, Sarah. "The Responsibility of the Writer as Participant in the World Community." *Zora Neale Hurston Forum* 3, no. 1 (Fall 1988): 34–39.

Australia Tarver

Yerby, Frank Gavin   (1916–1991)

One of the most prolific African-American writers, Frank Yerby is also the first African American to become a millionaire writing fiction, selling more than 50 million hardback and paperback copies of his novels. During his 45-year career as a novelist, Yerby published 33 novels, almost one a year beginning in 1946; his novels, many of them best sellers, were translated into 14 languages. Three of his novels, *The FOXES OF HARROW, The Golden Hawk,* and *The Saracen Blade,* were also made into successful movies.

Frank Yerby, the son of Rufus Garvin and Wilhemina (Smythe) Yerby, was born into an influential black family in Augusta, Georgia, on September 5, 1916. The Yerbys lived in a two-story house on the corner of Eight and Hall Streets, just outside "The Terry," a large predominantly black residential area. Since Yerby's father worked as a hotel doorman in such cities as Miami and Detroit, he periodically traveled to and from Augusta; consequently, Yerby and his siblings were raised by their mother and aunts, all of whom were teachers. As a young boy, Yerby developed strong propensities for reading and tinkering with mechanical and electronic devices, and frequently he fabricated stories, which he told his aunts. On one occasion, when his Aunt Emily reprimanded him for inventing stories, his aunt Fannie remarked prophetically, "Oh, let him alone. He might be a writer some day" (Richardson Personal Interview).

The Yerby children attended Haines Institute, then a private black institution in Augusta consisting of both elementary and high school grades. Yerby, however, was the only one in his family to attend Paine College, a black undergraduate institution in Augusta, where he majored in English and was active in college organizations. Although he had shown promise as early as high school and had been encouraged by his teachers, Yerby's interest in writing blossomed in college, and he also received significant encouragement from a well-known black writer. "The late James Weldon Johnson," Yerby said later, "approved some verses of mine shown to him by my sister, then a student at Fisk University" (Rothe, 672). While an undergraduate at Paine College, Yerby wrote short stories, poetry, and editorials for the school paper, *The Paineite,* and published in such "little magazines" as *Challenge, Shard,* and *Arts Quarterly.* After graduating from Paine, he attended Fisk University, where he continued to write stories and poetry, some of which he published in *The Fisk Herald* and *New Anvil.* He received his master's degree in 1938 and enrolled the same year in the University of Chicago to pursue a doctorate degree.

While in Chicago, Yerby worked with the Federal Writers' Project of the Works Progress Administration (WPA), where he met other writers who would make their mark in American literature. The Chicago WPA Group included ARNA BONTEMPS, Saul Bellow, WILLARD MOTLEY, RICHARD

WRIGHT, MARGARET WALKER, Nelson Algren, and Katherine Dunham, among others. Though he was only with the Chicago WPA for nine months, Yerby concluded that his WPA apprenticeship was some of the best training he had received. Financial problems, however, forced him to discontinue his education and seek a teaching position, and his departure from Chicago took him back to the South, where he worked from 1939 to 1941, one year as an English instructor at Florida A&M University and another year at Southern University in Baton Rouge. While teaching at Southern University, Yerby also married Flora Claire Williams of Alabama, whom he had met the previous year. Since his marriage necessitated additional income, he left his teaching position and moved to New York; however, he was unable to find work in New York and moved a year later to Detroit, where he began work as a laboratory technician with the Ford Motor Company in Dearborn, Michigan, where he also renewed his lagging interest in writing.

Like most of his contemporaries, Yerby began his career writing protest stories. During the years he worked at the Ford Motor Company, he wrote the short stories he published and a protest novel he submitted to a *Redbook Magazine* literary contest. *Redbook* rejected Yerby's novel, but not without encouragement. "This is a lousy novel," wrote Muriel Fuller, "but you sure can write. Send me something else." The "something else" Yerby sent was "Health Card," which Fuller, deciding that it was not *Redbook's* kind of material, sent to *Harper's Magazine,* where it was published in 1944. Subsequently, Yerby published three short stories: "White Magnolias," "Homecoming," and "My Brother Went to College." After George Joel of Dial Press expressed only a slight interest in Yerby's protest novel, however, Yerby concluded that protest fiction had little priority with publishers and switched to popular fiction. He convinced Joel to let him attempt a fast-paced historical novel, and on the strength of the first 27 pages, he received a $250 advance. This was his first novel, *The Foxes of Harrow* (1946).

The Foxes of Harrow catapulted Yerby into national prominence as a writer, establishing his commercially successful popular fiction formula and initiating the meteoric rise and decline of his critical reception in America. Set in the antebellum South between 1825 and 1865, *The Foxes of Harrow* is a historical romance that chronicles the adventures of Stephen Fox, an Irish immigrant outcast who successfully rises from poverty to wealth in New Orleans society by less-than-admirable means. A throwback to the picaresque tradition, *The Foxes of Harrow* reveals Yerby's skillful adaptation and manipulation of the genre to create a vehicle for him both to write entertaining fiction and debunk Southern myths. Yerby's second novel, *The Vixens,* continues the pattern established in the first novel, and in such subsequent novels as *The Golden Hawk* (1948), *Pride's Castle* (1949), and *Floodtide* (1950), critics noted his success in manipulating the conventions of popular fiction. In 1951, he published *A Woman Called Fancy,* a novel most significant for his declaration of his inability to endure the racism of America. His expatriation therefore should not have come as a surprise when, in 1952, Yerby departed America for France without fanfare.

Though Yerby continued to churn out historical romances one after another, the critical attention paid to his fiction declined significantly during the late 1950s and early 1960s, and his concern about his critical reception prompted him to try his hand again at writing about contemporary issues. Therefore, in 1963, Yerby wrote *The Tents of Shem,* a civil rights novel about a black couple integrating an all-white neighborhood. Fearing that Yerby's protest novel would have neither the popular nor the financial appeal of his previous novels, his publishers advised against its publication. Yerby's new willingness to demonstrate his race consciousness, however, influenced his writing of two of his most important novels, *Speak Now* (1969) and *The Dahomean* (1971). Critics were quick to point out that *Speak Now,* Yerby's first treatment of an African-American protagonist, deserted the historical romance genre, but his next novel attracted significant critical acclaim. Probably his best novel, *The Dahomean* is a painstaking re-creation of 19th-century Dahomean culture in Africa and the story of Hwesu, an African prince who comes of age and is captured into slavery at the end of the novel. The sequel to *The Dahomean, A Darkness at Ingraham's Crest* (1979), which chronicles Hwesu's adventures in America, is a powerful indictment of American slavery. In the sequel, however, Yerby returned to the historical romance and his favorite subject, the American South; he continued to debunk the myths of the South until his death on November 29, 1991.

There is little doubt that Frank Yerby effected a compromise, however large or small, in becoming a popular fiction writer in America, but this compromise was obviously one he was willing to make. His continued success in popular fiction depended on his adhering to the fictional persona and formula he first established in *The Foxes of Harrow*. While Yerby's auspicious and unprecedented invasion of American popular fiction significantly expanded the literary canvas for African Americans, it simultaneously raised questions about Yerby's racial consciousness and commitment. Yerby, however, chose to maintain his artistic detachment, opting instead to write antiromantic novels that debunked the myths, legends, and historical inaccuracies of the past.

BIBLIOGRAPHY

Fuller, Muriel. Letter to James Hill, January 28, 1974.

Graham, Maryemma. "Frank Yerby, King of the Costume Novel." *Essence,* October 1975, pp. 70–71, 88–92.

Hill, James L. "Between Philosophy and Race: Images of Blacks in the Fiction of Frank Yerby." *Umoja* (1981): 5–16.

———. "An Interview with Frank Yerby." *Resources for American Literary Study* (Fall 1995): 206–239.

Richardson, Josephine. Personal interview. Augusta, Ga. January 23, 1974.

Rothe, Anne, ed. "Frank Yerby." In *Current Biography,* 672–674. New York: Wilson Company, 1947.

Turner, Darwin T. "Frank Yerby as Debunker." *Massachusetts Review* 20 (Summer 1968): 569–577.

Yerby, Frank. "How and Why I Write the Costume Novel." *Harper's,* October 1959, p. 146.

James L. Hill

Young, Al (1939–)

A musician, teacher, screenwriter, novelist, and poet, Al Young was born in Ocean Springs, Mississippi, near Biloxi, the son of Albert James and Mary Campbell Young. In his own words, he "spent childhood shuttling between southern & northern U.S. Started writing westerns, detectives & science fiction in notebooks around the age of 10. Began a 2-finger type in the 6th grade & turned out my own hectographed coming weekly mag *The Krazy Krazette* in jr. high" (quoted in Miller, 137). While living in Detroit from 1957 to 1960, Young attended the University of Michigan on a trial basis, but after earning a living playing his guitar and singing in local coffeehouses, he left to explore the "sad world," ebullient with war and civil strife. Before settling on the West Coast, Young was the coeditor of a small magazine named *Generations* and the founder of *Loveletter;* in northern California he became a co–founding editor with ISHMAEL REED of *Yardbird Reader* and attended Stanford University as a fellow in creative writing before receiving a bachelor of art degree in Spanish in 1969 from the University of California at Berkeley.

His collections of poetry include *Dancing* (1969), *The Song Turning Back into Itself* (1971), *Earth Air Fire and Water* (1971), *Geography of the Near Past* (1976), *The Blues Don't Change New and Selected Poems* (1982), *Heaven: Collected Poems* (1988), and *Straight No Chaser* (1994). Young's novels include *Snakes* (1970), *Sitting Pretty* (1976), *Who Is Angelina?* (1975), *Ask Me Now* (1980), and *Seduction by Light* (1988). His screenwriting credits include *Sparkle* (1976) and *Bustin' Loose* (1981). Young is equally well known for his memoirs of black musicians: *Bodies and Soul* (1981), *Kinds of Blue* (1984), *Things Ain't What They Used to Be* (1987), and *Mingus/Mingus: Two Memoirs* (1989), written with Janet Coleman.

To enter Young's world of poetry is to enter a world of music, dance, feelings, transcendence, and self-discovery, a declaration of the existential. These are venues for change, personal and communal. Many of these themes are central to "Dancing All Alone," rich with intertextual references and allusion to writer from Shakespeare and Machiavelli to T. S. Eliot.

> We move thru rooms & down the middle of
> freeways,
> myself & I.
> I am neither prince nor citizen
> but I do know what is noble in me
> & what is usefully vulgar.
> It is from this point that the real radiates.
> (Heaven, 39)

Dance and music dominate "The Song Turning Back into Itself": "This music is real / Feel the rhythm" (*Heaven,* 73).

Young's interest in "essence" and that which is noble rather than solely in racial consciousness and the construction of a black nation place him on the opposite end of the spectrum from many of his contemporaries who were engaged in the BLACK ARTS MOVEMENT led by AMIRI BARAKA and HAKI MADHUBUTI, who called for a more politically liberating and functional art. Young rejects this perspective outright in "A Dance for Militant Dilettantes," in which he ridicules the advice of a more revolutionary black writer for whom Western aesthetics has little or no value: "these honkies man that put out / these books & things / . . . they want them a militant nigger" (*Heaven,* 13).

The ultimate quest for spiritual wholeness centers Young's life and work. Resonant with Whitman in "Song of Myself," Young's speaker in "When I am Real" declares, "Love of life is love of God / sustaining all life" (*Heaven,* 23–24). The poet, Young has said, "is something of a magician or shaman" (O'Brien, 264). His poetry shows him trying to live up to this description.

Young uses his novel *Snakes* (1970), a bildungsroman, to explore the central place of music—BLUES, jazz, gospel, pop—in African-American life and culture. Yet, as critics have pointed out, in his first novel Young wanted to celebrate black culture rather than make his work solely a novel about life in the black ghetto. In fact, several publishers, thinking the novel was not black enough, rejected *Snakes.* Young describes his novel as a text that explores "what happens to [the central characters] under the influence of . . . localized success" (O'Brien, 267). *Snakes* is about the friendship among four teenagers and specifically about MC's quest for success through his band. MC, Jimmy, Shakes, and Billy achieve success, but it is ephemeral. In the end the band breaks up, and the members take different paths to their future lives. But *Snakes* is also about the love MC shares with his grandmother and about the richness of black language, whose complexity Young celebrates through his characters', particularly Shakes's (short for Shakespeare), use of black urban language. William J. Harris notes that "Al Young has captured much of the beauty and complexity of black life and black speech in his impressive and extensive oeuvre" (306).

Young's talents were recognized and rewarded early in his career. He has received a Guggenheim Fellowship, a Wallace Stegner Writing Fellowship, a Fulbright National Endowment for the Arts Fellowship, the PEN-Library of Congress Award for Short Fiction, the PEN-USA Award for Non-Fiction, two American Book Awards, the Pushcart Prize, and two New York Times Notable Book of the Year citations. From 1969 to 1976 Young was the Edward B. Jones Lecturer in Creative Writing at Stanford University. He continues to teach as a distinguished writer and guest lecturer at major universities across the country.

BIBLIOGRAPHY

Harris, William. "Al Young." In *Dictionary of Literary Biography.* Vol. 33: *Afro-American Fiction Writers after 1955,* edited by Trudier Harris and Thadious M. Davis, 300–306. Detroit: Gale Research Company. 1984.

Miller, Adam David, ed. *Dices or Black Bones: Black Voices of the Seventies.* Boston: Houghton Mifflin, 1970.

O'Brien, John, ed. "Al Young." *Interviews with Black Writers.* New York: Liveright, 1973.

Young, Al. *Heaven: Collected Poems 1956–1990.* Berkeley: Creative Arts Books Company, 1992.

Wilfred D. Samuels

Young, Kevin   (1970–   )

Kevin Young made an impressive entrance onto the African-American literary stage near the end of the 20th century. His first collection of poems, *Most Way Home,* won The National Poetry Series and the Zacharis First Book Prize from *Ploughshares.* Young, whose family hails from Louisiana, prefers not to claim or identify a specific birthplace. His poems suggest he is the product of a more universal mother, Mother Earth, who gives birth in a more inclusive American/global village—one that is simultaneously Quivira, Beanville, or East Jesus, places Young remaps, revisits, and rediscovers in his poems without, as TONI MORRISON writes in *Playing in the Dark,* "a mandate for conquest" (3).

In "Quivira City Limits," "somewhere outside Topeka," for example, Young's speaker has an epiphany that, like William Carlos Williams's speakers in "The Red Wheelbarrow" and "Spring and All," provides insight into and comments on modernity: "it suddenly all matters again, / those tractors blooming rust / in the fields only need a good coat / of paint. Red." However, Young's speaker moves beyond awe and admiration to critique 15th-century Spanish and 19th-century explorers, conquistadors, and colonialists—the empire-building behavior and greed of appropriators and settlers that resulted not only in the creation of a modern "New World" but also in the alienation of the worker from the land and, even more lamentable, the destruction of Native American Indian cultures, specifically that of the Quivaran Indians of Kansas, whose culture remains now only in museums. Desecrated soil and now-silent wheat fields where once buffalo thunderously roamed against majestic landscape have given way to tractors that bloom "rust / in the fields":

> when will all this ever be enough
> this wide open they call discovery,
> disappointed, this place my
> thousand bones carry, now call home.

In the end, Young's speaker's racial identity or ethnicity is intentionally blurred, even unimportant. He speaks as an American, a resident and citizen of "this place," as the progeny of all that preceded him: "my thousand bones . . . call home." Despite the history of devastation, exploitation, and appropriation, the speaker seems to say, he must embrace this American place, his legacy.

In "East Jesus" Young's speaker, much like Sinclair Lewis in *Main Street,* is concerned with locality, with Littletown, U.S.A., and specifically with the myth of the innocence, Christian conservatism, and provincialism that ostensibly dominates places located between "Boonies & Sticks," in the middle of nowhere, in East Jesus, U.S.A. Young's speaker becomes landscaper and cartographer, providing longitudes and latitudes of generic East Jesus, where "the water tower is about half- / empty, the only bar (next county / over) LA TAVERN & TACKLE SHOP / stay full." Despite the residents' visible subscription to religious and moral principles, evidenced by their weekly church attendance and posted sermon titles—"AVOID /SINS TRAGEDY LEARN SATANS / STRATEGY"—during the services parishioners "sit & pray & can't / . . . / hardly wait to make love or have that drink, hungering through / the sermons & shouts."

Like MELVIN B. TOLSON, AL YOUNG, RITA DOVE, and CARL PHILLIPS, Kevin Young speaks as an American with an American voice, within an American context, rather than solely as an African-American poet. This is not to say that he does not value and find complexity and meaning in African-American culture, as is clearly borne out by his second collection of poems, *To Repel Ghosts* (2002), which, based on the work of artist Jean-Michel-Basquiat, was a finalist for the James McLaughlin Prize from the Academy of American Poets. Young seems to call for a reenvisioning of the African-American literary landscape at the dawn of the 21st century, revisiting and revising LeRoi Jones/AMIRI BARAKA's *Home* in the title of his first collection. Young is a former Stegner Fellow in Poetry at Stanford; he is currently Ruth Lilly Professor of Poetry at Indiana University.

BIBLIOGRAPHY

Gabbin, Joanne V., ed. *Furious Flower: African American Poetry from the Black Arts Movement to the*

Present. Charlottesville: University of Virginia Press, 2004.

Morrison, Toni. *Playing in the Dark: Whiteness and the Literary Imagination.* Cambridge, Mass.: Harvard University Press, 1992.

Young, Kevin. *Most Way Home.* New York: William Morrow, 1995.

Wilfred D. Samuels

Youngblood, Shay (1959–)

A Columbus, Georgia, native, Youngblood received a bachelor's degree in mass communications from Clark-Atlanta University in 1981 and a master's degree in creative writing from Brown University in 1993. Youngblood has written poetry, plays, and fiction. Sidney Poitier selected her play *Shakin' the Mess Outta Misery* to become a screenplay for Columbia Pictures. Before making her living as a writer, she served as an agricultural informational officer for the Peace Corps in Dominica in the eastern Caribbean. She then worked as a freelance writer in Atlanta, New York, and Paris, France. She has taught creative writing at the Syracuse Community Writer's Project and playwriting at the Rhode Island Adult Correctional Institution for Women. She has also taught for Brown University and the New School for Social Research.

She is a member of the Dramatists' and Authors' Guild, the National Writers' Union, and the Writers' Guild of America. She has won the Hollywood NATIONAL ASSOCIATION FOR THE ADVANCEMENT OF COLORED PEOPLE Theatre Awards for best playwright, 1991, for *Talking Bones;* the Kennedy Center's Lorraine Hansberry Playwrighting Award, 1993, for *Square Blues;* and the National Theatre Award from the Paul Green Foundation, 1995. She was the Edward Albee Honoree at the 21st Century Playwrights Festival, 1993.

Youngblood's plays *Shakin' the Mess Outta Misery, The Big Mama Stories* (1992), and *Soul Kiss* (1998) demonstrate her fascination with coming-of-age stories. Youngblood's female protagonists must all find their places in the world and must come to understand their impact on their communities. While the first two texts use a more conventional bildungsroman format, in which the protagonist must learn lessons from the elders and be part of a traditional rite of passage, *Soul Kiss* is a story that shows what occurs when the protagonist ignores the elders and tradition. In *Shakin'* and *The Big Mama Stories,* Youngblood's characters Daughter and Narrator both lose their mothers but are adopted by grandmother and aunt figures. These elders share stories that appear as legend or myth to these young daughters and act as griots who teach oral narratives from in the past. These elders also use a ritual marking the beginning of womanhood or the onset of menstruation to enable the daughters to transition into adulthood while accompanied by others who have already "been to the river."

In *Soul Kiss,* Mariah, the protagonist, rebukes the advice of her elders and decides to find her transition into adulthood without the aid of family. Mariah goes in search of her missing father only to become involved in an inappropriate relationship with him because she has ignored advice of her aunts and he still fantasizes about Mariah's missing mother, whom she closely resembles.

Youngblood's works have been met with mixed reviews. Her writing style has been praised, but her character development has been found lacking by some critics.

BIBLIOGRAPHY

Matuz, Roger, ed. *Contemporary Southern Writers.* Detroit: St. James Press, 1999.

Peterson, Jane T., and Suzanne Bennett. *Women Playwrights of Diversity: A Bio-Bibliographical Sourcebook.* Westport, Conn.: Greenwood Press, 1997.

Weaver, Angela E. "Shay Youngblood." Women of Color, Women of Words. Rutgers University. Available online. URL: http://www.scils.rutgers.edu/~cybers/youngblood2.html. Accessed October 27, 2006.

Creative Loafing (1995). Available online. URL: http://bibliothekibhak_Gluden2.ac.atyoungblood.asp. Accessed January 8, 2007.

Daintee Glover Jones

Z

Zami: A New Spelling of My Name: A Biomythography   Audre Lorde (1982)

AUDRE LORDE's *Zami: A New Spelling of My Name* opens with the beautifully articulated question of spiritual and intellectual indebtedness: "To whom do I owe the power behind my voice, what strength I have become, yeasting up like sudden blood from under the bruised skin's blister?" (3). The entire text of this astonishing, genre-breaking biomythography devotes itself to revealing that indebtedness, informing the reader that "it is the images of women, kind and cruel, that lead me home." And home, for Lorde, is a self-invented yet entirely real country, Zami: "my journey to this house of myself" (46), "a Carriacou name for women who work together as friends and lovers."

Part autobiography, and part revisionist myth-making, *Zami* tells the story of "coming out blackened and whole," of Lorde's fully claiming the fierce beauty of black lesbian identity, of becoming a woman-loving woman, a poet, a creator of self-authored words and perceptions. Part memory, part dream, a collage of collective and personal myth—an interweaving of all of these—the text disrupts chronology, moves from feeling state to feeling state in a poetic voice in which Lorde's spiritual and erotic encounters are powerfully her own but participate also in a collective female, feminist, lesbian mythology. As M. Charlene Ball suggests, in naming *Zami* a biomythography, Lorde is "deliberately creating myth from her own life. . . . Myth can essentialize: it can appear to belong to a timeless realm that lies beyond history . . . [but] revisionist myth such as Audre Lorde's, . . . does the opposite; it challenges and displaces existing myth" (253). Ball describes the revisionist myth-making of Lorde and others by noting that "far from existing in a timeless world that makes palatable the oppressions of this world," such myth-making "transforms this world, their readers, and themselves" (Ball, 63–64). Thus the young Lorde finds who she needs in the goddess Seboulisa and lives several lifetimes in order to meet and claim her as the mirror of her mother: "I grew Black as my need for life, for affirmation, for love, for sharing—copying from my mother what was in her, unfulfilled. I grew Black as Seboulisa, who I was to find in the cool mud halls of Abomey several lifetimes later-and as alone" (58).

In the uncanny way that factual detail can often be more compelling than fiction, readers are introduced to the very young, legally blind Lorde as she discovers how to see by touch, by taste, by feel, by listening to the world around her, and most of all by smell—the pages are redolent with "cinnamon, nutmeg, mace . . . guava jelly, sweet-smelling tonka bean . . . pressed chocolate . . . wild bay laurel leaves" (14). Her newly acquired eyeglasses—received at age three—enable Lorde to trace the now-distinguishable letters of words with her fingers, leading to a determination there and then that she will learn to read. In spelling out her own artistic creation myth, Lorde begins with the women in her own family, her mother, and her sister Helen, whose stories—"filled with tough little girls who masqueraded in boys' clothing and always foiled the criminals, managing to save the day" (46)—inspire Lorde not only to believe that she can be a storyteller too but also to realize the power of language to enable conceptualization and to incite action—a thread that runs through the whole of Lorde's work, later articulated in the essay "The Transformation of Silence into Language and Action."

The chapter "How I Became a Poet" begins with two powerful observations: first, that Audre did not speak at all until she was four years of age, and second, that her feared and much-loved antagonist—her mother, Linda—was also a profound source of Lorde's language and vision: "out of my mother's mouth a world of comment came cascading when she felt at ease or in her element, full of picaresque constructions and surreal scenes. . . . I am a reflection of my mother's secret poetry as well as of her hidden angers" (32). Her mother's attempts to shield Audre from racism in Harlem and beyond—strangers' spittle, teachers' dunce caps, white children's predictable betrayals—often manifested itself in painful bursts of abrasive tough love, but juxtaposed to these memories are those of the eros of mother-daughter intimacy, an eros that has rarely been explored with as much beauty or unhesitating honesty as in *Zami.*

Her childhood memories, complex and erotically charged, give way to subsequent memories of lying between a lover's legs or the association of the sweet smell of mace and nutmeg with a lover's breath or skin. The memory of pounding garlic while menstruating, the "delicate breadfruit smell rising up from the front of my print blouse that was my own womansmell, warm, shameful, but secretly utterly delicious" gives way to the most taboo of fantasies: "years afterward when I was grown, whenever I thought about the way I smelled that day, I would have a fantasy of my mother, her hands wiped dry from the washing,

and her apron untied and laid neatly away, looking down upon me lying on the couch, and then slowly, thoroughly, our touching and caressing each other's most secret places."

Much of this biomythography is devoted to Lorde's recounting of the stories of her evolving lesbian identity, of the women who become her lovers, and most of all, of the woman she becomes—not surprising for a book whose dedication page is inscribed, "In the recognition of loving lies an answer to despair." In *Zami,* as well as in "Uses of the Erotic: The Erotic as Power" and indeed, all of Lorde's work, the erotic functions as the capacity for joy, "as the personification of love in all its aspects—born of Chaos, and personifying creative power and harmony" (*Sister Outsider,* 55). Refusing the split between personal and political, refusing romance, the stories of Lorde's relationships, like her love poems, insist on the primacy of self-empowering.

Ginger, the first woman Lorde makes love to, she describes as "gorgeously fat," with "skin the color of well-buttered caramel, and a body like the Venus of Willendorf" (136). Embracing Ginger's beauty, she sees her own. Eudora, too, introduces Lorde to a homecoming within herself, "the way to the Mexico I had come looking for, that nourishing land of light and color where I was somewhere at home" (170). The 19-year-old Audre bravely tells Eudora ("the most fascinating woman I had ever met"—and some 30 years her senior), "I want to sleep with you," and each of them is transformed. Audre's self-imposed notion of butch propriety drops like a kimono shyly removed: "When I told Eudora I didn't like to be made love to, she raised her eyebrows. 'How do you know?' she said, her eyes wrinkling at the corners, intense, desiring" (169). Eudora's fear that her body is no longer beautiful, in the aftermath of the pale keloids of radiation burns scarring her chest, is answered by Audre's unequivocal desire, her eyes speaking tenderness, her lips' urgent whisper that their lovemaking should take place "in the light." (To readers familiar with Lorde's own long struggle with breast cancer, written about so eloquently in *The Cancer Journals* and *A Burst of Light,* this passage is especially poignant, as is the section in which Lorde describes her early job at Keystone Electronics, scanning crystals with unshielded X-ray machines, chewing the crystals in her mouth to dispose of them without having to scan them in an attempt to obtain bonuses to overcome the poverty-scale wages she and other women of color were paid—almost certainly a major factor in the cancer that subsequently claimed her life.) And when alcohol and old unfinished business with a former lover result in Eudora's sending Lorde away, it is a newly resolved Lorde who departs: "I was hurt, but not lost. And in that moment, as in the first night when I held her, I felt myself pass beyond childhood, a woman connecting with other women in an intricate, complex, and ever-widening network of exchanging strengths" (175).

An important, painful relationship with Muriel offers Audre a lesson about separations, a subject that receives her poetic insights in the earlier volume of poems *The Black Unicorn* (1978). The conventional ideology of romance promotes the fear of abandonment by one's lover. *Zami* records the evolution of a black lesbian poet powerful enough to take on a relationship that repudiates utterly the conventional ideology of romance—as Lorde does in her relationship with Kitty/Afrekete, who at various points in the text is described as Lorde's lover (an actual black woman existing in real time and space) and is alluded to as an ancient Dahomeian mythological goddess; as aspects of Aphrodite, Persephone, Demeter, Athena, and other Greek goddesses; and perhaps most important, as aspects of Lorde herself.

Afrekete's beauty is associated with her magical apartment, framed by a murmuring, mysterious, glowing fish tank, its "translucent rainbowed fish" shaded by "pot after clay pot of green and tousled large and small-leaved plants of all shapes and conditions." Tar Beach, the rooftop of Afrekete's apartment, the "chief resort territory of tenement-dwellers," offers the lovers a place to make "moon, honor, love" to one another, their "sweat-slippery dark bodies, sacred as the ocean at high tide" (252) ride one another to the crossroads of joy, sleep, and the power of black women's love, poetry, community, and survival.

The goddess-like *"Afrekete, who came out of a dream to me"* (249) is not worshipped as an "other" or exoticized in the ways that black women's bodies frequently have been made an object of consumption for white men. Her beauty is a reflection of Audre's, their sexuality profoundly mutual, the images of coital love and penetration profoundly lesbian in their tenderness and passion, the descriptions themselves italicicized as if to suggest both their lyrical quality and their mythological aspect: *"There were ripe red finger bananas, stubby and sweet, with which I parted your lips gently, to insert the peeled fruit into your grape-purple flower"* (249). *Zami* closes with lines that could suggest Afrekete not just as lover but as an aspect of the self: "We had come together like elements erupting into an electric storm, exchanging energy, sharing charge, brief and drenching. Then we parted, passed, reformed, reshaping ourselves the better for the exchange. I never saw Afrekete again, but her print remains upon my life with the resonance and power of an emotional tattoo" (253).

In "A Letter to Audre Lorde," ESSEX HEMPHILL offers clear insights into the importance of what Lorde wrote in *Zami* and elsewhere:

> You gave us living, fire-breathing words capable of healing, tearing down, building up, braving the long nights and languishing days. You gave us words we could use wisely. Words we could depend on. You gave us, simply, your life as a lesson to guide our own lives through this maze of destitution and despair that some would call a country, a nation, a home.

BIBLIOGRAPHY

Alexander, Elizabeth. "'Coming out Blackened and Whole': Fragmentation and Reintegration in Audre Lorde's *Zami* and *The Cancer Journals*." *American Literary History* 6, no. 4 (Winter 1994): 695–715.

Ball, M. Charlene. "Old Magic and New Fury: The Theaphany of Afrekete in Audre Lorde's 'Tar Beach.'" *NWSA Journal* 13, no. 1 (2000): 61–85.

Hall, Lynda. "Lorde and Gomez Queer(y)ing boundaries and Acting in Passion(ate) Plays 'Wherever

We Found Space.'" *Callaloo* 23, no. 1 (2000): 394–421.

Keating, AnaLouise. *Women Reading Women Writing: Self-Invention in Paula Gunn Allen, Gloria Anzaldúa, and Audre Lorde.* Philadelphia: Temple University Press, 1996.

Morris, Margaret Kissam. "Audre Lorde Textual Authority and the Embodied Self." *Frontiers: A Journal of Women Studies* 23, no. 1 (2002): 168–188.

Raynaud, Claudine. "'A Nutmeg Nestled Inside Its Covering of Mace': Audre Lorde's *Zami.*" In *Life/Lines,* edited by Bella Brodzki and Celeste Schenck, 77–103. Ithaca, N.Y.: Cornell University Press, 1988.

Lynda Koolish

Zane (1967–)

A writer, novelist, publisher, Web site manager, businesswoman, and bookseller, Zane is the author of many of today's best-selling erotica novels. Given the raw sexual content of her work, Zane, married with children and the daughter of a schoolteacher and preacher, uses only her pseudonym and refuses to be photographed in order to protect the privacy of her family. Bored by her life as a salesperson working throughout North Carolina as well as by the book she was reading, Zane began writing erotica one night in her hotel. She sent the product to a friend, who began circulating the story like a chain letter. This eventually led the business-savvy Zane to set up her own Web site, where she published her creative work and corresponded with thousands of fans, mostly women, who enjoyed Zane's candid, simple, and realistic treatment of sex.

In 2000 Zane, who still manages her own Web site, Eroticanoir.com, which gets more than 1 million hits a year, inaugurated her official self-publishing business and company, Strebor Books, releasing her first collection of erotica short stories, *The Sex Chronicles: Shattering the Myth,* in which she sets out to debunk the myth that men are more sexual in nature than women and that women are sexually inhibited. Featuring female protagonists and characters who run the gamut from housewives to sorority girls, Zane divides the stories into three sections—"Wild," "Wilder," and "Off Da Damn Hook"—to present and support her premise and argument. In 2002 Zane followed her first collection of stories with a second, *Getting Buck Wild: Sex Chronicles 2,* Vol. 2. (2003) Together the books sold more than 250,000 copies by word of mouth alone.

Also published by Strebor Books, *Addicted* (2001), Zane's first novel, is typical of the genre—popularized by such writers as Terry McMillan (*Waiting to Exhale*), Bebe Moore Campbell (*Your Blues Aint Like Mine*), and rapper-turned-novelist Sister Souljah (*The Coldest Winter Ever*)—that she has helped redefine: "fictional works in which middle-class African American women work hard and play even harder, asserting both financial and sexual independence as they negotiate hectic jobs and frantic love lives" (Younge). Zoe Reynard, *Addicted*'s heroine, is a successful businesswoman with a loving and equally successful husband, three children, and a loving, protecting mother. On the surface Zoe's life seems ideal, but as the story continues the deep restraints and torments she confronts internally are revealed. She comes to believe she is addicted to sex, after taking on three extramarital affairs and dealing with her husband's lack of sexual openness. Zoe turns to a professional therapist when she begins to feel her life crumbling beneath her. During their private sessions, Zoe learns that she has concealed deeply hidden secrets about her childhood, including being raped. At issue as well is the fact that her husband's mother had been a prostitute. Zoe's infidelity comes back to haunt her and interfere in her professional, domestic life as well as endanger her safety. In addition to her two collections of stories and *Addicted,* Zane's *New York Times* best sellers include *Skyscraper* (2003), *Nervous* (2004), *Shame on It All* (2001), and *The Heat Seekers* (2003).

Zane's stories explode with sexual liberation and indulgence in sensual appetites. Her characters and stories are well developed with intricate plots and twists. She hurries to dispel the criticism that her work is merely pornography. "Porn is just straight sex," she has said. "My books have a story.

If you took the sex out of it, you'd still have the story" (Younge). In Zane's work there is little or no emphasis on race or gender, specifically womanist or feminist issues. "Any collective memory around struggle is minimized and status is determined by what we can buy" (quoted in Younge). Zane's books have been translated into several languages, including Swedish, Japanese, and Greek.

BIBLIOGRAPHY

Younge, Gary. "Little Black Books." *The Guardian.* September 18, 2004. Available online. URL: http://www.guardian.co.uk/weekend/story/0,3605,1305854,00.html. Accessed October 27, 2006.

Carlos Perez

BIBLIOGRAPHY OF SECONDARY SOURCES

Andrews, William, ed. *African American Autobiography: A Collection of Critical Essays.* Englewood Cliffs, N.J.: Prentice Hall, 1993.

Anglesey, Zoë, ed. *Listen Up! Spoken Word Poetry.* New York: Ballantine Publishing Group, 1999.

Awkward, Michael. *Inspiring Influences: Tradition, Revision, and Afro-American Women's Novels.* New York: Columbia University Press, 1991.

Baker, Houston A., Jr. *Blues, Ideology, and Afro-American Literature: A Vernacular Theory.* Chicago: University of Chicago Press, 1984.

———. *Modernism and the Harlem Renaissance.* Chicago: University of Chicago Press, 1987.

———. *Turning South Again: Re-Thinking Modernism / Re-Reading Booker T.* Durham, N.C.: Duke University Press, 2001.

Barksdale, Richard, and Keneth Kinnamon, eds. *Black Writers of America.* New York: Macmillan, 1972.

Bell, Bernard. *The Afro-American Novel and Its Tradition.* Amherst: University Press of Massachusetts, 1987.

Bennett, Michael, and Vanessa D. Dickerson, eds. *Recovering the Black Female Body: Self Representations by African-American Women.* New Brunswick, N.J.: Rutgers University Press, 2000.

Bone, Robert A. *The Negro Novel in America.* Rev. ed. New Haven: Yale University Press, 1965.

Bogle, Donald. *Toms, Coons, Mulattoes, Mammies, and Bucks.* New York: Continuum, 1990.

Bontemps, Arna Wendell, ed. *The Harlem Renaissance Remembered.* New York: Dodd, Mead & Co., 1972.

Boyd, Melba Joyce. *Wrestling with the Muse: Dudley Randall and the Broadside Press.* New York: Columbia University Press, 2003.

Branch, William B., ed. *Black Thunder: An Anthology of Contemporary African American Drama.* New York: Penguin, 1992.

Brawley, Benjamin. *The Negro in Literature and Art in the United States.* New York: Duffield, 1930.

Bruce, Dickson D., Jr. *The Origins of African American Literature, 1680–1860.* Charlottesville: University Press Virginia, 2001.

Butcher, Margaret Just. *The Negro in American Culture.* New York: Knopf, 1956.

Byerman, Keith Eldon. *Fingering the Jagged Grain: Tradition and Form in Recent Black Fiction.* Athens: University of Georgia Press, 1985.

Christian, Barbara. *Black Feminist Criticism: Perspectives on Black Women Writers.* New York: Teachers College Press, 1985.

———. *Black Women Novelists: The Development of a Tradition, 1892–1976.* Westport, Conn.: Greenwood, 1980.

Coleman, James W. *Blackness and Modernism: The Literary Career of John Edgar Wideman.* Jackson: University Press of Mississippi, 1989.

Collins, Patricia Hill. *Black Feminist Thought.* New York: Routledge, 1990.

Dance, Daryl Cumber, ed. *From My People: Four Hundred Years of African American Folklore.* New York: W. W. Norton, 2002.

———. *Shuckin' and Jivin': Folklore from Contemporary Black Americans.* Bloomington: Indiana University Press, 1978.

Davies, Carole Boyce. *Black Women, Writing, and Identity: Migrations of the Subject.* London: Routledge, 1994.

Davis, Arthur. *From a Dark Tower.* Washington, D.C.: Howard University Press, 1974.

Davis, Arthur P., J. Saunders Redding, and Joyce A. Joyce. *The New Cavalcade.* Vol. 2. Washington, D.C.: Howard University Press, 1992.

Davis, Charles T. *Black Is the Color of the Cosmos: Essays on Afro-American Literature and Culture, 1942–1981.* New York: Garland, 1982.

De Veaux, Alexis. *Warrior Poet: A Biography of Audre Lorde.* New York: Norton, 2004.

Dick, Bruce and Amritjit Singh, eds. *Conversations with Ishmael Reed.* Jackson: University Press of Mississippi, 1995.

Donalson, Melvin. *Black Directors in Hollywood.* Austin: University of Texas Press, 2003.

———, ed. *Cornerstones: An Anthology of African American Literature.* New York: St. Martin's Press, 1997.

Draper, James P., ed. *Black Literature Criticism: Excerpts from Criticism of the Most Significant Works of Black Authors over the Past 200 Years.* Detroit: Gale Research Inc., 1992.

Duvall, John. *The Identifying Fictions of Toni Morrison: Modernist Authenticity and Postmodern Blackness.* New York: Palgrave Macmillan, 2000.

Dyson, Michael Eric. *Reflecting Black: African-American Cultural Criticism.* Minneapolis: University of Minnesota Press, 1993.

Early, Gerald, ed. *Lure and Loathing: Essays on Race, Identity, and the Ambivalence of Assimilation.* New York: Penguin, 1993.

Erwin, Hazel, ed. *African American Literary Criticism, 1773–2000.* New York: Twayne Publishers, 1999.

———, ed. *The Handbook of African American Literature.* University Press of Florida, 2004.

Fabre, Michel. *From Harlem to Paris: Black American Writers in France, 1840–1980.* Urbana: University of Illinois Press, 1993.

Fontenot, Chester J., and Joe Weixlmann, eds. *Black American Prose Theory.* Studies in Black American Literature 1. Greenwood, Fla.: Penkevill, 1984.

Gabbin, Joanne V., ed. *Furious Flower: African American Poetry from the Black Arts Movement to the Present.* Charlottesville: University of Virginia Press, 2004.

Gates, Henry Louis, Jr. *Loose Canons: Notes on the Culture Wars.* New York: Oxford University Press, 1992.

———. *The Signifying Monkey: A Theory of African-American Literary Criticism.* New York: Oxford University Press, 1988.

Gates, Henry Louis, Jr., and Kwame Anthony Appiah, eds. *Alice Walker: Critical Perspectives Past and Present.* Amistad Literary Series. New York: Amistad, 1993.

Gates, Henry Louis, Jr., and Nellie Y. McKay, eds. *The Norton Anthology of African American Literature.* New York: Norton, 1997.

Gayle, Addison, Jr., ed. *The Black Aesthetic.* New York: Doubleday, 1971.

———. *Black Expressions.* New York: Weybright & Talley, 1969.

Gayles, Gloria Wade. *Conversations with Gwendolyn Brooks.* Jackson: University Press of Mississippi, 2003.

George, Nelson. *Hip Hop America.* New York: Penguin, 1998.

Greene, J. Lee. *Blacks in Eden: The African American Novel's First Century.* Charlottesville: University Press of Virginia, 1996.

Hakutani, Yoshinobu, and Robert Butler, eds. *The City in African American Literature.* Madison, N.J.: Fairleigh Dickinson University Press, 1995.

Harper, Michael S., and Robert B. Stepto, eds. *Chant of Saints: A Gathering of Afro-American Literature, Art, and Scholarship.* Urbana: University of Illinois Press, 1979.

Harper, Michael S., and Anthony Walton, eds. *Every Shut Eye Ain't Asleep: An Anthology of Poetry by Af-*

rican Americans since 1945. Boston: Little, Brown, 1994.

Hemphill, Essex, ed. *Brother to Brother: New Writings by Black Gay Men.* Los Angeles: Alyson Publications, 1991.

Henderson, Stephen, ed. *Understanding the New Black Poetry: Black Speech and Black Music as Poetic References.* New York: William Morrow, 1972.

Hernton, Calvin. *The Sexual Mountain and Black Women Writers.* New York: Anchor, 1987.

Hill, Patricia Liggins, ed. *Call and Response: The Riverside Anthology of the African American Literary Tradition.* Boston: Houghton Mifflin, 1998.

Hogue, Lawrence. *The African American Male, Writing and Difference.* Albany: State University of New York Press, 2003.

hooks, bell. *Black Looks: Race and Representation.* Boston: South End Press, 1992.

Hull, Gloria T. *Color, Sex, and Poetry: Three Women Writers of the Harlem Renaissance.* Bloomington: Indiana University Press, 1987.

Hunter, Michael B., ed. *Sojourner: Black Gay Voices in the Age of AIDS.* New York: Other Countries Press, 1993.

Hutchinson, George. *The Harlem Renaissance in Black and White.* Cambridge: Harvard University Press, 1995.

Jones, LeRoi, and Larry Neal, eds. *Black Fire: An Anthology of Afro-American Writing.* New York: William Morrow, 1971.

Kitwana, Bakari. *The Hip Hop Generation: Young Blacks and the Crisis in African-American Culture.* New York: Basic Civitas Books, 2002.

Koolish, Lynda. *African American Writers: Portraits and Visions.* University Press of Mississippi, 2001.

Larkin, Joan, and Carl Morse, eds. *Gay and Lesbian Poetry in Our Time.* New York: St. Martin's, 1988.

Levine, Lawrence W. *Black Culture and Black Consciousness.* New York: Oxford University Press, 1977.

Lewis, David Levering. *When Harlem Was in Vogue.* New York: Oxford University Press, 1979.

Locke, Alain L., ed. *The New Negro: An Interpretation.* New York: Albert and Charles Boni, Inc., 1925. Reprint with preface by Robert Hayden. New York: Atheneum, 1968.

Lowe, John, ed. *Conversations with Ernest Gaines.* Jackson: University Press of Mississippi, 1995.

Maguire, Roberta S., ed. *Conversations with Albert Murray.* Jackson: University Press of Mississippi, 1997.

Mahone, Sydne, ed. *Moon Marked and Touched by Sun: Plays by African American Women.* New York: Theater Communications, 1994.

McBride, Dwight., ed. *James Baldwin Now.* New York: New York University Press, 1999.

McKinley, Catherine E., and L. Joyce DeLaney. *Afrekete: An Anthology of Black Lesbian Writing.* New York: Doubleday and Co., 1995.

Mishkin, Tracy, ed. *Literary Influence and African American Writers, Collected Essays.* New York: Garland Publishing, Inc., 1996

Mitchell, Angelyn. ed. *Within the Circle: An Anthology of African American Literary Criticism from the Harlem Renaissance to the Present.* Durham, N.C.: Duke University Press, 1994.

Morrison, Toni. *Playing in the Dark: Whiteness and the Literary Imagination.* Cambridge, Mass.: Harvard University Press, 1992.

Nana-Ama Danquah, Meri, ed. *Shaking the Tree: A Collection of New Fiction and Memoir by Black Women.* New York: W. W. Norton, 2003.

Napier, Winston, ed. *African American Literary Theory.* New York: New York University Press, 2000.

Nielsen, Aldon. *Writing between the Lines: Race and Intertextuality.* Athens: University of Georgia Press, 1994.

O'Brien, John, ed. *Interviews with Black Writers.* New York: Liveright, 1973.

Peterson, Bernard L., Jr. *Early Black American Playwrights and Dramatic Writers.* New York: Greenwood, 1990.

Powell, Kevin. *Step into a World: A Global Anthology of the New Black Literature.* New York: Wiley & Sons, 2000.

Powell, Kevin, and Ras Baraka, eds. *In the Tradition: An Anthology of Young Black Writers.* New York: Harlem Rivers Press, 1992.

Quashie, Kevin Everod, Joyce Lausch, and Keith D. Miller. *New Bones: Contemporary Black Writers in America.* Upper Saddle River, N.J.: Prentice Hall, 2001.

Redmond, Eugene B. *Drumvoices: The Mission of Afro-American Poetry, a Critical Mission.* Garden City, N.Y.: Anchor Books, 1976.

Reid-Pharr, Robert F., ed. *Black Gay Man: Essays.* New York: New York University Press, 2001.

Rose, Tricia. *Black Noise: Rap Music and Black Culture in Contemporary America.* Middletown, Conn.: Wesleyan University Press, 1994.

Ruff, Shawn Stewart, ed. *Go the Way Your Blood Beats: An Anthology of Lesbian and Gay Fiction by African-American Writers.* New York: Henry Holt and Company, 1996.

Rushdy, Ashraf. *Neo-Slave Narratives: Studies in the Social Logic of a Literary Form.* New York: Oxford University Press, 1999.

Samuels, Wilfred, and Clenora Hudson Weems. *Toni Morrison.* Boston: Twayne Publishers, 1989.

Smith, Rochelle, and Sharon L. Jones, eds. *The Prentice Hall Anthology of African American Literature.* Upper Saddle River, N.J.: Prentice Hall, 1999.

Smith, Valerie, ed. *African American Writers.* New York: Collier, 1993.

Sundquist, Eric. *Cultural Contexts for Ralph Ellison's Invisible Man.* Boston: St. Martin's Press, 1995.

Troupe, Quincy, ed. *James Baldwin: A Legacy.* New York: Touchstone, 1989.

Turner, Darwin T., ed. *Black American Literature: Essays, Poetry, Fiction, Drama.* Columbus, Ohio: Charles E. Merrill, 1970.

———. *Black Drama in America: An Anthology.* New York: Fawcett, 1971.

———. *In a Minor Chord: Three Afro-American Writers and Their Search for Identity.* Carbondale: Southern Illinois University Press, 1971.

TuSmith, Bonnie, ed. *Conversations with John Edgar Wideman.* Jackson: University Press of Mississippi, 1998.

Walker, Alice. *In Search of Our Mothers' Gardens.* New York: Harcourt, 1983.

Ward, Jerry W., Jr., ed. *Trouble the Water: 250 Years of African American Poetry.* New York: Mentor, 1997.

Washington, Mary Helen, ed. *Invented Lives: Narratives of Black Women, 1860–1960.* Garden City, N.Y.: Anchor Press, 1987.

Major Works by African-American Writers

Allen, Jeffery Renard. *Rails under My Back.* New York: Farrar, Straus & Giroux, 2000.

Angelou, Maya. *I Know Why the Caged Bird Sings.* New York: Random House, 1969.

Baldwin, James. *The Amen Corner.* New York Dial, 1968.

———. *Another Country.* New York: Dial, 1962.

———. *Blues for Mister Charlie.* New York: Dial, 1964.

———. *The Fire Next Time.* New York: Dial, 1963.

———. *Giovanni's Room.* New York: Dial, 1956.

———. *Going to Meet the Man.* New York: Dial, 1965.

———. *Go Tell It on the Mountain.* New York: Knopf, 1953.

———. *If Beale Street Could Talk.* New York: Dial, 1964.

———. *Just Above My Head.* New York: Dial, 1978.

———. *Nobody Knows My Name. More Notes of a Native Son.* New York: Dial, 1962.

———. *Notes of a Native Son.* Boston: Beacon, 1965.

———. *The Price of the Ticket: Collected Nonfiction 1948–1985.* New York: St. Martin's, 1985.

———. *Tell Me How Long the Train's Been Gone.* New York: Dial, 1968.

Bambara, Toni Cade. *Gorilla, My Love, Short Stories.* New York: Random House, 1972.

———. *The Salteaters.* New York: Random House, 1980.

———. *The Sea Birds Are Still Alive: Collected Stories.* New York: Random House, 1977.

———. *Toni Cade Bambara. Deep Sightings and Rescue Missions: Fiction, Essays, and Conversations.* Edited by Toni Morrison. New York: Vintage, 1999.

Baraka, Amiri (LeRoi Jones). *The Baptism and Toilet.* New York: Grove, 1966.

———. *The Dead Lecturer.* New York: Grove, 1964.

———. *Dutchman and the Slave.* New York: Morrow, 1964.

———. *Preface to a Twenty-Volume Suicide Note.* New York: Corinth, 1961.

———. *The System of Dante's Hell.* New York: Grove, 1965.

Bradley, David. *The Chaneysville Incident.* New York: Harper & Row, Publishers, 1981.

Brooks, Gwendolyn. *Aloneness.* Detroit: Broadside, 1971.

———. *Annie Allen.* New York: Harper, 1949.

———. *The Bean Eaters.* New York: Harper & Row, 1971.

———. *Beckoning.* Detroit: Broadside, 1975.

———. *Bronzeville Boys and Girls.* New York: Harper, 1956.

———. *Family Pictures.* Detroit: Broadside, 1970.

———. *In the Mecca.* New York: Harper & Row, 1968.

———. *Maude Martha.* New York: Harper, 1953.

———. *Primer for Blacks.* Chicago: Black Position Press, 1981.

———. *Report from Part One.* Detroit: Broadside, 1972.

———. *Report from Part Two.* Detroit: Broadside, 1996.

———. *Riot.* Detroit: Broadside Press, 1970.

———. *Selected Poems.* New York: Harper & Row, 1963.

———. *A Street in Bronzeville.* New York: Harper, 1945.

———. *to disembark.* Detroit: Broadside Press, 1981.

———. *The World of Gwendolyn Brooks.* New York: Harper & Row, 1971.

Brown, Claude. *Manchild in the Promise Land.* New York: Simon & Schuster, 1969.

Butler, Octavia. *Adulthood Rites: Xenogenesis.* New York: Warner Books, 1988.

———. *Bloodchild and Other Stories.* New York: Four Walls Eight Windows, 1995.

———. *Clay's Ark.* New York: Warner Books, 1996.

———. *Dawn: Xenogenesis.* New York: Warner Books, 1987.

———. *Fledgling. A Novel.* New York: Seven Stories, 2005.

———. *Imago.* New York: Warner Books, 1989.

———. *Kindred.* Boston, Beacon, 1988.

———. *Mind of My Mind.* New York: Warner Books, 1994.

———. *Parable of the Sower.* New York: Four Walls Eight Windows, 1993.

———. *Parable of the Talents.* New York: Seven Stories, 1988.

———. *Patternmaster.* New York: Warner Books, 1976.

———. *Survivor.* New York: Warner Books, 1978.

———. *Wild Seed.* Garden City, New York: Doubleday, 1980.

Campbell, Bebe More. *Brothers and Sisters.* Berkeley, Calif.: Berkeley Publishing Group, 1995.

———. *What You Owe Me.* Berkeley, Calif.: Berkeley Publishing Group, 2002.

———. *Your Blues Ain't Like Mine.* New York: Ballantine Books, 1993.

Channer, Colin. *Satisfy My Soul.* New York: Ballantine Publishing Group, 2002.

———. *Waiting in Vain.* New York: The Ballantine Publishing Group, 1998.

Clifton, Lucille. *Blessing the Boats: New and Selected Poems 1988–2OOO.* New York: BOA Editions, 2000.

Cooper, J. California. *Homemade Love.* New York: St. Martin's, 1988.

———. *In Search of Satisfaction.* New York: Doubleday, 1995.

———. *The Wake of the Wind.* New York: Doubleday, 1998.

Danticat, Edwidge. *Breath, Eyes, Memory.* New York: Vintage Books, 1994.

———. *The Farming of Bones.* New York: Viking, 1999.

———. *Krik! Krak! Stories.* New York: Soho Press, 1995.

Datcher, Michael. *Raising Fences: A Black Man's Love Story.* New York: Riverhead Books, 2001.

Davis, Angela. *The Autobiography.* New York: International Publishers, 1974, 1988.

Derricotte, Toi. *Captivity.* Pittsburgh: University of Pittsburgh Press, 1989.

———. *The Empress of the Death House.* Twin Lakes, Wisc.: Lotus Press, 1978.

———. *Natural Birth.* Trumansburg, N.Y.: Crossing Press, 1983.

———. *Tender.* Pittsburgh: University of Pittsburgh Press, 1997.

Dixon, Melvin. *Trouble the Waters.* Boulder: University of Colorado Press, 1989.

Donalson, Mel. *Dancing on Quicksand.* Pasadena, Calif.: TCS Publications, 2007.

———. *Seekers and Saints.* Pasadena, Calif.: TCS Publications, 2007.

Dove, Rita. *American Smooth: Poems.* New York: W. W. Norton, 2004.

———. *Selected Poems.* New York: Knopf Publishing Group, 1993.

———. *Thomas and Beulah.* Carnegie Mellon University Press, 1987.

Due, Tananarive. *The Between.* New York: HarperCollins Publishers, 1995.

———. *The Good House.* New York: Atria Books, 2003.

———. *The Living Blood.* New York: Pocket Books, 2001.

Dumas, Henry. *Ark of Bones and Other Stories.* Edited by Hale Chatfield and Eugene Redmond. Carbondale and Edwardsville: Southern Illinois University Press, 1970.

———. *Goodbye Sweet Waters. New and Selected Stories.* Edited and with an introduction by Eugene Redmond. New York: Thunder's Mouth Press, 1988.

———. *Jonoah and the Green Stone.* Edited by Eugene Redmond. New York: Random House, 1976.

———. *Poetry for My People.* Edited by Hale Chatfield and Eugene Redmond. Carbondale and Edwardsville: Southern Illinois University Press, 1970.

———. *Rope of Wind and Other Stories.* Edited by Eugene Redmond. New York: Random House, 1979.

Eady, Cornelius. *The Autobiography of a Jukebox.* Pittsburgh: Carnegie-Mellon University Press, 1991.

———. *BOOM BOOM BOOM.* Brockport, N.Y.: State Street Press, 1988.

———. *Brutal Imagination.* New York: G. P. Putnam's Sons, 2001.

———. *The Gathering of My Name.* Pittsburgh: Carnegie-Mellon University Press, 1991.

———. *Kartunes.* West Orange, N.J.: Warthog Press, 1980.

———. *Victims of the Last Dance Craze.* Chicago: Ommation Press, 1986.

———. *You Don't Miss Your Water.* New York: Henry Holt, 1995.

Ellis, Trey. *Home Repairs.* New York: Simon & Schuster, 1996.

———. *Platitude.* New York: Vintage Books, 1988.

Ellison, Ralph W. *Flying Home and Other Stories.* Edited and with an introduction by John F. Callahan. New York: Random House, 1996.

———. *Invisible Man.* New York: Random House, 1952.

———. *Juneteenth.* Edited by John F. Callahan. New York: Random House, 1999.

———. *Shadow and Act.* New York: Random House, 1964.

Evans, Mari. *I Am a Black Woman.* New York: Morrow, 1970.

———. *Nightstar.* Los Angeles: UCLA Center for Afro-American Studies, 1981.

Forrest, Leon. *Meteor in the Madhouse.* Evanston, Ill.: Northwestern University Press, 2001.

Gaines, Ernest J. *The Autobiography of Miss Jane Pittman.* New York: Dial, 1971.

———. *Bloodline.* New York: Dial, 1968.

———. *A Gathering of Old Men.* New York: Knopf, 1983.

———. *In My Father's House.* New York: Knopf, 1978.

———. *Of Love and Dust.* New York: Dial, 1967.

George, Nelson. *Night Work.* New York: Simon & Schuster, 2003.

Giovanni, Nikki. *Black Feeling, Black Talk.* New York: Black Dialogue, 1967.

———. *Black Judgment.* Detroit: Broadside, 1969.

———. *Ego Tripping and Other Poems for Young People.* New York: Lawrence Hill, 1973.

———. *Gemini: An Extended Autobiographical Statement on My First Twenty-five Years of Being a Black Poet.* Indianapolis: Bobbs-Merrill, 1971.

———. *My House.* New York: Morrow, 1972.

———. *Re:Creation.* Detroit: Broadside, 1970.

———. *The Selected Poems of Nikki Giovanni: 1968–1995.* New York: William Morrow, 1996.

Glave, Thomas. *Whose Song? and Other Stories.* San Francisco: City Lights, 2000.

Golden, Marita. *Migrations of the Heart.* Garden City, N.Y.: Anchor Press, 1983.

Hansberry, Lorraine. *A Raisin in the Sun.* New York: Random House, 1959.

———. *The Sign in Sidney Brustein's Window.* New York: Random House, 1965.

Harper, Michael. *Dear John, Dear Coltrane.* Pittsburgh: University of Pittsburgh Press, 1970.

———. *Healing Song for the Inner Ear: Poems.* Urbana: University of Illinois Press, 1984.

———. *History Is Your Own Heartbeat.* Urbana: University of Illinois Press, 1971.

———. *Nightmare Begins Responsibility.* Urbana: University of Illinois Press, 1975.

———. *Song: I Want a Witness.* Pittsburgh: University of Pittsburgh Press, 1972.

Harris, E. Lynn. *Invisible Life.* New York: Consortium Press, 1991.

———. *I Say a Little Prayer.* New York: Doubleday, 2006.

Hayden, Robert. *A Ballad of Remembrance.* London: Breman, 1962.

———. *Heart-Shapes in the Dust.* Detroit: Falcon, 1940.

———. *The Lion and the Archer.* New York: Hemphill, 1949.

———. *Robert Hayden: Collected Poems.* New York: Liveright, 1985.

———. *Selected Poems.* New York: October House, 1966.

———. *Words in the Mourning Time.* New York: October House, l970.

Himes, Chester. *Cast the First Stone.* New York: Coward-McCann, 1952.

———. *Cotton Comes to Harlem.* New York: Putnam, 1965.

———. *If He Hollers Let Him Go.* New York: Doubleday Doran, 1945.

———. *The Primitive.* New York: New American Library, 1955.

———. *The Third Generation.* New York: World, 1954.

Hemphill, Essex. *Ceremonies: Prose and Poetry.* New York: Plume, 1992.

———. *Conditions: Poems.* New York: Be Bop Books, 1986.

Hopkinson, Nalo. *Midnight Robber.* New York: Warner Books, 2000.

Hughes, Langston. *Ask Your Mama: Twelve Moods for Jazz.* New York: Knopf, 1961.

———. *The Big Sea.* New York: Knopf, 1949.

———. *Fine Clothes for the Jew.* New York: Knopf, 1927.

———. *Five Plays by Langston Hughes* [*Mulatto, Soul Gone Home, Little Ham, Simply Heavenly,* and *Tambourines to Glory*]. Edited by Webster Smalley. Bloomington: Indiana University Press, 1963.

———. *I Wonder as I Wander.* New York: Knopf, 1956.

———. *Mulatto.* New York: Knopf, 1935.

———. *Montage of a Dream Deferred.* New York: Knopf, 1951.

———. *Not Without Laughter.* New York: Knopf, 1930.

———. *The Panther and the Lash.* New York: Knopf, 1967.

———. *The Selected Poems of Langston Hughes.* New York: Knopf, 1965.

———. *Simple Speaks His Mind.* New York: Knopf, 1950.

———. *Simple Takes a Wife.* New York: Knopf, 1953.

———. *The Ways of White Folks 1934.* New York: Knopf, 1934.

———. *The Weary Blues.* New York: Knopf, 1926.

Hurston, Zora Neale. *Dust Tracks on a Road.* Philadelphia: Lippincott, 1942.

———. *Jonah's Gourd Vine.* Philadelphia: Lippincott, 1934.

———. *Moses Man of the Mountain.* Philadelphia: Lippincott, 1939.

———. *Mule Bone* (with Langston Hughes), New York: Harper, 1931.

———. *Mules and Men.* Philadelphia: Lippincott, 1935.

———. *Seraphs on the Swanee.* New York: Scribners, 1948.

———. *Their Eyes Were Watching God.* Philadelphia: Lippincott, 1937.

Jackson, Major. *Leaving Saturn.* Athens: University of Georgia Press, 2002.

Jackson-Opoku, Sandra. *Hot Johnny (And the Women who Loved Him).* New York: Ballantine Books, 1991.

———. *The River Where Blood Is Born.* New York: One World, 1997.

Johnson, Charles. *Middle Passage.* New York: Atheneum Macmillan Publishing Company, 1990.

———. *Oxherding Tale.* Bloomington: Indiana University Press, 1982.

———. *The Sorcerer's Apprentice, Tales and Conjurations.* New York: Plume, 1994.

Jones, Edward. *The Known World.* New York: HarperCollins Publishers, 2003.

Jones, Gayl. *Corregidora.* New York: Random House, 1975.

Jordan, June. *Haruko! Love Poems.* London: Serpent's Tail, 1993.

———. *Kissing God Goodbye.* New York: Anchor Books, 1997.

———. *Living Room: New Poems.* New York: Thunder's Mouth, 1985.

———. *Naming Our Destiny: New and Selected Poems.* New York: Thunder's Mouth, 1985.

———. *Passion: New Poems, 1977–1980.* Boston: Beacon, 1980.

———. *Things That I Do in the Dark.* Boston: Beacon, 1981.

Kenan, Randall. *A Visitation of Spirits.* New York: Grove, 1989.

Kincaid, Jamaica. *Annie John.* New York: Farrar, Straus & Giroux, 1985.

———. *The Autobiography of My Mother.* New York: Farrar, Straus & Giroux, 1996.

Knight, Etheridge. *Born of a Woman: New and Selected Poems.* Boston: Houghton Mifflin, 1980.

———. *Poems from Prison.* Detroit: Broadside Press, 1968.

Komunyakaa, Yusef. *Copacetic.* Middletown, Conn.: Wesleyan University Press, 1984.

———. *Dien Cai Dau.* Middletown, Conn.: Wesleyan University Press, 1988.

———. *I Apologize for the Eyes in My Head.* Middletown, Conn.: Wesleyan University Press, 1986.

———. *Magic City 1992.* Hanover, N.H.: University Press of New England, 1992.

———. *Neon Vernacular: New and Selected Poems, 1977–1989.* Middletown, Conn.: Wesleyan University Press, 1994.

———. *Pleasure Dome: New and Collected Poems, 1975–1999.* Middletown, Conn.: Wesleyan University Press, 2001.

———. *Talking Dirty to the Gods.* Farrar, Straus & Giroux, 2000.

———. *Thieves of Paradise.* Hanover, N.H.: University Press of New England, c1992, 1998.

Larsen, Nella. *Passing.* New York: Knopf, 1929.

———. *Quicksand.* New York: Knopf, 1928.

Lewis, William Henry. *I Got Somebody in Staunton.* New York: Amistad, 2005.

———. *In the Arms of Our Elders.* Durham, N.C.: Carolina Wren Press, 1994.

Logue, Antonia. *Shadow-Box.* New York: Grove, 1999.

———. *Chosen Poems, Old and New.* New York: W. W. Norton, 1982.

———. *From a Land Where Other People Live.* Detroit: Broadside, 1973.

Lorde, Audre. *The Black Unicorn.* New York: W. W. Norton, 1978.

———. *The Cancer Journals.* Argyle, N.Y.: Spinsters, Ink, c1980.

———. *Undersong: Chosen Poems, Old and New.* New York: W. W. Norton, 1992.

———. *Zami, A New Spelling of my Name.* Trumansburg, N.Y.: Crossing Press, 1982. Memoir.

Major, Clarence. *All Night Visitors.* New York: Olympia Press, 1969.

———. *Configurations: New and Selected Poems 1958–1998.* Port Townsend, Wash.: Copper Canyon Press, 1999.

———. *Dirty Bird Blues.* San Francisco: Mercury House, 1996, 1997.

———. *Emergency Exit.* New York: Fiction Collective, 1979.

———. *My Amputations.* New York: Fiction Collective, 1986.

———. *One Flesh.* Kensington, Md.: Kensington Books, 2003.

———. *Painted Turtle: Woman with Guitar.* Los Angeles: Sun and Moon Press, 1988, 1996.

———. *Reflex and Bone Structure.* New York: Fiction Collective, 1975, 1982, 1996.

———. *Some Observations of a Stranger at Zuni etc.* Los Angeles: Sun and Moon Press, 1989.

———. *Such Was the Season.* San Francisco: Mercury House, 1987, 1990.

———. *Swallow the Lake.* Middletown, Conn.: Wesleyan University Press, 1970.

———. *Waiting for Sweet Betty.* Port Townsend, Wash.: Copper Canyon Press, 2002.

Marshall, Paule. *Brown Girl, Brownstones.* New York: Feminist Press, 1981.

———. *Daughters.* New York: Plume, 1992.

———. *Praisesong for the Widow.* New York: E. P. Dutton, 1984.

———. *Reena.* New York: Feminist Press, 1983.

———. *Soul Clap Hands and Sing.* Washington, D.C.: Howard University Press, 1961.

McKay, Claude. *Harlem Shadows.* New York: Harcourt Brace, 1922.

———. *Home to Harlem.* New York: Harper, 1928.

———. *Selected Poems.* New York: Bookman, 1953.

McMillan, Terry. *Disappearing Acts.* New York: Viking, 1993.

———. *How Stella Got Her Groove Back.* New York: Viking, 1996.

———. *Mama.* Boston: Houghton Mifflin, 1987.

———. *Waiting to Exhale.* New York: Viking, 1992.

McPherson, James Alan. *Crabcakes.* New York: Simon & Schuster, 1998.

———. *Elbow Room.* Boston: Little, Brown, 1977.

———. *Hue and Cry.* Boston: Little, Brown, 1969.

Miller, E. Ethelbert. *Buddha Weeping in Winter.* Red Wing, Minn.: Red Dragonfly Press, 2001.

———. *Fathering Words: The Making of an African American Writer.* New York: St. Martin's, 2000.

———. *First Light: New and Selected Poems.* Baltimore: Duforcelf, 1984.

———. *How We sleep on the Nights We Don't Make Love: Poems.* Willimantic, Conn.: Curbstone Press, 2004.

———. *Where Are the Love Poems for Dictators?* Washington, D.C.: Open Hand Publishers, 1986.

———. *Whispers, Secrets, and Promises.* Baltimore: Black Classic Press, 1988.

Morrison, Toni. *Beloved.* New York: Knopf, 1987.

———. *The Bluest Eye.* New York: Knopf, 1970.

———. *Jazz.* New York: Knopf, 1992.

———. *Love.* New York: Knopf, 2003.

———. *Paradise.* New York: Knopf, 1998.

———. *Playing in the Dark: Whiteness and Literary Imagination.* Cambridge, Mass.: Harvard University Press, 1992.

———. *Song of Solomon.* New York: Knopf, 1977.

———. *Sula.* New York: Knopf, 1973.

———. *Tar Baby.* New York: Knopf, 1981.

Mosley, Walter. *Cinnamon Kiss: A Novel.* New York: Little, Brown, 2005.

———. *Fear of the Dark.* New York: Little, Brown, 2006.

———. *Fortunate Son.* New York: Little, Brown, 2005.

———. *A Little Yellow Dog.* New York: W. W. Norton, 1996.

———. *The Man in My Basement.* Boston: Little, Brown, 2004.

Motley, Willard. *Knock on Any Door.* New York: Appleton-Century, 1947.

Murray, Albert. *Train Whistle Guitar.* New York: McGraw-Hill, 1974.

Naylor, Gloria. *Mama Day.* New York: First Vintage Contemporaries Edition, 1989.

———. *The Men of Brewster Place.* New York: Hyperion, 1998.

———. *The Women of Brewster Place.* New York: Viking Penguin, 1982.

Petry, Anne. *The Street.* Boston: Houghton Mifflin, 1953.

Phillips, Carl. *Pastoral Poems.* Saint Paul, Minn.: Graywolf Press, 2000.

———. *The Rest of Love.* New York: Farrar, Straus & Giroux, 2004.

———. *Rock Harbor.* New York: Farrar, Straus & Giroux, 2002.

Reed, Ishmael. *catechism of d neoamerican hoodoo church.* London: Breman, 1970.

———. *Conjure: Selected Poems, 1963–1970.* Amherst: University of Massachusetts Press, 1972.

———. *Flight to Canada.* New York: Random House, 1976.

———. *The Freelance Pallbearers.* Garden City, N.Y.: Doubleday, 1967.

———. *The Last Days of Louisiana Red.* New York: Random House, 1976.

———. *Mother Hubbard.* New York: St. Martin's 1982.

———. *Mumbo Jumbo.* New York: Doubleday, 1972.

———. *The Reed Reader.* New York: Basic, 2000.

———. *The Terrible Threes.* New York: Atheneum, 1989.

———. *The Terrible Twos.* New York: St. Martin's, 1982.

———. *Yellow Back Radio Broke-Down.* Garden City, N.Y.: Doubleday, 1969.

Rhodes, Parker Jewell. *Douglass' Women.* New York: Washington Square Press, 2002.

———. *Voodoo Dreams, A Novel of Marie Laveau.* New York: Picador USA, 1993.

Sanchez, Sonia. *A Blues Book for Blue Black Magical Women.* Detroit: Broadside, 1973.

———. *Homecoming.* Detroit: Broadside, 1969.

———. *homegirl & handgrenades.* New York: Thunder's Mouth, 1984.

———. *It's a New Day: Poems for Young Brothas and Sistus.* Detroit: Broadside, 1971.

———. *I've Been a Woman: New and Selected Poems.* Sausalito, Calif.: Black Scholar Press, 1981.

———. *Liberation Poems.* Detroit: Broadside, 1970.

———. *Love Poems.* New York: Third Press, 1973.

———. *A Sound Investment.* Chicago: Third World Press, 1980.

———. *We a Baddddd People.* Detroit: Broadside, 1970.

Sapphire. *Push.* New York: Vintage Books, 1996.

Senna, Danzy. *Caucasia.* New York: Riverhead Books, 1998.

Shepherd, Reginald. *Angel, Interrupted.* Pittsburgh: University of Pittsburgh Press, 2003.

———. *Otherhood.* Pittsburgh: University of Pittsburgh Press, 2003.

———. *Some Are Drowning.* Pittsburgh: University of Pittsburgh Press, 2003.

———. *Wrong.* Pittsburgh: University of Pittsburgh Press, 1999.

Tademy, Lalita. *Cane River.* New York: Warner Books, 2001.

Tervalon, Jervey. *All the Trouble You Need.* New York: Atria Books, 2002.

———. *Dead above Ground.* New York: Atria Books, 2000.

Thomas, Lorenzo. *The Bathers.* New York: I. Reed Books, 1981.

———. *Characters Are Few.* Berkeley, Calif.: Blue Wind Press, 1979.

———. *Dancing on Main Street.* Minneapolis, Minn.: Coffee House Press, 2004.

Thurman, Wallace. *The Blacker the Berry.* New York: Macaulay, 1929.

———. *Infants of the Spring.* New York: Macaulay, 1932.

Tolson, Melvin B. *A Gallery of Harlem Portraits.* Edited by Robert M. Farnsworth. Columbia: University of Missouri Press, 1979.

———. *Harlem Gallery: Book I, The Curator 1979.* New York: Twayne, 1965.

———. *Libretto for the Republic of Liberia.* New York: Twayne, 1953.

———. *Rendezvous with America.* New York: Dodd, Mead, 1944.

Toomer, Jean. *Cane.* Boni & Liveright, 1923.

———. *The Wayward and the Seeking: A Collection of the Writing by Jean Toomer.* Edited by Darwin T. Turner. Washington, D.C.: Howard University Press, 1980.

Touré, Askia M. *Dawn Song! The Epic Memory of Askia Touré.* Chicago: Third World Press, 2000.

———. *From the Pyramids in the Projects: Poems of Genocide and Resistance.* Trenton, N.J.: Africa World Press, 1989.

Walker, Alice. *By the Light of My Father's Smile.* New York: Random House, 1998.

———. *The Color Purple.* New York: Harcourt Brace Jovanovich, 1982.

———. *Good Night, Willie Lee, I'll See You in the Morning.* New York: Dial, 1979.

———. *In Love and Trouble: Stories of Black Women.* New York: Harcourt Brace Jovanovich, 1973.

———. *In Search of Our Mother's Gardens: Womanist Prose.* San Diego: Harcourt Brace Jovanovich, 1983.

———. *Meridian.* New York: Harcourt Brace Jovanovich, 1976.

———. *Possessing the Secret of Joy.* New York: Harcourt Brace Jovanovich, 1992.

———. *Revolutionary Petunias and Other Poems.* New York: Harcourt Brace Jovanovich, 1973.

———. *The Temple of My Familiar.* New York: Harcourt Brace Jovanovich, 1989.

———. *The Third Life of Grange Copeland.* New York: Harcourt Brace Jovanovich, 1970.

———. *You Can't Keep a Good Woman Down.* New York: Harcourt Brace Jovanovich, 1981.

Walker, Margaret. *For My People.* New Haven, Conn.: Yale University Press, 1942.

———. *Jubilee.* Boston: Houghton Mifflin, 1966.

West, Dorothy. *The Living Is Easy.* New York: Arno, 1969.

———. *The Wedding.* New York: Doubleday, 1995.

Whitehead, Colson. *The Intuitionist.* New York: Anchor Books, 1999.

Wideman, John Edgar. *All Stories Are True.* New York: Vintage, 1992.

———. *Brothers and Keepers.* New York: Holt, Rinehart & Winston, 1984.

———. *Cattle Killing.* Boston: Houghton Mifflin, 1996.

———. *Damballah.* New York: Avon, 1981.

———. *Fatheralong.* New York: Pantheon, 1994.

———. *Fever.* New York: Henry Holt, 1989.

———. *A Glance Away.* New York: Harcourt, Brace & World, 1967.

———. *Hiding Place.* New York: Avon, 1981.

———. *Hoop Roots: Basketball, Race and Love.* Boston: Houghton, Mifflin, 2001.

———. *Hurry Home.* New York: Harcourt, Brace & World, 1969.

———. *The Island Martinique.* Washington, D.C.: National Geographic Society, 2003.

———. *The Lynchers.* New York: Harcourt Brace Jovanovich, 1973.

———. *Philadelphia Fire.* New York: Henry Holt, 1990.

———. *Reuben.* New York: Henry Holt, 1987.

———. *Sent for You Yesterday.* New York: Avon, 1983.

———. *The Stories of John Edgar Wideman.* New York: Pantheon, 1992.

———. *Two Cities.* Boston: Houghton Mifflin Company, 1998.

Williams, John Alfred. *The Man Who Cried I Am.* Boston: Little, Brown, 1957.

Williams, Sherley Anne. *Dessa Rose.* New York: Morrow, 1986.

———. *Give Birth to Brightness: A Thematic Study in Neo-Black Literature.* New York: Dial, 1972.

———. *The Peacock Poems.* Middletown, Conn.: Wesleyan University Press, 1975.

———. *Someone Sweet Angel Chile.* New York: Morrow, 1982.

Wilson, August. *Fences.* New York: Plume, 1986.

———. *The Ground on Which I Stand.* New York: Theatre Communications Group, 2001.

———. *Jitney.* Woodstock, N.Y.: Overlook Press, 2001.

———. *Joe Turner's Come and Gone.* New York: Plume, 1988.

———. *King Hedley II.* New York: Theatre Communications Group, 2005.

———. *Ma Rainey's Black Bottom.* New York: Plume, 1985.

———. *The Piano Lesson.* New York: Dutton, 1990.

———. *Seven Guitars.* New York: Dutton, 1996.

———. *Three Plays.* Pittsburgh: University of Pittsburgh Press, 1991.

———. *Two Trains Running.* New York: Dutton, 1992.

Wright, Richard. *Black Boy: A Record of Childhood and Youth.* New York: Harper, 1945.

———. *Eight Men.* New York: World, 1961.

———. *Lawd Today.* New York: Avon, 1963.

———. *The Long Dream.* Garden City, N.Y.: Doubleday, 1958.

———. *Native Son.* New York: Harper, 1940.

———. *The Outsider.* New York: Harper, 1953.

———. *Savage Holiday.* New York: Universal, 1965.

———. *Uncle Tom's Children.* New York: Harper, 1947.

Young, Al. *Ask Me Now.* New York: McGraw-Hill, 1980.

———. *The Blues Don't Change: New and Selected Poems.* Baton Rouge: Louisiana State University Press, 1982.

———. *Heaven: Collected Poems, 1956–1990.* Berkeley: Creative Arts Book Co., 1992.

———. *Snakes: A Novel.* New York: Holt, Rinehart & Winston, 1970.

Young, Kevin. *Black Maria.* New York: Knopf, 2005.

———. *For the Confederate Dead.* New York: Knopf, 2007.

———. *Jelly Roll: A Blues.* New York: Knopf, 2003.

———. *Most Way Home.* New York: William Morrow, 1995.

———. *To Repel Ghost.* Cambridge, Mass.: Zoland Books, 2001.

LIST OF CONTRIBUTORS

Abdullah, Melina California State University, Los Angeles

Aljoe, Nicole University of Utah

Atiya, Donnette Hatch Hurricane, Utah

Atkins, Yvonne California State University, San Bernardino

BakenRa, Alim University of Illinois, Urbana-Champaign

Barlow, George Grinnell College

Bell, Alexander St. Louis Community College, Florissant Valley

Bell, Chris University of Illinois, Chicago

Birkhold, Matthew Temple University

Black, Ray University of Chicago

Bland, Janet University of Denver

Bozeman, Terry Spelman College

Briggs, Kindra University of Utah

Bruce, Marcus Bates College

Bunyan, Scott Mohawk College

Byerman, Keith Indiana State University

Carson, Warren University of South Carolina, Spartanburg

Celestino, James University of Utah

Chandler, Gena E. Virginia Tech

Cherry, Joyce L. Albany State University

Chidziva, Lewis Utah Valley State University

Coleman, Ronald G. University of Utah

Crawford, Malachai University of Missouri

Cronin, Gloria Brigham Young University

Cummings, Jerome Lake Charles, Louisiana

Davidson, Adenike University of Central Florida

Davis, France A. University of Utah

Demirtürk, E. Lâle Bilkent University, Turkey

Dickson, Ryan University of Utah

Dolinar, Brian Claremont Graduate University

Donalson, Mel California State University, Los Angeles

Dowling, Robert Central Connecticut University

Dunn, Stephanie Ohio State University

Ervin, Hazel Morehouse College

Feldman, Keith George Washington University

Fikes-Samuels, Detavio Stanford University

Fikes-Samuels, Michael Denver City College

Flora, Brian George Washington University

Ford, Naimah University of Missouri, Columbia

Galbus, Julia University of Southern Florida

Glover Jones, Daintee University of Houston

Green, Tara Southern University

Gregersen, Jeremy University of Oregon

Guzzio, Tracie Church State University of New York, Plattsburg

Hakutani, Yoshinobu Kent State University

Hankerson, Stephanie Powell Albany State University

Harris, La Shawn D. Howard University

Hart, Jay Weber State University

Hill, James Albany State University

Hollady, Hilary University of Massachusetts, Lowell

Hudson-Weems, Clenora University of Missouri, Columbia

Hunter, Jeannine F. University of Tennessee

Jacques, Geoffrey University of Massachusetts, Boston

James, G. Winston Brooklyn College

Janifer, Raymond Shippensburg University

Jennings, Brian Brigham Young University

Johnson, Linda University of Missouri, Columbia

King, Lovalerie Pennsylvania State University

Koolish, Lynda San Diego State University

Langley, April University of Missouri, Columbia

Lee Eddy-Sanders, Shauna Provo, Utah

Leiter, Andrew University of North Carolina, Chapel Hill

Lester, Neal Arizona State University

Love Jackson, Candice Tougaloo College

Ludwig, Erik University of Utah

McNeil, Elizabeth Arizona State University

Morgan, Kevin State University of New York at Albany

Mundy-Shephard, Rosemarie Albany State University

Murphy, Merilene M. University of California, Los Angeles

Muzorewa, Gwinyai P. Temple University

Newson-Horst, Adele University of Wisconsin, Oshkosh

Nichols, Keely Byars North Carolina State University

Nixon, Timothy K. George Washington University

Oventide, Robert Pasadena City College

Page, Philip California State University, San Bernardino

Pak, Christine University of Utah

Parentes, Cassandra Texas Christian University

Park, Jai Arizona State University

Pearson, Kim Hai University of Utah

Perez, Carlos University of Utah

Perkins, Dolen George Washington University

Perry, Michael Arizona State University

Pinson, Hermine Williamsburg University

Poindexter, Michael Sacramento Community College

Potter, Lawrence, Jr. Western Michigan State University

Rambsy Howard, II Southern Illinois University, Edwardsville

Ramey, Lauri California State University, Los Angeles

Rashid, Kamau University of Illinois, Urbana

Ratcliffe, Jeff Salt Lake City, Utah

Raynor, Deirdre University of Washington

Richards, Kaye University of Utah

Richards, Rondell Nelson University of Utah

Roberts, Rich University of Utah

Rodgers, Paul Henry Ford Community College

Rowden, Terry College of Wooster

Ruffin, Kimberly Bates College

Rutledge, Rebecka E. Miami University

Samuels, Wilfred D. University of Utah

Shelton, Vanessa University of Iowa

Simmons, Judy Dothard Los Angeles, California

Simpson, La Juan Morehouse College

Smith Pollard, Deborah University of Michigan, Dearborn

Tarver, Australia Texas Christian University

Tate, Beverly Pasadena City College

Taylor-Thompson, Betty University of Houston

Tettenborn, Eva Binghamton University

Tucker, Veta S. Grand Valley State University

Wallace, David University of Tennessee

Wanzo, Rebecca Duke University

Whalen-Bridge, John University of Singapore

Whitt, Margaret University of Denver

Wilcots, Barbara University of Denver

Williams, Dana A. Howard University

Woodard, Loretta G. Marygrove College

Young, Reggie University of Louisiana, Lafayette

Zumoff, J. A. University of Massachusetts, Boston

INDEX

O